International Directory of
COMPANY
HISTORIES

International Directory of

COMPANY

HISTORIES

VOLUME 14

Editor
Tina Grant

S<small>T</small>. J<small>AMES</small> P<small>RESS</small>

The paper used in this publication meets the minimum requirements of American National Standard for Information Sciences—Permanence Paper for Printed Library Materials, ANSI Z39.48-1984.

This book is printed on recycled paper that meets Environmental Protection Agency Standards.

Library of Congress Catalog Number: 89-190943

British Library Cataloguing in Publication Data

International directory of company histories. Vol. 14
I. Tina Grant
338.7409

ISBN 1-55862-342-6

Printed in the United States of America
Published simultaneously in the United Kingdom

Cover photograph courtesy of the Federal Reserve Bank.

10 9 8 7 6 5 4 3 2 1

CONTENTS _____

Company Histories

PREFACE _____

International Directory of Company Histories provides detailed information on the development of the world's largest and most influential companies. To date, *Company Histories* has covered more than 2500 companies in fourteen volumes.

Inclusion Criteria

Most companies chosen for inclusion in *Company Histories* have achieved a minimum of US$100 million in annual sales and are leading influences in their industries or geographical locations. State-owned companies that are important in their industries and that may operate much like public or private companies also are included. Wholly owned subsidiaries and divisions are presented if they meet the requirements for inclusion.

St. James Press does not endorse any of the companies or products mentioned in this book. Companies that appear in *Company Histories* were selected without reference to their wishes and have in no way endorsed their entries. Many of the companies were given the opportunity to participate in the compilation of the articles by providing information or reading their entries for factual accuracy, and we are indebted to many of them for their comments and corrections.

Entry Format

Each entry in this volume begins with a company's legal name, the address of its headquarters, its telephone number and fax number, and a statement of public, private, state, or parent ownership. A company with a legal name in both English and the language of its headquarters country is listed by the English name, with the native-language name in parentheses.

Also provided are the company's founding or earliest incorporation date, the number of employees, and the most recent sales figures available. Sales figures are given in local currencies with equivalents in U.S. dollars. For some private companies, sales figures are estimates. The entry lists the exchanges on which a company's stock is traded, as well as the company's principal Standard Industrial Classification codes. American spelling is used, and the word ''billion'' is used in its American sense of one thousand million.

Sources

The histories were compiled from publicly accessible sources such as general and academic periodicals, books, annual reports, and material supplied by the companies themselves. *Company Histories* is intended for reference use by students, business people, librarians, historians, economists, investors, job candidates, and others who want to learn more about the historical development of the world's most important companies.

Cumulative Indexes

An Index to Companies and Persons provides access to companies and individuals discussed in the text. Beginning with Volume 7, an Index to Industries allows researchers to locate companies by their principal industry.

ABBREVIATIONS FOR FORMS OF COMPANY INCORPORATION

A.B.	Aktiebolaget (Sweden)
A.G.	Aktiengesellschaft (Germany, Switzerland)
A.S.	Atieselskab (Denmark)
A.S.	Aksjeselskap (Denmark, Norway)
A.Ş.	Anomin Şirket (Turkey)
B.V.	Besloten Vennootschap met beperkte, Aansprakelijkheid (The Netherlands)
Co.	Company (United Kingdom, United States)
Corp.	Corporation (United States)
G.I.E.	Groupement d'Intérêt Economique (France)
GmbH	Gesellschaft mit beschränkter Haftung (Germany)
H.B.	Handelsbolaget (Sweden)
Inc.	Incorporated (United States)
KGaA	Kommanditgesellschaft auf Aktien (Germany)
K.K.	Kabushiki Kaisha (Japan)
LLC	Limited Liability Company (Middle East)
Ltd.	Limited (Canada, Japan, United Kingdom, United States)
N.V.	Naamloze Vennootschap (The Netherlands)
OY	Osakeyhtiöt (Finland)
PLC	Public Limited Company (United Kingdom)
PTY.	Proprietary (Australia, Hong Kong, South Africa)
S.A.	Société Anonyme (Belgium, France, Switzerland)
SpA	Società per Azioni (Italy)

ABBREVIATIONS FOR CURRENCY

DA	Algerian dinar	Dfl	Netherlands florin
A$	Australian dollar	NZ$	New Zealand dollar
Sch	Austrian schilling	N	Nigerian naira
BFr	Belgian franc	NKr	Norwegian krone
Cr	Brazilian cruzado	RO	Omani rial
C$	Canadian dollar	P	Philippine peso
DKr	Danish krone	Esc	Portuguese escudo
E£	Egyptian pound	SRls	Saudi Arabian riyal
Fmk	Finnish markka	S$	Singapore dollar
FFr	French franc	R	South African rand
DM	German mark	W	South Korean won
HK$	Hong Kong dollar	Pta	Spanish peseta
Rs	Indian rupee	SKr	Swedish krona
Rp	Indonesian rupiah	SFr	Swiss franc
IR£	Irish pound	NT$	Taiwanese dollar
L	Italian lira	B	Thai baht
¥	Japanese yen	£	United Kingdom pound
W	Korean won	$	United States dollar
KD	Kuwaiti dinar	B	Venezuelan bolivar
LuxFr	Luxembourgian franc	K	Zambian kwacha
M$	Malaysian ringgit		

International Directory of
COMPANY
HISTORIES

Aaron Rents, Inc.

Aaron Rents, Inc.

Suite 1100
309 E. Paces Ferry Road, N.E.
Atlanta, Georgia 30305-2377
U.S.A.
(404) 231-0011
Fax: (404) 240-6584

Public Company
Incorporated: 1962
Employees: 2,200
Sales: $229 million
Stock Exchanges: NASDAQ
SICs: 2511 Wood Household Furniture Except Upholstered;
2514 Metal Household Furniture; 2521 Wood Office
Furniture; 2522 Office Furniture, Except Wood; 5712
Furniture Stores; 5722 Household Appliance Stores; 5731
Radio, Television, and Consumer Electronics Stores; 7359
Equipment Rental and Leasing, Not Elsewhere Classified

Aaron Rents, Inc., rents residential and office furniture and
accessories, household appliances, consumer electronics, and
business equipment. Besides being one of the largest companies
in its industry, Aaron is distinguished as the only rental company that manufactures and reconditions its own furniture. The
company was operating about 230 showroom stores in 21 states
going into 1995 and was enjoying healthy growth.

Aaron Rents is the creation of entrepreneur R. Charles Loudermilk. Loudermilk was born in Atlanta, Georgia, in 1927—"On
the wrong side of the tracks," by his own admission. He attended Georgia Tech, had a tour in the Navy, and earned his
business degree from the University of North Carolina, before
accepting a job with Pet Milk Company and later the pharmaceutical and chemical giant Pfizer. While working for Pfizer
during the early 1950s, Loudermilk came across a small North
Carolina store that rented furniture and other merchandise. Eager to strike out on his own, Loudermilk drew on the concept
and started a rental business in 1955, borrowing $500 from
Trust Company Bank, while a partner invested another $500.

Loudermilk's first order was for 300 chairs. He and his partner
rushed to an army surplus store and purchased 500 chairs. They
delivered 300 of them to an auction in Atlanta and charged ten
cents per chair per day. "It was a hot day and the chairs didn't
stack well," Loudermilk recalled in company annals. "My

partner decided he didn't want to be in the rental business
anymore." After his partner bailed out, Loudermilk stuck with
his idea and continued to buy and rent furniture. Because he had
little money to invest in the business, he worked at his mother's
restaurant and poured virtually every nickel back into his rental
venture for seven straight years. Later, Loudermilk was able to
rent a small storefront and hire a woman to answer the telephones; he named the company Aaron Rents to ensure top
billing in the Yellow Pages.

Loudermilk gave his receptionist a catalog from a California
company and told her to buy rental equipment from it. When a
customer called or came in to rent some item she would simply
let them select pieces from the catalog. If an order came in for a
table or bed, for example, Loudermilk would drive down to
Sears, buy a piece similar to the one in the catalog, and deliver it
himself. Thus, Loudermilk got into renting party equipment and
sickroom gear, later moving into office and residential furniture.
"People said it was a gamble," Loudermilk recalled in the
November 21, 1983, *Forbes.* "It really wasn't. We never
bought the second item until the first one was rented."

Loudermilk spent the late 1950s nurturing the business at his
original Buckhead area store before branching out in the 1960s
with a second shop. A third store was opened in 1964 and rented
only furniture. By that time his inventory had grown to include
large outdoor tents. Interestingly, Loudermilk rented four tents
to civil rights marchers when they made their famous trek from
Selma to Montgomery, Alabama, in 1965. Two years later the
company opened an outlet in Baltimore, its first outside of
Atlanta. By 1969 Aaron Rents was generating a healthy $2
million annually from an inventory of about $3 million.

Besides furniture and party-related supplies, Aaron Rents outlets were eventually renting everything from corkscrews and
pillowcases to sofas and executive desks. The business was
relatively simple and straight forward. Loudermilk would purchase goods, rent them out, and depreciate them down to a value
of zero. Tax laws during the early 1970s allowed him to depreciate the entire value of the item over a period of three years; the
depreciated value was written off against income to reduce
taxes. Everything that he could get from the equipment in rent
or by selling the item after that was pure gravy.

Aaron Rents prospered during the 1960s and 1970s. By the mid-
1970s, in fact, the operation had expanded to include nearly 20
showrooms that were generating annual sales of about $10
million. That sales figure made Aaron the largest private company operating in the burgeoning U.S. furniture rental business.
Although Aaron's steady growth prior to the 1980s was admirable, it was meager in comparison to the rampant expansion the
company would achieve in the following 15 years. Several
factors contributed to that expansion. Importantly, in the late
1970s Loudermilk decided to focus his efforts on the residential
and office markets, rather than his traditional party and
sickroom segment. That decision resulted in a rapid climb in
sales. Thus, in 1982 Loudermilk sold off his party and sickroom equipment operations and dumped the proceeds into his
residential and business division.

In addition to shifting the company's focus, Loudermilk
achieved growth during the late 1970s and early 1980s through

new financing strategies. Rather than waiting until his goods had depreciated to reap his profits, he began taking less depreciation during the rental period and then barely breaking even on the resale of the furniture. A $200 desk, for instance, would be depreciated down to $100 and then marked up to $130 for resale. Simply put, he found a way to take his profits earlier. When the furniture was no longer rentable, Loudermilk would sell it alongside value-oriented new furniture in warehouse-style stores—they were called Aaron Sells Furniture—next to his rental shops. That way, he was able to attract customers that didn't want to rent but didn't have cash for expensive new furniture.

The overall strategy helped to boost the company's net income to a record $4.7 million in 1983 from sales of $55.4 million. By the end of that year Aaron Rents was operating a total of 92 stores in 14 mostly southern states. It was servicing 50,000 rental contracts worth an average of $48 monthly, giving Aaron roughly 15 percent of the $350 million furniture rental market. Loudermilk had become a multimillionaire. He spent his weekends on his 3,700-acre south Georgia plantation, where he tended his herd of purebred limousin cattle and perused his corn and soybean fields. When not at the plantation, he might be found hunting geese in Alaska or Scotland. Otherwise, Loudermilk worked to enlarge his rental empire.

Another important factor in Aaron Rents' tremendous expansion during the early 1980s was Loudermilk's strategy to add to the company's growth through acquisition. Loudermilk took Aaron Rents public in 1982 to raise expansion capital—although he had retained 42 percent of the company's stock as of 1983, which was valued at about $38 million. He used part of the money from the public offering to buy a few of his biggest private competitors. Most notable were the acquisitions of leading private rental companies Metrolease (Metropolitan Furniture Leasing), of North Carolina, and the Houston-based Modern Furniture Rental. Loudermilk bought Modern Furniture in July of 1983 for $6.5 million in cash before plunking down $4.5 million for Metrolease the following summer. Meanwhile, the rental industry in general was expanding, adding fuel to Aaron Rents' growth. Aaron Rents' annual revenues surged to a whopping $84 million in 1984, making it the largest rental company in the nation. Indeed, Aaron Rents surpassed the venerable industry leader GranTree, which had doubled its revenues from $41 million in 1977 to $82 million in 1984.

At the same time, Aaron Rents' bottom line was benefiting from in-house manufacturing operations. The company had started producing its furniture out of necessity in 1971 when Lockheed Corp. brought employees to Atlanta from all over the world to build a new plane. Manufacturers simply could not meet Aaron's demand for furniture to rent to the influx of workers, so Loudermilk decided to begin building the furniture himself. He purchased a local manufacturer called MacTavish Furniture Industries and was instantly in the furniture-making business. The decision to manufacture proved fruitful, and Aaron became the only company in the rental industry to exclusively build its furniture. The benefits were multifold. Not only did Aaron benefit from a dependable, low-cost furniture source, but it also saved money and time related to the repair and reconditioning of its old furniture. In addition, Aaron was able to control both

styling and price to suit the specific needs of its targeted customers.

Aaron continued to pursue acquisitions and to expand its furniture making operations during 1984 and 1985. By early 1986 the chain had ballooned to 154 stores in 20 states and annual revenues were topping a fat $100 million. Despite sales gains, however, earnings growth had stalled. The problem was primarily the result of the fast store expansion. New stores typically took 12 to 18 months to achieve profitability, so many of Aaron's outlets were still dragging down the bottom line. Loudermilk decided to slow the company's expansion and to focus on consolidating and streamlining existing operations. During 1986 and 1987 the company closed some Aaron Sells outlets, beefed up its management team, and launched a drive to cut costs and improve profit margins. Loudermilk took a break from day-to-day management of the company during those years, devoting much of his time to his duties as chairman of the Metro Atlanta Rapid Transit Authority and to his political interests.

The effects of management efforts at Aaron seemed apparent by 1988. Sales rose to $119 million and $132 million in 1987 and 1988, respectively, while net earnings climbed to $4.79 million and $5.54 million. However, the sales gains were partially the result of Loudermilk's October 1987 purchase of Ball Stalker Inc., an Atlanta-based manufacturer and distributor of upscale office furniture. Similarly, the profit increase was generated primarily by a cut in Aaron's effective corporate tax rate from 46 percent to 34 percent; the tax cut was ushered in with the renowned Tax Reform Act of 1986 (TRA). However, the TRA eliminated many of the depreciation benefits that Aaron had previously enjoyed. So, although earnings rose between 1987 and 1988, they were still low compared to previous projections, and the TRA promised to hurt future profits as well. Evidencing investor discontent with the situation, Aaron's stock price skidded from a high of $25.75 in 1984 to just $12 before the 1987 stock market crash, after which it plummeted to a low $6.50.

Realizing that his company was struggling, Loudermilk returned to day-to-day control of the company in 1987. He renewed the company's efforts to overhaul operations, cut costs, and boost margins. At the same time, Loudermilk continued to expand the Aaron network of stores. Early in 1988, in fact, he purchased furniture rental operations in Florida from Furniture Enterprises and Powell Furniture Rental, as well as a Jackson, Mississippi, store from competitor Cort Furniture Rental Corp. By late 1988 the company was operating 183 stores in 31 states. Before the end of the year, however, that number would be reduced as a result of the consolidation of several Aaron Sells outlets with adjacent Aaron Rents stores.

Importantly, Aaron followed in the footsteps of its chief competitors, GranTree and the highly successful Rent-A-Center, in 1987 when it entered the rent-to-own business. Under that program, customers were allowed to make regular payments over a pre-determined period—usually 18 or 24 months—to use furniture, appliances, electronics, and other goods. These payments differed from usual rent payments by being applied to the purchase price, and the consumer could own the item at the end of the rental period. By late 1988 Aaron was offering rent-to-own at 18 of its store locations, introducing a 12-month ownership plan—which caught on with customers—and Loudermilk was planning to expand the successful program throughout his network. The rent-to-own initiative was part of Loudermilk's push to focus on renting rather than selling furniture.

Facing flat market growth in the furniture rental industry, Loudermilk stepped up reorganization efforts in 1989 by eliminating distinctions between the rental, sales, and combination-store divisions. He replaced them with six geographical regions, each with a vice-president responsible for 10 to 20 outlets; previously, a single manager had been placed in charge of about 60 stores. Similarly, the office-furniture rental division, which comprised about 47 stores going into 1990, was reorganized into six geographical regions, each of which was headed by a vice-president. Finally, Loudermilk initiated a franchising campaign designed to increase Aaron's regional coverage with minimal capital cost to the company.

The reorganization was slow to take hold. In fact, Aaron suffered three consecutive years of declining sales and earnings beginning in 1989. Eventually, though, the company's financial performance recovered. Among Loudermilk's successful moves during the early 1990s was renting office equipment, not just office furniture. He had hesitated to rent equipment for several years because he felt that Aaron lacked the management expertise to handle that market segment. However, that move contributed to Aaron's turnaround, which began in 1992. Indeed, although Aaron's sales for 1992 (fiscal year ended March 31, 1992) grew tepidly to about $145 million, the company posted a profit of about $3.1 million—Aaron's first profit gain since 1988.

Encouraged by success with the Aaron Rental Purchase stores, which made up Aaron's rent-to-own business, Loudermilk began expanding the chain through both franchises and company-owned stores. As a result, revenues sailed to $158 million in 1993 before rocketing to about $186 million in 1994 (year ended March 21, 1994). Throughout the fiscal 1994 year Aaron added rental-purchase stores to its chain at a rate of one per week. The growth continued during 1995. By September 1995, in fact, Aaron was operating a total of 206 company-owned outlets and 33 franchised stores. Sales were booming. Revenues swelled 24 percent in fiscal 1995 to nearly $230 million as net income vaulted to a record $11.33 million. Aaron continued to benefit from its five furniture manufacturing plants in Georgia and Florida. Loudermilk, still in charge in mid-1995, expected to expand Aaron's production and showroom operations through the 1990s.

Principal Subsidiaries: Aaron Investment Company.

Further Reading:

Bork, Robert H., ''Money in the Mattress,'' *Forbes,* November 21, 1983, p. 108.
Danielson, Gilbert L., ''Aaron Rents, Inc., Names Ken Butler and Brian Stahl Division Presidents,'' *PR Newswire,* February 2, 1995.
Gilligan, Gregory J., ''Rent-to-Own Delivers to Aaron a New Direction, Higher Sales,'' *Richmond Times-Dispatch,* July 31, 1993, Section BUS.
Hallem, Jeanie Franco, '' 'Cooling It' Is New Motto for Aaron Rents,'' *Atlanta Business Chronicle,* February 24, 1986, p. 2B.
Robertshaw, Nicky, ''Aaron Rents Expanding with Six-Eight Stores,'' *Memphis Business Journal,* November 21, 1994, p. 3.
Schonbak, Judith, ''Aaron Rents Bounces Back,'' *Business Atlanta,* September 1988, p. 32.
——, ''Aaron Rents Launches New Venture,'' *Business Atlanta,* July 1992, p. 8.
Weiner, Daniel P., ''Aaron Rents Inc.,'' *Fortune,* November 25, 1985, p. 40.
Welch, Mary, '' 'Radical' Shift for Aaron Rents,'' *Atlanta Business Chronicle,* December 19, 1988, p. 6.

—Dave Mote

adidas®

Adidas AG

Postfach 11 20
D-91072 Herzogenaurach
Germany
0 91 32 84-0
Fax: 0 91 32 84-22 41

Private Company
Founded: 1948
Employees: 5,079
Sales: DM 3.29 billion
SICs: 2329 Mens'/Boys' Clothing Not Elsewhere Classified;
2339 Womens'/Misses' Outerwear Not Elsewhere
Classified; 2369 Girls'/Childrens' Outerwear; 3149
Footwear Except Rubber Not Elsewhere Classified

With about 25 percent of the world market going into the mid-1990s, Adidas AG is one of the largest athletic shoe suppliers in the world. The German-based company is the decisive leader in the global soccer shoe market, and also markets a wide array of sports apparel and accessories. Adidas was the undisputed leader in the world athletic shoe market until the late 1970s, when U.S. competitors captured increased market share. The privately held enterprise was working to regain lost ground in the mid-1990s and seeking to go public in 1996.

Adidas emanated from a bitter dispute between two brothers, Rudolph and Adi Dassler, in the small Bavarian mill town of Herzogenaurach. Rudi and Adi were born in 1898 and 1900, respectively, to Christofl and Pauline Dassler. Their home town of Herzogenaurach was a regional textile manufacturing center at the time, but during the early 1900s most of the mills converted to shoemaking. Adi was trained to be a baker, but those skills offered him little hope of finding a job in the final years of World War I. Instead, the Dassler family started a tiny shoemaking business in the back of Pauline's laundry. Adi began making shoes using materials from old helmets, tires, rucksacks, and other garbage that he could scavenge. Adi's sister cut patterns out of canvas, and the always innovative Adi built a shoe trimmer that was powered by a bicycle.

The company's first shoes were bedroom slippers that sported soles made from used tires. Adi, who had a lifelong love of sports, converted those slippers into unique light-weight gymnastics and soccer shoes with nailed-on cleats. Demand for those shoes allowed the family to build a factory in 1926, when output rose to about 100 pairs per day. Adi's brother and father both quit their jobs to work in the company.

The Dassler family's company received a major boost when their shoes were worn by German athletes in the 1928 Olympics in Amsterdam. Four years later, moreover, athletes clad in Dassler shoes won medals in the Olympics in Los Angeles. Then, in the 1936 Games, the world-renowned American sprinter Jesse Owens raced to victory in Dassler shoes. Owens's shoes featured two widely spaced stripes that wrapped over the ball of the foot, a design that became increasingly commonplace on the feet of athletes around the world.

Demand for Dassler shoes mushroomed during the early 1930s and continued until the start of the German offensive that led to World War II. During the war, the Dassler factory was commandeered for the production of boots for German soldiers. Both Adi and Rudi were reportedly members of the Nazi party, but only Rudi was called to service. Adi stayed home and ran the factory. Allied forces occupied the region at the war's end, and American soldiers even moved into the Dassler home. Christolf Dassler died about that time. Adi made friends with some of the American soldiers, and even made a pair of track shoes for a U.S. soldier who eventually wore them in the 1946 Olympics.

After the soldiers left, Rudi returned to Herzogenaurach and rejoined his brother. He had spent several years fighting and one year interned in an American prisoner-of-war camp. Just as they had been forced to do after World War I, Adi and Rudi scavenged for shoemaking material to rebuild their business in war-torn Germany. They used army tents for canvas and old American tank materials for soles. They paid their 47 workers with materials like firewood and yarn.

It was only a few years after Rudi's return that an infamous dispute broke out between the two brothers. Although the men kept the impetus for the fight a secret until their deaths, rumors swirled that the battle stemmed from disagreements related to the war. One story indicated that Rudi was upset that Adi had not used his connections with the Allies to get him out of the prison camp during the conflict. Whatever the reason for the feud, Rudi walked away from the family home and business forever in the spring of 1948, intent on starting his own shoe business. He took with him the company's sales force and control of a building that was to become a new factory. Adi kept most of the work force and the original headquarters offices and factory. From that time forward, the brothers never spoke a word to one another except in court. The businesses that they created represented one of the most intense rivalries in all of Europe.

When they split, Rudi and Adi agreed that neither would be allowed to use the Dassler brand name on their shoes. Rudi named his new company and shoes Ruda, while Adi named his Addas. Shortly thereafter, Adi changed the name to Adidas (emphasis on the last syllable) and Rudi, on the advice of an advertising agency, changed the name of his shoes to Puma. Adi altered the Dassler family trademark of two stripes by adding a third. He also adopted the slogan ''The Best for the Athlete'' as part of his marketing campaign. Rudi chose as his logo a cat's paw in motion.

For many years a signpost in the center of town had two arrows: one pointed to Adidas and the other to Puma, which faced Adidas on the opposite side of the River Aurach. Each company had its own soccer team, and employees from each company drank different beers. Enrollment at the two elementary schools in town was determined by the factory at which a child's father worked (Adidas employees' children attended one school, while Puma employees' children attended the other), and children learned early in their lives to look down on the competing shoe company.

Each shoe company's culture bore the mark of its founder. It may have been for that reason that Adi came to dominate the global athletic shoe industry. Both Rudi and Adi were intelligent and able. Puma eventually became a venerable and established shoe company throughout the global industry. But under Adi Dassler's guiding hand, Adidas grew during the mid-1900s to became the undisputed world shoe industry giant. Adi, known as shy and intelligent, was respected in his village. A natural athlete, inventor, and craftsman, Adi combined his interests to produce a number of breakthrough innovations that catapulted the company to prominence. By the time Dassler died in 1978, in fact, Adidas shoes were being worn throughout the world—more than any other sports shoe—by both professional and weekend athletes, and as casual footwear.

Adi was credited with numerous inventions during the late 1940s and 1950s, including the first shoes designed for ice and the first multi-studded shoes. Adidas is also credited with pioneering the now-commonplace practice among athletic shoe manufacturers of selling sports bags and athletic clothing bearing their brand name. Among Adi's most notable early contributions was his improvement of the soccer shoe. Prior to 1957, soccer shoes were designed as they had been for decades, with metal studs mounted in leather. These shoes were heavy, particularly when they got wet. Adi designed a new type of shoe that sported a nylon sole and molded rubber studs. The result was a more lightweight, durable shoe. Introduced in 1957, the revolutionary soccer shoe was eventually copied by other shoe companies, including chief-rival Puma.

Another of Adi's pivotal innovations, and the one that helped most to thrust the company into the global limelight, was the screw-studded soccer shoe, which allowed worn cleats to be replaced. The cleats were introduced in 1954 at the World Soccer Championships in Bern, Switzerland. Heavy rains during the first half of an important game turned the soccer field to a muddy mess by half-time. The West German national team members went to their locker room, removed their standard cleats, and installed longer cleats to get a better grip in the field. Adi watched as the West German team captured a 3–2 victory over the favored Hungarians, a triumph that was viewed by the German people as a symbol of their return from the ashes of war. Soon after that event, Adidas' shipments exploded from about 800 pairs to 2,000 pairs of shoes per day.

Two years later Adi started its successful and long tradition of naming one of its shoes after the Olympics. The shoe introduced at the 1956 Olympics was the Melbourne—the Games were held in that Australian city that year—the first to offer multiple studs. Adi's son Horst handled the promotion with a marketing strategy that won accolades abroad. He simply gave the shoes away to Olympic athletes, who wore them for a global audience. Athletes wearing Adidas won a whopping 72 medals that year and set 33 records. After that, Adidas scored another major marketing coup by signing agreements to supply entire sports teams with footwear, an agreement that ensured that Adidas equipment would be worn by many of the world's greatest athletes on both sides of the Iron Curtain. Other shoe and sports equipment companies eventually followed the company's lead, and contracts to supply free equipment to such high-profile athletes became highly competitive.

Adidas initiated a number of savvy marketing programs during the 1950s, 1960s, and 1970s, but the Olympics remained the centerpiece of its marketing strategy for several years. In the 1964 Tokyo Games, medals won by Adidas-shod competitors amounted to 80 percent of the total, as they captured all but 30 of the medals awarded. At the Montreal Olympics, Adidas outfitted all of the winners in hockey, soccer, volleyball, and women's basketball. Adidas shoes were worn by athletes who accounted for 83 percent of all medals awarded and a fat 95 percent of the track-and-field gold medals. Adidas became virtually dominant in the athletic shoe industry. Aside from its clever marketing and winning designs, moreover, it was considered the quality leader. Indeed, other shoemakers considered Adidas superior in machinery, craftsmanship, and materials.

Adidas's most lucrative strategic maneuver was its entry into the giant and blossoming U.S. athletic shoe market in the late 1950s. Adidas attacked that market at a good time. Its major competitors were manufacturers of canvas sneakers that bore names like Keds and P.F. Flyers. Adidas's high quality, well-designed shoes became explosively popular, first with more serious athletes, but finally with the mainstream weekend-athlete and casual-footwear markets. Puma also made a run in the United States beginning in the 1950s. Its shoes sold relatively well, but ultimately came to be regarded as inferior to Adidas in quality. In contrast, by the mid-1970s Adidas had become nearly synonymous with quality athletic shoes in the United States.

Adidas expanded globally during the 1960s and 1970s, maintaining its dominant position in the world sports shoe industry. By the late 1970s the company was churning out about 200,000 pairs per day and generating well over a half billion dollars in sales annually (the company was still privately owned, so revenue figures are speculative). Adidas operated 24 factories in 17 countries and was selling a wide range of shoes in more than 150 nations. In addition, the company had moved by that time into diverse product lines including shorts, jerseys, balls and other equipment, track suits, and athletic bags. The company had registered about 800 patents and was producing roughly 150 different styles of shoes. About 90 percent of all Formula 1 drivers, for example, raced in Adidas.

Throughout the company's rampant growth, its founder continued to lead and innovate. In 1978 the 77-year-old president introduced what he considered to be his greatest contribution ever to his beloved game of soccer. In recognition of the fact that players spent about 90 percent of their time on the field running rather than kicking the ball, Adi designed an ultralight soccer shoe with a sole resembling a sprint shoe. The shoe also featured an orthopedic footbed, a wider positioning of the studs to give better traction, and even a special impregnation treatment designed to counter the weight-increasing effect of the humid Argentinian climate. The shoes were first used in the World Cup in Argentina by almost every team in the competition.

Adi Dassler died shortly after he introduced his landmark soccer shoe in 1978. He had run the company and its predecessor for about 60 years and built it into the unmitigated giant of the world shoe industry. His death marked the end of an era at the company. Indeed, Adidas suffered a string of defeats in the late 1970s and 1980s that severely diminished its role in the world sports shoe industry. The company's loss of dominance was not solely attributable to Dassler's death, however. In fact, the athletic shoe industry became intensely competitive following his death, primarily as a result of aggressive U.S. entrants. The increased competition actually began after the 1972 Olympics in Munich, when a mob of companies decided to hop into the lucrative business. After having the industry mostly to themselves for years, Adidas and Puma suddenly found themselves under attack from shoe manufacturers worldwide.

Dassler had carefully arranged a management succession before his death. Family members remained in key management positions, but several professional managers were also brought in to take over key functions like marketing, production, and public relations. Unfortunately, the effort failed to keep the company vibrant. Adidas retained its lead in the global athletic shoe market for several years and remained dominant in its core European market into the 1990s. Importantly, though, it was soundly thrashed in the North American market by emerging athletic shoe contenders Nike Inc. and Reebok Inc. Those companies launched an almost militant marketing offensive on the North American sports shoe market during the 1980s that caught Adidas completely off guard.

Adidas, not used to such fierce competition, effectively cowered and helplessly ceded dominance of that important region. Incredibly, Adidas U.S. sales shrunk to a measly $200-million-plus by the end of the decade, while Nike's mushroomed to more than $2.4 billion. By that time, Reebok and Nike together claimed more than 50 percent of the U.S. athletic shoe market, compared to about three percent for Adidas. The Adidas brand name had become a fading memory in the minds of many aging baby boomers, and many younger U.S. buyers were virtually unaware of the brand. "This is a brand that has taken about five bullets to the head," said one observer in *Business Journal-Portland* in February 1993.

Adidas managed to maintain its lead in the soccer shoe market and even to keep a healthy 26 percent of the European market for its products. But the North American market became the core of the global athletic shoe industry and Adidas found itself scrambling to maintain respect worldwide. Besides increased competition, moreover, Adidas suffered during the 1980s and early 1990s from relatively weak management. To make matters worse, members of the Dassler family and relatives that still owned Adidas began fighting over control of the company. Amid increased competition and family squabbling, Adidas' bottom line began to sag. The organization lost about $77 million in 1989 before the family sold the entire organization for only $289 million. The buyer was Frenchman Bernard Tapie, a 47-year-old entrepreneur and politician.

From the beginning, analysts doubted Tapie's ability to turn the ailing company around. A perpetual showman, Tapie purchased the company partly for the attention he would get from the French people for securing ownership of a renowned German institution. Tapie had already gained notoriety as an entrepreneur and as a parliamentary head of the ruling Socialist Party. Tapie's promotional skills did little for Adidas. The company continued to lag and Tapie himself became embroiled in political and business scandals. Tapie stepped aside as chief of the company in 1992 and handed the reins to Gilbert Beaux. Tapie also started looking for a buyer for Adidas.

Under new management, Adidas looked as though it was beginning to turn the corner going into the mid-1990s. Of import was the company's 1993 purchase of U.S.-based Sports Inc., an enterprise that had been founded by Rob Strasser. Strasser was credited as the marketing genius that had helped to make Nike into the leading U.S. athletic shoe company. Strasser quit Nike in 1987 to form Sports Inc. When Adidas bought out his 50-person marketing venture, it named Strasser head of the newly formed Adidas America subsidiary. Strasser brought with him another former Nike executive, Peter Moore, with whom he hoped to regain some of Adidas' lost glory. "We'll compete from day one," he said in the *Business Journal-Portland* in 1993, "but it won't happen overnight."

Tapie finally found a buyer for Adidas in 1993. The company was purchased by a group of European investors for $371 million. Unfortunately, Strasser died late in 1993. Moore took over as head of the U.S. subsidiary. Adidas expected Moore to lead the company's turnaround on that continent and to help it eventually attain the kind of strength Adidas International still exerted in Europe and some other parts of the world. The company reported improving profits in 1994, which was largely the result of increased marketing efforts and product introductions in the United States as well as cost-cutting and reorganization efforts throughout its organization.

Principal Subsidiaries: Adidas America Inc.; Adidas North America Inc.; Adidas (Canada) Ltd.; LCS America Inc.; Erima Sportbekleidungs GmbH (Germany); Adidas Sarragan France S.a.r.l.; Adidas Espana SA (Spain); Adidas Portugal Lda (Portugal); Adidas Sport GmbH (Switzerland); Le Coq Sportif International SA (France); Adidas Austria AG; Adidas Benelux B.V. (Netherlands); Adidas Belgium N.V.; Adidas Budapest Kft. (Hungary); Adidas (U.K.) Ltd.; Adidas (Ireland) Ltd.; Adidas Norge A/S (Norway); Adidas Sverige AB (Sweden); Adidas Poland Sp.z.o.o.; Adidas CSFR Spol s.r.o. (Czech Republic); Adidas Moscow Ltd.; Adidas de Mexico S.A. de C.V.; Sarragan de Mexico S.A. de C.V.; Adidas do Brasil Ltda. (Brazil); Adidas Latin America S.A. (Panama); Ralber S.A. (Uruguay); Adidas Corp. de Venezuela; Adidas Hong Kong Ltd.; Adidas Singapore Pte Ltd.; Adidas Asia/Pacific Ltd. (Hong Kong); Adidas (Thailand) Co., Ltd.; Adidas Australia Pty Ltd.; Adidas New Zealand Pty Ltd.; Adidas (South Africa) Pty Ltd.

Further Reading:

Bates, Tom, "Adidas Names Moore to Replace Strasser," *Oregonian,* November 10, 1993.
Carter, Donna, "Mutombo's Shoes Take Off Worldwide," *Denver Post,* December 18, 1992, p. C1.

Colodny, Mark M., "Beaux Knows Adidas," *Fortune,* December 31, 1990, p. 111.

Fallon, James, "Adidas Sold for $370.48 Million," *Footwear News,* February 22, 1993, p. 39.

Francis, Mike, "Strasser Headed for Top of Adidas? One of the Founder of Sports Inc. May Become Head of Adidas U.S.A.," *Oregonian,* February 3, 1993.

"How Adidas Ran Faster," *Management Today,* December 1979, pp. 58–61.

Manning, Jeff, "Adidas, Sports Inc. Join Forces, Strasser Heads U.S. Operation," *Business Journal-Portland,* February 8, 1993, p. 1.

Mulligan, Thomas S., "Adidas to Put U.S. Market in Hands of Ex-Nike Whiz," *Los Angeles Times,* February 5, 1993, p. D2.

Silverman, Edward R., "Foothold in Sneaker War," *New York Newsday,* July 8, 1992, p. 31.

Strasser, J.B., and Laurie Becklund, *Swoosh: The Unauthorized Story of Nike and the Men Who Played There,* New York: Harcourt Brace Jovanovich, 1991.

Waxman, Sharon, "Tapie: The Flashy Frenchman Behind the Adidas Acquisition," *Washington Post,* July 22, 1990, p. H1.

—Dave Mote

╞ AIR NEW ZEALAND

Air New Zealand Limited

Quay Tower
29 Customs Street West
Auckland
New Zealand
64 9 366 2400
Fax: 64 9 366 2401

Public Company
Incorporated: 1949 as Tasman Empire Airways Limited
Employees: 9,618
Stock Exchanges: New Zealand
Sales: NZ$2.89 billion
SICs: 4512 Air Transportation Scheduled; 4522 Air
    Transportation Nonscheduled

Air New Zealand Limited is New Zealand's largest airline, that country's fifth largest public company, and one of the top 40 airlines (by annual revenues) in the world. In 1995 the airline was serving about 20 regional centers through its domestic operations and about 20 countries through its international division. In addition, the company was operating several subsidiaries involved in businesses ranging from cargo services and travel agencies to catering and engineering services. Operated as a government-owned airline from the 1950s through much of the 1980s, Air New Zealand established itself as the dominant national carrier, although its profit record was spotty. After bottoming out in the early 1980s, Air New Zealand was privatized beginning in the mid-1980s; healthy sales and profit gains ensued and even accelerated after the company became fully private in 1989. By the mid-1990s, Air New Zealand was generating close to US$1.5 billion in sales and transporting nearly 6.5 million passengers annually, making it the 40th largest airline in the world.

The company that became Air New Zealand was formed in 1939. It officially began operating in April 1940 as Tasman Empire Airways Limited, a joint venture that was registered as a limited liability company in Wellington, the capital of New Zealand. New Zealand's government originally owned 20 percent of the enterprise, while the remainder was held by regional airlines BOAC (38 percent) and Qantas (23 percent), and Union Airways of New Zealand (19 percent). The company started out as a specialty service, providing air service across the Tasman Sea (between New Zealand, Australia, and Tasmania) with

'flying boats.' Among the individual founders of the company was Sir Geoffrey Roberts, who became known as the "Father of Air New Zealand" by many of his associates. Roberts served as the company's first general manager until 1958, and then as a director and chairman of the company during the 1960s and 1970s.

In 1953 the governments of New Zealand and Australia became the sole owners of Tasman Empire Airways, each with a 50 percent share. The New Zealand government bought out Australia's half in 1961, though, and became the sole owner of the operation. In 1965 the name of the company was changed to Air New Zealand Limited to reflect its status as a national air service provider. Throughout the 1960s and 1970s, in fact, the government invested heavily to make Air New Zealand a leading airline in the South Pacific. The company expanded with destinations throughout the New Zealand/Australia region and South Pacific Islands, but also to other locales in Asia and the West. During that period, the company logged millions of miles flying over water and forged a worthy reputation in the global airline industry as a safe and competent carrier.

Air New Zealand benefited during the 1960s and 1970s from government ownership. Besides having easy access to investment capital, the airline enjoyed protection from competing carriers in its domestic market. Despite deep pockets and protected markets, however, Air New Zealand eventually began to suffer from limitations imposed by the vast bureaucracy that engulfed the enterprise. High operating costs and a stifling management environment were hurting the company's performance. Intensifying the strain was the government decision to merge Air New Zealand and National Airways Corporation. The government had created National Airways in 1947, a few years after Tasman Empire was formed. That government-owned operation was initiated to provide domestic air service, as well as regional services to other South Pacific Islands. The two airlines were merged into a single entity called Air New Zealand (ANZ).

The operations of National Airways burdened the resultant organization with even higher operating costs, such as big wages paid to union workers. The airline was losing money and, by the early 1980s, even the government recognized that something needed to be done to turn it around. To that end, in 1982 it brought in Norman Geary to serve as chief executive of the company and to whip the organization into shape. Geary succeeded Morrie Davis, who had been with Air New Zealand since the 1940s and had served as chief executive since 1975. Under Geary's direction, ANZ's financial performance began to improve. In fact, the company started posting profits in 1982 and continued to do so throughout the 1980s and into the early 1990s.

Geary was able to achieve gains at ANZ by reducing operating costs and boosting revenues. He accomplished that by convincing the government to back him up in key efforts, particularly related to labor negotiations, and by breathing new life into the company's marketing strategy. Soon after taking the helm, for example, he launched a route from Auckland to Los Angeles to London. He also purchased a new fleet of Boeing 747s and initiated an effort to boost ANZ's share of the Pacific tourist market. The government had sponsored studies that suggested that those moves would fail. Nevertheless, Geary was committed to the new strategy and was even able to get doubting bureaucrats to give him a chance.

As a result of Geary's efforts, ANZ rapidly improved. The new route to London, for example, sold out quickly, and Geary's efforts to boost profits from tourism paid off. Indeed, during the 1980s New Zealand became an increasingly popular destination for leisure travelers around the world. New routes, upgraded equipment, elimination of unnecessary overhead, and improved marketing helped the company to boost its number of passengers to more than four million annually by the mid-1980s. Meanwhile, operating profits rose to more than NZ$100 million. Geary was eventually credited with turning ANZ into an efficient, profitable carrier. In 1987, the last full year that Geary was in charge, ANZ's revenues increased to about US$800 million and total passengers served climbed to about 4.7 million (about 3.3 million international passengers and 1.4 million domestic).

Geary departed in June 1988 and was succeeded by R. James Scott. Scott was brought in to usher ANZ into a new era of privatization. Indeed, New Zealand's government had started privatizing much of the nation's air transport system in the mid-1980s, including airports and air traffic control systems. It also started moving ANZ toward privatization and preparing to open the New Zealand market to competition. To that end, it allowed a new air carrier called Ansett to begin operating in July 1987. Ansett began modestly with a single route. From there, however, the start-up expanded rapidly into other routes dominated by ANZ. It initially managed to snap up as much as 30 percent of the market in some of those routes and threatened to pose a formidable long-term challenge to ANZ's domestic operations; some observers speculated that the government's decision to allow Ansett to compete eventually played a role in Scott's leaving ANZ.

ANZ completed its privatization in 1989. Its new owners included Australian rival Qantas, as well as Japan Air Lines and American Airlines. Those three companies owned 35 percent of the company, and the Brierley's New Zealand investment firm controlled about 65 percent of the stock, much of which it had agreed to sell to the public. Thus, Air New Zealand was effectively free from government interference. With the domestic market increasingly open to competition and offering few growth opportunities, Scott planned to focus the newly private ANZ on international business. Tourism had been surging in New Zealand and surrounding areas, and Scott planned to boost the share of ANZ's revenues attributable to international traffic from about 60 percent in 1988 to about 90 percent by 1993.

Specifically, Scott wanted to turn ANZ into a "quality niche carrier" that dominated the markets and routes that it was most able to serve, rather than trying to compete with major international airlines in the most popular routes. ANZ's financial performance and passenger volume declined in 1990 and 1991, primarily as a result of diminished international traffic during the global economic downturn. But management undertook a number of new initiatives that buoyed the company. For instance, ANZ reached marketing agreements with major airlines that strengthened its commitment to the North American and South Pacific market; for example, services were added or aug-

mented in Dallas, Honolulu, Toronto, and Vancouver. Those agreements, according to Scott, represented ANZ's intent to double in size by the year 2000.

James McCrea replaced Scott as chief executive of ANZ in August 1991. McCrea had joined the airline in 1956, in the engineering division, and worked his way up to general manager of airline operations by 1982 and then to deputy chief executive in 1989. He worked closely with Scott to ensure that ANZ operated profitably and efficiently. As chief executive, McCrea continued to pursue many of his predecessor's goals, although he reduced ANZ's growth forecasts. Instead, he planned to steer ANZ on a course toward steady passenger growth and healthy profitability, largely by cultivating international tourism traffic. Importantly, the company began to promote what it termed "multidestinational regional tourism." In other words, it focused on encouraging leisure travelers to fly ANZ into New Zealand or some other South Pacific destination, and then on to other locations along ANZ's South Pacific network—Hawaii, Fiji, Tahiti, Western Samoa, the Cook Islands—during the same vacation.

ANZ prospered under new management during the early 1990s and into the mid-1990s. Passenger volume rose from about 4.8 million in 1991 to 5.8 million in 1994 and then to 6.4 million in 1995. During the same period, sales rose 30 percent to move toward the US$1.5 billion mark for fiscal year ended June 1995. More importantly, operating profits rebounded and vaulted to roughly US$150 million annually by 1995. The gains were primarily the result of increased leisure traffic, particularly in Asia, and new programs designed to take advantage of tourism growth. In 1992, for example, ANZ introduced a new service called "beyond Australia" with operations in Taipei, Bangkok, and Brisbane. In 1993 ANZ initiated service to South Korea. In 1994 and 1995, moreover, ANZ boosted the number of direct flights from Los Angeles to Sydney to five per week.

On a typical weekday in 1995, ANZ made 528 flights between 60 airports and 19 countries. In addition to its thriving airline business, ANZ managed to rack up profit gains from its diverse assemblage of subsidiaries and operating units. Among the most important of those entities was Air New Zealand Engineering Services, which alone generated about US$176 million in sales for 1994. Other profit centers included a pilot training center, travel agency, information systems services, and catering and cargo operations. Other operations included ANZ's domestic airline operations, which continued to face challenges prompted by deregulation and increased competition. For the mid- and late 1980s, ANZ management was planning to continue building its international leisure business with a focus on Asia, as well as to pursue its strategy of multidestinational regional tourism.

Principal Subsidiaries: The Mount Cook Group Limited; Air New Zealand Link; Jetset Travel and Technology Holdings Party Limited; Hotpack Reservations (NZ) Limited; United Travel Agencies Limited; Blue Pacific Tours Limited; Travel Industries Automated Systems Party Limited.

Further Reading:
"Air New Zealand: Flying in the Face of Disaster Warnings," *Business Week*, September 13, 1982, pp. 80, 84.

Davidson, Brian, ''Air New Zealand's Prickly Path to Privatisation,'' *Interavia,* February 1989, p. 130.

Hill, Leonard, ''Kiwis Widen the Niche,'' *Air Transport World,* November 1994, p. 87.

Mooney, Timothy, ''Air New Zealand Expands Its Role as Leading Carrier to Australia, New Zealand and South Pacific Island,'' *Business Wire,* January 25, 1991.

Morris, Kathleen, ''Air New Zealand: Friendlier Skies,'' *Financial World,* April 11, 1995, p. 15.

Woolsey, James P., ''Air New Zealand Sets Sights to Be Quality Niche Carrier,'' *Air Transport World,* July 1989, p. 66.

—Dave Mote

Amdahl Corporation

1250 East Arques Avenue
Sunnyvale, California 94088-3470
U.S.A.
(408) 746-6000
Fax: (408) 738-1051

Public Company
Incorporated: 1970
Employees: 7,400
Sales: $2.05 billion
Stock Exchanges: New York
SICs: 3571 Electronic Computers; 3572 Computer Storage
  Devices; 7372 Prepackaged Software

Amdahl Corporation is a leading manufacturer of large-scale data-processing systems. In addition, it produces data-storage subsystems, data-communications products, and software, and has an extensive educational service. Competing with International Business Machines (IBM), the world's leading manufacturer of large-scale computers, Amdahl has carved out its own niche with a focus on enterprise data servers, customer service, and consulting. Amdahl's customers include private and public corporations, financial institutions, governmental bodies, universities, and research foundations throughout the world.

Amdahl Corporation was founded on October 19, 1970, in Sunnyvale, California, by Gene M. Amdahl. Born in 1922 in South Dakota, Amdahl left his home state to pursue a doctoral degree in theoretical physics. With a knowledge of electronics gained in the Navy and a familiarity with computer programming garnered from a brief course, Amdahl designed and helped construct an early computer known as the WISC (Wisconsin Integrally Synchronized Computer).

In 1952 Amdahl joined IBM and became chief designer of the IBM 704 computer, which was released in 1954. In 1955 Amdahl and other systems designers began conceptualizing a new computer for IBM, which they christened the Datatron. IBM's Stretch, also known as the IBM 7030, was an outgrowth of the Datatron, a computer using new transistor technology. The name Stretch was not an acronym, but rather stood for "stretching the limits of computer technology development." Although Stretch was a financial failure for IBM, it was valuable as the precursor to the successful IBM System 360. In 1956 Amdahl left IBM; he worked at two other high-technology

firms before returning to IBM four years later. Amdahl later became the principal architect for the phenomenally successful System 360, which was introduced in 1964.

Amdahl was appointed an IBM fellow, and was thus free to pursue his own research projects. In early 1969, while director of IBM's Advanced Computing Systems Laboratory in Menlo Park, California, he began to investigate the company's cost-pricing cycle as it applied to a large computer they were developing. His team concluded that to make the computer pay for itself, IBM would also have to market two scaled-down versions of the advanced technology. IBM management insisted that Amdahl stay with the original plan to create only one large processor, while Amdahl recommended that they shut down the laboratory. The laboratory was closed in the spring of 1969.

Over the following few months, Amdahl reviewed the policies that prevented IBM from aiming at the high end of computer development and presented his analysis to IBM's top three executives. Although the officers agreed with his analysis, they maintained that it would not be in IBM's best interest to change direction. Amdahl decided to strike out on his own.

Amdahl submitted his resignation to IBM for the second time in September 1970 and founded Amdahl Corporation just a few weeks later. Amdahl took none of IBM's technical personnel with him when he left; he was joined only by young financial specialist Ray Williams and two secretaries. Amdahl and Williams determined that they would need between $33 million and $44 million to see a product to completion (in fact, it took $47.5 million). They had chosen a difficult year for raising money, as new capital-gains taxes and an advancing recession made venture capital scarce. Amdahl and Williams first took their business plan to investment bankers, who rejected their proposal because they felt that Amdahl Corporation could not effectively challenge IBM. The pair eventually received $2 million from Heizer Corporation, venture capitalists in Chicago, the day after spending the last of their own investment.

At the same time, three other young California computer companies—MASCOR (Multiple Access Systems Corporation, which was started by staff members who left IBM after the closing of the Advanced Computing Systems Laboratory), Berkeley Computers, and Gemini Computers—had gone bankrupt. Many of their employees joined Amdahl Corporation, forming an impressive technical team.

During Amdahl Corporation's first eight months, it continued the search for more capital. The needed funds came from Fujitsu, a leading Japanese computer manufacturer, which suggested a joint development program and licensing under Amdahl's patents. This 1971 agreement was accompanied by the $5 million investment that Amdahl needed to complete its second phase of development.

In 1972 Nixdorf Computers, a leading German computer manufacturer, agreed to invest $6 million if Nixdorf could represent Amdahl in Europe. Fujitsu also increased its investment, and U.S. investors began to appear. Amdahl amassed a total of $20 million to build a prototype computer and a production facility.

Also in 1972, IBM announced the debut of the 370, its first computer with virtual memory, a flexible, advanced memory technology. Amdahl had been developing a computer like the IBM 370, but without virtual memory, and IBM's introduction forced Amdahl to scrap its initial design.

Amdahl Corporation decided to offer stock publicly in early 1973, but could not find an underwriter. The company then experienced delays with the Securities and Exchange Commission until 1974, by which time the stock market had declined, so Amdahl returned to the private market.

In August 1974 Eugene R. White, a vice-president at Fairchild Camera and Instrument Corporation, was appointed president of Amdahl Corporation. Effecting changes that helped save the company, White laid off almost half the employees and concentrated on marketing efforts and field support services. He was also instrumental in negotiations with Fujitsu and Heizer to get the funding necessary to complete the company's first product.

In June 1975 Amdahl shipped its first computer, the Amdahl 470 V/6, to NASA's Goddard Spaceflight Center in New York. The computer competed directly with IBM's System 370 Model 168. The initial sale was followed by sales to the University of Michigan, Texas A & M University, and the University of Alberta. Massachusetts Mutual Life, Amdahl's first commercial customer, chose Amdahl's 470 V/6 over the IBM 370 when IBM raised its prices and delayed delivery. Other customers followed, including AT&T.

Determined to best IBM, Amdahl was the first truly plug-compatible manufacturer, or manufacturer whose products are compatible with both IBM hardware and software. Critics maintained that the Amdahl machines provided better performance for less money. IBM's machines were water-cooled, while Amdahl's were air-cooled, which decreased installation costs by $50,000 to $250,000. The use of LSI (large-scale-integration), many integrated circuits on each chip, meant the Amdahl 470 V/6 was one-third the size of IBM's 360/168; the V/6 also performed more than twice as fast and sold for about 10 percent less. Machine sales remained slow due to concerns over the company's survival, but by the spring of 1977 Amdahl had 50 units in place, seriously challenging IBM in large-scale computer placements. To improve its cash position, Amdahl decided to sell rather than lease its equipment. IBM responded by slashing prices, forcing Amdahl to follow suit.

In 1976 Amdahl successfully went public with its stock. With the new funds, the company converted its debt to equity, created substantial cash reserves, and found itself operating at a profit. Revenues climbed from less than $14 million in 1975 to $321 million in 1977, with net income of $48.2 million.

In response to the challenge from Amdahl, IBM announced several machine enhancements. Not until the announcement of its 3033 in 1977, however, did IBM come up with a competitor for the price/performance ratio of Amdahl's 470 V/6. Amdahl responded by announcing a new computer: the 470 V/7. About one-and-a-half times faster than IBM's 3033, it would cost only three percent more. A year later Amdahl had installed 100 of the machines.

Amdahl's loosely organized corporate structure was very unusual for such a high-revenue organization. Even after two years of full operation, Gene Amdahl and Gene White still spent much of their time in high-level sales—in fact, many customers insisted on meeting Amdahl personally before closing the deal. Any mention of a chief executive officer was intentionally omitted from the corporate bylaws, but in 1977 Amdahl did hire John C. Lewis as president. Lewis had previously served as president of the business systems and data systems divisions of Xerox Corporation, and had spent ten years in management at IBM. Gene White became deputy chairman.

In early 1979, IBM introduced a line of medium-sized computers called the 4300 series. This line, coupled with reports that IBM would soon be announcing the H-Series of large computers, prompted many Amdahl customers to lease rather than buy equipment in order to be able to shift to an IBM product later. This development created serious cash flow problems at Amdahl. Revenues dropped by $21 million in 1979, with a 64 percent drop in net income.

On September 1, 1979, Gene Amdahl resigned as chairman, a post he had held since 1970. Deputy chairman Eugene R. White became chairman of the board and chief executive officer, a post that had never before been filled. Staying on the board as chairman emeritus, Amdahl led a new technical excellence committee and focused on strategic development. Less than a year later he resigned from the board to form Trilogy Corporation, a computer company that would compete directly with Amdahl and IBM. Recognized as one of the world's leading innovators in computer design, Amdahl again put his creativity to work on a new venture.

In 1979 and 1980 Amdahl Corporation failed in two attempted mergers, first with Memorex Corporation, a manufacturer of computer data-storage equipment, and then with Storage Technology Corporation, a maker of printers and tape and disc storage subsystems. The failures were attributed to Fujitsu, Amdahl's largest shareholder, which feared losing its influence in a merger and sought to keep tight reins on proprietary technology. Fujitsu's demands were rejected by the merger partners.

In November 1980, IBM announced the 3081 processor, previously labeled the H-Series, which would offer twice the performance of IBM's top model, the 3033, upon its completion in late 1981. The industry waited for Amdahl's response. Six days later Gene White announced the 580 series, a computer with processors twice as powerful as the Amdahl 470 series and still compatible with it, which also featured a more compact body and greater energy efficiency. Amdahl's new product was not slated for shipment until April 1982, however, and did not actually ship until August 1982, causing a drop in net income. In addition, Amdahl's early 580 series processor had significant reliability problems and was lacking in some of the features of the new IBM product. Amdahl's competitive advantage was further eroded by a U.S. Justice Department decision to dismiss a 13-year-old antitrust suit against IBM, enabling the giant computer manufacturer to price its products more aggressively and move faster with new technologies.

To expand its market, in 1980 Amdahl completed the successful acquisition of Tran Telecommunications Corporation, a maker of digital data communication networks. In 1982 Amdahl branched into storage devices by offering a direct-access storage device supplied by Fujitsu. This enabled Amdahl to broaden its product base and provided a buffer against the vicissitudes of direct competition with IBM's large-scale computers. By 1988 Amdahl's sales of storage devices had grown to about 20 percent of total sales. To remain competitive in its fierce battle with IBM, Amdahl was spending 13 percent of total sales on research and development in 1983, while IBM spent only 6.3 percent.

In 1984 Amdahl developed UTS, its version of UNIX, the operating system developed by AT&T. Amdahl claimed that UTS, which was compatible with UNIX, operated 25 percent faster run on the Amdahl 580 than on IBM's product, and did so for a lower licensing fee. The developers of the operating system ensured its complete compatibility with IBM's control programs.

Amdahl introduced multiple domain feature (MDF) in late 1984. MDF enabled a computer to run two or more different operating systems concurrently, while also performing multiple tasks. In just over two years, 30 percent of the Amdahl 580 series sites used this feature, cutting costs on software, hardware, and personnel.

In 1984 Heizer decided to liquidate its Amdahl stock. Fujitsu bought the offering, expanding its holdings to about 49 percent. The Japanese firm was prohibited by mutual agreement from owning more than 49.5 percent of Amdahl's shares, and in 1990 Fujitsu held about 43 percent of the company's stock.

Over the years Fujitsu provided important components and subassemblies for Amdahl processors, including LSI logic chips and very large-scale integration emitter-coupled logic chips, which are essential to Amdahl products. Fujitsu also played an important role in the design and manufacture of peripheral products. The two companies worked closely in supporting each other in their respective technological developments.

In May 1985 a former IBM executive, E. Joseph Zemke, joined Amdahl as chief operating officer, sharing the Office of the President with president and CEO John C. Lewis. Zemke had most recently been president and CEO of Auto-Trol Technology of Denver, Colorado, and had been corporate director of marketing at IBM.

Amdahl's model 5890, introduced in October 1985 to compete directly with IBM's Sierra-class CPU, stood up against its IBM counterpart in reliability and technology and offered multiprocessor capabilities that enhanced the performance range of Amdahl processors. In late 1986, Amdahl began shipping its new model. The computers performed even better than advertised, and final quarter sales boosted revenues to nearly $1 billion. The success of the model 5890 was reflected in Amdahl's increased customer base. Between 1980 and 1985 its customer sites in the United States grew from 450 to 1,350, and it expanded internationally from 14 to 19 countries. The company also increased sales of its large-scale disc-storage products made by Fujitsu.

Continued shipment of its successful product lines during 1987 catapulted Amdahl's revenues to $1.5 billion, an increase of almost 56 percent over the previous year, and earnings jumped nearly 250 percent. The company upgraded its successful 5890 to keep abreast of improvements in IBM's 3090 computer. Its further commitment to UTS enhanced its strength.

John C. Lewis was elected chairman of Amdahl in May 1987, retaining the title of CEO. Joseph Zemke became president, but continued his duties as chief operating officer. Gene White, formerly chairman, again became vice-chairman.

For most of its existence, Amdahl had played catch-up to IBM's product announcements, but in May 1988, it took the initiative and announced a new product line, the 5990 processor. Orders poured in. IBM reacted quickly to defend its 69 percent of the U.S. large-scale computer market share, but the new processor— acknowledged as the fastest in the industry—not only out-performed IBM by almost 50 percent, but was also more compact and less costly. By the end of 1988, Amdahl had shipped more than 40 of its new mainframes. The price and performance features of Amdahl's products raised sales nearly 17 percent to $2.1 billion. IBM responded by discounting its systems. Amdahl announced its own discounts, and the decreased profit margin caused earnings to fall by 30 percent in 1989.

Amdahl's consistent ability to produce computers with a superior price/performance ratio helped keep the company competitive in a market dominated by IBM. Staying on the leading edge of technology and catering to its customers' needs launched Amdahl to over $2 billion in revenues in 1989. In February, Amdahl acquired Key Computer Laboratories, Inc., a company that was expanding globally, with 33 percent of its revenues coming from Europe and 8 percent from Asia and the Pacific region in 1989. In 1991 Amdahl introduced Huron, a successful new application development software, and established the Canadian Software Development Centre. The center was run by Huron's creator, Helge Knudsen.

As the 1990s progressed, the major threat to Amdahl's viability no longer appeared to be IBM, but the shrinking mainframe computer market. As smaller, cheaper, and more powerful machines became available, Amdahl found its sales slipping. Excessive costs forced the company to stop work on a mainframe Unix product that had long been underway. By September 1993, sales had collapsed. Amdahl's CEO Zemke was quoted in *Business Week* as saying, "It was like Death Valley." Amdahl shut down factory lines and cut back the work force three times that year. The company reported a net loss for 1993.

Analysts predicted that Amdahl's continued success would require stronger innovation. Amdahl's strategy was to offer its customers integrated packages combining its hardware technology with the industry's most advanced software, as well as stellar support and consulting services. Amdahl's maintenance, support, and consulting services made up 28 percent of revenues in 1993 and increased another 11 percent in the first quarter of 1994. Margins on those services were almost double the hardware margins, and Amdahl's service businesses were consistently given the highest ratings in the industry.

In the following year, Amdahl entered into new partnerships with three computer firms: Electronic Data Systems, nCube, and Sun Microsystems. The agreement with Electronic Data Systems spawned the Antares Alliance Group, a joint software development group 80-percent owned by Amdahl. Antares was formed to market Amdahl's Huron and research new software ideas and prototypes for business analysis and modeling programs. Helge Knudsen became director of the Antares Research Institute.

In 1994 Amdahl introduced the Xplorer 2000 series. The new product was the result of an alliance between Amdahl, Oracle, and Information Builders, Inc. The partnership was formed, according to *Software Magazine,* to explore opportunities to create "massively parallel database servers and software that will let customers process thousands of transactions per second and share data between MVS and Unix systems."

Later that year, Amdahl and Sun Microsystems introduced A + Edition, a group of extensions that allow Sun's symmetrical multiprocessing servers to perform more efficiently when a higher number of total possible servers are working. The software accomplished this by providing tuning for database applications with a large number of users and more evenly distributing the workload among the processors in the servers. While the new product was well received, some potential customers expressed concern about the cost for the value.

Businesses' need to downsize their information management, both in terms of money and space, may create a window of opportunity for computer companies that can produce products allowing companies to use their existing hardware and software more effectively. Software links, along with support and consulting services that allow users to manage huge amounts of data more efficiently, may be preferable to new equipment purchases. Although Amdahl's fortunes have fluctuated in a very volatile market, it has repeatedly emerged from near-extinction, and its tenacity and innovation may continue to pull it through over the long term.

Principal Subsidiaries: Amdahl Australia Pty. Ltd.; Amdahl Belgium S.A.; Amdahl Canada Limited; Amdahl Computer Systeme Gesellschaft m.b.H.; Amdahl Computersysteme Palais Lichtenstein; Amdahl Danmark Computer Systems; Amdahl Deutschland GmbH; Amdahl France S.A.; Amdahl Intl. Hong Kong; Amdahl International Management Services Limited (U.K.); Amdahl Ireland Ltd.; Amdahl Italia S.p.A.; Amdahl Nederland B.V.; Amdahl New Zealand; Amdahl Norge A/S; Amdahl Pacific Basin Operations (Thailand); Amdahl Pacific Services Pty. Ltd. (Australia); Amdahl Singapore; Amdahl Svenska AB; Amdahl Switzerland AG; Amdahl (U.K.) Ltd.

Further Reading:

Amdahl, Gene M., "The Early Chapters of the PCM Story," *Datamation,* February 1979.

Barker, Paul, "Developer of Huron Goes Back to His Roots," *Computing Canada,* March 30, 1994, p. 13.

Bozman, Jean S., "Amdahl, Sun Honor Promise with A +," *Computerworld,* October 3, 1994, p. 77.

Cancilla, Susan, "Amdahl, IBM Awake to Mainframe Revival," *Info Canada,* March 1995, p. IC2.

Hof, Robert D., "Amdahl Escapes 'Death Valley,' But Now What?" *Business Week,* May 16, 1994, p. 88.

Schmedel, Scott, "Taking on the Industry Giant," *Harvard Business Review,* March–April 1980.

Ubois, Jeff, and Vaughan, Jack, "Parellelizing DBs Come to Town," *Software Magazine,* June 1994, p. 24.

Uttal, Bro, "Gene Amdahl Takes Aim at I.B.M.," *Fortune,* September 1977.

—Ann T. Russell
updated by Katherine Smethurst

American Maize-Products Co.

250 Harbor Drive
Stamford, Connecticut 06902
U.S.A.
(203) 356-9000
Fax: (203) 359-1020

Wholly Owned Subsidiary of Eridania Beghin-Say, S.A.
Incorporated: 1906 as Western Glucose Co.
Sales: $441 million
Employees: 1,450
Stock Exchanges: American Chicago
SICs: 2046 Wet Corn Milling; 2048 Prepared Feeds & Feed
    Ingredients for Animals & Fowls; 2087 Flavoring Extracts
    & Flavoring Syrups, Nec

American Maize-Products Co. manufactures and sells products
derived from corn wet milling, such as corn sweeteners and
starches for use in the manufacturing processes of several industries. In the wet-milling process the starch component is either
dried for sale or processed further into other products. These
include high-fructose corn syrup, which is widely used as a
sweetener in the soft-drink industry. In the mid 1990s American
Maize was the only producer in North America and the largest
producer in the world of cyclodextrins, doughnut-shaped molecular structures produced from starch that had many applications. American Maize was acquired in 1995 by a French company, Eridania Beghin-Say, S.A., a unit of Montedison SpA and
the largest starch producer in Europe. Eridania then announced
it would sell 88 percent of American Maize's tobacco-products
subsidiary, Swisher International, Inc.

American Maize originated as Western Glucose Co. in
Hammond, Indiana, and was incorporated in Maine in August
1906. It produced two items: corn starch and corn syrup. Wil-
liam Ziegler acquired control of the company in 1907. Royal
Baking Powder Co. purchased a majority of the capital stock of
Western Glucose in January 1908 and changed its name to
American Maize-Products two months later. Royal Baking
Powder sold its holdings in American Maize to its stockholders
of record on October 11, 1928.

At the time of this sale American Maize was manufacturing
corn sugar, cereal sugar, refined corn oil, special starches, dextrins, and other corn products. Its plant in Hammond comprised
42 buildings and contained 645,000 square feet of floor space,
with a grinding capacity of about 35,000 bushels of corn per
day. The company had about 600 employees. Its assets were
valued at $7.5 million at the end of 1929. Net income increased
from $81,823 in 1927 to $1,558,440 in 1929. The company had
its headquarters in New York City.

American Maize continued to make a profit and pay dividends
during the Great Depression of the 1930s. By the end of 1933
the number of its employees had grown to about 1,000. Net
income rose from $60,586 in 1935 (the most severe year of the
Dust Bowl drought) to $777,663 in 1939. By the end of the
decade branch offices had been established in Atlanta, Boston,
Chicago, Los Angeles, Pittsburgh, St. Paul, and Seattle.

By 1950 American Maize was manufacturing a line of packaged
goods as well as syrups, starches, corn oil, and various chemicals derived from corn. The number of buildings at its plant had
grown to 47, with 789,149 square feet of office space, and
grinding capacity had increased to about 40,000 bushels of corn
per day. Branch offices had been added in Brooklyn and Buffalo. C. M. Armstrong, Inc., had been established as the company's sales agent in the chemical field. William Ziegler, Jr.,
was chairman of the board. Net sales grew from $10.1 million in
1940 to $25.4 million in 1949, and net income from $549,744 to
$782,432. The best year of the decade was 1946, when net sales
reached $28.6 million and net income $1,415,201.

The 1950s was an uneventful decade for American Maize. Its
plant capacity remained the same, and its mix of products
changed little. Net sales rose only from $28.4 million in 1950 to
$36 million in 1959, after reaching a decade-long high of nearly
$38 million in 1956. Net income, however, rose from a decade
low of $513,206 in 1951 to a high of nearly $2.4 million in 1958
before slumping slightly to $2.1 million in 1959. Reflecting
higher profits, the dividend per share increased in the late 1950s,
and investors bid up the stock from a high of $36 a share in 1955
to a high of $84 in 1959.

By the mid 1960s American Maize had moved aggressively into
the development of new products. A new class of carbohydrate
esters with a variety of nonfood as well as food uses, the starch
phosphates, were being produced by the company at a pilot
facility in Central City, Nebraska, from a special type of corn
grown under contract. Among these products was Ediflex, a
wholly digestible, water-soluble transparent packaging film. By
this time American Maize was manufacturing more than 100
different products. Although the food industry was taking 70
percent of its volume, it was also selling to the paper, textile,
adhesive, chemical, oil-well drilling, pharmaceutical, and fermentation industries. Net sales reached $50.7 million in 1965,
and net income $3.4 million.

In 1966 American Maize moved into the tobacco-products field
by acquiring Jno. Swisher & Son, Inc., a privately owned cigar
maker based in Jacksonville, Florida, for $36 million in cash.
Swisher, a tobacco grower in the South and producer of King
Edward cigars, the best-selling cigar in the United States, had
earned $2.9 million in 1965 on sales of $42.2 million. It became
a subsidiary of American Maize. In 1969 Swisher acquired
Boyer Brothers, Inc., a privately owned manufacturer of popular-priced cup candies, for 20,000 shares of newly created preferred stock.

By expansion and acquisition, American Maize had grown into a much larger company by 1970. Its plant comprised about 60 buildings on about 80 acres of land, and its grinding capacity had increased to 60,000 bushels of corn per day. Ediflex, made in Central City, was being shipped in rolls to a packaging plant in Saddle Brook, New Jersey. The company owned a warehouse in Beacon Falls, Connecticut, and leased warehouses in Pittsburgh and South Boston, Massachusetts. Swisher owned three cigar-manufacturing plants, a filler-tobacco preparation plant, and 4,400 acres of land in western Florida. Candy and related products were being manufactured in Altoona, Pennsylvania. William Ziegler, Jr.'s son, William Ziegler III, became chairman of the board in 1964.

Net sales reached $106.6 million in 1969. Corn processing accounted from 48 percent, tobacco for 47 percent, and candy for five percent. Of corn-processing sales, corn syrup and corn-syrup solids for the food and beverage industries accounted for about 45 percent, starches and dextrins used by the paper, textile, chemical-laundry, and food industries for 33 percent, and corn germ sold to other refiners for further processing and corn meal and feed sold to livestock-feed dealers for 22 percent. However, net income was only $3.4 million in 1969. The company's acquisitions had raised debt from zero to an estimated 39 percent of total capitalization by the end of 1971, the year the company also bought S.A. Schonbrunn & Co., a privately held coffee roaster, for $14.6 million in cash.

American Maize's program of diversification was based on its belief that the growth prospects of corn refining were limited, with sales growing an average seven to eight percent a year, and earnings perhaps ten percent a year at best. Its objective was to dilute sales based on corn milling to about 25 percent of total sales. The company's cigars were seen as soon outstripping corn products in both sales and profits. Its coffee brands, including Savarin, Medaglia d'Oro, El Pico, and Old Dutch, were well established and popular in the Northeast. Boyer, whose products included Mallo Cup and Smoothie, was thought to be the second-largest producer of cup candies in the United States. Chocolate manufacturing was added to its operations in 1971.

By the mid 1970s American Maize's earnings picture had improved. The company had profits of $9.2 million in 1974 on sales of $218.1 million. Ironically, however, that year corn processing, rather than the newer areas of company operations, accounted for more than 80 percent of operating profits. The Hammond plant increased to grinding capacity of 85,000 bushels a day in 1975 and was operating at 90 percent of this capacity. By contrast, cigar consumption was slipping, and the coffee operation lost $500,000 in 1974. William Ziegler III became American Maize's chief executive officer in 1975. The company moved its executive offices to Stamford, Connecticut, in 1979.

Despite its problems with diversification, American Maize was seeking a new area of profits in building materials. In 1974 it acquired Briggs and Lundy Lumber Cos. for about $3.7 million. Reestablished as the company's Lundy-Briggs Co., Inc., division, it operated building materials and home improvement centers in Pennsylvania and upstate New York. In 1978 American Maize acquired certain assets of Berwind Corp.'s Buchanan Building Supply division, a marketer of home-improvement supplies and

construction materials, for $5.2 million. A year later the company purchased Dill Enterprises, Inc., and its affiliate, Lloyd's of Connecticut Inc., for $7.5 million. This acquisition added 19 Lloyd Lumber stores in Connecticut and New York to the 20 similar stores in Pennsylvania and New York.

In 1975 American Maize joined with the Amalgamated Sugar Co. of Ogden, Utah, a major beet-sugar processing company, in a joint venture to produce high-fructose corn syrups. The resulting Amalgamaize Co. opened a 30,000-bushel-a-day facility near Decatur, Alabama, in 1977. The wisdom of this decision was manifest by 1980, when Coca-Cola Co. authorized its domestic bottlers to substitute high-fructose corn syrup for up to half the (more-expensive) sugar in Coca-Cola. Later Pepsi-Cola announced that it would also use high-fructose corn syrup as a partial substitute for sugar. During the five-year period that ended in 1979, corn processing accounted for 45.2 percent of American Maize's revenues and 51.5 percent of its profits. American Maize bought Amalgamated Sugar's half-share of Amalgamaize in 1983.

American Maize's sales reached a record $413.7 million in 1980 and its net income a record $10.7 million. Next to corn processing, cigar production was the largest source of company profits, with Swisher's gains in market share compensating for a 15-year-long decline in cigar consumption. Candy operations played a relatively insignificant role in the company's finances. Coffee's contribution to profits had been low and highly volatile because of the fluctuating price of the commodity. The company sold its Schonbrunn coffee subsidiary to Tetley Inc. for about $16 million in 1982 and its Boyer candy subsidiary to Consolidated Brands Inc. in 1984.

Building-materials supply stores, under the Briggs, Buchanan, and Lloyd names, were seen as a growth area for American Maize in the early 1980s. However, although accounting for about 25 percent of the company's sales volume in this period, they did not fulfill their promise, losing almost $500,000 in 1981 and about $1 million in 1982. In 1988, when this unit, Lloyd Home and Building Centers, accounted for revenues of $107 million, or nearly 20 percent of American Maize's total, the company took a $4 million restructuring charge, including $2 million for the writeoff of intangible assets. American Maize dissolved Lloyd in 1990 by closing or selling the remaining 17 stores, taking $20 million in losses.

American Maize formed Amalgamaize into a new subsidiary, American Fructose Corp., in 1983. It sold some of its common stock to the public in 1984, raising $20 million and leaving American Maize with a 68-percent share in the company. By then high-fructose corn syrup had become the largest volume product in the 100-year history of corn wet milling, and American Maize was completing an expansion program that would make the Decatur plant capable of producing 550 million pounds of the product (on a dry basis) per year. To raise production capacity even higher, American Maize acquired Amstar Corp.'s Dimmitt division in November 1984 for about $43 million in cash, giving American Fructose a second plant, in Dimmitt, Texas.

Meanwhile, production at American Maize's Hammond facility increasingly was being given to specialty starch and syrup products. In 1988 the first plant in North American was opened at Hammond for the production of cyclodextrins, biosynthetically produced starch-derived chemicals with broad application in the food industry to enhance taste, smell, texture, and color.

Swisher increasingly was giving attention to the more promising overseas cigar market, having acquired an exporter, Martin Bros. Tobacco Co., in 1980. European cigar consumption was rated at almost three times the level in the United States. In 1986 American Maize acquired the smokeless tobacco (chewing tobacco and snuff) business of the Helme Tobacco division of Culbro Corp. for about $67 million. It also purchased some assets of Universal Cigar Corp. for about $13 million. Tobacco products accounted for 24 percent of American Maize's sales volume of $547.5 million in 1988 and an impressive 71 percent of its operating income of $27.5 million that year.

By 1990 American Fructose's annual capacity to manufacture high-fructose corn syrup had grown to one million pounds. Roughly two-thirds of its sales of $155.4 million in 1988 came from this product, of which it held about eight percent of the market, and 26 percent of its fructose sales were to Coca-Cola. In 1993 American Maize acquired and merged American Fructose, paying $30.8 million in cash for about 11 percent of its shares and exchanging the rest of the shares for a like number of American Maize's class A common stock.

Problems with American Maize's home-improvement centers resulted in a deficit of $2.8 million in 1989. The company's net sales of $547.5 million in 1988 was not topped until 1994, and although net income recovered smartly during 1990–92, operating profits fell to only $214,000 in 1993. Mainly because of an accounting change for retirement benefits, it took a $31.2 million net-income loss that year. By then Ziegler's stewardship of the company was being challenged by his own sister. Ziegler had added the posts of president and chief operating officer to his responsibilities in 1989. A year later Helen Ziegler Steinkraus filed the first of a half-dozen lawsuits in four states aimed at removing her brother and bringing in new management. She won part of her objective when Ziegler agreed in 1992 to step down as president and allow his successor to run day-to-day operations.

During this battle it emerged that the family holding company controlling American Maize had an odd number of shares, and that Ziegler's trusts held one more share than his sister's trusts, which in turn gave him control of 47 percent of the company's Class B voting shares to go with another seven percent in his own name. Steinkraus and her family contended that this arrangement violated various wills. Her suit was rejected by a New York City court in 1994. Nevertheless, in March 1995, while Steinkraus's case was on appeal, the directors of American Maize accepted a $40-a-share, $430 million bid (later raised to $441.7 million) for the company by Eridania Beghin-Say S.A., a French agro-industrial concern. The directors planned to get around Ziegler's opposition by issuing new shares of Class B stock to put him in the minority.

Ziegler filed a lawsuit in Maine to block the issuance of the new shares and won a temporary blocking order in April 1995. The impasse ended in July, when Eridania overcame Ziegler's opposition by agreeing to sell 88 percent of American Maize's tobacco business, Swisher International, for $165 million to a group led by him and to loan him $20 million to finance the acquisition. According to a federal filing, an investor group had been prepared to offer $225 million for Swisher, which reported operating profits of $24 million—up 73 percent—in 1994. Eridania said it intended to retain the remaining 12 percent of Swisher.

American Maize had net income of $26.9 million in 1994 on net sales of $604 million. Of this total, corn processing accounted for 73 percent of net sales, or about $441 million, with tobacco products responsible for the remainder. Corn processing accounted for 65 percent of company profits, or about $17.5 million. The company's long-term debt was $264.7 million at the end of 1994.

The Ingredients Division, located in Hammond, was manufacturing all of American Maize's corn starches in 1995, extracting them from common, waxy, and high amylose and various new hybrid strains of corn. It also produced modifications of these starches by chemical or physical processes to make products designed to serve the particular needs of various food and industrial uses. Specialty starch products derived from waxy corn were being used as stabilizers, fillers, thickeners, and extenders in such products as canned and frozen foods, pie fillings, puddings, salad dressings, baby foods, soups, and snack foods. Waxy corn starches were also being used as adhesives by the gummed-tape industry.

In addition, the Ingredients Division was producing corn-syrup solids, maltodextrins, dextrins, and cyclodextrins. Corn-syrup solids and maltodextrins were being used in a variety of food applications, including dry-food and beverage mixes and microwaveable and convenience foods. Dextrins were being sold to the paper, adhesives, textile, and chemical industries for their sizing and adhesive properties. Cyclodextrins had many applications, including fragrance carrying, cholesterol removing, and drug delivery in the pharmaceutical industry. Corn germ, corn-gluten feed, and corn-gluten meal were byproducts of this division's operations. Corn germ was being sold for further processing into corn oil and corn-germ meal. Corn-gluten feed and corn-gluten meal were being sold for use in animal feeds.

The Sweetener Division, based in Chicago, was producing glucose corn syrups and high-fructose corn syrup. Corn syrups were being used in many foods and beverages for both sweetness and also such attributes as color, texture, and freezability. High-fructose corn syrup was being used primarily by the soft-drink industry as a sweetener. Sales to Coca-Cola accounted for about 14 percent of American Maize's revenues in 1994.

American Maize's wholly owned Hammond facility, located on about 113 acres, had a grinding capacity of about 85,000 bushels of corn per day in 1995. A construction program, expected to be completed by the end of 1996, was to increase grinding capacity by about 30 percent and corn-syrup capacity by about 50 percent. The leased Decatur facility had a grinding capacity of about 55,000 bushels per day. The part-owned Dimmitt facility also had a grinding capacity of about 55,000 bushels per day. American Maize was leasing its executive offices in Stamford, its Sweetener Division offices in Chicago, various storage and distribution facilities in various locations, and rail-transportation equipment.

Principal Subsidiaries: American Maize-Products Decatur Inc.; American Maize-Products Dimmitt Inc.; American Maize Technology, Inc.; AMP International Exporting, Inc. (Barbados); AMPCO Holding Corp.

Further Reading:

"American Maize-Products Company," *Wall Street Transcript,* September 10, 1984, p. 75,195.

Barrett, William P., "Soured Blood," *Forbes,* June 8, 1992, p. 126.

Gordon, Mitchell, "Higher Prices, Strong Demand Sweeten American Maize Profits," *Barron's,* January 12, 1976, pp. 62–63.

——, "Not Chickenfeed: American Maize-Products Sees Gains from Building-Supply Stores," *Barron's,* January 10, 1983, pp. 43–45.

Lesly, Elizabeth, "A Bittersweet Harvest for American Maize," *Business Week,* August 7, 1995, p. 31.

Lipin, Steven, "Single Share Shapes Furor in Family, Future of Firm," *Wall Street Journal,* March 7, 1995, p. C1.

Muldoon, Joseph B., "American Maize-Products," *Wall Street Transcript,* March 9, 1981, p. 60,781.

Nacmanie, Miron, "American Maize-Products Co.," *Wall Street Transcript,* February 21, 1972, p. 27,269.

Shalita, Barbara L., "Acquisition Route Means Growth for American Maize," *Investment Dealers' Digest,* January 9, 1967, pp. 26–27.

"Strong Prices, New Consumer Lines Spur American Maize-Products Net," *Barron's,* November 30, 1970, pp. 28–29.

Trovell, Thomas N., Jr., "High on Fructose," *Barron's,* September 15, 1980, pp. 48–49, 54.

Wyatt, Edward A., "The Rains Came," *Barron's,* June 12, 1989, pp. 15, 67.

—Robert Halasz

Amoco Corporation

200 East Randolph Drive
Chicago, Illinois 60601
U.S.A.
(312) 856-6111
Fax: (312) 856-2460

Public Company
Incorporated: 1889 as Standard Oil Company (Indiana)
Employees: 43,205
Sales: $29.32 billion
Stock Exchanges: New York Midwest Pacific Toronto Basel
 Geneva Lausanne Zürich
SICs: 1311 Crude Petroleum & Natural Gas; 2911 Petroleum
 Refining; 2869 Industrial Organic Chemicals Not
 Elsewhere Classified; 6719 Holding Companies Not
 Elsewhere Classified

Amoco Corporation is active in three main fields within the petroleum, natural gas, and chemical industries: exploration and production, petroleum products, and chemical products. Amoco is the largest producer of natural gas in North America, sells gasoline through more than 9,600 service stations in 30 states, and produces such chemical products as polymers, fabrics, fibers, and chemical feedstocks. It currently searches for oil and natural gas in 25 countries, a much more targeted exploration operation than in previous years.

Amoco has been in business since 1889, though it was known as Standard Oil Company (Indiana) until its name was changed in 1985. The company was formed outside Whiting, Indiana, a location chosen by John Rockefeller's Standard Oil Trust as a refinery site close enough to sites in the growing midwestern market to keep freight costs low, yet far enough away to avoid disturbing residents.

From the beginning, the Whiting facility was organized as a self-supporting entity, planning for long-term expansion. Though refining was its main activity, it also constructed oil barrels for transportation and manufactured an oil-based product line consisting of axle grease, harness oil, paraffin wax for candles, and kerosene produced from the crude oil. The oil itself flowed to Chicago and other midwestern cities via two pipes originating in Lima, Ohio. Land transportation began on the refinery's grounds, at a railroad terminal belonging to the Chicago & Calumet Terminal Railroad, a company over which a

Standard Oil interest had gained control. This terminal's placement gave the company exclusive use of the tracks, access to the West and the Southwest, and a direct route that eliminated the expense of switching tolls.

Standard (Indiana) had no direct marketing organization of its own. After the Standard Oil Trust was liquidated in 1892 by order of the Ohio Supreme Court, the 20 companies under its jurisdiction reverted to their former status and became subsidiaries of Standard Oil Company (New Jersey). The functions of Standard Oil (Indiana) were then expanded to include marketing.

The company's capitalization was increased from $500,000 to $1 million, which was divided into $100 shares. Standard Oil still owned about 54 percent of Standard (Indiana). Standard (Indiana) used the extra cash to buy Standard Oil Company (Minnesota) and Standard Oil Company (Illinois), formerly P.C. Hanford Oil Company, an oil-marketing organization in Chicago. The extra capital expanded Standard's sales territory, which was broadened even further when the property of Chester Oil Company of Minnesota was bought. Other acquisitions followed, and by 1901 the company was marketing through its own organization in 11 states.

At first, Standard (Indiana) had few competitors in the petroleum-product market. It enjoyed about 88 percent of the business in kerosene and heavy fuel oil. After competition began to grow, Standard (Indiana) fought back with strategically placed bulk storage stations and subsidiary companies in competitive areas that cut prices and drove competitors out. Earnings rose from $605,781 in 1896 to a high of almost $4.2 million in 1899, but the company's competitive practices and its growing market share made it the target of government agencies. In 1911, after a court battle lasting almost three years, Standard Oil Company (New Jersey)—the parent company to Standard (Indiana) and other Standard companies—was ordered to relinquish supervision of its subsidiaries.

Gasoline sales had risen from 31.6 million gallons to 1.57 billion between 1897 and 1911. Once independent, Standard (Indiana) began to cater to the burgeoning automobile market, opening a Minneapolis, Minnesota, service station in 1912. Chicago's first service station opened in 1913, and by 1918, there were 451 altogether. Together with growing sales of road oil, asphalt, and other supporting products, the automotive industry provided one-third of all Standard (Indiana) business.

To get as much gasoline out of each barrel of crude as possible, Standard formulated the cracking process, which doubled the yield by separating the oil's molecules, by means of heat and pressure, into a dense liquid plus a lighter product that would boil in gasoline's range. The possibility of cheaper gasoline and a new line of petroleum-based products made the method attractive to other refiners, who licensed it, accounting for 34 percent of the company's total profits between 1913 and 1922.

With the end of World War I, company chairman Colonel Robert Stewart's top priority was to find a secure source of crude oil, to meet the rapidly expanding demand for gasoline and kerosene. Before the war, Standard had depended on the Prairie Oil and Gas Company for its supply, but military needs diverted Prairie's crude to the refineries along the Atlantic seaboard. To obtain a reliable source of crude oil, Stewart acquired 33 percent of Midwest Refining Company of Wyoming, in 1920. A half interest in the Sinclair Pipe Company was purchased in 1921, for $16.4 million in cash, improving transportation capacity. Sinclair's 2,900 miles of pipeline ran from north Texas to Chicago, encompassed almost 6,000 wells, and ran through oil-rich Wyoming.

Standard bought an interest in the Pan American Petroleum & Transport Company in 1925. The interest, costing $37.6 million, was the largest oil consolidation in the history of the industry, giving Standard (Indiana) access to one of the world's largest tanker fleets and entry into oil fields in Mexico, Venezuela, and Iraq. In 1929 Standard (Indiana) acquired another chunk of Pan American stock through a stock swap, bringing its total ownership of Pan American to 81 percent.

Pan American also introduced Standard to the American Oil Company, of Baltimore, Maryland. Started by the Blaustein family, American Oil marketed most of Pan American's oil in the eastern United States and was 50 percent-owned by Pan American and 50 percent-owned by the Blausteins. The Blausteins were initiators of the first measuring gasoline-pump and inventors of the high-octane Amoco-Gas that reduced engine knocking.

Though expensive, these investments proved to be sound; by 1929, the Depression notwithstanding, Standard Oil (Indiana) was second only to Standard Oil (New Jersey) as a buyer of crude oil. Equally profitable as a supplier, the company's net earnings for 1929 were $78.5 million after taxes.

In 1929 Stewart was followed as CEO by Edward G. Seubert, who continued to strengthen Standard's crude oil supply. With an eye to future supply security, Seubert shifted the emphasis to buying and developing crude oil-producing properties like McMan Oil and Gas Company, a 1930 purchase that provided 10,000 barrels daily. Also in 1930, Standard acquired both the remaining 50 percent interest in the Sinclair Pipe Line Company and the Sinclair Crude Oil Purchasing Company for $72.5 million, giving it control over one of the country's largest pipeline systems and crude oil buying agencies. These subsidiaries now became the Stanolind Pipe Line Company and the Stanolind Crude Oil Purchasing Company; they were joined in 1931 by the Stanolind Oil & Gas Company, a newly organized subsidiary absorbing several smaller ones.

In 1929 a retail venture called the Atlas Supply Company, which was co-organized with five other Standard firms, had been organized to sell automobile tires and other accessories nationwide. The Great Depression, however, made competition fierce by the end of 1930. Even worse conditions threatened after the largest oil field in history was found in east Texas in late 1930. The new field caused production to rise quickly to a daily average of 300,000 barrels in 1931, glutting the market. Ruthless price-cutting followed. Standard (Indiana) did not engage in this practice, preferring instead to curtail exploration and drilling activities. As a result, only 49.9 billion barrels were produced in 1931, as against 55.1 billion the year before, and the company's 13 domestic facilities operated well below capacity. The 45,073 employees worked on construction projects, and accepted wage cuts and part-time employment to minimize layoffs. The flow of cheap crude oil continued, often in excess of limits set by state regulatory bodies; gas sales were accompanied by premiums like candy, ash trays, and cigarette lighters. Track-side stations, where gasoline was pumped from the tank car into the customer's automobile, posed another price-cutting threat. Also prevalent were cooperatives organized by farmers, who would buy tank cars of gasoline for distribution among members to save money. These conditions caused 1932 earnings to reach only $16.5 million—down from $17.5 million in 1931.

In 1932 Standard decided to sell Pan American's foreign interests to Standard Oil (New Jersey). These properties cost Standard Oil (New Jersey) just under $48 million cash plus about 1.8 million shares of Standard Oil (New Jersey) stock.

By 1934 the worst of the Depression was over. Activities in Texas led the Stanolind Oil & Gas Company to the Hastings field, which held 43 producing wells by the end of 1935. Also in 1935, more oil-producing acreage in east Texas came with Stanolind Oil & Gas Company's $42 million purchase of the properties of Beaumont-based Yount-Lee Oil Company, an acquisition that helped Stanolind Oil & Gas to increase its daily average production to 68,965 barrels.

During the 1930s overproduction began to threaten, and federal and state governments tried to curb oil production with heavy taxes. Standard felt the bite in Iowa's 1935 chain-store tax, which could not be justified by their service stations' profit margin. The company therefore turned back leased stations to their owners, and leased company-owned stations to independent operators, to be operated as separate outlets. By the following July, all 11,685 Standard (Indiana) service stations were independently operated and the company was once more primarily a producer distributing oil at wholesale prices. This move spurred the newly independent entrepreneurs, whose increased sales helped to achieve a net profit for Standard of $30.2 million for 1935.

When Standard reached its 50th year in 1939, during World War II, its research chemists were working to improve the high-octane fuels needed for military and transport planes. Standard's engineers cooperated with other companies to build the pipelines necessary for oil transportation. By 1942, the "Big Inch" pipeline carried a daily load of 300,000 barrels of crude from Texas to the East Coast, where most of it was used to support the war effort. Loss of manpower and government steel restrictions curbed operations, yet the company produced 47 million barrels of crude and purchased about 102 million barrels from outside sources. Other wartime products from Standard plants included paraffin wax coatings for military food rations, toluene (the main ingredient for TNT), butane, and butylene for aviation gasoline and synthetic rubber.

On January 1, 1945, Seubert retired as president and chief executive officer of the company. He left behind him 33,244 employees, sales of crude oil topping the 1944 figure by 37.1 percent, and a gross income of $618.9 million. Seubert was succeeded as chairman and CEO by Robert E. Wilson, formerly president of Pan American Petroleum & Transport Company, and Alonzo W. Peake became president. Peake had been vice-president of production.

The management style instituted by Wilson and Peake differed from the centralized, solo authority Seubert preferred. The two men split the supervisory authority, with no overlap of direct authority. Wilson was responsible for finance, research and development, law, and industrial relations, while Peake's commitments included refining, production, supply and transportation, and sales and long-range planning. Responsibility for operating subsidiaries was split between the two. The result was a decentralized organization, making for swifter, more cooperative decision-making at all levels.

In 1948 Stanolind Oil & Gas formed a foreign exploration department to head exploration attempts in Canada and other countries. The new team spent more than $98 million by 1950, with Canada and the Gulf of Mexico its prime targets.

By 1952 Standard Oil (Indiana) was acknowledged as the nation's largest domestic oil company. It possessed 12 refineries able to market its products in 41 states, plus almost 5,000 miles of crude oil gathering lines, 10,000 miles of trunk lines and 1,700 miles of refined product pipelines. By 1951, gross income had reached $1.54 billion.

In 1955 Peake retired as president, to be succeeded by former Executive Vice-president Frank Prior, who inherited the problem of a decrease in allowable production days in the state of Texas, as a result of additions to oil reserves in the state. The rising amount of imported oil was another problem that arose during Peake's tenure. The total had swelled from 490,000 barrels per day in 1951 to 660,000 barrels in 1954.

Nevertheless, cheaper international exploration costs spurred Standard (Indiana) to again become active in the growing foreign oil arena that it had all but left in 1932 when it sold Pan American's foreign interests. To handle international land leasing and joint ventures, the company organized Pan American International Oil Corporation in New York, as a subsidiary of Pan American Petroleum. Foreign operations included exploration rights for 13 million acres in Cuba, obtained in 1955; a subsidiary company formed in Venezuela in 1958, for joint exploration of 180,000 acres together with other companies; and 23 million acres obtained for exploration in Libya.

The traditional oil-industry profit arrangement for international activities had been an even split between the company and the host government, though several firms had quietly bent the guidelines. Standard (Indiana) broke openly with this custom in a 1958 deal with the National Iranian Oil Company (NIOC), in which Standard (Indiana) split the profits evenly, then gave NIOC half of its own share, to which it added a $25 million bonus.

The late 1950s also saw domestic reorganization. In 1957 the company consolidated nine subsidiaries into four larger companies. Stanolind Oil & Gas Company became Pan American Petroleum Corporation, consolidating all Standard Oil (Indiana) crude oil and natural gas exploration and production. American Oil Pipe Line Company, a former subsidiary of American Oil, was merged into Service Pipe Line Company—which had been known as Stanolind Pipe Line Company until 1950—focused on oil transport. Crude oil and natural gas purchasing operations were combined to form the Indiana Oil Purchasing Company; and Amoco Chemicals Corporation consolidated all chemical activities into a single organization. Total income for 1957 was about $2 billion.

In 1960 company President John Swearingen succeeded Prior as chief executive officer, the chairmanship being left vacant. Swearingen turned both domestic and foreign operations over to subsidiaries, making Standard Oil (Indiana) entirely a holding company. Operating assets were transferred to the American Oil Company, into which the Utah Oil Refining Company was also merged. American Oil's responsibilities now included the manufacture, transport, and sale of all company petroleum products in 45 states, though limited marketing operations in three other states were also maintained. This consolidation allowed the company to develop a national image and provided more efficiency in staff use and storage and transport flexibility. Coverage being national, the company was able to advertise nationally and demand better rates from ground and air transporters.

Standard (Indiana) also became concerned with product trade names. The 1911 breakup had left several former Standard (New Jersey) subsidiaries in different areas of the country with the Standard Oil name and rights to the associated trademarks. American Oil thus had the right to use the Standard name only in the 15 midwestern states that had been the company's original territory. Thus, in 1957, the word "American," together with the Standard Oil (Indiana) logo, was used in all other states. Since a five-letter name was easier for motorists to note, in 1961 the company began to replace the brand name American with Amoco, the name first coined by American Oil's original owners for the high-octane, anti-knock gasoline that had powered the Charles Lindbergh trans-Atlantic flight. Familiar within the company since the 1945 organization of the Amoco Chemicals Corporation, "Amoco" was used increasingly on products and by subsidiaries, until, by 1971, major subsidiaries everywhere had "Amoco" in their names.

In 1961 Standard's total income reached almost $2.1 billion, yielding net earnings of $153.9 million. Continuing with methodical reorganization, Swearingen oversaw the expansion and modernization of the company's domestic refining capacity as well as 11 of its 14 catalytic cracking units. An aggressive marketing program featured large, strategically placed retail outlets, plus the addition of Avis car-rental privileges to the credit-card services that had been in operation since the early 1930s. By the end of 1966 there were 5.5 million card holders, encouraging American Oil to go national with its motor club.

Because only 8 percent of its assets were located overseas, Standard (Indiana) still lacked a large foreign market for crude oil. Swearingen moved swiftly to close the gap. By 1964 foreign explorations were taking place in Mozambique, Indonesia, Venezuela, Argentina, Colombia, and Iran. Refining and marketing were also flourishing, through the acquisition of a 25,000-barrel-per-day refinery near Cremona, Italy, and about 700 Italian service stations. About 250 service stations were also opened in Australia in 1961, along with a 25,000-barrel-per-day refinery. Other foreign refineries were to be found in West Germany, England, Pakistan, and the West Indies. In 1967 Standard began production in the Persian Gulf Cyrus field, by which time the huge El Morgan field in the Gulf of Suez was producing 45,000 barrels daily.

The market for Standard's chemical products also increased during the mid-1960s. To keep pace with demand for the raw materials used in polyester fiber and film, the company built a new facility at Decatur, Alabama, in 1965, adding another in Texas City, Texas, a year later. There were also 641 retail chemical-fertilizer outlets in the Midwest and the South. The popularity of polystyrene for packaging also grew. All these advances ensured profitability; overall chemical sales rose to $158 million by the end of 1967, on total revenues of almost $3.6 billion.

Fuel shortages and the wave of OPEC price rises, nationalizations, and takeovers of the early 1970s underlined the importance of oil exploration. Swearingen's strategy was to accumulate as much domestic exploration acreage as possible before other companies acted, while organizing production in developing foreign markets that were not too competitive.

To capitalize on concern about air pollution, the company introduced a 91-octane lead-free gasoline in 1970 at a cost in excess of $100 million. Though motorists were initially reluctant to accept the 2¢-per-gallon price rise, the 1973 appearance of catalytic converters on new cars assured the success of the fuel.

Environmental matters came to the fore again in 1978, when an Amoco International Oil Company tanker, the Amoco *Cadiz* suffered steering failure during a storm and ran aground off the French coast, leaking about 730,000 gallons of oil into the sea. The huge oil spill cost $75 million to clean up, and left its mark on the area's tourist trade as well as its ecosystem. The French government brought a $300 million lawsuit against Amoco that eventually led to an $128 million judgment against Amoco. Amoco appealed the ruling, but the U.S. Circuit Court of Appeals in Chicago not only upheld the judgment but also increased it to $281 million. Amoco chose not appeal this ruling and paid the French government $243 million and the affected Brittany communities $38 million.

In late December 1978 the Shah of Iran was overthrown, and Standard (Indiana) hurriedly closed its Iranian facility and evacuated American staff members after all American employees of Amoco Iran Oil Company received death threats. The year 1978 had seen record-breaking production in Iran, and its loss resulted in a 35 percent production decrease in the company's overseas operations. Despite these turbulent events, net income was $1.5 billion in 1971, on total revenues of $20.197 billion.

By the end of the 1970s, chemical production accounted for about 7 percent of company earnings. To gain more visibility with consumers, Standard (Indiana) began to stress end-product manufacture as well as the production of ingredients used in manufacturing processes. The trend had begun in 1968, when polypropylene manufacturer Avisun Corporation was purchased by Amoco Chemicals Corporation from Sun Oil Company. The $80 million price tag included Patchoque-Plymouth Company, maker of polypropylene carpet backing. By 1986 a 100-color line plus improved stain resistance made Amoco Fabrics & Fibers Company's petrochemical-based Genesis carpeting a serious competitor of the stain-resistant carpeting offered by du Pont. Other strategies focused on market stimulation for basic industrial products. Since this required specialized marketing skills, the company divided its chemical operations among four subsidiaries.

In 1983 John Swearingen retired as chairman of the board. In his stead came Richard W. Morrow, who had been president of the Amoco Chemicals Corporation from 1974 until 1978, before assuming the Standard (Indiana) presidency in 1978. In 1985 Standard Oil Company (Indiana) changed its name to Amoco Corporation. Morrow also presided over the 1988 acquisition of Dome Petroleum, Ltd. of Canada, which was later merged into Amoco Canada. Dome, owning 28.7 million acres of undeveloped, arctic-region land, improved Amoco's oil and gas reserves. The Dome purchase was hard-won, costing Amoco $4.2 billion. Other chances to expand oil and gas exploration in 1988 came with the acquisition of Tenneco Oil Company's Rocky Mountain properties, for approximately $900 million.

Amoco Corporation began the 1990s with record revenues of $31.58 billion and net income of $1.91 billion. By 1990, the need for raw materials had expanded internationally, moving strongly towards Europe and the Far East. Joint ventures in Brazil, Mexico, South Korea, and Taiwan met the growing demand for polyester fibers, helping to generate about 35 percent of business overseas.

H. Laurence Fuller took over as chairman in 1991 amidst a downturn in Amoco profits owing to weakening demand for petroleum products and reduced prices caused by the recession. Revenues fell to $28.3 billion in 1991 and to $26.22 billion in 1992, while net income declined to $1.17 billion and $850 million, respectively. Fuller aimed not only to turn around the company's fortunes but also to overtake Exxon, the top U.S. oil company, in profitability. Fuller began this effort with a 1992 restructuring intended to reduce costs and improve efficiency. 8,500 employees were axed—16 percent of Amoco's work force—contributing to $600 million in savings. Exploration operations were cut back from a wildcatting strategy spread out over more than 100 countries to a targeted search for oil and gas in 20 countries with proven reserves. China became a prime target area; after establishing an offshore drilling operation in 1987, Amoco signed a deal in 1992 to become the first foreign company to explore the mainland, thought to hold more than 20 billion barrels of oil.

This restructuring served as prelude to an even larger reorganization effort initiated in 1994. 4,500 more jobs would be cut over the next two years, with projected savings of $1.2 billion each year. Amoco's organizational structure was completely overhauled. The three major subsidiaries—Amoco Production Company, Amoco Oil Company, and Amoco Chemical Company—that had been responsible for the three major areas of operation were replaced by a decentralized structure with 17 business groups divided into three sectors: exploration and production, petroleum products, and chemicals. A Shared Services organization was created to share the resources of Amoco's support operations.

Amoco's chemical operations were overhauled during these restructurings by shedding such weak areas as oil well chemicals and by increasing expenditures in fast-growing areas such as polyester. One result was that profits from Amoco's chemical sector increased from $68 million in 1991 to $574 million in 1994 thanks in large part to its 40 percent share of the world market in paraxylene and purified terephthalic acid, both used to make polyester, the demand for which grew dramatically, especially in Asia.

New product expenditures were also bolstered during this period. With demand for alternative and cleaner-burning fuels on the rise, Amoco introduced Crystal Clear Ultimate, a cleaner-burning premium gasoline, and test-marketed compressed natural gas for use by fleet operators. Also tested were shared service stations which offered Amoco gas and fast food from (McDonald's and Burger King), or such services as dry cleaning (DryClean U.S.A.). These tests were so successful that Amoco planned to roll out 100 such units in 1995 at a cost of $100 million. Amoco also embarked in 1994 on a drive to become a leader in natural gas-powered electricity generation. That year it created Amoco Power Resources Corporation to pursue this venture and purchased a 10 percent interest in electricity facilities in Trinidad and Tobago.

With the cost of oil and gas exploration soaring and lean operations not able to withstand the failure of a risky venture, more and more oil companies turned to joint ventures in the early and mid-1990s to spread the risk. Amoco was a member of a ten-company consortium that signed an agreement in 1994 with the Republic of Azerbaijan to develop oil fields in the Caspian Sea. Also in 1994 Amoco joined with rivals Shell Oil and Exxon to finance a $1 billion offshore oil platform in the Gulf of Mexico, to be the world's deepest. And in 1995 Shell and Amoco created a limited partnership to develop oil fields in the Permian Basin area of west Texas and southeast New Mexico.

Under Fuller's guidance, Amoco seemed well-positioned to challenge Exxon for the top spot in U.S. petroleum. Revenues had once again surpassed $30 billion by 1994 and net income had rebounded to $1.79 billion. Amoco's lean and targeted operation and its reinvigorated chemical sector provided it with a strong position from which to grow in the increasingly competitive 1990s.

Principal Subsidiaries: Amoco Company; Amoco Leasing Corp.; Amoco Pipeline Co.; Amoco Power Resources Corporation; Amoco Properties Inc.; Amoco Realty Co.; Amoco Research Corp.; Amoco Technology Co.; AmProp Finance Corp.; Solarex Corp.; Amoco Canada Energy Ltd.; Amoco Canada Petroleum Co. Ltd.; Amoco Canada Resources Ltd.; Amoco Holding G.m.b.H. (Germany); Amoco Chemical (Europe) S.A. (Switzerland); Amoco Chemical (UK) Ltd.

Further Reading:

Chelminski, Rudolph, *Superwreck: Amoco, The Shipwreck That Had to Happen,* New York, Morrow, 1987, 254 p.
Cook, James, "First-Rate Company," *Forbes,* May 1, 1989, pp. 84–85.
"Corporate Restructuring '90s Style: Merge and Purge, Lean and Mean," *National Petroleum News,* September 1994, pp. 16–18.
Dedmon, Emmett, *Challenge and Response: A Modern History of Standard Oil Company (Indiana),* Chicago: Mobium Press, 1984, 324 p.
Fairhall, David, *The Wreck of the Amoco Cadiz,* New York: Stein and Day, 1980, 248 p.
Giddens, Paul Henry, *Standard Oil Company (Indiana): Oil Pioneer of the Middle West,* New York: Arno Press, 1976, c1955, 741 p.
Mack, Toni, "Catching up to Exxon," *Forbes,* March 13, 1995, pp. 64, 66.
Melcher, Richard A., Peter Burrows, and Tim Smart, "Remaking Big Oil: The Desperate Rush to Slash Costs," *Business Week,* August 8, 1994, pp. 20–21.
Therrien, Lois, "Amoco: Running Smoother on Less Gas," *Business Week,* February 15, 1993, pp. 110–112.
"Whittle-Down Economics," *Oil and Gas Investor,* November 1992, pp. 43–46.

—Gillian Wolf
—updated by David E. Salamie

AMP Incorporated

P.O. Box 3608
Harrisburg, Pennsylvania 17105-3608
U.S.A.
(717) 564-0100
Fax: (717) 780-6130

Public Company
Incorporated: 1956
Employees: 30,400
Sales: $4.03 billion
Stock Exchanges: New York Boston Cincinnati Midwest
    Pacific Philadelphia
SICs: 3678 Electronic Connectors; 3643 Current-Carrying
    Wiring Devices

AMP Incorporated is the world leader in electrical and electronic connection devices and interconnection systems, claiming 19 percent of the $19 billion worldwide interconnections market. Boasting more than 100,000 types and sizes of products in its line and a reputation for dependable customer service and high quality, AMP has long enjoyed steady growth through heavy research and development spending and aggressive global expansion. More recently AMP has turned to acquisitions as an additional growth generator, starting with small moves but eventually embarking on the major 1995 acquisition of M/A Com Inc., a deal that also moved AMP into the area of wireless interconnection components—one of several industries related to AMP's core products that AMP expanded into during the 1980s and 1990s.

The founder of AMP was Uncas A. Whitaker, a former employee of Westinghouse Electric and the Hoover Company who held degrees in mechanical and electrical engineering and law. In 1941, after two years as a senior engineer for American Machine & Foundry in New York, Whitaker decided to start his own company. Aircraft Marine Products, as the company was called, specialized in solderless, uninsulated electrical connections for aircraft and boat manufacturers: a short metal tube with a ring on the end and a crimping tool. The device allowed electricians to make quick, removable wire connections without a heating element or flux. It was simple, unique, and very popular.

From a small office in New Jersey, Aircraft Marine established supply contracts with some of the largest industrial manufactur-

ers in the world. Less than three months after the company was created, the United States entered World War II. Companies such as Boeing, Consolidated Vultee, Ford, and Electric Boat redirected their production toward the war effort, developing new products and accelerating output. More than ever before, warplanes, battleships, and field equipment incorporated electrical devices, and increasingly these were assembled with solderless connections.

With its business thriving from war production, Aircraft Marine soon moved to a larger facility in Glen Rock, Pennsylvania. It then moved its headquarters to Harrisburg in 1943, after winning over the city's chamber of commerce, which did not want new business in the city, complaining about inadequate housing. A fire at the Glen Rock plant and the trauma of relocation overshadowed the introduction of the preinsulated terminal, an improved version of AMP's existing product that left all but the terminal ring exposed—an improvement that reduced the incidence of shorted circuits.

Much of U.S. industry saw lucrative contracts terminate with the end of the war. Many of Aircraft Marine's customers went bankrupt, were acquired, or were forced into mergers; in general they were compelled to reduce the scale of their operations drastically. Aircraft Marine, however, needed little product conversion in order to adapt to the postwar economy, because its connections were versatile components rather than more specialized finished products. Still, the transition was stressful for Aircraft Marine. It was able to survive the sudden drop in orders through drastic austerity measures and additional underwriting from Midland Investment Company, its primary benefactor. Whitaker was bitter after the company's experience with military contracts and procurement controls.

Aircraft Marine reentered the commercial market with another new product, the strip-formed terminal. During 1952 the company created a marketing unit called AMP Special Industries and established sales of existing products, and the introduction of connectors for pin and sockets, coaxial cables, and printed circuits resulted in unprecedented growth. Expanding through sales-led growth rather than by acquisition, Aircraft Marine added subsidiaries in Australia, Britain, the Netherlands, Italy, Japan, Mexico, and West Germany during the 1950s.

Aircraft Marine changed its name to AMP Incorporated upon incorporation as a public company in 1956. The company thereafter raised additional capital through share offerings. AMP improved and expanded its plant space and began a more ambitious research and development effort. Having demonstrated brisk and stable growth, AMP was listed on the New York Stock Exchange in October 1959.

Whitaker relinquished the company presidency to George A. Ingalls in 1961. Although he remained chairman, Whitaker wished to emphasize a more democratic form of leadership. He assigned many of his own managerial responsibilities to other managers and slowly removed himself from the company's daily operations.

AMP made a conscious decision during the 1960s against diversification into a wider range of products. Instead, management elected to concentrate on the "passive components" market it had come to dominate. AMP had experienced 15 percent annual growth for a decade beginning in the mid-1950s and anticipated an increasingly difficult "active component" market in the ensuing decades. Indeed, though Japanese electronics manufacturers were developing new capabilities in active components—particularly transistors—they neglected to take advantage of trade regulations that would have allowed them to establish an enduring position in passive components. As a result, AMP became the largest passive component manufacturer in Japan.

AMP continued to make frequent management changes; presidents and chief executives served only for about five years before changing jobs. Whitaker, however, served as chairman until his death in 1975. His death neither interrupted the company's business nor caused a management battle for power. Under the leadership of Joseph D. Brenner, AMP maintained its stable course but devoted increasing sums of money toward research into new "semipassive" systems.

Products that materialized from this intensified effort included more advanced coaxial connections for the growing cable-TV market, fiber-optic terminals for improved telecommunications systems, and more durable membrane switches. To some extent, however, AMP did not take full advantage of military sales. Much like Whitaker, Brenner refused to seek Pentagon sales because the government negotiated special prices on the basis of margin. This necessitated inspection of AMP's books—something Whitaker viewed as interference in the company's business. Instead, AMP was, in effect, a secondary supplier; it sold to companies that did hold Pentagon contracts. Insulated from the vagaries of defense procurement, AMP was better able to maintain stable growth, which continued at an annual rate of about 16 percent.

Walter Raab, a CPA with nearly 30 years of service to AMP, was named chairman and CEO upon Brenner's retirement in 1982. A cautious planner in the mold of his predecessors, Raab presided over AMP during a delicate period. Major customers, such as IBM, Ford, and Digital, sought to cut supply costs by reducing stocks and numbers of suppliers. AMP and its principal competitors, Molex and Thomas & Betts, were expected to benefit most. Already the largest suppliers to the industry, they were most likely to survive. In fact, they stood to gain market share as smaller suppliers were eliminated.

AMP invested heavily in the development of integrated subassemblies and new automated application methods. The system was originally conceived for use in automotive manufacturing. The installation of automotive wiring harnesses, or electrical systems, was complex and labor-intensive. Subassemblies, however, were simple and cut down on person-hours. AMP had to wait more than ten years, however, before auto manufacturers were willing to incorporate the system into production. In 1985 components customers suddenly initiated a drastic reorganization—they switched to automated subassemblies in a very short period. AMP, the least affected, suffered an 18 percent drop in sales, but it recovered quickly as new products were brought on line.

Recognizing the potential sales that came with U.S. military expansion under the Ronald Reagan administration, AMP created a special group that was open to Pentagon scrutiny and designed to engage in government sales. Still, less than five percent of its sales came from the military. In late 1987 both AMP and Molex purchased shares in Matrix Science Corp., a defense-oriented connection manufacturer. In early 1988 AMP then acquired Matrix outright for $120 million. Even with this move, however, military sales would lessen in importance in the coming years. By 1994 less than three percent of AMP's sales came from the military.

In the late 1980s and early 1990s AMP continued to expand internationally. The company opened plants and/or set up subsidiaries in Singapore, South Korea, and Taiwan in 1987; in Brazil, France, Germany, India, Italy, Japan, and Taiwan in 1992; and in China, the Czech Republic, Hungary, Poland, and Turkey in 1994. All AMP foreign subsidiaries were staffed only with locals and had their own engineering and production facilities in order to quickly respond to the needs of the local customers.

During this period, AMP also expanded overseas through acquisitions and partnerships. The firm acquired the Swiss-based Decolletage S.A. St.-Maurice in 1989 and SIMEL S.A., a leading supplier of connections for the European power utility market based in France, in 1994. AMP also entered into a joint venture, the AMP-AKZO Company, with Akzo N.V. of the Netherlands in 1990.

By 1994 AMP could boast of 185 facilities operating in 36 countries, with plans for further expansion in the mid- and late 1990s (including Indonesia and Vietnam). Through its global strategy, AMP continued to decrease its dependence on sales in the United States and achieved a remarkably diverse geographic distribution: only 42 percent of 1994 sales came from the United States (down from 63 percent in 1984), with 31 percent from Europe (up from 20 percent in 1984) and 22 percent from the Asia/Pacific region (up from 13 percent in 1984).

Thus solidifying its position in electrical and electronic connectors through international channels, AMP began to expand more aggressively into related industries. Much of this growth would come (at least initially) through acquisitions rather than through the company's traditional reliance on internal growth through large R&D expenditures. Among the areas into which AMP expanded were cables and cabling systems (1991 acquisition of Precision Interconnect Corporation), fiber-optic connectors (1992 acquisition of Optical Fiber Technologies), piezoelectric plastic film sensors (1993 acquisition of Elf Atochem Sensors), and wireless communications equipment (1995 acquisition of M/A-Com Inc.).

The acquisition of M/A-Com was perhaps the most significant and was certainly the largest of the many AMP acquisitions in the 1990s, resulting from a stock swap that cost AMP about $270 million plus the assumption of $75 million in M/A-Com debt. Based in Lowell, Massachusetts, M/A-Com had posted 1994 sales of $342 million and brought AMP immediate entry into the wireless communications components market—but at a cost some analysts thought too high. M/A-Com became a wholly owned subsidiary of AMP, and M/A-Com management felt it would now have access to capital desperately needed to stay competitive in the fast growing wireless market.

Two other strategies AMP adopted during this period were subsystems development and the use of independent distributors. With the former, AMP reacted to demands of customers who increasingly wished to acquire complete subsystems rather than components that required assembly. Increasing its use of independent distributors and cooperative affiliates, AMP found more marketing channels and potential for greater sales. By 1994 AMP already generated 14 percent of its sales through nondirect channels, double the seven percent figure of 1984.

Guided by James E. Marley, chairman, and William J. Hudson, chief executive officer and president, AMP's aggressive international expansion and moves into related industries and subsystems development came at a time when its traditionally healthy sales growth had slowed. From 1989 to 1993 the company averaged only 5.3 percent in annual growth in net sales. The results for 1994 were much improved, however, as AMP increased its sales 16.7 percent and topped $4 billion for the first time. In addition to increasing expenditures on acquisitions, AMP continued to spend heavily on R&D—with $456 million in total research, development, and engineering expense for 1994, 11.3 percent of net sales. With such sizable investments in the future, AMP seemed well positioned to meet two of its main goals: consistent sales growth in the nine to 14 percent range and $10 billion in annual sales by early in the 21st century.

Principal Subsidiaries: ACSYS Incorporated; AMP-AKZO Company (50%); AMP Packaging Systems, Inc.; Carroll Touch, Inc.; Connectware, Inc.; Kaptron, Inc.; M/A-Com Inc.; Microwave Signal, Inc.; Precision Interconnect Corporation; Raylan Corporation; The Whitaker Corporation; AMP S.A. Argentina C.I.Y.F.; AMP do Brasil Ltda.; AMP of Canada, Ltd.; AMP de Mexico, S.A.; AMP Österreich Handelsges M.b.H. (Austria); AMP Belgium; AMP Czech s.r.o. (Czech Republic); AMP Danmark; AMP Finland OY; AMP de France S.A.; AMP Export Ltd. S.a.r.l. (France); SIMEL S.A. (France); AMP Deutschland G.m.b.H.; AMP of Great Britain Ltd.; AMP-Holland B.V.; AMP Ireland Limited; AMP Italia S.p.A.; AMP Norge A/S (Norway); AMP Polska Sp. z.o.o.; AMP Portugal, Lda.; AMP Española, S.A.; AMP Svenska AB (Sweden); AMP (Schweiz) A.G. (Switzerland); Decolletage S.A. St.-Maurice (Switzerland); AMP Turkey; Australian AMP Pty. Ltd.; AMP Shanghai Ltd. (People's Republic of China); AMP Products Pacific Ltd. (Hong Kong); AMP India Private Limited; AMP (Tools) India; AMP (Japan), Ltd.; Businessland Japan Company, Ltd.; Carroll Touch International, Ltd. (Japan); AMP Products (Malaysia) Sdn. Bhd.; New Zealand AMP Ltd.; AMP Philippines, Inc.; AMP Singapore Pte. Ltd.; AMP Korea Limited (South Korea); AMP Taiwan B.V.; AMP (Thailand) Limited.

Further Reading:

Cohn, W. H., *The End Is Just Beginning,* Carnegie-Mellon Press, 1980.

Barton, Michael, *Life by the Moving Road: A History of the Harrisburg Area,* Woodland Hills, Calif.: Windsor Publications, 1983.

Erdman, Andrew, "Staying Ahead of 800 Competitors," *Fortune,* June 1, 1992, pp. 111–12.

Hinchberger, Sharon, "Fortune 500 Manufacturer Develops Global Strategy," *Central Penn Business Journal,* January 7, 1994.

Hwang, Suein L., "AMP Inc. Agrees to Buy M/A-Com in Stock Deal," *Wall Street Journal,* March 13, 1995, pp. B6(W)/B7(E).

Lappen, Alyssa A., "Worldwide Connections," *Forbes,* June 27, 1988, pp. 78, 80, 82.

Poist, Patricia, "AMP Quietly Masters an $18 Billion Market," *York Daily Record,* April 18, 1993.

Zinter, Aaron, "Pa. Firm Agrees to Acquire M/A-Com," *Boston Globe,* March 11, 1995, p. 61.

—updated by David E. Salamie

Applebee's International Inc.

4551 W. 107th Street
Overland Park, Kansas 66207
U.S.A.
(913) 967-4000
Fax: (913) 341-1694

Public Company
Incorporated: 1983
Employees: 8,700
Sales: $208.53 million
Stock Exchanges: NASDAQ
SICs: 5812 Eating Places; 5813 Drinking Places; 6794 Patent
Owners and Lessors

Applebee's International Inc. franchises and operates a national chain of restaurants under the Applebee's Neighborhood Grill & Bar name. The eateries proffer moderately priced, high-quality fare for all ages in a friendly, informal atmosphere. After expanding rapidly during the late 1980s and early 1990s, Applebee's was operating more than 560 restaurants in 43 states, one Canadian province, and the island of Curacao in July 1995.

Restaurateur William Palmer and his wife opened the first Applebee's restaurant—named T.J. Applebee's—in Atlanta in November 1980. Offering a unique menu and comfortable atmosphere, the Atlanta eatery was a success. Palmer's goal with Applebee's was to create a neighborhood-like pub and restaurant where patrons could order high-quality food at a relatively low price. Specifically, he hoped to provide an alternative for all ages to fast-food restaurants, steakhouse franchises, and similar chains, which Palmer believed were offering relatively impersonal service and mediocre fare. The concept, while simple, was so successful that T.J. Applebee's began to get the attention of larger food companies. To that end, Creative Food 'N Fun Co. purchased the concept from Palmer in 1983; Creative Food 'N Fun Co. was a subsidiary of the giant holding company W.R. Grace & Co.

W.R. Grace hoped to use its deep pockets to parlay the T.J. Applebee's concept into a large chain of franchised restaurants. Grace, through its wholly owned Creative Food 'N Fun Co. subsidiary, set up a separate Applebee's Division in Kansas City to operate the newly incorporated Applebee's. Palmer was kept on board as president of Applebee's. Between 1983 and 1985 Palmer added new Applebee's outlets in the Atlanta area.

In addition, Applebee's began franchising the concept to other regional restaurant developers.

Among Applebee's first regional franchisees was Burton 'Skip' Sack, who purchased the New England franchise rights to Applebee's restaurants in 1984. His experience was representative of other Applebee's franchisees during the late 1980s and early 1990s. Sack had started out as a bus boy at Howard Johnson's, where, over a 22-year-period, he progressed to senior vice-president of the company. He left HoJo's in 1983 and bought the Red Coach Grill chain of eateries. When his first Applebee's restaurant was an instant success, he sold off his Red Coach restaurants and concentrated on developing more Applebee's outlets. During the late 1980s Sack developed a small network of Applebee's outlets in various parts of New England. "We waited a year and a half to see if it was just a fluke," Sack said in the May 3, 1993, *Union Leader,* adding that "In 1988, we opened our second restaurant in Franklin, Massachusetts, and it did even better." By 1993 Sack was operating about 15 outlets that were generating earnings of nearly $18 million annually, and he was planning to open several more stores.

Sack and other Applebee's franchisees generally prospered during the late 1980s and early 1990s. Perhaps the most successful franchisee, however, was Tom E. Dupree Jr. Dupree opened his first Applebee's restaurant in 1986 and rapidly expanded his chain to become the leading franchisee in the system. "We felt it [the Applebee's concept] hit all the demographic shifts dead center," Dupree explained in the July 5, 1994, *Atlanta Constitution.* "People are tired of plastic drinks and cardboard food," he noted. Dubbed 'Apple South,' the Atlanta-based company that Dupree created through which to operate his restaurants generated huge sales gains throughout the late 1980s and early 1990s. Indeed, between 1986 and 1991, Dupree opened 52 new outlets. Incredibly, he doubled that number during the next two years by expanding its chain to more than 100 stores. Furthermore, average per-store sales steadily increased.

Applebee's major growth spurt began in 1988, after W.R. Grace sold the company. Grace had succeeded in bringing new franchisees into the system but had only achieved moderate growth and profitability. Even by 1986, total revenues from franchise fees and other sources were less than $5 million. And, despite the success of individual stores, Applebee's lost money every year between 1985 and 1988, with the exception of a small surplus in 1986. Recognizing that Applebee's had much greater potential were Abe J. Gustin Jr. and John Hamra. Hamra was serving as chairman of Applebee's board at the time. In 1988 Gustin and Hamra decided to buy the company from W.R. Grace and try their hand at owning and managing the organization. The Applebee's organization was comprised of 54 units at the time, most of which were franchises. As intimated above, that number would surge during the next few years.

Hamra and Gustin were well suited to run Applebee's. Hamra was already acting as chairman, so he had the connections and expertise to pull-off the buyout. Gustin, though, would be the driving force behind Applebee's stellar gains during the next five years. He had started his career as a teenager, toiling in his brother's Birmingham, Alabama, barbecue hut. After that, he served a 15-year stint with Schlitz Brewing Co., where he started out driving a beer truck and worked his way up through the marketing side of the company. In a 1993 article in the *Nation's Restaurant News,* Gustin discussed the impact of his mentor at Schlitz, Tom Rupus: "Tom Rupus, vice president of sales when I was at Schlitz, had a huge impact on the direction of my career. . . . He told me, 'I don't care what you're doing; you're gonna look like a businessman.' So I used to ride in the beer trucks and unload beer in a suit and tie."

Gustin was hired away from Schlitz by ABA Distributors, a wholesale beer distributor in Kansas City, where he served as chairman, president, and director. From there, he moved into food service as chairman of Juneau Holding Co., a Kansas City-based owner and operator of 18 Taco Bell Restaurants. Gustin wanted to expand his Taco Bell chain but was told that the company wasn't issuing any more territory rights. That's when he began considering the up-and-coming Applebee's. Gustin flew to Atlanta, checked out the Applebee's concept, liked what he saw, and worked out a deal to become the organization's third franchisee. Gustin also took the advice of then-chairman John Hamra, and began selling off his Taco Bell holdings. He opened his first Applebee's in 1986. The success of that store prompted him to open six more outlets during the next several months. Then, in January 1988, he teamed up with Hamra to buy Applebee's from W.R. Grace.

Under new ownership, revenues at Applebee's soared 500 percent to more than $24.21 million during 1988. Likewise, net losses for the year plunged from $877 million in 1987 to $47 million in 1988. The increase was largely the result of new restaurants; the Applebee's chain grew to 88 units by the end of 1988 and then to 110 stores by mid-1990. To sustain that growth, Gustin and Hamra had taken Applebee's public early in 1990. Cash from the initial public offering was used to reduce some of the $10 million in debt incurred while acquiring the Applebee's chain from Grace. After the offering, Gustin announced that Applebee's would soon be opening an additional 70 franchise units, news which boosted Applebee's stock price. Unfortunately, the investment capital needed to open the outlets failed to materialize and only 39 of the restaurants were opened.

Scrambling in 1990 to raise capital in a recessionary economy, Gustin was finally able to get a loan guarantee from Bell Atlantic, and the cash flow resumed. He recruited new franchisees to add to the company's existing base of about 50, and the Applebee's chain began to sprawl across the United States. In 1990, in fact, Applebee's was selected by *Barron's* as a small company with a five-year high-growth potential because of its management strategy and vision. Adding credence to that assessment was the fact that revenues, which were comprised primarily of franchise-related fees, surged to $38.2 million in 1989, $45.13 million in 1990, and then to $56.5 million in 1991. More importantly, net income rose to $5 million in 1992 from $1.8 million in 1990. Going into 1993, Applebee's was operating about 200 outlets, roughly 85 percent of which were franchised and 15 percent of which were owned by Applebee's International.

The reasons for Applebee's success were several. The foundation of the company's strategy was its neighborhood theme, which influenced all operating decisions in the organization.

The Applebee's menu depicted a doormat that read 'Welcome to the Neighborhood,' on the cover, and the restaurants were designed to project a comfortable, neighborly environment. Franchisees were encouraged to get involved with local charities and neighborhood events, and to personalize their restaurants in some way to keep them from looking like a chain restaurant that could be found in any other city in the nation. The benefit of the neighborhood strategy was that it cultivated repeat business from the local population. In fact, the Applebee's outlets targeted the crowd that would prefer to frequent a local mom-and-pop restaurant than the typical impersonal chain.

As part of the effort to personalize the restaurants, Gustin empowered individual franchisees and restaurant managers to make decisions about how their restaurants operated and even what type of food they served. Two of the core required menu items were barbecued riblets cut from the tip of the tenderloin, and fajitas. The restaurants also typically offered chicken wings, burgers, lasagna, soup and salad, sirloin steak, apple honey cobbler, and cheesecake. In addition, each restaurant featured a full bar, where Applebee's special apple margarita were served. Aside from those staples, franchisees were allowed to experiment with their menus and emphasize foods popular in their particular market. Furthermore, Applebee's wait staff was highly trained to respond to customer's specific needs, and staffers were taught a special ten-step serving process. Importantly, the restaurants were set up to ensure that most people were served their meal within 15 minutes of ordering.

Applebee's growth rate accelerated in 1993 and 1994. By exploiting the company's proven management and operating formula, and by attracting new investment capital, Gustin was able to grow the chain at an average pace of more than 100 restaurants annually. During this time, Hamra retired, and Gustin became chairman, chief executive, and president. "My original vision was that there could be as many as 500 Applebee's," Gustin said in the September 20, 1993, *Nation's Restaurant News.* "Now we're targeting 1,200 to 1,500," he added. To help him expand the company, Gustin hired such seasoned executives as Ken Hill, chief operating officer, and George Shadid, chief financial officer. They and other team members rallied going into the mid-1990s to expand the Applebee's chain of eateries to more than 500 going into 1995.

As the number of franchised and company-owned stores rose, so did Applebee's' sales and profits. Indeed, revenues more than doubled in 1993 to $117 million before lurching to a big $208 million in 1994. For the same years, net income vaulted to $9.5 million before nearly hitting $17 million during 1994. Applebee's continued to expand at a speedy clip in 1995, and by the middle of the year was boasting about 575 outlets in 43 states, one Canadian province, and the island of Curacao. Although the size of the organization had changed, the goals of the individual restaurants had not; "It helps for people to know they can bring the kids, have a drink if they like, and be served their food within 15 minutes of ordering," Gustin said in the July 1995 *Ingram's.* "People also want to walk out without feeling they've left their wallets behind them," he observed.

Principal Subsidiaries: Innovative Restaurant Concepts, Inc.; Pub Ventures of New England, Inc.; Applebee's of Pennsylvania, Inc.; Applebee's of Michigan, Inc.; Applebee's of Minnesota, Inc.; Apple Vermont Restaurant, Inc.; Applebee's of New Mexico, Inc.; Applebee's of New York, Inc.; Applebee's of Texas, Inc.; Applebee's Neighborhood Grill & Bar of Georgia, Inc.; Applebee's of Nevada, Inc.; Gourmet Systems of California, Inc.; Gourmet Systems of Kansas, Inc.; Gourmet Systems of Nevada, Inc.; Gourmet Systems of Minnesota, Inc.; Gourmet Systems of Tennessee, Inc.; Gourmet Systems, Inc.

Further Reading:

Cauley, Lauree, "Applebee's Capitalizing on Pittsburgh's Neighborhoods," *Pittsburgh Business Times & Journal,* June 11, 1990, Sec. 2, p. 15.

Ezell, Hank, "Apple South a Casual Success," *Atlanta Constitution,* July 5, 1994, p. D1.

Kaberlin, Brian, "New Special on Applebee's Table: Buy Big Franchisee," *Kansas City Business Journal,* November 15, 1991, p. 1.

Kaberlin, Brian, and Adam Feuerstein, "Palmer May Rejoin Applebee's International," *Atlanta Business Chronicle,* December 2, 1991, p. 3A.

Keegan, Peter O., "Abe J. Gustin Jr.: 'Risk-Taking' Type of Guy," *Nation's Restaurant News,* September 20, 1993, p. 122.

Plyler, Tami, "Applebee's Recipe for Expansion," *Union Leader,* May 3, 1993, Business Sec.

Saponar, R.C., "Applebee's to Go Public Wednesday," *Nashville Business Journal,* September 18, 1989, p. 3.

Smith, Margaret, "Corporate Report 100: Serving Success," *Ingram's,* July 1995, p. 45.

Walkup, Carolyn, "Applebee's Nabs Lucrative Slice of Small-Town American Pie," *Nation's Restaurant News,* October 30, 1989, p. 3.

—Dave Mote

Arby's Inc.

6917 Collins Avenue
Miami Beach, Florida 33141
U.S.A.
(305) 621-7223
Fax: (305) 351-5192

Wholly Owned Subsidiary of Triarc Companies, Inc.
Founded: 1964
Employees: 82,000
Sales: $1.8 billion
SICs: 5812 Eating Places; 6794 Patent Owners & Lessors

A subsidiary of Triarc Companies, Inc., Arby's Inc. is a leading global fast-food restaurant chain with more than 2,800 restaurants worldwide. Arby's is distinguished within the industry by its menu, which features roast beef sandwiches. The chain expanded rapidly during the 1970s and 1980s by franchising. In 1995 the Arby's chain included about 330 company-owned stores and more than 2,500 franchise outlets.

Arby's emanated from the brainstorm of brothers Leroy and Forrest Raffel. The Raffels operated a food-service equipment business in Youngstown, Ohio, in the early 1960s, and had noticed the huge boom taking place in the burgeoning fast-food industry. It had been only about ten years since Ray Kroc had purchased the national rights to franchise the McDonald brothers' hamburger operation, and Burger King was already jumping into the franchising game with its knock-off of the McDonalds formula. Leroy and Forrest, both in their 30s, wanted to get in the flourishing industry early with their own fast-food concept, but sought an angle that would separate their restaurants from the emerging group of McDonald's look-alikes. They finally settled on a menu featuring roast beef sandwiches.

The Raffels opened their first restaurant on July 23, 1964. They named the store R-B, which was a derivative of "Raffel brothers." The tiny restaurant sported ten seats and an attention-grabbing yellow roof, and employed a staff of 20 people. The first menu offered "slow-cooked" roast beef sandwiches for 69 cents, extra-large iced tea, and soft drinks. The R-B concept was a hit with customers, and the brothers quickly moved to open five more stores before the end of 1965. After that, growth was rampant. By mid-1967 there were more than 100 R-B outlets pushing roast beef sandwiches and tea. Before 1970, through the magic of franchising, the brothers had grown the chain to a whopping 300 outlets in 37 states. The menu by then had been expanded to include different roast beef sandwiches and various side items.

The concept for Arby's, as it later became called, was a bigger success than even the Raffel brothers had imagined. It seemed clear to them and other fast-food industry observers that the chain was destined to join the ranks of the fast-food mega-giants like McDonalds and Burger King. To make that quantum leap, however, the brothers needed cash. They had gotten by during the late 1960s with bank loans and help from individual investors. To sustain growth in the 1970s, they would have to take the company public. They registered for an offering in 1970. The new issues market was thriving at the time and the Raffels expected to generate a big cash war chest through the offering. Unfortunately, a Securities and Exchange Commission accounting rule change made at the time forced Arby's to delay its offering until April.

In an incredible twist of fate, Arby's initial public offering (IPO) was rescheduled for April 24. It was on that day that the new issues market virtually collapsed. Stunned, the Raffel quickly aborted the stock sale. As a result, they were left stranded without the money that they had expected to garner from the offering. Suddenly, they were in a position in which they were unable to pay their bills. The banks that had previously loaned money to Arby's quickly swooped in to protect their investment. They effectively took over the company, fired 125 of the 150 employees who staffed the firm's headquarters, and slashed services to the franchisees that were operating the Arby's outlets. Frustrated franchisees, feeling duped by their parent company, stopped paying royalties. In November 1970 the company was forced to file for Chapter 11 bankruptcy.

Despite the blistering setback, the Raffels managed to regain control of Arby's five months after the company entered bankruptcy. They spent the next few years restoring it to profitability and getting back to the place they were at before the failed IPO. They also tagged on a number of new franchised outlets. By 1975 they were operating nearly 500 outlets throughout the United States. Still, the Raffels needed more money for expansion. Rather than attempt another stock offering, they decided to find a larger company with which they could merge. The parent company could then fund their expansion.

In 1976 the Raffels reached an agreement with Royal Crown Cola to sell the Arby's chain for $18 million. Arby's, still under the direction of Leroy and Forrest, continued to flourish under the Royal Crown umbrella. Another 300 units were added to the chain between 1976 and 1979. Importantly, Arby's generated big profits and solid sales gains during this period. In 1979 Royal Crown moved its prosperous Arby's subsidiary to Atlanta. The Raffel brothers decided it was time to jump ship. They retired as millionaires, leaving a legacy of more than 800 Arby's restaurants scattered throughout the United States.

Arby's languished under new management. Indeed, the chain quickly spiraled into decline after the Raffels left, and by 1983 incompetent management had left the enterprise directionless and floundering. Unit sales slumped to a sloppy $600,000 annually at a time when some other chains were boasting a unit average of more than $1 million. Arby's was rapidly losing stature as a contender in the fast-food industry. Fortunately, a new management team was able to turn the ailing enterprise around. In 1984 Royal Crown (along with its Arby's subsidiary) was bought out by Miami financier and feared corporate raider Victor Posner through his DWG Corp. Posner tapped Leonard Roberts to serve as chief executive of Arby's.

The 40-year-old Roberts came to Arby's from Ralston Purina's Foodmaker fast-food division. A fast-food industry veteran, Roberts quickly implemented much-needed changes at Arby's and turned a critical eye to the Arby's menu. Under Royal Crown's ownership, Arby's had started offering conventional burger fare in an attempt to compete with the hamburger chains. He scaled back items that could be found in almost any fast-food restaurant and returned the menu to its traditional niche of roast beef. He then began supplementing that foundation with specialty items like deli sandwiches, chicken cordon bleu sandwiches, and roast chicken. Roberts also tightened Arby's quality standards and began hunting for new franchisees.

Roberts' overall strategy proved successful. During the mid-1980s Arby's raced near to the front of the fast-food pack, opening hundreds of stores throughout North America and even a few in Europe. At the same time, per-store sales increased, partly because the company launched an aggressive advertising campaign and pioneered unique customer service concepts like accepting credit cards and allowing customers to order by computer. By 1989 the Arby's chain had ballooned to 2,100 restaurants that were capturing annual sales of more than $1 billion, figures that made Arby's the twelfth-ranked fast-food chain in the industry.

While Arby's achieved huge gains during the late 1980s, however, trouble was brewing behind the scenes. Roberts had become dissatisfied with Posner's control. He felt that Posner was hindering Arby's growth by bleeding its cash flow, rather then reinvesting income to expand the chain at a faster rate. At one point, according to Roberts, Posner had withheld bonuses from middle managers for two straight years. In fact, several of Posner's holdings were in trouble and he had been taking cash from the profitable Arby's subsidiary to keep them afloat. Furthermore, Posner himself was in trouble. He pleaded no contest to tax evasion in 1987 and received a $7 million fine and five years probation. Shortly thereafter he became the target of an insider trading investigation.

Posner was also considering moving the Arby's headquarters to his holding company's base in Miami—a move with which Roberts disagreed. Weary of his clashes with Posner, Roberts decided to back a bid by a group of franchisees to buy out the Arby's chain for $200 million. When Posner rejected the bid, Roberts publicly criticized him. Incensed, Posner fired Roberts and replaced him with Irving Riese, who, along with his brother Murray, owned interests in about 500 restaurants. The appointment infuriated many Arby's franchisees, who felt that Reise's ownership of competing fast-food stores constituted a conflict of interest. Posner and Riese relented and Frank Belatti accepted the chief executive slot.

After Roberts left, Arby's began to flounder as it had when the company's founders had bailed out a decade earlier. Partly because of Posner's ongoing involvement with the company's

operations—Posner decided in 1990 to go ahead and move the company to Miami in 1991, for example—many of the company's top executives bolted. The vice president of international development, for instance, quit just as Arby's launched an aggressive campaign to expand abroad. Other abandoned posts included vice-president of franchising, executive vice-president of operations, and vice-president of administration. With the company's management structure gutted, Arby's languished.

Some industry observers placed the blame for Arby's early 1990s demise squarely on Posner's shoulders. Although his past business successes had earned him a reputation as a savvy financier, critics charged that the 70-year-old magnate was losing his touch by the late 1980s. They contended that he essentially used Arby's as a cash cow during the late 1980s and early 1990s, collecting franchise fees and dumping them into his portfolio of holdings. Indeed, by the early 1990s Arby's was just one of a group of Posner's holdings that were worth an estimated $26 billion. He owned companies, real estate, and securities throughout the world.

Posner's life and business exploits comprised an intriguing tale. He started out working in his Russian-immigrant father's grocery store in Depression-era Baltimore. He dropped out of high school and used his savings to start building low-cost housing. By the time he was 25 he was a millionaire. He began buying up vast amounts of real estate up and down the east coast. He eventually began buying companies at a rapid pace, and, according to critics, running many of them into the ground. "He was a horrendous manager," said childhood friend and attorney Ira Elegant in the *Herald* in 1994. "He'd drain the companies until there was nothing left."

Posner's fortunes began to change in the mid-1980s. Legal problems mounted as years of questionable business practices were placed under a microscope by federal and state investigators. Among many other lawsuits, shareholders sued Posner and son Steven in 1990 for plundering the giant DWG holding company. While Posner claimed to have trouble paying creditors and employees, he had drawn out $31 million in compensation and charged an average of $474 each day in meal expenses during 1991 alone. The lawsuit eventually led to the demise of Posner's empire. In 1993 a New York federal district judge banned Posner and his son from any further involvement with public companies, and he forced the Posners to give up control of their remaining holdings and to repay ill-gotten gains. Posner became critically ill with an abdominal aneurysm in 1994, while his son, facing massive debts, was forced to give up his Bentley and Ferrari (he was able to keep his Lamborghini).

Posner's financial downfall left his companies, including Arby's, looking for new owners. Triarc Companies Inc. was created as a successor to the failed DWG Corp. It effectively purchased the assets of Arby's and RC Cola. Named as president and chief executive of Arby's was Don Pierce, who had formerly overseen three PepsiCo-owned food chains, including the venerable Taco Bell. Pierce immediately intensified Arby's expansion drive, which had continued during the early 1990s despite the Posner turmoil. He also began revamping the outlets to evoke a Montana "big sky" feeling of the Old West. He was helped by a new management team that was now free of the detrimental influence of Posner. Shortly after taking the helm, Pierce moved the company's headquarters to Fort Lauderdale.

Arby's continued to expand through franchising during the early 1990s. By 1993, in fact, Arby's was operating more than 2,600 outlets in the United States, Canada, Asia, the Middle East, Mexico, Latin America, Europe, and the Caribbean. During 1994, under Pierce's direction, the company added another 200 stores to bring the global total to about 2,800. As a result, total store sales vaulted from $1.52 billion in 1992 to about $1.8 billion during 1994. Meanwhile, profitability improved and management made plans to continue to expand Arby's globally and to increase per-store earnings. Among other achievements, Arby's opened the largest Arby's store in the world in 1995. Located in Tulsa, the 3,000-square-foot restaurant was expected to generate $1.5 million in annual receipts.

Principal Subsidiaries: Arby's U.K. Limited (United Kingdom).

Further Reading:

Cohen, Laurie P., "Posner Clan Feuds Over Empire's Spoils," *Herald,* October 14, 1994, p. 1.

Hartnett, Dwayne, "Arby's Giant: Tulsa Home of Huge Restaurant," *Tulsa World,* April 30, 1995, p. B1.

Henterly, Meghan, "Arby's Saddles Up New Image," *Cincinnati Enquirer,* September 12, 1994, p. D1.

McKenna, Jon, "Key Executives Defect From Arby's Inc.," *Atlanta Business Journal,* February 25, 1991, 5A.

Robertshaw, Nicky, "Under New Ownership, Arby's Targets Memphis for Significant Expansion," *Memphis Business Journal,* October 17, 1994, p. 1.

Sokler, Lynn, "Arby's to Relocate Headquarters," *PR Newswire,* July 29, 1993.

Stine, Mark, "Arby's Roast Beef Sandwich Chain Rolls Out in the UK," *Business Wire,* November 16, 1992.

Wax, Alan J., "The Beef at Arby's: Discord, Turmoil," *Newsday,* September 24, 1989, p. 60.

Widmer, Laura, "Arby's Inc. Names Chief Financial Officer," *PR Newswire,* June 2, 1995.

—Dave Mote

AT&T Istel Ltd.

P.O. Box 5
Grosvenor House
Prospect Hill
Redditch
Worcestershire B97 4DQ
United Kingdom
(01527) 64274
Fax: (01527) 63360

*Wholly Owned Subsidiary of American Telephone and
    Telegraph Company*
Incorporated: 1979 as BL Systems
Employees: 1,648
Sales: £125 million
Stock Exchanges: London
SICs: 7379 Computer Related Services, Not Elsewhere
    Classified; 4899 Communication Services, Not Elsewhere
    Classified

AT&T Istel Ltd. is the British information technology subsidiary of American Telephone & Telegraph Company (AT&T), the world's largest telecommunications group. Originally established as a subsidiary computer services firm for the automaker British Leyland, Istel quickly went on to provide information technology to other companies in a variety of industries. After separating from British Leyland, the company operated independently for a few years before seeking an alliance with AT&T.

Originally called BL Systems, the company was created to provide British Leyland with reliable, state-of-the-art information technology services. The idea of a separate information technology company for this purpose was conceived in 1977 by John Leighfield, who later became the new company's chairman and chief executive. When the plan was approved in 1978, all British Leyland's mainframe computers were unified in one data center at Redditch, joined via a microwave communications network—the first such private network in Europe—to the automotive manufacturing sites. The new center was finished in February 1979, and BL Systems came into official existence the following June.

BL Systems was intended to serve the full complement of systems, computing, and telecommunications needs of its parent company, and was not encouraged to actively seek commercial activities outside the firm. As early as March 1980, however, BL Systems took on its first outside client, developing the See Why package, a color graphics, interactive simulation system, for Alcan Aluminium.

Thereafter, BL Systems quickly established for itself a corporate identity separate from that of its parent company, with headquarters and staff consolidated at two locations, Grosvenor House and Coventry.

In November 1980 BL Systems inaugurated the first private videotex service—the Stocklocator system—for the BL dealer network. This system, later called Infotrac, was based on a leased-line data communications network. At the completion of its first full year of operation, BL Systems' revenues stood at a very respectable £25.7 million.

In February 1981 BL Systems served its first foreign customer, Heineken, which used the company's data center for remote testing while changing its own computer systems. BL Systems' See Why package won the British Computer Society's Software Innovation award in October. The following month the company celebrated the installation of its 100th disc drive. After the first stage of the U.K.'s deregulation of telecommunications, BL Systems was granted the first Value-Added Network Services license, which permitted the company to initiate Comet, Britain's first electronic mail service. The number of BL Systems employees had risen to 1,000, and by the end of the year revenues stood at £27.4 million, with £1.9 million of this attributable to outside customers. By the end of 1982, revenues reached £29.5 million, and the equipment in BL Systems' data center was valued at £20 million.

As BL Systems began to recognize the increasing importance of outside clients to its business, the company focused on attracting and retaining outside customers. To that end a 1983–87 five-year plan was established, with the goal of attaining 30 percent of the company's revenue from outside sources by the end of the decade.

In January 1983 BL Systems engaged in a joint venture with Atlantic Computers to found the Failsafe business unit, which provided contingency preparation and rescue services for computer failures. In April BL Systems launched a U.S. office in Boston called Istel Inc. to sell the popular See Why package. The year's other achievements included the foundation of BL Systems' Travel Service, its first facilities management project, for Homeview, and the assignment to manage an EEC-sponsored project to create the ground rules for computer-integrated manufacturing (CIM).

In 1984 BL Systems changed its name to Istel, making known its intentions to become a significant player in the fast-growing field of information technology, rather than simply a support function to the automotive industry as represented by BL. By mid-year—and several years earlier than originally targeted—the company surpassed its goal of achieving 30 percent of its revenue from outside clients.

Istel's first sale to a National Health Service (NHS) customer was made in 1984, when the company provided the Herefordshire District Health Authority with the Star tendering and review system. This marked the first step toward what would become a prominent role in the health sector. Later in the year the company made its first acquisition, Business Science Computing, which it purchased from British Steel.

In 1985 Istel defined its objectives, significantly altering its corporate structure to create specialized marketing divisions to court particular markets and sectors. That year the company also established Istel Automation to sell CIM systems to the manufacturing industry and launched InView, a highly successful data communications link between insurance companies and their retail markets. At the end of the year, Istel's revenues stood at £49.7 million, with £14.6 million of that attributable to non-BL customers.

Significant changes were heralded for Istel in 1986. The government announced plans to sell British Leyland (which had been renamed the Rover Group) to British Aerospace, and to spin off Istel as a separate company, preferably through a management-led employee buy-out. As preparations were made for the company's new status, Istel continued to grow, securing its first £1 million order (from Horizon Holidays), and providing its first sale to the Royal Air Force. The company's revenues jumped to £60.8 million by the end of the year.

In June 1987 a £1.8 million share offer was made to employees and proved very popular, being oversubscribed almost three times. Such confidence was clearly justified, as the company's revenues rose by nearly £10 million that year over the previous year. In 1988 the newly independent Istel developed separate operating divisions for its business: Istel Financial Services, Istel Commercial Services, and Istel Motor Industry Services. Other achievements for the year included the establishment of Istel Visual Interactive Systems; several acquisitions (of Viewtel, Abbey Business Consultants, Mycrom, and Deritend Computers); and the opening of an office in Edinburgh.

Believing that Istel would be better positioned for growth if it operated under the aegis of a larger, like-minded firm, Istel's board of directors searched for months for a suitable parent company. Finally, in October 1989, a deal was struck with AT&T, and the renamed AT&T Istel began a new era.

The alliance quickly proved advantageous to Istel, allowing it access to many new opportunities within AT&T's large, international client pool. Even as economic recession worsened, Istel continued to grow, opening two new business units in the United Kingdom: AT&T Istel Global Messaging Services Lim-

ited and AT&T Istel Computer Services Limited. By the end of 1990 revenues had reached £131 million.

The following year Istel made its first international acquisition, of the Dusseldorf-based Infoplan, giving the company an important foothold in continental Europe. Meanwhile, in its domestic market, the company stepped up its contracts with the NHS, largely in the field of facilities management, and acquired Belmin Systems, a provider of electronic purchasing systems for local and central government agencies.

As the 1990s progressed, Istel continued to expand and became increasingly associated with the health industry. In 1994 the company outmaneuvered intense competition to win contracts for management systems for two hospitals in Dublin. In 1995 important contracts were signed with West London's Hillingdon Hospital, the West Dorset General Hospital NHS Trust, the Norfolk and Norwich Health Care NHS Trust, and the Camden and Islington Community Health Services NHS Trust. The company had not severed ties with its former parent, Rover Group, which remained Istel's single biggest customer in the mid-1990s.

AT&T Istel thus retains ties with its original, loyal customers, has developed a specialty in the health care sector, and is continually on the lookout for new opportunities in the many industries that require information technology services. With its impressive record of steady growth backed by the strength of its new parent company, the world's largest telecommunications group, AT&T Istel appears well positioned to continue as a technological and financial success story.

Principal Subsidiaries: Al Deritend Ltd.; AT&T Istel GmbH (Germany); AT&T Istel Inc. (U.S.A.); Belmin Systems Ltd.; Facilities Management Services Ltd.; InView Ltd.; Viewtel Holdings Ltd.

Further Reading:

''AT&T Istel Wins Pounds 2m Hospital Pay Deal,'' *Birmingham Post,* February 24, 1995.
''Health Tonic for AT&T Istel,'' *Birmingham Post,* November 2, 1994.
History of AT&T Istel, 1979–91, Redditch: AT&T Istel, 1992, 7 p.
''RHA Sorts Out Deal to End Scandal of Computer Cash,'' *Birmingham Post,* November 18, 1994.
''Rover Old Boys Win Pounds 5m Project,'' *Birmingham Post,* March 31, 1995.

—Robin DuBlanc

Atlas Van Lines, Inc.

1212 St. George Road
Evansville, Indiana 47711
U.S.A.
(812) 424-4326
Fax: (812) 421-7125

Wholly Owned Subsidiary of Atlas World Group, Inc.
Incorporated: 1948 as Atlas Van-Lines, Inc.
Employees: 460
Sales: $294.9
SICs: 4212 Local Trucking Without Storage; 4213 Trucking
    Except Local; 4731 Freight Transportation Arrangement

The fifth-largest moving company in the United States, Atlas Van Lines, Inc., derives the majority of its revenue from helping corporate customers relocate. With approximately 600 agents in North America and 800 agents worldwide, the company generated nearly $300 million in annual revenue during the mid-1990s, a total that positioned it as one of the leaders in the household goods moving industry, ranking behind only North American Van Lines, United Van Lines, Allied Van Lines, and Mayflower Transit Co.

As they had for the past decade, members of the Independent Movers' & Warehousemen's Association gathered together in 1947 for their annual convention to discuss topics of mutual interest. In attendance were long-distance movers from across the country who had made the journey to French Lick, Indiana—the site of that year's convention—to be among their peers and discuss the nuances of their industry, the awkwardly named household goods moving industry. Over the course of the previous half century, the household goods moving industry had evolved from the entrepreneurial efforts of commercial freight operators who supplemented their paychecks by helping people move from one residence to another. Horse-drawn wagons that hauled coal, ice, groceries, and other goods were used in their off-hours to move furniture, clothes, and other household goods, marking the beginning of moving such objects as a commercial enterprise. Eventually, some of these part-time enterprises developed into full-time, full-fledged businesses.

Soon, the business of transporting household goods depended on wagons and then motor-powered trucks operating exclusively as moving company carriers. As the new century un-

folded and the decades passed, a host of small, locally operating moving companies were organized across the country, collectively forming what was then called the transfer and storage industry. Moving companies were governed by a federally empowered regulatory body, the Interstate Commerce Commission, and were represented by their own national association, the Independent Movers' & Warehousemen's Association Inc. Despite having a national association and being governed by a regulatory commission, the companies comprising the household goods moving industry were relatively weak, primarily because each was confined to a limited service area which tended to place a ceiling on their financial growth.

For several years prior to the 1947 convention, some members of the Independent Movers' & Warehousemen's Association had discussed removing this barrier to their growth by establishing a national operating organization. At French Lick talk turned to action, and a small group of movers began mapping plans to create a national operating organization. The following year, in 1948, 33 movers banded together in a cooperative effort to realize their common goal, creating a new long-distance moving company named Atlas Van-Lines, Inc.

Incorporated on May 19, the newly created, agent-owned company made its first move toward acquiring operating authority throughout the country two weeks later, when its directors purchased operating authority for direct service within 36 states and the District of Columbia. With head offices in Chicago, Atlas Van-Lines began its inaugural year of operation with the ability to direct service throughout the eastern half of the United States. For the next three decades the company would strive to secure operating authority throughout the rest of the country, an objective that would propel its growth and dictate its acquisitive strategy, eventually creating one of the nation's largest companies in the household goods moving industry.

The company derived much of its business during its quest for nationwide operating authority from military personnel moving from one location to another, the most itinerant segment of the country's population during the cold-war era. This constant source of business helped Atlas Van-Lines record $365,000 in sales after its first year of operation, a total that would climb to $1 million the following year. From the outset, the company's directors implemented a recruiting program to attract more agents, hoping to increase the company's ranks and, in turn, drive its annual sales total upward. In order to gain access to additional regions in the country, the company's annual revenue volume needed to grow, which it did during the early and mid-1950s, climbing to roughly $5 million by 1957.

At this point, Atlas Van-Lines was making enough money to finance another acquisition and continue the pursuit of its goal to obtain operating authority in the 48 contiguous states. With the acquisition of Howard Van Lines in 1958, which was renamed Atlas Van Service, Atlas Van-Lines gained access to Utah, Nevada, Arizona, New Mexico, and California, extending the company's service territory from coast to coast. On the heels of this acquisition, the company moved its corporate headquarters in 1960 from Chicago to Evansville, Indiana, where the directors of Atlas Van-Lines would orchestrate the geographic expansion of the agent-owned company into the 1990s.

At the time of the move from Chicago to Evansville, annual sales were discouragingly stagnant, hovering around $8 million for the preceding three years. In order to boost revenues for the continued expansion of the company, Atlas implemented a public relations campaign, the highlight of which was a *New York Times* article in 1962 that described Atlas Van-Lines' revival of Evansville's economy. Two years later the company took further steps to draw public attention to Atlas Van-Lines: the company's board of directors voted to double from one percent to two percent the advertising and sales development fund deduction taken from agents' settlement accounts, thereby enabling the company to expand its advertising program to include national print media.

Although the acquisition of Howard Van Lines in 1958 had extended Atlas Van-Lines' service territory from coast to coast, areas within the United States still remained where the company maintained no operations, particularly in the Rocky Mountain region and in the Pacific Northwest. During the early 1960s, while advertising efforts were increased to cover the entire country, the company's directors set their sights on obtaining operating authority in those regions where Atlas Van-Lines held no operating authority. In 1962 the company purchased the authority owned by Golden Van Lines of Colorado, giving it the opportunity to add new agents from the independent moving companies located in Idaho, Montana, Utah, and Wyoming. In 1964 Atlas Van-Lines acquired various interstate operating authorities by purchasing three companies that added Washington, Oregon, part of Idaho, and part of North Dakota to the company's growing map of regions served by Atlas Van-Lines vehicles.

Much had been achieved during the 1960s toward extending Atlas Van-Lines' geographic coverage across the United States, but the company also established an international presence during the decade, beginning with its acquisition of Torrance, California-based International Sea Van Inc. in 1959. Through this subsidiary, Atlas Van-Lines began shipping household goods overseas, then in 1960 began shipping to international markets through the air, giving the company two conduits for its service to foreign markets.

Late in the decade, the directors of Atlas Van-Lines made another pivotal move when they organized and hosted an industry forum for corporate traffic and transportation managers. Held in 1967, the Forum, which became an annual event, focused on tailoring moving services for relocating corporate clientele, a small but burgeoning market that 20 years later would provide the bulk of the company's business. Since its formation, Atlas Van-Lines had subsisted primarily on relocating military personnel, a market that would continue to drive the company's growth as it entered the 1970s. However, during the 1980s and 1990s, moving employees of major corporations would overtake military relocations as government defense spending waned. Eventually, corporate relocations would account for roughly two-thirds of Atlas Van-Lines' business. By addressing this new market in 1967, Atlas tapped an essential source of future revenue, gaining an early lead on its competition as the company entered the 1970s.

In 1974, the day arrived when Atlas Van Lines (the company dropped the hyphen from its name in 1971) could finally boast that its authority extended throughout the contiguous United States. On September 13, the company achieved its goal after 26 years of pursuing operating authority throughout the contiguous 48 states. Hawaii and Alaska were added to the company's service territory in 1976 and 1981 respectively, making Atlas Van Lines one of the few genuine national moving companies in the country.

Atlas Van Lines achieved its long-sought-after goal of blanketing the country with its moving vans a few short years before the household goods moving industry was dramatically reshaped by federal deregulation. Until 1980, the Interstate Commerce Commission wielded extensive control over moving companies like Atlas, dictating whether a moving company could go into business, what goods it could haul, where it could operate, and how much it could charge for its services. When the federal government deregulated the household goods moving industry through the Motor Carrier Act of 1980, the industry underwent radical and sudden changes. The number of moving companies in the country nearly doubled during a four-year span, jumping from 18,045 in 1980 to 30,481 in 1984, an increase that greatly intensified competition and sent service prices cascading downward.

The inaugural year of deregulation also marked the beginning of a new era at Atlas Van Lines. Since its inception in 1948, the company had been privately owned and tightly held by its agents, who had watched over its development from a fledgling enterprise into the sixth-largest moving company in the United States. In search of capital to finance further expansion, however, the agents decided to offer Atlas Van Lines stock to the public in 1980.

Four years after going public the company became the object of a hostile takeover. Contrans Acquisitions, Inc., a Toronto, Canada-based company led by a former Atlas Van Lines president, announced its intention to purchase control of Atlas Van Lines in May 1984. The hostile takeover attempt came as a shock to Atlas directors, forcing them to act quickly if they were to keep Contrans from gaining control. In October 1984, the potential takeover by Contrans was avoided when Wesray Transportation, Inc., an affiliate of Wesray Group, purchased Atlas Van Lines for $71.6 million., thereby thwarting Contrans' unsolicited advances toward Atlas Van Lines.

Forced into the arms of Wesray, Atlas Van Lines now found itself owned by another company after 36 years of independence. The transition was difficult for Atlas directors, agents, and employees, who struggled with Wesray's focus on the profitability of the company rather than the service and support it provided. Exacerbated by contrary operating philosophies, the relationship between Wesray and Atlas soured, formally ending four years after it began when Atlas Van Lines agents purchased the company in a leveraged buyout.

Returned to independence and private ownership during its 40th anniversary year, Atlas Van Lines attempted to put the troubled years of the 1980s behind it. The dramatic changes in the household goods moving industry engendered by deregulation had proven to be a formidable challenge to many moving companies across the country, but Atlas Van Lines, despite its difficult years in the middle of the decade, had emerged from the first ten years of deregulation buoyed by encouraging success. Transportation and handling of trade show exhibits and sophisticated electronic equipment had developed into a promising business that complemented the company's mainstay business of relocating corporate clientele, giving Atlas Van Lines the means with which to build a strong business for the future.

Financially, however, the company's performance was discouragingly lackluster, a problem the directors of Atlas Van Lines hoped to solve as the company entered the 1990s. Despite an economic recession during the early 1990s, Atlas recorded stable financial growth, becoming the fifth-largest moving company in country early in the decade. Annual revenue jumped from $217.5 million in 1992 to nearly $295 million in 1994, the year shareholders agreed to establish a new holding company, Atlas World Group, Inc., for Atlas Van Lines and its seven subsidiaries.

Encouraged by the success recorded during the first half of the decade, Atlas Van Lines exited the mid-1990s firmly positioned as a leader in the household goods moving industry. In 1995 the company recorded its fifth consecutive year of record earnings, a feat that harkened back to the robust growth registered during the 1960s and 1970s and fueled hoped for success in the future.

Principal Subsidiaries: Atlas Terminal Company; Atlas Van Lines International Corp.; Atlas Van Lines Ltd. (Canada); Atlas Van Lines of Texas, Inc.; Atlas World Class Travel, Inc.

Further Reading:

"Atlas Soars in Customer Poll," *Evansville Press,* September 29, 1994, p. 18.
"Atlas Stockholders Agree to Form Holding Company," *Evansville Courier,* September 22, 1994, p. 6C.
Atlas Van Lines, *Atlas Van Lines: Moving On,* Phoenix: Heritage, 1994.
"Atlas World Posts Record Profits 5th Straight Year," *Evansville Press,* March 8, 1995, p. 20.
Kroeger, Mark, "From the Home Office in Evansville, Here's the List," *Sunday Courier,* January 2, 1994, p. 1E.
Muller, E. J., "Encouraging Carriers to Go for the Gold," *Distribution,* August 1992, pp. 82–88.
"Relocation: Things Companies Pay For," *Inc.,* January 1993, p. 42.
Sword, Doug, "Gee Whiz!," *Indiana Business Magazine,* February 1992, pp. 11–15.

—Jeffrey L. Covell

Bank of Mississippi, Inc.

One Mississippi Plaza
Tupelo, Mississippi 38802
U.S.A.
(601) 680-2000
Fax: (601) 680-2261

Wholly Owned Subsidiary of BancorpSouth, Inc.
Incorporated: 1876 as Raymond, Trice & Company
Employees: 1,195
Total Assets: $1.7 billion
SICs: 6022 State Commercial Banks

The Bank of Mississippi, Inc., is one of the strongest and most influential chains of state banks in America's deep South. Since statewide banking was first permitted in Mississippi in 1986, the bank has opened more than 80 branches from Biloxi to Vicksburg. The Bank of Mississippi also has very strong ties to local communities throughout the state; over 85 percent of the bank's shareholders are residents of Mississippi, and bank management has designated community programs, such as community college scholarships and educational loans to students, a high priority.

Mississippi was the heart of the Confederacy during the American Civil War. By the end of the war the state was in economic chaos, particularly since a Union Army blockade had prevented supplies of food and necessary materials from reaching the state and its economic lifeline, the cotton trade, had been brought to a complete halt. In order to rebuild the local economy, the Mississippi state legislature voted to grant a rare perpetual charter to Raymond, Trice & Company, the forerunner of the Bank of Mississippi, on March 31, 1876. Established in the small town of Verona, the bank was situated in the back room of a store.

Raymond, Trice & Company immediately began to grant loans to landowners to expand their operations, launch new enterprises, and buy horses and equipment, and to the community to fund schools and rebuilding projects. By 1886 the bank was granting loans and doing business over a wider and wider area, and its shareholders decided to move the bank to Tupelo in order to take advantage of the better communications between the town and rural communities. The company was renamed the Bank of Lee County, and shortly afterward the Bank of Tupelo.

The Bank of Tupelo grew with the state of Mississippi. The states that had seceded from the Union during the Civil War were nearly healed by the turn of the century, and cotton fields all over Mississippi were yielding profitable crops. The Bank of Tupelo merged with the Bank of Nettleton in 1904 and with the Fulton Bank in 1906, providing the Bank of Tupelo with a stronger presence in northeastern Mississippi. The bank continued to open offices, and by the end of the 1920s the Bank of Tupelo was regarded by many of its customers as the most stable financial institution in Mississippi.

Then the Great Depression swept across the United States. President Franklin Delano Roosevelt completely revamped the banking industry, attempting to establish policies that would ultimately reinvigorate U.S. financial institutions, but many banks went bankrupt before the new policies could be implemented. The Bank of Tupelo, however, with a conservative loan program and cautious management, was able to survive the worst years of the Depression.

In addition to the problems caused by the Great Depression, the Bank of Tupelo also confronted challenges specific to the southern United States. The place of agriculture in southern life began to diminish in importance during the mid-1930s, as individual cotton farms gave way to large combines. At the same time, the region was faced with inadequate rural housing, the regular flooding of the Mississippi, which displaced thousands of people, and the growing and obvious need for serviceable roads and highways. Management at the Bank of Tupelo regarded all of these problems as part of the bank's responsibility to address. Loans were made to rebuild homes destroyed by floods, and the bank joined forces with other financial institutions to help fund adequate housing for families in rural areas of northeastern Mississippi.

With the coming of World War II, the Bank of Tupelo sold war bonds to help finance the U.S. war effort. After the war, in pursuit of a stronger regional economy, the Bank of Tupelo joined forces with other Mississippi financial institutions, local development organizations, and such federal agencies as the Appalachian Regional Commission and the Tennessee Valley Authority. These groups laid plans for a strong economic foundation across northeastern Mississippi. The Bank of Tupelo helped cultivate the growth of small business ventures, retail stores, utility companies, and local school systems. By 1949 the bank was expanding once again, and acquired both the Merchants & Farmers Bank of Ecru and the Bank of Sherman.

For 30 years the Bank of Tupelo had been guided by President J. P. Nanney, whose leadership propelled the bank from the status of a local institution to a regional powerhouse. His cautious financial policies, combined with his commitment to developing an industrial base for the area (he was twice elected mayor of Tupelo), were in large part responsible for the bank's success. By the early 1950s Nanny had hired J. C. Whitehead, Jr., as his hand-picked successor. Whitehead, who had graduated from Mississippi State University and whose father had been president of the Fulton Bank since the early 1920s, began his career at the bank as a trust officer. When Nanney died in 1959, Whitehead became president of the bank.

During the 1960s, under Whitehead's leadership, the Bank of Tupelo entered a period of unprecedented growth. One of Whitehead's first priorities was to increase the bank's loan/deposit ratio. In just a few short years, Whitehead had increased the ratio from 21 percent to an impressive 60 percent. This development provided the bank with the capital necessary to make loans to encourage the growth of various industries in northeastern Mississippi. At the same time, Whitehead proposed that the bank change its name to better reflect the concerns of the state as a whole. After exhaustive discussion among the bank's managers, the name "Bank of Mississippi" was finally chosen.

The bank continued to prosper in the 1970s, initiating acquisitions and mergers that resulted in many new financial associates. Customer services were upgraded and communication among the bank's many offices was improved. Most importantly, the bank sharpened its focus on business and industrial development. The bank joined forces with the Community Development Foundation, the Lee County Soil & Water Conservation District, and the Tombigbee River Valley Water Management District to encourage local entrepreneurs and attract national companies. The results of the consortium's efforts were dramatic, yielding economic gains throughout the state. Employment and wages increased, the tax base expanded, and citizens across the state gained greater access to a wider variety of services and products.

One of the most important of the bank's many activities during this period was its involvement in and support of the state of Mississippi's educational system. The bank supported programs within the public school system, encouraged and helped to develop curriculum at the community college level, provided loans and scholarships to students attending state universities, and contributed to educational programs at leading colleges and universities throughout the state.

Until restrictions were removed in 1986, Federal law prohibited statewide banking, with bank activities constrained to a one-hundred mile radius from a bank's main administrative headquarters. With the repeal of restrictions, the Bank of Mississippi expanded its presence across the state. Under a new president,

Aubrey B. Patterson, Jr., the Bank of Mississippi merged with First Mississippi National. This merger resulted in the bank's gaining greater access both to the Gulf Coast and Jackson markets, and provided the bank with the largest market share in the region of Hattiesburg. A short time later, the bank acquired both the American Bank of Vicksburg and the Bank of North Mississippi. With these acquisitions, the Bank of Mississippi was able to serve communities from the Gulf of Mexico to the Tennessee state border.

By 1990 the Bank of Mississippi had grown to more than 70 offices and branches operating in more than 40 cities and towns. A new administration and operations facility was constructed for the bank's main headquarters in Tupelo, and a highly sophisticated telecommunications system between branches was put in place. On a daily basis, deposits were collected by air transportation and put into the Federal Reserve Bank located in Memphis.

In the early 1990s the Bank of Mississippi was acquired by BancorpSouth, Inc., a large regional banking institution. The terms of the acquisition stipulated that the Bank of Mississippi would remain a relatively autonomous financial institution. Within a few years, with the financial help of BancorpSouth, the Bank of Mississippi had expanded its network of branch locations in the state.

Further Reading:

"BancorpSouth in Accord to Add Wes-Tenn Bancorp," *New York Times,* June 17, 1995, p. 19.
"BancorpSouth's Net Income Surged 31%," *American Banker,* May 24, 1995, p. 9.
Cline, Kenneth, "Strong Nonbank Units Help Diversify the Earnings System" and "A Tupelo Honey," *American Banker,* October 12, 1994, p. 4.
——, "Loan Growth Boosts 3 Southeastern Regionals," *American Banker,* October 17, 1994, p. 8.
"LF Bancorp to Be Acquired in $29.3 Million Stock Swap," *Wall Street Journal,* August 17, 1994, p. B4.
Patterson, Aubrey, *Bank of Mississippi, Inc.,* Newcomen Society: New York, 1990.

—Thomas Derdak

Banner Aerospace, Inc.

300 West Service Road
Washington Dulles International Airport
Washington, D.C. 20041
U.S.A.
(703) 478-5790
Fax: (703) 478-5795

Public Company
Incorporated: 1956 as Banner Hardware Jobbing Co.
Employees: 550
Sales: $222.38 million
Stock Exchanges: New York
SICs: 5088 Transportation Equipment & Supplies; 3452
   Bolts, Nuts, Rivets & Washers; 3562 Ball & Roller
   Bearings

Banner Aerospace, Inc., calls itself "the world's largest independent stocking distributor of aircraft hardware inventory," with over 300,000 distinct products. Its product line can be categorized into two groups, rotable products and hardware. Rotable products include jet engines, engine parts, flight data recorders ("black boxes"), radar and navigation systems, instruments, landing gear, and hydraulic and electrical components. Hardware includes bearings, nuts, bolts, screws, rivets, and other fasteners. Banner sells its products to commercial airlines, air cargo carriers, original equipment manufacturers, and other distributors. More than one-third of its sales are made internationally.

The company had a low profile until the mid-1980s, when Jeffrey J. Steiner assumed control and began using it as an investment and takeover vehicle. In the latter half of that decade, Banner's rapid-fire, junk-bond-financed acquisitions earned it a reputation as "the KKR (Kohlberg, Kravis, Roberts and Co.) of public companies." Following a 1989 merger and subsequent reorganization, Banner Aerospace was 47.2 percent owned by the Fairchild Corporation. Although Banner Aerospace is legally a successor to Burbank Aircraft Supply, Inc., its history can more accurately be traced through Banner Industries, Inc.

Samuel J. Krasney has been credited with saving Banner Industries from bankruptcy in 1968 and slowly building the Cleveland company into a major player in the secondary aerospace parts industry. Although some sources designate him as Ban-

ner's founder, others trace the company's history to 1925. According to *Moody's Industrial Manual*, the original Banner Hardware Jobbing Co. was incorporated in 1956. Its name was abbreviated to Banner Industries in 1960, and the firm was reincorporated in 1970 under that name.

Krasney planned to grow through acquisition; however, many of his early purchases proved to be missteps. Patterson Industries, Inc., was acquired in 1968 and divested in 1973; Misceramic Tile, Inc., was bought in 1969 and sold four years later; and Advance Foundry was purchased in 1969 and sold in 1975.

The 1970s brought better fortunes. The 1972 acquisition of Thompson Aircraft Tire Corp. established Banner as the exclusive distributor of Japanese-made Bridgestone aircraft tires. By the mid-1980s, tires and retreads contributed one-fifth of the company's annual sales, and Thompson ranked as the largest independent retreader of aircraft tires in the world. In 1973 Banner bought Burbank Aircraft Inc., a subsidiary that would grow to become the group's largest revenue generator. The California-based company ranked as one of the most important distributors of aircraft fasteners, fittings, and electrical components in the global aircraft industry. Krasney's methodical acquisition strategy proved successful, and the group ended the 1970s with record earnings.

During the early 1980s, forays into manufacturing and trucking proved poorly timed. The company's trucking subsidiary, Lee Way Holding Co., fell into Chapter 11 bankruptcy in 1985. This transport company had been formed through the 1977 merger of the newly acquired Lovelace Truck Service, Inc., with Commercial Motor Freight, Inc. (acquired in 1969). The deregulation of the interstate trucking industry was cited as the cause of the subsidiary's failure. Throughout the early 1980s, the $100 million company was unable to surpass 1979's earnings record of $5 million. Banner dipped into the red at least once during this period, in 1982. Thomas Jaffe of *Forbes* speculated that Banner's difficulties made it a prime takeover candidate.

They also took a heavy toll on CEO Krasney. After three rounds of heart surgery, Krasney decided to rid himself of the problematic company. He reduced his stake in Banner from 38 percent to 28 percent in 1983 with the sale of 400,000 shares to the venture capital fund Warburg, Pincus Capital Corp. Two years later he sold most of his remaining interest in Banner to Jeffrey J. Steiner for $15 million. Steiner also picked up Warburg, Pincus's shares, raising his stake to 39 percent by mid-1988.

Steiner brought a cosmopolitan air to Banner. Born in Austria, he spoke four languages and maintained residences in London, Paris, St. Tropez, Palm Beach, and New York. As a child during World War II, Steiner had fled with his Jewish father and Turkish mother from Austria to his mother's homeland. He later earned a degree in textile engineering from Britain's Bradford Institute of Technology. After graduation, he planned to work in the United States for one year, then go home to his family's textile business. Plans changed when the young sales trainee at Texas Instruments quickly advanced through the corporate ranks to become president of subsidiaries in France, Mexico, and Switzerland. By the time he was 25, Steiner had earned a position on Texas Instruments' management committee.

After ten years at Texas Instruments, Steiner returned to Europe to found Cedec S.A., a turnkey engineering firm headquartered in Paris. Steiner began dabbling in investing on the side, concentrating primarily on the European energy market in the 1970s. Then, in 1981, he decided to cash out of Europe and try his hand at the American investment scene. Banner proved to be the opportunity he was looking for.

As chairman and CEO, Steiner oversaw financing and acquisition planning from his Manhattan office, while Krasney continued to make a significant contribution to Banner's day-to-day activities as vice chairman and chief operating officer in Cleveland. A hard-working risk-taker, Steiner took his cues from corporate raiders like Carl Icahn and Nelson Peltz. In partnership with Icahn in the early 1980s, Steiner amassed stakes in Marshall Field, Uniroyal Co., and Phillips Petroleum Co. According to *Business Week,* Steiner hoped his Banner Industries would grow like ''Peltz's Triangle Industries Inc., which [had] built a $3 billion empire using Drexel [Burnham Lambert Inc.] financing to buy old-line industrials it then tries to fix up.'' Through Banner, Steiner began to ''trade subsidiaries like a stockbroker with a blind account,'' in the words of Robert McGough of *Financial World.*

Steiner, who was elected chairman and chief executive officer late in 1985, acquired Solair Inc., a broad-based aircraft equipment supplier with about $10 million in annual sales, by the end of 1986. The new leader took Banner into the world of junk-bond financing in 1987 with the acquisition of Rexnord Inc., a diversified manufacturer of oil pipeline and refining equipment, water pollution control systems, and aerospace fasteners. The total $825 million price tag dwarfed Banner's $149 million annual sales, but Drexel Burnham Lambert prepared a successful financing package. Krasney candidly acknowledged to *Crain's Cleveland Business* that he ''never in a thousand years would have done something this big.''

Within less than two years, Steiner liquidated $825 million worth of Rexnord's assets, including the subsidiary's research and development operations, Bellofram Corp., Mathews Conveyor Co., Railway Maintenance Equipment Co., and Fairfield Manufacturing Co., in order to meet Banner's $3.2 million monthly interest charges. Steiner also cut a deal with former employer Texas Instruments Inc. for the divestment of Rexnord Automation Inc., raising $65 million with this transaction alone. The sales recouped Rexnord's purchase price, yet allowed Banner to retain 40 percent of Rexnord's earning power. Steiner characterized his strategy to *Financial World* as ''a combination of industrial restructuring and LBOs.''

The acquisitions spree powered a 39 percent growth rate from 1984 to 1989, ranking Banner among *Fortune*'s 25 fastest-growing companies. By 1989, Steiner increased Banner's net worth fourfold to $160 million and the firm had amassed more than $1 billion in assets. Annual sales volume tripled from $128 million in 1985 to $433 million in 1989, and net income multiplied to about $50 million. Although $525 million in debt was retired during the period, the company was still highly leveraged, with about $620 million in outstanding junk bonds.

Instead of using Banner's cash flow to settle these obligations, Steiner continued to leverage the company's borrowing power

to finance new deals. Banner acquired Indianapolis-based rival PT Components late in 1988 for an estimated $175 million cash. Steiner merged the formerly privately held PT Components—one of the leading manufacturers of power transmission parts in the United States—with Rexnord's mechanical power division and sold about 60 percent of the resulting Rexnord Corp.'s shares to outside investors.

Banner acted as ''white knight'' to Fairchild Industries in 1989, when it rescued the company from a year-long hostile assault from the Carlyle Group, a Washington, D.C. merchant bank. The $265 million cash transaction increased Banner's consolidated annual revenues by more than 100 percent to almost $1 billion.

The merged companies underwent a complicated reshuffling in the ensuing months. Banner Industries and Fairchild were united under the name the Fairchild Corporation in 1990. Although Fairchild was the larger of the two, the ''new'' Fairchild was legally considered a successor to Banner Industries.

The Banner name was not retired: Steiner reorganized Banner Industries' Aerospace Distribution Group as Banner Aerospace Inc. in 1990. This ''new'' company's legal predecessor and primary subsidiary was Burbank Aircraft Supply. Samuel J. Krasney was named Banner Aerospace's CEO, president, and chairman.

The Fairchild deal became the capstone of a precarious pyramid of leverage that began to crumble in the early 1990s. Defense cutbacks, increased competition, and general economic difficulties depressed the aviation industry. The downturn cut into cash flow when both Banner and Fairchild needed it most. By late 1990, Banner/Fairchild's cash flow barely covered its expenses. In August 1990 Fairchild sold about 53 percent of Banner Aerospace's equity to outside investors. Fairchild divested other subsidiaries to raise the funds needed to meet its debt payments.

Banner Aerospace's sales and earnings increased from $218.59 million and $15.98 million in 1990 to $264.44 million and $19.03 million in 1991, but began to decline in 1992. Sales declined to $205.12 million by 1994 and Banner lost a total of $14.84 million in 1993 and 1994. The closure of two subsidiaries—Banner Aeronautical Corp. and Aero International Inc.—accounted for $11 million of that deficit. Banner also blamed intense price competition for its red ink.

After a quarter-century with Banner, Samuel Krasney retired in September 1993. The firm's 17-person headquarters was moved to Chantilly, Virginia, and Krasney was succeeded by Jeffrey Steiner, who engineered a quick turnaround in 1994. Banner squeaked out of its losing position with a $475,000 profit and an optimistic outlook in fiscal 1995.

Principal Subsidiaries: Adams Industries, Inc.; Aerospace Bearing Support, Inc.; Aircraft Bearing Corporation; BAI, Inc.; Burbank Aircraft Supply, Inc.; DAC International, Inc.; Dallas Aerospace, Inc.; Georgetown Jet Center, Inc.; Matrix Aviation, Inc.; NASAM Incorporated; PacAero; Professional Aviation Associates, Inc.; Solair, Inc.

44   Banner Aerospace, Inc.

Further Reading:

Ashyk, Loretta, "Just Like Any Guy?" *Crain's Cleveland Business,*
    March 9, 1987, p. 1.
Giesen, Lauri, "Banner Sells off Rexnord R&D Unit to Pay Down
    Debt," *Metalworking News,* July 13, 1987, p. 4.
Gordon, Mitchell, "Put Out the Pennants," *Barron's,* April 28, 1986,
    p. 54.
Jaffe, Thomas, "Happy Landing," *Forbes,* October 21, 1985, p. 210.
Jones, Sam L., "Fastener Industry Riveted by Sudden Talk of
    Mergers," *Metalworking News,* October 31, 1988, p. 1.
Livingston, Sandra, "Banner to Take Over Fairchild," *Plain Dealer,*
    May 9, 1989, p. 1D.
McGough, Robert, "Banner Industries: Do Your Homework," *Finan-
    cial World,* October 16, 1990, p. 20.

Phillips, Stephen, "Banner Aerospace to Relocate," *Plain Dealer,*
    August 12, 1993, p. 1E.
"PT Components Acquired by Banner Industries," *Industrial Distribu-
    tion,* September 1988, p. 15.
Sabath, Donald, "Banner Aerospace Loss Due to Air-Transport
    Woes," *Plain Dealer,* May 27, 1993, p. F2.
Schiller, Zachary, and Kathleen Deveny,"The Next Takeover Artist
    You Meet Could Be Jeff Steiner," *Business Week,* February 9,
    1987, p. 33.
Taub, Stephen, "The KKR of Public Companies?" *Financial World,*
    March 21, 1989, p. 14.

—April Dougal Gasbarre

Barings PLC

8 Bishopsgate
London
Greater London EC2N 4AE
England
(011) 71 280 1000
Fax: (011) 71 283 2633

Wholly Owned Subsidary of ING, B.V.
Incorporated: 1762
Employees: 1,728
Operating Revenues: £307 million
Stock Exchanges: London
SICs: 6790 Miscellaneous Investing

Barings PLC, sometimes referred to as the ''Queen's Bank,'' has one of the most illustrious and dramatic histories in the banking industry. The company grew to importance during the Napoleonic Wars by financing Britain's military campaigns, and after Napoleon's downfall, Barings helped arrange France's financial recovery. Known as the sixth great European power during the 19th century, the company was also involved in the American purchase of Louisiana from France in 1803, the refinancing of the Bank of England in 1839, and the reconstitution of the Banque de France in 1849. Barings faced a crisis in 1890 when speculative expansion brought the company's liabilities to more than 21 million pounds sterling, and while the bank was rescued by the Rothschild family and the Bank of England, Barings never again reached the pre-eminent position it once held. The latest dramatic chapter in Barings' history was written in 1995 when investment speculations by a lone manager in the company's Singapore office led to losses of over £1 billion, frantic but unsuccessful attempts by the British banking community to save the bank, and ultimately the acquisition of the firm by a Dutch financial services group, ING.

The great financial house of Barings was founded in 1762 by two sons of an English country gentleman who had made a fortune in the wool manufacturing trade. The younger son, Francis, soon rose to leadership of the firm and began to arrange some of the most important financial transactions of the period. As Governor of the East India Company, Francis Baring underwrote many imports to Britain from all over the world, including such new and highly sought-after items as coffee, cocoa, tea, and tobacco. From the Far East, the bank financed the importation of porcelain artifacts for the aristocracy. In Russia, Francis Baring was active in arranging trade agreements between the rising merchant class and businessmen from Western Europe. When the American colonies revolted against British rule in 1776, Baring was at the forefront of the prominent and influential individuals who advocated peace with the colonists.

Francis Baring's second son, Alexander, succeeded him in the business. Alexander traveled to the newly independent United States and purchased large amounts of land in Maine and Pennsylvania which eventually brought millions to the firm. On his journey he also married Anne Bingham, the daughter of Senator William Bingham of Pennsylvania. Bingham was at that time the richest man in the United States, and Anne's dowry amounted to $900,000, a staggering figure in those days. The marriage also brought with it important connections in the American banking industry.

Under the leadership of Alexander, Barings bank was involved in one of its most important and far-reaching transactions: sustaining the British effort to defeat Napoleon. From 1898 through 1814 Alexander Baring gave repeated assurances to William Pitt the Younger, Britain's prime minister during the lengthy struggle with France, that money would continue to be available for the country's military campaigns. At the same time, Alexander Baring also conducted business with Napoleon, arranging the sale of France's Louisiana Territory to the United States in 1803. While he was criticized in Britain for helping Napoleon raise money to continue war with England, Baring's primary intent was to assist President Thomas Jefferson expand the boundaries of the newly formed United States. Following the in tradition of his father, Alexander Baring protested against the measures the British government brought against the United States during the War of 1812.

After Napoleon had been defeated at the battle of Waterloo by the Allied forces under the command of Wellington, Baring thought that the future of Europe was dependent upon a French economy that was financially healthy. In consultation with British diplomats, the Barings bank therefore decided to provide an enormous indemnity loan to France. The French prime minister, Richelieu, and the French foreign minister, Tallyrand, regarded this loan as having guaranteed the peace of Europe. When the British, French, Austrian, Prussian, and Russian representatives met at the Congress of Vienna in 1815 to draw up the peace treaty for Europe that remained in force until World War I, they all concurred that Barings bank was the sixth great European power and without its assistance no peace treaty would have a lasting effect.

For his service to the British nation, Alexander Baring was knighted by the royal family and dubbed Lord Ashburton. As Lord Ashburton, he continued arranging important financial transactions not only in Europe, but in Asia and the United States as well. One of his last acts before he retired was arranging the settlement, in association with the renowned American orator and New Hampshire senator Daniel Webster, of the disputed boundaries between Maine, New Brunswick, and Quebec. Upon his retirement, he brought into the firm two men who he thought would maintain its reputation, honesty, and credibility. Thomas Baring, Alexander's nephew, became head of the bank's international operation, while Joshua Bates of Massachusetts was placed in charge of the company's American and Canadian interests.

During the early and mid-nineteenth century, under the direction of the new leadership, Barings bank enhanced its reputation in international finance. In Europe, during the financially unstable years of the late 1830s and 1840s, Barings was the strongest bank operating on the Continent. In 1839, when the Bank of England ran into difficulties, Thomas Baring was there to shore up the fortunes of Britain's national bank. In 1847, under similar circumstances, the firm came to the rescue of the Banque de France. Yet Barings was most influential in its transactions involving the United States. Barings functioned as the agent and banker for the federal government and numerous state governments. Barings assisted the Bank of the United States and an untold number of private firms, and was one of the major financial backers of the burgeoning American railroad industry. In 1848, after the Mexican War, Barings arranged and financed the purchase of Texas by the U.S. government from Mexican officials. During the American Civil War, Barings underwrote the purchase of Alaska from Russia by the U.S. government. Although the transaction was ridiculed at the time as ''Seward's Folly,'' in mockery of Abraham Lincoln's secretary of the interior, William H. Seward, Barings had the foresight to see the enormous potential of this acquisition.

Barings ran aground financially in 1890, but the seeds of disaster were planted in 1824. Barings had collaborated with Adrian Hope and Company, a Dutch banking firm, to provide loans to the new nation of Argentina. This transaction was the first of many between Barings and the South American country. Over the years, Barings became more and more involved in the economy of Argentina, financing a wide variety of projects, including railway lines, harbor construction, grand hotels, and even bathhouses. Nothing seemed too small or too large for Barings to finance. In fact, the company had developed such strong ties to the Argentine government that at one point managers from England were actually running the Argentine National Bank. By 1888, however, exclusively through Baring bank activities and transactions, Argentina had run up a debt in an amount that began to cause concern within the British financial community. In 1890 it was discovered that Barings was responsible for almost all Agentinian loans, which totaled a staggering figure of 38 million pounds sterling. Argentina defaulted on the loans, and Barings reported over 21 million pounds sterling in liabilities. Government ministers decided that if Barings failed, English credit would be damaged along with the company; as a result, the Bank of England initiated a bond sale to Russia and arranged a loan from the Banque de France. Called the Baring Guarantee Fund, the financing saved the historic banking firm from ruin.

Although Barings was rescued from the ignominious fate of liquidation, from the time of the debacle in the 1890s the bank never regained its pre-eminent status in the international financial community. In 1906 the company withdrew from all transactions on the North American continent and did not conduct any activities in the United States for eight decades. Under the watchful eye of industry regulators and the management at the Bank of Britain, Barings was no longer trusted to handle large financial transactions, either domestically or internationally.

The bank's influence as a major global financier had been completely undermined by the problems in Argentina, and the firm's management was relegated to looking after relatively small accounts of London businesses and wealthy country gentlemen.

During the 1920s and 1930s, Barings continued to labor under the stigma of its past mistake. The lack of opportunity to make or arrange large financial transactions led the bank's management into the only field it could pursue—financial advice and consulting. Since the company was only involved in stock and bond consulting to a limited degree, the worldwide depression of the 1930s, which damaged many banks, did not significantly affect Barings. This backhanded stroke of good fortune led to the gradual repair of the company's reputation, and during the late 1930s, and throughout the decade of the 1940s, Barings developed its financial consulting services.

With its reputation nearly rehabilitated after 50 years, and with the approval of ever-watchful English banking industry regulators and the management of the Bank of Britain, Barings was chosen by the newly crowned Elizabeth II in 1952 as one of the guardians of the royal fortunes. Her Majesty and the royal family had always been impressed with the prestige and tradition of one of the pillars of Britain's long-lost mercantile empire, and the choice of Barings seemed natural to many people. In addition to the Queen's fortune, a significant amount of the royal family's assets, including those of her son Charles and Princess Anne, were place under the control of management at Barings. Barings advised the Queen well, and soon the royal fortune was increasing dramatically during the 1960s and 1970s. Members of the royal family were so pleased with the consulting services at Barings that Prince Charles decided to establish his own charity with the bank. Called the Prince's Trust, the money was used to create programs for economically deprived teenagers.

By the 1980s, Barings was considered one of the models of merchant management in Britain and was given greater and greater opportunity by the Bank of Britain and industry regulators to pursue more profitable ventures. Corporate finance, convertible bonds, and fund management were stable but not very lucrative business activities for the bank, so management at Barings decided to re-enter the international banking arena. For the first time in 80 years, the company moved into American finance scene and began to advise medium-sized U.S. firms on restructurings, partnerships, and mergers. One of the company's most important transactions during this time involved the arrangement of a joint venture between SmithKline Beckman and Nova Pharmaceuticals. In addition, management decided to expand its financial services, and opened a stock brokerage operation in Tokyo to take advantage of the highly profitable bull market in Japan during the mid-1980s. Not long afterward, Barings Securities Ltd. was established to use the gains from its Tokyo office to set up operations around the Pacific Rim, Latin America, and continental Europe. Barings PLC was once again playing upon the international stage as it had done during the 18th and 19th centuries.

During the early and mid-1990s, Barings quickened the pace of its international brokerage operations. Offices in Tokyo, Singapore, London, and the rest of the world expanded dramatically, with new employees hired and promoted rapidly. One of these newcomers was a young man named Nick Leeson. Leeson, the son of a plasterer who was raised in one of the public housing projects of north London, dropped out of high school and took his first job as a bank clerk. His rise within the financial services industry was nothing less than meteoric. Later he worked for Coutts & Company, a prestigious London bank, and then took a job with the American investment firm of Morgan Stanley. The position Leeson held at Morgan Stanley helped him win a job at Barings in 1989. By 1992 Leeson had accepted a promotion to the Singapore office where Barings was expanding its trading operations.

In 1993 approximately 20 percent of the firm's total profits were brought in by Barings Futures group, of which Leeson was a major participant. The young man had developed a reputation for spotting small differences in the value of futures on the Osaka and Singapore exchanges, and made millions for his company by taking advantage of the spread. Barings was so pleased with Leeson's performance that his salary was increased to $350,000. He soon became manager of the Singapore office and grew used to living the luxurious lifestyle of an international financier, driving a Mercedes, owning a yacht, and taking advantage of an unlimited travel expense account. As he reported more profits, the company managers in London granted him more authority. Leeson became so powerful that London managers allowed him to assume total control over the trading desk and the settlement operation, which meant that he not only made the trades but kept the books.

During late 1994 and early 1995, Leeson immersed himself in the highly speculative world of buying and selling futures contracts. He began to lose enormous amounts of money but, because of his control over the Singapore office, was able to keep the figures from being accurately reported to London headquarters. On Tuesday, February 21st, the unimaginable happened. Due to reckless trading on the futures market, Leeson had gambled away over $1 billion, more than twice the total capital available at Barings. Suddenly, the venerable 233-year-old bank of Britain's glorious imperial days was insolvent. Leeson hopped on a flight to Malaysia and then traveled to Germany, where he was arrested. Losses at Barings soared to $1.3 billion by the end of the debacle.

The international financial community reeled, and both the British government and private sector looked frantically for a savior for the bank. Barings was the most important of all the

Queen's banks, and its failure would result in a loss of $100 million for the royal family. Fortunately, in June 1995, ING, one of the largest Dutch financial services companies, bought Barings at the fire-sale price of just over $1 billion. Not content to wait for publication of an investigative report by the Bank of Britain, ING immediately fired 21 high-ranking managers at Barings who were believed to be aware of Leeson's trading activities.

Under the direction of ING, Barings will be reorganized into a much more efficient and streamlined investment services firm. Not surprisingly, ING's strategy includes a comprehensive evaluation of the operations and accountability systems Barings has in place, and will alter those if necessary. The once-proud bank will undoubtedly survive, but only ING management knows in what shape or form. Once again, the history of Barings has come full circle.

Further Reading:

"The Barings and the Rothschilds," *Fortune,* April 1948, p. 97.
"Broking Trouble: Barings," *Economist,* October 3, 1992, pp. 4–86.
Chau-Eoan, Howard G., "Going for Broke," *Time,* March 13, 1995, pp. 40–47.
"ING Group Fires 21 Top Executives at Barings," *Time,* May 15, 1995, p. 27.
Johnson, Maureen, "Break-the-Bank Trader Talks," *Chicago Sun-Times,* September 17, 1995, p. 20.
Kaye, Stephen D., "Ripples from a Fallen Bank," *U.S. News & World Report,* March 13, 1995, pp. 68–70.
Lawson, W. R., "An Averted Crash in the City," *Fortnightly Review,* December 1890, pp. 932–45.
Levinson, Marc, "An Evil Is upon Us," *Newsweek,* March 13, 1995, pp. 49–50.
Pederson, Daniel, and Michael Elliot, "Busted!" *Newsweek,* March 13, 1995, pp. 37–47.
——, and Carol Hall, "God Save the Royal Fortune," *Newsweek,* March 13, 1995, p. 40.
Reier, Sharon, "Flying Dutchman: Why Aad Jacobs Decided Holland's ING Would Buy Barings," *Financial World,* June 20, 1995, pp. 28–30.
Shortt, George E., "The House of Barings and Canada," *Queen's Quarterly,* October 1930, pp. 732–43.
Willoughby, Jack, "The Sixth Great Power Returns," *Forbes,* February 20, 1989.
"Who Lost Barings?" and "Baring Not Quite All," *Economist,* July 22, 1995, pp. 16 and 66.

—Thomas Derdak

BATES WORLDWIDE

Bates Worldwide, Inc.

405 Lexington Avenue
New York, New York 10174
U.S.A.
(212) 297-7000
Fax: (212) 986-0270

Wholly Owned Subsidiary of Cordiant plc
Incorporated: 1940 as Ted Bates & Company, Inc.
Employees: 6,500
Gross Billings: $5 billion
SICs: 7311 Advertising Agencies

Bates Worldwide, Inc. is one of the leading advertising agency networks in the world with 185 offices in 65 countries and annual billings in excess of $5 billion. Headquartered in New York City, the company organizes its owned and affiliated agencies into four regions: Bates Americas, Bates Asia-Pacific, Bates Europe, and Africa. The company provides its 2,200 clients with a full range of marketing communications services. Formerly known as Backer Spielvogel Bates Worldwide (BSB), the company's name was changed to Bates Worldwide in 1994, as Chairman and CEO Michael Bungey sought to strengthen Bates' global network and reputation. Although Bates had strong local agencies throughout the world, it was known by different names in different countries, and Bungey's objective, as reported by Penny Warneford in *The Australian*, was "to create an international brand out of the agency so that multi-national advertisers would hire and retain the services of the agency around the world, knowing that each of its offices stood for the same standards."

The emphases on brand name and international marketing were traditions that went back to the Bates agency founder Theodore L. Bates, who established Ted Bates & Company in 1940. A 1924 graduate of Yale University, Ted Bates worked in advertising for several years, serving as a vice-president and director at Benton & Bowles before forming his own agency. Ted Bates began with two clients, Colgate-Palmolive-Peet and Continental Baking, and four brands to advertise: Colgate Dental Cream, Palmolive Shaving Cream, Hostess Cup Cakes, and Wonder Bread. Within the agency's first six months, gross billings stood at $5 million, an accomplishment largely attributed to the Unique Selling Proposition (USP) developed by Ted Bates and Rosser Reeves, the agency's chief creative officer.

USP focused on identifying a unique feature of each product and connecting it in the minds of consumers with the brand name. Moreover, early USPs emphasized the potential health benefits of a product. One early company publication described how the agency contracted with five leading universities to undertake dental research in discovering some new quality in Colgate Dental Cream. Conducted by recognized authorities, the tests continued for many months and provided the medical proof for the USP message: *The Colgate Way Stops Tooth Decay Best.* That declaration, repeated thousands of times in every medium, sent Colgate sales soaring in the United States. In another example, an advertising campaign for Continental Baking told consumers that *Wonder Bread Helps Build Strong Bodies 12 Ways.* The USP principle would later be applied in Bates ads for Minute Maid Orange Juice (*Better For Health Than Oranges Squeezed At Home*) and Royal Puddings (*Give More Food Energy Than Sweet, Fresh Milk*).

After ten years and a world war, the agency was working with 41 of its clients' brands, its billings approached $28 million, and, by one estimate, sales of the four original brands promoted by Bates had increased by 368 percent. With the agency doing so well, Ted Bates surprised the advertising industry in 1948 by dissolving the incorporated firm and converting the business to a partnership. Fourteen senior officers became members with equal shares, equal rights, and equal responsibilities.

During the 1950s, Bates and Reeves were the first to take advantage of the advertising potential of television. "Advertising," Reeves wrote, "is the art of getting a Unique Selling Proposition into the heads of the most people at the lowest cost," and television offered the best way to do that. While most of their competitors had announcers reading ad copy and holding up the product, Bates introduced unique spot commercials, such as one for Anacin that featured hammers pounding on the heads of headache sufferers. As Paul Foley, of the Interpublic Group of Companies, later told the *New York Times,* Bates's "use of television in the early days developed a whole new advertising form."

Always looking for new ways to get USPs to more people, Bates was also quick to realize the potential of overseas markets. Europe was beginning to recover from the economic devastation of World War II, and a few American companies began setting up overseas branches or entering joint ventures. In 1956, Bates set about building an international network. Three years of negotiations with Hobson & Partners, Ltd, one of England's most successful agencies, resulted in the establishment in London of Hobson, Bates & Partners, Ltd. in 1959. This arrangement provided Bates' American clients with a fully operative overseas office and gave British clients access to the American market. Within a single year, Hobson's billings leaped from $5.4 million to $14.2 million.

The Bates agency was growing as well, adding both M&M/Mars and Nabisco, Inc. to its client base in 1954. In 1959, when Chase Manhattan Bank became a client, the agency began moving beyond its traditional packaged consumer goods accounts into services.

Such growth prompted Ted Bates to change the company's ownership structure again. In 1955 he dissolved the partnership and reconverted the company to a corporation. With several hundred employees on the payroll, a corporate structure made it easier to create appropriate levels of responsibility. Ownership in the corporation's stock was limited to Bates employees, and Ted Bates became honorary chairman of the board as well as chairman of the executive committee. Rosser Reeves became vice-chairman and eventually chairman and CEO. Bates continued to direct the agency's expansion into Europe, Southeast Asia, and Australia. When Bates died in 1972, Ted Bates & Company was among the five largest agencies in the world.

The company continued to prosper, developing a huge network of global offices and promoting its products with USPs. A new slogan, "Think Global. Act Local," introduced in 1984, reflected the company's philosophy that local affiliated offices should take full advantage of the economies of scale and resources of a worldwide network while responding to the local culture and market to sell messages.

In 1986, Saatchi & Saatchi plc purchased the company, then called Ted Bates Worldwide, for $450 million and merged it the following year with another U.S. agency, Backer & Spielvogel Advertising, which it had acquired for $65 million. In the first years after the merger, Backer Spielvogel Bates Worldwide (BSB) prospered, winning such clients as Wendy's, CPC International, and Burroughs-Wellcome. In fact, in 1988 BSB was named the top ad agency in Europe. However, Saatchi & Saatchi required BSB to drop its large, long-time Colgate business to avoid potential conflicts of interest with the clients that Saatchi & Saatchi retained at the time.

Under new parentage, Bates' tradition of research continued. In a 1990 *American Demographics* article, Rebecca Piirto reported that the agency had invested more than $2 million in Global Scan, an annual worldwide customer lifestyle study that analyzed markets and consumer desires in 17 different countries. Identifying five global "psychographic" personality types—strivers, achievers, pressureds, adapters, and traditionals—Global Scan helped agencies like BSB recognize cultural and economic differences that could make or break an international ad campaign. The companies could therefore tailor their advertising strategies to suit consumer preferences and ideals.

The company had also developed several other proprietary systems, including Brand Essence, a study that identified and refined distinctive and competitive brand positionings; Ad Scan, a pre-testing method of the relevance of advertising before production; and Brand Scan, which evaluated advertising over time and provided information on its real effect and cost.

However, the late 1980s and early 1990s also brought severe challenges to BSB's parent, Saatchi & Saatchi, which was debt laden following its acquisitions and began losing new business bids. While Saatchi & Saatchi worked to recover and underwent several management shake-ups, BSB remained a core asset for the company.

In January 1993, CEO Carl Spielvogel named Michael Bungey president and chief operating officer of Bates Worldwide. The following year Bungey became CEO and assumed the position of worldwide chairman at the end of the year when Spielvogel retired.

Bungey had been with BSB for several years, having served as chairman of BSB Europe as well as chairman and CEO of BSB Dorland in London; he had a reputation for winning new accounts. "I learned how to do new business because I started an agency and we didn't have any business," Bungey told Stuart Elliot in a 1993 *New York Times* article. He was referring to Michael Bungey & Partners which he started in 1971 and which eventually became part of BSB Dorland. In 1987, Bungey set out to build a creative reputation for Dorland and to develop new international business. By 1992, the company finished first among 20 top British agencies ranked on net billings gains, despite the unexpected loss of its $35 million Rover car account.

As chairman of BSB Europe Bungey restructured the company's European network. The local offices, the former Ted Bates affiliates, "were a mass of unwieldy local agencies still largely controlled by their local manager-founders," according to Noreen O'Leary in *ADWEEK*. Tim Corrigan, a BSB colleague, told O'Leary, "Michael has successfully changed the management of every single agency and created a whole new culture and new ways of doing things."

In assuming the worldwide position, "Michael's challenge now is no less than to take an organization built around a cult of personality and make it into the integrated global marketing concern it was always envisioned as," a Saatchi colleague told O'Leary. After moving from London to New York City, Bungey spent much of 1993 meeting with key clients, familiarizing himself with the New York office, and mapping out plans for the company's future. He established an account planning department and promoted Frank Assumma to president of Bates USA.

Bungey also began a year-long research of clients, prospective clients, and agency management regarding the company's brand identity, resulting in the name change to Bates Worldwide in 1994. Every agency within the Bates network was expected to include the name Bates in its name to adopt a single brand name on a global basis. "The name change signals that Bates is now a reconstituted agency. In the past few years, they haven't been top of mind when you think of major agencies. Now they're becoming a contender," said Arthur Anderson, managing partner of agency search consultancy Morgan, Anderson & Co. of New York, in a 1994 *Advertising Age* article.

With regard to new business, Bungey aimed at adding more global company accounts. He told Warneford in *The Australian* that multinational advertisers "rather than local national advertisers represent the future for agencies as the number of advertiser companies shrinks worldwide and national companies are swallowed by multinationals." Moreover, O'Leary reported that Bungey had targeted "clients that already worked with the company in one or more countries—brands like Mercedes, Avis, Chanel, Estée Lauder, Nissan, 3M and Goodyear—as well as international business from marketers like Energizer, British American Tobacco and Electrolux which have not already aligned themselves with agencies on a regional or global basis." Bungey also reemphasized the Bates Unique Selling Position, a strategy that had been downplayed somewhat under BSB. During 1994, key agencies, including AC&R, McCaffrey & McCall, and CME/Houston became part of Bates Worldwide.

By the end of 1994, things had improved considerably at Bates USA. As reported in *ADWEEK,* the agency won a bid for Warner-Lambert business valued at $70 million as well as Miller's estimated $40 million Lite Ice beer account. The $60 million Texaco account was transferred to Bates and Miller and North American Phillips made new media-buying assignments. As a result, Bates USA business increased by more than $200 million.

Bates Worldwide showed record growth in 1994, and was ranked seventh among the top 20 U.S.-based agency networks by *ADWEEK,* with total worldwide billings of $5 billion, an 8 percent increase over 1993 billings. This figure included $850 million in new business, such as the Compaq business for Europe, Africa, and the Middle East awarded to Bates Europe and British American Tobacco Company's Lucky Strike account and global creative assignment.

With regard to creativity, in 1993 and 1994 Bates won over 400 creative advertising awards worldwide at the top ten regional competitions. At the International Advertising Festival at Cannes, Bates ranked number two in 1995, with ten awards. Furthermore, two Bates agencies, Bates Hong Kong and Delvico Bates, placed in the top ten overall standings.

Bungey continued to expand the company while restructuring its organization. During 1994, Bates added new agency affiliations to the network in Argentina, Bangladesh, Chile, Croatia, Fyrom (formerly Macedonia), India, Israel, Latvia, Mexico, Pakistan, Paraguay, Peru, Slovenia, Sri Lanka, Turkey, Costa Rica, El Salvador, and Panama. Structurally, each of the regional directors in the company's four regions reported directly to Michael Bungey.

Bates Americas, headquartered in New York, included Bates North America (USA and Canada) and Bates Latin America, and had 700 million consumers. With 38 offices in 13 countries and billings of $1.7 billion, it handled 333 brands and had nine clients in four or more countries. During this time, Bill Whitehead became chief operating officer of Bates North America, as well as president and chief operating officer of Bates USA. Dan Reid was chairman of Bates Latin America.

Bates Asia-Pacific, headquartered in Sydney, had 31 offices in 14 countries, with 3.3 billion consumers. The region had $900 million in billings, advertising 762 brands. Nineteen of its clients were in four countries or more, and it had the most member agencies in a local country's list of top five agencies. The largest non-Japanese based agency network in the Asia-Pacific region, Bates was the first international advertising agency to be granted a license in Vietnam. Alex Hamill was regional director of Bates Asia-Pacific and chairman of George Patterson Bates in Australia.

Bates Europe, headquartered in London, had 85 offices in 29 countries, including a growing network of 13 offices in Central Europe and Russia. It had 1.1 billion consumers and billings of $2.5 billion, advertising 1,373 brands. Twenty-three clients were in four or more countries. Jean de Yturbe was chairman of Bates Europe and chairman and CEO of Bates France.

By 1995, Bates Worldwide also included several specialty shops with particular areas of expertise: HealthCom, with offices in London, Milan, New York, Canada, Australia, and Spain; Bates Alliance, specializing in retail advertising; Bates Direct for direct marketing; BKS/Bates Entertainment, for TV programming development, production, marketing and distribution; Bates Manhattan, specializing in prestige, fashion and luxury advertising; and Decision Shop, a strategic research consultancy in London.

At the beginning of 1995, parent company Saatchi & Saatchi Company PLC changed its name to Cordiant plc and named Michael Bungey to its board of directors. Unfortunately, in February of that year, Bates Worldwide lost its 40-year old account with Mars, Inc., a $360 million billing. That loss led to some reduction in staffing levels in Bates' offices around the world. In June, both *USA Today* and the *New York Times* reported that Cordiant, in efforts to cut costs, was considering combining the financial, technological, and back-office operations of its two U.S. agency networks, Bates Worldwide and Saatchi & Saatchi Advertising Worldwide.

By mid-1995, however, Bates Worldwide had already recorded nearly $500 million in new business for the year. This included the Coles Myer media buying account, the largest media win in the history of Australian advertising, as well as the Jamont pan-European advertising program, Eurocard, and Optus Vision. Despite the Mars loss, the benefits of Bungey's rebranding effort were evident in the new business won in 1994 and 1995, especially from multinational and global companies. By mid-decade, Bates Worldwide, with a single, cohesive presence worldwide, its USP strategy, and its creative reputation, appeared well-positioned to take advantage of the increasing significance of the merging markets of Southeast Asia and Latin America as well as to benefit from improving economic conditions in Europe and North America.

Further Reading:

"Backer Spielvogel Bates Worldwide Plans New Office in China", *Advertising Age,* February 24, 1992, p. 49.

Barrager, Dave, "Global News: Shops Bet on Vietnam As Next Asian Boom," *ADWEEK Eastern Edition,* February 8, 1993, p. 17.

"BAT Strikes Bates Lucky," *ADWEEK Eastern Edition,* January 16, 1995, p. 5.

Burrett, Tony, "Patterson is Now A Global Role Model," *AdNews,* November 11, 1994.

"Cordiant Explores Cuts in Operations," *New York Times,* June 12, 1995, p. D7.

Elliott, Stuart, "The Media Business: Advertising, Wendy's Return to Britain Convinces Backer Spielvogel of the Importance of a Global Focus," *New York Times,* April 9, 1993.

Fahey, Alison, "An Asian Addition, Bates Gains a Place on Coke's Roster," *ADWEEK Eastern Edition,* July 17, 1995.

Farrell, Greg, "Corner Office: A Firm Hand," *ADWEEK Eastern Edition,* November 21, 1994, p. 21.

Garcia, Shelly, "Bates Bites The Bullet," *ADWEEK Eastern Edition,* February 27, 1995, p. 5.

O'Leary, Noreen, "Bungey Jumping," *ADWEEK Eastern Edition,* September 27, 1993, pp. 30–40.

Piirto, Rebecca, "Global Psychographics," *American Demographics,* December 1990, p. 8.

"Saatchi & Saatchi Advertising," *ADWEEK Eastern Edition,* January 25, 1993, p. 12.

"Ted Bates, Ad Agency Founder, Dies," *New York Times,* June 1, 1972, p. 46.

Warneford, Penny, ''Bungey Jumps Into the Hot Seat at BSB,'' *The Australian,* December 30, 1993, p. 20.

Wells, Melanie, ''Michael Bungey, Building Backer's Confidence As New President,'' *Advertising Age,* March 15, 1993, p. 42.

Wells, Melanie, ''BSB Sharpens Its 'Global Focus','' *Advertising Age,* June 7, 1993.

——, ''Bungey Pushes BSB Ahead into Bates Worldwide Era,'' *Advertising Age,* May 30, 1994, p. 35.

——, ''Cordiant Looks to Trim Costs,'' *USA Today,* June 9, 1995, p. B2.

Wentz, Laurel, et al, ''Backer Takes Top Ad Agency Spot in Europe,'' *Advertising Age,* September 12, 1988.

—Ellen D. Wernick

BECKMAN

Beckman Instruments, Inc.

2500 Harbor Boulevard
P.O. Box 3100
Fullerton, California 92634-3100
U.S.A.
(714) 871-4848
Fax: (714) 773-8543

Public Company
Incorporated: 1934 as National Inking Appliance Company
Employees: 5,880
Sales: $888.6 million
Stock Exchanges: New York
SICs: 3826 Analytical Instruments; 3841 Surgical & Medical
   Instruments

A leading designer, manufacturer, and marketer of laboratory instruments, Beckman Instruments, Inc., sells a broad range of diagnostic products and laboratory systems to customers who conduct basic scientific research, new product research, and diagnostic analysis of patient samples. With operations in more than 20 countries and more than half its sales generated outside the United States, Beckman ranks as global leader, able to keep ahead of its competition by making groundbreaking discoveries in the field of laboratory analytical systems.

At the heart of Beckman's success lies a legacy of scientific innovations that propelled the company's growth, enabling it to carve a distinct and respected position in its industry. From the outset, Beckman earned a reputation as an important contributor to scientific progress, investing considerable time and money to develop new products representative of signal advancements in the scientific instrument field. As time progressed, additional pioneering efforts resulted in groundbreaking products, further bolstering the company's reputation, but underpinning Beckman's growing stature within the scientific instrument industry was also a concerted, aggressive approach to marketing. These ingredients for success were instilled in the company's corporate culture by Beckman's founder, Dr. Arnold Orville Beckman.

For his life's work, Beckman was awarded the National Medal of Technology in 1988, a remarkable achievement for a black-smith's son who began his working career in an occupation entirely divorced from science and technology. Born in 1900 in Callum, Illinois, Beckman began playing the piano at nickelo-

deons in nearby Bloomington, Illinois at age 13, working after school and at night to fulfill his ambition to become a jazz musician. Furthering his education, however, took a firmer and more lasting hold on the young Beckman, leading him the shelve his musical aspirations and apply to the University of Illinois, where he earned B.A. and M.A. degrees in chemical engineering.

After leaving the University of Illinois, Beckman began working for Bell Laboratories in 1923, then two years later decided to return to school to pursue a Ph.D. at the California Institute of Technology. Beckman remained at the California Institute of Technology to teach chemistry after obtaining his degree, then began supplementing his salary from the university by working as a consultant. In this capacity Beckman was hired to devise a special ink for the National Postal Meter Company, a project that soon developed into the National Inking Appliance Company, an enterprise 10 percent-owned by Beckman and 90 percent-owned by the National Postal Meter Company.

The name National Inking Appliance Company was short-lived, lasting only from its adoption in November 1934 until April 1935, when the company was renamed National Technical Laboratories. Beckman continued to teach at the California Institute of Technology for six years after forming National Inking Appliance Company, dividing his energies between teaching chemistry and running his company until 1940. His company had already demonstrated considerable success by the time it gained its new name, introducing its first commercial product, the pH Meter, in 1935. Designed by Beckman, the pH Meter measured the acidity or alkalinity of almost any solution, combining electronics and chemistry to create a product that was the first of its kind. Although the pH Meter sold for $195, far more than the product it competed against—litmus paper—which cost a few cents per vial, orders for the more expensive and more sophisticated pH Meter grew steadily. By the late 1930s, as sales of other scientific apparatus declined with the lingering economic depression, sales of Beckman's pH Meter rose substantially, providing the financial fuel to fund the development of the company's next product, the DU Spectrophotometer.

Introduced in 1941, the DU Spectrophotometer represented Beckman's next hallmark product, a scientific instrument that used the pH Meter as an amplifier for a photoelectric cell to determine the intensity of various wavelengths in a spectrum of light. For this purpose, the Beckman DU Spectrophotometer represented a substantial improvement over competing products on the market at the time, increasing the accuracy of analysis and reducing analysis time by a considerable margin. Previously, hours or even weeks were required to conduct such an analysis, but the DU Spectrophotometer produced more accurate results in a matter of minutes.

By the time the DU Spectrophotometer was introduced, annual sales had topped $250,000; slightly more than a decade later the company generated more than $20 million a year in annual sales, recording growth that testified to the heavy demand for the company's products. Beckman Instruments was adopted as the new name for the company in 1950, by which point the company had firmly established itself as a leading manufacturer of analytical instruments used by both science and industry. As he had from the outset, Beckman took his profits and plowed them back into the company, enabling Beckman Instruments to fund research and maintain a steady stream of new products. This focus on the development of new products and the exploration of new technological possibilities gave the company a diverse product line, ranging from small liquid crystal displays to large process monitoring systems.

By the 1960s, after Beckman had gone public in 1952 and gained admittance to the New York Stock Exchange in 1955, the company's diverse products were competing in industrial, medical, educational, space, and defense markets. During the latter part of the decade the company began to shift away from defense and space exploration, which were subject to the vagaries of the federal budget. The company's president, William Ballhaus, explained to *Forbes,* ''We wanted to develop a market where we could succeed or fail on our own, not because somebody cut the budget.'' To Ballhaus, Dr. Beckman, and the rest of the company's management this meant placing a greater emphasis on clinical and medical markets, which were growing rapidly as mounting malpractice suits were forcing doctors to increase the number of diagnostic tests they performed.

In 1965 medical research and clinical products accounted for 25 percent of Beckman's sales volume, a proportion that would climb to 33 percent by 1969 and 40 percent by 1974. This growth was driven largely by the introduction of new products introduced during the late 1960s, including the Beckman Protein Peptide Sequencer, an instrument used for the determination of protein structures, and the Beckman Glucose Analyzer, an instrument that quickly measured blood sugar in samples as small as 10 microliters. Like the pH Meter and DU Spectrophotometer before it, the Beckman Glucose Analyzer represented a substantial improvement over existing technology, completing in less than three minutes what had previously taken 30 minutes.

With instruments such as the Protein Peptide Sequencer and the Glucose Analyzer entering a burgeoning market, Beckman reaped the rewards. Annual sales, which had hovered around $130 million for five years—raising concerns about the company's continued financial growth—responded vigorously as the number of diagnostic tests performed in the United States increased from 2.9 billion to five billion between 1971 and 1975.

By the end of 1975, annual sales neared $230 million, thanks to the company's successes in both the medical and industrial sectors. Beckman's industrial products included a broad range of process control instruments, air and water pollution control instruments, and industrial research products, which combined generated nearly as much money for Beckman as its medical products. Together, medical and industrial products accounted for nearly 80 percent of the company's sales volume and provided much of its financial growth approaching the 1980s. Two other business segments rounded out the company's product line during the latter part of the 1970s. Scientific research contributed 16 percent to Beckman's annual sales, and defense-related business accounted for another six percent, considerably less than a decade before.

In 1982, the company was acquired by SmithKline Corporation, ending nearly a half century of independence. The merger

between SmithKline and Beckman created SmithKline Beckman Corporation, a company that operated until the summer of 1989 when it agreed to merge with Beecham Group PLC. At the time, the Beckman unit of SmithKline Beckman Corp. was not performing well, as the federal government and large insurance companies began applying stricter control over health care costs. Medical equipment makers like Beckman were negatively affected by mounting concern over health care costs, leading the architects of the merger between Beecham Group and SmithKline Beckman to consummate their agreement without the assets that formerly composed Beckman, and the company was spun off.

On its own again after seven years, Beckman emerged from under the SmithKline corporate umbrella with its sales and profits roughly split between foreign and domestic markets, and comprising two primary business units: a bioanalytical systems group, which served the basic research market, and its diagnostic systems group, which focused on the clinical laboratory field. Revenues were roughly split between these groups. Despite the losses suffered from the clamp down on health care costs, the company was in better shape than a cursory assessment revealed. Though known primarily as a manufacturer of sophisticated equipment, Beckman derived roughly half of its sales and a greater portion of its profits from consumables, or the reagents and disposable items used by equipment operators. Unlike the company's medical equipment and instrument product line, these consumable products were not adversely affected by increased scrutiny of health care costs.

As the company entered the 1990s, the consumable side of its business provided a stable source of income, holding the company in good stead as it prepared to contend with greater governmental pressure to reduce health care costs. Reductions in government research spending plagued the company during the early 1990s, until management began focusing on increasing sales to private-sector biotechnology and pharmaceutical companies through Beckman's bioanalytical division. A promising new line of diagnostic instruments and eventual corporate-wide cost-cutting measures contributed to the company's resurgence as well, raising annual sales to $888.6 million in 1994 and lifting its net earnings to $42.2 million.

As the company charted its course for the future, management emphasized increasing efficiency and productivity, both in the types of systems designed for Beckman customers and in reducing internal operating expenses. Though questions about the health care industry in the United States clouded the company's prospects, Beckman's outlook was bolstered by its strong strategic positions in diagnostics and biotechnology systems. In 1995, the company pursued acquisitions and marketing alliances to augment its business focus on the chemistry of life.

Principal Subsidiaries: Beckman Analytical S.p.A.; Beckman Eurocenter S.A.; Beckman Instruments Pty. Ltd. (Australia); Beckman Instruments, Inc. (Canada); Beckman Instruments, Inc. (Naguabo); Beckman Instruments Espana S.A.; Beckman Instruments France S.A.; Beckman Instruments GmbH; Beckman Instruments, Inc. (Ireland); Beckman Instruments, Ltd. (Japan); Beckman Instruments, Ltd. (United Kingdom); Beckman Instruments International S.A.; SmithKline Diagnostics, Inc.

Further Reading:

Armour, Lawrence A., "Just What the Doctor Ordered," *Barron's,* December 14, 1964, p. 3.

"Beckman Gets Customers to Design Its Product," *Business Week,* August 17, 1974, p. 52.

"Beckman Instruments Taps Medical Field in Big Way," *Barron's,* November 3, 1975, p. 59.

"Beckman on Exchange," *New York Times,* November 8, 1955, p. 43.

Bedingfield, Robert E., "Along the Highways and Byways of Finance," *New York Times,* November 27, 1955, p. F3.

Boffey, Philip M., "Major Benefactor of American Science," *New York Times,* November 5, 1985, p. C3.

Carey, John Gerald, "The Health Sciences Stock Index," *Wall Street Transcript,* February 9, 1970, p. 19,536.

Joffe, Thomas, "Fishing with the Basses," *Forbes,* March 1, 1993, p. 144.

"Keep Doing What You're Doing," *Forbes,* May 1, 1976, p. 21.

King, Thomas R., "Stake in Beckman Instruments Held by Bass Group," *Wall Street Journal,* February 5, 1992, p. 16.

Koenig, Richard, "SmithKline Sets Pretax Charge, 1,600 Job Cuts," *Wall Street Journal,* September 28, 1988, p. 3.

Smith, Marguerite T., "These Health-Care Stocks Can Prosper Even in the Face of Cost Cutting," *Money,* July 1990, pp. 55–57.

Smith, Randall, "SmithKline Merger Terms Give Control of New Concern to Beecham Chairman," *Wall Street Journal,* April 13, 1989, p. A8.

Wyatt, Edward A., "Beckman's Back," *Barron's,* September 11, 1989, p. 17.

—Jeffrey L. Covell

BELOIT CORPORATION

Beloit Corporation

1 St. Lawrence Avenue
Beloit, Wisconsin 53511
U.S.A.
(608) 365-3311
Fax: (608) 364-7013

Wholly Owned Subsidiary of Harnischfeger Industries, Inc.
Incorporated: 1858 as The Merrill and Houston Iron Works
Employees: 7,500
Sales: $712.8 million
SICs: 3554 Paper Industries Machinery

Beloit Corporation is the world's leading manufacturer of papermaking machinery. An estimated 70 percent of the world's newsprint, writing, and printing-grade paper is produced on machines made by Beloit, as is an estimated 50 percent of the world's napkins, paper towels, and tissues. Besides manufacturing paper and paperboard machines, the company has a substantial business rebuilding these machines and providing parts and service. Beloit also produces equipment and systems for pulp manufacturing, paper stock preparation, deinking, and recycled fiber and wood chip processing. The company has the industry's largest installed equipment base and operates plants in the United States, Italy, England, Brazil, Poland, and Canada. Beloit licensees also operate plants in Australia, China, France, Italy, Japan, Spain, and India. Beloit's machines are considered the "Cadillac" of the industry; the company is responsible for many major advances in papermaking technology, and its machines hold numerous records for speed.

The company was founded in 1858 in Beloit, Wisconsin, by partners Orson E. Merrill and George Houston. Their firm, The Merrill and Houston Iron Works, principally manufactured a waterwheel that had been developed by George Houston, but it also made iron products including saws, augers, spokes, iron and steel castings, and horseshoe nails. The Merrill and Houston Iron Works got its first order for papermaking machinery from Orson Merrill's brother, who owned a paper mill on the nearby Rock River. He had bought his paper machine in New England, but rather than order parts from the eastern manufacturer he asked if Merrill and Houston could make them. Soon other area paper mills also placed orders for parts, and by 1862 Merrill and Houston was building complete paper machines. The company continued to produce its waterwheels and other iron products while it built several paper machines a year, from four in 1862 to 14 in 1884.

In spite of this steady business, The Houston and Merrill Iron Works ran into financial difficulties. The company changed hands several times until it landed in receivership in 1882. The plant continued to operate in order to pay off its debts. The assets of the company were sold to a Janesville, Wisconsin, businessman in January 1885 for $20,000. Later that year, four employees of Merrill and Houston formed an association to lease back from the purchaser most of the plant and property. Under the name Beloit Iron Works, the former employees put the plant back in business. Fred Messer, who had been a superintendent at Merrill and Houston, became president, and the other officers of the new company included a lathe operator, a draftsman, and a former boss erector. These four, along with ten employees, turned the company around. In its first year Beloit Iron Works had sales of nearly $20,000, and by 1889 the company employed 100 people. Beloit filled many orders for paper machine parts and soon advertised that it could build a complete paper machine every 30 days.

By 1889 Beloit's officers had bought back all the property of the old Houston and Merrill company. Orders for parts, rebuilds, and new paper machines came from all over the Midwest, Canada, and even Texas. Beloit built and installed a paper machine at the Chicago World's Fair of 1893 and won a United States Columbian Award. This exposure bolstered Beloit's reputation in the United States, and its name became known abroad as well. The company plowed money back into the plant in order to keep up with changing technology. Its paper machines became larger and faster, and around the turn of the century they sold for between $25,000 and $30,000 each. Beloit sold a machine to Japan in 1897, two to China in 1900, and the company continued to lead the industry over the next dozen years.

The paper industry grew rapidly, and sales at Beloit increased. The company expanded its facilities and modernized its tools and machine shop in the 1920s to make ever larger machines. The first paper machines the company had made had been only 30 inches wide; the machines of the 1920s were wider than 160 inches. As sales surged, Beloit became a large employer, with a peak of 550 workers in 1930. Alonzo Aldrich, one of the original four founders of Beloit Iron Works and president since 1889, presided over the good times. Aldrich died in 1931, and the presidency passed to his son-in-law, Elbert Neese Sr., who had been a manager at Beloit since 1916. The first year of his presidency coincided with the nadir of the Great Depression. Orders were next to nothing, and over two-thirds of Beloit's workers were let go. But the company recovered gradually, and by 1937 it employed more workers than in 1930. When the United States entered World War II, Beloit turned its production from paper machines to machines for war materials. It built lathes and boring mills, even engines for the Navy. Beloit workers became unionized for the first time, becoming members of the International Association of Machinists.

After the war Beloit went back to manufacturing papermaking machines. The company added buildings and equipment to make newer machines that broke existing records for speed and production. As Beloit returned to prosperity, it began to expand.

In 1949 Beloit opened a sales office in Paris. About one-fifth of Beloit's shipments were overseas in the 1950s, and the company began to acquire plants abroad. In 1957 Beloit bought an Italian operation, which it named Beloit Italia SpA. Further international expansion included a plant in England, Beloit Walmsley Ltd., in 1960; a Canadian branch in 1962; and a Spanish operation in 1963. In the United States Beloit opened sales offices in Portland, Oregon, and Mobile, Alabama, in the 1950s and acquired several paper equipment manufacturers in Pennsylvania.

While continuing to expand internationally in the 1960s with new projects in Poland and India, Beloit began to diversify its product line somewhat. The company changed its name in 1962 from Beloit Iron Works to Beloit Corporation in order to reflect its changing business. Beloit experimented with manufacturing machinery for use in the plastics industry and other nonpaper industries. The company eventually deemed these diversification projects unsuccessful. When the paper industry slowed down between 1970 and 1972 Beloit had very few orders to fill. Though business picked up dramatically in the next two years, surging inflation in 1974 had dire effects. That year the company lost money for the first time since its reorganization in 1885. However, Beloit quickly recovered and entered one of its most profitable periods beginning in 1975.

Elbert Neese Sr. had died in 1961, and he was succeeded as president by Harry Moore. Moore was president until 1974, when Elbert Neese Jr. took the post (Moore was elevated to chairman). Beloit continued to diversify, acquiring a farm, an insurance company and a railroad in the 1970s. Though these were ultimately unsuccessful projects, creating a financial drain, Beloit still made significant advances in its core business—paper machinery. Beloit's Jones Division in Dalton, Massachusetts, expanded its facilities in order to research new paper industry technology such as refiner mechanical pulp production and newspaper deinking. In 1977 Beloit developed computer-aided drafting and computer-aided manufacturing (CAD/CAM) technology to automate its machinery design process. Because Beloit's papermaking machines were custom built, the design process for each order required sometimes thousands of drawings, and so the CAD/CAM development increased the company's productivity enormously. Beloit also acquired more businesses in the 1970s, including the Lenox Machine Company, which manufactured winders and sheeters for the paper industry, and another specialized paper industry manufacturer, the Rader Companies. In 1977 Beloit spent $12 million to acquire the Roll Covering Division of Raybestos Manhattan, which became Beloit Manhattan. This company chalked up about $8 million in sales, but it suffered very little from the ups and downs of the business cycle that affected Beloit, a big advantage. Manhattan's acquisition added stability to Beloit, and in less than ten years Manhattan's sales were close to $50 million. Beloit also acquired minority shareholdings in some of its overseas plants in the 1970s, and in 1978 it began construction on a manufacturing division in Brazil, Beloit-Rauma.

Elbert Neese Jr. became chairman of Beloit in 1984, with Thomas McKie succeeding him as president. Then, in 1985, Neese announced the Neese family wished to sell the Beloit Corporation. The business had been closely held for more than a century. When plans for the sale were announced, over 30 companies in the United States, Europe, and Japan expressed an interest. After only a few months, a deal was struck with Milwaukee-based Harnischfeger Corp., a maker of mining and earth-moving equipment. Harnischfeger paid $175 million for Beloit Corp. At the time, Beloit had sales of $483 million, with 18 plants in five countries and 6,300 employees. Harnischfeger boasted 1985 sales of $484 million. Harnischfeger's president and chief executive officer, William W. Goessel, had spent 32 years as a Beloit executive before he moved to Harnischfeger in 1982, and so he understood Beloit's business very well. After the acquisition by Harnischfeger, Beloit restructured its operations to concentrate more closely on pulp and paper industry equipment. Shortly after the sale to Harnischfeger, Beloit's Japanese licensee, Mitsubishi Heavy Industries Ltd., bought a 20 percent interest in Beloit.

John A. McKay became Beloit's new president in November 1986. The next year, Beloit formed a strategic alliance with Measurex Corp., an industrial process control company, to develop online computer controls and computer integrated manufacturing systems for the paper industry. Paper machine technology was advancing rapidly, and consumers were demanding higher-quality products. The alliance with Measurex allowed Beloit to offer its customers highly sophisticated control systems using artificial intelligence. Beloit also spent millions of dollars on research and development and maintained three research centers: a main one in Rockton, Illinois, another in Pittsfield, Massachusetts, and a third in Bolton, England.

The late 1980s saw a boom in the paper industry. Paper companies were making record profits, and Beloit employed two shifts of engineers to keep up with equipment orders. Because Beloit had so much equipment installed around the world, it also had a large and profitable business in spare parts and rebuilds. The company reinvested much of its profit in upgrading equipment. Harnischfeger spent close to $26 million in 1987, mostly to restructure, retool, and modernize Beloit plants. The Beloit, Wisconsin, plant was gutted and refitted with new machine tools; the Beloit Manhattan facility and a plant in Canada were similarly modernized. Beloit also overhauled its spare parts operation. By 1987 Beloit's spare parts storage area was completely computerized and running without a single human worker inside the area. Beloit's customers had computer access to the spare parts inventory and could place an order directly with the storage area for immediate automatic retrieval and shipping. The first year this system was in place Beloit's spare parts business increased 40 percent. The company installed the system in its Canadian and European plants as well.

Business in the late 1980s was so good that it created a backlog, and orders took 18 months to fill. The price for a new paper machine was close to $50 million, though only a few years earlier the price had been between $10 and $15 million. Not surprisingly, 1988 was a record year for Beloit. Sales increased 42 percent over the previous year, to $697 million. The company handled approximately 45 major rebuild projects and had a similar number of orders for new equipment. Beloit had five divisions worldwide capable of making a complete paper machine, and each was working at top capacity. Beloit had about $952 million in bookings for 1988 and, including Beloit's licensees, bookings topped $1 billion. Beloit also handled its first project in the Soviet Union and explored the China market through a joint venture. The company continued to plow money back into plants, investing another $12.7 million in facilities and equipment in Wisconsin. New tools enabled Beloit to produce paper machines over 400 inches wide, as its customers were requiring.

Beloit continued to expand its manufacturing capabilities in the 1990s. In 1991 the company acquired an 80 percent equity in a Polish paper machine manufacturer, which it renamed Beloit Poland S.A. in 1993. Beloit also acquired a Wisconsin manufacturer of refiner plate in 1992 and entered a joint venture in 1994 with a German paper machinery manufacturer, Jagenberg AG. Beloit also acquired a paper machine optical alignment and inspection services company, OASIS Inc., in 1994.

Beloit had experienced trouble with patent infringement from European competitors, and in the 1980s it had filed patent infringement suits . After almost ten years in various courts, the lawsuits were resolved in Beloit's favor. In May 1993 Beloit was awarded $17.2 million in damages after a federal court found a German manufacturer, J. M. Voith GmbH, had infringed Beloit's paper drying technology patents. And in November 1994 Beloit was awarded $7.9 million in damages in a patent infringement case involving a Finnish competitor, Valmet Corp.

Recycling became an increasingly important part of the paper industry in the 1990s, and Beloit positioned itself to take advantage of this trend. The company began constructing small paper mills, called minimills, to make recycled paper out of used corrugated boxes. Beloit had long been a leader in deinking and recycling technology. The challenge of the minimills was that they generally had to be located in an urban area in order to be close to a used paper source, limiting access to the large amounts of water that traditional mills used for processing. Beloit opened a recycling minimill in Montville, Connecticut, in 1994 and built another near Oswego, New York. Beloit also entered a consortium of three companies in 1994 to construct and operate urban minimills. The consortium pooled the resources of Hoffman Environmental Systems, a company that developed no-discharge water technology, as well as Ogden Projects, which ran the completed mills, and Beloit, which built

the recycling machinery. This was expected to be an area of rapid expansion for Beloit in the future.

Principal Subsidiaries: Beloit Canada Ltd./Ltee.; Beloit Industrial Ltda. (Brazil); Beloit Poland S.A.; Beloit Technologies Inc.; BWRC, Inc.; Beloit Italia SpA (Italy); Beloit Lenox Europe GmbH (Germany); Beloit Walmsley Limited (United Kingdom); J&L Fiber Services, Inc.; Optical Alignment systems & Inspection Serv., Inc.; Sandusky International Inc.

Further Reading:

Ahn, C. R., "Spare Parts and Service Simplified by Computerized Ordering System," *Pulp & Paper,* September 1987, pp. 107–10.

"Alliance: Industry Suppliers Try Unique Approach to Consolidation," *Pulp & Paper,* August 1987, pp. 172–76.

"Beloit Sold for $175 Million to Harnischfeger," *Pulp & Paper,* April 1986, p. 21.

"Beloit Wins Valmet Appeal; Sues Voith, Chesapeake," *Pulp & Paper,* March 1985, pp. 35–37.

"Customized CAD/CAM's Aid Machinery Manufacturer's Drawing Ability," *Pulp & Paper,* September 1987, pp. 72–73.

Evans, John C. W., "Beloit-Jones Research Center Boasts Latest in TMP Equipment," *Pulp & Paper,* April 1976, pp. 116–17.

"Harnischfeger Acquires Beloit," *Wall Street Journal,* April 1, 1986, p. 6.

"Harnischfeger Expects Lower Fiscal '93 Profit Than Analysts Predict," *Wall Street Journal,* January 14, 1993, p. B4.

"Harnischfeger Industries, Inc.: Beloit Unit Wins $7.9 Million in Patent-Infringement Case," *Wall Street Journal,* November 29, 1994, p. B6.

"Harnischfeger to Sell 20% Holding in Unit to Japanese Concern," *Wall Street Journal,* October 27, 1986, p. 11.

"Harnischfeger Wins Damages," *Wall Street Journal,* May 25, 1993, p. C22.

Kansas, Dave, "Mills for Recycled Paper Head to the Big City," *Wall Street Journal,* January 21, 1994, p. B1.

Patrick, Ken, "Beloit's Future Looks Bright, Steady Growth Expected by Harnischfeger," *Pulp & Paper,* May 1986, pp. 66–69.

—— "Expansion Pace Puts Heavy Demands on Manufacturers," *Pulp & Paper,* April 1989, pp. 74–77.

"TC: Valmet Didn't Infringe U.S. Patent," *Pulp & Paper,* June 1984, p. 39.

—A. Woodward

Biogen Inc.

14 Cambridge Center
Cambridge, Massachusetts 02142
U.S.A.
(617) 252-9200
Fax: (617) 252-9617

Public Company
Incorporated: 1978
Employees: 500
Sales: $156.34 million
Stock Exchanges: NASDAQ
SICs: 2834 Pharmaceutical Preparations; 2835 In Vitro and
   In Vivo Diagnostic Substances

Biogen Inc. develops, manufacturers, and licenses drugs for human healthcare through genetic engineering. A pioneer and key player in the dynamic and volatile biotechnology industry, Biogen has distinguished itself as one of the few biotech companies to remain independent and to achieve profitability. Biogen entered the mid-1990s rife with cash and with a number of drugs in its research and development pipeline.

Biogen is considered one of the pioneers of the young biotechnology industry. It got its start in 1978 when mental giant Walter H. Gilbert, a Nobel prize-winning biologist who was teaching at Harvard at the time, decided to try developing his research into marketable products. Biotechnology, as it was known in the mid-1970s, was still in its infancy. The discovery of the structure of DNA, which led to the understanding of the process by which proteins are produced by cells, had occurred in 1953. But it wasn't until the early 1970s that more rapid progress ensued. Importantly, in 1973 two U.S. scientists discovered the process of recombinant DNA, whereby a piece of DNA is snipped from one gene and spliced into another gene. The significance of that discovery was that it proved that scientists could genetically alter microorganisms and, importantly, produce mass amounts of proteins that naturally occurred only in small quantities.

Walter Gilbert had been a major contributor to the development of recombinant DNA technology during the 1970s, and he had earned his Nobel prize as a result of his research in that area. Subsequent related breakthroughs during the mid- and late 1970s indicated that scientists would eventually be able to use gene-splicing and cloning techniques to create various 'wonder'

drugs and products that could, among other benefits, cure cancer and many other diseases or create perfect produce and livestock with fantastic characteristics. Despite the promise of the technology, a recognizable industry that could develop such drugs and take them to market was slow to form. Before 1980, in fact, only a few significant biotech start-ups had appeared: Cetus (founded in 1971); Genetech (1976); Genex (1977); Biogen (1978); Centocor (1979); and Amgen (1980).

Biogen, like its biotech peers, was able to capitalize on the belief of some investors during the late 1970s that biotechnology was going to radically impact many areas of industry, medicine, food, energy, and agriculture. Although Biogen and some other companies made significant contributions to the burgeoning field of biotech, it was not until the 1980s that the industry boomed. The growth was largely the result of a U.S. Supreme Court ruling that genetically engineered bacterium could be patented. For many, that ruling suggested the possibility of unimaginable wealth for biotech innovators. As a result, millions of dollars poured into the industry, primarily through venture capital but also through the sale of publicly traded stock. Companies that showed promise, like Biogen, benefited the most.

Biogen launched a number of research initiatives during the late 1970s and early 1980s related to a variety of healthcare drugs. Some efforts fizzled, but, unlike many other biotech start-ups, Biogen eventually succeeded in generating some marketable products. The two biggest winners were a hepatitis B vaccine and alpha interferon. The hepatitis B vaccine was, as its name implies, a vaccine for hepatitis B, a blood-borne disease that causes a serious infection of the liver and substantially increases the risk of liver cancer; more than 250 million people worldwide still suffered from chronic hepatitis B virus infections in the early 1990s. Biogen eventually obtained patents in several countries related to its hepatitis B antigens produced by genetic engineering techniques, and the drug—marketed by Smith-Kline Beecham and Merck—became a big seller. In many countries, in fact, infants are commonly vaccinated against Hepatitis B using Biogen's drug.

Alpha interferon was an even bigger source of revenue for Biogen. Alpha interferon is a naturally occurring protein produced by normal white blood cells. Biogen developed and patented a process of producing vast amounts of the protein using recombinant DNA techniques. Its alpha interferon compound became the first genetically engineered drug to receive market approval in the United States. Biogen's alpha interferon, also known as Intron A, was eventually being sold by licensee Schering-Plough in more than 60 countries to treat a variety of conditions including hepatitis B, hepatitis C, genital warts, Kaposi's sarcoma (an AIDS-related cancer), and hairy-cell leukemia.

Biogen racked up major points in the research and development game during the early 1980s, and positive press brought tens of millions of dollars into its coffers. Like most biotechnology companies, though, Biogen was burning through the cash as fast, or faster, than it poured in. Chief Executive Gilbert, in his quest for new genetically engineered drugs, established a global research and development network during the early 1980s that sported operations in Zurich, Geneva, Belgium, Germany, and the United States. Although impressive and sometimes effective, the organization eventually became unwieldy and lacked focus. Some critics charged that despite his scientific prowess, Gilbert lacked business skills. The company was a great place to do research, but it had yet to show a profit. By 1984, in fact, Biogen had racked up a stunning $100 million in losses and was teetering on the edge of bankruptcy.

Gilbert managed to keep Biogen afloat during the early 1980s by licensing other companies to manufacture, market, and distribute its drugs. To make ends meet, he also started selling Biogen's patents. Some criticized the move as representing a sell-out of the company's technological achievements; Biogen's original goal, in fact, had been to both develop and manufacture its inventions. Instead, the company had essentially become a research boutique that supplied drug companies in Europe, Japan, and the United States with technology. In the end, however, Gilbert's licensing and selling was credited with saving the company from total bankruptcy. Indeed, many of Biogen's scientifically-savvy biotech start-up peers were effectively forced out of business—often through merger or acquisition—because of financial difficulties.

By 1985 Biogen was using an estimated $100,000 each day in research costs. Furthermore, royalty revenues had slid to less than $20 million annually because the company had sold some of its patents. Biogen investors were fed up; the company's directors had already, in fact, pulled Gilbert from the chief executive slot and had been searching for a replacement for more than a year. Finally, in 1985, they hired James L. Vincent. Vincent graduated from Duke University, where he had been recruited to play football but didn't because of a neck injury. He earned his MBA at Wharton before joining Bell Telephone Company of Pennsylvania. From there he served in various positions including president of Texas Instruments-Asia, chief operating officer at Abbott Laboratories, and president of Allied Health and Scientific Products Company. He was known as a hard-charging, imposing, and capable manager.

Biogen began a radical restructuring and turnaround under Vincent's command. Soon after arriving at Biogen, Vincent sold or closed the European operations and brought in some new managers. Importantly, he also began working to recover some of the patents that the company had sold off during the early 1980s. By the time Vincent arrived, in fact, Biogen had sold off nearly 90 percent of its patents. Vincent succeeded in negotiating with companies to get or buy back most of those patents. By 1989 Biogen had regained control of 90 percent of all of its original patents. As Vincent got back the rights to the company's technology, he started licensing them to other manufacturers. The result was that the company's royalty revenues increased and Biogen's balance sheet gradually began to move back toward solvency.

The impact of Vincent's efforts were slow to materialize. Biogen lost more than $70 million between 1985 and 1988, and gross revenues actually plummeted to a low of about $8.5 million in 1987 after net income dipped to a $28 million deficit in 1986. But Biogen started to spring back in the late 1980s. Sales reached $28.5 million in 1989, and the company posted its first-ever profit—a $3.2-million surplus. Revenues surpassed $50 million in 1990 and then hit $61 million in 1991, by which

time the company was generating net income of more than $7 million annually. That growth was partly attributable to new additions to Biogen's product line. By 1991 the company was selling through licensees several different drugs that were generating global sales of about $600 million annually: Intron A Alpha Interferon; Hepatitis B vaccine; Hepatitis B diagnostics; and Gamma Interferon (used to treat renal cell carcinoma).

Biogen benefited in 1992 from heady gains in sales of several of its drugs, particularly alpha interferon. The company stunned analysts, in fact, by reporting revenues of $123.8 million for the year and an increase of more than 500 percent in its net income to $38.3 million. And the company expected those gains to continue in the near future. Furthermore, Biogen had several new products in its research and development pipeline that had the potential to add big sums to its bottom line. The most promising of its drugs going into the mid-1990s was Hirulog, a blood thinner derived from leeches. Hirulog, which acted as a direct inhibitor of Thrombin (the main enzyme that coagulates blood), was designed to provide immediate relief to people with severe and sudden chest pains, and to prevent clotting complications after veins were opened up through balloon angioplasty or coronary bypass surgery. Biogen had invested heavily in Hirulog and was trying to gain FDA approval to market it.

The Hirulog project represented Biogen's drive to become a manufacturer and marketer, rather than just a developer and licensor, of drugs. Simultaneously, Biogen was seeking approval for a drug that it had developed and wanted to manufacture called interferon beta-la (the trade name of which was Avonex), designed as a treatment for relapsing multiple sclerosis. Both drugs were in the final stages of clinical testing in mid-1994. If approved, they would usher Biogen into a new era as a full-fledged pharmaceutical company that developed and sold its own drugs and products. Moreover, Vincent had been beefing up Biogen's management and sales force to prepare for their approval. To that end, in January 1994 he had conducted a major coup by recruiting James R. Tobin to Biogen's management ranks to serve in the newly created position of president and chief operating officer.

The 49-year-old Tobin had previously spent 21 years at pharmaceutical giant Baxter International Inc., where he rose from a financial analyst to president of the company. Tobin received his masters degree from Harvard Business School before joining Baxter. He was apparently being groomed to assume the chief executive position at Baxter when he decided that he was looking for a different kind of challenge. Tobin was considered a heavy hitter in the pharmaceutical industry, and his move to Biogen gave that company a new respect in the industry. Tobin's job at Biogen would be to shepherd the company from a licensor to a manufacturer and marketer of drugs. Shortly before he arrived, Biogen posted record revenues of $136.5 million for the year and net income of about $32.5 million.

Biogen entered 1994 with high hopes. Its dreams were temporarily stalled, however, by a string of setbacks. In the fall of 1994, Biogen announced that it was discontinuing its efforts to bring Hirulog to market because of disappointing test results. That news was greeted by shareholder lawsuits alleging securities violations for stopping work on the drug. Then, early in

January 1995, news came that German pharmaceutical giant Schering AG announced plans to produce interferon beta-la, Biogen's other breakthrough drug, using the same method as Biogen. Biogen, however, maintained that it had access to all patents necessary to market Avonex interferon beta-la. Nevertheless, the news sent Biogen's stock price tumbling $7 to $35.37, which was down from a high of $55.75 before the Hirulog setback.

Largely because of write-offs related to Hirulog, Biogen posted a net loss of $4.9 million from revenues of $156.34 million. The company's problems were exacerbated early in 1995 when pricing changes in Japan of the alpha interferon that Biogen developed and licensed to Schering-Plough Corp. contributed to a significant reduction in first-quarter profits. That news affected the company's stock price negligibly, though, as Biogen's balance sheet easily withstood the hit. Indeed, Biogen's gains during the early 1990s had put it in excellent financial shape. The company entered the mid-1990s cash-rich and among the healthiest biotechnology companies in the country. It was still generating revenues from licensing its marketable drugs, and some of those products were positioned well to benefit from market changes. It also had a number of promising products in development, although they had not yet progressed past the clinical, or final, stage of pre-market testing.

Moreover, in December 1995, Biogen announced that the FDA had unanimously approved Biogen's Avonex interferon beta-la drug for treating relapsing forms of multiple sclerosis. Studies had found that Avonex was, in the words of Biogen CEO Jim Vincent, "the first and only drug to show in a blinded clinical trial that it slows the progression of [MS] disability as well as reduces the frequency of exacerbations." The approval represented a major event in Biogen's history as well as in the history of the biotechnology industry.

Further Reading:

Brandel, William, "Businessperson of the Year: How Biogen's Jim Vincent Got Biotech to Turn a Profit," *New England Business,* January 1991, p. 16.

Gendron, Marie, "Biogen Pushes Ahead to Develop New Multiple-Sclerosis Treatment," *Boston Herald,* January 25, 1994.

Hower, Wendy, "Antsy Investors Eye Biogen's Drug Trials," *Boston Business Journal,* July 20, 1992, p. 6.

Prince, Cathryn J., "Patent Deal Rocks Biogen," *Boston Business Journal,* January 13, 1995, p. 1.

——, "Tobin: The Direct Approach," *Boston Business Journal,* January 13, 1995, p. 20.

Rosenberg, Ronald, "Biogen Bets on the Leach: Biotech Company Seeks Approval of Drug Expected to Capture a Chunk of $500 Million Market for Blood Thinners," *Boston Globe,* November 17, 1992, p. 39.

——, "Royalty Drop Slashes Biogen Profits," *Boston Globe,* April 28, 1995, p. 69.

——, "Tobin Hired by Biogen a 'Coup,' " *Boston Globe,* January 20, 1994, p. 33.

Shao, Maria, "Growth—The Globe 100; Biogen Inc.," *Boston Globe,* May 17, 1994, p. 56.

Syre, Steven, "Biogen Faces Patent Hurdles," *Boston Herald,* January 21, 1995, p. 17.

—Dave Mote

BOOKS-A-MILLION

Books-A-Million, Inc.

402 Industrial Lane
Birmingham, Alabama 35211
U.S.A.
(205) 942-3737
Fax: (205) 945-1772

Public Company
Incorporated: 1964 as Bookland
Employees: 1,180
Stock Exchanges: NASDAQ
Sales: $172.3 million
SICs: 5942 Book Stores

Books-A-Million, Inc., is the fourth-largest book retailer in the United States, with combined annual sales of $172.3 million in fiscal 1995. The company operates 124 stores in 17 southeastern states. Of these, 50 are Books-A-Million superstores, which offer more than 3,000 magazine titles, 68,000 book titles, and 75 newspaper titles, as well as collectibles, cards, and gifts. Thirty-one are smaller Bookland stores, which are more traditional book stores: they offer books and periodicals and are primarily targeted to regional markets too small to support a superstore. The remainder are Bookland combination stores, which offer a complete selection of cards and gifts in addition to the books and periodicals sold by traditional Bookland stores. They are located in small towns and target regional markets.

Books-A-Million's roots go back to a humble newspaper stand constructed in 1917 by 14-year-old Clyde W. Anderson, who had dropped out of school to support his family upon the death of his father. The young man's first job was delivering newspapers in his hometown of Florence, Alabama. Shortly after he began selling newspapers, a large group of construction workers from the North came to town to build the Wilson Dam. When they mentioned to the young newspaper boy that they missed reading their hometown newspapers, Anderson contacted northern newspaper publishers and made a deal with the railroad to have the papers delivered to Florence. Using old piano crates, Anderson built a newsstand, and business was soon booming. Within a few years, he and his brother were able to invest their profits in a bona fide book shop.

In 1950 Clyde W.'s son Charles C. Anderson inherited the book store and expanded it into a chain of stores called Bookland. During the 1970s, Bookland expanded rapidly as shopping malls sprang up across the American landscape, and by 1980 Anderson operated 50 stores located primarily in shopping malls throughout the Southeast. Charles C. also established a book and periodical distribution business. When his sons Charles, Jr., and Clyde B. were old enough, they began working in the wholesale business and book store, respectively.

In the mid-1980s Bookland doubled its size when it bought Gateway Books, a chain of stores based in Knoxville, Tennessee. According to the young Clyde B. (who had moved into senior management after graduating from the University of Alabama), many Gateway stores were poor performers. Within two years, Bookland had closed 27 of 50 Gateway stores, a move that left the company with many excess books and store fixtures. These three factors—excess books, excess fixtures, and a young executive with big plans—combined to become the driving forces behind the company's move into superstores.

In 1988 the youngest Anderson led the company to open an 8,000-square-foot store in a shopping center in Huntsville, Alabama. By his own account, the store—furnished in part with fixtures and stock from the abandoned Gateway stores—was a flop. "It was one of my early learning experiences," he reported in an interview with *Birmingham* magazine. Shortly afterward, however, the company opened a second superstore under the name Books-A-Million. The new superstore was located just down the street from the first one, but this time with 30,000 square feet of selling space, as opposed to 8,000. "We did very successfully from day one," Anderson told *Birmingham* magazine.

The company made the decision to expand into the superstore format at the right time. In other regions of the United States, larger book retailers, such as Barnes & Noble and Crown Books, had already begun to switch to the superstore format and were beginning to squeeze out smaller stores. The concept behind superstores was to establish specialty shops with an enormous selection of goods and prices comparable to, or lower than, department store sale prices. Bookstores weren't the only retail businesses to explore this concept. Instituted by Toys 'R' Us in the early 1980s, the formula quickly spread into home furnishings (with Bed Bath 'N Beyond), electronics (with Circuit City) and do-it-yourself home improvement (with Builders Square).

Books-A-Million superstores sought to purchase books at high volume and pass the savings on to customers. To draw customers, bargain books—sold at 40 to 90 percent of publisher's suggested retail prices—were placed prominently in the front of the stores and updated weekly to keep bargain hunters coming back. In addition, the weekly top ten best sellers were offered for up to 40 percent off the publishers' suggested retail price, while paperbacks were offered at up to 25 percent off suggested retail prices.

Books-A-Million distinguished itself from its competitors by maintaining a regional focus at a time when national chains threatened to homogenize book selling. Individual Books-A-Million stores were given the freedom to launch marketing campaigns for books of particular interest to customers in their own markets. For example, books published by the *Birmingham News* on topics like the University of Alabama's successful football season or the death of a local race-car celebrity received special campaigns, as did *The Firm,* a first novel by Mississippi author John Grisham, which became a national best-seller and feature film. Books-A-Million was also one of the few book superstores to target medium-sized cities; its competitors most often chose to open new stores in larger metropolitan areas.

Bookland began opening new superstores at a rate of about ten per year while continuing to operate its smaller stores. Most of the company's 50 Bookland stores were located in shopping malls with department store anchors such as Sears and J. C. Penney's, or discounters like Wal-Mart or Kmart. Some of these were maintained according to their original format; others were converted to combination stores.

In a 1994 interview with *Retailing Today,* Anderson explained the reasons behind the decision to develop combination stores: "We're from a small town and we wanted a concept that would work in a small town. We found that some of these small towns couldn't support just a book store. But if you could have a combination book and something else—we developed a combination books and cards—that the economies of that may work."

In 1992 the company changed its name to Books-A-Million, Inc., and went public on the NASDAQ exchange, selling 2.6 million shares at $13 per share. (A secondary stock offering in October 1993 sold 1.25 million shares at $23 per share.) That year, Clyde B. Anderson became CEO. His father remained chairman, and Charles Anderson, Clyde's brother, took over the family's wholesale book and periodical distributorship.

The Anderson brothers proved to have a knack for marketing. "Get to know your customers and give 'em what they want," was Clyde's philosophy as told to *Forbes.* A prime example of his strategy occurred in 1993, the year the University of Alabama upset Miami in the Sugar Bowl. Although *Sports Illustrated* had decided not to feature the event as its cover story, the Anderson brothers convinced the magazine's editors to print 200,000 special editions of the magazine, put Alabama running back Derrick Lassic on the cover, and add additional stories about the Alabama victory. Books-A-Million bought all 200,000 copies of the special commemorative edition and within a month sold all of them, bringing in $900,000 and an estimated profit of $200,000.

By 1993 Books-A-Million operated 113 stores in cities and small towns across the southeastern Unites States. As the company grew, Anderson continued to expand the concept of a superstore. In addition to positioning itself as a bargain book outlet, Books-A-Million began developing the concept of bookstore-as-entertainment. Events such as book signings and readings (especially by Southern authors) became regular features, along with book-buying clubs and special discount cards. The company also strove to develop its customer service: book searches, special orders, and free gift wrapping encouraged customer loyalty. In 1993 about ten Books-A-Million stores contained espresso bars, which contributed to the store's image as a place to sit and enjoy books. Even the stores' hours of operation, from 9 a.m. to 11 p.m., encouraged visiting the store

and browsing. "It's a very exciting place to be in our superstores," Anderson boasted to *Forbes.*

Books-A-Million also instituted a number of programs aimed at encouraging reading among children. By 1994 many stores contained separate Kids-A-Million departments, colorful sections that offered a large selection of gifts, books, and videos for children. Weekly story hours were held, and the company supported local schools by offering discounts on library material and ordering bulk shipments of books on classroom reading lists.

In fiscal 1994 Books-A-Million had a profit margin of .046, the highest in the book superstore business, on net sales of $123.3 million. The company operated 84 Bookland stores and 29 superstores and was continuing to expand rapidly. By December 1994, the company operated 43 superstores across the southern United States. New stores were reported to cost $825,000 to build, but in 1994 start-up costs were recouped in less than one year.

Twenty more superstores were opened in fiscal 1995. Books-A-Million preferred to build its new superstores in regional shopping centers that had anchor tenants such as Toys 'R' Us or discount clothing chains like Marshalls and T. J. Maxx. Less desirable locations were shopping centers with upscale neighboring tenants such as the Talbott's clothing chain, or, on the opposite end, bargain factory outlets. In 70 percent of Books-A-Million's markets the company had no strong competitors; in the remaining 30 percent, its main competitor was Barnes & Noble. Some analysts feared that Books-A-Million superstores were pulling customers from its own Bookland stores, but Anderson told a group of investors in 1995 that sales erosion was minor and was "more than offset by efficiencies in advertising and transportation costs." Sales in fiscal 1995 grew to $172.4 million, and net income grew to $8.1 million from $5.6 million in 1994. Same-store sales increased 13.8 percent for superstores and 6.4 percent for all stores.

The future success of Books-A-Million is contingent upon the company's ability to control costs, and in this Books-A-Million leads all other book superstores, in part due to its close relationship with the Anderson family's distributorship. Books-A-Million has also carved out a unique position as a regional retailer in a trade increasingly dominated by national players. These factors combine to make near-term prospects for the company quite promising.

Principal Subsidiaries: Book$mart; American Wholesale Book Co.

Further Reading:

Stern, William M., "Southern Fried Reading," *Forbes,* June 20, 1994, p. 91.
Teitelbaum, Richard S., "Companies to Watch: Books-A-Million," *Fortune,* January 25, 1993, p. 105.
Williams, Roy, and Mick Normington, "Anderson Family Values," *Birmingham News,* February 26, 1995, p. 1D.

—Maura Troester

Borg-Warner Automotive, Inc.

200 S. Michigan Avenue
Chicago, Illinois 60604
U.S.A.
(312) 322-8500
Fax: (312) 461-0507

Public Company
Incorporated: 1987
Employees: 8,500
Sales: $1.2 billion
Stock Exchanges: New York
SICs: 3711 Motor Vehicles and Passenger Car Bodies; 3714
    Motor Vehicle Parts and Accessories; 3728 Aircraft Parts
    and Auxiliary Equipment, Not Elsewhere Classified; 3568
    Mechanical Power Transmission Equipment, NEC

Not to be confused with its former parent (Borg-Warner Corp.) or ex-sibling (Borg-Warner Security Corp.), Borg-Warner Automotive, Inc. is one of the world's leading developers and suppliers of automotive parts and systems. The company maintained ten American operations and several more in Canada, Germany, Italy, Japan, Korea, and Wales in the mid-1990s. Known primarily for supplying powertrain components to major automakers in Detroit and Europe, Borg-Warner Automotive broadened its horizons in the 1990s by making deals in China, France, Italy, and India to produce parts for increasingly popular light truck and sport-utility vehicle models and new engine and transmission designs in North America and Europe. The company has undergone significant changes over the years, but Borg-Warner Automotive's manufacturing skill and reputation have allowed it to not only weather the breakup of its corporate family, but to triumph first as a private, then as a newly public, independent company in 1993.

Borg-Warner's history was as complex and interesting as one of its powertrain assemblies: a cluster of components (in this case, small, specialized auto parts manufacturers) harmoniously working to power a highly successful industrial giant. To tell the story of Borg-Warner Automotive, one must trace the formation of several disparate manufacturers in the United States and abroad. The first of these was Morse Equalizing Spring Company of New York, founded in 1880, which patented the rocker joint. In 1901 Warner Gear of Muncie, Indiana, was

formed, and the next year, Marvel-Schebler Carburetor Company began operations in Flint, Michigan. A fourth company, Long Manufacturing, came on line in Chicago to manufacture automobile radiators, while a fifth company, Borg & Beck, was organized in 1904. All of these companies figured in the development of Borg-Warner Automotive.

By 1906 Morse manufactured a line of automobile chains that were soon licensed for sale in England and Germany. Then came the production of automotive timing chains, followed quickly by Warner Gear's development of the industry's first manual transmission. In 1910 Long Manufacturing moved from Chicago to Detroit while a sixth rookie in the auto game, Mechanics Machine Company of Rockford, Illinois, began producing transmissions in 1911. Over the next several years, Morse built a new facility in England as Warner Gear fashioned a growing reputation for quality.

By the 1920s, Borg & Beck's sturdy yet inexpensive clutch was mass produced in millions of cars while Mechanics Machine Co. developed a universal joint with continuous lubrication, an innovation that rendered the former model (which had to be greased every 500 miles) obsolete. At the same time, Warner Gear standardized its manual transmissions and introduced the T64, at nearly half the cost of its predecessors. In the young yet burgeoning auto industry, each of the aforementioned companies was busy developing a specialized product line, unaware that they would be united under the banner of Borg-Warner in a sweeping merger in 1928. Borg & Beck, Marvel Carburetor, Mechanics Universal Joint (renamed from Mechanics Machine in 1925) and Warner Gear became the Borg-Warner Corporation. The following year, Morse Chain (an auto timing and industrial chain producer at this time) and Long Manufacturing joined the new company at the same time that the Norge firm (including its Detroit Gear subsidiary) was acquired.

The next decade brought several technological firsts for both Borg-Warner and the industry: Warner Gear pioneered the "synchronizer," a device that made a manual transmission's gear teeth mesh together with ease for smooth shifting; Morse Chain brought out its first roller chain; and Borg-Warner's self-contained overdrive transmission was introduced to immediate success as Chrysler and 11 other automakers quickly placed orders. Borg-Warner Automotive Service Parts Division was also launched in the 1930s, and in 1936, to emphasize Borg-Warner's commitment to and enthusiasm for auto racing, the company commissioned a sterling silver trophy for the Indianapolis 500 (the first was presented to Louis Meyer). As the decade neared its close, Stieber Rollkupplung GmbH (the predecessor to Borg-Warner GmbH) was founded in Munich in 1937.

In the prewar 1940s Borg-Warner created its Spring Division (to supply automatic transmission parts), began working on transfer cases, and soon directed its attention to World War II production needs. Among its contributions were Morse Chain's drives for Navy tug boats and jeeps built with Warner Gear's transmissions. After the war, Warner Gear's technology briefly lent itself to the medical field in 1949, producing iron lungs. It then returned to auto parts in 1950 with three revolutionary developments—the torque converter, a three-speed automatic transmission, and a new-fangled clutch that would become one of the company's biggest sellers worldwide. Automotive sales for the company reached over $200 million. Among the first automakers to jump at Borg-Warner's newest innovations were Studebaker and Ford. The latter was so enamored of Borg-Warner's transmissions that it signed a five-year exclusive contract with Borg-Warner in 1951 for the production of automatic transmissions.

As the 1950s continued, Borg-Warner expanded its operations in several new directions. Not only did the company venture into South America, creating Borg & Beck do Brasil, but it also built new facilities in Simcoe, Ontario, and Letchworth, England. The English facility was soon producing Warner Gear's overdrive units and the Model D.G. automatic transmission. In 1956 the T10 four-speed high performance manual transmission was introduced in the Chevrolet Corvette to wide acclaim. As Marvel-Schebler tinkered with a fuel injection system, Borg-Warner built (and patented) the first retractable seat belt restraint system and developed a line of paper-related wet friction components.

To broaden its international operations, Borg-Warner acquired Coote & Jurgenson, an Australian transmission producer for autos and tractors in 1957. Three years later, Brummer Seal Company was merged into Borg-Warner's Spring Division. The next year, 1961, was the beginning of a new era—though few recognized it as such—as James F. Bere joined the company as head of the Borg & Beck subsidiary. In 1962 Borg-Warner expanded into Mexico, and into Asia in 1964 and 1965 with two Japanese joint ventures (NSK-Warner and Tsubakimoto-Morse).

As the company's varied units continued to devise new product innovations (the "Hy-Vo" chain, Flex-Bands, and the aluminum Model 35 automatic transmission), Bere nimbly climbed the corporate ladder and was named as group vice president at age 42. Yet he ruffled feathers the following year when he openly discussed, in detail, the financial data of each of the company's ten divisions, a practice not done before at decentralized Borg-Warner. As a result, insiders were shocked when Chairman Robert S. Ingersoll announced Bere as his new president in 1968, promoting him over four company veterans. Instead of being fired for his boldness, Bere had begun a trend: rather than keep profits and losses shrouded in a need-to-know fog, he had been open and honest about company performance. Yet with Bere's frankness came bleak consequences: the closure of underperforming subsidiaries to relieve and strengthen assets that had been forced to carry their weight. Though Borg-Warner diversified into chemicals, plastics, industrial products, financial assistance, and eventually even into security and armored car services, its automotive division had remained a constant, usually contributing upwards of 50 percent of Borg-Warner's total revenue.

In 1969 Aisin-Warner was formed as another joint venture with Japan to build automatic transmissions, including the advanced Model 35, which was now distributed to 30 automakers for use in over 100 vehicles ranging from Nissans to Jaguars. The following year Borg-Warner acquired the Massachusetts-based Nu-Era Gear and improved on its automatic transmission by

developing the Model 45, which was soon manufactured in new facilities in Australia and South Wales. Marvel-Schebler expanded by merging with Tillotson Carburetor in 1971, the same year that Borg & Beck christened a new plant in Michigan.

In 1972, just four years after his surprise appointment as president, Bere became CEO when Ingersoll left the company and the United States to become an ambassador to Japan. The next year, Borg-Warner introduced its full-time, four-wheel drive (4WD) transfer cases using Hy-Vo drive chains, while its newest manufacturing operation opened in Ireland. Over the next several years came two new major innovations (the Model T50 five-speed transmission and continuously variable transmission for commercial vehicles); further expansion (new plants in Arkansas and New York and renovation of Warner Gear's Indiana facility); the issuance of 2,000,000 common shares of Borg-Warner stock; and Bere's election as chairman of the board (in 1975).

When Borg-Warner celebrated its 50th anniversary in 1978, its automotive profits had reached $98 million. The next year, overall sales topped $2.7 billion as the company headed into the tumultuous 1980s. Although U.S. auto production fell by 25 percent in 1980, Borg-Warner kept its losses to a respectable 16 percent decline, a good amount below the national average. This was due in part to its continuing improvement of the T4 and T5 manual transmissions and its production of new, lightweight transfer cases. Yet transfer cases took a giant technological leap in the 1980s with the introduction of sport utility vehicles and light trucks like the Ford Ranger.

Buoyed by steady sales of transmissions and transfer cases, the company experimented with electronic sensors, silicon technology, and non-asbestos friction materials. Borg-Warner also tightened its focus by selling Morse Industrial and its automotive service parts divisions in 1981. Three years later, the company consolidated its many automotive operations under the umbrella of Borg-Warner Automotive, Inc., setting up international headquarters in Troy, Michigan. Sales for the newly named automotive conglomerate topped $1 billion in 1984. By 1985 Borg-Warner Automotive employed 10,000 people and began using high volume laser-cutting in its Frankfort, Illinois, plant. It also produced its one-millionth T5 manual transmission that year, while continuing its consolidation (Warner Gear was renamed Transmission Systems, Borg & Beck was renamed Clutch Systems, and Marvel-Schebler became known as Control Systems).

In 1986 Borg-Warner experienced a changing of the guard: after 25 years of service, Bere stepped down as CEO (remaining chairman of the board) and was succeeded by Richard J. Doyle as president and CEO. Doyle's first year at the helm was marked by several highs, including an exclusive contract to manufacture its new Model 1356 transfer cases for all of Ford's light trucks and sport utility vehicles. Additionally, the company opened sales offices in Frankfurt, Sao Paulo, Seoul, and Tokyo and signed a licensing agreement with Nanjing Motor Works of Beijing, boosting international sales to a record high of 30 percent of its $3.4 billion in revenue.

Yet for all of Borg-Warner Automotive's success, there was a steep price—the interest of corporate raiders Irwin Jacobs and Samuel Heyman in the fast-and-loose leveraged buyout (LBO) haven of the 1980s. After spending $680 million, Jacobs and Heyman each possessed 10 percent of the company, to the shock and dismay of Borg-Warner's board. Determined to squelch not only Jacobs' and Heyman's takeover attempt but any future opportunists as well, Borg-Warner's brass decided to take the company private. Turning to Merrill Lynch Capital Partners, an LBO fund, Borg-Warner's board was supposed to offer stockholders $43 per share. Instead, the directors decided to wait, hoping Jacobs and Heyman would lose interest.

Instead, in March 1987, Heyman bought Jacobs' holdings and offered stockholders $46 a share in a hostile takeover bid. Borg-Warner again turned to Merrill Lynch, but Heyman's offer had upped the ante to a buyout valued at over 20 times the company's earnings. In May, Merrill Lynch completed one of the ten biggest LBOs of the decade for $4.4 billion ($3.4 billion from banks and $1 billion from junk bond sales), establishing 51 percent ownership in the now-private Borg-Warner.

The 65-year-old Bere assumed the CEO role again to oversee the company's breakup. The already daunting task was made more difficult by the onset of Black Monday, a dramatic plunge in the stock market. The drop substantially affected the sales of the chemical and plastics division (sold to General Electric for $2.3 billion) and Borg-Warner Acceptance Corp. (sold to TransAmerica for $782.5 million). What was left was Borg-Warner Security ($1.3 billion in revenue for 1989), and its subsidiary, Borg-Warner Automotive (BWA), with sales of $958 million in 1989 and earnings of $93 million. Sales fell to $920 million in 1990 as a result of an industry slump.

Around this time, transfer case technology branched into heavy duty and all-wheel drive for several models from General Motors. BWA also developed the new 1354 model for Ford Explorers and Ranger trucks, while the "touch drive" model was installed in all F-series trucks. This year also marked the appointment of Donald C. Trauscht, a 23-year company veteran, as president of BWA, and by 1991 over one million model 1354 transfer cases had been installed in F-series trucks along with Borg-Warner's automatic locking hubs, now the industry standard.

In the early 1990s BWA offered the industry's first three-year/36,000-mile warranty on transfer cases and debuted its latest technological breakthrough—the "Torque-on-Demand" transfer case capable of automatically shifting from two- to four-wheel drive when necessary. This innovation led to another sole-source agreement with Ford for the rest of the decade. Meanwhile, the T56 six-speed manual transmission became standard in Chrysler's Viper sportscar and new Ford Mustangs, and international operations were expanded in Japan and China. 1993 saw the appointment of Siegfried P. Adler as president of BWA, as Trauscht was elevated to president and CEO of the unit's parent company, Borg-Warner Security. That year Borg-Warner Automotive, Inc. was spun-off into an independent company with J. Gordon Amedee as chairman and CEO.

Closing the year with $985.4 million in sales (and a net loss of $97.1 million due to spin-off accounting charges), up from 1992's $926 million (and a net loss of $12 million), BWA pointed to a number of milestones as evidence of its continued vitality: production of its three-millionth T5 manual transmission and four-millionth transfer case for Ford; the signing of a "life of the product" pact with General Motors for its advanced "Maji-Band" brake band assembly for automatic transmissions; and a new five-year contract with SsangYong Motor Company for manual transmissions and transfer cases.

In July 1994, John Fiedler was named president and CEO of Borg-Warner Automotive after serving Goodyear's North American Tire division for 30 years. The company, poised for a renaissance as the automotive industry boomed, was now comprised of four subsidiaries: Automatic Transmission Systems, Control Systems, Morse TEC (Chain Systems) and Powertrain Systems. The latter unit, propelled by transfer cases—the darling of the sport utility vehicle and light truck industry—grew by over 12 percent to account for 40 percent ($550.7 million) of 1994's total $1.2 billion in revenues.

When Fiedler came on board, one of his first pronouncements was his intention to double BWA's revenues by the end of the 1990s, implement a slew of cost reductions, improve productivity, increase foreign investments, and form more joint ventures both in and out of North America. Fiedler also hinted that he and BWA's directors were in an acquisitive mood: "We're in an excellent position to grow and we're going to raise some eyebrows," he told Barron's in August 1994, after posting an impressive 25 percent sales gain for the first half of the year, way over the industry's 11 percent overall increase.

Finishing 1994 with sales of $1.2 billion and a net profit of $64.4 million, Borg-Warner's future was increasingly bright. Figures from the first half of 1995 remained firm—despite cutbacks by Detroit's Big Three (Ford, Chrysler, and GM)—with all divisions posting double-digit increases. Powertrain Systems posted $291.6 million in sales ($265 million in 1994), while Automatic Transmission Systems added $219.5 million (it posted $180.2 million in 1994). Borg-Warner finished the first half of 1995 with total net sales of $683.8 million (a 24 percent overall increase from the same period in 1994). Picking up the slack from Detroit was steady growth in demand in Asia and Europe, as BWA's trademarked Morse Gemini Chain System and Torque-on-Demand transfer case (only two of the company's 1,900 active domestic and foreign patents) continued their phenomenal success.

Principal Subsidiaries: Automatic Transmission Systems Corporation; Control Systems Corporation; Morse TEC Corporation; Powertrain Systems Corporation.

Further Reading:

Bautz, Mark, "Wall Street Newsletter," *Money,* June 1995, pp. 68–72.
Benoit, Ellen, "A Survivor," *Forbes,* April 21, 1986, pp. 100, 104.
Bere, James F., "The Director as Servant and Leader," *Directors & Boards,* Spring 1991, pp. 7–8.
Borss, Marcia, "A Debtor With Options," *Forbes,* November 26, 1990, p. 64.
Byrne, Harlan S., "Lean Machine," *Barron's,* August 15, 1994, p. 19.

Crown, Judith, ''Borg-Warner Faces Life After CEO Bere,'' *Crain's Chicago Business,* January 13, 1992, pp. 1, 29.

Flaherty, Robert J., ''Now the Real Test Begins,'' *Forbes,* February 18, 1980, pp. 134, 138.

''Follow-Through,'' *Forbes,* March 3, 1980, p. 12.

Gornstein, Leslie, ''Open Road for Borg-Warner Exec,'' *Crain's Chicago Business,* July 11, 1994, pp. 22–23.

Lowe, Frederick H., ''He's a Big Sports Fan,'' *Chicago Sun Times,* January 29, 1995.

Nathans, Leah, ''Hot for Glory,'' *Business Month,* January 1989, pp. 55–59.

Saxon, Wolfgang, ''James F. Bere, 69, A Chicago Leader and Corporate Chief,'' *New York Times,* January 4, 1992, p. 27.

Spragins, Ellyn, ''Healthy Smokestacks,'' *Forbes,* August 15, 1983, pp. 58–59.

—Taryn Benbow-Pfalzgraf

Boston Celtics Limited Partnership

151 Merrimac Street
Boston, Massachusetts 02114
U.S.A.
(617) 523-6050
Fax: (617) 523-5949

Public Company
Incorporated: 1986
Employees: 60
Sales: $52 million
Stock Exchanges: New York
SICs: 7941 Sports Clubs, Managers & Promoters

Operator of the Boston Celtics basketball team, Boston Celtics Limited Partnership represents the financial, managerial, and broadcasting power behind arguably the most successful franchise in the history of sports, the Boston Celtics, a team that has won an unprecedented 16 national championship titles during the 1950s, 1960s, 1970s, and 1980s and counts among its players many of basketball's legendary figures. Sixteen Celtics players were inducted into the Naismith Memorial Basketball Hall of Fame between 1960 and 1987, with Larry Bird, Kevin McHale, and others certain to add to that prestigious total once eligible for consideration. The team won 11 championship titles during a 13-year span, including eight in a row, accomplishing a feat unparalleled in American major professional team sports. Celtics players from the past included the best to ever play the game of basketball; its owners and coaches were among the most revered, most despised, and most controversial figures in sports history. By all measures, the Celtics represented a legacy of success and captivating lore. Its storied history, its decades of dominance in the National Basketball Association, and the idiosyncratic personalities who created the franchise's success combined to create a unique Boston Celtics mystique—one that defied duplication and one that distinguished the organization from all others in professional sports. Yet the magnitude of the corporate entity behind the basketball team and the amount of revenue directly derived from the team belied the significance and wealth of success the Celtics represented.

Boston Celtics L.P. occupied a singular position both in corporate America and among the roster of team owners in the National Basketball Association. In terms of annual revenue the company ranked well below the thousands of medium-sized companies scattered across the country, generating less than $100 million per year in revenue. Paradoxically, yet indicative of the enormous business professional sports represented during the 1980s and 1990s, the company derived relatively little from the sale of game tickets, making the majority of its money—more than 70 percent—from advertising, television, cable, and radio fees. Financially, Boston Celtics L.P. was supported by much more than the Boston Celtics, yet it was nothing without the Boston Celtics and the widespread interest created by the team.

As owner of the Boston Celtics, Boston Celtics L.P. assumed its position of control relatively late in the team's history, beginning its corporate life in 1986, 40 years after the team was formed. Considering that the Celtics recorded 16 league championships during the 40-year span bridging the team's creation and the formation of Boston Celtics L.P., nearly all of what Boston Celtics L.P. represented during the mid-1990s was owed to the owners, players, and coaches who created the Celtics dynasty between 1946 and 1986, none of whom could have made the contributions they did without the dogged efforts of the team's founder, Walter Brown.

Owner of the Boston Bruins hockey team and the fabled Boston Garden, Brown cared little and perhaps knew even less about the game of basketball when he and a small group of arena operators gathered in New York City in 1946 to organize the Basketball Association of America. Like others in attendance, Brown was primarily concerned with keeping his arena filled with paying spectators, something that had proven hard to accomplish during the winter nights in Boston. Brown had made various attempts to keep the turnstiles spinning at Boston Garden when the Bruins had the night off, booking the Ice Follies, Ringling Brothers and Barnum & Baily Circus, a Notre Dame football game, midget auto races, rodeos, women's softball games, and book shows, but he was in search of a steady attraction and went to New York to create one.

Basketball seemed an odd choice considering the game enjoyed little popular support, particularly in Boston, where the population was devoted to baseball and hockey. Basketball, in fact, had been eliminated from the Boston city school system in 1925, nearly two decades earlier. Nevertheless, Brown and his cohorts—all of whom, except one, owned hockey teams—organized the 11-member Basketball Association of America in the Commodore Hotel on June 6, 1946, and Brown left New York with a basketball franchise, as yet unnamed.

After considering several team names, including "Whirlwinds," "Unicorns," and "Olympics," Brown opted for "Celtics," hoping to grab the attention of Boston's large Irish population. John Davis "Honey" Russell was hired as the first Celtics coach, and the team soon began its inaugural season, losing its first game 59–53 to the Providence Steamrollers, the first of many losses during the franchise's fledgling years. The Celtics were 22–38 after their first season, and, despite Brown's expectations of packing his arena with adoring fans, the team never filled half the seats in the Boston Garden, averaging only 3,608 people per game. The Celtics posted a losing record the following year yet made the playoffs. But more important to the team's future was its financial condition, as the losses mounted for Brown and the company he led, Boston Garden Arena Corporation.

A coaching change was made before the 1948–1949 basketball season, with Alvin "Doggie" Julian taking over for Honey Russell, but his impact was negligible and the Celtics again recorded a losing season, winning 25 games and losing 35. By this point the financial condition of the team was grave. During its third season, the Celtics lost $100,000, bringing the total loss for its first three seasons to $350,000. Shareholders of the Boston Garden Arena Corporation wanted out and urged Brown to fold the franchise, but Brown persevered, convincing the disgruntled stockholders to give the Celtics franchise one more year to prove its financial viability. The following season was the worst in the franchise's short history, as the Celtics posted a dismal 22–46 record; the team's record was 89 victories and 147 losses during the first four years. As a result, attendance had declined and the franchise lost another $100,000, bringing its total loss for four years of operation to nearly $500,000. Boston Garden Arena Corporation stockholders were no longer receptive to Brown's pleas after the fourth season and they sold their stakes in the franchise to Brown, leaving the disheartened founder saddled with debt and in charge of the failing Celtics.

To stave off a complete collapse of the franchise, Brown sold his home and other private investments, keeping the Celtics in business for another season. As later became apparent, Brown's decision to keep the team afloat, despite no obvious sign that the team's future would be any more successful than its past, was an immensely beneficial one. Two new faces arrived for the 1950–1951 basketball season: coach Arnold Jacob "Red" Auerbach, who was hired as the Celtics third head man in five years, and guard Bob Cousy, who would convert his harshest critic—his new coach—into one of his staunchest supporters. Red Auerbach, age 32 when Walter Brown named him coach of the Celtics, would be chiefly responsible for creating the celebrated Celtics mystique that would intimidate opposing players and draw legions of Celtics fans into the Boston Garden for generations to come. With his ever-present victory cigar clamped in his mouth, Auerbach would guide the Celtics through the team's much heralded glory years, orchestrating the action from courtside for the next 16 seasons, then wielding his managerial control for decades afterward. Under Auerbach's glare, the other new arrival—Cousy—would develop into one of the game's greatest players, transforming the Celtics organization from a perennial loser into the most successful franchise in the history of professional basketball.

Together, Cousy and Auerbach righted the floundering Celtics, who posted a 39–30 record during the 1950–1951 season—the team's first winning season—and advanced to the playoffs. Perhaps more important, average attendance rose 2,000 per game during the season, enabling Brown to begin recouping his losses and beat back the financial pressures that threatened the franchise's existence.

The Celtics advanced to the playoffs each of the next five years, but a championship title—the hallmark of a sports organization's success—eluded the franchise. In retrospect, the Celtics were missing one key player, and that player, Bill Russell, arrived in camp in the autumn of 1956. The acquisition of the 6'10" Russell took the Celtics franchise over the top; during his rookie year (1956–1957) attendance rose by an average of 2,500 fans and the Celtics won their first league championship. After losing the championship series the following season to the St. Louis Hawks (whom Boston had defeated to take their first championship), the Celtics captured an amazing eight titles in a row, ranking as the National Basketball Association's preeminent franchise between the 1958–1959 and 1965–1966 seasons.

Walter Brown died in 1964, near the end of the Celtics' string of championship titles, marking the end of one era and the beginning of another as the reins of ownership, which had remained with Brown for nearly 20 years, passed from hands to hands. The connection between Walter Brown and the Celtics franchise had been resolute; when the bond was severed, it was not long before a series of owners took over and dissolved the familial nexus between owner and franchise. Following Brown's death, Lou Pieri, who had been co-owner with Walter Brown since 1950, and Marjorie Brown took charge of the Celtics organization for a year, then a succession of corporate owners, incongruous with the Celtics-Walter Brown era, assumed control: National Equities, 1965–1968; Ballantine Brewery, 1968–1969; Trans-National Communications, 1969–1971; Investors' Funding Corporation, 1971–1972; and Leisure Technology, 1972–1974.

Two years after Brown's death, another Celtics era ended when Red Auerbach relinquished his coaching duties and Bill Russell took over, becoming the first African-American to either coach or manage a major professional sports team. Under Russell, the Celtics won two more championship titles (1968 and 1969); the team went on to win two more league titles during the 1970s with Tom Heinsohn, a former Celtics player, coaching the team. Ownership of the franchise during the mid- and late 1970s had devolved to Los Angeles film producer Irv Levin, who, in 1978, traded the Celtics franchise to John Y. Brown and Harry Mangurian in exchange for the Buffalo Braves franchise, which Brown and Mangurian owned. Aside from the peculiarity of trading one franchise for another, the deal between Levin and Brown/Mangurian was notable for another reason: the arrival of John Y. Brown to the Celtics organization put in place an owner who would ignite a bitter, intrafranchise feud and engender the Celtics' most contentious year in its history.

Auerbach, who continued to embody the Celtics mystique and direct the franchise as its general manger, disliked John Y. Brown intensely, particularly because Brown had ignobly obtained the revered Celtics franchise through a swap. Even more irksome to the longtime Celtics coach and general manger was Brown's disregard for his authority. As part of the franchise swap, several Celtics players were sent to the Braves franchise, the first time a player transaction had been made without Auerbach's knowledge since his arrival in 1950, nearly 30 years earlier. Angered, Auerbach began discussions with the New York Knicks about a job with the franchise and was offered a four-year contract as president of the rival organization for a salary that would make him the highest paid National Basketball Association executive ever.

Auerbach relented, opting to remain in Boston after listening to advice from his wife and gaining assurances from Brown that he would not be excluded from future decisions affecting Celtics players. Less than a year later, Brown traded three first-round draft picks to the New York Knicks for Bob McAdoo without consulting Auerbach, bringing the running feud between the two to a climatic tumult. Enraged, Auerbach approached Brown and informed the Celtics owner that if he did not sell the team within two weeks he—Auerbach—would leave. Two weeks later,

Brown sold his interest in the team to Harry Mangurian; Brown then went on to successfully run for governor of Kentucky.

Against the backdrop of this public dispute between Brown and Auerbach, the Celtics franchise had drafted a 6′9″ forward from Indiana State University named Larry Joe Bird in 1978. Bird would establish himself during the 1980s as one of the greatest players in the history of the game, and with the addition of Kevin McHale and Robert Parish (both of whom were acquired through a complicated trade involving Bob McAdoo), the Celtics franchise had formed the nucleus of a team that would win three national championships during the 1980s, extending the winning tradition into a fourth decade.

As the drive toward winning three championships during the decade gained momentum, ownership of the franchise once again changed hands when, in 1983, Harry Mangurian sold the team to Don Gaston, Paul Dupee Jr., and Alan Cohen for $17 million. The new owners were intent on transforming the Celtics franchise into a major, profitable business, rather than treating it like a prestigious, self-aggrandizing asset, as many of the owners who followed Walter Brown had done. Gaston, Dupee, and particularly Cohen wanted more from their acquisition and began looking for a way to substantially build on their investment. Ticket prices were raised, but the three owners were in search of a way to realize more dramatic financial gains. In 1985 Cohen learned of such a way from David Stern, commissioner of the National Basketball Association.

Following Stern's suggestion, Gaston, Dupee, and Cohen formed a master limited partnership named Boston Celtics L.P. that enabled the three owners to avoid paying a substantial percentage of taxes on revenue the franchise generated and provided for the distribution of shares of Boston Celtics stock to the public, a first for a professional sports franchise. In 1986, 2.6 million Celtics shares, representing 40 percent of the team, were offered to the public at $18.50 per share, from which the three owners earned $44.74 million in proceeds. After the public offering, Gaston owned 32.5 percent of the Celtics, Dupee owned 14.7 percent, and Cohen owned 11.8 percent, more than enough to continue with their ownership unchallenged by all others.

The formation of Boston Celtics L.P. and the sale of Celtics stock had given the three owners much, yet the proceeds gleaned from the public offering were not sufficient to keep Gaston, Dupee, and Cohen from searching for other ways to capitalize on their investment. In 1985 the Celtics franchise sold its television rights in a five-year deal to an independent UHF station, WLVI-TV, which immediately increased the station's estimated value from $50 million to $75 million, giving the three owners tangible evidence of the financial worth of their organization and the magnitude of revenue others were earning from their franchise. In order to redirect the broadcasting revenues into their pockets, Gaston, Dupee, and Cohen began hatching plans to acquire their own broadcasting entities, and in late 1987 the opportunity arrived.

After WFXT-TV became available the Celtics franchise purchased it for $10 million and formed Boston Celtics Communications Limited Partnership, a sister company to oversee the broadcasting business of the Celtics organization. The Celtics then sold their own station the broadcasting rights to air Celtics

games for $30,000 per game during the preseason, $150,000 per game during the regular season, and $200,000 per game during the playoffs. When WEEI-AM was acquired by Boston Celtics Communications L. P. in 1989, the three partners worked out a similar arrangement, giving the Celtics franchise radio broadcasting fees ranging between $1.4 million and $2.5 million per year.

By the beginning of the 1990s, as the Celtics' dominance on the basketball court began to wane, Gaston, Dupee, and Cohen stood over a genuine sports empire, with revenue pouring in from the Celtics on the court and the Celtics over the airwaves. When Mangurian sold the Celtics in 1983, the team was generating roughly $8 million in revenues per season. After going public in 1986, the franchise's annual revenue volume rose dramatically, more than tripling as the team's coffers swelled from broadcasting and licensing contracts and increased ticket prices. Financial growth continued into the next decade, thanks to the formation of Boston Celtics Communications L. P. and its two primary assets, WEEI-AM and WFXT-TV, boosting Boston Celtics L.P.'s annual revenues to $30 million in 1990. By 1993, the company was generating more than $80 million annually.

By the end of the 1993 fiscal year, both Larry Bird and Kevin McHale had retired from the team, with Bird making his exit before the 1992–1993 season and McHale leaving after the 1992–1993 season. Their departures marked the end of yet another era in Celtics history, raising concern over the team's future and its ability to win additional championship titles. In 1994, the company sold its radio station, and the following year it sold the television station WFXT for accumulated proceeds of about $105 million.

There was no doubt where future Celtics teams would play their home games, however. The franchise played its last season at the Boston Garden during the 1994–1995 basketball season and began its 1995–1996 campaign at the new and larger FleetCenter, where both the Celtics and Boston Celtics L.P. hoped to establish a winning and lucrative tradition.

Principal Subsidiaries: BCCLP Holdings Corporation; Boston Celtics Communications LP (99%); Boston Celtics Broadcasting LP (99%); WEEI-AM (ABC Radio Network).

Further Reading:

Araton, Harvey, and Filip Bondy, *The Selling of the Green,* HarperCollins: New York, 1992, 271 p.
"Fox Gets Celtics Station," *New York Times,* July 12, 1995, p. D5.
Hackney, Holt, "Boston after Bird," *FW,* November 27, 1990, p. 68.
Hammonds, Keith H., "For Celtics Fans, It's Wait Till Next Fiscal Year," *Business Week,* June 27, 1988, p. 89.
McLaughlin, Mark, "Win or Lose, Celtics' Performance Has Little Effect on Price of Stock," *New England Business,* June 20, 1988, p. 48.
Ryan, Bob, *The Boston Celtics: The History, Legends, and Images of America's Most Celebrated Team,* Addison-Wesley: New York, 1989, 224 p.
Shaughnessy, Dan, *Ever Green,* St. Martin's Press: New York, 1990, 259 p.
Webber, Alan M., "Red Auerbach on Management," *Harvard Business Review,* March/April 1987, p. 84.

—Jeffrey L. Covell

British Airways PLC

P.O. Box 10
Speedbird House
Heathrow Airport
Hounslow, Greater London TW6 2JA
England
81 759-5511
Fax: 81 897-1889

Public Company
Incorporated: 1924 as Imperial Air Transportation, Ltd.
Employees: 50,060
Sales: £7.177 billion (US$9.78 billion)
Stock Exchanges: London
SICs: 4500 Transportation by Air; 4725 Tour Operators

British Airways PLC is the largest international airline in the world. It is based at Heathrow Airport in London, the busiest international airport in the world, and has a global flight network through such partners as USAir in the United States, Qantas in Australia, and TAT European Airlines in France. Via its own operations and those of its alliance partners, British Airways serves 95 million passengers a year using 441 airports in 86 countries and more than 1,000 planes.

British Airways' earliest predecessor was Aircraft Transport & Travel, Ltd., founded in 1916. On August 25, 1919 this company inaugurated the world's first scheduled international air service, with a converted de Havilland 4A day bomber leaving Hounslow (later Heathrow) Airport for London and also Le Bourget in Paris. Eight days later another company, Handley Page Transport, Ltd., started a cross-channel service between London's Cricklewood Field and both Paris and Brussels.

That same year Britain's advisory committee for civil aviation proposed plans for establishing a world airline network linking Britain with Canada, India, South Africa, Australia, and New Zealand. Because airplanes capable of crossing wide stretches of water were not yet available, the committee recommended that first priority be given to a route to India operated by state-assisted private enterprise.

Progress was made quickly. Before the end of the year the British government was operating a service to Karachi and had established a network of 43 Royal Air Force (RAF) landing strips through Africa to the Cape of Good Hope. Meanwhile,

strong competition from subsidized foreign airline companies had forced many of the private British air carriers out of business. By March 1921 all British airline companies had suspended their operations. The government responded with a pledge to keep the British companies flying, using its own form of subsidization.

In January 1923 Parliament appointed the Civil Air Transport Subsidies Committee to form a single British international air carrier from existing companies. On March 31, 1924 the Daimler Airway, British Marine Air Navigation, Instone Air Line, and Handley Page merged to become Imperial Air Transport.

In 1925 Imperial Airways operated a number of European routes while it surveyed a route across the Arabian desert from Cairo to Basra in present-day Iraq. The airline was faced with a number of problems on this route. The desert was featureless, making it easy to get lost. Water stops and meteorological and radio stations were difficult to maintain. Basra was a major terminal on the route to India. However, on January 7, 1927 the Persian government forbade Britain the use of its airspace, blocking all flights to India. Negotiations reopened the airspace two years later, but not before generating a demand for longer range aircraft.

Passengers flying to India flew from London via Paris to Basel, where they boarded a train for Genoa. A flying boat then took them on to Alexandria, where they flew in stages to Karachi. The passage to India, previously three weeks by sea, had been reduced to one week by air.

Imperial Airways service to Calcutta was established in July 1933, to Rangoon in September, and to Singapore in December. In January of the following year the Australia's Queensland and Northern Territories Air Service (Qantas) inaugurated a route linking Singapore with Brisbane. The passage to Australia could be completed in twelve-and-a-half days.

A commercial service through Africa was opened in 1931 with flying boats linking Cairo with Mwanza on Lake Victoria. In April 1933 the route was extended to Cape Town, the trip from London taking ten-and-a-half days. An east-west trans-African route from Khartoum in the Sudan to Kano in northern Nigeria was established in February 1936. This route completed a world network which linked nearly all the countries of the British Empire.

The primary source of revenue on the network was not from transporting passengers but mail. Nevertheless, an increase in demand for more passenger seating and cargo space generated a need for larger airplanes. Britain's primary supplier of flying boats, the Short Company, developed a new model, designated the C-class, with 24 seats and weighing 18 tons. Since it had an increased range and flew 145 miles per hour, it was able to simply bypass "politically difficult areas." The Short C-class went into service in October 1936. A year later Imperial Airways made its first trans-Atlantic crossing with a flying boat equipped with extra fuel tanks. However, it was Pan Am, with more sophisticated and updated Boeing airplanes, which was first to schedule a regular trans-Atlantic service.

Imperial Airways was formed with the intention of being Britain's "chosen instrument" for overseas air service. On its

European services, however, Imperial was competing with the British Continental airlines and an aggressive newcomer called British Airways. British Airways was created in October 1935 by the merger of three smaller airline companies. Three months later the company acquired a fleet of Lockheed 10 Electras which were the fastest airplanes yet available. The competition from British Airways threatened the "chosen instrument" so much that in November 1937 a Parliamentary committee proposed the nationalization and merger of Imperial and British Airways. When the reorganization was completed on November 24, 1939, the British Overseas Airways Corporation (BOAC) was formed.

The creation of BOAC was overshadowed by the declaration of war on Germany the previous September. The Secretary of State for Air assumed control of all British air services, including BOAC. Within a year Italy had entered the war and France had fallen. Britain's air routes through Europe had been eliminated. British flying boats, however, continued to ferry personnel and war cargo between London and West Africa with an intermediate stop at Lisbon in neutral Portugal. The air link to Khartoum maintained Britain's connection to the "Horseshoe Route," from Cape Town through East Africa, Arabia, India, and Singapore to Australia. When Malaya and Singapore were later invaded by the Japanese, BOAC and Qantas opened a nonstop service between Ceylon and Perth in Western Australia. BOAC transported ball bearings from neutral Sweden using a route which was dangerously exposed to the German Luftwaffe. BOAC also operated a service for returning flight crews to North America after they delivered American- and Canadian-built aircraft to the Royal Air Force.

When the war ended BOAC had a fleet of 160 aircraft and an aerial network that covered 54,000 miles. The South American destinations of BOAC were assigned to a new state-owned airline, British South American Airways (BSAA), in March 1946. Similarly, the European services were turned over to British European Airways (BEA) on August 1, 1946. After the war Britain reestablished its overseas services to the nations of its empire. Some of the nations which had recently gained their independence from Britain received advice (and often finance) from BOAC.

In order to remain competitive with the American airline companies, BOAC purchased Lockheed Constellations, the most advanced commercial aircraft of the day. They were later joined by Boeing 377 Stratocruisers and Canadair Argonauts (modified DC-4s). BEA operated generally smaller airplanes and more frequent flights between the British Isles and Continental Europe. In 1948 it joined other Allied airline companies in the airlift to Berlin during the Soviet blockade.

Following a series of equipment failures at BSAA, the Civil Aviation ministry declared that the company should reemerge with BOAC. On July 30, 1949, BSAA was absorbed by BOAC. Even though its passenger load had steadily increased, BOAC accumulated a debt of £32 million in the five years from 1946 to 1951. Much of this was due to "recapitalization," or purchasing new equipment; the British-built Handley Page Hermes and de Havilland's DH Comet 1, the world's first jetliners, were delivered to BOAC.

In January 1954 one of BOAC's Comets exploded near Elba in the Mediterranean. Another Comet crashed near Naples only 16 days after an investigation of the first crash was concluded. As a result, the Comet's certificate of airworthiness was withdrawn and a full investigation was ordered. In the final report it was determined that the Comet's pressurized cabin was inadequately designed to withstand low air pressures at altitudes over 25,000 feet. When the airplane reached that altitude it simply exploded. The cabin was strengthened and the jet reintroduced in 1958 as the DH Comet 4.

The company was forced to purchase propeller-driven DC-7s to cover equipment shortages when delivery of its Britannia turboprops was delayed in 1956. When the Comet reentered service BOAC found itself with two undesirable fleets of aircraft which were later sold at a loss of £51 million ($122 million).

South American operations were suspended in 1954 when the Comet was taken out of service. Operation of the route with shorter range aircraft was too costly. At the insistence of Argentina and Brazil, which claimed Britain had "lost interest" in South America, the routes were reopened in 1960. That same year the first of 15 Boeing 707 jetliners was delivered to BOAC.

British European Airways used a wide variety of aircraft for its operations and remained a good customer for British aircraft manufacturers. In 1964 the company accepted delivery of the first de Havilland Trident 1, a three-engine airliner capable of speeds up to 600 miles per hour. A few years later, when the company expressed an interest in purchasing a mixed fleet of Boeing 727s and 737s, it was instructed by the government to "buy British" instead. BEA complied, ordering BAC-111s and improved versions of the Trident.

BOAC's cargo traffic was growing at an annual rate of 27 percent. Nevertheless, a sudden and unexplained drop in passenger traffic during 1961 left many of the world's airline companies with "excess capacity," or too many empty seats to fly profitably. At the end of the fiscal year BOAC's accumulated deficit had grown to £64 million. The losses, however, were underwritten by the British government, which could not allow its flag carrier to go bankrupt.

BOAC and Air France agreed to commit funds for the buildings of a supersonic transport (SST) in 1962. In June the company became associated with the Cunard Steamship Company. A new company, BOAC-Cunard Ltd., was placed in charge of the trans-Atlantic air services in an attempt to capture a larger portion of the American travel markets.

The British government published a "White Paper" (a statement of government policy) which recommended a drastic reorganization of BOAC. In response, the company's chairman, Sir Matthew Slattery, and the managing director, Sir Basil Smallpiece, resigned. Britain's minister for aviation appointed Sir Giles Guthrie as the new chairman and chief executive officer. Under Sir Giles BOAC suspended its unprofitable services and rescheduled its equipment purchases and debt payments. After the financial situation had improved, the company continued to purchase new equipment and expand its flight network. In April of 1967 BOAC established its second around-the-world route and opened a new cargo terminal at Heathrow.

The company's sister airline, BEA, had been paying close attention to consumer marketing for vacationers. In 1967 the company created a division called BEA Airtours Ltd., offering complete travel packages to a number of vacation spots. In May 1969 BOAC opened a passage to Japan via the North Pole. The route was shortened even further when the Soviet Union granted BOAC landing rights in Moscow and a Siberian airlane to Tokyo.

On March 31, 1972, after six years of record profits, BOAC announced that it no longer owed any money to the government. Later, on July 17, following several recommendations on further reorganization of the state-owned airline companies, management of BEA and BOAC were coordinated under a new government agency called the British Airways Group. On April 1, 1974 the two companies were merged and renamed British Airways. A second reorganization of the internal management structure took place in 1977.

The first British Airways' Concorde was introduced in 1976. Jointly manufactured by British Aerospace and the French firm Aerospatiale, the supersonic Concorde was capable of carrying 100 passengers at the speed of 1,350 miles per hour at an altitude of 55,000 feet. A seven-hour flight from New York to London was nearly reduced to half the time by the Concorde. British Airways employed additional Concordes on a number of international services, most notably London-Singapore, which was temporarily suspended through 1978 due to "political difficulties."

In 1980 Prime Minister Margaret Thatcher appointed Lord (John) King as the new chairman of British Airways. His stated assignment was to prepare the airline for privatization (sale to private stockholders). Lord King's first move was to adopt aggressive "American-style" marketing and management philosophies. As a result, he initiated a massive campaign to scale down the company and reduce costs. More unprofitable air services were terminated, and a staff reduction (begun under Lord King's predecessor, Roy Watts) was continued. A British Airways official told *Business Week* magazine that, "we had too many staff but couldn't get rid of them because of the unions." In order to utilize the excess labor, the company was forced to remain large. Lord King established a better relationship with labor, which had become more agreeable to layoffs and revisions of work rules. In three years the work force was reduced from 60,000 to 38,000 without a strike.

On July 11, 1983, no fewer than 50 senior executives were fired. The company's chief executive officer, Colin Marshall, hired in their place a team of younger executives (mostly with nonairline business backgrounds). The new executive staff initiated a series of programs to improve punctuality and service at the airline, whose BA acronym stood in many customers' minds for "Bloody Awful." They hired Landor Associates, a successful San Francisco-based design firm with considerable experience with airlines, to develop an entirely new image for British Airways. The result was controversial. The British Airways coat of arms and portion of the Union Jack on the airplane's tail fin was bound to upset the more politically temperamental countries of the third world which the company serves. The familiar "Speedbird" logo which dates back to the days of

Imperial Airways was removed despite employee petitions to retain it.

British Airways also recognized a need to replace older airplanes in its fleet with more modern and efficient equipment. The company's Lockheed TriStars were sold to the RAF for conversion into tankers, and the BAC-111s were sold because they would violate new noise regulations. British Airways leased a number of airplanes until new purchases could be made after the privatization.

The company was plagued by its decision to retain separate European and overseas divisions. The result was a perpetuation of the previous management regimes of BEA and BOAC. To rectify this problem the operation was further divided into eight regional groups involved in three different businesses: cargo, charter, and tours. Each of the eight groups has increased autonomy and responsibility for its business and profitability.

The Laker Airways Skytrain, an initially successful cut-rate trans-Atlantic airline, was forced to close down due to what its chairman, Freddie Laker, claimed was a coordinated attack by a number of airlines to drive the company into bankruptcy. Laker charged the companies, which included British Airways, with violations of antitrust laws. He later settled out of court for $48 million, but in a subsequent civil suit British Airways was also required to issue travel coupons to passengers who claimed they were hurt by the collapse of Laker Airways.

Ironically, in the mid-1980s the company began advocating the deregulation of European air fares in the belief that it could compete more effectively than its rivals. But Air France and Lufthansa in particular were reluctant to participate, claiming that deregulation would endanger the delicate market balance which took so many years to establish.

In 1985 British Airways was made a public limited company, but all its stock was retained by the government until such time that it could be offered to the public. The privatization of British Airways (which was limited to a 51 percent sale) was delayed by a number of problems. The company's chief domestic rival, British Caledonian, opposed British Airways' privatization claiming that the company already controlled 80 percent of the domestic market and was too large to compete against. But British Airways' most significant obstacle to privatization involved reducing the debt that it accumulated during the 1970s, and increasing the company's profitability. In February 1987 the privatization was finally consummated when 720.2 million shares of British Airways stock were sold to the public for one billion pounds ($1.47 billion).

British Caledonian, or BCal, was formed in 1970 through the merger of Caledonian Airways and British United Airways. For many years, BCal was British Airways' only large domestic competitor, fighting vigorously under the direction of Sir Adam Thompson for more favorable operating rights from the British government. When Britain's Civil Aviation Authority recommended the reallocation of British Airways routes to BCal in 1984, Lord King threatened to resign. Instead, British Airways was instructed to trade its profitable Middle East routes for some of BCal's less profitable Latin American destinations. The Middle Eastern routes became much less popular during 1986 as a result of regional tensions and falling oil prices. BCal, which had been generating a fair profit, started to lose money and was faced with bankruptcy.

In July 1987 British Airways acquired BCal for £237 million in stock. The new airline had almost 200 aircraft, and combined British Airways' 560,000-kilometer route structure with BCal's largely unduplicated 110,000-kilometer network, forming one of the largest airline companies in the world. Several smaller independent British airline companies unsuccessfully challenged the BA/BCal merger on the grounds that the new company would dominate both London's Heathrow and Gatwick airports, forcing them to relocate to the less accessible and underdeveloped field at Stansted.

With its dominance of the home market secure for the time being, British Airways aggressively expanded in Europe, North America, and the Pacific Rim over the next several years, aiming to become a global airline. Its first foray into the lucrative U.S. market came in 1988 when it formed a marketing alliance with United Airlines designed to feed customers from one carrier to the other and vice versa. This partnership set the pattern for British Airway's expansion—it would not be based on forming new airlines outside England or acquiring them, but rather through strategic alliances. Nevertheless, this first partnership collapsed a little more than two years later when United became a direct competitor to British Airways once it had gained access to Heathrow in 1991, along with American Airlines. The two strongest airlines in the United States had purchased the Heathrow rights from the floundering Pan Am and TWA, immediately increasing competition in British Airways' home market.

While the alliance with United was still operating, British Airways suffered losses in Europe in 1990 and 1991 because of the Gulf crisis in the Mideast. Shortly after, in July 1991, it entered into an alliance with Aeroflot in Russia to create a new airline called Air Russia. After several false starts over the next few years, this venture never got off the ground. Additional proposed alliances failed in 1992 for other reasons. Officials from British Airways and KLM Royal Dutch Airlines held extensive discussions about a merger in 1991 and 1992, but talks broke down over the valuation of the two firms. Later in 1992, British Airways attempted to purchase 44 percent of USAir Inc. for $750 million. American, United, and Delta Air Lines (the U.S. "Big Three") vigorously lobbied against the deal and demanded enhanced access to the British market if the deal was to be approved by the U.S. government. In December the purchase was blocked.

That same month the first in a string of alliances was struck when the airline paid $450 million for 25 percent of Qantas, the Australia-based international airline. In 1993, British Airways gained a 49.9 percent stake in the leading French independent carrier TAT European Airlines, then launched a start-up in Germany called Deutsche BA with 49 percent ownership. Through these alliances, British Airways had enhanced its position in the Pacific Rim and Europe. It now refocused its attention across the Atlantic where it restructured its offer for a piece of USAir into a $400 million purchase of 25 percent of the company. This alliance received U.S. government approval. The government also approved a code-sharing arrangement that enabled the partners to offer their customers a seamless operation when they use both airlines to reach their destination.

While all this dealmaking was going on abroad, British Airways faced an embarrassing and potentially costly fight at home with Richard Branson's upstart Virgin Atlantic Airlines. Since starting operations in the early 1980s, Virgin had made some inroads against British Airways primarily by focusing on customer service, something "Bloody Awful" BA had neglected for years. Branson filed suit against British Airways in 1991 alleging that British Airways had smeared Branson and his airline and conducted "dirty tricks" such as spreading rumors about Virgin's insolvency. In 1993 the suit was settled out of court with British Airways offering a public apology and paying £500,000 to Branson and £110,000 to Virgin. The case also led to the resignation of Lord King. Second-in-command Colin Marshall took over as chairman. Further litigation followed between the two rivals, most seriously a $1 billion antitrust suit brought by Virgin in the United States. Various suits damaged British Airways' reputation and led to comments such as the following from the *Economist:* "BA now looks . . . like an anxious, overbearing giant trying to squash a feisty little rival."

With its Virgin difficulties continuing, British Airways' overseas partners suffered huge losses: in 1993 Qantas lost $271 million, while in 1994 TAT lost $60 million and USAir lost $350 million. The situation at USAir was so grim that British Airways declared that they would hold back an additional $450 million investment in the firm until the carrier was in the black. In May 1995 British Airways was forced to take a $200 million charge to write down the value of its USAir investment.

Even though British Airways was struggling with its alliance strategy, the real test of its global strategy lay ahead with the long-awaited 1997 deregulation of the European airline industry. It approached that date as one of the most profitable airlines in the world, despite the faltering alliances, and had been in the black every year since privatization.

Principal Subsidiaries: British Airways Capital Ltd. (89%); British Airways Finance BV; British Airways Holidays Ltd.; Caledonian Airways Ltd.; Qantas Airways Ltd. (25%, Australia); TAT European Airlines S.A. (49.9%, France); Deutsche BA L.m.b.H. (49%, Germany); Air Russia (31%); Bedford Associated, Inc. (U.S.); British Airways (U.S.); Galileo International Partnership (14.6%, U.S.); USAir Group, Inc. (24.6%, U.S.).

Further Reading:

Banks, Howard, *The Rise and Fall of Freddie Laker,* London: Faber, 1982, 155 p.

Campbell-Smith, Duncan, *The British Airways Story: Struggle for Take-Off,* London: Hodder and Stoughton, 1986, 327 p.

Corke, Alison, *British Airways: The Path to Profitability,* New York: St. Martin's Press, 1986, 145 p.

Dwyer, Paula, "Air Raid: British Air's Bold Global Push," *Business Week,* August 24, 1992, pp. 54–60.

Dwyer, Paula, and Keith L. Alexander, "Sky Anxiety: Faltering Partners Are Shaking British Airways' Strategy of Global Alliances," *Business Week,* March 21, 1994, p. 38.

Gurassa, Charles, " 'BA Stood for Bloody Awful'," *Across the Board,* January 1995, pp. 55–56.

Kindel, Stephen, "Economies of Scope," *Financial World,* September 14, 1993, pp. 42–43.

Lynn, Matthew, "Battle of the Atlantic," *Management Today,* November 1991, p. 48.

Palmer, Jay, "The British Are Coming: By Slashing Costs, Selling Comfort and Forging Alliances, British Airways Has Made Itself a Contender in the Battle to Rule the Skies," *Barron's,* December 12, 1994, pp. 29–34.

Penrose, Harald, *Wings Across the World: An Illustrated History of British Airways,* London: Cassell, 1980, 304 p.

Wada, Isae, "Going Global: BA Chief Executive Outlines Carrier's Expansion Plans," *Travel Weekly,* September 6, 1990, pp. 1–3.

"We Are Flying into Turbulence," *Economist,* March 4, 1995, pp. 64–66.

—updated by David E. Salamie

Brother Industries, Ltd.

15-1 Naeshiro-cho
Mizuho-ku
Nagoya 467
Japan
(052) 824-2511
Fax: (052) 821-7628

Public Company
Incorporated: 1934 as Yasui Sewing Machine Company.
Employees: 3,980
Sales: ¥218.58 billion (US$2.2 billion) in 1994
Stock Exchanges: Tokyo Osaka Nagoya
SICs: 3579 Office Machines, Not Elsewhere Classified; 3639
    Household Appliances, Not Elsewhere Classified; 3542
    Machine Tools, Metal Forming Types; 3552 Textile
    Machinery; 3541 Machine Tools, Metal Cutting Types;
    3931 Musical Instruments

Brother Industries, Ltd., is one of the world's top manufacturers of electronic office machines. Although faxes, word processors, printers, copiers, and other office equipment constituted nearly two-thirds of Brother's annual sales by the early 1990s, the company also produced industrial and household sewing machines, household appliances, and machine tools. By the mid-1990s, the company's products were manufactured and distributed in countries around the world, yet over half of its annual sales continued to be generated at home in Japan. Brother has managed to remain competitive in the fast-paced electronics industry by developing innovative devices for its diverse markets. The company's sales grew steadily through the early 1990s, from about US$1.3 billion in 1992 to over US$2.2 billion in 1994. Net income declined from US$6.7 million in 1992 to a loss of US$9 million in 1993, but the company bounced back with a US$39.6 million profit in 1994. Although publicly held, Brother Industries continued to be led by a member of the founding Yasui family, Yoshihiro Yasui, into the early 1990s.

The company was founded in 1908 by two brothers to repair imported sewing machines. Then known as the Yasui Sewing Machine Company, the firm launched Japan's first domestically produced sewing machine under the Brother label in 1928.

Yasui's early sewing machines were industrial models used in the manufacture of straw hats. The company launched its first

household sewing machine in 1932. The growing firm was incorporated two years later and continued to refine its sewing machines throughout the period between the World War I and World War II, adding advanced capabilities like lock stitching and buttonholing, for example.

Renamed Brother Sales, Ltd., in 1941, the company began to apply its accrued expertise in motors and manufacturing to diversification during the postwar era. Some of the side projects, like a 1956 motorcycle named the "Darling," turned out to be dead ends. But in 1954 the company launched a series of small and large home appliances that soon grew to include electric washing machines, irons, mixers, fans, and refrigerators. Brother augmented its home apparel line with its first knitting machine during this period as well.

Brother rode the wave of Japanese imports into the United States in the postwar era, as its high-quality products were quickly recognized by consumers in there and around the world. The company established a U.S. marketing subsidiary, Brother International Corporation, in 1954 and established European sales operations three years later to guide overseas expansion.

The 1960s and 1970s witnessed concurrent moves into industrial machine tools and the electric, and then electronic, office machines that would become Brother's largest product group. The company launched its first portable typewriter in 1961 and changed its name to Brother Industries, Ltd., the following year. Cash registers, calculators, and adding machines filled out the office machine segment over the course of the 1960s. At the same time, Brother applied electronics technology to its line of home appliances, offering tape recorders and stereos in the mid- and late 1960s, microwave ovens in the 1970s.

Brother's mechanical know-how combined with emerging electronics to result in the world's first high-speed dot matrix printer in 1971. By 1981 Brother's Information Systems Division carried one of the largest lines of printers. Continuous innovation in the typewriter segment throughout the 1970s culminated in the 1980 launch of an electronic office typewriter.

The company founded its Office Equipment Division in 1981 to market a new generation of electronic and computerized typewriters, fax machines, and word processors. By 1983 sales in this segment of Brother's business surpassed its traditionally dominant sewing machine sales. In order to compete with personal computers, Brother added editing screens and memory to its electronic typewriters and launched a word processor in 1987. The company's line of printers diversified widely from its base in traditional impact models (dot matrix and daisy wheel) to nonimpact technologies like thermal transfer and laser delivery systems by the end of the 1980s. Brother applied its expertise in printing and computing to new lines of copiers and fax machines in the latter years of the decade and added specialty office machines, including Japanese-language word processors and memory devices, during this period. The innovative P-Touch Electronic Labeling System enjoyed extraordinary popularity, selling more than 1 million units within just three years of its 1988 launch.

Notwithstanding its wide-ranging diversification, Brother continued not only to manufacture but to refine its historical product lines. The company applied computerization to industrial and home sewing machines as well as knitting machines. Brother produced its ten-millionth typewriter in 1980 and its ten-millionth knitting machine three years later.

One of Brother's sales strategies has been to keep prices as low as possible, especially on equipment that has been superseded by newer technologies. The typewriter was a prime example. Brother's U.S. subsidiary came under fire from its primary U.S. competitor, Smith-Corona Corp., in the mid-1970s for using this competitive tactic. Smith-Corona accused Brother of "dumping" typewriters—selling them below "fair market value" in order to capture market share—in violation of the Antidumping Act of 1921. In 1979 the U.S. federal government agreed and started adding punitive duties (58.7 percent) to each typewriter imported into the United States.

Brother had begun overseas production with the 1978 launch of a Taiwanese sewing machine plant. In order to avoid high import tariffs, the company began to establish factories in the United Kingdom, United States, Malaysia, and Ireland. While Brother was busy moving factories and assembly plants to its primary markets, Smith-Corona started moving its production out of the United States in an effort to cut labor costs. By the early 1990s Smith-Corona was not manufacturing any typewriters in the United States.

In 1991 Brother proved that turnabout is fair play when it charged Smith Corona with dumping its portable typewriters from a factory in Singapore. Although its case was dismissed on the grounds that it was not a U.S. company, Brother's U.S. subsidiary won on appeal. This time, Smith-Corona was told to fight fair or face fines. Brother and Smith-Corona called a truce in early 1994, agreeing to drop their complaints and legal actions against one another. Smith-Corona, which by this time was partly owned by the British firm Hanson plc, succumbed to Brother's competitive onslaught (as well as other inexorable market forces), and sought Chapter 11 bankruptcy protection in 1995.

Even though markets and prices for typewriters and word processors shrunk throughout the 1980s, Brother continued to enjoy growth. The company's continued success hinged on its flexibility, which in turn was grounded in the company's research and development efforts. As manual typewriters gave way to electric, and then electronic, typewriters (and eventually to word processors and personal computers), Brother aggressively stayed at the forefront of each trend. Similar changes transformed the printer market, which evolved from impact methods like the daisy wheel into newer nonimpact technologies like inkjet, bubble, and laser printers.

In the early 1990s Brother continued to parlay synergies between its diverse business segments into innovative new products. By combining specialized software with its electronic sewing machines, for example, the company created home sewing models that could design and automatically sew embroidery. The application of inkjet printing technology to the apparel business resulted in the "P's" system, which printed clothing and other patterns directly on the fabric, eliminating a full step in the production process. Brother hoped to apply computer integrated manufacturing to ever higher levels of apparel production in the mid- to late 1990s by creating software that facilitated design of apparel factories as well as the clothing itself.

Brother applied its communications skills to an entirely new field, entertainment, in the early 1990s as well. The company utilized integrated services digital network (ISDN) technology to create JOYSOUND, a multimedia, online, networked karaoke system. This newfangled jukebox offered full instrumentations of over 3,000 popular songs through an online computer network, which many bar and nightclub owners subscribed to, eliminating the need to maintain an expensive and space-consuming laser-disc collection. The company also developed TAKERU, a system that distributed personal computing software online. The company was also among the first to launch one of the newest generation of network computers. These inexpensive devices permitted the most basic and popular functions, including access to online services and electronic mail, PC compatibility, and word processing. They sacrificed memory capacity to keep costs low; Brother's Power Note, for example, sold for just under US$300.

Brother's sales grew steadily through the early 1990s from about US$1.3 billion in 1992 to over US$2.2 billion in 1994. But a global recession squeezed profits during this period. Net income declined from US$6.7 million in 1992 to a loss of US$9 million in 1993, but the company rebounded with a US$39.6 million profit in 1994. Although Brother appeared to have prevailed over one of its primary rivals, Smith-Corona, the Japanese firm would continue to struggle against adverse market forces. For example, Brother was expected to pursue economizations in manufacturing, in part by whittling its wide-ranging product lines down to core products. Slow-growth areas like home appliances and machine tools appeared to be likely candidates for reduction or outright elimination.

Principal Subsidiaries: Brother International Corp.; Brother Real Estate, Ltd. (55%); Taiwan Brother Industries, Ltd. (Taiwan); Brother Industries (Aust.) Pty. Ltd.; Brother Industries (U.K.) Ltd. (United Kingdom); Brother Industries (U.S.A.), Inc. (United States); Brother International Corp. (U.S.A.) (United States); Brother International Corp. (Canada) Ltd. (Canada); Jones Sewing Machine Co., Ltd. (U.K.) (United Kingdom); Brother International (Nederland) B.V. (Netherlands); Brother International G.m.b.H. (Germany) (Germany); S.A. Brother International (Belgium) N.V. (Belgium); Brother International G.m.b.H. (Austria) (Austria); Brother Handels A.G. (Switzerland); Brother Internationale Industriemachinen G.m.b.H. (Germany); Brother International Corp. (Ireland) Ltd. (Ireland); Brother International (Europe) Ltd.; Brother France S.A. (France); Brother Industries Technology (Malaysia) Sdn. Bhd. (Malaysia); Brother America Inc. (United States); Brother Finance (U.K.) Limited (United Kingdom); Elgin Brother Industrial Ltda. (Brazil); Brother International Corp. (Europe) Ltd.; Brother (U.S.A.) Inc. (United States).

Further Reading:

"Brother Wins Another," *Television Digest,* February 15, 1993, p. 17.
Mullins, Brody, "Smith-Corona in Chapter 11," *Insight on the News,* August 7, 1995, p. 32.
Plotkin, Hal, "Competitive Advantage," *Inc.,* December 1993, p. 44.
"Who's Dumping What?" *Television Digest,* April 22, 1991, p. 16.

—April Dougal Gasbarre

Brown and Williamson Tobacco Corporation

1500 Brown & Williamson Tower
Louisville Galleria
P.O. Box 35090
Louisville, Kentucky 40232
U.S.A.
(502) 568-7000
Fax: (502) 568-7107

Wholly Owned Subsidiary of B.A.T. Industries PLC
Incorporated: 1906
Employees: 5,800
Sales: $3.50 billion
SICs: 2111 Cigarettes; 2131 Chewing & Smoking Tobacco

Brown and Williamson Tobacco Corporation, a subsidiary of London-based B.A.T. Industries PLC, is the third largest manufacturer and marketer of cigarettes in the United States. With leading brands like Kool and Viceroy, the company was selling more than 90 billion cigarettes annually in 1994. B.A.T. merged Brown and Williamson and The American Tobacco Company in 1994, which boosted Brown and Williamson's market share from 11.3 to 17 percent.

Brown and Williamson (B&W) was founded in 1894 in the tobacco heartland of Winston-Salem, North Carolina. The business was started by George Brown and Robert Williamson, who formed a partnership before incorporating the company as Brown & Williamson Tobacco Company in 1906. In the beginning, B&W concentrated on specialty products like Bloodhound, Brown & Williamson's Sun Cured and Red Juice chewing tobaccos. After establishing those successful brands during the early 1900s, B&W assumed a leadership position in the pipe tobacco segment when it purchased the Sir Walter Raleigh brand. That brand had been marketed on a regional basis by the J.G. Flynt Tobacco Company since 1884. B&W purchased it in 1925 and began distributing it nationally. Sir Walter Raleigh eventually became one of B&W's hallmark brands.

About the same time that it began marketing Sir Walter Raleigh pipe tobacco, B&W moved into the burgeoning cigarette market. Cigarettes had been a relatively small segment of the tobacco market prior to the turn of the century. They had first become popular with women during the 1800s as an alternative to cigars and plug, twist, and pipe tobacco. After cigarettes were issued to U.S. soldiers during World War I, though, demand began to escalate. B&W launched an aggressive drive into the cigarette industry following the war. Strong sales of cigarettes and other tobacco products created healthy profit growth at B&W, which caught the eye of outside investors. In 1927, London-based B.A.T. Industries PLC purchased B&W to operate as one of its subsidiaries. B.A.T. expanded B&W's name to Brown and Williamson Tobacco Corporation in 1927, and in 1928 and 1929 added extensive manufacturing facilities in Louisville, Kentucky. At that time, B&W moved its headquarters from Winston-Salem to Louisville.

B&W made its mark on the cigarette industry during the 1930s with a number of brands and products. Importantly, B&W introduced Kool brand cigarettes, which were the first menthol cigarettes marketed nationally in the United States. B&W also began selling Viceroy cigarettes, which were eventually credited with popularizing the filter-tip. Both Viceroy and Kool became mainstay brands for B&W and helped to make it a growing force in U.S. tobacco. Besides those brands, B&W brought out Bugler and Kite cigarette tobacco in the mid-1930s. B&W's Bugler Thrift Kit was the first roll-your-own kit sold in the country. B&W achieved another first with the introduction of the economy-priced pack of cigarettes. Dubbed Wings, the brand sold for just ten cents per pack (compared to 15 cents for most other brands at the time), making it a big hit during the Great Depression. Wings was also the first cigarette package to utilize an outer wrap of moisture-proof cellophane.

Innovation and market growth buoyed B&W throughout the 1930s and 1940s. In fact, the legion of smokers in the United States spiraled upward after World War II and during the 1950s. At the same time, new influences began to shape the tobacco industry. Reports citing potential health risks associated with smoking cast a shadow on the industry. The results of the reported health risks were that tobacco taxes were increased, advertising channels for cigarette marketers were reduced, and smokers' preferences began to change. Among the most notable changes in preferences during the 1950s and 1960s was the switch to filter-tipped cigarettes. B&W, a pioneer in the filter-tip segment, responded with filter-tip versions of most of its cigarettes. Furthermore, B&W introduced the first filter made of cellulose acetate, which became a feature of its Viceroy Kings brand.

Despite negative health reports, smoking increased throughout the 1950s and most of the 1960s. By the mid-1960s more than 40 percent of the entire U.S. population was smoking cigarettes regularly. B&W benefited not only from increased smoking, but also from market share gains. Its most successful brand was Kool, which had struck gold in certain market niches, becoming the "king" of the menthol market. Studies also indicated that Kool dominated the African American market, about 70 percent of which smoked menthol cigarettes. By the early 1970s, Kool was controlling a whopping ten percent of the entire U.S. cigarette market. Augmenting the highly successful Kool brand during the early 1970s was a line-up of new low-tar brands, including Kool Milds, Viceroy Extra Milds, and Raleigh Extra

Milds. Those brand introductions helped B&W grab a 17 percent share of the entire U.S. cigarette market by the mid-1970s.

Although B&W enjoyed some significant successes during the late 1960s and early 1970s, it also began to face some serious internal and external challenges. Importantly, in the late 1960s the percentage of Americans who smoked began to decline. The descent was largely a corollary of a 1964 Federal Government mandate that required manufacturers to post health warnings on cigarette packages and advertisements. Subsequent government controls, most notably the 1971 ban on television advertising, exacerbated the dilemma and the share of smokers began to decline gradually; by the early 1990s, the percentage would fall to about 25 percent. Another blow came in 1983, when cigarette taxes vaulted 100 percent. That increase, moreover, was followed by a string of tax increases that devastated the domestic cigarette industry.

Although the share of the U.S. smoking population declined during the late 1960s and early 1970s, the actual number of cigarettes sold continued to grow at a heady clip. Total U.S. cigarette consumption grew from about 500 billion in 1965 to nearly 650 billion by 1980. Unfortunately, according to some critics, B&W failed to take full advantage of the increased industry volume. The problem was largely attributable to stalled growth of its core Kool brand. In 1975 B&W's Kool began to lose market share to such rivals as Salem. Importantly, B&W had failed to translate its successful "Come to Kool" advertising campaign from television to print following the Federal ban on cigarette television advertising. B&W tried during the early 1970s to attract younger smokers to Kool by associating the brand with jazz music, but kids were favoring rock 'n roll. Meanwhile, competing brands like Newport employed more successful marketing tactics and managed to steal Kool market share.

Between 1975 and 1985, Kool's share of the total cigarette market plunged from 10.3 percent to less than seven percent. B&W tried to supplant lost sales with other products, but it achieved only moderate success. In 1981, for example, B&W introduced a new low-tar cigarette called Barclay, investing $100 million in the product launch to get Barclay off to a good start. Unfortunately, B&W had understated Barclay's tar content, and the Federal Trade Commission forced the company to revise the ads. Barclay's growth stagnated following the ad change. B&W's successes during the early and mid-1980s included product introductions geared for the value segment of the cigarette market, which began surging following big tax increases in the early 1980s. But gains in that niche failed to generate growth. In fact, B&W's total share of the U.S. cigarette market toppled from 17 percent in 1976 to about 12 percent ten years later.

For the first time since the turn of the century, cigarette purchases began declining in the early 1980s. Indeed, sales volume in the United States slipped steadily during the 1980s from nearly 650 billion cigarettes in 1980 to about 500 billion in 1990. That trend, combined with lagging market share gains at B&W, mandated a new strategic direction for the company. To that end, B&W promoted Thomas E. Sandefur Jr. to president of the company in 1984. The 45-year-old Sandefur was a to-

bacco industry veteran, having worked for R.J. Reynolds Tobacco Co. from 1963 to 1982. He joined B&W with the understanding that he would eventually become head of the company. From 1982 to 1984 Sandefur worked to grow B&W's international operations as senior vice-president of international marketing. Sandefur worked under Chief Executive Raymond J. Pritchard (a native of Wales and former B.A.T. Industries executive) but was a major influence on the company's strategic direction.

Sandefur was known as capable, demanding, and shrewd. He grew up in Perry, Georgia, and earned a business degree at Georgia Southern College. Recruited by R. J. Reynolds as a salesman, he moved quickly up the corporate ladder on the marketing side of the business. Among his successes at R. J. Reynolds was a line of hugely successful low-tar brands including NOW and Camel Lights. Impressed by his success at Reynolds, B&W lured Sandefur away in 1982 and began grooming him for the top spot. Sandefur was also known as a tobacco hard-liner who vehemently opposed government regulation of his trade. And he was known for trying to keep a very low public profile, despite occasional appearances (in caricature) in the Doonesbury comic strip. Even in his work for civic organizations—he was active in a number of civic organizations, particularly the Boy Scouts—Sandefur tried to minimize his public exposure.

When Sandefur took the helm in 1984 he initiated his drive to turn the company around. Specifically, he launched an aggressive bid to increase B&W's shipments overseas, where cigarette sales were growing, and to boost B&W's efforts in the surging U.S. low-priced cigarette segment. Toward the latter goal, B&W began marketing as value-oriented brands Viceroy, GPC Approved (a plain label brand), Raleigh Extra, and Richland, among others. On the international front, B&W moved aggressively into cigarette markets in Asia, Africa, South America, the Middle East, Europe, Japan, and Puerto Rico. Meanwhile, Sandefur and other B&W executives continued to battle the army of Federal bureaucrats assaulting the tobacco industry. In April 1994, Sandefur and other tobacco industry executives were brought in front of a Senate subcommittee, interrogated, and lambasted for their role in promoting smoking. Sandefur and other executives reportedly denied that cigarettes were addictive at the hearing.

Despite government entanglement, Sandefur managed to boost B&W's performance during the late 1980s and early 1990s. International sales, for example, bolted 150 percent between 1986 and 1991 and B&W's control of the U.S. cigarette export business surged to 20 percent. By 1991, in fact, B&W's international business represented a full 45 percent of the company's total sales volume. B&W also assumed a leading role in the value-priced cigarette segment, with 21.2 percent of the total market in 1991. Meanwhile, B&W continued to innovate by introducing the first super-slim cigarette—Capri—in 1988. Throughout the late 1980s and early 1990s, moreover, B&W restructured its operations and management as part of an overall effort to cut costs and streamline operations. The net result was that B&W managed to hoist revenues to about $3.5 billion by the early 1990s and to increase profit margins.

When CEO Pritchard retired in 1993, Sandefur assumed full leadership of the company. He continued to restructure, expand internationally, and chase the value market. In 1994, in a major industry merger, B.A.T. (B&W's parent company) acquired The American Tobacco Company and integrated its operations into those of B&W. American Tobacco, which was once the unmitigated behemoth of the U.S. tobacco industry, controlled about seven percent of the U.S. cigarette market. Thus, the acquisition gave B&W a total of more than 18 percent of the U.S. market in 1995, making it the third largest cigarette manufacturer and marketer in the United States. American Tobacco owned well-known brands including Lucky Strike, Pall Mall, Misty, Montclair, Tareyton, and Private Stock. Those bolstered B&W's successful brands, which in 1995 included Kool, GPC, Capri, and Viceroy. In addition to cigarettes, B&W marketed loose cigarette tobacco, pipe tobacco, plug chewing tobacco, and snuff.

Further Reading:

The Brown and Williamson Story; A Retrospective, Louisville: Brown and Williamson Corp., September 1995.

Fitzgerald, Tom, "Brown & Williamson Announces Changes Relating to American Tobacco," *PR Newswire,* December 22, 1994.

Louis, Arthur M., "The $150-Million Cigarette," *Fortune,* November 17, 1980, pp. 121–122.

Otolski, Greg, "Sandefur to Succeed Pritchard as Chief of B&W Tobacco," *Courier-Journal,* January 13, 1993, p. B10.

Otolski, Greg. "The Tangled Trail of B&W's Documents," *Courier-Journal,* April 2, 1995, p. A1.

Pomice, Eve, "Kooling Off," *Forbes,* November 17, 1986, p. 230.

Wolfson, Andrew, "B&W Chairman Little-Known, and Likes it That Way," *Courier-Journal,* June 19, 1994, p. A1.

—Dave Mote

BRUSHWELLMAN

Brush Wellman Inc.

17876 St. Clair Avenue
Cleveland, Ohio 44110
U.S.A.
(216) 486-4200
Fax: (216) 383-4091

Public Company
Incorporated: 1931 as Brush Beryllium Co.
Employees: 1,833
Sales: $345.9 million
Stock Exchanges: New York
SICs: 3339 Primary Nonferrous Metals Nec; 3369 Nonferrous Foundries Nec

Brush Wellman Inc. is the world's leading producer of pure beryllium and beryllium products. The vertically integrated company is justifiably proud of its investment of time and money in the development of beryllium. Once characterized as a "mystery metal," this rare material has been adapted for applications ranging from watch springs and golf clubs to spacecraft, and, in large measure as the result of Brush Wellman's efforts, has come to be considered a "miracle metal." The company's perseverance through decades of criticism that it was not performing up to its potential began to pay off in the 1980s, when broader, more stable markets brought long-held expectations of bumper profits to fruition.

Beryllium was discovered by Louis Nicolas Vauquelin in 1798 and isolated by Friedrich Wöhler and Antoine Bussy thirty years later. It was known for many years as "glucinium," a name based on its sugary taste. Although beryllium occurs in many minerals, most of them are rare. Beryl rock, which contains the highest concentrations of beryllium (11 to 15 percent), has long been the primary source of this material. Beryl rock's clear varieties are the gems aquamarine and emerald.

Blue-gray in color, beryllium boasts a unique combination of characteristics. It is 30 percent lighter than aluminum, but is stronger (by weight) than steel. Beryllium maintains integrity of shape and strength over extremes of heat and cold and has a high capacity for heat absorption.

Brush Wellman was founded by Charles Baldwin Sawyer and Bengt Kjellgren in 1931 as the Brush Beryllium Company. Sawyer and Kjellgren had begun their work with beryllium in 1921 at Cleveland's Brush Laboratories. This research facility was founded by and named for Charles F. Brush, inventor of an early electric generator called the Brush arc dynamo. Experiments on the conductivity of metals led to the development of an extraction process that used heat and pressure to separate beryllium from beryl ore. One of several companies spawned by research conducted at the Brush Laboratories, Brush Beryllium was created to develop marketable applications for beryllium.

In its early years, the company concentrated on producing pure beryllium. The metal's strength and reliability made it a prime candidate for military applications. Defense sales gained volume and significance with the advent of World War II. Brush Beryllium played a role in the development of atomic energy, missiles, aircraft, and rockets.

Boosted by defense and later aerospace contracts, Brush Beryllium's annual sales multiplied quickly, from $4.5 million in 1955 to $18 million by 1960. Metals and Minerals Division chief Stephen Zenczak later told *Fortune*'s John Quirt that "in 1960 beryllium was an absolutely magic word and we were up on cloud nine." High demand obliged Brush, then led by Robert W. Biggs, to seek stable sources of beryl ore.

Up to that point, Brush Beryllium had been dependent upon imported beryl ore, which it processed into beryllium. Most of the world's beryl rock can be found in Brazil, but as a 1984 *Forbes* article noted, procuring the material was "like hunting for four-leaf clovers or panning for gold." In fact, Brush relied on Brazilian "prospectors" to collect the surface-level pieces of rock. The only other known global sources of commercial-grade beryl rock were located in the U.S.S.R. and China, a factor that imbued the drive for a stable (preferably domestic) source of beryl with national security implications.

The discovery of bertrandite, another beryllium-bearing ore, in Utah's Topaz-Spor Mountains in the early 1960s opened the door to vertical integration at Brush Beryllium. Taking a great calculated risk, Brush bought the right to explore and mine 12,500 publicly owned acres in Utah for $3 million. At the time, company executives weren't even sure that beryllium could economically be culled from bertrandite. Due to the highly speculative nature of the venture, they initially retained only a 30 percent stake in the independent company known as Beryllium Resources. Reassured that their bet was well placed, Brush Beryllium bought the remaining shares in 1962 and made the operation into the Geological Exploration & Mining Division.

A $16 million on-site processing unit converted both imported and freshly mined materials into beryllium hydroxide concentrate. From there, the materials were transported to the company's plant in Elmore, Ohio, where they were pulverized into a powder before undergoing a "thermal shock" process that transformed the substance into solid, malleable forms. This lengthy process was further complicated by the fact that beryllium powder is explosive, toxic, and possibly carcinogenic. These factors engendered the regulatory scrutiny of the Occupational Safety and Health Administration and the Environmental Protection Agency. Nevertheless, consistently high demand for the strategic metal driven by the Cold War "space race" more than compensated for these intricate and costly production requirements throughout the 1960s.

The early 1970s brought cutbacks in the space program. Consequently, Brush Beryllium attempted to reduce its reliance on defense and aerospace through diversification, acquiring three businesses in northeast Ohio between 1971 and 1975. The most significant purchase during this period was S. K. Wellman, a manufacturer of industrial brakes and clutches. In honor of its $13.5 million investment, the parent company changed its name to Brush Wellman Corp. in 1971. Two years later, Brush Wellman spent $5.5 million on Sawyer Research Products, Inc., the world's leading producer of specialty cultured quartz crystals. The 1974 acquisition of Bucyrus Blades, Inc., manufacturer of blades for bulldozers and snowplows, added to Brush's stable of niche companies.

This diversification program never lived up to expectations. Altogether, the new businesses contributed less than 20 percent of Brush Wellman's annual revenues, and their profit margins were only about one-third as high as those generated by beryllium. Perhaps most telling, the new businesses failed to safeguard the parent from a post-Vietnam War decline in demand; profits dropped from $8 million in 1973 to $3.8 million by 1975.

Instead of simply seeking new avenues for diversification, Brush Wellman re-evaluated the beryllium market. Under the guidance of Henry G. Piper, who succeeded Robert Biggs as chief executive officer in 1978, the company developed new beryllium-based products and undertook an aggressive marketing campaign. Most of the growth was generated by copper-beryllium alloys. Adding proportionally small amounts of beryllium to copper (often less than three percent) produced a material that conducts electricity and heat well, is resistant to corrosion, wear and fatigue, and is strong yet malleable.

Although copper-beryllium alloys have been used in an astonishing array of products ranging from eyeglasses to submarine cable, Brush Wellman's chief target became the electronics market, where conductivity, reliability, and durability are paramount. By focusing its efforts there, Brush threw its hat into the fast-paced electronic connector market, which generated more than $3.7 billion in total annual sales by 1983. A study by Stephen F. Hager of Unimar Group Ltd. cited in the September 24, 1984, issue of *American Metal Market* asserted that well over two-thirds of this industry's products were developed after 1960. Brush Wellman's connectors were used primarily in computer, automotive, and telecommunications equipment. Beryllia ceramic, an oxide form of beryllium, quickly created another new product group. This material's capacity to diffuse heat can help extend the life of electronic circuitry in wireless telephones and automotive controls.

Brush Wellman's sales more than doubled to $190.2 million from 1975 to 1981 and its net income quintupled to $19.3 million during that period. By that time, pure beryllium only constituted about five percent of sales. The company divested its quartz and industrial brake businesses in the early 1980s (but kept the Wellman surname) and invested instead in increased beryllium capacity and more closely related acquisitions. In 1982 Brush Wellman paid $46.68 million for Technical Materials, Inc. (TMI), a manufacturer of specialty metal strip that incorporated varying combinations of copper, nickel, stainless steel, and precious metals. The late 1986 acquisition of Wil-

liams Gold Refining Co. provided TMI with a source of high-purity precious metals.

Brush Wellman also worked to widen the appeal of beryllium-based products by developing lower-cost materials in the 1980s. Introduced in 1986, the company's patented Brush Alloy 174 used significantly less beryllium (.15 to .5 percent, compared to 2 percent) and cost about half as much as its standard copper-beryllium alloys. This material offered higher conductivity, strength, and durability than the copper and bronze alloys it was created to supplant. During this same period, Brush Wellman began expanding its geographic reach, establishing distribution centers in Germany, Great Britain, and Japan.

The new strategy paid off in the early 1980s. Brush Wellman's sales grew at an average annual rate of 15 percent from 1978 to 1988, a pace that outstripped the overall connector industry. This statistic indicated that the company was both capturing business from more traditional manufacturers and creating new markets for its high-end products. By the mid-1980s, over two-thirds of Brush Wellman's sales were made to the electronics market. David Carey of *Financial World* estimated that the company held "70 percent of the market for alloys and 80 percent of the one for ceramics" by 1988.

Ever-increasing demand made continued supply a concern. According to John Quirt, the company estimated that its Utah reserves would last until the turn of the twenty-first century. Brush continued to supplement its domestic source with imports and initiated a Resource Recovery program that recycled beryllium and copper from scrap.

Despite its foresight and market savvy, Brush Wellman was pummeled by economic recession in the late 1980s. Even the Defense Department's beryllium stockpiling program could not prevent a four-year slump that began in 1988. Sales declined by nearly 23 percent, from $345.84 million in 1988 to $267.47 million in 1991, and the company went from a net surplus of $32.5 million to a $44 million deficit. The financial results reverberated in the front offices. CEO Raymond A. Foos, who had succeed Henry Piper in 1988, was asked to resign in 1990. Piper resumed his duties as interim CEO until 1991, when Brush Wellman's board brought in Gordon D. Harnett to take the reins. Harnett had advanced to senior vice-president of specialty chemicals at B. F. Goodrich Co. before accepting the leading role at Brush Wellman.

Harnett continued a restructuring plan undertaken in 1989. The strategy's two main goals, increased productivity and market development, were achieved through several methods. Brush Wellman used attrition, early retirement, and layoffs to reduce its payroll by 18 percent from 1988 to 1991. Concurrent inventory reduction programs, capacity increases, and a retooling raised quality and service while reducing costs. These tactics helped Brush Wellman regain its profit margins without raising prices. The company's market development strategy included a shift from the stagnating mainframe computer market to the fast-growing personal computer segment. And although Brush Wellman's overall employment level shrank, the company increased its sales force by 40 percent.

From 1989 to 1994, the company reduced its sales to the aerospace and defense market from 29 percent of the total to 14 percent, with automotive electronics, telecommunications, and consumer products filling the gap. International sales increased to more than one-third of the company's total revenues. Perhaps most importantly, the company's bottom line recovered as a result of the reorganization plan. Sales reached a record $345.9 million in 1994, and net income recovered to a level not seen since 1989. However, the $18.6 million profit did not even approach the record $39.1 million set in 1984. Given the company's commitment to continuous improvement at all levels, there was no reason to believe that this milestone would not be surpassed in the mid-1990s.

Principal Subsidiaries: Brush Wellman GmbH; Brush Wellman (Japan), Ltd.; Brush Wellman Ltd.; Brush Wellman (Singapore) Pte. Ltd.; Technical Materials, Inc.; Williams Advanced Materials Inc.; Williams Advanced Materials Pte. Ltd.

Further Reading:

Burgert, Philip, "Beryllium Copper Draws Capital for Electronics," *American Metal Market,* September 24, 1984, p. 5A.
Byrne, Harlan S., "Brush Wellman Inc.," *Barron's,* February 1989, p. 41.
Carey, David, "Brush Wellman: Takeover Enigma," *Financial World,* May 3, 1988, p. 14.
Gleisser, Marcus, "Brush Wellman Tells Story of Growth," *Plain Dealer,* February 4, 1982, p. B6.
Koshar, John Leo, "Brush Wellman: A Firm Alone in its Field," *Plain Dealer,* May 18, 1980, p. E1.
Leibowitz, David S., "Dull, Dull, Dull," *Financial World,* June 13, 1989, p. 104.
Prizinsky, David, "Brush Wellman Sweeps Aside Poor Sales Years," *Crain's Cleveland Business,* October 3, 1994, p. 2.
Quirt, John, "Fat Years at Brush Wellman," *Fortune,* June 15, 1981, p. 148.
Regan, James G., "Brush Wellman to Restructure," *American Metal Market,* December 28, 1989, p. 5.
Rose, William Ganson, *Cleveland: The Making of a City,* Cleveland: World Publishing Co., 1950.
Stavro, Barry, "Back to the Atom," *Forbes,* June 18, 1984, p. 182.
Trainor, Kenny, "Brush Wellman's Growth, Strategy, Financial Strengths Cited," *American Metal Market,* October 13, 1989, p. 4.
Troxel, Thomas N., "Metal Winner: Beryllium Demand Spurs Expansion at Brush Wellman," *Barron's,* January 14, 1985, p. 55.
Van Tassel, David D., and John J. Grabowski, *The Encyclopedia of Cleveland History,* Bloomington: Indiana University Press, 1987.

—April Dougal Gasbarre

Business Men's Assurance Company of America

P.O. Box 419458
Kansas City, Missouri 64141
U.S.A.
(816) 753-8000
Fax: (816) 751-5572

Wholly Owned Subsidiary of the Generali Group
Incorporated: 1920
Employees: 800
Sales: $607 million
SICs: 6311 Life Insurance; 6321 Accident & Health
   Insurance

Insurance and financial services company Business Men's Assurance Company of America (BMA) is a member of the Generali Group, one of the world's largest insurance organizations. BMA serves individuals and business owners through the sale of life and disability insurance, annuities, and employee benefit programs. The company is one of the country's top professional life reinsurers and offers investment products and services through subsidiaries as well.

The founder of BMA was W. T. (Tom) Grant. Grant grew up in Ellinwood, Kansas, the son of a homesteader who headed west after the Civil War. The Grant family had a long history, traceable back to Peter Grant of Inverness, Scotland, who in 1651 had been sent to the Massachusetts colony by Oliver Cromwell because of his support for Charles I. Growing up on a farm, Grant developed the characteristics that had long been associated with his lineage—hard work, self-reliance, independence, and frugality. One of Grant's tasks at his father's farm was to milk 20 cows a day.

Grant first became a bank clerk after graduating from high school. He was fired not long after he started when a stockholder thought his weekly salary of $5 was too high. For a short time Grant sold fire and hail insurance to farmers, but he decided to attend the Paris Exposition in 1900. After his return to the United States, Grant attended law school at the University of Kansas and was so highly regarded by his fellow students that he was elected president of his class. Rather than practice as a lawyer, however, Grant went back into the insurance business. At the age of 26, the young man was appointed a general agent

for National Life of USA, an insurance organization that sent him to work in Colorado, Montana, and Pennsylvania before asking him to settle in Kansas City, Missouri, and establish a sales organization in the region.

One day in 1908, Grant received a flyer from Traveling Men's Accident Association suggesting that traveling men needed accident insurance coverage. Impressed by the flyer, Grant made a number of sales calls and immediately saw that accident insurance policies garnered a significant amount of sales appeal. Soon the young man began to think about forming his own insurance company. Grant was well aware of the changes occurring during the early years of the 20th century and that such technological developments as the automobile would create new markets for the insurance industry. However, in order to start his own insurance firm, Missouri state laws required that any new mutual assessment association have a fund equal to the maximum benefit of the contract ($5,000). This state requirement meant that Grant had to put up $5,000 in cash or policies at $10 per policy for a company that did not yet exist. A remarkable salesman, in a very brief period of time Grant procured 531 applications for insurance to meet the state's law for granting a charter.

In June 1909 the charter was granted by the state of Missouri, and the Business Men's Accident Association immediately opened its doors to customers. For the next two months, applications began to arrive on a regular basis. Suddenly, in September of the same year, a policyowner was killed in a Texas train accident. The money that the company had collected as premiums had been used to pay for operating expenses, and the firm was unable to pay the policy. The firm faced a tough decision: either pay the claim and go out of business or refuse to fulfill its obligation to the policyholder and ruin its reputation. Grant's new insurance company came under intense scrutiny. Fortunately, the firm's board of directors guaranteed a bank loan to cover the claim. When news spread that the company had paid the policyowner's claim, new applications for insurance policies at Business Men's Accident Association came pouring in. The company had successfully weathered its first major crisis.

The company's reputation for standing by its policyholders grew, and by the end of 1909 applications had more than tripled. But another crisis loomed after the addition of health insurance policies in 1911. The years at the end of World War I saw a flu epidemic unparalleled in U.S. history. Thousands of people were stricken and died, and claims made by policyowners strained the resources of the firm to its limit. Although the company suffered extensive losses, it met every customer claim that was presented. In 1918, Business Men's Accident Association reported a total of $1.234 million in premium income. Having surpassed Grant's goal of one million, the company was ranked first in the field of disability income.

Business Men's Accident Insurance changed its name to Business Men's Assurance Company of America (BMA) in 1920. The firm reported $150,000 worth of capital, with $50,000 established as a surplus. At the time, BMA reorganized as a stock life company. Shares were distributed to the employees, along with the opportunity to make additional money through dividends and stock splits. The goal of selling over $1 million worth of life insurance for one month was set and achieved. Grant was not a man to stand still, however. He implemented an expansion program during this time and opened the company's first branch office in San Francisco in 1922 and a second office not long afterwards, in Salt Lake City, Utah. Applications for health and life insurance policies were pouring in, and by the end of the decade BMA was operating 13 offices in 30 states across the United States.

Although the 1930s began auspiciously, with the company moving into its first solely owned headquarters, the happy occasion was undermined by the debilitating economic effects of the depression. Every person and every business across the United States, including BMA, was affected by the worst economic crisis ever to hit the nation. Grant immediately saw the difficulties posed by the onset of the depression and implemented severe cost-cutting measures to keep the company afloat. Disability claims reached staggering numbers due to high unemployment. Grant responded by cutting policies altogether and by reducing accident and health premium income by half. Operating expenses were reduced by cutting all salaries 10 percent, and a new, extremely aggressive sales strategy for life insurance policies was implemented to offset losses in accident and health premiums. One of Grant's most original ideas for collecting premiums occurred during this time when he set up a program, approved by the Federal Reserve Bank, to collect insurance premiums directly from the checking account of a policyholder. Called the Automatic Renewal Plan, it was the forerunner to today's system of electronic funds transfers from one bank account to another. By 1934, even though the company found itself amid the height of the depression, Grant's cost-cutting measures and sales strategy were wildly successful. During its 25th anniversary celebration, the company achieved a goal of selling over $100 million worth of life insurance.

BMA prospered during World War II. Immediately before the war, the firm became involved in the reinsurance business, and it received contracts from other companies. The firm was also intensely involved in the development of medical and hospital insurance and began to offer policies in both fields when Blue Cross and Blue Shield were established. From 1941, the first year of the war, until 1945, the company continued to develop this area of business, but it wasn't until after the war that a department was created to handle all aspects of reinsurance. Grant was the driving force behind the company's postwar move to expand into the reinsurance business, clearly recognizing the financial rewards of being involved in the field. His contacts throughout the Midwest helped BMA to develop into one of the country's premier reinsurance companies.

The founder of BMA, Tom Grant, died on November 29, 1954, at the age of 76, after attending a violin recital at the Kansas City Conservatory of Music. Grant's handpicked successor, J. C. Higdon, had already worked at the company for years and continued the general strategy that the founder had set. This included the sale of an extremely large variety of health and life insurance policies. With such a wealth of offerings, BMA salesmen had more opportunities to provide potential policyholders with better coverage at lower prices. Plans like Life Income at 65, Retirement Income, and the Junior Accident Plan, which cost a mere $6 annually, helped drive company sales upward. By 1955, Business Men's Assurance Company reported that it

had achieved its longtime goal of having $1 billion worth of life insurance in force.

The Grant family always played a large part in the development of BMA, and in 1960 this tradition continued with the selection of W. D. Grant, the founder's son, as president and chief executive officer. Graduating from the University of Kansas and earning an MBA at the Wharton School of Finance at the University of Pennsylvania, Bill Grant started working at the firm in 1941. With the coming of World War II, Grant served in the U.S. navy as a officer in the Atlantic fleet. Upon his return to the United States after the war, Grant immediately resumed his responsibilities at BMA and worked his way up to vice-president by 1951. In 1956, he became executive vice-president and, in 1960, assumed the position his father had held since the company started operations in 1909.

One of the first decisions made under Bill Grant's administration was to design and construct a new company office building. Uncharacteristic for a president of an insurance firm, Grant was intimately involved in the design and construction process from beginning to end. Grant insisted that the new offices not only consider functionality but also create a work environment that was comfortable and relaxing. BMA contracted the famous Chicago design firm of Skidmore, Owings & Merrill to do the work. When the building was completed the design firm suggested that the interior spaces be decorated with modern art, but Grant rejected the proposal for sound reasons. Grant was well aware that the building was near the beginning of the Sante Fe Trail, one of the old wagon roads filled with legends of the Old West—pioneer trains, cowboys, and Native Americans. Looking for a way to pay homage to and preserve that heritage, Grant collected Native American artifacts and famous Western paintings by renowned artists such as Peter Hurd and Frederick James. The result was one of the most stunning examples of American architecture and interior design created during the 1960s. The American Institute of Architects gave the BMA Tower its award for outstanding high-rise construction of 1963. Both the building and its interior have become so famous that they are included in many artbooks used throughout the world by students learning the elements of architecture and interior design.

For BMA the decade of the 1960s was one of expansion and acquisition. Under Grant's direction, the company began to purchase and manage numerous real estate ventures across the United States. The firm also acquired television stations in Kansas City, Denver, Colorado, Sacramento, California, and Portland, Oregon. Along with acquisitions in the field of oil and gas exploration, the company expanded in the area of venture capital. In 1967, Business Men's Assurance Company established the first U.S.-owned insurance firm in Australia. Grant's expansion and diversification strategy provided nearly 40 percent of the company's total profits by the end of 1969.

The 1970s were not as good to the company as was the previous decade. Rising costs for medical and hospital care affected the entire insurance industry, and BMA was not immune from this ominous trend. In order to help reduce the increasing rate of medical expenditures, the company developed programs in the areas of health assessment and wellness. The company's most important strategy during this time was to keep health insurance affordable for employers and employees alike. However, by the late 1970s and early 1980s, record inflation and skyrocketing interest rates exacerbated the problem. The sale of new life insurance policies began to wane, and the cost of meeting the claims of individual health insurance plans increased. Profitability decreased as a result. Traditional life insurance policies were no longer practicable either for BMA or for its customers, and new policies such as interest-sensitive contracts were developed.

During the late 1980s and early 1990s, BMA repositioned itself in the insurance market. Moving away from medical and hospital insurance, the firm offered mainstream life and annuity programs. In addition, BMA began to concentrate more on the grey-collar and blue-collar markets in an attempt to attract more customers. Yet BMA still suffered declining profits, and in late 1989 the board of directors sought a buyer for the company's insurance operations.

In 1990, the company's insurance operations were acquired by Assicurazioni Generali, an international insurance holding company located in Trieste, Italy. Managers at Generali were very enthusiastic about the trends in the U.S. insurance market and supported BMA in its expansion into different and nontraditional insurance markets. With the Generali Group's encouragement, the company continued its foray into fields other than medical insurance by entering the Guaranteed Investment Contract (GIC) market and by purchasing Jones & Babson, a no-load funds firm based in Kansas City that managed approximately $2 billion worth of investors' money. In late 1994, BMA sold all its existing group and individual medical insurance business, in order to focus fully on financial services, life reinsurance, and non-medical insurance products.

By the mid-1990s, BMA reported over $1.5 billion in total assets. The company offered a wide range of products, from individual life, disability, and annuities to group dental, disability, and life insurance. The purchase of the company by the Generali Group had stabilized its financial position and allowed BMA management to concentrate on increasing its margin of profitability. With able management and the continued support of the Generali Group, BMA can confidently face the ups and downs of the U.S. insurance market.

Principal Subsidiaries: Jones and Babson, Inc.; BMA Financial Services, Inc.

Further Reading:

Grant, W. D., *Aiming High,* Newcomen Society: New York, 1984.
Holliday, Kalen, "Business Men's Buys a Mutual Fund Firm," *American Banker,* October 12, 1993, p. 15.
Koko, Linda, "BMA Repositions Portfolio Toward a Full Product Line," *National Underwriter Life & Health-Financial Services Edition,* August 31, 1992, pp. 9–12.
——. "BMA Seeks Brokers With Flex Term," *National Underwriter Life & Health-Financial Services Edition,* August 23, 1993, pp. 7–8.
——. "DI Plan Plays At 5 Different Levels," *National Underwriter Life & Health-Financial Services Edition,* October 18, 1993, pp. 29–32.
Ward, John L., "An In-Depth Look at the Life-Health Insurance Industry: Past, Present, and Future," *Business Economics,* October 1993, pp. 21–25.

—Thomas Derdak

Carmike Cinemas, Inc.

1301 First Avenue
Columbus, Georgia 31901-2109
U.S.A.
(706) 576-3400
Fax: (706) 576-3471

Public Company
Incorporated: 1982
Employees: 9,000
Sales: $327.6 million
Stock Exchanges: New York
SICs: 7832 Motion Picture Theaters, Except Drive-In; 5812
   Eating Places

Carmike Cinemas, Inc. is the largest movie theater chain by number of screens and theaters operated in the United States. The company operates 2,330 motion picture screens in 32 states. Carmike's theaters are located mainly in smaller cities, where they are frequently the only movie venues in town. By operating primarily in these secondary markets, Carmike has avoided the rugged competition for city and suburban viewers engaged in by most other big movie exhibitors. Nearly all of the company's theaters are multi-screen facilities, and their highest concentration is in the South and the Midwest, although expansion is taking place in just about every part of the country entering the mid-1990s. Because it specializes in smaller markets—usually with populations under 200,000—and often has a regional monopoly in those places, Carmike has sometimes been called "the Wal-Mart of the theater industry."

Carmike's swift rise to prominence among movie exhibitors was the work of the Patrick family, a clan with a history in the theater business. Company chairman Carl Patrick Sr. was an executive with Martin Theaters, a Columbus, Georgia-based chain owned by another family. In 1969 Martin was purchased by Atlanta tycoon J.B. Fuqua, and it became part of Fuqua Industries. Although Patrick initially wanted his two sons, Michael and Carl Jr., to stay away from the movie theater industry, Michael had other ideas.

While still a student at Georgia State University, Michael Patrick worked at the Rialto Theater in Atlanta, taking tickets and making popcorn. Shortly after that he accepted a job with Martin. Eventually, Carl Sr. became president of Fuqua Industries, while Michael worked his way up to head of the com-

pany's movie theater division. When Fuqua decided to shed the division in 1982, the father and son team took hold of the theater chain in a leveraged management buyout. They then named the new company Carmike, a combination of the first names of brothers Carl Jr. (who became a director, but remained uninvolved in company operations) and Michael.

With Carl Sr. as chairman and chief executive, and Michael running the company's operations as president, Carmike embarked on a program of expansion at a time when many theater chains were holding back, fearful that movie-going was giving way to home video and cable television. In 1983 Carmike acquired Video Independent Theatres, Inc., adding 85 screens to the 265-screen base with which it had emerged from the Martin buyout. The company grew by building new theaters as well, adding 27 screens in 1982 and 18 in 1983 through its own construction projects. Carmike's strategy was clear from the outset. Patrick sought out smaller cities that he believed were underserved by movie theaters. Upon finding a good candidate, he then either purchased and expanded the existing theater or built a new multi-screen facility, often adjacent to the local mall. Using this method, Carmike expanded quickly throughout the South.

Carmike's management has credited a great deal of the company's success to I.Q. Zero, its unique computer system. Early on, Patrick realized that the small markets in which he was operating would not allow him much slack in controlling operating costs. To address this problem, he commissioned some Columbus, Georgia, friends to create a hardware and software package that would allow Carmike management to monitor the expenses and revenue of each Carmike theater to the most minute detail. The result was I.Q. Zero, a system unlike any other that exists in the industry. At the end of each business day, I.Q. Zero sends box office, concessions, and other types of information to company headquarters in Columbus. Using I.Q. Zero, the company can access sales figures for a particular size of a particular brand of candy at one theater in Tennessee with the touch of a button. I.Q. Zero is also capable of alerting theater managers when their sales per person ratio has fallen below acceptable levels as determined by top management. By providing this kind of information, I.Q. Zero has helped Carmike keep a tight rein on costs by substituting technology for management personnel wherever possible.

The company's growth spurt continued unchecked through the middle of the 1980s. Although no existing theater chains were acquired in 1984 or 1985, Carmike built 55 new screens of its own during those two years. 1986 was an especially eventful year for Carmike. That year, the company acquired Essantee Theatres, Inc., adding 209 screens to its growing empire. In addition, 54 new screens were constructed. The Patricks took Carmike public in October of 1986, with an initial over-the-counter stock offering, although the Patrick family retained about three-fourths of the company's voting stock. In the mid-1990s, the family held roughly 59 percent of the company's stock.

However, the company also met with some challenges in 1986. Like many of its competitors, Carmike split markets in order to keep the upper hand in negotiations with movie studios for the rights to show new pictures. When this practice was ultimately deemed illegal, Carmike ended up paying a $325,000 fine for an antitrust violation. In spite of the scrutiny of regulators, Carmike carried on with its strategy of finding smaller-sized cities in which it could have a virtual monopoly on first run movies; the company was able to attain that status in some 60 percent of the markets in which it operated. The other key element in Carmike's approach was to show movies with the broadest possible appeal, carefully avoiding anything that could by construed as an art film.

By 1987 Carmike was earning $3 million on revenue of $84 million. The company continued to add screens by the dozen, and by 1988 the chain consisted of 670 screens in 216 movie theaters in 135 cities, still mostly located in the South, where it had already become the biggest movie exhibitor in the region. Nationally, Carmike was fifth largest in terms of number of screens by this time. While the four theater chains that remained larger—General Cinema, United Artists Theatre Circuit, Cineplex Odeon, and AMC Entertainment—continued to butt heads with each other over the movie-going dollars generated by America's major population centers, Carmike sailed along by itself, opening multi-screen complexes in smaller markets, of which there seemed to be an endless supply.

Carmike brought another existing chain, the 116-screen Consolidated Theaters, Inc., into the fold in 1989, while adding another 35 screens of its own construction. Patrick also took his first vacation since launching the company. The company continued to prosper, with revenues approaching the $100 million mark, by bringing Hollywood's biggest, most mainstream movies into the sleepy towns of middle America. Because it maintained monopoly or near-monopoly positions in most of its markets, Carmike was able to negotiate better rates from movie distributors than could many of its competitors. Patrick was in a position, according to the *Wall Street Journal's* Anita Sharpe, to tell Hollywood, "Either you play Carmike Cinemas or Blockbuster Video." The company found savings in other areas as well. Its small town costs for constructing new theaters ran less than half of what such projects cost in prime suburban locations. And although ticket prices were lower at Carmike Cinemas than in big market theaters, Carmike's high-tech systems allowed it to expand the chain without adding large numbers of home office employees.

As the 1990s began, Carmike's approach still ran contrary to that of its major competitors: while they were trying to become "leaner and meaner," Carmike was still looking for new turf. Consequently, the 154 existing screens the company acquired in 1990 came from two of its biggest rivals, Cineplex Odeon and United Artists. On top of that, 24 new screens were constructed. With nearly 1,000 total screens in about 175 different markets, Carmike was established as a major force in the movie theater industry. Meanwhile, Hollywood studios were emphasizing the kinds of films that Carmike's customers favored—action movies featuring big-name stars. The Rambo-type movies went over especially well at the many Carmike theaters located near military facilities.

Over the next couple of years, Carmike picked up additional screens cast off by the likes of American Multi Cinema (AMC). Its biggest single leap in size came in 1991 with the addition of 353 screens in the form of a joint venture with Excellence

Theaters. Carmike bought out its partners in that project two years later. By 1992 the company was operating 1,400 movie screens—twice the number it had in its possession only three years earlier—and posting revenues of $172 million. After buying out its joint venture partners in the Westwynn Theatres chain (formerly called Excellence) in 1993, Carmike was probably the third largest movie chain in the country, trailing only United Artists and AMC. The company also absorbed Manos Enterprises, a chain with 80 movie screens. That year, the company's revenue jumped to $242 million. As the chain continued to expand, Patrick and his team found ways to wring even more savings out of the I.Q. Zero system. The system took over yet more tasks formerly performed by humans, allowing management to reduce corporate overhead costs to a mere 2.5 percent of operating revenues, down from the four percent level the company had maintained for several years.

By the middle of 1993, Carmike had established a presence in 23 states in the South, Southwest, and Midwest. The company's 388 theaters contained a total of 1,560 screens. Again in 1994, Carmike picked up screens from other chains, built theaters of its own, and had a record year in just about every category. During 1994 the company acquired 178 screens from Cinema World, bought another 48 screens from General Cinema, and built five new complexes holding 43 screens. Carmike also added 15 new screens to complexes already in operation. Part of the financing for all of this growth came from a public offering of $58 million worth of newly issued common stock, after which the Patricks still held the majority of voting interest in the company.

Buoyed by its five new acquisitions between the beginning of 1994 and the middle of 1995, Carmike narrowed the size gap between itself and industry leader United Artists considerably. By July 1995, the company had 2,223 screens in its empire, less than 100 screens fewer than the number operated by United Artists.

Meanwhile, Carmike's success in getting middle America to come to the movies made Patrick something of a guru among Hollywood executives. Top managers at entertainment companies such as Disney, Twentieth Century Fox, and Time Warner frequently turned to Patrick for projections about how certain films would do at the box office. Mogul Ted Turner consulted Patrick before his Turner Broadcasting System bought production companies New Line Cinema and Castle Rock Entertainment. By knowing the tastes of his small-town audience, Patrick was occasionally even able to make hits out of movies that were poorly received in big cities.

Many movie industry analysts have considered Carmike the best-managed theater chain in the country for several years. The company's ability to churn out profits year after year while its competitors struggle to streamline and stem their losses seems to support this opinion. Like all theater chains, however, Carmike is at the mercy of Hollywood. If the studios do not make movies that people want to see, the exhibitors suffer along with the producers. Carmike has clearly shown, though, that it is among the best at bringing in customers, regardless of the competition posed by VCRs, cable television, and high school football, and in spite of Hollywood's occasional inability to supply quality products. As long as people in small towns continue going to the movies, Carmike will continue to build and buy theaters to serve that market.

Principal Subsidiaries: Wooden Nickel Pub, Inc.; Eastwynn Theatres, Inc.

Further Reading:

Barrett, William P., "A Wal-Mart for the Movies," *Forbes,* August 22, 1988, pp. 60–61.

Blickstein, Jay, "Small-Town Dixie Chain on Exhib Fast Track," *Variety,* March 30, 1992, p. 51.

"Box Office Bonanza," *Forbes,* March 27, 1993, p. 19.

Byrne, Harlan, "Carmike Cinemas: *Jurassic Park* Could Help It Have a Dino-Mite Year," *Barron's,* June 28, 1993, pp. 39–40.

Hawkins, Chuck, "The Movie Mogul Who Thinks Small," *Business Week,* July 2, 1990, p. 37.

"Now Playing, Carmike," *Forbes,* March 27, 1995, pp. 160–161.

Pendleton, Jennifer, "Chain Sees Possibilities in Midst of Recession," *Variety,* March 30, 1992, p. 51.

Reingold, Jennifer, "Carmike Cinemas: It Always Plays in Peoria," *Financial World,* March 14, 1995, pp. 20–22.

Sharpe, Anita, "Last Picture Show," *Wall Street Journal,* July 12, 1995.

—Robert R. Jacobson

Casco Northern Bank

P.O. Box 678
Portland, Maine 04104
U.S.A.
(800) 452-8762
Fax: (207) 776-7454

Wholly Owned Subsidiary of KeyCorp
Incorporated: 1933
Employees: 664
Total Assets: $1.2 billion
SICs: 6021 National Commercial Bank

Known as "The Bank of Maine," Casco Northern Bank has over $1 billion in assets and many offices throughout the state of Maine and has undergone many changes during its long history. During the 1970s the firm gained a national reputation for offering some of the most innovative banking services in the industry, including NOW accounts, the first such service in Maine that provided interest on checking accounts. At the beginning of the 1980s, however, Casco suffered along with the rest of the banking industry and was forced to undergo a series of major changes, including mergers and the acquisition and reselling of the firm by major bank holding companies.

Casco's incorporation and charter started in 1933, but its history actually extends back to 1824 with the formation of the Casco Bank in Portland, Maine. Initially chartered and operated as a state bank, the coming of the U.S. Civil War and the passage of the National Bank Act in 1865 convinced the firm's shareholders to relinquish their status as a state bank and operate as the Casco National Bank. In 1866 the bank was completely destroyed by a fire that swept across Portland, and almost $2 million in both currency and notes were lost. Shareholders voted to rebuild the bank the same year.

Casco National Bank prospered during the next 30 years and built a reputation among farmers and merchants in Portland. In 1897 the shareholders voted to merge with Mercantile Trust Company, a much smaller banking concern. The merger brought to Casco numerous branches in tiny towns across the state, including offices in such locations as Bridgton, West Buxton, Norway, South Paris, South Berwick, and Buckfield as well as four additional offices in the city of Portland. Renaming itself the Casco Mercantile Trust Company, the new operation conducted business under the auspices of the state charter of

Mercantile Trust. Other mergers and acquisitions followed, and by 1900 the bank reported assets in excess of $23 million and deposits of nearly $20 million. The bank grew slowly but steadily during the early years of the 20th century, increasing both the amount of its assets and customer deposits. In the 1920s Casco Mercantile Trust Company was widely regarded as one of the most stable and reliable banks in the region.

However, with the stock market crash of 1929 and the Great Depression, deposits for the bank began to decrease at an alarming rate and by 1932 had fallen from $19 million to $14 million, with continuing decline. Casco Mercantile was in trouble, and other banks in the Portland area started donating money to keep the bank solvent. In early 1933 the state's bank regulators recognized that nearly all the banks in Maine had exhausted their liquid assets, and more depositors were clamoring for their money every day. In March 1933 the governor of Maine, Louis J. Brann, preempted President Franklin Delano Roosevelt's federal Bank Holiday by ordering the closure of banks throughout the state.

After the Bank Holiday, only four banks in Portland were able to reopen and conduct business under their old state charters: Portland Savings, Maine Savings, Portland National Bank, and Canal National Bank. Casco Mercantile Trust Company, First National Bank, and Fidelity Trust Company were unable to reopen and thus were forced into liquidation. Approximately $10 million of depositor money was part of what the bank could not cover. A lengthy and very painful liquidation process ensued, ultimately taking over five years to settle. Similar events occurred in every city and small town across the United States.

After the demise of Casco Mercantile Trust Company, a group of young businessmen and established bankers became convinced that a new bank was needed to serve the rural areas surrounding Portland. Since most of the banks reopening were in the city itself, this group regarded a newly organized bank as a necessity for people living in the countryside. There was a significant obstacle ahead of them, however: state law required that a new bank raise $200,000 of capital with an additional $100,000 in surplus. This compounded the group's desire to open a new bank, and it had to convince investors that there was, in fact, a need for bank branches in outlying rural localities where other banks had failed and that the bank would hire able management. This second criterion was especially important due to the erosion of depositors' trust in how deposits were managed prior to the Bank Holiday.

In six short months the group of 25 businessmen and bankers, under the dynamic and persevering leadership of Leonard Timberlake, the former president of Casco Mercantile Trust Company, was able to raise the state-required funds. On December 11, 1933, the new Casco Bank & Trust Company opened its doors as a state-chartered bank. During the same day, the bank also opened branch offices in Limerick, South Paris, Buckfield, Woodfords Corner, Bridgton, South Portland, and West Buxton. Everyone was surprised, as the venture was thought to be an impossibility by the more conservative banking elements in the state. Banking services had been restored in many rural areas.

The founding directors of the bank, as well as the state's regulatory authorities, assumed that Timberlake would become president of the newly formed enterprise. Unfortunately, his name had been indelibly connected to the failure of Casco Mercantile Trust Company and its loss of millions of dollars. Thus a new president was required, one who had an unblemished record and a proven track record in business. Although without experience in banking, H. Herbert Sturgis was chosen as the first president of the new Casco Bank & Trust Company. In spite of the fact that Sturgis had served on the board of directors at Casco Mercantile, there were no residual effects. He was widely respected and admired in rural areas, where his lumber company operated. To Sturgis's credit, many of the bank's first customers were people who knew or had some connection with Sturgis.

Sturgis left the daily operations of the bank to Timberlake, who stayed on as vice-president. During the first full year of business the bank attracted many new depositors and not a few had received liquidation payments from Casco Mercantile. Commercial loans were also in high demand, and with careful consideration the bank management developed a successful lending program. By June 1935 the bank's total assets had grown from $300,000 to over $11 million. In addition, the bank was growing so rapidly that management decided to open another bank office in Fryeburg.

The late 1930s were anxious years for the new bank. The traumatic Bank Holidays remained in the minds of Casco's board of directors, and the membership insisted that all loans be submitted to the board for approval—even loans as small as $25. Real estate loans could not be more than 50 percent of appraised property values, which were also determined and approved by the board of directors. In addition, the total amount of real estate mortgages could not exceed one-third of the entire amount of the bank's savings accounts. As the bank prospered and assets rose steadily, however, the directors gradually gave more authority to the bank's management. By the end of the 1930s the president, vice-president, and treasurer were given $500 worth of unsecured loan authorization. Moreover, the board of directors granted management at the bank practical authority to conduct operations without its direct approval, and from that time forward it properly concerned itself with the role of setting policy.

Casco's president, Herbert Sturgis, died in March 1943. The bank's board of directors was convinced that Timberlake was the man to replace Sturgis, especially since the passage of time had lessened the perception that Timberlake was responsible for the mismanagement of the bank before the Bank Holidays in the early 1930s. The new president assumed his duties in 1943 and continued in this capacity until 1955. Timberlake's strategy included cautious but steady expansion. Assets climbed to $41 million, and 13 new branch offices were opened under his administration. Among all the services that Casco provided, Timberlake focused on consumer loans to individuals. Committed to delivering high-quality and reliable banking services to the bank's customers, Timberlake pushed the consumer loan program to approximately $5 million, its residential mortgage program to over $7 million. In fact, loans to individuals constituted more than 60 percent of Casco's total loan portfolio.

Halsey Smith became president upon Timberlake's retirement. Brought to the bank by Timberlake in 1951 and groomed as his successor, Smith was only 34. He assessed the strengths and weaknesses of the bank and decided to implement a strategy that revamped much of the informal nature of Casco's operations and business. He extended the loan program to take advantage of the growing business sector in Maine and continued the expansion strategy established by Timberlake. The First-Auburn Trust Company, along with its branch network in New Auburn, Gray, and Brunswick, was acquired in 1960, and a total of 17 new branch offices were opened throughout southwestern Maine. Assets climbed to $115 million by 1969, and Casco Bank was the recognized leader in the southwest region of the state.

In the fall of 1970 Casco moved into its newly built facility in Portland, and it centralized administrative and managerial operations. Wendell L. Phillips replaced Smith as president and aggressively pursued untapped markets throughout Maine. Within two years the bank grew from the fifth-largest to the second-largest in Maine, helped by the acquisition of Northern National Bank, located on Presque Isle. Having penetrated the northern and southern regions of the state, management determined to make inroads across central Maine as well. Under Phillips, Casco initiated many new banking services, including NOW accounts and Passbook Plus. These two innovative banking services brought millions of new depositor dollars into the bank.

John M. Daigle replaced Phillips as president and led the institution through volatile years within the banking industry. With a background as senior accountant at Arthur Andersen & Company and many years of service at Casco as controller and treasurer, Daigle was well prepared for the trials ahead. At the beginning of the 1980s the U.S. economy went into recession, with increasing inflation, escalating prices, and a loss of business in the commercial sector. Having experienced uninterrupted growth and expansion for nearly two decades, the bank tailspinned, and profits dropped by one-third. Daigle's response was to merge with Northern National, a bank partner with Casco for years. Named Casco Northern Bank, the new organization was better able to compete in the deregulated banking atmosphere. By the mid-1980s Casco seemed to have revived. Assets approximated $735 million in 1984, and 56 branch offices served people throughout Maine. As most commercial banks in the state lost market share Casco increased total deposits.

The recession within the banking industry was lengthier than anticipated, however, and Casco management decided to merge with Bank of Boston, a huge bank holding company focusing on the New England region. Boston's investment helped stabilize Casco's condition and provided the bank with enough capital to continue opening new branch offices. By the mid-1990s, however, Bank of Boston decided to sell Casco Northern Bank. As it turned out, Bank of Boston was never a significant presence in retail markets in Maine and shifted its focus to the wealthier urban areas in southern New England.

In early 1994 KeyCorp, a Cleveland-based holding bank with over $61 million in assets, offered to purchase both Casco Northern Bank in Maine and the Bank of Vermont. Through its Portland subsidiary, Key Bank of Maine, the deal was finalized for a purchase price of $198.5 million. With the purchase, Key Bank of Maine took control of $3.5 billion in assets and became the second-largest bank in the state. With the addition of Casco's branch offices, Key Bank of Maine began to supervise operations of approximately 100 branch locations. Although the U.S. Department of Justice initially questioned KeyCorp's acquisition of Casco, the complaint was dropped after KeyCorp management agreed to sell a number of its branches in seven different areas within the state of Maine.

Under the new management, Casco National Bank was completely incorporated into KeyCorp. Long known as one of the premier banks serving the state of Maine, branches once owned by Casco National Bank continued to emphasize high-quality customer service in both rural and urban areas.

Further Reading:

Aber, Jack W., and William E. Jackson III, ''The Surprising Importance of Deposit Rate Flexibility,'' *Journal of Retail Banking,* Spring 1992, pp. 9–14.

Daigle, John M., *Casco Northern Bank,* Newcomen Society: New York, 1984.

Iida, Jeanne, ''Key Buying Maine, Vermont Units From Boston Bank,'' *American Banker,* June 27, 1994, pp. 2–5.

Oppenheim, Sara, and Sara Seiberg, ''KeyCorp's Maine Purchase Approved,'' *American Banker,* January 24, 1995, p. 4.

Racine, John, ''Big Acquisitions Create Opportunities to Purchase Branches,'' *American Banker,* January 23, 1995, pp. 18A-25A.

Seiberg, Jaret, ''Banks: Plan to Ease Tying Rules a Start, but Should Go Further,'' *American Banker,* January 26, 1995, p. 3.

—— ''Justice Dept. Withdraws Objection to KeyCorp Deal,'' *American Banker,* December 20, 1994, p. 2.

Vogelstein, Fred, ''Superregional Shows Clout,'' *American Banker,* March 10, 1992, pp. 1–10.

—Thomas Derdak

Cato Corporation

P.O. Box 34216
Charlotte, North Carolina 28234
U.S.A.
(704) 554-8510
Fax: (704) 551-7521

Public Company
Incorporated: 1946 as Cato Stores
Employees: 8,595
Sales: $476.2 million
Stock Exchanges: NASDAQ
SICs: 5621 Women's Clothing Stores

The Cato Corporation owns a chain of approximately 678 women's apparel stores in 22 U.S. states, primarily in the South and Southeast. The company operates through two principal divisions: the Cato division, which oversees 553 Cato and Cato Plus women's fashion stores, and the It's Fashion! division comprising a chain of 125 off-price stores offering family fashions and accessories. Offering wide selections at low prices, Cato's chain stores are largely based in "strip mall" shopping centers, and 40 percent are anchored by Wal-Mart stores. In 1994 the company earned $476.2 million in total revenues, with $463.7 million of the total in retail sales.

Cato has been a family business since its beginnings. Its founder, Wayland Henry Cato, made his start in retail in 1916, working a summer job in a general store in his hometown of Ridge Spring, South Carolina. Initially embarking on a career as a teacher, he took to retailing instead and became a top salesman, tenaciously capitalizing upon any opportunity to show customers merchandise. That fall he convinced his father to help him open their own dry goods store.

Cato's retail career was interrupted by a naval stint in World War I and a failed bootlegging episode in which he was abducted and nearly killed. He returned to his store in 1919, only to face another difficult challenge. Wholesale prices dropped substantially right after he bought a shipment of goods for his store, a development that made the products much cheaper at other stores that were able to take advantage of the drop. Unlike other merchants, however, Cato chose to sell the goods at cost, hoping to make a profit after buying additional products at the lower prices. Aggressive thinking like this kept the Cato store open when many others were folding.

After marrying in 1922, Cato and his wife, Annie Derham, agreed that their future lay outside Ridge Spring. He was employed by United Merchants and Manufacturers, where he managed a subsidiary known as Aiken Stores, Inc., a chain. Cato also helped negotiate for his employer the purchase of gas stations, coal yards, lunch counters, warehouses, and mill stores, including a Greenville, South Carolina, dress shop known as the Martha Park store. Under United Merchants and Manufacturers direction, Cato helped expand the Martha Park shop to 20 locations within a few years. Moreover, as part of his compensation as an employee of United Merchants and Manufacturers, Cato was given the opportunity to purchase a few shares in Aiken Stores, Inc.

After 23 years of service, Cato left United Merchants in 1946 to launch his own business. Together with his sons, Wayland Henry Cato, Jr., and Edgar Thomas, Cato founded Cato Stores as a Delaware corporation. (Edgar would return to journalism school after two years of helping with store construction.) The company was headquartered in Charlotte, an ideal location amid the many small textile, furniture, and tobacco towns of the Carolinas. Due to a dearth of building in the Depression and World War II, main street venues in county seats were difficult to find, but Wayland Sr. located two in the towns of Sumter and Mullins, South Carolina, sites of nearly-simultaneous grand openings. Three other stores were opened the first year; their revenues totalled $136,000.

Wayland Cato Sr. hired local women to manage the stores, including Della Parish, the manager of the neighboring Martha Park store in Gaffney, South Carolina, whom Cato had hired while working for United Merchants. Her dedication to the success of the venture—including performing alterations on her own time—helped safeguard its perilous early years. But Cato also made an unfortunate hiring decision in filling his merchandise manager position. The manager, who had plans for a ladies' apparel chain of his own, ordered elegant and expensive styles that did not sell in the poor, rural South. He resigned in 1947, and second-year earnings for seven Cato stores rose to $404,000.

The post of merchandise manager was filled in 1949 with Murray Turkel, a New Yorker. In spite of his northern origins, he and Wayland Cato Jr. quickly targeted the store's primary consumer—"juniors" sizes seven to 11, a younger, more fashion-oriented consumer than those of national department stores and local independent shops. Such a buying orientation made Cato stand out.

By 1948 Cato's seven stores garnered $700,000 in sales and $30,000 in net earnings. Sales hit $1 million the next year. For the next few years, sales per store would average from $80,000 to $100,000. Sales increases and store openings of two or three a year remained fairly constant, except during a recession in the mid-1950s. In 1956 Cato began using rudimentary punch card tabulating equipment in merchandising, the first retail chain in the Southeast to do so. The same year, a heart attack forced Wayland Cato Sr. to cut back his duties.

At the end of the 1950s, the company began to tinker with its formula, reflecting changing economic conditions. It began to investigate leases in shopping centers as well as Main Street locations, although the majority of its shops (90 percent in the mid-1970s) continued to be located downtown. In response to a competitor, Cato offered a charge program for customers on an experimental basis. The program was a success, and by the 1970s it accounted for over 20 percent of total sales, supplying the company with addresses for direct mail promotions as well. Several administrative changes took place in the maturing company in this era as well. Cato issued its first annual report and for the first time offered certain employees stock options. Wayland Cato Jr. was named president of the company in 1960, though he continued to share management duties with his father, as no single chief executive officer was named. His brother Edgar became a vice-president.

Wayland Cato Jr. had learned a great deal from his father. He was also a voracious reader who was particularly struck by *The Prince,* a treatise on power written during medieval times by Niccolo Machiavelli. In the company publication *A Commitment to Change* (1975), Wayland Cato Jr. called the book "the most accurate description of the world of power and influence I've ever read.... For it to make sense today, the reader has only to substitute the modern chief executive officer for the prince, the board of directors for the council to the prince, the executive vice president or general manager for the prime minister, and the corporate officers for the aristocrats."

Acquisition seemed an effective way to rapidly increase the company's growth, and its main competitor in the Southeast, Glamor Shops, Inc., interested the Catos very much. The 54 stores owned by Glamor Shops would more than double Cato's store holdings, and a loss in 1958 made its owners eager to sell. However, the soft economy and concerns over Glamor's drawbacks—particularly its expensive lease arrangements and relatively inefficient operations—scuttled the deal in 1962 after almost two years of negotiations. Still, Cato's aggressive approach to business openings enabled the company to nearly double its store total in under two years. The company diversified in opening "self-service" discount apparel and general merchandise stores in 1965. First known as C-Marts, the name was changed to Waco (a contraction of Wayland Corporation) to distinguish it from K-Marts, S-Marts, Wal-Marts, and the like. The stores sold a broader variety of merchandise aimed at the entire family, which required a correspondingly greater store area, typically 15,000 square feet. These Waco stores were later sold off or closed in the mid-1970s.

After a decade of strong performance, Cato went public in 1968, selling shares at $19 each. Mediocre preformance and stock prices over the next 12 years, however, prompted the company to go private in 1980, buying back shares at $13 each. In 1987, after five years of improved results, Cato was once again taken public. But, the cyclical business of retail fashion proved at times a cruel leveller of the company's ambitions. In the late 1980s, Cato alienated its customers somewhat in both its selection of merchandise and its pricing. Aware of a problem, Cato installed information systems powered by a gargantuan IBM mainframe to monitor distribution of goods. Cost cutting efforts, though, soon eliminated the mainframe as overkill. Overexpansion and a highly competitive environment compounded the company's misfortunes, however, and the company teetered towards bankruptcy, losing $10 million in 1990, when its stock fell to 56 cents a share. Nevertheless, co-founders Wayland

Cato, Jr., and his brother Edgar Cato guaranteed $1.5 million each to three banks in order to secure a $30 million line of credit, averting disaster.

The early 1990s proved to be a period of recovery and expansion, thanks partly to the company's decision to bring some new blood into the management. Under the direction of Wayland Cato, Jr., the company's chairman, CEO, and president, several key executive positions were filled with new, promising people. Linda McFarland Jenkins, a senior merchandising officer who had been displaced when Dillard Department Stores, Inc. bought the J.B. Ivey Co., was brought in as chief merchant of the Cato division. An outstanding success, she was given the position of company president as well and was eventually made chief operating officer.

Jenkins helped change the type of merchandise Cato stocked and the way they bought and sold it. As one company representative told *The Charlotte Observer,* Cato was marking up prices approximately five percent lower than the competition. Subsequently, twice as many items (16–18 percent) sold before being placed on sale. The company reduced the risk of being stuck with inferior overseas goods by buying through importers, and restrained itself from stocking too many identical items, which small town shoppers would avoid. The lower risks of both policies outweighed the higher costs. In addition, Jenkins decided that Cato was stocking fashions that were too traditional for Cato's small-town customers, who preferred items embellished with "zippers and bows and buttons," as she told *Business North Carolina* in 1991. Besides lowering prices and stocking different merchandise, Cato also closed almost 100 poorly performing stores and its New York buying office. These cutbacks eerily mirrored those of 1970, when around 150 of the company's 338 non-store employees were dismissed.

Among the other new appointments at Cato were David Kempert (executive vice-president, chief stores officer, Cato division); Howard "Skip" Severson (executive vice-president, and chief real estate and store development officer); John Cato (executive vice-president of the company and president and general manager of the It's Fashion! division); and Clarice Cato Goodyear (executive vice-president and chief administrative officer). Together with Jenkins, the new team was instrumental in Cato's turnaround.

In fact, the various changes instituted by Cato's new leadership produced such a strong turnaround in performance that the company was soon expanding once again. Within a year of its 56-cent low, the stock had risen to $9.50 a share. Despite closing 68 stores in 1991, earnings increased from a loss of almost $10 million in 1990 to a positive $9.5 million, almost a $20 million swing in earnings. After the divestment of poorperforming stores, Cato opened 129 new stores, relocated and expanded 48 stores, and remodeled an additional 48 in 1992 and 1993.

In 1992, the company reported earnings of $18 million, up $9 million from the prior year. Earnings again rose to $24.8 million in 1993, a record year. Cato stock peaked at $24.75 a share in 1993, but fell to $5.50 on earnings of $18 million the next year. While some analysts alleged that lower earnings figures had sent investors, including some board members, scurrying, the company ended the year with no long-term debt, working capital of over $94,000, and stockholders' equity of over $141,000.

Cato opened 80 Cato division stores in 1994—all of them carrying regular and plus-size clothing. It also expanded its selection, and began offering clothing for girls aged four to 14 in some stores, a unique innovation among women's clothing stores. To accommodate these contents, the new stores averaged 6,500 square feet. By contrast, a typical 1970 vintage store had 2,000 to 3,000 square feet. Also that year, the company opened 23 It's Fashion! stores, which averaged 3,000 square feet. The following year, Cato Corporation opened a total of 37 new stores (19 of them Cato stores and 18 It's Fashion! stores), while also relocating and expanded 29 existing stores and remodeling an additional 40 stores in the Cato division.

Principal Subsidiaries: CHW Corporation; Providence Insurance Company Limited.

Further Reading:

"After Dressing for Success, Cato Sheds Some Shares," *Business North Carolina,* July 1994, p. 10.

Bailey, David, "Cato's Repeat Business," *Business-North Carolina,* December 1991, p. 40.

"Cato Corp," *CDA-Investnet Insiders' Chronicle,* December 13, 1993, p. 3.

"Cato's Slip is Showing," *Business North Carolina,* January 1988, p. 54.

Childs, Terri, and Ilene Rosenthal, "SPA Announces Settlement in Copyright Infringement Suit," *Business Wire,* March 6, 1992.

Coleman, Kathleen, "Cato Pirated Software, Four Companies Allege," *Business Journal-Charlotte,* October 7, 1991, p. 4.

Coleman, Kathleen, "Insiders Sell as Stocks Hit Peaks," *Business Journal-Charlotte,* December 16, 1991, p. 4.

Curan, Catherine M., "Cato Sees Large-Size Cash Crop," *WWD,* March 16, 1994, p. 20.

Glickman, Clifford, "A Retail Strategy That Paid Off Big," *The Charlotte Observer,* September 2, 1991, pp. 1D, 6D.

Greene, Kelly, "Cato Expansion Plans Slowing as Sales Stall," *Business Journal-Charlotte,* April 3, 1995, p. 4.

Greene, Kelly, "Cato Makes Major Move Into Children's Clothing," *Business Journal-Charlotte,* March 28, 1994, p. 1.

McIntosh, Jay, "Cato Edges Into Profit Column After Six Months of Losses," *The Charlotte Observer,* June 1, 1988, p. 7B.

Pellett, Jennifer, "Women Retailers: Navigating Corporate America," *DM,* November, 1992, pp. 82–87.

Rublin, Lauren R., "Taylor-Made Portfolio: A Pro With a Special Touch Offers Five Potential Winners," *Barron's,* June 22, 1992, pp. 16–20.

Snow, Katherine, "Glass Ceiling Cracked at Cato," *Business Journal-Charlotte,* October 12, 1992, p. 1.

—Frederick C. Ingram

CCH Inc.

2700 Lake Cook Road
Riverwoods, Illinois 60015-3888
U.S.A.
(708) 940-4600
Fax: (708) 267-2987

Public Company
Incorporated: 1927
Employees: 5,100
Stock Exchanges: NASDAQ
Sales: $579 million
SICs: 2741 Miscellaneous Publishing; 7389 Business
   Services Nec; 7374 Data Processing and Preparation

Best known as the publisher of the *Standard Federal Tax
Reporter,* CCH Inc., publishes a wide array of topical law
reports for legal, accounting, and business applications. The
company markets over 600 products—including loose-leaf *Reporters,* magazines, casebooks, bound books, and electronic
products—which provide concise, detailed information on laws
and regulations enacted by federal and state governmental agencies. Since the early 1990s, CCH has been moving away from
print media, replacing its traditional black pressboard binders
with reports available on CD-ROM, floppy disk, audio cassette,
and online databases. CCH operates two primary businesses in
the United States: ProSystem fx, which develops and markets
tax preparation software for the accounting industry; and Legal
Information Services, which provides tax-related information
on corporate, credit, securities, and intellectual property matters. The company also has divisions in Canada, Europe, Asia,
Australia, and New Zealand.

The company's present organization is the result of a merger in
1927 between two competitors, Corporation Trust Co. and
Commerce Clearing House. The larger of the two, Corporation
Trust, was founded in 1892 by Oakleigh Thorne to publish
materials that aided lawyers in "organizing, qualifying, registering and representing" businesses under the varying state
laws of that time. Sales expanded as governmental legislation of
business activities became more complex, compelling even the
most knowledgeable lawyers and accountants to rely on guide-
books for accurate explanations. One of Corporation Trust's
first clients was the United States Steel Corp., and in 1903,
the company asked Corporation Trust to track and report on the

activities of various state and federal legislative bodies. The
company organized its first legislative reporting department,
and soon was selling reports to customers such as American
Tobacco Company (now American Brands Inc.), Prudential
Insurance, and American Telephone and Telegraph Company.

Ten years later, the company's growth took another giant step
when the United States government passed the Tariff Act of
1913, effectively instituting the nation's first income tax. While
the measure was being debated, Corporation Trust had published reports on the progress of various tax-related bills as they
passed through the House and Senate. The company established
its first income tax department and by December 1913 had
signed up 1,000 subscribers to its first *Income Tax Reporter*—a
400-page loose-leaf binder that summarized the Act and provided space for updates on tax laws as influenced by court and
administrative rulings. The tax department served as the breeding ground for what CCH called "the art of loose-leaf reporting," which led to the decision to report on legislative developments on a topic-by-topic basis.

Tax law reporting became a lucrative business for Corporation
Trust, but the company was not without competition. In 1913 a
professor and two students at New York University founded a
publishing house called Prentice Hall to publish an economics
book they had written. Soon Prentice Hall began publishing its
own guide books on the new tax laws, and also a binder on
income tax laws that seemed to be a knock-off of Corporation
Trust's binder system. The most essential development in the
history of CCH, however, was when a company called Commerce Clearing House published a bound income tax guide so
successful that the founder, William KixMiller, abandoned the
company's other business reporting to focus solely on income
tax guides. Demand for easy-to-read tax guides became even
greater as the U.S. government raised tax rates to prepare itself
for World War I. The economic constrictions of war forced
Corporation Trust to temporarily abandon its legislative reporting service and decrease the output of all other departments,
focusing strictly on income tax publications. By 1920 approximately 20 other competitors had entered the tax guide field.
Corporation Trust held the largest share of the market, but
Prentice Hall and Commerce Clearing House were rapidly gaining market share.

The postwar era remained highly competitive for legal and
business reference publishers, with Corporation Trust, Prentice
Hall, and Commerce Clearing House all seeking to exploit new
market niches. When Commerce Clearing House created the
Business Law Reference Reporter, Prentice Hall sued the company for copyright infringement. The protracted legal battle,
although ultimately inconclusive, severely damaged Commerce
Clearing House's financial reserves. In 1927, in order to preserve his business, KixMiller merged Commerce Clearing
House with Corporation Trust. The new corporation took the
name Commerce Clearing House, Inc., (CCH) although Corporation Trust (and the Thorne family) assumed the controlling
interest in the company.

By 1929 the two companies had effectively merged their operations under one roof in the burgeoning Printer's Row district of
Chicago. In 1930 the company reorganized itself as a corporation in the state of Delaware, with home offices in Chicago, and

opened its first company-owned printing operations. CCH acquired a total of eight separate "reporters," ranging in subject matter from the *Public Utility Index-Digest* to the *Motor Carrier Reporter*. Business was further boosted in 1933 with the enactment of President's Franklin D. Roosevelt's New Deal program, a transformation of government that created an enormous need for reporters to assist businesses in understanding the new laws. CCH created individual reporters covering labor, social security, liquor control, food and drug, securities, and bankruptcy regulations.

As the entry of the United States into World War II appeared imminent, CCH began publishing the *War Law Reporter* as well as an unprecedented number of publications on the federal tax code that helped decipher an enormous increase enacted in federal tax rates. When the United States entered World War II, the company devoted the majority of its efforts to publishing various federal, state, and local tax reporters, and company printing operations supported the U.S. Government with special publishing projects. The postwar years were profitable for CCH, despite a shortage of material goods that made expansion difficult. CCH established Commerce Clearing House, Canadian Ltd., in 1945 and a second editorial office in San Francisco in 1946. During this period business also expanded when several competing publishing houses went out of business and recommended CCH publications to their subscribers.

With the dawn of the Cold War, demand for CCH's war law reporting continued. In 1950, when the United States entered the Korean War, CCH was the first to come out with a reporter on the Defense Production Act of 1950 and subsequent "emergency controls." The company developed the *Emergency Business Control Law Reporters,* a flexible series of loose-leaf reports focusing on individual topics such a prices, materials, and market stabilization. CCH also created a publication in cooperation with the New York Stock Exchange, which set the stage for the company's later introduction of guides to the American, Pacific, Midwest, Boston, and Philadelphia stock exchanges.

In 1961 CCH went public on the NASDAQ exchange. The following year the company began venturing into European markets with the publication of *Common Market Reports* as well as a series on world tax rates published through a joint project with Harvard University. In 1963 the company began publication of a guide to British taxes for use by Canadian and American businesses. CCH benefitted once again from important governmental policy initiatives, publishing the *Employment Services Reporter* in 1964 as a means of assisting businesses in understanding the Civil Rights Act. The following year, when the Social Security Act was passed, the company published 3.8 million books explaining the intricacies of Medicare and Medicaid regulations. The company also grew through acquisition, acquiring National Quotation Bureau, Inc., in 1963 and Facts on File, a publisher of news summaries, in 1965, as well as a majority share in Computax Services Inc., a computerized tax preparation service. International expansion continued throughout the decade, and in 1968 CCH gained a foothold in Australia by founding Commerce Clearing House, Australia. Sales that year were $37.8 million.

The company continued to add new publications through the 1970s, focusing on its traditional areas of tax and business law,

as well as on emerging topics such as computer law, workplace safety regulations, and consumer safety reports. In 1974 CCH raised its holdings in Computax shares from just over 50 percent to 96 percent. Although the company had been unprofitable for several years, by 1973 Computax was the leader in the growing industry of computer-based tax preparation, preparing 700,000 returns per year. Throughout the 1970s Computax profits rose and fell as it struggled to keep abreast of changes in the computer industry that were prompting more and more businesses to prepare their tax returns internally.

CCH's tax publication division grew sharply during the late 1970s and early 1980s, fueled by increasingly complex tax measures such as the 1,200-page Deficit Reduction Act of 1984. CCH's *Standard Federal Tax Reporters* (to which subscriptions could be bought for $925 per year) dominated the market and enjoyed a strong reputation for quality and accuracy. Prentice Hall, the company's nearest competitor, held only a third of CCH's market share in tax publications, and the two had had virtually no new competitors since 1935. The company's balance sheet was so impressive it prompted *Fortune* magazine to declare that "the financial achievements of Commerce Clearing House have been nothing short of splendid." The company posted nearly $40 million in earnings in 1984 and held a cash reserve of $75 million.

CCH's sparkling performance was not long-lived, however. Net income slipped from $53 million in 1987 to $31 million in 1991, largely due to a lackluster performance by Computax, which prompted the division to lay off 150 of its 650 employees and consolidate its 31 tax-processing bureaus. Sales were slipping in CCH's publishing division as well, as CCH's core clients—law and accounting firms—had experienced financial difficulties in the late 1980s, prompting many to cancel their subscriptions to the *Standard Federal Tax Reporter*. Other long-time clients switched to online databases such as Westlaw and Lexis/Nexis for tax-related information. And a new competitor, Research Institute of America, had entered the field. Bankrolled by parent company Thompson Corp., Research Institute was able to capture market share with user-friendly products at low prices.

In 1991 Richard Merrill stepped down as chief executive and was replaced by a three-member executive committee consisting of Edward L. Massie, president of the publishing division, Ralph Whitley, head of Computax, and Oakleigh Thorne IV, the great-great grandson of the company's founder, who had moved up in the ranks after earning his MBA from Columbia University in the late 1980s. The three-man committee was assigned the task of restructuring the company's operations and marketing strategies, which had remained much the same in the company's 80-year history.

The three-member committee earmarked $86 million to position the company in the burgeoning market of electronic media. Many publications were made available on CD-ROM (a move that allowed all 36,000 pages of information in the *Standard Federal Tax Reporter* to fit neatly onto one disk), through a new online service called CCH ACCESS, and on audio cassettes and floppy disks. Under Whitley's direction, Computax's mail-in tax preparation services were replaced by a series of tax-compliance software packages that allowed accountants to file returns using their personal computers.

The restructuring of Computax led to the elimination of more than 1,500 jobs at its 31 bureaus nationwide. In addition, CCH eliminated 245 printing and shipping positions by closing printing plants in Chicago and Clark, New Jersey, and transferring operations to a plant in St. Petersburg, Florida, the company's most efficient operation. Other plants were converted into CD-ROM production facilities. The company posted a loss of $64.2 million in 1992, resulting from a one-time charge of $100.5 million related to the restructuring of its computer system and accounting for retiree benefits. Restructuring continued in 1993 as CCH sold Facts on File, Inc., and the National Quotation Bureau Co. to Smith McDonell Stone and Co., and purchased Matthew Bender & Co., parent company of Bender's Federal Tax Service, and eight state tax services and related tax publications, from Times Mirror Company.

Profits in 1993 were a slim $6.3 million; in 1994 they tripled to $18.9 million, fueled by gains at Computax and by Legal Information Services's electronic publishing ventures. This was still below the company's earnings of $40 million a decade earlier, but was not unusual given the difficulties many publishing firms experienced in the early 1990s. As it neared its 60th anniversary, CCH was seeking to transform itself from one of the nation's leading print providers of legal, tax, and business information into a leading player in the rapidly expanding field of electronic publishing.

Principal Subsidiaries: CCH Publishing Inc.; Legal Information Services; Computax Inc.; CCH Canada; CCH Europe; CCH Asia; CCH Australia; CCH New Zealand; Matthew Bender & Co; McCord Co.

Further Reading:

Bennett, Julie, "Ready for Combat: Business-Style Oakleigh Thorne IV Revels in Setting a New Course," *Chicago Tribune,* August 27, 1995.

Gruber, William, "After Taxing Times, Electronic Leap Pays Off for Publisher," *Chicago Tribune,* March 27, 1995, Bus. Sec.

"The Other Story About Windows 95: CCH Business Owner's Toolkit Debuts with the Microsoft Network PR," *Newswire,* August 23, 1995.

"Publisher to Issue New Stock," *Chicago Tribune,* March 29, 1991, Bus. Sec.

Randle, Wilma, "Job Cuts at Chicago Print Site," *Chicago Tribune,* June 5, 1993, Bus. Sec.

Sherman, Stratford P., "The Company that Loves the U.S. Tax Code," *Fortune,* November 26, 1984, p. 64.

Stern, William M., "Energy Transfusion," *Forbes,* February 14, 1994, p. 84.

Taylor, Marianne, "Hot Off the Presses—The Latest on Taxes," *Chicago Tribune,* August 11, 1993, Bus. Sec.

—Maura Troester

Centocor Inc.

244 Great Valley Parkway
Malvern, Pennsylvania 19355
U.S.A.
(215) 651-6000
Fax: (215) 651-6000

Public Company
Incorporated: 1979
Employees: 550
Stock Exchanges: NASDAQ
Operating Revenues: $67.2 million
SICs: 2835 Diagnostic Substances; 2836 Biological Products
   except Diagnostic

Centocor Inc. is a biotechnology company that develops and markets products to treat infectious, cardiovascular, and auto-immune diseases and cancer. It is also engaged in a number of other biotechnology research projects. Centocor, which was among the first start-ups in the biotechnology industry, entered the mid-1990s hoping to profit from products it had been developing and seeking to bring to market for more than a decade.

Centocor was founded in May 1979 by a group of scientists and entrepreneurs lead by Michael Wall. Wall graduated from the Massachusetts Institute of Technology with a degree in electrical engineering. Early in his career, during the 1950s, he worked for several electronics start-up companies. In the mid-1960s he switched to biology and, with some partners, founded a company called Flow Laboratories. In 1969 the group sold their company for $3 million to General Research Corp., a Virginia biomedical concern. General Research kept Wall on to help run the company for ten years. During that time he became interested in the burgeoning field of biotechnology.

Biotechnology can be simply defined as the manipulation of living organisms or biological components at the molecular, subcellular, or cellular level to create marketable products. Such products include bacterial and virus vaccines, toxoids, serums, plasmas, and various microbiological substances, as well as in vitro and in vivo diagnostic substances. The modern biotechnology industry was inspired by the 1953 discovery of the structure of DNA, which led to an understanding of the process by which proteins are produced by cells. It wasn't until the 1970s, however, that rapid progress was made in biotechnology.

In 1973 two U.S. scientists discovered the process of recombinant DNA, whereby a piece of DNA is snipped from one gene and spliced into another gene. This discovery demonstrated that scientists could genetically alter microorganisms and produce mass amounts of proteins that occur naturally only in small quantities. In the seven years following that breakthrough, a handful of biotechnology startups were formed to develop marketable biotech drugs and products. In 1975 researchers produced the first monoclonal antibodies, which are essentially cloned cells that can be used to attack foreign toxins, viruses, and cancer cells.

Inspired by major biotech breakthroughs, Wall left Flow General (or Flow Laboratories) in 1979 to start a biotechnology company called Centocor, planning to use biotechnology to develop diagnostic medical tests. The proposition was ambitious because the diagnostic testing market at the time was dominated by healthcare giants like Abbot Laboratories and Warner Lambert. Those companies generally developed proprietary tests to run on their own analyzers, which they sold to laboratories, blood banks, and hospitals. To compete directly in that market, Centocor might have to invest hundreds of millions of dollars to develop and promote its own analyzers.

Wall and fellow executives evaded the cost barrier by designing diagnostic tests that could be processed on other company's analyzers. Centocor then sold the tests to distributors, which were usually companies that sold their own analyzers. Abbott Labs, for example, eventually purchased Centocor's proprietary test for gastrointestinal and ovarian cancer. Centocor also kept costs down by minimizing in-house research expenses. In contrast to other biotech start-ups, which typically funded expensive original in-house research with venture capital, Centocor used its limited cash reservoir to piggyback off of discoveries made in university, government, and even private laboratories. When Centocor found a promising discovery for which it saw a marketable use, it would buy the technology and allow its in-house team of Ph.D.s, which numbered 25 by the mid-1990s, to develop the breakthrough into a marketable diagnostic test.

''You can have a garage full of Ph.D.s working on a project,'' Wall said of his research philosophy in the May 6, 1985, *Forbes,* ''and nine times out of ten some guy across the street is going to come up with the discovery that beats them all.'' Besides saving money on original research, Centocor's strategy also allowed it to reduce the time necessary to get its products from the laboratory to the marketplace. In the case of the ovarian cancer test that Centocor sold to Abbott, for example, Wall learned in 1981 that researchers at the Dana-Farber Cancer Institute in Boston had isolated antibodies that could detect ovarian cancer cells. Centocor began funding the project and two years later employed the antibody in a test kit utilized to detect cancer cells.

During the early 1980s Centocor succeeded in bringing products to market and looked as though it might show a profit, which was no small feat in the biotechnology industry. Indeed, the commercial biotechnology sector had exploded during the early 1980s, largely as the result of a Supreme Court ruling that allowed genetically engineered bacterium to be patented. The ruling ensured that biotech innovators would be rewarded for their efforts if they developed a commercially viable treatment or cure. Millions of dollars poured into the industry as investors sought to profit from the promised onslaught of wonder drugs that would soon spring from biotech labs. The reality by the mid-1980s, however, was that many biotech companies had succeeded in burning through millions of dollars in research and development cash without producing a single significant commercial product.

Centocor capitalized on the excitement about biotechnology during the early 1980s by offering its stock to the public in 1982, bringing $21 million to Centocor's balance sheet. The company showed its first meager profit in 1984, and by 1985 was generating about $20 million in annual revenues and $2 million in net income, although its revenues were coming from research contracts and investment income, as well from product sales. Furthermore, the company was still sitting on about $18 million of the cash captured in its initial public offering.

Centocor's future looked bright going into the late 1980s. In addition to expected sales gains for the two tests already on the market, Centocor had been developing and was preparing to introduce tests for breast, liver, and lung cancer, among other ailments. Importantly, Centocor was also engaged in the research and development of therapeutic products that used monoclonal antibodies to deliver such agents as radioisotopes and chemotherapeutic drugs. Although profits fluctuated, Centocor managed to post successive revenue gains during the late 1980s: sales grew to $27 million in 1986 before jumping to $55 million in 1988 and then to $72 million in 1989. As revenues swelled, so did the Centocor organization, adding a manufacturing facility in the Netherlands and bringing its global work force to more than 400 by the end of the decade.

Centocor's work force and facilities expansion during the late 1980s reflected the company's intent to evolve from a creator of diagnostic tests to a developer, manufacturer, and marketer of drugs. Indeed, Centocor management hoped to parlay its profitable base of diagnostic tests into a research and development engine for monoclonal antibody products. The goal was to patent pivotal new drugs and then manufacture and bring them to market, making Centocor a full-fledged pharmaceutical company. Products being developed by Centocor during the mid- and late 1980s included Myoscint, which could diagnose heart attacks, and Fibriscint, which could diagnose deep-vein blood clots. Centocor executives knew that if they could succeed in getting FDA and European approval for its drugs, the payoff could be huge.

Centocor's flagship research project during the late 1980s and early 1990s was Centoxin, a drug that the company had started developing in 1982. Centoxin was designed to treat gram-negative sepsis, a bacterial infection that kills 80,000 people annually in the United States alone. An estimated 200,000 cases of gram-negative infection is diagnosed each year in the United States. Symptoms of the infection are a fever and drop in blood pressure, which is often followed by septic shock that leads to organ failure and death. The infection is usually spawned by trauma like major surgery. Centocor was enthusiastic about Centoxin because the estimated market potential for the drug worldwide in the early 1990s was between $1 billion and $1.5 billion annually. The drug, therefore, promised to launch Centocor to the status of a major pharmaceutical company.

Having completed most of its in-house development and testing, the company began restructuring its operations in the early 1990s in anticipation of FDA and European approval of the breakthrough drug. In 1990 alone, Centocor increased the staff at its Malvern headquarters from 340 to more than 500. To fund growth and investment in Centoxin, the company set about raising hundreds of millions of dollars in cash through stock offerings and by selling investment interests. It used much of the cash to begin building a large sales network and manufacturing facilities to sell Centoxin and its other drugs. By 1992 the Centocor organization encompassed a work force of about 1,500, including 300 salespeople and staff at production facilities in the United States and Europe.

Primarily because of costs related to the Centoxin project, Centocor posted income deficits of more than $300 million in 1990 and 1991, combined. The company was, apparently, betting its future on the success of Centoxin. Unfortunately, in April 1992 Centocor nearly lost that gamble when the FDA said that Centocor's data for Centoxin didn't demonstrate the drug's effectiveness. Executives were stunned. Realizing the urgency of the situation, a committee of directors headed by Chairman Wall quickly restructured the company's management. Among other major changes, James E. Wavle, Jr., president and chief executive of the company, resigned. Centocor spent the next few years shuttering idle production facilities and releasing two-thirds of its 1,500-member work force.

The delay in getting Centoxin to market meant that the company had, at least temporarily, lost its chance to join the ranks of the big pharmaceutical companies. "What they are giving up is the possibility of being an independent, fully integrated pharmaceutical company," said analyst David Webber in the May 4, 1992, *Philadelphia Business Journal.* Centocor management acknowledged the setback but countered criticism, claiming that the company had other products in its research pipeline and would eventually find a way to get its investment back out of Centoxin. Still, investors were alarmed. In January 1993 Centocor announced that it had halted its crucial clinical trial on Centoxin and had also ceased selling the drug in Europe, where the drug had been approved for some applications. The announcement brought a spate of shareholder suits alleging false claims and misrepresentation by the company.

Centocor posted ugly income deficits of $196 million, $74 million, and $127 million in 1992, 1993, and 1994, respectively. Meanwhile, the company's market value plunged from $2.3 billion to a meager $250 million. Centocor management refused to concede defeat. The company had still had $150 million in cash to get it by after the Centoxin blow was dealt in 1992. Besides slashing costs, Centocor quickly entered into an alliance with pharmaceutical giant Eli Lilly, which paid $50 million for a five-percent stake in the company. Lilly also agreed to help Centocor get Centoxin through the approval process. Centocor relinquished the worldwide marketing rights to Centoxin in exchange for half of the drug's future profits. It also effectively promised to give Lilly the marketing rights to another of its major drugs, ReoPro, if Centoxin failed to be approved.

Centoxin did fail to be approved. Surprisingly, test data eventually showed that patients taking Centoxin actually had a higher death rate than those taking a placebo. With Centocor on the brink of bankruptcy, Lilly threw its weight behind ReoPro, a cardiovascular drug used primarily in high-risk angioplasty. In June 1994 the FDA recommended ReoPro for approval. The drug, which would be marketed by Lilly, was expected to generate annual sales of $250 million by 1997. The accomplishment came just in time to save Centocor from collapse. In fact, in mid-1995 the company expected to show an annual profit for the first time since 1989. Buoyed by the success of its alliance with Lilly, Centocor began seeking other alliances to market its drugs.

In mid-1995 Centocor's major product initiatives included: ReoPro; CenTNF, a therapeutic product designed to treat rheumatoid arthritis and inflammatory bowel diseases; and Panorex, a cancer-fighting drug. The company was also developing and selling various diagnostic products and tests related to ovarian cancer, syphilis G, pancreatic cancer, breast cancer, gastric cancer, lung cancer, and other afflictions. With manufacturing operations in the Netherlands, the United States, and the United Kingdom, the company employed about 550 workers.

Principal Subsidiaries: Centocor B.V. (The Netherlands); Centocor U.K. Limited (United Kingdom); Nippon Centocor K.K. (Japan).

Further Reading:

Abelson, Reed, "Centocor Stock Rides Bio-Tech's Volatile Path," *Philadelphia Business Journal,* October 20, 1986, Sec. 1, p. 15.

Armstrong, Michael W., "Centocor Hoping to Raise Record Amount of Money," *Philadelphia Business Journal,* December 17, 1990, Sec. 1, p. 11.

——, "Centocor Revamps Operations to Fortify for Its Survival Fight," *Philadelphia Business Journal,* May 4, 1992, Sect. 1, p. 6.

——, "Embattled Centocor Hit with More Shareholder Suits," *Philadelphia Business Journal,* February 1, 1993, Sec. 1, p. 15.

——, "Passing on Youthful Retirement, He Opted for a Biotech Start-Up," *Philadelphia Business Journal,* August 3, 1992, Sec. 1, p. 4.

Bamford, James, "Refocus: How a Near-Death Experience Forced Centocor into Strategic Alliances," *Financial World,* April 11, 1995, p. 68.

Chambers, Pat Pfeiffer, "Two Area Firms Ready for Biotech Boom," *Focus,* July 15, 1987, Sec. 1, p. 17.

Marcial, Gene G., "Inside Wall Street: Centocor Not Yet in Recovery," *Business Week,* July 4, 1994, p. 80.

Teitelman, Robert, "Searching for Serendipity: Centocor Combs University Labs for Technology," *Forbes,* May 6, 1985, p. 80.

—Dave Mote

Chemical Banking Corporation

270 Park Avenue
New York, New York 10017-2070
U.S.A.
(212) 270-6000
Fax: (212) 270-2613

Public Company
Incorporated: 1968
Employees: 42,130
Total Assets: $187.85 billion
Stock Exchanges: New York London
SICs: 6712 Bank Holding Companies; 6022 State
   Commercial Banks; 6021 National Commercial Banks

The Chemical Banking Corporation, a multibillion dollar bank holding company, began as a division of a New York City chemical manufacturer during the early 19th century. The company grew steadily through its long history, then more dramatically in the late 1980s and early 1990s when it became a superregional bank with holdings in New York, New Jersey, and Texas, in addition to maintaining its position as a money-center bank. In 1995 Chemical merged with the Chase Manhattan Corporation to form, under the Chase Manhattan name, the largest bank in the United States.

In the early 1820s a state-chartered bank in New York could not open its doors unless the New York State Assembly approved its charter. In those days, the legislature was hostile to banks, and obtaining a state charter could be difficult. Legislators were somewhat more inclined to grant charters to banks that were part of another business. When three New York City merchants—Balthazar P. Melick, Mark Spenser, and Geradus Post—decided to form a bank in 1823, they used a proven tactic to obtain their charter. On February 24, 1823, Melick, Spenser, and three other merchants incorporated the New York Chemical Manufacturing Company, headquartered in New York, to produce a variety of chemicals. The following year they successfully petitioned the New York State Assembly to allow the chemical company to amend its charter to permit the company to conduct banking activities. Chemical Bank was thus formed as a division of the New York Chemical Manufacturing Company on April 24, 1824, with Melick as its first president.

The bank initially served New York's mercantile community. At the time there were only 12 banks in New York City.

Chemical Bank flourished in this relatively open market and soon offered older banks, like City Bank of New York (later Citibank), stiff competition. By 1829 Chemical had more than $216,000 in deposits, $20,000 reserved in specie, and retained earnings of more than $4,000. The chemical manufacturing division was also profitable, earning $50,000 a year by 1832.

In 1831 John Mason was selected to be the bank's second president. Mason, one of the wealthiest landowners in the city, was also president of the New York Harlem Railroad Company. In 1839 Isaac Jones became the third president of Chemical Bank upon Mason's death. In 1844 John Quinton Jones became the fourth president of Chemical Bank. Jones started working for the company as an agent of the chemical division and eventually became cashier of the bank—the equivalent of general manager—during the presidency of his cousin, Isaac Jones. John Q. Jones is noted for developing the weakened bank into a very strong institution. Also in 1844, when New York Chemical Manufacturing Company's original charter expired, the chemical company was liquidated and the company was reincorporated as a bank only, in accordance with more liberal banking laws passed in 1838. By 1851 the directors had sold all of the chemical division's inventories and real estate holdings and distributed the proceeds as dividends to shareholders.

In 1853 Chemical became a founding member of the New York Clearing House, an association of banks formed to help members clear banking transactions. During the recession of 1857 many banks newly incorporated under the banking act of 1838 were hit hard. Eighteen New York City banks closed in a single day; some 985 banks throughout the country closed during a six-month period. Chemical Bank earned the nickname "Old Bullion" during the crisis by continuing to redeem bank notes in specie for several days after all other financial institutions had started issuing paper loan certificates.

Even as Chemical Bank earned a reputation for soundness and foresight among grateful corporate and individual customers during the crisis, it earned quite another among its peers. Other banks regarded Chemical as ruthless and uncooperative—for a time, the bank was even suspended from the New York Clearing House. Chemical had agreed in principle that clearing house members ought to band together to protect weaker banks during times of crisis yet it refused to pool its specie reserves to soften the effects of the recession (some historians speculate that Chemical Bank was able to continue to distribute specie after the general suspension only because its largest customers had privately agreed not to withdraw their deposits).

During the Civil War, the country experienced two more recessions, one in 1861 and another in 1863, which were followed by more bank closings. Because of Chemical's reputation for stability, its deposits increased dramatically with each of these later crises. By 1871 its deposits had climbed to $6.08 million. In 1865 the bank acquired a national charter under the National Bank Act of 1865 as the Chemical National Bank of New York. Chemical began issuing government-backed national bank notes, the forerunner to paper money. The bank gained two further advantages from its national charter: it became a depository of federal funds and the required reserves of other national banks, and its reputation for soundness was enhanced by the higher liquidity and solvency requirements set by the federal government.

In 1878 George J. Williams became president following Jones's death. Williams, who like Jones had served as president of the New York Clearing House Association, was arguably the most successful banker in the United States. Chemical grew rapidly under Williams's leadership during the turbulent decades at the end of the century. In the face of fierce competition, he made Chemical a major correspondent banker and built it into one of the largest and strongest banks in North America.

In 1903 Williams died and was replaced as president by Joseph B. Martindale. By 1907 the bank had lost its competitive advantage and was losing accounts at a rate of about 100 per year. When Martindale died in 1917 the bank was no longer among even the top 100 in the country. It had faltered in part because Martindale was extremely conservative at a time when other major New York banks were aggressively diversifying into securities and international markets.

Upon Martindale's death Chemical's board of directors made Herbert K. Twitchell president. Percy H. Johnston, a young Kentucky banker, became vice-president in 1917. Johnston turned the company around very quickly. First the bank stopped losing customers, then, between September and December 1917, deposits rose from $35 million to $63 million. By 1919 Chemical's stock had increased from a dangerous low to almost $200 per share.

Johnston was made president in 1920 and took the long overdue step of diversifying the bank's services. He set up a trust department and engineered Chemical's first merger, in 1920, with Citizens National Bank, a small but wealthy New York commercial bank. As a result of the merger, Chemical's assets rose to $200 million, its capital to $4.5 million, its deposits to $140 million. In 1923 Chemical established its first branch bank. Also in the early 1920s, Johnston recruited a new management team. These managers—Frank Houston, Harold Helm, and N. Baxter Johnson—guided the company through the mid-1960s.

In the late 1920s Johnston decided to expand the company's trust business. The bank was reincorporated as a state bank in 1929 under the name Chemical Bank & Trust Company because New York State granted broader trust powers than were available to national banks. By then Chemical had 12 branches in Brooklyn and Manhattan, and in 1929 it opened its first overseas office, in London. Later that year Chemical merged with the United States Mortgage & Trust Company. After the merger, Johnston became Chemical's first chairman and John W. Platten, formerly president of United States Mortgage, replaced him as president.

Also in 1929, Johnston established two affiliates. The first, Chemical National Company, Inc., bought, sold, and underwrote securities. The second, Chemical National Association, Inc., was formed as a holding company. During the Great Depression Johnston was able to maintain a strong capital position by merging the two affiliates into the bank and managing assets carefully. During the early 1930s, when about 8,000 banks failed and many others struggled to remain solvent, Chemical Bank's deposits actually rose by 40 percent. Deposits continued to grow during the late 1930s and early 1940s, reaching the $1 billion mark by 1941.

In 1946 Johnston retired, and the following year Chairman Baxter Johnson and President Harold Helm brought about a merger with Continental Bank and Trust Company. This merger was the first in a series that helped increase the bank's assets from $1.35 billion in 1946 to $15 billion by 1972. The most important of these unions was Chemical's 1954 merger with the Corn Exchange Bank Trust Company to form Chemical Corn Exchange Bank. The merger brought Chemical 98 additional branches throughout New York City.

In the late 1950s, under Helm (now chairman) and new President Isaac Grainger, Chemical began expanding international operations. In 1958 its first international subsidiaries were formed, and in 1959 the company's first full-service international branch opened in London. Also in 1959, Chemical merged with New York Trust Company, which had a large trust and wholesale-banking business. In the early 1960s Chemical began to expand into New York's suburbs, opening branches on Long Island and in wealthy Westchester and Nassau Counties.

In 1968 Helm and President William S. Renschard, appointed in 1960, followed a trend started by Citibank. They formed a bank holding company, Chemical New York Corporation, to facilitate expansion into other financial areas. In 1971 the company was internally restructured to decentralize the activities of the bank and clearly mark out areas of responsibility.

Chemical's international operations grew significantly in the late 1960s and early 1970s under the leadership of Donald C. Platten (the grandson of former president John W. Platten). Platten became president in 1972 and chairman in 1973. His strategy was not to build a large network of international branches, which would make the company vulnerable to fluctuations in foreign economies, but to concentrate on establishing branches in key international money centers. Chemical established offices in the Bahamas and Frankfurt in 1969; in Zurich, Brussels, and Paris in 1971; and in Tokyo in 1972. By 1977 Chemical had added branches in Milan, Singapore, and Taiwan. It also expanded its international operations by purchasing a 30 percent interest in a London merchant bank in 1977 and participating in several ventures with financial institutions in Austria, the Philippines, and other countries.

From 1972 through 1977 Chemical again experienced a period of consistent growth. The bank not only increased the number of operations it controlled, but also diversified the services it offered to both corporate and individual customers. One of Chemical's main objectives was to develop a broad base of fee-generating services that would be unaffected by interest rate fluctuations. Another was to earn a reputation as a progressive, result-oriented bank. Acquisitions continued during this period. In 1975 Chemical acquired Security National Bank, with its large Long Island branch network. Other important acquisitions at this time included several rural New York banks, a finance company with branches in 11 states, two investment-advisory firms, and a mortgage company. The company also formed a real estate-financing subsidiary, Chemical Realty Company, during this period and a wholesale bank in Delaware. One of Chemical's most popular innovations was ChemLink, a computerized system that enabled corporations to transfer funds anywhere and to have instant access to their funds worldwide.

In 1980 Platten and Chemical President Norborne Berkeley began restructuring the company's nonconsumer banking operations. Independent divisions were set up to operate the company's three largest sectors: multinational corporations, large domestic corporations, and middle-market businesses. This effort to streamline operations and cut out marginal businesses was necessary because, though Chemical had grown steadily during the past 30 years, it had failed to establish a niche in the industry and its overall performance had been unspectacular. What Chemical needed was to create a corporate image to distinguish it from other New York banks.

In 1982 Chemical made its first move to establish a corporate image. The company announced an agreement to merge with Florida National Banks of Florida, Inc., as soon as interstate banking between the two states was permitted. Platten and Chemical President Walter V. Shipley were immediately embroiled in a battle with Southeast Banking Corporation, a major competitor of Florida National Banks that wanted to pursue its own takeover bid. Following lawsuits, countersuits, and stockholder actions, the combat ended in a draw; Southeast would get the Florida National Bank branches and Chemical got the remainder of the company's business, giving it a foothold in the lucrative Florida market. This deal helped Chemical gain a reputation as a daring and slightly unconventional player in the financial world. In 1982 the bank also introduced Pronto, an electronic home banking system for consumers and small businesses. And in 1985 Chemical, AT&T, Bank of America, and Time, Inc., formed a joint venture called Covidea to provide electronic services.

In 1986 Chemical celebrated its tenth consecutive year of earnings growth by announcing another merger agreement, again with a company whose market was outside Chemical's traditional sphere of operations. This time the merger partner was a New Jersey bank holding company, Horizon Bancorp. Again, the actual merger had to wait until interstate banking between New York and New Jersey was allowed. The merger finally took place in January 1989, and Horizon was renamed Chemical Bank New Jersey. Meanwhile, Chemical turned to the acquisition of Texas Commerce Bankshares. This merger, effective in May 1987, was the largest interstate banking merger in U.S. history to date and allowed Chemical to expand into yet another major banking market. Texas Commerce was one of the largest bank holding companies in the Southwest, had the largest affiliate system in Texas, and was certainly the best capitalized of the major Texas banks.

As Chemical expanded through these mergers, it also suffered aftereffects from the crazed loan environment of the 1980s. Late in the decade Chemical was hit hard in loan losses from Third World borrowers, especially Argentina and Brazil. At the same time, the myriad, shaky real estate deals made in the United States in the 1980s came back to haunt Chemical (and many other banks). By 1991 Chemical's delinquent real-estate loans mounted to $1 billion out of the $6.7 billion total. With competition increasing in the banking industry, Chemical needed to take dramatic action to hold off its rivals.

Chemical's chairman and CEO, Walter V. Shipley, engineered just such a move with the 1991 merger of Chemical with Manufacturers Hanover Corp. Called the first major bank

merger among equals and the biggest bank merger in U.S. history to date, it brought together the nation's sixth- and ninth-largest banks into what became the nation's second-largest bank, behind only Citicorp, with assets of $135 billion. The merger also marked the beginning of an unprecedented era of bank consolidation that would see several mergers dwarf even the Chemical-Manufacturers merger.

The new institution retained the Chemical name, but it would initially be headed by Manufacturers chairman John McGillicuddy, who under the terms of the merger served as chairman and CEO of the new Chemical through the end of 1993, after which Shipley took over. Each of the banks boasted of large retail banking networks in New York; merged together, Chemical achieved cost savings by closing redundant branches and eliminating jobs. Over the next few years, 6,200 employees lost their jobs and $750 million in costs were cut each year. While assets grew slowly, reaching $149.89 billion in 1993, Chemical improved its profitability through these cost savings, increasing its return on assets from 0.3 percent in 1990 to 1.11 percent in 1993 and its return on equity from 5.94 percent in 1990 to 16.7 percent in 1993.

Chemical also sought to improve its strengthening operations and pull out of markets where it could not compete in the heightened competitive climate of banking in the 1990s. The bank bolstered itself in Texas when it purchased the assets of the failed First City Bancorp in 1992 and added Ameritrust Texas Corporation in a $130 million 1993 deal. With such moves, Chemical became the leading corporate bank in Texas.

Yet Chemical trailed retail banking competition in upstate New York. In 1992 it decided to abandon that market and sold its upstate branches to Fleet Bank of New York. Chemical also pulled out of New Jersey in 1995, a market it had entered only nine years earlier. Early in 1995 it sold 84 branches in southern and central New Jersey to PNC Bank Corp. for $504 million. In 1993 Chemical had received permission from the Federal Reserve to underwrite corporate bonds, and the bank aimed to become a major underwriter of below-investment-grade debt within a few years.

While Shipley returned to the helm and Chemical's merger with Manufacturers paid dividends, the U.S. banking industry was undergoing consolidation at a frenzied pace. In the first six months of 1995, for example, 100 bank mergers were announced with a total value of $37.7 billion. With competitive pressures reheating, Shipley turned again to the merger strategy to keep Chemical near the top of the banking industry. In late August 1995 Chemical and the Chase Manhattan Corporation announced a $10 billion stock-swap merger. This largest bank merger in U.S. history to date created the top U.S. bank with assets of $297 billion and a bank with $20 billion in equity to invest, the fourth-largest amount in the world. The new institution took the Chase Manhattan name, with Shipley serving as chairman and CEO and Chase's chairman Thomas G. Labrecque acting as president and chief operating officer.

The Chemical-Chase merger was similar to the Chemical-Manufacturers merger in that the two banks had numerous overlapping areas of operations that could serve as bases for cost cutting. Over the next three years the new Chase planned to eliminate 12,000 employees and $1.5 billion in costs. Managing this megamerger will surely dominate the operations of Chase/Chemical throughout the rest of the 1990s.

Principal Subsidiaries: Albuquerque Capital Management, Inc.; Bach Holding Corporation; Brown & Company Securities Corporation; CBC-U.S.A. Inc.; Chatham Ventures, Inc.; Chem-Advertising, Inc.; ChemSel, Inc.; Chemical Bank; Chemical Bank, National Association; Chemical Bank & Trust Company of Florida N.A.; Chemical Business Credit Corp.; Chemical Capital Corporation; Chemical Equity Incorporated; Chemical Financial Management Corp.; Chemical Financial Services Corporation, Ltd.; Chemical First State Corporation; Chemical Futures, Inc.; Chemical Futures Management, Inc.; Chemical Futures & Options, Inc.; Chemical International Securities Corp.; Chemical Investments Inc.; Chemical Mortgage Securities, Inc.; Chemical New Jersey Corporation; Chemical New Jersey Holdings, Inc.; Chemical New York, Inc.; Chemical Real Holdings, Inc.; Chemical Realty Corp.; Chemical Securities Inc.; Chemical Technologies Corporation; The Chemical Investment Group Ltd.; The CIT Group Holdings, Inc.; Manufacturers Hanover Trust Company; Manufacturers Hanover Venture Capital; MH Leasing International; New York Switch Corporation (12.62%); Offshore Equities, Inc.; The Portfolio Group, Inc.; Pronto, Inc.; Texas Commerce BancShares, Inc.; Van Deventer & Hoch; Bank of New Providence, Limited (Bahamas); SA Manufacturers Hanover Bank NV (Belgium); Court Square Financial, Ltd. (Bermuda); Banco Norchem, S.A. (Brazil); Chemical Administracao e Consultoria Economico Financeira Ltda. (Brazil); Chemical Commercio e Servicos Ltda. (Brazil); Noroeste Chemical S.A. Arrendamento Mercantil Norchem (Brazil); Chemical Bank Canada; Manufacturers Hanover Bank Canada Ltd.; Chemical Bank & Howard de Walden Limited (Channel Islands); Chemical Custody (Guernsey) Limited (Channel Islands); Chemical Investments (Guernsey) Limited (Channel Islands); Manufacturers Hanover Banque Nordique (France); CB Beteiligungs Und Verwaltungsgesellschaft MbH (Germany); Unterstuztungs Gesellschaft MbH der Chemical Bank (Germany); Chemical Asia Ltd. (Hong Kong); Manufacturers Hanover Asia Ltd. (Hong Kong); Chemical Trust and Banking Company Limited (Japan); Manufacturers Hanover Ltd. (Japan); Libmar Three, Inc. (Liberia); Libmar Four, Inc. (Liberia); Libmar Six, Inc. (Liberia); Marpan One, Inc. (Panama); Marpan Two, Inc. (Panama); Chemco Finance Singapore Limited; Chemical Securities Singapore Pte. Ltd.; Manufacturers Hanover Trust Company, Seoul Branch (South Korea); Chemical Servicios Financieros, S.A. (Spain); Manufacturers Hanover Trust, Sweden; Manufacturers Hanover (Suisse) S.A. (Switzerland); Manufacturers Hanover Trust Company, Geneva Branch (Switzerland); Manufacturers Hanover Trust Company, Zurich Branch (Switzerland); Chemical Bank (U.K.) Holdings Limited; Manufacturers Hanover Executor & Trustee Co. Ltd. (U.K.); Manufacturers Hanover Export Finance Ltd. (U.K.); Manufacturers Hanover Finance Ltd. (U.K.); Manufacturers Hanover Leasing Corporation, U.K. Representative Office; Manufacturers Hanover Ltd. (U.K.); Manufacturers Hanover Property Services Ltd. (U.K.).

Further Reading:

Bennet, Robert A., "A Second Act for Walter Shipley," *United States Banker*, March 1994, pp. 24–28.
Chemical Bank, 1823–1983, New York: Chemical Bank, 1983.
Hammer, Joshua, and Bruce Shenitz, "The New Giant on the Block," *Newsweek,* July 29, 1991, pp. 36–37.
Hartley, Tom, "Chemical Banking President Plotting Firm's Growth," *Business First of Buffalo,* May 31, 1993, p. 13.
History of the Chemical Bank, 1823–1913, New York: Chemical Bank, 1913.
Holland, Kelley, "Why the Chemistry Is Right at Chemical," *Business Week,* June 7, 1993, pp. 90–93.
Holland, Kelley, and John Meehan, "Wow! That's Some Bank," *Business Week,* September 11, 1995.
Jackson, N. Baxter, *"Old Bullion": One Hundred and Twenty-Five Years on Broadway,* New York: Newcomen Society, 1949.
Marshall, Jeffrey, "Bank M&A's Long Hot Summer," *United States Banker,* October 1995, p. 12.

—updated by David E. Salamie

Choice Hotels International Inc.

10750 Columbia Pike
Silver Spring, Maryland 20901
U.S.A.
(301) 593-5600
Fax: (301) 680-4062

Wholly Owned Subsidiary of Manor Care, Inc.
Incorporated: 1981
Employees: 2,150
Operating Revenues: $138 million
SICs: 6794 Patent Owners & Lessors

Choice Hotels International Inc., a subsidiary of Manor Care, Inc., is the world's second largest franchise hotel chain, overseeing more than 3,400 hotels and 400,000 rooms in 34 countries. Choice is also the fastest-growing hotel chain, adding nearly one hotel each day in 1994. Hotels in the Choice chain operate under seven market-segmented brand names (Clarion, Quality, Comfort, Sleep, Econo Lodge, Rodeway, and Friendship), ranging from economy to luxury, with special attention to business travelers and senior citizens. While Choice, through Manor Care, owns a number of hotels, its business primarily provides marketing, reservations, and quality assurance programs to its franchisees in return for a three to eight percent licensing fee.

Although Choice Hotels International was formally incorporated in 1981, its origins reach back to 1941, when a group of independent motel owners and operators in Florida formed the nonprofit Quality Courts United membership corporation in response to a negative perception of motels that was prevalent at the time. The rise of the automobile and the development of the first highways had brought growing numbers of roadside tourist camps, later known as motels, to serve the increasingly mobile American population. By the 1930s, however, motels had already gained a reputation as hideouts for criminals and other undesirables, prompting J. Edgar Hoover to write in *American* magazine that "a majority of the 35,000 tourist camps in the U.S. threaten the peace and welfare of the communities upon which these camps have fastened themselves and all of us who form the motoring public." The members of Quality Courts United sought to improve their image—and protect their businesses—by establishing and maintaining quality standards. The corporation also provided promotion and advertising services

for its members. In 1963 Quality Courts United incorporated as Quality Courts Motels, Inc., and began a more formal, franchise-based relationship with its members.

One of these members was Stewart Bainum, a former plumbing contractor, who had entered the construction business in the 1950s and built a nursing home in 1960. In 1963 Bainum franchised his first motel with Quality Courts Motels. By 1968 Bainum operated eight nursing homes, incorporating them as Manor Care, Inc., while grouping five motels, franchised with Quality Courts Motels, under the name Park Consolidated Motels, Inc. In that year, Bainum merged Park Consolidated with Quality Courts, becoming president and chief financial officer of a company which by then represented 410 franchised and 12 company-owned motels. With most of its motels concentrated in the eastern United States, Quality Courts moved to expand into the rest of the country and Canada. Within two years, Quality Courts operated franchised motels in 33 states, and began its first international operations, opening an International Division in Brussels and its first hotel in Bonn. At the same time, Quality broadened its business with the purchase of Revere Furniture and Equipment company, a seller of motel furnishings, and Contempo Associates, which focused on motel interior design.

With plans to expand throughout Europe, Quality changed its name in 1972 to Quality Inns International. The oil embargo of 1973, however, disrupted these plans. The effects of the gas shortage were particularly severe on the motel business, as the numbers of automobile travelers dropped dramatically, to the point that Quality saw its survival threatened. In response, Quality put international expansion on hold, halted new construction, dropped its unprofitable properties, and concentrated instead on developing its franchising business. Several years would pass before the company fully recovered from the embargo and resulting recession. By 1977 Quality counted itself as the tenth-largest motel chain in the United States. The purchase in the following year of the Royale Inns of America chain, as well as a joint venture with a Mexican bank to open 40 motels in Mexico, brought the number of Quality owned or franchised motels to 286. By the end of the decade, Quality had become the seventh-largest motel chain, posting record profits and increased dividends and announcing plans to grow by an additional 225 properties in the United States and Canada.

Until this time, Manor Care and Quality had been operating as separate businesses. In 1980 Stewart Bainum merged the two companies, with Manor Care purchasing Quality for $37 million. The company reorganized in the following year. Manor Care, Inc., became a holding company with three subsidiaries: Quality Inns, Inc., which oversaw Manor Care's own hotels; Quality Inns International, Inc., which directed the company's franchise operation; and Manor Healthcare Corporation, which operated the company's nursing home and health care-related businesses. The departure of Quality Inns president Joseph W. McCarthy in June 1980 left Quality without a president for nearly six months. At this time, Bainum appointed Robert C. Hazard and Gerald W. Petitt to head Quality. Together, "the Bob and Jerry Show," as they called themselves, would dominate the growth of Quality for the next fifteen years, raising its value from $15 million in 1981 to more than $500 million in 1995.

Hazard and Petitt met in 1967 at International Business Machines Corporation, where they worked in the data processing division. Their introduction to the hotel business came when they designed a hotel reservation system with the American Express Company. Reservation systems had by then become a critical element of the travel industry, and the development of computer technology had already proved a significant factor in the growth of the airline industry. When Hazard and Petitt were hired by Best Western in 1974, their first step was to implement what was then the most advanced reservation system in the country. Soon after, Best Western posted dramatic increases in its reservations, and Hazard and Petitt were named Best Western's chief executive officer and chief operating officer, respectively. By 1976 Best Western had become the world's largest hotel chain, beating out Holiday Inn, whose hotel in Beirut had been destroyed by terrorists in that year. As Petitt told the *Wall Street Journal,* the bombing "put us over the top as the nation's largest chain. We got a press release out immediately."

At Best Western, Hazard and Petitt, apart from developing what has been called a controversial management style, gained insights into the hotel business that they would bring to Quality several years later. Standardization of the hotels, in which customers could expect consistency in both room design and quality of services, as well as low prices, were factors that distinguished Best Western hotels from other economy motels and from higher-priced chains such as Holiday Inn. To ensure quality, Hazard and Petitt instituted stricter and more frequent inspections of Best Western hotels.

Relations with hotel operators were not as cordial, however, and, in 1980, Hazard and Petitt left Best Western to join Quality, which by then controlled 339 hotels. At Quality, Hazard and Petitt were promised 10 percent of net profits, prompting them to embark on a rapid expansion of the chain. Within three years, Quality doubled the number of its hotels, adding two to three new franchises per week. Quality also resumed its international expansion, principally through the Crest hotel chain, a European affiliate.

When Hazard and Petitt arrived at Quality, the chain's reputation for quality and cleanliness was rather low. Given free rein by Manor Care, the team instituted stricter quality standards and tougher inspections. Many hotels were dropped from the chain in the following years for failing to meet Quality's standards. Standardization of hotel amenities, room design, and furnishings was also stepped up. A long-running advertising campaign, begun in 1983 and featuring celebrities jumping out of suitcases, proved successful in drawing customers to Quality hotels. Hazard and Petitt brought a further development to the industry as a whole when they introduced segmenting to their line of hotels. Quality hotels were initially divided along three market-specific lines: Quality Royale, which would later become Clarion and included higher-priced and luxury hotels; Quality, in the mid-priced market; and Comfort, in the economy market. A quality-control system was instituted at this time, eliminating twenty motels from the chain. In addition, Quality initiated its own reservation system. Other innovations included the introduction of non-smoking rooms, all-suite hotel formats, and rooms adapted to senior citizens, which featured large-button phones and in-room coffee makers.

Between 1981 and 1990 the Quality line of hotels grew to include seven brand names, each targeted toward a specific market segment. Clarion Hotels, Suites, and Resorts were marketed to the upscale and business traveler, featuring boutiques, 24-hour business centers, and other amenities. Comfort Inns and Suites were limited-service hotels designed for the luxury-budget traveler, based on the "all-suite" concept. These hotels have generated some criticism, as the "suites" were often no more than long rooms divided in two by a partition wall. Quality Inns, Hotels, and Suites targeted the traveler in search of mid-priced, full-service accommodations. Sleep Inns, which were originally to be called McSleep Inns—a name abandoned after McDonald's Corporation threatened to sue for trademark infringement—appealed to the luxury-budget segment; unlike other segments, where older hotels were converted to meet segment requirements, Sleep Inns franchises featured entirely new construction. During the 1980s, Quality also acquired the brand names Rodeway, Econo Lodge, and Friendship, each targeting different areas of the budget and economy market. As reported in the *Wall Street Journal,* Robert Hazard referred to this segmenting approach as "seven ways to make more money." For a time, Quality became the leading hotel chain in the world. However, the segmenting concept also proved successful for other hotel chains, and Quality lost its lead to Hospitality Franchise Systems, Inc., which operated Howard Johnsons and Days Inn among its six chains.

The 1980s saw further international expansion. In 1985 Quality purchased a majority share in England's Prince of Wales Hotels, PLC, although it would sell its stake again two years later. This purchase, however, gave Quality a base from which to expand into the rest of Europe, and, by the end of 1986, Quality was represented in the United Kingdom, Belgium, Germany, Italy, and Switzerland, as well as in New Zealand, Mexico, and Canada. As the 1980s drew to a close, Quality had moved into Ireland, France, and India, and had instituted its Quality Suites, Comfort Suites, and Sleep Inn lines. Also developed during this time was the Clarion Hotels and Resorts line, begun as a chain of 37 resorts in a joint venture with the Associated Inns and Restaurants Company of America. Purchases in 1990 included the 148-motel Rodeway Inns International chain for $15 million, as well as the 615-motel Econo Lodges of America and 85-unit Friendship Inn chains for $60 million, completing the company's seven-brand marketing strategy.

In order to reflect its new diversity, Quality Inns International changed its name to Choice Hotels International in 1990. In exchange for a percentage of gross room revenue, Choice franchisees were linked to Choice's reservation system, which comprised 23 reservation centers worldwide. Customer calls, including those from travel agents and airlines, were routed through a toll-free number; operators then guided customers to one of the seven brand names. Franchisees further benefited from the national advertising provided by Choice, and by the company's quarterly quality inspections, which helped to maintain a reputation for quality and consistency throughout the chain. Choice also began assisting franchisees in acquiring financing and in construction. In addition, Choice began offering incentive programs to franchisee employees, including health care programs, in an effort to attract new employees and reduce turnover. These programs were instituted in part as a result of a dispute with the Immigration and Naturalization Service, which had alleged that some Quality motels had employed undocumented workers, underlining the shortage of available personnel.

The U.S. growth of Choice slowed somewhat, along with the hotel industry as a whole, when overbuilding, coupled with the economic recession of the early 1990s, forced many hotels throughout the industry to close. During this time, as much as one-third of Choice's hotels were losing money, and several filed for bankruptcy. Choice's aggressive sales techniques were also criticized by some of its franchisees, who charged Choice with oversaturating the market by building one Choice brand next to another. Choice defended itself by pointing out that each brand appealed to a different market segment, and thus, different customers. Such charges, which extended into other franchise businesses, prompted calls for legislation to control the franchise industry.

By 1992 Choice's five economy brands had captured 25 percent of the U.S. economy hotel market, and the company had grown to include 2,800 franchises and 12 company-owned hotels. By that year, Choice was also represented by 350 international hotels. As the growth of the hotel market in the U.S. market slowed, Choice increased its international expansion efforts. In 1993 Choice bought the failing Inovest, a large French chain of economy hotels, increasing its holdings with 144 French motels and 19 motels in six other European countries. In that same year, Choice began a joint venture with the largest Canadian motel chain, Journey's End Corporation, with 120 properties. Joint ventures provided Choice with established properties as it increased its international efforts, and deals were announced with Friendly Hotels PLC of England, and Eco Hotels of Italy, among others. Partnerships in Mexico and Singapore added another 60 hotels to the Choice chain. During the 1990s, Choice expanded into South America and the former Soviet Union, and began plans to expand into China as well.

In early 1995 Hazard and Petitt were promoted to Manor Care's board of directors, and Don Landry was appointed as CEO and president of Choice. Landry, who had been president of Manor Care's hotel division, oversaw the consolidation of that division with Choice International. While Choice's past emphasis had been on increasing its number of franchises, forecasting as many as 10,000 hotels by the year 2000, a refocusing of Choice's mission for the future was, as Landry told *Lodging Hospitality,* "to be the market leader serving those who serve travelers."

The new focus of the company looked forward to creating new relationships with travel agents and other travel industry businesses. Partnerships were developed with food service companies, bringing such partners as Pizza Hut, Metromedia Steakhouses, and Oh la la! into Choice hotels, providing added

service without raising licensing fees. Differentiating the Choice product line, so that each brand represented a clear and separate market, became more important than simply increasing the number of hotels in the Choice chain. A reengineering of its brands, as well as the phasing out of the Friendship brand, were part of an effort to heighten awareness of each brand. In 1995 Choice combined customer satisfaction ratings with quality-inspection scores for the first time, arriving at a new minimum standard for its franchisees. Also in 1995, Choice initiated its own World Wide Web home page, becoming the first major hotel chain to offer real-time room rates and reservations through the Internet. Plans were made to add 200 hotels in China and another 200 hotels in South America over the next two decades. Preparing to enter the next century, Choice showed no sign of slowing down.

Further Reading:

Callan, Kathleen, ed., "A Sleeping Giant," *Success,* November 1994.
"Choice Eyes Ex-Soviet Republics for Expansion," *Travel Weekly,* September 22, 1994, p. E14.
"Choice Hotels Continues to Pursue Expansion Overseas," *Travel Weekly,* October 12, 1992, p. 70.
"Choice Hotels' Web Site Posting Affords Direct Res Access," *Travel Weekly,* June 22, 1995, p. 27.
Dahl, Jonathan, "Kings of the Road," *Wall Street Journal,* November 28, 1994, p. A1.
Diamond, Kerry, "A Clearer Picture," *Travel Agent,* May 22, 1995.
Eardley, S., "Momentum Builds for Choice's Europe Growth," *Hotel and Motel Management,* April 5, 1993, p. 1.
Gatty, B., "Choice Takes Bullish Approach," *Hotel and Motel Management,* March 9, 1992, p.1.
Hasek, G., "Alliances Spur Choice Expansion," *Hotel and Motel Management,* November 21, 1994, p. 3.
——, "Choice Deals Could Add 400 Hotels," *Hotel and Motel Management,* April 3, 1995, p. 1.
——, "Choice Unveils Radical Plans," *Hotel and Motel Management,* April 24, 1995, p. 1.
Lincoln, L., "Choice Targets Mid-Market Niche in Thailand Expansion," *Travel Weekly,* May 17, 1993, p. 62.
MacDonald, J., "Linking Together," *Hotel and Motel Management,* May 9, 1994, p. 14.
McDowell, Edwin, "Innkeeper Expands in Europe," *New York Times,* June 12, 1993, p. L37.
"Now's the Time to Think Globally," *Lodging Hospitality,* March 1993, p. 18.
Prakash, Snigdha, "Looking Abroad for Hotel Expansion," *Washington Post,* October 19, 1992, p. B6.
Rowe, Megan, "Choice Chooses Change," *Lodging Hospitality,* May 1995.
Thomas, C., "Cutting Costs in Comfort," *Hotel and Motel Management,* March 22, 1993, p. 39.
Wolchuk, S., "How Choice Uses Franchising to Grow Worldwide," *Hotels,* April 1992, p. 52.

—M. L. Cohen

The Chubb Corporation

15 Mountain View Road
Warren, New Jersey 07061
U.S.A.
(908) 903-2000
Fax: (908) 580-3430

Public Company
Incorporated: 1882 as Chubb & Son
Employees: 10,000
Sales: $5.7 billion
Stock Exchanges: New York
SICs: 6231 Security and Commodity Exchanges; 6311 Life
    Insurance; 6324 Hospital and Medical Service Plans; 6331
    Fire, Marine and Casualty Insurance; 6552 Subdividers
    and Developers, Not Elsewhere Classified; 6719 Holding
    Companies, Not Elsewhere Classified; 8748 Business
    Consulting Services, Not Elsewhere Classified

The Chubb Corporation operates as a holding company for an
internationally diversified group of companies whose core business is in commercial, personal property, casualty, health, and
life insurance. The company has further diversified since its
founding with the addition of real estate development, consulting, and financial subsidiaries. Chubb is best known as a provider of specialty insurance policies for upscale clients, including both individuals and organizations. In the mid-1990s, the
company was the fourth largest insurer in the United States and
among the top fifteen worldwide. Consistently a top performer
in the industry, Chubb moved into the late 1990s with a reputation as a reliable and prestigious insurer.

Chubb was formed over a century ago with the partnership of
Chubb & Son, a New York underwriter of cargo and ship
insurance formed by Thomas Chubb and his son, Percy Chubb,
in 1882. The venture was initially funded with $100,000 col-
lected in $1,000 portions from each of 100 prominent mer-
chants. Soon after its formation, Chubb & Son was one of the
100 founders of the New York Marine Underwriters (NYMU).
Chubb first operated as a representative of NYMU and Sea
Insurance Company Limited of England. In 1901 NYMU,
Chubb's principal property and casualty affiliate, was reorganized as Federal Insurance Company.

During its first 40 years of business, Chubb & Son grew
quickly, acting as an agent for several insurers. The company
established itself as a respected underwriter of insurance for

ships and cargo. During the 1920s the company explored new
areas. In 1921 Chubb & Son began to represent U.S. Guarantee
Company. Through that company, Chubb began to underwrite
fidelity, surety, and casualty insurance. In 1923 Chubb opened
its first branch, in Chicago. In March 1929 Chubb and another
transportation insurance agent, the Marine Office of America,
organized Associated Aviation Underwriters, the largest aviation insurance-underwriting group in the United States. Seven
companies represented by Chubb and eight insurers represented
by the Marine Office joined to form the association. During the
Depression Chubb's growth slowed as the insurance industry
suffered. Nevertheless, in April 1930 Chubb & Son bought a
9,000-square-foot plot in Manhattan to house its companies and
allow room for expansion. In 1939 Chubb founded Vigilant
Insurance Company, a wholly owned fire and marine subsidiary. During World War II the economy recovered and Chubb &
Son's business began to grow more quickly.

In December 1941 Chubb gave employees with more than six
months of service their first Christmas bonuses. The workers
each received half of their bonus in cash and half in war bonds.
Also in December 1941, Chairman Charles A. Seibert, a 55-
year veteran of the company, announced his retirement.

Chubb's growth continued apace. The company acquired The
Colonial Life Insurance Company of America in 1957, and in
1959 Chubb & Son reincorporated under the laws of New York.
In 1967 the company's management formed The Chubb Corporation to act as a holding company. Chubb & Son became a
wholly owned subsidiary of The Chubb Corporation, as did
Chubb & Son's subsidiaries. The property and casualty companies within the Chubb group of insurance companies fell under
the management of Chubb & Son, the branch responsible for the
company's domestic property and casualty insurance companies and U.S. branches of foreign insurers. The primary property and casualty insurance company managed by Chubb & Son
remains Federal Insurance Company.

The Chubb Corporation saw many changes in the late 1960s. In
July 1967 Chubb acquired Pacific Indemnity Corporation of
Los Angeles. In November 1967 Pacific Indemnity president
and chief executive officer Carl Fisher was elected senior vice-
president and director of Chubb. In January 1969, First National
City Corporation—now Citicorp—agreed to acquire The
Chubb Corporation. In April 1969, however, the two corporations confirmed that the Department of Justice was examining
the antitrust implications of the merger. Later that month, the
two companies agreed to postpone the merger until the summer
of 1969 in order to allow the Department of Justice to complete
its study of the transaction. On June 13, 1969, the Department of
Justice announced its intention to bring suit to bar the acquisition. Three hours later First National City Corporation canceled
the planned merger.

In September 1969 William M. Rees, then president of The
Chubb Corporation, was elected chief executive officer, and
became responsible for all operations excluding investment.
Investment responsibilities and general corporate policy and
development remained with Chairman Percy Chubb II.

In 1970 Chubb acquired Bellemead Development Corporation,
a Delaware real estate company with land holdings primarily in
New Jersey and Florida. This acquisition was Chubb's first

major move into the real estate field. Chubb confirmed that its real estate consultants placed a value of more than $25 million on Bellemead's properties if sold individually on the open market.

In 1971 Chubb acquired United Life & Accident Insurance Company and founded Chubb Custom Market. Chubb Custom Market became involved heavily in the entertainment industry. The subsidiary specializes in insurance for the film industry and has insured such movies as *E.T. The Extra-Terrestrial, Tootsie, The Verdict,* and *Missing.* When Dustin Hoffman developed laryngitis and was unable to perform for three days during the filming of *Tootsie,* Chubb covered the additional expense. In addition to insuring films, Chubb Custom Market provides entertainment coverage for television productions, special entertainment events, and Broadway shows. In 1983 Chubb insured 75 percent of the productions on Broadway. Chubb's coverage was popular because of its comprehensive nature, which included theft, injuries, and equipment failure.

On June 9, 1971, American Financial Corporation, a Cincinnati, Ohio-based financial holding company, sold 875,000 shares of Chubb stock to Salomon Brothers in a transaction valued at more than $54 million. American Financial had begun to acquire the stock in 1969 and had planned to attempt a buyout of Chubb. Salomon Brothers resold the shares, which represented a 14 percent stake in Chubb, to the public later in the day. In 1973 Chubb, through the international division of Chubb & Son, joined First National City Corporation's subsidiary, FNC Comercio, in buying a majority interest in Companhia de Seguros Argos Fluminense, a Brazilian multiple-line insurance company.

The Chubb Corporation formed Chubb Life Insurance Company of America in 1978 to serve as an intermediate holding company for life insurance subsidiaries. In 1981 the company began to consolidate the activities of The Colonial Life Insurance Company of America and United Life & Accident Insurance Company at Chubb Life's headquarters in Concord, New Hampshire. This consolidation was completed in 1984.

In 1983 The Chubb Corporation completed and relocated to a new head office on 185 acres in Warren, New Jersey. The following year, Chubb focused its efforts on growth in its international division. The company sought to increase its international property and casualty insurance business and to expand its worldwide coverage for U.S. multinationals. The company's strategy for distinguishing itself was not to offer universal contracts or preformulated programs, but instead to create policies tailored to meet the needs of its clients. Chubb set a goal of maintaining 20 percent annual growth of its international business. Also in 1984, Chubb acquired Volunteer State Life Insurance Company of Chattanooga, Tennessee, and discontinued its money-losing medical-malpractice insurance policies.

During the summer of 1987 a nine-person delegation from the People's Republic of China spent two days at the company's Warren, New Jersey headquarters. The company's relations with China dated to before World War II, when Chubb owned and operated the Cathay Insurance Company. The delegation, consisting of government officials and representatives from the People's Insurance Company of China, studied Chubb's safety and loss control problems. Also in 1987, Chubb acquired Sover-

eign Corporation, a life insurance holding company. Profits were significantly lower that year due to higher catastrophe losses from the Chicago rainstorms, Edmonton tornadoes, and a hurricane in Bermuda.

Through a New York firm called Good Weather International Incorporated, Chubb began advertising rain insurance in ten states in May 1988. Drought insurance was also offered to midwestern farmers by the Chubb subsidiary, Federal Insurance. Chubb usually reserved the authority to approve each policy that its independent agents sold, but in this case Good Weather was given the authority to approve Chubb policies. Because rain insurance was a small part of Chubb's business— Chubb issued $5 million of coverage to approximately 200 farmers in 1987—the company set a total limit of $30 million of coverage. Response was moderate until early June, when lack of rain threatened farmers with the most serious drought in over 50 years. On June 14 and June 15, 1988, Good Weather received over 6,600 applications seeking $275 million worth of coverage, and applications kept coming after the deadline. While farmers worried about the drought, Good Weather and Chubb worried about the flood of applications. The figures were not totaled until the end of June. In the confusion, agents had signed up at least $350 million of coverage for nearly 9,000 farmers. The drought continued, and on July 15 Chubb notified 7,616 farmers that they had been denied coverage. In a goodwill effort, Chubb offered to return double the original premiums to farmers who had applied on June 14 or 15. The effort was unsuccessful, and by 1991 many lawsuits filed by these farmers remained unresolved. After this experience, Chubb decided to discontinue drought insurance.

In July 1988, Dean R. O'Hare, chairman and chief executive officer of The Chubb Corporation and Federal Insurance Company since May, was elected chairman and chief executive officer of Chubb & Son. In August 1988 Chubb agreed to let American National General Agencies Incorporated (ANGA) take over its entertainment insurance underwriting responsibilities on the East Coast. Headquartered in Los Angeles as a wholesale entertainment insurance broker, ANGA branched into New York to assume the underwriting function for production risks through Chubb Custom Market.

In 1989 Chubb took great measures to reestablish a positive corporate image. This time, its efforts were successful, and 1989 was a good year for the company overall. In April 1989 Chubb Life Insurance of America joined The Geese Theatre Company, a non-profit touring theater group working exclusively in prisons, in establishing a theater residency program in Concord, New Hampshire. Chubb generated more good press later that year when it won the Insurance Marketing Communications Association Special Award from members. The competition was mounted to recognize and award superior marketing communications work in the property and casualty industry.

Hurricane Hugo and the California earthquake had a significant impact on Chubb's 1989 domestic earnings. Although earnings still increased, the catastrophes took a substantial bite out of profits. International operations continued to contribute greatly to the company's financial success, and revenues from international operations that year approached $500 million, about 12.5 percent of the year's $4 billion total. Chubb worked to increase its international activities and set a goal of generating 25 percent of total revenue from international operations by the year 2000.

The softening of the property and casualty insurance market in the early 1990s affected Chubb less than some of its competitors. The company's focus on specialty products helped Chubb outperform the industry through those years. Chubb had showed great improvement in life and health insurance during 1989 and anticipated that earnings would continue to increase as group health operating conditions improved. At $4.2 billion, earnings for 1990 reached a new high, setting the company's fifth consecutive year of record earnings. The success was attributed to conservative underwriting, a large network of branch offices (71 with plans to open 4 more), and a solid balance sheet. With the failure of many large financial institutions shaking public confidence in the late 1980s, a clear ability to cover liabilities with liquid assets became essential to maintaining a reliable reputation; Chubb fulfilled this requirement well.

At the same time, a downturn in the economy and unfavorable regulatory conditions began to reveal potential vulnerabilities in Chubb's real estate and commercial insurance businesses. Commercial overbuilding in the 1980s glutted the market, and regulatory scrutiny following the Savings and Loan bank failures led banks to curtail real estate lending. Unable to counteract these changes, Chubb's real estate holdings and development ventures began to lose money. Chubb said in its 1990 annual report that it saw these market conditions as more than a cyclical downturn and that it would begin to view real estate holdings as long-term investments. The company predicted that conditions in the real estate market would even worsen as companies economized on space as a result of consolidating and downsizing their operations. In fact, Chubb reported a steady decline in net income from real estate after 1989 and a loss of about $2 million a year in 1993 and 1994.

Potential changes in regulations in the environmental and health care arenas from the administration of President Clinton and from state legislatures presented challenges for Chubb and the insurance industry in general. On the environmental side, uncertainties relating to toxic waste and asbestos claims made on policies written decades earlier posed an increasingly larger threat to profitability. Chubb began to lobby actively for regulatory reform, hoping to narrow the widening judicial interpretations of such regulations as Superfund toxic waste clean-up rules. In 1994, Chubb settled its most costly asbestos exposure from an insurance policy issued in 1956 to Fibreboard Corporation by Pacific Indemnity Corporation, a subsidiary of Chubb. Pacific Indemnity entered into a global settlement agreement in 1993 that set up a $1.525 billion trust for future claims and to which Pacific Indemnity would contribute $538 million, the rest to come from Continental Casualty Company. The agreement was pending court approval at the end of 1994.

New legislation in New York and New Jersey significantly changed the way the company would handle health insurance in that region. The legislation created community-based rating and limited restrictions on pre-existing conditions. Whereas other insurers left that market, Chubb restructured its offerings, encouraging clients to move to managed health care policies, and remained effective in the region, which accounted for 80 percent of Chubb's group health business.

In the mid-1990s Chubb increased its international expansion and accelerated the growth of its domestic network. The company's London branch, at the center of the world insurance market, had doubled in size since its formation in the early 1980s. In 1993, Chubb added offices in Birmingham, Reading, and Manchester to take advantage of profitable opportunities in more local business. When the company determined that London lacked the service-oriented insurance products required for that city's growing affluent population, personal insurance—which represents 23 percent of Chubb's total business—was highlighted. In Germany, the new opportunities created by the formation of the European Community and the deregulation of the European insurance industry led Chubb to promote its commercial lines. As a commercial powerhouse, Germany provided an attractive new market for foreign insurers. In 1993, Chubb opened five more offices in new locations: Des Moines, Iowa; Buffalo, New York; Miami; Vancouver; and Hamilton, Bermuda.

In 1994, premiums from international business passed 20 percent of the total, approaching the goal of 25 percent for the year 2000. Offices were opened in Beijing, Hamburg, Munich, London, and Glasgow. In the United States, Chubb opened a new office in Fresno, California. By 1995, the company had grown from 20 domestic branches in 1965 to 89 branches worldwide. The company estimated hiring 1,300 new underwriters a year for the next five years. Some analysts questioned if the quality of operations could be maintained at such a high growth rate in a soft market. By choosing markets and products carefully, Chubb felt it was well positioned to compete in the new global marketplace.

Principal Subsidiaries: Bellemead Development Corporation; Chubb & Son Inc.; Chubb Capital Corporation; Chubb Custom Insurance Company; Chubb de Colombia Compania de Seguros, S.A.; Chubb de Chile de Seguros Generales, S.A.; Chubb de Mexico, Compania Afianzadora, S.A. de S.V.; Chubb Indemnity Insurance Company; Chubb Insurance Company of Australia, Limited; Chubb Insurance Company of Canada; Chubb Insurance Company of Europe, S.A. (Belgium); Chubb Life Insurance Company of America; Chubb Securities Corporation; Chubb Services Corporation; The Colonial Life Insurance Company of America; Federal Insurance Company; Great Northern Insurance Company; Pacific Indemnity Company; Personal Lines Insurance Brokerage, Inc.; Vigilant Insurance Company.

Further Reading:

"Chubb Corporation: It's an Ill, Dry Wind," *Economist,* September 3, 1988, p. 76.
Fefer, Mark D., "Chubb: How to Win in a Land of Losers," *Fortune,* August 23, 1993, p. 80.
Hutton, Cynthia, "How Chubb Got Soaked on Drought Insurance," *Fortune,* September 12, 1988, p. 10.
Kirk, Don, "Germany Imports New Style Market," *Business Insurance,* November 7, 1994, p. 35.
Liscio, John, "Chubb Corp.," *Barron's,* December 28, 1987, pp. 33–34.
Mack, Gracian, "At the Top of His Game," *Black Enterprise,* March 1995, pp. 84–87.
Moreau, Dan, "Chubb Thinks Small, But All Its Little Pieces Add Up," *Kiplinger's,* May 1995, pp. 38–40.

—Leslie C. Halpern
updated by Katherine Smethurst

CIANBRO

Cianbro Corporation

P.O. Box 1000
Hunnewell Square
Pittsfield, Maine 04967
U.S.A.
(207) 487-3311
Fax: (207) 487-3734

Private Company
Incorporated: 1949
Operating Revenues: $150 million
Employees: 1,500
SICs: 1622 Bridge Tunnel Elevated Highway Construction;
    1611 Highway and Street Construction

Although Cianbro Corporation is one of the smaller construction firms in the United States, its influence on trends within the industry has been significant. The company focuses primarily on bridge and elevated highway construction projects, as well as civil, mechanical, piping, and electrical and instrumentation heavy industrial projects. Specifically, Cianbro projects have included the Piscataqua River Bridge between New Hampshire and Maine; the Great Bridge Bypass in Chesapeake, Virginia; the recycled fiber facility at Bowater in Maine; and the paper machine and groundwood mill at Madison Paper in Maine. Cianbro is also proud of its employee-management relations and its unique open-shop, non-union philosophy. Most companies with open shops are regarded with suspicion for their union-busting image, but Cianbro management tries to avoid conflicts with organized labor by promoting rigorous safety practices and by reducing employee exposure to stressful job conditions. This efficient worker-management relationship has contributed to the company's reputation for completing projects on time and under budget.

The foundation for Cianbro Corporation was laid by Ralph Cianchette during the 1930s. Cianchette opened a bridge building firm in Pittsfield, Maine, in the mid-1930s, and contracted most of his projects within the immediate region. Cianchette's four sons each started working at the firm as soon as they reached the age of 15. The company grew steadily but slowly until the start of World War II, when all of Cianchette's production crew, including his sons, were drafted into the U.S. military forces. Unfortunately, this unexpected interruption came in the middle of a major construction project, a bridge at Kittery Point,

Maine. Cianchette's disappointment was exacerbated by the fact that he had to finish the bridge at the price set before the onset of the war with almost no crew and with materials that were impossible to procure because of the government's strict rationing policy. He finally completed the bridge in 1943, but closed shop immediately afterwards and became Somerset County's deputy sheriff.

After World War II, the oldest of the Cianchette brothers, Carl, decided to revive his father's construction business. From his father he purchased a six-inch pump, a two-bag cement mixer, and some wheelbarrows. He also bought an army trailer and a Willys jeep that had been adapted for civilian use. Carl's first project, the Pittsfield Woolen Yarn building, was completed in 1946 for a total of $8,000. With Carl as sole owner of the company, sales for 1946 totaled $46,000. As the company grew during the next few years, brothers Ken, Ival, and Chuck became involved in its operations, and in late 1949 the four men incorporated their construction firm as Cianchette Brothers, Inc.

By 1950 company revenues jumped to approximately $200,000. The onset of the Korean War, which caused a massive buildup in the United States military, also brought a contract for the Cianchette Brothers to expand the facilities at Loring Air Force Base. After the Loring Air Base project was completed in 1951, the company then signed contracts with the state of Maine to build bridges and highways. In 1955 the company reported for the first time that sales had surpassed the $1 million mark, but it was during the late 1950s that Cianchette Brothers made even more significant strides in its development.

In 1958 the company acquired a machine shop located in Pittsfield which one of the brothers, Ken, turned into a veritable construction design house. A talented designer with a liberal dose of imagination, Ken Cianchette designed the well-known Chinbro Beam Clamp. This product, which was also patented, was used especially for heavy bridge steel. Another product he designed and patented at this time was the Chinbro Pipe Grab, which was used in handling all types of sewer and water pipes.

Even armed with these innovative designs, however, the company did not make large profits. The brothers soon discovered that Japanese companies, which had initially purchased the pipe grab in large quantities, came up with a production technique that allowed them to copy it for much less money than it cost to import the product. The brothers also recognized that the demand for beam clamps was less than they anticipated. Consequently, although these new products significantly affected the construction industry, the brothers were extremely disappointed that their innovations did not result in greater revenues.

To compensate for these unfulfilled expectations, the brothers decided to enter the ready-mix concrete business. Locating their new operation in Pittsfield, the company purchased a number of concrete mixers and a homemade batch plant, and began marketing their new service to customers. The new ready-mix concrete venture began to thrive from the very beginning and helped increase company revenues to $1.5 million by 1960.

Business operations grew slowly during the early years of the 1960s, and company revenues amounted to a little over $3 million by the middle of the decade. Many of the company's projects at this time involved cleaning rivers and streams. In

1967, the company acquired the E.C. Snodgrass Company of Portland, Maine, which provided Cianchette Brothers with highly trained personnel capable of helping Cianchette Brothers gain a larger share of the heavy industrial market. The acquisition also brought a number of projects that Snodgrass had not yet completed at the S.D. Warren paper mill in Westbrook, Maine, and led to the development of a comprehensive paper mill construction service.

In 1969 the company made another important acquisition—Hornbrook, Inc., based in Madawaska, Maine. The purchases of Hornbrook, a small road-building firm, and Snodgrass gave Cianchette Brothers a statewide presence. With most of its contracts in Maine, and a few in Vermont and New Hampshire, the company's sales jumped to $18 million by the end of the decade.

The company changed its name to Cianbro Corporation in the early 1970s, a decade that marked some of the company's best years. It finished work on one of its largest projects, the Piscataqua River Bridge situated between Kittery, Maine, and Portsmouth, New Hampshire. Other major projects completed during this period included the natural gas pipeline for Northern Utilities Company and the giant crane at the Bath Iron Works. The crane, operating on a base constructed by Cianbro Corporation, was reported to be the largest ever used in the Western Hemisphere.

All of the projects completed in the early 1970s were done under budget and sooner than anticipated. The company also added various acquisitions to augment its growing ready-mix concrete business, including the purchase of C.M. Page of Orono, Maine, in 1972; R.K. Brown of North Waterford in 1973; and Foster Sand & Gravel of Farmington in 1974. The company was so successful in the management of its projects and the expansion of its ready-mix concrete operations that the recession of the early 1970s hardly affected its revenues. Sales shot up to $32 million by the end of fiscal 1975, and reached $70 million by 1980.

One of the important elements that contributed to Cianbro's success was the emphasis the company placed on management-employee relations. To attract qualified personnel and encourage worker commitment to the firm, management made it a priority to arrange an attractive package of financial rewards. In 1965 the company established a profit sharing plan for employees who met the eligibility requirements. Cianbro's contribution to this plan in the first year of its existence was $30,000. Throughout the late 1960s and early 1970s, the company continued its contributions to the plan. In 1977 management decided to create a stock ownership trust that would allow eligible employees to purchase Cianbro stock. In 1981 the company made a $5 million contribution both to the profit sharing plan and to the stock ownership trust. By 1985 employees owned over 40 percent of the company's stock.

By 1981 Cianbro's sales increased to just over $100 million. During the same year, the company finished its two largest projects undertaken in Maine up to that time. The first project, the construction of a paper mill contracted by Madison Paper Industries of Madison, Maine, was completed under budget and ahead of schedule. The second project involved the construction

of a bio-mass boiler at the paper mill of S.D. Warren Company in Westbrook, Maine. Like the work at Madison Paper Industries, this project was also completed ahead of schedule and under budget.

Unfortunately, by the mid-1980s, the company was rocked by a recession in the construction industry. As new construction projects within the state of Maine became harder to procure, management at Cianbro made the decision to expand into other geographical regions. The company's first acquisition was a site development contracting company located in Tampa, Florida. By 1985 the firm's Florida operation had contracts worth over $20 million, and the prospects for future growth in the state looked very promising. A second acquisition, the N.C. Monroe Construction Company, was made at approximately the same time. Monroe Construction, situated in Greensboro, North Carolina, was involved in constructing commercial and high-rise buildings. The acquisition gave Cianbro access to a concrete building frame system, used primarily for apartment buildings, which was patented and licensed nationwide. The purchase of Monroe Construction also helped Cianbro expand its influence into North and South Carolina and into the state of Texas (with a focus on apartment buildings).

As the recession eased its grip on construction activities in Maine, Cianbro was able to win new contracts. Projects involving paper mill facilities and bridge building were the most plentiful, while a rather unusual project called for the company to reconstruct a dam for the Central Maine Power Company. Having learned a hard lesson about diversification, however, management was not about to cut back its efforts to expand into other states. Consequently, new projects outside Maine remained one of management's priorities. In the mid-1980s, Cianbro was engaged in a wide range of work, including maintenance and construction at a power plant in Maine, rebuilding a food processing facility in New Hampshire, finishing hydro-electrical construction projects in Vermont and New York, building a large warehouse in Connecticut, replacing a bridge in Maryland, resurfacing the Woodrow Wilson Bridge in Virginia, constructing a flood control dam in Florida, and completing a comprehensive $25 million water treatment project for the district of Washington, D.C.

During the late 1980s and early 1990s, Cianbro continued to expand its construction operations in the Northeast and Mid-Atlantic regions of the United States. In addition, the company entered into some rather unique arrangements in order to maintain its profitability. Ranging far from the field of construction building and management, the company entered into a joint venture with E.C. Jordan Company and D.W. Small & Sons. Under the agreement, Cianbro management planned to produce 25 million gallons of ethanol for use in gasoline as an octane enhancer. Although this project initially showed great promise, it did not generate the kind of revenues Cianbro expected.

A second project, even more far ranging than the first, was the development of the Martian Bigfoot, the biggest sphagnum peat moss harvesting machine ever made. The machine, designed by Ken Cianchette, was manufactured at the company's fabrication shop in Pittsfield, Maine. Fifteen times larger than any other comparable machine, the Martian Bigfoot possessed an enormous harvesting capacity—approximately 500 cubic yards of peat in one sweep. The machine was used primarily in Russia by entrepreneurial farmers.

Cianbro Corporation also made significant strides during the early 1990s in a comprehensive improvement of its administrative capabilities and organizational structure. The company installed a Computer Project Management Cost Control and Scheduling System (CIPREC), a highly sophisticated, state-of-the-art program created by IBM that incorporated all the latest developments in cost control mechanisms and project scheduling. This program, designed to combine systems by Systonetics and Cal Comp with those of Cianbro, allowed the company to provide it as a service to its customers.

By 1995, Alton E. Cianchette, the son of one of the founding brothers, had assumed the position of chief executive officer of the company, while Chuck Cianchette remained company chairman. Although the leadership of Cianbro was being passed from one generation to the next, the continuity in strategy and employee relations remains intact. For this reason alone, Cianbro Corporation's future is full of promise.

Principal Subsidiaries: Cianbro Realty Corporation; N.C. Monroe Construction Company.

Further Reading:

Brown, James P., "The Amazing Brothers Cianchette," *Down East: The Magazine of Maine,* 1984, pp. 74–120.
Cianchette, Ival R., *Cianbro,* New York: Newcomen Society, 1983.
Cohn, D'Vera, "Metro Road Project Halted By Complaint of Pollution," *Washington Post,* May 11, 1994, p. B2.
Korman, Richard, "Cianbro Puts Worker On a High Moral Plane," *Engineering News Record,* November 28, 1994, pp. 24–27.
Rosta, Paul, "Calamities Have Little Cost Impact," *Engineering News Record,* June 27, 1994, pp. 34–38.
Stewart, Larry, "Finding People To Fix And Run The Machines," *Construction Equipment,* July 1994, pp. 36–42.

—Thomas Derdak

CMS ENERGY

CMS Energy Corporation

330 Town Center Drive, #1100
Dearborn, Michigan 48126
U.S.A.
(313) 436-9200
Fax: (313) 441-0402

Public Company
Incorporated: 1987
Sales: $4 billion
Employees: 10,013
Stock Exchanges: New York
SICs: 4911 Electric Services; 4923 Gas Transmission and
  Distribution; 1311 Crude Petroleum and Natural Gas; 6719
  Holding Companies

CMS Energy Corporation is a diversified energy company with businesses engaged in electric and gas utility operations. The company's primary subsidiary, Consumers Power Company, is Michigan's largest utility and the fourth largest gas and electric utility in the United States. In addition to its regulated utility business, CMS is one of the world's top independent power producers with ownership interests in 31 power plants on three continents. Through its subsidiary, CMS Nomeco, CMS is also a producer of oil and natural gas with over 1,000 active wells in eight countries.

CMS Energy's main subsidiary, Consumers Power Company, holds an important place in the history of the power industry in the United States. Founded in 1910 through a merger of a variety of gas, electric and electric trolley companies, Consumers Power was at the forefront of the development of the large utilities that marked the business world of the turn of the century. By the 1960s, Consumers Power had established itself as an old, dependable, solid utility company. As the largest utility in Michigan, the company had paid regular and substantial dividends for some 50 years.

Although when Consumers was founded, hydro power had been the main energy source in Michigan, by the 1950s coal-powered turbines were delivering 80 percent of the state's power. It was Consumers Power's efforts to develop alternate sources of electric power that would land the company on the verge of bankruptcy and would lead to the founding of CMS Energy. The period after World War II was one of optimism for American industry and science; nuclear power appeared poised to

become the pollution-free, cheap energy source of the future. Consumers Power was quick to jump on the nuclear bandwagon, building first an experimental nuclear plant at Big Rock, Michigan, and then the much larger commercial Palisades plant. In spite of technical difficulties in the operation of the Big Rock plant and serious cost overruns in the construction of Palisades, in 1970 Consumers embarked on the construction of a third nuclear reactor at Midland, Michigan. The Midland facility was originally scheduled to open in 1975 at a cost of about $500 million. Nine years and $3.5 billion later, Consumers Power pulled the plug on the still unfinished plant.

The Midland debacle plunged Consumers Power into a state of crisis. Stock prices plummeted from a high of $55 before Midland to only $5.00 a share in 1985. Income, which had already been dwindling, now fell to a net loss of $270 million. Financial analysts were suggesting that bankruptcy might be the most attractive option for the beleaguered utility. To make matters worse, Dow Chemical had made massive investments in the ill-fated plant in an agreement to buy excess steam to be used in its chemical processing. The giant chemical company was now suing Consumers Power, alleging mismanagement and a cover-up on the part of the utility. The Michigan Public Service Commission, the regulatory agency that oversees utility rates, authorized an emergency $99 million rate increase fearing that bankruptcy of Michigan's largest utility would wreak havoc with the already suffering Michigan economy. The commission was reluctant, however, to let rate payers bear the full burden of the Midland fiasco, and Consumers was faced with the need for massive reorganization to deal with its huge debt burden.

In 1985, Consumers Power hired William T. McCormick, Jr. to head the reorganization of the troubled company. McCormick, who held a doctorate in nuclear physics from MIT, had extensive experience dealing with regulators and politicians from years spent as a lobbyist in Washington. This experience would be crucial in the new CEO's handling of the Consumers Power reorganization.

McCormick's first move was to create a holding company for Consumers Power. In May 1987, shareholders of Consumers Power approved a reorganization plan in which shares of Consumers common stock were converted into shares of CMS Energy Corp. common stock, and Consumers Power became a subsidiary of the new energy company. The creation of CMS Energy offered several advantages to the utility. Charges of mismanagement had severely damaged the reputation of the 75-year-old firm, and McCormick felt that starting afresh with a new name and management team could only improve investor confidence. More importantly, the new energy corporation could expand into non-regulated energy related ventures without putting its regulated utility business at risk. McCormick moved quickly to cut costs and free up cash to retire preference stock and to refinance the company's crippling debt load. By 1987, the new management had succeeded in paying off or refinancing some $3 billion in debt, reducing CMS' fixed charges by $67 million.

It was McCormick's solution for the Midland plant fiasco that would prompt both the most plaudits and the most controversy for the newly born energy corporation. It was clear that it would be impossible to salvage the nuclear capacity of the project but even with the new cost cutting plan and rate hikes it would be equally unrealistic to expect to recover from the burden of taking the $3.6 billion loss that abandoning the project would entail. "Some people jumped all over us for suggesting anything other than abandoning the plant," McCormick stated in a 1988 article in *Forbes,* "but we projected we would need additional capacity by the early 1990s when we could get the cogeneration plant into operation, and everyone realized that it would be senseless to throw these usable assets away." Under McCormick's plan the non-nuclear facilities of the plant would be converted to a gas-fired 1,370 megawatt cogeneration plant, salvaging about $1.5 billion worth of existing facilities. Of course completing the conversion would cost an additional $500 million but McCormick had a solution for raising these funds.

McCormick managed to convince Dow Chemical that they should once more join forces and operate the new Midland project as a joint venture. The cogeneration plant would provide steam for Dow's processing needs and electricity to be sold to CMS' subsidiary, Consumers Power. Dow Chemical, along with a number of smaller companies with a vested interest in the survival of the plant, was to control 51 percent of the newly formed Midland Cogeneration Venture. CMS Energy, in turn, swapped $1.5 billion of abandoned Midland assets for a 49 percent interest in the cogeneration facility plus $1.2 billion in notes. CMS' equity in the venture was deliberately kept below 50 percent so that the the new power plant would be governed by the federal Public Utilities Regulatory Policy Act (PURPA), which gave independent power producers certain advantages in selling power to utilities provided they were not more than 50 percent-owned by a public utility. Under PURPA, public utilities were required to buy power from the independents for the avoided cost of producing this power by the utility itself, which would usually entail a higher price than would be attainable on the wholesale market. Part of the agreement between CMS and its Midland partners specified that Consumers would buy the bulk of Midland's power at this higher PURPA rate, thereby securing a market for the cogeneration project's energy. More importantly, McCormick planned to use the cash generated by the notes to fund CMS' investment in its non-regulated energy business.

By 1987, with reduced costs and the non-cash credits from Midland, CMS' earnings rebounded to $262 million. Investors, charmed by McCormick's innovative ideas and persuasive rhetoric, returned to the CMS fold and stock prices once again rose to almost $40 by 1989. But not everyone was happy with the new plans for Midland. Regulators who had already bailed out the company by agreeing to large rate hikes were angered that the cash from the Midland deal was to be used to grow CMS through diversification rather than to be passed on to subsidiary Consumers Power and its customers. CMS' use of PURPA to allow Consumers to pay higher-than-market rates for the cogeneration plant's energy also came under fire by the Michigan Public Service Commission, which would agree to let Consumers pass on the higher PURPA costs to its customers for only about half of the energy that Consumers had already agreed to buy from the Midland venture. To make matters worse, an industrial coalition calling itself ABATE was also determined to block the higher rates and appealed in federal

court to strip Midland of its qualification to operate under PURPA.

After seven years of lawsuits, countersuits, and appeals by CMS, its partners in the Midland Cogeneration Venture, ABATE, the Michigan Public Service Commission, and the Michigan Attorney General, many of the issues surrounding the Midland plant still remained unresolved. The Michigan Public Service Commission's limits on recoverable costs, as well as rulings reducing recoverable write-offs of the abandoned nuclear facilities at Midland, saw CMS posting substantial losses for three years in a row from 1990 through 1992. With shrunken dividends and an uncertain future investors once again shied away from CMS stock and share price dropped to only $15.

In 1993, CMS Energy finally reached an agreement with the Michigan Public Service Commission that would allow Consumers to recover from its rates 915 of the 1,240 megawatts of energy the company had agreed to buy annually from the Midland partnership. This compromise, although still under appeal by ABATE, finally allowed CMS to emerge from the Midland quagmire and to once again become a profitable enterprise. Record electric sales by Consumers, as well as a boom in foreign independent power production, boosted CMS' revenues to $3.6 billion in 1994. The resolution of a host of regulatory issues allowed net income to return to $179 million although this was still short of pre-1990 levels.

In spite of the troubles with the Midland venture, CMS Energy stuck to their plan of diversification, albeit at a slower pace than McCormick would have liked had the cash from Midland been forthcoming. Back in the 1960s, Consumers Power had created a subsidiary, the Nomeco Oil and Gas Company, to manage the development of oil and gas reserves needed to operate Consumers' utility business. With only eight employees, Nomeco was originally intended only to build domestic reserves of oil and gas for the company's use and was not envisioned as a revenue producer. As part of McCormick's new vision for the company, CMS expanded the mandate of this subsidiary to include significant independent production of oil and gas to be sold on the open market for immediate earnings. By the early 1990s the subsidiary had producing wells in the United States, Australia, Colombia, Equatorial Guinea, and New Zealand with proven reserves of 60 million net equivalent barrels and almost 100 employees. As the resolution of Midland related disputes began to free up cash in the mid-1990s, CMS was able to further expand its oil and gas production, acquiring four gas and oil production companies in Michigan, Africa and Colombia, and beginning production in the huge oilfields of Ecuador. By 1995 proven reserves had almost doubled to 113 million barrels, and revenue from Nomeco was close to $90 million.

In the late 1980s, CMS formed two subsidiaries, CMS Gas Marketing and CMS Gas Transmission and Storage, to take advantage of Consumers Power's expertise in gas procurement and handling. These service-based companies were one of the early successes of CMS' program of expansion, making a respectable $4 million in net income on revenues of $42 million by 1991. The opening of the Grands Lacs Market Center in St. Clair, Michigan, in 1994 was a important step for CMS as it would provide a major storage and exchange point for buyers and sellers through the United States and Canada. CMS' gas service companies would continue to contribute substantially to CMS' recovery in the mid-1990s, with revenues reaching $145 million by 1994.

One of McCormick's most ambitious plans for CMS Energy was the development of its independent power production business. McCormick believed that the power industry in the United States was moving inexorably towards less regulation and more competition, and he was determined to put CMS Energy at the forefront of this movement. A subsidiary, CMS Generation, was founded in 1986 with the aim of furthering the independent power production business. CMS' cash flow problems of the late 1980s and early 1990s severely restricted the growth of this business sector, however, as the heavy investment needed to acquire or build new plants was simply not available. To make matters worse, one of the few investments the new subsidiary was able to make was Oxford Energy Co., a tire burning power plant that went bankrupt in 1992, costing CMS $31 million. It was not until 1993 that CMS Generation was able to produce even modest revenues for its parent company, with its acquisition of a New York waste wood burning electricity plant as well as its first foreign plant in Argentina. It would be this foreign investment that would finally pay off for CMS' independent power unit.

Growth in the domestic independent power production sector was much slower than analysts like McCormick had predicted, with 1994 estimates coming in at only about one percent annually through the year 2020. International markets, however, surged in the mid-1990s. Many countries in Latin America, Asia, and Eastern Europe were faced with power shortages yet could not afford to expand and run their own generating systems. Governments began to look at large American and European power companies as potential partners in building their power infrastructures. With limited competition in these markets, returns on investment could be up to double those in the domestic power market.

In 1994, CMS entered this market on a large scale, founding new joint projects in Argentina, the Philippines, India, and Morocco. Revenues doubled from the previous year and, even more importantly, high rates of return meant that net income from these operations quadrupled from 1993. At $20 million,

this income represented the largest contribution to CMS' bottom line from the company's non-utility businesses. 1994 was also an important year on the domestic front for CMS Generation as they began the process of acquiring HYDRA-CO, the independent power subsidiary of Niagara Mohawk Power, although earnings from this acquisition would not be incorporated into CMS finances until the following year. The addition of HYDRA-CO's plants would bring CMS Generation's total number of U.S. plants to 25, making CMS one of the nation's top five independent power producers. In spite of the serious problems of the 1980s and early 1990s, by 1995 CMS seemed poised to emerge as an important player on the international energy scene.

Principal Subsidiaries: Consumers Power Co., NOMECO Oil & Gas Co., CMS Generation Co., CMS Gas Marketing, CMS Gas Transmission and Storage.

Further Reading:

Bush, George, *Future Builders: The Story of Michigan's Consumers Power Company,* New York: McGraw-Hill, 1973.
Cook, James, "So Near, But Maybe Not So Far," *Forbes,* September 19, 1988, pp. 128–130.
Egan, John, "Out of the Briar Patch," *Financial World,* October 29, 1991, p. 26.
Maher, Tani, "Power Games," *Financial World,* October 3, 1989, pp. 30–31.
Mitchell, Russell, "Dow and Consumers Power are Lovey-Dovey Again," *Business Week,* October 27, 1986, p. 90.
——, "The $4 Billion White Elephant on Bill McCormick's Back," *Business Week,* June 9, 1986, p. 64.
Norman, James R., "Reined In," *Forbes,* August 16, 1993, p. 70.
Tice, David W., "Less There Than Meets the Eye: A Hard Look at CMS Energy's Financials and Earnings," *Barron's,* October 16, 1989, pp. 15, 20–24.
——, "Risky Venture: A Utility's Cogeneration Project Still Has Woes Aplenty," *Barron's,* October 21, 1991, pp. 24, 38.
Whitman, Martin J., "Virtues of Bankruptcy: For Nuclear Utilities, There May be Many," *Barron's,* May 6, 1985, pp. 16–18, 43–45.
Woodruff, David, "Plugging into the Power Surge Abroad," *Business Week,* August 15, 1994, pp. 100, 102.

—Hilary Gopnik

Cobra Electronics Corporation

6500 West Cortland Street
Chicago, Illinois 60635
U.S.A.
(312) 889-8870
Fax: (312) 889-1678

Public Company
Incorporated: 1961 as Dynascan Inc.
Employees: 239
Sales: $82.1 million
Stock Exchanges: NASDAQ
SICs: 3661 Telephone and Telegraph Apparatus; 3825
  Instruments to Measure Electricity; 3663 Radio and TV
  Communications Equipment; 3651 Household Audio and
  Video Equipment

Cobra Electronics Corporation designs and markets consumer electronics products like cordless telephones, telephone answering machines, citizen band radios, and car stereos. Its products are built to specification by manufacturers in East Asia.

Cobra was founded as Dynascan in 1961 by electronics engineer Carl Korn, who served as president, and Samuel Horberg, who became chief financial officer. The two had worked together in the electronics field since 1947, and they had formed another company in 1954. Dynascan initially sold electronic testing equipment like oscilloscopes and television testing equipment. It soon added a limited range of remote-controlled materials handling tools under the brand name Telemotive. They were used to operate cranes used for mining, construction, and shipping.

The U.S. government delegated radio spectrum for a citizens band in 1958, and in 1963 Dynascan took advantage of the new market by bringing out its first citizens band radio. CBs were still an obscure medium, used by some hobbyists and truckers. Dynascan initially manufactured its own CB radios but switched to importing lower-priced models manufactured by two Japanese companies, Toshiba and Uniden, in 1971, around the time CBs became more popular with a wider public. Dynascan's Cobra brand CB radios caught on, propelling the company to sales from sales of $13.8 million in 1973 to sales of $102 million in 1976, with gross profits of $15 million.

Part of the popularity of CB radios proved to be a fad, however. And just as the fad was fading, the Federal Communications Commission abruptly increased the number of channels CBs could use to 40 from 23. Overnight, 23-channel CB radios became obsolete, and Dynascan was caught with a large inventory that no one wanted. A large number of other CB manufacturers suffered from the same conditions and several went out of business. But Dynascan sold its inventory through dealer promotions and could rely on earnings from its other equipment and tools to carry it through the crisis.

The firm moved to lessen its dependence on CBs. It introduced a line of sound products for cars that included speakers, amplifiers, stereos, and cartridge and cassette players. Dynascan's engineers designed these products after thorough market research. The products were then manufactured in East Asia. The firm's products had a good reputation and were considered a higher-quality option to lower-priced competing products like the Radio Shack and Realistic lines manufactured by Tandy. The firm sold its Cobra products via a two-step distribution network composed of 90 wholesale distributors who in turn sold to 10,000 local outlets. The Cobra line of audio products accounted for 74 percent of 1977 revenues; the other 26 percent came from the firm's industrial products.

In 1979 Dynascan introduced another important product: cordless telephones. Like CB radios, they were still something of a novelty item when the firm introduced them, but demand soon exploded. Dynascan aggressively sought market share for its Cobra telephones and earned $17 million in 1983 on sales of $173 million. In four years the firm's stock rose to 35 from 3.5, making it worth $165 million.

Once again the fad came to an end. Cordless telephone sales in the United States plunged from $850 million in 1983 to $325 million in 1984. Once again caught with a large inventory, Dynascan lost $31 million in 1984. The firm had to borrow large amounts of money to remain solvent. It postponed raises and froze hiring for six months.

As a result of these boom and bust cycles, Korn rethought the firm's priorities and decided to focus on merchandising rather than manufacturing. Because it imported products from Asian manufacturers, the company's investment lay in inventory and receivables rather than the high fixed costs of owning a factory. Korn forced out the firm's president, Frank DiLeo, and in April 1985 replaced him with Jerry Kalov, a turnaround specialist who was signed to a ten-year contract. Kalov had already saved the speaker company JBL Inc. in the 1970s as well as the stereo maker Jensen International Inc. Dynascan began a three-year plan geared toward profits rather than sales volume.

When another of its products caught on, this time the Cobra radar detector, Dynascan refused to overextend itself. Kalov was unwilling to invest too much of the firm's capital in inventory, even if it meant passing up some sales. Rather than emphasizing total sales, the firm' management began pushing all of its product lines, giving it a broader base and, it hoped, less vulnerability to business cycles. Cordless telephone sales began increasing again, and Cobra had become the leading brand of CB radio. The firm was also manufacturing telephone-answering machines and corded telephones. It ended its losses in 1985 and made a small profit the following year.

Dynascan began placing more emphasis on creating new products. In October 1986, it introduced a line a line of high-frequency radio scanners that enabled users to listen to radio bands used by the police. It also began producing some of its phones with decorator colors, responding to consumer demand for more choices. Neither of these introductions cost very much because they were extensions of existing products.

By the end of 1986, Dynascan had experienced seven consecutive quarters of stronger profits. It had $20 million of debt and working capital of $47 million. Feeling that it had successfully turned around its own consumer electronics operation, Dynascan decided to do the same for companies with similar businesses. In late 1986, it bought 51 percent of Marantz Co., a manufacturer of high-quality audio and video equipment based near Los Angeles, for about $15 million. Although its products were well known and respected, Marantz had lost $1.6 million in 1985 on sales of $50 million and hadn't made a profit in five years. Like Dynascan, Marantz ordered its products to specification from manufacturers in the Far East.

In 1987 and 1988, Dynascan worked to expand its lines of telephones and answering machines, feeling it had a tiny percentage of a huge market. The firm used an in-house sales staff but also used independent manufacturers' representatives to market its products to retail outlets like catalog showrooms and electronics stores. A line of precision test and measuring equipment was sold to electronics distributors for use by schools, electronic service technicians, and electronics firms. It monitored its suppliers via a subsidiary, Dynascan AK, and had buying offices in Hong Kong and Tokyo.

Continuing its attempts to expand, in 1988 Dynascan bought Lloyd's Electronics, a money-losing manufacturer of low-end clocks and portable stereos based in New Jersey.

With consumer electronics increasingly competitive, Dynascan began stressing its own research and development. Around 1985, the firm was spending about 1.5 percent of sales on R&D, or $2.18 million per year. The firm had not been known as an inventor, usually copying the technology of others and adding a few innovations. But in 1988, the firm introduced the first cordless answering machine, which proved popular with consumers and retailers. It then introduced the first cordless telephone that did not require an exterior antenna. Competitors asserted that the Intenna, which used a built-in antenna, would suffer from poor reception, but Dynascan initially had trouble meeting demand for the popular phone. With a price under $100, the Intenna also got Dynascan into the discount distribution network that its high-end cordless phones had prevented it from entering.

These successes were tempered by losses. Though 1988 sales rose 12 percent to $213.8 million, income fell ten percent to $7.2 million because Lloyd's and Marantz continued to lose money. Lloyd's proved difficult to turn around. For not much more money, consumers could buy name-brand products like Sony, and Lloyd's continued to be unprofitable. Dynascan introduced a new Marantz line in 1989 aimed at the high end of the market. Called Century, the new line won approval from the trade press, but, with some components costing over $1,000, it proved too expensive for Marantz's dealer base. As a result, Marantz continued to lose money. Finally, in October 1990, Dynascan announced it was selling Marantz to Dutch electronics conglomerate Philips N.V. for $8 million.

The early 1990s was a difficult time for Dynascan. Revenue shrunk, and the firm lost money four years in a row, losing $5.7 million in 1992 on sales of $117.7 million, for example. In 1992, Kalov became president, and he began cutting costs by shrinking the corporate staff by one-third and shutting down the firm's Tokyo office. He also moved the firm's products into corporate phone centers, the Fingerhut and Spiegel catalogs, and home shopping networks, which brought higher profit margins and fewer product returns. Many Cobra products, such as a cordless telephone that used a scrambler to give users privacy, required explanations to make consumers understand their benefits. Consumers did not receive such explanations while shopping in the aisles of discount stores, and so they either failed to buy the product or returned it later. In 1993, to emphasize its successful lines of Cobra products, the firm changed its name to Cobra Electronics Corp. In 1994, Cobra expanded its retail presence by signing an agreement to sell its Cobra line through Sears, Roebuck and Co. stores.

In 1994 the struggling company hired Stephen M. Yanklowitz as chief operating officer in hopes of turning itself around. Yanklowitz had no background in the consumer electronics industry. Instead, he was hired for his marketing skills. As executive vice-president of Western Publishing he had marketed children's books and software. He had also served as the president of a firm that marketed porcelain and china sculptures, and as general manager of the Crayola products division of Hallmark Cards, where he added new products to the line.

Yanklowitz's arrival beefed up the firm's marketing muscle and gave Kalov more time to work on expanding Cobra's product line. Kalov visited defense contractors, looking for technologies with applications in the home electronics market. Some of the more advanced technologies used in cordless phones had their origins in military communications.

"We're a little company and we can't afford to develop this stuff in our back room," Kalov told *Crain's Chicago Business* in September 1994. "We've got to get hold of some of these emerging technologies in other ways."

Cobra continued to reshape its management to strengthen its new emphasis on marketing. In 1994, Charles Stott, who had a background in product development, became the firm's new vice-president of operations. John Pohl, an experienced consumer-marketing executive, became vice-president of marketing in early 1995.

New products included two radios geared toward car travelers needing inexpensive communications for emergencies, as well as new CB radios that automatically alerted drivers to predicted weather emergencies. The CBs signaled users to tune into National Weather Service channels whenever it sent out an alert signal. To better stay in touch with consumers, the firm expanded its customer-service hotline, which received 400,000 calls in 1994. Cobra also began using focus groups and quantitative market research. It began plans to expand its consumer advertising and promotions, direct-marketing programs, and point-of-purchase techniques.

The firm was profitable the first two quarters of 1994, but, largely because of problems with product availability, it lost money the following two quarters and had a loss of $1.5 million for 1994. Sales volume declined because of Cobra's switch from low-margin, high-volume distribution. Also due to this switch, the firm redesigned old products and introduced new ones more quickly than in the past, causing some problems with the firm's contract manufacturers.

Further Reading:

Anderson, Veronica, ''Cobra Electronics Not Snake-Bitten by Losses,'' *Crain's Chicago Business,* May 31, 1993.

Henry, David, ''Death Wish,'' *Forbes,* October 20, 1986.

Murphy, H. Lee, ''Inventing, Manufacturing: New Roles for Dynascan,'' *Crain's Chicago Business,* May 8, 1989.

——, ''Dynascan Testing Kalov's Turnaround Touch,'' *Crain's Chicago Business,* November 5, 1990.

——, ''Flagging Cobra Taps Marketing Vet,'' *Crain's Chicago Business,* September 26, 1994.

Stouffer, Paul W., ''Turnaround Encore?'' *Barron's,* December 22, 1986.

—Scott M. Lewis

Colgate-Palmolive Company

300 Park Avenue
New York, New York 10022-7499
U.S.A.
(212) 310-2000
Fax: (212) 310-3284

Public Company
Incorporated: 1923 as the Eastern Operating Company
Employees: 32,800
Sales: $7.59 billion
Stock Exchanges: New York Amsterdam Frankfurt London
   Paris Zürich
SICs: 2844 Toilet Preparations; 2841 Soap & Other
   Detergents; 2048 Prepared Foods, Not Elsewhere
   Classified

Colgate-Palmolive Company's growth from a small candle and soap manufacturer to one of the most powerful consumer products giants in the world is the result of aggressive acquisition of other companies, persistent attempts to overtake its major U.S. competition, and an early emphasis on building a global presence overseas where little competition existed. Today the company is organized around five core segments—oral care, personal care, household surface care, fabric care, and pet nutrition—that market such well-known brands as Colgate toothpaste, Irish Spring soap, Softsoap liquid soap, Mennen deodorant, Palmolive dishwashing liquid, Fab laundry detergent, Soupline/Suavitel fabric softeners, and Hill's pet food.

In 1806, when the company was founded by 23-year-old William Colgate, it concentrated exclusively on selling starch, soap, and candles from its New York City-based factory and shop. Upon entering his second year of business, Colgate became partners with Francis Smith, and the company became Smith and Colgate, a name it kept until 1812 when Colgate purchased Smith's share of the company and offered a partnership to his brother, Bowles Colgate. Now called William Colgate and Company, the firm expanded its manufacturing operations to a Jersey City, New Jersey, factory in 1820; this factory produced Colgate's two major products, Windsor toilet soaps and Pearl starch.

Upon its founder's death in 1857, the firm changed its name to Colgate & Company and was run by President Samuel Colgate until his death 40 years later. During his tenure several new products were developed, including perfumes, essences and perfumed soap. The manufacture of starch was discontinued in 1866 after a fire destroyed the factory.

In 1873 Colgate began selling toothpaste in a jar, followed 23 years later by the introduction of Colgate Ribbon Dental Cream, in the now-familiar collapsible tube. By 1906 the company was also producing several varieties of laundry soap, toilet paper, and perfumes.

While the Colgate family managed its manufacturing operations in New York, soap factories were also opened in 1864 by B. J. Johnson in Milwaukee, Wisconsin, and in 1872 by the three Peet brothers in Kansas City, Kansas. In 1898 Johnson's company introduced Palmolive soap, which soon became the best-selling soap in the world and led the firm to change its name to the Palmolive Company in 1916. The Peets, who sold laundry soap mainly in the Midwest and western states, merged their company with Palmolive in 1926. Two years later the company that resulted from that merger joined with Colgate & Company to form Colgate-Palmolive-Peet, with headquarters in Jersey City.

Although Palmolive's management initially assumed control of the combined organization, the Colgate family regained control of the company after the 1929 stock market crash and installed Bayard Colgate as president in 1933. The firm adopted its present name in 1953 and moved its offices for domestic and international operations to New York City in 1956.

Between 1914 and 1933 the company began establishing international operations, with subsidiaries in Canada, Australia, Europe, and Latin America. It also built upon its strategy of growth by acquisition, buying up a number of smaller consumer product companies over the next two decades. These acquisitions did little to close the gap between Colgate and its archrival, Procter & Gamble, a company that had been formed in the 1830s and had by now assumed a commanding lead over Colgate in selling detergent products in the United States.

In 1960 George H. Lesch was appointed Colgate's president in the hopes that his international experience would produce similar success in the domestic market. Under his leadership, the company embarked upon an extensive new product development program that created such brands as Cold Power laundry detergent, Palmolive dishwashing liquid, and Ultra Brite toothpaste. In an attempt to expand beyond these traditional, highly competitive businesses into new growth areas, Colgate also successfully introduced a new food wrap called Baggies in 1963. As a result of these product launches, the company's sales grew between eight and nine percent every year throughout the 1960s.

Lesch assumed the chairmanship of Colgate, and David Foster became president in 1970 and CEO in 1971. Foster was the son of the founder of Colgate-Palmolive's U.K. operations. He joined the company in 1946 as a management trainee and rose through the sales and marketing ranks both in the United States and overseas.

During the 1970s, as environmental concerns about phosphate and enzyme detergent products grew, the company faced additional pressure to diversify beyond the detergent business. In response to this pressure, Foster instituted a strategy that emphasized internal development via a specialized new venture group; joint ventures for marketing other companies' products; and outright acquisitions of businesses in which Colgate could gain a marketing advantage over Procter & Gamble. In 1971, for example, the company began selling British Wilkinson Sword Company razors and blades in the United States and other countries. In 1972 Colgate-Palmolive acquired Kendall & Company, a manufacturer of hospital and industrial supplies. It was originally hoped that the Kendall acquisition would bolster the pharmaceutical sales of Colgate's Lakeside Laboratories subsidiary, which had been acquired in 1960. The partnership never materialized, however, and Lakeside was sold in 1974. The Kendall business proved to be one of Foster's most successful acquisitions. Within two years, the subsidiary was producing sales and earnings results well above the company's targeted goals.

In 1971 the U.S. Federal Trade Commission enacted restrictions on in-store product promotions, such as couponing. In response to these restrictions, Foster began to employ other tactics designed to enhance Colgate's visibility in the marketplace. Two such programs awarded money to schools and local civic groups whose young people collected the most labels and box-tops from selected Colgate products. Under Foster, Colgate-Palmolive also began to sponsor a number of women's sporting events, including the Colgate-Dinah Shore Winner's Circle, a women's professional golf tournament. Foster chose women's sports in an effort to appeal to Colgate-Palmolive's primarily female customer base. He even went so far as to have Colgate buy the tournament's home course, the Mission Hills Country Club in Palm Springs, California, so that he could supervise the maintenance of the greens.

In 1973 Colgate acquired Helena Rubinstein, a major cosmetics manufacturer with strong foreign sales but a weak U.S. presence. Believing that its marketing expertise could solve Rubinstein's problems, Colgate reduced both the number of products in the company's line and the number of employees in its workforce, increased advertising expenditures, and moved the products out of drugstores and into department stores. The following year the company acquired Ram Golf Corporation and Bancroft Racket Company, and in 1976 it bought Charles A. Eaton Company, a golf and tennis shoe manufacturer.

Although total U.S. sales of consumer products appeared to be slowing by the end of 1974, particularly in soaps and detergents, Colgate's international sales continued to carry the company forward. It maintained its leadership position abroad through new product development geared specifically to local tastes throughout Europe as well as through its involvement in the growing markets of less-developed countries in Latin America, Africa, and Asia.

Foster's diversification strategy initially improved earnings, but Colgate's domestic sales, market share, and profit margins were beginning to soften. This was due, in large part, to an economic recession and an advertising cutback the company had made in an attempt to boost earnings. Colgate was consistently losing the marketing battle in personal-care products to Procter & Gamble. It had no leading brands and few successful new product introductions because of reduced spending for research and devel-

ment. In an effort to remedy this problem and broaden its product mix, Colgate moved into food marketing in 1976 with the acquisition of Riviana Foods, a major producer of Texas long-grain rice with its own subsidiaries in the pet food, kosher hot dog, and candies businesses. The Riviana acquisition, however, did not live up to the company's expectations. Along with purchasing a successful rice-milling business, Colgate found that it had also saddled itself with two unprofitable restaurant chains and a low-quality candy company. In 1977 declines in the price of rice seriously eroded Riviana's cash flow.

Helena Rubinstein created additional headaches. Whereas other cosmetic manufacturers had moved their products from department store distribution to higher-volume drugstores, Colgate's management elected to keep Rubinstein products in department stores even though stores' demands for marketing support eroded the company's margins so severely that it lost money on every cosmetic item sold. Colgate finally sold the business in 1980 to Albi Enterprises.

David Foster had become chairman in 1975. In 1979, embattled by a series of marketing failures and the pressures of an acquisition strategy that yielded more losers than winners, Foster suddenly resigned, citing ill health. Colgate president and chief operating officer Keith Crane was appointed as Foster's successor. A 42-year Colgate employee, Crane quickly instituted a new management structure consisting of several group vice-presidents, reunited all domestic operations under one group, and realigned division managers in an attempt to promote a more cohesive organization. Consumer advertising and product research were given renewed emphasis to support the company's basic detergent and toothpaste lines.

Over the next two years, Crane sold a number of Foster's acquisitions that no longer fit with the company's long-term strategic plan, including Hebrew National Kosher Foods, which had been part of the Riviana purchase; Ram Golf; and the Bancroft Racket Company. Crane also put the Mission Hills Country Club up for sale and withdrew Colgate's sponsorship of the sporting events his predecessor had nurtured.

Also during the late 1970s and the 1980s, Colgate found itself named as a defendant in two lawsuits. In 1981 the company lost a suit brought by United Roasters, who successfully argued that Colgate had violated the terms of a contract between the two firms for Colgate to market Bambeanos, a soybean snack produced by United Roasters, and was awarded $950,000. The following year the company was sued by the federal government for alleged job discrimination. According to a complaint filed with the U.S. Equal Employment Opportunity Commission, Colgate had failed or refused to hire people between the ages of 40 and 70 since 1978 and had also deprived employees in that age group of opportunities for promotion.

By the end of 1982 Crane also experienced problems at Colgate. Several attempts at new product development never made it out of the test-market stage. Increased advertising expenditures for a limited number of major brands produced only temporary gains in market share while slowly killing off other products receiving little or no media support. Even Fresh Start detergent, one of the most successful new products to come out of the Foster era, was having problems retaining market share. Thus while Procter & Gamble's sales and margins were increasing, Colgate's were on the decline. To make matters worse, the strong dollar overseas hurt Colgate's international sales, and changes in Medicare policy weakened Kendall's business.

In 1983 Crane relinquished the title of president to Reuben Mark, one of the company's three executive vice-presidents and a member of Crane's management advisory team. Mark also assumed the position of chief operating officer at that time; one year later he succeeded Crane as CEO. Mark built upon his predecessor's restructuring efforts in an attempt to increase profits and shareholder value. Between 1984 and 1986 several inefficient plants were closed, hundreds of employees laid off, and noncore businesses sold including the remnants of the Riviana Foods acquisition, except for the Hill's Pet Products subsidiary.

In an attempt to refocus the company's marketing and profitability, Mark developed a set of corporate initiatives intended to address business areas ranging from production-cost reduction to new product development, with a heavy emphasis on motivating employees and involving them in company decision making. In response to the implementation of these ideas, the company's U.S. toothpaste business enjoyed a boost with first-to-the-market introductions of a gel toothpaste and a pump-type dispenser bearing the Colgate brand name. Similar U.S. market share gains were earned by new and improved versions of its Palmolive and Dynamo detergents and Ajax cleaner.

With the company's turnaround firmly under way, business units managed by key executives were formed to develop plans for the company's major product categories. The purpose of each plan was to identify how products under development could be best introduced in domestic and international markets. Two years into this strategic reorganization, coinciding with Mark's appointment as chairman in 1986, Colgate confronted an embarrassing controversy.

Since the early 1920s Hawley & Hazel Chemical Company had marketed a product called Darkie Black and White Toothpaste in the Far East. Colgate had acquired a 50 percent interest in this company in 1985. The following year, the Interfaith Center on Corporate Responsibility, a coalition of Protestant and Roman Catholic groups, demanded that Colgate change what it deemed to be the product's racially offensive name and packaging, which depicted a likeness of Al Jolson in blackface. The company acknowledged the criticism and agreed to make the necessary changes.

Colgate also continued to seek out growth areas in its personal-care product and detergent businesses. In 1987 it acquired a line of liquid soap products from Minnetonka Corporation, the first transaction the company had made in the personal-care area in several years. Building upon its success in launching an automatic dishwashing detergent in liquid form ahead of its competitors, the company also beat Procter & Gamble to the market with a laundry detergent packaged in a throw-in pouch called Fab 1 Shot, although this product failed to sustain consumer interest or reach sales expectations over the long term.

Buoyed by product development breakthroughs and a renewed commitment to consumer products marketing, Colgate sold its Kendall subsidiary and related health care businesses in 1988 to

Clayton & Dubilier. The sale enabled Colgate to retire some debt, sharpen its focus on its global consumer products businesses, and invest in new product categories. Moreover, Mark's global approach enabled the company to maintain its overall profitability despite not having a leadership position in the United States. And though Colgate lagged behind Procter & Gamble in the toothpaste category, for example, it held a commanding 40 percent share of the toothpaste market worldwide.

Mark's strategy appeared to pay off handsomely. By the end of the third quarter of 1989 Colgate's international operations performed strongly while the profitability of its U.S. operations rose, due mostly to manufacturing-cost economies and greater control over promotional and sales expenses. Not yet ready to concede the U.S. market for personal-care products to Procter & Gamble, though, Colgate acquired Vipont Pharmaceutical, a manufacturer of oral-hygiene products, toward the end of that year. Vipont's products, several of which Colgate had already been marketing overseas, enabled Colgate to strengthen the market position it had recently established with the introduction of a new tartar-control formula toothpaste.

Colgate continued to make significant acquisitions in the early and mid-1990s while it attempted to gear up its product development program, which had been unable to develop and introduce more than a few new products each year. In 1991 Colgate acquired the Murphy-Phoenix Company (whose top brand was Murphy's Oil Soap) to bolster its household care segment. That same year, Mark initiated a restructuring aimed at improving the firm's profitability and gross margins, which lagged behind the industry leaders. A major part of the effort was the elimination or reconfiguration of 25 factories throughout the world and an eight percent reduction in the workforce. Consequently, Colgate took a $243 million charge in September 1991, which reduced significantly the firm's net income for the full year.

Colgate's most dramatic acquisition to date came in 1992 with the $670 million purchase of the Mennen Co., which added to its personal care line the top U.S. deodorant brand, Mennen Speed Stick, and the number-two baby-care brand, Baby Magic. In addition, Colgate gained footholds in skin-care and hair products, and the Mennen brands gained the power of Colgate's worldwide distribution and marketing reach. This major acquisition was followed in 1993 by the purchase of S. C. Johnson Wax's liquid hand and body soap brands, which enabled Colgate to become the worldwide leader in liquid soap.

Gross margins steadily improved in the early 1990s, reaching 48.4 percent by 1994 (up from 39.2 percent in 1984). This provided Colgate with additional funds for research and development and advertising. The North American sector also experienced gains in gross margins, which resulted in part from pricing increases on Colgate detergents. In turn, this cut into overall North American sales, which declined eight percent from 1993 to 1994. Mark's strategy was to turn North American sales around through new product introductions such as a variant of Irish Spring soap and an extension of the Murphy's Oil Soap brand into a Murphy's Kitchen Care line of all-purpose cleaners. Under the leadership of Lois D. Juliber, who formerly headed up new product development, the North American sector was able to introduce several products within a short span for the first time.

A hidden jewel within the Colgate empire in the 1990s has been its pet foods sector, Hill's Pet Nutrition. The worldwide leader in therapeutic and specialty wellness pet food, Hill's enjoyed a compound annual growth rate of 14.6 percent from 1989 to 1994. During this period the market for premium pet food increased dramatically in Europe and Japan, with Hill's snatching a substantial portion of this growth. Overall, pet foods were one of Colgate's leading profit generators, boasting gross margins of 55 to 60 percent.

Early in 1995 Colgate made another major acquisition with the $1.04 billion purchase of Kolynos Oral Care from American Home Products, which gained it the Kolynos toothpaste brand, the top brand in Brazil and a leader in several other Latin American countries. This purchase pushed Colgate's share of the Latin American oral-care market from 54 percent to 79 percent.

In September 1995 Colgate announced another major restructuring of its operations to close or reconfigure 24 additional factories and cut 3,000 more employees (more than eight percent of the workforce). Mark said the action was necessary to finance new growth initiatives; Colgate took a $369 million charge as a result. The results in 1995 were also affected by a deepening recession in Mexico, which had accounted for 11 percent of sales and 20 percent of profits in 1994.

By 1995 Colgate's global presence as a consumer products company extended to 194 countries, with leading positions for several of its key brands. Colgate will likely continue to aggressively defend these positions, increase market share of its trailing brands whenever possible, and seek additional brands and product types within its primary product sectors through acquisitions and a revitalized product development program.

Principal Subsidiaries: Murphy-Phoenix Company; Softsoap Enterprises, Inc.; Colgate-Palmolive S.A.I.C. (Argentina); Colgate-Palmolive Pty. Ltd. (Australia); Colgate-Palmolive (Barbados); Colgate-Palmolive Belgium; Colgate-Palmolive Ltda. (Brazil); Colgate-Palmolive Canada; Javex Manufacturing Co. (Canada); Colgate-Palmolive CIA (Colombia); Colgate-Palmolive (Central America), Inc. (Costa Rica); Colgate-Palmolive C.I.S.A. (Cote d'Ivoire); Colgate-Palmolive A/S (Denmark); Colgate-Palmolive, Inc. (Dominican Republic); Colgate-Palmolive Del Ecuador, S.A.; Colgate-Palmolive (Central Amer-ica), Inc. (El Salvador); Colgate-Palmolive (Fiji) Ltd.; Colgate-Palmolive France; Hill's Products (France); Colgate-Palmolive A.B. (Germany); Colgate-Palmolive Gmbh (Germany); Colgate-Palmolive (Hellas) S.A. (Greece); Colgate-Palmolive (Central America) S.A. (Guatemala); Colgate-Palmolive (Guyana) Ltd.; Colgate-Palmolive (Central America), Inc. (Honduras); Colgate-Palmolive (Hong Kong) Ltd.; Hawley & Hazel Chemical Co., (Hong Kong) Ltd.; Colgate-Palmolive (India) Ltd.; Colgate-Palmolive (Ireland); Colgate-Palmolive S.p.A. (Italy); Viset (Italy); Colgate-Palmolive Co. (Jamaica) Ltd.; JCR (Japan) Ltd.; Colgate-Palmolive (E. Africa) Ltd. (Kenya); Colgate-Palmolive (Malaysia) Sdn. Bhd.; Colgate-Palmolive, S.A. De C.V. (Mexico); Colgate-Palmolive (Morocco); Colgate-Palmolive Nederland (Netherlands); Colgate-Palmolive Ltd. (New Zealand); Colgate-Palmolive (Central America) (Panama); Colgate-Palmolive Philippines Inc.; Colgate-Palmolive Portuguese Ltda. (Portugal); Colgate-Palmolive (Eastern) Pte. Ltd. (Singapore); Colgate-Palmolive Ltd. (South Africa); Colgate-Palmolive S.A.E. (Spain); Colgate-Palmolive AB (Sweden); Colgate-Palmolive AG (Switzerland); Colgate-Palmolive (Thailand) Ltd.; Colgate-Palmolive (Caribbean), Inc. (Trinidad & Tobago); Colgate-Palmolive (Tunisia); Colgate-Palmolive Ltd. (U.K.); Colgate-Palmolive, Inc. (Uruguay); Colgate-Palmolive Co. Anonima (Venezuela); Colgate-Palmolive (Zambia) Ltd.

Further Reading:

Foster, David R., *The Story of Colgate-Palmolive: One Hundred and Sixty-Nine Years of Progress,* New York: Newcomen Society in North America, 1975.
Hager, Bruce, ''Can Colgate Import Its Success from Overseas?,'' *Business Week,* May 7, 1990, pp. 114, 116.
——, ''Colgate: Oh What a Difference a Year Can Make,'' *Business Week,* March 23, 1992, pp. 90–91.
Kindel, Stephen, ''The Bundle Book: At Reuben Mark's Colgate, Attention to Small Details Creates Large Profits,'' *Financial World,* January 5, 1993, pp. 34–35.
Morgenson, Gretchen, ''Is Efficiency Enough?'' *Forbes,* March 18, 1991, pp. 108–9.
Nayyar, Seema, ''Colgate Buys Its Way Back into the Game,'' *Adweek,* February 17, 1992.
Rudnitsky, Howard, ''Making His Mark,'' *Forbes,* September 26, 1994, pp. 47–48.
Sasseen, Jane A., and Zachary Schiller, ''For Colgate-Palmolive, It's Time for Trench Warfare,'' *Business Week,* September 19, 1994, pp. 56–57.

—updated by David E. Salamie

COM/Energy®

Commonwealth Energy System

One Main Street
Cambridge, Massachusetts 02142-9150
U.S.A.
(617) 225-4000
Fax: (617) 225-4481

Public Company
Incorporated: 1926 as New England Gas & Electric
    Association
Operating Revenues: $978.6 million
Employees: 2,169
Stock Exchanges: New York Boston Pacific
SICs: 4911 Electric Services; 4924 Natural Gas Distribution;
    4961 Steam & Air Conditioning Supply; 6512 Operators
    of Nonresidential Buildings

Commonwealth Energy System (COM/Energy) is a public utility holding company with four subsidiaries operating in Massachusetts. Three are engaged in the generation, transmission, and distribution of electricity, and the fourth in the distribution of natural gas. COM/Energy also owns a steam distribution company, a liquefied natural-gas and vaporization facility, and five real-estate trusts.

Commonwealth Energy System was the name adopted in 1981 for what had been formerly the New England Gas & Electric Association. New England Gas & Electric was founded on the last day of 1926 as an unincorporated trust to control various gas and electric companies. The oldest of these was the Worcester Gas Light Co., formed in 1849 after winning a contract to provide gas street lighting along Main Street in Worcester, Massachusetts. Another early member of the future system, New Bedford Gas Co., was incorporated in 1850. It absorbed New Bedford Electric Light Co. in 1888 and Edison Electric Illuminating Co. of New Bedford in 1890. This consolidated utility became New Bedford Gas & Edison Light Co. in 1891. Yet another early unit was Cambridge Electric Light Co., organized in 1886 as one of the first electric utilities in the United States.

At the time of its founding New England Gas & Electric was affiliated with the Associated Gas & Electric system through ownership and control of its common shares by important stockholders and officials of Associated Gas & Electric Co. Associated was one of the eight great systems that, with only a few exceptions, controlled all private gas and electric companies in Massachusetts. In 1928 Associated served 50 cities and towns in the state with an aggregate population of 788,000. By the use of the holding-company device, a relatively small investment could result in control of properties many times greater in value. Associated's capital structure was characterized as early as 1927 as "a financial nightmare," and the company was placed in bankruptcy by the federal Securities and Exchange Commission in 1940.

Before federal legislation enacted in 1935 broke up a number of far-flung combines, New England Gas & Electric owned public electric utilities in New Hampshire, Maine, and the maritime provinces of Canada as well as Massachusetts. In 1930 the system owned and operated nine steam, internal-combustion, and hydroelectric generating stations in Massachusetts, New Hampshire, Nova Scotia, and Prince Edward Island. Its gas plants, which at this time provided manufactured rather than natural gas, served Worcester, Cambridge, New Bedford, and a number of smaller Massachusetts communities. In 1929 New England Gas & Electric served 115,204 electric and 141,343 gas customers. Gross earnings came to $14.5 million that year and gross income to $2.2 million.

Service to Canada ended when New England Gas & Electric divested itself of four utility subsidiaries during 1935 and 1936. By 1940 the New Bedford Gas & Edison Light Co. subsidiary was accounting for more than half of the system's electricity sales, followed by Cambridge Electric Light Co. New Hampshire Gas & Electric Co., serving chiefly Portsmouth, was third in sales of electricity, followed closely by Plymouth County Electric Co. and Cape and Vineyard Electric Co., the latter serving the island of Martha's Vineyard and most of Cape Cod. The system's gas sales were chiefly by its Worcester, Cambridge, and New Bedford subsidiaries. Steam for heating was being sold to ten Cambridge customers by Cambridge Steam Co. Gross income came to $2.8 million in 1939 and net income to $298,424.

Except for the divestiture of electric service to Calais, Maine, the scope of New England Gas & Electric's operations remained the same in the 1940s. In 1950 it was providing electric service to about 151,000 customers in 77 communities and gas service to about 169,000 customers in 39 communities. There was no direct competition in kind from any privately or municipally owned public utility. New England Gas & Electric had taken a 36-percent stake in Algonquin Gas Transmission Co., a company formed in 1949 for the purpose of building natural-gas pipeline. The system's total operating revenues rose from $19.4 million in 1944 to $31.2 million in 1950. Net income rose from $520,864 to more than $2.3 million over the same period.

In 1954 New England Gas & Electric sold its New Hampshire Electric Co. subsidiary and New Hampshire's subsidiary, Kittery Electric Light Co., to Public Service Co. of New Hampshire, thereby restricting its operations to Massachusetts. Because of consolidation, by 1960 only seven operating subsidiaries remained in the system: Cambridge Electric Light Co., Cambridge Gas Co., Cambridge Steam Corp., Cape and Vineyard Electric Co., New Bedford Gas & Edison Light Co., Plymouth County Electric Co., and Worcester Gas Light Co. Electric and gas service now was being provided to 41 communities each. Operating revenues increased from $34 million in 1951 to $52 million in 1959, while net income rose from $2.4 million to $3.8 million during the same period.

New England Gas & Electric fully entered the atomic age in 1968, when the Yankee nuclear power plant began operations in Rowe, Massachusetts. The system took a combined interest, through a consortium, of 15.5 percent in four such plants. The others were Connecticut Yankee of Haddam, Connecticut; Maine Yankee of Wiscasset, Maine; and Vermont Yankee of Vernon, Vermont, all of which became operational in 1972. The Rowe facility was closed in 1992.

In 1966 New England Gas & Electric's operating revenues reached $75 million, and net income was $7.2 million. One of the system's assets was the rise in the year-round population of Cape Cod from 37,000 in 1940 to an estimated 85,000 in 1965. A new subsidiary, Canal Electric Co., formed in 1966, was completing a 560-megawatt oil-fired electric generating station in Sandwich, at the eastern end of Cape Cod Canal. This facility soon was providing 70 percent of the system's electrical capacity, three-quarters of which was being sold to other utilities. In Cambridge, an influx of diverse industries and research institutes was increasing sales volume. A new superhighway promised to attract industry to Worcester.

The system's electric service was in 1967 reaching about 200,000 customers in 41 communities, while natural gas was being distributed to 177,000 customers in 44 communities, ten of which were also being served by the system's electricity. Natural gas was being supplied to companies under long-term contracts with Tennessee Gas Transmission Co. as well as by Algonquin Gas Transmission Co. Among the 40-odd Cambridge Steam customers, the best-known were Harvard University and the Massachusetts Institute of Technology.

In 1971 preliminary agreement was reached for the purchase of a still-uncompleted liquefied natural-gas facility at Hopkinton, Massachusetts, in a joint venture with Air Products and Chemicals, Inc. This facility, which became operational in 1972, gave the system a gas surplus during periods of extreme weather that was also available for sale to other gas companies. COM/Energy bought out its partner in 1985, but Air Products and Chemicals continued to operate and maintain the facility under contract.

Commonwealth Gas Co. (COM/Gas) was formed in 1971 by the merger of the Cambridge and Worcester gas companies. In the same year Cape and Vineyard was merged into New Bedford Gas & Edison Light. This subsidiary was renamed Commonwealth Electric Co. (COM/Electric) in 1981. Meanwhile, Canal Electric was constructing another large oil-fired generating plant in Sandwich, this time in partnership with Montaup Electric Co. It became operational in 1976.

New England Gas & Electric's record income of $9.6 million in 1967 was not matched until 1971 because of a combination of factors, including higher interest expenses and increased local taxes. But by 1981, when New England Gas & Electric Association was renamed Commonwealth Energy System, operating revenues had reached $512.5 million and net income $26.9 million. The number of customers receiving electric service in the system's 41 communities had reached about 267,900. The

number of communities receiving gas had reached 47 (of which 12 also received electricity from the system), and the number of customers had reached about 194,600. Also in that year, COM/Gas purchased the gas business and assets of New Bedford Gas & Edison Light, subsequently Commonwealth Electric Co. (COM/Electric).

COM/Energy weathered the petroleum shortages and price hikes of the 1970s and early 1980s and the waning of nuclear power as an alternative generating fuel better than most public utilities. Between 1984 and 1988 it had the third-best annual average return on equity among 24 Northeast utilities, with 17 percent. It had the second-lowest percentage of debt to equity among the 24 in this period, at 75.5 percent.

In the early 1990s, however, COM/Electric came under fire from the Massachusetts Department of Public Utilities for its rates, which were second-highest in the state and among the highest in the country. An audit commissioned by the department in 1991 recommended 62 changes, including stricter budgeting and control processes, more competitive bidding and monitoring of outside service vendors, and major improvements in customer service. In 1993 the state's Division of Energy Resources responded to a Cambridge Electric request for a ten-percent rate hike by asking it and COM/Electric to explore mergers with two competing utilities. State officials were said to feel that Massachusetts's eight electric companies were too many and that high electric rates were a factor in the high cost of doing business there.

The typical COM/Electric residential customer was using about 500 kilowatt hours of electricity a month in early 1993 and paying $70 a month. The average cost of 14 cents per kilowatt-hour compared to a typical charge of 11 cents per kilowatt-hour by other state electric utilities. In April 1993 COM/Electric announced that it was laying off between 150 and 175 employees in all departments to cut costs. The COM/Energy system also, in 1995, curtailed power purchases from a costly cogeneration plant in Lowell, Massachusetts, and bought out a contract to purchase power supplies from a plant in Pepperell, Massachusetts.

COM/Electric announced a four-year, $10.8-million rate cut in April 1995, which it attributed to its "aggressive cost-cutting" efforts. However, an official in the state attorney general's office said some of the reduction was owed to customers because of "power outages due to management mistakes" and attributed some of the rest to accounting matters that had nothing to do with cost-cutting. As part of the deal with the attorney general's office, COM/Electric agreed to refund to customers half of any earnings above 9.5 percent of revenues through 1998.

COM/Energy's operating revenues rose from $835.8 million in 1990 to $978.6 million in 1994. Of the 1994 total, 65 percent came from electricity, 33 percent from gas, and two percent from steam. Net income grew from $22.6 million to almost $49 million in this period. Consolidated long-term debt was $418.3 million at the end of 1994.

The system had 356,697 electricity customers at the end of 1994, of which residential customers numbered 311,153. Of its 8.4 million megawatt-hours of electricity sales in 1994, residential sales comprised 21 percent; commercial sales, 24 percent; industrial sales, five percent; other sales, five percent; and wholesale sales to other systems, 45 percent. Of 231,609 natural gas customers at the end of 1994, 211,075 were residential. Of 47.4 billion BTUs of gas sales in 1994, residential sales accounted for 45 percent; commercial sales, 23 percent; industrial sales, nine percent; other sales, four percent; and interruptible and other sales, 19 percent.

COM/Energy system companies owned electric-power generating facilities with capability of 1,046.5 megawatts at the end of 1994. Cambridge Electric Co. had two steam electric-generating stations in Cambridge with a capability of 76.5 megawatts. Canal Electric Co., which did not serve retail customers, owned and operated the 560-megawatt oil-fired steam-generating unit (Unit No. 1) at Sandwich, Massachusetts, and operated and half owned the similar 584-megawatt unit (Unit No. 2) at Sandwich. Three-quarters of Unit No. 1's capacity was being sold to neighboring utilities under long-term contract. Canal Electric also had a minor ownership interest in the Seabrook (New Hampshire) 1 nuclear power plant, from which it received 40.5 megawatt capability, and COM/Electric had a minor interest in Central Maine Power Company's oil-fired Wyman Unit 4, from which it received 8.8 megawatt capability. COM/Electric's 60 megawatt New Bedford steam electric-generating plant closed in 1993.

Through equity ownership in Hydro-Quebec Phase II, a Canadian waterpower project, Canal had an entitlement of 67.9 megawatts of electricity. From four nuclear units an additional 140.7 megawatts were available to the COM/Energy system, which had an equity interest in the Connecticut Yankee, Maine Yankee, and Vermont Yankee units, but not in the fourth, the Pilgrim nuclear power plant in Plymouth, Massachusetts. COM/Energy and its units also purchased and exchanged power with other companies in order to reduce its reliance on oil. Of COM/Energy's retail energy generation in 1994, 38 percent was fueled by natural gas, 25 percent by nuclear power, 24 percent from oil, two percent from hydro (waterpower), and 11 percent from waste-to-energy and other sources.

COM/Energy sold its interest in Algonquin Gas Transmission Co. to Texas Eastern Corp. in 1986 for $56.3 million. Prior to a federal order that became effective in 1993, COM/Gas purchased most of its natural gas from either Algonquin or Tennessee Gas Pipeline Co. Following the order, which required interstate pipelines to unbundle existing gas sales contracts into separate components, it turned to third-party vendors for gas while continuing to purchase transportation, storage, and bal-

ancing services from Tennessee, Algonquin, and other companies. Hopkinton LNG Corp., another COM/Energy subsidiary, had a liquefaction plant and three above-ground storage tanks in Hopkinton, Massachusetts, and a satellite vaporization plant in Acushnet, Massachusetts, with additional storage capacity. The system's gas properties included 2,761 miles of gas distribution lines at the end of 1994.

COM/Energy Steam Co. was purchasing steam produced by Cambridge Electric in connection with the latter's generation of electricity and was also producing steam itself. In 1994 it distributed steam to 20 customers in Cambridge and to Massachusetts General Hospital in Boston, but in 1995 MIT, its largest customer, turned to cogeneration. During 1994 the company sold a record 1.5 billion pounds of steam. COM/Energy Services Co. provided essential services to the system and its subsidiaries, including executive and financial management, accounting, data processing, and legal and other services.

Among COM/Energy's five real-estate subsidiaries in 1995, Darvel Realty Trust held Riverfront Office Park in Cambridge, while COM/Energy Research Park Realty planned to develop another parcel in Cambridge. COM/Energy Freetown Realty held 596 acres of land in Freetown, Massachusetts, but was planning to sell it.

Principal Subsidiaries: Cambridge Electric Light Co.; Canal Electric Co.; COM/Energy Acushnet Realty; COM/Energy Cambridge Realty; COM/Energy Freetown Realty; COM/Energy Research Park Realty; COM/Energy Steam Co.; Commonwealth Electric Co.; Commonwealth Gas Co.; Darvel Realty Trust; Hopkinton LNG Corp.

Further Reading:

Ackerman, Jerry, "Utility to Cut Power Purchases," *Boston Globe,* November 29, 1994, pp. 45, 49.
Biderman, Charles, "Rate Hikes, New Plant Enhance Outlook for New England G&E," *Barron's,* March 8, 1971, pp. 31, 34.
Blanton, Kimberley, "2 Utilities Urged to Explore Mergers," *Boston Globe,* February 4, 1992, pp. 41, 45.
"Brisk Expansion in Service Area Fuels Gains for New England G&E," *Barron's,* December 18, 1967, pp. 28, 30.
Sit, Mary, "Audit Asks ComElectric Changes," *Boston Globe,* October 10, 1992, p. 23.
——, "Commonwealth Electric to Lay off at Least 150," *Boston Globe,* April 14, 1993, p. 35.
Zitner, Aaron, "How Many Officials Does It Take to Cut Electric Bill?" *Boston Globe,* April 13, 1995, pp. 69, 79.

—Robert Halasz

Computer Data Systems, Inc.

1 Curie Court
Rockville, Maryland 20850
U.S.A.
(301) 921-7000
Fax: (301) 948-9328

Public Company
Incorporated: 1968
Employees: 3,400
Sales: $205.9 million
Stock Exchanges: NASDAQ
SICs: 7374 Data Processing & Preparation; 7372
   Prepackaged Software; 5045 Computers, Peripherals &
   Software

Computer Data Systems, Inc. does 90 percent of its computer service business with federal and state governments, primarily in setting up and operating data processing systems for its client agencies and selling its own prepackaged software to them. Computer Data Systems (CDSI) grew from humble beginnings in 1968 with four employees to become one of the nation's top 25 government contractors in 1995 with a staff of 3,400 at 22 locations across the United States. In the 1990s, the company ranked among *Forbes* magazine's 200 best small U.S. companies for four years in a row.

In providing computer systems, products, and expertise to its clients, CDSI contracts for the establishment and day-to-day operation of data processing systems. Projects range from developing a prototype online fingerprint identification system for the U.S. Immigration and Naturalization Service, to implementing and operating the Federal Direct Student Loan Program for the U.S. Department of Education, to developing a computer system for the state of Georgia that responds to 25,000 calls a month from travelers seeking information.

In an industry where the people change almost as fast as the technology, most of CDSI's respected senior management has been with the company for more than ten years, and its top executives have been at CDSI for decades. Clifford M. Kendall, one of the four CDSI founders in 1968 and the company's first vice-president of finance, served as president and chief executive officer for 20 years before moving to chairman of the board. Gordon S. Glenn, his successor as president and CEO, joined the company back in 1971 as a computer programmer for a

U.S. Navy contract and worked his way up to the company's top operating position. Glenn took pride in the continuity of senior management. "We like to get them, work with them and promote from within," he told *Washington Technology* in 1995. By that year, all 25 of the company's officers had been promoted from within its ranks.

In the brutally competitive government contracting arena, CDSI achieved strong revenue and earnings growth over the years by sticking close to its target markets and leveraging its expertise in financial and management computer systems from one project to another.

CDSI was founded and incorporated in 1968, in Rockville, Maryland, just outside of Washington, D.C. One year after its founding, it became the first Washington, D.C.,-area company to be listed on the National Stock Exchange. In 1970, the young firm opened its first regional office in Florida and formed a subsidiary, Computer Data Systems International, Ltd., to support its new clients in Western Europe. The following year, CDSI developed automatic information management systems for the state of Florida, the U.S. Navy, and the National Science Foundation.

By 1971, the staff had grown to 100 and profits exceeded $9,000. And the following year, with new clients that included the U.S. Environmental Protection Agency, the U.S. Department of Health and Human Services, and several labor unions, revenues were up 27 percent and profits tenfold, to $98,000.

New clients in 1973 included the World Bank and the U.S. Department of Agriculture. Revenues reached $2.3 million and the company formed another subsidiary, the National Institute for Public Services, Inc., to focus on the information-processing requirements of credit unions. The next year, revenues were up by 40 percent and the project backlog exceeded $3.8 million. In 1975, CDSI acquired Electronic Composition, Inc., an automated typesetting and photocomposition firm.

The company paid its first cash dividend in 1976, as its business volume increased for the eighth consecutive year, and it established a full-service corporate data center. In 1977 CDSI acquired Forlines and Associates, a firm specializing in financial systems, and its software products that included the Builders Information System, the Law Firm Accounting System and the Financial Accounting and Reporting System (FARS) which became one of CDSI's mainstay software offerings in the years ahead. The company celebrated its tenth anniversary in 1978 with 100 clients and a nine percent rise in revenues.

CDSI began its second decade by adding two mainframe computers to its corporate data center, as revenues again increased to more than $8 million. In 1980, the company tailored its FARS accounting software so that it could be used by federal government agencies and recorded its best year in its history, with revenues up 71 percent to $14.8 million.

CDSI won a three-year, $40-million contract with the General Services Administration (GSA) in 1983 and formed Computer Data Systems Sales, Inc., to compete in the expanding turnkey systems marketplace. Its Debt Management and Collection System software was implemented for the Department of Housing and Urban Development's Title 1 program. In its 15th consecutive year of revenue increases and 13th of profitability, CDSI had 1,500 employees supporting 200 clients at 29 sites around the world.

In 1984, CDSI completed construction of a new corporate headquarters in Rockville. Other major projects included the operation of a 70,000-square-foot fulfillment warehouse for the Federal Emergency Management Agency. The next year, CDSI signed two new GSA contracts with a total value of $54 million over four years. In 1986, it licensed its FARS accounting software to the Interstate Conference of Employment Security Agencies. In 1987, it won a $22.8-million Navy project and a $11-million project for the Department of the Interior, both lasting three years.

During its early years, CDSI focused primarily on the professional services side of its business—providing technological expertise and specialized software to its clients, mostly in the area of financial management and accounting. In 1987, the fast-growing company set up a new division to pursue larger projects in which it would integrate its own software and services with hardware and software from other vendors.

The company marked its 20th anniversary in 1988. That year it acquired Group Operations, Inc., in a deal that added a suite of software "productivity tools" to CDSI's offerings. The so-called tools—actually specialized software for analyzing and writing computer programs—were used to re-engineer and re-structure old programs, making them more efficient and easier to keep current.

The year 1989 was a blockbuster for CDSI. Contract awards totaled $500 million, paced by a $158-million, five-year contract to support the Department of Energy's Office of Information Technology Services and Operations. Company revenues were up by 59 percent to more than $105 million.

In 1990, CDSI demonstrated its capability to handle large, multidisciplined projects with the addition of the Defense Department's civilian medical claims processing system, which would grow in three years to encompass 55 separate computer systems running on a network that linked six regional data centers which processed more than 18 million health claims a year. Another contract win involved work for the U.S. Naval Weapons Center, and the company's Transportation Management System was deployed during Operation Desert Storm in the Persian Gulf.

By 1991, CDSI had become GSA's largest information services contractor, and its financial and management offerings supported 20 federal and 24 state government agencies. That year, the company centralized its sales and marketing efforts previously handled by senior managers in each of its specialized areas, into a single business development group.

CDSI celebrated its 25th anniversary in 1993, its best year yet with record revenues of $180.9 million, up 27.7 percent, and net income of $5.5 million, an increase of 56.8 percent. More than 3,600 CDSI employees supported 185 contracts in 42 states.

In December of that year, CDSI won its largest contract ever, a $376 million project to handle the data processing for the Education Department's Federal Direct Student Loan program.

Although the profitability of the contract got off to a slow start because of up-front investments in hardware, it began to improve as the number of schools participating in the loan program headed upwards from 105 to a projected 1,500. And as the volume of student loans increased, so did CDSI's revenue and profit from the program.

Other new business in 1993 included contacts with the Justice and Housing and Urban Development departments totaling $28.1 million. And the company sustained its excellent record in recompeting for its contracts that re-opened to bidding as their terms expired, winning awards from the Defense, Justice, Transportation and Army departments.

As the company moved into its second quarter century, it entered a pivotal period in the evolution of its technology, its marketplace and its business. In terms of technology, the large, expensive mainframe and midrange computers that had dominated government data processing operations since the 1960s were being challenged by networks of low-cost personal computers that could perform many of the same tasks. The software for mainframe computers, in which federal automation contractors like CDSI had invested so much effort and money over the years, had to be adapted to run on the new "client/server" local area networks of personal computers. The new PC networks were very attractive to government agencies because they cost less than the big mainframes and were easier to use and maintain.

The government contracting marketplace of the early 1990s, meantime, was in turmoil. Defense expenditures flattened in the post-Cold War period as the armed services downsized ranks, triggering consolidations in the defense aerospace industry. And political, fiscal and downsizing pressures constrained spending by civilian agencies, as well.

CDSI sustained some short-term business setbacks itself in 1994, losing its bids to continue servicing three contracts that it originally had won in 1988 when its competitors in the new bidding cut their profit margins to wrest the projects away. But the company regarded these as the normal ups and downs of the government contracting business, and CDSI's net income for 1994 was a record $7.73 million, an increase of 40.3 percent over the previous year on revenue of $205.9 million.

Despite cost pressures on government, the outlook for the federal automation industry was healthy in the early 1990s, according to computer industry analyst William Loomis, who followed CDSI. "If the government is going to cut back employees, the thinking is that they'll need more computers to increase productivity," he told *Warfield's Business Record,* noting that "If so, growth in that area will continue, even if the government does downsize."

Changing times provide profitable opportunities for businesses able to exploit them, and in the early 1990s CDSI began positioning itself to capitalize on the downsizing trends in computer technology and government by aggressively investing for the future.

The company revamped its proprietary FARS financial software, which was originally developed in the 1980s for big IBM mainframe computers, to run on the client/server networks of the 1990s that typically mixed hardware from different manufacturers. The new version was designed to be portable between different brands of hardware and easily tailored to different computing environments.

It upgraded its corporate data processing facility to increase its capacity to handle the processing work from clients. It established internal research and development organizations, called "centers for excellence" to focus on its core technologies of financial management, networking, quality, software development methodology and imaging technology.

Like other government contractors, CDSI sought to broaden its services to other markets, but the federal government continued to be its bread-and-butter business. "We want to expand in the commercial state and local markets," Glenn told *Washington Technology* in 1995, adding, "we don't want to rely on the federal government too much, but it still will be the biggest player in information technology."

Principal Subsidiaries: Computer Systems Data Sales, Inc.

Further Reading:

Day, Kathleen, "Computer Data Systems Loses a GSA Contract, *Washington Post,* August 2, 1994, p. D4.
Endoso, Joyce, "CDSI Looks Ahead and Keeps Its Eyes on the Prize," *Washington Technology,* February 9, 1995.
Hosinki, Joan M., "System Integration's Big Leagues Beckon CDSI," *Government Computer News,* November 6, 1987, p. 114.
Kerber, Ross, "On Computer Data's 25th Anniversary, a Bid to Be Stronger," *Washington Post,* July 26, 1993, p. E11.
McCarthy, Shawn P., "Give Up Your Mainframes, Financial Systems Vendors Say," *Government Computer News,* March 6, 1995, p. 46.
Monroe, John Stein, "CDSI Retools for High-Tech Services," *Federal Computer Week,* July 26, 1993, p. 32.
Myers, Randy, "Surviving the Whims of Government Contracting," *Warfield's Business Journal,* July 2, 1993 p. 1.

—David M. Linton

Consolidated Products Inc.

36 S. Pennsylvania Street
Indianapolis, Indiana 46204
U.S.A.
(317) 633-4100
Fax: (317) 633-4106

Public Company
Founded: 1981
Employees: 7,712
Sales: $161 million
Stock Exchanges: NASDAQ
SICs: 5812 Eating Places; 6794 Patent Owners and Lessors

Consolidated Products, Inc., is a holding company that operated 152 restaurants in 11 states going into 1995. The company's primary holding was the venerable Steak n Shake chain of 1950s-style restaurants. That division encompassed more than 140 units in the Midwest and Southern United States, only 23 of which were franchised. Consolidated posted healthy sales and profit gains during the early 1990s as a result of new store openings and improved per-store sales.

Consolidated Products was formed in 1981 by Kelley & Partners, Ltd., a New York-based limited partnership headed by E. W. Kelley. Kelley created Consolidated as a vehicle to purchase a controlling interest in Franklin Corp., the Indianapolis, Indiana-based company that owned Steak n Shake. Franklin had purchased Steak n Shake in the late 1960s and subsequently moved its headquarters to Indianapolis. Franklin expanded the chain rapidly during the early and middle 1970s, significantly increasing both sales and profits. By the late 1970s, though, it became clear that Steak n Shake had grown too quickly. Starved for cash, Franklin finally found a white knight in Kelley & Partners' Consolidated Products.

When Kelley purchased Franklin, he took control of one of the oldest restaurant chains in the United States. Indeed, the first Steak n Shake shop was opened in 1934 by Gus Belt. Belt's original store was located at 1219 Main Street in the central Illinois town of Normal. In that shop he invented the seared steakburger that was destined to become famous locally and in parts of the Midwest. The patty was made from 100 percent pure ground beef that included fine cuts of T-bone, strip steak, and sirloin. Belt also pioneered the concept of cooking food in front of the customer, which later became commonplace in

many restaurants throughout the nation. Belt's Steak n Shake restaurant quickly caught on and he expanded during the 1940s and early 1950s into other parts of Illinois and into St. Louis, Missouri. In 1954 he extended nationally with stores in Indianapolis and Daytona, Florida.

Belt died in 1954, and his wife, Edith—her picture still hangs in the original Steak n Shake in Normal—took over. She continued to run the company successfully until the late 1960s, when she sold out to Franklin Corp. During her reign, in fact, Steak n Shake established much of the loyal following that would carry it into the 1980s. The restaurant exemplified the stereotypical 1950s burger restaurant: Waiters and waitresses wore black pants, white shirts, bow ties, and white hats and tennis shoes. Carhops provided curb service—patrons flashed their headlights for service and ate from a tray hinged on their rolled down window—while the older crowd usually went inside to eat.

Besides its famous seared steakburgers, Steak n Shake made a name for itself during the 1940s and 1950s with its thin-cut french fries, famous homemade chili, and "tru-flavor" shakes. During the 1960s and 1970s, Steak n Shake distinguished itself from the emerging fast food crowd that turned to disposable packaging and processed and frozen foods. In contrast, Steak n Shake continued to serve meals on white china with flatware, and it eventually became one of the only chain restaurants in the country to still make its milkshakes the "right" way, with a vanilla ice cream base and syrup flavoring. Steak n Shake also became known for its advertising slogans, which included: In Sight It Must Be Right; Famous for Steakburgers; and TAK-HOMASAK, which referred to Steak n Shake's carryout meals in throw-away wrapping.

Steak n Shake thrived during the early 1970s under the wing of Franklin Corp. Franklin tagged a number of new stores onto the chain throughout the Midwest and parts of the southern United States. When the enterprise began to stumble in the late 1970s, Franklin backpedaled and sold or closed unprofitable stores. The company also ceased paying dividends in an effort to stem a rising tide of red ink. Because Steak n Shake was Franklin's sole revenue source, the company was gasping when Kelley came along in 1981. Kelley, through the newly formed Consolidated Products, provided a much-needed injection of cash into the chain that helped it hurdle a difficult point during the late 1970s and early 1980s.

Kelley was 64 years old when he purchased a controlling interest in Steak n Shake. He was born on a farm outside of Kokomo, Indiana, and had been raised in a family of farmers and entrepreneurs. Prior to forming Consolidated, Kelley had accrued broad business experience in both small and large organizations, and as an entrepreneur. By the early 1990s his credits would include reviving the ailing Steak n Shake, bringing Grey Poupon to the U.S. market, developing ingredients for Lean Cuisine dinners and Klondike ice cream bars, and overseeing a snack company and a large agribusiness in Indiana and Florida. His associates and managers, several of whom went on to run major companies on the New York Stock Exchange, attributed much of his success to his emphasis on long-range planning. Kelley also devoted a significant amount of his time to social causes, including the founding of the Tipton Foundation, which was established to better the quality of life in small communities.

Although Kelley's investment saved the company from going under, Steak n Shake continued to languish during the early 1980s. The chain needed more than a small influx of cash to help it recover from a period of neglect that began in the mid-1970s. By the early 1980s the chain had lost its luster and was lagging important trends in the marketplace. Its old black and white exterior-tile buildings looked antiquated, and the traditional curbside service was losing its appeal against the speedy fast food drive-thrus at competing burger chains. Furthermore, Steak n Shake had strayed from the important concepts that had made it famous. Many of the stores had moved the grill to the back of the kitchen to hold down noise, for example, whereas other stores had replaced the bright white interior tile with a drab beige, giving them a coffee-shop appearance.

Steak n Shake struggled during 1982 and 1983, and then began experiencing losses in 1984. After five consecutive quarters of losses, Kelley decided to shake up the organization. To that end, he hired James Williamson, Jr., in 1985 to act as president and chief executive of Consolidated. Williamson had previously served as president of the large convenience store chain Circle K. Williamson's goal was to restore the three basic elements that had made the chain so successful: clean stores, hot food, and friendly service. His first move was to revamp the menu. He yanked items that were ordered infrequently and took a long time to prepare, and adjusted the menu to feature the famed seared steakburgers. Williamson then went to work on the restaurants themselves. He brought back the original clean black and white tile, but added red awnings and accents to give the stores some punch. He also jettisoned curb service and began installing drive-thrus. Finally, he moved the kitchen back out into the dining area and brought back the applicable slogan, "In Sight It Must Be Right."

Steak n Shake reached bottom in 1985 when it lost $567,000. From that point on, however, both sales and profits surged. Much of the growth was attributable to the addition of drive-thru service, which grew to account for a full 30 percent of company sales by the late 1990s. However, the updated appearance and menu also contributed to the company's recovery. Furthermore, Steak n Shake was benefiting from a program Kelley launched in 1984 to weed out poorly performing stores and supplant them with new restaurants in better locations. Between 1985 and 1989 he shuttered 25 restaurants and built about 20 new company-owned or franchised units. By 1989 the Steak n Shake chain consisted of about 120 outlets mostly in the Midwest. In that year, Consolidated garnered net earnings of $4.3 million on revenues of $99.8 million.

Revenue gains during the late 1980s also reflected Kelley's addition of a new division to Consolidated. In 1985 Kelley purchased restaurants held by Wheel Restaurants Inc. and Sweeney Specialty Restaurants. He then formed a division called Consolidated Specialty Restaurants, Inc., to operate a diverse group of eateries ranging from full-service theme restaurants to coffee shops. By 1989 the division was sporting 16 locations that included Carlos Murphy's, Santini's, The Charley Horse, Big Wheel, Jeremiah Sweeney's, and more. Williamson was planning to convert several of the units into Santini's or into Charley Horse restaurants, the latter of which was a concept born in suburban Chicago. Although the specialty division boosted Consolidated's sales, it was failing to bring in profits and became a drag on the company's bottom line during the late 1980s and early 1990s.

Williamson left Consolidated and was replaced by Stephen Huse in May of 1990. Huse was an Indiana restaurateur. Among other credits, he cofounded the Noble Roman's pizza chain in the 1970s and later started Huse Food Group, a holding company with various restaurant interests. Among his first moves was a controversial recapitalization in October of 1990; Consolidated borrowed $23.8 million to provide shareholders, many of whom were insiders, with cash dividends. The move was designed to buoy the company's lagging stock price. Then, in 1991, Huse launched a franchising initiative that he believed would allow Steak n Shake to expand rapidly nationwide. To that end, Steak n Shake Inc. signed an agreement with an Atlanta-based company owned by Kelley's son that transferred five Atlanta Steak n Shakes into that company's hands. The same company also agreed to open 50 new stores in the Atlanta and Charlotte, North Carolina, areas during the next 10 to 15 years. Huse hoped to reach similar agreements with area franchisers in Indiana, Ohio, Illinois, and Kentucky.

Huse never got the opportunity to push his franchising strategy; he resigned late in 1991. Kelley temporarily filled the void. Although he had been disappointed by what he viewed as a slow start for Steak n Shake's franchising campaign, Kelley remained committed to the concept. "We'll see franchising come through, come Hell or high water, because it's in the long-term interest of the company," Kelley said in the February 24, 1992, *Indianapolis Business Journal.* Also under Huse's leadership, Steak n Shake began using television advertising, which ultimately turned out to be a smart move for the chain. Meanwhile, the Specialty Restaurants division continued to suffer. Kelley was trying to convert several of the division's 14 units into a new concept called Hardwood Grill, but the overall division still struggled for profits.

Kelley eventually replaced Huse with Alan B. Gilman, a retail industry veteran who had served as chief executive at New York's Abraham & Straus and president of Murjani International, a marketing company. Gilman, under Kelley's direction, remained focused on the goal of increasing franchising and intensifying existing marketing programs. Between 1992 and 1993 the number of franchised Steak n Shakes increased from 16 to 23, while the total number of outlets rose from 104 to 118. More importantly, marketing campaigns and an improving economy significantly boosted per-store sales. Revenues climbed from $115 million in 1991 to $126 million in 1992, and then to $158 million in 1994. Moreover, net earnings more than doubled during the same period to about $7.17 million in 1994.

Going into 1995, Consolidated was operating a total of 141 Steak n Shake restaurants in Missouri, Indiana, Illinois, Michigan, Georgia, Florida, Ohio, Kentucky, Iowa, Arkansas, and Kansas. Management was pursuing an aggressive growth plan designed to more than double the number of outlets to 315 by 1999. Of 171 new restaurants planned for development, 78 were expected to be franchises. Improving per-store profits throughout the early 1990s and going into 1995 added validity to the plan. Meanwhile, Consolidated Specialty Restaurants reduced its holdings to 11 units, all but three of which were operating under the Colorado Steakhouse banner by 1995. That division continued to produce lackluster returns.

Principal Subsidiaries: Steak n Shake, Inc.; Consolidated Specialty Restaurants, Inc.

Further Reading:

Aramian, S. Sue, ''Consolidated Elects New President,'' *PR Newswire,* July 13, 1992.

''Consolidated Elects President,'' *Indianapolis Business Journal,* July 20, 1992, p. 8.

Harton, Tom, ''Steak n Shake Is on a Roll, but Stock Price and Specialty Restaurants Can't Keep Up,'' *Indianapolis Business Journal,* December 1989, p. 3.

MacKenzie, Coral, ''Enhanced Stock, But Bigger Debt Load: Consolidated Products Recap Has Changed the Balance Sheet,'' *Indianapolis Business Journal,* March 4, 1991, p. 5.

Murphy, Scott, ''Indiana's Entrepreneurs of the Year: Master,'' *Indiana Business,* September 1993, p. 65.

Parent, Tawn, ''Franchising Stalls at Consolidated Products,'' *Indianapolis Business Journal,* February 24, 1992, p. 3A.

——, ''Steak n Shake Signs Franchise Agreement to Add 50 Stores,'' *Indianapolis Business Journal,* June 24, 1991, p. 1A.

Partington, Marta, ''Steak n Shake: 'Famous for Steakburgers' for 56 Years,'' *Indiana Business,* April 1990, p. 37.

Romeo, Peter J, ''Steak n Shake Tosses Salads: Rollout Spices Two-Year Turnaround Strategy,'' *Nation's Restaurant News,* April 11, 1988, p. 116.

—Dave Mote

Consumers Power Co.

212 W. Michigan Ave.
Jackson, Michigan 49201
U.S.A.
(517) 788-0550
Fax: (517) 788-0258

Wholly Owned Subsidiary of CMS Energy Corp.
Incorporated: 1910
Employees: 9,382
Sales: $3,340 million
SICs: 4939 Combination Utility Not Elsewhere Classified

Consumers Power Co., a subsidiary of CMS Energy Corp. since 1987, is the largest utility company in Michigan and the fourth largest in the United States; it has provided electricity and gas to Michigan homes throughout the 20th century and services six million people across the state.

The Consumers Power Company was formed in 1910 through the merger of the properties of the two largest Michigan power company owners, W. A. Foote and the partners Anton G. Hodenpyl and H. D. Walbridge. Through the Commonwealth Power holding company, Foote controlled almost all the electric utilities in western Michigan including the Jackson, Albion, Kalamazoo, Battle Creek, Plainswell, and Grand Rapids electric companies. Foote also had interests in a number of "traction lines," the electric trolley systems that were one of the most important customers for his electric power. The long-time partners Hodenpyl and Walbridge, in turn, controlled most of the gas companies in eastern Michigan, along with some electric power facilities and traction lines. The Hodenpyl and Walbridge interests also extended into New York, Pennsylvania, Illinois, and Indiana, where the partners had been consolidating gas, electric, and tram lines into multiutility "railway and light" companies. The merger of the properties of these entrepreneurs into the Consumers Power Company created the largest utility company in Michigan and formed the basis for what was to become, for a brief period, one of the most important utility conglomerates in the United States.

The primary source of power for these pioneering electric utilities was the swift-flowing rivers of Michigan. They had been crucial in the earlier development of the state, providing transportation for the logging industry that had opened up western Michigan. By the late 1800s, however, both the cus-

tomers for wood products and the supply of timber had dried up, and the rivers, surrounded by decimated forest land, had lost their commercial value. W.A. Foote, a miller by trade, had been accustomed to harnessing water to run his flour mill. When a local entrepreneur asked him if he could set up a small electric dynamo in his flour mill, Foote became intrigued by the potential of this new way of exploiting water power. In 1885, Foote sold his mill and entered the electric utility business. Like all electric companies at that time, Foote's first plants in the towns of Adrian and Jackson were small in scale and were intended only to generate enough electricity to power street lights and some residential and business lighting. These needs could be met by local hydro- or coal-powered generators, but as electric trolley cars became more and more popular the demand for plentiful and (even more important) consistent electric power began to exceed the output of small local power plants. In 1898, William Foote, with the help of his engineer brother, James, undertook construction of the first large-scale dam in Michigan along the Kalamazoo River. Although at first beset by problems of power loss because of the then daunting 25 miles of wire needed to stretch to the nearest town, the Trowbridge dam and its successors, the Rogers and Croton dams, provided the bulk of the electric power in western Michigan for the next 30 years.

While W. A. Foote was building his tiny electric empire in western Michigan, the partners Anton Hodenpyl and Henry D. Walbridge were buying up local gas and traction line companies and merging them into larger interregional concerns. Gas power was the older cousin of the lighting industry. By the turn of the century gas companies had already had some fifty years of experience in lighting the streets and homes of America, and whereas electric power was still a risky venture, gas companies had a secure financial basis. Gas not only had the advantage of being first on the scene, but residential customers preferred its soft light to the harsh glare of the incandescent bulbs. Financiers rather than engineers, Hodenpyl and Walbridge operated out of a New York City office from which they controlled an ever-growing network of utilities and electric railway companies. The turn of the century was the heyday of the electric transportation industry in the United States. Not only had local tram lines become an essential part of town life, but "interurbans"—the intercity electric railways—were increasingly stealing the business of the more expensive and dirtier steam locomotives. With the internal combustion engine still only a novelty, the clean, comfortable interurbans seemed to be the wave of the future. Even old railroad barons like Cornelius Vanderbilt were convinced that control of the electric railways was essential to continuing in the train business. In 1906 Vanderbilt offered Hodenpyl and Walbridge an astounding $1 million for their New York area traction lines. The partners quickly accepted the offer, thereby obtaining the much needed capital to expand their acquisition of utilities.

It was by the unlikely means of a small-time Michigan lumberman, Edward Loud, that the Foote and Hodenpyl-Walbridge interests became merged. Loud had been slowly buying up lands along the Au Sable River with the long-term plan of shoring up his family's crumbling lumber business by selling the power of the swift Au Sable current. Loud discussed his plans for a dam with Foote, and though both men were convinced that the project had merit, neither had the capital necessary for such a large undertaking. In 1908, Hodenpyl-Walbridge

& Company's attention was drawn to the Au Sable, and so they invited Loud to New York to discuss a possible purchase. Foote saw his chance to merge some of the Hodenpyl-Walbridge capital, his company's technical expertise in hydropower, and Loud's Au Sable holdings. It soon became apparent that the benefits of this limited deal could be extended to the entire operations of the two utility firms, and by 1909 the merger had been completed.

The birth of Consumers Power, however, was not without complications. The same financial pressures and incentives that had given rise to the company had caused mergers and buyouts to spring up throughout the utilities industry. Critics were beginning to question the wisdom of allowing control over such an essential service to be concentrated in the hands of so few. Michigan politicians responded to this concern by giving the already existing Railroad Commission additional jurisdiction over electric rates and utility securities. This meant that any new offer of securities in connection with the founding of Consumers Power would have to be approved by the commission. There was no particular reason to believe that this approval would not have been given in the long run. The financiers, however, did not relish the idea of an intensive and lengthy public investigation of the assets and earnings of the myriad of small utility companies involved in the merger. They chose instead to simply bypass the commission by incorporating Consumers Power as a holding company in the state of Maine. The new company would have control over Foote's old operating company, Commonwealth Power, as well as the other Michigan utilities held by Foote or Hodenpyl-Walbridge. Consumers Power would in turn be controlled by a super-holding company to be called the Commonwealth Power Railway and Light Company, which also controlled a variety of utility and electric railway companies in other states. This system of nested holding companies not only allowed the financial management of these diverse companies to be under the control of a single group of men, it permitted the operating companies to retain their independence to raise funds through stock offerings.

World War I was a turning point for Consumers Power and its holding company, Commonwealth Power Railway and Light. Not only had the war sapped capital needed for the construction of large hydro dams and electric railway lines, but the automobile was making serious inroads into the electric railway business. The electric interurbans, which had seemed the great new trend in transportation through the first two decades of the century, suddenly seemed awkward and expensive when compared to the gasoline-powered automobile. Thus the electric railway business that had provided the bulk of Commonwealth Power's profits during the height of W. A. Foote's presidency had dropped to a distant third behind electricity and gas by the early 1920s. The decline in the electric railway had serious repercussions for Consumers Power, which had relied on the interurbans for the bulk of their electric power sales.

Under the leadership of B. C. Cobb, Consumers Power took two important steps in securing a future despite this harsh climate. Because the company could no longer rely on major sources of capital, they began to offer preferred shares to all of their customers. By the end of 1920, 6,378 shares had been sold and the tradition of broad public ownership of utility stocks had been established. It was more difficult to respond to the lost sales caused by the decline in the electric railway. Electricity and gas were still seen primarily as sources of light. Consumers Power realized that it would have to create the market for its utilities by promoting new uses for the power it provided. The company began an intensive effort, including theatrical demonstrations and a bevy of traveling salesmen, to introduce the many gadgets and appliances that could be powered by electricity. Thanks in part to these promotional campaigns (as well as an aggressive new spate of acquisitions), net income grew from $4.2 million in 1922 to $14.3 million in 1929.

By the early 1930s Consumers Power's holding company, Commonwealth Power, divested of its failing electric railways, had acquired a large number of smaller utility companies. In a race to become one of the major players in the utilities field, Commonwealth Power, now called Commonwealth and Southern, had bought and operated properties in Michigan, Illinois, Ohio, Indiana, Alabama, Georgia, Mississippi, Florida, and Tennessee. It was the last acquisition that brought Commonwealth Power into its most bitter confrontation with the Franklin D. Roosevelt administration.

The utilities industry was increasingly becoming consolidated in the hands of fewer and fewer large holding companies, and the newly elected Democratic government was determined to diminish the power of these corporate giants. The battle over utilities monopolies came to a head when Roosevelt signed a bill granting control over electric power production and distribution to the publicly owned Tennessee Valley Authority. This placed a publicly owned utility in direct competition with Commonwealth and Southern's Tennessee Electric Power Company, and it brought Consumers Power's president, Wendell Willkie, into direct confrontation with the Roosevelt administration. After a long, drawn-out battle and several trips to the U.S. Supreme Court, Willkie admitted defeat and sold Tennessee Electric to the TVA. The war over utilities, however, had just begun. Willkie's campaign to halt public ownership of utilities had been very public and very vocal, prompting high-level Republicans to recruit the longtime Democrat to run against Roosevelt in the 1940 presidential race. Willkie's electoral defeat by the immensely popular incumbent set the final stage for the dissolution of the giant privately owned utilities.

The Public Utility Act of 1935 had called for the dissolution of all utility holding companies that could not show that they controlled a regionally distinct and internally integrated system of operating companies. Commonwealth and Southern argued that the management of Consumers Power and its other operating companies was internally consistent and compact and that the holding company met the requirements of the law. Interpretation of the Public Utility Act was fraught with difficulties, however, and it would take six years—and Willkie's defeat—before the Securities and Exchange Commission reached a final decision as to the fate of Commonwealth and Southern. In 1941 the ax finally fell and the holding company was ordered to divest itself of either Consumers Power or its southern operations. World War II would delay the enforcement of this decision, but in 1946 Commonwealth and Southern was dissolved and Consumers Power, under the direction of Justin R. Whiting, was left as an independent gas and electric utility company.

The postwar years were a boom period for Michigan industry. Given the abundance of large, new factories in need of Consumers Power electricity, kilowatt-hour sales nearly doubled between 1945 and 1955. Michigan's new employment opportunities also gave rise to a surge in population, and Consumers Power residential sales boomed. Most of the increased sales were due to an almost eightfold increase in the use of gas furnaces over the same period. Although gas heating had been available since the turn of the century, the manufactured gas that Consumers Power supplied to its customers produced comparatively little heat per unit burned, making gas heating prohibitively expensive. In the mid-1930s natural methane gas had been used in small areas on an experimental basis; it was found that, with its higher heat value, gas costs for home heating could be cut by about 50 percent. By 1945 Consumers Power had converted entirely to natural gas and quickly made up for (and then far exceeded) the number of customers it had lost in the amount paid per household. During this same period a number of acquisitions of smaller regional utilities allowed Consumers Power to extend operations over most of central Michigan, from the northern tip of Michigan's Lower Peninsula to the Ohio border.

In response to the increased demand for electricity and gas in the 1950s and 1960s, Consumers Power undertook the construction of a large number of new production, storage, and distribution facilities. Although hydro had delivered the bulk of Michigan's electric power for the first decades of the century, it soon became impossible to meet the demands of a growing population, given the limited number of dams that could be built on Michigan's waterways. Coal-powered, steam-driven turbines became the only viable alternative. Thus the two existing coal-powered facilities were enlarged and three new coal plants were built during this period. These five plants, all named after important past executives of the company, would continue to provide about 80 percent of Consumers Power electric power through the mid-1990s.

When Consumers Power gave up manufactured gas in favor of natural gas it traded its production problem for one of supply. Throughout the 1930s and 1940s the company's main source for natural gas had been the Panhandle Eastern Pipeline Company, which piped gas from the resource-rich panhandle region of Texas, Kansas, and Oklahoma to population centers in the Northeast. In the 1950s this source was supplemented by supplies from the Trunkline Gas Company, with its wells in the Gulf Coast area (it later became Consumers Power's largest gas source). The company also exploited local Michigan wells, but these could never produce what was needed for heating homes through the bitter Michigan winters. The problem of seasonal demand was ingeniously solved by using the Michigan gas fields as huge natural storage tanks into which excess gas could be pumped during the summers, when demand was low. This system of gas storage would remain an essential component of the company's gas distribution system through the end of the century.

The ever-growing problem of energy supply created the biggest challenges for Consumers Power executives throughout the 1960s and 1970s. As the supply of coal shrank and prices rose, Consumers began to look seriously toward other ways of producing electricity. In the 1950s scientists and the public were

determinedly seeking a peaceful use of the enormous potential of atomic power. In a 1950s replay of the turn of the century, when it seemed electric trains would dominate transportation in the 20th century, nuclear power seemed poised to become the solution to the world's energy problems. Under the directorship of James H. Campbell, Consumers Power teamed up with Detroit Edison, the second largest utility in Michigan, to build an experimental "breeder" reactor; then in 1958 it built a small boiling-water reactor at Big Rock Point, Michigan. The Big Rock project was initially fraught with technical difficulties and cost overruns, but this was expected given the pioneering nature of the enterprise. As senior vice-president Robert Allen put it in the official history of the company, "Big Rock had a tremendous facility for demonstrating things in a negative way." By the late 1960s Consumers Power felt it had learned enough about nuclear power generation to build a larger, and hopefully profitable, nuclear reactor: It was the Palisades nuclear plant that would mark the end of Michigan's honeymoon with nuclear power and the beginning of Consumers Power's financial problems.

Big Rock had been built with little controversy, but by the 1960s public awareness of potential environmental problems with nuclear power had grown. Consumers Power was confronted with considerable organized objection to the Palisades plant from environmentalists concerned with the discharge of hot water from the plant into Lake Michigan. Construction cost overruns, the delays caused by the environmental intervention, and the environmental safeguards that were eventually added to the plant ended up costing Consumers Power millions more than had been budgeted. By 1971 the effect of the Palisades debacle, in addition to soaring energy costs, seriously affected Consumers stock, which fell to $30 per share from a high of $54. To make matters worse, the Michigan Public Service Commission refused to authorize a large rate increase to offset these costs.

Even before the completion of the Palisades plant plans had been under way to construct a second nuclear facility at Midland, Michigan; in spite of the problems at Palisades the company decided to go forward with this huge project. The Midland facility was originally scheduled to open in 1975 at a cost of about $500 million. Ten years and $3.5 billion later, Consumers Power pulled the plug on the still unfinished plant. If Consumers Power found itself in trouble with investors in the early 1970s because of the Palisades overruns, by 1984 the ill-fated Midland project caused a crisis. Shares bottomed out at $5 and the company suspended the common stock dividend. Investors bailed out in droves and *Barron's* was suggesting that bankruptcy might be an attractive option. The monumental cost overruns were blamed in part on mismanagement. The reputation of the 75-year-old company was at an all-time low. In 1985 William T. McCormick Jr. was hired to save the beleaguered utility.

McCormick's first move was to restructure Consumers Power and create a holding company, CMS Energy, to manage the utility. With the holding company McCormick could expand the company's nonregulated energy business and take risks that might be considered inappropriate for a publicly regulated utility. His next priority was to try to salvage some of the $4 billion white elephant at Midland. Dow Chemical had previously agreed to buy steam and energy from Midland and in 1984 had filed suit against Consumers, alleging mismanagement and cover-ups by Consumers management. Clearly, McCormick needed to make peace with Dow to get Midland and Consumers on their feet again. He reached a deal with the giant chemical company whereby Midland would be converted to a natural gas cogeneration plant that would produce steam, which would be used for Dow's chemical processing needs, as well as electricity, which would be sold to CMS's primary subsidiary, Consumers Power. Forty-nine percent of the venture was to be owned by CMS, and 51 percent by a group of investors led by Dow. With this structure the Midland Cogeneration Venture (MCV) would be governed by the Public Utilities Regulatory Policy Act (PURPA), which allows independent power producers to sell their power to utilities for the avoided cost of production by the utility.

The Midland Cogeneration Venture was plagued by years of lawsuits and disputes with regulators over the amount and cost of the energy to be provided to Consumers Power and its customers. By 1994 CMS Energy had reached an agreement in principle with most concerned parties that allowed Consumers Power to buy a substantial portion of MCV's energy output at the avoided cost of production. The difference between the original contract with MCV and this agreement would, however, result in substantial ongoing losses for the utility in the purchase of this energy. McCormick's restructuring and the authorization of substantial rate increases by the Michigan regulators succeeded in restoring Consumers Power to profitability. Continuing troubles with Midland, as well as cost increases surrounding the decommissioning and waste disposal at its nuclear facilities, would, however, continue to depress CMS stock price and dividends into the late 1990s.

Further Reading:

Bush, George, *Future Builders: The Story of Michigan's Consumers Power Company,* New York: McGraw-Hill, 1973.

Egan, John, "Out of the Briar Patch," *Financial World,* October 29, 1991, p. 26.

Norman, James R., "Reined in," *Forbes,* August 16, 1993, p. 70.

Tice, David W., "Less There Than Meets the Eye: A Hard Look at CMS Energy's Financials and Earnings," *Barron's,* October 16, 1989, pp. 15, 20–24.

Whitman, Martin J., "Virtues of Bankruptcy: For Nuclear Utilities, There May Be Many," *Barron's,* May 6, 1985, pp. 16–18, 43–45.

—Hilary Gopnik and Donald McManus

Consumers Water Company

Three Canal Plaza
Portland, Maine 04101
U.S.A.
(207) 773-6438
Fax: (207) 761-7903

Public Company
Incorporated: 1926
Employees: 640
Revenues: $401 million
Stock Exchanges: NASDAQ
SICs: 4941 Water Supply; 6719 Holding Companies, Not
    Elsewhere Classified

Consumers Water Company is one of the best managed utilities in the United States. The company owns, through its subsidiaries, eight water utilities in six states, including Maine, Ohio, Illinois, New Jersey, New Hampshire, and Pennsylvania. Serving nearly a quarter of a million people, the company's water systems provide an average daily production of more than 77 million gallons. Strongly adhering to the belief that all its customers deserve safe, clean water, Consumers Water has committed large sums of money to developing state-of-the-art filtration and disinfection systems to meet the stringent requirements of the federal Safe Drinking Water Act. The company's concern for the environment is just one of its successful endeavors. As every investor knows, utility companies almost always distribute dividends on a regular basis. Consumers Water Company is no exception. Consumers has one of the longest records of uninterrupted dividend growth and distribution in the United States.

Consumers Water Company began its existence under the most auspicious circumstances imaginable. Incorporated on February 18, 1926, the firm's original board of directors included George F. and Vernon F. West, partners in George F. West & Son, a well-known and highly successful water utility construction and management firm; Herbert Payson and Harold C. Payson, partners in H.M. Payson & Company, the largest and most influential underwriter of utility firms in America at that time; William B. Skelton, a lawyer who previously served as chairman of the Maine Public Utilities Commission; Philip Burgess, one of the principals from an engineering firm that designed water utility pumping stations and other facilities for the water utilities

industry; and James W. Coburn, a businessman with extensive experience in accounting. Vernon F. West was chosen to serve as the company's first president and, with the talented support of all the other board members, immediately began to implement a strategic acquisitions policy.

During the first year of the firm's existence, management acquired four utility companies, including Kankakee Water Company located in Illinois, Penobscot County Water Company situated in Maine, Shenango Valley Water Company in Pennsylvania, and Beaver Valley Water Company, also located in Pennsylvania. In 1927 and 1928, four more utility companies were acquired and then, after a brief period of consolidation, another five utility firms were purchased during 1930. The last acquisition of the year, in December, was the Springfield City Water Company in Springfield, Missouri. A number of the companies purchased by Consumers Water were already owned or controlled by H.M. Payson & Company or George F. West & Son. Since most of these companies were purchased for stock, by the end of 1930 the firm counted over 100,000 outstanding shares of stock. Most of this stock was held by the Wests, while the remaining shares were held by other individuals sitting on the company's board of directors.

When the Great Depression affected almost every aspect of American life in the 1930s, Consumers Water Company was hard hit by the economic instability that wreaked havoc on businesses throughout the country. In 1932, the company reduced salaries of employees making more than $20 per week by ten percent, and during the same year the firm was forced to defer the payment of a quarterly dividend on preferred stock. Yet Consumers Water Company also had a stroke of good fortune at approximately the same time. The Dartmouth Real Estate Company, a mid-sized, family-operated development firm, had arranged to lease two large warehouse facilities to A&P Company. When Dartmouth Real Estate was unable to meets its obligations to A&P, management at Dartmouth turned to the people at Consumers Water Company for help. In exchange for 50 percent ownership of Dartmouth's stock, management at Consumers Water Company agreed to help the real estate firm fulfill its financial obligations in the deal with A&P. One of the arrangements between Dartmouth and Consumers Water involved the option for Dartmouth to buy back its stock. Unfortunately for Dartmouth, since the Depression lasted the entire decade, the option for the repurchase of the stock expired before the Dartmouth owners could exercise their option. By the end of the decade, Consumers Water Company knew that it was only a matter of time before total ownership of Dartmouth Real Estate was finalized. When management completed the deal, the acquisition of Dartmouth had the effect of doubling the size of the firm.

Consumers Water Company weathered the Great Depression better than many other businesses. The company recorded a slight profit every year during the decade of the 1930s, and was also able to use this money to upgrade and improve its properties. When World War II began, the company was confronted with a whole new set of problems which were as daunting as those experienced during the previous ten years. During wartime, utility rates within the United States were frozen. Fortunately, however, the costs of almost all of the materials needed by various utilities were also frozen. The overwhelming problem faced by Consumers Water Company was to find the necessary material to repair and maintain the facilities owned by the firm. Of equal importance was the ability to find the manpower to work for the company since almost every able-bodied young man was serving in the United States Armed Forces. Under these circumstance, Consumers Water Company did as much as it could to provide reliable and continuous service to its customers.

The postwar years were very similar to the war years for the company. During the late 1940s and early 1950s, Consumers Water Company continued to provide service for its customers on a reduced scale. Although labor was no problem, the procurement of materials remained difficult even after the war was finished. As the country began to adapt itself to a peacetime economy, however, Consumers also began to gradually recover. By the early 1950s, after Harold C. Payson replaced Vernon F. West as president, the company was poised to take advantage of its rapidly improving financial status.

In the mid-1950s, Springfield City Water Company contributed half the company's earnings and also contained half of its investment. According to a previous agreement with the city government, the city had the option to purchase Springfield at a fair price. After the sale had been concluded, Consumers Water Company reported a profit of nearly $3.5 million, which suddenly doubled the value of the company's stock. Since Consumers had already divested many of its holdings, only five utility firms were still under company management, the board of directors was faced with the decision of either liquidating the firm and distributing the profits or plowing the money from the Springfield sale back into additional acquisitions of water utility companies. The management at Consumers Water Company decided to implement an aggressive acquisitions policy.

A cautious group of investors, and with Fletcher W. Means assuming the position as president in 1957, it wasn't until 1959 that the company made the first step in its new acquisition policy. The company's first acquisition in almost 30 years was the Camden and Rockland Water Company. Additional purchases followed rapidly over the next five years, including Newport Water Company, Wilton Water Company, Wiscassett Water Company, and Damariscotta Water Company, each located in Maine. Consumers also expanded into other eastern states with acquisition of water utility companies in New York and New Jersey. During the latter years of the 1960s, the company purchased two more water companies in Maine, and other water utilities in New Jersey and Pennsylvania.

With such an aggressive acquisitions strategy, the company grew rapidly during the late 1960s. Yet under the leadership of Fletcher Means, and his successor John White, there was every attempt to implement a decentralization policy throughout the company's operations. The subsidiaries owned by Consumers each had their own local president and board of directors. Composed primarily of local community and business leaders, these subsidiaries were granted a large degree of autonomy. At the same time, Consumers Water Company headquarters in Portland, Maine, made sure that standardization and uniformity were practiced in such areas as accounting methods, personnel practices, and customer service procedures. This decentralization policy worked especially well since local people were directly involved in the decisions of a utility company that provided service to thousands of customers.

In 1973, the company purchased Ohio Water Service Company, and over the next few years the consolidation of its services and facilities into Consumers' preoccupied and engaged most of management's time. During the late 1970s, however, management thought that the firm's earnings and dividends were not keeping up with inflation and, in order to rectify this situation, hired a consulting firm to come up with a possible solution. The recommendation made by the consulting firm was to diversify the holdings of Consumers Water Company into non-utility businesses. Having already done this once with the acquisition of The Dartmouth Company during the 1930s, management developed a strategy to purchase companies that would augment the manufactured housing business.

The first acquisition under this new strategy was Burlington Homes of New England, one of the leading manufacturers of modular and mobile homes. The second purchase was Schiavi Homes, Inc., the biggest retail operation involved in the sale of mobile homes throughout New England. Management at Consumers Water Company saw the purchase of these two companies as an opportunity to pursue an organizational plan of vertical integration. With both Burlington Homes and Schiavi under its control, the non-utility business of Consumers Water Company shot up from ten to 30 percent. Unfortunately, however, the quality of Schiavi products did not meet Consumers' expectation, and the company was sold during the mid-1980s.

Yet immediately after the diversification into manufactured housing, Consumers Water Company resumed its aggressive acquisitions plan involving water utilities. In 1984, the company purchased a wastewater utility plant north of its facility in Kankakee, Illinois; in 1985, the company purchased Roaring Creek Water Company in Shamokin, Pennsylvania; in 1986, the company acquired Inter-State Water Company in Danville, Illinois; and in 1987, the company bought Woodhaven Utilities Company in Illinois, and Califon Water Company in New Jersey.

During the late 1980s, Consumers Water Company decided to create its own subsidiaries in the field of manufactured housing. Still pursuing a grand organization strategy of vertical integration, management at Consumers created Arcadia Company, a firm involved in the development of manufactured housing communities. Arcadia's first project was a 205-unit apartment community in Taunton, Massachusetts. Another subsidiary, C/P Utility Services Company, was also added to the firm's non-utility holdings in a joint venture. Located in Hamden, Connecticut, C/P Utility provided a whole range of technical services, not only for water utilities but other industries as well, including meter installation, corrosion control, and leak detection. Buying out its partner in the joint venture, C/P Utility recorded $8.7 million in revenues by 1992. Later, in 1995, C/P Utility changed its name to Consumers Applied Technologies, Inc. to better reflect its involvement in the consulting and technical services of water conservation, corrosion control, distribution system evaluation, and environmental engineering.

In the early 1990s, the assets and properties of the Dartmouth Company were liquidated and Consumers Water, while maintaining a modest diversification program, decided that the firm should emphasize the ownership and operation of water utilities rather than non-utility holdings. The company underwent a series of mergers and acquisitions, and in 1994, the company's divested itself of its homebuilding interest, Burlington Homes of New England, Inc.

During the late 1980s and early 1990s, Consumers Water Company along with the rest of the water utility industry was placed under stringent federal requirements of the Safe Drinking Water Act. The passage of this act by the United States Congress raised many fears within the industry that water utility companies would not be able to comply with the requirements of the act due to older water distribution systems and the ever-growing pattern of increased water consumption. When a severe drought swept the eastern coast of the United States during the late 1980s, many water utility companies were hit hard by the capital expenditures needed to implement systems for water rationing. But Consumers Water Company had kept pace with developing technologies within the water utility industry and was able to meet the demand caused by the drought, and the requirement of the Safe Drinking Water Act, without any difficulty.

Into the 1990s, the management team at Consumers Water Company has remained remarkably stable. John White served as president of the company from 1966 to 1984, and was then replaced by John Van C. Parker, who was in turn succeeded by Peter L. Haynes. The long tenure of company presidents is not only indicative of stable management but careful and sound decision-making. With such able people guiding the company into the future, Consumers Water Company will remain one of the most efficiently operated utility firms in the United States.

Principal Subsidiaries: Consumers Pennsylvania Water Company; Consumers Maine Water Company (92.1%); Consumers New Jersey Water Company (97.1%); Consumers Ohio Water Company; Consumers Illinois Water Company; Consumers New Hampshire Water Company; Consumers Applied Technologies, Inc.

Further Reading:

DeStaebler, Douglas C., "Water Utility Industry," *The Value Line Investment Survey,* November 12, 1993, p. 1416.
Leach, Mark, "Unassigned Stocks," *The Value Line Investment Survey,* May 15, 1992, p. 1419.
Levenson, Maurice, "Water Utility Industry," *The Value Line Investment Survey,* February 10, 1995, p. 1417.
Parker, John Van C. Parker, *Consumers Water Company,* New York: Newcomen Society, 1988.
Sivy, Michael, "Consumers is Actively Acquiring Firms in the Price Range of $2–$5 Million," *Wall Street Journal,* April 28, 1982, p. 39.
——, "Hot and Cold Running Dividends Promise Total Returns of 9% or More," *Wall Street Newsletter,* November 1994, p. 64.

—Thomas Derdak

Corby Distilleries Limited

1002 Sherbrooke Street West
Suite 2300
Montreal, Quebec H3A 3L6
Canada
(514) 288-4181
Fax: (514) 288-6715

Public Company
Founded: 1859 as Corbyville Mills & Distillery
Employees: 170
Sales: US$69.1 million
Stock Exchanges: Toronto
SICs: 2084 Wines, Brandy, and Brandy Spirits; 2085
   Distilled and Blended Liquors; 5182 Wine and Distilled
   Beverages

Based in Montreal, Corby Distilleries Limited markets a full range of domestically produced distilled spirits and liqueurs as well as imported cognac, scotch, gin, and a variety of wines. Leading brands marketed and distributed by Corby include Lamb's, Wiser's, and Canadian Club. The company boasts a legacy of success dating back to the 1870s.

The enterprise that would become Corby Distilleries was started in the mid-1800s by entrepreneur, politician, and English immigrant Henry Corby. Corby, in search of adventure and opportunity, had sailed to the New World in 1832 with his new bride. After arriving in Quebec, the couple sailed up the St. Lawrence River into Lake Ontario. They eventually reached Belleville, a town located at the mouth of the Moira River that had been settled in 1816. The 26-year-old Corby and his wife were impressed by the beauty of the area and chose to remain in the town. Corby invested what little money he had in merchandise for a tiny food shop. He soon added a bakery to the store, which allowed him to put to use skills he had developed as an apprentice baker in London.

Within a few years Corby had established himself as the leading baker in the little town of Belleville. Besides growing his business, Corby and his wife managed to have three children. Corby also joined in the 1837 Rebellion as a volunteer in a rifle company. After a brief stint of service he returned to Belleville and contracted to provide supplies to troops encamped in the village. Tragedy struck shortly thereafter. Two days after Christmas, Corby's wife and three children were enjoying a sleigh ride on the bay. The sleigh broke through the ice and all four drowned. Corby subsequently married the sister of his first wife, a common practice at the time. She eventually bore 12 children before she died and Corby married a third time. Corby later purchased Massassago Point, where his first family had drowned, and turned it into a public resort as a memorial.

In 1838 Corby sold his bakery and grocery business and purchased the steamer "Queen," which he captained as a transport between Belleville and nearby Kingston. After four years he left that business and became involved in the buying and selling of grain. In 1857 he started a milling operation in nearby Corbyville. This business was the precursor to Corbyville Mills & Distillery. The mill started out offering a grain cracking service to farmers in the area, who brought in wagon loads of corn which they would take home with them after Corby ground it. In 1859 Corby expanded his operation, making arrangements with farmers wherein they left extra grain which he distilled into whiskey and sold back to them as a sideline business. The liquor sideline grew steadily until, in the 1870s, the mill became secondary to Corby's distillery operation.

Corby was heavily involved in politics as well as business. He was chosen as mayor of Belleville for a two-year term that began in 1867. He was then elected to the Canadian Provincial Parliament. Meanwhile, the distillery business continued to thrive and Corby's fine whiskeys became much more widely known. By the late 1870s the aging Corby was prepared to begin turning over the business to his sons. Best suited among them to run the company was Henry Corby Jr., the second-oldest son. Henry Corby died in 1881 and the younger Corby assumed leadership. Henry Corby Jr. (also known as H. Corby) brought a new level of energy and business expertise to the enterprise. Under his able hand the company flourished into a leading regional distillery.

H. Corby built a suite of offices on Main Street in Belleville and a new warehouse. He also was quick to institute the practice of bottling whiskey rather than sell it in barrels. For a number of years large barrels of whiskey were brought into Belleville by horse-drawn cart from Corbyville for bottling. A bottling operation was eventually established in Corbyville. Crates of the bottled whiskey were then transported to the Belleville warehouse, from which they were loaded onto rail cars and shipped throughout Canada. As the rail system expanded across the country during the late 1800s and early 1900s, the Corby name spread throughout the country and became known as a high-quality whiskey. Corby also began importing Scotch whiskey, and for a while the company became involved in the tobacco trade.

Like his father, H. Corby became known as a philanthropist and politician. He, like the senior Henry Corby, was a captain in the volunteer fire department. He also donated large sums of money to the Belleville hospital and the St. Thomas Anglican church. As Belleville grew, Corby was a major donor and leader for a variety of improvement projects. He also served two full terms and part of a third in Parliament. In addition, Corby became an avid traveler and ventured to Egypt, Europe, and many Pacific islands. Company annals relate an incident that occurred in Nice, France, on one of his trips. Corby encountered a small wines and spirits shop. In jest, he asked the owner if he had any of that "good Corby's whiskey." The dealer rummaged around and, to Corby's surprise, found a dusty, 15-year-old bottle of Corby's whiskey that Corby purchased as a souvenir.

By the early 1900s Corby had amassed a sizable fortune and was ready to retire. His opportunity came one day in 1905 when a tobacco trader named Mortimer Davis called on him. During the course of their conversation Corby expressed his desire to leave the business and devote more of his time to travel. Through the sale of bonds issued for a newly formed corporation call H. Corby Distillery Co., Ltd., Davis managed to buy out Corby and take control of the company in 1907. Corby spent the remainder of his life traveling and relaxing. He died in Honolulu in 1918 at the age of 67 and was survived by his wife and three daughters.

Unfortunately for Davis, the distillery was destroyed by fire shortly after he purchased it. The facility was quickly rebuilt, however, and Davis eventually parlayed his new company into a top Canadian distillery. In fact, Davis had already become a respected name in the regional tobacco industry before he purchased Corby. He would later be remembered as a major influence on the Canadian whiskey business and would even be knighted because of his important industrial contributions to the British Empire. His influence in the liquor industry spread throughout Canada, England, and the United States, partly as a result of war-time contributions. Indeed, during World War I Corby Distillery suspended production of liquor and converted entirely to the manufacture of alcohol, much of which was shipped to the United States to make synthetic rubber and other materials. The company also produced millions of gallons of industrial alcohol for shipment to the United States during World War II.

In 1918 Canadian Industrial Alcohol Company Limited, a holding company, purchased H. Corby Distillery Company Limited. Canadian Industrial made subsequent acquisitions as well and emerged as a major player in the alcoholic beverages and industrial alcohol industries. One of the most important of these purchases was Robert McNish & Company Limited of Glasgow, Scotland, the bottler of the renowned Scotch whiskey Grand McNish. Canadian Industrial also acquired J.M. Douglas & Company Limited, a major import company, and Wiser's De Luxe Whiskey. For about 30 years Corby operated under the umbrella of its parent, Canadian Industrial. During that period Corby flourished as a leading manufacturer and distributor of Corby whiskeys and other beverages.

By 1950, in fact, the Corby Distillery facilities had ballooned to include over 80 buildings on about 23 acres. The company's wine storage capacity had grown to include ten rack warehouses, each of which could store 15,000 to 50,000 barrels of whiskey and gin. After the completion of a modern "continuos" still in 1950, Corby boasted a production capacity of over four million gallons of grain and molasses spirits per year—the grain spirits were used to make whiskey and gin, while the molasses distillates were utilized in the manufacture of industrial alcohols. Because of Corby's growing importance, Canadian Industrial chose to change the name of the holding company in 1950 to H. Corby Distillery Co. Ltd. (the name was changed again in 1968 to Corby Distilleries Ltd.).

Thus, in 1950 Corby became the parent company of a wide range of alcoholic beverage and industrial alcohol operations that distributed products throughout North America, in Europe, and in other regions. In 1951 Corby moved its headquarters into 1201 Sherbrooke Street West, a mansion in Montreal that was built in the 1890s. The structure had originally been built as a home for Montreal banker James Baxter. The residence was purchased to house the executive offices of Thomas Robertson Limited in 1900 and was redesigned by renowned architect Stanford White, who also designed Madison Square Garden in New York. Corby purchased the structure, completely renovated it, and opened its offices there in 1951. The grand opening of the structure was attended by both Canadian and U.S. dignitaries. The building became a government-protected historic property in 1974.

By the mid-1970s the Corby umbrella encompassed a variety of companies and products and managed a wide distribution network located primarily in North America. Top-selling brands included Corby whiskeys, Wiser's whiskeys, and Lamb's rums, as well as a number of products imported through the J.M. Douglas subsidiary. During the 1980s Corby expanded steadily through increased sales and the acquisition of other brands. During that period, sales ballooned into the area of US$90 million annually as Corby assumed control of more than 25 percent of the entire Canadian spirits and imported wines market. By the late 1980s Corby was generating more than US$80 million in annual sales, employing a work force of about 570 people, and maintaining the business's fiscally sound base; the company had managed to achieve steady growth throughout the 1970s and 1980s without accruing any long-term debt.

Corby's financial performance began to wane in the early 1990s. Revenue declined about 15 percent between 1990 and 1994 (year ended February 28), although profits remained strong. Much of the decline in sales was attributable to ongoing tax increases related to alcoholic beverages in Canada. Indeed, the tax environment had become a problem for the alcoholic beverage industry: the Canadian government was slapping a whopping 83 percent duty on domestic spirits. As a result, the consumption of alcoholic beverages began to gradually decline. Worse yet, a sophisticated smuggling network had developed to bring alcohol into Canada from the United States. Going into the mid-1990s it was estimated that one of every four bottles of liquor consumed in Canada was smuggled into the country illegally on the black market.

Corby managed to sustain healthy profits during the industry downturn of the early and mid-1990s by slashing costs, restructuring, and adjusting its product mix. The company eliminated much of its work force, sold off its executive offices, closed several of its less productive manufacturing facilities, and even began entertaining offers for its Corbyville plant. The latter move represented Corby's transition from manufacturing to marketing and distribution. In addition, the company added a number of new brands and products to its portfolio, strengthening its market diversity. It added the Canadian Club, Ballantine's, and Kahlua brands in the early 1990s, for example, and began marketing lines of ready-to-drink cocktails. The net result of Corby's overall effort was an increase in net earnings, despite lower sales and a decline in the company's total assets.

Corby Distilleries entered the mid-1990s with control of about 27 percent of the Canadian spirits and imported wines market. Corby marketed nine of the 25 leading brands of spirits sold in Canada and enjoyed a leading position in major categories like whiskey, rum, gin, Scotch whiskey, vodka, cognac, liqueurs, brandy, and tequila. Popular brands marketed and distributed by Corby in 1995 included Canadian Club, Wiser's, Lamb's, Kahlua, Beefeater, Salvador's, Hennessy, and Courvoisier, among others. The company's 1995 annual report cited government regulations and taxation as a major determinant of the company's long-term success.

Principal Subsidiaries: Meaghers Distillery Ltd.; McGuinness Distillers Ltd.

Further Reading:

Brent, Paul, "Taxes, Hard Times Fuel Underground Economy," *Financial Post,* June 26, 1993, p. 6.

Heinrich, Erik, "Corby Shares Advance Despite Six-Month Loss," *Financial Post,* October 9, 1991, p. 15.

Shalom, Francis, "Illegal Booze Costs US $1 Billion: Distiller—Head of Corby Says Industry Hurt by Moonshine Smuggled from U.S.," *Gazette,* June 25, 1993, p. 7D.

—Dave Mote

Corporation for Public Broadcasting

901 E. Street, NW
Washington, D.C., 20004
U.S.A.
(202) 879-9600
Fax: (202) 783-1039

Private Company
Founded: 1967
Operating Revenues: $282.4 million
Employees: 115
SICs: 4833 Television Broadcasting Stations

The Corporation for Public Broadcasting distributes government money to public television and radio stations and to organizations that create programming for them. While nearly all of its funding comes from Congress, it is not a government agency.

During the 1960s, during a period of intense scrutiny and criticism of television, a report by the Carnegie Commission outlined measures to improve the quality of television by increasing the quantity of educational programming. The report recommended that funding for public television be increased and that an organization be formed to funnel funding to public broadcasting stations. Initially, this funding was to come from a tax on television sets like that used in Great Britain. Partly because of opposition from television manufacturers, the funding source was changed to Congressional appropriations.

A large number of public radio and television stations already existed. The earliest had been founded by universities around 1917. The first radio station run by a nonprofit community group was started in Berkeley, California, in 1949 by the Pacifica Foundation. The first noncommercial television station began broadcasting in Houston in 1953. In 1962 the federal government began helping to fund educational television through the Educational Television Facilities Act.

CPB was founded by the Public Broadcasting Act of 1967, with the support of President Lyndon Johnson and most of Congress. The Act set up the CPB as a government-sponsored corporation whose funding came through the Department of Housing, Education, and Welfare through the Office of Education. The CPB was allowed to make its funding requests directly to Congress. Because it was not set up as an independent agency or given

long-term financing, the CPB was required to continually approach Congress for funding approvals—an arrangement that has influenced much of its history.

Under the terms of the Public Broadcasting Act, the CPB set up a fifteen-member board of directors that was appointed by the president with the consent of the Senate. This board could not have more than eight members from the same political party as the president, and its members were forbidden from engaging in political activity. With the sponsorship of President Johnson, the CPB was highly centralized under its first president, John Macy, and first chairman, Frank Pace, and it enjoyed a great deal of autonomy in decision making.

As part of its mandate to create an interconnected system of broadcast stations and to distribute and sponsor programming, the CPB quickly set up two further organizations: the Public Broadcasting Service, established in 1969 to create and distribute television programming, and National Public Radio, created in 1970 to handle radio news and features. While CPB set up PBS and NPR, they were never its subsidiaries. The CPB received money from Congress and distributed it to PBS and NPR, as well as to independent producers who created programming for public broadcast stations. Many of the programs now most closely associated with public television, including *Mister Rogers' Neighborhood* and *Sesame Street,* appeared between 1968 and 1970.

The CPB's vulnerability to political pressures became apparent after Richard Nixon was elected president in 1968. By 1971 the Nixon Administration was in conflict with the CPB over controversial programming, perceiving anti-Administration bias in such programs as *Washington Week in Review, Bill Moyers,* and *The Great American Dream Machine.* The documentary *Banks and the Poor,* which alleged that many major banks discriminated against poor customers, also alienated members of Congress by displaying a long list of the names of members of the House and Senate who had ties to the banking industry.

Soon public broadcasting was being denounced by Vice President Spiro Agnew, local stations were being encouraged to be more autonomous, and Nixon vetoed the CPB's appropriations bill for 1973. CPB bowed to pressure from the administration, agreeing to restructure itself and its dealings with other parts of the public television system.

A "partnership agreement" established between CPB and PBS removed the Corporation from many programming decisions it had formerly made, giving these powers to PBS and individual stations. CPB was left to finance technical operations by means of a contract with PBS. CPB, in turn, took over from PBS the right to review controversial programs to make certain that they were balanced and fair. Further, the share of its funding that CPB gave as unrestricted grants to public broadcasting stations rose to 50 percent. This meant less power for CPB and more for local stations. CPB was rewarded for its capitulation to political pressure with an increase and stabilization of its funding, but had less control over what was done with this money. The Corporation's appropriation rose from $23 million for 1971, to $35 million for 1972 and 1973, and to $47.5 million for 1974.

As a result of these changes, CPB President John Macy resigned, as did many of his top aides. The changes also led to growing friction between the Corporation and PBS.

Over the next few years, the CPB was criticized by members of Congress, and by some of its own supporters, for not hiring enough minorities to meet the requirements of civil rights legislation. Of 29 managerial positions in 1975, only two were held by minorities. President Gerald Ford largely ignored the CPB during his two-year term, while Congress raised CPB appropriations to $103 million for 1977 (appropriations were usually allocated two years in advance).

The CPB had an easier time during the Carter Administration than during the Nixon and Ford Administrations. The Public Telecommunications Financing Act of 1978 returned some of the CPB's autonomy, eliminating the Office of Telecommunications Policy, which had overseen many aspects of the CPB, and setting up a separate account for the Corporation within the U.S. Treasury. As another result of the act, the CPB gave its grants for the production of programs directly to the producers of the programs. To do this, the CPB created the Program Fund, which defined the criteria for winning such grants and made the awards. Finally, the act opened the Corporation's board meetings to the public, and mandated that CPB annually submit a plant to Congress laying out its objectives for the next five years.

In 1978 President Carter tried to win $1 billion over a five-year period for CPB, but the plan met with opposition in Congress, partly because many in Congress felt the Corporation's mission was still confused, and also because it had a poor record of hiring minorities and women.

In 1979 the Carnegie Commission released another report on public television. This time the Commission urged that Congress spend $1 billion a year on public television—and also recommended that another organization be created to take the place of CPB. The report was critical of CPB, claiming that it was partly responsible for creating an unwieldy bureaucracy that wasted money that might have otherwise gone to programming. With Congress unwilling to pass President Carter's far more modest budget, the Carnegie recommendations went nowhere.

Nevertheless, CPB continued to fund the expansion of the public broadcasting network. In 1979, for example, it played a key role in financing the linking of 192 public radio stations to a satellite. This allowed National Public Radio to distribute its programming via satellite instead of via telephone or audio tapes that had to be mailed to stations. Approximately 20 percent of public radio programming was produced nationally, and could now be distributed more quickly and with better audio quality.

With the election of President Ronald Reagan in 1980, the U.S. government entered a period of budget cutbacks. The 1983 appropriation for CPB was quickly reduced to $137 million from $172 million, reversing a six-year trend of increases in CPB's budget. The Corporation was forced to make layoffs, and shrank its managerial force from 134 in 1982, to 102 in 1983, and to 92 in 1984.

Meanwhile Congress cut the CPB board from 15 members to 10, and required that two of these board members come from public television and radio stations. Congress also mandated that 25 percent of the CPB budget go to the Program Fund and instructed the Corporation to begin finding other sources of funding. Ten public television stations were allowed to try limited commercial advertising to help pay their bills.

In 1983, with National Public Radio facing a $9.1 million debt, Congress charged the CPB with putting the organization on a sound financial footing. Negotiations over a bailout loan were tense, as the two organizations vied for control of NPR's primary asset, its equipment. Finally, in late July, the Corporation gave NPR a $500,000 advance to meet its payroll. Further loans followed, with the proviso that ownership of NPR's equipment be shifted to a group of independent trustees to prevent their potential seizure by creditors. NPR also agreed to cut costs, raise the fee it charged member stations, and increase its contributions from listeners.

President Reagan's CPB board appointments were often controversial. In 1984 he chose the former head of the organization Women for Reagan-Bush, Sonia Landau, to replace Sharon Rockefeller, who had been appointed by President Carter, as chair. Rockefeller remained on the CPB board, however, and she and Landau quickly engaged in a heated public debate, with Rockefeller and some other directors charging that Reagan appointees had politicized the CPB. Edward J. Pfister, president of the Corporation during Carter's term, resigned from the board after it voted to cancel a trip he was to make to Moscow to investigate the suitability of some Soviet television programs for American broadcasting. He, Rockefeller, and others alleged that the trip was canceled for political reasons, while the Landau faction said it was canceled to avoid wasting taxpayer money. When Landau's term expired in 1986, Reagan reappointed her, but the Senate declined to act on her nomination, and William Lee Hanley, Jr., an oil company executive, was eventually elected chair. At about the same time, Martin Rubenstein became the second CPB president in two years to resign over policy differences with the Corporation's board.

In 1987 Congress ordered CPB and PBS to settle their differences. The two organizations reached a compromise the following year in which the Corporation took responsibility for new programs and authority for the Independent Television Service and the Minority Initiatives production group, both of which had been created by Congress the previous year. CPB agreed to split its remaining programming money with PBS. The agreement was an attempt to streamline public broadcasting, allocating more money to programming and less to administration.

The 1990 appropriations bill once again restructured how the CPB allocated its money. The bill ordered the Corporation to form the Independent Production Service and give it a budget of $6 million a year. It also gave $3 million for minority programming, and specified that 25 percent of CPB's interest income go to public radio and the other 75 percent to public television. Finally, the bill ordered the Corporation to spend no more than $10.2 million on its administration, plus, in following years, either four percent or the percent rise in the Consumer Price Index, whichever was greater.

In 1992 Senate conservatives attempted to reduce the CPB budget by nearly $400 million over a three-year period. They contended that the programs shown on public broadcasting reflected a liberal bias and were sometimes obscene. The conservatives were defeated by a vote of 75–22, and a $1.1 billion authorization was voted for 1994 to 1996.

By 1994 the public broadcast community for which CPB provided funding had grown to 629 radio stations and 351 television stations. The Corporation's allocation for fiscal 1995 was $285.6 million. Its administrative costs were $13 million, or 4.5 percent of its budget. It made $143.5 million in community service grants directly to local television stations and $44.6 million in community service grants to radio stations. Grants for national programming for radio and television totaled $67 million, and were the largest single source of financing for public television and radio programs. About six percent of its budget, or $17 million, went to general system support, which included training and technological research and development. The CPB and public broadcasting received praise in some quarters because of the educational and cultural value of some of its programming, as well as the low level of violence compared to that of commercial broadcasting.

However, despite Congress's own criticism of violence in commercial broadcasting, congressional hostility to the CPB had never been higher. Some members of Congress called for the privatization of the CPB, asserting that the government should not be supporting broadcasting, and that the diversity of programming the CPB was created to foster was now being provided by cable television stations. They argued that public broadcasting could survive on greater private and corporate donations (particularly with more advertising allowed by corporation underwriters), and the marketing of characters from popular programs like *Sesame Street* and *Barney & Friends.*

The mood on the local level was sometimes similar to that in Congress. In 1994 New York Mayor Rudolph Giuliani began drawing up plans to sell two of the city's public broadcast outlets, WNYC-TV and WNYC-FM, prompting the CPB to warn him that it would seek millions of dollars in reimbursement costs if the city went ahead with the sale.

The Congressional elections of 1994 turned CPB's situation from bad to worse as the Republican Party gained control of both the House and the Senate. Attempting to cut federal spending—and objecting to what many saw as liberal or immoral programming—Congress soon directed the Corporation to look for ways to completely replace its federal funding with other sources of revenue. Representative Peter Hoekstra of Michigan introduced a measure to eliminate the CPB's funding for 1998.

The CPB, along with public television and radio leaders, began a major grass-roots effort against a funding cutoff. CPB president Richard Carlson formed a task force with executives from PBS, NPR, and other organizations to increase public support. PBS stations began airing commercials warning that its programming might disappear if the CPB's funding were cut off.

The Corporation hired Lehman Brothers Inc., a New York financial firm, to investigate possible sources of new revenue. Lehman looked at ways to cut costs throughout public broadcasting, by methods including limiting funding to one public broadcasting station in each market. It also considered generating revenue by marketing toys from popular public broadcasting programs, selling broadcast spectrum, and increasing the amount of corporate sponsorship. Lehman's report concluded that all of these means together could not replace federal government funding, leaving the Corporation's future murky.

Further Reading:

Brown, Les, "Carnegie Unit Urges a Billion a Year for Public TV," *New York Times,* January 23, 1979, pp. A1, B17.
——, "Carter's Five-Year $1 Billion Plan for Public Broadcasting Opposed," *New York Times,* March 4, 1978, pp. A1, A44.
Ferretti, Fred, "Corporation for Public Broadcasting Seeks Funds," *New York Times,* February 3, 1970.
Gerard, Jeremy, "Public TV's Plan: Cut Red Tape, Diversify Shows, *New York Times,* November 20, 1989, p. C18.
Gould, Jack, "Major Programing Shake-Up Hits Educational TV," *New York Times,* April 9, 1969, p. A1.
——, "Pace and 12 Others Named by President to Public TV Board," *New York Times,* February 18, 1968, p. A1.
Lashley, Marilyn, *Public Television,* Westport, Conn.: Greenwood Press, 1992.
McAvoy, Kim, "Public Broadcasters Go on Offense," *Broadcasting & Cable,* December 19, 1994, pp. 48–49.
Molotsky, Irvin, "Public Broadcasting Is Airing Its Linen," *New York Times,* August 11, 1985.
Oneal, Michael, and Richard Melcher, "Dead End for Sesame Street?," *Business Week,* June 19, 1995, pp. 66–68.
Rathbun, Elizabeth, "House Makes CPB Cuts," *Broadcasting & Cable,* March 20, 1995, p. 15.
——, "The Selling of Public TV," *Broadcasting & Cable,* February 13, 1995, pp. 43–45.
Schwartz, Tony, "Public TV Faces Financial Crisis," *New York Times,* November 13, 1980, pp. A1, C34.
Tolchin, Martin, "Public Broadcasting Wins Senate Battle for Federal Money," *New York Times,* June 4, 1992, pp. A1–B10.

—Scott M. Lewis

D&K Wholesale Drug, Inc.

8000 Maryland Avenue
Suite 1190
St. Louis, Missouri 63105
U.S.A.
(314) 727-3485
Fax: (314) 727-5759

Public Company
Incorporated: 1987
Employees: 185
Sales: $319 million
Stock Exchanges: NASDAQ
SICs: 5122 Drugs, Proprietaries & Sundries; 6719 Holding
   Companies Not Elsewhere Classified

D&K Wholesale Drug, Inc. is one of the rising stars in the regional wholesale drug distribution industry. With sales approaching $320 million in fiscal 1995, the company provides its services to customers in 17 states, primarily in the Midwest and south central United States. From warehouse facilities located in Cairo, Illinois, and Lexington, Kentucky, D&K Wholesale Drugs distributes a wide range of pharmaceuticals, beauty aids, and health products to such diverse customers as large chain drugs stores, independent pharmacies, both small and large hospitals, and other specialists that provide health care services.

D&K Wholesale Drugs was founded as a holding company in 1987 by Hord Armstrong, III and his cousin, W. VanMeter Alford, Jr. After graduating from Williams College in 1963, and attending New York University's business school the following year, Armstrong started his career in business with the Morgan Guaranty Trust Company, and in a short period of time was elected assistant treasurer. In 1977, he left Morgan Guaranty to serve as first vice-president at White Weld & Company, and when White Weld was acquired by Merrill Lynch in 1978, Armstrong left to become treasurer of Arch Mineral Corporation, a coal mining operation. By 1981 he had been appointed vice-president and chief financial officer of Arch Mineral.

In the late 1980s, Armstrong, Alford, and a group of investors decided to form D&K in order to acquire two pharmaceutical distributors: Delta Wholesale Drug, Inc. and W. Kelly Company. Delta, based in Cairo, Illinois, was a small but highly successful regional wholesale pharmaceutical distributor that sold primarily to large drug store chains. Kelly, a Kentucky-

based company founded in 1941, sold pharmaceuticals to independent drugs stores in the central southern states. D&K Wholesale Drugs—so named for the "D" in Delta and the "K" in Kelly—was established as a private company in 1987. Armstrong became the company's chairman, chief executive officer, and president. Alford, who had previously served as president and general counsel for Diamond Shamrock Company, an energy resources firm, assumed the positions of president, chief operating officer, secretary, and director.

Together, Delta and Kelly initially comprised the entire working operations of D&K Wholesale Drugs, but within a short period of time Armstrong and Alford had initiated a comprehensive plan to revise the direction of both companies. The new strategy included a plan to increase service capabilities, incorporate new product lines for distribution, and expand into nearby geographical areas.

During this time, the wholesale drug industry was beginning to flourish. In ten years, from 1980 to 1990, industry sales increased from just over $6 billion to nearly $31 billion. Demographic, medical, and social trends fueled this dramatic increase. In 1980, within the United States, there were 72.5 million people over the age of 45; by 1990, there were over 81 million people who had passed this age. This part of the population, according to studies analyzed by Armstrong and Alford, tended to have more disabilities and chronic illnesses than younger segments of the population. At the same time, government health insurances and private insurance companies initiated cost containment procedures that strongly advocated use of pharmaceutical treatments rather than in-hospital curative techniques such as surgeries. The owners of D&K were convinced that these trends would continue for some time into the future.

Furthermore, new drug therapies developed by large pharmaceutical manufacturers required a wider distribution network than ever before, due to the increase in the amount of drugs being purchased. As a result, these large companies began to rely more heavily on wholesale drug distributors in order to sell their products. From 1980 to 1990, the percentage of drugs sold through drug wholesalers jumped from 57.3 to 75 percent. In addition, the number of pharmaceutical wholesale companies dropped from 139 to 84, primarily because of large wholesalers acquiring smaller firms to create more efficient economies of scale. Those firms which sold pharmaceutical items, including regional drug stores chains, mail order companies, grocery stores with pharmacies, and small, independent pharmacies, were the focus of D&K's marketing strategy. Armstrong and Alford thought that if they could provide a highly efficient and highly personal service approach to capitalize on the trends in health care treatment, then their new company was assured of success.

D&K's management proved correct. From 1987 to 1989, the company's net sales jumped to $79.3 million. The following year, the company increased its sales force, and immediate results were seen in sales, particularly in Cincinnati, Louisville, and the entire state of Iowa. With contracts through a mail order prescription company, as well as with a midwestern hospital chain, the company's net sales figures continued to increase. By 1991, net sales had increased a hefty 25.6 percent to $129 million, and the following year, Armstrong took the company public.

In 1992, the company's net sales increased by 12.6 percent to $145.2 million. This increase in sales was largely due to the success of D&K's marketing team in the Louisville, Cincinnati, and Iowa locations. Net sales also increased due to contracts with a large hospital chain, a mid-sized drug store chain, and a number of large grocery chains which housed pharmacies on their premises. This new business more than offset the loss of sales amounting to over $14 million that had been garnered from a mail order prescription company the previous year.

With the added revenues, management decided that this was an appropriate time to upgrade and improve upon the company's operational services. Consequently, D&K installed a state-of-the-art computerized inventory management system, while also installing and implementing new computer equipment and various software programs to improve efficiency. Management expanded the company's delivery system by using company vehicles and establishing regional transfer centers that provided quicker deliveries over a wider geographical area. In addition, the company centralized its marketing, finance, and purchasing departments, and hired new staff to help with information systems, delivery of products, and sales.

By 1993, D&K had established two large distribution centers and five transportation depots to serve a 14 state area, including Indiana, Illinois, Iowa, Missouri, Kansas, Oklahoma, Arkansas, Mississippi, Alabama, Tennessee, Kentucky, Ohio, West Virginia, and Virginia. The company arranged a two-year contract with Medicap Pharmacies, Inc., in Des Moines, Iowa, to supply products to over 90 independently operated drug stores within the group. The sales from this agreement alone were expected to reach approximately $40 million by the end of the two-year period.

At the same time, D&K joined an association called the Independent Drug Wholesalers Group (IDWG), which was made up of 55 wholesalers doing business from coast to coast. The association was formed in order to pool resources and compete more effectively within a limited market. One of the most successful developments to come out of the association was its own proprietary brand of generic drug called ALIGEN. D&K arranged to market ALIGEN products and other generic pharmaceuticals developed by the Independent Drug Wholesalers Group so that it could capitalize on the increasing market share of these products.

During 1994, the company made significant steps in positioning itself to capture a larger share of the wholesale distribution market. In June, D&K acquired selected holdings of Malone & Hyde, Inc., a Memphis-based subsidiary of the Drug Distributors Unit of Fleming Companies, Inc. The purchase included all the pharmaceutical inventory and all the non-prescription inventory of Malone & Hyde Drugs, Inc. that was meant for the Super D Drug Store chain, a 118-store retail drug operation. Through this acquisition, the company also assumed the supply contract, estimated at approximately $50 million annually, between Super D Drug Store and Malone & Hyde. As a result, D&K became the primary provider of over-the-counter pharmaceuticals and prescription drugs to the entire Super D Drug

Store chain. By the end of fiscal 1994, net sales had passed the $200 million mark and had risen to $211.2 million, an increase of nearly 26 percent over the previous year's figures.

After its successful incorporation of the assets of Fleming's Malone & Hyde Drug Distributors unit, management at D&K began to look for additional acquisition prospects. In October 1994, the company acquired the Northern Drug Company of Duluth, Minnesota. D&K purchased all of Northern's common stock at the discount price of $5 million and began to assume control of Northern's operations and distribution network almost immediately. Northern, with annual net sales of $60 million, was a full-service wholesale drug company with over 200 customers located throughout Minnesota, Michigan, and Wisconsin. Nearly 80 percent of Northern's customers were independent drug stores, with the remaining 20 percent of sales coming from two large hospital accounts.

Continuing its very first acquisition plan, in March 1995 D&K acquired Krelitz Industries, Inc. Krelitz, a wholesale drug company based Minneapolis, with annual sales over $100 million, was purchased by D&K for $1.4 million in both cash and stock. Krelitz operated through Twin City Wholesale Drug Company, one of the leading regional distributors to hospitals, clinics, and various other retail stores. The company's most important contract was with the Minnesota Multi-State Consortium, a managed care business that provided Krelitz with over $30 million in sales annually. As a bonus, along with its purchase of Krelitz, the acquisition also included a subsidiary called Viking Computer Services, Inc., which provided highly sophisticated computerized systems and software for companies within the pharmaceutical wholesale distribution industry, including inventory control, pharmacy disbursement, computerized order entry, and innovative payment processing systems.

Fiscal 1995 was a watershed year for D&K. Net sales increased an incredible 51.5 percent over the previous year to $320 million. In just seven years, net sales had jumped from $79.3 million to the 1995 figure. In addition, the company's net income increased from a loss of $38,000 in 1991 to a gain of $1.4 million by 1995. Earning per share also increased from five cents in 1992 to 54 cents per share by the end of fiscal 1995. All of these factors gave encouragement to D&K management, and plans for further expansion were under way.

During the late 1980s and early 1990s, there was a movement within the industry to consolidate operations and develop more efficient economies of scale. This consolidation led to the emergence of six leading drug wholesale companies, each with net sales amounting to over $4 billion. These six companies held approximately 80 percent of the drug wholesale market in the mid-1990s. A second tier of about 40 drug wholesale companies, among which D&K counted itself, also emerged, each with less than $2 billion in net sales. In 1995, D&K management believed that it would be one of the second tier companies to participate in the consolidation of drug wholesalers at that level.

Principal Subsidiaries: Northern Drug Company; Krelitz Industries, Inc.; Viking Computer Services, Inc.

Further Reading:

Carey, John, ''Getting Drugs To Market In Half The Time,'' *Business Week,* August 24, 1992, p. 36.

Cutaia, Jane H., ''Swallowing A Bitter Pill,'' *Business Week,* January 11, 1993, p. 82.

Morris, Gregory, ''The Squeeze is on in Pharmaceuticals,'' *Chemical Week,* August 12, 1992, p. 23.

Schwartz, Ronald M., ''Pryor: Get Greed Out Of The System,'' *American Druggist,* January 1994, pp. 22–28.

Weber, Joseph, ''A Miraculous Recovery For No-Name Drugs,'' *Business Week,* May 24, 1993, p. 126.

Weber, Joseph, ''Withdrawal Symptoms,'' *Business Week,* August 2, 1993, pp. 20–21.

—Thomas Derdak

Dannon Co., Inc.

120 White Plains Road
Tarrytown, New York 10591-5522
U.S.A.
(914) 366-9700
Fax: (914) 366-2805

Wholly Owned Subsidiary of Groupe Danone S.A.
Founded: 1942; incorporated as Dannon Milk Products, Inc.
Sales: $600 million
Employees: 700
SICs: 2023 Dry, Condensed & Evaporated Dairy Products

Dannon Co., Inc., popularized yogurt in the United States in the 1950s and has remained the nation's leading producer of yogurt. Originally marketed as a no-frills health food, Dannon yogurt achieved success in fruit-filled and sweetened varieties. The brand is sold throughout the United States by a network of more than 50 groups of food brokers.

Yogurt has long been a staple in the diet of Balkan and Near East peasants. A product formed from milk into the consistency of custard by fermentation in the open air, it was popularized in western Europe soon after 1900 by Elie Metchnikoff, a Nobel laureate who attributed the long life of Bulgarians to one of the two bacteria that converted milk into yogurt. Although Metchnikoff's hypothesis has not been borne out by further investigation, yogurt is a nutritious, vitamin-rich food. It can be eaten by the estimated 50 million Americans who have difficulty in digesting milk, and studies have suggested that it can aid in the prevention of gastrointestinal infections.

By virtue of his position as director of the Pasteur Institute in Paris, Metchnikoff conferred credibility on yogurt as a health food. Its consumption spread to western Europe, especially France (where even in the 1980s eight times as much yogurt was being eaten per person as in the United States). A Spanish businessman, Isaac Carasso, obtained cultures from Bulgaria and the Pasteur Institute. He began to manufacture yogurt in Barcelona in 1919 for sale through pharmacies. As business expanded he established a French branch in the 1920s. His son Daniel, for whom he named the product Danone, directed the French operation.

Daniel Carasso came to the United States in 1942 with Joe Metzger, a Swiss-born Spanish businessman, and Metzger's son Juan. They purchased a small yogurt factory in New York City and continued production using the family formula but changing the name from Danone to Dannon. At first Dannon Milk Products turned out only 200 half-pint glass jars a day of the obscure product for small numbers of ethnic Turks, Arabs, and Greeks and, in Juan's words, "health-food fanatics." Juan Metzger, who washed out the returnable jars every day, later recalled in a *People* interview, "We only sold $20 worth a day, but even then we were the bigger of the two companies in the business."

In order to publicize yogurt, Dannon's founders hired an advertising firm. Samples were distributed in quality restaurants, airports, and places where international travelers congregated. Soon radio comedians were poking fun at the product. In one week the Metzgers counted 24 jokes about yogurt on the air, mostly ridiculing its claims to foster longevity. "What was the best one?" Joe asked his son. "Well," replied Juan, "there was the one about the 97-year-old woman who died, but the baby lived."

Although the American public of the 1940s seemed to find yogurt's exotic name and origin hilarious, it was slow to accept the product. In that era "health food" generally was regarded as a preoccupation of wacky cultists, based largely in southern California. Moreover, the tart, sour natural flavor of yogurt was not to the liking of the American public. Around 1950, however, Dannon found the key to wider acceptance by adding a layer of strawberry preserves to the bottom of the container. The company slogan changed from "Doctors recommend it," to "A wonderful snack . . . a delicious dessert." A low-fat yogurt was introduced later to soothe the qualms of weight-conscious customers.

Before long a fleet of 55 leased trucks was supplying virtually every New York supermarket and delicatessen with Dannon yogurt. Celebrities like Bernard Baruch, Danny Kaye, Adlai Stevenson, Judy Holliday, and Kim Novak admitted to liking it. Waxed cups replaced the glass jars. Dannon moved from the Bronx in 1952 to a larger facility in Long Island City, Queens. In 1958 Juan Metzger said, "We knew we were over the hump two years ago, when Bob Hope told a joke about yogurt and nobody laughed."

Daniel Carasso returned to Europe in 1948. Joe Metzger became president of Dannon Milk Products, Inc., in 1952, moving up to chairman of the board in 1959, when Juan Metzger became president. By then Dannon was producing yogurt in six flavors, comprising half to three-quarters of the yogurt made in the United States, and generating annual sales of about $3 million. In 1959 the company was acquired by Chicago-based Beatrice Foods Co. for between $3 million and $3.5 million in stock. Metzger continued to head its Dannon yogurt subsidiary and became its chairman of the board in 1965.

By 1967 Dannon came in 10 varieties. The company was selling about 30 percent of the 100-million half-pint cups of yogurt being purchased annually in the United States. Automation had dramatically increased production, but the basic method of making yogurt continued almost unchanged: bacteria converted the sugar in pasteurized low-fat milk, causing it to thicken and become yogurt. Shipping depots had been established in Boston, Detroit, Philadelphia, and Washington because Dannon, which claimed to be the first company to achieve national distribution for perishable foods, would not trust delivery of its product to anyone else.

To broaden its customer base, Dannon added rock 'n' roll shows to its radio outlets and distributed "Go Yogurt" buttons to schoolchildren. An airplane-borne streamer spread the message, "Yannon Dogurt—oops / Dannon Yogurt" to crowds at Brooklyn's Coney Island. Dannon later shot the first American television commercial made in the Soviet Union. It featured an 89-year-old native of the Caucasian republic of Georgia eating Dannon yogurt while a background voice said, "And this pleased his mother very much. She was 114."

By 1981 U.S. yogurt sales had reached 1.3 billion containers a year, with Dannon accounting for one third. There were plants in New Jersey, Florida, Ohio, Texas, and California as well as New York City. The number of flavors had grown to 15, including apricot, Dutch apple, boysenberry, and coffee, although strawberry remained the most popular. Frozen yogurt and a premixed yogurt called Melange had also been successfully introduced. In 1981, however, Dannon reluctantly abandoned direct delivery to West Coast stores, because retail chains there insisted the product be sent to their refrigerated warehouses.

In 1981 Dannon was acquired from Beatrice by BSN-Gervais-Danone, a Paris-based company that partly stemmed from the original Carasso yogurt venture and had grown into one of France's largest conglomerates. BSN paid a hefty $84.3 million in cash for the company, which earned about $3.7 million on sales of about $130 million in fiscal 1981, but a BSN spokesman told *Advertising Age,* "To buy back the name we own around the world, all over Europe, in South America and Japan, is something we were prepared to pay for."

By 1985 the U.S. yogurt market had grown to about $1 billion, but Dannon's share had fallen to about 21 percent. For three years the company's advertisements had been urging the public to "Get a Dannon body," but now it was adding new, richer yogurt products to stay ahead of the competition, which now consisted of 125 other brands. During 1984 and 1985 the company brought to market a French-style blended yogurt called Dannon Extra Smooth, another French-style breakfast yogurt with nuts and raisins, and the extra-fruity Dannon Supreme, a dessert yogurt with higher fat content and more sugar. Dannon's president told a *Wall Street Journal* interviewer, "We'll never grow if we're only a medicine for diet nuts," while the president of its advertising agency said, "Dannon sat back on its heels for a long time; now we plan at least three new products a year."

These new products, aided by a doubling of the advertising budget to $12 million in 1985, lifted Dannon's market share to 26 percent in 1986. For the first time the company began advertising on network television and doing trade promotion, as well as consumer advertising, in order to make sure it received enough shelf space in supermarkets. Minipacks of six cups were introduced in 1985. By Dannon's silver anniversary in 1992 the company was selling two million cups a day in dozens of varieties and flavors.

Consumption of yogurt dropped in 1989 and recovered only marginally in the following years. To stimulate sales, Dannon in 1992 began test-marketing Sprinkl'ins, a yogurt for children filled with fruit, sugar, and mix-in candy bits. An employee at Grey Advertising, Dannon's agency, told a *New York Times* reporter, "Yogurt hasn't been very kid-friendly in the past because the taste was too sour. This is a way of creating a new generation of yogurt eaters." The inside of the package holding four small cups of Sprinkl'ins was printed with games and puzzles.

Nutritionists had nothing good to say about Sprinkl'ins; one compared it to junk food because of its high sugar content. Children, however, responded enthusiastically. Nationally introduced in 1993, Sprinkl'ins had sales of $43.9 million that year. In 1994 the company introduced Dannon Danimals, a new yogurt line decorated with pictures of wild elephants and bears. Dannon promised to donate 1.5 percent of the sale price to the National Wildlife Federation.

At the same time Dannon was increasing the sugar content in its product line, it was running print ads encouraging people to substitute yogurt for oil, sour cream, milk, or eggs in preparing food. These ads included recipes for lower-calorie versions of desserts like brownies and included a toll-free number. It was also testing Instead, a sour-cream alternative, and was considering expansion of its own branded yogurt cheese into other areas.

Dannon introduced no fewer than 23 new products in 1994 and 11 more in the first part of 1995. Its share of the $1.6 billion U.S. market for refrigerated spoonable yogurt reached 37 percent in early 1995. In April of that year the company won two Edison Awards for product innovation: a silver for its new Pure Indulgence frozen yogurt and a bronze for Sprinkl'ins. Grey Advertising won an award from the Advertising Research Foundation for a campaign that, according to the foundation's president, "clearly moved the needle on sales." The campaign, introduced in July 1994 with the theme "Taste Why It's Dannon," showed spots with such scenes as a woman watching the fattening treats on a dessert cart transformed into their Dannon Light counterparts.

Among the new 1994–95 products were Tropifruta, aimed at the Hispanic market, Dannon Light dessert flavors like creme caramel and banana cream pie, and Double Delights, which combined fruit toppings with Bavarian cream or cheesecake yogurt. "For years it was 'health, health, health,' with consumers," Dannon marketing executive Robert Wallach told *Brandweek.* "Now they're swinging back to moderation, looking to balance taste with health."

In 1994 the Dannon Co. was 89.32-percent owned by Groupe Danone, the new name adopted by what had been BSN-Gervais-Danone. Dannon's corporate headquarters moved from New York City to White Plains in the 1980s and to Tarrytown in 1994. The streamlined manufacturing system consisted of only two production plants: in Minster, Ohio, and Fort Worth, Texas. The research-and-development center, in Minster, was scrutinizing freshly made yogurt for quality, developing new products, and selecting and studying the bacteria used in making yogurt for optimum taste and texture. Dannon's distribution network carefully timed delivery to store shelves for optimal freshness and quality.

Further Reading:

''Dannon Fattens up on Nothing but Yogurt,'' *Business Week,* September 9, 1967, pp. 82, 84, 86, 89.

''Dannon Yogurt: Its Cups Overfloweth,'' *Nation's Business,* March 1981, p. 89.

Fannin, Rebecca, ''Dannon's Culture Coup,'' *Marketing & Media Decisions,* November 1986, pp. 59–60, 64–65.

Foltz, Kim, ''Dannon's Bet: Yogurt 'Just for Kids,' '' *New York Times,* May 1, 1992, pp. D1, D9.

Neiman, Janet, ''Dannon Buyer Eyes U.S.,'' *Advertising Age,* June 29, 1981, pp. 1, 80.

Rowes, Barbara, ''This Yogurt King Has Turned a Sour-Tasting Snack into a Sweet Story of Success,'' *People,* November 10, 1980, pp. 121–22.

Spethmann, Betsy, ''Dannon: Kudos on Taste,'' *Brandweek,* May 15, 1995, pp. 18, 20.

Stewart-Gordon, James, ''Yogurt's March from Fad to Fashion,'' *Reader's Digest,* December 1968, pp. 158–62.

—Robert Halasz

Dauphin Deposit Corporation

Dauphin Deposit Corporation

213 Market Street
P.O. Box 2961
Harrisburg, Pennsylvania 17105-2961
U.S.A.
(717) 255-2121
Fax: (717) 231-2615

Public Company
Incorporated: 1905 as Dauphin Deposit Trust Co.
Employees: 2,300
Total Assets: $5.1 billion
Stock Exchanges: NASDAQ
SICs: 6712 Bank Holding Companies; 6022 State
    Commercial Banks

Dauphin Deposit Corporation is one of the most successful mid-sized bank holding companies in the country, overseeing the operations of over 100 branch banking offices throughout central Pennsylvania, as well as two non-bank financial subsidiaries. Dauphin Deposit's continued expansion can be attributed to a history of conservative banking practices, careful acquisitions, and strong leadership.

Dauphin traces its history to the opening of the Harrisburg Savings Institution in Harrisburg, Pennsylvania, on September 28, 1835. With $50,000 in start-up capital, the bank was founded by several prominent men of Dauphin County and established on the site of a tavern on Market Street in downtown Harrisburg. The savings institution recorded $10,762.01 in deposits and $22,595 in assets after its first day of business, and after seven months, the bank paid its first dividend to stockholders. It was a promising start for an institution that would survive a Civil War, a Great Depression, two World Wars, and the ever-changing regulatory environment and competitive economic climate of the 1990s.

Among the first deposits at the Harrisburg Savings Institution was that made by James McCormick, a founder who entrusted $1,000 to the fledgling bank. McCormick would thereafter establish a stronger interest in Harrisburg Savings, and, although he was neither an officer nor a trustee in these early days, he would eventually become bank president in 1840. The McCormicks were one of Harrisburg's foremost families. Descendants of Irish immigrants who settled in Dauphin County, the McCormicks were successful in such business ventures as the law,

publishing, land development, railroads, iron and steel, and eventually, banking.

The first years of the bank were a time of perseverance and change. Just two years after the bank opened, the country was hit with an economic crisis: the Panic of 1837, caused by overtrading and careless speculation of public lands, stock, and property. Pennsylvania banks were hit especially hard when incomes from new canals and turnpikes fell below expectations and revenues from the railroad lagged. Several banks failed during this time, and payment in specie was suspended and not fully resumed in Pennsylvania until early 1841. Nevertheless, Harrisburg Savings Institution withstood the Panic, and in fact, built a larger office during this time.

Under James McCormick's leadership, Harrisburg Savings became known as Dauphin Deposite Bank in 1845, with an extended charter and increased capitalization. (The 'e' was dropped from Deposite in 1859.) McCormick managed the bank until his death in 1870, when son Henry was named president for a short term. Another son, James McCormick, Jr., took over in 1874 and retained the position into the early part of the 20th century. From 1874 to 1905 the bank operated as a private institution, as directed by the estate of the first James McCormick, with the founder's sons and son-in-law James Donald Cameron serving as trustees.

In 1905, the bank was incorporated in Pennsylvania as the Dauphin Deposit Trust Company. During this time, as banking in Harrisburg became more complex, local banks and trust companies approved the creation of a clearing house, and Dauphin Deposit would figure prominently in its management. Moreover, Dauphin Deposit announced that it would become a member of the Federal Reserve System, as business grew and the city of Harrisburg as well as its school districts became depositors at the bank. The bank also reported holdings that included city water bonds, Pennsylvania Canal bonds, Pennsylvania Railroad bonds, and Northern Central Railroad bonds.

Another change in leadership occurred in 1908, when William K. Alricks, the founder's son-in-law, became president of the bank. He would serve until his death in 1912, when Donald McCormick, son of the younger James McCormick, began his term as president. Donald McCormick remained in this position for 33 years and was the last of the family to manage the bank.

By 1919, Dauphin's holdings included bonds of several railroads, including the Atchinson, Topeka & Santa Fe; Chicago B&O; Northern Pacific; the Pennsylvania Railroad; and the Reading Co. The number of stockholders at Dauphin also expanded, from three in 1905 to around 20 by 1925.

Dauphin Deposit survived the Great Depression under the strong, conservative McCormick family leadership. In fact, the bank maintained a reputation for stability during this time, assisted in part by some strategy on the part of Donald McCormick, who made sure that customers had a clear view of the stacks of currency that arrived daily at the bank. Regarding their own operations as secure, McCormick and the board of directors were reportedly reluctant to comply when President Franklin D. Roosevelt ordered all banks to close in 1933. Later, McCormick would occasionally refuse to reopen accounts closed by wary customers during the bank emergency.

When Dauphin Deposit celebrated its 100th anniversary in 1935, the Harrisburg *Evening News* featured a commemorative supplement, with pictures of the founding family and a statement by Donald McCormick citing that growth had resulted in more than $10.5 million in deposits and nearly $25 million in trust funds.

During World War II, many Dauphin Deposit employees served in the U.S. armed forces, prompting Donald McCormick to establish a company newsletter to help keep those employees serving abroad apprised of bank activity. When McCormick died in 1945, leadership passed for the first time to a non-family member, Harper W. Spong. A new era thus began at Dauphin Deposit, one in which the bank would prosper and expand geographically.

In the mid-1950s and into the 1960s, Dauphin Deposit entered into a series of mergers, acquiring the Market Street Trust Company of Harrisburg, the Penbrook Banking Company, the Carlisle Trust Company, and Peoples Bank in Steelton. Interestingly, the Carlisle Trust Company, which came on board with Dauphin in 1957, was said to have established the concept of the Christmas Club (a program through which customers put away money for use during the holiday season), having initiated such a program in 1909 for local schoolchildren. Dauphin Deposit also began establishing branch banks in Dauphin County during this time, as well as in the Pennsylvania counties of Cumberland, Lebanon, and York. The Camp Curtin Trust Company of Harrisburg, the Lemoyne Trust Company, Peoples National Bank of Hanover, and The First National Bank of Lebanon were also eventually acquired by Dauphin Deposit during this time.

Other developments included expansion of the bank's headquarters, still located on Market Street in Harrisburg. At this site, Dauphin erected its first time-and-temperature clock in 1958. The bank would eventually become the world's largest user of time-and-temperature equipment; over the next 20 years, such devices became familiar landmarks and reference points for many central Pennsylvanians driving or walking by the bank branches. Unfortunately, by 1977 Dauphin would be forced to curtail its use of the energy-consuming clocks in the face of the national energy crisis.

In May 1965 Dauphin's board decided to withdraw from the Federal Reserve System, a move it deemed necessary in achieving greater flexibility in operations. The trust department was restructured into the Financial Services Division, reflecting the broader scope of services Dauphin offered its customers. Also, an employee training and education system was developed to encourage employees to better their skills and knowledge of the industry. Toward that end, the bank established a tuition reimbursement plan and programs that allowed employees to attend various banking association courses and seminars.

Under the leadership of John D. Wickert, Dauphin Deposit reorganized in 1977, forming a holding company called the Dauphin Deposit Corporation to oversee the operations of the Dauphin Deposit Bank and Trust Company. Other subsidiaries of the new parent were Dauphin Life Insurance Company and Dauphin Investment Company.

The reorganization, and all the paperwork and record keeping that it engendered, prompted management to seek out more

efficient administrative systems, and Dauphin Deposit took advantage of technological innovations of the time. In fact, Dauphin Deposit was among the first banks to utilize the central information files, postronic bookkeeping machines (through which balances and account numbers were automatically microencoded), automatic reading of checks through microencoding, electronic booking machines, data processing, and digital switchboards.

By the mid-1980s, Dauphin was reporting total assets of $2.3 billion, net income of $20.8 million, deposits of $1.94 billion, and total loans of $1 billion. Dauphin Deposit's growth was also evident through its stock performance. One hundred shares of Dauphin stock purchased in 1950 at a cost of $5,000, for example, would become 1,766 shares valued at a little over $60,000 by 1985, a figure that did not include the cash dividends paid out in the interim. Moreover, Dauphin Deposit was able to boast having paid uninterrupted dividends nearly since its inception.

In addition to its dividends, another long-standing Dauphin tradition was its commitment to the communities it served. Community projects taken on during the company's early years included a campaign for a safe water supply, the establishment of a hospital and dispensary in Harrisburg, and an effort to fund the rebuilding of the city of Chambersburg, which was torched by Confederate soldiers during the Civil War. Public service was still a bank concern in modern times, as Dauphin Deposit contributed to various charities and cultural events. Moreover, in 1980 the bank signed a "new beginning" agreement in response to charges that it had not done enough for inner-city residents. Specifically, Dauphin established a lending goal of $5 million to certain urban areas over a three-year period; provided extensive credit counseling for low- and moderate-income city residents; and offered a "good neighbor" discount of one percent on prevailing interest rates for home improvements and mortgage loans to Harrisburg residents. A Federal Reserve Board compilation of housing loans in the city in 1982 found that Dauphin Deposit had made 217 of the 441 loans that year. In 1984, the Urban League of Metropolitan Harrisburg honored the bank with its third annual Equal Opportunity Day Award.

During the 1980s, Dauphin Deposit continued to expand its market area. Mergers during this time included The Peoples National Bank of Shippensburg and Southern Pennsylvania Bank of York. In 1983, the Bank of Pennsylvania, based in Reading, was acquired, along with its holding company, Bancorp of Pennsylvania. Creating new services to meet the changing needs of banking customers, Dauphin responded to customer demands for easy, convenient banking services. New products included automated teller machines, credit cards, certificate of deposits, checking accounts with no minimum balance requirements, and home equity loans. Dauphin Deposit also developed an international unit to handle international transactions such as trade financing and providing letters of credit.

The late 1980s and early 1990s were a time of regulatory change, lending fads, volatile capital markets, and a slowing economy. But Dauphin Deposit consistently outperformed bank holding companies with assets in the $3 to $10 billion range through a prudent business strategy and continued acquisition.

Some analysts attributed the bank's continued success in part to the economic strength of the central Pennsylvania area it served.

In 1987, Dauphin Deposit acquired Colonial Bancorp and announced an agreement to acquire The Farmers Bank and Trust Company of Hummelstown. Collectively, these acquisitions brought $275 million is assets. Later, a new 13-story corporate headquarters was built in downtown Harrisburg.

1991 was a landmark year for Dauphin Deposit. Earnings rose for the 20th consecutive year. The September 1991 issue of *United States Banker* ranked Dauphin Deposit third among the nation's second hundred largest banking companies, based on the company's performance in relation to the average equity/asset ratio and the average return on assets. *Money Magazine* reported in March 1991 that Veribanc, a bank rating agency, placed Dauphin Deposit among the safest banks in the United States.

More important to the bank's health perhaps was the 1991 acquisition of Hopper Soliday and Co. Inc., a Pennsylvania securities broker/dealer and the largest underwriter of general obligation municipal bonds in the commonwealth. With this purchase, Dauphin Deposit became only the fourth U.S. bank approved to underwrite corporate debt and the first mid-size bank in the country to break into the niche market of brokering. According to Dauphin Deposit's 1992 annual report, Hopper Soliday, in the first 18 months of affiliation, returned over 60 percent of the initial investment that the corporation made to acquire it.

In the August 1991 issue of *ABA Banking Journal,* Christopher R. Jennings, then-president of Dauphin Deposit Corporation, commented on the corporate vision: "Dauphin has concentrated on building capital and keeping its asset quality high. We have tried to create what we believe is the prototype of the smaller regional bank that can survive. Still, we believe that we have to increase our size through acquisition in order to make the economies work properly."

Other important acquisitions in the 1990s included the agreement to merge the FB&T Corporation and its major subsidiary

Farmers Bank and Trust Company of Hanover, Pennsylvania. With assets of $648 million, FB&T expanded the Dauphin's franchise into Maryland and Pennsylvania counties where it had not had a presence before. In addition, Dauphin Deposit acquired Valley Bancorp, based in Chambersburg, which reported annual total assets of $324 million.

In addition, on July 1, 1994, Dauphin Deposit Bank acquired Eastern Mortgage Services, a full-service mortgage banking company, which originated, serviced, and sold first and second residential mortgage loans of varying types primarily to the eastern Pennsylvania and New Jersey mortgage markets. By the end of 1995, Eastern Mortgage was expected to expand to include 17 offices in six states.

Looking ahead to the 21st century, some industry analysts regarded Dauphin's profitability, strong capitalization, and relatively small size as providing an attractive acquisition package for larger banking companies. However, Dauphin remained independent in the mid-1990s, and its continued growth and strong leadership was likely to ensure a prosperous future.

Principal Subsidiaries: Dauphin Deposit Bank and Trust Company; Hopper Soliday & Co. Inc.; Dauphin Life Insurance Company; Dauphin Investment Company; Farmers Mortgage Corporation.

Further Reading:

"Alaska Shows the Way," *United States Banker,* September 1991, pp. 43–44.
Borowsky, Mark, "Dauphin Deposit Corp.'s Waiting Game," *Bank Management,* June 1992, pp. 51–54.
Cocheo, Steve, "Too Many Banks?" *ABA Banking Journal,* August 1991, pp. 29–32.
Cocheo, Steve, "Underwhelmed by Underwriting," *ABA Banking Journal,* September 1992, pp. 53–54.
"National Bancorp of Alaska Wins Again," *United States Banker,* August 1992, pp. 42–47.
Sharfman, Bern, *Dauphin Deposit: The First 150 Years,* Harrisburg, Penn.: Dauphin Deposit Bank and Trust Company, 1985, 95 p.

—Beth Watson Highman

The David J. Joseph Company

300 Pike Street
P.O. Box 1078
Cincinnati, OH 45201
U.S.A.
(513) 621-8770
Fax: (513) 381-7071

Wholly Owned Subsidiary of SHV Holdings, N.V.
Incorporated: 1920
Employees: 725
Sales: $1.5 billion (est. 1994)
SICs: 5093 Scrap & Waste Materials

With an estimated 19 percent of the domestic market, The David J. Joseph Company is widely recognized as America's oldest and largest scrap iron and steel company. The company also ranks at the top of the global scrap heap. In addition to its core scrap processing and brokerage business, the company leases and markets refurbished railroad equipment.

The David J. Joseph Company (DJJ) stood at the forefront of a highly fragmented, but slowly consolidating, industry in the mid-1990s. At that time, an estimated 4,000 companies operated America's $8 billion scrap metal industry. The business could be separated into three segments: collection, processing, and brokerage. The vast majority—up to 90 percent—of DJJ's business was concerned with scrap brokerage; the firm's 14 domestic and international trading offices would buy processed material from other companies and sell it to steel producers. DJJ primarily dealt in ferrous (iron- and steel-based) metals, but it also dealt in nonferrous materials. Although proportionately small, DJJ's scrap processing operations were impressive. The company's 17 scrap processing and mill service facilities across the United States scrapped railcars, shred autos, and managed scrap inventory. Company policy precludes publication of annual tonnage figures, but DJJ's volume has been estimated at over 5.3 million tons.

The company's history can be traced back to the mid-19th century, when German immigrant Joseph Joseph started a textiles business in Cincinnati. Swept up in the industrial revolution, the founder launched a scrap iron business in 1885. The railroad and construction industries helped increase demand for steel—and in turn boosted the scrap business—throughout the late 19th century.

Known in the late 1800s and early 1900s as the Joseph Joseph & Brothers Company, the family business diversified vertically and horizontally. The Indiana Rolling Mill Co. subsidiary was eventually merged into Republic Iron & Steel, a leading steelmaker in the early 20th century. The founder also created the Railway Supply Company and the Ohio Falls Iron Company.

Although each of the founder's five sons earned positions in management, it was the youngest who rose to the top. David Joseph first started working at the scrap brokerage in 1897 at the age of 11. The future company namesake rejoined the firm in 1905 after earning degrees from the Franklin Institute and Harvard University. He advanced to leadership of scrap operations by the time he was 30. Following the 1920 dissolution of Joseph Joseph & Brothers, the David J. Joseph Co. was formed to pursue the scrap iron business.

The development of the open-hearth furnace in the early 1900s both improved the quality of steel and encouraged consumption of scrap metal. Although steel manufacturers used "home scrap" from their own operations, the burgeoning auto industry's voracious appetite drove the expansion of the purchased scrap business.

Nonetheless, the scrap business remained a risky proposition ruled by the cyclical dictates of supply and demand. Scrap dealers played the odds, stockpiling material when prices dropped and selling when demand drove prices up. Scrap collection grew so efficient that an analyst for *American Metal Market* characterized the market as "demand-driven," asserting that "scrap is bought, not sold." A 1995 company publication noted that DJJ dealers occasionally "resorted to barter, taking finished steel in the attempt to make a profit." Given the structure of the industry, DJJ evolved into a brokerage. It established contracts with steelmakers that required the firm to find scrap supplies to meet steelmakers' needs.

The speculative nature of the scrap iron business was exacerbated by the Great Depression, which in the United States shut down over half of the capacity for steel production. According to a company history, David Joseph didn't let the national financial crisis stand in the way of a good deal. The 1933 purchase of 16,000 Southern Railroad railcars and engines is an oft-cited case in point. DJJ shipped a whopping 625,000 tons of scrap to Great Britain four years later. Large, risky transactions such as this helped DJJ rebound in the mid-1930s.

DJJ's close ties to the railroad business developed into an enduring, but lesser-known, segment of the family company. Railcars were an abundant source of scrap steel. DJJ's railcar scrapping developed proprietary burning equipment for wood-lined boxcars. The firm not only scrapped railroad equipment, it also refurbished railcars. Some of these were drafted for use in a company-owned fleet that transported scrap across the country; others were sold or leased to railroads and businesses. This auxiliary operation eventually developed into DJJ's Railroad Equipment Division, which had facilities in Illinois, Nebraska, Colorado, Tennessee, Florida, Kentucky, Virginia, Georgia, Texas, and Utah by the late 1980s. This division maintained a fleet of nearly 10,000 general-purpose railcars by the mid-1990s.

By the early 1940s DJJ was generally acknowledged to be America's largest scrap iron broker; it also ranked as a top scrap iron and steel exporter. David J. Joseph Jr. joined the family firm in 1938 and assumed the presidency in 1945. In contrast to his father, the Yale alumnus was better known for his managerial techniques than his trading prowess. DJJ expanded with the steel industry throughout the postwar era.

The Joseph family divested ownership of its namesake company to SHV Holdings, N.V. of The Netherlands in 1975. SHV was a worldwide global trading conglomerate with interests that included wholesaling and energy. David J. Joseph Jr. accepted the presidency of SHV's North American Holding Corporation and remained in that capacity for seven years. He retired in 1982.

James R. Breth was elected to DJJ's presidency in 1980. He had started as a broker in one of the firm's southern offices, advancing to office manager in 1960. He became vice-president of trading in 1976. In 1986, the veteran trader was elected chairman.

Technological advances and structural changes in the steel industry benefited DJJ in the 1980s and early 1990s. Just as open-hearth furnaces had changed the face of the steel industry at the turn of the century, the development of the electric-arc furnace in the 1960s spurred another revolution. The electric-arc furnace used scrap iron and steel—instead of the traditional mix of iron ore, limestone, and coke—to make a limited range of steel products. Compared to conventional integrated mills, the "minimills" that evolved around electric-arc furnace technology were faster, more efficient, more versatile, and more productive than their dominant counterparts. At the same time, steel mills striving for increased efficiency reduced their production of "home scrap," thereby raising their need for purchased scrap. Thus, even as U.S. steel production declined in the late 1970s and early 1980s, demand for purchased scrap iron and steel increased.

The minimill segment of the steel industry fit well with DJJ's own decentralized strategy. Its regional markets and emphasis on autonomy echoed DJJ's corporate culture. DJJ had the foresight to forge close ties with two of the most important minimills in the United States, Nucor Corp. and Florida Steel Corp. Established in 1967, North Carolina-based Nucor had grown into the largest and most profitable producer in the minimill sector. DJJ enjoyed valuable exclusive brokerages with Nucor and Florida Steel.

DJJ's internal technological advances created efficiencies and improved profitability as well. Perhaps most noteworthy was the company's information system that linked company traders, and technology facilitated the coordination of orders and supplies.

The vast majority of DJJ's post-World War II business was conducted domestically, but in recognition that the United States was the world's largest exporter of scrap, the company reentered international markets in 1985 and created an international division two years later. With the support of its globally influential parent, DJJ expanded its geographic reach through exports to Canada, Mexico, and overseas markets. In 1993, DJJ expanded railcar leasing, repair, and remarketing into Mexico through a joint venture with Servicios Financieros Quadrum S.A.

DJJ also expanded through acquisition in the late 1980s and early 1990s. After a six-year hiatus, the company reentered the nonferrous segment of the scrap business with the purchase of United Iron & Metal Co., a Baltimore firm. The 1991 acquisi-

tion of Frank H. Nott Inc., a private, family-owned company founded in 1887, further expanded DJJ's nonferrous activities.

Two publicized attempts to expand DJJ's processing activities through acquisition were inexplicably aborted, however. In 1992, the company initiated the $18 million purchase of three southern scrap yards from Proler International Corp. The deal was abandoned within months of its announcement with no public explanation. Less than a year later, the proposed acquisition of Ferrous Processing & Trading Co., a major Detroit-area scrap yard, fell through. Later in 1993, DJJ was able to acquire two ferrous scrap shredders from the bankrupt CF & I Steel Corp.

Although DJJ's processing operations remained limited in the early 1990s, the company was not sheltered from the environmental pitfalls of this aspect of the scrap business. Scrap processing entails handling and disposition of the hazardous by-products of everything from automobiles to medical equipment. As a result, it is regulated by state and federal environmental and worker safety agencies. In 1993, DJJ's Tampa, Florida, scrap yard discovered two cancer therapy devices containing radioactive material. (Both components were found before any harm was done.) DJJ has also been involved in a Tampa-area Superfund cleanup ordered by the U.S. Environmental Protection Agency. These events dramatically illustrated some of the risks associated with the scrap industry.

DJJ got a new leader in 1992, when Louis F. Terhar Jr. advanced to president and chief executive officer. Terhar had been with DJJ a scant three years. James Breth stayed on as chairman.

Industry analysts were divided over the prospects for the domestic and international scrap markets in the mid-1990s and beyond. Some predicted that rising global minimill capacity and production would fuel scrap steel shortages. That was good news for scrap dealers, who anticipated higher prices. Other analysts, however, forecast that rising scrap prices would simply revitalize the more traditional integrated production methods. Given the support of its parent, its historical performance, and its strong ties to the minimill sector, DJJ's position appeared impervious to market shifts.

Further Reading:

"The David J. Joseph Company," Cincinnati: The David J. Joseph Company, 1995.
"David J. Joseph Co. Celebrates Centennial," *American Metal Market,* January 10, 1986, p. 17.
Kruglinski, Anthony, "DJJ's McMillan: A Good Time for Selling and Profit-Taking," *Railway Age,* August 1995, p. 10.
Marley, Michael, "Clues to 'Hot' Scrap Uncovered," *American Metal Market,* April 14, 1993, p. 2.
——, "No Scrap Shortage Foreseen," *American Metal Market,* October 26, 1994, p. 2.
——, "World Scrap Shortage Seen; Supply Tightness and Higher Prices May Not Ease," *American Metal Market,* March 23, 1995, p. 1.
"Volatile Scrap Market Predicted," *American Metal Market,* July 15, 1988, p. S26.
Worden, Edward, "Exec Foresees 'Crunch' Due to Prices," *American Metal Market,* April 4, 1995, p. 9.
Wulff, Stephen W., "Scrap's Quality Now Major Concern," *American Metal Market,* December 7, 1989, p. 14.

—April Dougal Gasbarre

DAY RUNNER.

Day Runner, Inc.

2750 West Moore Avenue
Fullerton, California 92633-2565
U.S.A.
(714) 680-3500
Fax: (714) 680-0542

Public Company
Incorporated: 1980 as Harper House, Inc.
Employees: 598
Sales: $121.8 million
Stock Exchanges: NASDAQ
SICs: 2741 Miscellaneous Publishing

Day Runner, Inc., is America's leading developer and manufacturer of paper-based personal organizers. The company produces and markets a wide variety of organizers and planners, as well as refills and other accessories, ranging from student planners to sophisticated systems for busy executives. The original Day Runner System, available in several different materials and sizes, remains the company's biggest seller. The product line has since been expanded to include FactCentre Organizers and 4-1-1 Student Planners on the lower end and the PRO Business System for professionals in a higher price range. Day Runner has also added to its line a software product for personal computers designed to work in conjunction with a paper-based system.

Altogether, the company has sold about 21 million planners and organizers since 1980, the year it was founded. They can be found in 17,000 retail stores throughout the United States, as well as in Europe and the Far East. As of fall 1995, more than 11 million people were using Day Runner products to keep their lives in order.

Day Runner was established as Harper House, Inc., in 1980. The personal organizer that became the company's flagship product was conceived by Boyd and Felice Willat, film production coordinators in Hollywood. The Willats discovered that the simple planners on the market at that time were not up to the task of organizing the frantic schedules they kept in both their work and social lives. To meet their own needs, they designed an organizer that combined the functions of calendar, address and telephone book, and personal planner. Reasoning that other people were probably having similar problems managing their hectic lives, Harper House put its first generation of Day Runner personal organizers, called the Day Runner System, on the market in 1982, targeting the growing numbers of young, ambitious professionals and entrepreneurs with family responsibilities and numerous outside interests.

Initially, Day Runner organizers were marketed mainly in gift stores, as something of a novelty item for executives. It quickly became clear, however, that the Day Runner had market potential far beyond what could be called a novelty. A key shift in strategy came in the mid-1980s, when Harper House began emphasizing ''productivity'' in its promotion of the Day Runner line, and the organizers began appearing in office supply stores rather than gift shops. Soon Day Runner organizers were being purchased by a much broader range of people, including executives, blue-collar workers, and students.

By 1987 Harper House had annual sales of $11 million. As the decade rolled on, consumers continued to flock to office supply stores to buy Day Runners. Over the years, the Day Runner System was offered in a growing array of styles. Users could choose between loose-leaf and spiral formats; vinyl and leather; and snap, Velcro, and zipper closures. The systems could also be personalized by choosing from a variety of refills, calendar formats, and accessories. All versions of the system shared Day Runner's trademark burgundy and gray page design, and featured the company's characteristic colored tabs.

As the name Day Runner began to achieve a high degree of recognition in the growing personal organizer market, Harper House made the decision to adopt it as its corporate name in 1988. Company revenues continued to soar over the next few years. By 1989 Day Runner's sales had grown to $26 million, with net income reaching $2.3 million. The impressive increase in the company's sales during this period was fueled in part by its appearance in low-cost office product superstores, such as Office Depot and Staples. Around this time, competition began to emerge from electronic organizers, like Sharp Co.'s Wizard. Although electronic gizmos like the Wizard and similar products made by Casio and other companies sold reasonably well, they did not make much of a dent in the market for paper-based planning systems at the time.

Day Runner entered the 1990s on a strong note. By early in the decade, the personal organizer market had blossomed into a $500 million business, with Day Runner in the lead among companies doing primarily retail business. Since the other leading planner companies sold their wares through different channels—Franklin Quest Co. at its own time management seminars and Day-Timers by direct mail—competition was relatively scarce. By 1991 Day Runner's sales had grown to $53 million, a 500 percent jump over a period of just four years. That year the company rolled out a new line of products, called the FactCentre. First introduced as one model, the FactCentre was essentially a more economical version of the original Day Runner System, with sections for calendars, addresses, and notes. The line was eventually expanded to include specialized models for business people (Personal Organizer), purse carriers (Compact Organizer & Memo Planner), home planning (Home Manager), and school (Student Organizer & Planner). Suggested prices for the various FactCentres ranged from $10 to $65.

1992 was a particularly eventful year at Day Runner. In March the company went public, with an initial offering of 1.4 million shares. By this time, there were about 80 different Day Runner organizers for customers to choose from, and about 6,000 stores from which those organizers could be bought. At the root of the company's ongoing growth was the idea that each individual had different planning needs, and these differences could be translated into subtly different organizer products. In order to assess exactly what these differing needs were, the company sought out feedback from customers. As its base of potential customers broadened, Day Runner began selling its goods in large discount chains, such as Fred Meyer, Inc., and Wal-Mart. The target market throughout these mass marketing efforts was usually the 25 to 49 age group with better-than-average incomes and busy lifestyles.

Day Runner also introduced its first organizer computer software, Time Plus, in 1992. Designed to be used in conjunction with a paper-based personal organizer, Time Plus duplicated the most worthwhile features of existing planner software in a more user-friendly format. Day Runner's system, for DOS-based IBM-compatible computers, offered automatically updated to-do lists, special abbreviations to ease database manipulation, and the ability to print out updated address book entries, project notes, and other features on sheets that could then be popped into a conventional Day Runner organizer.

In spite of a fourth-quarter slump that saw Day Runner's newly offered stock sink to around $8 a share (from a high of $21.75 shortly after it began trading), company sales soared again in 1992, reaching $71 million for the year. Day Runner Chairman Mark Vidovich attributed the slump to poor sales at smaller independent dealers. Large wholesalers, the company's bread and butter, continued to sell Day Runner products at a brisk pace. By this time Day Runner controlled at least half of the retail market for personal organizers.

Day Runner emphasized mass market channels even more as the 1990s continued. New outlets for Day Runner products in 1993 included Payless Drug Stores, Revco, and Kmart. During 1993 the company sold over three million organizers and planners and about 12.5 million refills. Two new products were introduced during the year. The PRO Business System, designed for business managers, took the standard Day Runner concept to new levels of sophistication. New wrinkles offered by the PRO Business System included a seven-ring format, graphics for locating specific sections more easily, a built-in solar-powered calculator, and, in some models, a slide-out panel that turned the organizer into a miniature desk top.

The other new Day Runner product launched in 1993 was the d'Affaires, a line of organizers with an elegant look. The d'Affaires was designed to be sold in departments stores, luggage shops, leather goods stores, and other specialty retailers. This new look featured beige pages and brown ink in a soft leather binder. Like the classic Day Runner organizer, the d'Affaires was offered in a variety of page sizes and book thicknesses. Along with the addition of the PRO Business System and d'Affaires lines, the company also expanded the Fact-Centre line.

For 1993 Day Runner reported sales of nearly $82 million, about one-fourth of which came from mass market sources. That figure was held down somewhat by a wave of closings and consolidations among independent office supply dealers. Nevertheless, net income took a healthy jump to $5.6 million, a company record. A number of other developments took place during 1993. James E. Freeman, formerly president and chief operating officer of Stuart Hall Co., was named to the newly created position of chief operating officer at Day Runner. An East Coast distribution facility was opened as well. Perhaps more importantly, the company increased its focus on operations outside North America by creating Day Runner International Ltd., a wholly owned subsidiary based in the United Kingdom. Sales to foreign customers during the year amounted to $3.5 million.

As the 1990s progressed, more new products were unveiled. The 4-1-1 line of student planners, first introduced for the 1994 back-to-school season, was aimed at the student market from junior high through college. Available in both loose-leaf and wire-bound formats with youthful styling, the 4-1-1 line included places for phone numbers, class notes, class schedules, and personal information. Day Runner was recognized by the Calendar Marketing Association for its innovative design work on the 4-1-1 system. Fueled by the company's success at seeking out new market segments and targeting new products accordingly, Day Runner's sales reached $97 million in 1994. As Day Runner continued to parlay its dominance in the personal organizer market—which it had largely created—into profits, the business media began to take notice. Both *Forbes* and *Business Week* included Day Runner on their lists of America's best small companies in 1994.

In 1995 Day Runner introduced a Day Runner Planner for Windows. The new Planner software combined all of the most popular Day Runner functions, including calendars, phone books, to-do lists, project planners, and expense reports into an easy-to-use system whose graphics resembled the classic look of the paper-based Day Runner organizer. Other features made possible by the software included auto-dialing and audible alarms. Pre-formatted, hole-punched paper for printing out sheets generated by the software were also made available. For those customers who did not already use Day Runner organizers, a special package that included both the Planner software and a paper-based organizer was offered at a bargain price.

For the fiscal year ending in June 1995, Day Runner's sales increased by 26 percent to $121.8 million. During 1995 Freeman was given the additional title of president in addition to his role as chief operating officer. Day Runner was also cited again by the Calendar Marketing Association, this time receiving that organization's Gold Award for the page design of its PRO Business System.

Principal Subsidiaries: Day Runner de Mexico, S.A. de C.V.; Day Runner International Limited.

Further Reading:

O'Brien, Timothy L., "Fast Track: Personal Organizer Firm's Days Are Full—Of Cash," *Wall Street Journal,* October 14, 1992, p. B2.
——, "Day Runner Stock Falls 28% as Sales Slip Below Forecast," *Wall Street Journal,* December 23, 1992, p. C11.
Petruno, Tom, "A Stock Offering That Should Fit in Your Schedule," *Los Angeles Times,* February 28, 1992, p. D3.
Teitelbaum, Richard S., "Companies to Watch: Day Runner," *Fortune,* June 15, 1992, p. 123.
Whitmyer, Claude F., "Discovered: A Time Manager That Works," *The Office,* October 1992, p. 26.

—Robert R. Jacobson

DDB NEEDHAM WORLDWIDE

DDB Needham Worldwide

437 Madison Avenue
New York, New York 10022
U.S.A.
(212) 415-2000
Fax: (212) 415-3562

Wholly Owned Subsidiary of Omnicom Group
Founded: 1925 as Maurice H. Needham Co.
Gross Billings: $6.7 billion
Employees: 6,726
SICs: 7311 Advertising Agencies

DDB Needham Worldwide is one of the largest advertising firms in the world, with 183 offices representing over 1,200 clients in 75 countries. It was formed in 1986 through the merger of Doyle Dane Bernbach and Needham Harper Worldwide.

Doyle Dane Bernbach was founded in New York City in 1949 by Ned Doyle, Maxwell Dane, and William Bernbach, who acted as president. Bernbach and Doyle had worked together at Grey Advertising during the mid-1940s; Dane had been running his own small advertising firm. DDB initially had 13 employees and $500,000 in billings. Its first ads were done for Ohrbach's department store and appeared in New York daily newspapers. Initially, most of the company's clients used small budgets to promote little-known products, but it became one of the most influential firms in advertising history.

DDB quickly became known for stylish advertisements that relied on catchy slogans and witty humor rather than the repetition and hard sell used by many competing firms; its "soft-sell" approach stood out. By 1954 the firm had grown sufficiently to expand to the West Coast by taking over Factor-Breyer, a Los Angeles agency. Gradually it built spin-off DDB/West around it.

In 1960 the agency won the account of Avis, then the number-two auto rental company. Bernbach penned the slogan, "We Try Harder Because We're Number 2." In 1961 DDB opened its first international office in West Germany, where an important client, Volkswagen, was based. One of the firm's more memorable slogans, done for Volkswagen, was "Think Small," and featured a tiny photograph of a Volkswagen Beetle surrounded by blank space. Ads like this were widely imitated,

bringing the firm international acclaim and new clients. In 1966 the firm signed Mobil Oil, a major client for the next two decades with advertising budgets in the tens of millions of dollars.

Meanwhile, the firm continued to build its overseas network. Its London office was particularly strong and employed leading creative talents during the 1970s. In 1968 the firm named Bernbach chairman and chief executive officer; in 1976 it named him chairman of the executive committee. Under his leadership DDB often ignored rules followed by other agencies, relying on instinct and brainstorming sessions rather than research and marketing plans. It also tried to keep creative personnel separated from business pressures that account executives and clients fretted over. This philosophy won and kept many of the most creative people in advertising as employees.

However, this successful formula collapsed after Bernbach's death in 1982. Some personnel became arrogant and difficult to manage; many clients left, as did some high-profile talent. The firm's earnings fell to $7.6 million that year, a 30 percent decline from the year before. By 1986—despite worldwide billings of about $1.67 billion, 3,400 employees, and 54 offices in 19 countries—some industry observers thought the firm was in serious trouble.

Needham Harper Worldwide started in Chicago in 1925 as Maurice H. Needham Co. It had two clients, with billings totaling $270,000. Billings reached $500,000 in 1928, and the following year the firm reorganized as Needham, Louis and Brorby, Inc. Billings reached $1 million in 1934, the same year the agency signed Kraft Foods. Hollywood was becoming the center of the production of network radio programs, and NL&B opened a Hollywood office to produce clients' programs, which included "Fibber McGee and Molly," and "The Great Gildersleeve."

In 1951 the agency opened a New York office to concentrate on the rapidly expanding television industry. To strengthen its still weak New York base, the firm merged with Doherty, Clifford, Steers and Shenfield in 1965 and changed its name to Needham, Harper & Steers. In the meantime, the much stronger Chicago office was adding clients like the Morton Company, Household Finance Corporation, and General Mills. In 1966 NH&S won the Continental Airlines account and opened a Los Angeles office to handle it. The firm soon added Frigidaire to its client list.

In 1972 the agency opened an office in Washington, D.C. It initially handled advertising from local McDonald's owner/operator co-ops, but soon it was winning government, media, and local retail clients. The firm was successful in the late 1970s, and in 1978 it was named Advertising Agency of the Year by *Advertising Age*. In 1980 NH&S started an Issues & Images division to concentrate on corporate, government, and association advertising.

Keith L. Reinhard, who had headed the agency's Chicago office, became president in 1982 and made improving the New York office one of his primary goals. Despite some successes, the firm was struggling in New York. The jingle-based advertisements that had won clients like McDonald's in the Midwest were not working well in the New York market. In June 1982 the firm restructured, citing the preparation for future growth. NH&S became the holding company for three smaller companies: Needham, Harper & Steers/USA, Inc., had offices in New York, Chicago, Los Angeles, and Dayton, Ohio; Needham, Harper & Steers International, Inc., became responsible for all NH&S operations outside of the United States, operating in 32 world markets; NH&S/Issues & Images, Inc., became a separate corporation including NH&S/Washington and the public relations firm of Porter, Novelli & Associates, which had offices in Washington and Los Angeles.

In 1984 NH&S bought the DR Group, Inc., a large direct-response advertising company with offices in New York, Boston, and London. Because of client conflict problems, in May 1984 the New York office of NH&S/Issues & Images became a separate, unaffiliated company called Biederman & Company. The Washington office of Issues & Images became a division of NH&S/USA. The public relations arm of Issues & Images was renamed Needham Porter Novelli. Soon after, the agency ended its holding company experiment and consolidated back to one company, now called Needham Harper Worldwide, Inc.

The company expanded its California presence in 1985 with the purchase of Lane & Huff Advertising, based in San Diego; Needham Porter Novelli bought the Public Relations Board, Inc., of Chicago. As it approached its merger with Doyle Dane Bernbach, Needham Harper had its headquarters in New York, with major offices in Chicago, Los Angeles, and Washington and secondary offices in Phoenix, Sacramento, San Diego, and Baltimore.

During the mid-1980s many public companies were snatched up in hostile takeovers, and public advertising firms, including the weakened Doyle Dane Bernbach, worried about their futures. Though their positions were stronger, Needham Harper and another large firm, BBDO, also worried about being taken over. Led by Needham head Keith Reinhard and BBDO president Allen Rosenshine, in 1986 the three firms—DDB, Needham Harper, and BBDO—agreed to merge into the Omnicom Group, which would act as a holding company. BBDO remained a separate company, but DDB and Needham Harper merged further into a new company called DDB Needham Worldwide. Needham Harper had been weak in New York and Europe, precisely where DDB was strong, and DDB had wanted to strengthen its Midwest operations. Together the two companies boasted clients like General Mills, Amtrack, GTE Telcom, Volkswagen, and Chivas Regal Scotch, with billings of $2 billion. Strategically the merger made sense, but getting employees and their different styles to mesh proved difficult.

That task was spearheaded by Reinhard, who became president of the new firm. He soon found that the DDB New Yorkers resented the merger and considered him a country bumpkin, since he had grown up in Indiana and worked in Chicago. Morale was low in New York because of the years of decline following Bernbach's death; it fell further as a result of layoffs. The staff of the former DDB was cut to 700 from 1,100. Both firms had London offices, which heard of the merger via facsimile, and each office started telling newspapers it would head the combined agency. Reinhard made six trips to London, fired most of the Needham managers, and put DDB managers in charge. Critics charged that the merger had no creative vision,

and the New York office signed no new clients; many employees started to leave for other agencies.

Problems also arose because of competing accounts held by Needham and DDB. For example, because of DDB's historic ties to Volkswagen, Needham's Los Angeles office, which had the $100 million Honda Motor account, was spun off as Rubin Postaer & Associates; the $32 million RJR Nabisco account, which had been DDB's, was let go because of Needham's General Mills account.

After a period of introspection, which included reading William Bernbach's writings about advertising, Reinhard decided the new firm should be a creative leader but for larger clients, leaving truly adventurous advertising to smaller competitors. He started using teams for each client project, including employees from media buying and account planning in addition to the usual creative staff and market researchers. The teams were to stress relevancy, originality, and impact. Many industry observers felt that incorporating media planning into the creative process was an important innovation, and the firm became known for it.

In the fall of 1987, with a creative direction chosen, Reinhard replaced executive creative director John Noble, who had been a divisive advocate of DDB methods, with the team of Jack Mariucci and Robert Mackall. They managed the firm's 105-person creative department. Copywriters and art directors were not assigned to specific clients but rather were used by the department's six creative directors as needed. The staff learned to work together and the firm's talent flight stopped. It began to win important new accounts like the $42 million campaign for Sears's Discover credit card. The firm grossed $358.5 million in 1987 on billings of $2.6 billion.

In 1988 the firm continued to win new accounts, like the $18.5 million contract to create advertisements for the New York State Lottery and a $25–30 million account for a global campaign for Seagram's Martell cognac. It also won a Clio award for a print ad created for Colombian coffee. As with any ad agency, it also lost accounts such as the $20 million Hasbro account. But the firm was now rolling, and it was the leading U.S. advertising agency in 1989 in terms of newspaper media billings.

In a move that raised eyebrows throughout the advertising industry and beyond, DDB Needham offered in 1990 to guarantee the results of its advertising, making its compensation for an ad campaign partly related to the client meeting its sales goals. For three years the firm had been test marketing parts of the program, which called for a bonus of up to 33 percent or a discount of up to 30 percent on firm charges. Advocates claimed the plan would result in more accountability and many clients liked it; critics pointed out the difficulty of scientifically proving the effect of advertising on sales. In any event, few clients signed up.

Meantime, the U.S. economy and the economies of many of its trading partners were in recession, leading to a drop in advertising billings. Accordingly, the firm lost the accounts of some important clients like Clorox, Campbell's Soup, and Maybelline. Still, the firm scored some victories. It won the $40 million Reebok shoe account and the $12.5 million Canon 35-mm camera account. Nevertheless, the early 1990s proved to be a difficult time for the firm: it laid off 29 of 700 employees at its New York office in mid-1991, 45 more in mid-1992. In 1993 it dropped from being the third-largest agency in the United States to sixth-largest, with revenues declining to $229 million on sales of $1.9 billion.

In May 1992 the firm brought in Andy Berlin as president of the New York office. Berlin had been CEO of Goodby, Berlin & Silverstein, a San Francisco agency, which he left because the firm would not grow fast enough for his ambitions.

At the beginning of 1993 DDB Needham announced that it would no longer take, at least temporarily, any new business. Already possessing a good-sized roster of longtime clients, the firm felt it best to make certain their needs were met rather than seek new business—and thereby risk alienating favored customers who could feel slighted. One reason for this move was the rumblings of dissatisfaction from Volkswagen. Berlin personally took over supervision of the U.S. portion of the account, which had $50 million in billings (the account had been supervised by DDB's Troy, Michigan, office). Even with the extra attention, however, in March 1993 Volkswagen put its $100 million German account up for review.

At the same time, the firm moved forward with a plan to centralize its media buying. In September 1992 DDB combined about $200 million worth of national television buying from the Chicago and New York offices. It opened a branch called USA Media, which bought airtime for all of Needham's U.S. offices.

Tensions persisted. The Chicago office, which long had a base of packaged goods manufacturers that preferred conservative advertising, was luring high-profile executives from other firms to begin flashier, higher-profile ad campaigns that might win awards and new clients. But the effort was lagging by mid-1993, and billings in the Chicago office had actually been

declining slightly for the past several years. The office lost the $20 million Audi account and the $25 million American Dairy Association account, and the creative talent that had come up with cutting-edge ads for gym shoes had a harder time selling boxes of cereal.

DDB Needham restructured the office, but laying off 14 percent of the workforce there badly hurt morale. Other advertising agencies were going through similar problems, but DDB Needham's management kept on the Chicago office—still its largest and most profitable. Starting around the beginning of 1994 things came together for the Chicago office, and it won new clients including Helene Curtis, S. C. Johnson, and Budweiser. Billings grew to $670 million, up about $75 million from 1993. The advertising industry in general was recovering from the lean years of the early 1990s, and DDB Needham's clients in package goods, health care, and telecommunications were buying more advertising. At the end of 1994 DDB Needham won an important new account when Sony Europe chose it for a $120 million ad campaign.

Further Reading:

Borden, Jeff, "Once an Ad Agency Star, Needham Loses Its Shine," *Crain's Chicago Business,* June 21, 1993.
Lafayette, Jon, "Still Awaiting Liftoff," *Advertising Age,* October 26, 1987.
McFadden, Robert D., "William Bernbach, Advocate of the Soft Sell in Advertising, Dies at 71," *New York Times,* October 3, 1982.
Mussey, Dagmar, "DDB Needham Wins $120M Sony Europe," *Advertising Age,* December 12, 1994, p. 1.
Sherrid, Pamela, "The Bernbach Legacy," *Forbes,* June 20, 1983.
Sloan, Pat, "DDB Needham Selects its First U.S. President," *Advertising Age,* November 1, 1993, p. 2.
Stern, Aimee L., "A Merger Clicks, Painfully," *New York Times,* July 16, 1989.

—Scott M. Lewis

Del Webb Corporation

Del Webb Corporation

6001 North 24th Street
Phoenix, Arizona 85016
U.S.A.
(602) 808-8000

Public Company
Incorporated: 1960 as the Del E. Webb Corporation
Employees: 1,800
Sales: $803.12 million
Stock Exchanges: New York Pacific
SICs: 6552 Subdividers and Developers, Not Elsewhere
    Classified; 1521 Residential Building Construction

Once known for its hotels and casinos, Del Webb Corporation is one of the largest residential developers in the United States as a result of its success in planned retirement communities.

The life story of its founder, Delbert E. Webb, reads like a screenplay: fame and fortune pursue the simple boy. According to his official biography, he liked to boast of knowing every president since Franklin Delano Roosevelt on a first-name basis. Starting early in his career, he met such baseball greats as Ty Cobb, later Mickey Mantle, Joe DiMaggio, and Yogi Berra. As a golfer, he walked a course with Bing Crosby, Bob Hope, Barry and Robert Goldwater, as well as Howard Hughes. Later, after Webb's death, legendary crooner Frank Sinatra would buy a share in the company.

Several times in his life, Delbert E. Webb found his fate unpredictably refracted through circumstance. His scholarly career was cut short in high school when in 1915 financial setbacks afflicted his father, the president of a California gravel company. After completing his freshman year, Del Webb fell back on two boyhood occupations: baseball, which he had been playing semiprofessionally since age thirteen, and carpentry. For the next 12 years he moved about California, working as a carpenter exclusively for companies with baseball teams, on which he could also earn extra money. A severe bout with typhoid fever (he lost 105 pounds, from 204) truncated his major league ambitions; in fact, he could not work at all for a year.

Phoenix, in spite of its depressed economy, attracted Webb, like many others in search of a healthful climate. Eager to return to the ball field, Webb violated a league residency requirement,

which he had missed by one day. Unable to play and unwilling to do anything halfway, he ended his baseball career forever in 1928 and began concentrating on construction full-time. He soon was moonlighting as a contractor. His first major jobs came from the Bayless family of grocers, who originally hired him, according to one source, after a wayward superintendent skipped town during a project. Webb's competence and personability, as well as such windfalls as rebuilding the local Sears store after a fire, kept his small business active through the stock market crash of 1929.

Although strongly identified with his work on grocery stores, Webb during this time eagerly sought public sector jobs, such as schools, dormitories, and the 1938 addition to the Arizona capitol building. George W. P. Hunt, Arizona's first governor, commissioned Webb to build his distinctive pyramid-shaped tomb. Webb also completed several landmark buildings for Phoenix businesses and an unprofitable dance hall joint venture. With some audacity, a tiny branch office was opened in Los Angeles in 1937 to accommodate a high school project there; the geographic influence of his company gradually grew.

Del Webb's reputation gained stature from such challenging and prestigious projects, and through his own personal influence he had established himself as one of Arizona's largest contractors by World War II. However, he still hadn't attained the capital required for the bonding requirements of large federal projects. The White Miller Construction Company, a road-building firm, entered into a joint venture with Webb, helping him meet bonding requirements and also supplying certain types of expertise. The arrangement soon showered the Del E. Webb Construction Company with dozens of government jobs, including three major military bases; civil projects such as gas stations kept coming. President Roosevelt's controversial internment of Japanese Americans created a challenging order for quick construction of a huge relocation camp the size of an entire city. Webb completed the project at breakneck speed.

The new scale of operations required Webb to make several changes. In 1941, the company moved out of its severely cramped quarters into a spacious new building. The company also built itself at every building site portable office buildings, standardized in order to smooth administration. Del Webb organized personnel and procedures in a similar fashion. His travel and shoulder-rubbing demanded increasing amounts of his time, so in 1943 he appointed L. C. Jacobson, a trusted employee, to look after the home front, making him a 25 percent partner.

Concern over the cyclical nature of construction spurred the company to diversify in the postwar economy. It bought Master Products, a leather goods and filing equipment company, and invested in photography and petroleum. Webb bought a share in the New York Yankees in 1945. He gave away greatly coveted Yankees game tickets to potential clients as premiums, which allowed him to bask in a constellation of influence. After 20 years, however, the ball club was sold to CBS for $14 million. Later diversions into sports included sponsoring an Indy race car in the early 1960s.

Webb's defense work brought him into contact with one of the most unique Americans of the century, the secretive tycoon

Howard Hughes. The Del Webb Company was hired to build an addition to the Hughes Aircraft Company plant in 1950. The scarcity of materials during the Korean War proved another hurdle successfully cleared, which boosted the company's reputation. Webb built several plants for Hughes.

The company constructed apartments and hospitals, including the mammoth St. Joseph's in Phoenix, built at the beginning of the 1950s, a decade of explosive growth for Phoenix. It also entered into a new area of operations—planned communities—beginning with the 700-unit Pueblo Gardens on the outskirts of Tucson. San Manuel, a company town built for Magma Copper Company, followed. It required Del Webb to build streets, stores, parks, and infrastructure as well—all in the middle of the desert.

The company's out-of-state work also thrived during the postwar period, as manufacturers expanded out of their old facilities (Kraft Foods) or ordered new facilities to reduce cross-country freight costs (Pabco Floor Covering; Self-Locking Carton Company). Del Webb's matchmaking skills helped produce a joint venture that foreshadowed the ''industrial ecology'' movement by decades. The Self-Locking Carton Company harmonized operations with the Diamond Match Company in the Integrated Forest Products Manufacturing Plant in Red Bluff, California, resulting in a pinnacle of efficiency. Besides egg cartons (made of newsprint recycled at the plant) and matches, paper plates and lumber were also produced at the factory, itself partly made of wood.

Numerous hotels were also built and cofinanced by Del Webb during this period, including Webb's own Highway House motel chain. The firm's expansion required increasing amounts of capital, and on December 8, 1960, the company was incorporated as the Del E. Webb Corporation in an offering worth $12 million. This year also marked the dawn of a brilliant new phase in Del Webb's history: the opening of the first Sun City and the beginning of its full-force involvement in residential and commercial property development.

Ben Schleifer, a Russian émigré, is credited with developing the first community designed for senior citizens, Youngtown, northwest of Phoenix. A number of executives shuttled the concept through the Del Webb Corporation, where it grew quite different from Schleifer's community. Sun City would offer a relatively affluent generation of retirees ''activity, economy, and individuality,'' according to Tom Breen, one of the project's first sponsors. Built around the remains of a 20th-century ghost town, Marinette, Arizona, the project featured a recreation center, golf course, swimming pool, and shopping center—all finished before the first houses were sold. New Year's Day 1960 was the day of the impressive grand opening; turnout was ten times the expected 10,000, and 237 houses (worth over $2.5 million) were sold in the first weekend. Sales steadily surpassed expectations, and the community grew. Eventually a hospital was built, providing another important selling point. Other Sun Cities soon sprouted up across the Sun Belt: first a small, 150-unit community in Kern City, California, then one south of Tampa, Florida, in 1962. However, these clones did not meet the success of the original, in part due to lower visibility (the Tampa location was somewhat isolated from the main thoroughfares). A fourth Sun City between San

Diego and Los Angeles actually outperformed its model but suffered setbacks due to a strike.

The success of the complicated project, a work of many hands, enhanced Del Webb's personal reputation even more, garnering him a *Time* magazine cover and a place as spokesman for his vision of active retirement living. In spite of this type of popular identification, the company continued to pursue government contracts such as missile silos. The company began to venture into the international arena, losing money on Central American infrastructure projects. The Del Webb Corporation located its new headquarters in a glittering 17-story building, the first erected in what was to become a new financial center for Phoenix.

In the 1960s, hotel and casino development also became a highly visible part of Del Webb's blend of projects. The company had built one of the early Las Vegas hotels, the Flamingo, in 1946.

One of its owners, mobster Bugsy Siegel, was murdered in Beverly Hills just weeks after its grand opening. According to Webb, he didn't know his client's notoriety when he began the project. But he noted Siegel paid for the work quickly, in cash. The Flamingo was designed to astonish visitors when it was built, but its 100 rooms seemed quaint after Del Webb built the 1,000-room Sahara two decades later. Observers noted the casino business gained a measure of respectability from Del Webb's presence. The company headquartered its Hotel Group in the Thunderbird Hotel after acquiring it in 1964.

Gaming and leisure, enhanced by convention activity, dominated Del Webb's balance sheet and seemed an expanding industry. The company developed casinos and resorts outside of Las Vegas, including the Sahara Tahoe, the Mountain Shadows and TownHouse in Arizona, and the Fresno TowneHouse. Nevertheless, the group's most prestigious properties, such as the Mint in Las Vegas and the Primadonna Club in Reno, were located in Nevada.

By 1978 Del Webb was known as the largest gaming company in the world. Its success in this arena made it an attractive takeover target for Frank Sinatra, his attorney Milton Rudin, and newspaper publisher Harry Greenspun. However, the Hotel Group met its Waterloo in New Jersey with the purchase of the President Hotel site on the Atlantic City boardwalk and the purchase of a share in the Claridge Hotel. The President Hotel was nearly full when Del Webb took over with plans of building a new casino in its place, and plans for relocating the residents caused some initial public relations problems. Billing itself as ''a corporation with a conscience,'' the company helped elderly residents find alternative housing and provided some financial assistance. Although the building was emptied six months later with the company's image intact, financing difficulties scuttled the plan and the building was sold.

Del Webb kept the Claridge Hotel after dipping deeply into its considerable credit (including the first revolving credit for a developer) for its restoration. However, the effort was besieged by increasing interest rates and construction costs. A bloated (compared to Nevada's) and seemingly hostile bureaucracy stalled the casino's licensure in a costly investigation of dozens of executives. The Claridge was sold in October 1983 as part of a company-wide belt-tightening that laid off thousands at Sun City and sold many other properties.

To organize this restructuring, Robert K. Swanson was elected president and chief operating officer in 1981, after the retirement of Bob Johnson, a company veteran who had served as president for three years and served as CEO after Del Webb himself left the post in 1973 (remaining as board chairman). Johnson had succeeded Webb as chairman of the board as well as president when the health-conscious Webb—his desk sported a "No Smoking" sign—died on July 4, 1974, due to complications related to cancer treatment. Johnson also headed the Del E. Webb Foundation, a charitable organization founded in 1961.

Swanson sold several recreational properties in order to cut the company's massive debt. Philip J. Dion joined Del Webb in 1982 as senior vice-president for finance, a critical position. Eventually, he and Swanson came to believe that the company's best chance for survival lay in dissolving the casino and hotel group, which, until the New Jersey venture, had been profitable. Fortunately, the success of most of these properties helped them sell, as did a recovering economy. Del Webb also took advantage of a unique tax loophole allowing it to buy millions of dollars worth of tax losses from Alaska Native Corporations, benefiting the company by $27.5 million between 1985 and 1987.

However, in 1987, crisis struck again after the stock market crashed in late October. Robert Swanson retired and Phil Dion took over almost immediately as chief executive officer. Again, a plan to reduce debt by liquidating assets was enacted, and the company began concentrating exclusively on its retirement communities, since the hotels and casinos would require too much capital to maintain. The property management division of the company was also liquidated.

The Del Webb Corporation emerged from these difficulties as a more focused company, and its Sun City developments performed well. The original met its goals of 25,000 dwelling units and 50,000 residents in 1978, reaching a cost of nearly $1 billion. Sun City Las Vegas proved even more profitable than the wildly successful original. By 1995 over 50,000 residences had been built in seven developments in five states. A new development with a more affordable product line—the Sun City MacDonald Ranch—was planned for the Las Vegas area. However, a weak economy dampened the success of its southern California project, Sun City Palm Desert.

In the 1990s the company expanded upon its core business, venturing into less exotic areas than its previous diversification efforts. Coventry Homes, acquired in 1991, competed in the conventional residential construction market, and Terravita, located in North Scottsdale, offered a planned community setting to people of all ages. Both performed well. In fiscal 1995 Coventry boasted 921 closings, an annual increase of 57 percent. More than half of the available Terravita homes (723) were sold within a year and a half of the development's opening in November 1993. A similar, but much larger, planned community known as the Villages at Desert Hills was planned for Phoenix.

Del Webb seemed well prepared for the 21st century. In 1995 annual net orders rose almost 400 units to 4,534; revenues leaped almost $300 million to $803 million. At the same time, the average sale price for its new homes grew 18 percent. A $45 million common stock offering in August 1995 helped reduce the company's debt. The fastest-growing segment of the U.S. population in the 1990s—adults aged 55 and over—was predicted to peak in 2010 as the baby boom generation reached retirement age. As Phoenix and Las Vegas, the company's home territories, continued in their above-average rates of growth, Del Webb entered a new frontier with Sun City Hilton Head, located near the South Carolina coast.

Principal Subsidiaries: Coventry Homes.

Further Reading:

Byrne, Harlan S., "Del Webb Corp.," *Barron's,* August 31, 1992, p. 33.

"Competitive Positioning (Best Building Company)," *Professional Builder,* October, 1994, p. 102.

"Del Webb Corporation Announces Proposed Common Stock Offering," *PR Newswire,* July 25, 1995, 725LA028.

"Del Webb Reports Record Earnings for Fiscal Year 1995; Company Also Sets Records for Sales Orders, Closings, and Backlog," *PR Newswire,* July 25, 1995, 725LA020.

Donohue, Gerry, "Gearing Up for the Recovery," *Builder,* May 1992, p. 214.

Edmondson, Brad, "Here Comes the Sun King," *American Demographics,* December, 1989, p. 40.

Finnerty, Margaret, *Del Webb: A Man. A Company.* Flagstaff, Arizona: Heritage, 1991.

"Grandchildren Teach Us Patience," *PR Newswire,* August 25, 1995, 8235LAFNS1.

Schine, Eric, "A Dare in the Desert: 5,500 Retirement Homes," *Business Week,* December 9, 1991, p. 94.

Weiss, Gary, "Del Webb Could Swim Against Tide," *Business Week,* October 5, 1992, p. 122.

—Frederick C. Ingram

Department 56, Inc.

One Village Place
6436 City West Parkway
Eden Prairie, Minnesota 55344
U.S.A.
(612) 944-5600
Fax: (612) 943-4500

Public Company
Incorporated: 1984
Employees: 205
Sales: $217.9 million
Stock Exchanges: New York
SICs: 5199 Gifts & Novelties

Department 56, Inc. is a leading designer, importer, and distributor of collectibles, giftware, and holiday merchandise. The company is perhaps best known for its collection of hand-crafted, ceramic and porcelain miniature villages. Also popular, however, are other holiday and home decorative accessories, which include a line of porcelain and pewter figurines known as Snowbabies. In fact, Department 56's product line consists of more than 2,000 different items; the company typically introduces approximately 600 new items each year, while discontinuing items from previous seasons, a practice that enhances the collectibility of Department 56 products. Manufacturing of Department 56 items is contracted to facilities in Asia and Europe, and in the mid-1990s, Department 56 giftwares were available in some 19,000 gift and department stores across the United States.

Department 56 was founded by Edward R. Bazinet, who worked in the early 1970s as a manager at the Minneapolis-based Bachman Holdings, Inc., a retailer of floral, gift, and garden items. Bazinet was in charge of a wholesale gift imports department at Bachman Holdings, which, for accounting purposes, was dubbed department 56. When Bazinet decided to strike out on his own and form his own company in 1976, he named his company Department 56. Bazinet served as chairman and chief executive officer, while Todd L. Bachman was named president and vice-chairman. Headquarters were established in Eden Prairie, Minnesota.

Appealing to collectors of Christmas decor, the new company's first offerings centered on its Original Snow Village Collection, which was introduced in 1977. The Original Snow Village

comprised small, hand-painted, ceramic pieces nostalgically recollecting small-town American winter scenes. Some of the little buildings and houses featured miniature electric lights inside, the wires for which were meant to be hidden underneath blankets of plastic snow. The unique design and quality of each piece in the Village series appealed to customers, who spotted them in gift and department stores and began acquiring them in order to recreate entire miniature villages in their homes.

Over the next seven years, the popularity of Department 56 gift items increased steadily, and in 1984, Department 56 was formally incorporated, being owned and operated by Bachman Holdings and ed bazinet international, inc. That year, the company introduced a variation on its Snow Village theme: The Heritage Village Collection. The first pieces in this collection became known as the Dickens Village and comprised porcelain homes, buildings, and accessories for recreating a Victorian Christmas village. Porcelain, as opposed to ceramic, allowed for greater detail, and porcelain's translucence gave a warmer visual effect to the pieces when lit. The Dickens Village series also offered tiny figurine representatives of characters from Dickens's "A Christmas Carol." Moreover, Department 56 obtained a license from the Dickens estate to use the famous Charles Dickens signature initials on some of the products. With the addition of finer detail and quality, the collectibility of Department 56 products rose dramatically.

1986 was an important year for new product introduction at Department 56. That year, two new series were added to the Heritage Village Collection: the New England Village (with such pieces as covered bridges, town halls, and sleighs, recalling winter scenes in rural American towns) and The Alpine Village (with farmhouses, churches, and clock towers reminiscent of hamlets in the Swiss Alps).

Another important introduction in 1986 was that of the Snowbabies. Snowbabies were figurines of toddlers bundled in fuzzy-looking snowsuits; they were made entirely of porcelain bisque, which was also hand applied onto the little snowsuits, creating the impression that snow crystals had fallen on the babies as they played outdoors in the snow.

The Snowbabies series reportedly took six years for designers Kristi Jensen Pierro and Bill Kirchner to perfect, and the concept could be traced back to the late 1800s. Although some collectors disagree on their origin, two theories have emerged. One is that the concept originated with explorer Admiral Robert Peary and his wife Josephine. The couple, residing in Greenland in 1893, had a daughter, whom the Eskimos referred to as "Ad-Poo-Mickaninny," or "snow baby," because of her white skin. The child was named after an Eskimo woman friend, who made the baby a one-piece snowsuit. Josephine Peary later wrote two children's books about a snow baby, and, as an adult, daughter Marie Peary published an autobiography in 1934 entitled *The Snowbaby's Own Story*. Others, however, trace the snow baby to 19th century Germany, where "tannenbaumkonfekt"—small dolls made from sugar, flour, and a gum thickener—were a popular holiday decoration. The candy figurines became so popular that commercial confectioners could not keep up with the demand. One confectioner reportedly commissioned a German company to create "snow babies" out of hand-whipped bisque, and other German manufacturers were quick to adapt the designs. The bisque figurines remained popular in Germany through the 1930s.

Department 56 Snowbabies represented considerable crafts-manship and labor on the part of the company's overseas manufacturers. Each design was transformed into a clay model, from which several molds were cast. The final production mold was then filled by hand with a hand-blended mixture of clay and water. All accessories, such as backpacks, wings, and stars were then attached to the dried, hardened figurine by hand, as were the fine grains of bisque known as snow crystals. Finally, facial features and coloring were applied by hand to each figurine. The popularity of the Snowbabies later prompted Department 56 to publish a hard-bound book featuring poetry and stories on the adventures of the Snowbabies.

From 1988 to 1991, Department 56 focused primarily on ex-panding designs and production within their popular collec-tions. Toward that end, it began issuing specialized pieces that would appeal to the vocations and hobbies of consumers. For example, the company introduced a vet and pet shop model for pet owners and veterinarians, a bank or brokerage house for those with financial interests, and a post office that might appeal to mail carriers. Moreover, the Snowbabies collection was ex-panded to include tree ornaments, picture frames, music boxes, and water globes featuring the popular characters. Snowbabies also became available in pewter. Finally, the company en-hanced the Heritage Village Collection (offering the Christmas in the City and Little Town of Bethlehem series of collectibles) and introduced such new lines of collectibles as Mercury Glass tree ornaments, Winter Silhouette figurines, and Merry Makers porcelain monk figures.

Department 56 relied on independently-owned foreign manu-facturers, located primarily on the Pacific Rim, for the manufac-ture of their collectibles. To oversee quality control and the export of products, the company formed a wholly-owned sub-sidiary, Department 56 Trading Co., Ltd., based in Taiwan. The company believed that its relationship with its foreign manufac-turers was crucial to its competitive position in the industry, enabling it to develop and produce detailed, high-quality prod-ucts, while keeping prices affordable for customers.

In the early 1990s, Department 56 went through a period of reorganization. In October 1992, the company entered into an agreement to acquire all outstanding stock held by Bachman Holdings, Inc. and ed bazinet international, inc. Department 56 was then organized and acquired by a private investment firm, Forstmann Little & Co. for $270 million. The following year, Forstmann Little Partnerships and the company's management took Department 56 public, with an initial offering of 5.29 million shares at $18 each. Leadership throughout the reorgani-zation remained with Bazinet and Bachman.

Early in 1994, a second public offering was made of 5.8 million shares at a little over $27 each. The company was clearly thriving. In fact, since 1989, the company had experienced average annual net sales growth of 25 percent, while net sales averaged a 39 percent annual growth rate.

The financial success of Department 56 was attributable to several factors. First, the company had a large number of repeat sales. In a study conducted by the company, it was learned that 60 percent of Department 56 customers received their first Village piece as a gift. Of these, 70 percent continued to build their collection, acquiring two to three new pieces each year. In fact, Department 56 had build a following of an estimated 200,000 collectors. In addition, the company regulated the availability of its products, creating greater demand. While many Department 56 products were available in the mid-1990s through approximately 19,000 gift retailers, mail houses, and department stores, only 6,000 retailers were authorized to dis-tribute the Village Series and Snowbabies products.

Success was also heightened by the collectors' market the com-pany was helping to foster. As Village Series and Snowbabies designs were retired, they began trading in secondary markets at prices higher than the original retail prices. Although Depart-ment 56 did not participate as a purchaser or seller in the secondary market, the company certainly benefitted from the publicity and the potential collectibility of its new lines. Ac-cording to a 1993 article in *Fortune* magazine, one of the most highly-prized Department 56 items became a miniature mill produced in a limited quantity of 2,500 and originally selling for $35 in the mid-1980s; a little over ten years later, the mill sold on the collectors' market for as much as $6,500. To insure authenticity, each Department 56 item was clearly marked with the series name, title, year of introduction, and company logo.

In 1994, Bachman left Department 56, returning to Bachman's Inc. to serve as chairman and CEO. He was replaced by Susan Engel, who assumed the positions of president and chief operat-ing officer at Department 56. A graduate of Cornell University and Harvard Business School, Engel had extensive experience in marketing and management, which she gained through em-ployment at J.C. Penney's and Booz, Allen and Hamilton, before becoming president and CEO of the Champion Products division of Sara Lee Corp. It was Bazinet's hope that Engel would help Department 56 build its lead in the giftware market. Commenting on her move to Department 56 in a 1995 *Gifts & Decorative Accessories* magazine article, Engel observed ''It's hard to look at this company and not get really excited about it. . . . Both the products and the displays were so inviting, I knew this was something I could do.''

Gaining licenses from Coca-Cola and Walt Disney Co. in the mid-1990s, Department 56 began offering collectibles incorpo-rating these popular logos and themes. Soon consumers were able to build collections from the Disney Parks Series, including Mickey's Christmas Shop, antique shops, a fire station, and other Mickey and Minnie Mouse accessories. Long-time collec-tors of the Snow Village series were offered a new Coca-Cola bottling plant and delivery truck to add to their villages. More-over, by concealing motors in the bases of village accessories, Department 56 began offering ''animated'' pieces, including the Village Animated Skating Pond, with skating figures gliding over a ''frozen pond,'' and the Village Animated All Around the Park, with adults and children strolling through a snowy, tree-lined park.

To promote their items and raise money for charitable causes, Department 56 held a national holiday decorating program called ''Homes for the Holidays'' in 1995. There, retailers of Department 56 items offered decorating ideas, free seminars, and demonstrations for decorating the home during the holiday season. In conjunction with this event, Department 56 raised money for Ronald McDonald Houses through corporate contributions, fundraising raffles, and auctions. Olympic skater Dorothy Hamill was chosen as the event's national hostess, being a loyal collector of Department 56 items herself.

Although the giftware and decorative accessories was a highly fragmented and seasonal industry—with most sales occurring around major holidays, especially Christmas, and thousands of companies competing in the industry with a wide variety of products—it also represented a promising niche market, with estimated growth of 10 to 14 percent annually. And Department 56 maintained an enviable position in the market, holding an eight percent share of the collectibles segment, in which the industry leader held about a 16 percent share. In 1994, Department 56 reported sales of over $217 million, an 18 percent increase over previous year. Given its consistent finan-

cial growth and the popularity of its products, Department 56 seemed well poised to maintain its strong position in the industry.

Principal Subsidiaries: FL 56 Intermediate Corp.; ed bazinet international, inc.; D 56, Inc.; Browndale Tanley Limited; Department 56 Trading Co., Ltd. (Taiwan)

Further Reading:

"Forstmann Little to Acquire Collectibles Firm," *HFD-The Weekly Home Furnishings Newspaper,* October 19, 1992, p. 85.
"People Watching," *HFD-The Weekly Home Furnishings Newspaper,* September 26, 1994, p. 71.
Labate, John, "Department 56," *Fortune,* December 12, 1994, p. 243.
Werner, Holly M., "Meet Susan Engel," *Gifts & Decorative Accessories,* June 1995, p. 158.

—Beth Watson Highman

Deutsche Bank A.G.

Taunusanlage 12
60262 Frankfurt am Main
Germany
(4969) 71500
Fax: (4969) 7150-4225

Public Company
Incorporated: 1870
Employees: 73,450
Total Assets: DM 631.74 billion
Stock Exchanges: Berlin Bremen Düsseldorf Frankfurt
    Hamburg Hanover Munich Stuttgart Vienna Antwerp
    Brussels Paris Luxembourg Amsterdam Basel Geneva
    Zurich London Tokyo
SICs: 6000 Depository Institutions

Deutsche Bank A.G. has weathered two world wars, three depressions, and a divided Germany to become one of the world's leading financial institutions and one of the ten largest banks in the world in the mid-1990s. It has positioned itself as a Europe-wide universal bank (one that offers a variety of services) and a global investment bank.

Deutsche Bank was founded in Berlin on March 10, 1870 with the approval of the king of Prussia. The company opened its doors for business a month later under the directorship of Georg von Siemens, with five million thalers in capital.

The company's creation coincided with the unification of Germany. After Germany's victory in the Franco-German War, France was required to pay an indemnity of FFr 5 billion, which greatly stimulated German industry, trade, and consumption. Deutsche Bank naturally assumed a position of leadership in the country's expanding economy. The founding of the Second German Reich in 1871 led to another important development: the thaler was replaced by the mark, a new currency based on gold.

Within two years, the bank had established domestic branches in Bremen and Hamburg and expanded into eastern Asia with offices in Shanghai and Yokohama. In 1872 it opened a London branch, and capital stood at 15 million thalers.

Many joint-stock banks, including Deutsche Bank, had been created in the wake of the liberalization of requirements for starting new companies, but many failed within a few years. During the financial crisis of 1873–75 it appeared that the entire economic system was on the verge of collapse; small shareholders as well as wealthy business people were ruined, and in Berlin alone nearly 50 banks filed for bankruptcy.

But Deutsche Bank, because of its concentration on foreign operations, was largely unscathed by the financial panic. With its assets intact, the young bank began to make significant acquisitions, including Deutsche Union-Bank and the Berliner Bankverein. These purchases transformed Deutsche Bank into one of Germany's largest and most prestigious banks.

In 1877 Deutsche Bank joined a syndicate of leading private banks popularly known as the "Prussian consortium." The bank was also employed by the government for the issue of state loans, and it grew rapidly in both influence and assets. By 1899 it was able to offer to float, without help from other financial institutions, a 125 million mark loan for Prussia and, at the same time, a 75 million mark loan for the German Reich.

Throughout the 1880s and 1890s Deutsche Bank was a leader in electrical development. It helped to form finance and holding companies and issued bonded loans and shares for the construction of dynamos, power plants, electric railways, tramways, and municipal lighting systems. By 1897, there were 750 power plants located across Germany. The bank also invested in the Edison General Electric Company in the United States and began to build a power plant in Argentina.

During the same period, the bank was a driving force behind railway development. In 1888, Deutsche Bank obtained a concession to build an east-west railway to open up Asiatic Turkey. A decade later, 642 miles of the Anatolian railway were in operation in Turkey, from Constantinople through Eskisehir to Ankara, and from Eskisehir to Konya. At the same time, in the United States the bank participated in the financial reorganization of Northern Pacific Railroad. All of this, of course, was done in addition to contributing significantly to the development of Germany's own extensive network of surface and underground railways.

The continuity of bank operations was uninterrupted when von Siemens died in October 1901. At Deutsche Bank, like most other German banks, all decisions are made by the board of directors, and the board customarily takes credit for the company's successes. The firm has no official chairman, but selects one board member to act as "spokesman." Thus the absence of von Siemens had little effect on the bank, since management by consensus is the bank's guiding principle.

By the early years of the 20th century, the company had acquired the Bergische-Markische Bank, the Schlesischer Bankverein, and interests in the Hannoversche Bank, the Oberrheinische Bank, and the Rheinische Creditbank, and in Italy, participation in the founding of Banca Commerciale Italiana. The bank's capital was now more than six times the amount it was founded with.

The bank then entered a period of consolidation and growth: it built up its sub-branches; improved and extended customer services; paid particular attention to the deposit business; and promoted checks for personal use. In association with numerous regional banks, Deutsche Bank also became involved in a wide range of business activities, including transportation, coal, steel, and oil, as well as railways and electrification. Shortly before World War I, with 200 million marks in capital backed by a 112.5 million mark reserve and deposits and borrowed funds of 1.58 billion marks, the *Frankfurter Zeitung* called it the world's leading bank.

Deutsche Bank weathered the many economic problems during World War I; at the end of the conflict, the bank had offices at 182 locations throughout Germany, and a staff of nearly 14,000. But with the war lost, the German empire gone, and the transition from monarchy to democracy threatened by revolution, Allied demands for reparations totaling 132 billion gold marks pushed the German banking system to the brink of ruin. By 1923, one gold mark was worth 1 trillion paper marks.

In 1929, as financial chaos loomed, Deutsche Bank merged with its 20-year rival, the Disconto-Gesellschaft. At the time of their merger the banks were the two largest in Germany; combined, their capital, reserves, and deposits were each at least twice as large as that of any competitor. The merger, designed to cut administrative costs by closing competing operations, was very successful, and the resulting bank had enough capital and reserves to withstand the economic crisis. Before the collapse, Deutsche Bank and Disconto-Gesellschaft had handled about 50 percent of all business conducted by Berlin banks. By 1931, the bank was relying heavily on its undisclosed reserves and had twice reduced capital, but it remained solvent and required no government aid.

Under orders from the National Socialist government that came to power in 1933, unemployed workers were put to work under a ''reemployment'' plan. At first, the government only concentrated on projects that were meant to counteract the high unemployment rate; the autobahns were the chief showpiece of this strategy. But by 1936, a significant percentage of industrial production had been switched to the manufacture of weapons and munitions and ''reemployment'' had become ''rearmament.'' Deutsche Bank supported the program through the purchase of government securities.

During World War II, the government financed its budget deficit by printing new money, a misguided practice that quickly led to spiraling inflation. The problem was artificially suppressed by questionable banking measures; more treasury paper began to appear among the bank's assets. Deutsche Bank's enormous losses were made known only when Germany surrendered to the Allies in April 1945.

After the war, Allied occupation authorities investigating possible war crimes committed by German banks found that Deutsche Bank and its rival Dresdner Bank bore substantial responsibility for the war through their lending to the Nazi government, their purchase of government securities, and the influence that they exerted over large industrial concerns through their shareholdings and corporate directorships. Both banks also had close ties to SS chief Heinrich Himmler and other Nazi officials, had exploited conquered nations by seizing the assets of their financial institutions, and had helped disenfranchise Jews in Germany. Four directors (including one Nazi Party member) and two executives of Deutsche Bank were arrested by the Allied authorities, but were never tried.

After lengthy negotiations with the occupying forces, Deutsche Bank's ten regional institutions were formed into three banks: Norddeutsche Bank A.G., Rheinisch-Westfalische Bank A.G., and Suddeutsche Bank A.G. served the northern, central, and southern areas of West Germany respectively. In 1957, these three banks were again reorganized, this time to form a single Deutsche Bank A.G. with corporate headquarters in Frankfurt. At the time of its reunification, the bank employed over 16,000 people and its assets totaled 8.4 billion marks. Hermann J. Abs, the strategist behind the reorganization of the bank and one of the key figures in West Germany's financial recovery, became its spokesman.

In the 1960s Deutsche Bank concentrated on improving services for its smaller depositors. The bank launched programs for personal loans of up to DM 2,000 and medium-sized loans up to DM 6,000 for specific purchases, as well as an overdraft facility of up to DM 1,000 for consumers. Other services included personal mortgage loans, improvements in savings facilities, and the establishment of a eurocheque system. By the end of the decade, the bank had become the largest provider of consumer credit in West Germany.

Under the direction of Abs, Deutsche Bank began to reestablish its international operations (it had lost all of its worldwide holdings after the war). It first reopened offices in Buenos Aires, Sao Paulo, and Rosario, Argentina, and then in Tokyo, Istanbul, Cairo, Beirut, and Teheran. In 1968, Deutsche Bank joined the Netherlands' Amsterdam-Rotterdam Bank, Britain's Midland Bank, and Belgium's Societe Generale de Banque in founding the European-American Bank & Trust Company in New York. And in 1972 Deutsche Bank founded Eurasbank (European Asian Bank) with members of the same consortium.

When Hermann Abs retired in 1967, his place as spokesman was taken by Karl Klusen and Franz Heinrich Ulrich, who became co-spokesmen. Abs had wielded such a great concentration of economic and financial power that a special law limiting such influence was named after him—''Lex Abs'' reduced the number of supervisory-board seats a single person could hold simultaneously in West Germany.

During the 1970s Deutsche Bank became the dominant financial institution in West Germany. Under the guidelines of the ''universal banking'' system in place in Germany for more than a century, commercial banks are allowed to hold unlimited interests in industrial companies, underwrite and trade securities on their own, and play the foreign currency markets, in addition to providing credit and accepting deposits. Deutsche Bank took advantage of this rule during the 1960s and 1970s by investing in a wide range of industrial companies. In 1979, the bank held seats on the supervisory boards of about 140 companies, among them Daimler-Benz, Volkswagen, Siemens, AEG, Thyssen, Bayer, Nixdorf, Allianz, and Philipp Holzmann.

But the bank's extraordinary influence in West Germany aroused concern about the extent of the bank's instruments in other companies. As a result of these concerns, Deutsche Bank began to reduce its industrial holdings in the 1970s. This trend, however, was briefly interrupted in 1975 when Middle Eastern concerns flush with petrodollars supplanted the big banks as a source of capital investment. At the request of Chancellor Helmut Schmidt, Deutsche Bank purchased a 29 percent interest in Daimler-Benz from industrialist Friederich Flick to ensure that it would stay in German hands, with the understanding that the bank would resell the shares once the crisis had passed. Deutsche Bank already owned 25 percent of the famed automaker. In December of that year, it resold the shares to a consortium that included Commerzbank, Dresdner Bank, and Bayerische Landesbank.

During the 1980s, Deutsche Bank made major expansions in its foreign operations, both in commercial banking and investment banking. It opened its first U.S. branch office in New York in 1979, and by 1987 had bought out all its partners in the Eurasbank consortium and renamed it Deutsche Bank (Asia), providing 14 more branches in 12 Asian countries. At nearly the same time, the company's capital-markets branch began operating and trading in Japanese, British, and American securities. By the end of 1988, the bank had approximately 7.2 million customers at 1,530 offices, more than 200 of them outside of West Germany.

In 1980 Deutsche Bank was the only one of the West German Big Three banks to turn a healthy profit. Unlike Commerzbank and Dresdner Bank, the other two of the Big Three, Deutsche Bank did not overexpand, but remained cautious in the face of high interest rates and continued recession. In 1984 it acquired a 4.9 percent stake in Morgan Grenfell, the British securities firm; in 1985 it bought scandal-plagued industrial giant Flick Industrieverwaltung from Friederich Flick, with the intention of taking it public; and in 1988 it acquired a 2.5 percent interest in the automaker Fiat. Another sign of Deutsche Bank's aggressive pursuit of foreign markets is the fact that in the wake of the stock market crash in October 1987, at a time when massive layoffs were taking place in the securities industry, its American securities affiliate, Deutsche Bank Capital Corporation, expanded its work force. In 1988 Deutsche Bank entered the treasury securities market at a time when many foreign firms were leaving. Two years later, the U.S. Federal Reserve recognized Deutsche Bank Government Securities Inc. as a primary dealer of government securities.

At home, Deutsche Bank took a large and controversial step toward becoming a one-stop financial service center in 1989 when it created its own insurance subsidiary to complement its commercial and investment banking businesses. Immediately, it was considered a strong rival for the Allianz Group, the West German-based company that was Europe's largest insurer.

Wilhelm Christians and Alfred Herrhausen became Deutsche Bank's new co-spokesmen in 1985. When Christians retired in early 1988, Herrhausen was appointed sole spokesman for the bank. Following Herrhausen's assassination by terrorists on November 30, 1989, Hilmar Kopper became spokesman.

In the late 1980s and early 1990s, Deutsche Bank bolstered its investment banking arm through additional acquisitions, aiming to become a global investment bank. After acquiring the Toronto-based investment bank McLean McCarthy Ltd. in 1988, it purchased the remainder of Morgan Grenfell in 1989 for $1.5 billion. It also took a more aggressive approach to the

North America market. In 1992 Deutsche Bank North America was formed—with John A. Rolls as chief executive officer—to coordinate and manage all of Deutsche Bank's North American operations, including those in investment banking which included McLean McCarthy and C. J. Lawrence Inc., the latter a U.S. investment bank acquired in 1986. The following year Deutsche Bank Securities Corporation was formed to specifically manage such areas as investment banking, securities transactions, and asset management services.

At the same time it aimed to become a global investment bank, Deutsche Bank also pursued a strategy of extending its position as a universal bank beyond Germany. Initially, it focused on Western Europe. But with the fall of communism throughout Eastern Europe in 1989 and 1990, Deutsche Bank sought to become a Europe-wide universal bank. To that end, in 1986 it had acquired Banca d'America e d'Italia S.p.a. from the Bank of America for $603 million (in 1994 this bank was renamed Deutsche Bank S.p.A.). In 1993 Deutsche Bank increased its presence in Italy when it purchased a majority interest in Banca Popolare di Lecco. That same year, the bank purchased Banco de Madrid in Spain, later integrated into Deutsche Bank, S.A.E. By 1994 Deutsche Bank operated 260 branches in Italy and 318 branches in Spain, and in both countries it was the largest foreign bank.

Following German reunification, Deutsche Bank quickly capitalized on the opportunity by entering into a joint venture with Deutsche Kreditbank to begin to restake its claim to eastern German territory. By 1994, Deutsche Bank had more than 300 branches in eastern Germany. It also opened offices elsewhere in Eastern Europe: Bulgaria, the Czech Republic, Hungary, Poland, and Russia.

The early 1990s were a time of rising fortunes for Deutsche Bank as net income more than doubled from DM 1,025 billion in 1990 to DM 2,243 billion in 1993. This trend was reversed in 1994 when a series of problems hit within a short period. First the bank suffered huge losses from loans of DM 1.2 billion it had made to a property group run by Jurgen Schneider, which collapsed in early 1994. Then two firms in which Deutsche Bank had invested heavily ran into trouble—Balsam filed for bankruptcy and Metallgesellschaft (MG), an engineering conglomerate, nearly collapsed after losing $1.33 billion on speculative oil trades. Kopper provoked additional controversy and public resentment when he called bills amounting to $33 million that the Schneider property group owed to construction workers "peanuts." Early in 1995 the former head of MG sued Deutsche Bank over who was responsible for MG's downfall. Also in early 1995, Deutsche Bank's ties to the Nazi government of Hitler were dredged up when East German files were made public for the first time.

The losses it suffered in 1994 forced Deutsche Bank to increase its loss reserves which contributed to a reduction in net income to DM 1,360 billion. In 1995 Deutsche Bank made significant moves to further establish itself as a global investment bank. Deutsche Bank North America acquired ITT Commercial Finance Corporation for $868 million to strengthen its presence in asset-based lending. The acquisition was immediately renamed Deutsche Financial Services Corporation. Later in 1995 Deutsche Bank consolidated all of its investment banking operations into Morgan Grenfell under a new unit, Deutsche Morgan Grenfell, based in London and headed by Ronaldo Schmitz. The move shifted more than half of Deutsche Bank's business to London control rather than that of Frankfurt, a shift that the *European* called a "corporate revolution."

In the mid-1990s Deutsche Bank held a strong position in Europe as a universal bank—though not equally strong in each country—and was rapidly gaining ground on its global rivals in investment banking. With very deep pockets, Deutsche Bank was equipped to sustain its two-prong strategy and to become stronger through additional acquisitions and expansions.

Principal Subsidiaries: ALD AutoLeasing D G.m.b.H.; Bonndata Gesellschaft für Datenverarbeitung m.b.H.; Bonnfinanz A.G. für Vermögensberatung und Vermittlung; DB Export-Leasing G.m.b.H.; DB Research G.m.b.H. Gesellschaft für Wirtschafts- und Finanzanalyze; Deutsche Asset Management G.m.b.H.; Deutsche Bank Bauspar-A.G.; Deutsche Bank Lübeck A.G.; Deutsche Bank Saar A.G.; Deutsche Centralbodenkredit-A.G.; Deutsche Gesellschaft für Fondsverwaltung m.b.H.; Deutsche Gesellschaft für Mittelstandsberatung m.b.H.; Deutsche Grundbesitz-Investmentgesellschaft m.b.H.; Deutsche Immobilien Leasing G.m.b.H.; Deutsche Immobilien Anlagegesellschaft m.b.H.; Deutsche Immobilienvermittlungs-Holding G.m.b.H.; Deutscher Herold Allgemeine Versicherungs-A.G.; Deutscher Herold Lebensversicherungs-A.G.; Deutscher Herold Rechtsschutzversicherungs-A.G.; DWS Deutsche Gesellschaft für Wertpapiersparen m.b.H.; Frankfurter Hypothekenbank A.G.; GEFA Gesellschaft für Absatzfinanzierung m.b.H.; GEFA-Leasing G.m.b.H.; Globale Krankenversicherungs-A.G.; Grunelius KG Privatbankiers; Lebensversicherungs-A.G. der Deutschen Bank; Lübecker Hypothekenbank A.G.; Morgan Grenfall G.m.b.H.; Roland Berger & Partner Holding G.m.b.H.; Schiffshypothekenbank zu Lübeck A.G.; Deutsche Bank (Austria) A.G.; DB (Belgium) Finance S.A./N.V.; DB Bourse S.N.C. (France); Deutsche Bank France S.N.C.; DB Vita Compagnia di Assicurazioni e Riassicurazioni sulla Vita S.p.A. (Italy); Deutsche Bank Factoring S.p.A. (Italy); Deutsche Bank Fondi S.p.A. (Italy); Deutsche Bank Leasing S.p.A. (Italy); Deutsche Bank Securities SIM S.p.A. (Italy); Deutsche Bank Società per Azioni (Italy); Deutsche Bank Luxembourg S.A.; DB Investment Management S.A. (Luxembourg); Europäische Hypothekenbank S.A. (Luxembourg); Deutsche Bank de Bary N.V. (the Netherlands); DB Leasing - Sociedade de Locação Financeira Mobiliária, S.A. (Portugal); Deutsche Bank de Investimento, S.A. (Portugal); DB Gestión Sociedad Gestora de Instituciones de Inversión Colectiva, S.A. (Spain); DB Securities Sociedad de Valores y Bolsa, S.A. (Spain); DB Vida Compañía de Seguros y Reaseguros, S.A. (Spain); Deutsche Bank Credit, S.A. (Spain); Deutsche Bank, Sociedad Anónima Española (Spain); Deutsche Bank (Suisse) S.A.; Deutsche Bank Gilts Ltd. (U.K.); Deutsche Sharps Pixley Metals Ltd. (U.K.); Morgan Grenfall & Co. Ltd. (U.K.); Morgan Grenfall Asset Management Ltd. (U.K.); Morgan Grenfall Development Capital Ltd. (U.K.); D.B. Investment Management S.A. (Argentina); Deutsche Bank Argentina S.A.; Deutsche Bank Argentina Sociedad de Bolsa S.A. (Argentina); Deutsche Bank S.A. - Banco Alemão (Brazil); Deutsche Bank (Canada); Deutsche Bank Securities Canada Limitied; Morgan Grenfall (C.I.) Ltd.; Deutsche Bank Financial Products Corp. (U.S.); Deutsche Bank Futures Corp. (U.S.); Deutsche Bank Sharps Pixley Inc. (U.S.); Deutsche Bank Trust Company (U.S.); Deutsche Credit Corp. (U.S.); Deutsche Financial Services Corporation (U.S.); Deutsche Financial Services Holding Corporation (U.S.); Deutsche Morgan Grenfell/C. J. Lawrence Inc. (U.S.); Deutsche Sharps Pixley Metals Inc. (U.S.); Bain & Company Ltd. (Australia); Deutsche Bank Capital Markets (Asia) Ltd. (Hong Kong); Deutsche Bank (Malaysia) Bhd.; Deutsche Bank (Asia Pacific) Ltd. (Singapore); Morgan Grenfall Asia Holdings Pte. Ltd. (Singapore).

Further Reading:

Brady, Simon, "Deutsche Makes Its Mark," *Euromoney,* June 1992, pp. 24–28.
Brierley, David, "Corporate Revolution in the Air as Deutsche Moves to London," *European,* July 21, 1995, p. 17.
Delamaide, Darrell, "The Deutsche Bank Juggernaut Will Keep on Rolling," *Euromoney,* January 1990, p. 32.
Duyn, Aline van, "A Truly Universal Bank," *Euromoney,* September 1994, p. C30.
Fallon, Padraic, "The Battle Plans of Hilmar Kopper," *Euromoney,* January 1994, p. 28.
Fisher, Andrew, "Tough Guy at the Bank," *Financial Times,* November 21, 1994, p. FTS4.
Fuhrman, Peter, "A Faster Ship in a Richer Sea," *Forbes,* November 26, 1990, pp. 40–41.
Gall, Lothar, *Die Deutsche Bank, 1870–1995,* Munich: Beck, 1995.
Grigsby, Jefferson, "Deutsche Bank uber Alles," *Financial World,* May 15, 1990, pp. 42–43.
Kantrow, Yvette, "John Rolls' Grand Plan," *Investment Dealers' Digest,* August 29, 1994.
Kraus, James R., "Changing to Make Its Mark," *American Banker,* September 20, 1994.
Muehring, Kevin, "The Kopper Era at Deutsche Bank," *Institutional Investor,* December 1990, pp. 136–139.
"New Dreams at Deutsche Bank: Germany's Grandest Bank Has a New Vision of Its Future—A Rather More Modest One Than in the Past," *Economist,* June 22, 1991, pp. 79–81.
Rescigno, Richard, "The View from Deutsche Bank," *Barron's,* November 18, 1991, pp. 8–12.
Seidenzahl, Fritz, *100 Jahre Deutsche Bank,* Frankfurt: Deutschen Bank, 1970.
Zweig, Phillip L., "Deutsche Bank Goes on the Attack," *Business Week,* July 17, 1995, pp. 83–84.

—updated by David E. Salamie

Discount Drug Mart, Inc.

211 Commerce Drive
Medina, Ohio 44256-1398
U.S.A.
(216) 725-2340
Fax: (216) 722-2990

Private Company
Incorporated: 1969
Employees: 1,500
Sales: $260 million
SICs: 5122 Dairy Products Stores; 5331 Variety Stores; 5912
   Drug Stores & Propriety Stores; 5411 Drug Stores; 5451
   Grocery Stores; 8082 Pharmaceutical, Home Health Care
   Services

Discount Drug Mart, Inc. operates a chain of discount drug
stores located exclusively in Ohio and primarily in the greater
Cleveland area. A commitment to provide customers with low
prices and one-stop shopping were key elements in the company's growth, which brought revenues to an estimated $260
million by 1994. In fact, Discount Drug Mart was among the
largest privately held retailers in the greater Cleveland area,
ranking 15th on the Arthur Andersen Greater Cleveland 100
rankings in the late 1980s.

Discount Drug Mart was founded by Parviz Boodjeh, a pharmacist and successful businessman. In the early 1960s Boodjeh
and two other partners introduced the Jay Drug chain of stores
in the Cleveland area. This successful operation caught the eye
of executives at Cook United, another discount retailer based in
Cleveland, and was purchased by Cook for an undisclosed sum
in the mid-1960s. Boodjeh remained on board with the new
corporate parent for a short time but soon grew disenchanted
with a management style he deemed impersonal and again
struck out on his own.

Specifically, Boodjeh believed that retail centers should provide
low prices and a diverse product line that would allow customers to fill most of their shopping needs in one stop. Boodjeh's concept also focused on maintaining the friendly and
personal service generally attributed to smaller, hometown drug
stores. In 1969, he established the first Discount Drug Mart in
Elyria, a western suburb of Cleveland. Discount Drug would
soon prove Boodjeh's most successful retail enterprise, garnering a loyal customer following.

At the first Discount Drug store, customers could have prescriptions filled, purchase toiletries, and find grocery and gift items.
In fact, the first store even carried durable good items such as
lawn mowers and vacuum cleaners. Soon, however, Boodjeh
found that customers would return these items when they
needed repair, burdening his fledgling store with a service he
was not interested in providing. So he opted to add to his store's
shelves the hardware and parts needed to fix such items and
found that this enhanced his recipe for success. Boodjeh's concept of one-stop shopping was well received, paving the way for
three additional stores by 1973.

Discount Drug's wider array of product selection required more
space than that of competitors' stores, which averaged from
8,000 to 12,000 square feet. Indeed, Discount Drug required
almost twice that amount of space, presenting a particular challenge for Boodjeh as he sought to expand his chain. However,
the misfortune of a local supermarket chain in the Cleveland
area in the mid-1970s proved a boon to Discount Drug; tough
economic times for the A&P supermarket chain left a host of
empty stores in Cleveland. In 1975 Boodjeh leased five of these
stores, more than doubling the chain of outlets to nine, each
averaging around 16,000 square feet. Also during this time,
Discount Drug announced its entrance into the Cleveland drug
store market.

In the early 1980s, Boodjeh began standardizing the merchandise offerings among his growing chain and commissioned an
architect to develop a store design on which all Discount Drug
stores would be based. A 22,000 square foot model was produced and adopted, and this design was later modified and
enlarged to 24,000 square feet, making room for new product
lines and a video rental business.

Also during the 1980s, computer technology helped the chain
distinguish itself as an innovator, with such in-store additions as
electronic price scanners, which not only facilitated the check
out process but also generated reports to management on product sales and reordering needs. Discount Drug also turned to
computers to help map out new store displays. Using a plano-
gram (known in the industry as a Pegman), Discount Drug
computers showed store managers where and how products
should be displayed.

By the late 1980s, Discount Drug was recognized as one of the
hardest working chains in the country. In 1989 it ranked 34th in
sales according to a Chain Store Guide list of the top 100 drug
chains. Moreover, industry figures showed the chain sold more
than $300 worth of merchandise per square foot.

However, the early 1990s brought intense competition to the
industry. Discount Drug was still smaller than the Ohio drug
store chains of Revco and Phar-Mor, and even these chains
were being threatened by the superstore concept as championed
by Kmart, Wal-Mart, and Target, which were all expanding at a
breakneck pace.

In response, Boodjeh eschewed the aggressive marketing strategy of his competition, remaining content with gradual, steady
growth averaging three to five new stores per year. Such conservative growth proved a successful strategy. Moreover, instead
of looking to grow in areas that already featured competitors'
stores, he focused on pinpointing locations that needed a dis-

count drug retailer. Each new Discount Drug site was carefully selected to meet his specific criteria: it had to be close to the street and located near other successful businesses to ensure customer draw. And in order to keep company assets available for further expansion, Boodjeh sought out developers to purchase the land, build the store, and then lease the property to Discount Drug.

Also unlike many other retail chains, Discount Drug kept corporate costs exceptionally low. Located on the industrial southwest side of Medina, Ohio, Discount Drug headquarters were modestly furnished throughout with linoleum floors, metal desks, and a common "bullpen" room that served as office to Boodjeh and other company executives. Without the managerial "ivory tower," Discount Drug fostered a sense of community and cooperation among its executives and work force.

Finally, Boodjeh made sure that Discount Drug management remained in touch with the customer. Having observed that retaining many levels of management tended to distance the decision makers from the community they served, he established a corporate policy requiring all supervisors to spend a minimum of three days a week in each of their respective stores. In fact, Boodjeh himself served as store pharmacist one day a week at one of the chain's outlets.

Such conservative strategies helped Discount Drug fare well despite the increased competition of the 1990s. "We're just a small fish in a big pond," explained Discount Drug vice-president of finance, Tom McConnell, in the *Akron Beacon Journal*. McConnell added that "to compete against those (bigger) chains, we just have to provide better service and be price competitive, which is tough because we're smaller . . . we just have to work harder."

The success of the Discount Drug chain was attributed not only to Boodjeh's vision and his sensitivity to customer needs, but to the people who worked in the stores. The family-type atmosphere Boodjeh nurtured and maintained throughout the company's 25-year history fostered a low rate of employee turnover, and employees were also encouraged to take on more responsibility and move up in the company.

Several members of Boodjeh's family also played active roles in the management of the company in the early 1990s. Three of Boodjeh's sons were store supervisors and members of the management team: Don Boodjeh, vice-president of advertising; David Boodjeh, vice-president of operations; and Douglas Boodjeh, heading up two of the company's newest business ventures, IPS, Inc. and IPS Network, Inc.

IPS (Immediate Pharmaceutical Services) and IPS Network were launched in 1987 to carry the Discount Drug name into the burgeoning health care market. IPS outlets were set up in physicians' offices, enabling patients to fill prescriptions on the spot. Moreover, in 1994 IPS expanded its offerings to include mail order prescription services. This move was prompted by the spiralling cost of health care in America; like its competitors, Discount Drug perceived that customers were demanding a less expensive option to having prescriptions filled at pharmacies. Mail order prescription services were both cost effective and convenient for the customer, who could have a scrip filled at Discount Drug and then mail order the refills. After forming an alliance with other local drug stores, IPS Network successfully contracted with insurance companies and corporations to gain its share of this growing market.

As Discount Drug Mart marked its 25th anniversary, corporate growth strategy remained conservative, including no plans to expand nationwide. While company management was focused on sustaining Discount Drug's legacy of growth and profitability, the corporate vision remained the same as when the first Discount Drug doors opened: serve customers with low prices and friendly service.

Principal Subsidiaries: IPS, Inc.; IPS Network, Inc.

Further Reading:

Board, Katie, "Small Chains Battle for Retail Drug Slice," *The Akron Beacon Journal,* July 2, 1990, pp.
"Discount Drug Mart Thrives on Gradual, Steady Growth," *The (Cleveland) Plain Dealer,* October 25, 1988, pp.

—D. Muniak

Eastman Chemical Company

100 North Eastman Road
P.O. Box 511
Kingsport, Tennessee 37662
U.S.A.
(423) 229-2000

Public Company
Incorporated: 1993 as Eastman Chemical Company
Employees: 17,495
Sales: $4.32 billion
Stock Exchanges: New York
SICs: 2821 Plastic Materials & Resins; 2823 Cellulosic Man-
    Made Fibers; 2869 Industrial Organic Chemicals, Nec;
    2819 Industrial Inorganic Chemicals, Nec

Founded in 1920 as a subsidiary of the Eastman Kodak Company, Eastman Chemical Company was spun off as an independent company by Kodak in 1994. Eastman Chemical produces a
wide range of plastics, chemicals and fibers—more than 400
products in all—but is most heavily supported by two products,
polyethylene terephthalate (PET) resin and cellulose acetate
filter tow, which together contribute roughly 40 percent of the
company's total revenues and 50 percent of its earnings.

When the First World War broke out in 1914, George Eastman
watched the supply of essential materials arriving from European producers to his company, the Eastman Kodak Company,
slow to a trickle. The ramifications were nearly disastrous. The
company had grown dependent on European manufacturers for
many of the raw materials required to sustain its operations,
particularly photographic paper, optical glass, and gelatin, without which Eastman's photography empire would shrivel into
insolvency. Also of great importance and in short supply during
the war years were the numerous chemicals crucial to the
photography company's production processes, including methanol, acetic acid, and acetone. As the war dragged on, Eastman's predicament grew increasingly severe, and film production at Eastman Kodak's manufacturing facilities in Rochester,
New York, nearly ground to a halt.

Determined to ensure Kodak's future self-reliance, Eastman
decided the most prudent solution was to develop an independent supply of chemicals. Accordingly, after the conclusion of
the war, Eastman and other Kodak delegates began searching
for a suitable location for a Kodak-owned and operated chemi-

cal production facility. As Kodak employees were scouting the
country, a resident of Kingsport, Tennessee, named J. Fred
Johnson was conducting a nationwide search of his own, hoping
to sell a half-built wood distillation plant to an interested party.
Johnson, an employee of the Kingsport Improvement Company,
was attempting to revitalize Kingsport's economy, which had
thrived during the war but was limping along at the war's
conclusion, bereft of the business generated by the manufacturing industries that had temporarily established operations in
Kingsport for war-related work.

One company that had come to Kingsport during the war was
the American Wood Reduction Company, which had contracted
with the federal government to construct a wood distillation
plant for making methanol and other related chemicals. Before
the plant was finished, however, the war ended and American
Wood Reduction cut its ties to Kingsport, leaving a lone
watchman to stand guard over the partly constructed facility.
After the retreat of American Wood Reduction, Johnson began
his search for an industrial concern that could use the idle wood
distillation plant.

By 1920 Kodak and Johnson had found each other, and a group
of Kodak representatives led by Perley S. Wilcox, a future
chairman of Kodak and an employee since 1898, arrived in
Kingsport to examine the half-built wood distillation facility
Johnson was eager to sell. Finding it to their liking, the Kodak
group pushed for its acquisition, and later that year George
Eastman authorized the purchase of the plant and surrounding
acreage for $205,000. Wilcox was named director and general
manager of the new company, becoming the first leader of
Tennessee Eastman Corporation, a Kodak subsidiary.

Shortly after the construction of the wood distillation plant was
finished, the solitary watchman who had guarded an architectural skeleton was replaced by more than 300 Tennessee Eastman employees, who were put to the task of meeting Kodak's
substantial chemical needs. Kodak's Rochester facilities required 40,000 gallons of methanol per month, in addition to
other necessary chemicals such as acetic acid and acetone.

Tennessee Eastman delivered its first shipment of methanol to
Rochester in July 1921. The company generated $35,000 in
sales after its first year, but its total production fell short of
Kodak's chemical needs for the next several years. In addition,
the Kingsport plant was unprofitable and would remain so long
after its production volume was raised to a sufficient level.

By the mid-1920s Tennessee Eastman was satisfying Rochester's monthly methanol needs, but weak profits continued to
hound Tennessee Eastman for another decade. To improve
profitability, the company began marketing the by-products
created from the Kingsport plant's distillation processes, including charcoal, tars, wood preservatives, and other process
wastes. Charcoal powder and wood tar were combined to form a
charcoal briquette that the company sold as cooking and household fuel, transforming the 300 railroad cars of charcoal dust the
company produced each month into a money-making sideline
business. Other by-products from the Kingsport plant were also
marketed, including coal tars and various derivatives of acetone, which were marketed to sugar refineries, as well as
lumber.

Process economy started Tennessee Eastman down the road toward profitability and provided a springboard for diversification into segments of the chemical industry exclusive of Kodak's needs. Sales in 1930 were $1.95 million, with acetic anhydride and lumber ranking as the company's two major products. During the 1930s, Tennessee Eastman began to make pivotal contributions to its parent company's Rochester facilities, beginning with its manufacture of cellulose acetate in 1930. Kodak had experimented with using cellulose acetate as a film base back in 1907, striving to replace flammable nitrocellulose with a non-flammable alternative. The company's innovation quickly became the industry standard.

Perhaps more important, Tennessee Eastman distinguished itself as a leader and pioneer in the chemical industry through its production of acetate yarn. An experimental acetate yarn plant had been constructed in 1928, and by 1931 the Kingsport-based facility had begun large-scale production, churning out 287,000 pounds of yarn that year alone. Within a decade, Tennessee Eastman's acetate yarn was recognized throughout the textile industry as the best quality yarn on the market, securing the company's economic stability for the next two decades and paving the way for the development of other mainstay products.

One year after large-scale production of acetate yarn had begun, Tennessee Eastman began producing Tenite cellulosic plastics, which were used for radio parts, toys, telephones, and automobile steering wheels. That year, 1932, also was the first year Tennessee Eastman's trade sales exceeded its sales to Kodak.

By 1940 Tennessee Eastman was recording nearly $30 million in annual sales, an exponential increase from the $1.95 million generated 10 years earlier. The increase had been fueled largely by the company's production of acetate yarn, which by this point was Tennessee Eastman's single major product, as it would be a decade later, when annual sales stood at $130 million. Kodak organized an additional chemical subsidiary in 1950, Texas Eastman Company, then formed Eastman Chemical Products, Inc., in 1953 to serve as the marketing arm for both Texas Eastman and Tennessee Eastman. Tennessee Eastman, meanwhile, had undergone a name change, switching its corporate title from Tennessee Eastman Corporation to Tennessee Eastman Company in 1951. Although the name change was minor, a significant development occurred contemporaneously that dramatically altered the company's future. During the early 1950s, Tennessee Eastman developed cellulose acetate filter tow, which was used in cigarette filters, giving the company a product that drove sales upward for the next half century and supplanted acetate yarn as its mainstay product.

With filter tow sales leading the way, Tennessee Eastman registered $244 million in annual sales in 1960, continuing to record exponential leaps in annual revenues decade by decade. In 1968 the Eastman Chemicals Division of Eastman Kodak Company was formed, bringing together the various chemical concerns within Kodak's corporate structure and unifying them as a division. When it was organized, the chemicals division included Tennessee Eastman, Texas Eastman Company, Carolina Eastman Company, Eastman Chemicals Products, Inc., and the following related marketing organizations: Holston Defense Corporation, Ectona Fibers Limited, Bay Mountain Construction Company, and Caddo Construction Company.

With this collection of companies banded together, annual sales generated by the division shot upward, swelling to $588 million in 1970, a revenue total derived largely from the production of filter tow and polyester fibers. Late in the decade, the Eastman Chemicals Division introduced polyethylene terephthalate (PET) resin, used to make plastic containers. The addition of PET to the division's product line helped annual sales exceed $2 billion by the beginning of the 1980s.

In 1990 Kodak reorganized its chemicals division, renaming it Eastman Chemical Company. Annual sales by this point exceeded $3.5 billion, ranking the company among the largest chemical concerns in the world. With large market shares in PET and cellulosics, Eastman Chemical entered the 1990s as the jewel of the Kodak empire. Kodak, on the other hand, was not faring as well. As the decade progressed, debt began to mount, and Eastman Chemical was put in the awkward position of supplying cash to its debt-heavy parent, a reversal of roles for the former captive chemical supplier that complicated its corporate priorities and hobbled its investments in chemical operations.

As a result, Kodak spun off its chemical subsidiary to Kodak shareholders on the first day of 1994, creating the 10th largest chemical company in the country. As part of the spin-off, Eastman Chemical was also saddled with $1.8 billion in long-term debt. By the end of its first year as an independent company, however, Eastman Chemical had whittled its debt down by $600 million, reducing its ratio of debt to total capital from 63 percent to 48 percent during a 12-month span.

Intent on expanding internationally, Eastman Chemical moved toward its future as an independent chemical supplier supported by four core product groups: container plastics, specialty polyester packaging plastics, coatings materials for paints and solvents, and filter tow. With its quick success in paring its once heavy debt to a more manageable level and its commanding lead in the global market for PET resin and cellulose acetate filter tow, Eastman Chemical appeared destined for profitable years ahead.

Further Reading:

"Eastman Chemical," *Rubber World,* August 1995, p. 6.
"Eastman Growth Strategy Includes a Global Reach," *Chemical Marketing Reporter,* November 14, 1994, p. 24.
Hunter, David, "Eastman's Deavenport in the Driver's Seat," *Chemical Week,* June 29, 1994, p. 36.
Kiesche, Elizabeth, "Prospects for Success of Fresh Chemical Spinoffs Look Mixed," *Chemical Week,* January 5, 1994, p. 20.
McCall, Ron, *Eastman Chemical Company: Years of Glory, Times of Change,* Rochester: Eastman Kodak Company, 1990, 69 p.
Miller, James P., "Eastman Chemical Co. Is Developing Its Own Image," *Wall Street Journal,* November 14, 1994, p. B3.
Prince, Greg, "Summer Vacation? No Way!," *Beverage World,* August 1991, p. 48.
Sparks, Debra, " 'We Have to Show Them': There's a Lot Below the Surface at Eastman Chemical—Too Bad Wall Street Can't See It," *Financial World,* May 10, 1994, p. 37.

—Jeffrey L. Covell

Edmark Corporation

6727 185th Avenue N.E.
Redmond, Washington 98052
U.S.A
(206) 556-8400
Fax: (206) 861-8998

Public Company
Incorporated: 1970
Employees: 156
Sales: $22.71 million
Stock Exchanges: NASDAQ
SICs: 2741 Miscellaneous Publishing; 7372 Prepackaged
  Software

Edmark Corporation is a developer and publisher of educational software and educational print materials for the consumer and education markets. Engaged in the development of multimedia educational software since 1992, Edmark has garnered more than 65 important industry design awards heralding the company's innovative approach and its software's educational value. Edmark's software products, targeting end-users ranging in age from two to 14, are organized into "families" and sold to a customer base largely comprising software distributors and retailers and educational institutions. In addition to being sold throughout the United States, Edmark's software is produced in several languages and sold in more than a dozen other countries. Edmark additionally publishes print materials for special-needs students that are marketed to educational institutions.

Edmark was founded in 1970 as a developer and publisher of school print materials and established its headquarters in Redmond, Washington. During its first 15 years Edmark focused its operations on print materials for the special education market, becoming well regarded within its niche despite slow-growing sales, which did not break the $1 million mark until 1985.

During the latter half of the 1980s Edmark made several moves to diversify its product line and enhance its revenues. In 1985 the company began developing and publishing Apple II software programs for special education students, and soon afterwards the company entered the preschool market. With the company expanding its product range, in 1986 Edmark went public. As part of the company's expansion into computer-based educational materials, Edmark's chief executive, Tom Korten, orchestrated the acquisition of the TouchWindow prod-

uct line in 1988. Often referred to as the "Touchscreen," the product sat atop a computer monitor and for all practical purposes replaced a computer's keyboard, making computer use for special-needs students much easier. Having acquired the TouchWindow from the Personal Touch Corp. for $126,500, Edmark expanded on its new product by developing TouchWindow software for Apple computers.

In 1988 Edmark hired Sally G. Narodick to serve as a consultant and help develop a new strategic plan for the company. Narodick, who had started her own consulting firm a year earlier after relinquishing a senior vice president's post at Seattle's largest bank, Seafirst, brought to Edmark a background that included masters degrees in both business and education. Narodick suggested Edmark become an educational technology business that made learning fun and embark on a gradual entrance into the consumer software market. She based her recommendation on three trends: a rising birth rate (due to baby boomers having babies), increasing numbers of home computers, and a slow-growing special education market in which sales to schools would not support substantial growth.

With multimedia software as its targeted product of the future, between 1989 and 1991 Edmark made several moves to finance its entrance into the preschool and early childhood consumer and education markets and to build a software development team that could produce quality products. At Narodick's suggestion, Edmark restructured its corporate board in order bring on Seattle investor W. Hunter Simpson, and in early 1989 both Simpson and Narodick became directors. After serving as a consultant for Edmark for less than two years and a director for six months, Narodick was named chairman and chief executive of Edmark in October 1989, signaling the beginning of the company's transformation from a special education print materials publisher to a multimedia educational software publisher.

Narodick took over the helm of Edmark at a time when its revenues were $2.5 million and the company was principally a publisher of special-education workbooks for schools. In 1990 Edmark began expanding its management and development teams in order to initiate a new strategic plan centered around multimedia software. To that end, in October 1991 Narodick hired Minnesota educator and award-winning software developer Donna Stanger as vice-president of product development. Stanger brought to Edmark 20 years of experience as a teacher and more than a dozen years as a developer of computer-based curriculum materials and educational software. Stanger placed Edmark in the fairly rare position as a software company with two females in lead executive roles. The Minnesota teacher insisted that she be accompanied by a team of three younger male programmers—whom she had worked with since those programmers were in high school. (Stanger referred to herself as the team's "den mother.") Although Edmark's balance sheet included $1.9 million in recently generated equity capital, just a year earlier the company had been forced to reduce staff and salaries because of a cash shortage. Nonetheless, Narodick took the financial risk and hired the four-person team despite the fact that the group had never developed a consumer product before and it increased Edmark's 25-person payroll by 20 percent.

For the 1992 fiscal year (ending June 30, 1992, and thus including the previous 1991 holiday season) Edmark earned

$364,000 on sales of $6 million, compared to earnings of $265,000 a year earlier on sales of $4.3 million. As Edmark was closing its books on its 1992 fiscal year, the company debuted two consumer demonstration products: *Millie's Math House*, a preschooler numbers and math program targeting a market niche with little competition, and *KidsDesk*, a desktop utility program that safeguarded the files of parents (making them feel more secure about investing in children's software) and allowed children to open their own setup folder and files.

In 1992 Edmark secured distribution or sales arrangements for its new products with Egghead Software, Ingram Micro (the industry's largest distributor), and a handful of other computer software retailers and catalogs. In October 1992 Edmark released *KidsDesk* and *Millie's Math House*, which combined received 29 important industry design awards during the next three years and an initial highly favorable review from *The Wall Street Journal* prior to the 1992 holiday season.

For the 1993 fiscal year ending in June of that year, Edmark earned just $125,000 on sales of $8.7 million. To enhance sales and distribution efforts, in 1993 Narodick hired Daniel Vetras as vice-president of consumer sales and Paul Bialek as vice-president of finance and administration. Vetras was a native of the same Massachusetts town as Narodick and a sales veteran who had worked for both Digital Equipment and Lotus Development Corporation. Bialek's experience included work as a senior audit manager for the international accounting firm KPMG Peat Marwick, which served as Edmark's independent auditors.

For the 1993 holiday season Edmark doubled its software product line with the release of *Bailey's Book House*, a reading skills program, and *Thinkin' Things Collection 1*, which introduced a critical thinking product line. The company also released an updated version of *KidsDesk*. However, Edmark entered the 1993 holiday season with several factors working against it: a limited marketing budget, only four software products appearing in less than 2,000 outlets, and an insufficient sales tracking system that resulted in sold-out shelves in some retail outlets and products stuck in storerooms in other outlets.

Edmark entered 1994 seeking additional financing to expand distribution channels and gain a presence in superstores and mass-merchandising outlets, as well as to fund stepped-up product development. As a result, in February 1994 Edmark—for the third consecutive year—returned to investors for capital. Narodick courted Doug Mackenzie, a partner in the venture capital firm Kleiner Perkins Caufield & Byres, who agreed to lead an equity investment of $5.5 million, paying the going-market price of $10 a share. (Mackenzie later joined the company's board.) Despite the increased funding, the company braced for an annual loss stemming from increased development and marketing expenses, and it lost $1.9 million on sales of $11.6 million in the 1994 fiscal year.

For the 1994 holiday season Edmark doubled its product line for the second straight year. The company's four new releases included *Sammy's Science House*, a program designed to build fundamental science skills and the third program in the company's early-learning family, and *Thinkin' Things Collection 2*. Edmark also expanded its age market through the debut of a

new family of interactive story-writing programs for six-to-12-year-olds, the Imagination Express Series. That year the company released that series' first two titles, *Destination: Neighborhood* and *Destination: Castle*. *Destination: Neighborhood* featured materials for children to create interactive stores, poems, and journals describing their real and make-believe experiences; *Destination: Castle* provided children with a medieval kingdom setting for the same.

In order to enhance name recognition of Edmark products, in mid-1994 Narodick hired Mark McNeely—a former chairman of a leading Seattle advertising agency that was known for building brand names—to lead an expanded marketing program. Entering the 1994 holiday season, Edmark's distribution channel had more than doubled, having expanded to 5,000 outlets that included book stores, toy stores, office superstores, and mass-merchandisers, such as Wal-Mart and the Price Club. Edmark also added a much-coveted distributor, Comp USA, the computer superstore chain, which signed a purchase order for Edmark's entire line and agreed to jointly fund marketing programs and Edmark's presence at industry expositions.

In 1994 Edmark also took steps to improve its product visibility in stores and to address stock outages. A new tracking system was initiated, and Vetras hired part-time field merchandisers, mothers with young children, in 10 major metropolitan areas to help with in-store demonstrations. Edmark also initiated a holiday promotion in which KidsDesk was packaged as a free bonus with all other Edmark products. The package contained registration cards for a $10,000 savings bond contest that expanded the company's customer mailing list to more than 150,000 user names.

In December 1994 Edmark entered into a strategic alliance with Harcourt Brace School Publishers, a division of Harcourt Brace & Company. The publisher of educational materials agreed to collaborate on the development of educational software and to develop new lines of multimedia software, including products based in part on technology used in Edmark's Imagination Express software. Harcourt agreed to pay Edmark a one-time $1 million licensing fee as well annually co-fund research and development costs, beginning with a $347,500 contribution in 1994.

During the 1995 fiscal year Edmark doubled its work force and its number of software titles (after more than doubling its development funding to $4.6 million, up from $2.1 million in 1994 and $450,000 in 1993), in addition to nearly doubling its distribution outlets to 9,000. These efforts translated into sales that nearly doubled, rising 95 percent to $22.7 million and generating record earnings of $2 million. The largest jump in Edmark's revenues came from multimedia software, with sales to the consumer market growing from $3.3 million in 1994 (and $1.5 million in 1993) to $10.9 million in 1995. Slightly more than half of all consumer sales were of CD-ROM products, with the majority of those released just prior to the 1994 holiday season. Sales of multimedia software to the education market also rose dramatically, from $934,000 in 1994 (and $130,000 in 1993) to $3.4 million in 1995. Sales of special-education products for 1995 were $7.1 million, a slight decrease from the previous year and nearly the same as 1993 sales.

Edmark attributed much of its increasing success to a healthy market for its products and the fact that the company was well positioned to capitalize on a growing industry. In 1995 Edmark qualified for listing on the Nasdaq National Market, and between mid-1994 and mid-1995 the company's stock value mushroomed 800 percent from a first quarter 1994 low of $6.50 to more than $50 a year later. The value in Edmark's stock signaled Wall Street's increasing interest in companies producing CD-ROM software, particularly children's educational programs. Edmark's success did not go unnoticed in business publications; between May and August 1995 the small but growing company was the subject of feature articles in *Business Week, Inc.,* and *The Wall Street Journal.* With its stock value rising, in August 1995 Edmark split its common stock 3-for-2 and completed a secondary public offering of 1.1 million shares (639,000 of which were sold by the company), generating $22.5 million in proceeds. Following the offering Edmark's management and board members owned approximately 36 percent of the company. The proceeds from the public offering, along with a $2 million line of available credit, were expected to be sufficient to meet the company's financial outlays through fiscal 1996.

For the 1995 holiday season, Edmark planned to release new versions of most of its multimedia titles for Microsoft Corporation's Windows 95 operating system. Edmark also expected to have products from its collaboration with Harcourt released before the close of 1995 and a total of 13 titles on retail shelves. New offerings anticipated to make their first holiday season appearance included *Trudy's Time & Place House*, a new early learning series program to build time-telling, mapping, and direction skills; *Thinkin' Things Collection 3*, the third in Edmark's critical thinking skills series of programs; and two new interactive story-making programs offering new landscapes, *Destination: Rain Forest* and *Destination: Ocean.*

As it moved through the 1996 fiscal year, Edmark expected to add 5,000 new outlets for its software (including more book stores, mass-merchandisers, and toy stores) and to expand its work force by about a third. With just three percent of the $600 million educational software market in 1995, the company recognized it had room to grow, and analysts were suggesting sales could reach $40 million for the 1996 fiscal year.

The market for educational software also held potential for significant growth, with home computer ownership expected to continue to increase for the foreseeable future. Edmark expected its partnership with Harcourt to generate an expanded share of the educational software market, which was growing increasingly competitive with such companies as Microsoft and Disney moving into the field. That field's landscape was also being modified in the mid-1990s with new exclusive distribution agreements that were placing distribution firms in a position to dictate what chains would pay for products and how products would be displayed, with larger players able to exert more leverage than smaller ones.

As it entered 1996, Edmark maintained its goal of publishing high-quality educational products and was banking on distinguishing itself from larger competitors through its award-winning products. Given that repeat business in the educational software market required upgrading software and expanding product lines, Edmark continued its strategy of introducing consumers to its families of software at a young age in hopes that customers would progress from one title and one product series to the next. With Edmark's distribution and marketing prowess beginning to equal its product quality by the mid-1990s, the company appeared well positioned for continued growth, particularly in consumer market sales. Although the mid-1990s appeared to be more a time of market growth than industry consolidation, a shakeout in the industry appeared inevitable, and Edmark recognized it was increasingly being viewed as an attractive acquisition target.

Further Reading:

Baker, M Sharon, "Edmark Has High Hopes for New Holiday-Season Offerings," *Puget Sound Business Journal,* November 4, 1994, p. 6.

Baker, Molly, "Edmark Charms the Kids and the Street," *The Wall Street Journal,* May 30, 1995, pp. C1, C7.

Erickson, Jim, "Edmark's Earnings Up but Stock Goes Down," *Seattle Post-Intelligencer,* October 20, 1995, pp. D1, D5.

Geballe, Bob, "Edmark: Software Killer with a Woman's Touch," *Seattle Weekly,* October 18, 1995, pp. 23–27.

Murphy, Anne, "The Link," *Inc.,* June 1995, pp. 58–66.

Yang, Dori Jones, "The Pied Piper of Kids' Software," *Business Week,* August 7, 1995. pp. 70–71.

—Roger W. Rouland

were empty Mothers' Oats oatmeal boxes, and the young entrepreneur eventually went out of business as demand exceeded supply. Nutter also earned money building fish and lily ponds made of concrete and rocks, as well as popular water fountain bird baths—creative projects that whetted his appetite for success.

Nutter entered the University of Kentucky with plans to one day preside as president over a company he had started from scratch. He planned to work his way through school and exit with a mechanical engineering degree. With all the experience he had gained following his father around commercial power plants since his early childhood, he felt he could pass the State of Ohio Stationary Engineer's test. At the age of 21, upon completion of his sophomore year, he acted on his convictions and dropped out of college. Nutter traveled to Dayton, Ohio, determined to take the State of Ohio examination necessary to earn a stationary engineer's license. "Don't even waste your time trying," he was told.

Yet Nutter was determined, and did in fact become the youngest person in Ohio history to pass that test. The accomplishment was no small news and was featured in a Hamilton, Ohio, newspaper, prompting a job offer from the Hamilton-based Hooven-Owens-Rentschler Company, where Nutter became assistant to the chief engineer.

During this time, according to Nutter, the company had purchased two second-hand coal pulverizers, whose parts were shipped completely disassembled and piled into two railroad coal cars. The company's chief engineer assigned his favorite crew to tackle the difficult assembly assignment, but no progress was made. Too ready and willing to pester his boss with ideas to improve plant operations, Nutter was, in retribution, assigned the task of assembling the machines himself with no instructions. With a little assistance from a maintenance carpenter, Nutter grouped the parts by appearance and gradually assembled the complex machines, much to everyone's surprise. However, shortly thereafter, the chief engineer concocted a reason to fire Nutter. As Nutter was leaving the plant, Gordon Rentschler, the company's CEO, asked Nutter where he was going. "I've just been fired," Nutter explained; "well then," Rentschler replied, "you've just been rehired. Come along with me."

Nutter kept his job, but soon became bored with machine assembly and found work as a stationary engineer at Procter and Gamble, where he hoped to eventually fill a retirement vacancy as chief engineer. His anticipated course of action was foiled, however, when the position was offered to a young mechanical engineering graduate. "I knew right then that I'd traveled as far as two years of college could take me," Nutter explained, adding that "with a borrowed trailer stacked high, reminiscent of the *Grapes of Wrath,* I left for Lexington."

Nutter packed his belongings and headed for the University of Kentucky. When the college dean told Nutter he couldn't enroll in classes in the middle of a semester, Nutter simply ignored the statement and advised the dean that he would need a job for food, tuition, and books. The dean complied. At the university, Nutter worked 30 to 40 hours per week in addition to the many hours he spent studying, and under such a difficult schedule, his

Elano Corporation

2455 Dayton-Xenia Road
Dayton, Ohio 45434
U.S.A.
(513) 426-0621
Fax: (513) 426-7181

Wholly Owned Subsidiary of General Electric Company
Incorporated: 1951
Employees: 550
Sales: $80 million
SICs: 3444 Sheet Metal Work; 3312 Stainless Steel; 3356 Titanium and Titanium Alloy Bars, Rods, Billets, Sheets, Strip, and Tubing

Elano Corporation is one of the most successful manufacturers of castings, pipings, tubings, and various other components used primarily by the aerospace industry. Under the direction of founder Ervin J. Nutter, Elano became one of the first to employ new and highly sophisticated technology, despite its small-business roots. In fact, the company has been recognized as one of the best of the small manufacturers in the United States and has garnered many quality-control awards, including the Air Force "Zero Defects Award," General Motors' "Certificate of Excellence," and General Electric's "Outstanding Performance Award."

Elano Corporation was established by Ervin J. Nutter. Like many other companies, Elano's history is intimately related to the background, interests, and determination of its founder. Nutter came from a family of entrepreneurs. His grandfather, John Nutter, had traveled west to Wyoming and established one of the territory's first wagon freight hauling businesses. Nutter's father, Ervin F. Nutter, who gained a reputation for his construction and operation of large commercial power plants, eventually became chief engineer of McGregor Golf Equipment Company and was attributed with the development of state-of-the-art golf ball processing. Nutter's mother, Carrie McDavid, was among the first women to earn a teaching degree from the University of Kentucky, Nutter's eventual alma mater.

Ervin J. Nutter was born in Hamilton, Ohio, in 1914. While in high school, he constructed, in his words, "a nice little business erecting radio antennas and manufacturing radio crystal sets," which helped his neighbors receive station KDKA in Pittsburgh. Among the materials he used, in short supply at the time, grades suffered. However, during Nutter's final semester, the dean of the engineering college bet Nutter a new hat that he couldn't achieve all As for the term. Nutter later was pleased to recall that the dean lost that bet, adding "God bless him, I know he *wanted* to lose."

Upon graduating from the University of Kentucky, at the height of World War II, Nutter received a framed copy of Kipling's poem "If" from his mother, a leather briefcase from his father, and a new hat from the dean. Moreover, the dean took Nutter to a local bank and co-signed a note for $200 to pay expenses for Nutter's move from Lexington to Dayton, Ohio.

At an advanced civilian's salary, Nutter accepted a position at Dayton's Wright Field, one of the most important aviation research and development laboratories operated by the U.S. government. While designing, building, and operating laboratory equipment, he learned the intricacies of modern aviation.

Nutter rose fast at Wright Field and was soon the only civilian branch chief in the laboratory, where he was placed in charge of environmental testing for the Air Force. During his spare time, Nutter assisted his friend and future Elano partner, Captain Lee Otterson, by designing an aerial spraying device capable of covering huge areas with DDT, a new insecticide. "It seemed like a strange project," Nutter later confessed, "until I found out we were losing more troops to malaria than to combat in the South Pacific." Knowing Nutter's background in thermodynamics and flow of fluids, Otterson confided the details and, off the record, asked for suggestions. Nutter worked evenings for weeks on the project, eventually designing a device to hang under the belly of a B-25; with the bomb bay full of tanks, the plane was capable of spraying a gallon of the liquid over an acre of ground. Nutter was granted his only patent for the invention, obtained by the Air Force, and was commended for helping eliminate malaria-carrying mosquitoes, which saved countless lives.

V-J Day arrived and Otterson, now a major, formed a unique verbal partnership with Nutter that gave birth to a new company, the Agricultural Aviation Company (Ag Aviation), which was the precursor to Elano Corporation. According to their plan, Otterson returned to his home in California to operate a rice farm, while Nutter remained in Dayton to open an engineering firm. The sole purpose of the enterprise was to design and manufacture an aerial spraying device for small aircraft. Still employed at Wright Field, Nutter contributed a portion of his salary to hire the company's first employee, Bob Calvert, a mechanical engineer, Air Force captain, and former classmate of Nutter. Otterson pitched in numerous small loans from his farm income, once the rice was harvested, all of which Nutter would later repay.

"About that time," Nutter recalled, "the family moved from Dayton to Trebein Road in Beavercreek. We had a couple of acres, a nice home with a single-car garage, a small barn with a chicken house, and an old, two-room tenant house which later became Elano's first plant." Having made an early decision that Ag Aviation would not accept government contracts due to the complexity of paperwork involved, Nutter nonetheless changed his mind when the Air Force asked for a bid on spray devices for its smaller aircraft. Under Bob Calvert's direction, Ag Aviation landed the contract.

With virtually no equipment, Nutter converted his spacious back yard into an impromptu manufacturing facility, supervised by Calvert. The old tenant house became plant No. 1, equipped with less than $400 worth of machinery. The government was so pleased with the spray device that it asked Nutter to provide a bid for volume production. However, Ag Aviation lost the contract when a team of inspectors deemed his makeshift facility incapable of producing the large production volume required by the Air Force.

Nevertheless, another line of business was emerging at Ag Aviation. "Our first line of products came quite by accident," Nutter recalled. "One day while I was in the office of the manager of Overlook Homes, a World War II housing project, he showed me a worn kitchen faucet stem. He told me that he would have to buy a whole new faucet, since parts for wartime-built plumbing fixtures were not available. Sensing a national market, we mailed our first advertisement to every government housing project in the United States, eventually building the plumbing replacement parts business into a $10,000-a-month operation." Specifically, a need existed for swing spouts for kitchen sinks. When bending metal tubing into the shapes necessary for such a swinging spout presented a challenge, Nutter designed a special tube bender. Nutter would later note that "the bending of those kitchen swing spouts was the key that unlocked the door to the future of Elano Corporation.

As the company grew, Nutter expanded his manufacturing operations into a cow barn and a garage located at his home. However, as his family's life was constantly disrupted by the operations, Nutter moved the facilities to the basement of Marshall Brothers' Garage on Dayton-Xenia Road. When a salesman calling at the little plant saw the company's bent tube production, he asked to represent the company. The salesman said that General Electric was having a difficult time purchasing critical jet engine parts, particularly those involving curved, tubular, stainless steel. Nutter had the answer.

His company's improved and relocated manufacturing site passed a government survey team's inspection, and on August 20, 1951, the company won seven GE contracts totaling $25,025. Ag Aviation was renamed Elano Corporation, a name coined from the initials of Nutter and partner Lee Otterson.

Within four months of the first contract with General Electric, Elano had backlogged a quarter of a million dollars in additional business. To expand his operations, Nutter secured bank loans, which he paid off early. Throughout the remainder of the 1950s, Elano grew at an enormous rate. As more and more orders were taken for tubings and engine components, the company's reputation for product quality and reliability also grew. General Electric contracted the small rural community business to produce engine components for some of the most famous aircraft during the Cold War, including the J-79, the F-4, the J-93, and the C-5A transport.

Mutual dependency led to mutual success. In Erie, Pennsylvania, GE had developed a powerful diesel engine to power its line of railroad locomotives, and Nutter was tapped to help GE develop an exhaust system capable of withstanding the high temperatures and vibration of the new engine. Nutter met with GE's engineering staff in Erie, and returned home with a preliminary design—a sophisticated, stainless steel manifold with a state-of-the-art bellows system that utilized three sheets of thin stainless steel that would withstand a 2,500 horse power engine. Ironically, at the time he made the trip, Nutter didn't realize that GE's chief competitor, General Motors, was also in the locomotive business. Upon parking his Cadillac on the GE lot, Nutter received a humorous but nonetheless serious suggest that he not park a GM car on GE property. "Needless to say," Nutter quipped, "I didn't have a bit of a problem parking a Lincoln on that lot the next time I was in town." Nutter's manifold design, manufactured by Elano, was, by 1996, withstanding a 4,000 horse power engine.

During the early and mid-1960s, Elano Corporation, under the leadership of Nutter and Otterson, had grown large enough to merit an acquisitions and expansion program. The company's first purchase came in 1966, when it bought Acme Screw Products, a firm that specialized in machine components. In just a few years, sales for Acme Screw Products grew from $500,000 to over $3 million. Elano East, an engineering firm in Rowley, Massachusetts, was also created in 1966 and specialized in developing prototypes for aircraft engine companies throughout New England.

With expansion and acquisition in place, Elano braced for a period of unparalleled growth in the 1970s. Nutter purchased Otterson's company share in 1972, channeling profits into future development. Not long after establishing a quality name for itself as a major defense contractor, Elano developed a highly sophisticated device for suppressing infrared radiation in helicopter engines, which helped prevent heat-seeking enemy missiles from honing in and destroying the aircraft. The company also created its own laboratory at this time, Enlo Incorporated, to develop, design, and manufacture aerospace industry castings and hardware.

In a somewhat unusual personal move, Nutter created KBJ Ranch, an agricultural business that devoted itself to specialized crop development and sophisticated cattle-breeding methods. Nutter teamed up with Ohio State University and built a complete medical operating room for cattle. Scientific research there, performed by staff at Ohio State, produced such findings as a record 35 pregnancies from a single conception and eventually produced approximately 50 state and national champion cattle. Nutter also eventually teamed up with former classmate David Scott, CEO of Allis Chambers, to help pioneer no-till crop planting equipment, widely used into the 1990s. As Nutter's work gained recognition, he was installed as a Fellow in the Engineers' Club of Dayton, and was among the first four University of Kentucky School of Engineering graduates to be enshrined in that school's Hall of Distinction.

Discussing the key to Elano's success, Nutter observed that the company's achievements could be traced to "the truest principles of our country's free enterprise system . . . privilege based upon responsibility, dignity based upon justice, and rewards based upon individual effort." He added, "These principles all apply to Elano, for it was built on individual initiative through the continuing hard work of many."

The 1980s continued an upward growth swing at Elano, due to its solid partnership with GE. A 1985 agreement to sell Elano to GE at the height of Elano's success was not an easy decision for Nutter, who, growing older, had become mentally and physically exhausted by the company's daily demands. Yet he retired, content that he had parlayed a childhood dream into a rich, lifelong endeavor. Acknowledging the hard work of others at the company, Nutter noted "one may leave a legacy of achievement, but that achievement will be remembered only if it serves the needs of others."

Elano endured a comprehensive reorganization under its new managers at General Electric, who revamped the firm's business operations. Under GE's direction, the company began to focus exclusively on marketing and selling aerospace industry products and increasing sales to the international market.

In the early and mid-1990s, Elano Corporation was producing tubular and sheet metal components, bracket assemblies for jet engines, and fittings, connectors, and vacuum casting for the aerospace industry. Its tubular components were designed and manufactured specifically for fuel, air, and oil lines of high-performance aircraft. The company also formed an extremely lucrative repair-service unit for aircraft engines. Elano is regarded as one of the most reliable U.S. manufacturers of quality components for the aircraft and aerospace industries. Moreover, General Electric has made a commitment to Elano's research and development facilities, and the result has been a wealth of new aerospace component designs.

Further Reading:

CorpTech Directory of Technology Companies, CorpTech: Boston, 1995, Vol. 3, p. 61.

Nutter, Ervin, *Elano Corporation,* Newcomen Society: New York, 1982.

—Thomas Derdak

Exar Corp.

P.O. Box 49007
San Jose, California 95161-9007
U.S.A.
(408) 434-6400
Fax: (408) 435-1712

Public Company
Founded: 1971
Employees: 500
Sales: $159.47 million
Stock Exchanges: NASDAQ
SICs: 3674 Semiconductors and Related Devices

Exar Corp. designs, develops, and markets analog, digital, and mixed-signal integrated circuits for use in telecommunications, data communications, microperipherals, consumer electronics products, and other goods. The circuits are sold primarily to other manufacturers who install them in various electronic systems and equipment. Exar grew rapidly during the late 1980s and early 1990s by introducing cutting-edge products and acquiring other companies.

Exar started out as a small subsidiary of the Japanese semiconductor manufacturer Rohm Company Ltd. of Kyoto, Japan. Rohm was founded in Japan in 1954. Rohm became involved in the electronics components industry and eventually began designing and manufacturing integrated circuits, which were originally developed in the United States. Rohm established the subsidiary in the United States in 1971 as a way of strengthening its presence in North American markets and getting access to U.S. technology. Throughout the 1970s and early 1980s, Exar was led by Rohm expatriates from Japan that came to the United States. During that time, Exar existed as a relatively small designer and manufacturer of analog and integrated circuits—a sort of U.S. sister company for Rohm.

Following Exar's inception and through the early 1980s semiconductor components replaced vacuum tube gear as the fundamental building blocks used in electronic equipment. Semiconductor components were classified as either discrete devices, such as an individual transistor or diode, or integrated circuits, which incorporated numerous transistors and other elements to create a much more complicated circuit. On an integrated circuit (IC), the elements were fabricated on a small chip of silicon, which was then encapsulated in ceramic, metal, or plastic. Pins

sticking out of the IC allowed it to be connected to a circuit board, which held the circuits that controlled the entire electronic device.

The semiconductor industry that developed during the 1970s and early 1980s could basically be divided into two categories: digital and linear, or analog. Digital circuits performed the functions of storing, switching, or translating data that was expressed in binary form (as 0 or 1). Linear circuits, in contrast, monitored and influenced continuously varying signals. Thus, they were used to monitor, condition, amplify, and transform varying properties like temperature, pressure, weight, light, sound, or speed. Both Rohm and Exar researched, developed, and manufactured digital and linear circuits for various applications. An important part of Rohm's business, for example, became the design of custom circuits for automated manufacturing equipment that was custom-engineered for the fabrication of specific products.

Rohm and Exar both benefited from their alliance during the 1970s and early 1980s. The companies regularly exchanged technical information and key personnel, and partnered on certain product designs, process technologies, and manufacturing procedures. Besides sharing technical information and personnel, Rohm benefited from Exar's access to the U.S. market. For example, Exar acted as a proxy for Rohm by purchasing certain equipment for Rohm in the United States and by negotiating certain supply and purchase agreements with U.S. companies. Exar also allowed Rohm to tap into some of the best and brightest engineers in America's high-tech talent pool. On their side, Exar benefited from Rohm's deep pockets, which it used to finance the development of new products. Exar also profited by having many of its circuits and components manufactured in Japan at Rohm's highly efficient manufacturing facilities.

Semiconductor markets flourished during the 1970s and early 1980s. Importantly, many Japanese manufacturers began to assert themselves in the global semiconductor market, which was traditionally controlled by U.S. producers. By the early 1980s Rohm was generating annual revenues of roughly $300 million annually, and Exar was doing about $25 million in sales. By that time, Exar had successfully carved out a niche producing custom analog integrated circuits. It also manufactured a range of both custom and standard analog and digital integrated circuits for industries ranging from telecommunications and computer peripherals to industrial controls and scientific instrumentation. About 33 percent of Exar's revenues were still attributable to Rohm, but it was steadily increasing sales to other companies.

Healthy semiconductor markets combined with proprietary technology developed by Rohm and Exar pushed Exar's sales and profits much higher during the early and mid-1990s. Indeed, sales shot from $22 million in 1982 to $39 million in 1984, and then to a whopping $57 million in 1985. Net income grew nearly ten-fold during the same time frame to $4.2 million. At the same time that Exar was achieving those gains, the United States began pressuring many Japanese manufacturing sectors, in effect, to reduce their profile in the U.S. market. The pressure was especially high in the semiconductor industry, where the Japanese were rapidly consuming U.S. global market share. Partly because of that pressure, Rohm made the decision in 1984 to begin minimizing its ownership interest in Exar.

In 1985 Exar went public, selling shares valued at $11 each. The offering reduced Rohm's stake in the company to 68 percent. It also brought about $14 million into Exar's coffers. "We're the first Japanese company to be a full-blooded American company," said Nubuo Hatta, president of Exar. "We have U.S. products, people, and, now, financing." The offering had the added benefit of increasing Exar's ability to attract talented engineers, who often wanted stock options as part of their pay package. Although Rohm reduced its ownership in Exar, the two companies planned to sustain their long-running relationship with few changes. Top managers were still Japanese, for example, and Rohm was able to select a majority of the company's board of directors.

For a variety of reasons, Exar began to flounder in 1985. Markets for some of Exar's key technologies, for example, drooped in the mid-1980s. The most prominent factor contributing to Exar's decline, though, was its decision to purchase Exel Microelectronics, Inc. Exel was a privately held manufacturer of advanced semiconductor products. Exar viewed the $6.5-million purchase as a way to get access to new technology as well as Exel's chip fabrication facility. After Exar purchased the company it discovered that the fabrication facility needed heavy capital investments. The plant was not fully utilized for a few years, and Exar suffered heavy losses in 1987 and 1988. Exar's revenues dipped to $52.5 million in 1986. Sales bobbed back up to $56.4 million in 1987, but the company posted a disappointing $7.9 million net loss. In 1988, moreover, Exar suffered a crushing deficit of $12.8 million on sales of $69.14 million.

To stem the tide of red ink, Rohm stepped in to help. It purchased 81 percent of Exel for $40 million and within about a year it purchased the remaining assets of the company for about $6.5 million. The buyout allowed Exar to recoup all of its original investment as well as its losses. In addition, Exar continued to benefit from technology contributed by Exel. Some of that technology, in fact, proved extremely lucrative for Exar during the late 1980s and early 1990s. Exar stepped up its research and development efforts during that period and found itself well positioned to take advantage of thriving markets for cutting-edge semiconductor technologies like EEPROM (electrical erasable programmable read-only memory) and ASICs (application specific integrated circuits).

Surging markets and leading technology helped Exar enlarge its revenue base from less than $70 million in 1988 to about $90 million annually by 1990, about $6 million of which was netted as income. That increase reflected an increase in wafer services to Rohm, as well as a 21 percent increase in the sale of custom semiconductors and a 17 percent jump in sales of telecommunications products. The turnaround in income reflected across-the-board revenue improvements in both existing and new products. Early in 1989, for example, Exar introduced the first low-power, single-supply read/write amplifier circuit for the disk-drive market. That and other product introductions carried the company to unprecedented profitability by the mid-1990s.

Meanwhile, parent Rohm continued to reduce its stake in Exar. In 1990 Rohm sold 1.65 million shares to Exar, which diminished its ownership share of the company to about 46 percent. Then, in 1992, Rohm removed Hatta, its Japanese chief executive. Exar's board hired a new head for the company: George

Wells. Wells was born in Scotland and received his bachelor's degree in physics from the University of Glasgow, where he also studied nuclear physics for two years. After college he went to work for Fairchild Camera and Instrument from 1969 to 1980 before laboring in various management positions at ITT and GTE. Wells then served as the head of General Electric's global semiconductor operations from 1983 to 1985 before acting as vice-chairman for LSI Logic between 1985 and 1992.

Exar continued to thrive under Wells' leadership. As soon as he arrived, Wells launched an aggressive quality initiative. He also began repositioning the company's product line to emphasize high-margin, high-growth products, particularly in the areas of communications, document imaging, and consumer and other computer applications. Among the most promising technologies that Exar was developing in the early and mid-1990s was mixed-signal chips, which combined digital and linear functions. Because the market was relatively specialized, the major chip producers had paid little attention to it. The chips were more complicated and more expensive to produce, but they had the effect of reducing the board size and lowering manufacturing costs for equipment manufacturers. Thus, buyers of the chips were able to produce ever smaller components with greater numbers of functions.

Going into 1993, Wells had reorganized the company's high-tech "logic" products into five categories that reflected the diversity of its markets: 1) advanced consumer products, such as camcorders; 2) data communications products, like computer modems (importantly, Exar claimed to have introduced the first integrated fax/data modem that allowed both send and receive fax capabilities at 9600 bauds per second); 3) mass storage devices, like chips used in personal computer hard disk drives; 4) telecommunications—for example, Exar had created a chip that made "caller identification" possible; and 5) embryonic specialty products, such as chips that operated remote control car locks. By focusing on those high-tech niches, Exar was able to raise its revenues to $113 million in 1991, $140 million in 1992, and then to about $146 million in 1993. The company's net income, moreover, grew from $7.15 million to $13.7 million during that time.

By 1994 Exar was rife with cash from surging sales and profits. Rather than sitting on the surplus, Wells decided to invest it by acquiring other companies that complemented his strategy of cultivating high-margin, high-profit semiconductor technologies. To that end, Exar purchased Origin Technology in May of 1994. Origin was a pioneer in automatic speech recognition technology that was applicable in a range of consumer and telecommunications markets. Three months later, Exar bought Micro Power Systems Inc., which was a leader in the development of high-performance data-acquisition circuits. The $25 million addition was a major boost to Exar's flourishing mixed-signal division. Early in 1995 Exar purchased Startech Semiconductor Inc., which designed and marketed application-specific semiconductors for a range of markets. A few months later Exar bought Silicon Microstructures, Inc., a leader in the production of micron-sized mechanical parts etched in silicon for use in high-tech sensing devices.

Rohm completely eliminated its ownership affiliation with Exar in 1994. The two companies continued to do business with each other, however. After experiencing record sales and income growth, Exar ran into turbulence in 1994, largely because of its rampant acquisition campaign but also because of problems related to its existing hard-disk chip business and an economic slowdown in Japan. Sales stagnated at about $160 million in the fiscal year that ended March 31, 1995, and earnings plunged to a negative $11.08 million. Despite the loss, Exar management remained optimistic. Wells attributed the loss to fallout from the company's final transition from commodity-like goods to high-margin products. In fact, Exar's strength in key growth technologies, its proven research and development expertise, and its meager debt load suggested a positive long-term outlook for the semiconductor manufacturer.

Principal Subsidiaries: Exar International, Inc.; Exar IC Design, Ltd. (United Kingdom); Exar Japan Corp. (Japan); Origin Technology, Inc.; MPS Holdings, Inc.; Micro Power Systems, Inc.; Startech Semiconductor Inc.; Silicon Microstructures, Inc.

Further Reading:

Guire, Ronald W., "Exar Announces Termination of Its Hard Disk Drive Product Line," *PR Newswire,* May 25, 1995.

——, "Exar Announces Year-end Results—Net Income Up 26 Percent," *PR Newswire,* May 5, 1993.

——, "Exar Corp. Financial Results," *Business Wire,* May 23, 1989.

Heins, John, and Marc Beauchamp, "Shogun Bonds and Yankee Equity," *Forbes,* December 16, 1985, p. 120.

Hyatt, Joshua, "Japanese Publicly Break with Tradition," *Inc.,* March 1986, p. 19.

Matsumoto, Craig, "Cash-Rich Exar Goes on Buying Spree, Purchases Two Firms," *Business Journal-San Jose,* June 20, 1994, p. 26.

Neumeier, Shelley, "Exar," *Fortune,* December 16, 1991, p. 106.

Palmer, Jay, "If You Can't Beat 'Em . . . ; Japanese Connection Pays Off for Exar," *Barron's,* December 14, 1992, pp. 20–22.

Rosen, Neal, "George Wells Named President of Exar," *PR Newswire,* June 30, 1992.

Stern, Theodore J., "CNC Tooling Renews the Industrial Revolution," *Eastern Pennsylvania Business Journal,* June 1992, p. 34.

—Dave Mote

Fastenal Company

2001 Theurer Boulevard
Winona, Minnesota 55987
U.S.A.
(507) 454-5374
Fax: (507) 454-6542

Public Company
Incorporated: 1968
Employees: 1,600
Sales: $162 million
Stock Exchanges: NASDAQ
SICs: 5072 Hardware

Fastenal Company sells nuts, bolts, and other industrial and construction supplies. Going into 1995 it offered 37,000 different parts at each of its 330 company-operated stores throughout the United States and Canada. Besides its Fastenal stores, the company has also begun operating FastTool and Fastenal/Fast-Tool outlets, which offer an array of tools and safety supplies. Fastenal has been distinguished by more than 15 years of rapid, steady growth.

The idea for Fastenal was conceived by 11-year-old Robert (Bob) A. Kierlin. When Kierlin assisted his father at the family's auto supply shop in Winona, Wisconsin, he noticed that customers typically drove from store to store looking for fasteners that they needed for particular jobs. If a hardware store didn't have the right nut or bolt, the owner would often send the customer to the Kierlins' store, and vice-versa. In many instances, Bob noted, the fastener simply couldn't be found and the buyer would have to place a special order and wait. "I wondered if you could put together a store with all the parts," Kierlin recalled in the November 9, 1992, *Forbes.*

The idea stuck with Kierlin. After graduating from high school in 1957 he went on to major in mechanical engineering at the University of Minnesota, where he later earned his M.B.A. After college Kierlin accepted a job with IBM in nearby Rochester. He worked as a financial analyst for about ten years, but was itching to start his own business. According to Kierlin, the opportunity came when he missed an interview for an international position because of a late plane. Instead of getting the job, he ended up starting the company he had envisioned as a boy.

With some effort, he was able to persuade an IBM co-worker, Jack Remick, to help him pursue his goal of selling nuts and bolts. Also joining Kierlin were former high-school buddies Michael Gostomski, Dan McConnon, and Steve Slaggie. Slaggie, Kierlin, and McConnon had graduated from Winona Cotter High School in 1957, and Gostomski had followed in 1958. The five partners ponied up $30,000 and rented a 20-foot-wide storefront in Winona. The group's first dispute was over what to name the store. Someone suggested "Lightning Bolts," but two of the founders were so opposed to the name that they threatened to take their money and leave. The men finally settled on Fastenal. Remick hand-painted the store sign, which one day would be framed and hung in the company's headquarters offices.

The founders' goal with Fastenal was to devise a means of making all kinds of nuts and bolts readily available to the general consumer. The group tinkered with various solutions, including an idea for a nuts and bolts vending machine. They finally settled on a retail strategy to stock a store with thousands of fasteners that would serve as a dependable one-stop shop. Most of the initial planning was done during the weekends and other times when the group could get time off from work. "It was almost like a hobby," Remick reminisced in the November 1994 *Corporate Report-Minnesota.*

The first Fastenal shop opened its doors in 1967 on Winona's Lafayette Street. Despite sluggish sales, the group opened a second outlet in Rochester a few years later, thinking that the larger city might provide the customers that the Fastenal concept needed. It soon became clear to the partners, however, that the venture was a flop. The partners were delivering nuts and bolts in a 1949 Cadillac and having to periodically chip in $1,000 from their savings just to keep the company afloat. "The ship almost went under," Slaggie recalled. "We'd look at the income statement and say, 'We lost how much money?' and then order a round of Budweisers. There was so much red ink."

The group finally determined that their retail strategy was flawed. Rather than targeting the general consumer, they decided to focus on the commercial market. It turned out that price was much less of a factor than timeliness for that market segment, because contractors and companies often lost money searching or waiting for a particular part. Kierlin and his partners discovered that there was a great need for a service that could quickly provide the fastener or part that a buyer needed. The change turned out to be exactly what the stores needed to become profitable, and Kierlin left IBM in 1973 to run Fastenal full time.

Kierlin continued to improve Fastenal's strategy during the 1970s and gradually began expanding with new stores. The concept became relatively simple: the partners would open outlets in small to medium-sized towns like Winona and Rochester, where price competition tended to be lower than in large cities, which had special fasteners and parts more readily available. As a result, Fastenal was able to generate profits on the basis of reliability and quick service. The company also targeted towns that had healthy manufacturing and construction industries, seeking to become those customers' one-stop shop for fasteners and related parts. The stores stocked a large selection and promised prompt delivery of any item that wasn't on the shelf. Later, Fastenal even began manufacturing custom parts that couldn't be found on the market, at a manufacturing and distribution plant established in Winona.

Fastenal branched out during the early 1980s. Importantly, in 1981 Fastenal purchased the inventory and customer list of the fastener lines of Briese Steel in Rochester. That move spurred growth, first into La Crosse, Wisconsin, and then throughout the upper Midwest. By the early 1980s Fastenal was operating more than 30 company-owned stores. Although all of the original founders contributed to the venture's growth, Kierlin was always the driving force; in fact, the other founders, with the exception of Slaggie, went on to start their own small companies while remaining part-owners in Fastenal. Kierlin focused aggressively on customer service and used his financial background to keep tight control on the company's finances.

Kierlin was a singular personality. His cluttered office in Winona housed a telescope that he used to bird watch (Winona is perched along a scenic stretch of the Mississippi River about 100 miles south of Minneapolis). He rarely wore a tie to work and was known for his informal style, as well as a unique salary plan. Even when his company became a publicly traded, multi-million-dollar corporation, he paid himself only $120,000 annually, which was less than he paid several of his employees. And, unlike other chief executives who received low salaries, he paid himself no incentive bonus of any kind. Instead, he was content to watch his ownership interest in Fastenal grow along with the company. Also unusual was the fact that no employees had their own parking spaces and everyone, including Kierlin, received the same vacation benefits.

Beneath his casual exterior, Kierlin was an aggressive capitalist and ideologue with little patience for the methods of government or organized labor. He also held a fierce commitment to education. In a book that he self-published in the early 1990s, *The Unified Theory of Life,* Kierlin condemned the state of public education. ''Increasingly,'' he wrote, ''ownership of what goes on at the public schools resides not with the parents, nor even with local voters, but rather with state legislatures and state departments of education. . . . 'Experts' impose their beliefs on what schools should teach and how the schools should teach them. The sense of omniscience leads the 'experts' to get into the minutiae of school schedules, start-times, extra-curriculars and hot-lunch programs.''

Kierlin backed his rhetoric financially. In 1987 he and the other Fastenal cofounders set up the Hiawatha Education Foundation to help Cotter, their alma mater, and other area Catholic schools. Within six years the foundation had contributed a whopping $25 million. Much of that was used to transform Cotter into a world-class, technology-rich institution that was ultimately attracting hundreds of boarding students from around the country and even the world. The Cotter campus was moved to the closed College of St. Teresa, where ceilings were lowered to house computer networking infrastructure. In addition, a $2 million sports complex was built that incorporated six indoor tennis courts. Because of the Foundation's endowment, tuition to the school was a measly $1,225 by the mid-1990s, and each graduate was entitled to a college scholarship ranging from $500 to $7,000.

Kierlin continued to expand Fastenal at a rapid rate. By 1985 the chain had grown to a total of 35 company-owned stores. That number grew to 45 in 1986 and 58 in 1987. To generate cash for more expansion, Fastenal's founders took the company public in 1987. The stock jumped from $9 to $15 by year's end, making the Fastenal initial public offering the most successful of the 627 conducted during the year of the October 1987 crash. Fastenal tapped the proceeds of the sale to add new outlets to its burgeoning chain. 17 shops were added in 1988, 28 in 1990, and 32 in 1991. By 1992 Fastenal was operating 200 stores throughout the industrial heartland of Pennsylvania, Ohio, Michigan, and Minnesota, but also as far away as Texas, New York, the Dakotas, and West Virginia.

Fastenal's gains were the result of Kierlin's profitable strategy and constant adaptation to markets. By the early 1990s each Fastenal store was offering a huge 30,000 items. Four thousand of those were stocked, while the rest could be delivered within 24 hours from regional distribution facilities in Winona, Indianapolis, and Scranton (Pennsylvania). Store operators were trained to find the answer to any question posed to them by a customer, as service was the centerpiece of the Fastenal strategy, and any parts that Fastenal employees couldn't track down could be custom manufactured in the Winona plant. The stores were typically able to garner profit margins of between 50 percent and 80 percent, which was far above the industry average of about 37 percent. Costs were kept low by locating shops in low-rent districts and minimizing other overhead.

As Fastenal carried its successful strategy into small and medium-sized towns throughout the United States and into Canada, sales and profits surged. Even per-store sales continued to climb, despite economic recession in the early 1990s. Fastenal's revenues grew from $11.6 million in 1985 to $20.3 million and $41.2 million in 1987 and 1989, respectively, while net earnings climbed from $818,000 to $4.3 million. Between 1989 and 1992, sales doubled to $81.3 million as net income climbed to $8.83 million. In 1992 Fastenal opened a fourth distribution center in Dallas and agreed to purchase a fifth in Atlanta. It also entered its 29th state. Kierlin and the other co-founders, who still owned a combined 45 percent of the company, had become millionaires.

The reason for Fastenal's proliferating base of customers was readily apparent: customers were willing to pay a premium for a dependable service that could save them a lot of money. About 50 percent of Fastenal's sales during the early 1990s came from manufacturing companies, while another 30 percent came from the construction industry. As an example, a contractor paying employees $30 per hour in wages and benefits couldn't afford to have a project held up by the lack of a special fastener for a piece of equipment—and he knew he could find it at Fastenal. In one instance, a Ford plant's assembly line was shut down by a breakdown that required a few dozen special bolts. Ford's regular supplier told the company it would have to wait until Monday—three days later. ''Meanwhile, its costing them something like $50,000 an hour to have this line not operating,'' Slaggie said in the March 11, 1992, *Successful Business.* ''They called us and the part is an oddball, something we don't have in stock. We had them fax us the blueprint for the machine and we determined we could make it. . . . We had them finished Sunday afternoon.''

Amazingly, Fastenal moved through the early 1990s with virtually no long-term debt, while expanding at a rampant pace. New stores were added from the East Coast to the West Coast, and the company opened up a sixth distribution center. The total number of Fastenal outlets grew to 256 in 1993 and 324 by the end of 1994. With solid gains in existing store sales, company revenues increased to $110 million in 1993 and $161 million in 1994. After posting record net earnings of $11.9 million in 1993, Fastenal's net income surged to $18.7 million in 1994.

Fastenal entered 1995 with 330 stores in 44 states, each of which offered 37,000 different items, and the company planned to add 150 outlets to the chain within the next few years. Some of the stores were called FastTools. Positioned next to Fastenal shops, FastTools carried the same concept to the tool market by offering about 3,000 different power and hand tools and safety products. The company was also experimenting in 1995 with a small Fastenal/FastTool combination store for small towns with 5,000 to 8,000 residents. The company planned to build 500 to 1,000 of those stores over the long term. By 1995 only two of the original founders were with the company: President and Chief Executive Kierlin and Treasurer Steve Slaggie. They and the other co-founders, all of whom were board members, were still the principal shareholders of the company, which remained based in Winona.

Principal Subsidiaries: Fastenal Canada Company.

Further Reading:

Barrett, William P., ''Bob Kierlin Versus the Shorts,'' *Forbes,* November 9, 1992, p. 204.

Burcum, Jill P., ''Winona's Fastenal Bolts Past $100-million Mark,'' *Corporate Report-Minnesota,* November 1994, p. 22.

Buttweiler, Joe, ''Fastenal Was Best IPO Performer,'' *Minneapolis-St. Paul CityBusiness,* February 8, 1988, Section 1, p. 16.

Ciccantelli, Meg, ''Corporate Capsule: Fastenal Co.,'' *Minneapolis-St. Paul CityBusiness,* November 26, 1993, Section 1, p. 21.

Croghan, Lore, ''The Wal-Mart of Nuts and Bolts,'' *Financial World,* July 18, 1995, p. 51.

McLeod, Reggie, ''Fastenal's Success Boon to Schools: Winona Firm's Founders Aid Private Education,'' *Successful Business,* August 29, 1989, Section 1, p. 30.

Parker, Walter, ''Fastenal Corp. Founders Remake a Tiny World-Class High School,'' *Knight-Ridder/Tribune Business News,* December 12, 1993.

Storm, Sheila, ''Fastenal to Add New Stores,'' *Successful Business,* December 9, 1991, Section 1, p. 1.

Swalboski, Gran, ''Booming Fastenal Driven by Service,'' *Successful Business,* March 11, 1991, Section 1, p. 22.

Youngblood, Dick, ''Fastenal Co. Doing Well by Sticking to Nuts and Bolts,'' *Star Tribune,* September 27, 1993, Section BUS.

—Dave Mote

Fidelity Investments Inc.

82 Devonshire Street
Boston, Massachusetts 02109
U.S.A.
(617) 570-7000
Fax: (617) 476-7356

Private Company
Incorporated: 1946 as Fidelity Management and Research
   Company
Employees: 15,800
Total Assets: $373.6 billion
SICs: 6282 Investment Advice

Fidelity Investments Inc. is one of the world's most successful retail investment services firms, offering its customers one of the widest ranges of mutual funds in the industry as well as discount brokerage and institutional and trust services. Innovation, in particular, has played a key role in the company's progress. However, the investment community has raised many an eyebrow at the way Fidelity's leaders have led the company through uncharted areas: the company was first, for example, to offer mutual funds with check-writing services; first to offer hourly updates on the net value of a mutual fund; and first to offer same-day trading of fund shares. Fidelity was privately owned and based in Boston and not the Mecca of financial services, New York. Although set apart from its competitors, the company, with more than 21 million individual and corporate customers, was the largest mutual fund manager in the United States, and it was the second largest discount brokerage firm with nearly 4 million accounts and over $157 billion in customer assets.

The Fidelity Fund was created in 1930, not a booming time for an investment industry reeling from the stock market crash of 1929 and heading into the Great Depression. In 1943, Boston lawyer Edward C. Johnson II bought the fund, which had $3 million in assets under management, and became its president and director. In 1946, Johnson formed Fidelity Management and Research Company, the predecessor of Fidelity Investments, to serve as an investment adviser to the Fidelity Fund. He also established the Puritan Fund, the first income-oriented fund to invest in common stock.

In an era when investment management was dedicated to preserving capital, Johnson's objective was to make money—and

make money he did. His strategy was not to buy blue-chip stocks but to buy stocks with growth potential. Johnson believed the management of a mutual fund should rely on one person's instincts and knowledge instead of management by committee. He was the first to put an individual in charge of a fund. One of Johnson's earliest, and most successful, fund managers was Gerry Tsai, a young, inexperienced immigrant from Shanghai whom Johnson hired as a stock analyst in the early 1950s. Tsai began running the Fidelity Capital Fund in 1957, buying speculative stocks like Polaroid and Xerox. His performance gained him fame and customers, and in less than ten years he was managing more than $1 billion. Tsai left Fidelity in 1965, when Johnson reportedly told him that he planned to turn the company over to his son. Edward C. Johnson III (Ned) graduated from Harvard in 1954, served in the army for two years, and worked at a bank before joining his father's company in 1957. Between 1961, when Ned became manager of the newly established Trend Fund, and 1965 the Trend Fund ranked first among growth funds.

The 1960s were a decade of growth for the U.S. economy and for Fidelity. In 1962 the company established the Magellan Fund, which eventually became the largest mutual fund in the world. The firm also launched FMR Investment Management Service Inc., in 1964, for corporate pension plans; the Fidelity Keogh Plan, a retirement plan for self-employed individuals, in 1967; and, to attract foreign investments, established Fidelity International the following year in Bermuda. In addition, it formed Fidelity Service Company in 1969 to service customer accounts in-house, one of the first fund groups to do so.

Ned Johnson succeeded his father as president of Fidelity Investments in 1972, around the time that the market began to take a turn for the worse and investors began to abandon stocks and equity funds and return to the security of savings accounts. That same year the Johnsons formed FMR Corporation to provide corporate-administration services to other Fidelity companies.

During Ned Johnson's first two years as president of Fidelity Investments, the financial market was virtually dormant, and assets shrank by more than 30 percent to $3 billion in 1974. Ned Johnson needed a way to reverse the firm's course and he found it in the money market fund. These new funds used investor deposits to make very short-term loans. Because the principal was never really at risk and only the interest fluctuated, money market funds turned out to be a great investment, but Johnson knew that unless the new funds offered the same liquidity and service as savings accounts, they would never be truly competitive. Consequently, in 1974 he established Fidelity Daily Income Trust (FIDIT), the first money market fund to offer check writing, a revolutionary—and instantly successful—idea.

While his father had remained devoted to mutual funds, Ned Johnson explored new aspects of the business. In 1973 Johnson began to integrate the company vertically by taking over back-office account-processing functions from banks that handled the job for most mutual funds. He also turned to direct sales rather than sales through brokers, enabling Fidelity to cut costs. However, this also meant that at a time when Fidelity was low on cash (due to a bad market) it was spending millions on computers, advertising, and telephones.

In the mid-1970s the company created the Fidelity Group Individual Retirement Account (IRA), as well as the Fidelity Municipal Bond Fund—the first no-load, open-ended fund in the United States to invest in tax-free municipal bonds. In 1977, the year his father retired, Ned Johnson became chairman and CEO of Fidelity and Peter Lynch began managing the Magellan Fund, which by then had assets totaling $22 million.

After the United States abolished fixed-rate brokerage commissions in 1975, Fidelity became the nation's first major financial institution to offer discount brokerage services when it formed Fidelity Brokerage Services Inc., in 1978. In 1979, Fidelity Institutional Services was formed to manage relationships with corporate clients. Along with the rest of the country, Fidelity enjoyed the bull market during the 1980s, a decade of considerable growth for the firm; assets under management grew from $3 billion in 1974 to $13 billion in 1981. Between 1980 and 1983 Fidelity launched several new products: the Tax-Exempt Money Market Trust, the nation's first no-load, tax-free money market fund; Fidelity Money Line, to provide electronic fund-transfer services nationwide; the Ultra Service Account, the only asset-management account offered by a mutual fund organization; and sector funds, which featured separate portfolios specializing in specific industries.

The firm also spun off several subsidiary companies, each run by a president who ultimately reported to Johnson. They included Fidelity Systems Company; Fidelity Management Trust Company; Fidelity Marketing Company; Fidelity National Financial (one of only three publicly owned title insurers in the United States); and Fidelity Investments Southwest, a remote-operations center in Dallas, Texas, part of a state-of-the-art telephone network. After introducing telephone switching, a service allowing customers to change funds over the telephone, the company opened another remote-operations center in 1986 in Salt Lake City, Utah.

The firm also unveiled same-day trading of its 31 Select Portfolio funds, which enabled investors to get quotes on an hourly basis and redeem or purchase shares between 10:00 a.m. and 4:00 p.m. rather than waiting until after 4:00 p.m. to get a fund's closing net asset value. By 1986 Fidelity had 2,800 employees, 104 mutual funds, $50 billion in assets under management, and more than 2 million customers—400,000 of them in the $4 billion Magellan Fund. Between 1977, when Peter Lynch first took over Magellan, and 1987 the fund's shares had grown by more than 2,000 percent, outperforming all other mutual funds and making Lynch the industry's most successful and aggressive fund manager.

Because Lynch didn't invest heavily in conservative stocks and kept very little liquid capital, the Magellan Fund was hit hard by the crash that shook Wall Street on October 19, 1987. Caught off-guard, Fidelity was forced to sell shares heavily in a plummeting market to meet redemptions. On that day alone, nearly $1 billion worth of stock was sold. By the end of the week, Fidelity's assets had dropped from $85 to $77 billion. Still, almost all of the firm's equity funds beat the market on Black Monday. In 1988, the year following the crash, Fidelity's revenues were down a quarter and profits were 70 percent lower. Determined never to suffer another Black Monday, Johnson cut personnel by almost a third (from a precrash high of 8,100) and

began sharpening the company's international presence and to enter the lucrative insurance field. In 1989, with more than $80 billion in assets under management, the firm had captured about 9 percent of the entire mutual fund industry; a year later these figures leapt to nearly $119 billion in assets with over 35 million mutual fund transactions in 1990, the year Peter Lynch surprised the industry by resigning from the Magellan Fund to spend more time with his family and write (he rejoined the company as a part-time adviser in 1992). Replacing Lynch was Fidelity's OTC portfolio manager Morris Smith, who with Lynch's advice increased the fund to $13 billion by 1991, making it the world's largest mutual fund.

As the 1990s progressed, Fidelity continued to break new ground and attract more clients, both individual and corporate, to its growing retail, institutional, and brokerage businesses. Consumer retirement products like IRAs, SEPs, Keough plans, and college programs continued to fare well; corporate 401(a), 401(k), and 403(b) retirement plans (the first and third for nonprofit organizations) climbed to record highs. Numbers consistently bore out Fidelity's status as a maverick: in 1991 assets under management reached $156 million for nearly 10 million customers; in 1992 clients topped 12 million and assets rose to just shy of $190 million; and in 1993 assets jumped to $258 million for an ever-expanding client base of over 16 million.

Two keys to Fidelity's wild growth were constant innovation, an ongoing reliance on research (with its own Management & Research division) and the intuition of its fund managers. At Fidelity, fund managers were increasingly known as trailblazers or young turks (just as Ned Johnson himself was regarded in the 1970s), boldly going where few before them had even considered. For years, risky, aggressive investments paid off handsomely for the company's programs, including the famous Magellan Fund, which had swollen to $25 billion in 1993, until a combination of factors including rising interest rates and market volatility contributed to substantial reversals in 1994. Several of its divisions suffered serious setbacks in high-risk bond investments such as emerging-nation debt and derivative securities when the peso nosedived in December 1994.

In addition to Fidelity's losses in 1994, the company struggled to maintain consumer confidence after several incidents had sullied its reputation. The first occurred with the 1992 conviction of former portfolio manager Patricia Ostrander for accepting bribes from Drexel Burnham Lambert's Michael Milken in the late 1980s. Then came three revelations in 1994: the deliberate transmission of day-old prices for about 150 mutual funds; a company reversal after stating that the Magellan Fund would pay a year-end distribution, when in fact it would not; then another gaffe when incorrect 1099-DIV forms were mailed to shareholders of two international funds. Yet despite these problems and negative economic factors, Fidelity still managed to beat over 83 percent of its fund competition, posted increases for most of its business units, and raised assets under management to $297 billion, a climb of nearly 15 percent for 1994.

In January 1995 Thomas J. Steffanci, head of the Fixed-Income unit, resigned, followed by Robert Citrone, manager of Fidelity's prominent emerging markets segment. When company veteran Fred L. Henning Jr., one of Fidelity's most conservative fund managers, was named to succeed Steffanci, industry wags attributed the resignations as fallout from the company's losses in 1994. In the wake of its troubles in 1994, Fidelity's investments became less aggressive in 1995, steering away from derivatives and developing-nation debt and retreating, as Henning told the *Wall Street Journal,* to ''predictable'' though lower returns. Yet even as Fidelity took a more cautious approach to investing in the mid-1990s, the company was still among the most innovative in the industry by expanding its online services from the simplistic Prodigy to the extensive reaches of the Internet's World Wide Web.

As Fidelity approached its 50th anniversary in 1996, the third generation of the Johnson family, 34-year-old Abby Johnson, a director of the FMR Corp. and manager of Fidelity's OTC Portfolio (with assets nearing $2 billion), had clearly proven herself as an investment manager on the move. Though Ned Johnson and Abby herself remained mum about her possible succession to the family's throne, insiders believed she would one day run Fidelity's sprawling empire of 48 businesses, 21 million customers, and $506.1 billion in total customer assets.

Principal Subsidiaries: Advanced MobileComm, Inc.; Boston-Coach; Charitable Gift Fund; COLT (City of London Telecommunications); Community Newspaper Company; Fidelity Accounting and Custody Services; Fidelity Brokerage Services; Fidelity Brokerage Services, Inc.; Fidelity Brokerage Technologies Group; Fidelity Capital; Fidelity Capital Markets; Fidelity Capital Technology; Fidelity Distributors Corporation; Fidelity Fund Guide; Fidelity Institutional Retirement Services Company; Fidelity Investment Advisor Group; Fidelity Investments Brokerage Firm; Fidelity Investments Canada Limited; Fidelity Investments Dealer Services; Fidelity Investments Institutional Group; Fidelity Investments Institutional Services Company; Fidelity Investments Life Insurance Company; Fidelity Investments Preferred Services; Fidelity Investments Retail Customer Service; Fidelity Investments Retail Distribution Company; Fidelity Investments Retail Group; Fidelity Investments Retail Marketing Company; Fidelity Investments Southwest Company; Fidelity Investments Tax-Exempt Services Company; Fidelity Management Trust Company; Fidelity Personal Trust Services; Fidelity Properties, Inc.; Fidelity Security Services, Inc.; Fidelity Service Co.; Fidelity Systems Company; Fidelity Trust Company; FMR Corp.; FMR Kentucky, Inc.; FMR Texas, Inc.; J. Robert Scott; National Financial Correspondent Services; National Financial Services Corporation; Strategic Advisors, Inc.; Wentworth Gallery Ltd.; World Trade Center Boston; *Worth* Magazine.

Further Reading:

Blumenthal, Karen, ''Fidelity Sets Vote on Scope of Investments,'' *Wall Street Journal,* December 8, 1994, pp. C1, C2.

Callan, Sara, ''Fidelity's Head of Emerging Markets Quits,'' *Wall Street Journal,* January 30, 1995, p. B2.

Clements, Jonathan, ''Fidelity Investments Plans to Move into Advice-Giving,'' *Wall Street Journal,* December 9, 1992, pp. C1, C18.

Fleming, Charles, ''Liberté, Egalité, Fraternité, Fidelity: Fund Manager Targets France, Again,'' *Wall Street Journal,* June 17, 1994, p. B6.

''The Heir Who Opened a World of Choices to Small Investors,'' *Money,* October 1992, p. 151.

McGough, Robert, ''Fidelity Investments Says Peso's Plunge Led to Dividend Mix-Up at Two Funds,'' *Wall Street Journal,* February 2, 1995, p. A4.

—— ''Fidelity Sold Morrison Stock Preceding News,'' *Wall Street Journal,* February 3, 1995, p. A4.

—— ''Fixed-Income Chief Resigns at Fidelity,'' *Wall Street Journal,* January 24, 1995, pp. C1, C2.

—— ''Manager of Fidelity Dividend Fund May Be Following in Her Dad's Footsteps,'' *Wall Street Journal,* November 23, 1993, pp. C1, C20.

McGough, Robert, John R. Emshwiller, and Sara Calian, ''Mutual Muddle: Deliberate Mispricing at Fidelity Highlights Lax Controls on Quotes,'' *Wall Street Journal,* June 23, 1994, pp. A1, A3, A6.

Pae, Peter, ''Fidelity Expands Fledging Business in Credit Cards,'' *Wall Street Journal,* April 10, 1992, p. B3.

''Personal Investing: How to Invest for a Slowdown,'' *Fortune,* February 20, 1995, p. 117.

''Portfolio Talk: Stocks That the Magellan Fund is Buying Now,'' *Fortune,* May 3, 1993, p. 34.

Rebello, Joseph, ''Fidelity Puts a Conservative at Bond Helm,'' *Wall Street Journal,* May 4, 1995, p. A4.

Sandberg, Jared, ''Fidelity Investments Plans to Provide Financial Information on the Internet,'' *Wall Street Journal,* February 14, 1995, p. B4.

Smith, Geoffrey, ''The Daughter Also Rises: How Fast and How Far Will Abby Johnson Go at Fidelity,'' *Business Week,* July 17, 1995, pp. 82–83.

Suskind, Ron, ''Peter Lynch Rejoins Fidelity As Part-Timer,'' *Wall Street Journal,* December 21, 1992, pp. C1, C15.

—Kim M. Magon
—updated by Taryn Benbow-Pfalzgraf

First Nationwide Bank

135 Main Street
San Francisco, California 94105
U.S.A.
(415) 904-1100
Fax: (415) 904-1157

Wholly Owned Subsidiary of First Nationwide Holdings, Inc.
Incorporated: 1982 as First Nationwide Financial
   Corporation
Employees: 3,500
Assets: $15 billion
SICs: 6035 Federal Savings Institutions; 6712 Bank Holding
   Companies

With more than 150 branches in seven states and assets of about $15 billion, First Nationwide Bank was among the largest savings and loan institutions in the United States going into the mid-1990s. The bank provides a full range of consumer financial services, including banking, loan, and investment services. Beginning in the mid-1980s, First Nationwide expanded rapidly and then contracted just as quickly before it was sold by Ford Motor Co. in 1994.

First Nationwide Bank was incorporated as a publicly traded company in 1982 as First Nationwide Financial Corporation. However, the bank's roots can be traced to January 14, 1885. On that day, Citizens Building & Loan Association opened for business in San Francisco with $50,000 in assets. Despite economic turbulence that marred the period, the burgeoning savings and loan survived and even managed to expand during the late 1800s and early 1900s. In 1906 the company's facilities were ravaged by the infamous earthquake. Despite the giant setback, Citizens scrambled to resume business within three weeks—not a single depositor lost any funds as a result of the tragedy. By 1925 Citizens was boasting deposits of $1 million.

Citizens was slammed by the stock market crash of 1929 and the ensuing Great Depression. Unlike many of its peers, it managed to emerge intact, and then to benefit from federal legislation in succeeding years that was enacted to stabilize the historically volatile banking industry. Citizens was granted a federal charter in 1935, in fact, and changed its name to Citizens Federal Savings and Loan Association. Citizens distinguished itself in 1945 by making the first GI home loan in California to a returning World War II veteran, and again in 1953 when it

became the first association to convert from a federal mutual charter to a state stock charter. In 1955, moreover, Citizens opened its first branch office. That branch, opened in a nearby San Francisco neighborhood, signaled the start of a long period of growth during the 1960s and 1970s.

Indeed, Citizens became involved in a series of mergers and acquisitions during the 1960s and 1970s that completely changed the face of the tiny building and loan association. Importantly, in 1962 Citizens merged with First Federal of San Jose, resulting in an organization with a whopping $200 million in assets. Similarly, Citizens was absorbed in 1973 by United Savings and Loan. The combined institution was incorporated as a holding company named United Financial Corporation of California. By the end of the 1970s, United Financial was controlling nearly $3 billion in assets. In 1980, though, that holding company was acquired by National Steel Corporation as part of that company's effort to diversify out of the steel industry.

After being integrated into United Financial and then National Steel Corporation for nearly a decade, Citizens was restored as a separate entity in 1981. Citizens was converted back to a federal charter and renamed First Nationwide Savings. It became the first U.S. savings and loan institution to cross state lines when, with federal assistance, it acquired failed savings and loans in Florida and New York. Those acquisitions boosted First Nationwide's asset base to a big $6.9 billion going into 1982. During that year, National Steel reduced its ownership share to 82 percent and effectively spun off the unit as First Nationwide Financial Corporation, a publicly traded financial institution with $7.2 billion in assets and 140 branches in three states. Thus, in just two years Citizens had been completely transformed from a regional savings and loan into a multi-state, multi-billion-dollar entity with offices on both coasts.

The evolution of the giant First Nationwide during the early 1980s reflected a trend of consolidation in the financial services industry that gained momentum in the early and mid-1980s. The emerging paradigm at the time was that financial "supermarkets" would eventually dominate the financial services and banking landscape; many people believed that giant, diversified, national financial networks, which would benefit from economies of scale made possible by new information technology, would take the place of local and regional financial institutions. Because it was the first savings and loan to expand nationally, First Nationwide was considered on the cutting edge of the financial supermarket trend. For that reason the company caught the eye of automobile giant Ford Motor Company.

Ford purchased First Nationwide Financial Corporation, along with some bank branches in Hawaii, in 1985 for $493 million. By that time, the savings and loan was sporting 177 branches in four states and a portfolio with about $11.6 billion in assets. Ford management viewed the buyout as a diversification with vast potential. Ford would buy up troubled savings and loans across the nation and then assemble them into a cohesive, efficient financial supermarket—the first truly nationwide thrift in the United States. In 1986 Ford changed the name of First Nationwide Savings (the chief subsidiary of First Nationwide Financial Corporation) to First Nationwide Bank, a federal savings bank. Ford also acquired new branches from a troubled thrift in Ohio.

Ford's foray into the booming financial services industry initially appeared to be a savvy move. First Nationwide posted a healthy $102 million profit in 1986 and was successfully building its network. In 1987, in fact, First Nationwide Bank opened new branches in Michigan, before expanding aggressively into Illinois, New Jersey, and Denver in 1988. During 1988 First Nationwide doubled its assets to an impressive $29 billion, making it a leader in the national thrift industry. While it was buying up savings and loans, Ford was also expanding its banking operations into retail stores. Ford partnered with K-Mart discount stores to eventually open about 200 First Nationwide offices in 13 states across the nation.

Unfortunately, First Nationwide's financial performance failed to keep pace with its growth. After peaking in 1986, the thrift's profits stalled. Company executives explained that the profit plunge was temporary and expected, given the poor financial condition of the savings and loans that it had purchased. However, the problems actually ran much deeper. In fact, by 1988 First Nationwide had ballooned into an unwieldy, loosely connected amalgamation of troubled financial institutions. As a result, First Nationwide's profits began to plummet. At the same time, the savings and loan industry itself was beginning to totter from deep-rooted structural problems that would eventually result in the infamous and costly U.S. savings and loan debacle of the late 1980s.

By late 1988, Ford management realized that First Nationwide was in trouble. In an effort to turn the operation around, Ford brought in a new chief executive, John Devine, to replace Anthony Frank. Devine had joined Ford straight out of business school in 1967 and worked as a financial executive on the automotive side of the business. Devine took the helm in September of 1988. He immediately began paring the thrift's assets and working to restructure the unruly operation. Importantly, Devine junked the lagging K-Mart outlets. Although the number of First Nationwide K-mart branches had swelled to about 200, they were only serving about 8,500 households and had generated a pitiful $200 million in combined deposits—less than the total deposits of just one of the company's larger non-retail branches.

After lopping off the retail outlets and eliminating some of the network's less successful branch operations, First Nationwide was left with about 250 full-service branches in 15 states and an ATM network of 25,000 automated teller machines sprinkled across the country. Total assets dropped to about $26 billion; the bank's parent, First Nationwide Financial Corporation, had a total of $34 billion in assets, $8 billion of which were attributable to smaller savings and loan subsidiaries. Still, Devine's efforts were insufficient to turn the ailing thrift around. As a real estate depression intensified and federal regulations affecting the thrift industry proliferated, First Nationwide's profits deteriorated. Devine responded by cost-cutting, laying off employees, and selling more assets. Nevertheless, the company began losing money in 1991.

During 1992 and 1993 Devine continued to sell off chunks of First Nationwide, while expanding very cautiously into more profitable regions of the United States. By early 1993 the number of states in which the bank was operating had been decreased from fourteen to ten, and the total number of branches had fallen to 225. Before the end of the year, the bank's assets had declined to a total of $17 billion and its network was serving only eight states. Although management vowed that it had not thrown in the towel, it appeared that Ford's dream of building the first nationwide financial supermarket had become a nightmare.

Even by the early 1990s, Ford might have completely jettisoned First Nationwide Financial Corp. and all of its subsidiaries had it been able to elicit an amount even close to what it had invested in the project. Instead, it continued to invest more money, hoping that the operation would recover. It didn't. By the end of 1993, First Nationwide was still the country's fourth largest savings and loan institution, but it held that status in a floundering industry. Frustrated with ongoing problems, Ford management decided to sell First Nationwide.

Ford found a buyer for First Nationwide Bank early in 1994. The company was purchased by Dallas-based First Madison Bank for a total of $1.1 billion—Ford took a $440 million write-off and retained $1.2 billion of the thrift's bad loans. It was the largest transaction in the history of the savings and loan industry. First Madison was a thrift founded in 1993 by financier Ronald O. Perelman. Perelman created the thrift with assets left over from the sale of First Gibraltar, his troubled thrift that he sold to BankAmerica Corp. in 1993. Perelman was attracted to the deal by First Nationwide's giant $6 billion portfolio of single-family-home loans, but also by its operations in California and Florida. Perelman appointed Gerald J. Ford, former head of First Gibraltar, as chief executive at First Nationwide. He also dropped the First Madison name in favor of First Nationwide.

When Perelman bought First Nationwide, the thrift had 180 branches in eight states and $15.5 billion in assets. Going into 1995, the thrift had 156 branches in seven states: California, Florida, Michigan, New Jersey, New York, Ohio, and Texas. It also had 22 residential lending offices and five satellite offices in six states, and was originating residential loans in a total of 35 states through its wholesale lending operations. With a work force of 3,500, First Nationwide Bank was the seventh largest savings and loan institution in the nation. It provided a full range of consumer banking services, including consumer loans, investments, savings and checking accounts, and, through its First Nationwide Mortgage Corporation subsidiary, mortgage loans. A healthier loan portfolio and increasing efficiency suggested improved performance for the thrift in the future.

Principal Subsidiaries: First Nationwide Mortgage Corporation.

Further Reading:

Anderson, Mark. "First Nationwide Cuts Again," *Business Journal-Milwaukee,* November 28, 1994, p. 1.
Carlsen, Clifford, "Automaker Turned Banker Takes Helm," *San Francisco Business Times,* February 8, 1991, p. 12.
Johnson, Stephen L., "First Nationwide Bank to Close Operations in K-Mart Stores," *Business Wire,* February 10, 1989.

Kraul, Chris, and Donald W. Nauss, ''Ford to Sell Unprofitable Thrift Unit to Dallas Firm,'' *Los Angeles Times,* April 15, 1994, p. 1D.

Risen, James, ''Investor Perelman Still Benefits From 1988 Deal,'' *Los Angeles Times,* September 19, 1994, p. 1D.

Rose, Barbara, ''Bumpy Road Hurts Ford's Local S&L,'' *Crains Chicago Business,* March 8, 1993, p. 1.

Sands, David R., ''Banking Network Will Quit K-Mart,'' *Washington Times,* February 13, 1989, p. 5B.

Sedgwick, David, ''First Nationwide Faces Credit Downgrade,'' *Detroit News,* January 23, 1991, p. 1F.

——, ''Ford Taps Controller for Top Slot: Devine to Succeed Seneker, Whose Exit May Mean More Outsiders on the Board,'' *Detroit News,* September 21, 1994, p. 1E.

——, ''Losses Drive Ford to Consider Selling First Nationwide,'' *Detroit News,* November 18, 1993, p. 1E.

Shingler, Dan, ''Ford's S&L Subsidiary Takes Flight at Cardinal,'' *Crains Cleveland Business,* January 21, 1991, p. 1.

Willoughby, Jack, ''Ford's Toughest Remodeling Job,'' *Financial World,* December 10, 1991, p. 58.

—Dave Mote

Foodmaker, Inc.

9330 Balboa Avenue
San Diego, California 92123
U.S.A.
(619) 571-2121
Fax: (619) 571-2101

Public Company
Incorporated: 1966
Employees: 25,000
Sales: $1.05 billion
Stock Exchanges: New York
SICs: 5812 Eating Places; 6794 Patent Owners & Lessors

Foodmaker, Inc., is the operator and franchisor of Jack in the Box restaurants, the fifth-largest fast-food hamburger chain in the United States. In addition to the 1,220-unit Jack in the Box chain, which has restaurants spread throughout the western and southwestern United States, Hong Kong, and Mexico, Foodmaker holds a 39 percent equity position in Family Restaurants, Inc., which operates 663 restaurants throughout the United States, including Chi-Chi's Mexican Restaurants, El Torito, Carrows, Coco's, and Charley Browns.

Foodmaker, Inc.'s, predecessor was Foodmaker Co., a foodservice company that had created numerous successful specialty restaurant chains, including Oscar's, Hamburger House, Family Tree, and The Jolly Ox. Foodmaker Co.'s greatest success was Jack in the Box, a unique chain of fast-food restaurants that enabled customers to drive up to a menu board, place their order, and drive away with their food in roughly three minutes. Situated on top of the menu board, with a microphone concealed inside, was the company's symbol, a large jack-in-the-box. Foodmaker Co.'s fast-food concept was notable for its speed of service and its drive-through, rather than drive-in, format.

Jack in the Box had evolved from a car-hop restaurant opened in 1941 as Topsy's Drive-In. Over the next several years, as the drive-in restaurant concept began to enjoy increasing popularity, Topsy's Drive-In was expanded to four locations and renamed Oscar's, then renamed Jack in the Box in 1950, when its first drive-through unit was opened in San Diego. The chain expanded to 24 units by 1961 and to 182 units by 1966, the year that Foodmaker, Inc., was established.

Throughout Jack in the Box's formative years, Foodmaker Co. had prepared all of the chain's food products except dairy items and hamburger buns, providing for the daily delivery of food to each individual restaurant. In 1965, however, Foodmaker Co. spun off its restaurant division, including Jack in the Box, and its commissary and specialty restaurant division, which included Hamburger House, Family Tree, and The Jolly Ox. The former was incorporated in July 1965 as Jack in the Box, Inc. In September 1966 Foodmaker, Inc., was incorporated, and four months later it acquired the commissary and specialty restaurant business of Foodmaker Co. The result after the confusing corporate reshuffling was Foodmaker, Inc., operator of 27 specialty restaurants located throughout Southern California, and Jack in the Box, Inc., owner of roughly 200 Jack in the Box restaurants.

Shortly thereafter Foodmaker, Inc., merged with Jack in the Box, Inc., and Foodmaker, Inc., began providing exactly the same preparation, purchasing, and delivery services to Jack in the Box restaurants that Foodmaker Co. had previously provided. By the time the dust had settled from the renewed alliance, the chain of fast-food drive-throughs had established a solid foundation after a decade and a half of growth. Offering a menu that included hamburgers, cheeseburgers, french-fries, onion rings, fried chicken, fried shrimp, tacos, apple turnovers, and soft drinks, Jack in the Box had proved its popularity with the American public, prompting Foodmaker, Inc., to map out an ambitious expansion plan. Between 1966 and 1973, Foodmaker management proposed to open 450 to 500 additional Jack in the Box restaurants, more than tripling the size of the chain.

Such optimism pervaded Foodmaker's management in 1966 for several reasons. Since the inception of the Jack in the Box concept and the chain's swift expansion throughout the Southwest, only two units had failed, an enviable record made more remarkable by the potentially risky practice of leasing Jack in the Box restaurants to independent entrepreneurs. Designated leasees rather than franchisees, independent Jack in the Box operators purchased all their food from Foodmaker, paid rent to Foodmaker based on the sales their restaurant generated, and kept the remainder of the money their particular unit produced as income.

Much of Foodmaker's growth was due to its methodical approach to managing the Jack in the Box chain. Everything, including the preparation of food, the selection of restaurant sites, the screening of prospective leasees, and the staffing of individual Jack in the Box units was done methodically and efficiently. Once successfully past a preliminary screening, leasees were subjected to a battery of tests conducted by a psychologist, then provided with a location for their Jack in the Box that from 1965 forward was selected by a computer. After seven months of training, Jack in the Box operators were required to stay in close contact with Foodmaker management through daily and weekly accounting summaries. Foodmaker's control over the chain went further, including at least three onsite inspections per week, giving Foodmaker the ability to maintain quality standards, monitor performance, and plot further growth with precision. Well organized and enjoying gratifying success, the Foodmaker organization drew the attention of much larger companies, and within two years of its incorporation Foodmaker became a subsidiary of Ralston Purina Co.

During the 1970s, Foodmaker led the Jack in the Box chain toward its most prolific growth, but as the decade progressed, the chain began to increasingly resemble its larger competitors, particularly the industry giant, McDonald's. Jack in the Box began to struggle during the latter part of the decade, and its expansion into East Coast markets was at first cut back from original estimates, then halted altogether. By the end of the decade, Jack in the Box restaurants were being offered for sale in increasing numbers, forcing Foodmaker to respond quickly in order to effect a turnaround.

The decade ended on an explosive note in 1979 when Foodmaker management signaled a dramatic shift in marketing strategy by blowing up the chain's symbol, the jack in the box clown, in television commercials. Jack in the Box announced that it would no longer compete for McDonald's target customer base of families with young children. Instead, Foodmaker would attempt to attract older, more affluent customers with what it touted as a higher-quality, more upscale menu, which attempted to satisfy the changing tastes of aging Baby Boomers.

In accordance with this new marketing strategy, Jack in the Box restaurants were remodeled and redecorated with designs intended to attract older, more affluent patrons. Most important, the chain's menu was greatly expanded, transforming Jack in the Box from a limited-menu hamburger operation that had been unsuccessfully competing against McDonald's into a chain of restaurants boasting a diverse menu at a time when few fast-food operations offered more than what had become the standard menu for the industry. Menu diversification became the key to success during the 1980s, driving annual sales upward as the decade progressed.

After Foodmaker's new strategy had recorded encouraging success for several years, Ralston Purina came out with its own new strategic plan, announcing in 1985 that it would only continue to own companies that were number one in their respective markets. Despite Foodmaker's progress during the first half of the decade, Ralston Purina's edict meant that Foodmaker was slated for divestiture. Foodmaker's management arranged a $435 million buy-out of the company, returning Foodmaker to private ownership after 18 years as a subsidiary of Ralston Purina.

Once again on its own, Foodmaker continued to distinguish itself from other fast-food chains with its varying, expanding menu. Under Foodmaker's direction, Jack in the Box was introducing at least two new menu items per year at a time when the chain's competitors were simplifying their menus, and was recording big success with such items as Chicken Fajita Pita, Hot Club Supreme Sandwich, Ultimate Cheeseburger, and a line of "finger foods" that included egg rolls, deep-fried shrimp, and fried chicken strips. During the late 1980s the chain's menu offered more than 40 items. By 1987 sales reached $655 million, the chain boasted 897 restaurants, and Foodmaker went public.

With Jack in the Box once again demonstrating the strength it had shown during the 1950s and 1960s, Foodmaker began looking for another growth vehicle for the company. In 1988 Foodmaker acquired Chi-Chi's Inc., based in Louisville, Kentucky, for $235 million. The acquisition gave Foodmaker a chain of roughly 200 Mexican dinner restaurants to complement its primary money earner, Jack in the Box.

Believing the stock market had significantly under-valued its stock, Foodmaker management returned the company to private ownership after the acquisition of Chi-Chi's. Over the course of the next two years sales generated by the Chi-Chi's chain doubled, jumping from $25 million to $50 million, while the Jack in the Box chain continued to perform admirably. In 1990 the 1,000th Jack in the Box unit was opened in Yorba Linda, California, marking the end of a ten-year period that saw the chain emerge from the formidable shadow cast by McDonald's and establish a distinct image. Looking ahead, Foodmaker management anticipated opening 60 new Jack in the Box units per year and 20 new Chi-Chi's restaurants per year during the early 1990s, confident that the previous decade of growth would continue unabated into the 1990s.

The onset of a national economic recession, however, dashed the company's expectation of an encouraging start in the new decade. In 1991 the company suffered an 81 percent decline in net earnings, while annual sales remained flat, hovering at $1.15 billion. Once again, Foodmaker went public, hoping to raise money to continue expanding its two chains. Despite the lackluster performance recorded during 1991, the company management announced an ambitious plan in October 1992 to spend between $60 and $100 million over the next decade on international expansion, delineating plans to develop roughly 700 Jack in the Box units in the Far East, Southeast Asia, and Latin America. Two months later, the company suffered a disastrous blow when a customer, six-year-old Lauren Rudolph, suffered three heart attacks and died. Her death was caused by a foodborne bacteria known as E. coli, the origin of which was linked to the consumption of a tainted and undercooked Jack in the Box hamburger.

Within a month three more Jack in the Box customers died—all young children—while more than 600 people in five Western states fell ill, arousing nationwide fear of an E. coli bacterial epidemic and a pervasive distrust of the Jack in the Box chain. Foodmaker lost $98.1 million the following year and another $39.6 million in 1994, while sales slipped to $1.24 billion in 1993 and $1.05 billion in 1994. In the wake of the E. coli epidemic, the Chi-Chi's chain of 237 Mexican restaurants was sold to Restaurant Enterprises Group Inc. for $270 million in cash and equity, as Foodmaker attempted to recover from the massive image problem engendered by four dead customers and hundreds others left with lasting health impairments and the need for organ transplants.

In early 1994 Foodmaker settled four wrongful-death lawsuits stemming from the E. coli outbreak, paying the victims' families an unspecified amount. The company launched a comprehensive food safety program immediately after the E. coli outbreak, but by May 1995 had yet to record a profitable quarter since the tragic death of the four children. Not surprisingly, sales and performance levels enjoyed by Jack in the Box before 1993 continued to elude the chain during the mid-1990s, causing considerable concern for the future.

An aggressive attempt to achieve a recovery was underway as Foodmaker plotted its future course for the late 1990s and into the next century. In 1995 the company resurrected its clown mascot in national television commercials, bringing the old symbol of Jack in the Box back in a series of advertisements featuring a blue-suited executive wearing a spherical clown head. Foodmaker earmarked $35 million for remodeling Jack in the Box units by the spring of 1995, with the remodeling of franchise units slated to follow in the ensuing 18 months. Whether Foodmaker and Jack in the Box could fully restore their tarnished image remained to be seen.

Principal Subsidiaries: Family Restaurants, Inc. (39%); Jack in the Box.

Further Reading:

Alva, Marilyn, "Foodmaker Set to Turn Its Back on Wall Street," *Nation's Restaurant News,* September 12, 1988, p. 1.

Farrell, Kevin, "Jack Goodall, Chairman, CEO, Foodmaker Inc.," *Restaurant Business,* May 1, 1990, p. 162.

"Foodmaker, Inc.," *Barron's,* February 15, 1988, p. 88.

"Foodmaker Plans Foreign Expansion," *Nation's Restaurant News,* October 12, 1992, p. 14.

"Foodmaker Settles Claim from 1st of 4 E. Coli Deaths," *Nation's Restaurant News,* February 28, 1994, p. 18.

Howard, Theresa, "Public Offerings to Slash Foodmaker's Debt Costs," *Nation's Restaurant News,* December 23, 1991, p. 14.

"Jack-in-the-Box Says Acquisition Would End Any Interest Conflict," *Wall Street Journal,* May 9, 1967, p. 23.

Martin, Richard, "Foodmaker Revives 'Jack' to Aid Turnaround Efforts, *Nation's Restaurant News,* January 30, 1995, p. 20.

——, "Ralston Purina Cuts Its Ties to Food Service," *Nation's Restaurant News,* October 20, 1986, p. 3.

Papiernik, Richard L., "Chi-Chi's Sale, New Ads Fail to Cure Foodmaker's Woes," *Nation's Restaurant News,* May 1, 1995, p. 14.

"Prospects Are Popping at Jack-in-the-Box," *Investment Dealers' Digest,* April 25, 1966, p. 34.

"Ralston Purina Agrees to Acquire Foodmaker," *Wall Street Journal,* January 9, 1968, p. 32.

Saxton, Lisa, "Jack-in-the-Box Parent Files Suit Against Vons," *Supermarket News,* February 15, 1993, p. 29.

Slatter, John, "Skeleton at the Feast?," *Barron's,* October 3, 1966, p. 11.

Warner, Rick Van, "Foodmaker Wins Chi-Chi's: $230M Deal Spawns Powerful New Company," *Nation's Restaurant News,* March 7, 1988, p. 1.

—Jeffrey L. Covell

Formosa Plastics Corporation

39 Chung Shan 3rd Road
Kaohsiung
Taiwan
(02) 712-2211
Fax: (02) 712-5287

Public Company
Founded: 1965
Employees: 3,345
Sales: NT $27.16 billion (US $1.29 billion)
Stock Exchanges: Taiwan
SICs: 2865 Cyclic Crudes and Intermediates; 2869 Industrial
   Organic Chemicals, Not Elsewhere Classified.

A pioneer of the Taiwanese plastics industry, Formosa Plastics
Corporation is the world's largest producer and processor of
polyvinyl chloride (PVC). In the mid-1990s, the company
ranked as Taiwan's largest non-government enterprise and a
significant contributor to the country's gross national product.
Formosa Plastics Corporation is the keystone of a characteristi-
cally Asian interlocking group of public and private companies
managed by the Wang family (no relation to the clan behind
Wang Laboratories, Inc.). Under the direction of its octogenarian patriarch, Chairman Yang-Chung Wang, the Formosa Plastics group generated a multi-billion-dollar family fortune.

Other primary businesses in the group included Nan Ya Plastics
Corp., Formosa Chemicals & Fiber Corp., and Formosa Plastics
U.S.A. Although technically separate, these businesses are often treated as a group in trade journals. (Header includes information on Formosa Plastics Corporation alone.) Taken together,
the Formosa Companies make up a system of vertical integration that includes everything from oil wells to petrochemical
processors and plastic bag manufacturers. Each unit releases its
financial information separately (if at all). Sales for each of the
companies broke down as follows: Formosa Plastics Corp., $1.3
billion (1994); Formosa Chemicals & Fiber, $976.63 million
(1993); Formosa Plastics U.S.A., $1 billion (1993 est.); Nan Ya
Plastics, $2.94 billion (1994). The company has grown with the
plastics industry virtually from the postwar birth of the petrochemical industry to plastic's entrenchment as a commodity by
the mid-1980s.

The hallmarks of the Formosa Plastics empire—vertical integration, emphasis on commodities, and efficient production—

were established and enforced by founder Y. C. Wang. Armed
only with an elementary education, Wang took his first job
selling and delivering rice for ten dollars a month at the age of
15. Shut out of the lucrative timber industry by the then ruling
Japanese, the teenager started his own rice shop with $200
borrowed from his father in 1932. Wang soon moved from
retailing to milling and put in long hours to compensate for the
privileged status of his Japanese competitors. Undaunted by the
World War II destruction of his operation, Wang built a bigger
mill. The postwar ouster of the Japanese opened up the timber
market to competition, and it was in lumber that Wang made his
first fortune.

With $500,000 from his timber business and a $680,000 loan
from the American economic aid mission, Wang licensed Japanese plastics technology and founded Formosa Plastics in 1954.
He later joked to *Forbes*'s Andrew Tanzer that at the time
"he didn't even know what the P in PVC stood for." PVC is
fabricated from ethylene, a petrochemical. First used in its
plastic or flexible form for "wonder" fabrics like polyester and
imitation leather, the substance's hard resin form was later used
for everything from construction materials to computers.

Applying his innate knack for making commodity products to
the new business, Wang increased production from five tons per
day to 20 tons per day, thereby lowering his unit costs.
Undaunted by a dearth of local customers, he created downstream businesses of his own to transform the raw PVC resin
into more consumer-oriented products. The first was Nan Ya
Plastics. Founded in 1958, this resin processor would consume
over half of Formosa Plastics's annual output by molding the
PVC resin into building materials like pipe, flooring, and window frames, as well as packaging material and a plethora of
other products. The Wang family's third major enterprise was
born of the patriarch's cost-cutting fervor. In the early 1960s,
Nan Ya started manufacturing an imitation leather that required
a woven backing. Instead of buying expensive imported cotton,
Wang formed Formosa Chemicals & Fiber Corp. to produce
rayon fibers from timber waste.

Strictly speaking, these three businesses—Formosa Plastics,
Nan Ya Plastics, and Formosa Chemicals & Fiber—are not
affiliated. They are, however, widely recognized as part of a
powerful system of vertical integration. The Wang family owns
at least 20 percent of each company's stock, and each of the
companies holds a one percent to four percent stake in the other
two. Taken as a whole, the group stands as one of the few (if not
the only) mass producers of the four synthetic textile fibers—
rayon, nylon, polyester and acrylic—in the world. This status
has given the Formosa group excellent economies of scale and
consolidated its influence in the petrochemical industry.

Formosa gathered steam over the late 1960s and throughout the
1970s, maintaining strictly domestic operations and building up
a potent export trade. By the mid-1980s, all but 15 percent of
Formosa Plastics' production was exported.

Wang began to expand its production internationally in the
early 1980s, investing over $200 million in U.S. production
facilities from 1981 to 1985. These strategic acquisitions illustrated Wang's oft-praised knack for buying low, when commodities industries were at the bottom of their periodic cycles,

then whipping them into shape in time for an upswing. His first noteworthy move was the 1981 acquisition of a money-losing vinyl chloride monomer (VCM) plant in Baton Rouge, Louisiana. From 1978 to 1981, this subsidiary of Imperial Chemical Industries had reportedly lost $80 million. In exchange for taking on the business's $27 million debt, Wang got his first U.S. plant. He immediately began to bring the factory into line, turning excess real estate into $42 million in cash. He cut the payroll by over 44 percent, yet increased production by 35 percent, thereby bringing the company into the black within less than five years.

Wang applied the same principles to his $12 million purchase (also in 1981) of a PVC plant in Delaware from Stauffer Chemical. A near 50 percent decrease in the payroll and a 30 percent increase in production helped cut monthly losses of $2 million by 90 percent within four years. In 1983, Wang acquired Manville Corp.'s bankrupt PVC pipe operations for $20 million cash and a $10 million note. As if on cue, the construction market recovered in 1984 and the business earned a $5.5 million profit.

In all, Wang bought 14 American PVC processors from 1980 to 1988. His 1988 acquisition of over 200 oil wells, a gas processing plant, and a pipeline company from Aluminum Company of America (Alcoa) extended Formosa U.S.A.'s vertical line of production upward, to the plastics industry's most vital need: petroleum.

While other leading petrochemical firms failed in the PVC business, Wang maintained strong profitability. Sympathetic observers have attributed his success to hard work and determination; others have characterized him as ruthless and driven. In spite of his advanced age, Wang worked long hours (reportedly 100 per week) and expected his employees to work similar hours (from 48 to 70 hours a week). Although his intimate knowledge of virtually every aspect of the group's far-flung operations was admirable, it could also be labeled "micromanagement." Writing in 1983 for Forbes, Arthur Jones noted Wang's daily (including Saturdays and Sundays) meetings with the managers of Formosa's hundreds of divisions. The combination of long hours and Wang's "relentless interrogations" were blamed for a high rate of nervous ailments dubbed "the Formosa Plastics syndrome" by local doctors.

The chairman's own children provided first-hand testimony of his "stranglehold" on the business. Daughter Charlene joined her in-laws, the Chiens, to create First International Computer Inc. in the early 1980s. In 1994, she told Pete Engardio of Business Week that she chose the computer industry because it was "something he [Y. C. Wang] knew nothing about." Son Winston told Fortune's Louis Kraar that he'd "never seen a decision made by anybody except the chairman."

Even Wang's philanthropic endeavors had an edge: Named for Y. C. Wang's father, the wholly owned Chang Gung Memorial Hospital Foundation owned one-third of Formosa Chemicals & Fibers and six percent of both Formosa Plastics and Nan Ya. The wholly owned Ming-Chi Institute of Technology also held significant stakes in the group.

But perhaps the most highly criticized aspect of Wang's business conduct was his handling of environmental considerations.

In a lengthy 1985 profile of the Wang empire for Forbes, Andrew Tanzer quoted one competitor who asserted that "[Wang] doesn't play by the rules. If he gets caught polluting or evading taxes, he bargains with the [Taiwanese] government."

Wang tried to import those methods to the United States, but ran into slightly more formidable roadblocks in the form of both federal environmental regulation and citizen action groups. The state of Delaware sued Wang on 30 air pollution counts in 1984 and later shut down his plant there for two weeks. From 1984 to 1990, Formosa U.S.A.'s Texas plant in Point Comfort racked up no less than 40 citations from the Texas Air Control Board, resulting in well over $600,000 in fines. In 1988, when the first federal Toxics Release Inventory named Calhoun County—home of the Point Comfort plant—America's most polluted county, the focus on Formosa intensified.

Nevertheless, Wang applied for permission to make a $1.5 billion addition to Point Comfort's ethylene capacity that fall. A seemingly endless string of roadblocks delayed the project. Wastewater violations brought record-setting fines from state and federal agencies. Texans United, a local environmental group, labeled Formosa "an international environmental outlaw." Published (but not necessarily substantiated) accusations of bribes, pay-offs, kickbacks, and shakedowns further tarnished Formosa's image. The project was also plagued with legal disputes over construction contracts and worker safety. In 1992, Formosa and a group of its critics agreed to set up a Technical Review Committee that included company and community representatives. The new plastics and processing plants were completed and were cleared for production by state and federal agencies later that year. The company was finally able to begin production of PVC, polypropylene, and related chemicals in the fall of 1993. The same year, Formosa announced plans to fully integrate its North American PVC business.

Back in Taiwan, Formosa had encountered similar delays in the initiation of a $9.4 billion complex that would produce 450,000 metric tons of ethylene and 225,000 tons of propylene each year to supply over 20 downstream plants. The first phase of the project was a $3.3 billion naptha cracker slated to begin production in 1998. This plant alone was expected to increase Taiwan's fiscal growth by one percent annually during construction and 1.5 percent annually by the end of the decade. Formosa borrowed $5.5 billion to fund the complex, which was projected to produce over $7 billion in annual revenues by 1998. Although thwarted in the early 1990s by bureaucratic delays, Formosa Plastics announced plans to build three additional plants on the banks of China's Long River in 1994.

Faced with a maturing PVC market in the mid-1980s, Wang established a research and development division and began investigating opportunities for diversification. He considered cement and pharmaceuticals, but focused instead on specialty chemicals for the fast-growing computer industry. Son Winston convinced his father that computer components fit in with the company's long-term strategy by virtue of their rapid commoditization. Although Wang had long eschewed joint ventures, Nan Ya sought the help of the Hewlett-Packard Company for technical advice in the creation of its circuit board plant. In keeping with Wang's previous successes, Nan Ya moved to vertically integrate the new operation by producing the chemicals needed to manufacture the circuit boards.

Speculation regarding the pattern of succession at Formosa began in the mid-1980s and continued through the mid-1990s in spite of the fact that the octogenarian Chairman Wang showed no signs of slowing down. At five years his junior, brother Y. T. Wang served as president of both Formosa Plastics and Formosa Chemicals & Fiber and appeared to be a likely candidate to assume the top seat. The brothers' many Western-educated children, who were involved in the business both at home and abroad, constituted a third tier of leadership. Y. C.'s son Winston and Y. T.'s son William had advanced to executive positions at Nan Ya. Winston was regarded as the driving force behind Nan Ya's diversification into semiconductors, LCD screens, and other electronic components. Other family interests were dominated by Y. C.'s progeny. Daughter Susan Wang held the title of assistant to the president at Formosa U.S.A., but according to a 1993 *Chemical Week* article, she was "widely acknowledged to have operational charge of the U.S. business." As previously mentioned, daughter Charlene was a top executive at First International Computer (FIC), a leading manufacturer of IBM clones and computer mother-boards that generated $600 million in annual sales by the mid-1990s. In November 1993, Formosa and FIC pooled $2.3 million to rescue Everex Systems, a California manufacturer of "high-end" personal computers, and Wang installed daughter Cher at its head. With such a deep pool of potential successors, the Wang legacy appeared secure in the mid-1990s.

Principal Subsidiaries: Everex Systems; Formosa Heavy Industries Co. Ltd.; Formosa Petrochemical Co., Ltd.; Formosa Plastics Corp., U.S.A.; J-M Manufacturing Co., Inc.; Mailao Harbor Administration Co., Ltd.; Tai Shih Textile Industry Corp.; Yungchia Chemical Industries Co., Ltd.

Further Reading:

Engardio, Pete, and Margaret Dawson, "A New High-Tech Dynasty?" *Business Week,* August 15, 1994, p. 90.
"Formosa Plastics Fined Record Sum Under RCRA," *Chemical Marketing Reporter,* March 4, 1991, p. 3.
"Formosa Wins Water Permit in Face of Newspaper Attack," *Chemical Marketing Reporter,* July 5, 1993, p. 7.
Jones, Arthur, "Wealth in Taiwan," *Forbes,* December 19, 1983, p. 127.
Kraar, Louis, "They Love the Getting, Not the Spending: The Overseas Chinese," *Fortune,* October 12, 1987, p. 162.
——, "Ten to Watch Outside Japan," *Fortune,* Fall 1990, p. 25.
Morries, Gregory D. L., "Formosa Plastics Labors to Clean Up Its Image," *Chemical Week,* June 23, 1993, p. 18.
Richards, Don L., "Formosa Flap," *Chemical Marketing Reporter,* April 16, 1990, p. 5.
Simon, Ruth, "Taiwan's U.S. Strategy," *Forbes,* May 29, 1989, p. 43.
"Taiwan's Sixth Naptha Cracker Gets Green Light," *The Oil and Gas Journal,* July 12, 1993, p. 39.
Tanzer, Andrew, "Y.C. Wang Gets Up Very Early in the Morning," *Forbes,* July 15, 1985, p. 88.

—April Dougal Gasbarre

General DataComm Industries, Inc.

1579 Straits Turnpike
Middlebury Connecticut 06762-1299
U.S.A.
(203) 574-1118
Fax: (203) 758-8507

Public Company
Incorporated: 1968 as C.P. Johnson Associates
Employees: 1,823
Sales: $211 million
Stock Exchanges: New York
SICs: 3661 Telephone & Telegraph Apparatus

General DataComm Industries is a leading provider of multimedia networks and telecommunications equipment used by businesses, telephone companies, and governments worldwide. The company is involved in all aspects of its telecommunication networks, from designing, manufacturing, and marketing its products, to offering installation and maintenance services as well.

General DataComm was founded by Charles P. Johnson, a native Chicagoan who had trained as an electronics technician when he joined the Navy in 1945. After the war, he worked for the telephone company during the day, while he attended Northwestern University in the evenings on the GI Bill. He then worked as a transmission engineer at Illinois Bell and a sales manager for Kellogg Switchboard, a subsidiary of ITT. While at Kellogg he went up against AT&T in selling equipment to independent telephone companies, a challenge that honed his sales skills and taught him the intricacies of the telecommunications market.

After working for another electronics company and a data communications company, Johnson decided to start his own firm, C.P. Johnson Associates in 1968. Using his own funds, he rented 25,000 square feet of office space for his fledgling company, a work space obviously far too large but valuable in establishing the credibility he needed in the industry. His first few employees were industry contractors, hired on as consultants, who had experience developing telecommunications networks for the military, and from the beginning the firm planned to design and manufacture equipment for complete network systems.

Working quickly, Johnson developed a business plan, raised $1.5 million in venture capital, and reincorporated as General DataComm (GDC). A decision by the Federal Communications Commission during this time had opened up the market for telecommunications, enabling customers to connect their own computer equipment to telephone lines. Johnson, who thoroughly knew the business and its technology, also proved an excellent salesman. He realized that large manufacturers of telecommunications equipment, like AT&T, made all of their products to the specifications of their most demanding clients, which meant that it was better and more expensive than most customers needed. So GDC made products that were slightly less sophisticated and much less expensive. GDC soon won a large multiplexer order from Shell Oil Co., and with Shell on its client list, the new GDC was able to attract business from smaller companies.

GDC's multiplexers made it possible to send many circuits simultaneously over a single connection, decreasing the need for many telephone lines. Eventually, GDC also moved into producing modems, which sent digital data over telephone lines. Thus, GDC's customers were businesses with computer data they needed to send over the telephone.

In its own manufacturing system, GDC stressed standardization. The firm's modular design and interchangeable parts made it easy to customize equipment for clients. This kept manufacturing costs low and was another reason why the firm could undersell rivals like AT&T, which did not stress standardization. GDC also developed technical improvements that made its products easier to use and service. For example, it was the first company in its field to put light emitting diodes on its equipment to aid in diagnosing breakdowns.

By 1973 GDC was reporting revenues of $6.8 million. The company was also spending about 13 percent of revenues on research and development, as it was in the midst of converting all of its products to large scale integrated circuitry. This process put a number of discrete components onto a single chip, reducing costs and the power demand of its products. By the late 1970s, GDC was spending about eight percent of sales on research, hoping to keep its manufacturing costs the lowest in the industry. Its largest customers were AT&T rivals like Bell of Canada, which accounted for 12 percent of sales, and GTE, at 16 percent.

Facilitated by its practice of producing interchangeable parts, GDC was able to quickly develop new products. In fact, by the end of 1977, GDC was manufacturing more than 200 types of data transmission equipment using fewer than 2,000 different components, a ratio that far outshone its industry rivals. In 1977 GDC bought a 150,000 square foot plant in Danbury, Connecticut, for about $2.7 million, or about eight-years rent on the facility it had been leasing about 16 miles from there.

By 1979, GDC's $41.4 million in sales made it the fourth largest data transmission equipment company in the United States, ranking second in number of units sold. In fact, the company's sales had been growing at 30 percent a year since 1974, and Johnson noted in a *Forbes* interview that he would not want the firm to grow any faster because it might then become more unwieldy. Even so, this growth forced the firm to carry a lot of debt and to make several stock offerings to raise cash.

During this time, GDC primarily made low- and medium-speed equipment and systems, leaving the high-end equipment to rivals like AT&T. The company sold its products to three market segments: the common-carrier market, which consisted of independent telephone companies, specialized common carriers, Western Union, and railroads; the business systems market, with customers ranging from Fortune 500 companies to small businesses; and the international market, including businesses and telephone companies in Canada, Europe, Latin America, and the Far East.

In 1980 a Federal Communications Commission decree affecting the telephone companies caused that market to shrink. To compensate, GDC moved to increase its share of the business market. It increased its business sales force to 175 from 32, and put more money into developing high-speed equipment. Still, company growth slowed somewhat, as it reached sales of $57.6 million in 1981, up from $53.6 in 1980. Sales grew to $60.7 million in 1982.

At the beginning of 1984, the telecommunications market changed drastically with the break up of AT&T. Suddenly the regional Bell operating telephone companies became potential customers. Sales soared to $145.7 million in 1984 as GDC signed on Ameritech and Bell Atlantic as customers. Nevertheless, domestic business users were becoming GDC's biggest customers, accounting for 55 percent of sales in 1986. Domestic telecommunications carriers only accounted for 15 percent of sales, while international customers accounted for 30 percent. GDC was particularly strong in Canada and Britain where it had direct sales staffs.

Other changes in the data communications and telephone markets were prompted by rapid breakthroughs in technology. GDC began providing some of the equipment used by businesses for video conferencing and in 1986 came out with 20 new products, but due to economic recession and weak computer sales, GDC's sales declined in 1986. The company responded with a boost to its sales staff, and cost-cutting measures that included a ten percent reduction of paid work hours during the first quarter. The telecommunications market continued to change rapidly, with increased use of fiber optic cable, satellites, and microwave radio, which bypassed telephone company facilities; GDC scrambled to keep up with the changes.

The firm established a Network Services Group in 1986 which combined network engineering, program management, systems integration, and field service. Believing that network management was an important long-term market, the company named its customer network service Meganet and stressed GDC's ability to offer its customers a wide range of network services from a single vendor. A new 360,000-square-foot plant in Naugatuck, Connecticut, finished in 1986, focused on problems relating to customer network requirements.

Sales recovered in 1987, but 1988 was again a tough year for the firm. As sales declined and the firm lost $15.7 million, management decided to restructure. Still, GDC continued to win new business from companies like Hongkong Bank. It used the firm's Megaswitch multiplexer as the backbone of an interna-

tional network that sent information between the bank and subsidiary offices via satellite and fiber optic cable. GDC installed over 600 high-speed modems at more than 300 locations in a three-month period for McDonnell Douglas as part of a nationwide network built for the Veterans Administration. Moreover, the State of Colorado was building a communications network using a full line of GDC products.

In 1989 GDC agreed to develop telecommunications technology with Japan's Hitachi Ltd. The firms worked on adapting GDC's multiplexers to a new technology called Integrated Services Digital Network, which carried voice, data, and video transmissions over a single phone line. Hitachi already operated a private information network in Japan that used some of GDC's multiplexers. Later that year, GDC installed one of the world's first multiplexer networks with ISDN capabilities. ISDN was expected to rapidly become an important technology as computers and video information became more central in communications. GDC also signed a three-year multimillion dollar deal with TRT, the data communications group of N. V. Philips, under which Philips resold the firm's multiplexers in Europe under the Philips name.

In the late 1980s and early 1990s, local area networks (LANs), which linked personal computers together, were rapidly becoming an important communications method, especially with the growing prevalence of personal computers. In 1990 GDC entered the LAN bridge business, becoming part of a technology that otherwise could have been a threat to its network business. The firm also reached an agreement with Alcatel Network Systems to use that company's Synchronous Optical Network interface, a standard for fiber optic networks that controlled channel bandwidth. GDC quickly moved multiplexers using the interface to market, selling from $28,000 to $180,000.

In 1991 the firm increased its presence in Europe when it bought Eurotech France, a telecommunications equipment company. Later in the year, France's Société Général bank built an international network around GDC multiplexers, also using the firm's voice compression technology. With the Mexican economy expanding, the firm also bought a majority interest in General Telecomm of Mexico. McDonald's Corporation, Citicorp, and other companies placed orders to create or upgrade multimedia networks.

Global communications systems were changing rapidly from analog to digital, but not always in ways that GDC had predicted ten years earlier. Rather than relying on centralized, mainframe computers, corporations were creating and sharing information over LANs. Accordingly, GDC began working on methods for customers to use the low-speed copper wires that most businesses already had in place. The firm also announced that it would develop multimedia networks for business customers and governments. Because such networks dealt with large volumes of video and voice information going through a variety of interconnected networks, GDC worked on several strategies and products, putting special emphasis on a high-capacity backbone switching architecture.

The firm continued to work with and develop products for major telecommunications companies, including products designed to hook up to corporate LANs via analog phone lines. Although many telecommunications firms had installed fiber optic lines in large parts of their systems, copper cables were still present throughout their systems, especially in the final links to customers' premises. Telcos were therefore very interested in methods of using copper cables efficiently, and GDC hastened to oblige them, producing equipment to send high-speed digital signals over copper.

An important component of the firm's multimedia network strategy was to move into Asynchronous Transfer Mode Technology (ATM), which was a wide-area network technology, one that GDC believed would not only succeed in the corporate world, but would eventually be used for interactive home entertainment. ATM governed the switching and transmission of information, dividing it into 53-byte information cells that could carry data, video, image, and voice information. In 1993, GDC introduced Apex, an ATM-supporting backbone switch for corporate local area networks. The firm also bought Netcomm Limited of Basildon, England, an ATM technology firm, for about $7.5 million in cash and stocks. Netcomm became GDC's Advanced Research Centre Limited. Apex switch manufacture was transferred to GDC's Connecticut factory. The switches were soon used for the world's first international ATM service, which ran between London and New York City. They were also used for the first ATM networks in Eastern Europe and China. All told, GDC had shipped about 240 ATM switches and related products to customers in 15 countries by the end of

1994, making it one of the leading ATM firms. It seemed the firm's ATM strategy might pay off.

Principal Subsidiaries: General DataComm, Inc.; General DataComm Systems, Inc., General DataComm, Ltd. (Canada); General DataComm Limited (UK); Eurotech France SARL; General DataComm SARL (France); General Telecomm S.A. de C.V. (Mexico); General DataComm Pte Lrd. (Singapore); General DataComm Pty. Limited (Australia); General DataComm de Venezuela C.A.; General DataComm Leasing Corporation; DataComm Service Corporation; General DataComm Advanced Research Centre Limited (UK); General DataComm Industries GmbH (Germany); General DataComm CIS (Russia); General DataComm China, Ltd.; General DataComm Do Brasil LTDA, S.C.

Further Reading:

Biggs, Jean A., "Who's Afraid of Ma Bell?," *Forbes,* June 23, 1980, pp. 132–34.
"Development Agreement with Hitachi is Signed," *Wall Street Journal,* January 11, 1989, p. B4.
Johnson, Charles P., and James McNabb, "General DataComm Industries, Inc.," *Wall Street Transcript,* January 23, 1978, pp. 49, 552–53.
Karpinski, Richard, "General DataComm Throws Hat in ATM Ring," *Telephony,* February 1, 1993, pp. 14, 16.

—Scott M. Lewis

Good Humor-Breyers Ice Cream Company

909 Packerland Drive
P.O. Box 19007
Green Bay, Wisconsin 54307
U.S.A.
(414) 499-5151
Fax: (314) 727-2021

Wholly Owned Subsidiary of Unilever, Inc.
Incorporated: 1993
Employees: 2,300
Sales: $500 million
SICs: 2024 Ice Cream & Frozen Desserts

In 1993 Good Humor and Breyers Ice Cream, two companies famous for their ice cream and frozen novelty dessert products, joined to form Good Humor-Breyers Ice Cream Company. As the largest American producer of these consumables, the company offers several popular product lines under such favorite brand names as Breyers, Good Humor, Klondike, Popsicle, and Sealtest. With an increasingly health conscious consumer base, Good Humor-Breyers has also developed new lines of fat free and sugar free ice cream. Moreover, the company remains committed to its role as an industry innovator, developing patented processes used to produce such products as Viennetta, a ready-to-serve dessert of layered ice cream and chocolate.

Breyers Ice Cream Company

Breyers Ice Cream Company is the oldest ice cream producer in the United States. In 1866, before the invention of the telephone, the start of the modern Olympics, and the construction of the Golden Gate Bridge, William A. Breyer decided to produce a relatively new concoction called ice cream. With the American economy recovering from the recent Civil War, Breyer was out of a job and, worried about how to support his family, hit upon the idea of selling a dairy product made out of cream, pure cane sugar, nuts, fresh fruits, and other natural flavorings.

Unable to rent a store to sell his ice cream, Breyer began to make and sell his product from his kitchen in Philadelphia. At first he sold ice cream to his neighbors and people living in the nearby community. As the reputation of his ice cream grew, he added different flavors and ingredients to expand his product line. With demand for Breyer's ice cream growing by the month, the entrepreneur purchased a horse and wagon to sell his products on the streets of Philadelphia. Breyer also purchased a large dinner bell, which he fitted on the wagon and sounded along his route to announce the arrival of his ice cream.

By 1882 Breyer had saved enough money to open a retail ice cream store. Not surprisingly, demand for his ice cream grew even more rapidly. People from every neighborhood in the city were soon traveling to Breyer's store on Frankford Avenue. Breyer made all the ice cream in the back of his store and sold it across the counter and by means of horse drawn wagons. The more the public tasted Breyer's ice cream, the more they wanted, and in quick succession Breyer opened up five more retail ice cream stores in different areas of the City of Brotherly Love.

Philadelphia mourned the loss of William A. Breyer when he died late in 1882. Luckily for all the new ice cream lovers, his wife Louisa assumed control of the business with the help of her sons Frederick and Henry. For the next 14 years, Louisa Breyer devoted herself to the success of her husband's business. The retail stores flourished with sons Frederick and Henry as owners and supervising managers. Eventually, the family was overwhelmed by the increasing demand for Breyer's ice cream. No longer able to supply their customers by making ice cream in the small back room of their original store on Frankford, Louisa, Frederick, and Henry opened the family's first wholesale manufacturing plant, in Philadelphia.

As the old century gave way to the new one, Breyer's ice cream was in demand more than ever. By 1904 the family's wholesale manufacturing plant was inundated with orders for ice cream, and the family opened a second manufacturing plant on Cumberland Avenue. In an important innovation in the history of the product, the company began to freeze ice cream by using brine rather than salt and ice. This allowed manufacturers to lower the cost of producing the dessert.

With Louisa Breyer having already passed away, and Frederick dying in 1907, Henry became the sole owner of the firm. In 1908 he incorporated the business as Breyer Ice Cream Company. Soon afterward, he introduced the Breyer Pledge of Purity. Under the name of Henry Breyer, this pledge personally guaranteed that each container of Breyers product included all natural ingredients and the best ice cream available.

Breyer's ice cream grew more popular with each passing year. In 1914 the company announced that it was producing one million gallons annually, an accomplishment that was considered almost impossible at the time. Henry Breyer was a master organizer, and he arranged for the company's products to be delivered throughout Philadelphia and nearby communities by whatever means of transportation were available, including trolley freight, auto express, boat, railway express, and a vast collection of horse-drawn delivery wagons. With sales always increasing, the Breyer's Ice Cream Company factory on Cumberland Street needed more space. Rather than building a new plant, Henry Breyer continued to expand the firm's existing facilities. By 1918 the plant on Cumberland Street occupied an entire city block.

Even with the expansion of its space, the plant was operating both day and evening shifts. Henry Breyer brought together architects and designers to construct the largest ice cream manufacturing factory in the world. Opened in 1924, the plant operated at full capacity from its very first day. Confident that sales of Breyer's ice cream would continue to increase, Henry built new manufacturing plants in New York in 1925 and New Jersey in 1927. The Breyer's name was put up on the lights over Broadway Avenue in New York City to celebrate the opening of the manufacturing plant.

During the late 1920s, the company was incorporated into the National Dairy Products Corporation (NDPC), a holding company for famous brand-name products. Operating as a new division within NDPC, Breyers Ice Cream was able to take advantage of the marketing tools at National Dairy's disposal. As the 1920s came to a close, Breyers was still selling more ice cream than any other firm in the United States; however, the Great Depression of the 1930s, and the death of Henry Breyer in 1936, took a toll on the company, and sales decreased substantially.

With the onset of World War II, interest in Breyers ice cream products seemed to revive, and there was a resurgence in production. Working at Breyers during this time was also a distinct pleasure. During the late 1940s and early 1950s, Breyers held a daily ice cream break for its employees, with a different flavor each day. On Mondays the employees received novelty treats, such as hot buttered pecans or buttered almonds.

During the 1960s, Breyers ice cream was sold only in ice cream parlors, soda fountains, delis, and other service establishments. Operators at Breyers took orders over the phone, picked up the orders at the warehouse, placed them on a dolly, and had the ice cream delivered to the customers. Increased sales of ice cream led the NDPC to purchase Sealtest Ice Cream Company and merge it with Breyers; Sealtest had long been another favorite with American consumers.

By the early 1970s, the National Dairy Products Corporation had renamed itself Kraftco Corporation and begun to distribute Breyers in Florida and Georgia. By 1976 Kraftco Corporation had shortened its name to Kraft, Inc., and by the mid-1980s the company began to distribute Breyers ice cream to states throughout the midwestern and western United States. Even with increased distribution, Breyers remained committed to its Pledge of Purity. On one occasion, in order to make its mint chocolate chip ice cream all natural, the firm removed the green coloring that most people associated with the flavor of mint. Although customers were shocked when they opened containers labeled Breyers Mint Chocolate Chip and discovered what looked like vanilla ice cream, Breyers stuck by its pledge and refused to change the color.

Although Breyers' sales were good and the company introduced a new line of frozen desserts, including Light Ice Milk and frozen yogurt treats, Kraft management decided to sell Breyers Ice Cream Company to Unilever, Inc., an Anglo-Dutch multinational corporation that was operating such well-known consumer products companies as Lipton, Lever, and Cheeseborough. Unilever relocated Breyers headquarters to Green Bay, Wisconsin, and merged the firm with Gold Bond-Good Humor

Ice Cream Company to create Good Humor-Breyers Ice Cream Company in 1993.

Good Humor Ice Cream Company

The Good Humor Ice Cream Company was created in 1920 by Harry Burt, a candy maker working in Youngstown, Ohio. Burt had already created what he called the "Jolly Boy Sucker," however, he was unhappy with the name and changed it to the "Good Humor Sucker." Burt was an early advocate of health food and believed that his Good Humor Sucker not only tasted great, but was healthy food, too.

Burt soon added ice cream treats to his candy store. While working late in his store one summer evening, Burt created a chocolate coating for ice cream. The inventor gave a sample treat to his young daughter Ruth, who loved it; however, she told her father that the treat was too sloppy to eat.

Burt put wooden sticks in the ice cream to use as handles, at the suggestion of his son, Harry Jr. The wooden sticks became solidly frozen into the ice cream due to the ice crystals formed from the residue of water in the wood handles. Without delay, father and son went to sign an affidavit for his invention of the Good Humor Bar.

A natural genius in marketing, Burt hired 12 trucks to transport the Good Humor Bar to his customers' doorsteps, attaching bells on each of the trucks to draw attention to the product. Soon sales of Good Humor Bars were skyrocketing in Youngstown. As the reputation of the treat spread, Burt expanded his operation into Detroit and then Chicago. When Burt refused to be bullied by gangsters in Chicago who demanded protection money, they blew up some of his trucks with dynamite. The enormous publicity Burt garnered from the failed intimidation tactics helped make Good Humor ice cream Chicago's favorite dessert.

The coming of the Great Depression during the 1930s did not prevent Good Humor's distribution from expanding across the United States. Burt hired and intensively trained men who lived up to the image the Good Humor Ice Cream Company wanted to portray. Clean, white uniforms and a cheery manner became trademarks of the Good Humor Man. The qualifications for becoming a Good Humor Man included the ability to be friendly with children and look after their safety. Burt was so successful in molding the image of the Good Humor Man that by the 1950s such virtues as enthusiasm, dedication, friendliness, dependability, and honesty had come to be associated with his ice cream company. Newspaper reports of the local Good Humor Man rushing a baby to a hospital for treatment and breaking up a counterfeit money operation in Long Island, New York, only added to the image.

In 1961, Good Humor was purchased by Thomas J. Lipton, a subsidiary of Unilever, the Anglo-Dutch conglomerate. With Burt gone and the company now managed by non-family members, Good Humor Ice Cream Company went through a period of significant change. While the Good Humor Bar remained the company's primary product, such items as the Chocolate Eclair Bar and Strawberry Shortcake Bar were added to a growing product line. With the changing demographics of urban America, the friendly Good Humor Man who drove slowly through neighborhoods ringing his bells also began to disappear. As a result, the company focused more on selling its ice cream in supermarkets and grocery stores, and by the 1980s, the company was experiencing increased competition.

Unilever decided that what was lacking was critical mass, so in 1989, it acquired Gold Bond Ice Cream based in Green Bay, Wisconsin, and with it, the Popsicle family of frozen novelties, a major force in the market. The new company, Gold Bond-Good Humor, was poised to take a powerful leadership role in the category.

In 1993, Gold Bond-Good Humor capped off its aggressive acquisitions by adding Klondike to its impressive brand base. And, in that same year, the Gold Bond-Good Humor company took over Breyers Ice Cream Company to make Good Humor-Breyers the largest American producer of both ice cream and frozen novelties.

By combining Good Humor with Breyers Ice Cream Company, Unilever brought their most promising ice cream products under a single distribution and marketing strategy, a move that paid off in the early 1990s as the company became America's leading producer of ice cream and frozen novelties. By that time, the Good Humor-Breyers family also included the Klondike, Popsicle, and Sealtest brands, each of which had a long history of producing high quality, popular frozen dessert products. As the twentieth century drew to a close, Unilever man-

agement hoped that its Good Humor-Breyers Ice Cream Company could capture an even larger share of the $10 billion ice cream and frozen dessert market in the United States. With its popular brands and the strong financial backing of Unilever, the likelihood of increased success for Good Humor-Breyers is very realistic.

Further Reading:

Bauer, Bob, "Good Humor-Breyers Adds 50 Items," *Supermarket News,* February 6, 1995, p. 32.

Benjamin, Ben, "In the Ice Cream R&D Trenches," *Food Processing,* September 1993, p. 95.

Elliot, Stuart, "Four Agencies Get Big Food Accounts," *New York Times,* February 13, 1995, pp. C7, D7.

——, "Ogilvy & Mather Named to Breyers Account," *New York Times,* June 7, 1994, p. C4.

Martinez, Julia C., "Kraft Names Frozen Desserts Division after Long-Running Breyers Ice Cream," *Philadelphia Inquirer,* August 23, 1993, p. 8.

Ramirez, Anthony, "Good Humor-Breyers Accounts," *New York Times,* October 31, 1994, p. C7.

Rosenbaum, Gail, "Novel Ideas: Two Good-Humored Brits in Green Bay Keep the Novelty Market on Its Toes," *Dairy Foods,* June 1992, p. 39.

Spethmann, Betsy, "Brand Builders," *Brandweek,* February 20, 1995, p. 18.

Warner, Fars, "Good Humor Pulls into Supermarkets," *Adweek's Marketing Week,* March 9, 1992, p. 6.

—Thomas Derdak

Gould Electronics, Inc.

35129 Curtis Boulevard
Eastlake, Ohio 44095-4001
U.S.A.
(216) 953-5000
Fax: (216) 953-5050

Wholly Owned Subsidiary of Japan Energy Corporation
Incorporated: 1928 as Gould Storage Battery
Employees: 3,000
Sales: $280 million
SICs: 3497 Metal Foil & Leaf; 3674 Semiconductors &
Related Devices

Gould Electronics, Inc., is a designer and manufacturer of materials and components for use in the electrical and electronics markets. Headquartered in Eastlake, Ohio, the company is a wholly owned subsidiary of Japan Energy Corporation, a diverse corporation with interests in petroleum, specialty metals, electronics, biotechnology, and pharmaceuticals. Following an extensive history in the automotive battery market, Gould diversified during the 1970s and 1980s, but incurred significant debt that led to its acquisition. In 1993, Gould Inc. was liquidated and a new company called Gould Electronics, Inc., was established.

The origin of Gould Electronics dated to the late 1800s. Charles J. Gould started a small foundry to forge couplers for railroad cars. During its early years, Gould Coupler was a successful business and continued to add other products to its line, including batteries for railcars. When a fire destroyed Gould's plant in 1895, he rebuilt his business on a much larger scale and established a town around his factory. The new community of Depew was founded on 1,300 acres outside Buffalo, New York, and named after Chauncey Depew, president of New York Central Railroad and Gould's biggest customer.

The growing market for storage batteries prompted Gould to expand his product line and change the business name to Gould Storage Battery Corporation. Gould produced storage batteries for use by trains, electric utilities, subways, elevators, and farms. Gould also became a principal supplier of submarine batteries to the United States Navy. In addition, Gould developed a battery for the rapidly growing automotive industry. By 1930, the company had become an established name in the battery industry and was one of the largest manufacturers of industrial batteries in the country.

Over 900 miles away in St. Paul, Minnesota, another company was carving a successful niche in the battery business during this time. The Electric Manufacturing Company was originally a distributor of electrical accessories, but after a man named Lytton J. Shields bought the company, he guided it into the automotive battery distributorship business. Realizing that the real success came from the manufacturing end of the business, Shields pursued an affordable way to make lead grids and connectors for batteries. After two years of research, the company went into battery production and was renamed the National Lead Battery Company.

Unfortunately, the combination of a small customer base, a fire which destroyed the battery factory, and a recession after World War I left National Lead Battery Company with great financial problems. Shields was faced with the difficult decision of whether to close the business or to rebuild. A legend said that Shields and his associates decided to toss a coin: heads, they would rebuild; tails, they would give up. According to the story, heads was tossed.

Shields began to build his business again with determination. To increase sales, Shields needed a customer with a national business presence. He pursued Sewell Avery, then president of Montgomery Ward, and arranged a meeting with him to visit National Lead Battery. Shields hired men to work just for the afternoon of the very important meeting and had only enough materials to keep the production line moving for a few hours. The staged production line was convincing and Avery signed a contract with National Lead Battery. This first national customer helped National Lead Battery emerge from financial ruin.

The battery company's next big success came when it developed a way to produce replacement batteries for $5 to $10. At this time, replacement batteries normally retailed for as much as $40. As a result of its significantly lower prices, National Battery received national contracts with Goodrich, Goodyear, and Phillips, making it one of the largest producers of replacement batteries. Shields established plants throughout the country and pursued growth through a series of acquisitions during the 1920s. Taking ''Lead'' out of its name, the company was known simply as National Battery.

In 1930, a patent brought the companies of Gould Storage Battery Corporation and National Battery together. Always looking for new business opportunities, Shields' interest was drawn to a fiberglass method of insulating battery plates for which Gould Storage Battery Corporation held the patent. Shields saw an application for this process in the production of automotive batteries. The ambitious Shields acquired Gould Storage Battery Corporation for $225,000. The fiberglass separator batteries were perfected for automobiles, and, in 1936, Shields introduced a significant advancement in the industry. The Kathanode Glass-Klad battery was guaranteed to last ''as long as you own your car.'' At his death in 1936, Shields left behind a national company with branches in 16 cities and seven plants across the country.

However, in the late 1930s, competition in the replacement battery continued to increase, while demand did not. To continue to build the company, Shields' successor, Albert H. Daggett, expanded the business into the industrial battery market. With the advent of World War II, the industrial division of National Battery grew into a major supplier of batteries for submarines and aircraft. Industrial battery sales doubled, and, after the war, the company had sales of almost $25 million and earnings over $890,000. In addition, the acquisitions of other battery manufacturers doubled the size of the company; in 1948 revenues grew to $50 million and earnings to $3.1 million. The company also changed its name to Gould-National Batteries, Inc., to capitalize on Gould's past focus in the industrial market.

Gould-National Battery struggled during the 1950s and 1960s. Costs grew faster than margins in replacement batteries, and the industrial market slowed after the war. In an effort to increase market share, the company began to diversify. In 1958 Gould-National acquired from White Machine Works a group of companies that manufactured parts for internal combustion engines. This purchase began Gould-National's presence in automotive engine manufacturing, a presence the company developed further by acquiring another engine parts manufacturer called Wilkening Manufacturing Company in 1960. Wilkening Manufacturing Company developed a patented heat-shaping process for making piston rings and later provided equipment rings for aircraft engines. With the acquisition of Cyclone Filter Corporation, Gould-National entered the air and fuel filter markets, expanding their business to make it a supplier to store brands like Montgomery Ward. The company also branched out of the industrial battery business to develop a presence in the alkaline battery and rechargeable battery markets.

In the late 1960s demand for automotive batteries continued to decrease because improvements in technology and the use of alternators had extended battery life twofold. Earnings at Gould-National also continued to fall, and the company needed to reevaluate its business strategy. After the retirement of Daggett, the board hired William T. Ylvisaker as the new chief executive officer. In his new position he worked to eliminate debt, sell unprofitable businesses, reduce inventories, and decentralize division operations. Ylvisaker's other goal was to diversify and move the company away from its reliance on the battery market. Following this strategy, Gould-National merged with Cleveland-based Clevite Corporation. Clevite Corporation manufactured precision automotive parts, batteries, and electronic systems and components. The merger resulted in Gould, Inc. In 1969, the company reported total sales of $342 million and earnings over $12 million. Other smaller acquisitions, which included a maker of heating equipment parts, a smelter and refiner of lead, and a maker of specialized electric motors, helped Gould to diversify. Another major acquisition in 1976 helped Gould strengthen its position in electronics: I-T-E Imperial Corporation focused on distribution, transmission, and control of electricity, and manufactured hydraulics and fluid power systems.

From 1969 to 1976, Gould acquired 20 companies, including makers of electronic controls, computer output devices, battery-related equipment, medical instrumentation, and electronic test and measurement equipment. It transformed itself into a major electronics company, ranking in size among the top 150 U.S. corporations. Gould now had 35,000 employees and sales of $1.2 billion. Its markets had grown throughout the United States and into Japan and Europe. Its business mix was 55 percent electric, 30 percent industrial, and 15 percent batteries. The

company moved into a new corporate headquarters in Rolling Meadows, Illinois, just outside of Chicago. In Ylvisaker's final step in transforming Gould into a high-tech electronics company, he divested Gould's industrial group of businesses and sold the company's battery operations. Money from these sales was used to further strengthen the business as an electronics company. Gould's electronic business now made up 75 percent of sales.

The rapid transition from batteries to electronics did come at a cost to the company. According to a 1987 article in *Industry Week,* Gould divested businesses from 1980 to 1984 with more than $1 billion in earnings. Although the revenues reached a high of $2.2 billion in 1980, the following years Gould found itself losing money. Over half of Gould's upper management left in the late 1970s because of personality conflicts with Ylvisaker, and in 1984 David Simpson, president and chief operating officer, resigned. He was replaced by James McDonald, a former IBM manufacturing executive.

McDonald was hired to reorganize the company and strengthen its financial position. During the late 1980s, Gould had more than $270 million in losses caused by excessive spending and failed business ventures. According to *Forbes* magazine in 1987, Ylvisaker bought a Florida real estate development in the late 1970s and invested over $80 million in the property to build a polo club, one of his favorite interests. However, interest rates rose and land values dropped, contributing to almost $50 million in losses for Gould on this speculation. Gould also incurred additional losses in its defense business. Ylvisaker replaced former Gould defense executives with his friends. His inexperienced colleagues badly underestimated production costs on a contract with the Air Force. They also bid on a fixed-price contract to produce a field radio for the Navy and Marines before plans for the project were completed. Gould never did produce a radio. To help lessen this debt, Gould sold its defense contracting business. Under McDonald's guidance, Gould also reduced employment by more than 9,000 people, cut corporate staff by over 50 percent, sold two corporate aircraft and three corporate apartments. By 1986, the board encouraged the resignation of Ylvisaker, and, after he stepped down, McDonald took over his position.

After four years of divestment and reorganization, Gould had brought in billions of dollars and paid off or established reserves for almost all its debt, making it an attractive company to purchase. The buyer emerged through a joint venture with Gould. In 1988, Nippon Mining Co. Ltd. had become Gould's agent for selling fuses in Japan, and the two companies later formed a computer marketing alliance. Nippon Mining Co. Ltd. was Japan's largest non-ferrous metals smelting company with annual sales of $6.5 billion. Nippon offered to buy Gould for over $1 billion dollars, a purchase price double the book value of Gould. The deal was too good for stockholders to resist, and Gould took the offer immediately. McDonald resigned from the position of chairman and CEO just hours after the acquisition, as one of the largest stockholders in Gould with over 240,000 shares. McDonald was replaced by a veteran Gould executive named C. David Ferguson.

The acquisition of Gould made Nippon Mining into a major electronics companies. It became one of the 50 largest non-U.S.

electronics companies in the world. Nippon was particularly interested in Gould's copper foil production capability. Gould was the world leader in copper foil production, offering the largest selection of standard and specialty copper foils. Nippon had studied the world market's growing demand for copper foil, which was used in the production of circuit boards, and saw great potential in Gould's foil production plant in Eastlake, Ohio. As a result of this focus, Nippon moved Gould's headquarters to Eastlake.

Nippon Mining merged with Kyodo Oil Company in 1992 and formed Nikko Kyodo Co. Ltd. Investing $150 million in Gould, Nikko Kyodo concentrated its efforts on restructuring Gould and renovating its copper foil production facilities in the United States. However Nikko Kyodo had overestimated the demand for copper foil and circuit materials. Prices fell and Nikko Kyodo was forced to cut Gould's workforce from over 7,000 people down to just 2,600. In addition, Nikko Kyodo sold Gould's minicomputer business. According to a 1993 article in *The New York Times,* Gould had not made a profit since it was acquired and in 1992 lost $70 million. The financial problems that burdened Gould during the 1980s apparently continued even after new management tried to revive its balance sheet.

After consecutive years of operating losses, Gould Inc. was liquidated in 1993. It was estimated that Nikko Kyodo would need approximately 90 billion yen ($857 million) to pay off the debts incurred by Gould Inc. and its U.S.-based holding company called Nippon Mining U.S. Inc., which was also dissolved. Nikko Kyodo stated that they did not regret buying Gould because the area of high-technology remained their main focus for the 21st century. The company also reported that, as the computer market recovered, they expected copper foil demand for circuit boards to increase. With capital of $630 million, Nikko Kyodo established two new companies in the United States to take over the business of Gould Inc.: Gould Electronics Inc., still headquartered in Eastlake, was formed to continue production of copper foil for printed circuit boards, and Gould Instrument Systems Inc., based in Valley View, Ohio, was established to make test and measurement equipment. Although Gould Electronics and Gould Instrument Systems were newly formed, their roots definitely were well established in the history of Gould.

In December 1993 Nikko Kyodo changed its name to Japan Energy Corporation, to reflect the company's commitment to energy supply, new business growth, and technological development. According to Japan Energy Corporation's 1994 annual report, the businesses transferred to Gould Electronics and Gould Instrument Systems had promising growth areas and good operating performance in their first stage of operation.

Further Reading:

"Ex-IBM Exec. Replaces Gould President," *Electronic News,* July 23, 1984, p. 60.
Furukawa, Tsukasa, "Gould to Pan Out; 2 Firms to Be Formed," *American Metal Market,* September 13, 1993, p. 5.
——, "Gould Unit Divided by Parent," *American Metal Market,* February 8, 1994, p. 6.
——, "Nippon Mining Plans to Invest $150M in Restructuring Gould," *American Metal Market,* April 29, 1992, p. 5.
"Gould Intends to Sell Its Battery Operation," *American Metal Market,* April 14, 1983, p. 1.
Greenberg, Jonathan, "Getting Rid of a Good Thing," *Forbes,* May 9, 1983, p. 112.
Moskal, Brian S., "Old Story—with a Twist: Mini Super Is a Key Product for Electronics Maker," *Industry Week,* May 4, 1987, p. 46.
"A New President to Fit Gould's New Shape," *Business Week,* July 30, 1984, pp. 78–79.
Oneal, Michael, "Gould Is So Thin You Can Hardly See It," *Business Week,* August 29, 1988, p. 74.
——, "McDonald's the Name, Fixing Gould Is the Game," *Business Week,* July 28, 1986, pp. 77–78.
Pollack, Andrew, "$865 Million Write-Off Over Gould," *New York Times,* September 8, 1993, p. D3.
Weiner, Steve, "Taking the Pledge," *Forbes,* June 29, 1987, p. 41.
A Young Company with Deep Roots—A History of Gould Inc., Rolling Meadows, Ill.: Gould Inc., 1984.
Zipper, Stuart, "Gould Agrees to $1B Takeover by Nippon Mining," *Electronic News,* September 5, 1988, p. 11.
——, "Gould Reorganizes After Sale," *Electronic News,* October 10, 1988, p. 23.

—Beth Watson Highman

healthcare services. He acted as president and chief executive of that company's European operations for nine years and last served as president of the overall holding company, American Medical Holdings, Inc. Burleson left American Medical Holdings in 1989, shortly before he created GranCare. Burleson was joined by Roy Christensen. Christensen had founded Beverly Enterprises, the nation's largest nursing home operator.

GranCare was created with the help of venture capital funding. The enterprise started out with annual revenues of $92.6 million garnered from 39 health care centers that supported about 5,200 beds. During 1991 the company managed to snare a few other small nursing home operators, which provided insight into its central goal. Management hoped to eventually acquire a broad network of nursing home facilities and related care enterprises. The goal was to improve their profitability by achieving economies of scale related to paperwork and administrative tasks, purchasing, and other operational burdens. To that end, GranCare completed its first major acquisition in 1991 when it bought 23 nursing homes from ARA Living Centers Inc. By late 1991, after consolidating all of its operations, GranCare was operating 60 long-term healthcare facilities that supported nearly 8,000 beds.

GranCare generated revenues of about $175 million in 1991, $3.8 million of which was net earnings. Those figures thrust the fledgling start-up to the ranks of a mid-size corporation in little more than a year after its inception. Because of the acquisitions, however, GranCare had accrued a heavy load of debt. To diminish its liabilities and generate more cash for acquisitions, GranCare offered its stock to the public in November of 1991. The company sold 2.7 million shares at $10.25 each, which pumped nearly $27 million into its coffers. Capital from that and subsequent offerings would be used by GranCare during the next few years to transform the company into a leading U.S. provider of care for the elderly.

During the first part of 1992 GranCare worked to streamline its operations. It squelched its acquisition program, with the exception of a few additions to its network of nursing homes and the integration of four institutional pharmacies. By mid-1992 the California-based company was operating 68 nursing homes in California, Wisconsin, Colorado, Arizona, Illinois, and South Dakota, as well as the four pharmacies. GranCare's extension into the pharmacy business reflected an important aspect of Burleson's long-term strategy. As he built GranCare's nursing home network he planned to establish divisions within the company that would provide specialty medical services to and through the facilities. The pharmacies supplied prescription drugs, administered computerized medical records, provided consulting services to GranCare customers, supplied wound care, and offered intravenous therapy services. The division also sold medical goods, including orthotic and prosthetic equipment.

Late in 1992 GranCare made its second major acquisition. It purchased Professional Health Care Management Inc. of Ann Arbor, Michigan. That buyout brought 17 long-term health care facilities into its network, which added approximately 2,500 beds to GranCare's total. It also tagged a fat $65 million onto its revenue base. As a bonus, the acquisition added to GranCare's rehabilitation services and gave it an ownership interest in an

GranCare, Inc.

One Ravinia Drive, Suite 1500
Atlanta, Georgia 30346
U.S.A.
(404) 393-0199
Fax: (404) 698-8199

Public Company
Incorporated: 1990
Employees: 15,000
Sales: $549 million
Stock Exchanges: New York
SICs: 8051 Skilled Nursing Care Facilities; 8052 Intermediate Care Facilities; 8059 Nursing and Personal Care Facilities, Not Elsewhere Classified

GranCare, Inc., is a leading U.S. provider of comprehensive healthcare services for the elderly. The company operates nursing care facilities and pharmacy operations and provides services related to contract management, home health care, and assisted living. After its formation in 1990, GranCare grew explosively through mergers and acquisitions. By mid-1995 the organization boasted, among other credits, 17,400 beds in its healthcare network.

Although it was incorporated in 1990, GranCare is the successor to American Medical Services, Inc., a nursing home company formed in the late 1960s. American Medical grew slowly before it acquired a string of nursing homes in the 1980s. During the 1980s, in fact, the operation expanded at a rate of about 20 percent to 30 percent annually. Transworld Corp., a hotel and food services company based in New York City, purchased the operation in 1986 for approximately $93 million. By 1987 American Medical was operating 30 nursing homes in four states: 11 in Wisconsin, 14 in California, 4 in Colorado, and 1 in Illinois. The company was generating annual sales of about $90 million by the late 1980s.

In 1990 American Medical Services merged with a small nursing home outfit called HostMasters; the resulting company was called GranCare. These three major changes—the buyout of American Medical, the merger, and the formation of GranCare—were spearheaded by Gene E. Burleson, who became chief executive of GranCare. The 49-year-old Burleson was a healthcare industry veteran. From 1974 to 1989 Burleson worked for American Medical International, Inc., a provider of x-ray services operation. Shortly before the buyout, GranCare acquired an interest in five skilled nursing centers and two retirement centers. Also in 1992, GranCare launched a home health care operation to provide skilled nursing services, therapy, and home health aides. GranCare sold off three of its facilities during the year, giving it a year-end total of about 85 locations in seven states with 11,389 beds.

GranCare generated sales of $373 million in 1992 and $13.2 million in net income. The gains were largely the result of the sheer size of the company's network of nursing homes and care centers. Importantly, though, these numbers also reflected healthy gains in GranCare's specialty medical services and pharmacy divisions. Specialty medical services, which included services like rehabilitation therapy and skilled nursing care, accounted for about 20 percent of total company revenues in 1991. In 1992 that figure rose to more than 40 percent and would continue to grow to 50 percent by 1994. At the same time, GranCare's pharmacy division increased its sales to about $93 million in 1992. The importance of the add-on profit centers was that they generally offered greater profit margins than traditional nursing home fees.

GranCare intensified its acquisition drive in 1993. In January Burleson purchased Coordinated Home Health, Inc., Coordinated Nursing Services, Inc., and Infusion Plus, Inc. Those additions served to bolster GranCare's thriving specialty medical services. Also in January, the company bought out Colter Village, which consisted of a retirement center and a skilled nursing facility. A few months later GranCare picked up Bella Vita, a 126-bed skilled nursing facility in Colorado, and Pacific Therapies, Inc., which provided physical, occupational, and speech therapy services. In April GranCare added Patient Therapy Systems Inc., a therapy bed and services company, and four skilled nursing facilities located in Wisconsin. Other 1993 acquisitions included Brim Medical Equipment and Supplies, Inc., an enteral and urological supply company. Those purchases helped push GranCare's 1993 sales past the half-billion-dollar mark.

Also boosting GranCare's sales during 1993 were important additions to its flourishing pharmacy division. In June GranCare bought Winyah Dispensary, LTC, which served the institutional market for pharmaceuticals. Then, in September, GranCare purchased Medication Delivery Systems, Inc., another institutional pharmacy. Finally, in December GranCare made a major acquisition when it scooped up CompuPharm, Inc. Because of the size and name recognition associated with the new holding, GranCare renamed its pharmacy division CompuPharm. Going into 1994, GranCare's CompuPharm subsidiary consisted of a coast-to-coast network of 13 pharmacies that were serving institutions containing 57,000 beds.

GranCare's expansion and profits during the early 1990s were the result of management's long-term strategy of building a formidable nationwide network of healthcare services for the elderly. Its success was augmented, however, by demographic trends that were shaping the industry. Most notable among those trends was the growth in the number of Americans aged 65 and over. As the size of that segment of the population grew during the early and mid-1990s, so did GranCare's potential client base. In 1990 the percentage of Americans aged 65 to 74

that were receiving long-term care was about 1.4 percent. The share for the 75 to 84 age group was more than six percent. Those figures were expected to grow at an increasing rate through the turn of the century. For example, the U.S. census bureau estimated that the number of people aged 75 and over would increase from about 13 million in 1990 to about 17 million, or 6.1 percent of the population, by the year 2000.

Thus, GranCare was building its network for a rapidly growing market. Furthermore, it was taking advantage of the trend away from hospital care and toward managed and home care, which would allow it to benefit disproportionately from emerging demographic trends. To that end, GranCare planned to increasingly shift its focus from traditional nursing home care, in which patients typically stayed for years, to post-acute care, which typically ranged from a few days to a few weeks. GranCare offered the advantage of lower costs at its facilities, compared to inpatient hospital costs.

GranCare continued to buy new companies in 1994, though at a slower pace. Most of its acquisitions were additions to its profitable pharmaceutical division. In March it purchased PPCP, Inc., another institutional pharmacy services company. Similarly, Burleson oversaw the buyout of Merit Pharmacy, Inc., about a month later. In July, GranCare picked up Long Term Care Pharmaceutical Services Corporation, an institutional pharmacy services company in Indiana. That major buyout was followed by the acquisition of Ricketts Drug, Inc., in Virginia. GranCare also acquired interests in seven South Carolina long-term healthcare facilities. At the same time, the company initiated a restructuring effort designed to consolidate and streamline operations and shake up top management. The company jettisoned several nonperforming units, including its rehabilitation operation. Christensen resigned as chairman—he was replaced by Burleson—and GranCare's chief financial officer resigned. Finally, GranCare's headquarters were relocated to Atlanta, Georgia.

GranCare boosted sales to about $550 million in 1994, about $15.2 million of which was net income. Thus, in four years it had enlarged its revenue base more than five-fold. However, the headiest growth was yet to come. In April of 1995, GranCare purchased Cornerstone Health Management, a contract management firm based in Dallas, Texas. That company specialized in the implementation and management of geriatric specialty programs, including post-acute skilled nursing and mental health services. Importantly, that purchase increased GranCare's toehold in the rapidly growing contract management industry. By mid-1995 GranCare would be operating 105 contract management programs (through which it contracted to provide specialty services) in acute care hospitals in 20 states.

Much more important than the Cornerstone buyout was GranCare's announcement in May that it was going to acquire Indiana-based Evergreen Healthcare, Inc. Evergreen was the largest company GranCare had ever bought; it operated 64 long-term care facilities with more than 7,500 beds in nine midwestern and southeastern states. The organization was similar to GranCare in that it offered subacute, rehabilitation, and pharmacy services. It also provided specialized services for diseases like Alzheimer's and Huntington's through five dedicated units. The acquisition was completed in July, making GranCare the sixth largest publicly traded long-term care facility in the United States. Because of that merger, GranCare's revenues in 1995 were expected to surge into the $750-million range. "This virtually doubles our size, and it gives us a more significant presence in the Southeast," said Kay Brown, GranCare senior vice president, in the May 4, 1995, *Atlanta Constitution.*

By mid-1995 GranCare was operating 137 nursing care facilities with 17,500 beds located in 15 states. About 70 percent of its revenues were coming from skilled nursing care services and subacute care, which included rehabilitation therapy, dietary, therapeutic, and other services. About 22 percent of its sales were attributable to pharmacy services, which had expanded to include 24 full-service institutional pharmacies and three satellite offices. Contract management fees accounted for about four percent of sales, while home healthcare and assisted living services each made up about one percent. Although the company was shouldering a relatively heavy debt load, Burleson planned to sustain his strategy of growth through acquisition, and to capitalize on demographic and industry trends in the long-term care industry.

Principal Subsidiaries: CompuPharm, Inc.

Further Reading:

Brown, Ken, "GranCare Announces Reorganization, Corporate Relocation," *PR Newswire,* August 17, 1994.

Burleson, Gene E., "Athans Joins GranCare as Chief Operating Officer," *PR Newswire,* November 4, 1993.

——, "GranCare to Acquire 17 Facilities Representing 25 Percent Capacity Increase," *PR Newswire,* September 17, 1992.

Cole, Benjamin Mark, "Fledgling Nursing-Home Operator GranCare Goes Public, Immediately Bucks Bear Market," *Los Angeles Business Journal,* December 2, 1991, p. 29.

Conroy, William, "American Medical Buys Illinois Nursing Home for $4.6 Million," *Business Journal-Milwaukee,* May 18, 1987, p. 25.

DeWitt, John, "Nursing Giant Aims to Expand, Fine-Tune Focus," *Arizona Business Gazette,* November 17, 1994, p. 1.

GranCare, Inc., New York: Smith Barney, July 28, 1995.

GranCare, Inc.—Teamed Up and Ready to Roll, New York: Salomon Brothers, July 1995.

Gross, Neil, "Kiss That Old Patient Goodbye," *Business Week,* June 26, 1995.

Miller, Andy, "GranCare Buying Nursing Home Firm," *Atlanta Constitution,* May 4, 1995, p. 1E.

—Dave Mote

Grand Metropolitan PLC

20 St. James's Square
London SW1Y 4RR
England
71-321-6000
Fax: 71-321-6001

Public Company
Incorporated: 1934
Employees: 87,163
Sales: £8.12 billion (US$12.49 billion)
Stock Exchanges: London
SICs: 6790 Miscellaneous Investing

Grand Metropolitan PLC is primarily in the business of producing and selling brand name food and alcohol products, but also retains holdings in vision care and fast food from its more diversified days. It is one of the top three wine and spirits companies in the world and is an international food giant as well. Brands controlled by Grand Metropolitan include Bailey's, Burger King, Green Giant, Haagen-Dazs, Old El Paso, Pillsbury, Progresso, and Smirnoff.

Born in 1910, Maxwell Joseph left school at the age of 16 to begin a career with local real estate agents in north London. He was paid the equivalent of six dollars per week for selling houses and other property. Shortly after mastering the intricate sales techniques and valuation skills of a successful realtor, Joseph established his own property firm in 1926. That firm has grown to be Grand Metropolitan, now one of Britain's largest and most diversified companies.

Throughout the late 1920s and the 1930s, Joseph attempted to purchase properties that would bring a high return when resold by his firm. Because the English economy was in the midst of a depression, however, there were few prospective buyers and even fewer who could offer the kind of money that would meet his profit criteria. The advent of World War II further deflated Joseph's hopes for a prosperous business.

Joseph's firm finally began to move toward success after the War, with the purchase of the damaged Mandeville Hotel in the Marylebone district of London in 1946. Throughout the 1950s and 1960s Grand Metropolitan expanded through the development and purchase of new hotels. Joseph later admitted that he bought these hotels for "chicken feed." "Between 1950 and 1965," he said, "there wasn't a real estate man in the country who knew the value of hotels." Joseph did; moreover, he understood what they would be worth in the future.

Grand Metropolitan's base of operations widened as Joseph continued to purchase more profitable and more prestigious hotels. The first such acquisition was London's Mount Royal Hotel, acquired in 1957 for $2.8 million. Grand Metropolitan quickly followed that takeover with purchases of a number of other luxury hotels throughout Europe. In Paris, Joseph purchased the Lotti Hotel; in Cannes, the Carlton Hotel; and in Copenhagen, the Hotel d'Angleterre. By the end of the 1960s, Grand Metropolitan had established a significant presence in the European hotel industry.

Because of the financial success of the Grand Metropolitan hotels, Maxwell Joseph felt confident enough to embark on a new strategy of diversification. He initiated the purchase of Express Dairies in 1969. The two-part purchase was completed in 1970 with approval from the shareholders of Grand Metropolitan and the former owners of Express Dairies. Because this purchase had received firm shareholder support, Grand Metropolitan went on to purchase Berni Inns, Ron Nagle, and Truman Hanburg. Of these varied acquisitions, the Truman Hanburg deal was the most significant because it was Grand Metropolitan's first brewery. This particular acquisition also involved the largest takeover deal in Britain up to that time—the purchase price amounted to £400 million.

Seeking a financially equivalent takeover in 1972, Joseph purchased the Watney-Mann brewery. His purchase of Watney was fully justified in terms of company strategy. Grand Metropolitan already had a 49 percent stake in Carlsberg, a Danish brewer. Stanley Grinstead, the deputy chairman of Grand Metropolitan, and Maxwell Joseph were concerned that although they owned almost half of Carlsberg, they had no control over what brands were brewed. At the time, Carlsberg brewed only the Carlsberg and Tuborg brands of beer. Grand Metropolitan felt that if it wished to expand in the beer market, it must acquire and control a less parochial beer company such as Watney-Mann.

Despite the future positive effects that all of these extensive purchases could have produced, Grand Metropolitan had incurred a large debt, particularly as a result of the purchases of Truman Hanburg, Express Dairies, and Watney-Mann. There were management failures at Watney-Mann which exposed Grand Metropolitan to severe financial losses. Furthermore, the company's expansion into Italy and France could not be effectively controlled from London. The company learned that it had to send special advisers into the foreign country in order to establish partnerships and gain a share of the market—but that, too, was a costly lesson.

In 1974 the company's debt peaked at £528 million, and Grand Metropolitan was forced to sell some of its smaller businesses to decrease that debt. For example, Joseph decided to sell the Royal Manhattan Hotel of New York and close the Vandenheuvel Brewery, which was one of Watney-Mann's three breweries in Belgium; neither enterprise had been particularly profitable. To further decrease debt, Grand Metropolitan also sold its shares in Carlsberg beer for £5.39 million. By these and other similar moves, Grand Metropolitan began to reduce debt substantially and to reposition itself for a more careful acquisition strategy.

Grand Metropolitan's 1977 purchase of a 20 percent share in Pleasurama, a casino operator, was one of its most important of the decade. Pleasurama and Grand Metropolitan already operated a joint venture, the A.M Casino, an enterprise located in Grand Metropolitan's Ritz Hotel in London. With the Pleasurama purchase, Joseph increased shareholder's equity above the level of debt for the first time since 1969.

Joseph had passed the usual retirement age of 65 in 1975, but he had refused to relinquish his chairmanship. He continued to distrust younger and less experienced associates with business decisions, and he insisted on personally approving all major transactions. Under Joseph's guidance, Grand Metropolitan embarked in the late 1970s on a second series of acquisitions in which "leveraged buyouts," takeovers that incur huge debt, were carefully avoided. Occasionally, too, Joseph disposed of companies that were, in fact, profitable. Grand Metropolitan had purchased the Savoy Hotel Group from Trafalgar House in 1978. The Savoy Group was profitable, but it yielded only a 2 percent return. Joseph sold the Savoy Group to the Rothschild Investment Trust for £8.4 million, and Grand Metropolitan subsequently invested in other higher-yielding businesses.

For many years the Liggett Group, an American tobacco and liquor company, distributed Grand Metropolitan's J&B brand Scotch whisky in the United States. In 1980, on reported sales equivalent to $6.2 billion, Grand Metropolitan made a $415 million tender offer for Liggett—a move that also signalled a change in Joseph's attitude toward the American market, which he had in the past avoided. In purchasing Liggett, Grand Metropolitan would also gain control of Austin Nichols, a Liggett subsidiary well-established in the American liquor market. Shortly after Grand Metropolitan had made its bid, however, Liggett sold Austin Nichols to Pernod Ricard for $97.5 million. The Paddington Corporation, the Liggett subsidiary responsible for marketing J&B Scotch, therefore became Grand Metropolitan's main concern in the tender offer.

Liggett's management was strongly opposed to a takeover by Grand Metropolitan, fearing above all that Joseph would replace them with managers from Grand Metropolitan. As Liggett mounted a legal battle to thwart Grand Metropolitan, Standard Brands entered a competing bid of $513 million. Determined to succeed, Grand Metropolitan raised its tender offer to $590 million—a price that Standard Brands could not top and Liggett shareholders could not refuse.

In a separate, less successful bid, Grand Metropolitan failed to gain control over the Coral Leisure Group during 1980. The company's bid, valued at £85 million, was opposed by many shareholders who lacked confidence in Coral's ability to generate profit or future growth. Yet the decision to abandon Coral was, in effect made by the English Monopolies Commission, which ruled against the takeover.

The continued involvement of the Monopolies Commission in Grand Metropolitan's affairs brought to light an increasingly urgent shortcoming in the company's position: Grand Metropolitan had overemphasized its growth within Britain. With nearly 90 percent of its profits generated domestically, Grand

Metropolitan would face other charges of monopoly control over certain markets if it continued to invest in British enterprises. The company's overexposure within the British economy became problematic in 1980, when the country entered a period of recession. In response, Grand Metropolitan inaugurated three- and four-year management plans, intended to improve short-term planning until the company could diversify geographically.

Grand Metropolitan achieved greater financial stability in 1981, largely due to Liggett's success in selling Bailey's Original Irish Cream and J&B Scotch in the United States. Increased sales of these products justified larger advertising budgets for them, which, in turn, helped to maintain their increased market shares. In order to derive greater profits from liquor sales in Britain, Grand Metropolitan attempted to enter the retail liquor business. But because the British government did not permit producers and distributors of liquor to own retail outlets, Grand Metropolitan was forced to adopt a different strategy: the company subleased its bars and restaurants to "outside" management, and thus circumvented the restrictions, while drawing at least a portion of the profits earned from retail liquor and food sales.

By 1982 Grand Metropolitan owned 66 hotels in Europe and the Middle East. That year, the company agreed to purchase the Inter-Continental Hotel chain, consisting of 110 hotels, from Pan American World Airways in exchange for $500 million, Grand Metropolitan's Forum Hotel chain, and several other smaller hotel properties. The Monopolies Commission, however, became so involved in this transaction that Grand Metropolitan at last decided to end its concentration on European markets. Thereafter, the company redirected investment capital to the largely unrestricted markets of the United States, where it established an American subsidiary called GrandMet USA Inc. This company was given direct responsibility for the operations of Liggett and three new companies: Western Dairy Products, in California; Express Foods Inc., in Vermont; and Dry Milks Inc., in Kentucky.

In Britain, Grand Metropolitan divested itself of both marginally performing subsidiaries and companies the operations of which were considered peripheral to Grand Metropolitan's core industries. CC Soft Drinks Ltd., a subsidiary that bottled and distributed Coca-Cola in southern England, was sold to the Coca-Cola Export Corporation in 1984. The following year Grand Metropolitan sold its Express Dairy subsidiary to Northern Foods for £51 million. Northern Foods subsequently purchased four other Grand Metropolitan dairies and a distributor, reducing Grand Metropolitan's share of the dairy market by one-third. Proceeds from these divestments were used to strengthen Grand Metropolitan's hotel and entertainment division, which in 1985 purchased the profitable Mecca Leisure group for £95 million.

During 1985, however, Grand Metropolitan again altered its corporate strategy. Because they correctly anticipated the phenomenal growth of health care services in the United States, the company's board decided to make investments in that industry a company priority. Grand Metropolitan acquired Quality Care Inc., a large home health care and medical equipment company, and soon afterwards purchased an interest in Pearl Health Services. After it was taken over by Grand Metropolitan, Pearl established a large chain of dental and eye care centers intended to exploit opportunities in the American market for medical services in shopping malls and retail thoroughfares.

Grand Metropolitan appointed a new chief executive officer, Allen Sheppard, in 1987. Under the guidance of Sheppard and his heir apparent, CEO George J. Bull (who had spent three decades at the International Distillers & Vintners Ltd. subsidiary), Grand Metropolitan would over the next several years reposition itself again, this time to focus on its core business of branded food and alcohol. Operations outside these areas were to be sold off when financially tenable. Health care was one of the first to be deemphasized even though the company had only recently entered the field. Sheppard believed that opportunities in this industry had already been exploited and advocated the sale of Quality Care before the industry became unprofitably competitive.

In March 1987 Grand Metropolitan bolstered its liquor holdings by acquiring Heublein Inc. from RJR Nabisco for $1.3 billion. Heublein had lost many of its nonbeverage operations while a subsidiary of RJR Nabisco, but its beverages included such brands as Smirnoff vodka, Arrow liqueurs, Harvey's Bristol Cream sherry, and Guinness Stout—brands now controlled by Grand Metropolitan. The firm exited from another business in 1988 when it sold the Inter-Continental Hotel chain to Seibu Saison for 52 times earnings.

Flush with money from the hotel sale and needing to do something with it to avoid being taken over itself, Grand Metropolitan sought an acquisition that would enhance its food sector. It settled on the troubled U.S. food giant Pillsbury Company. Since Pillsbury's management had developed a plan to turn the company around and wanted the chance to implement it, they fought Grand Metropolitan's takeover bid. A few months later, however, in December 1988, Grand Metropolitan increased its bid to $66 a share (a total of $5.68 billion in cash), an offer that Pillsbury reluctantly accepted. This huge takeover brought a host of important brands to the Grand Metropolitan fold, including Pillsbury bakery items, Green Giant frozen vegetables, Haagen-Dazs ice cream, and the Burger King fast-food chain.

Ironically, Grand Metropolitan essentially adopted the brand-revitalization and restructuring plan proposed by Pillsbury's ousted executives, although perhaps in much more aggressive fashion. Within a year, $150 million in expenses had been eliminated, 3,350 jobs were cut, $140 million was invested in Pillsbury plants, advertising was increased, and quality-improvement and new product development programs were bolstered. Haagen-Dazs and Burger King were separated from Pillsbury and became distinct subsidiaries. Burger King had struggled along with the rest of Pillsbury, so Grand Metropolitan increased advertising and promotions and quickly introduced a broiled chicken sandwich which had been in the development stage for years but was never introduced under Pillsbury. Within a few months of introduction the chicken sandwiches were selling at a clip of a million a day, already half the number of popular Whopper burgers sold per day.

Grand Metropolitan also aimed to take the Pillsbury brands global. Under Pillsbury, Burger King never had the resources to expand internationally. Less than a year after purchasing Pillsbury, though, Grand Metropolitan had acquired the Wimpey hamburger chain in England, then converted 150 of them into Burger Kings. France and Hungary were also targeted for expansion. The Green Giant and Haagen-Dazs brands were also slated for ambitious international growth over the next several years.

With its absorption of Pillsbury incomplete and its holdings not yet reduced to the food and alcohol core, Grand Metropolitan struggled during the early 1990s partly because of restructuring costs, such as the $700 million spent in 1993 and 1994, but also to falling alcohol sales. Consumption of liquor was dropping in the United States and elsewhere during this period, hurting sales of all the major alcohol companies. To make up for lost sales, many companies turned to price increases and an emphasis on premium brands, which helped Grand Metropolitan until it suffered the blow of losing the distribution rights to Absolut vodka and Grand Marnier liqueur. Grand Metropolitan was particularly vulnerable since its alcohol sector provided a disproportionate amount of its profits. For instance, in 1993 alcohol generated only 42 percent of its sales revenue but 54 percent of its operating profit. As a result, companywide sales which had peaked at £9.39 billion in 1990 dropped to £8.12 billion by 1993, and net income which had peaked at £1.07 billion in 1990 had fallen to £413 million by 1993.

Contributing to the company's difficulty was the heavy debt it still held from the Pillsbury takeover, amounting to $4.2 billion in 1993. To reduce this load and to further concentrate the firm's holdings, Grand Metropolitan shed additional businesses in 1994 and 1995. In 1994 it sold the Chef & Brewer pub chain for $1.1 billion and its Alpo pet food unit to Nestlé for $510 million. The following year it sold its Van de Kamp's frozen seafood and frozen dessert business to an investment partnership for $190 million. Rumors also surfaced in 1995 that Burger King would be spun off, and further speculation held that the Pearle Vision Center chain would be sold once it returned to profitability. Earlier in 1995, however, Grand Metropolitan had gone shopping again, this time netting Pet, Inc. for $2.6 billion, gaining such brands as Old El Paso Mexican food products and Progresso soups, and seemingly entrenching itself further into the branded food business.

To many observers, Grand Metropolitan remained in the mid-1990s a puzzle whose pieces did not all quite fit together. The company was certainly much less of a conglomerate than in the past, but had not yet fully committed itself to branded food and drink products. Sheppard retired in January 1996 and Bell became chairman, which appeared to indicate that Grand Metropolitan would stay the course and continue to concentrate on its core businesses.

Principal Subsidiaries: GrandMet Foods UK; Grand Metropolitan Community Services-UK; Grand Metropolitan Estates; Grand Metropolitan Information Services Ltd.; Inntrepreneur; International Distillers & Vintners Ltd.; Memory Lane Cakes Ltd.; Peter's Savoury Products; Burger King Corporation (U.S.); Green Giant International Inc. (U.S.); The Haagen-Dazs Company Inc. (U.S.); Heublein Inc. (U.S.); Pearle Inc. (U.S.); The Pillsbury Company (U.S.).

Further Reading:

Cuff, Daniel F., "De-Cluttering a British Conglomerate," *New York Times,* March 12, 1989, p. F9.

Flynn, Julia, and Laura Zinn, "Absolut Pandemonium: As Liquor Sales Fall, Companies Are Battling for Premium Brands," *Business Week,* November 8, 1993, pp. 58–59.

Flynn, Julia, Lois Therrien, and Gail DeGeorge, "A Grand Design for Grand Met," *Business Week,* December 20, 1993, pp. 58–59.

Grand Metropolitan PLC Annual Reports, London: Grand Metropolitan PLC, 1934–94.

Howard, Theresa, "Lord Allen Sheppard: Chairman, Grand Metropolitan PLC, London," *Nation's Restaurant News,* January 1995, pp. 192–193.

Jaffe, Thomas, "Pillsbury's New Doughboys?," *Forbes,* October 31, 1988, p. 174.

Papa, Mary Bader, "Run, Doughboy, Run," *Corporate Report-Minnesota,* July 1990, p. 39.

Reader, W. J., *Grand Metropolitan: A History, 1962–1987,* Oxford: Oxford University Press, 1988.

—updated by David E. Salamie

Great Lakes Chemical Corporation

One Great Lakes Boulevard
P.O. Box 2200
West Lafayette, Indiana 47906-0200
U.S.A.
(317) 497-6100
Fax: (317) 497-6234

Public Company
Incorporated: 1933 as McClanahan Oil Company
Employees: 7,000
Sales: $2.11 billion
Stock Exchanges: Los Angeles New York San Francisco
SICs: 2819 Industrial Inorganic Chemicals, Not Elsewhere
    Classified; 2869 Industrial Organic Chemicals, Not
    Elsewhere Classified; 2879 Pesticides and Agricultural
    Chemicals, Not Elsewhere Classified; 2899 Chemicals and
    Chemical Preparations, Not Elsewhere Classified; 2992
    Lubricating Oils and Greases

Great Lakes Chemical Corporation is one of the world's largest
manufacturers of bromine and brominated chemical products.
Bromine, an acrid red liquid which irritates the skin, mixes
easily with hundreds of organic compounds, producing thousands of toxic and non-toxic chemicals. Although bromine
compounds are not its only products, Great Lakes Chemical
relies heavily on bromine for much of its revenue.

Great Lakes Chemical was originally founded as an oil and gas
exploration company called the McClanahan Oil Company. Its
founder, W. L. McClanahan, established the company to take
advantage of a growing oil industry centered near Mount Pleasant in central Michigan. The company remained small for many
years, restricted both by competition from larger companies and
limited oil reserves in Michigan.

In 1946 Charles Hale, a geologist and Wall Street financier,
became the largest shareholder of the McClanahan Oil Company and later assumed its presidency. As part of his goal to
create a natural resources conglomerate, Hale engineered the
company's acquisition of the Great Lakes Chemical Corporation in March of 1948. Great Lakes Chemical held titles to oil
and gas reserves, as well as some bromine wells near Filer City,
Michigan. In May of 1950 the two companies merged to form
the Great Lakes Oil & Chemical Company.

During the 1950s Great Lakes expanded its petroleum interests
by purchasing the Olds Oil Corporation in December of 1951
and the Cleveland Oil Company in October of 1952. These
companies were later merged with Great Lakes Oil & Chemical
as part of a program to rationalize production. The company's
ability to compete in its traditional petroleum markets began to
erode during the late 1950s. Faced with impending bankruptcy,
Great Lakes was forced to alter substantially its business
strategies.

Earl T. McBee, a professor of industrial chemistry at Purdue
University and a consultant to Great Lakes since 1953, advocated the company's gradual withdrawal from the petroleum
industry, favoring instead the expansion of its bromine operation. Charles Hale agreed with McBee and in 1957 authorized
the sale of the company's oil properties in California. Through
the sale of additional California real estate during 1960, Great
Lakes raised enough capital to purchase a 50 percent share of
Arkansas Chemicals Inc., which owned several bromine-rich
brine wells in Arkansas. As a result, Great Lakes became a
major bromine products company by gaining a stake in the best
deposits before the industry leader Dow Chemical could do so.

The company changed its name to Great Lakes Chemical Corporation on May 9, 1960, and continued its reorganization
process by attempting to diversify into financial services. The
venture was unsuccessful, however, and was discontinued in
1963.

At the time, the largest application for bromine was ethylene
dibromide, an additive to leaded gasoline. Ethylene dibromide,
however, was a simple commodity chemical with a low profit
margin. In an effort to create a line of more profitable specialty
chemicals, Great Lakes Chemical devoted 5 percent of its sales
to develop new bromine compounds in a joint venture with PPG
Industries. Applications were found for bromine in a wide variety of products, including biodegradable soil fumigants and
herbicides, dyes, cleansing powders, synthetic rubber, refriger-
ants, photographic papers, and flame-retardant additives for
plastics.

In 1969 Great Lakes Chemical purchased the Cavedon Chemical Company and the Microseal Corporation, in addition to
Lunevale Products Ltd. of Lancaster, England. The following
year Great Lakes Chemical formed a joint venture with Pechiney Ugine Kuhlmann of France called Sobrom. Sobrom was
established to develop brominated soil fumigants for the European market. The company increased its presence in France in
1972 when it formed another company called Microfral with
Compagnie Français des Lubricants. Through these companies,
Great Lakes Chemical enlarged its marketing network on an
international scale.

In 1973, Earl McBee died of a heart attack. He was succeeded
by Emerson Kampen, an employee of many years who gained a
reputation for strong central management. Kampen continued
many of McBee's policies, including that of cooperation with
French companies. In February of 1976 Great Lakes Chemical
agreed to form an American joint venture with Pechiney Ugine
Kuhlmann called the Forex Chemical Corporation, which was
established to develop fire extinguishing compounds.

In the latter half of the 1970s, other chemical manufacturers accidentally released bromine fire retardants into rivers, causing cattle to be poisoned in Michigan and raising questions about the safety of these retardants in children's pajamas. Great Lakes Chemical maintained that its bromine products were safe, but it was forced to observe costly new regulatory measures imposed on the industry.

Great Lakes Chemical had become highly profitable, taking advantage of higher demand and new applications for bromine. The company nearly doubled its brine reserves near El Dorado, Arkansas, when it purchased the bromine operations of Northwest Industries' Velsicol subsidiary in 1981. In doing so, Great Lakes Chemical prevented competitors like Dow and Ethyl from increasing their bromine assets. The Federal Trade Commission, however, filed suit to prevent the takeover on antitrust grounds. After several years of litigation the matter was finally settled in March of 1984, when the FTC agreed to permit the takeover on the condition that Great Lakes would license its technologies to PPG Industries, in order to make it a "viable competitor."

In 1984 the federal government banned ethylene dibromide for non-fuel uses. As a result of the ban, Great Lakes Chemical only lost 2 percent of profits; however, the increased use of unleaded gasoline during the late 1970s forced the company to de-emphasize production of ethylene dibromide.

To compensate, Great Lakes Chemical chose to expand into biotechnology and in 1982 took control over the Enzyme Technologies Corporation. Another promising area for expansion was oil field chemicals. Clear fluids containing bromine salts are effective agents in flushing oil out of the ground. In July of 1982 Great Lakes purchased a fluids company called Mobley Chemical and in October acquired a 63 percent share of the Oilfield Service Corporation of America.

In September of 1983 Great Lakes Chemical purchased the Inland Specialty Chemical Corporation for $10 million. The acquisition marked the entry of Great Lakes into the area of electronic chemicals, where it sought to apply its halogen-based X-ray resist technology to semiconductors.

The company's expansion belied an internal problem: the leadership of Emerson Kampen was repeatedly called into question and described as "abusive" by senior managers. As a result of Kampen's refusal to delegate greater authority, five vice presidents resigned from Great Lakes Chemical between 1975 and 1984. One of those vice presidents was Kenneth Karmel, who left in 1982 to head Ethyl's new Bromine Chemicals Division. Fearing that its industrial secrets would be compromised, Great Lakes Chemical challenged Karmel's contract with Ethyl in court.

By the mid-1980s, Great Lakes Chemical claimed to be the largest producer of bromine products in America, largely through the benefit of licensing agreements with other companies. Although bromine chemistry accounted for over 80 percent of Great Lakes' products, Great Lakes management denied that the company was dependent on one product. The company had several hundred different products and efforts to diversify continued.

Over the next five years, Great Lakes continued its domestic and international expansion by making seven more acquisitions. In April of 1985 the company purchased the remaining shares of Enzyme Technology Corp. in exchange for Great Lakes shares worth approximately $331,000 and all of the outstanding stock of Purex Pool Products, Inc., for almost $21 million. The Purex acquisition marked the establishment of a new specialty in recreational water treatment products. This investment was further developed with the purchase in 1990 of Bio-Lab, Inc., a manufacturer of swimming pool and spa products, for $55.4 million in cash.

In 1986, the company acquired Pentech Corp. and QO Chemicals, Inc., a furfural specialty chemicals group, for $121.6 million in cash. In the same year, Great Lakes purchased a 15 percent interest in Huntsman Chemical Corp. and an additional 25 percent interest in January 1987. In January 1995, Great Lakes divested 23 percent of its stake, retaining enough to maintain friendly customer relations. Great Lakes received a $130 million cash dividend that put the company in an even better position to continue its program of expansion through acquisition. In March of that year, the Huntsman family bought back all remaining shares owned by Great Lakes.

In 1989, Great Lakes acquired a 51.15 percent interest in Octel Associates and its operating company Associated Octel Company, Limited, for $198 million. That interest was raised to 87.82 percent when Great Lakes purchased Shell U.K. Limited's 36.67 percent interest. This acquisition was a major advancement in Great Lakes' strategy to keep "a specialty chemical orientation, leveraging strong raw materials positions, being a low-cost manufacturer, and developing high performance products." Octel Associates was the world's largest supplier of motor fuel compounds and Europe's leading producer of key raw materials.

Great Lakes grew internationally over the next few years with the acquisition of Degussa AG's chemical manufacturing facility in Konstanz, Germany; Bayrol Chemische Fabrik GmbH; LOWI, a German-based manufacturer of polymer stabilizers; and Societé Française d'Organo-Syntheses, a polymer additives and specialty polymer producer. By 1994, Great Lakes was in the number two position in the $2 billion polymer stabilizers market. The acquisition of Bayrol had given the company access to the European and Mediterranean markets. With Bio-Lab's presence in Canada, New Zealand, and Australia, and the acquisition of Aqua Chem to strengthen U.S. market penetration, Great Lakes was well represented in all the key markets for water treatment products.

In 1994, Emerson Kampen stepped down due to serious medical complications and was succeeded by senior executive Robert McDonald as chief executive officer and by board member Martin Hale as chairman. In the 20 years of Kampen's tenure, the company had grown more than a hundredfold in annual revenue. His strategy of taking a "disproportionate share of the growth markets for bromine-based chemicals, both domestically and internationally" had made the company successful and continued to be its dominant principle.

By 1994, the company described itself as having operations in one dominant industry segment, but as being diversified within that segment. Great Lakes announced a reorganization dividing the company into six autonomous business units by product type: flame retardants, intermediates and fine chemicals, petroleum additives, polymer stabilizers, specialized services and manufacturing, and water treatment. Each group would include its own manufacturing, research and development, and marketing functions. The company had grown to hold plants at 32 locations in 14 states and eight foreign countries, with operations around the world. More than half of net sales to unaffiliated customers were derived from transactions with foreign companies.

Great Lakes' bromine capacity represented 20 percent of the world's supply in 1992. By 1995, capacity constraints were preventing the company from accepting profitable business. Strong markets for flame-retardant products encouraged Great Lakes to invest $60 million in enhancing bromine derivative production capacity. An estimated additional $40 million dollars were earmarked to enhance bromine production capacity in the United States and abroad.

Principal Subsidiaries: Bayrol Chemische Fabrik GmbH; Bio-Lab, Inc.; Chemische Werke LOWI Beteiligungs GmbH & Co.; Chemol RT (78%); E/M Corporation; Four Seasons Industrial Services, Inc.; Great Lakes Chemical (Europe), Ltd.; Great Lakes Chemical France S.A.; Great Lakes Chemical International, Inc.; Great Lakes Chemical Italia S.r.l.; KAO-Quaker Co., Ltd. (50%); Octel Associates and The Associated Octel Company, Limited (87.8%); Octel Chemicals Limited; OSCA, Inc.; WIL Research Laboratories, Inc.

Further Reading:

Breskin, Ira, ''Great Lakes to Expand Capacity,'' *Chemical Week,* February 22, 1995, p. 8.
''Great Lakes Restructures,'' *Chemical Marketing Reporter,* May 30, 1994, p. 13.
''Huntsman Buys Back Voting Shares,'' *Chemical Marketing Reporter,* March 27, 1995, p. 7.
Rotman, David, ''Great Lakes Cuts Stake in Huntsman, Gets Hefty Dividend,'' *Chemical Week,* January 4–11, 1995, p. 20.

—updated by Katherine Smethurst

Greenwood Mills, Inc.

P.O. Box 1017
Greenwood, South Carolina 29648
U.S.A.
(803) 229-2571
Fax: (803) 839-7500

Private Company
Incorporated: 1889
Employees: 7,000
Sales: $525 million
SICs: 2211 Broad Woven Fabric Mills, Cotton

Greenwood Mills, Inc. is one of the oldest, most successful textile businesses in the United States. Part of the company's success, and what distinguishes Greenwood Mills from many other companies within the United States, is that the firm's management has cultivated a work force of uncommon stability. Hundreds of employees come from the third and even fourth generation of families associated with the firm. Indeed, in 1980 Greenwood Mills proudly reported that nearly 20 percent of all its employees had worked for the company more than 25 years.

The company was founded as the Greenwood Cotton Mill in 1889 by William Lowndes Durst. The mill was located in Greenwood, South Carolina, and Durst, a wealthy farmer and merchant, became the firm's president. Within a year of its establishment Greenwood Cotton Mill employed 75 people, processed approximately five bales of cotton per day, and produced such items as sheetings and cotton print cloth. When Durst died in 1902, he was replaced by his brother W.L. Durst, president of the Bank of Greenwood. He managed the company well until the financial panic that swept across America in 1907. The panic resulted in Greenwood Mills' near bankruptcy. A youthful cashier in Durst's bank by the name of James C. Self, who had impressed the Greenwood Mills board of directors, was suddenly elected president, presumably to preside over the liquidation of the company.

When Self assumed his position as president, Greenwood Mills was financially strapped, unable to purchase cotton to run its operations or pay its employees. Faced with outdated equipment and with the company deeply in debt, Self decided to visit the Draper Corporation in Boston, Massachusetts, to purchase new equipment for a comprehensive modernization and revitalization of the company. He first met with Eben Draper, brother of chief executive George Draper. Impressed with the young man's commitment and sincerity, Eben Draper promised to refit Greenwood with entirely new equipment. When George Draper returned from an extended trip, however, he immediately reversed his brother's decision. Self returned to Boston and confronted George Draper with the words, "... in the South, sir, we do what we promise." Taken aback, George Draper approved the sale of equipment, and Greenwood Mills was on its way to success.

In 1913 Self hired J.B. Harris as the company's general superintendent. Harris soon became Self's most valued employee, and helped the company with every aspect of its operations. By 1916 the company's financial stability had reached a point where it was able to purchase new Draper looms, build a nearby church for its workers, begin a night shift, and count over 250 employees on its payroll. Still an employee of the Bank of Greenwood, at this time Self decided to leave the bank and devote all his time to the development of Greenwood Mills.

During the early 1920s, as a financial crisis within the American economy began to push the price of cotton lower and lower, Self started to purchase as much cotton as the coffers of the company would allow. When the price of cotton fell all the way to 11 cents per bushel, the company's warehouses were packed with cotton. Suddenly, as the country's financial crisis stabilized and cotton rose to 30 cents per bushel, Self was vindicated in his purchases. With brisk sales bringing increasing revenues, Self acquired the Ninety Six Cotton Mill and later purchased the Grendel Mill Number 2 in Greenwood, which he renamed Mathews. These acquisitions brought more business to the company, and soon Greenwood Mills was regarded as one of the most financially sound businesses in the southern part of the United States.

Greenwood Cotton Mills weathered the Great Depression of the 1930s by relying upon its previously built-up financial base. By 1935 the company was operating three shifts per day, and Self was able to purchase all of Greenwood's stock, thereby becoming its sole owner. Two years later, the Mathews plant was expanded. Within a short time it developed into the leading producer of fabrics made from spun rayon. All these developments combined to prepare the company for the demands of World War II.

Although the company had been highly successful before the Second World War, the war added to Greenwood's prominence within the textile industry. Contracted by the U.S. Army to produce special poplin cloth for the armed services, the Mathews mill was the sole operation in the entire country that successfully met the Army's strict specifications. During the course of World War II, the Mathews mill and the Ninety-Six mill produced over 100 million yards of cloth for the armed services, more than any other company within the American textile industry. By the end of the war, Greenwood Cotton Mills had received four awards from the Army for the high quality of its cloth.

After the war, the company changed its name to Greenwood Mills and initiated a comprehensive restructuring and modernization program. Mathews mill and Ninety Six mill were incorporated into the restructuring effort, and a new plant named in honor of J.B. Harris was built close to the Mathews facility. This expansion was achieved without incurring any debt. At the same time, Self arranged for the construction of a living community for employees of the Harris plant. Comprised of well-built brick homes, a school, and a shopping center, the Harris Community was the last mill village planned and constructed by management for company employees in the United States.

Self also created a not-for-profit foundation which funded many charitable projects during the 1950s, including the construction of the Self Memorial Hospital in 1951. In 1952 Self was honored as ''Man of the South'' for his business accomplishments and his community involvement. In 1953 he supervised the last plant built under his leadership of the company, the Durst facility. The Durst plant was unusual since it was the only cotton print mill cloth facility built in the United States for over 30 years, and many experts within the industry believed such a mill to be out-of-date and financially risky. But Self's confidence was justified—the mill developed into one of the largest producers of 100-percent cotton print cloth fabric during the 1950s.

In 1955 James C. Self died and was succeeded as president by his son, Jim Self, who immediately embarked upon an aggressive expansion strategy. Beginning in 1960, Greenwood Mills added eight plants in less than eight years. The most important of these included the Sloan plant, located at the Ninety Six facility, which was one of the first mills to make one fabric. In 1962 the company built the Adams plant, also located at the Ninety Six facility. Two years later the Chalmers plant was added to the company's growing list of textile mills. The Chalmers plant soon grew into a leading producer of cotton corduroy.

In 1965, for the first time, Greenwood Mills acquired a company outside the immediate location of Greenwood, South Carolina. The company purchased the Joanna Cotton Mills located in Joanna, South Carolina. Greenwood's management rearranged and reconstituted Joanna's facilities into four plants which focused on specific fabric areas, and a single yarn plant. In 1968 the company acquired Fabric Services, a Orangeburg, South Carolina, operation owned by Monsanto Company. This finishing and dyeing business provided Greenwood Mills with the ability to sell its own finished fabrics. Previously the company had contracted dyers and finishers on a free-lance basis to finish its products. Greenwood renamed its new purchase the Liner plant, in honor of a retiring vice president.

During the 1960s and 1970s, the public's demand for brighter colors necessitated more sophisticated technology to evaluate color in the dyeing process. A Greenwood Mills vice president in engineering, Lyle C. Wilcox, invented the spectrophotometer as a response to this challenge within the textile industry. The spectrophotometer was a computer scanning piece of equipment that assured the color scheme integrity of a piece of cloth. Holding the patent to this process, Greenwood licensed the new technology to such diverse customers as Communications Corporation and Ford Aerospace.

The company continued its expansion program throughout the 1970s. In 1972 the company opened a marketing office in London, England, in order to regularly assess the European textile industry. At approximately the same time, distribution agents were contracted in Canada, South America, Africa, Australia, and various other countries in the Pacific Rim. In 1973 Greenwood Mills purchased the Edisto plant in Orangeburg. Owned by M. Lowenstein and Sons, the plant was a major producer of both knitted and textured woven fabrics in the southern part of the United States. Four additional plants of Inman Mills, situated in Spartanburg, South Carolina, were also purchased during the mid-1970s. With its expansion strategy completed for the moment, the company took a break and announced a comprehensive consolidation and modernization program amounting to $65 million. This program involved all phases of Greenwood's operations, including the purchase of over 500 state-of-the-art air jet looms, a new corduroy finishing plant, and a modernized weaving facility.

In the late 1970s, Greenwood Mills returned to the past in order to make its present operation more efficient. Along with other cotton factories, Greenwood Mills developed a way to make the shipment of cotton more cost effective. New locks on the Arkansas River provided access all the way to the Mississippi, and company management decided that barging cotton from Pine Bluffs, Arkansas, to Chattanooga, Tennessee, and then transporting by truck to Greenwood, South Carolina, was a more reliable and less expensive shipping process than those that were currently in place. In October 1979, a barge loaded with 2,360 bales of cotton departed Pine Bluff and arrived in Chattanooga 25 days later. Valued at a cost of more than $750,000, the shipment of cotton by barge was the first of its kind in the South since the turn of the century.

Throughout the 1980s, Greenwood Mills continued to improve and upgrade its manufacturing plants. With over 20 facilities operating under the name of Greenwood Mills and revenues climbing, the firm was one of the most financially stable in the entire American textile industry. Along with its sound financial position, the company also maintained a solid relationship with its employees. Contracts agreed upon between Greenwood management and the textile workers union were generally achieved to everyone's satisfaction without lingering resentment or acrimony.

During the late 1980s and early 1990s, the company began to experience what every textile manufacturer feared most—increased competition from foreign countries. Textile manufacturers and clothing companies located in the Pacific Rim and South America were able to pay low wages to employees and make minimal capital investments. They were thus increasingly able to undersell American and European companies. As the market share for Greenwood Mills, along with many other firms, started to erode, the company fought back by cutting its prices and reducing its overhead. These measures, however, were not enough to remain competitive.

As a result of the increasing competition from foreign textile companies, in 1993 management at Greenwood Mills decided to build a clothing facility overseas. The strategy was to take advantage of the lower cost in wages and the generally less expensive operating overhead available overseas. The company arranged a low cost loan of $77 million through the International Finance Corporation, and made plans to construct a denim plant in Pakistan. Before the deal could even be formalized, however, intense criticism from American textile manufacturers and clothing companies rained down on Greenwood Mills. Chief executive officers and presidents of such companies as Akrwright Mills, Cheraw Yarn Mills, and Parkdale Mills vigorously objected to Greenwood's plan by pointing out that it would divert jobs overseas and hurt the domestic textile industry. At the same time, the decision made by Greenwood management was supported by the U.S. Department of State. Government officials maintained that the project was more beneficial than harmful because it was in agreement with American foreign policy efforts to lessen the dependence of developing countries on U.S. aid by encouraging the construction of more indigenous-based industries. With the backing of the federal government, Greenwood Mills adhered to its original plan of constructing a new plant in Pakistan.

Greenwood Mills remained under the leadership of the Self family in the early 1990s. James C. Self's two sons, James C. Self Jr. and W. Matthew Self, assumed direct supervision of the company when the elder Self decided to step down. A tragic automobile accident in May 1995, however, resulted in the death of James C. Self Jr., and Matt Self was named president.

Principal Subsidiaries: Greenwood Cotton Company; Greenwood Development Company; Greenwood Mill, Inc.; Greenwood Warehouse Company; Lindale Manufacturing, Inc.; Greenwood Mills Marketing Company.

Further Reading:

Barrett, Joyce, ''Greenwood Hit On Plan To Build Pakistan Plant,'' *Women's Wear Daily,* July 28, 1993, p. 13.
''Greenwood CEO Killed On Highway,'' *Women's Wear Daily,* May 9, 1995, p. 2.
''Greenwood Mills, Inc.,'' *Textile World,* February 1992, p. 10.
''Greenwood Mills,'' *HFD-The Weekly Home Furnishings Newspaper,* May 23, 1994, p. 34.
''Greenwood Obtains Funds For Asian Deal,'' *Daily News Record,* June 30, 1993, p. 10.
''Greenwood, Pakistan Firm In Denim Venture,'' *Women's Wear Daily,* June 30, 1993, p. 14.
Pfaff, Kimberly, ''Weaving Toward Success In 1993,'' *HFD-The Weekly Home Furnishings Newspaper,* June 8, 1992, pp. 34–40.
Self, James C., *Greenwood Mills, Inc.,* Newcomen Society: New York, 1980.

—Thomas Derdak

Harbert Corporation

P. O. Box 1297
Birmingham, Alabama 35201
U.S.A.
(205) 987-5500
Fax: (205) 987-5568

Private Company
Incorporated: 1949 as Harbert Construction Corporation
Employees: 500
Sales: $100 million
SICs: 1311 Crude Petroleum & Natural Gas; 4939
   Combination Utilities; 6531 Real Estate

After a long and successful history primarily in the construction and mining fields, Harbert Corporation has evolved into three main businesses: real estate, cogeneration, and investment management. In 1993, the company sold its construction interests to Bill Harbert—the founder's brother and a key player in developing the international operations of the corporation—as well as to the Engineers & Constructors division of Raytheon. Thereafter, Harbert Corporation focused on serving the market for alternative energy and cogeneration plants, as well as on its commercial real estate and investment management interests, under the leadership of the founder's son Raymond Harbert.

Headquartered in the Riverchase area of Birmingham, Alabama, Harbert was founded by John Murdoch Harbert III, in 1949. After returning from service in the U.S. Army during World War II, Harbert entered Alabama's Auburn University to study engineering. Upon graduation in 1946, he started his own construction business. In the postwar economic boom, construction was a highly competitive business. At that time, according to a company publication, "58,600 other new contractors also entered the business in the United States. The same year, nearly 47,000 went out of business."

Harbert purchased a few pieces of surplus Army construction equipment, which he kept in a small yard beside his one-room office. The company's first project was to build a bridge near Prattville, Alabama, which cost around $45,000 to construct. Subsequent jobs consisted primarily of small bridges and roads, the labor for which was contracted out. Harbert was soon joined by his brother Bill L. Harbert, and two other engineers, and before long the upstart company boasted a staff of between 25

and 30. In 1949, the company was incorporated in Birmingham, Alabama.

A reputation for integrity, good work, and the ability to meet contract specifications led to increased business on a grander scale. Harbert projects during the 1950s included construction of highways, dams, and bridges. By the end of the decade, the Harbert Corporation had experienced rapid growth, with a work force of 7,000 and an equipment inventory of over 3,000. During this time, Harbert accepted a contract to build a natural gas pipeline in Florida, and thus its experience and expertise diversified. In fact, the pipeline was also significant in that it represented the first transmission of natural gas to consumers in Florida's industrial and residential communities. Constructing the pipeline in Florida opened Harbert management's eyes to the potential for real estate development in that state, and Harbert soon acquired some land in Sarasota, where it built a shopping mall and residential community. This represented the company's first foray into real estate and land development.

Diversification began to center on the country's demand for energy and natural resource exploitation. Accordingly, Harbert's business interests expanded to include coal mining in Kentucky and construction contracts in Central and South America. The corporation also purchased a large limestone quarry near Paducah, Kentucky, and assumed responsibility for laying 2,000 miles of pipeline for intrastate gas use in Florida through the Five Flags Pipeline Company, which Harbert developed, owned, and operated.

During this time, the accomplishments of Harbert's founder began to receive national notice. John Harbert was named Marketing Man of the Year in Alabama in 1967 and was cited by *Engineering News-Record* as one of the ten outstanding construction men of the year. In 1969, he was presented the first Silver Hard Hat Award by the Construction Writers' Association. While his company thrived, he devoted considerable time to several projects that he felt might benefit from his experience and beliefs. He established a writing center at nearby University of Montevallo and gave generously to his alma mater, Auburn University, providing its campus a laboratory, office and instructional building for the school of engineering.

Of course, Harbert's primary focus continued to be his corporation, which was expanding in a number of ways. The company established a new subsidiary, Harcon Barge Company, which oversaw a network of barge transports in the Tennessee, Ohio, and Mississippi rivers. Natural gas transmission operations in Florida also continued to grow. Furthermore, the company's emphasis on heavy equipment management skill was on the rise. A three-and-a-half-mile portion of the Tennessee Tombigbee Waterway was constructed by Harbert in Mississippi. In 1973 Harbert redesigned a newly purchased facility, The Harriman Coal Terminal, which was later expanded to transload barges, according to a company publication "at an average rate of 400 tons per hour."

In 1981, Harbert began selling off its mining operations. Its coal mines, towing barges, and other coal-related properties were sold to Standard Oil for around $400 million. With this lucrative deal, the company began to focus instead on oil exploration, acquiring the Plumb Oil Company in Houston and forming its own Harbert Energy Corporation. Two years later, in fact, John Harbert reportedly joined Texas oil magnate T. Boone Pickens in a hostile takeover bid for Gulf Oil Co. Although the bid was unsuccessful, Harbert's stockholdings were worth millions when Chevron succeeded in taking over Gulf Oil. Harbert would again team up with Pickens in an effort to take over the Diamond Shamrock Corporation in 1986. With a keen eye for such profitable opportunities, Harbert gained inclusion on the *Forbes* magazine list of the 400 wealthiest Americans in 1984. And, of course, his foresight and industry know-how was of benefit to Harbert Corporation.

Land development and construction continued apace, most notably perhaps on Birmingham's Riverchase development, begun in 1974 and completed in the 1980s. The planned community included single and family dwellings, the Riverchase Galleria, and offices—aesthetically pleasing buildings of granite and glass set beside a serene lake. The Riverchase Galleria Mall proved one of the company's most ambitious construction projects and boasted one of the largest shopping centers in the United States, parking decks, a four-star hotel, and an office building. Another such plaza, completed in 1989, was the AmSouth/Harbert Plaza in downtown Birmingham's financial center, a 32-story, 630,000 square foot facility which housed retail space, a three-level underground parking garage and office space. At the same time, the company continued to build major bridge structures including two interchanges between Miami and Ft. Lauderdale, Florida, that represented the first such contract package ever awarded by the State of Florida.

In 1987, Forbes estimated Harbert's annual sales at over $500 million. Such figures were bolstered by Harbert's expansion into securities and investment banking, as the company formed another subsidiary, Harbert Capital Services, to serve that market. Moreover, the company's energy and waste management interests grew, engendering the formation of Harbert Cogen Inc., which operated small power plants, the acquisition of GWF Power Systems and Combustion Power Co., and the birth of Harbert Resource Recovery Inc., a joint venture with a French waste management company.

In 1990, John Harbert stepped down from his position as company president, and his son Raymond became president and CEO of Harbert Corporation. Under his leadership, the company began to refocus in three areas: energy, commercial real estate, and portfolio investment strategy. The company's prospects in the field of oil exploration had proved disappointing, and in 1992, Harbert sold its oil and gas assets. Nevertheless, the energy industry, bolstered by the passage of the Public Utility Regulation Policies Act (PURPA) back in 1978, was thriving, and Harbert was poised to take advantage of the increase in demand among the alternative energy and cogeneration/independent power plant markets.

In 1993, the engineering division of Raytheon acquired the assets of Harbert's construction interests for an undisclosed amount, signalling an end of an era at Harbert. Two years later, the company's founder, John Harbert, died. He had led his company for more than 45 years, and was always proud of the "family atmosphere" he fostered among his employees. No matter how large the corporation became, Harbert had tried to maintain a personal interest in every employee, offering educational incentives that encouraged self-improvement and personal fulfillment. He was regarded as an inspiration to the Birmingham community at large.

In the mid-1990s, Harbert Corporation was working to accelerate, according to company literature, "its shift from low margin, labor-intensive businesses to focus on investment opportunities that allow it to utilize its operational and investment expertise to exploit market inefficiencies."

Principal Subsidiaries: Harbert Realty Services, Harbert Power Corporation, The Harbinger Group, Inc.

Further Reading:

"Air-Driven Unit Goes on Line," *Engineering Record,* October 7, 1991, p. 16.

Flynt, Wayne, *Mine, Mill & Microchip,* Northridge, Calif.: Windsor Publications, Inc., pp. 334–335.

Normington, Mick, "Harbert: Wide learning, Great Energy," *The Birmingham News,* April 1, 1995, p. 10A.

Powers, Mary, "Raytheon Puts Harbert in Its Peace Portfolio," *Engineering Record,* June 28, 1993, p. 12.

"Business Brief—Raytheon Co.: Unit Buys Assets of Business from Harbert International," *Wall Street Journal,* June 21, 1993, p. A2.

—Loretta Cobb

The Hartstone Group plc

1 Saint Andrew's Court
Thame
Oxfordshire OX9 3GG
United Kingdom
(01844) 261544
Fax: (01844) 261560

Public Company
Incorporated: 1985 as Glamar Group plc
Employees: 4,190
Sales: £363 million
Stock Exchanges: London
SICs: 6711 Holding Companies; 2251 Women's Full Length
& Knee Length Hosiery; 2252 Hosiery, Not Elsewhere
Classified; 5137 Women's, Girls' & Babies' Clothing &
Accessories; 5199 Non-Durable Goods, Not Elsewhere
Classified

The Hartstone Group plc is a leading manufacturer in the international leathergoods and hosiery markets, supplying products both under its own brand names and for retailers' own-label brands. From modest beginnings as a Leeds-based hosiery firm in the 1970s, the company became what the *Observer* called a "glamour stock" between 1989 and 1993, expanding rapidly through aggressive acquisition to become a significant force in its chosen markets. Serious financial troubles in 1993 caused a corporate shake-up and forced Hartstone to rethink its strategy. Today the company is pursuing a more moderate growth policy in its bid for success in the leathergoods and hosiery industries of the United Kingdom and abroad.

The company that was to become Hartstone began in 1975 as a small women's hosiery distribution firm based in Leeds. Incorporated ten years later as Glamar Group plc, the company remained much the same until 1989, when Glamar became the basis of an ambitious attempt at corporate empire-building. The metamorphosis began with a senior management buyout of the company, led by Stephen Barker, who became chief executive and chairman. Under his direction, the new management embarked upon a dramatic course of acquisition. Targeting the hosiery and leathergoods markets, the company (renamed the Hartstone Group in 1990) began scooping up small firms at an unprecedented rate. The accessories industry was extremely fragmented, and Hartstone aimed to integrate these small busi-

nesses into a coherent, rationalized whole that would benefit from greatly increased market share, economies of scale, and stronger purchasing power. Between 1989 and 1993 Hartstone acquired approximately 20 companies at a cost of about £200 million.

By 1993 Hartstone had achieved a formidable position in the hosiery and leathergoods markets. Some of the company's most significant interests were in the United States, where it owned Etienne Aigner and Michael Stevens, both acquired in 1991. The former designed, sourced, and distributed women's shoes and leather accessories for the North American market. A well-known brand since the 1950s, Etienne Aigner was the fourteenth-most-recognized designer brand among American consumers. Producing moderate-priced shoes and moderate- to higher-priced handbags and small leathergoods, the company sold its products primarily through department stores, including Macy's and Lord & Taylor, and also through its own retail stores located in out-of-town centers. The latter were outlets for the firm's lower-priced lines and discounted last-year's lines; while margins on such items were necessarily lower, the retail stores were useful for clearing out older stock and improving awareness of the Etienne Aigner brand. Nonetheless, Hartstone did not want to devalue the brand, and carefully limited its agreements to sell its products through discount stores.

Etienne Aigner had a customer base in the southeastern United States and under Hartstone's direction was expanding into the central and western regions of the country. When Hartstone purchased the company, its products were traditional in design and targeted at women between 40 and 50 years old. Hartstone introduced a more contemporary look in order to appeal to women between 20 and 40 and began licensing the brand name to manufacturers of other products, such as shirts, ties, and fragrances.

Hartstone's other principal U.S. acquisition was Michael Stevens, a designer, sourcer, and distributor of leather, vinyl, and fabric handbags and small leathergoods. With lower-priced goods than Etienne Aigner, Michael Stevens enjoyed approximately 30 percent of the market in handbags priced between $20 and $40. The company sold products primarily under its own name (accounting for some 80 percent of sales), but also marketed goods under the brand names Valerie Barad and Sereta, and in addition furnished some retailers with own-label products. Selling mostly through chain stores, Michael Stevens controlled approximately six percent of the American market in handbags and four percent in small leathergoods.

Hartstone's U.K. and European leathergoods businesses operated under the umbrella of Hartstone Leathergoods Ltd. The group included Symphony International, a producer of lower-priced synthetic handbags; Jade Accessories, a manufacturer and importer of low- and medium-priced leather and synthetic handbags and belts, marketed through department stores and chain stores; Lanca, a mid-priced branded range; the more exclusive Triad, producing handbags, briefcases, travel bags, purses, and wallets; and the Luggage Company, a designer, sourcer, and distributer of synthetic suitcases, briefcases, and travel cases. In Spain Hartstone owned Cima, a manufacturer of top-of-the-line leathergoods that sold both under its own name and under such prestigious brand names as Christian Dior and

Lladro. Rubo Lederwaren, a Dutch firm acquired in 1991, distributed leathergoods in the Netherlands and Belgium.

Hartstone's hosiery division was equally extensive and international. The company's 1991 purchase of Aznar gave it one of Spain's largest manufacturers of hosiery, producing the women's brands Marie Claire and Cherie, as well as Kler, a popular brand of men's socks. Aznar International, a 1993 acquisition, added to Hartstone's product line underwear, lingerie, nightwear, and swimwear, principally for the Spanish market. Ipko-Amcor and Werner, brought into the group in 1990, were the company's Dutch and German producers respectively of hosiery and socks. Cogetex, in France, enjoyed 30 percent of the domestic market in women's hosiery. Hartstone sold its Well brand primarily in French supermarkets and hypermarkets, and as hypermarkets expanded into Holland, Germany, Spain, and Italy, Well hosiery products penetrated these markets as well.

In the United Kingdom, Hartstone occupied a strong position as the second-largest supplier of women's hosiery in the country. Most of Hartstone's products (some 70 percent) were offered as own-label brands by chain stores, although the group also produced its own brands, including the well-known Bear Brand label. The company offered stores' own-label socks for such prominent outlets as Boots, Marks & Spencer, and Tesco, as well as the Bridgedale brand, a line of outdoor socks. Hartstone moved into casual wear with its 1990 purchase of Pamplemousse, which expanded into France and Holland from its base in the United Kingdom.

In May 1992 Hartstone was able to announce a 200 percent rise in profits, with sales up 245 percent to £240 million. It was an impressive tribute to the tactics of the "whiz-kids who took over Hartstone . . . and turned it into a go-go stock," according to *Investors Chronicle.*

It was also a short-lived triumph, as one year later it became apparent that Hartstone was in serious trouble. In the course of one dramatic day, Hartstone issued a profits warning (its second in three months), announced that the company had breached certain covenants of its lending agreements, and accepted the resignation of chief executive and chairman Stephen Barker.

The company had extended itself too far, too fast: according to *Investors Chronicle,* Barker had "failed to put in place sufficient management systems at Hartstone to control the sprawling empire." The company's lenders imposed a standstill and Hartstone was forced to scramble to secure new lending agreements to keep it afloat—a process that Shaun Dowling, the company's new chairman, described as "exhausting, time-consuming and very costly negotiations, shuttling between the United Kingdom and the United States, trying to reconcile and resolve the positions of different lenders and their respective advisers." It was reported that at one point in the negotiations Dowling was forced to pledge £50,000 of his own money, and when the cost of the refinancing was finally assessed, it came to a hefty total of £13.6 million.

With a restructured management team and a radically altered board of directors, Hartstone set about retrenching. It became apparent that the company could not sustain both its leathergoods and hosiery divisions at their current level. Deciding to concentrate on the leathergoods division, Hartstone jettisoned Cima, Cogetex, and Pamplemousse, among many other businesses. In a break with its past, the company also sold the original Glamar hosiery firm.

In its leathergoods division, Hartstone reorganized its business to reduce waste and increase profitability—at a cost to the company of some £10 million. Hartstone renewed its focus on its own branded products, while at the same time strengthening its reliance on made-to-order products for selected well-known, high-quality retailers' own-label brands, which was a lower-risk enterprise. The company established more cautious financial policies, emphasizing cost-effectiveness and operational efficiency, cutting central costs, curtailing borrowing, and improving its central controls.

Chairman Dowling explained the previous trouble thus to shareholders: "It is now evident that the speed of [Hartstone's] growth was not balanced by the imposition and maintenance of effective controls by central management. . . ." This explanation was given in a 1994 document asking for a two-for-one rights issue which was to raise £30 million, half of which was needed to repay some of the debt demanded by the company's creditors. On hearing this news, the *Mail on Sunday* commented caustically that Hartstone "knows how to get up shareholders' noses"; be that as it may, the shareholders unanimously agreed to the rights issue, and although only 45 percent of the available shares were taken up, enough money was raised to satisfy the company's lenders.

Meanwhile, former chief executive and chairman Stephen Barker instituted proceedings against Hartstone for a compensation package of £400,000 for loss of office. The company paid him £60,000, but denied that Barker was entitled to more. Eventually, advised that it would lose a legal battle over the matter, Hartstone settled out of court, giving Barker a total of £280,000.

In June 1995 Hartstone experienced what the *Financial Times* called a "sharp swing back into the black," showing profits of £4.7 million as compared to 1994's losses of £70.7 million (although much of that loss, it should be noted, was attributable to exceptional costs arising from restructuring, closures, and disposals). Hartstone's chairman commented drily that his company was "just about respectable" now.

With its resources admittedly insufficient to actively pursue dominance in both its leathergoods and hosiery divisions, Hartstone has chosen to concentrate on building the former. (In the mid-1990s the company's intentions were to retain the more established, reliable elements of its hosiery interests, although there was some speculation among financial analysts that Hartstone might in the future decide to devote itself entirely to leathergoods.) As Hartstone continues to enhance the promotion of its branded goods, the company hopes to move increasingly into licensing arrangements whereby these brand names may be used by suppliers of related products. As part of a longer-range plan, as the brands become more established, the company intends to seek international expansion, for both its American and British operations.

Principal Subsidiaries: Aznar Industrial SA (Spain); Aznar SA (Spain); Etienne Aigner, Inc. (U.S.A.); Hartstone Leathergoods Ltd.; Ipko-Amcor BV (Holland); Michaels Stevens Ltd. (U.S.A.); Rubo Lederwaren BV (Holland).

Further Reading:

"Barker Takes Action as Hartstone Loses £72m," *Daily Mail,* July 16, 1994.

"Firm Hands at the Helm," *Investors Chronicle,* May 19, 1995.

"Going the Rights Way," *Mail on Sunday,* July 31, 1994.

"Hartstone Acts to End Payout," *Daily Telegraph,* July 16, 1994.

"Hartstone Hosiery Sale to Courtaulds Textiles," *Financial Times,* January 29, 1994.

"Hartstone Investors Back Rights," *Times,* August 9, 1994.

"Hartstone May Drop Euro Tights," *Observer,* January 9, 1994.

"Hartstone £71m in the Red and Calls for £30m," *Financial Times,* July 16, 1994.

"Hartstone £280,000 Settles Row with Former Chairman," *Daily Telegraph,* June 16, 1995.

"Hartstone Rejoins the Dividend List," *Financial Times,* June 16, 1995.

"Hartstone Sells French Arm to Courtaulds for £45m," *Independent,* January 29, 1994.

"Make or Break," *Investors Chronicle,* July 22, 1994.

"60 Jobs Secured in Madison Hosiery MBO," *Yorkshire Post,* May 10, 1994.

"Untimely Horror Story," *Investors Chronicle,* June 4, 1993, p. 16.

—Robin DuBlanc

Harza Engineering Company

233 S. Wacker Drive
Chicago, Illinois 60606
U.S.A.
(312) 831-3000
Fax: (312) 831-3999

Private Company
Incorporated: 1920
Employees: 860
Operating Revenues: $120 million
SICs: 8711 Engineering Services

Located in the heart of Chicago, Harza Engineering Company is the premier water resources development firm in the Midwest. The company has a long history of successful projects in the United States and abroad, including the Derbendi Khan Dam, built in Iraq in 1963, which was at that time the world's tallest rock-fill dam; the Reza Shah Kabir Dam in Iran, one of the tallest thin-arch dams ever built; and the Guri Project in Venezuela, the largest hydroelectric facility in the world.

The founder of Harza Engineering Company, Leroy Francis Harza, was a student of Professor Daniel W. Mead, chairman of the Department of Civil Engineering at the University of Wisconsin at Madison. In the early years of the 20th century, Mead had established one of the first independent engineering consulting practices. According to Mead, dams and power plants should be designed and their construction supervised by experts in engineering, who should have no financial interest in the facilities. Only impartial engineering expertise could assure safe and economical facilities.

Working in Mead's design office, Harza learned about running an engineering consulting practice. In 1912, after graduating from Wisconsin, Harza moved to Portland, Oregon, to set up his own practice. Unfortunately, there was little demand for consulting engineers in the American Northwest, and the young man was forced to take a job in Chicago with a construction firm that was part of the Insull Group of utilities. Yet Harza was still convinced that there was potential for an independent engineering consulting practice, so he approach Samuel Insull to convince him of the benefits. Insull, an influential man in Chicago, was impressed by Harza's enthusiasm and agreed to help him form Harza Engineering Company.

During the 1920s Harza Engineering concentrated on designing dams. Its assignments included the Dix Dam in Kentucky, which, as the tallest rock-fill dam in the world at the time, provided the company with needed publicity. In the wake of this project, Harza Engineering was contracted for new projects across the country, and the firm grew in both total revenues and staffing. Under the Middle West Utilities Company, which was owned by Samuel Insull, Harza Engineering was contracted to build dams and electrical power plants for the rural electrification program initiated by Franklin D. Roosevelt's New Deal administration. However, by the end of 1932, at the height of the Great Depression, business came to a grinding halt. In one year the firm shrank from a total of 50 employees to just one— the owner himself.

Harza suffered a heart attack in 1933. As he recovered, so did the fortunes of his company. Harza Engineering was contracted by the Loop River Public Power Authority in Nebraska, and Harza Engineering began to build hydroelectric power plants funded by the federal government's PWA program. Additional assignments were soon forthcoming from the Army Corps of Engineers, who were responsible for constructing large flood control projects and power plants on rivers throughout the United States. One of the company's most lucrative contracts during this period came from the South Carolina Public Service Authority, which contracted Harza Engineering to design and construct the Santee Cooper project, the largest power plant in the state, at a cost of more than $50 million. By the end of the decade, Harza Engineering Company was employing almost 200 people.

With the entry of the United States into World War II, most of the company's engineers were called to active duty, and the firm gradually shrank until only the owner and a secretary remained. One of the bright spots during the war was the company's first overseas contract. Before the war, the government of Uruguay had arranged for the German government to design and build a hydroelectric dam in their country, but the Germans were prevented by the British blockade of Montevideo Harbor from delivering the generating equipment. Harza Engineering Company was called upon by the United States government to supply Uruguay with American equipment, and the company was subsequently contracted by Uruguay to make sure that all the equipment was correctly installed.

After the war, Harza was determined to return to the full range of activities that the company engaged in before the hostilities. The rural electrification program was resumed, and the market for electrical power increased across the United States. Soon the company was contracted to design and supervise the construction of hydroelectric dams in Wisconsin and Washington state. By 1947 Harza Engineering was once again fully operational and sound enough financially to significantly increase the number of its employees.

During the postwar period, the company also built upon its experience in Uruguay to attain many overseas contracts. The reconstruction era of the late 1940s was the heyday for engineering companies that designed large dams harnessing hydroelectric power, and Harza took advantage of numerous international opportunities. New projects were initiated in Taiwan, Iraq, Pakistan, Ethiopia, Jordan, the Philippines, Iran, and India.

By the early 1950s approximately half the company's projects were located overseas.

After L. F. Harza died during the early 1950s, his successors at Harza Engineering continued to carry out the founder's vision. The company gained a worldwide reputation for quality, reliability, and honesty, and many developing countries sought its engineering services for important and sensitive projects. In 1951, for example, the company was contracted to design a flood control system for the Meric-Evros River that forms the boundary between Greece and Turkey. This extremely sensitive assignment involved an exchange of land and a reconfiguration of the actual boundary between the two countries, and Harza Engineering was required to balance the amount of land transferred to within one-tenth of an acre. In 1953 the company was asked to design a master plan for the irrigation of land adjacent to the Jordan River in the Kingdom of Jordan. That same year the company was also contracted to design a water control plan and construct a storage dam for the Tigris River in Iraq. During the mid and late 1950s Harza Engineering was asked by the government of Iran to design three dams, one of which would serve as the major water supply to Tehran, in addition to functioning as a source for irrigation and hydroelectric generation.

From 1958 to 1962 Harza engineers were working for Vietnam, Laos, Cambodia, and Thailand to conduct a hydrologic study on the Mekong Delta. At approximately the same time, after India had gained its independence from England, the Indian government diverted the water from rivers in the Indus Basin system for use exclusively in India, denying over three million people in Pakistan access to the water. The United States and the industrialized nations of Western Europe provided more than $2 billion to the Pakistan government for the development of other water sources to offset the loss of the Indus Basin headwaters; Harza Engineering was appointed as the engineering consultant to the Pakistan government. The Mangla Dam in Pakistan is one result of the company's efforts in that country.

Throughout the 1960s and 1970s Harza Engineering was heavily involved in providing engineering services in Iran. Projects included a multi-purpose dam for the Karun River in southern Iran, which became a 650-foot arch dam providing hydroelectric power of over one million kilowatts. Downstream, Harza Engineering designed a complex but highly efficient irrigation distribution system for arid land. Unfortunately, when the Islamic Revolution overthrew the Shah of Iran, Harza Engineering Company was asked to leave the country. The firm had already completed its major projects, which were in full operating condition at the time of the revolution; however, the company was unable to collect its fees for the work completed. Harza Engineering appealed to the international tribunal in The Hague, Netherlands, but the company's claims were never resolved.

In the late 1970s the company worked extensively in Latin America. In 1979, under the auspices of the Kissinger Commission, Harza Engineering was asked to design a plan for flood control, irrigation, and drainage in the Sula Valley in northern Honduras. Covering 258,000 acres, the project was of great benefit to farmers in the surrounding area. The company also designed all of the hydroelectric generating plants in El Salvador.

Major projects in the United States during these years included the controversial Tunnel and Reservoir Project (TARP) in Chicago. Chicago has combined sewers, where flood runoff and domestic sewage flow along the same sewers to treatment plants. When the city experiences extreme rainfall, excess water, including sewage, is dumped into the Chicago River or Lake Michigan. Harza Engineering was asked to find a solution to the problem and continued to work on it into the mid-1990s. Other major domestic projects included a water supply to Denver, a pumped-storage project in Bath Country, Virginia, and a hydroelectric generation project in Susitna, Alaska. The Susitna project included the design and construction of the highest rock-fill dam in North America.

The early 1990s brought economic recession, which hit the engineering field hard. Although Harza Engineering had grown into one of the largest and most prestigious firms in the industry, it did not escape the effects of the downturn. Amid keen competition, management at the company chose to consolidate its services with those of another firm in order to cultivate more contracts. As a result, Harza Engineering merged with Kaldveer & Associates, a consulting firm in the field of geotechnical engineering. In 1992 the company was listed as the 22nd largest engineering firm in the international market, and 13th overall in the specialized power engineering market.

By the end of 1993 the recession had nearly come to an end, and Harza Engineering concentrated on improving its international market share. Since the market for engineering consulting services in the Middle East was essentially saturated, the firm turned toward opportunities in China, Latin America, and Eastern Europe. With the demise of Communism, many nations in the former East Bloc began to contract specialized engineering consulting firms for help in rebuilding their infrastructure. Harza was at the forefront of this development. By 1995 the company had moved from 13th to 10th on the list of companies in the field of power engineering consulting.

Further Reading:

"Design: Country Borders Are No Limit," *Engineering News Record,* July 24, 1995, pp. 34–38.

Hannan, Roger J., and William G. Krizan, "Stage Set for New Global Opportunities," *Engineering News Record,* April 6, 1992, pp. 37–40.

"Harza Engineering Company," *Electrical World,* August 1992, p. 30.

Harza, Richard D., *Harza Engineering Company,* Newcomen Society: New York, 1984.

Schriener, Judy, "Focus Is on Outside Borders," *Engineering News Record,* May 30, 1994, p. 18.

——, "Is That Optimism in the Air?" *Engineering News Record,* October 26, 1992, p. 17.

Tulacz, Gary J., "Asia Continues to Power International Design Quest," *Engineering News Record,* April 3, 1995, pp. 76–78.

——, "Firms Make Best of Dreary Times," *Engineering News Record,* October 4, 1993, pp. 32–48.

—Thomas Derdak

Health O Meter Products Inc.

24700 Miles Road
Beford Heights, Ohio
U.S.A.
(216) 464-4000
Fax: (216) 464-5629

Public Company
Founded: 1919 as Continental Scale Works
Employees: 993
Sales: $69.45 million
Stock Exchanges: NASDAQ
SICs: 3596 Scales and Balances, Except Laboratory; 3634
   Electric Housewares and Fans; 6719 Holding Companies,
   Not Elsewhere Classified

Health O Meter Products Inc. designs, manufactures, markets, and distributes a comprehensive line of consumer and professional products. As of 1995, it was the leading U.S. producer of weighing instruments, including bathroom, kitchen, and diet scales. It was also the top manufacturer of automatic drip coffeemakers through its venerable Mr. Coffee subsidiary. Health O Meter purchased Mr. Coffee in 1994, increasing its sales more than fourfold.

Founded in 1919, Health O Meter was a pioneer in the personal scale industry. The Germans introduced the first household, or bathroom, scale in the early 1910s. The Juraso, named after German inventors Jas Raveno and son, incorporated a small mirror suspended on chains at a forty-five degree angle to allow users to read the dial while standing on the scale. The scale became a popular novelty item and was selling worldwide within a few years. Importantly, Chicago's Marshall Field's department store began carrying the scale in 1913. At the same time, household kitchen scales were gaining in popularity, and a number of U.S. and European companies had entered that market. Thus, when World War I started and the supply to the United States of Juraso bathroom scales was cut off, Marshall Fields began looking to U.S. kitchen scale manufacturers for a replacement.

Marshall Field's new bathroom scale would ultimately be designed and manufactured under the direction Mathias C. Weber, superintendent of the Chicago Scale Company. Weber had come to the United States as a teenager in 1906 from his native Hungary. His background as a scale mechanic helped to land

him a job in New York working on commercial scales for $16 per week. He soon developed a reputation within the industry as a talented mechanic and tradesman. He was even called on by the New York City Bureau of Weights and Measures, at the age of 21, as a technical expert to give advice. In 1912 Weber was lured away by another scale manufacturer, Osgood, to manage its service department. Two years later he was hired by Chicago Scale Company as superintendent of operations—Chicago Scale's president had ordered a subordinate to hire "the best scale man in the country."

Shortly after Weber started his job at Chicago Scale, Marshall Fields approached the company about supplying a bathroom scale to replace the Juraso. "Theirs was an ordinary, ball-bearing action mechanism. I had conceived a superimposed parallelogram platform scale using a spring suspension, something I later patented," Weber recalled in *The Housewares Story*. "And we also made a big change in the arrangement of the dial. . . . I happened to glance at the speedometer on the [car] dashboard . . . 'That's it!' I shouted . . . 'we'll place the dial in such a position that it can be easily read when you're standing on the scale.' " The innovative scale was introduced in 1917 and marketed at a price of $7.50—about $2.50 less than the Juraso. "We got a letter [from the maker of the Juraso] warning us of the serious consequences if we copied their scale! We had a good laugh and went back to work."

For some time Weber had considered starting his own scale business. At home, he had even developed a new scale that he called the "Health-O-Meter." Through his barber, Weber met a wealthy investor named Irving King Hutchinson. In 1919, Irving, Irving's brother Alfred, and Weber formed the Continental Scale Works to begin manufacturing Weber's design. That same year they began building and selling the Health-O-Meter model no. 100. The scale had a cast-iron frame and incorporated an accurate rack and pinion system with hardened bearings. Selling for $16, the scale was finished in white, weighed 20 pounds, and stood eight inches tall. Its accuracy was guaranteed to within one pound.

The scale was quickly accepted in the marketplace and Continental's sales surged. The demand growth was partly attributable to the dieting fad that began in the United States following World War I. Prior to World War I, most people measured their weight at novelty machines that cost a penny. After the war, though, a slim figure was considered fashionable for women and the concept of an at-home scale was appealing. Continental Scale Works also benefited from Weber's inventive product introductions. In 1921, for example, Weber patented the horizontal clock-face scale dial. In addition, he patented the doctor's-type beam scale, which eventually became a standard fixture in doctor's offices and medical facilities throughout much of the world.

Continental, with its patented Health-O-Meter line, became the leading household scale manufacturer in the world during the 1920s and 1930s. It gradually lost much of its market dominance, however, as imitators introduced similar scales. Among the best-known imitations was the short-lived "Princess" scale, which was a low-platform scale developed by a young German immigrant named Carl Burkhardt. Burkhardt was working for Narlor Heather Company of Indiana when that company introduced his Princess scale design in 1934. Narlor unveiled the low-slung scale at a home show in Chicago. Incredibly, the scale was priced at only $1.25. It became the talk of the home show, and Narlor won a huge order for 50,000 of the scales from Sears, Roebuck and Company. When Weber was finally able to examine the scale, he was dismayed to discover that its internal mechanism was a direct copy of the one he patented for the Health-O-Meter. After a difficult fight, Weber succeeded in getting a court order to stop the company from selling the Princess.

Throughout the 1920s, 1930s, and 1940s Weber spent a significant amount of his time and resources working to protect his patents. Other scale makers did, however, introduce their own innovations and competition in the industry intensified. For example, despite its early demise, the Princess scale did become an important influence on the bathroom scale industry because of its unique low-profile design. During the 1930s, in fact, scalemakers worked to distinguish their scales from the growing herd of models by focusing on fashion. The high, box-like scales were eventually replaced by low platform designs that were offered in a number of colors, shapes, and styles. Continental met market demands with new and better scales and remained an industry innovator and leader for several years.

During the post-World War II U.S. economic and population boom, demand for bathroom scales rocketed and sales of Health-O-Meter scales increased. By the 1960s, in fact, bathroom scales had become a common fixture in American homes. By the early 1970s, moreover, Americans were purchasing more than 6 million bathroom scales annually. The bathroom scale market began to slow in the 1970s, though, and by the late 1970s had reached a level of zero growth. As competition in the bathroom scale arena heated up during the 1960s and 1970s, Continental focused its resources on the less crowded market for beam scales sold to doctor's offices and other commercial markets. Meanwhile, another company that would become an important part of the Health O Meter story was taking shape: North American Systems.

North American Systems was founded in 1968 by Vincent Marotta and Samuel Glazer. Shortly thereafter, they began to market their Mr. Coffee automatic drip coffee maker. The company got in early on the move away from percolator and other types of coffeemakers and toward more convenient drip and filter coffeemakers. By 1975 North American was the leading U.S. manufacturer of drip-type coffeemakers. As the drip concept was popularized in the late 1970s and early 1980s, the company rode a wave of success as the leading supplier. In fact, to many consumers the brand name 'Mr. Coffee' was synonymous with the drip coffeemaker. Mr. Coffee gradually suffered a reduction in its fat share of the coffeemaker market as a slew of competitors entered the industry. Competition became particularly intense during the early and mid-1980s, when low-cost foreign producers began undercutting prices on Mr. Coffee's domestic, union-manufactured machines.

Despite increased competition, the company retained its industry lead with a 30 percent share of the drip coffee market and continued to post sales and profit gains into the mid-1980s. By 1986, the still privately held North American Systems was generating roughly $120 million in annual sales. North American was purchased from Marotta in 1987. John Eikenberg, with the help of New York investment firm McKinley Allsopp Inc., bought the company through a leveraged buyout. Eikenberg, who became president of the enterprise, was a 26-year veteran of the housewares industry. He had formerly served as president of RevereWare Group and, among other credits, headed the National Housewares Manufacturing Association. He was working as a private consultant prior to the Mr. Coffee LBO. After taking control, Eikenberg quickly changed the name of the company to Mr. Coffee and made clear his intent to exploit the popular Mr. Coffee brand name in other segments of the housewares market.

Mr. Coffee languished under the control of Eikenberg and McKinley Allsopp. Sales dropped to about $102 million in 1988 during the management transition, partly because the bungled LBO had left the once financially healthy Mr. Coffee laden with more than $80 million of debt. Mr. Coffee got a $55 million loan from Chrysler Capital Corp. early in 1988 but still was unable to pay its bills. A stock offering later in the year allowed the company to avert disaster, but Mr. Coffee still posted a pitiful $7.6 million net loss for the year. In 1989, Peter Howell, another housewares industry insider, was promoted to chief executive to turn the situation around. Sales jumped to $128 million in that year and net income recovered to a positive $1.07 million. Also in 1989, Mr. Coffee began to introduce new products, including The Quick Brew microwave coffeemaker and the Iced Tea Pot, a teamaking device. Mr. Coffee's profits leaped to $5.7 million in 1990 from sales of $173 million.

Like Mr. Coffee, Continental also experienced turbulence during the 1980s—Continental became Lee-Continental Corp. after investment company Thomas H. Lee Co. purchased a major interest. Indeed, the scale market stagnated in the early 1980s and remained that way throughout the decade. By the early 1980s Health O Meter had, in effect, become a semi-successful manufacturer of high-end scales for doctors' offices. Annual sales were mired in the $15 million range, and growth prospects appeared negligible. Health O Meter had long ago ceded dominance of the bathroom scale market, which had become dominated by Sunbeam-Oyster and by Illinois-based Counselor Co., a division of Newell Co., in the mid-1980s. Attempting to boost sales and earnings, Health O Meter purchased some other companies through leveraged buyouts in 1984 and 1988, which expanded its presence in markets for household scales and timers. The LBOs were conducted under the direction of Lawrence Zalusky, who became president of the company in 1984.

By expanding into new markets, lowering prices, and chasing the mass retail market, Zalusky managed to regain some of Continental's old glory. Sales rose at an approximate rate of 19 percent annually, reaching a respectable $46 million by the early 1990s. Much of the gain was the result of Continental's reemergence as a leader in bathroom scales. Importantly, in 1989 Continental borrowed an idea from a successful scale importer to design the Bigfoot bathroom scale. The Bigfoot series of bathroom scales featured speedometer-like, oversized readouts that were an instant hit. Within three years the Bigfoot scales were accounting for about 30 percent of Continental's revenues. Continental's gains in the bathroom scale industry were made largely at the expense of Counselor Corp. Counselor suffered a long slide in the market that was capped by the loss of most of its giant K-Mart account to the increasingly competitive Continental.

Despite sales gains, Continental suffered net losses in both 1990 and 1991. The company went public in 1992 as Health O Meter Products Inc. as part of an effort to raise cash. Zalusky used the $30 million in proceeds to pare the company's debt and, among other things, invest in new marketing and product development. By early 1993 Health O Meter was boasting a dominant 60 percent of the U.S. scale market and was also enjoying success with new overseas operations. Meanwhile, Mr. Coffee stumbled again in 1991 and lost money. However, completely revamped coffeemaker lines combined with successful new product launches helped the company to raise annual sales and profits to $175 million and $6.68 million, respectively, by 1993.

In 1993, Thomas H. Lee Co., the same investment enterprise that owned 35 percent of Health O Meter, engineered the purchase of a controlling interest in Mr. Coffee. The $135 million deal resulted in Health O Meter taking over the operations of Mr. Coffee. The merger also entailed restructuring Health O Meter's debt and a $19 million stock offering designed to bring cash into the newly formed concern. Lee moved Health O Meter's corporate offices to Mr. Coffee's headquarters in Ohio and named Howell president of the new concern—Zalusky became a director on the board. Lee planned to combine the two companies to benefit from economies of scale related to both administrative and manufacturing activities. The company also planned to reduce expenses at Mr. Coffee by increasing automation and overseas manufacturing, among other initiatives.

Combined sales for Health O Meter and Mr. Coffee during 1994 approached $250 million and were rising steadily going into 1995. By 1995, Health O Meter was employing a work force of about 1,000 in all of its operations. Its two primary divisions were Mr. Coffee and Health O Meter/Pelouze. The latter division comprised a wide array of mechanical and digital scales, massagers, and timers for home use, as well as high-end scales for professional use. Those goods were sold primarily through discount merchandise chains, but also through catalogs, department stores, and mail order companies. The larger Mr. Coffee Division still emphasized drip coffeemakers and teamakers, but during the early 1990s also branched out into various kitchen appliance products, including water filters, potato baking devices, juicers, food dehydrators, and breadmakers. Although the company was still battling a relatively heavy debt load from the Mr. Coffee acquisition, improving sales and cash flow boded well for Health O Meter's short-term future.

Principal Subsidiaries: Health O Meter Inc.; Mr. Coffee.

Further Reading:

Colodny, Mark M., ''Mister Mr. Coffee,'' *Fortune,* March 25, 1991, p. 132.

Liebecik, Laura, ''New Mr. Coffee Chief Brews Plans for Products, Markets,'' *Discount Store News,* August 24, 1987, p. 34.

Lifshey, Earl, *The Housewares Story: A History of the American Housewares Industry*, Chicago: National Housewares Manufacturers Association, 1973.

Mooney, Barbara, ''Mr. Coffee Comeback Perks Along: New Products and IPO Both Are Doing Well,'' *Crains Cleveland Business,* July 9, 1990, p. 1.

——, ''Mr. Coffee Looks for Wake-Up Cup,'' *Crains Cleveland Business,* January 27, 1992, p. 3.

Murphy, H. Lee, ''Health O Meter Set to Weigh in with Home Health Care Items,'' *Crains Chicago Business,* April 20, 1992, p. 52.

——, ''Health O Meter Weighing Ohio,'' *Crains Chicago Business,* September 12, 1994, p. 4.

Oloroso, Arsenio Jr., ''Spending Adds Weight to Scale Firm's Profits,'' *Crains Chicago Business,* May 31, 1993, p. 18.

Prizinsky, David, ''State Tax Break OK'd for Mr. Coffee,'' *Crains Cleveland Business,* May 1, 1995, p. 3.

—Dave Mote

HealthSouth Rehabilitation Corporation

2 Perimeter Park South
Birmingham, Alabama 35243
U.S.A.
(205) 967-7116
Fax: (205) 969-4719

Public Company
Incorporated: 1984 as Amcare, Inc.
Employees: 27,000
Sales: $1.13 billion
Stock Exchanges: New York
SICs: 8011 Offices & Clinics of Medical Doctors; 8049
    Offices of Health Practitioners Not Elsewhere Classified;
    8069 Specialty Hospitals, Excluding Psychiatric; 8093
    Specialty Outpatient Facilities, Not Elsewhere Classified

HealthSouth Rehabilitation Corporation is the leading provider
of medical rehabilitation services in the United States with
approximately 40 percent of the total market. Through about
450 outpatient and 100 inpatient facilities (in late 1995), Health-
South offered physical, occupational, and respiratory therapies,
as well as speech language pathology, sports medicine, neuro-
rehabilitation, and nursing care. The enterprise was expanding
rapidly in the mid-1990s by acquiring other companies.

HealthSouth was the brainchild of Richard Scrushy. Scrushy
grew up in Selma, Alabama, and earned a degree in respiratory
therapy from the University of Alabama, Birmingham. By the
age of 30 he had advanced to vice-president at Lifemark Corp.,
a Houston-based health care management firm. At Lifemark,
Scrushy witnessed first-hand the changes sweeping the health
care industry. The dominant trend was toward a reduction in
reimbursement dollars available to traditional medical practi-
tioners. Corporations and insurance companies were trying to
cut health care expenditures while, at the same time, costs in the
medical field were rising. ''I saw the squeezing of reimbursement in the health care system and I wanted to take advantage of
that change,'' Scrushy said in a June 1990 article in *Forbes*.
''My idea,'' he added, ''was to provide high-quality hospital-
type rehabilitation services in a low-cost setting.''

Scrushy got his chance to start his rehabilitation company in
1984, when Lifemark Corp. was purchased by Los Angeles-

based American Medical International. Armed with a plan,
Scrushy lacked only the money to get started. His break came in
a Houston restaurant, when a Citicorp venture capitalist over-
heard Scrushy outlining his business plan and eventually offered a $1 million grubstake, giving birth to what would become
HealthSouth. Scrushy convinced four of his Lifemark associates to break ranks with him and move to Birmingham to build
the company's first outpatient facility. Their company was incorporated in January 1984 as Amcare Inc. before its name was
changed to HealthSouth in May 1985.

Scrushy got into the rehabilitation industry at a good time.
During the early 1980s people began to view rehabilitation as a
means of reducing medical expenses. Specifically, rehabilitation could be used to minimize unnecessary, expensive
surgeries. It also helped injured workers get back to their jobs
more quickly, thus eliminating expensive worker's compensation and disability costs. As health and insurance professionals
began to recognize those benefits, the use of rehabilitation
services soared. Between 1982 and 1990, in fact, rehabilitation
expenditures increased at an average annual rate of about 20
percent and the number of outpatient rehabilitation centers
soared. That industry growth contributed to healthy gains for
HealthSouth throughout the decade.

Perhaps more important than general industry expansion for
HealthSouth during the 1980s was Scrushy's and his fellow
managers' unique operating strategy. When HealthSouth got
started in 1984, rehabilitation centers were stereotyped as drab,
institutional-like facilities with generally mediocre staff.
Scrushy wanted to change that image. Borrowing from health
clubs, he designed his rehab centers as bright, open-spaced,
mirrored rooms with trained physical therapists and sporty
equipment. The centers more closely resembled high-priced
health clubs than traditional hospital-styled rehab centers, and
doctors became increasingly willing to send patients to a
HealthSouth facility for treatment. Scrushy added a few more
HealthSouth outlets and by 1985 was generating nearly $5
million in annual revenues.

HealthSouth added new rehab centers to its chain throughout
the mid- and late 1980s. Because of the company's unique
recipe for success, its centers became known as effective and
cost-efficient, and as models for other companies in the rehab
industry. Rather than focusing on a specific rehab niche, such as
head or spinal injures, HealthSouth differed from many of its
competitors in that it targeted the larger market for less expensive, general outpatient rehabilitation services. HealthSouth's
facilities were built around a large gymnasium, in which some
patients rode exercise bikes while listening to rock music. Old
and young people worked out side-by-side, often with the help
of a therapist, while others enjoyed physical, occupational, or
speech therapy in private treatment rooms. Some of the machines were even hooked to computers that fed reports to
doctors about how patients were responding to treatment.

HealthSouth appealed to the medical community by offering a
number of rehabilitation programs tailored for different ailments. At the urging of Dr. Scott Burke, a Denver spinal
rehabilitations specialist, HealthSouth designed a program to
treat back problems. Becoming widely used, the whole package—incorporating stretching, aerobic conditioning, anatomy

education, and work simulation exercises—took about four weeks and cost a total of only $3,700, which was much less than the patient might otherwise spend on unnecessary surgeries and hospital costs. HealthSouth also began offering special services for the lucrative sports rehabilitation market. To that end, HealthSouth eventually launched an entire sports division with separate facilities and prominent doctors. Dr. Jim Andrews, one of HealthSouth's most renowned surgeons, treated such celebrities as Bo Jackson, Jane Fonda, and Charles Barkley, among others.

While HealthSouth kept the doctors and patients happy with state-of-the-art facilities, it stayed on the good side of the insurance companies by minimizing overhead and treatment costs. It saved money on construction, for example, by using the same basic floor plan and architecture for all of its outpatient centers, including the same carpeting, wallpaper, and furniture. Because the centers processed so many patients—about 15 to 20 per hour, or roughly 200 a day at many HealthSouth facilities—the average cost of a visit was kept at a low $50 to $90. Insurers didn't blink at the cost, because it was much less expensive than traditional treatment. A study conducted by Northwestern National Life Insurance Co. estimated that every $1 spent on rehabilitation saved about $30 on disability benefits.

By 1988 HealthSouth was operating a network of 21 outpatient facilities, 11 inpatient facilities, and seven rehabilitation equipment centers in 15 states, making it a leader in the U.S. rehabilitation industry. Sales had spiraled upward at an average of more than 100 percent annually since 1984, peaking at $75 million in 1988. Revenues shot up to $114 million in 1989 and then to $181 million in 1990, about $13 million of which was netted as income. In fact, HealthSouth managed to post successive profits every year after 1985. Besides increasing its customer base at existing centers, the company grew by purchasing other rehab and health care companies and restructuring them to fit into the HealthSouth organization. It was in December 1989, for example, that Scrushy jumped into the sports rehab business when he paid $21 million for a 219-bed general hospital in Birmingham that specialized in orthopedic surgery and sports medicine.

By the mid-1990s, HealthSouth was operating 14 inpatient and 31 freestanding outpatient rehabilitation centers in 21 states. The company continued to add new general rehabilitation centers to its chain in 1991 and 1992. Meanwhile, its specialized sports business flourished and it enjoyed success with its new orthopedic hospitals that featured leading surgeons. By 1992 HealthSouth had established itself as one of two leaders in the U.S. rehabilitation industry. Its chief nemesis was Continental Medical Systems Inc., of Pennsylvania. Continental, with $20 million in net earnings in 1991 compared to $22 million for HealthSouth, generated most of its profit from rehabilitation service contracts with hospitals, schools, and nursing homes. Like HealthSouth, it operated inpatient and outpatient rehab centers across the country.

Continental and HealthSouth nearly merged in 1992. The resulting company would have been a $2 billion concern had the deal not fallen through. Instead, HealthSouth remained independent and went on to become the largest provider of rehabilitative services in the nation. It attained that status through an aggres-

sive merger and acquisition agenda advanced during the early and mid-1990s. Chief among its acquisitions was the purchase of National Medical Enterprises Inc. in December 1993. That pivotal buyout added 31 inpatient rehabilitation facilities and 12 outpatient rehabilitation centers to HealthSouth's portfolio, boosting the total number of outpatient centers in its chain from 126 at the end of 1992 to 171 going into 1994. Evidencing the effectiveness of HealthSouth's strategy was a substantial improvement in the performance of National Medical's facilities in the two years following the acquisition.

HealthSouth's revenues for 1993 surged impressively to $575 million and the company assumed the industry lead. Health-South achieved its dazzling gains during the early 1990s, in part, by focusing on rehabilitating people who were injured rather than chronically ill. That was the primary growth market, because employers and insurance companies were eager to get those people out of the health care system. HealthSouth's Workstart program was a good example of its core service. The Workstart plan was designed to get most workers back on the job after surgery or an injury within 30 days at an average cost of just $2,700. The program was ideal for employers because HealthSouth, using advanced testing and statistical analysis, was able to determine the extent of the patients' pain and injury. Among other benefits, that kind of analysis discouraged faking or exaggerating the extent of injuries to take advantage of disability payment programs.

HealthSouth stepped up its acquisition program in 1994 and 1995 by absorbing a number of new companies. Two major purchases included the September 1994 acquisition of ReLife Inc. and the February 1995 buyout of NovaCare, Inc.'s inpatient rehabilitation hospital division. ReLife brought 31 inpatient rehabilitation facilities and 12 outpatient centers that added roughly $119 million in annual revenues to HealthSouth's income statement. That and other acquisitions helped to push HealthSouth's sales past the $1 billion mark to $1.13 billion in 1994. Furthermore, net income vaulted to $53.23 million and the company's stock price raced to a record level. Following the NovaCare acquisition, the company's total network rose to more than 425 facilities located in 33 states.

HealthSouth sustained its aggressive growth drive throughout 1995, snapping up several smaller competitors. Importantly, in October 1995 HealthSouth announced that it had agreed to purchase the rehabilitation services operations of Caremark International for $127 million in cash. The Caremark operations consisted of 123 outpatient rehabilitation facilities that were generating about $80 million in annual revenues. That gave the company a total of about 440 outpatient facilities and about 40 percent of the total rehabilitation market. Also notable was the early 1995 acquisition of Surgical Health Corporation, which represented HealthSouth's diversification into an entirely new market: outpatient surgery services. HealthSouth also bought Diagnostic Health Corporation, which offered outpatient imaging services. Going into 1996, HealthSouth, still under Scrushy's leadership, was the U.S. leader in rehabilitation services and sports medicine and one of the top providers of outpatient surgery services.

Principal Subsidiaries: HealthSouth Medical Center, Inc.; Sports Therapy and Advanced Rehabilitation Training, Inc.;

Physician Practice Management Corp.; Disability and Impairment Evaluation Centers of America, Inc.; HealthSouth Doctors' Hospital, Inc.; Hospital Health Systems, Inc.; HRC Day Care, Inc.; Doctors' Health Service Corp.; Doctors' Scanning Associates, Inc.; Doctors' Home Health, Inc.; Doctors' Medical Equipment Corp.

Further Reading:

Brown, Valerie D., "HealthSouth Corporation Acquires Therapy Group," *Springfield Business Journal,* July 24, 1995, p. 3.

"HealthSouth Adds Facilities in Three States," *PR Newswire,* June 25, 1993.

Paris, Ellen, "Straighten That Back! Bend Those Knees!" *Forbes,* June 11, 1990, p. 92.

Tanner, Anthony J., "Health South Rehabilitation Corp. to Build 151-Bed Facility in Michigan," *Business Wire,* October 24, 1988.

Yardley, Jim, "The Road to Recovery," *Atlanta Constitution,* February 20, 1992, Sec. B.

Young, Randy, "HealthSouth Puts Injured Workers Back on Wellness Track," *San Antonio Business Journal,* June 26, 1989, Sec. 2, p. 17.

—Dave Mote

Heilig-Meyers Co.

2235 Staples Mill Road
Richmond, Virginia 23230
U.S.A.
(804) 359-9171
Fax: (804) 254-1493

Public Company
Founded: 1913
Operating Revenues: $1.15 billion
Employees: 12,510
Stock Exchanges: New York Chicago Pacific
SICs: 5712 Furniture Stores; 5719 Miscellaneous Home
   Furnishings Stores; 6411 Insurance Agents, Brokers and
   Service

The Heilig-Meyers Co. has been described as the Wal-Mart of home furnishings. Partly by acquisition, partly by expansion, Heilig-Meyers grew so rapidly in the 1970s and 1980s that in 1986 it became the largest publicly traded home-furnishings retailer in the United States. It passed the $1 billion mark in annual revenues in 1994. By May 1995 Heilig-Meyers had 662 stores in 24 states and Puerto Rico. Most of these were in small towns more than 25 miles from a metropolitan market. Heilig-Meyers was selling not only furniture and accessories, but also bedding, small appliances, consumer electronics, jewelry, and seasonal goods. An important source of income was in-house credit. About 80 percent of its sales had been made on credit, principally through installment sales. It also offered insurance with its credit sales.

Heilig-Meyers was founded in 1913, when W. A. Heilig and J. M. Meyers opened a home-furnishings store in Goldsboro, North Carolina. These two Lithuanian immigrants had entered the retail business in 1911 by peddling piece goods to farmers settled around Goldsboro. The two men drove a horse and wagon over dirt roads to deliver merchandise, or even traveled on foot with the furniture on their backs.

In-house credit, along with effective cost controls, allowed Heilig-Meyers to survive the Great Depression. In its only year in the red, 1931, the company still only lost $5,000. By 1934 Heilig-Meyers had added stores in Kinston and Wilson, North Carolina. A fourth store opened in Raleigh in 1936 and a fifth in Rocky Mount, North Carolina in 1939.

The collaboration between Heilig and Meyers ended in 1946 with the Meyers family retaining control of the stores in Goldsboro, Wilson, and Rocky Mount. J. M. Meyers turned over direct management responsibility to his sons Hyman and Sidney. Hyman became president and general manager, and Sidney became director of merchandising. Their father continued, however, to be involved daily with all aspects of the business until his death in 1968.

Company headquarters were moved to Richmond, Virginia, in 1951.

By this time Heilig-Meyers had developed its operational philosophy of focusing on small towns and rural areas for its growth. Because newspaper circulation was limited in such locations, management chose to base its advertising on direct mail. The limited customer base meant that the company could not grow if it confined itself to selling furniture. Soon items such as jewelry, electronic goods, small appliances, lawn mowers, and bicycles were being offered as well. In 1965, when Heilig-Meyers had 14 stores, mostly in eastern North Carolina, it opened a central warehousing facility in Rocky Mount.

Heilig-Meyers had 19 stores early in 1970, when it merged with the nine-store chain of Thornton Stores of Suffolk, Virginia. George A. Thornton, Jr., founder of Thornton Stores, became chairman of the board of the combined company, a position he held until his death in 1980. Heilig-Meyers had 41 stores when it went public in 1972 to finance further expansion. The officers, besides Thornton, were Hyman Meyers, president, and Sidney Meyers and Nathan Krumbein (brother-in-law of Hyman and Sidney Meyers), vice-presidents. Heilig-Meyers had revenues of $22.1 million and net income of $1.5 million in 1972. In 1974, when it operated 55 stores in North Carolina, South Carolina, and Virginia, it had net income of $1.7 million on revenues of $34.4 million.

Part of Heilig-Meyers's subsequent growth in the 1970s came by acquisition. The company purchased the assets of Granite Furniture Co. of Mount Airy, North Carolina, in 1975, and Bruce's Furniture Stores of Easley, South Carolina, in 1979. It also bought furniture stores in Richmond, Danville, Virginia, and Kershaw, South Carolina. By 1980 there were 72 stores. Revenues had risen to $81.5 million and net income to $5.1 million. Management considered, but ultimately rejected, a 1979 proposal from an unidentified company to buy Heilig-Meyers for about $36 million in cash and notes. Two years later it turned down a $43.9 million offer from Citicorp Capital Investors Inc. of Chicago and Founders Equity Inc. of Washington.

The Meyers brothers and Krumbein sold much of their stock in 1983 and retired the next year, but remained directors. They turned over the management to two trusted executives still in their thirties, William DeRusha and Troy Peery, Jr.. DeRusha, the company president, subsequently became chairman and chief executive officer. Peery advanced from treasurer to senior vice-president and secretary and later became president and chief operating officer. DeRusha and Peery still held these posts in 1995.

DeRusha won an award and high praise from the *Wall Street Transcript* in 1984 for his management. A leading industry specialist cited Heilig-Meyers for "the number one management team in the industry." He credited the previous management with having put into place a successful system of how the stores should be run, down to the smallest detail. Another industry analyst said that in 1982, a year of severe economic recession year, "Their earnings only flattened when others typically went down 20, 30, 50 percent. They've never closed a store in their 72-year history as a result of nonperformance.... What we could say has changed is that they've adopted a more rapid expansion program."

The Heilig-Meyers system of operation called for placing stores in communities of 50,000 or less, where competition from other retailers was limited to local stores. After saturating the market in Virginia, North Carolina, and portions of West Virginia, the company turned in the 1980s to South Carolina, Georgia, Alabama, Mississippi, and Tennessee for expansion. In fiscal 1985 (ending March 31, 1985), when there were 127 stores, net income reached $11.7 million on revenues of $167.9 million. A board of investment analysts told the *Wall Street Transcript* in 1985 that Heilig-Meyers had become "the premier investment play in the retailing side of the [home furnishings] business.... They have established a tremendous record—20 percent compounded growth rate in earning and 15 percent compounded growth rate in sales."

Part of this growth was by acquisition. In 1984 Heilig-Meyers bought a Bristol, Tennessee, furniture company and a West Virginia supply company that it merged into a subsidiary. The purchase of 14 Royal Jackson stores in 1985 for $9.3 million opened up the Mississippi and Alabama markets. In 1986 the company bought the 74-unit Sterchi Bros. Co. for $44 million. These acquisitions brought Heilig-Meyers's total to 216 stores in 175 towns.

Although Heilig-Meyers was selling household goods ranging from VCRs to bicycles and lawn mowers, in addition to furniture, DeRusha told a interviewer for *Dun's Business Month* in 1986 that "We're really in the distribution and credit business." Some 90 percent of the company's 300,000 customers were using its credit plans to make purchases on time, paying annual financing charges of up to 24 percent. Income from credit came to 16 percent of total revenues. In defense of the company's practices, DeRusha pointed out that many of its customers could not pay cash, that there was no minimum monthly payment or penalty for late payment, and that it offered delivery within a week plus a unique repair service.

Heilig-Meyers placed great emphasis on its intensive training program of three to five years for developing its store managers. Once promoted to this level, company personnel were earning $32,000 to $38,000 a year, with an incentive program based on store performance that could double their salaries. As a result, the Heilig-Meyers manager was the highest-paid person in some towns.

In 1987 Heilig-Meyers purchased 22 stores in North Carolina, South Carolina, and Georgia from Reliable Stores Inc. for about $22 million in cash. It was also planning to open 20 to 25 new stores during the year. By early 1988 the company had 258 stores in 11 states, with its reach extending into Florida and Kentucky. Revenue came to $303.5 million in fiscal 1988, and

net income to $15.5 million. The following year revenue grew to $351.6 million and earnings to $17.1 million. By the fall of 1989 the 277-store chain had entered the Midwest for the first time, in Ohio.

In February 1990 Heilig-Meyers bought 34 stores and warehouses in Tennessee, Kentucky, West Virginia, and Virginia from Reliable Stores for about $35 million. Over the next year it also acquired six stores from Holthouse Furniture Corp. and nine from The Furniture Center, Inc., for $5,639,000 and $10,621,000, respectively. Revenues reached $447.8 million in fiscal 1991, and net earnings $18.3 million. Later in 1991 the company bought five more Furniture Center stores for $2,782,000 and 42 stores from WCK, Inc., for $14,384,000.

By 1992 Heilig-Meyers had set a goal of 50 new stores a year. In that year it acquired 13 stores from Gibson McDonald Furniture Co. for $13,736,0000, four stores from Reichart Furniture Corp. for $739,000, and 14 stores in Pennsylvania and West Virginia from Wolf Furniture Enterprises for $6,799,000. Of Heilig-Meyers's 401 stores, 60 percent were less than four years old. There were five distribution facilities, each designed to serve between 90 and 125 stores within a 200-mile radius.

Heilig-Meyers purchased McMahan's Furniture Co. for $65 million in 1993. This acquisition added 92 stores: 65 in California, 12 in Arizona, seven in New Mexico, four in Texas, three in Nevada, and one in Colorado. The company entered the Chicago area by purchasing 11 L. Fish stores. This acquisition of Fish's four downtown and seven suburban stores was a departure from the company's traditional focus on smaller markets, but DeRusha said they were a good geographic fit for Heilig-Meyers, which had been expanding in the Midwest. Also in 1993 the company began sponsoring a racing team in NASCAR motor-racing competition.

Noting that about 80 percent of its sales were being made on company credit cards, an industry analyst declared in late 1993 that Heilig-Meyers had emerged in recent years as the country's most profitable furniture retailer. Its market capitalization of $1.6 billion was said to be the biggest in the business. The only question was whether the chain, with 470 stores, was running out of room to expand at its recent annual profits growth rate of 30 percent. After Heilig-Meyers reported sales up 31 percent and profits up 45 percent in fiscal 1994, a professor at American University wrote that the company recorded installment purchases in revenues before sales were final and glossed over a negative cash flow of $75 million. Heilig-Meyers's treasurer replied that "The whole report is completely erroneous and full of inaccuracies."

There was no change in the Heilig-Meyers strategy in 1994. It announced plans to open 70 to 90 stores during fiscal 1995, exclusive of acquisitions. Seventy-seven stores were added during 1994, including eight acquired Nelson Bros. units in the Chicago area, bringing the total to 647. Near the end of 1994 Heilig-Meyers announced plans to acquire Puerto Rico's largest-volume furniture retailer, Berrios Enterprises, for $85 million. The deal gave Heilig-Meyers 17 more stores and its first presence outside the U.S. mainland.

For fiscal 1995 (ending February 28, 1995), Heilig-Meyers reported that sales had reached $956 million and total revenues

$1.15 billion, an increase of 33 percent over the previous fiscal year. Net earnings were $66.8 million, up 21 percent. The company planned to open at least 50 new stores and to aggressively seek acquisitions that could take it beyond the 700-store mark in 1995. By then a sixth distribution center had opened in Moberly, Missouri, to serve its stores in Illinois, Iowa, and Missouri, and a seventh, in Fontana, California, to serve its California stores. According to company executives, expansion would continue to center primarily on small-town markets in the Southeast and Midwest. The company's long-term debt was $370.4 million at the end of fiscal 1995, up from $248.6 million at the end of fiscal 1994. Dividends had been paid in every year since 1975.

In 1995 Heilig-Meyers stores generally ranged in size between 10,000 and 30,000 square feet. The company owned 80 of its stores at the end of fiscal 1995, leasing the rest. Prototype stores, first introduced in fiscal 1993, featured the latest technology in display techniques and construction efficiencies. Existing stores were being remodeled on a rotational basis, with 38 remodeled in fiscal 1995 and about 50 slated for renovation in fiscal 1996.

During 1995 about 59 percent of Heilig-Meyers's sales were derived from furniture and accessories; 12 percent from jewelry, small appliances, seasonal goods, and miscellaneous items; 11 percent from consumer electronics; 10 percent from bedding; and 8 percent from appliances. These percentages had not varied significantly over the past three fiscal years. There were distribution centers in Orangeburg, South Carolina; Rocky Mount, North Carolina; Russellville, Alabama; Mount Sterling, Kentucky; Thomasville, Georgia; Moberly, Missouri; and Fontana, California. Three were owned by the company and the others leased, as was the corporate headquarters in Richmond. A fleet of trucks operated by the company delivered merchandise to each store at least twice a week.

Service centers in Fayetteville, North Carolina, Moberly, and Fontana provided repair services on virtually all consumer electronics and mechanical items sold in Heilig-Meyers stores. These centers had the capacity to process 500 repair jobs a week and were also authorized to perform repair work under certain manufacturers' warranties. Most repair orders had a turnaround of one week.

Heilig-Meyers was accepting major credit cards in all of its stores and, in addition, offering a revolving credit program featuring its private-label credit card. The company was extending credit for terms up to 24 months, with the average installment term about 17 months. During fiscal 1995 finance income amounted to about 17 percent of total revenues. Heilig-Meyers also offered property and life insurance, and in some states disability insurance, with its credit sales.

Monthly direct-mail circulars reaching about ten million households accounted for about half of Heilig-Meyers's advertising expenses in fiscal 1995, while television and radio commercials, produced centrally, were aired in almost all of the company markets.

Principal Subsidiaries: Heilig-Meyers Furniture Co.; HMPR, Inc. (Puerto Rico); MacSaver Financial Services, Inc.; MacSaver Insurance Co., Ltd (Bermuda).

Further Reading:

Buchanan, Lee, "Heilig-Meyers Sees 700 Units," *Furniture/Today,* November 14, 1994, pp. 1, 18.

Craft, Leslie, Jr., "What's in Store for Heilig-Meyers?" *Furniture/Today,* October 5, 1992, p. 16.

Engel, Clint, "Heilig-Meyers to Buy 17 Puerto Rican Units," *Furniture/Today,* December 26, 1994, pp. 1, 51.

——, "Heilig-Meyers Hones Strategy," *Furniture/Today,* March 27, 1995, pp. 1, 46.

Epperson, Wallace W., Jr., "Heilig-Meyers Co.," *Wall Street Transcript,* December 3, 1984, p. 76114.

"Furnishings/Residential & Commercial," *Wall Street Transcript,* September 16, 1985, pp. 79200–79202.

Hackney, Holt, "Heilig-Meyers: The Vulture Play in Home Furnishings," *Financial World,* December 8, 1992, pp. 18–19.

Levy, Robert, "Heilig-Meyers: Selling Big in Small Towns," *Dun's Business Month,* June 1986, pp. 56–57.

Schroeder, Michael, "The Sherlock Holmes of Accounting," *Business Week,* September 5, 1994, p. 48.

—Robert Halasz

Hermès S.A.

24, rue de Faubourg Saint Honoré
F-75008 Paris 08
France
(40) 17 47 17
Fax: (40) 17 47 18

Public Company
Founded: 1837
Employees: 2,700
Sales: Ffr 3.4 billion (US$694.2 million)
Stock Exchanges: Paris
SICs: 2300 Apparel & Other Textile Products; 3160
   Luggage; 3170 Handbags & Personal Leather Goods; 3870
   Watches, Clocks & Parts; 3110 Leather Tanning &
   Finishing; 3150 Leather Gloves & Mittens; 3910 Jewelry,
   Silverware, & Plated Ware; 5600 Apparel & Accessory
   Stores

Known as "one of the world's most elegant businesses,"
Hermès S.A. is a manufacturer and marketer of upscale luggage, apparel, and accessories. From a 19th-century foundation
in leather goods, the company (pronounced "air-may") diversified into silk goods (about 36 percent of sales in the early
1990s), ready-to-wear clothing (12 percent), and perfume (7.5
percent). Its ongoing dedication to family ownership and management, impeccable craftsmanship, and careful protection of
the brand's mystique set Hermès apart from many of its French
luxury goods compatriots.

With or without the venerable trademark, Hermès products are
distinguished by their uncompromising quality, a concept summarized in a family credo: "Que l'utile soit beau" ("That the
useful be beautiful"). By the mid-1990s Hermès was one of the
few French luxury goods manufacturers to remain under family
control. The firm made its first public stock offering in 1993 but
retained over 80 percent of its equity in the hands of 56
members of the Hermès family, six of whom owned 5–10
percent stakes. The familial stranglehold on control led Mimi
Tompkins of *U.S. News & World Report* to dub the company
"one of Paris' best-guarded jewels."

In the 1980s and early 1990s the business was led by Jean-Louis
Dumas, a fifth-generation descendant of the founder. Stanley
Marcus, chairman emeritus of Neiman-Marcus, has called
Dumas "one of the brightest retailers in the world." He's been

credited with building Hermès's worldwide retailing empire by
directing an intense program of geographic expansion. Although more than 50 percent of annual sales were still generated
in Europe in the early 1990s, the Asia/Pacific region contributed
nearly one-third of annual revenues, and the United States
pitched in 11 percent of yearly turnover. Hermès enjoyed average annual sales increases of 23 percent from 1984 to 1994 but
expected that heady growth to slow to single-digit percentages
in the mid- to late 1990s.

Hermès's trademark caléche, or horse-drawn carriage (based on
a drawing by Alfred de Dreux), harkens back to its original
wholesale saddlery business. Founded in 1837 by Thierry
Hermès, the firm gained renown as a producer of one-of-a-kind
saddlery for European noblemen. It has even been rumored that
coronations were sometimes postponed for years until Hermès
could create original carriage designs.

The functional and decorative "saddle stitch" used by Hermès
craftsmen to join pieces of leather would come to represent the
branded goods' quality and simple elegance. When executed by
hand (as it was throughout Hermès's history), the technique
involved punching holes through multiple layers of leather, then
alternating needles at either end of a beeswaxed linen thread
through the holes in a figure-eight pattern. The company continued to custom-make saddles, investing 20 to 40 hours in each,
throughout the 19th and 20th centuries.

Thierry's son Emile-Charles moved the family business to 24,
rue du Faubourg St. Honoré—a site that would become one of
Paris's most prized pieces of real estate—and launched retail
sales before the turn of the 20th century. He sold his stake in the
business to brother Emile-Maurice in 1922.

Faced with the ascent of the automobile and corresponding
obsolescence of the carriage, Emile-Maurice began to diversify
into travel- and sport-related leather goods, but he never abandoned Hermès's "horsey heritage." Saddlebags gave way to
luggage, wallets, and handbags. The famous Hermès "Kelly"
bag, named in the 1950s after Princess Grace (née Kelly) of
Monaco, who was often photographed with the accessory,
started out as a specialty 19th-century saddlebag and was reintroduced as a handbag in the 1930s. The attention to detail that
had become a family hallmark was applied to every new
Hermès product. The construction of each Kelly bag, for example, required 18 man-hours, and each purse was made by a
single artisan. This association with royalty and celebrities—
the Hermès "Constance" purse was a favorite of Jacqueline
Kennedy Onassis—helped burnish the brand image. Although
the company introduced a dozen new handbag styles each year,
these two designs remained in consistent demand, perhaps because of their association with these two international icons.

In the early 1900s Emile-Maurice bought a two-year patent on a
Canadian invention, the fermeture éclair (zipper), and brought it
back to France. The closure became so closely associated with
Hermès products like handbags, jockey silks, and leather gloves
that Frenchmen came to call it a fermeture Hermès. One oft-
repeated "zipper story" finds the Prince of Wales, a well-
known fashion plate, requesting a zippered leather golfing
jacket, thereby inaugurating the Hermès line of leather apparel.

The family launched ready-to-wear clothing, leather-banded watches, and leather gloves in the 1920s as well.

Emile-Maurice passed the family business on to his son-in-law, Robert Dumas. Dumas directed the design and production of the first Hermès carré, or scarf, in 1937. The custom-ordered accessory, called "Jeu des Ombinus et Dames Blanches," featured white-wigged ladies playing a popular period game. Over the years the scarves became ingrained in the French culture as a traditional heirloom. Although scarf production slackened in the mid-20th century, by the mid-1980s Hermès was unveiling a dozen new designs each year.

Like the production of leather goods, Hermès scarf-making process was totally dedicated to the pursuit of quality. Vertical integration was an important factor in that cause. By the early 1990s Hermès oversaw the entire process, from the purchase of the raw Chinese silk at auction, its spinning into yarn, and its weaving into a fabric twice as strong and heavy as that found in most scarves. Hermès scarf designers would spend years composing new prints, which were individually screen-printed with vegetable dye. In the process, each color is allowed to dry for one month before the next is applied. Hermès artisans would choose from a palette of over 200,000 colors; the most complicated design featured 40 colors. Hand-rolling and -hemming the scarves, which consumes a half-hour each, completes the process.

Notwithstanding this painstaking process, Hermès managed to put out two new scarf collections each year. Some designs reflected annual themes, like "the road" (1994) or "the sun" (1995), while other perennial favorites remained in circulation for decades. Scarf motifs have ranged from germane—the French Revolution, French cuisine—to the unexpected, like the flora and fauna of Texas. Some observers considered the scarves to be collectible works of art. Overall scarf volume multiplied from 250,000 in 1978 to 500,000 in 1986 and 1.2 million in 1989.

Hermès's union of quality materials and time-consuming handcraftsmanship was reflected in its high retail prices. By the mid-1990s one Hermès scarf commanded $245, a tie cost $115, and a Kelly purse set its owner back about $3,500. High demand added another element to the cost: customers were known to wait more than a year for orders to be filled.

Over the decades Hermès also earned a reputation for creating unique custom articles. Urging clients to "faites nous rêver" (make us dream), Hermès designers and craftsmen fashioned unusual special orders. The custom items ranged from the functional, like a calfskin fly-fishing tackle box, to the frivolous, like an ostrich-skin Walkman case. These limited-edition novelties didn't come cheap, either: indulgences like $175 chewing-gum holders made of leather, $1,000 silk kites, $20,000 alligator golf bags, and $12,500 mink jogging suits were out of reach for most of the world's consumers.

During the 1970s some observers feared that Hermès's profitability was being sacrificed on the altar of quality. Its own dedication to classic, natural materials—silk and leather—and modest styles clashed head-on with the era's love-affair with newer man-made materials—like plastic and polyester—and sexy fashions. Hermès's five percent annual sales growth rate lagged France's 15 percent inflation rate in the 1970s, and at one point, the company's workrooms—familiarly called "la ruche" (the beehive)—fell silent during a two-week lapse in orders.

When Robert Dumas died in 1978, his son, Jean-Louis, assumed the company's top post. The younger Dumas had worked as a buyer for Bloomingdale's before returning to the family firm in 1964, and this "outside" experience may have been the catalyst for the sweeping turnaround he engineered in the 1980s.

His multifaceted strategy expanded and revitalized the product line, strengthened the brand's youth appeal, extended vertical integration, and targeted the United States and Asia as fertile ground for growth. Dumas hired two young clothing designers, Eric Bergére and Bernard Sanz, to revive the apparel line. They added kinky new garments like python motorcycle jackets and ostrich-skin jeans that were characterized as "a snazzier version of what Hermès has been all along." A 1979 French advertising campaign that featured a young, denim-clad woman accessorized with an Hermès scarf introduced the branded goods to a new generation of consumers. As one writer noted in 1986, "Much of what bears the still-discreet Hermès label changed from the object of an old person's nostalgia to the subject of young peoples' dreams." By 1990 Hermès had expanded its array of merchandise to include 30,000 different items.

Dumas also revived the Hermès passion for vertical integration, which brought quality control at all phases of production under the family's watchful eyes. For example, Hermès had launched a line of "art de vivre"—giftware and home furnishings—in 1954. In the 1980s Dumas strengthened the company's hold on its suppliers, acquiring major stakes in such prestigious French glassware, silverware, and tableware manufacturers as Puiforcat, St. Louis, and Perigord. These tactics positioned tableware as one of Hermès's most promising business segments for the late 1990s.

The company's explosive growth—annual sales multiplied from about $50 million in 1978 to $460 million by 1990, and its net profit grew even faster—had as much to do with changing consumer values as with Dumas's revitalization. The trend of the 1960s and 1970s toward synthetic materials reversed, and a wave of conspicuous consumption engrossed consumers, especially Japanese and American "nouveau riche." Although demand for luxury goods stalled somewhat in the early 1990s, the global market surged from $4 billion in 1988 to nearly $6 million in 1994, according to France's luxury trade group, the Comité Colbert.

Dumas took advantage of the resurgence in Hermès's popularity by boosting store locations and licensed boutiques in America, Japan, Asia, and the Pacific Rim. The number of Hermès-owned stores quadrupled from 15 in 1978 to 60 in the early 1990s, as the total number of outlets worldwide grew to more than 225.

U.S. sales tripled from $20 million in 1986 to nearly $60 million in 1988 under the direction of Chrysler Fisher, an American. Hermès had first entered the U.S. market in the 1930s, when its products were offered at Lord & Taylor's New York store. The company later pulled out of the United States, only to relaunch a line of ties at Neiman-Marcus in the 1960s. Fisher, a former Neiman-Marcus executive, tailored Hermès to the convenience-oriented American consumer with the addition of a toll-free number, a customer-service department, and direct mail. When Fisher resigned in January 1993, Laurent Mommeja, a sixth-generation Hermès descendant, took over and announced plans to double U.S. sales by 1998.

Under pressure from some factions in the extended family, Hermès made its first public stock offering in June 1993. The equity sale generated more excitement than the semiannual sales at Hermès's flagship store: the 425,000 shares floated at Ffr 300 (US$55) each were oversubscribed by 34 times. Dumas told *Forbes* magazine that the equity sale helped lessen family tensions by allowing some members to liquidate their holdings without squabbling over share valuations among themselves. By 1995 the shares were trading at Ffr 600.

Perfume has been one of the few Hermès ventures to struggle. This business segment was launched by Jean Guerrand, a son-in-law of Emile-Maurice, with "Eau d'Hermès" in 1951. The business was elevated to subsidiary status in 1961 concurrent with the introduction of "Calèche" perfume (named for the company's carriage trademark). By 1993 Comptoir Nouveau de la Perfumerie was generating about Ffr 200 million ($40 million) in annual sales. Although the company's line of fragrances for men and women had captured seven percent of global perfume sales, its annual losses mounted in the early 1990s. This segment's sales peaked at Ffr 254 million in 1990 and declined to Ffr 200 million by 1994, while losses bloomed from Ffr 1.4 million in 1992 to about Ffr 30 million by 1994.

The very nature of the product may provide insight into Hermès's struggle to make it viable in the 1990s. While the vast majority of Hermès products are carefully fashioned to endure a lifetime of use, perfume is a mass-produced product with a decidedly ephemeral effect. Nevertheless, the retailer launched "24, Faubourg," a scent named for the address of the company's flagship store, in 1995 and 1996. Hermès hoped that the light, fresh fragrance would appeal to a younger customer than its more traditional perfumes and recapture the essence of luxury that had infused its perfume business with success in the 1950s and 1960s. In the meantime, the company sought to achieve profitability by contracting its excess manufacturing capacity to others in the mid-1990s.

Hermès's 1994 revenues totaled Ffr 3.43 billion, 20 percent more than the previous year's mark, and net increased 38 percent to Ffr 290 million. A growing advertising budget was partially credited with sales spurts in leather goods, watches, scarves, and other silk products. Same-store sales grew a whopping 16 percent.

Dumas planned to boost profits by reducing the number of Hermès "concessionaires" or franchisees. Specifically, Dumas planned to cut Hermès's total number of venues from 250 to 200 and to expand the number of company-owned stores from 60 to 100. This strategy would bring more control of venue under family hands. Although this move was expected to cost the company Ffr 200 million in the short term, it would increase long-term profit potential. With over Ffr 500 million in cash on hand, Hermès could afford the investment.

Although observers inside and outside Hermès expected the luxury goods company to continue to enjoy annual sales and profit increases, they also forecast that the rate of increase would slip into single-digit percentages. Dumas himself expected "unfavorable exchange rates" and high marketing expenses for "24, Faubourg" to reduce profit growth to about ten percent in 1995 and 1996.

Further Reading:

Berman, Phyllis, "Mass Production? Yech!" *Forbes,* September 22, 1986, p. 182.
Brubach, Holly, "The Hunger for Hermès," *Atlantic,* December 1986, p. 92.
Dryansky, G. Y., "Hermès: Quality With a Kick," *Harper's Bazaar,* April 1986, p. 218.
Hornblower, Margot, "As Luxe as It Gets: The Bold Scion of Hermès Gives an Old World Firm Fresh Pizazz," *Time,* August 6, 1990, p. 52.
Michael, Jane Wilkens, "Family Ties," *Town & Country Monthly,* June 1992, p. 53.
Reynolds, C. P., "Hermès," *Gourmet,* February 1987, p. 42.
Rotenier, Nancy, "Tie Man Meets Queen of England," *Forbes,* September 13, 1993, p. 46.
"Scarves Everywhere," *New Yorker,* January 30, 1989, p. 24.
Tompkins, Mimi, "Sweatshop of the Stars," *U.S. News & World Report,* February 12, 1990, p. 51.
Weisman, Katherine, "Bag War: Hermès Must Pay Bugatti for Use of Its Name," *Women's Wear Daily,* January 30, 1995, p. 9.
——, "Hermès: Scents Were Off in Otherwise Robust '93," *Women's Wear Daily,* June 1, 1994, p. 16.
——, "Hermès Sees Growth Slowing After Strong '94," *Women's Wear Daily,* June 1, 1995, p. 2.

—April Dougal Gasbarre

The Hillhaven Corporation

1148 Broadway Plaza
Tacoma, Washington 98402
U.S.A.
(206) 572-4901
Fax: (206) 502-3934

Public Company
Incorporated: 1955 as Hillhaven, Inc.
Employees: 42,000
Sales: $1.57 billion
Stock Exchanges: New York
SICs: 8051 Skilled Nursing Care Facilities; 5912 Drug Stores
& Proprietary Stores

One of the largest diversified health care providers in the United States, The Hillhaven Corporation owned, leased, and managed nearly 300 nursing centers in 33 states during the mid-1990s. In addition to its considerable presence in the nursing home market, which the company helped transform during the late 1940s and 1950s, Hillhaven managed 19 retirement housing and assisted living centers and 59 pharmacy outlets. From its inception in 1946, the company has been regarded as a pioneer in providing care for the elderly, contributing greatly to the advances made by the nursing home industry during the latter half of the 20th century.

When Tacoma, Washington-based Hillhaven was incorporated in 1955 it represented a new and progressive force in the nursing home industry, a company distinguished from all other competitors by its innovative approach to caring for the elderly. Chiefly responsible for creating the company's unique perspective, which later would be adopted by nursing home operators throughout the country, helping to transform the quality of the nation's nursing facilities, was Ted B. Hill, Hillhaven's founder.

Born in 1923, Hill was raised in Rock Rapids, Iowa, where he remained until he completed high school. After graduation, he moved across the country to Tacoma, a small city 30 miles south of Seattle, where he began working as an optometrist, biding his time and saving his money before he made a business investment that would change his life and an antiquated U.S. industry.

As his savings grew so did his entrepreneurial inclinations, one building in intensity and the other in volume, until he saw an advertisement one day that listed a nursing home for sale. Hill bought the frame structure with his savings, hired a friend to manage it, and convinced his wife to handle the bookkeeping; he continued to work as an optometrist, spending his weekends taking care of maintenance work at his new nursing home.

Soon after buying the nursing home, which years earlier had been occupied by an affluent family, Hill made a disheartening discovery, one that dampened his hopes for a prosperous new business. When Hill purchased the frame structure, he acquired a typical 1940s nursing home: a multistory structure identical in nearly all respects to an ordinary home. He had also inherited the ills of the U.S. nursing home industry. Narrow doorways, high, claw-footed bathtubs, and stairways were common features in nursing homes during the first half of the 20th century—Hill's nursing home was no exception—but for the elderly and disabled high bathtubs made bathing difficult, narrow corridors made wheelchair access impossible, and flights of stairs represented formidable barriers restricting movement, particularly in an emergency situation such as a fire.

Hill quickly realized the inadequacies of his newly acquired nursing facility, but instead of abandoning the nursing home industry as the focus of his entrepreneurial efforts he searched for a solution and in 1946 devised one. That year, Hill reportedly mortgaged everything he and his wife owned, convinced a friend to do the same, and raised enough money to build the first specifically designed nursing home in Washington State. Hill's creation was tailor-made for the elderly and disabled, a $100,000 structure outfitted with numerous features for the residents who would soon occupy it, including handrails along the corridors and adjacent to bathtubs, toilets, and showers, call-buttons in washrooms, and showers large enough to admit wheelchairs.

Then only 23 years old, Hill had made a definitive move in the nursing home industry, albeit one that drew little recognition. What little attention he did receive was largely negative, particularly from nursing home proprietors in the Pacific Northwest who predicted that the capital and operating costs of his nursing home would necessitate exorbitant rates. The design and layout of Hill's facility, however, realized substantial efficiencies, enabling him to charge the same rates as he had at his first, outmoded nursing home.

Initially, Hill's financial condition was precarious, with each dollar earned plowed back into his nursing facility or set aside to pay bills, but by 1949, three years after the completion of his first modern nursing facility, Hill was able to finance the construction of another facility in Olympia, Washington, although he had not yet decided to build a chain of nursing homes. Hill's second creation was a one-story facility, a rarity among the nursing homes scattered across the country at the time and one of the chief characteristics that would distinguish Hillhaven as an innovative leader in the industry.

After another three-year break between new nursing home construction, Hill began to generate a profit, giving him the money and the inducement to begin contemplating the establishment of a nursing home chain for the first time. The following year, in November 1953, he completed the prototype for the nursing home empire that would develop in the decades ahead: a

U-shaped, one-story facility in Hoquiem, Washington. Two months later another Hillhaven facility was opened in Bremerton, Washington; then in May 1955, one month after Hillhaven, Inc., was incorporated, Hill moved beyond Washington's borders for the first time and established a Hillhaven home in Portland, Oregon.

Over the course of the next three years, Hillhaven continued to expand, both geographically by entering into the California nursing home market and in terms of the number of housing units it managed. By 1958, Hillhaven began to attract the attention it had earlier lacked, particularly when the company was hailed as a progressive nursing home innovator in a 1958 *Readers' Digest* article. The company by this point operated 10 Hillhaven homes in Washington, Oregon, and California, all of which, like the nursing facility in Hoquiem, were U-shaped, one-story structures. The facilities averaged 57 beds per home, were constructed without ramps or steps, and avoided much of the institutional bleakness that was characteristic of more conventional nursing homes. But despite the many improvements, Hillhaven rates were commensurate with competing nursing homes, running between $6 and $7 per day in Washington and $10 to $11 per day in California.

As Hillhaven's management looked forward from 1958 with the expectation of increasing the number of nursing homes under its control and expanding geographically, two factors bolstered the company's optimism, one of which was closely familiar to those about to orchestrate the growth ahead; the other would only be discovered in retrospect. Hillhaven offered a unique, refreshing, and more accommodating approach to providing care to the elderly—this the company's leaders knew—but unbeknownst to those at the top was the explosive growth the nursing home industry would record in the years ahead. Historically, the nursing home industry had never been very large, representing only a $200 million industry in 1950, or 1.6 percent of total U.S. health care expenditures. By the end of the 1950s nursing home expenditures had risen to $500 million, increasing exponentially as Hillhaven began its vigorous expansion program, but the industry's most meteoric growth was yet to come.

During the 1960s, nursing home expenditures spiraled upward from $500 million to nearly $5 billion by 1970, a period during which Hillhaven developed a total of 32 new facilities in 10 states. Nursing home expenditures would continue to escalate during the 1970s, driving Hillhaven's revenues upwards and positioning the company as one of the preeminent nursing home companies in the nation. To take advantage of rising nursing home expenditures, which by the mid-1970s had eclipsed $10 billion, Hillhaven's management predicated the company's growth on providing diversified services to the elderly, expanding upon the rudimentary services established by Hill. During the decade the company became the first multifacility, long-term care provider to nationally implement a broad range of rehabilitative services, which placed an emphasis on abilities rather than disabilities through speech and occupational therapy programs and restorative nursing.

In 1973 the company formed the Hillhaven Foundation to establish an independent organization devoted to conducting education, demonstration, and research in geriatrics; four years

later, through the Hillhaven Foundation, it opened the first freestanding hospice in the United States at Tucson, Arizona. Designed to provide services to terminally ill patients and their families, the Tucson hospice opened the same year Hillhaven acquired First Healthcare, a 21-facility chain of nursing homes that strengthened the company's national presence in a market that was becoming increasingly lucrative. Nursing home expenditures had increased from $4.7 billion in 1970 to $10.1 billion in 1975, then quickly doubled over the next five years, reaching $20.6 billion by 1980, or 8.3 percent of total U.S. health care expenditures. As one of the country's largest long-term care providers, Hillhaven shared in the growth of its industry, becoming one of the key competitors in a market that began to attract the attention of large health care corporations.

Not surprisingly, the meteoric rise of the nursing home industry sparked outside interest and several large health care corporations sought to join the fray, hoping to secure a portion of what was becoming an increasingly larger market. As one of the largest companies in the industry, Hillhaven represented a coveted catch for whichever company could control it, and in 1979 Los Angeles-based National Medical Enterprises, Inc., did just that, acquiring the company before the growth of the nursing home market peaked.

With National Medical serving as its parent company, Hillhaven entered the 1980s propelled by the growth of the nursing home market. During the first two years of National Medical's ownership, nursing home expenditures climbed resolutely from more than $20 billion to $27.3 billion, providing ample justification for its acquisition of Hillhaven and spurring management to plot ambitious expansion plans. By the middle of the decade, Hillhaven was the second-largest investor-owned nursing home in the United States, controlling slightly more than 400 nursing homes and 21 senior housing projects, which ranked the company a distant second to Pasadena-based Beverly Enterprises, owner of more than 1,000 nursing homes.

Looking forward, Hillhaven's management planned to be more selective in its expansion throughout the country, deciding to invest only in new locations where the company was likely to attract more private-pay patients rather than those who relied on Medicaid, as nursing home expenditures began to record less prolific gains than they had during the previous two decades. Despite the more prosaic growth of the nursing home market, optimism remained high at Hillhaven, with the company's management anticipating 15 percent annual growth for the remainder of the decade through the construction of new facilities, acquisitions, and conversion of existing facilities that focused on providing specialized services.

By the late 1980s, however, profits for investor-owned nursing home chains were declining, as the nursing home industry struggled with labor shortages, regulatory restrictions, and mounting competition. Hamstrung by fixed reimbursement and escalating operating costs, Hillhaven was hobbled by the onset of troubled times; profits fell sharply, dropping from $76.4 million earned from $989 million in revenue in 1987 to $44.1 million on $1 billion in revenue in 1988. The following year, while Hillhaven continued to suffer from the pernicious conditions characterizing the nursing home industry during the late 1980s, National Medical announced in January that it was spinning off Hillhaven into a separate, independently operated company. A year later, in January 1990, the spin-off was completed, leaving Hillhaven, with its management intact, as an independent, investor-owned operator of nearly 350 skilled-nursing facilities spread across 37 states. Also included in the spin-off was a 120-unit chain of pharmacies and 24 retirement housing centers, which Hillhaven now owned as it entered the 1990s and fought to stop its late 1980s retrogressive slide.

With its independence restored, Hillhaven faced a difficult road ahead. Many of the company's nursing homes were recording lackluster results, exacerbating the harmful effects of intense competition and escalating operating costs that were crippling the nursing home industry. Saddled with debt, Hillhaven responded to the challenges it faced by streamlining its operations and establishing operating and financial criteria that each of its facilities were required to meet. During the four years following its spin-off from National Medical, Hillhaven eliminated 77 nursing centers, 87 pharmacies, and eight retirement centers that were not achieving the operating and financial goals it had established in 1990. Additionally, Hillhaven cut its headquarters staff by 20 percent and refinanced more than $500 million of its $731 million in long-term debt, which, combined with its facility closures, enabled the company to recover from its precarious position and look ahead once again with optimism.

Whereas Hillhaven was streamlining its operations during the early 1990s, the nursing home industry was beginning to consolidate, with several large health care providers joining forces to compete in the contentious 1990s. Hillhaven was not excluded from the industrywide trend, and in January 1995 Horizon Healthcare Corporation, a nursing home chain based in Albuquerque, New Mexico, made a $1.4 billion offer for Hillhaven and its 287 nursing homes. Hillhaven's management rejected the offer, wishing to remain independent, but in March 1995 Horizon increased its ante, offering $1.8 billion for Hillhaven. Later that month, the deal collapsed when Hillhaven refused to accept Horizon's offer before the specified deadline, but it was not long before another, much smaller health care company attempted to merge with Hillhaven, submitting an offer that would succeed and create one of the nation's largest health care providers with more than $2 billion in revenues.

In April 1995, Hillhaven accepted a buyout offer valued at $1.9 billion from Vencor, Inc., a Louisville, Kentucky, operator of 35 long-term, intensive-care hospitals with $400 million in annual revenue. The proposed merger, which stipulated that Hillhaven's management remain intact—something the proposal from Horizon did not—was regarded by pundits as a complementary marriage between two organizations whose fa-cilities, once combined under one corporate umbrella, would create a prodigious, integrated health care force. Roughly 65 percent of Hillhaven's nursing homes were located in states where Vencor operated hospitals, allowing the two merged companies to enjoy a significant boost in business through patient referrals.

On September 27, 1995, Hillhaven and Vencor announced that shareholders of both companies had separately approved the acquisition of Hillhaven by Vencor, thereby clearing the last obstacle barring the proposed merger. As Hillhaven prepared for its imminent merger into Vencor, prognostications for future growth were favorable. In 1995 there were more than 12 million Americans aged 75 or older, a number that was projected to reach 17 million by the end of the 1990s. With this estimated increase in Hillhaven's core customer base fueling optimism, the company moved forward, ready to strengthen its position in the nursing home industry.

Principal Subsidiaries: Medisave Pharmacies, Inc.

Further Reading:

''Hillhaven-CNA Financial Accord,'' *Wall Street Journal,* May 28, 1975, p. 36.
''Hillhaven Marks 30 Years of Nursing Home Growth,'' *Daily Journal of Commerce,* April 12, 1985, p. 3.
''Hillhaven Reports Record First Quarter Operating Results,'' *PC Newswire,* September 22, 1995, p. 92.
''Hillhaven to Become Independent Jan. 31,'' *Modern Healthcare,* January 8, 1990, p. 10.
Hodder, Ian, ''Hillhaven's Healthy Recovery,'' *Washington CEO Magazine,* August 1994, p. 11.
Loehwing, David A., ''Recovery in Nursing Homes,'' *Barron's,* March 26, 1973, p. 3.
Myerson, Allen R., ''Hillhaven Agrees to Vencor's Buyout Offer,'' *New York Times,* April 25, 1995, p. D2.
——. ''$1.5 Billion Is Bid to Create Big Nursing Home Chain,'' *New York Times,* January 27, 1995, p. D1.
Neurath, Peter, ''Hillhaven May Seek a Better Offer, Analyst Says,'' *Puget Sound Business Journal,* February 3, 1995, p. 9.
Osterland, Andrew, ''Acquire, Then Digest: Vencor,'' *Financial World,* June 20, 1995, p. 20.
Rudensky, Maria, ''Hillhaven Aims to Grow by Developing Facilities for Specialized Services,'' *Modern Healthcare,* September 26, 1986, p. 108.
''Vencor, Hillhaven Make Challenging Match,'' *Modern Healthcare,* May 1, 1995, p. 3.
''Vencor Will Acquire Hillhaven,'' *Wall Street Journal,* September 28, 1995, p. B2.
Wagner, Lynn, ''Nursing Homes Buffeted by Troubles,'' *Modern Healthcare,* March 18, 1988, pp. 33–38.

—Jeffrey L. Covell

Holson Burnes Group, Inc.

582 Great Road
North Smithfield, Rhode Island 02896
U.S.A.
(401) 769-8000
Fax: (401) 769-0752

Public Company
Incorporated: 1989
Employees: 600
Sales: $130 million
Stock Exchanges: NASDAQ
SICs: 2499 Wood Products Nec

Holson Burnes Group, Inc., is the largest designer, manufacturer, and distributor of photo albums in the United States, and the second largest designer and distributor of photo frames. The company was created in 1989 by the merger of two companies, making it the only major U.S. supplier of both frames and albums to all major retail distribution channels. In the mid-1990s Holson Burnes was battling fierce international competition with new product introductions and by acquiring other companies.

The Holson Burnes Group, Inc., was created in 1989 to purchase the outstanding shares of stock of The Holson Company and Charles D. Burnes Co., Inc. Holson was a leading U.S. designer and manufacturer of photograph albums and Burnes a leading producer and supplier of photo frames. At the time, both companies were owned by Bain Capital, a venture capital investment group based in Boston, but they were operating separately. In 1988 the chief executives of the two companies investigated a merger or joint venture to build on each company's strengths. Burnes had a strong presence in department and specialty stores with its picture frames, and Holson had a strong presence in mass-merchandise chains with its albums. By teaming up, each company would benefit from access to a new market and distribution channel. Both companies had good management, strong brand identities, and large and established customer bases.

In 1988 Charlie Gordon, the chairman of Burnes, and Thomas E. Hoffmeister, the recently appointed head of Holson, approached their parent company, Bain, about the possibility of a merger. Bain executives were enthusiastic, in part because the two executives were a good match: Hoffmeister had a financial

and operating background and Gordon had spent most of his career in sales and marketing. ''We went to Bain Capital and asked permission to merge,'' Hoffmeister recalled in the August 24, 1992, *Providence Business News,* ''and their reaction was 'Hallelujah, we wouldn't have forced it, but we always felt the companies belonged together, and if you guys are for it, we'll do it.' '' Thus, in 1989 Bain merged the two enterprises to create the unified Holson Burnes. Soon after the merger, Holson Burnes began introducing Burnes albums to department and specialty stores. Then, late in 1990, the company began selling Holson frames to mass merchants like Wal-Mart, Kmart, and Drug Emporium.

Burnes had been founded in 1917 by Charles D. Burnes. His company gradually accumulated the second-largest share of its market in the United States by creating new products, including the clear acrylic photo cube, which could hold six photographs, and the collage frame, which consisted of a framed matte with multiple cut-outs for several photographs. Burnes established itself in the high-margin specialty store and department store segments with major accounts like J. C. Penney, Sears, Dillards, and May Department Stores. Holson was founded in 1942 by Abraham Holson, an immigrant bookbinder who invented the modern photo album, as well as the magnetic page and the pocket page album. During the 1970s and 1980s the company became a major supplier to discount giants like Wal-Mart, Kmart, Price Costco, Target, Eckerd Drug Stores, and Staples.

By the mid-1980s Holson and Burnes were each generating roughly $30 million annually and enjoying relatively healthy profits. Both companies were benefiting from steady, strong growth in the photo processing industry, which served as an important indicator for album and frame sales. Photo processing receipts in the United States began increasing in the early 1980s and grew during the mid-1980s at rates of roughly ten percent annually. Between the early 1980s and early 1990s, in fact, the industry grew at an average annual rate of nearly seven percent, leading similar gains in the frame and album business.

At the same time, however, low-cost imports were providing a strong challenge, particularly at Holson. Although Holson was still a family-owned company in the early 1980s and did not release sales and profit data, Holson family members made it clear that competition from abroad was hurting their business. They charged that manufacturers in Korea and Hong Kong were dumping cheap photo albums into the U.S. market at a loss as part of a long-term strategy to put American competitors out of business and take over their market share. In January 1985 Holson and three other U.S. album manufacturers filed suit against the dumpers with the Federal Trade Commission.

To win the suit, Holson had to prove that its production operations were efficient and up to date, and that it planned to continue modernizing its facilities over the long term. At the time, Holson was manufacturing 435 different styles of photo albums, and its manufacturing facilities were highly automated and efficient by industry standards. In October 1985 the U.S. companies won their suit, and the federal government imposed duties on incoming albums to ensure competition. Although the duties helped stop the dumping, two major U.S. album producers had already filed bankruptcy and a third had stopped operating, and even after the duties were in place, the imports remained lower in price than domestic products.

Partly because of the import problem, the Holson family sold out to Bain Capital in 1986; however, the Holson Company, which was still managed by family members, continued to have problems under the Bain umbrella. To return the organization's competitive edge, Bain called in a series of consulting teams, including one from Price Waterhouse. Among the members of the Price Waterhouse team was Hoffmeister. Bain asked Hoffmeister to join Holson as head of the company in 1988 to effect a turnaround.

Hoffmeister shook up Holson's management team, replacing key executives. He also refocused the company's attention from camera and specialty store customers to larger retailers, who were demanding better service. "The story I like to tell is my first meeting with Sears," Hoffmeister recalled in the August 24, 1992 *Providence Business News.* "The people at Sears looked at us and said, we want you to know that your company stinks. . . . And we kept Sears. In fact, we didn't lose any major customers in that period, because we made commitments to them, we fixed it, and we didn't commit to what we couldn't do."

Shortly before Hoffmeister assumed the helm at Holson, Bain purchased Burnes, which was owned by Hallmark at the time. Burnes was in relatively good financial shape, under the leadership of Chairman Charlie Gordon, who had been running Burnes for several years. During the next year, Gordon and Hoffmeister independently recognized the potential benefits of a cooperation between the two organizations. When Bain gave the go-ahead to a merger, they moved quickly to form Holson Burnes Group, Inc., and to begin cross-marketing their products. In 1990 Holson Burnes also acquired Terragrafics, a leading supplier of high-end picture frames to specialty and department stores that was generating about $15 million annually. This purchase rounded out Burnes's strengths in the middle and upper-middle segments of the industry.

In 1990, the first full year that Holson and Burnes operated as a single entity, sales were $88 million. In 1991, the first full year that Holson Burnes and Terragrafics operated as a unit, sales jumped to $112. During the first few years Hoffmeister and fellow managers worked to streamline the company, eliminate overlap, cut production costs, and jettison poorly performing units. Largely as a result of reorganization expenses, Holson Burnes posted net losses in both 1990 and 1991. To help make up for the losses and to reduce the company's debt load, Bain took the company public in 1992, raising about $30 million.

The company's stock price shot up from about $15 to $19 after the offering, in part due to the 1992 introduction of the 'Showbox' photo viewer. Invented in Switzerland in 1987 and extremely popular in Europe, the Showbox was a photo frame that held 40 photographs, loaded very easily, and allowed a user to quickly shuffle through and view the photos without touching them. Although analysts expected the company to ship $13 million to $15 million worth of Showboxes for the year, Holson Burnes sold only $10 million worth of the Showboxes and posted a $12.35 million net loss. The company was left with excess inventory and forced to lay off some workers. By February 1993 Holson Burnes's stock price had plunged to just $4 per share.

Hoffmeister left the company in 1993 and Gordon became chairman and chief executive officer. Over the next two years the company struggled to gain control of its inventory and finances. Although revenues remained around the $130 million mark, profits improved markedly, to $3.2 million and $6.8 million in 1993 and 1994. In March 1995 Holson Burnes announced an agreement to buy Heritage Springfield, a Massachusetts-based distributor of photo albums to mass merchants. A month later the company announced its intent to acquire M. W. Carr, a leading supplier of frames to specialty stores. The two companies were expected to bring about $28 million of additional annual revenue to Holson Burnes, establishing the company as the leading U.S. manufacturer and supplier of photo albums and the second-largest producer of photo frames.

Principal Subsidiaries: The Holson Burnes Co.

Further Reading:

Barnes, Steven W., "Holson Burnes Group Reports Fourth Quarter and Year End Results," *Business Wire,* February 17, 1995.
DeMaio, Dan, "Malcolm Lloyd: CEO Frames a New Picture for Holson Burnes," *Providence Business News,* November 29, 1993, Sec. 1, p. 2.
——, "Picture This: Holson Burnes to Offer Shares to the Public," *Providence Business News,* April 20, 1992, Sec. 1, p. 7.
——, "Thomas E. Hoffmeister—Holson Burnes: Northern RI's Biggest Unknown Employer," *Providence Business News,* August 24, 1992, Sec. 1, p. 2.
Hiday, Jeffrey L., "Holson Burnes Net up 60 Percent in Quarter," *Providence Journal-Bulletin,* October 24, 1992, Sec. D, p. 2.
"Holson Burnes Will Acquire Album Maker," *Providence Journal-Bulletin,* March 18, 1995, Sec. B, p. 16.
Kehoe, Ann-Margaret, "Holson Burnes Group Agrees to Buy Two Rivals," *HFN The Weekly Newspaper for the Home Furnishing Network,* April 17, 1995, p. 58.
Levin, Derek, "Trade Restraints Aid Photo Album Manufacturer," *Vermont Business,* March 1986, Sec. 1, p. 47.
Smith, Gregory, "IPO Flops as Earnings Take Plunge," *Providence Journal-Bulletin,* March 11, 1993, Sec. E, p. 1.

—Dave Mote

Hughes Supply, Inc.

20 North Orange Avenue
Orlando, Florida 32801
U.S.A.
(407) 841-4755
Fax: (407) 872-1895

Public Company
Incorporated: 1947
Employees: 2,800
Sales: $802.45 million
Stock Exchange: New York
SICs: 5063 Electrical Apparatus and Equipment; 5074
    Plumbing and Hydronic Heating Supplies; 5075 Warm Air
    Heating and Air Conditioning; 5085 Industrial Supplies

Hughes Supply, Inc. is a wholesale distributor of a broad range of materials, equipment, and supplies to the construction industry. Their major product lines include electrical, plumbing, and electrical utility equipment; building materials; water and sewer products; heating and air conditioning equipment; and pipes, valves, and fittings. In fact, in the mid-1990s, Hughes Supply was distributing more than 95,000 different products from 5,000 different manufacturers through over 170 wholesale outlets. Major suppliers to Hughes Supply included Rheem, American Standard, Charlotte Pipe, Grinnell, Mueller, and Square "D".

Although little information is available on the company's early history, by 1928, Hughes Supply was operating in Orlando, Florida, having been founded by Clarence Hughes and his son Russell Hughes. In its early days, the company focused on distributing electrical supplies and equipment for use in residential construction in the Orlando area. The company weathered the Great Depression, and by 1939 had opened its first wholesale outlet outside of Orlando, in Gainsville. Steady success prompted the opening of another outlet in 1941, this one in Daytona.

From 1941 through 1944, as the country prepared and eventually entered World War II, material shortages forced the company to shift the focus of its operations to wartime production. In fact, Hughes Supply opened a manufacturing plant that produced casings for artillery shells, and that plant continued operations round the clock until the end of the war.

Returning to its distribution business after the war, Hughes Supply added a line of plumbing supplies to its product line, as electricians were starting to perform both electrical and plumb-

ing work. Postwar economic and building booms benefitted Hughes Supply, as new housing starts led to increased demand for electrical and plumbing supplies. The company was incorporated in the state of Florida in 1947 and continued to operate from its three distribution locations in Orlando, Daytona and Gainesville.

In 1949 the company diversified its business, establishing long-distance trucking operations through which it hauled Florida produce north and returned with vendor materials. This trucking operation would later prove very profitable in the 1980s, when the trucking industry was deregulated.

During the 1950s, Hughes Supply expanded and set up wholesale outlets in other areas of Florida where there was little competition: St. Petersburg, Lakeland, Sarasota, Clearwater, and Venice. In the 1960s Hughes Supply continued its expansion in Florida with five more wholesale outlets. During this time the company also broadened its product line to include electric utility supplies and equipment, industrial supplies, tools and contractor supplies, in addition to its staple plumbing and electrical supplies.

In 1970, Hughes Supply was taken public, offering 350,000 shares of common stock at an initial price of $17.60 per share. In its first year as a public company Hughes Supply achieved approximately $45 million in sales, and net income of $1.2 million. In 1973 Hughes Supply's sales volume reached $100 million.

In 1975 Florida suffered the worst year in construction business since World War II. Hughes Supply's sales suffered accordingly, dropping by 30 percent in one year. The company was forced to reduce personnel, cutting back from 1,100 employees in June 1974 to approximately 800 by January of the following year. In spite of the downturn in business, however, the company remained profitable, earning $865,000 in fiscal 1975.

The Florida construction market began to recover soon thereafter, and Hughes Supply's sales increased to $80 million. During this time, Hughes Supply celebrated its 50th anniversary in 1978 by hosting a trade show for its customers and vendors. This show had the distinction of being the largest show of its type organized by a single company in its industry to date.

At this time, Hughes Supply was still operating exclusively in Florida, and nearly all of the company's business was related to residential construction. However, Hughes Supply management was well aware of the impact of economic downturns on the residential construction market and regarded itself as particularly vulnerable to such downturns. So, the company's management decided to implement a strategy designed to minimize some of this vulnerability and, at the same time, set the business on the path to aggressive growth in the next few years. Their new three-part strategy was to diversify its product line and geographic scope, reduce dependence on residential construction, and capture more of the local construction dollar.

Hughes Supply expanded its business initially by opening new wholesale outlets in other Florida locations. Throughout the 1980s, however, the company began a series of acquisitions, the first of which was The Marbut Company, based in Georgia, in 1981. Marbut added heating and air conditioning supplies and equipment to Hughes Supply's product line, as well as geographic expansion into Georgia. Initially Hughes Supply sought out companies with strong local markets, with annual sales in the $5–15 million range. By 1982 Hughes Supply's sales had reached $200 million.

In 1985 Hughes Supply acquired Carolina Pump & Supply Corporation with its 11 branches in North and South Carolina. CP&S specialized in the distribution of water systems, as well as water and sewer equipment, in the Carolinas. Two more companies were bought by Hughes Supply in 1987: Paine Supply in Mississippi, a plumbing and HVAC distributor, and USCO, a plumbing wholesaler in the Carolinas. These two acquisitions brought the total number of Hughes Supply outlets to 75 in five southeastern states.

By January 1988 Hughes Supply's sales volume had reached over $400 million, and Hughes Supply opened the Hughes Training Center in Orlando for company personnel. In 1988 Hughes Supply acquired Stop Supply, Inc., a wholesale distributor of HVAC equipment and supplies in Tennessee and Kentucky, and Mills & Lupton Supply Company, an electric utility and industrial supply company operating in Tennessee and Georgia.

Hit by the national recession of 1991–1992, Hughes Supply's sales dropped by 12 percent for the fiscal year ending January 1992, and the company recorded its first ever loss. That year, Hughes Supply responded by effecting a number of internal changes and restructuring its operations; by January 1993, the company had returned to profitability.

In 1993 Hughes Supply acquired Alabama Water Works, a wholesaler of water and sewer equipment in Alabama. Electrical Distributors, Inc., the largest single-house distributor in Georgia, was acquired in the same year. Sales reached the $600 million mark by January 1994.

By the mid-1990s the average Hughes Supply wholesale outlet accounted for $5 million in annual sales, and a gross profit of approximately $1 million. It carried about $600,000 in inventory and $600,000 in trade receivables. Each outlet employed about 17 people in sales, warehousing, administration, and as truck drivers. Approximately one half of total sales volume was accounted for by companies acquired since 1981.

Indeed, Hughes Supply had made over 26 acquisitions since that time, with a strategy of seeking out companies with a product line and/or geographic coverage that would fill out its product line and geographic area of operations. Later acquisitions targeted larger companies with a strong market presence in selected product lines and geographic areas.

Analysts expected Hughes Supply's strategy of growth by acquisition to continue. In addition to targeting companies with new locations and complementary product lines, Hughes Supply also began seeking higher profit margin product lines, and diversification from new residential and commercial construction to a larger proportion of the repair and replacement business. A new product line, swimming pool supplies, was introduced in 1994. Pool supplies typically had a higher profit margin than Hughes Supply's other product lines, and Florida represented a significant market for these products.

By 1995, Hughes Supply was overseeing distribution outlets throughout the southeastern United States, and even in some parts of the Midwest, chiefly Indiana and Ohio. The company remained largely a family-run business. David H. Hughes served as chairman of the board and chief executive officer, and other members of the Hughes family were directors of the company. In 1995, however, Stewart Hall was named president at Hughes Supply, and he immediately set to work making internal reorganizations and streamlining divisions and subsidiaries.

Since going public in 1970, the company sustained a 12 percent annual compounded growth rate in sales, mainly due to its planned strategy of geographic and product diversification through aggressive acquisition. Nevertheless, the company remained highly dependent on the construction industry; roughly 55 percent of sales were to the commercial and municipal markets, and the remainder to the residential market. Moreover, Hughes Supply's business was highly cyclical, with its dependence on the new construction market. Still, to offset the effects of this cyclicality, the company had become more focused on the less cyclical sectors of construction activity, namely multi-family housing, public works, commercial construction, and industrial supplies.

Analysts estimated the size of the U.S. market for construction material and building supplies to be over $100 billion in the mid-1990s. Nearly all of Hughes Supply's competitors operated with only a limited product line or in one or two product groups with a smaller inventory. In a June 1995 report, analysts at Smith Barney stated that "in a highly fragmented market, Hughes' economies of scale provide advantages over smaller competitors." The same analysts also found that Hughes Supply's financing costs of five percent were substantially below those of most of its competitors, a critical factor in a business that made 90 percent of its sales on a credit basis.

No single manufacturer or supplier accounted for more than seven percent of Hughes Supply's total purchase volume in the fiscal year ended January 27, 1995. Hughes Supply served more than 45,000 electrical, plumbing, and mechanical contractors and subcontractors, electric utility companies, and municipal and industrial accounts. No single customer accounted for more than one percent of total annual sales. Less than one percent of sales are retail, and the growth in home center retailers, which served small contractors as well as do-it-yourselfers, was not expected to affect Hughes Supply's wholesale business which remained focused on large contractors.

Principal Subsidiaries: XSMC, Inc.; Carolina Pump & Supply Corp.; USCO Inc.; Paine Supply of Jackson, Inc.; Hughes Aviation, Inc.; One Stop Supply, Inc.; Mills & Lupton Supply Company; Twin-T of the Carolinas, Inc.; H Venture Corp.; HHH, Inc.; HSI Corp.; Electrical Distributors, Inc.; Alabama Water Works Supply, Inc.; Swaim Supply Company, Inc.; Olander & Brophy, Inc.; Port City Electrical Supply, Inc.; Elec-Tel Supply Company.

Further Reading:
"Business Briefs," *Wall Street Journal,* July 1, 1993, p. B4.
"Hughes Supply Sets Credit Pact," *Wall Street Journal,* June 2, 1993, p. C17.
"Who's News: Hughes Supply Inc.," *Wall Street Journal,* March 25, 1994, p. B6.

—Judith Harley

Ibstock plc

Lutterworth House
Lutterworth
Leicestershire LE17 4PS
United Kingdom
(01455) 553071
Fax: (01455) 553182

Public Company
Incorporated: 1899 as Ibstock Collieries Ltd.
Employees: 3,681
Sales: £235 million
Stock Exchanges: London
SICs: 6711 Holding Companies; 3251 Brick & Structural
   Clay Tile; 5031 Timber, Plywood, & Millwork; 5111
   Printing & Writing Paper

Ibstock plc is one of the largest brick manufacturers in the United Kingdom and operates manufacturing facilities in the United States and Europe as well. From its modest origins in early nineteenth-century coal mining, Ibstock grew to achieve a prominent and respected position in the brickmaking industry of the late twentieth century. While Ibstock is perhaps best known, according to company publications, "for its wide range of high quality facing bricks which meet architects' and designers' creative requirements," Ibstock also supplies the building industry with clay roof tiles and pavers, architectural stoneware, and terracotta products.

Ibstock was established in 1825 when William Thirlby, a farmer and lacemaker, started mining operations on his land at Ibstock, near Leicester. Within a few years his business was prosperous, serving local customers from a plentiful bed of coal. By the 1830s the mining site, which had grown to over 100 acres, was producing supplies of fire clay and clay suitable for making brick. Over the next ten years a primitive brickworks was developed, but bricks were strictly a by-product of the primary business of the colliery, with only the lowest-quality coal relegated to brickmaking. The sideline grew over the years as mechanization replaced the old, time-consuming processes by which brick was made. Nevertheless, brick's continuing low status at the colliery was apparent in the company's sales figures for 1879: coal accounted for £27,000, brick for £2,991.

In the early years of its existence the colliery changed ownership several times. In 1875 Samuel Thomson became managing

director, and the business soon became a family dynasty; under Samuel Thomson's son, also Samuel, Ibstock Collieries was incorporated as a private limited company in 1899.

Brickmaking began to assume a greater importance at Ibstock at the beginning of the twentieth century, as bricks became a popular choice of the building industry. By the start of World War I Ibstock was producing some three million bricks a year. After the war, coal mining became an increasingly problematic industry. Miners' coalitions were demanding better working conditions and higher pay, and were prepared to back up these demands with strikes. The government, which had taken control of the country's coal mines during the war (though Ibstock, due to its smaller size, had remained independent), continued to impose price controls on the industry. In 1921, when the government returned the mines to their owners, workers' wages dropped dramatically, prompting further labor unrest. In addition, foreign competition, particularly from Poland and Germany, was intense.

As a result of these internal and external pressures, in 1928 Ibstock decided to close the pits and elevate the company's sidelines of brick-, tile-, and pipemaking to center stage. An appraisal undertaken in 1933 showed that the company was capable of producing three million bricks and five million tiles and pipes per year, which was adequate for a subsidiary product, but not for a primary line of business.

Ibstock set about creating a more extensive works with modern equipment, including a Monnier kiln (the first such to be used in Britain), a novel tunnel kiln that fired bricks loaded on cars that moved through the kiln. Requiring a substantial investment of £8,000, the technological advance increased production capacity to nine million bricks a year. Reflecting its new direction, Ibstock Collieries changed its name to Ibstock Brick & Tile Company in 1935.

World War II curtailed Ibstock's growth, and for a while after the war production was limited by shortages of labor and materials. By the 1950s, however, Ibstock was positioned for further expansion, which the company fueled with an aggressive sales strategy. Unlike other brick manufacturers, who sold their wares exclusively to building products merchants, Ibstock targeted brick users directly. By employing an active sales network to pinpoint architects, for example, and persuade them to use Ibstock bricks, the company was able to gain an edge on the competition.

Over the next few decades, Ibstock grew steadily by investing in further automation. In 1959 work commenced on a new 20-chamber Staffordshire kiln, bringing annual output to 41 million bricks, and the installation of yet another kiln soon afterward (bringing Ibstock's total to four) increased that number to 56 million.

During the 1960s Ibstock began expanding rapidly. Led by a fourth-generation scion of the Thomson family, Paul Hyde-Thomson (the family surname had been modified years before to include an earlier chairman's wife's maiden name), and flush with capital from a stock market flotation in 1963, Ibstock acquired in quick succession several smaller firms, including Himley Brick, Aldridge Brick, Tile & Coal Company, Burwell Brick, Shawell Precast Products, and Superbrix. The aggressive acquisition strategy gave Ibstock a greater range of products, increased its geographical representation, and enlarged its production capacity: by 1967 the company had six manufacturing plants and an annual capacity of 130 million bricks.

Not all the acquisitions proved successful. Burwell was unprofitable, and was retained only until 1971; Shawell, renamed Ibstock Precast, was abandoned in 1977; and Superbrix, makers of bricks from inferior grade sandline, rather than clay, was in retrospect a poor choice for a company that prided itself on producing quality products.

Nevertheless, Ibstock continued to thrive, and in 1970 the company effected an important merger with the privately owned international wood pulp agency Johnsen, Jorgensen and Wettre. While the two companies had virtually no common ground, Ibstock wanted Johnsen's healthy cash reserves to finance further expansion, and Johnsen believed that Ibstock could invest that capital to the companies' mutual advantage. Thus the company became Ibstock Johnsen, with the two operating divisions kept separate.

Ibstock immediately embarked upon a new round of acquisitions, buying Roughdales Brickworks, North Eastern Bricks, Nostell Brick & Tile, and the Cattybrook Brick Company in 1971 and 1972. Because the company was reluctant to extend itself further domestically—fearing that in doing so it would compromise its position at the more exclusive end of the U.K. market—Ibstock looked abroad for further acquisitions.

The company's first overseas acquisition came in 1973, with the purchase of the Dutch facing brick manufacturer Van Wijcks Waalsteenfabrieken, followed closely by another Dutch company, Maatschappij tot Exploitatie van Steenfabrieken Udenhout, voorheen Weyers. These moves catapulted Ibstock to the position of sixth-largest brickmaker in the Netherlands.

The mid-1970s saw severe setbacks in Ibstock's home market, with labor unrest by British miners, OPEC's stranglehold on oil prices and the consequent energy crises, and the general economic downturn all having an adverse impact on Ibstock's domestic operations: profits were running approximately ten percent lower than normal. The company continued its overseas expansion, moving into Belgium in 1977 with the acquisition of Tuileries et Briqueteries d'Hennuyeres et de Wanlin and reinforcing its position in the Netherlands with the purchase of Steenfabriek De Ruiterwaard. With six factories in Holland, capable of producing 154 million bricks a year, combined with exports from its U.K. operation to fill Dutch orders, Ibstock controlled about seven percent of the Dutch market.

Ibstock next contemplated the potential rewards of the huge American market. In 1978 the company bought Marion Brick, based in Ohio, a significant purchase which boosted the company's turnover by a quarter and raised total production by one-half. Ibstock had an annual brick production of 400 million in the United States and Europe, and 250 million in the United Kingdom. The 1979 purchase of the Pennsylvania Glen-Gery Corporation increased the company's U.S. total to 500 million bricks a year and gave Ibstock approximately five percent of the U.S. facing brick market.

It quickly became apparent, however, that Ibstock's proud new empire was built on shaky foundations. Profits dwindled in Holland, evaporated in Belgium, and proved increasingly precarious in America. As Ibstock's chairman at the time, Paul Hyde-Thomson, later candidly explained: "In the U.K. we were doing well but the rest looked appalling, with Holland still haemorrhaging and the U.S. in a mess. . . . We did not have sufficient resources and, on top of everything, the market collapsed on us. I had made a mess of it. We had been too bold in purchasing more capacity than we had in the U.K."

Ibstock sold its Belgian operations in 1980, but conditions continued to worsen in the company's other markets. Faced with falling demand and stiff competition in the United States, Ibstock offset cost increases by charging higher prices to customers and carrying on with production as normal, stockpiling its unsold excess. This strategy was completely at odds with initiatives put into practice by Ibstock's American rivals, who drastically reduced prices and closed unneeded capacity. Ibstock's strategy only exacerbated an already grave situation. At the same time, sales levels in Holland were also dropping severely amid fierce competition. In 1981 Ibstock showed a profit of only £175,000 on revenues of more than £60 million.

It was a boost to the company's morale, if not to its bottom line, that it won the Royal Society of Arts Presidential Award for Design Management in recognition of the high standard of its brickwork, its varied spectrum of products, its marketing successes, and its design advisory service. The honor did not alleviate the company's financial difficulties, however, and it came as little surprise to observers that Ibstock found itself vulnerable to a takeover bid. The would-be buyer was London Brick, then the leader in the U.K. brick industry. While many within Ibstock were in favor of the alliance, others were opposed, making the proposal divisive within the company. Matters were then complicated by the appearance of a second bidder, the building materials group Redland. Both offers were subject to approval by the Monopolies and Mergers Commission (MMC), and while that body deliberated, Ibstock acted.

The company managed to divest itself of its unprofitable Dutch operations. At the same time, the U.K. side of the business began to show improvement, and while activities in the United States were still problematic, there was reason to believe the market might recover in the future. In short, Ibstock redeemed its flagging fortunes so far that by the time the MMC approved an alliance with London Brick (Redland had earlier withdrawn its offer), the larger company had to increase its bid from the £27 million it had proffered in December 1982 to £51.7 million in August 1983. By then, however, Ibstock was in a far stronger position and felt confident that it could proceed independently: the bid was rejected.

Freed of its disappointing European operations and with the U.K. business reassuringly steady, Ibstock turned its attention to the United States, where it set about revitalizing its affairs through a new, streamlined management structure, a renewed emphasis on an active, aggressive sales force, and the creation of a more visible public profile. In pursuit of the latter goal Ibstock opened a brickwork design center in Baltimore, an idea taken from the company's similar, successful centers in the United Kingdom. A kind of brickwork multimedia resource headquarters, the center provided designers with information about new brick technology and design innovation via a reference library, design equipment, brick samples, conference and audio-visual facilities, and staff experts in architectural design and structural engineering. Ibstock offered technical seminars for designers and users of brick. The company soon opened other, similar centers in Washington, D.C., New York, and Philadelphia.

In the United Kingdom Ibstock was expanding again, building new design centers, commissioning new kilns, and widening its range of available facing bricks with the introduction of new colors, shapes, and textures. The activity paid off: by the end of 1984 total revenues, split evenly between the United States and the United Kingdom, were up by 25 percent to £110 million, representing the sale of 653 million bricks. Pre-tax profits, nearly double those of the year before, reached £12.4 million.

Encouraged, Ibstock returned to a policy of expansion. Its U.S. subsidiary Glen-Gery acquired Hanley Brick, New Jersey Shale, and Midland Brick, diversified into clay paver products with the purchase of Capital Concrete Pipe Company, and moved further into concrete products with the acquisition of Kerr Concrete Pipe Company and Gomoljak, a concrete block and masonry distribution company. By the end of the 1980s, Ibstock's American operation was the fourth-largest brick producer in the United States and accounted for approximately 20 percent of the company's profits.

From the relative triumph of the late 1980s, Ibstock moved to losses in the early 1990s: £27.6 million in the red in 1992 and £18.7 million in 1993. Much of the loss was ascribed to reorganization costs and plant closures, particularly of the troubled Portuguese arm of the wood pulp business, Companhia de Celulose do Caima. The company began to divest itself of the wood pulp division, which had once been so lucrative that it could finance the rest of the group's expenditures. As late as the end of the 1980s the division was bringing in 30 percent of the group's profits, but by 1995 Ibstock had dropped "Johnsen" from its name and announced its intention to dispose of its by

then 56.3 percent interest in Caima because of the extremely cyclical nature of the woodpulp business.

In 1994 Ibstock was back in the black again, expanding both through the acquisition of Centurion Brick and Scottish Brick and through increased production. The following year the company secured a deal to purchase the brick business of Tarmac, a construction and building materials group. The move was expected to give Ibstock control of approximately 19 percent of the U.K. market. With figures varying, it was unclear whether the deal would make Ibstock the country's second-largest brick manufacturer or a strong third.

While Ibstock's history of fluctuating fortunes is testimony to the volatile nature of the brick industry, it seems clear that Ibstock has secured itself a steady and prominent place in the industry. Further domestic expansion may be difficult as the U.K. industry has become very tightly consolidated over the years; analysts note that the United States may provide more promising opportunities for expansion.

Principal Subsidiaries: Glen-Gery Corp. (U.S.A.); Ibstock Building Products Ltd.; Johnsen, Jorgensen & Wettre Ltd.

Further Reading:

Cassell, Michael, *Dig It, Burn It, Sell It! The Story of Ibstock Johnsen, 1825–1990,* London: Pencorp Books, 1990, 193 p.
"Hammered by Recession," *The Times,* April 20, 1994.
"Ibstock in Brick Talks with Tarmac," *Independent,* April 7, 1995.
"Ibstock Pays £65m for Tarmac Brick Interests," *Daily Telegraph,* May 13, 1994.
"Ibstock Set to Buy Tarmac Brick Side," *Financial Times,* May 12, 1995.
"Ibstock to Sell Its Stake in Portuguese Forestry Group," *Financial Times,* March 15, 1995.
"Reduced £19m Loss at Ibstock Johnsen," *Financial Times,* April 20, 1994.

—Robin DuBlanc

Illinois Bell Telephone Company

225 West Randolph Street
Chicago Illinois 60606
U.S.A.
(312) 727-9411
Fax: (312) 207-1601

Wholly Owned Subsidiary of Ameritech Corporation
Incorporated: 1881
Employees: 15,678
Revenues: $3.28 billion
SICs: 4813 Telephone Communications, Except
Radiotelephone

Illinois Bell Telephone Company is the legal name of what has generally been known as Ameritech Illinois since 1993. The firm is the largest provider of local telephone service in the state, and recently has been at the forefront of new technologies such as fiber optics and digital switching. It serves about 80 percent of the population of Illinois.

Illinois Bell was founded as the Chicago Telephonic Exchange in June 1878. It was originally part of the American Bell System, which later became American Telephone and Telegraph (AT&T). Chicago Telephone's agreement with American Bell allowed it to operate in Chicago and nearby parts of Illinois and Indiana. The firm's first move was to open a central telephone exchange in Chicago. At this time, use of the newly invented telephone was spreading rapidly in Illinois and throughout the rest of the United States. The Chicago Telephonic Exchange merged with a competing firm to form the Chicago Telephone Company in January 1881.

As a result of this growth, the firm began using five-digit telephone numbers in 1889, and had to expand its numbers again in 1892. In the 1890s the firm began installing automatic switches that could connect calls without the assistance of an operator. The first of these went operational in 1892 at Fort Sheridan, an army base north of Chicago. Long-distance service to New York began in 1892 out of a special office on Quincy Street in Chicago. At this time a private residential telephone cost $8 a month.

With the telephone quickly assuming an important role in American society, Chicago Telephone continued to grow rapidly. By 1905 it operated 100,000 telephones in the city of Chicago alone. As a result of this growth, the firm built a new headquarters in 1912 at 212 W. Washington Street in Chicago, adjoining its former headquarters building on Franklin Street. The two buildings together constituted the largest telephone building in the world. In 1920 the firm began to grow through acquisition, buying the Illinois properties of the Central Union Telephone Company. With this purchase and its already existing territory, Chicago Telephone operated in almost all of Illinois as well as Lake and Porter counties in Indiana. The company acknowledged its statewide presence by changing its name to Illinois Bell.

With ever more subscribers, the company began using seven-digit telephone numbers in 1921. The firm grew throughout the 1920s, until the start of the Great Depression in 1929. The Depression slowed growth for Illinois Bell and most other utilities, as customers hurt by the hard economic times of the period cut back on telephone use and delayed ordering new telephone lines.

World War II produced shortages for civilian telephones, parts, and wires because the needs of the U.S. armed forces received first priority. The war also increased the nation's reliance on telecommunications, however. The economy began growing again during the war, and after the war ended in 1945, Illinois Bell kept busy filling back orders that could not be filled during the war.

In the late 1940s and early 1950s, a period of tremendous economic growth for the United States, many Americans began moving to the suburbs and having children. These factors created an unprecedented demand for telephones, a demand so strong that in 1952 the firm installed nearly one new telephone a minute. In the mid-1950s Illinois Bell put direct distance dialing (DDD) into effect. This service used area codes and seven-digit telephone numbers, allowing customers to make long-distance calls without operator assistance. DDD began in 1955 with Waukegan and Highland Park, Illinois, two of the first cities in the United States to begin using the new system. It reached Chicago in 1961 and was available across the entire state of Illinois by 1969. At that time, Illinois had five area codes. In another first for the company, in 1959 Elgin became the first city in the United States to use touch-tone dialing.

With the enormous growth of the phone system after World War II, better switching methods were needed to keep up with the volume of calls. Fortunately, advances in the new area of transistor technology made an all-electronic switch possible. Electronic switches decreased switching time to minute fractions of a second, and later made new services possible. The first electronic switching office was tested in Morris in 1960.

At the same time, Illinois Bell and other companies in the Bell system introduced new services. In 1961 wide area telephone service (WATS) gave business customers the ability to make unlimited numbers of calls within a given calling zone for a standard price. The zone could range from the size of Illinois to the entire United States. Another innovation, the Centrex system, enabled customers at large businesses to receive and send calls directly, without having to go through an office switchboard. In 1967 Illinois Bell, which had grown to serve 5.5

million customers by this time, moved into a new headquarters at 225 W. Randolph in Chicago.

In 1970 Illinois Bell put out the dial tone first system, which allowed pay-phone customers to call the operator or information without using a coin. In 1971 the firm introduced the first services made possible by electronic switching: call waiting, speed calling, call forwarding, and three-way calling. At first these services were limited to Oswego and Aurora, but they were soon offered in the entire state of Illinois.

In 1975 Illinois Bell finally served all of Illinois: it bought telephone operations in the last few counties it had not previously served (in southwest Illinois) from Southwestern Bell. At the same time, the utility sold its Indiana properties to Indiana Bell.

Three years later, Illinois Bell began working with a new wave of important telephone technologies. First, it began testing advanced mobile phone service (AMPS) in the Chicago area. The firm also began testing a 1.5-mile fiberoptic system in Chicago, laying it below the streets. In 1981 it connected the Schaumburg-Hoffman estates area using fiberoptic cable, the first such connection in the United States.

It was around this time that events in the American legal system began to have an impact on Illinois Bell. AT&T and the Bell system had been accused of being a monopoly at various points during most of their history. In 1974 the U.S. Department of Justice filed a civil anti-trust suit against AT&T, formally accusing it of being a monopoly. The suit dragged on for years and was finally settled in 1982, when AT&T agreed to divest itself of all of its Bell operating companies, including Illinois Bell. As a result, on January 1, 1984, Illinois Bell became a subsidiary of Ameritech Corporation, one of seven new regional Bell operating companies that acted as holding companies for groups of the local Bells. Also included in Ameritech were Indiana Bell, Ohio Bell, Wisconsin Bell, and Michigan Bell. The reorganization was planned well in advance and resulted in little service disruption or change in the day-to-day operations of Illinois Bell.

Meanwhile, the firm continued its constant adoption of new technology. In 1982 it set up the first digital switching system in the world in Seneca. Digital switches were faster and of a higher quality than electronic switches. Just as important, they made possible another wave of new telecommunications services. Computers were assuming a vital place in modern communications and commerce, and digital switches allowed computer technology to be integrated with the telephone system. In 1984 Illinois Bell became the first telephone company to offer public switched digital service (PSDS), wherein customers could transmit digital information over existing phone lines at 56,000 bits per second.

In 1985 Illinois Bell carried out the first commercial trial of a technology called integrated services digital network (ISDN). This system encoded information (including the human voice) digitally, allowing customers to send voice, video, and digital data simultaneously over a single phone line. In the late 1980s Illinois Bell installed its five-millionth access line and noted that it had installed 50,000 miles of optical fiber, making its fiber network one of the largest in the world. Illinois Bell had

become one of the foremost technology users among U.S. local telephone companies.

The utility's sailing was not all smooth, however. A May 1988 fire in a switching station in Hinsdale caused widespread problems. The fire destroyed most of the station, one of the four largest in the Chicago area. As a result, about 35,000 customers in southeastern DuPage County had no telephone service for over a month. Because the station was a long-distance hub for many in Chicago's south and southwestern suburbs, hundreds of thousands experienced disruptions to their long-distance service as well. Repairs were estimated to cost over $30 million. Illinois Bell was widely criticized because the Hinsdale station did not have the state-of-the-art fire suppressing equipment found at many small, independent companies.

In 1988 Illinois Bell won a $108.1 million contract with US Sprint to update the telecommunications network of the state of Illinois. The two companies connected the offices of state agencies in Chicago and Springfield to college campuses and other state government locations. The network included voice, data, and video connections to be installed over a seven-year period. Illinois Bell took care of the local portions of the network, while Sprint worked on the long-distance connections. Rivals AT&T and MCI Communications filed protests when the contract was awarded to Illinois Bell, but the state stuck with its original decision.

Also in 1988, the company launched a total quality management program after examining surveys that showed decreasing customer satisfaction. To cut payroll costs and improve customer service, in 1990 Illinois Bell trimmed over 1,000 positions from the ranks of its management. It also consolidated customer sales and service into a single department.

As information services became more important to the U.S. economy, Illinois Bell's parent company, Ameritech, requested in 1992 that the Illinois Commerce Commission change the way Illinois Bell was regulated so that Ameritech could invest $3 billion in its data-carrying infrastructure over a five-year period.

In September 1993, Ameritech retired the Illinois Bell brand name. Bills for local telephone service were delivered with the name Ameritech at the top, rather than Illinois Bell, while Ameritech's Illinois operations were referred to in the press and in marketing efforts as simply Ameritech Illinois. However, the company's legal name remained Illinois Bell. The same switch was carried out at the other state Bells in the Ameritech group, so that Ameritech could promote the Ameritech name.

While the change was in some ways superficial, it reflected Ameritech strategies with the potential to profoundly impact Illinois Bell and its local phone service. Parent company Ameritech wanted to get into the highly profitable long-distance telephone market. The 1983 consent agreement that led to the breakup of AT&T had specifically barred the regional Bells from competing in the long-distance market, while AT&T was to stay out of the local market. But Ameritech proposed allowing competition in its local markets if regulators would allow it to compete in the long-distance arena. The motivation for this was strategy was simple: while local telephone service was profitable and safe, revenues were not growing quickly. For instance, Illinois Bell revenue grew from $2.98 billion in 1992 to $3.08 billion in 1993 to $3.28 billion in 1994. Further, the utility actually reported a net loss in income for 1994 of $402.2 million, primarily because of its discontinuance of regulatory accounting practices, and a loss of $175.2 million in 1992.

Ameritech initially proposed relinquishing its monopoly on local phone service in Chicago in return for access to the long-distance and cable television markets. That plan was rejected by state and federal regulators, who insisted that Ameritech first give up its local monopoly. They further stipulated that Ameritech only gain access to the long-distance market after competition existed in its local markets. With this goal in mind, Ameritech began offering competitors the right to purchase access to the Illinois Bell local network at wholesale prices that they could, in turn, sell to potential customers. Soon Illinois Bell was looking at potential competition from AT&T, the largest long-distance company, and MCI, the number-two long-distance company. It already faced competition in Chicago from four smaller companies, including Teleport Communications Group and MFS Communications, which had built their own fiber-optic loops in downtown Chicago to compete for the business market in that area.

An April 1995 agreement between Ameritech, AT&T, and the U.S. Department of Justice, would have created two areas—one of which was Illinois Bell's Chicago territory—in which the local telephone market would be opened to competition in return for access to the long-distance market. Before this agreement was approved by the U.S. District Court, a separate congressional attempt to rewrite U.S. telecommunications law ensued. Some versions of congressional telecommunications legislation offered the local Bells access to the long-distance market without giving up their local monopolies.

Meanwhile, Illinois Bell's market was changing in other ways. For years the firm had an earnings cap placed on it by the Illinois Commerce Commission. In October 1994 the Illinois Commerce Commission voted to allow Illinois Bell to keep whatever profits it could earn after putting into effect a price-regulation formula based on inflation and other indices. As part of the ruling, Illinois Bell reduced rates by $93 million a year on

certain services and put a five-year cap on basic residential telephone service rates. The same month, a federal appellate court ruled in favor of Ameritech in a suit over whether or not the Bells could offer cable television services. Originally forbidden from doing so by the Cable Communications Policy Act of 1984, the ruling allowed Illinois Bell to begin construction of a digital video network on which it planned to offer cable television services.

As a result of these changes, by the mid-1990s, Illinois Bell was in the midst of a quickly evolving market. It hoped to soon enter the long-distance and cable television markets, but its ability to do so depends in large measure on the contents of various congressional bills. In the meantime, local competition had already appeared in the form of small independents with their own fiberoptic loops in downtown Chicago. Sprint Communications Inc., working with Chicago-area cable companies, was also conducting tests with a eye to offering residential telephone service over cable television wires in 1996. Cellular telephones offered rival communications companies another point of competitive access to the local telephone market as well.

Further Reading:

''Illinois Telephone History,'' Independent Telephone Pioneer Association, 1991.

''News of the Week: Bell Focuses on Customers,'' *Telephony,* April 9, 1990, pp. 18, 22.

McCaughna, Dan, and Tasia Kavvadias, ''Illinois Bell Center Hit by Fire Was a Crucial One,'' *Chicago Tribune,* May 10, 1988.

O'Shea, Dan, ''Illinois Bell Program Stirs Regulatory Ire,'' *Telephony,* March 22, 1993, pp. 8–9.

Van, Jon, ''For Whom Bill Tolls—Now It's Ameritech,'' *Chicago Tribune,* August 10, 1993.

——, ''State Panel Places Call for Local Phone Rivalry,'' *Chicago Tribune,* April 8, 1995.

Winter, Christine, and Rob Karwath, ''Phone Office Lacked Best Fire Protection,'' *Chicago Tribune,* May 15, 1988.

Winter, Christine, ''Illinois Bell, Sprint Keep $108 Million State Job,'' *Chicago Tribune,* September 9, 1988.

—Scott M. Lewis

Immunex

Immunex Corporation

51 University Street
Seattle, Washington 98101-2936
U.S.A.
(206) 587-0430
Fax: (206) 587-0606

Public Company
Incorporated: 1981
Employees: 750
Sales: $144.33 million
Stock Exchanges: NASDAQ
SICs: 2836 Biological Products Except Diagnostic; 6794
    Patent Owners & Lessors

Immunex Corporation is a biopharmaceutical company that develops, manufacturers, and markets therapeutic products for the treatment of cancer, infectious diseases, and autoimmune disorders. The company more than doubled its revenue base between 1992 and 1993 as a result of a merger with Lederle pharmaceutical units of American Cyanamid Company. However, in the mid-1990s, Immunex was still trying to achieve profitability after investing heavily in research and development since its inception in 1981.

Immunex was formed during the start of the biotechnology craze of the early 1980s. Biotechnology, as it was known in the mid-1990s, was born in the early 1950s when the structure of DNA was discovered; that revelation lead to the understanding of the process by which proteins are formed. Subsequent breakthroughs, particularly in the early 1970s, showed that it was possible to genetically alter microorganisms and, importantly, produce mass amounts of proteins that naturally occurred only in small quantities. A handful of companies pioneered the commercial biotechnology industry during the middle and late 1970s, but it wasn't until the early 1980s that a horde of competitors jumped into the game. The pivotal turning point came when the U.S. Supreme Court ruled that genetically engineered bacterium could be patented. For many, that ruling suggested the possibility of fantastic profits for biotech innovators.

Eager to make their mark in the burgeoning commercial biotechnology industry were scientists Steven Gillis and Christopher Henney. Henney, a Ph.D., was internationally recognized for his research in immunology. Gillis also had a doctorate—in

biological sciences from Dartmouth College—and was recognized for his contributions related to immunology research. Gillis and Henney believed that they possessed the expertise to develop a method of producing large quantities of certain hormones that showed promise in fighting infection. So, at the urging of Seattle patent attorney Jim Uhlir, they formed Immunex as a means of developing and commercializing their techniques and drugs.

Joining the duo was Steve Duzan, an entrepreneur who owned an industrial ice-making machine business at the time. Duzan had become intrigued by the emerging biotechnology industry after being introduced to Gillis and Henney. While prior to joining their start-up he had virtually no experience in medical-related industries, he did know how to raise investment capital, and he was known as a tenacious, hard-driving manager. At the age of 34 Duzan had arranged the leveraged buyout of the Washington-based Cello Bag Co. Inc. Then, in 1980, he engineered the sale of the company to ARCO Chemicals, Inc. He used cash from that deal to purchase North Star Ice Equipment Corp., a small manufacturer of ice-making machines that exported much of its output to the Middle East. Duzan overhauled that company's manufacturing operations and managed to improve its profitability.

Duzan was looking for another company to buy when he met Gillis and Henney. Instead, he helped them to form a completely new company called Immunex. Gillis and Henney, naturally, managed the scientific side of the business, while Duzan went to work finding capital to fund Immunex's cash-hungry research and development operations. As it turned out, many of the entrepreneurial skills that Duzan had learned in his previous business exploits were well-suited to the seat-of-the-pants biotechnology sector. For the first six months Duzan worked without a salary while he scrambled to secure investors. "Immunex was the penniless new kid on the block going up against these giants like Hoffman-LaRoche and Kodak," recalled Stephen Graham, an attorney at Immunex's law firm, in a July 21, 1991 *Business Journal-Portland* article. "But time and time again," he added, "when Steve looked at a transaction with those people, he would decide what a relatively little guy had a right to expect. And then he would double it. And then he would go out and get it."

While Duzan labored to find cash to fuel Immunex's product development engine, Gillis and Henney oversaw an ambitious research effort to generate various immune system stimulants and related technologies. Their goal was to develop a breakthrough drug, or drugs, that would allow Immunex to become a full-fledged pharmaceutical company that developed and manufactured its own products. But that pivotal product proved elusive for Immunex's research team. The company's pursuits did succeed, however, in producing a number of valuable technologies and products that earned the company respect in the biotechnology industry. Specifically, Immunex discovered and cloned a long list of genes producing substances that could work in the human body to stimulate various blood cells to fight cancer, heal wounds, and prevent auto-immune diseases like arthritis and diabetes.

Among Immunex's most important products during the mid-1980s were its Interleukin drugs and GM-CSF (Granulocyte

Macrophage Colony Stimulating Factor). Those products were essentially immune system proteins that acted as hormones in the body, with each hormone commanding only specific types of cells. Each class of cells could be stimulated to respond with antibodies, enzymes, and other substances that multiplied and attacked infection. For example, Immunex's centerpiece drug, GM-CSF (marketed as 'Leukin'), was a blood-growth stimulator that enhanced the body's production of white blood cells. Leukin could fight infection in cancer patients whose white blood cells had been destroyed during bone marrow transplants. It also had potential applications related to chemotherapy.

Although Immunex was at the technological forefront in its niche, the company faced numerous roadblocks to success. Chief among its hurdles was the Food and Drug Administration (FDA) drug approval process. To shepherd a drug through the intimidating FDA gamut, a company typically had to invest millions of dollars completing its own tests and striving to comply with Federal regulations. The obvious risk was that the drug would fail to meet FDA approval and the company would be stuck with the loss. For a smaller company like Immunex, failure could be virtually devastating. To help bring their drugs and technologies to market, therefore, many biotech start-ups sought other avenues to profit. Common routes included selling or licensing proprietary technology to large pharmaceutical companies, or partnering with bigger competitors to develop and market new drugs.

Immunex managed to stay solvent and continued to fund its research and development arm during the 1980s by, in essence, selling its technology to companies that had the financial backing to take it to market. Some analysts criticized the strategy because it effectively turned Immunex into a ''research boutique'' and represented a diversion from the company's goal of becoming a true pharmaceutical company that marketed its own drugs. But the tactic was necessary to keep the company afloat given the volatile environment of the biotechnology industry. A critical juncture for the company came in 1983, shortly after the company had gone public to raise cash through an initial public stock offering. For no apparent reason related to Immunex's performance, the company's stock price plunged from $11 to $4. The price remained suppressed while biotech investors questioned the viability of the entire industry.

Unable to generate acceptable proceeds from the sale of more stock, Duzan arranged a number of deals that benefited Immunex. He negotiated with some large American and European drug companies, selling marketing and manufacturing rights to most of the major immune-system stimulants that it had cloned. Those agreements included high-profile products like GM-CSF and its Interleukin drugs. Although forfeiting company rights to some of that technology, Duzan was credited with swinging deals that, in the long-term, worked in Immunex's favor. For example, in selling marketing rights for GM-CSF to German pharmaceutical manufacturer Behringwerke AG, Duzan won a concession to oversee clinical trials for Leukine. That move later made it possible for Immunex to become a true pharmaceutical company, rather than just a research lab that collected royalties from its inventions.

Throughout the 1980s Immunex developed a number of promising technologies, most of which it sold or licensed to other companies. As fees and royalties income increased, revenues rose steadily to about $2.4 million in 1985, $11.3 million in 1987, and $23.3 million by 1989. But profits remained elusive, as the company continued to pour millions into research and development. Investors had generally been patient with Immunex because the company had been so successful at developing new products. But that patience gradually wore thin as they watched the company spend millions without ever successfully taking a drug to market. Immunex managed to post meager profits in 1988 and 1991, but those surpluses were insignificant compared to big losses in other years. Indeed, between 1985 and 1990 Immunex lost nearly $30 million.

Despite ongoing losses, it seemed as though Immunex had turned the corner toward profitability going into the early 1990s. In a series of bold and complex deals initiated in 1989, Duzan reacquired, sold, and swapped the rights to a number of its drugs. The end result was that Immunex, by 1990, was in a position to possibly begin marketing its own technology. ''In this business you've got to become a marketing organization,'' Duzan said in a April 15, 1990 Seattle Times article. ''Because that's the only way you can get enough cashflow to sustain your research.'' The most significant result of Duzan's wheeling and dealing was that Immunex managed to reacquire the U.S. co-marketing rights to GM-CSF and certain Interleukin drugs from its German partner Behringwerke AG. The move was risky because GM-CSF had not been approved for use in the United States by the FDA.

Investors finally had something to cheer about when, in March 1991, Immunex won FDA approval to market Leukin (GM-CSF) in the United States to treat bone marrow transplant patients. The company's shares rocketed to a record high of $59 following the announcement, and Immunex initiated an aggressive marketing program to sell the product. Shortly after the approval, Immunex was selling Leukine through a 50-member sales team organized to market the product to oncology specialists. At the same time, Immunex continued to invest millions of dollars into new drugs. Chief among its research projects in the early 1990s was Pixie 321, a synthetic molecule that was designed to incorporate the properties of Leukine and Immunex's Interleukin 3 (a cancer-fighting compound). Duzan hoped to sell that and other drugs through its own sales force.

Despite notable successes during the late 1980s and early 1990s, Immunex continued to disappoint some analysts and investors. The company chalked up heavy losses, largely related to research expenses, totaling $78 million in 1992. The company had hoped to offset that deficit with increased sales of Leukin, but its marketing effort failed to live up to some analysts' hopes. The problem was partially attributable to a product similar to Leukin that was introduced by competitor Amgen. Amgen received approval for its drug, Neupogen, in 1992. Whereas Leukin had been approved for the bone marrow transplant market, Neupogen was approved for use in the much larger chemotherapy market. The result was that shipments of Neupogen bolted to $290 million in 1993, while revenues from Leukin topped out at less than $23 million. ''One company operates in an ocean, the other in a pond,'' surmised Deborah Wardwell, a Seattle stock analyst, in the August 8, 1994 Seattle Times.

Encountering a fate similar to that experienced by many other biotech companies, Immunex was bought out. In June 1993 American Cyanamid purchased the company and merged it with its Lederle Oncology unit to form a new, publicly traded company still known as Immunex. Lederle Oncology was a leader in the immunology industry and had about a half dozen proprietary products in its drug portfolio. Lederle, with its more established marketing network, seemed like a natural complement to Immunex's powerful research operations. The merger initially failed to produce the desired results, however, because Lederle's products didn't sell as well as expected. That problem, combined with less-than-stellar gains with Leukin, created investor disappointment with Immunex. The stock price slipped to $30 before dropping to less than $15 per share in 1994.

Frustrated, American Cyanamid brought in a new chief executive to replace Duzan, who had been accused of alienating Wall Street with his brusque nature and questionable management decisions regarding Leukin. Specifically, he had been criticized for allowing Amgen to steal more than 90 percent of the market for Leukin. Gillis, who was heading up Immunex's research operations at the time, stepped in as a temporary president and CEO for a few months until American Cyanamid appointed Edward Fritzky to the position. (Cofounder Henney had left Immunex in 1989 to start his own consulting company.) Fritzky came to Immunex from American Cyanmid's Lederle Laboratories division. He had overseen the launch of six new products in that division and, at the age of 45, was considered a seasoned veteran in the pharmaceutical industry.

Interestingly, American Cyanamid was bought out by American Home Products in mid-1994, making the latter company the majority owner of Immunex. Fritzky remained president and CEO of the company, however, and sustained his efforts to turn Immunex into a development and marketing powerhouse in its pharmaceutical niche. Unfortunately, profits continued to evade Immunex going into the mid-1990s, amidst a string of setbacks. In September 1994, for example, cofounder Steve Gillis resigned his post to pursue other research goals. More importantly, the FDA refused to approve Leukin for use in the $500 million chemotherapy market that was dominated by Amgen. The stunning news sent Immunex's stock price tumbling 20 percent to less than $13 per share by May 1995. Nevertheless, management remained optimistic, given the company's proven research capabilities, pipeline of high-potential drugs, and ongoing efforts to get FDA approval to use Leukin in chemotherapy applications.

Principal Subsidiaries: Immunex Manufacturing Corporation; Immunex Carolina Corporation; Receptech.

Further Reading:

Cushing, William G., "Immunex Founder Stephen A. Duzan Named High-Tech Entrepreneur of the Year," *Business Wire,* February 10, 1989.
Dowell, Valoree, "Immunex Appoints Steven Gillis Acting Chairman and Chief Executive Officer," *PR Newswire,* September 17, 1993.
——, "Immunex Founder Resigns, Continues as Consultant," *PR Newswire,* September 29, 1994.
Grunbaum, Rami, "Energetic CEO's Goal: Deliver on Immunex Promise," *Puget Sound Business Journal,* April 22, 1994, p. 1.
——, "Stephen Duzan: Immunex Chairman Puts Young Company in the Big Leagues," *Business Journal-Portland,* July 22, 1991, p. 12.
Gupta, Himanee, "Immunex's 1st Product Brings Profit," *Seattle Times,* July 26, 1991, p. C10.
Heberlein, Greg, "Immunex Chief Rolls with the Punches," *Seattle Times,* August 8, 1994, p. E1.
——, "Merger Boosts Immunex Stock," *Seattle Times,* August 18, 1994, p. D1.
Lalonde, James E., "Betting On a Blockbuster: Wall Street Now See 'Transformed' Immunex," *Seattle Times,* April 15, 1990, p. E1.
——, "Immunex Founder Resigns," *Seattle Times,* August 2, 1989, p. G10.
Lim, Paul J., "Immunex Reassures Investors," *Seattle Times,* April 27, 1995, p. D3.
Milburn, Karen, "Immunex Cools Expectations," *Puget Sound Journal,* April 24, 1989, p. 10.
Price, Margaret, "Immunex: Tempest in a Test Tube?" *Financial World,* November 17, 1987, p. 18.

—Dave Mote

Indiana Bell Telephone Company, Incorporated

240 N. Meridian Street
Indianapolis, Indiana 46204
U.S.A.
(317) 265-2266
Fax: (317) 265-5564

Wholly Owned Subsidiary of Ameritech Corp.
Incorporated: 1920 as Indiana Bell Telephone Company
Employees: 5,700
Operating Revenues: $1.17 billion
SICs: 4813 Telephone Communications Except
   Radiotelephone

Indiana Bell Telephone Company, Incorporated, is the Indiana corporate legal entity for Ameritech Corporation, which provides a wide variety of advanced telecommunications services in Indiana. As that state's dominant local telecommunications company, Indiana Bell serves 64 percent of Indiana's population and 28 percent of its geographic area through 1.9 million telephone lines. The company has been known to its customers as Ameritech since 1993, when Indiana Bell, Ohio Bell, Michigan Bell, Illinois Bell, and Wisconsin Bell took the name of Ameritech as part of that company's new initiatives to make Ameritech's new market-driven structure and unified brand identity more visible to its 13 million customers in its five-state region. However, the Indiana Bell name is still used in connection with state regulatory matters, and Indiana Bell continues to own current Indiana Bell assets in the state.

Indiana Bell was one of five state-based Ameritech Corp. subsidiaries that were formerly part of American Telephone & Telegraph Company (AT&T) prior to AT&T's 1982 court-ordered divestiture of local phone service operations. In accordance with a consent decree arising out litigation preceding the AT&T breakup, Indiana Bell provides two principal types of services: local exchange and intra-LATA (short-haul long distance) toll service and network access in Indiana. In 1990 Indiana Bell dissolved its board of directors and in 1993 became known to its customers as Ameritech

Indiana Bell was incorporated in 1920 to operate Bell Telephone System local toll lines and telephone exchanges in Indiana. Indiana Bell's roots, though, can be traced to the last quarter of the 19th century and the birth of phone service in Indiana, which arrived in the state less that two years after Alexander Graham Bell's 1876 invention of the telephone. In 1877, after a telephone demonstration at the Indiana State Fair, the only two existing phones in the state were moved to downtown Indianapolis for the purposes of a practical test. The local coal operation Wales & Company connected the two phones, one placed at the company's office and one at its coal yard, by means of a telegraph line. In 1877 another local coal dealer, Cobb & Branham, applied for and received Indianapolis City Council permission to construct a permanent telephone line to run between its office and coal yard.

Indiana's first telephone company, Indiana District Telephone Company, was organized in December 1878. In January 1879 Indiana District Telephone received Indianapolis City Council permission to erect telephone poles and wires on public property, and two months later Indiana District Telephone, utilizing Bell patented equipment, established the state's first telephone exchange at the corner of Washington Street and Virginia Avenue. In 1880 the company was reorganized as Telephone Exchange Company of Indianapolis, and that same year the second telephone company in Indianapolis, Western Telephone Company, was founded. In 1883 Central Union Telephone Company, a Bell System operation and the direct predecessor of Indiana Bell, was created. During the 1890s competition in the Indiana telephone industry intensified, and new companies, acquisitions, and mergers proliferated. By the turn of the century, Indiana had over 600 independent telephone companies, and many telephone customers in the state had at least two phone companies from which they could choose; as a result, many telephone users found it necessary to have a phone from each service provider in order to communicate with customers of each telephone firm.

The creation of the Indiana Bell forerunner, Central Union Telephone, eventually resulted in the merger of it and the other two existing Indianapolis-based exchanges as well as the acquisition of the majority of telephone exchanges existing in Indiana, Illinois, and Ohio. In February 1920 Indiana Bell Telephone Company, organized to centrally own and operate telephone exchanges and local toll lines of the Bell Telephone System in Indiana, was incorporated; two months later Indiana Bell acquired the Indiana properties of Central Union Telephone, formerly operating in three states, and the properties of Indianapolis Telephone Company, which had been created in 1898. AT&T, which funded the acquisition of Central Union, took control of the stock of Indiana Bell Telephone.

The series of mergers that created Indiana Bell in 1920 were completed by July of that year after Indiana Bell had also acquired and consolidated the properties of United Telephone Company of Bluffton, Indiana; Citizens Telephone Company of Kokomo, Indiana; Indiana Union Telephone & Telegraph Company of Fowler; and Southern Telephone Company of Indiana. Edgar S. Bloom was named the first president of Indiana Bell, which established its headquarters in an eight-story red-brick building formerly serving as the Central Union Telephone headquarters. The newly consolidated company, launched with $15 million in capital, initially controlled the operation of 90 exchanges and 30,000 miles of long distance circuits and served 170,000 Indiana telephones through nearly 5,000 employees.

In 1921 Curtis H. Rottger was named president and served the company through the remainder of the decade. Indiana Bell's early growth-through-acquisition strategy was evidenced during the 1920s by the 1925 purchase of two small telephone operations, Citizens Telephone Company of Edinburg, Indiana, and the Indiana properties of Louisville Home Telephone Company. In July 1929 Indiana Bell acquired the physical property and other assets of several telephone service companies it already owned, including those operating in the Indiana communities of Columbus, Danville, Clinton, Martinsville, Michigan City, Bloomfield, and Rockville.

In 1930 James R. Carroll succeeded Rottger as president. That same year the building housing Indiana Bell's headquarters was relocated in an engineering feat that received global acclaim. The 11,000-ton building was moved 52 feet south and 100 feet west—all in 30 days while telephone service and business operations continued without interruption. Indiana Bell's territorial expansion continued in the 1930s with the acquisition of telephone operations in the Indiana towns of Albany, Rosedale, Lawrence, Lebanon, and Dugger.

Indiana Bell's expansion drive was cooled by World War II and resumed in 1946 with the common stock acquisition of a small telephone concern, West Newton Telephone Company. By that time the company's revenues had grown to more than $28 million, including $16 million from local services. In 1946 William A. Hughes was named president and served for two years before being succeeded by Harry S. Hanna, who remained president until 1960. In 1948 Indiana Bell constructed its first addition to its headquarters, adding five floors to its facility.

In 1950 Indiana Bell acquired the outside plant of Mt. Summit Rural Telephone Company. By 1951 annual local service revenues had grown to more than $32 million, while total revenues topped $50 million, and the company earned more than $6 million for the first time. After receiving Federal Communications Commission (FCC) authorization, in 1952 Indiana Bell acquired through the estate of J. T. Detchon a group of telephone companies that included the Noblesville Telephone Company, Browning Telephone Corp., Central Telephone Company, Sims Telephone Company, Daleville & Middletown Telephone Company, Citizens Telephone Company, and Union Telephone Company. In 1956 the company changed its named to Indiana Bell Telephone Company, Incorporated.

In 1960 Roy C. Echols was named president, and for the next eight years he guided the company through a period of facility expansion, technological advancements, and financial growth. During the same period the number of independent telephone companies fell below 100 for the first time since the 19th century. Indiana Bell added a 14-story annex to its headquarters in 1961 and a 20-story annex and eight-story addition six years later. During the early 1960s Indiana Bell began relying on increasingly larger public sales of debentures, as well as financial advances from parent AT&T, for expansion purposes; the company issued $20 million in debentures in 1963 and sold $25 million worth of public debt two years later, in part to pay off advances from AT&T.

Technological advances for Indiana Bell during the decade were highlighted by the 1965 completion of a program to convert all company phone exchanges to dial service. In 1968 the company introduced the Bell System's first 9-1-1 emergency calling system, which connected emergency callers to a central dispatcher serving fire, police, and rescue agencies. By mid-decade Indiana Bell's earnings had topped $25 million on revenues of more than $89 million, and by 1967 revenues from local services alone topped $100 million as total revenues grew to more than $180 million. In 1968 Thomas S. Nurnberger succeeded Echols as president.

In January 1970 Indiana Bell went back to the public debt market, selling $80 million of debentures which left the company with four issues of long-term debt totalling $165 million. In 1971 the company followed up with $100 million offering—generating enough popularity to put a temporary stop to a drop in the price of seasoned corporate bonds—and used proceeds to help fund its expansion program, repay AT&T advances, and pay off short-term debt. For the 1971 year, the Indiana Bell offering was one of about a dozen public debt sales by Bell System operating companies, whose debt offerings that year totalled more than $1.5 billion.

By 1973 Indiana Bell had completed a program to install direct distance dialing service for all of its customers, and by 1978 touch-tone service was available to all of the company's customers. In need of additional office space to replace that which had given way to additional telecommunications equipment, Indiana Bell constructed a 20-story office building at 220 N. Meridian, Indianapolis (just south of the original Indiana Bell headquarters at 220 N. Meridian), which was completed in 1975. In 1976 the company, as part of a program to consolidate Indiana Bell and Illinois Bell operations within the respective state territory of each, began serving 11 exchanges in Lake County, Indiana, that Illinois Bell had served since 1920. The exchanges transferred to Indiana Bell included those in Crown Point, East Chicago, Gary, Hammond, Highland, and Merrillville.

Expansion and technological advances translated into continued and consistent financial growth for Indiana Bell in the 1970s, and in 1975 annual revenues climbed above $400 million for the first time as income topped more than $50 million for the second consecutive year. In early 1977 Indiana Bell and three other AT&T operating subsidiaries, in an innovative and unusual financial move to save the companies an aggregate $60 million, offered to repurchase at premium prices high-cost old debentures from public holders. The offer was made to acquire the debentures before their first redemption date in order to trim interest expenses and hold down telephone rates and was made at a time when long-term interest rates were falling and market prices of long-term debt outstanding were rising. In late 1977, following the early redemption offer, Indiana Bell sold $90 million worth of new debentures. By the end of 1977 Indiana Bell's annual earnings had climbed to more than $84 million, on revenues of $572 million, and by the end of the decade the company's annual income was more $100 million.

In 1982 the U.S. Department of Justice (DOJ) brought to a close a 13-year-old antitrust suit against Indiana Bell's parent, AT&T, which had grown into the world's largest corporation. In a landmark decree designed to demonopolize the telecommunications industry and allow for equal access to long distance exchange facilities, the DOJ ordered AT&T to divest itself of its 22 operating subsidiaries, which were divided among seven newly created regional holding companies, which became known colloquially as Baby Bells.

Between 1970 and 1983 Indiana Bell named eight new presidents: David K. Easlick, James E. Olson, John W. Arbuckle, D.C. (Bud) Staley, William L. Weiss, Philip A. Campbell, William P. Vititoe, and Ramon L. Humke, who was named president in 1983 after Vititoe left to head up Michigan Bell. In 1983, Indiana Bell's last year as part of an AT&T-controlled local telecommunications system, Indiana Bell earned $137.8 million on revenues of $942 million. The regional telephone holding company formed from AT&T units in the Midwest was named American Information Technologies Corp., or Ameritech, and included Indiana Bell, Illinois Bell, Michigan Bell, Ohio Bell, and Wisconsin Bell. Headquartered in Chicago, Ameritech began operating as Indiana Bell's parent in 1984. That same year William L. Weiss, who had once served as president of Indiana Bell, returned from a stint as president of Illinois Bell to serve as Ameritech chairman and CEO.

Ameritech began its existence touting a high-tech communications system and was the first Baby Bell to start a cellular mobile phone service, in the Chicago area. From its outset, Ameritech—exemplified by Indiana Bell—was considered to have one of the most favorable regulatory environments to operate in, with only Ohio Bell in the Ameritech territory facing a stringent regulatory climate. Indiana Bell's favorable working relationships with state regulators, coupled with the company's tight control over finances, helped the Ameritech subsidiary enjoy favorable ratings on its debentures during the mid-1980s.

By 1984 Ameritech and other regional holding companies and their operating subsidiaries were already facing off against AT&T in competition for the fast-growing market for business systems, known as private branch exchanges, or PBXs. At the heart of PBX competition was equipment manufacture; while AT&T marketed its own PBX systems, the Baby Bells and their local operating concerns sold those made by AT&T's principal rival, Northern Telecom Ltd., or those from other manufacturers. In 1986 Indiana Bell launched its Integrated Information Network (INN), which represented a transition toward the cutting-edge integrated services digital network (ISDN) technology, and INN that year helped the company land two five-year contracts, worth about $22 million total. Those contracts were with pharmaceutical giant Eli Lilly & Co.—at the time one of Indiana Bell's top five customers, generating more than 45 million voice calls per year—and U.S. Steel's Gary, Indiana, plant. In securing the contracts, Indiana Bell went up against competition that included AT&T's voice-data PBX systems and services that bypassed local networks such as that of Indiana Bell.

In 1987 Indiana Bell debuted an enhanced 9-1-1 service, in Hammond, that allowed vital information about callers' locations to be displayed on a computer screen at a public-safety answering facility. In 1988 Indiana Bell, in competing for PBX business, became the first company in the country to offer an office-based automatic call distribution system service. In 1989 Ameritech began consolidating marketing operations into one division, Ameritech Services; Ramon Humke assumed the

duties of president of that operation and was succeeded as Indiana Bell president by Richard C. Notebaert. The consolidation represented the first in a series of steps by Ameritech that eventually led to consolidation of numerous business functions under the Ameritech Services moniker, including auditing, financial services, and marketing.

In 1989 Indiana Bell surpassed $1 billion in revenues for the first time and earned more than $155.3 million. August 1989 brought labor concerns to several Baby Bells, including Ameritech, which was struck by 40,00 members of the Communications Workers of America, who joined 160,000 other members striking three Baby Bells. After 17 days, Ameritech workers in five states began returning to work. Indiana Bell and Michigan Bell were the last to reach agreements with striking workers. Upon returning to work, employees received nine percent wage increases over three years as well as improvements in profit sharing plans, pension job-training programs, and family care packages.

In 1990 Indiana Bell achieved its "most successful win during its 70-year existence," according to *Telephony,* when it was chosen to coordinate the quickest installation of a statewide lottery network in American history. In helping to establish the Indiana lottery, Indiana Bell was responsible for the installation of a private-line lottery network that included phone lines to 1,200 lottery sales sites and the coordination of 800 more sites. Indiana Bell received a five-year guarantee to provide a constant two-way communications system between the lottery's central system and each of its 2,000 terminals, and the lottery in its first year became one of the company's largest customers, generating an average of $1,500 in ticket-purchase transactions each minute.

By 1990 Indiana Bell's number of lines had grown to 1.6 million. Since 1984, the company had grown at a rate of 285 percent, tops among Ameritech operating companies. Only 38 independent telephone companies remained in Indiana by 1990; in addition, along with Indiana Bell, three other major companies were operating in the state: GTE North, Contel, and United Telephone of Indiana. Despite the falling number of independent telephone companies, Indiana Bell faced heightened competition from well-funded independent companies utilizing fiberoptic technology. As a result of this and similar competitive threats in other states, Ameritech entered the 1990s with plans to construct fiberoptic cable rings in major market areas, including Indianapolis. In 1991 Indiana Bell, through its Ameritech parent, was among the first telecommunications operations in the country to be involved with experiments to transmit telephone and cable TV signals to homes over the same fiberoptic lines in Columbus, Indiana.

To reduce overhead and remain competitive with nonunion independent operations and large long-distance companies, during the early 1990s Ameritech and Indiana Bell made several rounds of reductions in its work force. In 1991 Indiana Bell unveiled one of the first programs that allowed PBX systems to install a location-identification system that could determine a caller's station number and specific address. In 1992 Indiana Bell participated in the Ameritech rollout of voicemail service by introducing it in Indianapolis. Other custom-calling features Indiana Bell introduced and expanded upon during the early

1990s included Call Waiting, Call Forwarding, Three-Way Calling, Speed Dialing, Call Screening, Caller ID, Automatic Callback, and Repeat Dialing.

To improve its telecommunications infrastructure, between 1988 and 1992 Indiana Bell spent more than $1 billion, and in the process, the company completed a program of computerizing all of its switching facilities. The company also boosted to about 60 percent the number of its lines served by the faster and more reliable digital call-handling systems, replacing older analog equipment. By the end of 1992 Indiana Bell had installed 54,000 miles of fiberoptic cables, which were capable of transmitting substantial volumes of data and were more resilient to water damage than traditional copper cables.

During an 18-month period in 1992 and 1993, William Weiss guided Ameritech through a major corporate reorganization aimed at making the corporation more competitive by reducing the size of the work force and focusing marketing efforts on customer products rather than geographic territories such as that under Indiana Bell's domain. In May 1992 four top Ameritech executives resigned or retired during a management shakeup. Thereafter Notebaert was named to head up Ameritech Services and Thomas J. Reiman replaced Notebaert as Indiana Bell president. By the end of 1992 Ameritech's staff had been cut by nearly 25 percent from its size a decade earlier, with the majority of those cuts made between 1990 and 1992.

In March 1993 Ameritech, after months of analyzing its operations, unveiled a restructuring plan that set the stage for the company to enter other markets. The reorganization plan was unique for a regional telecommunications corporation in that it proposed entrance into the areas previously barred to the seven Baby Bells, including long-distance service and cable television operations. Ameritech additionally announced intentions to diversify into interactive video services, including home office services, healthcare networks, public safety systems, electronic libraries, and home security. The Bell names of Indiana Bell and the other four Ameritech operating subsidiaries were all but eliminated as they began operating under the Ameritech name and logo, although continuing to exist as legal entities.

In exchange for an entrance into the long-distance market, Ameritech proposed opening up local phone service to competition. In line with this proposal, in May 1993 Indiana Bell asked the Indiana Utility Regulatory Commission to change the way the company's earnings were regulated, allowing the company to funnel its profits into construction of a telecommunications network that would be more competitive, in exchange for regulation of basic service rates. In addition, Indiana Bell offered to connect with fiberoptic cables all interested government centers, schools, and hospitals by the end of the decade and freeze basic rates until late in the decade.

In 1994 Weiss relinquished his titles of Ameritech chairman and chief executive to another former Indiana Bell president, Richard Notebaert. That same year Kent Lebherz succeeded Reiman as Indiana Bell president. Job cuts continued at Ameritech and Indiana Bell in 1994 and 1995, and Ameritech planned to further reduced nonmanagement workers by 6,000 by the end of 1995.

In mid-1994 Indiana Bell was granted basic rate price regulation approval in exchange for reductions and a short-term cap on basic rates and its agreement to link schools, public safety agencies, and government centers to fiber-optic technology. Following this approval, Indiana Bell rolled out a host of new services, including discount calling plans, customized telephone networks featuring abbreviated dialing between multiple locations, intercom calling, six-port teleconferencing, and specialized billing reports for business customers. Indiana Bell also unveiled toll restriction services allowing residential customers to block out all outbound long distance calls except those to 800 area codes, and pay-per-use repeat dialing and automatic callback services.

Before the close of 1994 all five of Ameritech's Bell operating subsidiaries had received basic service price regulation approval in exchange for profit deregulation, making Ameritech the first regional telecommunications concern to completely replace profit regulation. In another step to fulfill its reorganization proposals, in late 1994 Ameritech won approval from the Department of Justice to provide trial long-distance service in Chicago and Grand Rapids, Michigan, beginning in 1995. In late 1994 Ameritech also won necessary federal approvals to provide a commercial television delivery system in its five-state territory and announced plans to construct a cable network to deliver television signals to customers, with that network expected to serve six million customers by 2001.

Indiana Bell's own network by the end of 1994 included more than 65,000 miles of fiberoptic cables, with all of the company's access lines being served by computerized call-handling systems and three-quarters of those served by digital systems. Due to restructuring charges, Indiana Bell lost $83.7 million in 1994 on revenues of $1.17 billion; a year earlier the company had earned $163.2 million on revenues of $1.4 billion.

Ameritech entered 1995 as a much different company than that which had came away from the AT&T breakup. The regional corporation was offering information services, such as high-speed access to the Internet for businesses; was building a $4.4 billion interactive video communications network to provide competitive alternatives to cable television; was preparing to take on its former parent and others for long-distance business; was operating overseas; and was offering a full range of telephone services, including custom-calling features and cellular and paging services. During its evolution, Ameritech had formed partnerships with the likes of Walt Disney Company and Random House, while its competition had grown to include AT&T and MCI as well as Time-Warner, Telport, and Jones Intercable.

In August 1995 the United States House of Representatives approved legislation representing a major overhaul of the country's telecommunications laws, which would allow Ameritech and other regional telecommunications companies to provide long-distance service and allow long-distance companies such as AT&T to provide local phone service. In June 1995 the U.S. Senate had approved similar legislation, with the differences between the two pieces of legislation slated to be worked out in the fall of 1995. President Bill Clinton threatened to veto the legislation if approved; however, amendments and the wide margins by which both bills passed led analysts to suggest the president might sign modified telecommunications legislation.

As the nation's lawmakers were debating changes in telecommunications laws, the Communications Workers of America were threatening to strike Ameritech and three other Baby Bells in early August 1995. The most contentious issue involved job security in the light of Ameritech's plans to use increasing numbers of temporary workers and move more work to outside contractors. At the same time, Ameritech was negotiating with 11,500 members of the International Brotherhood of Electrical Workers, which, with the CWA, represented about 40,000 Ameritech employees. By mid-August Ameritech had staved off a strike threat and reached an agreement with both the CWA and the IBEW that granted workers a 10.9 percent wage increase over three years and job security provisions that would protect CWA members from involuntary layoffs. According to the *Chicago Tribune,* pending telecommunications legislation may have dampened Ameritech's drive to get a better deal from its union workers, as the company may have wanted to avoid undue attention. ''But if the competition in local phone service comes to pass and non-union competitors steal lucrative business, Ameritech may one day insist on a confrontation with unions,'' according to the *Tribune.*

As Indiana Bell moved toward the close of 1995, Ameritech continued its move to focus operations around customer-product groups rather than geographic areas and pending legislation that would further muddy the territory of the regional Bells. Historically Indiana Bell had been a stronghold in the Midwest for both AT&T and Ameritech, with both companies having frequently drawn upon executive talent developed at Indiana Bell when looking for leaders for the parent corporation. Indiana Bell had also been run with tight controls over finances and remained profitable, prior to the loss in 1994 due to restructuring costs, and had maintained favorable relations with state regulating authorities. But as Indiana Bell moved toward 1996 with federal regulation pending that could allow greater competition in Indiana, the 75-year-old Indiana Bell certainly faced a rapidly changing telecommunications industry.

Further Reading:

Carnevale, Mary Lu, ''Ameritech Inc. Begins Reorganization with Departure of Four Top Executives,'' *Wall Street Journal,* June 1, 1992, p. A3.
——, ''Ameritech, Union Set Tentative Pacts and Strike Ends,'' *Wall Street Journal,* August 31, 1989, p. B4.
——, ''Changing Market Forces Baby Bells to Clean House,'' *Wall Street Journal,* June 17, 1992, p. B4.
Cauley, Leslie, ''Ameritech Seeks Backing to Enter Long-Distance Line,'' *Wall Street Journal,* December 12, 1994, p. B5.
Dooms, Tracy M., '' 'Beginning of the End': Indiana Bell Says Monopoly Jeopardized by Upstart IDA,'' *Indianapolis Business Journal,* August 19, 1991, p. 1A.
Edwards, Ken, ''Indiana Bell Wins Big with Hoosier Lottery,'' *Telephony,* July 30, 1990, pp. 36–40.
Hawkins, Phil, ''Four AT&T Units Offer Premium Prices for $630 Million of High-Cost Old Debt,'' *Wall Street Journal,* January 24, 1977, p. 25.
History of Ameritech in Indiana, Indiana Bell Telephone, Incorporated, 1995.
''Indiana Bell's New Service Nails Two Major Contracts,'' *Telephony,* April 21, 1986, pp. 13, 98.
Joyner, Tammy, ''Ameritech Signals New Line on Future,'' *Detroit News,* March 24, 1993, p. E1.
Kukolla, Steve, ''Ameritech's Cable Entry Will Be under Microscope,'' *Indianapolis Business Journal,* January 9, 1995, p. 5.
Kukolla, Steve, ''Indiana Bell One of Strongest Ameritech Subs,'' *Indianapolis Business Journal,* April 4, 1994, p. 1.
Kukolla, Steve, ''Indiana Bell Parent Ameritech Dials up Reorganization Plans,'' *Indianapolis Business Journal,* March 1, 1993, p. 5.
Kukolla, Steve, ''Notebaert Exit Follows Pattern for 'Farm Club' Indiana Bell,'' *Indianapolis Business Journal,* June 8, 1992, p. A4.
Lopez, Julie Amparano, and Mary Lu Carnevale, ''Phone Firms Are Becoming Poles Apart: Bells, in Varying Degrees, Diverge and Diversify,'' *Wall Street Journal,* February 9, 1990, p. B5.
Rao, Srikumar S., ''The Painful Remaking of Ameritech,'' *Training,* July 1994, pp. 45–53.
Ricci, Claudia, ''Regulators' Influence Is Increased,'' *Wall Street Journal,* November 17, 1983, p. 25.
Tai, Pauline, ''Indiana Bell Debentures Priced to Yield 8.20% Are Sold Out Quickly,'' *Wall Street Journal,* August 4, 1971, p. 17.
Van, Jon, ''Ameritech, Union Reach Accord: CWA Wins Job-Security Provisions; Pact with IBEW Reportedly Near,'' *Chicago Tribune,* August 11, 1995, pp. 1, 3.
Van, Jon, ''Labor Troubles on Hold? Ameritech Fight May Be Warmup,'' *Chicago Tribune,* August 12, 1995, pp. 1, 3.
White, Eileen, ''Former Operating Units Fight AT&T for Business,'' *Wall Street Journal,* December 17, 1984, p. 26.

—Roger Rouland

Intuit Inc.

P.O. Box 3014
Menlo Park, California 94206
U.S.A.
(415) 322-0573
Fax: (415) 592-8324

Public Company
Incorporated: 1983
Employees: 1,228
Sales: $194 million
Stock Exchanges: NASDAQ
SICs: 7372 Prepackaged Software

Intuit Inc. was the leading maker of personal finance software in the world going into the mid-1990s. Its flagship product, Quicken, dominated the market with a share of about 70 percent and was the most popular software program of any kind in the world. In addition to Quicken, Intuit sold QuickBooks, a small business payroll processing program, and QuickPay, an add-on application that calculated deductions and printed payroll checks. Other Intuit programs helped to file tax returns electronically and conduct electronic commerce. After a failed merger with software behemoth Microsoft in 1995, Intuit was pioneering the electronic financial services industry.

Intuit is the brainchild of entrepreneur Scott Cook, who cofounded the company with Tom Proulx in 1983. Cook, then only 23 years old, had moved to Northern California in 1980 and was working in banking and technology assignments for the consulting firm Bain & Co. One night he and his wife, Signe, were sitting at their kitchen table in San Francisco paying their bills. It occurred to Scott that there must be a better way to manage their household finances and automate the hassle of bill paying. Inspired to start his own software company, he went to Stanford University to place an advertisement for a programmer. When he got to the campus, he stopped a passing student, Tom Proulx, for help in locating a bulletin board. Proulx, it turned out, had done some programming and agreed to write a simple check-balancing program for Cook. In his dorm room he created the first Quicken program, which he and Scott used to launch Intuit.

Cook's idea for a check-balancing program was unique, but he was only one of many people trying to break into the burgeoning personal computer software market at the time. According

to many of his associates, it was his background, intellect, and enthusiasm that separated him from the rest of the pack. Cook earned degrees in both math and economics at the University of Southern California (USC). (He credited summer internships with the Federal Government with encouraging him to go into business rather than the bureaucratic public sector.) Also at USC, Cook took it upon himself to resurrect the school's ailing ski club. He rented out a cabin at the nearest ski area and charged club members a mere $1 per night to stay. The club became one of the most successful organizations on campus and played an important role in getting him accepted into Harvard's graduate business school. Indeed, Cook was one of only a handful of students to enter Harvard straight out of undergraduate school, and was the youngest member of his 800-member class. "When I look back, that ski club success, as much as anything, led me to believe that I could start a successful company," Cook explained in 1992 to the *Business Journal-San Jose.*

Cook was snatched up by the Cincinnati-based marketing giant Procter & Gamble immediately after he graduated from Harvard in 1976, and was placed in charge of the Crisco shortening brand. At P&G he met co-worker Signe Ostby, his future wife. In 1980 the couple moved to California for its climate, with Scott taking the consulting job with Bain and Signe becoming vice-president of marketing at Software Publishing Corp. During the next few years Scott gained important experience related to banking and technology while Signe learned about marketing software. Meanwhile, Tom Proulx labored in his dorm room creating the first version of Quicken. After polishing up the program the pair launched Intuit in 1983.

While Proulx contributed the technical expertise to the original Quicken program, Scott drew on his consumer marketing background to ensure that the program would meet a real need in the marketplace. He conducted numerous telephone interviews and focus groups, for example, in an effort to determine exactly what households needed financially and what features were most important to potential customers. Co-workers called his emphasis on customer input fanatical, and Cook's fixation eventually became well known within the software industry. The application resulting from this research allowed people to enter data on screens that looked much like a check and a checkbook. The data was automatically processed, thus eliminating much of the tedium of balancing a checkbook.

Cook and Proulx started Intuit in Proulx's basement with a single product and seven employees. Cook originally planned to sell the software through bank branches, a strategy that soured when he realized that banks were poorly equipped to sell prepackaged software. Moreover, because Intuit was only one of several companies trying to market a personal financial software program, Cook was unable to find a retail distributor that would take his unknown product. By 1985 the company was struggling to stay afloat. Three employees left when Cook and Proulx became unable to pay salaries. The other four, still believing in their product, kept working for six months without any pay.

Cook remained surprisingly upbeat and helped to buoy the Intuit team during their initial struggles. Whenever Proulx's wife would come down into the basement to see how things were going, Cook would tell her that they couldn't be better. "The truth is that things couldn't be worse," Proulx recalled in 1995 to the *San Francisco Business Times.* "Years later he told me that in 1985, when we were out of money, if someone had agreed to buy the company from him to pay off his loans, he would have done it." In fact, Cook was more than $300,000 in debt and was facing a long 30 years of trying to pay off those obligations if his venture failed. "I never had any doubt that he would eventually succeed," Proulx added. "A large part of my belief was from having been propagandized by Scott."

By 1986 Cook and Proulx were beginning to see some light at the end of the tunnel. Importantly, the Apple version of Quicken was getting positive attention in the trade press, and sales were slowly picking up. Recognizing the power of such trade articles to generate sales, they made a pivotal decision that turned the company around. Instead of selling the programs through banks, they would sell them directly to customers through advertisements. In a risky move that could have quashed the entire venture, Proulx coaxed a reluctant Scott into placing $125,000 worth of advertisements, despite the fact that they had only $95,000 left in the bank. Cook wrote the ads himself, drawing on his marketing experience at Procter & Gamble. He emphasized the benefits of the program as opposed to its features, unlike most software ads of the time. "End financial hassles" was the key benefit touted in Cook's ads.

The advertising campaign was a success, and from that point forward Intuit's fortunes improved. Still, the company lacked a broad retail distribution channel and was only one of a growing number of personal financial software applications hitting the surging PC market. In an effort to expand his advertising efforts and boost Quicken's exposure, Cook approached more than 30 venture capital firms during the mid-1980s. All of them turned him down, including one represented by his former Harvard roommate. Nevertheless, Cook and Proulx persisted. Cook determined that word-of-mouth critiques of his program and customer loyalty would become the most valuable advertising tools at his disposable. For that reason, he decided that customer service and input would take top priority throughout the entire company.

Stories of Cook's obsession with customer service abound. Once, while visiting the office of a software association, Cook walked by a clerk entering data on one of his programs. He immediately stopped to interview her about the application, and later incorporated one of her suggestions into a version of the program. When Cook preached customer service to his employees at a meeting in 1988, he told them that he wanted Intuit's service to improve to the point where customers would become "apostles" for Quicken by purchasing other Intuit products and telling their friends about Intuit's offerings.

By the late 1980s Intuit was clearly on the fast track to success. In just a few years sales of Quicken exploded, and the program became one of the best-selling personal financial applications. Intuit suddenly had little problem securing more financing. Several well-known venture capital companies, including Sierra, Technology Venture Investors, and Kleiner Perkins Caufield and Byers, were willing to back Intuit's efforts to expand its retail distribution. Thus, during the late 1980s and early 1990s Quicken became one of the top-selling software applica-

tions in the world, surpassed only by industry staples like WordPerfect and Lotus 1-2-3. Sales climbed to $55 million in 1991 from just $20 million three years earlier, and Intuit's work force more than doubled in 1991 to about 425 employees.

Intuit broadened its scope in 1991 when it introduced QuickPay, a software program designed to help small businesses process their payroll. The $60 program, which was designed to work in conjunction with Quicken, was readily accepted by many users of Quicken. Intuit followed that introduction in 1992 with QuickBooks, a full-featured small-business bookkeeping program that provided an easier and less-expensive alternative to traditional accounting software. It was priced at about $140 and was also designed to work in cooperation with both Quicken and QuickPay. By 1992, Quicken (at a retail price of $70) was dominating the market with a powerful 70 percent share of the personal financial software market. Much of that success was attributable to the company's emphasis on customer satisfaction: one 1992 survey showed that 85 percent of all Quicken users had recommended the program to at least one other person.

Having established its dominance in the market for stand-alone personal and small-business financial software, Quicken started looking at the much bigger picture. Indeed, Cook and his associates believed that Intuit's future was in providing a means of electronically linking customers with banks, brokers, and other businesses, and in providing various electronic financial services to the public. To that end, Intuit struck a deal with Visa that allowed Quicken users to download credit card statements directly onto their computers and into Quicken. In 1993 Intuit spent $243 million to purchase ChipSoft, which allowed customers to file tax returns electronically. Intuit scored again later that year when it bought out the National Payment Clearinghouse Inc., a processor of electronic transactions, for $7.6 million.

Cook realized in 1993 that Intuit was evolving from an entrepreneurial start-up company to an established corporation. The company had even gone public by that time on the OTC market, and was rapidly adding employees and facilities in the wake of ongoing acquisitions and surging sales. Early in 1994 Cook selected 53-year-old William V. Campbell to serve in the newly created post of president and chief executive officer. Campbell, a former Apple executive, was skilled in building organizations. In addition to his background in the computer industry, he had also served as the head football coach at his alma mater, Columbia University. Campbell would oversee the day-to-day operations at Intuit while Cook, as chairman of the board, would continue to spearhead the company's strategic plans.

By the mid-1990s Intuit was drawing attention from a much larger suitor, with software giant Microsoft eyeing Intuit as a possible takeover target. To Microsoft, Intuit represented an entry into the only major software category in which it did not have a significant presence. Microsoft was competing successfully with its own personal financial program, Microsoft Money. By 1994, though, that application was serving only 22 percent of the market, compared to Quicken's walloping 70 percent. Furthermore, Intuit owned other programs of interest to Microsoft, such as TurboTax, MacInTax, and ProSeries, all of which were geared for the personal and small-business tax-return-preparation market. Finally, Intuit had valuable experience related to conducting computerized transactions over telephone lines.

Microsoft, with Cook's cooperation, attempted a buyout of Intuit in 1995. Critics and Microsoft competitors balked, claiming that the merger was anti-competitive and would give Microsoft too much power in the software industry. To Cook's dismay, the Justice Department tried to block the deal, which would have been the largest merger in the history of the software industry. Both Microsoft and Intuit fought the Department's efforts, and Microsoft even offered to sell off its Money program. Nevertheless, the $2 billion deal eventually collapsed. With that, Microsoft CEO Bill Gates renewed his efforts to make Microsoft Money a contender. Microsoft hired away a top Intuit salesman and launched a revamped version of Money to be used with Microsoft's long-awaited new operating system, Windows 95.

Like Microsoft, Intuit turned its attention back to its growing array of products following the failed merger. The company was still trying to digest the flurry of product and company acquisitions completed during the early 1990s. To that end, Intuit was working to consolidate and streamline its information systems and operational and financial controls. Even though the company's fiscal year was shortened by two months in 1994,

revenues surged to about $194 million. In the long term, Intuit was positioning itself to become a leader in the burgeoning electronic banking and financial services industries.

Principal Subsidiaries: ChipSoft; Intuit Ltd. (United Kingdom); Intuit Deutschland GmbH (Germany); Wintax Software Corporation (Canada).

Further Reading:

Buck, Richard, ''Intuit Stock Tumbles on Microsoft Ruling,'' *Seattle Times,* February 16, 1995, p. C1.

Crosariol, Beppi, ''US Fights Microsoft's Takeover of Intuit,'' *Boston Globe,* April 28, 1995, Section 1, p. 1.

''Intuit Corporate Profile,'' *Business Wire,* October 2, 1992.

Krey, Michael, ''Scott Cook: Intuit Co-Founder Got up to Speed at USC Ski Club,'' *Business Journal-San Jose,* July 20, 1992, Section 1, p. 13.

Levine, Daniel S., ''Executive of the Year: After Bringing Bill Gates to His Knees, Scott Cook Plans to Revolutionize the Finance Industries,'' *San Francisco Business Times,* January 6, 1995, Section 1, p. 1.

Ross, Sheryl L., ''William Campbell Joins Intuit as President and CEO,'' *Business Wire,* April 11, 1994.

''Welcome Back to the Jungle, Intuit,'' *Business Week,* June 5, 1995, p. 4.

—Dave Mote

Irwin Toy Limited

43 Hanna Avenue
Toronto, Ontario M6K 1X6
Canada
(416) 533-3521
Fax: (416) 533-3257

Public Company
Founded: 1926 as Irwin Specialties
Employees: 240
Sales: C$111 million
Stock Exchanges: Toronto Montreal
SICs: 2321 Men's & Boys Shirts, Except Work Shirts; 2331
    Women's, Misses', & Juniors' Blouses & Shirts; 3942
    Dolls & Stuffed Toys; 3944 Games, Toys, & Children's
    Vehicles, Except Dolls & Bicycles; 5091 Sporting &
    Recreational Goods & Supplies; 5092 Toys & Hobby
    Goods & Supplies

Based in Toronto, Irwin Toy Limited is a leading Canadian
developer, manufacturer, marketer, and distributor of toys.
Irwin sells its own products and the goods of foreign companies, under license, to toy dealers in Canada, which accounts for
about 90 percent of company sales. It also licenses its products
to foreign companies and sells some products directly to the
United States. In the mid-1990s the family-operated company
was working to significantly expand its presence in the giant
U.S. toy market.

Although Irwin Toy was not incorporated until 1954, the company's beginning can be traced to the 1920s. It was 1926, to be
exact, when Samuel Irwin started a small business selling sou-
venirs out of his home. He eventually built up a healthy enterprise selling wholesale souvenir items to retailers. In 1949 Irwin
handed the relatively small venture off to his two sons, Arnold
and MacDonald (Mac). Under their tutelage the company became engaged in the toy wholesaling business. Indeed, they
began adding toys to the souvenir lines during the 1950s, and by
the 1960s were selling an array of traditional toys and sporting
goods like baseball bats and balls, dolls, and arts and crafts
items.

Throughout the 1950s and 1960s Irwin remained a completely
family-owned business. The company enjoyed healthy sales
gains during the postwar baby boom of the 1960s. In fact, the
company's toy sales eventually surpassed revenues from souve-

nirs. Arnold and Mac recognized that the growing market proffered potentially lucrative opportunities. Their relatively small
company lacked the resources, though, to fully take advantage
of thriving markets. So in 1969 they decided to take the company public. Their goal was to raise funds for expansion without
giving up control of the company. That and subsequent offerings helped Irwin to became a dominant player in the Canadian toy industry. The Irwin family maintained ownership of
more than 50 percent of the company and continued to do so
into the mid-1990s.

In addition to injecting growth capital into Irwin Toy, the 1969
initial public offering succeeded in starting an engaging tradition for which the company became known. At the first annual
shareholders meeting after the company went public in 1969,
Arnold Irwin noticed a man and his six-year-old daughter
sitting in the audience. After the meeting, Irwin went down to
speak with the pair and to find out why the man had brought his
daughter to the meeting. The gentlemen turned out to be the
senior financial officer of Imperial Oil. He had purchased shares
of Irwin for his daughter as a way to get her interested in
business. "The newspapers reported that and the child shareholders situation just grew from there," Arnold recalled in the
October 1984 issue of *Executive*. "The company never did
anything to encourage it." Parents throughout Canada began
buying Irwin shares for their children, and the annual shareholders meetings were soon packed with kids. Youngsters regularly accounted for about half of the audience, making for some
interesting meetings. "One young lady wanted to know why
she couldn't be a director," Arnold remembered about one
gathering. "She was quite disappointed that, at her first annual
meeting, she wasn't proposed to the board."

Following the stock sale and throughout the 1970s Irwin's toy
business surged and the organization established itself as one of
Canada's top toy companies. Irwin diversified during the decade, adding a wide array of toys to its lineup. It also became
involved in other businesses. Its Irwin Specialties division,
which was founded by Samuel Irwin in 1926, was selling about
5,000 different souvenir items. The Irwin Sports division marketed Rawlings sporting goods, and a unit dubbed Irwin Leisure
sold lawn furniture and barbecue grills and gear. By the late
1970s Irwin was generating a fat C$50 million annually in sales
from its diversified operations; about 75 percent of that revenue
was attributable to the import, manufacture, packaging, advertising, and distribution of toys. The company was primarily
manufacturing goods that had been developed in foreign countries. Profits at the end of the decade were in the C$1 million to
C$2 million range.

Although Irwin had racked up heady gains during the 1970s, its
period of greatest growth would come during the early 1980s.
Indeed, between 1980 and 1983 Irwin's revenues rocketed to a
whopping C$120 million annually. The reason for the rapid rise
was Irwin's entrance into the burgeoning home-video game
market. In 1980 Irwin sought and won the license to sell the
California-based Atari home-video line of game products to the
Canadian market. The license was a major victory for Irwin at
the time because Atari was a smash hit. Sales across North
America exploded during the early 1980s and Irwin watched its
sales and profits climb to record levels. It seemed as though
everybody with children owned an Atari system or knew some-

one who did. Sales in Irwin's toy division more than doubled within three years. To keep up with the growth, new staff was added and distribution capacity was increased. By 1983 Irwin was churning out a hefty C$5.1 million in profit annually.

The Atari fortunes were short-lived. In the mid-1980s other companies began offering their own video games to compete with Atari. As competition intensified, prices dropped. The price of the Atari system plunged from $220 to just $50 within a few years. Atari, as well as distributors like Irwin, were left holding the bag. To make matters worse, Atari was owned at the time by Warner Communication. Warner managed Atari poorly and severely overestimated demand. "So they ended overproducing the product, and all of a sudden it came to a dead end. . . . We took a pretty good rap on that one," Arnold Irwin recalled in the October 1988 issue of *Canadian Business*. "It's what happens when you're a $60-million company but start to believe you're a $120-million company. We were victims of our own success."

The Atari debacle forced Irwin to post its first net loss in seven years when, in 1985, it endured a $2.6 million deficit. Atari scrambled to replace lost revenues and to shore up losses. It reemphasized its leisure products, textile, and sporting goods lines and began chasing new growth opportunities in its core toy business. In fact, during the early and mid-1980s Irwin had realized several breakthroughs in its toy division aside from Atari. Importantly, Irwin attempted its first toy development venture. In 1984 Mike Bowling, a 20-year veteran of the Ford assembly line in Cincinnati, had an idea for a new toy—a doll of a wrinkled mutt packaged as a Humane Society foundling.

He brought the idea to Irwin, which dubbed the toy the Pound Puppy and sold the doll complete with adoption papers and instructions for care and handling. It was the first toy Irwin had developed in-house. Sales were slow at first, but by 1987 the line had been expanded to include five models that were ringing up sales of $8 million annually in Canada. Furthermore, in the United States, where Tonka had purchased the license to sell the toy, Pound Puppy shipments topped $150 million, of which Irwin kept between four and eight percent. Over a period of five years Pound Puppy generated sales of $300 million in 35 countries.

Thus, Irwin launched an important new profit center during the mid-1980s: product development. Among other efforts, in 1985 Irwin developed and started marketing a toy called Zaks (Ziegler's Animated Konstruction System). Zaks was invented by Calgary designer Jim Ziegler. Ziegler approached product manager Dave Irwin with his concept. In fact, Ziegler had built a virtually complete product that had required about $75,000 of his own money. Dave called on his brother George, and the two Irwins decided to give the toy a shot. Zaks was a hit during its first Christmas season, and Irwin was able to quickly sell licenses to companies in the United States and Australia. Other successful product development efforts at Irwin during the mid-1980s included Yawnie, a doll with a gaping mouth, and My One and Only, which was a line of guy dolls marketed to young girls as a sort of fantasy boyfriend.

The success of Irwin's product development initiative provided an important boost to the company during a rough period. In

fact, besides the Atari setback, Irwin was reeling from the loss of its contract to manufacture and market toys in Canada for Kenner Parker Toys Inc. of the United States. Prior to 1986 Kenner Parker toys had represented as much as half of Irwin's total annual toy sales. When Kenner ended the agreement in 1986 and bailed out of Canada, Irwin was left with a gaping hole in its toy business. Proprietary products helped to fill the void. Irwin managed to squeeze out a thin C$636,000 profit in 1986, despite the fact that sales had crumbled to just C$66.5 million. Sales careened back up to C$81.7 million in 1987 and then to a healthy C$93.7 million in 1988, about C$1.8 million of which was netted as income each year.

Although the mid-1980s were brutal for Irwin, management would later credit the difficult period with making it the successful company that it would become during the late 1980s and early 1990s. Having learned from the Atari and Kenner experiences, Irwin was able to avoid the pitfalls many other toy manufacturers encountered and to post relatively steady sales and profit gains in a notoriously volatile industry. Assisting Irwin Toys to success during the 1980s was the third generation of Irwins to fill the executive ranks. Of import was George Irwin, Mac's son. George, who had originally pushed for Irwin to branch out into product development, had started working for Irwin part-time in the 1960s. After getting his degree in economics from the University of Western Ontario, he started full-time in 1971 as a retail person; he visited stores and counted inventory. After stints as a territorial salesperson and product manager he became a vice-president in 1983. Other Irwins who eventually joined the executive ranks included George's uncle Bryan and cousin Scott.

Irwin sustained steady sales and income growth during the late 1980s. Revenues peaked at about C$95 million in 1990 while net income climbed to C$3.1 million. The gains were partly the result of successful new product introductions. One example was The Twins, a pair of electronic dolls that giggled when they were together and cried when they were apart. In 1991 George was elevated to president of the company. The promotion came just as the economy was diving into a recessionary slump. Sales dipped slightly but surged in 1992 and 1993. In fact, in 1993 (fiscal year ended January 31) Irwin's revenues soared back to C$120 million, the same level at which they had been during the Atari craze. Again, the increase was attributable to the video game industry. Indeed, Irwin realized big gains as a result of sales of Sega video games (Irwin had signed an agreement in 1987 to represent Sega Enterprises of Japan in the Canadian market).

Just as it had in the mid-1980s, the bottom fell out of Irwin's video game business. Irwin actually decided to end the relationship with Sega because of the high risks and relatively low profit margins characteristic of the video game business. Instead, the new management team announced its intent to focus on more traditional toy industry segments and to try to increase its exposure in the United States. Largely because of Irwin's exit from the video game business, sales tumbled to C$76 million in 1994, only C$617,000 of which was profit. Coming to Irwin's rescue in 1994 and 1995, though, were the Mighty Morphin Power Rangers. Irwin won the Canadian license to market the Power Rangers, which became toy world's biggest hit since the Teenage Mutant Ninja Turtles. Irwin's revenues whistled up to C$111 million in 1995 (fiscal year ended January 31), a record C$6 million of which was netted as income.

Going into the mid-1990s Irwin Toy was emphasizing its toy business, although it was still engaged in sporting goods, textile, and souvenir businesses. In the sporting goods arena, Irwin marketed Cooper baseball products and Winnwell hockey gear. Most of the company's toys were manufactured overseas or licensed to other companies for production, although Irwin maintained a small plant in Toronto. Irwin-developed products were being marketed, usually under licensing agreements with other companies, in 35 countries going into 1995. Chief among the company's long-term goals was to boost the percentage of revenues attributable to U.S. sales from ten percent to 50 percent.

Principal Subsidiaries: Irwin Sports Inc. (United States).

Further Reading:

Carter, Peter, "Guys & Dolls," *Canadian Business,* October 1988, p. 40.
Evans, Mark, "A New Field Marshal in Toyland," *Financial Post,* January 30, 1991, p. 35.
Girard, Daniel, "Back to Basics Play Products Are the Future for Irwin Toy," *Toronto Star,* June 16, 1993, p. 1F.
Heinrich, Erik, "Recession Proof Toys Boost Irwin," *Financial Post,* September 16, 1992, p. 4.
Siklow, Richard, "Irwin Looks for U.S. Acquisition," *Financial Post,* February 18, 1995, p. 15.
Walker, Dean, "When Fun's the Product, the Game Can Get Rough," *Executive,* October 1984, pp. 62–65.

—Dave Mote

JDEdwards®

J.D. Edwards & Company

8055 E. Tufts Avenue, Suite 1331
Denver, Colorado 80237
U.S.A.
(303) 488-4000
Fax: (303) 488-4880

Private Company
Founded: 1977
Employees: 1,900
Sales: $240.6 million
SICs: 7372 Prepackaged Software

J.D. Edwards & Company is a leading global designer of software for midrange computers. Its software is used by those involved with distribution, manufacturing, finances, human resources management, construction, public services, and other industries. In 1995 J.D. Edwards was supporting branch offices in Europe and Asia and shipping its software throughout the world. The company achieved consistent growth by researching and developing top-performing software applications.

The name J.D. Edwards was derived from the names of the company's three founders: Jack Thompson, Dan Gregory, and Ed McVaney. Before forming J.D. Edwards on February 1, 1977, in Denver, Colorado, all three men were working at the accounting and consulting firm of Alexander Grant and Company (Grant Thornton & Co.). The three had been working as consultants and accountants for several years before deciding to quit and form their own company. Together they shared a wealth of top-level accounting and computer expertise that they hoped could be parlayed into a successful accounting software company. The partners' main goal when they launched the venture was to produce standardized software applications that actually worked in a predictable and reliable way, making users more effective at their jobs.

Heading the group from the start was 36-year-old McVaney, whose wife had coined the J.D. Edwards name. He had earned his bachelor's degree in mechanical engineering from the University of Nebraska in 1964 before receiving his masters degree in business administration in 1966 from Rutgers University in New Jersey. His first job after college was as an operations research engineer and an electronic data processor specialist in the Bell system, where he worked while he was earning his

MBA. In 1966 he accepted a position as a consultant in manufacturing and electronic data processing for Peat, Marwick and Mitchell. He worked there until moving to Grant Thornton & Co. in 1970, where he became the partner in charge of data processing and consulting services. Among other skills, McVaney became intimately familiar with IBM's midrange computers, which are smaller than mainframes but more powerful than personal computers.

McVaney, Gregory, and Thompson started out in a small office with a copy machine as their only piece of equipment. "The copy machine was my first big decision," McVaney recalled in the June 10, 1992, *Denver Post*. "We decided to be bold and go for the $105 a month." They borrowed $10,000 to cover the cost of the copier and other miscellaneous expenses, and set about designing software tailored to the accounting and financial tasks with which they were familiar. While McVaney handled much of the management and marketing, Jack Thompson acted as the company's technical force. Meanwhile, Gregory wore a number of hats and eventually became known as the company's premier firefighter and the creator of the training department.

J.D. Edwards started out designing software for IBM small and medium-sized computers, particularly the IBM 34 minicomputer. During its first year in business, the fledgling company generated about $200,000 in revenues. To add more technical expertise to their staff, the three partners merged with another tiny software firm. From the start, the founders agreed that a large portion of their cash flow should be reinvested in research and development. As a result, the company was able to produce a number of successful business applications during the late 1970s and early 1980s, and sales and profits steadily increased.

IBM eventually discontinued its 34 system, largely because of objections from dissatisfied users. It replaced it with the 36 and 38 systems. At the same time, competing midrange computer manufacturers like Sun Microsystems were jumping into the market with their own advanced machines. J.D. Edwards made a pivotal strategic decision to stick with IBM and gear all of its applications for the 36 and 38 systems. "The question [among software companies] was which way IBM would go with new technologies in the mid-range market," McVaney said in the January 1990 *Colorado Business*. "At the time, what we did looked very chancy. We bet all our marbles that the 46-bit System 38 . . . would be the winning technology, and we were right." The System/38 became one of the dominant entries in its class and was a leading midrange platform for several years.

In betting on the System/38, J.D. Edwards redesigned every one of its applications in 1983 to be compatible with the System/38 platform. That meant that the company had to ensure that three million lines of code conformed to the standard. During that effort, Edward's technical staff pioneered the 'Clone' method for software development and design. In essence, Edward's Clone technique eliminated much of the labor involved with programming. Traditionally, Edwards and its competitors relied on programmers to write their new applications by taking several hours to compile each program line individually. One drawback of the conventional method was that each program or chunk of code bore the imprint of its writer. Under the system chunk of code bore the imprint of its writer. Under the system Edwards developed, 90 percent of a given program could be written with the aid of 'the Clone,' which was a computer-generated technique of standardizing code and eliminating quirks of individual programmers. The net result of the new software development method was that Edwards' productivity doubled. Importantly, the consistency of the company's applications increased and debugging became a much easier and faster task. Thus, the overall quality of Edward's programs were enhanced. During the mid-1980s Edwards would use the Clone to develop an array of specialized programs for a broad range of industries and tasks. The company built up a strong position in the oil and gas industry, for example, but was also selling its innovative accounting and financial applications to industries ranging from publishing to construction.

McVaney and fellow managers seemed to have made the right decision in focusing on the IBM System/38 in 1983: Sales growth was, indeed, brisk. However, IBM began to lose its edge in the midrange computer segment in the mid-1990s. At the time, the personal computer market was taking off and IBM was scrambling to assert itself both in that segment and in its traditional mainframe business. Meanwhile, it lagged in midrange technology, and competitors began chipping away at IBM's market share. To keep up with the competition, IBM started working on a next-generation System/38 called the AS400.

J.D. Edwards, like many other software companies, started investing early to have software ready for the AS400 when it was finally introduced. To the dismay of Edwards' staff, IBM almost decided to cede its market share in the midrange market and simply eliminate the entire AS400 project. As late as 1985, by which time Edwards' had dumped a whopping $23 million into AS400-related research and development, IBM was weighing its options. Disaster loomed. Fortunately for Edwards, IBM decided to complete the development of the AS400. As a result, by the time IBM introduced the technology a few years later, Edwards was among the companies most prepared to take advantage of the new market.

Even before the AS400 was introduced, J.D. Edwards was ringing up big profits from its cutting-edge applications for the System/38. By 1984 the firm was employing 60 people. Sales shot up 63 percent in that year before leaping another 50 percent in 1985, by which time J.D. Edward's work force had more than doubled to 130. "We are now in the position of having clients beating down our door," said Edwards's marketing manager Howie Miller in the March 24, 1986, *Rocky Mountain Business Journal.* To keep up with spiraling demand, Edwards expanded its sales offices to include nine cities by late 1986. Its revenue base made it one of the four top companies in the midrange applications industry. Edwards was gaining on those competitors, though, and its widely diversified client base gave it a strong edge against any downturns that might affect an individual market.

Edwards posted big gains throughout the late 1980s. New applications for the System/38 drove growth until 1988, when the AS400 was finally introduced. Edwards was able to hit the ground running when sales of the AS400 started taking off. Importantly, McVaney was surprised to find huge growth op-

portunities overseas. J.D. Edwards had dabbled with cross-border sales in the mid-1980s and found a willing market. In 1988, therefore, McVaney launched an aggressive international expansion program. Sales, particularly in Europe, exploded. By 1990 international sales were generating roughly 20 percent of the company's $77 million revenue base—a rise from just $38 million in 1989. Edwards opened an office in Belgium to serve Europe, a branch in Florida as its Latin America headquarters, and another office in Singapore to serve Asia.

Another big growth area for Edwards beginning in the late 1980s was the manufacturing industry. Although the company served a wide array of markets, it had postponed entering the giant manufacturing sector, which was considered among the largest (and most competitive) arenas in the midrange application market. Success in that industry helped the company to more than double sales in 1990 before pushing revenues to a lofty $130 million in 1991. Going into 1992, Edwards was the largest producers of IBM midrange software in the world and the 30th largest software designer in the entire United States. By then, its work force had swelled to an army of more than 1,000, only about half of which were employed at the company's Denver headquarters. What's more, the company had attained its status virtually debt free and without ever having gone public. Amazingly, the company had grown at an average rate of 60 percent a year since its inception in 1977.

Besides focusing on the IBM lines, part of the key to Edwards's success in the late 1980s and early 1990s was its research and marketing strategies. The company continued to direct a high 22 percent of its revenue stream into research and development of new products. In addition, rather than chasing after the really big fish, Edwards focused on what McVaney referred to as "the middle American business community." That group basically encompassed companies with $50 million or more in sales, which generally were still too small to have their own software development departments; Edwards customer base did, however, include General Motors, Kodak, and other large corporations. As the number of clients increased, so did the number of industries and specific applications. By the early 1990s J.D. Edwards was developing software solutions for industries ranging from health care, real estate, and government to food service, air travel, and finance. Most of the applications addressed various accounting, payroll, purchasing, and project-management tasks.

Among the biggest surprises for McVaney and fellow executives was the amount of international demand for Edwards's applications. By 1992 a full 32 percent of the company's sales were coming from overseas, and that percentage was quickly climbing. "People ask me if I envisioned we would have gotten this big, and I answer 'yes,'" McVaney said in the June 10, 1992, *Denver Post.* "But international sales have been astounding. That's humbling to me." By 1992 Edwards was selling its software packages translated into Dutch, Danish, Portuguese, Japanese, and Arabic, among other languages, and the company had opened offices in London, Brussels, France, Germany, and Australia. Other offices were scheduled to open in Asia and South America, as intimated above, as well as in other European countries.

J.D. Edwards sustained its stunning growth rate during 1993 and 1994. Sales grew to a fat $197 million in 1993 before bulging to $241 million during 1994. The company had maintained an average annual growth rate of about 54 percent since 1977. Evidencing its ongoing commitment to technological leadership, J.D. Edwards completed the development in 1994 of WorldVision, which was a PC-based software product designed to operate in the popular Windows software environment. The program was created to provide a more user-friendly, Windows-type environment for AS400 applications that would demand less training and make the applications easier to use. The company also released a new product geared for the emerging electronic commerce industry. J.D. Edward's sales continued to surge in the first six months of 1995 as its work force ballooned to 1,800. The company, which was still privately owned and debt free in mid-1995, expected to employ 2,000 people worldwide by the end of the year.

Further Reading:

Dowling, Mark, "J.D. Edwards Rises to Software Superstar on IBM's Coattails," *Denver Business Journal,* February 15, 1991, p. 3.

Hardman, Chris, "J.D. Edwards & Co. Sets Another Revenue Record for 1994," *Business Wire,* January 24, 1995.

J.D. Edwards & Company: A Corporate History, Denver: J.D. Edwards & Company, 1995.

"J.D. Edwards & Company; Welcome to the Skunkworks of Software Brilliance," *Colorado Business,* January 1990, p. 40.

Mullen, Frank, "J.D. Edwards Software Firm Has Avoided High-Tech Bust," *Rocky Mountain Business Journal,* March 24, 1986, p. 19.

Murrel, Guy, "New Windowing Product from J.D. Edwards Marks Next Step on Client/Server Migration Path," *Business Wire,* October 21, 1994.

Van Housen, Jon, "Edwards' Founder Had Vision," *Denver Post,* June 10, 1992, p. 1C.

—Dave Mote

Jim Beam Brands Co.

510 Lake Cook Road
Deerfield, Illinois 60015
U.S.A.
(708) 948-8888
Fax: (708) 948-0393

Wholly Owned Subsidiary of American Brands, Inc.
Incorporated: 1933 as James B. Beam Distilling Co.
Employees: 1,500
Sales: $1.27 billion
SICs: 2085 Distilled & Blended Liquors

Jim Beam Brands Co., a subsidiary of American Brands, Inc., is the largest domestically owned liquor company in the United States. Its namesake brand, the two-hundred-year-old Jim Beam, has long been the world's best selling bourbon, shipping more than five million cases in 1994, and remains the single largest contributor to Jim Beam Brands' nearly $1.27 billion in annual revenue. Since the 1980s, Jim Beam Brands has aggressively expanded its line to include more than 150 other labels covering almost every alcoholic beverage category. Despite years of decline in domestic consumption of distilled spirits, Jim Beam Brands remains one of the industry's fastest-growing and most profitable companies.

Shortly after the Revolutionary War, the newly formed United States government encouraged homesteaders to settle west of the Appalachian Mountains. Settlers were promised sixty acres of land in return for clearing the land and growing corn for at least two years. Among the homesteaders was Jacob Beam, a miller from Germany by way of Virginia, who in 1788 brought his family and his belongings—including a copper still—to Bourbon County, Kentucky. Beam and many other settlers found fertile lands, and clear, limestone-fed springs, and their corn grew well. Beam built a water mill to grind his and neighboring farmers' corn crops, taking a percentage of the grain in exchange. Because the grain did not keep long, and was difficult to transport, many farmers, including Beam, began to distill their surplus corn into whiskey. Whiskey, which did not spoil and was easy to transport, soon became an important part of the economy, and was often used as payment in place of the unstable currency of the day.

The whiskey these farmers made, with its high corn content and the amber color it drew from being stored in charred oak barrels, became known as bourbon, after Bourbon County. Jacob Beam's bourbon, made according to his own recipe, quickly achieved a wide reputation for its quality. In 1795 Beam sold a barrel of his bourbon in Washington County, Kentucky, taking cash for the first time. By then the word "distillery" had been coined, from the distilling process used for producing bourbon, and more and more farmers were establishing their own distilleries. By the start of the War of 1812, Kentucky alone boasted more than 2,000 distillers. After inheriting land from his wife's father, Beam moved his still and his family of twelve children to Washington County. Demand for Kentucky bourbon soon spread through the entire country.

Jacob Beam's son, David, took over the family's business in 1820, inheriting his father's recipe for bourbon. The United States was then entering the Industrial Age; the invention of the steam engine, the digging of the Erie Canal, and the construction of the first railroads made it easier to transport goods around the country. David Beam had ten children, who helped in running the family distillery. In 1850 David Beam's son David M. Beam took his father's place, distilling bourbon according to Jacob Beam's original recipe. Four years later, upon the death of his father, David M. Beam moved the distillery to Nelson County, Kentucky, close to the railroad, which had by then reached Kentucky. David M. Beam now called the distillery the Clear Spring Distillery. Beam continued to produce the family's bourbon throughout the Civil War. That bourbon would become most famous under the name of David M. beam's son, James Beauregard Beam, born in 1864.

James B. Beam entered the family business at the age of 16, and took over the distillery and its bourbon recipe 14 years later. During the later 1800s and into the new century, distillers were faced with growing pressures from bootleggers, the temperance movement, and increasing government regulations. In an effort to stop the bootlegging, or counterfeiting of known whiskey brands, Congress passed legislation in 1897 creating "bonded whiskey," which would become defined as whiskey that had been aged at least four years in a government-bonded warehouse. Bonded whiskeys were sealed with a green paper stamp. The liquor industry was brought under the control of the Federal Food and Drug Act of 1906. Three years later, whiskey types were given their first legal definitions. These same years saw waves of new immigrants arriving in the United States, and the Clear Spring Distillery continued to prosper through the first two decades of the twentieth century.

The rise of the temperance movement, in response to increasing problems associated with the abuse of alcoholic beverages, reached its peak in 1919, when Congress ratified the 18th Amendment. The following year, with the passage of the Volstead Act providing enforcement of the new law, the United States entered the Prohibition era. James Beam was forced to shut down his distillery. He turned instead to growing citrus in Florida and mining, but continued to guard the family's bourbon recipe.

Prohibition proved unenforceable, and was finally repealed by the 21st Amendment in 1933. James Beam built a new, modern distillery and, aided by his son T. Jeremiah Beam, returned to making bourbon. In that year, the James B. Beam Distilling Co. was incorporated in Clermont, Kentucky. Following his great-grandfather's recipe, Beam cultivated a new strain of yeast to replace the culture lost during Prohibition. Beam, then seventy years old, continued to run the company until 1946, when T. Jeremiah Beam was named president and treasurer. Upon James Beam's death the following year, T. Jeremiah became the Beam company's master distiller. The company's corporate offices were moved to Chicago in 1949, while its distilling operations were maintain in Clermont. With no children of his own, T. Jeremiah brought his nephew, Booker Noe, into the company in 1950. By 1954 the company had built a second distillery to meet the demand for its bourbon, which by then had occupied the country's number one selling position for nearly two decades.

Booker Noe became Jim Beam's master distiller in 1960. In 1964 bourbon was declared "a distinctive product of the United States" by congressional resolution. This meant that, by law, bourbon was required to be made from at least 51% corn, to be aged for a minimum of two years in charred white oak barrels, and to be produced in the United States. Three years later, American Brands bought the James B. Beam Distilling Co. from the Beam family, and acquired Jacob Beam's bourbon recipe. Booker Noe remained on as master distiller, using the yeast strain cultivated by James B. Beam. By then, the Beam family's business had grown to $113 million in annual sales.

Throughout its history, the company had maintained a single product. As a subsidiary of American Brands, however, the James B. Beam Distilling Co. began to expand its product line, adding brands in other categories during the 1970s and 1980s. New pressures had arisen for the liquor industry. Concerns over alcohol's effect on health led to legislation requiring warning labels on each bottle sold. Bans on television advertising were introduced, restricting liquor companies to print ads. At the same time, alcoholism became officially recognized as a disease, and programs such as Alcoholics Anonymous were created to help people stop drinking. So-called "white" liquors, such as vodka and gin, were becoming more popular. People were becoming increasingly more conscious of their health, further depressing alcohol consumption. At the same time, more and more states were leveling so-called "sin taxes" on alcoholic and tobacco products. Domestic sales of alcoholic beverages peaked in 1979, with nearly 200 million cases sold; ten years later, the figure had dropped to less than 160 million cases. Nevertheless, Jim Beam bourbon sales continued to rise: by 1983 it was the fifth-largest-selling whiskey brand, with sales of $125 million.

Jim Beam Distilling's product portfolio grew through a combination of new product development and acquisition of existing brands. The company introduced products such as Kamora decaffeinated coffee liqueur and mixes such as Jim Beam and Cola—geared to add younger drinkers to Beam's traditionally older customer base—and acquired brands such as Peter Heering cherry liqueur and Aalbord Akvavit vodka. By 1984, the company posted $246 million in revenues. Jim Beam bourbon sold more than four million cases, accounting for roughly one-fourth of all bourbon sales. Two years later, sales had slipped

slightly, to 3.8 million cases; by then, however, Jim Beam was the third-largest-selling liquor in the United States, behind Bacardi rum and Smirnoff vodka.

In 1987 Jim Beam Distilling tripled in size with American Brands' $545 million cash purchase of National Distillers & Chemical Corp.'s distilling division, which had sales of $580 million in 1986. Among the labels now included in Jim Beam Distilling's catalog were Windsor Canadian, DeKuyper cordials, and Gilbey's gin and vodka; also acquired were the bourbons Old Grand Dad, Old Crow, and Old Taylor. Together, the new labels added nearly nine million cases to the company's annual sales. To reflect its growing portfolio, the company changed its name to Jim Beam Brands Co. in 1988; its corporate headquarters were moved to a new location outside of Chicago. Through 1989, the company weathered a lawsuit (alleging that a pregnant woman's consumption of Jim Beam bourbon had caused birth defects in her child) that threatened the entire liquor industry. Beam was found not liable in May 1989.

Beam's acquisitions continued into the 1990s, with the $272 million purchase of the UK-based Whyte & Mackay Distillers, bringing that company's best-selling scotch whiskeys into its product line. In 1990, Beam's volume topped 15 million cases. The following year, Beam Brands paid Seagram $372.5 million for seven of its brand trademarks, including the strong sellers Ronrico rum and Wolfschmidt vodka. Jim Beam Brands, with sales of nearly 21 million cases, was now the second-largest distiller, behind the 27.5 million cases of leader IDV/Grand Met.

The recession of the 1990s, coupled with increases in taxes, the Middle East War, and the continued growth of the health and fitness movement, brought further declines in annual liquor consumption. Throughout the 1980s and the early 1990s, bourbon sales, for example, had dropped an average of five percent each year. This trend began to reverse in 1993, when only a two percent drop in sales was posted. Part of this reverse came from the growing popularity of small-batch and boutique bourbons. Maker's Mark had been producing a small-batch bourbon since the 1960s. Beginning in 1987 Beam began to market its own small-batch bourbons, under the names Basil Hayden's, Knob Creek, Baker's, and Booker's, the last by Booker Noe. Small-batch bourbons were produced in lots of less than one thousand barrels, in contrast to the one million or more barrels of other brands. Single-barrel bourbons, as the name implied, remained unblended, and were aged up to eight years. With prices ranging up to $50 per bottle, these bourbons borrowed the more sophisticated image of single-malt scotches, and in turn stimulated interest in the bourbon category as a whole.

By 1995, Jim Beam Brand's portfolio had grown to encompass nearly every category of distilled spirits. Its products were grouped under three divisions—Core Group; Imports and Specialties; and Value Brands Group—offering a brand for every taste and budget. Jim Beam bourbon, with five million cases sold in 1994, continued to be the company's flagship brand. And with Booker Noe, his son, and grandson presiding over Jacob Beam's original recipe, Jim Beam remained the world's most popular and best-selling bourbon brand.

Further Reading:

Bradley, John Ed, ''Whiskey Land, USA,'' *Esquire,* September 1987, pp. 205–12.

Fabricant, Florence, ''Boutique Bourbons Win Prestige at Home and Sales Abroad,'' *New York Times,* December 16, 1992, p. C3.

''Jim Beam Historical Backgrounder,'' Chicago: Jim Beam Brands Co., 1995.

Mather, Robin, ''Bourbon-Maker Keeps a Spirited Tradition Alive,'' *Detroit News,* May 17, 1994, pp. 7–8D.

Norris, Eileen, ''James Beam Not Resting on Its Bourbon,'' *Advertising Age,* July 17, 1985, pp. 31–32.

Perry, Charles, ''Drink American,'' *Los Angeles Times,* January 12, 1995, p. H11.

—M. L. Cohen

John B. Sanfilippo & Son, Inc.

2299 Busse Road
Elk Grove Village, Illinois 60007-6057
U.S.A.
(708) 593-2300
Fax: (708) 593-3085

Public Company
Incorporated: 1959
Employees: 624
Sales: $250 million (1995 estimate)
Stock Exchange: NASDAQ
SICs: 2068 Salted & Roasted Nuts & Seeds; 2099 Food
   Preparations Not Elsewhere Classified; 2064 Candy &
   Other Confectionery Products

John B. Sanfilippo & Son, Inc. is the nation's second largest distributor of full-line nut products, after the Planters Lifesavers division of RJR Nabisco. Sanfilippo processes, packages, markets, and distributes over 2,000 different products under the brand names Evon's, Sunshine Country, Flavor Tree, and Texas Pride, as well as for private-label distributors. It is the country's largest vertically integrated shelled and in-shell nut company.

Sanfilippo started as a small pecan shelling operation in Chicago, early in the 20th century. At the time, pecan shelling was a cottage industry, with hundreds of small shellers supplying larger processors, distributors, and retail channels. Chicago, the center of the pecan shelling industry, had as many as seventy pecan shelling businesses by the time of the Depression. The manual shelling work was typically performed by the large immigrant population, such as Gaspare Sanfilippo, of Sicily. By the time Sanfilippo's Sicilian-born son, John B., was ten, he too worked as a pecan sheller.

At the time, an individual pecan sheller processed about 45 pounds of shelled pecans daily, for which he or she earned around $6 a day. By 1922, the Sanfilippos were able to open their own pecan shelling business in a storefront on Chicago's Division Street. The company's output climbed to 40,000 pounds per month. For the next forty years Sanfilippo supplied a limited customer base of retail nut shops, distributors, and a number of large candy and other confectionery manufacturers. Pecan shelling remained their sole source of revenue.

John B.'s son Jasper entered the family business at the age of nine. In the early 1950s, when John B. fell ill, Jasper took a one-year leave of absence from college in order to manage the family business. After college, Jasper rejoined his father and, in 1959, they changed the name of the storefront business to John B. Sanfilippo & Son. Operations moved to a new building located on Montrose Avenue on the northwest side of Chicago.

The company began to diversify its product line as the pecan shelling industry itself began to change. The introduction of new machinery was making it possible to shell greater quantities of pecans; the growth of national distribution channels in the years following World War II made it possible for a single sheller to serve a wider area. The increased competition that resulted enabled processors and consumers to demand a higher degree of product consistency and quality. Many of the smaller shelling operations began to disappear as the industry consolidated into fewer, larger nut processors.

Jasper took over leadership of the company after John B.'s death in 1963. He was soon joined by his brother-in-law, Mathias Valentine. The company's sales in 1963 were $300,000. Sanfilippo stepped up its diversification, entering distribution deals with almond, walnut, and peanut shellers. The company organized a network of brokers to sell its products to the industrial channel, marketing to bakeries, candy manufacturers, and other confectioners. Sanfilippo also moved into retail sales, packaging its products under the "Prairie State" brand name.

The company enjoyed modest success through the 1960s. That changed in 1974 when H.H. Evon Co. of Chicago, which distributed nutmeats throughout the Midwest under the Evon's brand name, went bankrupt. Evon defaulted on its $90,000 debt to Sanfilippo. Rather than demanding a cash payment, Sanfilippo agreed to acquire the Evon's brand name, as well as the company's small fleet of Evon's delivery trucks and its Midwest distribution business. Sanfilippo dropped its Prairie State brand and began to market the bulk of its products under the Evon's name. The fleet of trucks allowed Sanfilippo to initiate the store-to-door distribution of its products beyond Chicago.

With the acquisition of the assets of Evon's, Sanfilippo entered a new era of sustained growth. At the same time, quality and consistency became even more vital for the company in view of increasing consumer sophistication and the growth of national brands such as Planters and Fisher Nuts. Differences in growing and storage conditions and variable shelling, roasting, and packaging processes among its many suppliers affected not only the taste and appearance of their product, but also the size grading. Thus, Sanfilippo sought greater control of the handling and quality of its raw products. By the end of the 1970s, Sanfilippo's growth allowed it to make its first move toward the vertical integration of its production process.

In 1980 Sanfilippo constructed a modern pecan processing facility, designed by Jasper Sanfilippo, in Elk Grove Village in Illinois. The company also moved its corporate headquarters to its processing complex. The 135,000-square-foot facility took two years and $9 million to build, and incorporated the latest technological advances, including a high degree of automation. The new facility allowed Sanfilippo to control the full range of manufacturing processes, from processing to packaging to distribution. It also allowed management to cut the cost and raise the profit margins in its processing operations. By 1984 its sales had reached $56 million.

The company's growth continued throughout the 1980s. In 1984 Sanfilippo entered the bulk foods market with its acquisition of Midwest Nut & Seed Co. The Elk Grove facility was expanded twice—in 1985 and 1989—to 300,000 square feet. Between 1985 and 1990, Sanfilippo's revenues doubled from $78.8 million to $152 million. In 1987 the company moved toward vertical integration in the "Runner-type" peanut market by constructing a 200,000-square-foot production and warehouse facility in Bainbridge, Georgia. This new plant featured complete continuous-line shelling, blanching, processing, and packaging capabilities, with a production capacity of 120 million pounds per year. It became the first and only peanut plant in the world capable of performing the entire production process.

By 1991 Sanfilippo's sales had topped $161 million. Production in that year reached 103 million pounds of peanuts, 37 million pounds of walnuts, pecans, and other nut products, and an additional 38 million pounds of other snack items. Those goods were shipped to more than 6,000 retail, wholesale, foodservice, industrial, and government customers across the country. Sanfilippo's 1980s expansion, however, had left it with some $58 million in debt and a high debt-to-equity ratio. Meanwhile, as the industry continued to consolidate, Sanfilippo eyed still more aggressive expansion plans for the 1990s.

Sanfilippo went public in 1991. Its initial public offering of $12 per share of restricted voting stock raised $22 million, much of which went to pay down its debt. A secondary offering made less than two years later, for $14.25 per share, added $31.5 million. With its debt-to-equity ratio lowered and newly available credit worth nearly $60 million, the company launched on a new period of expansion and acquisition.

Less than six months after its IPO, Sanfilippo paid $4.2 million for Sunshine Nut Co. of San Antonio, Texas, and that company's two retail brands, "Sunshine Country" and "Texas Pride," which generated $32 million in annual sales. In December of 1992 Sanfilippo moved Sunshine's operations to a newly constructed 50-acre, $11.2 million facility in Selma, Texas. Sanfilippo was then vertically integrated in Runner-type peanuts, pecans, and almonds; three of the five major nut types.

Next, Sanfilippo spent $9.5 million building a full-scale, in-shell processing facility in Garysburg, North Carolina, in order to expand into a fourth nut type, Virginia-type peanuts. The company followed this move in April 1993 with the $3.2 million cash purchase of California-based Crane Walnut Orchards, making it fully vertically integrated in each of the five major nut types and the country's largest vertically integrated supplier.

As it expanded through acquisitions, Sanfilippo invested heavily in upgrading its existing plants. The Elk Grove facility was expanded to increase its warehouse space and shipping/receiving capacity, with plans past 1995 for a total of 475,000 square feet. The company also built a $5.3 million plant in Arlington Heights, Illinois, and spent $12 million moving its pecan shelling operations closer to the main pecan growing region in

Texas. In addition, Sanfilippo spent $9.7 million redesigning its recently acquired Gustine, California, walnut facility, while each of the company's existing facilities were retrofitted with updated technology.

Much of Sanfilippo's production technology was designed, invented, and even patented in-house by Sanfilippo's team of industrial engineers. For the walnut plant, the engineering team adapted its pecan-shelling technology to enable it to crack each walnut, as opposed to the common industry practice of sending them through rollers that yielded significantly lower proportions of whole, and more valuable, walnut halves.

Sanfilippo also built the country's largest refrigerated walnut storage house, allowing it to slow the deterioration of the nutmeat, maintain consistency in flavor and color, and reduce the need for costly fumigation. In its Arlington Heights plant, Sanfilippo designed a fully automated production system, including a computer-controlled roasting system capable of processing up to 4,000 pounds per hour. The computer controls contained each of the different recipes stored in memory, allowing the automatic adjustment of such recipe variables as roasting time, temperature, and oil dressing. Sanfilippo also designed an oil filtration system, allowing it to recycle virtually all of the oil not absorbed by the product.

By the end of its three-year expansion effort, Sanfilippo had spent more than $55 million on its new and upgraded facilities. Between 1991 and 1993 the company's annual sales jumped to top $200 million. In the ten-year period 1985–1994, the company saw a compound annual growth rate of nearly 16 percent. In February 1994, Sanfilippo signed an agreement with Procter & Gamble to handle part of its Fisher nut line, then the number-two nut brand in the country. The Arlington Heights facility was built in response to that agreement.

Sanfilippo's expansion effort, coupled with a sluggish economy and declining retail sales, resulted in a sharp drop in earnings, down to $49,000 in 1994 compared to more than $6 million in 1992. And its revenues grew only slightly in that year. A bumper peanut crop, moreover, forced the company to take a $1 million writedown on its peanut inventory. However, the company's difficulties proved temporary and by the following year its financial position had significantly turned around.

In 1995, Sanfilippo closed two major deals to solidify its number-two industry position. In May of that year the company announced it had reached a ten-year agreement with SuperValu Inc.'s subsidiary, Preferred Products Inc., to supply all of its private-label SuperValu nuts, peanut butter, and coconut products. By then, Sanfilippo processed and/or packaged for 100 private labels, a market that had grown increasingly important as consumer demand for name brand products slowed. Nevertheless, Sanfilippo's Evon's brand continued to provide the majority of its revenues, and the company made plans to push deeper into name-brand retail sales.

A further boost to the company came with its September 1995 acquisition of nearly all of the assets of Procter & Gamble's Fisher Nut business. Fisher, with 1994 sales of $62 million, represented nearly five percent of the market, compared with Sanfilippo's 1.7 percent and Planters' leading 37 percent position in the $1.3 billion market.

Aside from nuts, Sanfilippo's product line included peanut butter, desiccated coconut, dried fruit, seeds, snack mixes, sesame snacks, chocolate and other candies, as well as branded items such as Tootsie Rolls and Jelly Belly jelly beans. Approximately 55 percent of the company's nearly $209 million in 1994 sales, in fact, were generated through its consumer products— another 31 percent came from its industrial sales, and the remainder from contract manufacturing, government, and food-service channels, with exports making up the smallest percentage of its business.

Sanfillipo's customers included the U.S. Department of Agriculture's Agricultural Stabilization and Conservation Service, the U.S. Department of Defense's Personnel Support Center, national franchises such as McDonald's, as well as airlines, hospitals, universities, schools, and retail restaurants. The company's products were distributed nationwide. However, the bulk of Sanfilippo's sales were concentrated in the eleven-state Midwest region, and distributed by its own 60-truck fleet. Sanfilippo operated ten state-of-the-art processing and packaging facilities in Illinois, Georgia, Texas, North Carolina, and California, and a distribution facility in Nevada. Sales were made through its own sales staff and a national network of close to 250 independent food brokers and distributors.

As Sanfilippo moved toward the late 1990s, it remained an independent, single-line company competing with highly diversified, global corporations. Its position as the technological leader in the industry, coupled with its integration of the entire production process, enabled it to achieve low costs, higher margins, and prices as much as 25 percent lower than its competitors, while maintaining strict control of quality. The Sanfilippo family continued to provide the company's leadership and hold 65 percent of its stock, with Jasper Sanfilippo serving as president and chief executive officer and Mathias Valentine as executive vice-president.

Principal Subsidiaries: Sunshine Nut Company, Inc.

Further Reading:

Paul Rogers, ''Shell Game,'' *Snack Food,* September 1995.
——, ''Peanut Better,'' *Snack Food,* June 1995.
Gary Samuels, ''Nuts to Planters!'' *Forbes,* January 17, 1994.

—Mickey L. Cohen

Johnson & Higgins

125 Broad Street
New York, New York 10004
U.S.A.
(212) 574-7000
Fax: (212) 574-7676

Private Company
Incorporated: 1899
Employees: 8,400
Sales: $1.009 billion
SICs: 6411 Insurance Agents, Brokers and Service

What do the *Titanic,* Boeing jets, the racehorse *Secretariat*'s bloodline, and industrialist Andrew Mellon's business properties have in common? At one time or another in its 150-year history, Johnson & Higgins brokered the insurance coverage for each of these disparate entities. With over 8,400 employees worldwide and $1 billion in annual revenues, Johnson & Higgins is the fifth-largest insurance brokerage firm in the world and the largest that is privately owned. In contrast to an insurance underwriter, which writes actual policies, Johnson & Higgins brokers deals between clients and underwriters for many types of coverage, including property, workers' compensation, management and professional liability, environmental impairment liability, aviation, and marine policies. The company's 120 offices service large and mid-sized organizations—mostly corporations—and count among their clients half of the companies on the *Fortune* 500 roster. Though Johnson & Higgins's roots are in marine insurance, and its lucrative history has depended largely on charging commissions on the deals it brokers, recent macroeconomic cost-cutting trends have forced the company to move toward a per-service, fee-based compensation structure. This is in line with its evolving character as a consulting operation that helps clients find ways to reduce risk and thus the cost of coverage. The company's leadership sees its current mission as one of applying Johnson & Higgins's demonstrable past success to a changing industry and world. Hence the choice of "Experience for Tomorrow" as the firm's sesquicentennial theme.

The year of Johnson & Higgins's founding, 1845, saw the admission of Florida and Texas into the Union, the first telegraph cable laid across the English Channel, and Edgar Allen Poe's publication of "The Raven." Trade between the East Coast and the rapidly developing Midwest inaugurated a shipping boom that made New York City a major port and doubled its population in the 1840s to 700,000. Amid this growth, two 24-year-old clerks at an insurance company in lower Manhattan, Walter Restored Jones, Jr., and Henry Ward Johnson, set out to test their mettle as the partnership of Jones & Johnson, Average Adjusters and Insurance Brokers. Though at that time marine insurance policies were often simple enough to fit on one page and the need for brokers was therefore slight, there was a great need for average adjusters. The term "average" in this context derives from the French word for a loss and refers to the practice of the various owners of a ship's cargo sharing the costs of a loss when cargo is sacrificed to save the ship during a storm. This practice originated over 3,000 years ago and became increasingly complex in the 19th century as large vessels carried the property of hundreds of different merchants. The average adjuster served as a disinterested party who would assess the value of the loss and determine the portion to be borne by each merchant.

The partnership dissolved in 1853, with Walter Jones leaving to go into business for himself. Company records do not reveal the reason for the split, but Henry Johnson continued operations and soon took on a 22-year-old employee, A. Foster Higgins, as his new partner. Newly formed as Johnson & Higgins on January 3, 1854, the business was successful enough a year later to commission a 97-foot wrecking schooner, the *Henry Ward Johnson,* to salvage damaged ships and cargo. This may have been the ship used in 1862 when Navy Secretary Gideon Wells retained Johnson & Higgins to raise the U.S.S. *Varuna,* which sank after successfully neutralizing four Confederate gunboats in the Battle of New Orleans. As much of an honor as this task was, the Civil War ended a shipping boom reflected by the four-fold increase in U.S. shipping tonnage from 1845 to 1861. This growth had been spurred in part by the California Gold Rush and the new Yankee clipper ships that had reduced the travel time from New York to San Francisco (around Cape Horn) from 200 to 100 days.

The shipping industry revived slowly in the years following the war, but Johnson & Higgins weathered the downturn and ended up getting a boost from the soft market. Reduced shipping business during the war had hurt American insurers and put British companies in a stronger position, allowing them to charge lower rates and attract American shippers. This complicated the process of securing overall coverage and thus increased American merchants' need for brokers like Johnson & Higgins to put deals together. These changes came at a time of shifting company leadership. A third partner, A. William Krebs, joined the two founders in 1874, and another came aboard when Henry Johnson died in 1881, two years after his election as the first chairman of the Association of the Average Adjusters of the United States. Though he remained a part owner, Andrew Higgins left the company in 1887 at the age of 56 to pursue interests in finance and Republican politics. He achieved notoriety for his cooperation with J. P. Morgan in resuscitating a major New York City bank whose speculative failures had caused a severe financial panic, as well as for his endorsement of Democrat Grover Cleveland when the Republican party backed the protectionist McKinley Tariff Act of 1890.

In 1899, with the number of second-generation directors totaling six, Johnson & Higgins took the unexplained step of incorporation. Richard Blodgett, in his commemorative company history, *Johnson & Higgins at 150 Years,* quoted the company's current general counsel as saying, "I can trace the evolution of our corporate charter and all the ownership arrangements with exquisite detail. But why our forebears incorporated the firm, I don't know." Blodgett explained the historical context: by the turn of the century most U.S. goods were produced by corporations, but professional services, such as banking, law, and insurance, tended to remain unincorporated.

In any case, the partners designed a unique charter that is still in place today and is a reason for the company's continued private status. Each year one or two directors retires at the age of 60 and the board replaces them with senior executives, who buy into ownership. Upon retirement directors relinquish their stock to the company in exchange for a dividend paid out over the next ten years based on the company's performance. This system keeps control of Johnson & Higgins in the hands of active executives rather than outsiders, as is often the case when a company's stock is left to family estates and then sold off. It also insures that retiring directors usher in the most able replacements to secure for themselves the highest possible dividend.

By the turn of the century Johnson & Higgins had expanded to eight offices in as many cities and had 75 employees. Kicking off this expansion—the magnitude of which wasn't repeated until the 1960s—had been the 1883 opening of the second office, in San Francisco. This came about when an agent dispatched to handle the claim for the loss of a passenger steamer at the mouth of the Columbia River liked the area and wanted to stay. The growing demand for fire insurance in the wake of the great Chicago fire of 1871 and another the next year in Boston contributed to the opening of other branches, the next being the Philadelphia office in 1885. Johnson & Higgins's earnings from fire insurance were small compared to that from its marine business—only 10 percent of the New York office's income in 1901—but this would change as the demand for marine policies lessened by 1950.

The *Titanic*'s disastrous maiden voyage in April 1912 took the world by surprise, famed as the luxury liner was for its superior design, which included a double bottom and a hull divided into 16 compartments, two of which could be punctured without compromising the ship's buoyancy. Johnson & Higgins was among the incredulous: calculating the risk of total loss to be very small, it had brokered the U.S. portion of the $5.6 million coverage at a nominal rate. All claims were paid within 30 days, though payments accrued only to the owners of the ship, not the survivors or the families of those lost. It was not until 1934, after other marine disasters, that U.S. law required minimum liability coverage. The *Titanic* disaster led to safety changes, however: no longer would teak grace a ship's decks and wood-burning stoves warm its staterooms.

As the United States belatedly entered "the war to end all wars" in 1917, Johnson & Higgins was a major broker of marine insurance and thus aided the government's efforts to insure merchant ships subject to attack. Congress established the Bureau of War Risk Insurance, whose three-member advisory board included only one broker, a Johnson & Higgins director. In the decade following World War I, the company continued its expansion with an office in Havana, its first

outside the United States and Canada. (This was expropriated in 1960 by Fidel Castro's revolutionary government.) More significantly, by buying Albert Willcox & Co. in 1923, Johnson & Higgins began to establish itself in the reinsurance brokerage business, wherein insurance underwriters sell to other underwriters the portions of policies in excess of their capacity. Four years later the company also made its first foray into the employee benefits business, which is today a significant and growing segment of the corporation.

The years of the Depression were difficult ones for nearly all U.S. businesses, with cutbacks and total failures resulting in a national unemployment rate of about 25 percent. Johnson & Higgins suffered from the downturn, but the challenges presented minimal risk to its long-term stability and had a relatively minor affect on its employees. Though it closed offices in Boston, Baltimore, and New Orleans, the company avoided any layoffs and even managed to hire a few people. Of course, management had to cut costs, but this consisted primarily of economizing on business travel and related expenses. The biggest sacrifice was company-wide pay cut of 10 percent, which was followed by another of 20 percent soon after. However, salaries were restored by 1936. Johnson & Higgins's directors managed to avoid layoffs by taking the rest of the necessary cuts from their share of earnings, which supplemented each director's $10,000 salary.

In a May 1933 letter, Johnson & Higgins president H. W. LaBoyteaux exhorted all employees to heed a recent fireside chat by President Roosevelt and keep up their spirits in trying times. In the middle of a 31-year presidency and a 42-year presence on Johnson & Higgins's board (the longest in company history), LaBoyteaux ran the company with the proverbial iron fist. A commanding personality and a breeder of thoroughbred racehorses, he had joined the company at 22 as an average adjuster and head of the Philadelphia office, soon moving to lead the San Francisco office. By 1905 LaBoyteaux was a director—the only one outside of New York—and five years later he held the second largest amount of company stock after president W. R. Coe. Accounts differ as to the exact nature of his ascendancy to the presidency—whether he was offered it or demanded it—but he had virtually absolute control, which he exercised in the form of unilateral decisions.

Johnson & Higgins launched its first advertising campaign in 1940 only after an ad firm convinced LaBoyteaux that it was necessary by conducting a survey of business leaders which revealed that a majority of them supposed Johnson & Higgins to be a stock brokerage firm. Initially hostile to the idea, the president took to it enthusiastically when he realized the faulty perception. LaBoyteaux's willingness to change was accompanied by a determination to change that which provided an obstacle to the company's expansion. In 1943 LaBoyteaux served on a panel that effected a change in New York state law allowing insurers to write policies for more than one line of business. When he died of a heart attack in 1947, he left behind two books on marine subjects, one on racehorses, and a highly profitable company still dominant in the marine insurance brokerage industry. LaBoyteaux's determination and clarity of purpose had a downside, however: insufficient attention paid to the non-marine aspects of Johnson & Higgins's business left the company struggling to adjust in subsequent years.

A former Johnson & Higgins manager of corporate communications described the company after World War II as attempting to rest on its laurels: "They owned the goose that laid the golden eggs and they thought it would keep laying those eggs forever." As the company celebrated its 100th birthday, it boasted fourteen offices (including those in Canada and Cuba), 500 employees, 20 partners, top-ranked marine and average adjusting businesses that contributed more than half the company's revenues, and a smaller but increasingly important non-marine business. One postwar development in the direction of expanding the non-marine divisions was Johnson & Higgins's first use of safety engineers to help clients reduce risks and thus their insurance costs. These loss control specialists and technical advisors are now a key element in the company's ability to retain its stature in an ever-changing market.

Further pushing the company to evolve was the wake-up call Johnson & Higgins received when a major competitor, Marsh & McLennan, went public in 1962. The financial disclosure accompanying the sale of stock revealed that the company had revenues double that of Johnson & Higgins. This came as a shock to Johnson & Higgins's directors, who wondered how a 50-year lead had been squandered. The answer was that Johnson & Higgins's dominance in marine insurance forced the competition to focus on other forms of insurance, which proved highly profitable in the post-war boom. The board was soon split over whether to follow suit and go public as well. Some argued that it was the only way to raise enough capital to stay competitive, while others countered that the company was sufficiently capitalized and should stick to proven practices. CEO Elmer Jefferson settled the dispute by hiring an investment banking firm to look at the company's financial situation and make a recommendation. By the time the firm made its recommendation that Johnson & Higgins go public, the issue had died down and a majority of the directors had decided to stay the course.

Beginning with an office in Rio de Janeiro in 1954, Johnson & Higgins embarked upon a major expansion into global markets at the behest of its president, Dorrance Sexton. Sexton foresaw enormous opportunities for an international brokerage firm as U.S. companies expanded overseas and were less willing to settle for whatever insurance policies were available locally. While Johnson & Higgins had some correspondent relationships with firms in Europe, brokerages were already established on that continent, so it concentrated its energies first on Latin America where there was greater need. Sexton, who took on the effort personally, found an American expatriate in Brazil who shared his vision and signed on to head the operations in that country. Starting with indigenous companies as its first clients, the office began making a profit in its second year and expanded rapidly, opening offices around the country. By the early 1980s the Brazil branch was Johnson & Higgins's third largest after New York and Los Angeles, and others had followed in nearly every South American country.

In 1962 Sexton made a historic trip to Europe, where Johnson & Higgins had many non-exclusive correspondent relationships with European firms. A major breakthrough came when Colgate solicited bids from both Johnson & Higgins and Marsh & McLennan for a large volume of business. Both companies had working relationships with the top German broker, Jauch &

Hübener, so Johnson & Higgins asked the latter to choose one. It chose Johnson & Higgins, and years later the relationship remains a profitable one for both companies. In an unexpected side effect, this increased international presence led to domestic business, as clients that Johnson & Higgins originally dealt with overseas, such as 3M, commissioned the firm to broker their domestic insurance policies as well.

Another boon came in the 1970s as foreign corporations increased their presence in the United States, and Johnson & Higgins's international clients enlisted its services for their U.S. business. All of this activity led the company's directors to seek a way to unify these partnerships with foreign insurance companies. A series of annual conferences gathering many of Johnson & Higgins's international partners strengthened ties and led the company in 1982 to form an alliance dubbed UNISON. While it was not a formal partnership, the UNISON name provided a common rubric that by 1995 united 12 firms with 7,000 employees in 60 countries. Expansion continued into new markets in Eastern Europe, Russia, and the Pacific Rim. By 1995 international business comprised about 20 percent of Johnson & Higgins's revenues, and the firm brokered international insurance policies for 75 of the largest 100 companies on the *Forbes* list.

Johnson & Higgins's UNISON network helped the company become the leading figure in a significant field of insurance that has emerged in the last two decades: captives. Captives are insurance companies formed specifically to underwrite the risks of a parent corporation. Instead of paying premiums to an independent underwriter, money flows to a company (the captive) owned by the parent. Part of the impetus for this new insurance arrangement—which is limited in scope, accounting for only six percent of U.S. property and casualty premiums in 1994—was companies' growing dissatisfaction with increasing premium rates. Also, in foreign countries deductibles were not always offered, forcing a corporation to pay for insurance from the first dollar of loss. One strategy was for a corporation to buy full coverage and then have the underwriter reinsure the first portion of the risk with a captive owned by the corporation.

The captive market received a boost in the hard insurance markets of the mid-1980s but then continued to grow even when conditions relaxed because companies had decided to assume more risk and thus purchase less insurance. Johnson & Higgins's CEO since 1990, David Olsen, described the shift as another instance of the company evolving to better serve its clients: "Our job as broker, as a problem-solver, is to say, 'If the traditional marketplace doesn't meet your needs, we'll solve them in another way.' And one of those ways is captives." By 1995 Johnson & Higgins managed 400 captives for its clients, primarily in Bermuda, whose favorable regulations, tax-free status, and skilled work force attracted many captives.

As it celebrates its 150th anniversary in 1995, Johnson & Higgins seems to have made a successful transition from an established broker of marine and other insurance policies to a provider of a full range of insurance consulting services demanded by its diverse clients. Its UNISON network allows the company to respond effectively to the growing internationalization of business and to capitalize on the opportunities that the newly opening economies in Eastern Europe, China, and elsewhere provide. A recent change in its leadership structure to include 19 managing principals—shareholders without the full voting privileges of directors—should help it retain the talent that has in the past been frustrated by a lack of ownership potential. Finally, a commitment to explore new technology—evidenced by a Computer World-Smithsonian award in 1993 for its InfoEdge communications system—will help Johnson & Higgins continue to embrace change as it approaches the 21st century.

Principal Subsidiaries: A. Foster Higgins & Co., Inc.; Henry Ward Johnson & Co., Inc.; Shipowners Claims Bureau, Inc.; Willcox Incorporated Reinsurance Intermediaries.

Further Reading:

"100 Largest Brokers of U.S. Business," *Business Insurance,* July 5, 1993, p. 3.

Blodgett, Richard, *Johnson & Higgins At 150 Years,* Johnson & Higgins, New York, 1995.

Fraser, Jill Andresky, "Business as Unusual," *Inc.,* August 1991, pp. 39–43.

Kessler, Andy, "Fire Your Sales Force—the Sequel," *Forbes,* April 11, 1994, p. 23.

Wilke, John R., "Computer Links Erode Hierarchical Nature of Workplace Culture," *Wall Street Journal,* December 9, 1993, p. A1.

—John F. Packel, II

KEMET

Kemet Corp.

P.O. Box 5928
Greenville, South Carolina 29606
U.S.A.
(803) 963-6300
Fax: (803) 963-6322

Public Company
Incorporated: 1987
Employees: 8,400
Sales: $473 million
Stock Exchanges: NASDAQ
SICs: 3675 Electronic Capacitors

Kemet Corporation is a leading global supplier of capacitors, which store, filter, and regulate electrical energy and current flow and are found in virtually all electronic products and components. Specifically, Kemet is the largest producer of solid tantalum capacitors in the world and the second largest maker of multilayered ceramic capacitors in the United States. Going into the mid-1990s the company was shipping 11.5 billion capacitors annually from factories throughout the United States and Mexico and was selling a total of 35,000 different products.

Kemet was created in 1987 when Union Carbide Corporation decided to jettison its "Kemet" capacitor manufacturing division. The capacitor industry was hurting at the time, and Union Carbide decided that the division no longer complemented its overall corporate goals. On April 1, 1987, the managers of the capacitor operation, with the cooperation of GE Capital Corp., bought out the subsidiary and renamed it Kemet Electronics Corporation. Kemet became a stand-alone company with Union Carbide as a 50 percent shareholder. Dave Maguire, the former leader of the unit, was named chief executive of the new company. Under his direction, Kemet accelerated its rate of investment in the burgeoning surface-mount capacitor business.

Maguire's decision to attack the surface-mount business was influenced by a number of trends that were emerging in the capacitor industry, an understanding of which provides insight into Kemet. Capacitors are among the most common components found in electronic circuits and are generally considered commodity items. They are named according to their dielectric, which is the material used to store and regulate the electricity. Different dielectrics include ceramic compounds, aluminum oxide, tantalum pentoxide, mica, plastic, paper, and even air.

During the 1970s and 1980s, tantalum and ceramic capacitors became widely used in electronics industries for integrated circuits.

Most capacitors are mounted on a printed circuit board, which contains other electronic devices. A capacitor can be mounted by inserting lead wire 'legs' extending from the dielectric through holes in the board, or by soldering the capacitor directly to the surface of the board. Capacitors used in the former technique are called "leaded" capacitors, whereas the devices utilized in the latter technique are known as "surface-mount" capacitors. Until the late 1980s leaded capacitors were considered conventional. In fact, not until the mid-1980s did surface-mount capacitors begin increasing in popularity with equipment manufacturers. A primary advantage of surface-mount devices is that they can be applied to both sides of a printed circuit board, whereas leaded capacitors can only be attached to one side. That feature allows electronics manufacturers to build smaller devices.

The market switch from leaded to surface-mount capacitors complemented Kemet's operations, because Kemet had long been a leader in the production of tantalum and ceramic capacitors; those two dielectrics are widely used with integrated circuits and possess characteristics that are particularly useful in surface-mount applications. In fact, Kemet, as a subsidiary of Union Carbide, had made the decision to target the tantalum capacitor industry shortly after Bell Laboratories invented the solid tantalum capacitor in the 1950s. The advantage of the tantalum dielectric was that it was useful in applications that required low-voltage semiconductors in electrical circuits. Kemet's decision was a prosperous one, as demand for high-tech tantalum capacitors mushroomed during the late 1950s and 1960s.

Kemet succeeded in the tantalum capacitor business for reasons dating back to the company's inception. Kemet was established as a division of Union Carbide in 1919. Union Carbide created the unit to purchase the assets of the Cooper Research Company of Cleveland, Ohio. Cooper had invented a promising high-temperature alloy shortly before the buyout, and Union Carbide believed that it could integrate the technology into some of its operations. The name "Kemet" was derived from the words "chemical" and "metallurgy." Kemet used the advanced alloy to create high-performance grid wires utilized in triode vacuum tubes; the grids were used to regulate the flow of current in triodes, which were the precursor to the transistor. In 1930 Kemet's product line was broadened to include barium-aluminum alloy getters, which were an essential element in all vacuum tubes.

Kemet benefited during the 1930s and 1940s from the deep pockets of its parent, Union Carbide. That financial backing allowed Kemet to develop automatic machinery that made possible the production of high-quality getters in the massive quantities that were needed to match the rapid expansion of vacuum tube demand. Indeed, vacuum tubes were the basic building block of the electronics industry during the period. Importantly, demand for vacuum tubes during World War II exploded as production of communication, radar, and other types electronic equipment boomed. Evidencing the importance of Kemet's role in the vacuum tube industry, the company supplied an estimated 80 percent of all the vacuum tubes consumed by the Allies during the war.

Kemet continued to prosper selling vacuum tubes during the postwar economic boom. Interestingly, Kemet carved out a niche as a supplier for early vacuum-tube computer equipment. Then, in the early 1950s, Bell Telephone Laboratories invented the transistor. It soon became clear that the highly compact and efficient transistor was going to rapidly displace the vacuum tube. Kemet management foresaw the shift and decided to change its direction accordingly. Bell Laboratories had also invented the tantalum capacitor. Tantalum is a white, malleable, metallic element. When processed, the metallic substance offers specific characteristics needed for certain capacitor applications. Because Union Carbide had experience in the fields of high-temperature metals and alloys, the solid tantalum capacitor was chosen as Kemet's second-generation product to complement existing lines and eventually provide an alternative route to growth.

Kemet got into the solid-state capacitor industry on the ground floor. Demand for its capacitors ballooned during the late 1950s and early 1960s, and the devices quickly supplanted vacuum tubes as the company's core product. To keep pace with growth, Kemet built a 50,000-square-foot capacitor manufacturing facility in 1962 in Greenville, South Carolina. The plant opened in 1963 and remained Kemet's key production facility for several years. The plant was still operating in 1995, by which time it had been expanded and about 450,000 square feet were being used. By the late 1960s Kemet had established itself as a leading U.S. capacitor manufacturer and the top producer of solid tantalum capacitors in the world.

In 1969 Kemet expanded its capacitor line to include multilayer ceramic capacitors. Kemet's sales continued to rise during the 1970s and into the early 1980s. Shortly after entering the ceramic capacitor industry, the company opened a new production facility in Matamoros, Mexico. The Cleveland plant was then phased out and all of its equipment and personnel were transferred to the South Carolina facility or to the Mexican plant. New plants were subsequently opened in Greenwood, South Carolina, and Columbus, Georgia, but the Georgia plant was later shuttered. Increased capacity allowed Kemet to make heady advances in the market for high-tech ceramic capacitors. When Kemet entered the industry in 1969 there were 35 U.S. producers competing in that segment. By 1974 Kemet was the second largest supplier of ceramic capacitors in the nation, a position that it would retain for the next 20 years.

Kemet's success up until the 1980s was largely attributable to its savvy use of advanced capacitor technology, although its gains partially resulted from the United States's domination of many of the industries that incorporated capacitors. That situation began to change in the 1970s, when foreign manufacturers, particularly in Japan, began vying for American market share. In fact, a number of Japanese and other Asian companies entered the electronic device industries during the late 1970s and 1980s and became tough competitors against companies like Kemet. Heightened competition placed downward pressure on prices and reduced profit margins. In the United States, the capacitor industry, like many other electronics sectors, became consolidated as companies joined forces to achieve economies

of scale. By the mid-1980s, only a handful of the several hundred companies that had competed earlier in the century remained.

Kemet managed to survive the industry shakeout for several reasons. Its sheer size was one important advantage. In addition, Kemet managed to keep costs down by having much of its more rudimentary assembly work done at its low-cost Mexican production facility. Still, by the mid-1980s production of most types of capacitors had essentially become a commodity business. Large producers pumped out billions of capacitors for pennies apiece, and the companies that could create them at the lowest cost usually had the edge. To make matters worse, original equipment manufacturers that purchased most of the capacitors were increasingly moving to Asia and other low-cost manufacturing regions, which had the effect of depleting some of Kemet's U.S. customer base.

By the mid-1980s the capacitor industry had lost its luster in the eyes of Union Carbide executives. Profit margins were under pressure from foreign competitors, and the value of shipments by the U.S. capacitor industry was declining. Union Carbide decided to sell the company by way of a management leveraged buyout in 1987. As described earlier, Union Carbide retained 50 percent of the newly formed Kemet Electronics Corporation until the company could get its feet on the ground, and former division head Dave Maguire took over as chief executive of the company. In 1990 Union Carbide completely divested itself of Kemet shares, and Kemet management and other investors, including Citicorp Venture Capital, completed the leveraged buyout. Not until 1992 did Kemet go public, as Kemet Corporation, with a stock offering on the NASDAQ over-the-counter market.

Maguire believed that Kemet, under Union Carbide's ownership, had failed to take advantage of opportunities in the market. Although Kemet was operating in a depressed U.S. industry, the company maintained certain strategic advantages that could exempt it from the malaise. Chief among those advantages was Kemet's position as a leader in tantalum and multilayered ceramic technology. Those two technologies were of vital importance in the trend toward surface-mount circuits. Immediately after taking the helm, Maguire launched an aggressive drive to increase capacity for producing surface-mount ceramic and tantalum capacitors. Indeed, during the next eight years Kemet would spend more than $175 million adding new production capacity—all of which was for surface-mount products.

In addition to redirecting Kemet's product mix, Maguire initiated a comprehensive quality program. During the early 1980s, U.S. and European producers had been left in the dust by Japanese competitors on the basis of quality. To recover lost ground, Kemet adopted a Total Quality Management plan designed to completely turn around its customer service and product quality. The effort worked. By the early 1990s Kemet was recognized as a global leader in quality. At least one analyst called Kemet's focus on quality and customer service obsessive and unsurpassed. Sales to what became one of Kemet's largest customers shot up more than eightfold during the late 1980s and early 1990s because of its quality and service, according to the buyer. In 1992 Kemet achieved registration to the stringent and respected ISO 9001 standards for quality. It also received Ford

Motor Company's Total Quality Excellence Award, which was considered among the most prestigious awards of its kind in the country.

Kemet's aggressive quality initiatives, combined with its emphasis on surface-mounted capacitors, supplied hefty sales and profit gains during the late 1980s and early 1990s, despite overall sluggishness in the U.S. capacitor industry. Indeed, demand for surface-mounted capacitors mushroomed during the period and Kemet was among the best-positioned companies in the world to exploit the demand. Kemet's revenues from the sale of surface-mount capacitors shot from about $30 million in 1988 to nearly $300 million in 1994, reflecting annual compounded growth of 36 percent during the seven-year period. Meanwhile, sales of leaded capacitors declined only slightly. The net result was that Kemet's sales mushroomed from less than $200 million in the late 1980s to about $475 million annually in 1994. Likewise, net income vaulted from a deficit in the mid-1980s to about $30 million annually by 1994.

Kemet entered 1995 as the largest manufacturer of tantalum capacitors in the world with 18 percent of that thriving market—up from third place in 1988. It was also the fourth largest global supplier of multilayered ceramic capacitors with about seven percent of that segment. By 1995 Kemet was churning out a whopping 11.4 billion capacitors annually from ten different manufacturing plants in the United States and Mexico, and was offering a total of 35,000 different types of capacitors. Regardless of the cyclical nature of the electronic device industry, Kemet was well positioned for both short- and long-term gains. Revenues from Kemet's surface-mount business, for example, were forecast to jump past $500 million annually by 1997.

Principal Subsidiaries: Kemet Electronics Corporation; Kemet de Mexico S.A. de C.V. (Mexico); Kemet Electronics S.A. (Switzerland); Kemet Electronics Asia Ltd. (Hong Kong).

Further Reading:

History of Kemet, Greenville, S.C.: Kemet Corporation, August 15, 1994.
Kemet, New York: Lehman Brothers, July 14, 1995.
Kemet Corporation, New York: Merrill Lynch, June 30, 1995.
Levine, Bernard, "Suppliers Restructure as Shakeout Accelerates," *Electronic News,* April 30, 1990, p. 30.
Spears, Glenn H., "Kemet Reports Record Sales and Net Income for Fourth Quarter End," *Business Wire,* April 25, 1995.
Spiegelman, Lisa L., "Adding Capacity to Meet Rising Demand," *Investor's Business Daily,* May 15, 1995.

—Dave Mote

Key Tronic Corporation

4424 N. Sullivan Road
Spokane, Washington 99216
U.S.A.
(509) 928-8000
Fax: (509) 927-5348

Public Company
Incorporated: 1969
Employees: 2,244
Sales: $207.4 million
Stock Exchanges: NASDAQ
SICs: 3577 Computer Peripheral Equipment, Not Elsewhere
   Classified

The world's largest independent producer of computer keyboards, Key Tronic Corporation manufactures a broad range of key, touch, and voice input devices from its production facilities in Spokane, Washington; Dundalk, Ireland; Juarez, Mexico; and Las Cruces, New Mexico. The company also produces goods through joint ventures in Asia. Founded in 1969, Key Tronic rose to the top of the keyboard industry during the 1970s, when the company captured the largest share of the worldwide market for keyboards. It then battled its way through the highly competitive 1980s and 1990s to reign as the dominant keyboard manufacturer in the world in the mid-1990s.

According to Lewis G. Zirkle, founder of Key Tronic Corporation, he had two choices after he was fired from Litton Industries in 1969, ''either go back East or go fishing.'' His words, spoken in the early 1980s before a group of financial analysts gathered in Seattle, were deceptive, however, because Zirkle did neither. Instead, he mortgaged his home, withdrew his life's savings—accumulated from working more than 30 years in the electronics industry—and rented space at the Spokane Industrial Park in Spokane, Washington, where he began his new entrepreneurial career at age 54. Zirkle's time in the electronics industry had included 24 years as part of General Electric's production management team. Throughout his three decades of involvement in the industry, he amassed valuable experience that he put to use in his new business venture, which he organized in the fall of 1969 and incorporated as Key Tronic Corporation.

Zirkle's aim was to manufacture electronic keyboards, products that were then intended for use with digital printers, cathode ray

tube display systems, and industrial control systems. As preparations for the start of the fledgling company were hastily made in October 1969, a modest start-up enterprise emerged. Zirkle helped build the walls to house the six employees he would soon hire. Inside the walls, the trappings were meager: Zirkle shared a desk with his secretary, the five other employees huddled around makeshift tables—sheets of plywood balanced atop wooden sawhorses—and all those employed by the company, including Zirkle, swept the floors and scrubbed the toilets. It was a dubious, sketchy start for a former electronics production manager nearing the twilight of his professional career, but in the years ahead another industry dependent upon the electronic keyboards Zirkle was preparing to manufacture would streak into the business world, recording explosive, worldwide growth that would catapult Zirkle's negligible enterprise with it. The mercurial popularity of personal computers, inoperable without electronic keyboards, proved a pivotal factor in Key Tronic's development. The inextricable connection between Key Tronic's product and the growth of the computer industry would fully redeem the sacrifices made in the fall of 1969 and make the company a formidable force in the years ahead.

By November 1969, Zirkle and his staff had completed the design of Key Tronic's first keyboard, which was then subjected to a battery of tests for the next six months. Once the company's keyboard design passed inspection, the first shipment of Key Tronic keyboards exited the company's rented offices in April 1970. As the 1970s unfolded, the popularity of capacitance keyboards like those designed and manufactured by Key Tronic fueled the growth of Zirkle's company, snatching business away from more expensive solid-state keyboards and drawing the attention of the all-important original equipment manufacturers that did not produce their own keyboards. As the orders poured in, Key Tronic rapidly grew, increasing its payroll to 200 by 1972. By April 1976, six years to the month after the first shipment of keyboards had left Key Tronic's headquarters, the company recorded its first million dollar sales month; two years later it was recognized for the first time as the leader in the keyboard industry.

In 1978, the year Key Tronic gained recognition as the largest company of its kind in the world, the keyboard industry represented an $80-million business. Key Tronic at this point was generating $23 million in annual sales, enough to give the company a narrow lead over its closest rival, Micro Switch, which recorded $22 million in 1978 sales. Three other keyboard manufacturers battled for the industry's third spot, each collecting about $10 million in annual revenues. Once it assumed the top position, Key Tronic remained the industry leader into the next decade, when the keyboard industry recorded its most prolific growth.

Annual sales at Key Tronic approached the $50 million mark as the 1970s drew to a close, while the number of workers employed at the company's facilities eclipsed 1,000. Both physical and financial growth continued into the early 1980s as personal computers began to emerge, marking the beginning of the computer industry's exponential growth of historic proportions.

In 1982 an important breakthrough occurred at Key Tronic when the company developed the low profile keyboard, a product that would become the industry standard and position Key

Tronic as an innovative leader in the global keyboard market. On the heels of this significant event, Key Tronic diversified its product line as the personal computer market began to take shape. The company introduced a range of input devices in 1984 to complement its mainstay low-profile keyboard line, including optical character recognition equipment, mice, bar code, and digitizing equipment.

Between the time that Key Tronic introduced its low-profile keyboard and the time that it embarked on its course of product line diversification, it became a publicly owned company. By this point in June 1983, the company had widened its lead over all other competitors in the industry, controlling by far the largest share of the market for keyboards that computer makers did not manufacture themselves. Annual revenues, which reached $80 million in 1983, experienced even greater growth as the company's line of mice, optical character readers, and other input devices entered the market and began to contribute to annual sales totals. In 1984—a year in which more than 1.5 million Key Tronic keyboards were manufactured and sold— company sales jumped to more than $125 million.

Although Key Tronic had sprinted to the lead in the keyboard industry during the 1970s, it now appeared that its most prodigious growth would occur during the 1980s. The company's revenue volume had nearly tripled during the first four years of the decade despite recessionary economic conditions. Encouraged by this success and determined to further widen its lead over other keyboard manufacturers, Key Tronic reacted to the promising financial results of 1984 by expanding geographically in 1985. The global leader in its industry for the previous seven years, Key Tronic became an international manufacturer in 1985, establishing a manufacturing facility in Ireland to carve a larger presence in the burgeoning European market for keyboards. That same year, the company opened a production plant in Taipei, Taiwan, extending its reach into the Far East. With these new overseas facilities and its manufacturing plants in the Spokane area primed for an anticipated increase in demand for keyboards, Key Tronic's management, still led by Zirkle, waited for the record-breaking financial results for 1985. Instead, the company experienced a grim downturn in its fortunes.

Annual revenues dropped for three straight years beginning in 1985, falling along with the volume of keyboards shipped from Key Tronic's five manufacturing facilities. Although the company still remained the industry leader during this period, it faltered, primarily because many of its largest original equipment manufacturers (including Wang Laboratories, Key Tronic's largest customer) trimmed their orders for keyboards.

The problem was not the quality of Key Tronic's keyboards, nor the attractive powers of another company's product; rather, Key Tronic was losing money because its customers were embroiled in an increasingly competitive industry that featured pernicious pricing battles and feverish attempts to cut costs. Competitive and pricing pressures would become much more severe in years ahead for computer manufacturers, foreshadowing and engendering similar conditions for keyboard manufacturers in the late 1980s and early 1990s. But even as far back as 1985, Key Tronic's financial performance was impacted by the affects of this heightened competition. For three years the company reeled from the effects of declining demand for its products, recording

successive drops in annual sales and keyboard shipments and watching its 14-year stretch of consistent growth grind to a halt.

During the company's three-year span of anemic performance, an extraordinary management change occurred wherein Zirkle began to cede some of his authority after nearly 20 years of wielding resolute control over Key Tronic via his positions as the company's chief executive officer, president, and chairman. In November 1987, Donald J. Meyers was named president of Key Tronic, leaving Zirkle, 72 years old at the time, with the chairman and chief executive posts. The selection of Meyers as president was heralded as the formal beginning of an orderly transition from Zirkle's leadership, but seven months later, after Key Tronic announced an $11 million loss in June for the 1988 fiscal year, Meyers abruptly departed, and with him an entire level of senior management, essentially stripping the company of all senior management except Zirkle. As industry pundits speculated about Meyers' sudden departure, theorizing that he had tried to lead the company in a direction Zirkle had chosen not to go, and that he had been too aggressive on the pricing of Key Tronic's products for Zirkle's liking. In any case, Zirkle returned to his familiar post of president. He continued to steward the company from his three-seated throne as president, chief executive, and chairman.

While this abortive leadership transition was being played out, Key Tronic effected an important engineering change by incorporating membrane technology into the design of its keyboards. When Key Tronic first began manufacturing keyboards, printed circuit boards were chemically etched and plated manually, a costly and laborious procedure outdated by the pricing pressures of the 1980s. Beginning in 1987, Key Tronic began printing circuits on flexible membrane layers, a technological advancement that enabled the company to substantially reduce the manufacturing costs associated with the production of its keyboards.

Membrane technology represented the keyboard industry's newest trend during the late 1980s, but Key Tronic's adoption of the cost-cutting technology offered no panacea to the mounting challenges the company faced in the difficult years ahead. Although Key Tronic's list of customers included computer industry stalwarts such as Compaq, Wang, Unisys, and AT&T, profit margins in the keyboard industry were becoming increasingly smaller, squeezing the financial vitality out of the company.

In late 1989 Zirkle attempted again to hand the managerial reins of Key Tronic to another individual. His son, Fred Zirkle, was named president of the company as it prepared to enter the 1990s. Less than two years later, however, the younger Zirkle departed abruptly as well, resigning from Key Tronic in August 1991 after citing differences with his father over business strategies. Meanwhile, in an attempt to restore the lost luster of its financial performance, Key Tronic announced its intentions in November 1990 to produce a 386SX laptop computer featuring an integrated KeyMouse pointing device. The new product was scheduled to debut in early 1991. The company's attempt to branch out into the manufacture of laptop computers was canceled, however, and in the wake of its abortive foray into laptop computer production, Key Tronic's financial losses continued.

Key Tronic reported a loss of $7.7 million in 1991 and another $7.5 million loss in 1992. Annual revenues slipped as well, falling from $141 million in 1991 to $124 million in 1992. Keyboard prices continued to plunge during the first years of the decade as well, a sign that arresting the company's slide would be difficult. Key Tronic's board of directors, which included Zirkle, voted for a management change, hiring Stanley Hiller Jr. in March 1992 to lead the company away from the brink of failure. Head of the Hiller Group, the management organization that took control of Key Tronic, Hiller had earned a reputation as a corporate healer by transforming money-losing companies into profitable enterprises. By cutting costs and improving products, Hiller had substantially improved the financial performance of oil-field equipment maker Reed Tool Co., moving company Bekins Co., and air-conditioner manufacturer York International Corp., achieving results he now sought to bring to Key Tronic.

Hiller trimmed operating and manufacturing costs, automated production, and revamped a stale product line, scoring his biggest success with a low-cost keyboard known by Key Tronic employees as Kermit. The development of Key Tronic's low-cost keyboard, which wholesaled for $14—compared to $18 for the industry average—was essential to the company's success in the 1990s. Japanese keyboard makers were flooding the market with inexpensive keyboards, a key factor in the 25 percent decline in keyboard prices between 1991 and 1992. Many U.S. keyboard manufacturers had exited the business as a consequence, leaving only a handful of domestic producers to compete against the formidable Asian manufacturers.

Thanks to Hiller's cost-cutting and labor-saving steps, Key Tronic began to demonstrate signs of a recovery by 1993. Profitability returned to the long-time leader in the keyboard industry after years of torpid financial performance. As if to demonstrate its new-found vitality, Key Tronic acquired Honeywell Inc.'s keyboard division in 1993 for $33 million, giving the company further ammunition to wage its war in the personal computer market. Although Key Tronic's net income fluctuated in the wake of Hiller's decisive changes, the company's annual sales rose strongly, jumping to $159.5 million in 1994 from 1993's $123.3 million total.

As the company prepared for the late 1990s and the beginning of the twenty-first century, Hiller's short reign came to end in 1995, his temporary, stopgap work completed. In July 1995, Key Tronic's board of directors elected a computer and electronics executive named Fred Wenninger as chief executive, president, and director of the company. With Wenninger in charge of the company's future, Key Tronic moved forward, hoping to retain its leadership position in an industry it had first dominated nearly 20 years earlier.

Principal Subsidiaries: KT Services, Inc.; KT FSC (Guam); Key Tronic Taiwan Corp. (Republic of China); Key Tronic Europe, Ltd. (Cayman Islands); KTI Limited (Ireland); U.S. Keyboard Company; Key Tronic Juarez (Mexico).

Further Reading:

Johnson, Wendy, ''Analysts Get Taste of Zirkle's Crusty Style,'' *Seattle Business Journal,* April 2, 1984, p. 4.

Levin, Bernard, ''Key Tronic Placed on the Block,'' *Electronic News,* June 30, 1986, p. 1.

Levin, Bernard, ''Major U.S. Firms Move Toward Rubber Keyboards,'' *Electronic News,* December 10, 1984, p. 54.

Mendelson, Edward, ''Key Tronic Combines Standard Keyboard with Windows-Specific Keys,'' *PC Magazine,* July 1995, p. 49.

McAllister, Celia, F., ''A Mouse-and-Keyboard Marriage Made in Heaven,'' *Business Week,* May 21, 1990, p. 148E.

Poor, Alfred, ''Keyboards Beyond the Ordinary,'' *PC Magazine,* August 1987, p. 99.

Skillings, Jonathan, ''Trio of Vendors Set to Heat Up 386SX Notebook PC Market,'' *PC Week,* November 5, 1990, p. 16.

Thorpe, Norman, ''Analyst Is Optimistic About Key Tronic's Future,'' *Puget Sound Business Journal,* September 26, 1988, p. 12.

—Jeffrey L. Covell

Kikkoman Corporation

1–5 Kanda Nishiki-cho, Chiyoda-ku
Tokyo 101
Japan
(3) 3233-5605
Fax: (3) 3233-5604
or
Kikkoman International, Inc.
50 California Street
Suite 3600
San Francisco, California 94111
U.S.A.
(415) 956-7750
Fax: (415) 956-7760

Public Company
Incorporated: 1917
Employees: 4,500
Revenues: Y 215 billion
Stock Exchange: Tokyo
SICs: 2099 Food Preparations; 2085 Distilled & Blended
     Liquors; 2035 Pickles, Sauces & Salad Dressings; 2087
     Flavorings, Extracts & Syrups

Kikkoman Corporation is the world's largest and most famous producer of soy sauce, yet the company has not been merely a single-product business. Kikkoman produced and distributed Manns Wine, one of the most popular labels in Japan, made health foods such as vegetable juices and brown rice under the Del Monte brand label, owned and operated the Colza restaurant chains along with the Nakanakaya chain of pubs, and also ran a wine garden in the heart of downtown Tokyo. The company is well known for its biotechnology research and turning laboratory results in highly successful commercial products. Pioneering efforts in the cultivation of microorganisms, genetic engineering, and the testing of food products has enable Kikkoman to grab hold of a significant portion of the market within the food industry.

Kikkoman Corporation was founded in 1917 in Noda, Japan, but the company's roots go back to the 17th century. Around 1650, a number of families began to produce food seasonings from the plants and crops of their small, intensely cultivated growing fields. One of these products was soy sauce, a concoction primarily made from soybeans that was used to enhance the flavor of countless dishes, from soup to skewers of chicken. Many of these family-operated businesses located their operation next to the Edo River, so that freshly made soy sauce could be delivered as quickly as possible to customers in the capital of Edo, present-day Tokyo. During the time that Japan was open to outside trade, Dutch ships from half a world away bought soy sauce in the city of Nagasaki. These Dutch traders shipped the soy sauce back to The Netherlands, where the new taste became the overnight sensation for the upper classes.

Over the years, some of the families who produced soy sauce grew in wealth, prominence, and influence and contributed many astute business leaders that helped develop Japan's economy into one of the strongest in the Orient. However, by the end of the 19th and beginning of the 20th centuries, there were over 1,000 soy sauce companies competing for a rather limited Japanese market. In order to ensure the survival of their businesses, eight families producing soy sauce and other food seasonings in Noda banded together and formed Kikkoman Corporation in 1917.

From the very beginning, the production of high-quality soy sauce was the cornerstone of Kikkoman's success. The ingredients of soy sauce and the method of its production have been the same for nearly 400 years. Soy sauce is made from three simple ingredients—soybeans, wheat, and salt. The soybeans, rich and full of protein, are first steamed and then mixed with wheat, previously crushed and roasted. This mixture of soybeans and wheat is then combined with something similar but not identical to yeast, which serves as a catalyst for the culturing process. The result is a dry mash, known as *koji*. According to the traditional brewing procedure, brine is next added to the *koji* in order to make *moromi*. Moromi is a strong, even potent concoction, which remains in fermentation casks or tanks. During fermentation, the *koji* acts as an enzyme and changes the protein of a soybean into an amino acid while also transforming the starch of the wheat into sugar. After a short time, the *moromi* turns a startling reddish brown, and lactic acid cocci and yeast activate all the combined factors that make and distinguish the flavor, color, and aroma of soy sauce.

Kikkoman Corporation not only maintained the traditional manner of making soy sauce but also continued the historical method of careful atmospheric and temperature control that enables the brewing processes to take place. In the old days, master brewers took extensive precautions in brewing the soy sauce and spent long hours monitoring its progress. Buckets known as *kakioke* and paddles called *kaibo* provided these brewing experts with all they needed to control the entire process. After four centuries, the quality-control process has been refined through the development and cultivation of microorganisms that make production much more efficient.

After its founding in 1917, Kikkoman Corporation became known as the biggest soy sauce producer in Japan. The company sold exclusively to consumers in Japan and, since virtually every person used some form of soy sauce during a meal, revenues grew rapidly during the 1920s. Kikkoman began to expand its product line at this time and produced such variations as soy sauces for meat, noodles, fish, and chicken. By the end of the 1930s the company had grown so large that a brand-new plant, named Goyogura, was constructed in Noda; it was specifically developed and designed to preserve the traditional manner and techniques of brewing soy sauce. The Goyogura plant was designated to produce soy sauce for the emperor of Japan and the entire imperial retinue.

During the early part of World War II, the company's Japanese market remained high, but as the war progressed there was less and less food to eat, and consequently the demand for soy sauce decreased. By the end of the war, the company's production facilities in Noda had almost come to a complete halt. The postwar years were harsh ones for the entire Japanese population. Food shortages, lack of fuel, and a ruined economy contributed to years of privation. However, with the help of the United States and other countries, Japan slowly rebuilt its country and economy.

Kikkoman revived its fortunes along with the rest of Japanese business in the late 1940s. By the early 1950s the company was selling large amounts of soy sauce and other seasonings both to the domestic market in Japan and to the new burgeoning markets around the Pacific Rim. In the Asia-Pacific region, countries like Australia, New Zealand, Malaysia, Taiwan, and Korea began to open their doors to Japanese companies like Kikkoman. Within a very short time, Kikkoman's soy sauce was used on many different kinds of food, including fried noodles, fried rice, barbecued beef, roasted lamb, fish, fowl, and the entire range of vegetables. Chefs in those countries began to notice how soy sauce awakened the flavor of food, and soon the popularity of the product had spread across the Pacific Ocean to the United States.

In 1957, the company took a big step in its international development by establishing Kikkoman International, Inc., in San Francisco, California. The company's first subsidiary outside of mainland Japan, Kikkoman International was a marketing operation that helped popularize soy sauce in the United States. Although interest started slowly, soy sauce soon found its way into the recipes of chefs at glamorous restaurants as well as into common lunchtime meals. Soy sauce began to be used on distinctly American cuisine such as hamburgers, Caesar salads, and barbecued baby pork ribs. As its presence in the United States grew and its share of the food seasonings market increased, Kikkoman began to introduce other items such as teriyaki sauce and tofu in order to stir Americans' imaginations. By the end of the 1950s, the company was firmly established on the West Coast of the United States, and sales of its products were increasing rapidly.

By the 1960s, Kikkoman Corporation was ready to initiate a major expansion program in both the domestic and international markets. In 1962, the company created Tone Coca-Cola Bottling Company, Ltd., a soft drink bottling company located near Tokyo. This venture signaled the company's entry into a market not directly related to soy sauce and food seasonings. In one of its most important decisions, Kikkoman arranged to produce and market a number of Del Monte products for the Japanese market. The first of these items included a variety of Del Monte juices and tomato products. Kikkoman's advertising campaign for Del Monte products caused the brand to become a household name throughout the Japanese islands. In 1964, Kikkoman formed Mann's Wine Company, Ltd., for the purpose of producing and distributing its own wine labels in Japan. To complement the formation of this company, management at

Kikkoman also created a laboratory in order to develop sophisticated technology that would allow the use of domestically grown grapes to produce distinctive and unique Japanese wines. In addition, Mann's Wine Company began to import various brandy and champagne labels to market for domestic consumption. The decade ended on a high note when Kikkoman invested in the Japan Food Corporation, a large trading firm that provided greater access to overseas markets.

The 1970s witnessed a continuation of the policies set by the company during the 1960s. The ever-increasing demand for its products led Kikkoman to design and construct its own U.S.-based manufacturing facility. Located in Walworth, Wisconsin, in the heart of the Upper Midwest, the plant began making soy sauce and other food products in 1972. During the same year, Kikkoman initiated its operation of a chain of restaurants located in major cities across West Germany. Named Kikkoman Daitokai (Europe) GmbH, the venture garnered immediately popularity. Kikkoman Daitokai was the company's entry into the restaurant business, and, since revenues were increasing rapidly, management decided to open a chain of similarly styled restaurants in Japan. The Colza restaurant chain began operating in 1974 in Tokyo, specializing in *teppanyaki*-prepared grilled foods, and the Kushi Colza restaurant chain opened during the same year, specializing in vegetables and various meats heated on skewers of bamboo. This style of food, called *kushiyaki,* is one of the most popular in Japan. Since the restaurant chain within Germany had performed so well from its opening in 1974 through 1979, the company established Kikkoman Trading Europe GmbH in Dusseldorf to take advantage of the growing demand for Japanese products such as soy sauce.

Kikkoman's markets in the Asia-Pacific region grew in importance during the 1980s. The use of so many different kinds of food seasonings in countries such as Korea, China, Malaysia, and Australia led the company to establish a production facility in Singapore, called Kikkoman (S) Pte. Ltd., in 1983. As consumer demand continued to grow, the company added a fully automated plant located in Chitose, Japan. Both the facility in Singapore and the one in Chitose made products for the Asia-Pacific region. The European arm of Kikkoman's operations also expanded during the 1980s. The company expanded its restaurant business by creating Kikkoman Restaurants S.A., a subsidiary based in Switzerland.

Perhaps the most important development during the 1980s was the company's commitment to laboratory research and development. Kikkoman established a state-of-the-art research facility that remains on the cutting edge of technological sophistication in the food industry. Kikkoman's laboratory focuses on applying biotechnology and enzymology to create new seasonings and foods. One of its most significant achievements includes the improvement of a proprietary microorganism employed in the production of soy sauce. Other accomplishments are just as impressive. Scientists have been able to create an enzyme that produces gallic acid, normally used within the semiconductor and pharmaceutical industries. Initially created for industrial production, this enzyme has developed into one of the company's most lucrative commercial products. Company researchers were also the first to isolate luciferase and produce it for industrial use. Luciferase is an enzyme that enables fireflies to glow, and scientists at Kikkoman's laboratory have used it to detect various microorganisms in water and food. Another recent research success involves the development of the *Oretachi* orange, a fruit that is resistent to cold temperatures. Based on cell-fusion techniques, this knowledge is being exporting by Kikkoman to help orange growers around the world.

In the 1990s, Kikkoman continued to expand its international operations. The company purchased the perpetual marketing rights for the Del Monte brand label covering the entire Asia-Pacific region, except for the Philippines. Since this agreement was reached in 1990, the company has made a concerted effort to increase sales throughout the region. During the same year, Kikkoman entered into a joint venture and established President Kikkoman, Inc., a soy sauce production facility based in Taiwan. The company also formed Kikkoman Trading (S) Pte. Ltd., a subsidiary that markets products made in both Japan and Singapore, in addition to the whole line of Del Monte products, to the countries around the Pacific Rim. In 1992, Kikkoman Australia Pty. Limited was formed to take advantage of the market demand in Australia and New Zealand. This Australian subsidiary has been able to help make Kikkoman's soy sauce the highest selling oriental food seasoning ingredient in the country.

From a relatively small regional business, Kikkoman Corporation has grown into one of the most successful of all the multinational organizations. The company's organizational structure, cost-effective production methods, research and development commitment, and uncanny ability to take advantage of new food industry markets should be a case study for any student pursuing a master's degree in business administration.

Principal Subsidiaries: Kikkoman Ajinomingei Co., Ltd.; Kikkoman Business Development Inc.; KMC Co., Ltd.; Kikkoman Restaurant, Inc.; Mann's Wine Co., Ltd.; Manns Wine Pub Co., Ltd.; Nippon Del Monte Corporation; Pacific Trading Co., Ltd.; Seishin Corporation; Sobu Butsuryu Co., Ltd.; Sobu Service Center Inc.; Tone Coca-Cola Bottling Co., Ltd.; Japan Food Corp. (Aust) Pty. Limited; Japan Food Canada Inc.; Japan Food (Hawaii), Inc.; JFC Hong Kong Limited; JFC International Inc.; Kikkoman Australia Pty. Limited; Kikkoman Daitokai (Europe) GmbH; Kikkoman Foods, Inc.; Kikkoman International Inc.; Kikkoman Restaurants S.A.; Kikkoman (S) Pte. Ltd.; Kikkoman Trading Europe GmbH; Kikkoman Trading (S) Pte. Ltd.; President Kikkoman Inc.

Further Reading:

"Company Profile," *Forbes,* January 7, 1991, pp. 267–68.
"Company Profile," *Forbes,* January 3, 1994, pp. S21–S22.
Conan, Kerri, "Soy Sauce," *Restaurant Business,* October 10, 1993, p. 97.
Kikkoman Corporation, Company Document, 1995.
"More Than Oriental," *Prepared Foods,* October 1992, p. 64.
Ryan, Nancy Ross, "All About Soy Sauce," *Restaurants & Institutions,* November 15, 1994, p. 83.
Takagawa, Michael K., "Kikkoman Adds Takagawa to Team," *Nation's Restaurant News,* August 3, 1992, p. 136.

—Thomas Derdak

King Ranch, Inc.

10055 Grogan's Mill Road, Suite 100
The Woodlands, Texas 77380
U.S.A.
(713) 367-7300

Private Company
Incorporated: 1934
Employees: 663
Sales: $250 million
SICs: 0212 Beef Cattle, Except Feedlots; 1311 Crude
    Petroleum & Natural Gas; 2711 Newspapers; 5211
    Lumber & Other Building Materials Dealers; 5083 Farm
    & Garden Machinery & Equipment; 5948 Luggage &
    Leather Goods Stores

King Ranch, Inc. operates one of the largest and most famous cattle ranches in the world. The King Ranch itself, which covers about 825,000 acres—slightly larger than the state of Rhode Island—on four separate divisions of land in South Texas known as the "Home Ranches": Santa Gertrudis, Laureles, Norias, and Encino. The company represents a colorful part of Texas history. From its beginnings in the mid-nineteenth century as a family cattle ranch, the company has evolved into a major multinational operation active in a variety of agricultural and energy-related activities. While it is perhaps most famous for its agribusiness segment (cattle breeding; horse breeding; farming; commodity marketing and processing; commercial hunting leases), King Ranch also explores and develops oil and gas properties through its King Ranch Oil and Gas, Inc. subsidiary. Other businesses in which King Ranch is involved include residential real estate and a smattering of retail and commercial ventures near its Texas home turf. A private company, King Ranch is owned by 60 or so descendants of company founder Captain Richard King, a legendary figure in the history of cattle ranching in the United States.

Captain King started up his ranch in 1853 in an area known at the time as the Wild Horse Desert or the Nueces Strip, bounded by the Nueces River on the north and the Rio Grande on the south. A steamboat pilot by trade, King had arrived in southern Texas about eight years earlier to run a shipping operation on the Rio Grande with partner Mifflin Kenedy. On a trip through the Wild Horse Desert, King noticed a promising piece of land along the Santa Gertrudis Creek. He quickly formed a partner-

ship with another friend, Texas Ranger Captain Legs Lewis. King purchased the land and he and Lewis launched the livestock operation that would eventually grow into the King Ranch.

In order to expand the ranch during its early years, King hired a lawyer to seek out the owners of the old land grants throughout the area. He then bought the parcels and annexed them to the ranch. King also began to buy and sell cattle in huge numbers. His buying trips frequently took him into Mexico. In 1854 King brought north not only all of the cattle from one particular Mexican village suffering through a drought, but all of the village's humans as well. These transplanted villagers went to work on the ranch. Their descendants, who became known as *kiñenos* (King's men), have formed the core of the King Ranch work force ever since.

The ranch managed to survive its early years in spite of a hostile environment created by the presence of bandits, unhappy Indians, and the usual assortment of rustlers, raiders, and ruffians associated with the Wild West. King split his time between his two businesses, steamboating and ranching, during this period. In 1858 King built the first ranch house at the Santa Gertrudis site on a spot suggested by his friend Robert E. Lee, a young Lieutenant Colonel at the time. During the Civil War, the ranch served as a depot for the export of southern cotton through Mexico, sidestepping the Union naval blockade. King and Kenedy also used their shipping enterprise to supply the Confederate army. By the end of the Civil War, thousands of head of cattle were roaming the ranch, which had grown to nearly 150,000 acres in size. In 1867 King began using the Running W brand to mark his cattle. The Running W eventually became one of the most widely recognized marks in the history of the cattle industry.

By the end of the 1860s, King Ranch longhorns were being sold in northern markets. In order for this to happen, the cattle had to be driven thousands of miles to railroad points as far away as St. Louis, and later, Abilene, Kansas. Between 1869 and 1884, over 100,000 head of cattle from King Ranch made the trip. Much of the livestock ended up in the Chicago stockyards; other destinations included new ranches springing up in Oklahoma, Nebraska, Colorado, Wyoming, and Montana, as the cattle industry of the West began to mature.

In 1884 a young lawyer named Robert Kleberg began handling the legal affairs of King Ranch. Kleberg quickly became an indispensable part of the ranch's operation. When King died in 1885, he left his entire estate to his wife, Henrietta. The ranch covered more than 600,000 acres by this time. Mrs. King, who outlived her husband by 40 years, made Kleberg the full-time manager of the ranch. Kleberg married King's daughter Alice the following year.

Under Kleberg's management, operations at the ranch were streamlined and made more efficient. Kleberg built fences to divide the sprawling ranch into more manageable units. He also began to cross his cowherd with Shorthorn and Hereford bulls, since the expansion of the railroad made the Longhorn's ability to walk long distances irrelevant. One by one, the problems of running a growing ranch were addressed. Annoying wild mustangs and donkeys were captured and shipped elsewhere.

Crews were assigned to slow the encroachment of mesquite brush, which was quickly displacing the favorable "climax grasses." During the horrible drought years of the 1890s, Kleberg experimented with various ways of getting water to the land. Finally, in 1899, an artesian well was drilled. This well, originating over 500 feet below ground, provided enough water to support all of the region's livestock and agriculture. Along the way, the city of Kingsville was incorporated, following the vision of Henrietta King.

During the first fifteen years of the twentieth century, King Ranch managed once again to thrive in the face of further droughts, wars with Mexican raiders, and Kleberg's failing health. As Kleberg became weaker, he passed on responsibility for running the ranch to his sons, Bob and Dick Kleberg. Along the way, the ranch's selective breeding efforts intensified. They began crossbreeding Brahman bulls native to India with their own Shorthorn stock. The result was a new breed, which they dubbed "Santa Gertrudis." The Santa Gertrudis cattle combined the beefiness of the British Shorthorns with the Brahmans' ability to withstand the hot climate of summertime Texas. King Ranch began selling Santa Gertrudis bulls to other ranchers in the 1930s, and in 1940 the United States Department of Agriculture recognized Santa Gertrudis as the first ever American-produced beef breed.

Henrietta King died in 1925, at the age of 92. Mrs. King's death brought about a web of complications stemming from the division of her estate, high estate taxes, and various debts. The onset of the Depression, which caused beef prices to drop to the century's lowest levels, made matters even worse. Robert Kleberg died in 1932, signaling a complete generational shift in the ranch's management. By that time, King Ranch had grown to well over a million acres in size and was home to 94,000 head of cattle and 4,500 horses and mules, the quality of which had become very high through selective breeding.

When Mrs. King's estate was finally untangled, Kleberg's widow, Alice, and her children consolidated as much of the ranch as possible by purchasing the properties of other heirs. In 1935 the Klebergs made King Ranch a corporation so that its future as a single entity would be more secure. Estate taxes had left the ranch with a $3 million debt, however, and for the next few years the company struggled to remain afloat, with Bob Kleberg acting as manager of its day-to-day operations. To get the company back in the black, Kleberg turned to petroleum. He negotiated a long-term lease for oil and gas rights on the entire ranch with Humble Oil and Refining Company, which later became Exxon. Meanwhile, brother Dick served the company from the outside as president of the Texas and Southwestern Cattle Raisers Association and, beginning in 1931, as a seven-term member of the U.S. Congress.

Beef was not the only thing King Ranch was able to breed successfully. As the company developed its Santa Gertrudis cattle, it also engaged in the King Ranch Quarter Horse program. Bob Kleberg, the driving force behind the program, also became interested in thoroughbred racing horses. In 1938 he bought Kentucky Derby winner Bold Venture as a foundation sire for the ranch's thoroughbred breeding program. He also bought a stake in the Idle Hour Stable in Lexington, Kentucky,

in 1946. That year, a King Ranch horse, Assault (a son of Bold Venture), won horse racing's Triple Crown.

During the 1940s and 1950s, a number of innovations improved production and kept King Ranch at the cutting edge of the cattle industry. These innovations included mechanized brush control methods, the identification of new and better grasses, and the development of better corrals for working cattle. Modern game management and preservation systems were also set up. In the 1950s the company went international. By 1952 the company was sending livestock to outposts in Cuba and Australia in hopes of boosting production by introducing Santa Gertrudis genes into the mix. In Australia, one of King's partners was Swift & Co., the biggest buyer of the ranch's U.S. beef output. The company eventually established a presence in Brazil, Argentina, and Venezuela, where the techniques developed to clear mesquite brush in Texas could be used on South American rain forest. Morocco and Spain soon followed as well.

Dick Kleberg died in 1955. His son, Dick Jr., had been playing an increasingly important role in company affairs since the 1940s, and in 1969 he was named chairman of the King Ranch board of directors. By the early 1970s, King Ranch controlled about 11.5 million acres of land worldwide. In 1974 Bob Kleberg died after managing the company's operations for more than half a century. The Kleberg family's choice to replace him as president and chief executive officer of the company was James H. Clement, the husband of Ida Larkin, one of Richard King's great-granddaughters (and Robert Kleberg Sr.'s granddaughters). In choosing Clement to lead King Ranch into the next generation, the family passed over Robert Shelton, a vice-president and King relative who had been raised by Bob Kleberg. This snub, combined with legal haggling over oil payments to family members, led to Shelton's departure from the company a few years later.

During the 1970s, Clement began to feel that the company had become unwieldy, and he started selling off chunks of King Ranch's overseas real estate. In 1976 Clement hired W.B. Yarborough to take control of King Ranch's oil and gas business. Yarborough, an independent petroleum operator and former Humble Oil geologist—not to mention the husband of Richard Kleberg Sr.'s daughter Katherine—decided to take on the task on a part-time basis. Four years later he became the first president of King Ranch Oil and Gas, Inc., a new wholly owned subsidiary formed to handle all of King Ranch's petroleum affairs.

Dick Kleberg Jr. died in 1979, and soon after that his son, Stephen "Tio" Kleberg, took over management of King Ranch South Texas, the company's core ranch operation. Under Tio Kleberg's guidance, the company continued to update its cattle, horse, and farming operations. More and more emphasis was placed on applying modern business principles to these tradition-bound endeavors. Meanwhile, as an outgrowth of the King Ranch Quarter Horse program, the company became involved in competition cutting—an arena event in which horses try to separate individual heifers from the herd—in the mid-1970s. Within a decade, through a combination of strategic horse purchases and the application of its fabulously successful breeding techniques, King Ranch had established a dynasty of champion cutting horses.

A management upheaval took place in 1987 when, within the span of half a year, Clement retired as president of King Ranch and Yarborough retired as president of the King Ranch Oil & Gas subsidiary. Clement was replaced by Kimberly-Clark CEO Darwin Smith, who became the first chief executive in company history with no familial ties to founder Richard King. Tio Kleberg continued to run the ranch's day-to-day operations. Smith's reign lasted only a year. After his departure, Roger Jarvis, who had been running the company's petroleum operations, was named president and CEO. Leroy Denman, a longtime company affiliate, was elected chairman of the board in 1990.

As the 1990s opened, King Ranch faced a number of questions. As income from both cattle and petroleum operations declined, the company was forced to look for other business areas in which to try its hand. In addition, the number of company shareholders had increased over the years through inheritances, and the very future of the ranch as a single entity was called into question. Although several King heirs wanted to break up and sell the ranch to turn a quick profit, the family decided to keep it intact.

Several new ways to generate revenue were found over the next few years. The company began actively exploring for oil and gas, rather than passively waiting for royalties on the oil and gas found on its property by others. Cotton farming was another area into which the company plunged with a fair amount of success. The King Ranch Saddle Shop, once exclusively a supplier of cowboy gear for the kiñenos, went into the retail clothing and luggage business. Parts of King Ranch's property were opened not only to hunters, who pay nearly $3 million a year to shoot at deer, turkeys, and other animals, but to tourists as well.

Another turnover in management took place in 1995. That year, Jack Hunt, formerly the CEO of California's Tejon Ranch, was named president and CEO of King Ranch. A couple months later, Abraham Zaleznik, a King Ranch director since 1988, replaced the retiring Denman as chairman of the board. By this time, the newer, nonagricultural businesses were accounting for more than half of the company's income, and Tio Kleberg was the only King descendant still actively working the ranch.

Although 60,000 head of cattle still graze King Ranch's sprawling acreage and the company remains a major force in the cattle industry, King Ranch has evolved into a distinct agribusiness and energy corporation. Both in the cattle business and in its other pursuits, the management and shareholders of King Ranch have expressed a commitment to the kind of experimentation and innovation that have helped the company thrive for so many years. The King Ranch name and its Running W brand, first used by Captain King 1869 when he became a sole proprietor, continue as one of the most widely recognized identities in the industry.

Principal Subsidiaries: King Ranch Holdings, Inc.; King Ranch Properties, Inc.; King Ranch do Brasil S.A. (Brazil); Big B Sugar Corp.; King Ranch Saddle Shop, Inc.; King Ranch Oil and Gas, Inc.; King Ranch Power Corp.; Kingsville Lumber Company; Robstown Hardware Company; Kingsville Publishing Company.

Further Reading:

''Biggest Ranch Jumps Some Oceans,'' *Business Week,* May 17, 1952, pp. 192–194.

Cypher, John, *Bob Kleberg and the King Ranch: A Worldwide Sea of Grass,* Austin: Tex., 1995.

Denhart, Robert Moorman, *The King Ranch Quarter Horses,* Norman, Oklahoma: University of Oklahoma Press, 1970.

''The Fabulous House of Kleberg: A World of Cattle and Grass,'' *Fortune,* June 1969.

Godwyn, Frank, *Life on the King Ranch,* New York: Thomas Y. Crowell, 1951.

''King Ranch,'' *Fortune,* December 1193, pp. 48–61; 89–109.

''The King Ranch: The Last Frontier Empire Confronts the Modern World,'' *Texas Monthly,* October 1980, pp. 150–173, 234–278.

Lea, Tom, *The King Ranch,* Boston: Little, Brown and Company, 1957

McGraw, Dan, ''A Fistful of Dollars,'' *U.S. News & World Report,* July 24, 1995, pp. 36–38.

Nixon, Jay, *Stewards of a Vision: A History of King Ranch,* Houston: King Ranch, Inc., 1986.

Paré, Terence, ''New Chairman Tenderfoot Takes Over,'' *Fortune,* August 1, 1988, p. 217.

''Today's King Ranch,'' *The Cattleman,* September 1995, pp. 10–32.

—Robert R. Jacobson

Kinney Shoe Corp.

233 Broadway
New York, New York 10279
U.S.A.
(212) 720-3700
Fax: (212) 553-2094

Wholly Owned Subsidiary of Woolworth Corp.
Incorporated: 1917 as G. R. Kinney Co., Inc.
Operating Revenues: $3.91 billion
Employees: 36,000
SICs: 3149 Footwear, except Rubber; 5661 Shoe Stores;
  5669 Miscellaneous Apparel and Accessory Stores; 5941
  Sporting Goods Stores and Bicycle Shops

Kinney Shoe Corp., a subsidiary of Woolworth Corp., is a century-old company that made its reputation as a family shoe store. In the 1970s it also established the popular Foot Locker athletic footwear and apparel stores. At the end of 1994 Kinney Shoe Corp. was operating an empire that comprised 826 Kinney shoe stores; 1,828 Foot Locker, 595 Lady Foot Locker, 136 Kids Foot Locker, and 32 World Foot Locker stores; 539 Champs Sports sporting-goods shops; 200 Athletic X-Press family athletic footwear and apparel stores; 76 Footquarters brand-name family shoe stores; and 61 Going to the Game! licensed athletic-team apparel stores. It also ran three shoe-manufacturing factories. In 1995 the Kinney holdings were divided into two Woolworth divisions, although Kinney retained its corporate existence.

Son of a bankrupt general-store proprietor in upstate New York, George R. Kinney spent more than a decade working as a clerk for footwear manufacturers and paying off his father's debts. In 1894 he invested his remaining savings in a retail shoe store in Waverly, New York. Bypassing jobbers and independent wholesale distributors, Kinney bought footwear in large quantities directly from factories and sold them at the lowest possible prices, but for cash only. Mindful of his father's policy of extending credit to customers, which became disastrous, Kinney generally held to the motto, "Shoes on the Shelf or Money in the Till."

During the following years Kinney opened a number of other shoe stores in New York and Pennsylvania, in collaboration with managers who bought shares in the enterprises and became partners. Kinney was the head buyer, purchasing shoes from

manufacturers for 80 cents a pair and discouraging his managers from selling them for more than 98 cents. The stores operated on month-to-month leases and were quickly closed if they were unprofitable. Clerks were paid poorly but were rewarded with profit sharing in the form of bonuses.

There were 15 Kinney stores in 1903, the year Kinney moved his headquarters from Wilkes-Barre, Pennsylvania, to Manhattan, where the previous year he had become the first retailer in New York City to sell shoes for under a dollar. Accordingly, Kinney's footwear had a steady working-class clientele. In Pennsylvania's anthracite coal-mining region, a Kinney stronghold, miners could buy shoes on time despite the company's usual cash-and-carry policy. Especially popular was the durable rubber-and-felt "Woonsocket boot," which kept feet warm and comfortable down in the mines for $2.98.

By 1914 the number of Kinney stores had grown to 40, with total sales of $3 million. By the end of 1916 George Kinney had built the largest footwear chain in America, with 56 stores stretching as far west as Illinois. The following year a closely held company called G. R. Kinney Co., Inc., was incorporated in New York, replacing the former combination of partnerships.

Kinney, who owned the largest number of shares in the new enterprise, died in 1919 and was succeeded as president by an old friend and long-time associate, Ed Krom. By that year there were more than 60 stores with combined annual sales of almost $14 million.

In order to keep footwear costs down and to maintain an adequate supply of merchandise, Kinney had decided before his death to enter the shoe-manufacturing businesses. Four factories were acquired in 1919, each specializing in a different line of footwear. The following year another manufacturer was purchased and a new plant built. A large warehousing and distribution center was opened in 1921 in Harrisburg, Pennsylvania. By 1926 Kinney factories were producing about 14,000 pairs of shoes a day and supplying 60 percent of the merchandise sold in Kinney stores. The company also was buying and selling hosiery from the largest mills in the eastern United States and had been selling shoe polishes, laces, and brushes almost from its inception.

During the growing prosperity of the 1920s Kinney found it possible to pass on higher manufacturing and raw materials costs to its customers. It repositioned itself as the "largest exclusive family footwear chain serving the middle class" with "popular-priced staple shoes of good quality," selling for as much as $5.98. The company also began placing national radio and print advertisements and bought the nationally famous Educator brand of corrective shoes from its Boston owners.

Between 1923 and 1929 Kinney opened 158 new stores, extending its reach to nearly every mid-sized city east of the Mississippi. In 1929 there were 366 Kinney stores in 38 states and 295 cities. The company employed more than 1,400 people and earned $933,549 on nearly $20.9 million in net sales. Its common stock, first listed on the New York Stock Exchange in 1923, reached a 1929 high of $44 a share, not topped until 1955.

The stock market crash of October 1929 ended this period of prosperity. Kinney stock, much of it bought on margin, fell to

50 cents a share. The following year Andre Mertzanoff, an astute investor, acquired a controlling interest in the company, but he soon found that Kinney's troubles were just beginning. By 1932 it had 60 more stores than in 1929 but, because of the general economic collapse, only half the volume of total sales. One week a Brooklyn store posted sales of just 25 cents. Kinney lost money in 1931, 1932, and 1933. Stock dividend payments were halted in 1931 and did not resume on common shares until 1946.

During the mid-1930s Kinney closed many unprofitable stores, dropping the total number to 321 by 1937. Many of the remaining stores were refurbished or moved to better locations. Management established cost controls and centralized purchasing for the factories and ordering for the stores, assigning each store a specific quota of every item in stock.

World War II posed different problems. The federal government sharply curtailed supplies of raw materials and imposed price ceilings and strict regulations on inventories and styles. Consumers were limited to one pair of leather shoes every six months. Kinney experimented with sole materials like rope, canvas, compressed paper, plastic scraps, and carpet bottoms. Its factories produced more than two million boots for the armed forces, about one-quarter of their total output. They also manufactured combat footwear for the Soviet Union.

After World War II and the subsequent population exodus to the suburbs, Kinney was quick to recognize and exploit the trend. It opened its first suburban store in Alexandria, Virginia, in 1947. Within five years the company had also opened five large stores in urban "strip centers"—rows of stores with big parking lots along main roads near new housing developments. In 1954 Kinney opened its first freestanding roadside store, in Berlin, Connecticut. These suburban stores had complete inventories of 1,000 styles in about 6,000 square feet of space, dwarfing the traditional downtown stores. In 1954 Kinney also entered the West Coast market for the first time. In October 1957 the company opened seven stores in one day in the Los Angeles area.

Kinney sold nearly 8.3 million, and produced nearly 3 million, pairs of shoes in 1955. It had 352 stores that year, net sales of $51.7 million, and net income of $1.7 million. All these figures were records. The price of its stock rose as high as $69 a share, compared to an average of $18 in 1951. Nevertheless, Kinney lacked the financial resources to expand further, and several large stockholders wanted to sell. In 1956 the company was purchased by Brown Shoe Co. of St. Louis, then the nation's fourth-largest shoe manufacturer and third-largest retailer. (Kinney was then the nation's eighth-largest retailer.) Brown produced several nationally advertised brands, such as Buster Brown, and supplied the Regal shoe stores.

The deal ran into opposition from the U.S. Department of Justice, which maintained that it would violate federal antitrust laws by giving Brown excessive market power. Brown spent millions of dollars fighting a federal lawsuit but eventually lost its case in the courts in 1962. In 1963 Kinney was sold by Brown to the F. W. Woolworth Co. for $45 million in cash and promissory notes.

During its years under Brown, however, Kinney continued to increase its number of stores and volume of sales, plowing its profits back into the operation. Outmoded manufacturing plants were replaced by new one-story, air-conditioned factories on the Brown model. In fiscal 1962 Kinney earned about $2.5 million on sales of just under $100 million and operated 570 stores.

Kinney was Woolworth's first acquisition since the variety store chain's formation in 1912. Renamed the Kinney Shoe Corp., it retained its own management and control over its finances. The company began to move upscale in 1964 with "Flings," a new in-house brand for young women. Soon it was opening 60 to 70 shoe stores a year. It also opened its first leased shoe departments in 1964, in Woolworth's Woolco discount stores. Within three years, the new Stylco division operated 100 leased departments. It also began to operate leased shoe departments in other discount stores.

In 1965 Kinney moved its retail operations into Canada, first in six Woolco stores and then in two shopping centers. In 1967 the company achieved its 24th consecutive year of record sales, opening 90 new retail units. A new factory for boys' shoes was opened that year in Romney, West Virginia, and a large new distribution center in Mechanicsburg, Pennsylvania. Kinney Shoes of Canada acquired its second factory. In 1969 it purchased two more Canadian shoe factories and the Montreal-based chain of H. Lewis and Sons. By the end of 1968 Kinney had 716 stores and 157 leased departments. That year it acquired two women's lingerie companies, which it held only briefly, and started a necktie manufacturing operation, which it sold in 1975. It also bought "Williams the Shoeman," Australia's oldest shoe chain.

By 1974 Kinney sales had reached $358 million a year. More than 90 percent of its retail sales came from suburban stores, compared to 100 percent from downtown locations 25 years earlier. Between 1971 and 1973, 136 U.S. regional shopping centers opened, and Kinney had retail units in 134 of these. On assuming the company's presidency in 1974, Richard L. Anderson announced his aim to have a unit in every major shopping center, with freestanding stores only to be built in areas with no shopping centers. He also vowed to build a new factory every two years, and to keep them filled throughout the year. In 1974 Kinney had 940 stores and was manufacturing 40,000 pairs of shoes daily in 11 domestic plants.

Also in 1974, Kinney opened its Foot Locker sports specialty division to retail branded athletic footwear and accessories, none of it under the Kinney label. Another new division was created for Susie's Casuals, a group founded in 1968 that comprised 85 women's boutiques in major mall locations. Kinney's sales reached $495 million for the fiscal year ended January 31, 1975. In 1976 it operated 1,449 stores and 291 leased departments in other stores.

Kinney dubbed itself "The Great American Shoe Store" in the 1970s, promoting itself through network television commercials featuring country-and-western singer Ken Berry. The company mounted an enormously successful publicity campaign around the Bicentennial in 1976, and sponsored Walking Tours of America and Great American Running Trails. In 1979 it launched the Kinney Cross Country Championships, the first national competition for high-school runners.

The first Foot Locker opened in 1974 near Los Angeles, with shoes for running, hiking, track and field, basketball, bowling, golf, roller skating, and ice skating. Within five years, some 70 Foot Locker stores were racking up a total of $20 million in sales. Meanwhile, Kinney's 14 manufacturing plants reached peak production of 53,000 pairs of shoes a day in 1978. The company's growth in this period was phenomenal, lifting it to fourth place among shoe companies in the United States. It passed the $1 billion mark in annual sales in 1980 and operated 2,115 stores that year, not counting 368 leased departments.

However, these figures obscured a pattern of shrinking sales growth and profit margins that began in 1979 and continued in the early 1980s. Kinney's operating profit margin rose steadily from 1976 to a peak of 12.9 percent in 1978, then declined to 10.6 percent in 1979 and 9.3 percent in 1980, when the company had operating income of $96 million. Sales per square foot in Kinney stores dropped 5.7 percent in 1980. Soon after, an increasingly troubled Woolworth for the first time began to draw on Kinney's profits to help pay its dividends. When Woolworth closed its Woolco operations in the United States in 1982, taking a $600 million loss, Kinney's Stylco division was also closed.

Kinney's best performer in this period was Foot Locker, which in mid-1982 was operating 316 units in the United States and Canada. By the following year, when Foot Locker had 522 stores, athletic footwear accounted for half of the company's sales. The first U.S. Lady Foot Locker store opened in 1982, selling women's athletic footwear, apparel, and accessories. Also in that year, Kinney recruited Fredelle, a Canadian boutique, to sell branded, high-fashion women's shoes in the United States. Kids Foot Locker was launched in 1986, and Athletic Shoe Factory (later Athletic X-Press) was acquired in 1984 to combat discounters. When running began to fall out of fashion in the mid-1980s, Foot Locker highlighted basketball, developing the "Foot Locker Slam Fest." And during 1987 and 1988 Kinney merged two sporting-goods chains it had acquired to create Champ Sports mall stores, offering apparel and footwear as well as athletic hardware and accessories.

Other Kinney segments were not doing as well. Its shoe stores, concentrating on leather shoes in the $25 to $40 range, had been criticized for lack of fashion direction and were not expanding rapidly in number. And a flood of imports, plus the rising popularity of athletic footwear, had taken its toll on Kinney's shoe-manufacturing operations. In 1989 only five shoe factories remained, all in Pennsylvania. By 1994, there were only three, turning out about 13,000 pairs a day. The rest of Kinney's shoe supply was coming from Asia.

By late 1991, the number of Kinney shoe stores was down to 1,312, with its sales for the year expected to be down three percent, to $688 million. Foot Locker, by contrast, had expanded to 1,352 stores in the United States and sales of $1.5 billion. Champs' sales had grown from $18 million in 1987 to an estimated $397 million in 1991. In 1992 some 300 underperforming Kinney shoe stores were dropped, and in 1993 another 300 were closed. Some of them were to be converted to specialty formats.

In 1994 Kinney was the largest of Woolworth's divisions, contributing $3.5 billion in sales and providing 60 percent of the parent company's profits. It was operating more than 4,500 stores. Foot Locker, with more than 1,700, had moved into Europe, Mexico, and Australia, with plans to expand into Asia, and was located in virtually every U.S. mall.

In February 1995 Woolworth split Kinney into two separate divisions. The Athletic Footwear and Apparel Division was given operation of more than 4,100 stores worldwide, including the Foot Locker group (which included Athletic X-Press) and Champs Sports stores. Kinney Shoe Corp. president and chief executive William DeVries was appointed to hold the same posts in this division. The Specialty Footwear Division was given operation of Kinney's manufacturing facilities and 655 stores in the United States under the names Kinney, Footquarters, Colorado (an outdoor-apparel chain), and Basics.

Principal Subsidiaries: Armel, Inc.; Janess Properties, Inc.; Kinney Service Corp.; Kinney Trading Corp.; Menlo Trading Co.; Robby's Sporting Goods, Inc.; Simpson's Ferry Leasing Corp.

Further Reading:

Follett, Dorothy, "Kinney May Turn Corner after Sluggish Growth," *Footwear News,* January 11, 1982, pp. 1, 8.
"F. W. Woolworth Plans to Acquire Brown Shoe Unit," *Wall Street Journal,* July 2, 1963, p. 26.
Gloede, Bill, "Retail Agency Believes Ads Should Convey Image," *Editor & Publisher,* September 20, 1980, pp. 18, 20.
Jaslow, Nancy, "Kinney Aim: Every Mall," *Footwear News,* September 23, 1974, pp. 1, 9.
McDermott, Kathleen, *Retail Revolutionary: Kinney Shoe Corporation's First Century in Footwear,* Cambridge, Massachusetts: The Winthrop Group, 1994.
Santora, Joyce E., "Kinney Shoe Steps into Diversity," *Personnel Journal,* September 1991, pp. 72, 74–77.
Wilner, Rich, "300 Kinney Stores Will Be Closed," *Footwear News,* October 18, 1993, pp. 2, 32.
"Woolworth Divides Kinney Shoe Unit, Names 2 New Chiefs," *Wall Street Journal,* February 16, 1995, p. B4.
Zinn, Laura, "Why 'Business Stinks' at Woolworth," *Business Week,* November 25, 1991, pp. 72, 76.

—Robert Halasz

KITCHELL

Kitchell Corporation

1707 E. Highland Avenue
Phoenix, Arizona 85016
U.S.A.
(602) 264-4411
Fax: (602) 631-9112

Private Company
Incorporated: 1950
Employees: 558
Revenues: $170 million
SICs: 1542 General Contractors—Nonresidential Buildings;
    1541 General Contractors Industrial Buildings

Kitchell Corporation is one of the most prominent construction companies operating in the western part of the United States. Among the ten largest private firms in Arizona, and one of the top 75 construction companies within the United States, Kitchell has tackled construction projects from Delaware to California. With most of its operations located in two states, Arizona and California, the company has carved out a number of highly profitable niche markets, including the construction of corrections facilities, retail stores and malls, advanced technology facilities, schools, and hospitals. Some of Kitchell's most high-profile projects are located in California, such as Scripps Memorial Hospital in La Jolla, and the Santa Barbara Research Center for Hughes Aircraft Company.

The founder of Kitchell Corporation, Sam Kitchell, was born in 1923 in Hingham, Massachusetts. Educated at Amherst College, Kitchell served in the U.S Navy during World War II as the commander of an anti-submarine boat. Soon after the war ended, he was hired by Anchorage Homes, a company that manufactured prefabricated houses. After two years the company went bankrupt and Kitchell was out of a job. When his wife had their third child, Kitchell decided that he needed a more stable position within the construction industry. After hearing that there was a construction boom in the southwestern part of the United States, he packed up his wife and children and traveled to Phoenix, Arizona.

At first, Kitchell worked for a local architectural firm as a supervisor of construction projects. He also worked for a building contractor for a time as an estimator before meeting a Phoenix businessman, James B. Phillips, who had sold a business and was looking for a new investment. Kitchell convinced

Phillips that the construction industry was a good place to invest, and the businessman provided $10,000 to begin a new construction company. The two partners incorporated Kitchell-Phillips Contractors, Inc. in January 1950.

For three months, no one in the company drew any salary. Kitchell worked as the firm's estimator and his wife served as the company's secretary. By the end of year, however, Kitchell and Phillips had negotiated contracts to build a number of Safeway retail stores and a few schools near the city of Phoenix. These negotiations resulted in sales amounting to $800,000. The two men were also aided by the onset of the Korean War. Kitchell-Phillips Contractors secured projects for the American military at Luke Air Force Base and the Yuma Army Test Station. The most important of these wartime contracts was the rehabilitation and improvement of the Tank Training Command. Located at Camp Irwin in the Mojave Desert in California, the size of the contract doubled to nearly $2 million by the end of 1952.

The 1950s were boom years for Kitchell Corporation. During this time, Kitchell instituted its first profit-sharing plan for employees. In 1953 the company entered the real estate development business by forming a partnership with Utah Construction and Mining Company. The partnership was formed specifically to develop and lease an office building in Phoenix for Mountain States Telephone and Telegraph Company. Kitchell pioneered the highly innovative lift-slab method of construction on this building. According to this methodology, all the concrete floor slabs would be poured in the basement, then lifted up to their final height and welded to steel columns. Another office building for Mountain States was constructed in Albuquerque, New Mexico, not long after the one in Phoenix had been tackled.

In 1955 the company started its involvement in retail development by building a shopping center, Park Central Mall, on what was then the northern edge of Phoenix's city limits. A year later Kitchell constructed the Motorola Research Laboratory, a highly sophisticated research facility that was the first building equipped with concrete tilt-slab walls in the state of Arizona. At approximately the same time, Kitchell started its first health care project, an expansion of Good Samaritan Hospital. Based in Phoenix, the Good Samaritan Group was so impressed with the results of the addition to the hospital that it contracted Kitchell to work on 12 more health care-related projects.

In 1957 Kitchell Corporation was contracted by Harry Lenart, a broker who made a fortune on Wall Street, to construct a small office building on the corner of Scottsdale and Camelback roads in the sleepy town of Scottsdale, Arizona. On an empty field that had been used by the local Jaycee club for years as a rodeo ground, Kitchell not only constructed the building for Lenart, but also constructed a grocery store and a Goldwaters department store (founded by Barry Goldwater). Later, Kitchell would build numerous other office buildings, retail stores, and parking facilities for Lenart. By the end of the 1950s, Kitchell Corporation had achieved a volume in construction activities that approximated a total of $6 million. With more contracts arriving all the time, and prospects for the construction industry in the 1960s looking even brighter than the 1950s, Kitchell Corporation purchased its own office complex near Sky Harbor Airport, just outside of Phoenix.

The 1960s began on a positive note for the company. Morgan Guaranty Trust Company of New York became interested in Kitchell's promising future and invested one million dollars in stock and convertible debentures. Morgan's assumption was that Kitchell's quick growth and future prospects would ultimately lead to a stock offering when the company went public. Thus a new holding company was formed, and the contracting operation became its wholly-owned subsidiary. Sam Kitchell then bought out his partner Jim Phillips and renamed the firm Kitchell Corporation. Along with all of these organizational changes, the company continued to look for additional development projects. One of the most important developments during this time included an agreement to become a regional franchisee of Rodeway Inns, a Phoenix-based motel chain. Kitchell soon became known as a developer of motels throughout Arizona, California, west Texas, and New Mexico.

By the mid-1960s, however, Kitchell was struggling. Two of the company's largest and most important contracting projects, the 91st Avenue Sewage Treatment Plant and the Maricopa County Complex, both located in Phoenix, were plagued by cost overruns and mismanagement. A strike by local construction workers that lasted nearly three months, coupled with a glut on the real estate market caused by overbuilding, only exacerbated Kitchell's financial worries. This progression of events forced the company to sell all its previously acquired assets in the Mountain States Telephone and Telegraph Company building, along with all its holdings in Rodeway Inns.

To improve the company's financial picture, Sam Kitchell implemented a reorganization of the company that included promoting many employees from within and hiring new talent from outside the firm. A strategy emphasizing project controls, accountability systems, and development programs for personnel was put into place with great effect. One of the significant changes to company operations involved the notion of hiring a contractor as a construction manager, a step that the company felt would help it meet project budgetary and schedule factors. Immediately the company began to return to profitable and sustained growth. By the late 1960s, Kitchell Corporation was once again involved in creating a new subsidiary to develop and manage hotels. Called Doubletree Inns, the company's new venture developed, constructed, and managed new hotels in the states of Arizona, California, and Washington.

By 1969, Kitchell Corporation had reversed its fortunes. The company reported new construction projects amounting to approximately $20 million, and was listed in the *Engineering News Record* as one of the 400 leading contracting firms in the United States.

During the early 1970s, Sam Kitchell repurchased the stock and debentures held by Morgan Guaranty. At the same time, the company acquired Arizona Refrigeration Supplies, an air conditioning and refrigeration business, for $400,000. Kitchell, who fell ill and required a triple coronary bypass in 1975, then offered the managing team of Arizona Refrigeration the option to buy a controlling interest in the company that had acquired it earlier. When Arizona Refrigeration concluded the purchase,

and after Kitchell Corporation had reacquired the remaining shares of stock owned by outside investors, employees became the sole owners of Kitchell Corporation.

Kitchell's construction management system was hugely successful, and led to numerous projects in the mid- and late 1970s. New high-technology clients such as Armour-Dial Laboratory, Honeywell, and Digital Equipment were added to the company's growing list of customers. Twelve of the largest hospital projects built in Phoenix during this time were contracted by Kitchell, as well as eight of the largest regional shopping centers in Arizona. Under the auspices of a newly formed contract consulting company, Kitchell CEM (Capital Expenditure Managers), the firm supervised the construction of fifteen school sites within the Amphitheatre School District in Tucson, Arizona.

In 1977 a division office of Kitchell Contractors was opened in Orange County, California, and one year later a real estate subsidiary, Kitchell Development Company, was created in order to implement a more comprehensive approach to the company's real estate development opportunities. By the end of 1978, company sales surpassed the $60 million mark. A year later, Kitchell Corporation reported that new construction work amounted to $145 million and that the company was listed as the 110th largest contracting firm in America. Also in 1979, Kitchell sold its controlling interest in Doubletree Inns, which boasted 2,300 hotel/motel rooms at the time.

During the 1980s, Kitchell Corporation developed a five-year strategic expansion plan. This plan included establishing a presence in the states of Washington and Texas. Initially, the company's Texas office achieved some notable success, but the foreclosure on an office building in downtown Dallas that Kitchell was constructing portended future difficulties. By 1984 the Texas office was closed and the company turned its attention to developing its operations in Arizona and California. Over the years, the California office had grown so large that management thought it wise to create two separate corporations, one in Arizona and one in California.

In 1980 Kitchell CEM won the first contract in over 20 years to build a correctional facility in Arizona. Kitchell's management performed so well during this project that Kitchell was asked to enter into a joint venture with a correctional planner from California to manage the state's prison expansion program. In 1984 Kitchell assumed control of the entire project. It methodically reduced the cost of correctional facility construction and the per-bed cost for the state of California. With U.S. federal courts requiring states to expand their prison facilities, the demand for Kitchell CEM's services grew proportionally. Soon the company was providing specialized services and systems, such as site studies, design review, and cost and schedule control measures, to help other state governments build and manage correctional facilities.

During the mid-1980s Kitchell Corporation was involved in highly prestigious construction projects such as Scripps Memorial Hospital in La Jolla, California, and the Mayo Clinic in Scottsdale, Arizona. The company was also involved in building numerous high-technology facilities for companies such as Burroughs, Hughes Aircraft Company, Motorola, and International Rectifier. Most of these high-tech projects were located in the state of California. The company was also contracted to remodel many of the retail malls that it had built during its earlier years, and in the late 1980s it renovated a well-known retail center in Salt Lake City, Utah, named Trolley Square. In 1988 and 1989, Kitchell Development Company expanded into the rapidly growing market for office and industrial parks. By the end of the decade, the company had ascended to become one of the 50 leading construction management firms in the United States.

Despite the onset of a real estate recession, the early 1990s were the most profitable ever for Kitchell Corporation. In 1990 Kitchell Contractors-Arizona built and managed a wide range of projects, including a renovation of a 1.5-million-square-foot shopping mall in Portland, Oregon, and the shops at Arizona Center for the Rouse Company in downtown Phoenix. Kitchell Contractors built the AMI Irvine Medical Center, the TRW Military Electronics Plant, and a high-tech facility for Western Digital Company in California. These contracts resulted in the company's most successful year of business in the state of California. Arizona Refrigeration Supplies, although it started out slowly, garnered over $35 million in sales by 1991, and its stores were spread across Arizona, Texas, California, Virginia, and New Mexico.

In 1993, Kitchell formed a strategic alliance with Hochtief AG, the world's 14th largest contractor. Headquartered in Essen, Germany, Hochtief garnered a 35 percent minority interest in Kitchell, while the remainder of stock continued to be held by employees.

The following year, Kitchell CEM won its 12th consecutive contract from the California Department of Corrections. This success led to new correctional facilities contracts in Idaho, Indiana, Iowa, Delaware, and Washington, as well as a host of projects with both city and county governments. Also in 1994, Kitchell opened a regional office in Las Vegas and a develop- ment office in California. It expanded its retail development projects to several other western states as well.

By 1995 Kitchell had consolidated its contracting operations in Phoenix rather than continuing a separate, full-service office in southern California. The company had a total of 558 employees, almost all of whom owned part of the company through an innovative profit sharing/stock option program. Regarded as well managed, Kitchell has been able to create certain market segments for itself within the construction industry. As long as management continued to provide such highly specialized construction management services for complex projects, its continuing success seemed assured.

Principal Subsidiaries: Kitchell Contractors Arizona; Kitchell Contractors-California; Kitchell Development Company; Arizona Refrigeration Supplies; Kitchell CEM.

Further Reading:

"A Coin Toss Determined The Winner," *Building Design and Construction,* May 1994, p. 8.

"Crime Bill Garners $7.9 Billion For Prison Construction," *Building Design and Construction,* November 1994, p. 14.

"Crime Bills Propose $4.2 Billion Minimum For Prisons," *Building Design and Construction,* July 1994, p. 12.

Ichniowski, Tom, "Tougher Times In Prisons," *Engineering News Record,* June 15, 1992, pp. 28–32.

"Jails Bursting At The Seams," *Engineering News Record,* June 13, 1994, p. 23.

Kitchell, Sam, *Kitchell Corporation: Building People, Building Success,* Newcomen Society: New York, 1991.

Olsen, Christopher, "Schools, Prisons Propel Public Building Construction," *Building Design and Construction,* January 1994, pp. 34–35.

Rosenbaum, David, B., "Plum Job Awarded Soon," *Engineering News Record,* April 10, 1995, pp. 18–19.

—Thomas Derdak

Knoll

Knoll Group Inc.

Water Street
East Greenville, Pennsylvania 18041
U.S.A.
(215) 679-7991
Fax: (215) 679-3904

Wholly Owned Subsidiary of Westinghouse Electric Corp.
Founded: 1938 as Knoll Furniture
Employees: 4,000
Sales: $576 million
SICs: 2269 Finishing Plants Not Elsewhere Classified; 2521
  Wood Office Furniture; 2522 Office Furniture Except
  Wood; 2541 Wood Partitions and Fixtures

Knoll Group Inc. is a leading U.S. manufacturer of office
furniture. Its products include chairs, wood casegoods, files and
storage mechanisms, and full office systems. Knoll also produces textiles on contract and markets computer support accessories. The company was selling its products through showrooms, sales offices, and dealerships in about 500 U.S.
locations. It also sells through independent dealers in Europe,
the Pacific Rim, and Latin America.

Knoll was founded in 1938 by Hans Knoll. Knoll, the son of a
German furniture maker, was living in New York at the time.
Hans, like his father, was a craftsman, but he believed that new
woodworking and manufacturing technology being introduced
at the time could be integrated with his skills. His primary goal
was to produce furniture that was elegant and functional but
also affordable. That design philosophy would be hugely successful for Knoll and would guide the company not only
through the 1940s but even into the 1990s. Knoll found a
willing local market for his furniture designs during the late
1930s and early 1940s.

Knoll's design philosophy was heavily influenced by the famous Bauhaus school of design that was becoming dominant at
the time. The Bauhaus was founded in 1919 by architectural
renegade Walter Gropius, who merged an art academy and an
arts-and-crafts school. He based the school on the canon that no
distinction should be made between fine arts and practical
crafts, including furniture. Furthermore, the school held that
modern art and architecture must be responsive to the aesthetic
and engineering needs of the industrial world. The Bauhaus
style, or ''International Style,'' adopted by Knoll and other

progressive designers was distinguished by minimal ornamen-
tation and an emphasis on simplistic beauty. Famed architect
Ludwig Mies van der Rohe was running the school shortly
before it was shut down by the Nazis in 1933. By that time,
however, its principles were being adopted worldwide. In fact,
many of the school's faculty immigrated to the United States
where they influenced designers such as Knoll.

In 1946 Knoll married designer Florence Schust. Schust had
been trained as an architect and would ultimately be recognized
as one of the most influential women in twentieth-century
design. The two formed Knoll Associates to help customers
realize the value of design in the modern office. Their major
breakthrough came shortly after they were married when they
were hired to design the Rockefeller family offices in Rockefeller Plaza. The job was heralded as a benchmark for office
designs of the day, and it became a springboard for Hans and
Florence into other high-profile office design jobs.

During the 1940s and 1950s Florence Knoll worked closely
with clients to design their spaces. Importantly, she pioneered
the concept of developing a relationship with the client and
designing to meet their needs. She began each project with a
series of intensive interviews of executives and support staff to
discover exactly what they needed. She would then use that
information to design spaces and to help Hans design the furniture. Although that type of partnering relationship became commonplace in the design field during the middle and late 1900s, it
was considered revolutionary at the time.

Hans Knoll remained focused on the manufacturing end of the
business. In 1945 he moved the company's production facilities
from New York to an old mill in East Greenville, Pennsylvania,
which is in the Upper Perkiomen Valley. That region provided a
skilled and dedicated labor force for Knoll's furniture operations for several years. Indeed, during the 1950s and 1960s
Knoll became known for its innovative designs and high-quality
office furniture. Besides its good reputation, Knoll benefited
from spiraling office furniture markets during the post-World
War II economic and population boom.

Throughout the 1950s, 1960s, and much of the 1970s, corporate
America built and furnished billions of square feet of office
space throughout the country. To exploit that surging demand,
Knoll expanded throughout most of the country with sales
offices, showrooms, and dealerships that emphasized contract
sales. Knoll's furniture designs evolved to keep up with a
changing office marketplace during that period, but innovation,
thoughtful design, and affordability remained its cornerstone
creed. Well-known designers that worked for Knoll included
Vico Magistretti, Kazhuhide Takahama, Warren Platner, and
Tobia Scarpa. In recognition of Knoll's contribution to modern
design, the world-renowned Louvre's Musée des Arts Deco-
ratifs in Paris staged a 1972 exhibit devoted solely to the
company's furniture.

Importantly, Knoll introduced its first open-office furniture system in 1973. The Stephens System, designed by Bill Stephens,
capitalized on the dominant trend during the 1970s and 1980s
toward open offices, as opposed to walled-in spaces. Despite
increases in open-office products, the overall office furniture
industry stumbled during the commercial construction drought

of the late 1970s and early 1980s. Although the market would recover, the downturn marked an end to the booming traditional office furniture markets of the mid-1900s when many corporations spared little expense in furnishing their offices. The office furniture industry bottomed out in the early 1980s. During that time, Knoll, still privately held, was bought out by floor-covering manufacturer General Felt Industries Inc. General Felt took Knoll public in 1983 (as Knoll International) in a stock offering that raised about $56 million. Unfortunately, Knoll languished under General Felt's control.

Knoll's problems during the 1980s were partially caused by evolving and volatile office-furniture markets. However, they were also the result of decisions made at General Felt, which was headed by Marshall Cogan and Stephen Swid. Cogan worked at CBS and investment firm Orvis & Co. before taking a job as an auto analyst in 1964 at Carter, Berlind & Weill. Interestingly, that entrepreneurial investment company flourished under the direction of talents like Rober Berlind (the successful Broadway producer) and Arthur Levitt, who became president of the American Stock Exchange. The company became the nucleus of Shearson, Leob Rhoades, which was sold in 1981 to American Express for $900 million. Cogan profited handsomely as an executive at the company, but was pushed out shortly after the American Express buyout.

Cogan teamed up with money manager Stephen Swid in 1982 to purchase the money-losing General Felt, a carpet underlay business. They quickly returned the company to profitability. A few years later they purchased Knoll with the intent of improving it as they had General Felt. Cogan and Swid, through General Felt, also purchased ''21,'' a high-profile New York restaurant. The partners' strategy seemed sound at first, but the hard-charging Cogan gradually got carried away. He tried to take over the Boston Red Sox, the prestigious Sotheby's auction house, and the respected Wall Street investment firm of L.F. Rothschild Unterberg Towbin. After those defeats, General Felt succeeded in buying steering wheel and dashboard manufacturer Sheller-Globe.

Knoll posted profits during its first few years under General Felt's wing, but the venerable furniture maker eventually got lost in the shuffle. Knoll retained its status as one of the largest contract office furniture manufacturers in the nation, but its profits began to slide in 1986. By that time, General Felt had amassed a mountain of debt and all of its companies were struggling. Knoll had supplied about 80 percent of the cash flow generated by General Felt's three holdings in 1985, but by 1986 Knoll was losing money. Swid wanted to settle down and focus on improving existing operations while Cogan was eager to do more deals. The two had a falling out and Cogan kicked out Swid. To make matters worse, Cogan infuriated investors late in 1986 when he offered to buy back shares of Knoll for $12 each—He had sold them in 1983 for $16. GFI finally did spend about $38 million to take Knoll private in 1986.

Despite Cogan's blunders, Knoll claimed some gains during the mid-1980s. In 1986, for example, the company tapped the cash from the public offering to pay for a $20-million expansion of the East Greenville manufacturing plant. In addition, Knoll introduced its successful KnollStudio collection in 1985. That line, which was designed for executive offices and residences,

integrated classic icons of modern furniture by renowned designers like Mies van der Rohe, Marcel Breuer, Harry Bertoia, and Eero Saarinen. New product introductions and increased production capacity allowed Knoll to take advantage of surging office furniture markets during the late 1980s. The industry became increasingly consolidated and competitive during that period, however, and the company was ill-prepared to deal with the inevitable slowdown.

The office furniture market finally did crash beginning in the late 1980s and during the early 1990s. New office construction levels plummeted throughout the nation. At the same time, cost-conscious companies began looking for ways to reduce costs, including those related to furnishings. With sales dropping, General Felt began looking for a buyer for Knoll. In 1990 Westinghouse purchased Knoll International for an undisclosed amount of cash, $112 million worth of stock, and assumption of the company's $111 million of debt. Shortly before buying Knoll, Westinghouse had bought out furniture makers Shaw-Walker and Reff Inc. in deals worth a combined total of about $250 million. In 1990, Westinghouse combined Knoll, Shaw-Walker, Reff, and Westinghouse Furniture Systems into a single subsidiary called Knoll Group Inc. The consolidation boosted Knoll's status from fourth to third largest contract office furniture manufacturer in the United States (behind Steelcase and Herman Miller).

Given the industry downturn, the operations of Knoll Group were bloated. To whip the new company into shape and to combat proliferating competition, Westinghouse initiated a reorganization of all of Knoll's operations. The effort was designed to cut costs, improve efficiency, and conform to evolving market demands for cost-efficient office systems. Knoll Group, under the direction of Chief Executive Maurice C. Sardi, immediately began laying off workers and shifting production. Two Pennsylvania manufacturing facilities were shuttered and about 20 percent of Knoll's work force was eliminated between 1991 and 1993. That brought the total number of employees to about 4,200, roughly 1,200 of whom worked at the East Greenville facility. At the same time, the company invested an average of about $30 million annually to update plants and product lines.

Lagging furniture markets in effect canceled Westinghouse's efforts to streamline its furniture operations. Sales increased to $673 million in 1991, but the company still posted a disappointing net loss in 1991 of more than $1 million. Deep industry discounting and stagnant markets contributed to a much greater loss in 1992 of about $15 million on diminished sales of $576 million. Frustrated and seeking a narrower definition of its own operations, parent company Westinghouse decided early in 1993 to sell off Knoll Group. However, Westinghouse had trouble finding a willing buyer and by late 1993 was still trying to dump the division. Sardi took early retirement late in 1993 and was replaced by 51-year-old Burton B. Staniar.

Under Staniar's leadership, Knoll continued to pursue two goals reflective of the new office furniture environment: developing products aimed at the value segment of the market and intensifying effort to reach the small business and individual consumer. To that end, Knoll revamped its offerings during the early 1990s and converted its contract showrooms into more visible, consumer-oriented sales centers. Knoll introduced a new line of stand-alone furniture for the home-office crowd with desks retailing for less than $1,000. It also introduced several new products geared for ergonomically conscious buyers and for disabled users. It also beefed up offerings in its core office environments furniture lines with, for example, more convenient and comfortable desks and storage units.

Knoll continued to lose money in 1994, although its losses were considerably less than those suffered in 1993. Westinghouse was also on the rebound and had even decided, early in 1994, not to sell Knoll Group. Significant new products being marketed in 1994 and 1995 included the Gehry Collection, which was composed of bentwood tables and chairs, and the propeller Table, a line of innovative conference and training tables designed with modern electronic technology in mind. In mid-1995 Knoll Group was employing about 4,000 people worldwide and supporting approximately 500 locations. Knoll's main goal, as it had been since Hans Knoll founded the company in 1938, was to be a leader in the production and sale of innovative, functional, affordable office furnishings.

Principal Subsidiaries: Knoll Group North America.

Further Reading:

Blake, Laura, "Knoll Dialing in Consumer Market," *Grand Rapids Business Journal,* May 24, 1993, p. 1.

——, "Staniar Cites Knoll Group's Improvement," *Grand Rapids Business Journal,* November 7, 1994, p. 1.

Dearning, Sean, "Knoll Group on the Selling Block," *Wood & Wood Products,* February 1993, p. 44.

Harrison, Kimberly P., "New Player Rolls into Local Office Furniture Market," *Crains Cleveland Business,* March 13, 1995, p. 4.

The Knoll Group: History, East Greenville, Penn.: The Knoll Group, Inc., 1995.

Luymes, Robin, "Furniture Firms Fight Big Slide," *Grand Rapids Business Journal,* December 30, 1991, Section 1, p. 2.

Shope, Dan, "Westinghouse Plans to Touch Up Knoll Before Selling the Company," *Allentown Morning Call,* October 24, 1993, Section BUS.

Slutsker, Gary, "The Sour Smell of Success," *Forbes,* January 26, 1987, p. 54.

von Hassell, Agostino, "Furniture Maker Picks TPEs for Arm Rests," *Plastics World,* August 1991, p. 15.

—Dave Mote

LA-Z-BOY®

La-Z-Boy Chair Company

1284 N. Telegraph Road
Monroe, Michigan 48162-3390
U.S.A.
(313) 242-1444
Fax: (313) 241-4422

Public Company
Incorporated: 1941
Employees: 11,149
Sales: $850 million
Stock Exchanges: New York Pacific
SICs: 5712 Furniture Stores; 2521 Wood Office Furniture;
2522 Office Furniture, except Wood; 2511 Wood
Household Furniture, except Upholstered; 2541 Wood
Office and Store Fixtures, Partitions, Shelving, and
Lockers; 2512 Wood Household Furniture, Upholstered

The La-Z-Boy Chair Company is the largest independent manufacturer of upholstered furniture in the United States and third overall in the manufacture of residential furniture. The La-Z-Boy company enjoys near-universal name recognition; its name, in fact, has become synonymous with the recliner. Major subsidiaries include La-Z-Boy Canada Ltd., La-Z-Boy Contract Furniture Group, Kincaid Furniture Company, Hammery Furniture Company, and England Corsair Furniture.

La-Z-Boy originated in a love of carpentry shared by two cousins, Edward Knabusch and Edwin Shoemaker, both of Monroe, Michigan. In the early 1920s, Knabusch was a carpenter at the Weis Manufacturing Company and spent his evenings repairing furniture as well as building novelty and custom furniture in a workshop set up in the family garage. Despite the fact that Shoemaker was being groomed by his father to take over the family farm, he was far more interested in carpentry and spent his free time in his cousin's new workshop.

In 1925, Knabusch's hobby became a full-time business when he left Weis Manufacturing to start his own business. His first project was to invent a new bandsaw guide. Because of his engineering aptitude, Shoemaker was hired by Knabusch and together they completed the project. Afterward, business increased significantly, spurring Knabusch to purchase new equipment. By March 1927, the business had expanded far beyond any expectations shared by the two cousins, and they decided to form a partnership under the name Kna-Shoe Manu-

facturing Company. Meanwhile, business continued to expand and the partners soon outgrew Knabusch's family garage. By the end of 1927, with the financial support of friends and family, a new factory was completed north of Monroe. Built in the middle of a cornfield that fronted a cow path, the site led many to say the two men were foolish to establish their factory so far from the city. However, their gamble paid off as rumors of a state highway became reality soon after; the old cow path became M--24 (Telegraph Road), a major north-south Michigan artery.

As a rule, the partners preferred to develop new designs rather than copying the products of other companies. One such design was the ''Gossiper,'' which was a telephone stand with a built-in seat. Although the ''Gossiper'' was an immediate success, a large manufacturer soon copied the design and sold it more cheaply than Knabusch and Shoemaker. Other products would follow, but none were as successful as the simple wood slat porch chair that reclined to follow the body's contour, whether sitting up or leaning back—the world's first La-Z-Boy recliner. Believing they had a winner, the two men sought to market the new chair. However, when Arthur Richardson, a buyer for the Lion Store, suggested that they upholster the new chair for year-round use indoors, they changed their plans. Lacking any upholstery knowledge, the partners called upon George Welker to assist in upholstery decisions.

To protect their new invention the men incorporated in 1929 as the Floral City Furniture Company, abandoning the Kna-Shoe name because people mistook the company for a shoe manufacturer. Through friends and family, the men raised $10,000 to secure the necessary patents and began production. The men attended their first furniture show in May 1929 and returned with more orders then they could fill.

As their innovative recliner became increasingly popular, the need for a name became apparent. The partners held a public contest to name the recliner, thus finding a name and generating further interest in their product simultaneously. In November 1930, the winning name, La-Z-Boy, was trademarked, and the patent for the new mechanism was issued in January 1931. Soon thereafter, the partners licensed the right to manufacturer the chair to existing companies. Floral City manufactured the metal recliner mechanism and retained the rights to manufacturer and sell the chair in Monroe County. At the same time, Floral City Furniture returned to repairing furniture and manufacturing novelty/custom furniture.

Flourishing during the depths of the Great Depression, the men redoubled their efforts in retail sales. In 1933, the first floor of their factory was converted into a showroom. To celebrate the opening of the showroom, a circus tent was set up in front of the store to display furniture. Soon, the ''Furniture Shows'' were drawing people from Detroit and Toledo. With Knabusch's keen marketing sense, the company's flamboyant shows helped to assuage the anxiety of a people caught in the grips of a horrible depression. While other companies frantically worked for quick sales, Floral City provided entertainment in addition to their high-quality products. Knabusch and Shoemaker were able to sell their wares in ever increasing numbers, while thousands of other businesses faltered and failed. Business was so successful that in 1935 the partners opened a new showroom.

By the late 1930s, problems with the licensing agreements and increasing costs to manufacture the reclining mechanism led Shoemaker to develop a new mechanism. Completed in June 1938, the new mechanism was so different from the original that all new patents were required. The licensing agreements came to an end in 1939, and all manufacturing operations returned to Floral City Furniture.

In order to separate the manufacturing and retailing functions, the La-Z-Boy Chair Company was incorporated in May 1941. A new factory designed by Knabusch and Shoemaker was completed on October 15, 1941, but the new facility would not produce La-Z-Boys until six years later due to America's entry into World War II. While Woodall Industries produced specialized plane parts in the new building, La-Z-Boy rented out garage space to produce seats for tanks, torpedo boats, turret guns, and armored cars.

At war's end, the company reverted to civilian trade, and production of La-Z-Boy recliners began at the new building in 1947. La-Z-Boy rode their solid reputation and the Baby Boom into the 1950s. The platform rocker was introduced in 1951. The company's most unusual promotion took place late in the decade. In 1959 the company built a loveseat designed to look like a car seat. Upholstered in mink, the loveseat was fitted with lights, horns, fins, and tires. Unlike the imaginative promotions of the depression era, which combined style with substance, and marketing with manufacturing, the loveseat was all style.

By the beginning of the 1960s, the company regained the balance of innovation and promotion that had marked the company's earlier successes. La-Z-Boy began a long-lived marketing campaign that used the support of such celebrities as Bing Crosby, Ed McMahon, Johnny Carson, Joe Nameth, Alex Karras, and most importantly, Jim Backus. Known for his role as the voice of the myopic cartoon character Mr. Magoo, Backus recorded more than 15,000 television and radio commercials for La-Z-Boy during the 1960s.

A burst of product innovation accompanied this successful advertising campaign. Late in 1960, the partners introduced the Reclina-Rocker. Unlike other recliners, this one formed an unbroken line of support from head to toe and utilized independent seat back and footrest mechanisms. The partners commented that "[the] chair was like magic. It sold well from the beginning. The problem was making enough of them." Other new products included the Reclina-Way wall chair, which allowed the chair to be placed very close to wall while maintaining the ability to fully recline; the La-Z-Touch recliner, which featured a massage system to reduce muscle tension and stress; and the Reclina-Rest reclining chair. In order to keep up with increasing production and to help the company expand into the national market, La-Z-Boy opened its first factory outside of Michigan in Newton, Mississippi, in 1961.

The renewed marketing efforts, along with the introduction of the Reclina-Rocker, helped La-Z-Boy's sales increase from $1.1 million in 1960 to $52.7 million in 1970. In March 1972, the company went public, and, in the first year, 600 people bought over 320,000 shares in over-the-counter trading. The company enjoyed continued success throughout the 1970s, experiencing new sales records every year except for 1975, de-

spite the shutdown of the partners' first company, Floral City Furniture, in 1974. By the end of seventies, La-Z-Boy operated nine manufacturing plants: two in Michigan, and one each in Arkansas, California, Mississippi, Missouri, South Carolina, Tennessee, and Utah. In addition, La-Z-Boy had established licensing agreements with plants in Canada, Germany, Italy, Japan, New Zealand, Great Britain, Mexico, and South Africa. In 1979, the company purchased Deluxe Upholstering Ltd., a company that had previously manufactured La-Z-Boy products under a licensing agreement, and formed La-Z-Boy Canada Ltd. as a subsidiary.

New products and improvements to old ones contributed to the company's continued success in the 1970s. The company introduced a sleeper sofa in 1977 that represented the first major departure from La-Z-Boy's popular recliners. Applying the same high quality and mechanical savvy to the new product, the sofa featured a removable back, allowing greater portability; an innerspring mattress unique to La-Z-Boy's sleeper sofa; a counterbalancing mechanism; and a patented weight distribution mechanism. At the same time, the company improved the immensely popular Reclina-Rocker by integrating the Reclina-Way's ability to be placed very close to the wall, thus creating in the Wall Reclina-Rocker.

In 1982, the company reached a major turning point when Patrick Norton of Ethan Allen, renowned for its marketing savvy, was made senior vice-president of sales and marketing. Norton recalled that upon arriving at La-Z-Boy he found "a company with great plants, a great name, and a great product but a bit short on marketing direction." Charles Knabusch, adopted son of co-founder Edward Knabusch, assumed the position of chairman of the board in 1985 and, with Norton's help, concentrated on improvements in five major areas.

First, they actively sought to attract women. The furniture was redesigned in the mid-1980s to attract female customers, and in the early 1990s ad campaigns began to target women. In 1991, the company launched the largest ad campaign in its history without using a single television spot. Instead, the campaign concentrated on magazines, especially upscale women's titles. Jim Krusinski, director of advertising and public relations, stated that "Women are our primary target audience," and that, in choosing home furnishings, "it's common knowledge that many women tend to go to the magazines for ideas." The new campaign was in stark contrast to past "television-oriented" campaigns featuring various celebrities. Krusinski added, "We won't go back."

Second, La-Z-Boy began diversifying product lines through acquisitions and internal product development. Beginning with Burris Industries in December 1985, a maker of high-end motion chairs, La-Z-Boy went on to acquire RoseJohnson Incorporated in January 1986; Hammary Furniture, a manufacturer of residential tables and upholstery manufacturer, in September 1986; and the Kincaid Furniture Company, a producer of solid wood dining and bedroom furniture, in January 1988. In all, La-Z-Boy spent about $80 million on these acquisitions and not without criticism.

In 1989, the company became a target of a hostile takeover by its largest institutional investor, Prescott Investors, which owned 5.6 percent of the shares. Thomas Smith, Prescott's leading general partner, charged that earnings and share value had not grown at an acceptable rate and placed much of the blame on La-Z-Boy's acquisitions. However, in the end, Prescott backed off and La-Z-Boy stood by the new acquisitions. In addition to these acquisitions, La-Z-Boy created a new division, the La-Z-Boy Contract Group, composed of three entities: La-Z-Boy Business Furniture, La-Z-Boy Healthcare, and La-Z-Boy Hospitality. By 1993, these divisions and other subsidiaries amounted to 30 percent of La-Z-Boy sales.

In addition to acquisitions, new product development within the company signaled a broadening perspective. La-Z-Boy expanded into stationary and motion modular furniture and continued to support the sleeper sofas introduced in the late 1970s. In 1980, La-Z-Boy's sales of $160 million were derived almost exclusively from recliners. By 1993, recliner sales amounted to 57 percent of the company's nearly $700 million in total sales.

Third, La-Z-Boy reevaluated its retail system. In the 1970s and 1980s, independently owned La-Z-Boy Showcase Shoppes were opened across the country. In-Store Galleries within Independent General Furniture Dealers displayed La-Z-Boy furniture in separate dedicated settings. At the same time, ineffective dealers unwilling to push the product were eliminated. By the late 1980s, 42 percent of all the La-Z-Boy dealers in existence in 1980 had been eliminated. In 1989, the company reached a major turning point in its retail operations when it opened the first La-Z-Boy Furniture Gallery. These superstores facilitated the display of a much larger and more diverse selection of La-Z-Boy furniture. By 1993, the company was operating 63 La-Z-Boy Furniture Galleries and planned to transform many La-Z-Boy Showcase Shoppes into Galleries. The La-Z-Boy proprietary retail system included 750 locations, accounting for about half of La-Z-Boy's upholstered furniture sales, and thousands of independent retail outlets, regional furniture chains, and a major nationwide retailer.

Fourth, technological innovations placed La-Z-Boy at the forefront of the furniture industry. In the late 1970s, the company automated its material requirements planning process, which greatly simplified the acquisition of materials, manufacturing processes, and distribution. By the late 1980s, La-Z-Boy had introduced computer-aided design (CAD) to expedite the research and development of products, enabling the company to cut the delivery time of new products by 60 percent. Additionally, La-Z-Boy adopted an Electronic Data Interchange to facilitate the electronic transmittal and tracking of orders. As a result, retail operations were able to reduce ordering time and to track the progress of an order more accurately. As of 1993, the company had implemented the La-Z-Boy Screen Test video catalog system that allowed customers to review every style, color, and fabric offered by La-Z-Boy at the touch of a button.

Finally, La-Z-Boy set its sights on globalization. Although La-Z-Boy had licensed its chairs internationally for thirty years, international sales amounted to only one half of 1 percent of La-Z-Boy sales by the early 1990s. However, with the opening of markets in Eastern Europe and the former republics of the Soviet Union, La-Z-Boy redoubled its efforts to market its recliners in Europe. More importantly, La-Z-Boy made its most significant move towards globalization when it developed recliners designed for smaller Asian body types in 1993.

Beginning in 1987, La-Z-Boy began trading on the New York Stock Exchange, and in 1990 the company moved into the Fortune 500 at number 496, reaching number 460 by 1994. In spite of an economic downturn in furniture sales from 1989 to 1991, La-Z-Boy enjoyed continued success. La-Z-Boy sales rose ten percent to $805 million in fiscal 1994, which represented the company's twelfth straight year of record sales. La-Z-Boy continued to be the number one manufacturer of recliners with over 30 percent of the market.

Principal Subsidiaries: La-Z-Boy Canada Ltd.; Kincaid Furniture Company; Hammery Furniture Company; La-Z-Boy Contract Furniture Group; England Corsair Furniture.

Further Reading:

Bary, Andrew, "Comfy Again: After a Deep Slump, the Furniture Industry Is Bouncing Back," *Barron's,* November 8, 1993, pp. 14–15.
Cortez, John, "La-Z-Boy Cozies Up to Print," *Advertising Age,* July 22, 1991, p. 41.
"In Memory of Edward M. Knabusch 1900–1988," *La-Z-News,* March 1988.
Jannsen, Albert B., *I Remember When. . . A History of La-Z-Boy Chair Company,* n.d.
Kolebuck, Frank, "Automating to Streamline, Producing to Recline," *Manufacturing Systems,* November 1991, pp. 30–32.
Kupfer, Andrew, "Success Secrets of Tomorrow's Stars," *Fortune,* April 23, 1990, pp. 77–84.
Nulty, Peter, "What a Difference Owner-Bosses Make," *Fortune,* April 25, 1988, pp. 97–104.
Schifrin, Matthew, "Rocking the Recliners," *Forbes,* October 16, 1989, pp. 194–96.
Slat, Charles, "La-Z-Boy: Gradually Going Global," *Monroe Evening News,* December 5, 1993, pp. 1–2E.
"Sleeper Joins La-Z-Boy Line," *Monroe Evening News,* February 14, 1977, pp. 1A, 14A.

—Bradley T. Bernatek

Lance, Inc.

P.O. Box 32368
Charlotte, North Carolina 28232
U.S.A.
(704) 554-1421
Fax: (704) 554-5562

Public Company
Incorporated: 1926 as Lance Packing Company
Employees: 5,916
Sales: $461.5 million
Stock Exchanges: NASDAQ
SICs: 2052 Cookies & Crackers; 2068 Salted & Roasted
  Nuts & Seeds; 2096 Potato Chips & Similar Snacks; 2064
  Candy & Other Confectionery Products

Lance, Inc. is one of the most profitable snack food makers in the United States. Lance snacks are ubiquitous in 35 states, particularly in the Southeast, and are found in vending machines, convenience stores, and, beginning in the 1990s, supermarkets. Although most of the $27 billion industry is dominated by PepsiCo's Frito-Lay, Anheuser-Busch's Eagle Snacks, and Nabisco, Lance has shown no signs of surrendering its distinct niche. It ''scooped'' the industry in 1988 by replacing the saturated fats in its products with vegetable oils. The company achieved net sales of $487.98 million in 1994.

In 1913 Philip L. Lance and his son-in-law, Salem A. Van Every, founded the Lance Packing Company. They offered roasted peanuts to area merchants, as well as peanut butter, which they packed by hand. The business began when a customer asked Philip Lance, primarily a coffee dealer, to obtain 500 pounds of Virginia peanuts. The customer soon withdrew from the deal, but Lance was unwilling to disappoint the farmer who sold them to him. He roasted small quantities of the nuts himself on his kitchen stove and packaged them in brown paper bags which he sold for five cents a bag to passersby in downtown Charlotte.

Confident of providing a nutritious, profitable food, Lance bought a mechanical roaster and moved the business out of his home. A mill allowed him to supply merchants with both peanuts and peanut butter, which he spread on crackers for customers to sample. This led to an innovation: the first packaged peanut butter cracker sandwiches. By now the company's predilection for peanuts and for single-serving packages was well

established. A soldier stationed at a nearby World War I training base provided the recipe for Lance's next snack food: peanut brittle.

After Philip Lance's death in an auto accident in 1926, Salem Van Every assumed control of the company and incorporated it. The company grew dramatically during this period, earning its first $1 million in sales in 1935 and the first $2 million in 1939. It began baking its own crackers in 1938, a change reflecting the increased scale of operations. Salem Van Every died that same year, and his son Phil became president.

While candy came to dominate the company's product line before World War II, wartime sugar rationing swayed Lance towards baked goods, specifically peanut butter sandwiches and cookies. The company's maintenance shop also helped the war effort by making certain tools, such as a wrench for attaching warheads to bombs. Phil Van Every's successor, his son, Philip Lance Van Every, brought a new management style to the company, hiring consultants and implementing a unique administration style called multiple management. However, the company reached a rare landmark in 1944, Lance's only year to date in which annual sales volume did not increase. This was undoubtedly precipitated by the austerity of wartime; postwar fortunes would rise again as new sales districts were organized and many operations were automated. Lance achieved an annual sales volume of $14 million in 1950, and the decade ended with annual sales at Lance of $26.5 million. A new line of packaged saltine crackers for institutional use introduced in 1953 proved an enduring success.

The 1960s brought many changes. The company, which had been 80 percent owned by the Van Every family, made a large public share offering on December 7, 1961. In order to further diversify, a committee was formed to locate potential acquisitions, and Bullock Manufacturing Company in Conyers, Georgia, was acquired to produce potato chips. Although the unit posted a loss that year, it offered Lance an entrance into the chip business. A record 87,000 accounts were opened in 1962 through 96 sales headquarters. Lance operated in 23 states at this point and was prompted to move its plant to a new 231-acre site. The next year, Lance set its record for lowest cost of delivery.

The last half of the 1960s was particularly productive for Lance, as the company spent $2.5 million to expand its Charlotte plant. After Bullock Manufacturing became profitable in 1968, Lance acquired Food Processors, Inc., a Wilson, North Carolina, sweet potato plant. The next year a distribution center in Greenville, Texas, was completed to facilitate service to the southwestern sales territories. Revenues in 1969 were $57.8 million, up from $26.5 million in 1960, while earnings per share increased from $0.72 to $1.81.

Since the company's beginning, all of its individually-packaged products, including the very first roasted peanuts, had sold for five cents each. On March 6, 1970, the last of the nickel merchandise was produced, and henceforth, the snacks would sell for a dime apiece. Nevertheless, the company continued to add new sales territories, totaling 1,111 in 1970.

The following year, a new vending machine was developed capable of carrying anything in the company's line of snacks.

To meet the increase in demand, the manufacturing area of the company's plants was increased to 485,000 square feet with the addition of a 15,000 square foot candy department. Plans were drawn for a new potato chip plant and a new baking plant in 1971. Over the next two years, the company sold Food Processors, Inc., and replaced the Georgia chip plant with a new 60,000 square foot facility in Charlotte. Another 25,000 square feet of space was added for truck maintenance and shipping functions. The same year, board chairman Phil Van Every retired and was replaced by Glenn Rhodes.

The company was shaken in 1973 by high materials costs and federal price controls. Newly acquired Tri-Plas, Inc., a plastic food container manufacturer, performed poorly at first. Another major cost was the energy required by the new factory space. In 1974, federal price controls were removed and the escalation in raw materials prices slowed. The company acquired more manufacturing capabilities: a 23,600 square foot plant in Arlington, Texas, for potato chip production and Hancock's Old Fashion Country Ham of Franklinville, North Carolina. Although demand was so high that sales expansion was limited for part of the year, 75 new territories were created, down from 125 the previous year. This came in spite of a price increase of the snack line from ten cents to 15 cents, which also required retooling of the vending machines.

In the mid-1970s, concerns over energy availability prompted Lance to install propane gas storage in its plants, providing increased energy sources. In 1976, a development and exploration partnership was formed with C&K Petroleum Co., Inc. of Houston, Texas, in order to deal with the extreme shortage of natural gas that had developed by that time. The company also made efforts to conserve as much as possible. Although unprecedented pork prices hurt Hancock Ham, the Tri-Plas subsidiary continued to grow. A.F. "Pete" Sloan succeeded the retiring Glenn Rhodes as chairman of the board.

Sales territory continued to grow in the late 1970s, expanding into New England and the Great Lakes. The company bought a 44,431 square foot factory 25 miles from Charlotte for its Tri-Plas subsidiary. Although rising energy costs remained a prime concern, increasingly expensive packing materials also spawned a major conservation effort. However, sales and earnings continued to rise, perhaps reflecting a new 20 cent snack price. Lance's Charlotte plant was expanded yet again, adding high-speed wrapping machines, and the Midwest Biscuit Company of Burlington, Iowa, was purchased. The new subsidiary supplied midwestern grocery stores with crackers and cookies, mostly under private labels. Lance also created an audiovisual studio dedicated to the production of training materials in 1979, and bought a new site for its Tri-Plas west coast operations in 1980.

The 1980s proved a challenging period from the beginning. Due to a dismal domestic harvest, peanuts had to be imported for the first time. In response to the shortage, the company's packaged salted peanuts were diluted with sesame sticks, and its Peanut Bar and Redskins snacks were temporarily dropped from the product line. Even after the next year's improved harvest, government price supports kept prices high. In March 1980 the suggested retail price of Lance snack increased a nickel to 25

cents. However, the combination of all these factors resulted in net sales of $249.3 million for 1980.

The company concentrated on construction in 1981, completing or starting a vending machine repair shop, an efficient peanut roaster room, and 52,000 additional square feet of shipping space in Greenville, Texas. Lance modernized its fleet with more efficient tractors and larger (45 foot) trailers. A new convenience pack of "Captain's Wafers," salted crackers commonly found at restaurant salad bars, helped Lance break into the supermarket market. Soon the snacks were packaged in groups of eight, which became known as Home Paks, for this market, in spite of some reluctance by Pete Sloan, who believed "a supermarket sale takes away a vending machine sale." (In the 1990s, "Club Paks" containing 18 snacks would be offered through mass merchandisers.) In spite of a lackluster economy, 1982 proved successful, owing partly to the sale of Hancock's Old Fashion Country Ham to Smithfield Packing Company.

In spite of increased competition, Lance continued to prosper for the rest of the 1980s. Net annual sales increased 9.4 percent in 1984 to $337.4 million, spurred by more generous incentives. New sales districts continued to be added, and several new snacks were developed. Lance did acquire a Melbane, North Carolina, granola producer, Nutrition-Pak Corporation, but by this time the market for granola bars had peaked, and the unit was closed in 1988. However, a taste for healthier snacks remained. A launch of reformulated snacks dubbed the "Snack Right" program coincided, more or less, with Lance's 75th anniversary. Saturated fats and cholesterol were the targets of this campaign. The company even changed the way it labeled nutritional information to specify the different types of fat (saturated, polyunsaturated, etc.) that were included. Manufacturing capacity continued to be increased in the areas of peanuts and potato chips, which also began to be packaged in "family size" bags.

Like the preceding decade, the 1990s began with serious challenges which Lance met successfully. Its large number of customers provided some protection from the recession. Its social concerns were focused on recycling programs throughout its facilities and offices. After his retirement in April 1990, chairman of the board and CEO Pete Sloan was succeeded by J.W. "Bill" Disher, elected chairman and president. Technological advances during this time included the successful implementation of automated route accounting, which, with the aid of hand-held computers, enhanced the productivity of sales representatives. Regional offices were consolidated into the central accounting department, and to remain competitive, new attention was given to marketing research and Leslie Advertising of Greenville, South Carolina, was retained to develop a new marketing plan. In 1990, chocolate bars, including some Mars brand products, were successfully tested in vending machines, and Lance began producing its own. Production capacity was increased with the purchase of a Columbia, South Carolina, plant, which began operations as Vista Bakery late in 1992.

The individual serving sector of the market, Lance's home ground since the beginning, has enabled the company to keep operations simple and provided a diversified clientele, tempering economic fluctuations. Moreover, the company has managed to keep costs down, earning the loyalty of its many blue-collar consumers, in part by usually only introducing new products when similar ones have proved successful for competitors. Although the company has traditionally relied on availability, not advertising, as a main marketing tool, it rediscovered television and radio advertising in the mid-1990s to support its expansion into the supermarket. A historically debt-free company, Lance seemed well poised to prosper in the next century.

Principal Subsidiaries: Midwest Biscuit Company; Vista Bakery, Inc.

Further Reading:

Anderson, Dick, "Getting There Second," *Southpoint,* June 1989, pp. 18–20.

Bary, Andrew, "Fresh Growth in Store," *Barron's,* February 16, 1992, pp. 23–24.

Hannon, Kerry, "Why Steal Your Own Sales?" *Forbes,* May 18, 1987, pp. 208–210.

Hiestand, Michael, "Lance Inc: 'We're Not in the Junk Food Business'," *Adweek's Marketing Week,* May 9, 1988, pp. 26–30.

"The History of Lance," Charlotte, N.C.: Lance, Inc., 1992.

James, Frank E., and Alix M. Freedman, "Lance Cuts Fat From Junk Foods to Sell Snacks as Healthier Fare," *The Wall Street Journal,* March 29, 1988, p. 36.

Kimbrell, Wendy, "Southern Powerhouse," *Snack Food,* February 1994, pp. 26–41.

Lahvic, Ray, "Snack Baker Captures Impulse Sales," *Bakery,* April 1988, pp. 70–78.

"Lance, Inc," *Wright Investors' Service,* October 23, 1991, pp. 3–5.

Price, Scott, "Lance's Big Cheese," *The Business Journal,* December 5, 1988, pp. 8–9.

Rickard, Al, "Lance Labels Tell It All," *Snack World,* April 1988, pp. 39–40.

Robinson, Russ, "Snack Maker Replaces Fat, Oils with Low-Cholesterol Substitute," *Greensboro, NC News & Record,* March 12, 1988, p. 4.

Sage, Earl R., and Linda E. Swayne, "Lance, Inc.," in *Cases in Strategic Management (2):* pp. 429–445.

Smith, Doug, "Counter Attack," *Snack Food,* October 1991, pp. 38–44.

——, "Lance's Anti-Recession Recipe," *Charlotte Observer,* July 29, 1991, pp. I1–I2.

Tippett, Karen, "The Conservative Flavor of Lance," *FW,* June 26, 1990, pp. 49–51.

"To Win Hearty Market Share, Lance Gets the Lard Out," *Business North Carolina,* October 1988.

"Value Added: Baking's Key to Prosperity," *Milling & Baking News,* November 29, 1988, pp. 24–35.

Van Every, Philip Lance, *The History of Lance,* New York: The Newcomen Society in North America, 1974.

—Frederick C. Ingram

Lawter International Inc.

990 Skokie Boulevard
Northbrook, Illinois 60062
U.S.A.
(708) 498-4700
Fax: (708) 498-0066

Public Company
Incorporated: 1958
Employees: 480
Stock Exchanges: New York
Sales: $191 million in 1994
SICs: 2893 Printing Ink; 2821 Plastics Materials & Resins;
  2816 Inorganic Pigments

Lawter International Inc. manufactures and markets specialty
chemicals for the printing ink industry. Its founder, William J.
Terra, is credited with developing a printing process that revolutionized the magazine industry and made weekly publications
such as *Life* and *Time* possible. In addition to its printing ink
vehicles and slip additives (which give printing inks their ability
to carry color onto a variety of surfaces), Lawter's core products
include fluorescent pigments and coatings, thermographic compounds (used to produce raised lettering on stationery), and
synthetic and hydrocarbon resin (used for printing inks, var-
nishes, and lining beverage cans).

Lawter sells to both large and small ink manufacturers such as
BASF, Dianippon Ink and Chemicals, Coates/Lorilleux, and
Toyo. The company devotes a good portion of revenues to
research and development and operates according to a cus-
tomer-driven marketing strategy, which strives to anticipate
customer needs. Headquartered in Northbrook, Illinois, Lawter
operates 18 plants located in the United States, Canada, China,
Denmark, England, Ireland, Italy, Singapore, and Spain. The
company reported record earnings in 1994 of $29.9 million on
sales of $191 million.

The success of Lawter International can be traced to the inquisi-
tive and ambitious mind of founder William J. Terra. Terra was
the son of an Italian lithographer who had emigrated to the
United States at a young age. In 1934, Terra was a researcher
with the Columbian Carbon Corp. of Philadelphia, Pennsylvania. Always interested in printing and the chemical properties of
ink, Terra persuaded the company's chief to permit him to lead
a research team to investigate an idea he had toyed while

studying chemical engineering at Pennsylvania State University. He believed that a specific formulation of ink compounds
might speed up the process of printing and drying ink. Within a
year, Terra's team had developed an ink compound that would
allow high-speed presses to print color magazines in 24 hours—
remarkably shorter than the 25 days previously required. The
discovery was a major development for the printing industry—
in fact, it was one of the first major changes for nearly a
century—and immediately revolutionized certain segments of
the industry. The first magazine to adopt the new process was
the *Saturday Evening Post*.

In 1936, R. R. Donnelley & Sons of Chicago won an important
contract to print a new weekly photo magazine called *Life* using
Terra's ink compounds; Columbian Carbon sent Terra to Chicago to supervise the printing. The magazine was successful
and Terra was promoted to head up the company's Chicago
plant. But Terra was ambitious and wanted to set off on his own.
In 1940, he borrowed $2,500 from a friend named John Lawson
and founded Lawter Chemicals to develop and market new
technologies for the printing industry.

The company manufactured printing ink vehicles and florescents at its new plant in Skokie, Illinois. Despite Terra's success
at developing new products, the company's early years were
difficult, and when World War II erupted Terra closed shop and
served in the U.S. Navy. Upon his return in 1945, he reopened
the company, but again business was sluggish. For ten years,
Lawter grew slowly. A second plant was opened in Newark,
New Jersey in 1954, yet Terra struggled. Then in 1955 Terra
was asked to join the executive management team of a major
chemical firm. The company offered him a salary of $27,000
per year—more than four times what Terra was then making.

Terra considered closing his company and accepting the post.
But after speaking with his wife, Adeline, he decided to engage
a management consulting firm to investigate whether Lawter
had a chance of success. "I still have the report," Terra said in
the *Chicago Tribune*. "In the final analysis, it said the product
line was good, the industry was excellent and the potential was
much better than average in every way. There was really only
one thing wrong, and that was the management. They went on
and outlined what entrepreneurs did wrong, that entrepreneurs
think they're so much better at every phase of a business than
everyone else, that they make the mistake of trying to do
everything themselves."

Terra took the consultant's advice and borrowed money to hire
a top research director as well as experienced marketing, financial, and advertising executives. Sales improved under the new
management team and by 1958, Lawter's cash reserves and
equity were strong enough to purchase Krumbhaar Chemical
Inc., a well-respected manufacturer of synthetic resins. A third
plant was quickly built in San Leandro, California. In 1959, the
company purchased a raw-materials supplier and established
Lawter Chemicals (Canada) Ltd., as a wholly owned subsidiary
to produce and market printing ink vehicles in Canada. By 1960
the company had a stong enough balance sheet to make its first
public offering.

By 1961, Lawter's printing ink vehicles, resins, and florescents
were being sold to manufacturers throughout the United States

and Canada as well as in Central and South America, Europe, Australia, the Philippines, Japan, and South Africa. Sales had grown from $1.7 million in 1967 to $3.7 million in 1961; earnings grew from $57,000 to $242,000. In 1962, the company opened its fifth production plant in Ontario, Canada, and one year later it established a European subsidiary to producing synthetic resins and printing ink vehicles in Belgium.

By 1965 net sales of $7.4 million were more than double 1961 figures, and earnings had tripled to $994,000. That year, the company made its third acquisition, American Lithographic Varnish Co., a manufacturer of printing ink vehicles that provided Lawter with an expanded product line, improved distribution, and stronger research and development capabilities. Research and development continued to play a strong role in the company's growth. By 1970, 65 percent of company sales were generated by proprietary goods created in Lawter's laboratories.

Lawter acquired two more companies in the early 1970s, Virkotype Corp., a thermographic printing business, and Stresen-Reuter International, the Illinois-based ink vehicles and synthetic resin division of International Minerals and Chemical Corp. During this time, Lawter's profits were affected by raw materials shortages that raised the cost of goods produced, but by 1974 Lawter was able to institute a significant price increase that began to cover the higher materials prices. The company achieved record sales of $40 million in 1974, with earnings of $5.6 million. The following year, sales dropped by 9.8 percent to $36 million, but earnings rose to $5.7 million, fueled in part by a stabilized market for raw materials.

Lawter continued its expansion in Europe, and by 1976 it operated six subsidiary plants in Canada, Belgium, Great Britain, The Netherlands, and Germany. In 1977, the company reported record earnings for the 20th consecutive year. Sales, too, reached a record level of $47.9 million. The following year, Lawter acquired Dyall Products Inc., a producer of ink additives and related products, for an undisclosed amount of stock and other securities.

Lawter's growth was—and continues to be—fueled by a combination of careful acquisitions and aggressive new product development. The company was quick to respond to changing conditions in the printing industry, introducing in 1979 the LO-CAL line of printing inks, which were formulated to reduce the amount of energy required for drying ink. The LO-CAL inks were also noteworthy because they were not photochemically reactive and thus did not convert to smog when exposed to sunlight.

Expansion through Europe continued into the 1980s, as subsidiaries were established in Spain, Denmark, and France. Sales reached $81.5 million, with earnings of $11.9 million. However, the decade was marked by uncertainties and difficulties. In 1981, an explosion at Lawter's Bensonville, Illinois, plant injured six workmen and destroyed a wing of the plant, causing a work stoppage of ten days and more than $150,000 in damage. Although sales in Europe grew briskly, profits gains were undercut by the strength of the U.S. dollar on overseas markets and a sharp increase in the European prices of raw materials in 1984. Despite this, Lawter remained optimistic, noting that 65

to 70 percent of the demand at its new European plants were from new customers.

In 1987, Lawter surprised the investment community by putting itself on the auction block, looking for a possible sale or merger. Analysts assumed the reason was because Terra, at age 76, wanted to sell out. Indeed, Lawter's founder had accepted the post of ambassador-at-large for cultural affairs in the Ronald Reagan administration and had moved to Washington, D.C., to fulfill his duties. Terra had also grown into an avid collector of American art, and in April 1987 he oversaw the construction of the Terra Museum of Modern Art, a $35 million facility in downtown Chicago that held the family's extensive collection of 20th-century American paintings.

By February 1988 Lawter had taken itself off the auction block, allegedly because of the October 1987 stock market crash, which cut the company's share price by almost 50 percent to $11.75 per share. Company officials also predicted "excellent prospects for 1988 and beyond" and set about to prove their predictions.

In 1991, the *Chicago Tribune* declared, "Lawter has become a hot performer in the past five years, raising sales and earnings by aggressive selling of new products." Earnings nearly doubled between 1985 and 1990, to $23.4 million on sales of $150 million. New products included Ultrex, an environment-friendly line of fast-drying ink vehicles using soybean oil in place of petroleum products, and Luminex, an easy-formulating vehicle that adds gloss to inks. In 1991 the company also acquired Ampac Powders & Wax Compounds. Lawter continued to outsell its competition in 1992, launching at least 11 new products and capturing record sales of $167.6 million.

The company seemed in excellent shape as it entered 1993. Although the printing trade in the United States was in a slump (magazines and direct-mail catalogs decreased circulation after years of strong growth), Lawter had been able to weather the downturn on the strength of its overseas sales—nearly 50 percent of overall sales. The company's balance sheet was strong, with sizeable cash reserves, and Lawter began shopping for another acquisition.

In August 1993 Lawter launched a hostile bid, offering $172.5 million for Hach Co., which was based in Loveland, Colorado; Hach was a manufacturer of laboratory instruments and kits used to analyze the chemical content of water. Lawter already owned 28 percent of Hach and, as Terra told the *Chicago Tribune* that year, hoped to take control of the company in order to "expand into a new dynamic market [on] a direct basis." The deal fell through, however, when the Hach family, which held a 47 percent interest in the company, refused to cede their shares. *Crain's Chicago Business* hypothesized that the proposed merger "may well have failed over a clash of executives personalities," noting that both Terra and Hach chairman Kathryn Hach-Darrow retained firm control of the companies they founded, despite their respective ages of 83 and 72. But the reason may simply have been that Hach management did not feel comfortable with the alliance. "From a technological standpoint, there are no synergies between the two companies," Hach's chief financial officer told *Crain's*. "And I don't think there would be marketing synergies, either. The two companies make very different products.''

Revenues rose to $172.2 million in 1993, but costs rose at an even quicker pace and net income dropped a whopping 81 percent to $5 million. The sharp decline in earnings was caused by volatile European currencies and low interest rates on the company's large investment portfolio. Lawter was well prepared to weather the earnings drop, however, and by 1994 sales had increased 10.9 percent to $191 million and earnings jumped to a record $29.4 million. In addition, in June 1994 Lawter acquired Cremona Resine, S.A., an Italian manufacturer of synthetic resins, and began construction of a state-of-the-art resin manufacturing plant in Pleasant Prairie, Wisconsin.

The Pleasant Prairie plant was to produce environment-friendly, water-based acrylic resin and would double the company's output of resins in the United States while replacing outdated plants in Bensonville and Addison, Illinois. Shortly after the new plant opened, an explosion occurred in one wing of the facility, causing minor injuries to two employees and extensive damage. By 1995 the Pleasant Prairie plant was in full operation, although restart costs impaired profits for the year. In 1995 Lawter commenced construction of a plant in Antwerp, Belgium, intended to produce printing ink vehicles, synthetic resins, and specialty additives for the European market; it was scheduled to go on line in late 1996.

Lawter seems to be in a strong position as it nears its sixth decade of operation. Company President Richard D. Nordman ''continues to develop his own management strategy and style'' as Terra begins to assume a less active role in the daily operation of the business. Although fluctuations in the price of raw materials (soybeans, resin oils, linseed, rosin, and dimer) have the potential to greatly affect the company's profit margins, Lawter has for the most part avoided great losses by diversifying its market base and by taking a buyer-oriented approach to selling its products. Lawter has always been a technology-driven company that tries to anticipate customer needs. Its sales force interacts with customers on a one-to-one level, which allows the company to customize products for individual customers and to more easily pass on increases and discounts in the price of raw goods used to manufacture its products.

In the future, the company plans to grow by improving efficiency, offering new product lines, and international expansion. As for acquisitions outside its line of business, such as the failed Hach merger, ''We have an open mind,'' Nordman told *Crain's Chicago Business* in 1994. ''We are prepared to step outside of graphic arts and resins. But we will do it carefully.''

Principal Subsidiaries: Ecovar, Inc.; Virkotype Corp.; Lawter International FSC, Ltd.; Lawter International (Australasia) Pty. Ltd.; Lawter International, N.V.; Lawter International (Canada) Inc.; Lawter International, Ltd., (Tanjin), P.R.C.; Lawter International, A.p.S.; Lawter Interntional, Sarl.; Lawter International, GmbH.; Lawter International, Ltd.; Lawter International (Italia), Srl; Lawter International, B.V.; Lawter Antilles, N.V.; Lawter International Products, Pte., Ltd.; Lawter International (Proprietary), Ltd.; Lawter International, S.A.

Further Reading:

''A Look at Lawter International,'' *American Ink Maker,* June 1993, pp. 90–101.

Killian, Michael, ''The Collector Daniel Terra Loves American Art So Much, He Spent a Fortune to Build a New Chicago Museum in Its Honor,'' *Chicago Tribune,* April 19, 1987, p. F4.

''Lawter Improves Resin Production with Conveyor Pilot Plant Testing,'' *American Ink Maker,* July 1981, p. 18.

O'Connor, Matt, ''Lawter Folds Up Its For-Sale Sign,'' *Chicago Tribune,* February 18, 1988, Bus. Sec.

O'Connor, Matt, ''Lawter International Hangs Out For Sale Sign,'' *Chicago Tribune,* September 29, 1987, Bus. Sec.

—Maura Troester

Lincoln Telecommunications

Lincoln Telephone & Telegraph Company

P.O. Box 81309
Lincoln, Nebraska 68501
U.S.A.
(402) 474-2211
Fax: (402) 436-4711

Wholly Owned Subsidiary of Lincoln Telecommunications
   Company
Incorporated: 1903
Employees: 1,422
Sales: $156.3 million
SICs: 4813 Telephone Communications Except
   Radiotelephone

Lincoln Telephone & Telegraph Company is one of the largest telephone companies operating in a contiguous geographical location. The company's activities are concentrated throughout the entire state of Nebraska and reflect growing trends within the telecommunications industry, including the consolidation of resources and the development of the cellular phone service market. A subsidiary of Lincoln Telecommunications Company, Lincoln Telephone and Telegraph Company is at the forefront in the cellular technology revolution.

In 1903, Charles and Frank Bills traveled to Lincoln, Nebraska, for the specific reason of establishing a new, independent telephone company that would compete with Nebraska Bell Company. Charles, an investment banker, and Frank, a businessman, knew nothing about the burgeoning telephone industry, so they approached Frank Woods for legal advice. Woods was a member of a prominent legal firm at the time, and he began to help make the necessary arrangements for the two brothers to begin their telephone business. In March of 1903, the company was incorporated, and two months later the board of directors decided upon the name Western Union Independent Telephone Company. One year later, the company began processing calls for its customers. At the same time, the company name was changed to Lincoln Telephone Company.

In the first of many pioneering moves throughout its history, Lincoln began processing calls for its customers through the innovative but unproved Strowger Automatic Dial System. This was Nebraska's first dial installation system and one of the largest west of the Mississippi River. No one outside the company, including the managers at Bell Telephone and other independent companies, thought that the new system would work. After Lincoln proved it successful, however, a nationwide dial service was not far behind. Unfortunately, Lincoln Telephone Company seemed unable to take advantage of its success. The company's operations were in shambles: money was short, equipment was unproved or needing repair, and the company had no established procedures for maintenance or construction.

When Frank Woods assumed the position of president of the company in 1905, he immediately initiated a comprehensive reorganization plan. He revamped the accounting methods, hired personnel experienced in the telephone industry, and borrowed money to pay short-term debts. The most difficult problem facing the new company, however, was the competition for customers with Nebraska Bell Company. Bell and independent telephone companies competed intensely for customers within the same town, given the unregulated and uncoordinated nature of the industry at the time. A customer of one phone company was unable to call the customer of another phone company unless both customers subscribed to services at both telephone companies.

Lincoln Telephone Company grew rapidly during the following years, but competition among Nebraska Bell and independent phone companies reached a frenzied peak by 1910. Initially, everyone believed that competition within the telephone industry was healthy and that it would prevent a monopoly of services. But competition had grown so keen, and the strife among companies so intense, that the public was soon clamoring for government officials to regulate the industry and require the interchange of services among the many telephone companies, especially for such services as local and long distance calling and intra- and interstate calling.

The president of Lincoln Telephone Company, Frank Woods, recognized that the infant telephone industry could only be saved by restricting competition and implementing comprehensive services. After two years of lengthy negotiations in which he was one of the most important participants, Woods helped to forge a deal among 13 independent telephone companies, including his own and Nebraska Bell Telephone. The deal included the elimination of local competition through a division of operating territories and the establishment of networks of interconnecting toll lines. For his own company, Woods worked out an agreement that included the purchase of all Nebraska Bell Telephone holdings within a certain area and the sale of all properties not within that same prescribed area. The exchange of properties led to Bell paying Lincoln $2,293,000, certainly the largest check Lincoln Telephone Company had received up to that date.

By 1912, the company had adopted a new name, Lincoln Telephone & Telegraph Company, and had also added over 40 Bell telephone exchanges. The firm was now well financed, with assets over $4 million, and was servicing over 46,000 telephones. Customer billings were delivered by mail rather than in person, and a stock purchasing plan was initiated for all the company's employees. By 1915, Lincoln Telephone & Telegraph was part of the telephone service that extended from the

American east to the west coast, commonly known as the transcontinental bridge.

When the American Congress declared war on Germany in April of 1917, however, the company's fortunes took a turn for the worse. Many Lincoln employees volunteered for the war effort, while others jumped to companies that offered higher wages. In 1918, the company was hit hard by a devastating flu epidemic that killed thousands of people across the United States. Finally, during the same year, the U.S. Postmaster General issued a proclamation that placed all wire communications under the control of the federal government for the remainder of the war. For Lincoln Telephone & Telegraph, this change severely restricted all of the company's business for reasons of national security.

When World War I ended, the company started upon an era of growth and prosperity. Although management was faced with a labor shortage and higher taxes, Lincoln expanded its telephone service subscription rate more than 50 percent. The company introduced pay telephones in 1923, and by 1925 Lincoln Telephone & Telegraph reported that it had the highest telephone saturation rate in the entire United States with 28 stations for every 100 people. In 1929, before the stock market crash, the company introduced the Model-T Ford as part of its telephone service repair and maintenance fleet. During the 25th anniversary dinner celebration of the company's founding, Frank Woods, still serving as president, received a telephone call over transatlantic cable from London. Charles G. Dawes, the American ambassador to England and a close friend of Woods, wanted to congratulate the founder on the success of Lincoln Telephone & Telegraph Company.

The prosperity of the 1920s came to a startling halt on Black Friday in the fall of 1929. The stock market crash on Wall Street ushered in a new era of economic hardship. Lincoln Telephone & Telegraph's high of more than 83,000 phones in service at the end year dropped precipitously to just over 62,000 by the beginning of 1933. Due to the drought and dust storms in the plains states that exacerbated the economic difficulties, telephone service for many families became a luxury too expensive to afford. Farmers who had fallen on hard times and who lacked the money to pay for phone bills made arrangements with Lincoln Telephone employees to trade eggs, corn, or chickens for an additional month's telephone service. Employee wages at the company were drastically reduced, and those workers that left were not replaced. Lincoln Telephone & Telegraph survived the worst years of the Great Depression, but the company had a long road to travel to regain the former prosperity it had lost.

By the end of the 1930s, the company was well on the way to a full recovery. Telephones in service increased to 64,000 and the firm's assets amounted to $15 million. In 1941, Lincoln Telephone & Telegraph collaborated with the Bell System in constructing a transcontinental toll cable through the company's portion of Nebraska. This cable was finished just in time to accommodate the huge increase in demand for telephone services that was brought on by the start of World War II.

Not surprisingly, the company's experience during the Second World War paralleled its experience during World War I. The

U.S. government placed restrictions on all forms of telephone installations, especially for individual residences, and any requests for conversions to dial were summarily rejected. Paper shortages during the war meant that no directories could be published, and additional shortages of such items as gasoline and rubber created problems for the company's motor vehicle repair and maintenance fleet. As in World War I, many young men left the company to serve in the armed forces, thus drastically reducing the number of employees and the firm's overall productivity. Although Lincoln Telephone & Telegraph added 2,235 new telephone stations during this time, the gains of the late 1930s seemed stalled by the war.

Yet when World War II finally ended in 1945, the company bounced back rapidly. In 1946, Frank Woods retired from his position as president of the firm and was replaced by his son, Thomas C. Woods, who had served in different capacities with Lincoln Telephone since 1923. Thomas Woods immediately implemented an aggressive modernization program that included expanding the company's facilities and hiring new personnel. By 1950, Lincoln Telephone & Telegraph installed its 100,000th telephone. When Frank Woods died in 1952, he knew that the firm would perform well under the leadership of his son. His confidence was borne out in just a few years. In 1958, when Thomas C. Woods died, the company's assets and profits were higher than ever before.

Throughout the 1960s and 1970s, leadership for Lincoln Telephone & Telegraph Company were provided by Thomas Woods, Jr., who succeeded his father as president, and Frank H. Woods, Jr., who was elected to fill the position of chairman of the board of directors, a seat his father, the founder of the company, had vacated upon his death in 1952. These two men guided the company during the revolutionary years within the telecommunications industry. During the late 1950s and early 1960s, the firm installed Nebraska's first direct distance dialing system and the first direct distance dialing system in the state that provided coast-to-coast telephone service. In 1968, under the direction of the grandson and son of the founder, the company installed the state's first 911 emergency number. In 1971, Lincoln Telephone & Telegraph Company started operation of Nebraska's first telephone exchange that was electronically controlled. One year later, the company implemented a plan to improve and upgrade all its services for customers living in rural areas. By the end of the decade, the firm had installed and was operating a long-distance digital switching system and was in the process of installing a state-of-the-art computerized directory assistance system, one of the first such systems used by a telephone company in the United States.

In the mid-1980s, Lincoln Telephone & Telegraph Lincoln management decided to create a holding company, Lincoln Telecommunications, in order to subsume all the expanding telephone operations under centralized control. The company also formed a long distance company, Lincoln Telephone Long Distance, and began to establish itself as a full-service communications firm.

In the mid-1990s, management at Lincoln Telecommunications, following the growing trend of consolidation within the industry, purchased Nebraska Cellular Telephone Company to augment the services already provided by Lincoln Telecommunications. The acquisition cost over $130 million and increased the company's cellular service area to cover the whole state of Nebraska. Management wanted to capitalize on the growing number of cellular customers. The purchase was also a response to a strategy already being carried out by America's three largest long-distance telephone companies, AT&T, MCI, and Sprint, to enter the cellular telephone market. Seeming to return to the local phone business, these three long-distance carriers threatened one of the most lucrative markets open to local telephone companies, such as Lincoln Telephone & Telegraph.

In the mid-1990s, Lincoln Telephone & Telegraph Company, under the auspices of its parent company, Lincoln Telecommunications, provided long-distance voice and data services, as well as cellular and paging services. The company's position within the regional cellular market was very strong, an advantage the company hoped to use against the competition from long-distance carriers entering the cellular telephone industry.

Further Reading:

"Accord Reached to Buy Rest of Nebraska Cellular Firm," *The Wall Street Journal,* March 23, 1995, p. 6B.
"Lincoln Telecom to Buy Nebraska Cellular," *The New York Times,* March 23, 1995, p. 4D.
Woods, Thomas C., *Lincoln Telephone & Telegraph Company,* Newcomen Society: New York, 1979.

—Thomas Derdak

Lintas: Worldwide

1 Dag Hammarskjold Plaza
New York, New York 10017
U.S.A.
(212) 605-8000
Fax: (212) 838-2331

*Wholly Owned Subsidiary of Interpublic Group of
    Companies Inc.*
Incorporated: 1987
Employees: 7,269
Gross Billings: $5.12 billion
SICs: 7311 Advertising Agencies

One of the largest advertising agencies in the world, Lintas: Worldwide operates in 50 countries through more than 160 offices. During the mid-1990s, Lintas: Worldwide collected more than $5 billion in billings by developing advertising campaigns for a host of clients, the two largest of which were Johnson & Johnson and Unilever. Although the agency's corporate roots stretch back in several different directions, befitting the acquisitive nature of the advertising industry, it essentially began in 1899 as an in-house advertising shop for Lever Brothers, a British-based soap manufacturer. When Lever Brothers developed into the diversified Anglo-Dutch giant Unilever, Lintas gained a massive client that would sustain the agency's growth for the rest of the century. From its mainstay Unilever advertising account, Lintas went on to win numerous other advertising accounts from multinational clients including Diet Coke, Mastercard, and IBM.

Beginning in the mid-1960s, advertising agencies in the United States began acquiring one another, each hoping to increase their volume of business and clientele by absorbing the advertising accounts of fellow agencies. Acquisitions were not new to the industry, but with increasing frequency from the mid-1960s forward, one agency melded with another, joining forces to secure a firmer grip on the advertising dollars spent by manufacturers to sell their products. An industry-wide trend was beginning to take shape as agencies began to acquire one another, engendering a national phenomenon that extended beyond domestic borders to include foreign advertising agencies and the billions of dollars involved in what eventually would become a genuine global economy. As the acquisitive trend gained momentum, growth achieved through internal means became less attractive to aspiring agencies than the more expeditious approach of achieving growth through external means; acquisitions, mergers, and consolidations yielded immediate growth with the signing of documents, enabling aggressive agencies to double or quadruple their billings overnight. Of the 92 largest U.S. advertising agencies in 1966, 41 were either owned by other agencies or out of the business by the beginning of the 1980s. From the 1980s to the mid-1990s, the industry trend toward consolidation continued, accelerating if anything, producing a closely knit cadre of market leaders, each of whom represented a combination of various agencies weaved together over the previous 30 years.

During this 30-year era of consolidation, Lintas: Worldwide was created, although its ancestral roots stretched back well before the U.S. advertising agency industry began to coalesce in the mid-1960s. Like other large agencies that blossomed during this period, Lintas represented an amalgamation of various agencies that had banded together during the consolidation of the advertising industry, but two primary predecessor agencies formed the core around which other agencies were added later. These two agencies were Lintas, the in-house advertising agency formed in 1899 by British soap maker Lever Brothers, and an advertising agency founded in 1946 named Sullivan, Stauffer, Colwell & Bayles.

Lintas, an acronym for Lever International Advertising Services, operated initially as a captive advertising organization with a clear and necessarily restricted objective: develop advertising campaigns for the products manufactured by Lever Brothers, which rose to prominence through its production of Sunlight, the world's first packaged, branded laundry soap. An early proponent of large-scale advertising, Lever Brothers relied heavily on Lintas to develop advertising campaigns for the company's various soap products, which were sold in Europe, Australia, South Africa, and the United States. Lintas, accordingly, focused exclusively on supporting its rapidly growing owner, but when Lever Brothers and the Netherlands-based Margarine Union merged in 1930, creating Unilever PLC and Unilever NV, Lintas essentially became an independent agency and began pursuing advertising accounts on its own, supplementing its advertising activities for Unilever with advertising work for other European companies. Although the London-based agency continued to rely heavily on business derived from its relationship with Unilever, its non-Unilever advertising work gradually increased, accounting for 20 percent of its business worldwide by the mid-1960s, when the agency claimed to be the largest advertising shop in Europe. Lintas by this time had offices in 26 countries, conducted its advertising in 49 languages, and had established a presence in nearly every sector of the world except the United States, where another agency it would soon join forces with had been operating for the previous 20 years. When these two agencies came together, the foundation for Lintas: Worldwide was created.

The other agency that would figure heavily into the creation of Lintas: Worldwide was Sullivan, Stauffer, Colwell & Bayles, founded in 1946 by Raymond Sullivan, Donald Stauffer, Robert Colwell, and S. Heagan Bayles. During the 20 years bridging its formation and its association with Lintas, Sullivan, Stauffer, Colwell & Bayles had developed into a more than $100 million advertising business, deriving all of its billings from the United

States and Puerto Rico, two of the few regions in the world where Lintas's considerable reach had not yet extended. Intent on expanding into the United States, Lintas first approached Sullivan, Stauffer, Colwell & Bayles in 1962, when the two agencies worked out an agreement that sent Lintas executives to Sullivan, Stauffer, Colwell & Bayles for training in Stateside advertising techniques.

This initial link between the two organizations worked well, with more than 300 Lintas executives receiving training from Sullivan, Stauffer, Colwell & Bayles officials by the decade's conclusion. In 1967 the bond between the two agencies was strengthened substantially when they completed a formal contractual agreement to cooperate on worldwide advertising accounts, combining their facilities to provide a global advertising and marketing service. The result of this agreement created SSC&B: Lintas International, which began to conduct advertising work for several companies including Esso in Africa, the Middle East, and Portugal, Monsanto Co. in Europe, and Simmons Co. in Paris.

Three years later, in January 1970, Sullivan, Stauffer, Colwell & Bayles shortened its corporate title, changing its name to SSC&B, Inc., one month before its relationship with Lintas was strengthened further. In February the two agencies were involved in the largest single acquisition in the history of the advertising industry when SSC&B, Inc., purchased a 49 percent interest in Lintas, thereby creating SSC&B-Lintas, the seventh-largest advertising agency in the world. With nearly $200 million in billings, SSC&B-Lintas represented a prodigious global advertising force, comprising Lintas's considerable international experience in marketing the foods, detergents, toilet goods, packaging, plastics, and chemicals produced by Unilever PLC and Unilever NV and the U.S.-based business of SSC&B, which had built its reputation on developing Cover Girl advertising campaigns for cosmetics manufacturer Noxell Co.

For its size, the merger represented a historic transaction in an industry that was beginning to consolidate, ranking as the largest acquisition ever until SSC&B-Lintas again became involved in a merger of unprecedented magnitude toward the end of the 1970s. During the 1970s, another large advertising agency, New York-based Interpublic Group of Companies, Inc., was doing its part to join the acquisitive trend sweeping through the advertising industry by absorbing several foreign and domestic advertising agencies in quick succession, purchasing six agencies between 1975 and 1977. In 1978 Interpublic directed a hungry look toward SSC&B-Lintas, announcing in November it intended to acquire the agency and 49 percent of SSC&B: Lintas International, the corporate entity formed by Sullivan, Stauffer, Colwell & Bayles and Lintas in 1967. Interpublic had been attracted by the overseas capabilities of SSC&B-Lintas, and when the transaction was completed in September 1979, Interpublic gained such capabilities, along with more than $1 billion in worldwide billings, which ranked as the largest merger in the advertising industry to that point.

Before its acquisition of SSC&B-Lintas, Interpublic already owned the country's second-largest advertising agency, McCann-Erickson Worldwide; the 15th-largest, Campbell-Ewald; the 30th-largest, Marschalk; and the 80th-largest, Erwin Wasey. Once SSC&B-Lintas was purchased, Interpublic added

the eighth-largest agency to its formidable portfolio, one that collected nearly $850 million in billings from a respectable client roster that included Johnson & Johnson, Noxell, Sterling Drug, Rowntree Mackintosh, and, of course, Unilever. The agency's long association with Unilever, however, had earned SSC&B-Lintas the reputation of a rather conservative and dull advertiser, an agency that was well disciplined but conservative in its approach to marketing products. Its association with Interpublic would quickly change this perception. Beginning shortly after its absorption by Interpublic was completed, SSC&B-Lintas scored a major victory by taking on a Diet Coke advertising campaign as a secret project in 1980. The project led to SSC&B-Lintas's "Just for the Taste of It" campaign, the success of which lent the agency the legitimacy its need to be regarded as a glamorous consumer-products advertiser capable of developing creative and effective advertisements.

While this pivotal advertising campaign was under way, Interpublic purchased the remaining 51 percent of SSC&B: Lintas International in 1982, creating SSC&B: Lintas Worldwide, an agency that emerged after the transaction with three times the billings of the old SSC&B-Lintas. The next major transaction occurred five years later when Interpublic merged SSC&B: Lintas Worldwide and another of its agencies, Campbell-Ewald Co., which had built its business on advertising accounts for General Motors. Once merged the two agencies became Lintas: Worldwide, an agency group comprising Lintas: International and Lintas: USA, which included Campbell-Ewald's New York offices and the former SSC&B-Lintas agency.

Despite some problems with integrating the two managements, the merger was widely perceived as a success, creating the eighth-largest advertising agency in the country as well as one of the fastest growing agencies. Before the merger, SSC&B: Lintas Worldwide was collecting $1.7 billion in billings; Campbell-Ewald was generating $584 million in billings. After their first full year together, the combined agency had grown 50 percent, achieving $3.3 billion in billings and accounting for 41 percent of Interpublic's $1.2 billion in 1988 revenues. Much of this growth was attributed to the agency's more aggressive approach after the merger to obtaining new business, which brought in $250 million in billings during the first year after the merger from several notable clients. Mastercard's advertising account was awarded to Lintas: Worldwide, as well as Princess Cruises's $35 million account, RJR Nabisco's Planters Life-Savers' $25 million account, and the much-coveted $70 million account awarded by IBM Personal Computer Co.

The addition of these new clients were important developments for an agency attempting to reduce its reliance on long-standing clients Johnson & Johnson and Unilever. As Lintas: Worldwide exited the 1980s and prepared for the 1990s, the agency was encouraged by its quick success in attracting new accounts and began pursuing a five-year plan to develop into a $6 billion advertiser, hoping to add new clients to its core Johnson & Johnson and Unilever business. The early 1990s, however, provided less encouraging results than the late 1980s, particularly in the United States, where the agency's subsidiary, Lintas: New York, suffered a precipitous drop in its billings. Between 1992 and 1994, Lintas: New York watched its billings slip from $750 million to $350 million, a deleterious plunge brought about by the departure of several important clients from the agency's business. During the two-year span, Lintas: New York lost advertising accounts for Mastercard, Diet Coke, Molson, Maybelline, and IBM, arousing considerable concern as to the agency's future.

To bolster Lintas's U.S. interests, Interpublic searched for an acquisition and in July 1994 acquired Ammirati and Puris Inc., a New York-based agency that had built its business on a two-decade advertising relationship with German car manufacturer BMW. Ammirati and Puris was then merged with Lintas: New York, creating Ammirati and Puris/Lintas, the formation of which was designed to arrest the further erosion of Lintas: New York's business.

As Lintas: Worldwide entered the mid-1990s, hoping to recover from the losses it suffered earlier in the decade, it named a new chairman and chief executive officer to steward the agency through the late 1990s and into the 21st century. Martin Puris, the former leader of Ammirati and Puris, was promoted to Lintas: Worldwide's two highest management positions in July 1995 after successfully completing the incorporation of Lintas's New York offices into Ammirati and Puris. With a new leader at the helm, Lintas: Worldwide moved ahead, hoping to keep pace with a growing industry and establish new accounts.

Principal Subsidiaries: Lintas, Inc.; Lintas USA, Inc.; Lintas Marketing Communications, Inc.; Lintas Proprietary Limited (Australia); Lintas Communications Pty. Limited (Australia); Lintas Werbeagentur Gesellschaft mbH (Austria); Lintas Brussels S.A. (Belgium); Lintas Chile S.A.; Lintas Praha Spol. s.r.o. (Czech Republic); Lintas Danmark A/S (Denmark); Lintas International Limited (England); Lintas Overseas Limited (England); Lintas Superannuation Trustees Limited (England); Lintas W.A. Limited (England); Lintas Oy (Finland); Lintas Make Direct Oy (Finland); Lintas Service Oy (Finland); Lintas-Paris; Lintas Deutschland GmbH (Germany); Lintas Direct GmbH (Germany); Lintas Frankfurt GmbH (Germany); Lintas Hamburg GmbH (Germany); Lintas Hong Kong Limited; Lintas Budapest Reklam es Marketing Kommunicacios Kft (Hungary) (90%); Lintas Japan K.K.; Lintas Milano S.p.A. (Italy); Lintas Mexico S.A. de C.V. (Mexico); Lintas World-wide Namibia Limited; Lintas Nederland B.V. (Netherlands); Lintas Warszawa (Poland); Lintas, Agencia Internacional de Publicita Limitada (Portugal); Lintas Puerto Rico, Inc.; Lintas Worldwide Private Limited (Singapore); Lintas Limited (South Africa); Lintas Korea, Inc. (South Korea); Lintas S.A. (Spain); Lintas AB (Sweden); Lintas A.G. (Switzerland); Lintas Taiwan Limited; Lintas Ltd. (Thailand) (80%); Grafika Lintas Reklam-cilik A.S. (Turkey) (51%); Lintas Limited (Zimbabwe).

Further Reading:

Alter, Stewart, "SSC&B Puts Punch in Visuals," *Advertising Age,* December 24, 1984, p. 3.

Bernstein, Peter W., "Here Come the Super-Agencies," *Fortune,* August 27, 1979, p. 46.

Dougherty, Philip H., "Advertising: The Agency Show Must Go On," *New York Times,* March 28, 1967, p. 73.

Farrell, Greg, "Fixing a Hole," *ADWEEK Eastern Edition,* April 24, 1995, p. 30.

Gay, Verne, "C-E Eyes Advance Buys with Multimedia Titans," *Advertising Age,* September 2, 1985, p. 1

Hill, Julie Skur, "Joint Venture?" *Advertising Age,* September 2, 1985, p. 1.

Kanner, Bernice, "Interpublic, SSC&B Plan to Wrap Up Merger in Sept.," *Advertising Age,* July 30, 1979, p. 2.

Konrad, Walecia, "The Quiet Combination Rocking Madison Avenue," *Business Week,* January 16, 1989, p. 54.

Lafayette, Jon, "Agency Nets Merge, Trim, Consolidate," *Advertising Age,* October 19, 1987, p. 2.

"The Largest Ad Merger," *Business Week,* November 20, 1978, p. 48.

Morgan, Richard, "A Year of Living Dangerously," *ADWEEK Eastern Edition,* August 9, 1993, p. 20.

O'Connor, John J., "679 Agencies Hit Income of $4.1 Billion," *Advertising Age,* March 19, 1980, p. 1.

"SSC&B, Lintas Officially Open Int'l Operation," *Advertising Age,* June 19, 1967, p. 1.

"SSC&B Merges into Oblivion," *Advertising Age,* October 19, 1987, p. 135.

Taylor, Cathy, "As Ill Winds Blow, Lintas Seeks to Right Itself," *ADWEEK Eastern Edition,* June 14, 1993, p. 2.

Tilles, Daniel, "Rover's Main Agency Acquired by Lintas," *ADWEEK Eastern Edition,* June 5, 1995, p. 14.

—Jeffrey L. Covell

Logica plc

68 Newman Street
London W1A 4SE
United Kingdom
(0171) 637 9111
Fax: (0171) 637 8229

Public Company
Incorporated: 1969
Employees: 3,416
Sales: £228 million
Stock Exchanges: London
SICs: 6711 Holding Companies; 3573 Electronic Computing
  Equipment; 7372 Computer Programming & Other
  Software Services; 7379 Computer Related Services, Nec

Logica plc is the leading independent computing services company in the United Kingdom, and the "most buccaneering and stylish" such company as well, according to the *Financial Times.* Since its inception in 1969, Logica has played an important role in the fast-growing field of information technology, building a solid reputation for advanced technical know-how and sophisticated, innovative application of that knowledge. The company's boasts an international portfolio of blue-chip clients, including British Airways, Chase Manhattan Bank, NATO, IBM, Ford, and the Stock Exchange of Hong Kong. Operating worldwide, with offices in 17 countries, Logica is prominent in its three related areas of expertise: consulting, software, and systems integration. Given such strong points, Logica's relatively poor financial performance since its flotation in 1983 has been puzzling to analysts and a disappointment to shareholders. In the mid-1990s, however, thanks to an organizational shake-up and a refocusing of corporate goals, Logica appeared to be on track to enjoy rewards commensurate with its talents.

Logica was founded as a private company in London in 1969 by Len Taylor and Philip Hughes, who left their employment at Scicon, a subsidiary of British Petroleum, to start their own enterprise. Building their original team largely from other former employees of Scicon, Taylor and Hughes soon established the fledgling Logica as a company known for its technical excellence in computer services. The company's first big coup came in the 1970s, when it was awarded a contract to design S.W.I.F.T., a transference network for the international banking

community. Thereafter Logica's growth was quick and consistent, and it built a portfolio of well-known and influential clients. Logica recognized the importance of an international approach from the beginning, establishing its first overseas subsidiary in 1973 in the Netherlands and quickly expanding into the rest of Europe, North America, and the Pacific Rim.

Logica had entered the computer services market at an ideal time, getting in on the ground floor of what was to become the phenomenal growth industry of information technology. Others saw the potential as well, and many similar firms were created at around the same time as Logica. Over the years, however, most of these rivals foundered or were absorbed into large, often foreign, companies, leaving Logica as one of the few, and certainly the dominant, independent U.K. computer services firms.

In the mid-1990s, the range of market sectors to which Logica lent its expertise was extremely diverse. The company prided itself on a cross-market, "multi-disciplined" approach, and over the years had built up specialties in several areas, most notably banking and finance, defense and civil governments, energy and utilities, telecommunications, space, transport, computing and electronics, and manufacturing.

Banking and finance have traditionally provided Logica's largest market (generating 32 percent of revenues in 1994), with the company's experience in the sector extending back to its earliest years. Logica was much in demand for payment systems and network services, an area in which the company had excelled since the pioneer days of S.W.I.F.T. Logica was also credited with the creation of CHAPS, the network for the United Kingdom's Clearing House Automated Payment System. Logica worked on trading and settlement systems for prominent international securities houses, clearing banks, fund and investment managers, and stock exchanges. Stock exchanges themselves were another area of expertise for the company, with Logica being called in to improve and streamline existing systems in London, Hong Kong, Switzerland, Norway, Denmark, Australia, and Italy, and involved in the development of new exchanges in Trinidad and Tobago, Hawaii, Kuala Lumpur, Chicago, and Kuwait.

Retail banking proved a busy and lucrative field for Logica; retail institutions have long been acutely aware of the advantages of increased automation, but not always sufficiently knowledgeable about information technology to implement the most effective system—or, crucially, to be able to integrate a new system with other systems in use. Logica completed some 300 projects harnessing information technology capabilities for retail banking use, including customer information, deposits, credit and debit cards, loans, and branch automation. Logica was also active in the financial sector in the areas of commercial loans and insurance.

Logica's work in the fields of defense and civil government ranged from fairly standard administrative and operational systems to specialized intelligence, weapon, and sensor systems. Logica undertook projects in communications, data processing, pattern recognition, image and signal processing, computer simulations, machine intelligence, monitoring, and surveillance for its government clients, which included the United Kingdom,

Australia, Belgium, the Netherlands, and the European Commission.

Logica also developed a specialty in energy and utilities. Many of the company's contracts in these fields arose from the needs of newly privatized companies, in the United Kingdom and elsewhere, which recognized the need for improved efficiency in a more competitive environment. For clients in the oil, gas, electricity, and water industries, Logica worked to supply and install systems for better customer service, asset management, maintenance, materials, logistics, and assessment of environmental concerns.

Logica's expertise in the telecommunications sector dates back to the 1970s, when the company developed the software for the first teletext system. In the mid-1990s Logica offered services and products in broadcasting and video technology, digital image storage media, data communications, control systems, intelligent scheduling, and studio automation. Among the company's more ambitious projects was a long-term venture with Ameritech that was begun in the early 1990s and scheduled to be completed by the year 2000. Logica was charged with developing an interactive, multimedia information and entertainment service that would allow Ameritech's six million customers to access shopping, games, news, education, movies-on-demand, and travel arrangements through their television sets.

In the field of space exploration, Logica created sophisticated experimental space systems for such clients as the British National Space Centre and the European Space Agency. The company's commercial applications included satellite control centers to provide information about the weather, forecasts of crop yields, and earth observation programs.

In transportation, Logica was involved in projects relating to traffic control systems via air, road, rail, and water. Speedwing Logica, established jointly with British Airways in 1990, was a provider of applications software and services to the international air transport industry. In addition, Logica helped with a number of high-profile transport projects including the Channel Tunnel, the London Underground, the Dutch highway network, and Bologna's public transportation service.

Logica found natural clients in computer companies such as IBM, Digital, AT&T, Tandem, and Microsoft, developing systems and applications software for use with those companies' hardware systems. In industry, Logica's experience encompassed the manufacturing, pharmaceutical, and automotive markets. Here the company supplied help with business applications including customer service, streamlined procedures, and systems integration for business operations from stock ordering through to distribution.

To each sector it serviced, Logica offered expertise in three areas: consulting, software, and systems integration. Some 25 percent of the company's revenues derived from consulting. Logica enjoyed a solid reputation for its consulting work, the result not only of years of experience in the field of information technology itself, but also of the company's thorough understanding of the business nature of the specialist sectors its served.

Detailed knowledge of its clients' particular business environments also aided Logica in providing software: many of the company's software applications, originally developed for a specific use by a particular customer, became available as generic packages which, depending on the individual case, could either by used as they came or modified to meet individual needs. Alternatively, Logica could supply products for entirely new applications, either developed in-house or by other computer companies.

Systems integration played an increasingly important role in Logica's business as clients, already possessing a computerized infrastructure, sought to make use of the latest technology to expand their automation. Logica's role was to harmonize new hardware, software products, systems applications, and developing technologies with existing capability, and serve as project manager for the whole operation.

Logica occupied a unique position as an independent computer services firm. Tied to no computer product vendor but conversant with the attributes of all, Logica was free to offer advice and aid in the implementation of the most suitable combination of hardware, software, and systems applications available.

Continuing research and development was obviously vital to maintain Logica's position in the forefront of information technology. The company's technology center in Cambridge, acting as consultant to the rest of Logica as well as directly to clients, fulfilled the allied functions of formulating new technologies and developing practical applications for these innovations. In 1994 the company's spending on research and development was £5.7 million.

With such a successful and varied portfolio to its credit, it is the more surprising that Logica was underperforming in the 1980s and early 1990s. Despite a proven track record of success, a strong reputation, and enviable relationships with its clients—in 1992, some 60 percent of the company's most lucrative contracts were with customers of at least fifteen years' standing—Logica had consistently shown a rather disappointing bottom line since its flotation in 1983: indeed, the company's share price remained static for the next 10 years. Logica's weakness was such that it was nearly scooped up by the American company Electronic Data Systems in 1985. The takeover was avoided, but conditions worsened in the late 1980s. An unwise acquisition in 1988 of the American banking and telecommunications company Data Architects, intended as a foothold in the American market, turned out instead to be what the *Financial Times* bluntly termed a "financial black hole." This setback, combined with the recession that swept the United Kingdom and elsewhere, damaged Logica, and matters were not improved by the departure of the firm's two founders.

But perhaps Logica's most severe drawback was its own mix of corporate strengths. Noted since its inception for its technical excellence, Logica was less well-endowed with business acumen. Financial commentators delighted in painting an amusing picture of Logica as a company populated by absent-minded computer nerds so immersed in the arcane joys of information technology that they neglected the "real world" of sound business principles and competitive spirit. In any case, it was an irrefutable and uncomfortable fact that Britain's largest independent computer services company, highly respected though it was, did not even figure in the European top 50 such companies.

In 1993 new chief executive Martin Read appeared, intent on what the *Financial Times* described as "injecting a cool measure of market realism into Logica's technological hot-house culture." Read immediately set about dramatically realigning and restructuring the company. "Logica is 25 years old," commented Read, "and could be described as having a mid-life crisis." One high priority was to transform Logica into a truly international concern. Although Logica had operated in international markets for years, with subsidiaries and representative offices worldwide, each country's Logica functioned as a separate entity; Read aimed to convert this system to a seamless, global whole, whereby technical expertise and staff experience could be accessed as, where, and when needed.

Unusually for a company in the throes of restructuring, Logica did not shed staff, although management layers were simplified and administrative functions trimmed. (Indeed, the company maintained—as it had maintained, even throughout the recession—a substantial annual intake of recent graduates: one key, many believe, to Logica's continued position at the forefront of technological advancement.) In the new global Logica, staff could expect to be assigned to any country where their skills would be most useful.

Another of Read's first moves was to beef up Logica's sales and marketing team, a needed effort, as the *Sunday Times* commented: "Logica can be a difficult firm to identify. It does almost no advertising. . . ." The company was also thought to suffer from a lack of focus, which promoted a tendency to become involved in too many small or dead-end projects when it should have been considering each project as a stepping-stone to other opportunities. Logica had pursued a short-term consulting job or single installation project with enthusiasm equal to that with which it greeted, say, a several-year contract involving customized applications and complex systems integration. Under Read's direction, the company began to refocus its priorities—for example, axing its involvement with healthcare in Italy, but making a push into new geographical areas such as eastern Europe and the Middle East, where opportunities for future growth were likely to arise.

Part of the new plan involved a policy of strategic acquisitions, and Logica made its first significant purchases in a number of years. In 1994 alone the company acquired Precision Software Corp., a Virginia-based provider of commercial loans systems to prominent banks; the software division of Houston's Synercom Technology Inc.; and the Dutch company Fray Data International. The acquisitions were designed to further Log-

ica's goal of widening its product offerings and consolidating its place in chosen geographical markets.

Logica's new strategies, calculated to promote a happy marriage of Logica's traditional technological distinction with a new, sharpened business instinct, soon showed signs of paying off. In 1994 the company's pre-tax profits were up 50 percent. Activities in the United States, unprofitable for years, returned to a small but heartening profit. Operations in the United Kingdom and continental Europe showed continued improvement.

Logica's refocused corporate philosophy is set forth in a document entitled *The Logica Way,* in which it is confidently proclaimed: "Working as one global company, there is no limit to what we can achieve." Logica's goal is therefore to pursue its interests in the global applications of technology. The company certainly has the experience, having completed some 10,000 separate projects in over 50 countries. In 1994, however, fully 50 percent of Logica's clients were based in the United Kingdom, and the company plans to redress this imbalance. Intending to concentrate on sectors that are more international in scope—finance, telecommunications, and space, for example—Logica intends to marshal its technical superiority and loyal client base to establish a worldwide network of service.

Principal Subsidiaries: Logica BV (Netherlands); Logica GmbH (Germany); Logica Informatik AG (Switzerland); Logica Limited (Hong Kong); Logica North America Inc. (U.S.A.); Logica Pte Limited (Singapore); Logica Pty Limited (Australia); Logica SA (Belgium); Logica Sdn Bhd (Malaysia); Logica Svenska AB (Sweden); Logica U.K. Limited.

Further Reading:

About Logica, London: Logica plc, 1994?, 8 p.
"All Systems Go in Software," *Independent,* September 16, 1994.
"Bearbull," *Investors Chronicle,* June 17, 1994.
"Doing It the Logica Way," *Independent,* March 23, 1995.
"Kudos for Read as Logica Scales £7m," *Observer,* March 12, 1995.
"Logica Embraces Corporate Positivism," *Observer,* April 23, 1995.
"Logica Learns to Sell Itself," *Sunday Times,* April 3, 1994.
"Logica on a High Note," *Evening Standard,* July 15, 1994.
"Logica Revamp Costs £2m," *Independent,* March 11, 1994.
"People: Mann's Long Stint at Logica Comes to an End," *Financial Times,* February 25, 1994.
"Shopping-Mad Logica Grabs £13.5m Profit," *Daily Mail,* September 16, 1994.
"UK Company News: Logica Advances to £13.5m," *Financial Times,* September 16, 1994.
"UK Company News: On Course against the Odds," *Financial Times,* May 31, 1994.

—Robin DuBlanc

Lotus Cars Ltd.

Hethel
Norwich
Norfolk NR14 8EZ
England
(95) 360 8000
Fax: (95) 360 8300

*Wholly Owned Subsidiary of 21 Invest International
   Holdings Ltd.*
Incorporated: 1955
Employees: 200
SICs: 3711 Motor Vehicles & Car Bodies; 8711 Engineering
   Services

Lotus Cars Ltd. is an international developer, manufacturer, and marketer of luxury sports cars. Lotus's market is small; the company's entire production run from 1957 to 1995 totaled just over 50,000 vehicles. Although the company's exotic and expensive cars have always been its most recognizable products, the company's most profitable operation during the mid-1990s was its engineering consultancy.

Lotus continued to bear the stamp of founder Anthony Colin Bruce Chapman, whose initials appear in the marque's logo, into the mid-1990s. Chapman's 35-year career has been highly praised. In a February 1987 *Motor Trend* article, Phillip Bingham described the designer and engineer as "a genius, an iconoclast, a bloody-minded pioneer, a tireless human dynamo, a legend second only to Enzo Ferrari." Chapman's automotive innovations included monocoque construction, ground effects, commercial sponsorship of Grand Prix racers, and more. Following the founder's 1982 death, Lotus went through four transitions in ownership, two of them within a span of 18 months.

The history of Lotus Cars Ltd. can be traced to postwar Britain's club racing movement. Unlike the better known professional racing circuits, club racing was an "everyman" competition often involving street-legal cars. Colin Chapman, who had started building race cars in 1947 at the age of 19, wanted to create a relatively inexpensive yet high-performance vehicle for the club racing market. His Lotus Seven, launched in 1957, met both these criteria. Chapman helped his weekend-racing confederates save money on their speedy toys by offering the Seven as a kit; Britain's high auto taxes did not apply to the box of auto

parts. When assembled, the tiny car had an 88-inch wheelbase and weighed 900 pounds, but it could achieve top speeds of 110 miles per hour. Its four main models were sold primarily in kit form and were offered by Lotus until 1973 (when the car's production rights were transferred to Lotus aficionado Graham Nearn, whose Caterham Cars continued to manufacture the vehicle through the mid-1990s).

Chapman founded the Lotus Engineering Company in 1952 and conceived Lotus Cars Ltd. three years later. Like the club racers he catered to, Chapman had more enthusiasm than capital. He borrowed £25 from girlfriend (later wife) Hazel Williams to build his first car. Although Lotus would eventually make him a millionaire, the company was known for its seat-of-the-pants operation. Lotus's headquarters and production were housed in a garage behind the Chapman family's Hornsey North London hotel from 1955 to 1959, when the company moved to a production facility at a converted World War II airfield.

Chapman's lightweight, sparse designs harked back to his days at engineering school, when he participated in an aeronautical internship with DeHavilland aircraft. For example, he adapted monocoque chassis construction, in which the body covering bears as much or more of the vehicle's stress as the frame, from aircraft design. His body shapes, like the wedge, also echoed elements of aircraft. Many of these ideas were applied to racing models, then adapted for street cars.

Although Lotus's racing arm remained separate from its passenger car segment, they shared, through Chapman, an emphasis on engineering and design. Team Lotus's racing successes helped maintain the high interest in Lotus street cars. The group won three Grand Prix World Championships in the 1960s, seven GP titles in 1963 alone. In 1965 Lotus won its first Indianapolis 500. The company added design awards to its racing titles during the 1960s as well. These included two consecutive prizes at the London Motor Show, as well as Colin Chapman's attainment of the Companion of the Order of the British Empire (CBE) for "Services to Export."

Lotus launched its first passenger car, the Elite, in 1957. The model combined aesthetics and performance in a package that sold more than 1,000 cars over the course of its five year production run. The Elite's successor, the Elan, would become an icon of the sports car segment. Introduced in 1962, this convertible roadster became Lotus's all-time best-seller. This classic sports car featured the sleek fiberglass body and pop-up headlamps that became industry standards. Its engine was based on Ford Motor Co.'s 1500cc block, which was modified to be more powerful. By the time the company ceased production of the Elan and its derivatives in 1973, it had sold over 17,000. A Lotus corporate release asserts that "the Elan became a legend; it was a sports car by which owners were judged."

The Europa was another successful model introduced by Lotus during the 1960s. Just under 9,900 of these cars, which were among the first to feature a race car-inspired mid-engine layout, were sold from 1966 to 1974. Lotus Cars launched its first model with four full seats, a revival of the Elite, in 1974. The car body featured glass reinforced plastic construction and was characterized as "the most luxurious and expensive Lotus road car to date." Lotus continued to garner design honors in the

1970s. Model year 1975 brought the Esprit and Eclat, which together won three medals at the Earls Court London International Motor Show. The Elite became Lotus's first car to be approved for exhibition in London's Design Center.

Racing victories and international exposure enhanced the Lotus mystique in the late 1970s. The Esprit made its feature-film debut in the James Bond thriller *The Spy Who Loved Me* in 1977. Factory visits from members of the royal family and Parliament also boosted the company's prestigious image. During the same time, Team Lotus was racking up a string of design and racing triumphs. Chapman revolutionized Formula One racing with the launch of ground effects or "skirts" in 1977. In 1978 Mario Andretti was behind the wheel of the Lotus 79 that brought home Team Lotus's sixth Driving Championship title.

But while the racing group flourished, the production group began to struggle. The mid-decade oil crisis raised gas prices and eviscerated the sports car market. Lotus's monthly production declined from a high of 200 in the mid-1960s to 100 in 1978 and a paltry 32 in 1981 as a global recession began to take effect. The automaker's North American marketing group crumbled in the late 1970s; from 1980 to 1983, Lotus didn't sell a single car in the United States, the world's largest sports car market. Employment dropped from 900 in 1970 to 300 in 1974. The company recorded losses in 1974 and 1981. In light of Lotus's poor fiscal standing, its banker, American Express, withdrew its financial backing in 1982.

When John Z. DeLorean asked Lotus to revamp his DMC-12, the $18 million engineering and design contract looked like a lifesaver. As it turned out, it was a mixed blessing. On the downside, Lotus's intensive concentration on the DeLorean distracted the company from developing its own new models for the 1980s. Worse, DeLorean Motor Co.'s 1982 failure and John DeLorean's subsequent arrest entangled Lotus in a damaging scandal. The British government embarked on an exhaustive search for millions in "lost" business grants and loans made to DeLorean Motor Co. (DMC). Both Chapman and Lotus were implicated in a government investigation of DMC. When the government assessed a punitive tax assessment of £80 million against Lotus, the tiny automaker opened its books to scrutiny, eventually clearing itself and avoiding the penalty.

These multiple pressures exacted a price. Lotus reached its nadir December 16, 1982, when founder and guiding light Colin Chapman died of a massive heart attack at the age of 54. According to the founder's will, Team Lotus, "the jewel in the crown," went to its earliest benefactor, Hazel Chapman. Given the strikes against it, most observers expected Lotus to fold. But thanks to a cadre of dedicated team members and a timely fiscal reorganization, the company survived. Ironically, part of the revival was credited to Lotus's work for DeLorean. Michael Kimberley, who had been managing director since 1977, later told *Motor Trend* that the research and development contract "established Lotus as a credible overall vehicle engineering consultancy company."

That capability attracted the attention of Toyota Motor Company, which led a 1983 refinancing and reorganization of Group Lotus Car Companies. (Although Lotus had gone public in 1968, Colin Chapman had refused to sanction the sale of company equity.) Other corporate investors included British Car Auctions, JCB, and merchant bank Schroeder Wagg. In exchange for Lotus's research and development proficiency, Toyota offered the British company cheaper mass-produced parts. With Toyota's backing, Lotus was able to increase production to 640 cars in 1983 and reenter the U.S. market through a private import and distribution operation called Lotus Performance Cars.

When Lotus was acquired by auto industry giant General Motors Corp. in 1986, many observers sounded the marque's death knell. But instead of being stifled by a bland corporate bureaucracy, Lotus retained its independence and gained the financial support it needed to continue. Lotus hoped that the big-name influence would help it triple its annual U.S. sales to 1,500 from 1985 to 1988. In 1987, *Motor Trend* proclaimed that "the company [was] in the midst of a glorious renaissance." But that was not to be. In a January 1986 interview with *Ward's Auto World,* Kimberly noted global overcapacity in the specialty car market and predicted that "the number of independent auto manufacturers will reduce considerably over the next 20 years." As the ensuing years progressed, that prophecy appeared to be coming true.

In 1989 Lotus revived its most popular model, the Elan, in hopes of recapturing the glory of the 1960s and early 1970s. But recession, a new U.S. luxury auto tax, and changing demographics combined to gut the luxury sports car market. In 1991, Lotus joined Mercedes-Benz, Jaguar, Porsche, Peugeot, and Sterling, laying off about 20 percent of its 1,500 British workforce. Lotus also tried to boost sales by offering rebates of $5,000 to $15,000 on the $40,000 to $90,000 Elans and Esprits. But instead of the 6,000 cars it had hoped to sell in 1991 and 1992, less than 3,857 Elans rolled out of showrooms, each one at a loss. The company tried to balance inventory levels with a five-week break in production, then ceased building the Elan altogether in June 1992. The *Economist* blamed a misguided application of mass-production techniques to the traditionally small-run company. According to a 1992 piece, Lotus "spent six years and £30 million [US$60 million] developing the Elan and building a new, partly automated factory." Lotus could not sell enough Elans to account for the expenditure. The company continued to offer its higher-priced Esprit Turbo but was compelled to give a 20 percent rebate on the model.

In the late 1980s and early 1990s, Lotus Engineering's research and development consultancy proved the more vital business segment. The value of its contracts grew at a blistering 60 percent annually, and this division employed over 400 by early 1987. Lotus earned contracts with some of the world's top auto manufacturers, including Chrysler, Toyota, Austin Rover, and Volvo. The engineering segment brought in over US$50 million annually by the early 1990s.

Corporate ownership of Lotus changed hands again in 1993, when Bugatti Industries acquired the marque from General Motors Corp. for $48 million. Bugatti's Grand Prix heritage meshed more logically with Lotus's culture and helped the subsidiary improve both its sports car operations and its fiscal position. On the heels of fiscal 1994's (ended August 31) $16.5 million loss, Lotus chalked up net income of $3.2 million on $81.3 million revenues for fiscal 1995. Production more than doubled over the same period, from 320 to 710. Employment levels also rebounded to 700.

The group entered a completely new segment, high-performance bicycling, in the 1990s as well, applying design concepts like monocoque and composite construction techniques to the new segment. In 1992, the company's biggest proponent on the competitive cycling circuit, Chris Boardman, won the Olympic 4000m Gold Medal on a Lotus Sport bicycle.

Although it was apparently successful, Lotus's union with Bugatti was short-lived. Bugatti sold Lotus to 21 Invest International Holdings Ltd., a merchant bank, in April 1995 for $58.3 million. Although 21 Invest was headquartered in England, its two primary shareholders were Italy's Bonomi and Benetton families. One of 21 Invest's principal investors, Alessandro Benetton, was also intimately involved with his namesake Formula One racing team and the United Kingdom's TWR, a successful exotic car manufacturer.

In spite of these connections, the new owners vowed not to combine their disparate auto interests and even hinted that they would ''bring in other investors or permit a buyout by management'' before the end of the century.

Further Reading:

Bingham, Phillip, ''Lotus: Living with the General,'' *Motor Trend,* February 1987, p. 48.
''Britain,'' *Ward's Auto World,* January 1985, p. 57.
''Britain,'' *Ward's Auto World,* January 1986, p. 41.
''Colin Chapman, 1928–1982,'' *Motor Trend,* April 1983, p. 117.
Feast, Richard, ''Turbulent Times for Group Lotus,'' *Automotive News,* January 24, 1983, p. 35.
Fox, Charles, ''The Legacy,'' *Car and Driver,* June 1987, p. 101.
Girdler, Allan, ''A Street-Fighter Racer,'' *Road & Track,* November 1984, p. 136.
Harvey, Chris, *Lotus: The Complete Story,* Somerset, England: Haynes, 1982.
Henry, Jim, ''Layoffs at Lotus, Mercedes Add to Europeans' U.S. Woes,'' *Automotive News,* September 9, 1991, p. 3.
Hutton, Ray, ''Aftermath at Lotus,'' *Car and Driver,* November 1992, p. 32.
Kurylko, Diana T., ''Lotus Vows to Stay in U.S.,'' *Automotive News,* June 22, 1992, p. 4.
Kurylko, Diana T., and Luca Ciferri, ''Bugatti Sells Lotus,'' *Automotive News,* April 3, 1995, p. 6.
''Lotus-Eater,'' *Economist,* June 20, 1992, p. 66.
Nagy, Bob, and Jack R. Nerad, ''Auto Biographies: 30 Giants Who Shaped a New Age,'' *Motor Trend,* November 1985, p. 100.
Nye, Doug, ''Movers & Shakers,'' *Road & Track,* September 1984, p. 52.
Smith, Ian H., *The Story of Lotus, 1947–1960: Birth of a Legend,* London: Motor Racing Publications, 1970.
Thompson, Steven L. ''Now Dasher, Now Dancer,'' *Car and Driver,* December 1989, p. 99.

—April Dougal Gasbarre

plates for the first iron-hulled vessel built in America, an early river steamboat.

After Lukens died in 1825 his widow, Rebecca, took over the business while rearing her young children. She thus became the first woman in the United States engaged in the iron industry and was the first female chief executive officer of an industrial company. She not only saved the mill from the threat of bankruptcy, but also made it the nation's chief manufacturer of boiler plate. Boiler plate from the mill was conveyed as far as England, where it was used to build some of the first railway locomotives. Later two sons-in-law of Rebecca Lukens, Abram Gibbons, Jr., and Dr. Charles Huston, became active in the firm, which became Gibbons & Huston in 1849. A new, steam-powered mill was built in 1870 and another mill added in 1890 that was believed to have been the largest mill in the United States at the time. The company began turning out steel as opposed to iron products in 1881.

Gibbons & Huston was renamed Charles Huston & Sons in 1881 and Lukens Iron & Steel in 1890, when it converted from a family partnership to a corporation. After Huston died in 1897, one son, Abram Francis Huston, succeeded him as president, while the other, Charles Lukens Huston, became works manager. During this period the firm became one of the largest producers of open-hearth steel and steel plates in the eastern United States. Sales offices were opened in Baltimore, Boston, Cincinnati, New Orleans, and New York. A massive new steam-driven mill built in 1903 could produce plates up to 136 inches wide, making it the largest plate mill in the United States. In 1917 and 1918 this was exceeded by a 204-inch facility, the world's largest plate mill. Expanded to 206 inches in 1919 and still in regular operation in 1990, it remained the largest plate mill in the world for more than 40 years.

The company was reorganized and reincorporated in 1917 as the Lukens Steel Co., with a greatly expanded capital structure of 270,000 shares of common and preferred stock. Abram F. Huston was succeeded as president in 1925 by his son-in-law Robert W. Wolcott. (In 1984 descendants of Charles Huston still owned 30 percent of the common stock.) The early 1920s were a period of retrenchment for Lukens after the high level of orders during World War I. The company lost money in 1922, 1924, and 1925. This was followed by a return to prosperity, and in fiscal 1929 Lukens posted net income of $876,563 on sales of nearly $20.4 million.

The Great Depression brought on a new period of economic struggle. Steel production fell from 446,774 tons in 1930 to 165,731 in 1932. Lukens lost money in the fiscal years 1931, 1935, and 1938, and probably also in 1932 and 1933, when it did not publish financial reports. The company survived this period by cost reductions, intensive sales efforts, additional services to companies such as partial fabrication before shipment, and innovative programs. In 1937 Lukens reached an agreement with the Steel Workers' Organizing Committee under which the company recognized union members for the purpose of negotiating agreements relating to wages, hours, benefits, and work rules.

In a landmark development, clad plate was introduced to the product line in 1930. The cladding process, which involves

Lukens Inc.

50 South First Avenue
Coatesville, Pennsylvania 19320-0911
U.S.A.
(610) 383-2504
Fax: (610) 383-3324

Public Company
Incorporated: 1890 as Lukens Iron & Steel Co.
Sales: $947 million
Employees: 3,600
Stock Exchanges: New York Boston Chicago Pacific
 Philadelphia
SICs: 3312 Steel Works, Blast Furnaces (Including Coke
 Ovens) and Rolling Mills; 6719 Offices of Holding
 Companies, Nec

Lukens Inc. is a holding company with subsidiaries that manufacture carbon-, alloy-, and clad-steel plates and stainless-steel sheet, strip, plates, hot band, and slabs. It owns the oldest continuously operating steel mill in the United States. In 1995 its subsidiary Lukens Steel Co. ranked as one of the three largest domestic producers of plate steel and the largest domestic producer of alloy plate, while its Washington Steel Corp. specialized in the manufacture and marketing of stainless-steel sheet, strip, plate, hot band, and slabs. Washington Specialty Metals Corp., the company's third principal subsidiary, was a leading distributor of flat-rolled stainless steel. Over a five-year period ending in 1993, Lukens ranked fourth in profitability among 24 public steel corporations, earning an annual average of 14.8 percent on equity.

The origins of Lukens go back to the early days of the Republic. By 1793 a young Quaker, Isaac Pennock had established the Federal Slitting Mill south of present-day Coatesville, Pennsylvania, to produce iron rods and strips. In 1810 Pennock and another Quaker, Jesse Kersey, established the Brandywine Iron Works and Nail Factory on the site of what is now Coatesville. By 1817 Pennock had purchased Kersey's interest in this facility and leased it to his son-in-law, Dr. Charles Lloyd Lukens. The following year this mill became the first in the United States to manufacture boiler plate—high-quality iron essential to the making of steam boilers. It soon established a fruitful and enduring association with the shipbuilding industry, providing permanent bonding of two or more different types of metal, soon became an important segment of Lukens' business. The applications of clad are practically limitless where protection against rust, corrosion, and abrasion are required and the use of a solid plate of nickel or stainless steel would be impractical and cost-prohibitive. Lukens now offers the most complete line of clad steels in the industry.

In 1940 Lukens was able to resume the payment of dividends, which had been suspended for two decades (except for 1927). Debt had been reduced and plant improvements were being made in preparation to meet demand arising from World War II. During the war the U.S. Navy constructed a finishing mill that Lukens then leased and operated. Lukens turned out battleship armor for the navy and light tank armor, antiaircraft-gun bases, and other fabricated steel parts for the U.S. Army. Average employment reached a record high of 6,166 in 1944, when a liberty ship was named for Rebecca Lukens. After an initial postwar slowdown, Lukens earned a record profit of $2.8 million in 1947, with net sales of $61.5 million and production of 578,461 tons of steel in 1948, both company records. Wolcott was succeeded as president by Charles Lukens Huston, Jr., a fifth-generation descendant of the company's founder, in 1949.

Military orders were also important for Lukens in the 1950s. The company supplied keel plates and other components for the aircraft carriers *Saratoga* and *Forrestal* and steel for the *Nautilus,* the first atomic-powered submarine. It supplied plates for the hull, flight deck, and plane launchers of the navy's first nuclear-powered carrier, the *Enterprise.* The navy completed an armor-plate plant at Lukens in 1956. Lukens also supplied eye bars to anchor the cable of the Verrazano-Narrows Bridge in New York harbor, plates for the Throgs Neck and Walt Whitman bridges in New York City and Philadelphia, respectively, and fabricated materials for the *Savannah,* the world's first atomic-powered commercial ship.

Lukens turned a profit during every year of the decade. Its greatest production of steel was 763,679 tons in 1953. Net sales reached a peak of $130.5 million in 1957 and net income a high of $10.2 million in the same year. A new steel-making facility, centered around a 100-ton electric furnace, was completed in 1958. By 1960 the Coatesville tract covered 725 acres and included 3.25 million square feet of floor space.

During the 1960s Lukens took part in other high-profile projects. The arched column supports for New York City's World Trade Center, begun in 1968, were fabricated from the company's plate steel. Lukens provided the steel for a specially designed ice-crushing bow installed in the *Manhattan.* This oil tanker, the largest built in the United States at that time, made a historic voyage through the Northwest Passage across Canada's Arctic to Alaska's Prudhoe Bay in 1969. A year earlier Lukens had purchased Natweld Steel Products, Ltd., of Toronto to serve the Canadian market as a subsidiary renamed Canadian Lukens, Ltd. In 1969, when the parent company earned $7.2 million in net income on net sales of $145.2 million, steel production reached 897,000 tons.

In 1970 Lukens completed construction of a $12.8-million strand-casting facility that shortened the process of producing steel slabs and reduced handling costs. Five years later, now

equipped with four massive electric furnaces, it phased out the last of its antiquated open-hearth furnaces. A new line of low-sulphur, high-purity steels of exceptional toughness and ductility was introduced in 1977. In 1974 Lukens produced a record 958,000 tons of raw steel and had record net sales of $283.4 million. That year Charles Lukens Huston, Jr., retired as chairman of the board, bringing an end to the family's continuous leadership of the firm since its founding by Isaac Pennock in 1810.

After posting a record net income of $12.9 million in 1978, Lukens began suffering from the economic problems of the late 1970s and early 1980s: double-digit inflation, high energy and employment costs, and high interest rates. In addition, the steel industry was grappling with greater competition from other metals and materials and from cheaper steel imports. Net income as a percentage of sales dropped from 4.2 percent in 1978 to 1.3 percent in 1980. U.S. plate sales—the heart of the company's business—dropped 11 percent in 1980 and 8 percent in 1981.

Under president and chief executive officer W. R. Wilson, Lukens began to move into other lines of business. In 1981 the company paid $66 million for General Steel Industries Inc., which, in addition to steel, produced crushing and conveying machinery, reflective highway signs, and protective coatings for oil and gas pipelines. Also in 1981, Lukens purchased a 3.6-mile stretch of track and switching yard from the Consolidated Rail Corp. (Conrail), incorporating it as a subsidiary called the Brandywine Valley Railroad Co.

In 1982 Wilson announced that Lukens planned to make two small acquisitions each year and one large acquisition every three years, with nonsteel revenue to reach half of all company annual revenue by 1989. That year the company removed ''steel'' from its name, becoming simply Lukens Inc. To reduce costs, the company reduced its work force by 22 percent between January and September 1982 and cut the pay of salaried employees by 10 percent. Lukens was able to make a profit of $1.5 million in 1982 while other steelmakers were incurring heavy losses in that recessionary year. In 1983, however, the company lost $14 million, its first plunge into the red since 1938.

In 1984 Lukens returned to profitability, earning net income of $4.7 million on sales of $416.4 million. Wilson was credited with reducing company costs by $50 million over four years, mainly by dismissing nearly half the white-collar salaried staff. A capital-improvement program had doubled steelmaking productivity. Also in 1984, Lukens settled a 13-year-old lawsuit by agreeing to pay 1,300 black employees $2.5 million in damages and agreeing to set a goal to fill at least 18 percent of its hourly and salaried positions with black workers.

Lukens lost $4.2 million in 1985 but earned an $8.7 million profit in 1986 and enjoyed net earnings of $21.7 million in 1987 on sales of $505.2 million. Its stock moved that year from a low of 14⅝ to a high of 58¾, registering the largest percentage gain on the New York Stock Exchange. Also in 1987, the corporate structure was reorganized, with the formation of a new holding company, Lukens Inc., incorporated in Delaware. Lukens Steel Co. became its wholly owned subsidiary. In 1988 Lukens did even better than the previous year, earning $33.4 million on sales of $605.3 million. Closing its third record year in a row, in 1989 Lukens earned $41.5 million on sales of $644.9 million.

Military orders were one reason for Lukens's turnaround. The company was providing alloy plate steel for such projects as the army's Abrams tank and the navy's Aegis class cruiser, ballistic-missile submarines, and aircraft carriers. In 1988 Lukens won the largest single order in its history, a $74 million contract to supply carbon and military alloy plate over five years for use in the construction of two Nimitz-class nuclear aircraft carriers, the largest warships in the world. The company enjoyed its fourth consecutive year of record profits in 1990, earning $44.1 million.

The financial health of Lukens encouraged the United Steelworkers to launch a walkout in October 1991 by more than 1,200 workers at the company's unionized Coatesville plant. The union sought to eliminate a common industry practice known as contracting out, under which nonunion workers are hired to perform duties not directly tied to making steel. The strikers did not gain their objective, as salaried employees kept the mill running at 85 percent of normal operations during the 105-day walkout.

To broaden its presence in the lucrative stainless-steel market, Lukens purchased Washington Steel Corp. in 1992 for $273.7 million. The acquisition gave Lukens enough volume to justify building a sophisticated new rolling mill adaptable to stainless and carbon products. This new system, called Steck Mill Advanced Rolling Technology (SMART), was installed at Conshohocken, Pennsylvania. It began operation in 1995 and was capable of producing stainless coil plate up to 102 inches wide, compared to the prior limit of 60 inches. For customers, this meant fewer welds, saving hundreds of dollars per ton of steel.

Meanwhile Lukens sold its Canadian subsidiary in 1988 and its GSI Engineering subsidiary in 1989, and was in the process of divesting its remaining nonsteel businesses. In 1994, under a new chairman and CEO, R.W. Van Sant, who had been installed in January 1992, Lukens divested Flex-O-Lite, producer of highway safety products and its related Services and Materials Co. division (acquired in 1986). Also in that year, Lukens sold its Ludlow-Saylor division, the South Central Railroad Co. (acquired in 1990), and Cathodic Protection Services Co. (purchased in 1985). In 1995 it sold Energy Coatings Co. to Dresser Industries Inc. The sale of these six industrial-products units brought Lukens more than $70 million and completed its divestiture process.

In 1995 Lukens Steel Group was producing raw steel from an electric-arc furnace at the Coatesville plant, with about 70 per-

cent of production continuously cast into slabs at this facility. Rolling and fabrication facilities were located at this plant and another in Conshohocken, Pennsylvania. The steel group also had a fabrication facility in Newton, North Carolina.

The Washington Stainless Group included Washington Steel Corp.'s melting, continuous casting, and hot-rolling facilities in Houston, Pennsylvania, and rolling and finishing facilities in Washington, Pennsylvania, and Massillon, Ohio. The Washington Specialty Metals Corp. had fabrication and distribution facilities in Wheeling and Carolstream, Illinois, and Lawrenceville, Georgia. There were additional distribution centers in Carrollton, Texas; Youngsville, North Carolina; Tampa, Florida; Brampton, Ontario; and Vaudreuil, Quebec.

Of Lukens's net sales of $947 million in 1994, Lukens Steel Group and Washington Stainless Group each accounted for roughly half of the total. Net earnings came to $22.2 million. Shipments totaled 711,800 tons in 1993, and long-term debt came to $209.7 million in September 1994.

Principal Subsidiaries: Allegheny Ore & Iron Co.; Brandywine Valley Railroad Co.; Lukens Development Corp.; Lukens Management Corp.; Lukens Steel Co.; Washington Specialty Metals Corp.; Washington Specialty Metals Inc.; Washington Steel Corp.

Further Reading:

DiOrio, Eugene L., *Lukens: Remarkable Past—Promising Future,* Coatesville, Pennsylvania: Lukens Inc., 1990.
Hicks, Jonathan P., "Strike at Small Steelmaker Poses a Big Test for a Union," *New York Times,* December 26, 1991, pp. D1, D7.
"How It Was Paid For," *Business Week,* April 18, 1959, pp. 60, 62.
"Lukens: Broadening Its Product Mix without Weakening Its Position in Steel," *Business Week,* September 6, 1982, p. 109.
"Lukens Looks for Wider Fields," *Business Week,* March 26, 1955, pp. 166–68.
"Lukens Makes a Specialty of Success," *Dun's Review,* July 1976, pp. 67–68.
"Lukens Steel: A Specialist Blankets a High-Margin Market," *Business Week,* December 11, 1976, pp. 127–28.
"Lukens and Wilson: A Touch of Steel," *Financial World,* July 11–24, 1984, pp. 32–33.
Magnet, Myron, "How to Grow in a Cyclical Business," *Fortune,* September 6, 1993, p. 78.
"Whatever Happened to Lukens Steel?" *Dun's Review,* July 1965, pp. 39, 68C, 70.
"What's Behind the Giddy Doings of Lukens Stock," *Business Week,* May 4, 1957, pp. 40–43.
Wolcott, Robert W., *A Woman in Steel,* Princeton, New Jersey: The Newcomen Society, 1940.

—Robert Halasz

Mannesmann AG

Mannesmannufer 2 4
Postfach 55 01
D 4000 Düsseldorf 1
Germany
(211) 820 2249
Fax: (211) 820 2554

Public Company
Incorporated: 1890 as Deutsch Österreichische
   Mannesmannröhren Werke Aktiengesellschaft
Employees: 127,000
Sales: DM 30.4 billion
Stock Exchanges: Düsseldorf Frankfurt Geneva Zürich Basel
   Vienna Paris
SICs: 3312 Blast Furnaces & Steel Mills; 3500 Industrial
   Machinery & Equipment; 3600 Electronic & Other
   Electrical Equipment; 4449 Water Transportation of
   Freight, Not Elsewhere Classified; 5051 Metals Service
   Centers & Offices; 1541 Industrial Buildings &
   Warehouses; 8711 Engineering Services

Mannesmann AG developed from a steel tube manufacturer
into a highly diversified group of companies with a worldwide
presence involved in machinery and plant construction, industrial drive and control systems, electrical and electronic engineering, automotive technology, and its traditional area, steel
tube production.

The history of Mannesmann began five years before the company's founding with a major technical achievement. In 1885,
the brothers Reinhard and Max Mannesmann invented a rolling
process for the manufacture of thick walled seamless steel
tubes, the so called cross rolling process, at their father's file
factory in Remscheid. Introducing the invention, they founded
tube mills between 1887 and 1889 with several different business partners, in Bous on the Saar (in the Bohemian Komotau),
in Landore, Wales, and at home in Remscheid. The machine
building industry was unable to supply the necessary plant for
the application of the rolling process, and the iron and steel
industry was not able to provide the necessary supplies of high
quality semi finished products. As a result, numerous other
inventions had to be made and long years of experiments passed
before the initial difficulties in the industrial exploitation of the
new process were overcome.

In 1890, a technical breakthrough was achieved with the brothers' invention of the pilger rolling process. The name was taken
from the analogous Luxembourg Echternach pilgrims' proces-
sion, as during the rolling process the prepierced thick walled
steel ingot was moved forward and backward and turned at the
same time in order to be stretched into a thin walled tube. The
combination of the pilger and the cross rolling processes became known as the Mannesmann process. On July 16, 1890, the
tube and pipe mills existing on the Continent were brought into
Deutsch Österreichische Mannesmannröhren Werke Aktiengesellschaft which had its headquarters in Berlin. Reinhard and
Max Mannesmann formed the first board of management but
left it in 1893. In that year the company headquarters was
moved from Berlin to Düsseldorf, at that time the center of the
tube and pipe industry.

From about this time, seamless medium sized steel tubes were
successfully produced and sold worldwide at a profit, by far
surpassing rival products in quality. It was thus possible to
reduce the loss of more than 20 million marks, that had accumulated during the company's first years of business, and eventually to pay the first dividend in 1906.

The success of Mannesmann's tubes alarmed competitors
grouped in associations and syndicates. Feeling their very existence threatened, they stopped supplies of large and small tube
sizes, for which seamless production was not yet possible, to
dealers selling Mannesmann tubes. In order to be able to supply
a complete range of products, Mannesmann built a factory
for the production of longitudinally welded tubes in the second
half of the 1890s; the company also acquired shares in companies involved in tube and rolled steel trading and pipeline
construction.

Mannesmann's position in the export business, which was important from the beginning of the company, was consolidated
and expanded by the acquisition of the British Mannesmann
tube mill in Landore, Wales, which had been founded by the
Mannesmann and Siemens families but had never overcome its
start up problems, and by the founding of a Mannesmann tube
mill with its own electrical steelworks in Dalmine, Italy. Since
the turn of the century, branch offices undertaking storage and
direct sales business, sometimes with tube processing workshops and pipeline construction capacities, were set up in cooperation with well established companies all over the world,
especially in South America, Asia, and South Africa.

Except for the works in Dalmine and Bous, which operated their
own small steelworks, Mannesmann continued to be dependent
on supplies of semi finished products from third parties; even
Bous had to buy scrap and pig iron. With the tendency towards
horizontal integration by means of increasing numbers of cartels and vertical integration in the formation of vertically structured coal and steel groups that mined their own ore and coal,
produced pig iron and crude steels, and converted them to
finished products, this dependence on suppliers began to endanger Mannesmann's existence. Accordingly the company's foremost strategic goal became to achieve self sufficiency in semi
finished products and thus to enable the company to determine
price, quality, and the actual delivery period. In the process, iron
ore and pit or hard coal mines, a lime works, a factory for the
production of refractory materials, and finally, in 1914, a plate

rolling mill with an open hearth steelworks at Huckingen on the Rhine were acquired. Plans for the expansion of the steelworks and the construction of blast furnaces were thwarted by the outbreak of World War I.

In the period that followed, the company was forced to employ emergency labor, to cope with changes in its range of products, and to make up for the loss of export business, which had formerly accounted for 60 percent of sales. The British Mannesmann Tube Company, with its works in Landore and Newport, was lost. The Italian subsidiary in Dalmine had to be sold under duress. The loss of the works on the Saar and in Bohemia could only be avoided by allowing French and Czechoslovakian companies to participate.

This was not a time to shape and realize long term corporate strategies. In the ten year period beginning in 1914, day to day problems required full attention. At the end of the war, plants had to be replaced completely or were, upon instant transfer to peacetime production, no longer usable.

Export contacts were reestablished, and machinery in the remaining works was replaced and expanded to compensate for the loss of production capacity. Although Mannesmann's major steelworks had not yet been built, this construction plan was by no means abandoned. Measures were carried out that efficiently supplemented the existing installations. The mining division was strengthened by the acquisition of another pit coal mine and of a coal trading company with its own inland fleet. The works harbor at Huckingen was expanded to accommodate seagoing vessels, and the works area was enlarged by the purchase of further land.

In November 1925, Mannesmann turned down the offer to take part in the formation of what was at the time the largest German coal and steel group, Vereinigte Stahlwerke AG, and decided to maintain its independence even in those difficult times. This decision resulted in the creation of a company owned semi finished product manufacturing unit. In 1927, Mannesmann began to build a blast furnace, the Thomas steelworks, and auxiliary plants and shops. Despite a few strikes, a general lockout, and delays caused by harsh winter weather, expansion proceeded so quickly that as early as May 1929 two blast furnaces, each producing 800 tons a day, the sinter plant, and the Thomas steelworks with four converters holding 30 tons each, went into operation. The steelworks already had numerous facilities which, not only in terms of technology but also in terms of safety standards and regard for the environment in general, were ahead of their time. With the blast furnace and the Thomas steelworks, the company integrated the ore and pit coal mines on one side with the steel and rolling mills on the other, and completed its development into a fully vertically structured coal and steel group, typical until the 1970s of the Ruhr industry. Mannesmann thus became independent of outside suppliers of semi finished products and was able to make full use of the advantages offered by the combination of mining and steelmaking.

To promote sales, the domestic marketing organization was made more efficient by the establishment of warehousing companies. Shareholdings in trading, production, and assembly businesses in many European and overseas countries were ac-

quired. The Landore works lost during the war was recovered. Holdings in a company for the construction of power supply plants in Berlin and in a pipeline construction firm in Leipzig were acquired, to promote Mannesmann's tube sales. The latter two participations marked the beginning of new activity for Mannesmann that has since developed into a group of companies operated by Mannesmann Anlagenbau AG. The participation in the family owned Maschinenfabrik Gebr. Meer in Mönchengladbach, founded in 1872, which had for many years successfully constructed rolling mills for the manufacture of seamless tubes and tube processing machines, did not represent an attempt to diversify, but resulted from the fact that the company could no longer design and build its own rolling mills as it had done since 1886. Since the task was now assigned to others, Mannesmann intended to make sure that new designs were not made accessible to competitors.

Technical developments in the period before the outbreak of World War II were characterized by the successful solution of problems in the manufacture of tubes of high alloy stainless steel and the successful application of the extrusion process and the introduction of a new rolling mill for the manufacture of thick walled seamless steel tubes. At the same time, the semi finished and heavy plate product lines were extended, with the contribution of newly acquired companies. The Depression and the ensuing economic boom, further invigorated by government job creating schemes, both affected the company. The production and sale of all Mannesmann products were governed by national, European, and international cartels, from the mid-1920s until the end of World War II.

The outbreak of World War II hit the company during a phase of plant replacement. The Bous works and its staff were moved to Düsseldorf. Production remained essentially unchanged, but to a far greater extent than in World War I, the works replaced their conscripted work force with unskilled workers, women, civilian foreign workers, and prisoners of war.

All works were bombed several times and suffered varying degrees of damage. With the Allies approaching, the plants were vacated and as far as possible protected against plunder by emergency crews. By order of the Allies, Mannesmann was liquidated and in 1952 divided into three independent groups of companies, one of them Mannesmann AG. By 1955, Mannesmann AG had absorbed the other two and more or less reestablished its former unity. Mannesmann was the first group in the coal and steel industry to be split up into independent smaller groups, convene a general meeting of shareholders, pay a dividend, have its shares quoted at the stock exchange, increase its share capital, issue a loan, and regain its former structure.

The Czechoslovakian works were lost, and the Bous works, reintegrated in the 1930s, were confiscated again and later brought into a French company in which Mannesmann's stake rose from 40 to 51 percent in 1959, and finally to 100 percent in 1985. The British Mannesmann company had already been sold in the 1930s.

Even before the company's future was definitely settled, it again began to build up extensive activities abroad. Between 1952 and 1955, Mannesmann founded its own steel and tube mills in Brazil, Canada, and Turkey, establishing its presence in several important markets. While the Canadian joint venture was divested in the early 1970s, the Turkish joint venture, small at the start, has been repeatedly enlarged. Companhia Siderúrgica Mannesmann S.A. in Belo Horizonte developed into the Brazilian group of companies that supplied Mannesmann products and services, in particular to the South American markets. Its range of products and services included rolled and drawn high grade and special steel products, steel wires and welding rods, steel tubes, steelworks and rolling mill machinery and equipment, compressors, excavators, plastics injection molding machines, hoists, hydraulic systems, and components for industrial drive and control systems. The group ran its own ore mines, and had eucalyptus plantations for charcoal production. Its marketing was carried out by an independent trading company, Mannesmann Comercial S.A., of Sao Paolo.

Other participations for example, in companies producing irrigation systems, forage silos, agricultural tractors and engines, and plastics tubes and pipes—turned out to be less successful. As their future prospects began to look unpromising, they were eventually given up. The traditional coal and steel companies, on the other hand, were since the 1960s exposed to growing international competition. In many countries, new large, low cost plants were constructed that aimed at the world market. International competition, frequently government supported, threatened to eliminate European producers.

With investment expenses rising steeply, it was doubtful whether Mannesmann would in the future be able to compete worldwide in tubes, rolled steel, and tube processing. The existing excess production capacity for steel tubes, rolled steel products, and pit coal left very little hope for continuing with satisfactory profits. As a traditional coal and steel group, Mannesmann's outlook was not promising.

Nevertheless, by the end of the 1960s, Mannesmann had broken from tradition and was looking for new ways to secure its future. Domestic ore mining came to a complete halt and coal mining interests were brought together in a unified company, the Ruhrkohle AG.

The gradual acquisition of G.L. Rexroth GmbH between 1968 and 1975 reflected the new trend of development. From modest beginnings, the company was expanded and internationalized to become the world leader in hydraulics. In addition to hydraulic components and systems, the company's range of products and services comprised pneumatics and linear motion technology, electric servo drives, gears, and couplings. Rexroth marked the beginning of the restructuring of the Mannesmann group. This first step was successful and pointed the way forward for the company.

In 1970, Mannesmann and Thyssen agreed on a division of labor; Mannesmann took over tube production and tube laying from Thyssen and transferred its own rolled steel production and sheet processing activities in Germany to Thyssen. The new Mannesmannröhren Werke became the world's largest producer of tubes. Despite capacity reduction and concentration on the most efficient plants, further drastic restructuring became necessary as market conditions turned out to be worse than even the most pessimistic forecasts had anticipated. When losses

reached almost DM 1 billion in 1986–87, the situation became temporarily very grave.

By 1988, the worst problems had been overcome. However, structural adjustment which, at the semi finished products level, led to cooperation with other long established steelworks, was not yet completed. Cross border cooperation between the European tubemakers was one way to preserve the European tube industry. Two forward looking strategies at Mannesmannröhren Werke were participation in a company for the production of hydride stores for the storage and transportation of hydrogen and development of purest gases, and in a company producing automotive components with manufacturing facilities in a converted former steelworks.

With the acquisition of Demag AG, a well established group with a rich and eventful history, Mannesmann strengthened its activities in machinery and plant construction during the first half of the 1970s. By the middle of the decade, about 30 percent of the company's external sales was coming from these divisions.

At the beginning of the 1980s, Mannesmann gained access to the growing electronics markets by acquiring Hartmann & Braun in 1981 and Kienzle Apparate GmbH in 1981 and 1982. Hartmann & Braun was an international company in the field of measurement, control, and automation engineering, with subsidiaries in Germany, in other European countries, and overseas. The change of emphasis in Mannesmann's range of products towards the processing industry, with its higher growth potential, proved successful. Mannesmann's second acquisition in this field, Kienzle, operated in data processing and supplies electronic systems for motor vehicles. Mannesmann had previously entered data processing both as a user and through its successful development of printers. Kienzle enabled Mannesmann to operate in the center of data processing. Originally Kienzle supplied only the German market; later it became international and established sales operations in other countries, some with local partners.

The acquisition of a majority holding in Fichtel & Sachs AG in 1987 and in Krauss Maffei AG in 1989 enabled Mannesmann to consolidate its leading position in the machinery and plant construction sectors. A key motive for the acquisition of Krauss Maffei was the possibility of expanding Demag's plastics machinery activities and thus ensuring, according to the standard set by Mannesmann, lasting success in world markets. Most of Krauss Maffei's other divisions process engineering technology, transport technology, foundry technology, automation technology, surface treatment technology, and defense technology offered good growth potential.

Following the Fichtel & Sachs investment, the group's total activities comprised, in addition to the highly cyclical plant business, a less cyclical mass market products business with closer proximity to consumers. In the latter business, foreign sales were gaining an increasing importance. In most of their fields of activity, the Mannesmann companies were of a size that enabled them to carry out the necessary development work, produce at competitive cost, and maintain extensive sales and service organizations.

In 1990, Mannesmann again broke new ground. Believing that in a highly developed economy the service sector would grow at an above average rate and that telecommunications would be a particularly promising service, a consortium headed by Mannesmann tendered for the license to construct and operate the private D2 cellular telephone network. The acceptance of the bid submitted by Mannesmann Mobilfunk GmbH was of major importance to Mannesmann. It provided the company with an opportunity to enter the service sector.

The change in Mannesmann's corporate structure was clearly reflected in the sales breakdown. In 1968, coal, steel, and tubes accounted for half of external sales, and machinery and plant construction for 16 percent. Twenty years later, the situation was very different: in 1989, machinery and plant construction and electrical and electronic engineering together accounted for 53 percent of external sales, and tube mills only 22 percent. At the same time overall sales had quintupled, rising from DM 4.4 billion in 1968 to DM 22.3 billion in 1989. In 1990, the 100th year of its corporate history, Mannesmann was a broadly diversified capital goods producer occupying a leading position in most of its fields of activity.

The 1990s brought several challenges, however. Commenting on the company's situation, Mannesmann's chairman, Werner Dieter, paraphrased a quote from German folklore: ''before he provides the remedy, God makes you sweat, and right now we are sweating quite a lot.'' For the first time since it was founded, in fact, Mannesmann was about to lose money on operations. Net profits hit a high of $315 million in 1989, dropped to half of that in 1991 and fell to break-even in 1992.

The problem that was afflicting Mannesmann was also hurting much of German industry during this time: uncompetitively high wages, a distended work force, and an over dependence on recession-hit markets in Germany and throughout Europe. German industrial wage rates climbed to nearly 50 percent above those in the United States and Japan, and Mannesmann was pricing itself out of business. Unfortunately, the tubing business from which the company grew became the conglomerate's least healthy division in the early 1990s, losing an estimated $40 million in 1992. Moreover, Mannesmann's auto parts, construction equipment, machine tool controls, and plant construction businesses all lost money in 1992. Among the only successes during this period came from the company's factory crane and conveyor business; Mannesmann was the largest supplier of such equipment in the world, with $1.2 billion in sales in 1992.

The company did, however, have the financial resources to help adapt to these economic problems. Under Dieter's leadership, Mannesmann determined a financial strategy to help them recover. First, the company began shifting Mannesmann's engineering work from high-cost Germany to the lower-cost, highly competitive United States. Toward that end, the company acquired Rapistan, a Michigan-based leading conveyor belt company. It also opened a large factory in Kentucky to produce automotive shock absorbers. Another move Mannesmann believed would help them through this time involved entering into the cellular technology market, and they established a new division to oversee such operations. Although high startup costs

for the division contributed to a fall in net earnings, Dieter predicted that the system would be making money by 1995, and analysts predicted that this market could carry Mannesmann well into the next century. If as many Germans as Americans were to subscribe to cellular phone service, Mannesmann's pretax profits might reach $1 billion a year within seven years, according to market analysts.

In 1994, the company returned to profitability with net income of DM 340 million after a loss of DM 513 million the previous year. Operating profits and sales also increased. Mannesmann credited its machinery and plant construction, automotive technology, and telecommunications divisions with the success. However, in an unusual turn of events for the leader of Mannesmann, Dieter came under investigation in 1994 for alleged fraud. Specifically, charges surfaced that he had used his position to channel lucrative orders from Mannesmann's Rexroth GmbH subsidiary to Hydrac GmbH, a components company owned by his family. It was also alleged that the components were sold by Hydrac at inflated prices. Dieter was replaced, and in 1995 he stepped down from the company's supervisory board, even though a review commissioned by Mannesmann could not conclude that he had in fact defrauded the company. Dieter had overseen Mannesmann's return to profitability, and it remained for the company's new leader to take the company forward into the 21st century.

Principal Subsidiaries: Mannesmann Demag AG; Mannesmann Rexroth GmbH; Krauss Maffei AG; Mannesmann Anlagenbau AG; Fichtel & Sachs AG; Hartmann & Braun AG (95.5%); Mannesmann Kienzle GmbH; Mannesmann Mobilfunk GmbH (51.3%); Mannesmann Handel AG; Mannesmann SA (Brazil).

Further Reading:

''Dieter Leaves Mannesmann,'' *American Metal Market,* March 1, 1995, p. 2.
Fuhrman, Peter, ''Struggling to Adapt,'' *Forbes,* April 26, 1993, p. 102.
''Inquiry Inconclusive on German Executive,'' *The New York Times,* June 23, 1995, p. D2.
''The Inside Stories,'' *Datamation,* June 15, 1988, p. 116.
Linsenmeyer, Adrienne, '' 'If There's a Seat at the Bar, Take It,' Says Mannesmann's Dieter. 'If Not, Knock Someone Off','' *FW,* July 23, 1991, p. 24.
''Mannesmann Group Revenues Decline,'' *American Metal Market,* December 16, 1986, p. 3.
''Mannesmann in Black,'' *The New York Times,* May 6, 1995, p. 18.
Morais, Richard C., ''Making Up for Lost Time,'' *Forbes,* November 21, 1994, p. 122.
''Old Dogs, New Tricks: Mannesmann,'' *The Economist,* October 5, 1985, pp. 71 (2).
''Producer Prices for Steel Pipe Seen Stabilizing; Mannesmann: End to 'Structural' Crisis Not in Sight,'' *American Metal Market,* September 7, 1987, p. 7.
Regan, James G., ''Mannesmann to Buy 51% VDO Adolf Stake,'' *American Metal Market,* October 25, 1991, p. 4.
Wessel, Horst A., *Kontinuität im Wandel 100 Jahre Mannesmann 1890–1990,* Gütersloh, Mannesman AG, 1990.

—Horst A. Wesse
—updated by Beth Watson Highman

Metromedia Companies

1 Meadowlands Plaza
East Rutherford, New Jersey 07073
U.S.A.
(201) 804-6400
Fax: (201) 804-6540

Private Company
Incorporated: 1955, as Metropolitan Broadcasting Corp.
Employees: 20,000 (est.)
Sales: $2 billion (est.)
SICs: 5812 Eating Places; 4813 Telephone Communications
Services; 7812 Motion Picture Producers and Studios

Metromedia Companies evolved over the course of its relatively brief history from a small, publicly held television and radio company into one of America's largest private partnerships. In 1995, the restaurant and communications conglomerate was controlled by John Kluge, an octogenarian multibillionaire. At that time, over half of Metromedia's holdings were concentrated in several budget steakhouse chains, including Ponderosa, Bonanza, Steak and Ale, and Bennigan's. Metromedia also has a significant stake in WorldCom Inc., a publicly held long-distance telephone service. The company owned a controlling stake in struggling Orion Pictures Corp. after rescuing it from bankruptcy in the late 1980s. In 1995, Metromedia returned to its roots with the acquisition of two Eastern European radio stations.

Chairman John Warner Kluge was the driving force behind Metromedia's formation and growth. Kluge (which means "smart" in German) earned a reputation for identifying promising businesses in their infancy—a knack he has modestly attributed to luck. The independent television stations he accumulated in the 1960s and 1970s formed the nucleus of America's fourth major broadcasting network, Rupert Murdoch's Fox group. His investments in the fledgling cellular telephone and paging industry in the early 1980s quickly grew into a multibillion-dollar stake. But in the early 1990s, media attention focused on his apparent loss of "the Midas touch," as his investments in budget steakhouses and film wallowed.

Kluge (pronounced "Kloo-gy") was born in Germany in 1914 and immigrated to the United States with his family in 1922. He fostered his money-making skills while on scholarship at Columbia University, both in the classroom and at the poker table.

By the time he graduated in 1937 with an economics degree, Kluge's combination of skill and luck helped him accumulate about $7,000 in winnings. (He has since gratefully bestowed over $100 million on his alma mater.) Upon graduation, Kluge went to work at Otten Brothers Co., a small paper company in Detroit. Within four years, he had doubled the firm's sales, earning a 30 percent share of the company as well as its presidency.

After serving in the Army during World War II, Kluge began investing his hoard, purchasing Silver Spring, Maryland's WGAY radio station in 1946 with a partner. Over the next decade, Kluge honed his business skills with a series of wide-ranging ventures. Although Kluge didn't seem enamored with any particular industry segment, several themes began to emerge. First, he was attracted to businesses with high cash flow and low capital requirements. In 1951, for example, he launched a food brokerage. Essentially a manufacturers' representative, he sold goods to supermarkets on a flat 3 percent commission. His brokerage eventually became the largest in the Baltimore-Washington, D.C., metropolitan area, and Kluge maintained a 25 percent interest in the highly profitable business through the early 1980s.

Another hallmark of Kluge's business strategy was his liberal use of debt. Metromedia routinely maintained a higher than average debt-to-equity ratio. Though this tactic was criticized—sometimes strongly—Kluge never got burned. He used leverage in many crafty ways, often as a means to another favorite end, tax avoidance. According to a 1984 *Forbes* article by Allan Sloan, examples of his anti-tax shuffles included "a complicated sale-leaseback of most of the company's outdoor advertising division [and the purchase of] depreciating rights to 100 million of New York City buses and subway cars." Kluge even moved Metromedia's headquarters from New York City to Seacaucus, New Jersey, to avoid the former metropolis's high taxes.

Examples of Kluge's strong contrarian bent have cropped up throughout his career. For example, whereas other venture capitalists shunned the hotel industry in the early 1990s, Kluge sunk at least $150 million in an aging Manhattan hotel. The most significant aspect of Kluge's contrarianism was that it was more often successful than not.

A final noteworthy facet of Kluge's strategy was his passion for cost-cutting. Although he spared no expense on his own lavish lifestyle, strict on-the-job cost controls were sometimes criticized as cheap. In her captious 1988 book *Too Old, Too Ugly and Not Deferential To Men,* Christine Craft, an anchorwoman at one of Metromedia's midwestern television stations, attributed a general lack of upkeep to corporate stinginess. Notwithstanding such criticism, Kluge's combination of strategies served him well.

The budding entrepreneur laid the foundation of what would become a billion-dollar media empire in 1959, when he and a group of investors bought Paramount Pictures' 24 percent interest in Metropolitan Broadcasting Corp. for $4 million. The company's interests included independent television stations in New York and Washington, D.C., (two of the country's leading markets) as well as four radio stations. After assuming leadership of the company, which had been spun off from Allen B. DuMont Laboratories in 1955, Kluge took it public, retaining a 12 percent stake. At the time, Metropolitan was generating about $12.4 million in annual revenues, but its profits were practically nil.

Renamed Metromedia, Inc., in 1961, the company specialized in independent television stations—those not affiliated with one of the three national broadcasting networks. Although some observers judged several of his purchases overpriced (especially since independent television was widely construed as a dead end), the stations were bargains in comparison with their network-affiliated counterparts. Once Metromedia accumulated the FCC-mandated limit of seven television stations, Kluge started "trading up" to stations in ever larger and more influential markets.

But Metromedia's upward climb was not uninterrupted. The company struggled through the 1960s, when many of Kluge's ideas proved too far ahead of their time to suit shareholders and analysts. Hoping to build a multimedia empire, he bought a magazine, bus and subway poster concessions, and attempted to form a fourth television network. (His concept, in fact, came to pass in the form of Rupert Murdoch's News Corp. Ltd.) The extra-curriculars exacerbated six particularly lean years that started in 1969. When, in 1971, one reporter snidely wrote that he had turned "a helluva company into a shelluva company," Kluge launched a rarely suspended personal press blackout. A mid-1970s recession took Metromedia to its 1974 nadir, when the company's stock sunk to $4.25 a share. Kluge tightened cost controls and shed the magazine and other extraneous holdings.

His notoriously good luck combined with Metromedia's retrenchment to pull the company out of its slump shortly thereafter. In 1976, advertisers loosened their purse strings to the benefit of independent as well as network television stations. Metromedia's revenues grew by one fourth that year, and its profits doubled. By 1980, the company's $450 million annual revenues were generating $55 million in profits.

Kluge the contrarian eschewed the hoopla surrounding cable television and focused instead on programming in the late 1970s and early 1980s. Although his own production efforts proved less than successful, Kluge was good at picking off top shows going into syndication. He even applied his contradictory logic to programming, employing "counter-programming"—instead of going head-to-head with network schedules, Metromedia stations slated something different, like putting a sitcom against the evening news. During this period, the company acquired the rights to perennially popular syndicated shows like *All in the Family* and *M*A*S*H*, as well as first-run syndicated programs like *Thicke of the Night* and *Too Close For Comfort.* Metromedia's success was reflected in its stock price, which skyrocketed from $4.50 in 1974 to over $500 by 1983.

By the early 1980s, Metromedia had stations in seven of the top ten markets: New York; Washington, D.C.; Los Angeles; Boston; Houston; Minneapolis-St. Paul; and Cincinnati. His stable of stations was outranked only by network holdings. The company also held the legal limit of 14 radio stations, The Foster & Kleiser billboard company (which had 42,000 billboards by

1982), the Harlem Globetrotters exhibition basketball team, and the Ice Capades figure skating show.

Kluge and a group of investors took Metromedia private late in 1984 with a $1.6 billion deal. The leveraged buyout (LBO) borrowed the vast majority of the money needed to pay off shareholders, pledging future cash flow and projected asset sales to retire the accumulated debt. The terms of the transaction offered public stockholders about $40 per share ($30 in cash and $10 in debt): an 80 percent premium over its normal trade. Although the deal went through, Kluge found himself in a difficult position—he was expected to begin liquidating Metromedia's holdings in order to meet the terms of his heavy debt load. However, he was met with a stagnant market, where low prices for his prime media properties compelled him to sit tight. With the help of famed (and later discredited) junk bond wizard Michael Milken, Kluge bought some time with a "more favorable" debt refinancing.

The Metromedia "garage sale" started in 1985, after Capital Cities Communications's acquisition of the American Broadcasting Corporation heated up the media market. The company raised $2 billion with the sale of six television stations to Rupert Murdoch and the seventh to the Hearst Corporation. In 1986, Metromedia added over $1 billion more to its coffers with the sale of the billboard subsidiary, nine radio stations, the Globetrotters, and the Ice Capades.

Kluge's contrariety helped boost that already massive payoff by billions. Against a prevailing opinion that gauged a ten-year payoff period for carphone investments, he had guided Metromedia's expansion into cellular telephony with a $300 million investment in 1983. Writing for *Forbes* in 1990, Vicki Contavespi called it "one of Kluge's best bets." He sold most of those properties to Southwestern Bell for $1.65 billion and divested the rest for $3 billion in 1990. Within less than two years, the LBO and subsequent selloffs transformed Kluge's 25-percent, $250-million interest in the publicly owned Metromedia into a multibillion personal fortune and made him America's second richest individual.

Kluge began using the proceeds of his media selloff to amass a restaurant empire. In 1988, Metromedia bought the Ponderosa Steak House chain from Asher Edelman. Edelman had bought the 20-year-old business barely a year before, but bailed out to relieve himself of the hefty debt incurred during the LBO. Kluge then bought Dallas-based USA Cafes, operators of Bonanza steakhouses, from the founding Wyly brothers for $83 million in 1989. These two chains formed Metromedia Steakhouses Inc.

The steak segment's top two chains were very different. Ponderosa was concentrated in the Midwest and was dominated by company-owned units. Bonanza's stronghold was in the southwest, and the chain had operated as a "pure franchiser," with only two company-owned locations. After an initial period of criticism—both from Bonanza franchisees and restaurant industry observers—several major Bonanza franchise owners converted to the Ponderosa format. There did not, however, appear to be a concerted effort to compel a wholesale changeover. Metromedia also acquired S&A Restaurant Corp., franchisers of the Steak and Ale and Bennigan's chains to his stable of steak shops. These more upscale steak restaurants were operated separately from the budget chains, as S&A Corp.

Although Kluge was said to have invested over $1 billion in the 1,000 units, they lost more than $190 million from 1989 to 1994. To top it off, by 1993 Ponderosa had slipped from number one to number two, and Bonanza dropped to sixth place in annual sales. Industry analysts blamed the problems on everything from high competition to scanty capital improvements, but no one seemed to know how to turn them around.

Kluge entered a completely different milieu in 1988, when Orion Pictures Corp. was threatened with a hostile takeover from Sumner Redstone's National Amusement Corp. Orion was then headed by Arthur Krim, who called on friend Kluge to act as a "white knight." Kluge's investment of $78 million not only staved off the threat, but gave him a 70 percent interest in the company by the end of the year. But in spite of producing award-winning films like *Platoon, Silence of the Lambs,* and *Dances With Wolves,* Orion ran into trouble in the late 1980s. A string of "box office bombs" combined with Orion's heavy debt load ($500 million debt to $485 million in annual sales) to drive the company into bankruptcy by the end of the 1991. Orion emerged from bankruptcy in 1992, but lost $250 million from 1990 to 1994.

In an effort to maintain the studio's viability, Kluge took the unusual step of merging it with Actava Group, maker of Snapper lawn mowers, and Metromedia Inc., the group's investment arm, to form Metromedia International Marketing Inc. in 1994. This company expanded into Eastern European radio with the early 1995 acquisition of stations in Moscow and Bucharest.

Notwithstanding his apparent missteps into steakhouses and moviemaking, Kluge had his fingers in other, perhaps more promising "pies" as well. In 1990, he bought into a venture called International Telcell, an Eastern European cable television business. He also re-entered the outdoor advertising segment with Metromedia Technologies, the world's only computerized billboard-painting company.

Having acquired International Telephone & Telegraph Corporation's long-distance service division in 1989, Kluge used it as the basis of a strike into the long-distance telephone industry. The September 1993 merger of Metromedia Communications Corp. with Atlanta's Resurgens Communications Group Inc. and LDDS Communications Inc. moved the resulting company into the top tier of long-distance providers, behind American Telephone & Telegraph Company, Sprint Communications Company L.P., and MCI Communications Corporation. With Kluge as chairman, the publicly held company (of which Metromedia Companies retained a significant stake) changed its name to WorldCom Inc. in mid-1995.

Some analysts speculated that Kluge would need to rid himself of the troubled restaurant and movie businesses to concentrate on the long-distance interests. But Joseph Weber of *Business Week* noted that "Metromedia's chief has often been quoted as saying he would be bored with just one business to worry about." There was no question that Kluge had the patience to wait out lean times—he juggled independent television stations that others derided as "dogs" for over two decades before cashing in. Whether the octogenarian still had the stamina to see these projects to profitability was another question entirely.

Although Kluge retained control of Metromedia into the mid-1990s (and the company had no mandatory retirement rule), his General Partner and Executive Vice President Stuart Subotnick emerged as a likely candidate for succession. Subotnick, who was nearly three decades younger than Kluge, had been with Metromedia since 1967. Thrust into the position of chief financial officer upon his superior's untimely death, Subotnick came to the fore in the early 1980s, when Kluge made him a member of his "office of the president" troika. In the late 1980s he had been one of the participants in Kluge's failed LBO venture. Some sources say that he has been a chief (albeit behind-the-scenes) negotiator since the early 1980s. His status as a trusted personal tax advisor to John Kluge, as well as his survival of several upper management purges, appeared to clinch his role as successor.

Further Reading:

Baldo, Anthony, "Orion: Is Kluge Dancing with Wolves?" *FW,* December 11, 1990, p. 14.
Bernstein, Charles, "Conglomerate Menace Stalks Chains," *Nation's Restaurant News,* August 14, 1989, p. 3F.
"Billion-Dollars-Plus Buyback at Metromedia," *Broadcasting,* December 12, 1983, p. 2.
Brooks, Steve, "Round Up: Can an East Coast Billionaire Corral a Herd of Restaurants into One Rugged Team?" *Restaurant Business,* October 10, 1992, p. 86.
Carlino, Bill, "Ponderosa Ropes Bonanza," *Nation's Restaurant News,* September 11, 1989, p. 1.
——, "Wild Ride May Not Be Over for Metromedia and Its Steak Chains," *Nation's Restaurant News,* February 25, 1991, p. 8.
Cohen, Laurie P., "The Man with the Midas Touch Meets His Match in the Nation's Steakhouses," *The Wall Street Journal,* January 3, 1994, p. 9.
Colodny, Mark M., "Jack Kluge's Other Divorce," *Fortune,* June 4, 1990, p. 265.
Contavespi, Vicki, "Tips From Winners in the Game of Wealth," *Forbes,* October 22, 1990, p. 32.
Craft, Christine, *Too Old, Too Ugly, and Not Deferential to Men,* Prima Publishing & Communications, 1988.
Heuton, Cheryl, "Kluge's Return to Radio," *MEDIAWEEK,* April 3, 1995, p. 14.
"Metromedia on a Roller Coaster," *Newsweek,* August 22, 1983, p. 48.
Noer, Michael, "Stu Is Running the Show," *Forbes,* October 24, 1994, p. 284.
Reed, Julia, "The Billionaire Who Just Won't Quit," *U.S. News & World Report,* June 28, 1988, p. 41.
Rudnitsky, Howard, "The Play's the Thing," *Forbes,* June 8, 1981, p. 71.
Sloan, Allan, "The Magician," *Forbes,* April 23, 1984, p. 32.
——, "Metromedia Revisited," *Forbes,* December 17, 1984, p. 32.
——, "Two Paths Diverged: Warren Buffett and John Kluge Investment Activities," *Forbes,* June 3, 1985, p. 40.
Sherman, Strat, "Why Metromedia's Stock Went From $4.25 to $175," *Fortune,* April 5, 1982, p. 96.
Weber, Joseph, "The Millstones at Metromedia," *Business Week,* March 1, 1993, p. 68.

—April Dougal Gasbarre

Michael Baker Corp.

420 Rouser Road
Coraopolis, Pennsylvania 15108
U.S.A.
(412) 269-6300
Fax: (412) 269-2534

Public Company
Incorporated: 1946 as Michael Baker, Jr., Inc.
Employees: 3,175
Operating Revenues: $437.2 million
Stock Exchanges: American Chicago
SICs: 1389 Oil & Gas Field Services, Not Elsewhere
    Classified; 1541 General Contractors—Industrial Buildings
    & Warehouses; 1542 General Contractors—Nonresidential
    Buildings Other Than Industrial Buildings & Warehouses;
    1611 Highway & Street Construction, Except Elevated
    Highways; 1622 Bridge, Tunnel & Elevated Highway
    Construction; 1623 Water, Sewer, Pipeline &
    Communications & Power Line Construction; 8711
    Engineering Services

Michael Baker Corp. is one of the oldest and largest profes-
sional-services companies in the United States, providing engineering, construction, and operations and maintenance services
worldwide. In the mid-1990s its primary services were engineering design for the infrastructure market, including highways and bridges; operation and maintenance of oil and gas
production facilities; construction and construction management services for building construction; and digital mapping,
airport design, and environmental engineering.

Michael Baker Jr. was born in 1912 in Beaver, Pennsylvania.
His mother died when he was only six weeks old and, as one of
12 children, he had, he later observed, "a constant desire to
express myself and get attention . . . and a terrible hunger for
affection." His father, a civil engineer, demanded strict dedication to church, duty, and hard work. Baker left home to study
engineering at Pennsylvania State University but had to drop
out after his freshman year because his father's business collapsed during the Great Depression.

After a year of drifting around the country looking for work,
Baker landed a job in Jamestown, Pennsylvania, as timekeeper
on the construction of a dam. Soon after, he struck out on his
own as a contractor but wound up penniless when he bid too low

on a land-clearance project. A $200 loan he solicited from a
Beaver benefactor enabled him to return to Penn State, and he
graduated at the top of his engineering class. Too restless and
ambitious to work for others, he tried contracting again but went
bankrupt before the end of 1939.

Undaunted, Baker launched the Michael Baker, Jr. consulting
firm in Rochester, Pennsylvania, in 1940. Willing to take any
job and backed by six-months' credit on his office rent, he
grossed $15,000 by year's end and was employing eight men. In
1941 his billings reached $84,000. Soon after the Japanese
attack on Pearl Harbor, Baker won an assignment to conduct
surveys of a defense property near Paducah, Kentucky, and
complete them in a near-impossible 60 days. Borrowing money
for the necessary equipment from the local bank, he assembled
25 survey parties and finished the task in 45 days. By the end of
World War II Baker had provided engineering services to 122
airfields extending from Brazil to Alaska. He also found time
to design the eastern part of Pittsburgh's Penn-Lincoln Parkway East.

After the war Baker expanded his focus to community planning,
aerial mapping, irrigation, hydroelectric projects, bridge design,
and other public works, and he established an architectural
association for the design of schools, hospitals, other public
structures, and industrial plants. In 1946 he incorporated his
firm as Michael Baker, Jr., Inc. Billings exceeded more than
$1.5 million in 1948, when net profit came to over $100,000. By
the end of 1949 the company had eight divisions offering engineering services ranging from architecture to water control.

One of these divisions was earmarked for international assignments. In 1951 Michael Baker was made the consulting engineer and construction administrator for Saudi Arabia. This post
entailed the design of harbor facilities, customs buildings, major
highway systems, airports, water supply and electrical systems,
a private hospital for the royal family, a $30-million air base,
and additions to the royal palaces. Baker also acted as purchasing agent for the king, and his firm was responsible for maintenance work in the king's harem, a signal honor.

Baker's billings reached $5.7 million in 1955, when the firm's
profits were $200,000. Roughly half of the work came from
highways, about one-sixth from defense projects, and about
one-tenth from foreign operations. The number of divisions had
grown to ten in 1957, when there were a dozen branch offices
and four foreign ones. In 1956 the company became consulting
engineer to the Pennsylvania Turnpike Commission and the
Delaware River Joint Toll Bridge Commission, positions it
retained into the 1990s. Michael Baker, a colleague told a
Fortune reporter in 1957, "can smell engineering work like a
bird dog smells game. And he's thinking about next year, while
you're still thinking about today." He personally reviewed
every proposal, project, bill, and billing.

In 1958, when *Engineering News-Record* ranked Baker as the
largest architectural-engineering firm in the United States, the
firm had 1,009 employees. In 1960 the company was awarded a
contract to design Pittsburgh's Three Rivers Stadium. In the
same year the Philippines awarded the firm contracts to design a
wharf and marine slipway for the port of Manila and to procure
dredging services. Baker surveyed and staked out a 236-mile

natural-gas pipeline route from Ohio to Pennsylvania in 1967. Its revenues came to $12.7 million that year, when net income was $543,387.

Baker became a publicly owned corporation in 1968, with 60 percent of the first-issued common-stock shares, however, in Michael Baker's hands. The shares, offered at $12 each, rose to nearly $20 during the year. A year later Baker had 13 divisions. It had developed a data bank in excess of 300 computer programs used in the location and design of highways and utilities, the analysis and design of structures, soil analysis, population projections, and traffic and revenue studies. About 61 percent of its revenues were coming from state and local governments and agencies, nine percent from the federal government, and the remaining 30 percent from private industry.

By 1972 Baker could boast of having designed more than 7,000 miles of highway, the Pennsylvania Turnpike tunnels, the Squirrel Hill and Fort Pitt tunnels in Pittsburgh, the Mississippi Memorial Stadium (as well as Three Rivers Stadium), the 44-story Wells Fargo Building in San Francisco, and Seattle's Space Needle. But volume dropped from $21.3 million in 1970 to $19.8 million in 1971, and net income from about $1 million to about $500,000. In 1972 the company lost $473,000 on contract income of $20.1 million. In that year the firm's name was changed to Euthenics Systems Corp., but in 1975 it became the Michael Baker Corp.

Baker's fortunes were restored by the Trans-Alaska Pipeline. It designed the 360-mile main state road from the Yukon River to the state's North Slope plus more than 200 miles of access road connecting it to the pipeline route. The firm also designed part of the 796-mile-long pipeline itself and a suspension bridge to carry the pipeline over the Tanana River. Between 1969 and 1979 350 employees spent 3 million labor hours on the project, which accounted for about 50 percent of the company's revenue and 90 percent of its profit.

There were other notable accomplishments in the 1970s, including the design of the New River Gorge Bridge in West Virginia, with the world's longest single-span steel arch. When oil began flowing through the Alaska pipeline in 1977, however, there was little more for Baker to do, and the drawbacks of dependency on a single project immediately became obvious. Company president William L. Shaw later explained to a *Management Review* reporter, "We looked around for something else to do, and all those long-time clients whom we had served for many years said, 'Where were you when we needed you?' " Contract income nosedived from $28.3 million in 1977 to $19.8 million in 1978, and the company lost money in both 1978 and 1979.

Michael Baker Jr. died in 1977 and was succeeded by Michael Baker III as the company's chairman and chief executive officer. A protracted period of instability ensued, in which dissatisfied shareholders twice tried to overturn the management. Canadian investors holding nearly 14 percent of the common stock contemplated a takeover in 1982, and Century Engineering Inc. of Towson, Maryland, made an offer in 1983, when the company lost $1 million and was faced with impending bankruptcy. Instead, Baker workers agreed in 1984 to buy nearly 40 percent of the company's outstanding common shares, through an

employee stock-ownership plan (ESOP), from Baker family members and a family trust for $8.9 million, or $9 a share. Shaw succeeded Baker as chairman and chief executive officer. Early in 1985 the ESOP raised its stake in the company to 70 percent.

In the last months of Baker's reign, Shaw conceded to *Management Review,* "morale was terrible . . . probably as low as I've ever seen it in this company." About 600 of the 1,000 employees had been laid off and "Michael III isolated himself from the employees and the clients. . . . Our strategy at that particular point in our life was to be in business for the next year." Baker not only had to attract new customers and lure back old ones but improve its reputation. Shaw admitted, "We didn't do anything on time, we didn't meet the schedules, we didn't meet the budgets, and our performance was lousy." Even a client as old as the Pennsylvania Department of Transportation vowed never to give the company another job.

Baker's reputation was also damaged by its dependence on government contracts. A 1991 *Barron's* article described the company founder as "basically a salesman rather [than] an engineer [who] built his business through political links and contributions to politicians, especially those who influenced the awarding of public works contracts." When the U.S. attorney for western Pennsylvania, Richard Thornburgh, a Republican, brought Michael Baker Jr. before a federal grand jury to question him about contributions to the 1970 campaign of Governor Milton Shapp, a Democrat, Baker took the Fifth Amendment. He said that the company recently had paid the Internal Revenue Service an additional $100,000 in taxes, and that he had paid an additional $27,000 for the years 1970 and 1971 but added that no criminal charges or fraud penalties were involved.

Baker's profitability, aided by a $1 million cost-control program and an expanding national economy, soon returned, and in 1986 the company for a second straight year won an award for financial management achievement from the Professional Services Management Association. In 1989 contract revenues passed $100 million and net income reached nearly $2.3 million. One important asset was the acquisition, at the end of 1986, of Intelcom Support Services, Inc., a Texas-based firm providing contract operations and maintenance services to military and other government installations. Expanding Baker's core business to operations and maintenance meant, according to Shaw, "multiyear contracts with excellent cash flows . . . not subject to the fluctuations you experience in the pure engineering design business."

Further acquisitions also expanded Baker's scope. In 1990 the company purchased MO Services, Inc., of Houston, a firm engaged in providing operations and maintenance services to oil and gas producers, utilities, and industrial customers. The next year it acquired certain assets of the former Mellon Stuart Co., an action that placed Baker in general contracting, construction, and construction management. This closed the gap between design and maintenance in company operations, and by late 1991 Baker was receiving half its revenues from construction. In 1993 Baker completed the acquisition of Overseas Technical Services International, which was providing operations and maintenance services worldwide to major oil and gas producers.

Between 1985 and 1990 Baker averaged annual growth of 20 percent. Employment rose to 2,040 in 1991, compared to only 420 in 1984. Shaw credited much of the company's success to its ESOP, which had a stake in the company valued at $28 million in mid-1991, compared to the initial $3 million in 1984. Employees, he said, rather than expensive consultants, not only identified Baker's acquisition targets but also participated in the ensuing acquisition process. "Previously, we had good engineers and scientists," the president of a Baker subsidiary told a *Wall Street Journal* reporter in 1991. "Now, we have good engineers and scientists who are also good businessmen."

Baker's outlook soured again, however, in 1993, when the company lost $15.1 million on revenues of $434.8 million. Shaw attributed Baker's problems to Intelcom, which began losing money in 1991 as a result of a misguided decision to branch into cable installation and housing renovation. Baker lost money again in 1994, more than $7.9 million on contract revenues of $437.2 million. The 1994 deficit arose from a $10 million pretax charge taken not only to deal with Intercom's problems but also projects by Mellon Stuart for government agencies in the Chicago area that became embroiled in claims and disputes. The company's stock lost 60 percent of its value in 1994. Long-term debt, however, fell from $7.7 million to under $4 million during the year. Baker's ESOP held 29 percent of Baker's common stock and 67 percent of the voting power at the end of 1994.

Effective in 1995, Baker converted its three groups—engineering, construction, and operations and maintenance—to five market-focused units—transportation, general buildings, civil, energy, and environmental. The general-buildings sector accounted for 43 percent of contract revenues in 1994; transportation, 22 percent; civil, 18 percent; energy, 10 percent; and environmental, 7 percent. Among the principal markets for the company's services in 1994, some 40 percent came from commercial, industrial, and private clients; 35 percent from various state governmental and quasi-governmental agencies; and 25 percent from the federal government.

Baker's corporate staff in 1995 was being housed in leased office space in Coraopolis, Pennsylvania. The company owned a 75,000-square-foot office building on a 175-acre in Beaver County, Pennsylvania. Office space also was being leased in 13 other states and in Guam, Abu Dhabi, and England.

Principal Subsidiaries: Aerial Map Service Co.; Baker & Associates; Baker Engineering, Inc.; Baker Engineering NY, Inc.; Baker Environmental, Inc.; Baker/MO Services, Inc.; Intelcom Support Services, Inc.; Mellon Stuart Construction, Inc.; Overseas Technical Service International; Umwelt Consulting GmbH; Weston Geophysical Corp.

Further Reading:

"Consulting Engineer Goes Public," *Engineering News-Record,* June 27, 1968, pp. 67–68.
Gordon, Mitchell, "Blueprint Calls for Sharp Rise in Earnings for Michael Baker," *Barron's,* May 5, 1975, pp. 46–47, 52.
Mason, Julie Cohen, "On the Road to Recovery," *Management Review,* April 1991, pp. 23–24.
Maurer, Herrymon, "Michael Baker of the Turnpikes," *Fortune,* July 1957, pp. 140–41, 145–46, 150, 152.
"Michael Baker CEO Resigns After Unusual $5-Million Loss," *Engineering News-Record,* September 27, 1993, p. 8.
"Michael Baker, Jr. Inc.," *Wall Street Transcript,* April 28, 1969, p. 16459, and February 10, 1972, pp. 27583–84.
"Michael Baker Losses Show Pitfalls of Plans," *Engineering News-Record,* January 2–9, 1995, p. 26.
Narisetti, Raju, "Worker Input Helps an ESOP—and a Company—Work," *Wall Street Journal,* July 12, 1991, p. B2.
Palmer, Jay, "Baker the Moneymaker," *Barron's,* December 16, 1991, pp. 18–19.

—Robert Halasz

Michigan Bell Telephone Co.

444 Michigan Avenue
Detroit, Michigan 48226-2557
U.S.A.
(313) 223-9900
Fax: (313) 496-9321

Wholly Owned Subsidiary of Ameritech Corporation
Incorporated: 1904
Employees: 12,761
Sales: $2.85 billion
SICs: 4813 Telephone Communications Except Radio; 4822
   Telegraph & Other Communications

Michigan Bell, a wholly owned subsidiary of Ameritech Corp.,
is the primary supplier of local telephone service in Michigan.
The company, in business since the turn of the century, was
controlled by the American Telegraph and Telephone Co. until
the break-up of the telecommunications giant in 1984. Since
1993, all of the company's merchandise and services have been
marketed under the Ameritech brand name, although the Michigan Bell name continues to be used for corporate filings. In
addition to providing local and intra-regional toll telephone service to 82 percent of Michigan residents, Michigan Bell now
offers a diverse set of services including data transmission, radio
and television transmission, voice mail, and billing services.

The honor for owning the first telephone in Michigan goes to a
Grand Rapids plaster company whose president was a close
personal friend of Alexander Graham Bell. Bell sent his friend a
pair of prototype telephones and a public demonstration of the
scientific marvel was held on August 4, 1877. The following
month, the first commercial telephone line was installed between a Detroit drugstore and its laboratory almost two miles
away. By October, a set of telephones were connecting the units
of the Detroit police department.

Given that Bell had produced the first working model of the
telephone only one year earlier, public acceptance of the new
technology occurred with amazing rapidity. The Bell Telephone
Company was officially incorporated in Boston on July 9, 1877
and by October of that year they had granted a license to the
Michigan Telephone and Telegraph Construction Company to
operate phone lines in the Detroit area. These early telephones
had to be directly connected to each other by wires strung across
rooftops as the system of telephone exchanges had not yet been
perfected. In addition to poor sound quality, the early Bell

phones had only one transmitter/receiver and people had a
difficult time adjusting to the new style of conversation. ''After
speaking, transfer the telephone from the mouth to the ear very
promptly,'' instructed one Bell telephone ad,''When replying to
communication from another, do not speak too promptly . . .
much trouble is caused from both parties speaking at the same
time. When you are not speaking, you should be listening.''
These difficulties were to be overcome fairly quickly but much
to Bell Telephone's distress, it was the giant Western Union
Telegraph Company that would be responsible for the introduction of both the first telephone exchanges as well as a technically superior telephone apparatus.

Although the Bell company, by then renamed The American
Bell Telephone Company, staunchly maintained that Western
Union was violating their patent, in 1878 the giant telegraph
company entered the telephone business by constructing a
series of local telephone exchanges in their telegraph offices
across the nation. The first Michigan exchange was opened in
August of that year in the Detroit office of the American District
Telegraph Company and a second exchange was opened the
following year in Grand Rapids. An enraged American Bell
sued Western Union over the patent infringement and in the fall
of 1879 an agreement was reached between the two companies
whereby Western Union gave up all its telephone patents and
facilities in exchange for 20 percent of telephone rental receipts
over the seventeen year life of the Bell patents. With the issue of
competition out of the way at least until the patents expired, Bell
set to work expanding its telephone system.

A large number of local telephone companies were founded in
Michigan over the next two years, each operating under an
American Bell license that allowed the company to control all
lines within a 15 mile radius of its central office. By 1880, Bell-
licensed telephone exchanges were in operation in almost all
major lower Michigan towns from Cadillac in the north to Port
Huron and Grand Rapids in the east and west. During the next
few years the challenge would be to connect these local exchanges. Not only were there serious technical difficulties in
extending telephone lines beyond the 15–20 mile limit, but the
distribution of fees between the local licensees was also problematic. The Michigan Bell Telephone Company was founded
in 1881 as a holding company that would control a number of
smaller licensees and facilitate interconnection. This company
would soon merge with the largest of the local concerns, the
Detroit based Telephone and Telegraph Construction Company,
which become the Michigan Telephone Company. By 1885
Detroit had long distance connections to all major towns within
a 100 mile radius including Saginaw, Flint, Lansing, Ann Arbor
and Toledo, Ohio.

In 1894 Alexander Graham Bell's telephone patent expired and
a whole new era of telephone competition was inaugurated.
While in certain areas of the East Coast the American Bell
Telephone Company managed to maintain control of most telephone services, in the Midwest a large number of hastily formed
independent telephone companies made major inroads into
Bell's market. Michigan was one of the centers of this growth in
non-affiliated companies and at the turn of the century many
Michigan cities including Detroit and Grand Rapids had two or
three competing telephone systems. Bell steadfastly refused to
let these independents connect to their lines so that customers
had to choose between companies and could not communicate

by phone outside of their system. Businesses were forced to subscribe to both companies if they wanted to be available to the full range of the citizenry. By 1898 the Michigan Independent Telephone Association could boast that their members operated 16,000 telephones in the state against 14,000 for American Bell.

The Bell System, now under the aegis of the American Telephone and Telegraph Corporation, responded to this new competition by consolidating its Michigan holdings into a single entity. The Michigan State Telephone Company was incorporated in 1904 as the successor to the Michigan Bell Telephone Company (in 1924 it would resume this earlier name), but now with control over all Bell telephone exchanges in the state of Michigan. The Bell System found itself in an awkward position during the first two decades of the century. Not only was Bell faced with an onslaught of competing companies but its refusal to allow the independents to connect to AT&T long distance lines had given rise to an anti-trust investigation by the federal Department of Justice. Forced to move cautiously for fear of generating public and government animosity, Michigan Bell bought only one small telephone company during this period. Public attitude towards the company would reverse itself, however, following a brief government takeover during World War I.

President Wilson's nationalization of the entire telephone system in 1918 was officially justified on the grounds of national defense, but was also clearly the result of growing public animosity towards the monopolistic practices of big business at that time. Governmental control of the more then ten million telephones then in operation was, however, an unmitigated disaster. Local phone rates rose sharply while revenues fell. By the time the federal government returned the telephone system to private ownership in 1919, revenues on the 261,000 telephones in the Michigan Bell system had fallen from $8 million to just under $5 million. After much public brow-beating over the failure of nationalization, by 1921 Congress was ready to pass the Graham Act, which formally exempted telephony from the Sherman Antitrust Act as far as consolidation of competing companies was concerned. At the same time, AT&T was ordered to allow independent companies to connect to Bell System lines, thus putting an end to the era of the multi-company town. AT&T lost no time in buying up its competitors. Between 1922 and 1932 Michigan Bell purchased 17 independent companies. By the end of this spurt of acquisitions 527,000 of the 623,000 telephones in Michigan were operated by Michigan Bell. This approximately 80 percent market share would remain virtually unchanged through the rest of the 20th century.

Of all of the Bell regional operating companies, Michigan Bell was the hardest hit by the Great Depression. Coming at the end of the largest period of growth for the company since its founding, the stock market crash and subsequent economic collapse saw Michigan Bell's earnings per share drop from $9.00 to only $1.30 in 1933. Business closings had caused 200,000 customers to cancel service and uncollectible accounts rose to almost $1 million. It was not until 1939 that revenues and the number of telephones in service would climb back to pre-depression levels.

Although the Graham Act was intended to resolve many of AT&T's conflicts with the federal administration, the 1930s was a period of growing animosity between Bell System's operating companies and the state commissions that regulated

them. Many state regulators complained that the license and equipment fees that parent AT&T charged to its operating companies were unreasonably high. Since local service rates were based on the operating companies' costs and earnings, it was claimed that these inflated fees were enriching AT&T stockholders at the expense of the local rate payers.

In Michigan, this issue became centered around inequities related to intrastate toll rates. The Michigan Public Service Commission balked at the inequity and ordered Michigan Bell to reduce its rates. Bell appealed to the Michigan Supreme Court but eventually lost its case and was forced to lower intrastate toll rates. This battle was to be repeated in the 1940s at a time when the Bell System throughout the country was seeking rate hikes after freezes during World War II. In 1944, the Michigan Public Service Commission made the unprecedented decision to order Michigan Bell to refund retroactively $3.5 million of its 1944 local service revenues. Although this decision was eventually overturned in court, extended litigation over the calculation of rates would continue into the 1950s. In 1952, the Public Service Commission finally prevailed when the Michigan Supreme Court ordered Bell to refund over $13 million in past revenues. Although squabbles between the company and the Commission over the setting of rates would persist into the 1960s and 1970s, serious debate about the nature of this regulation would not reappear until the early 1990s.

The 1960s and 1970s were a time of prosperity and growth for Michigan Bell. The number of telephones in operation which had reached a million by 1942 and two million ten years later, underwent the fastest rate of growth in Michigan Bell's history during this period. From 1960 to 1980, about 200,000 new telephones were added to the Michigan Bell system each year. Technological advances including electronic switching and direct distance dialing, which had first been introduced in Birmingham, Michigan in 1956, became important tools in dealing with the tremendous number of calls being placed. Although prevented by the FCC from straying too far away from telephony, Michigan Bell also entered the data communications field with private-line voice and teletype services. By 1983 annual revenues had surpassed $2 billion.

While Michigan Bell thrived, in 1974 parent AT&T became the object of a federal antitrust suit brought on in part by accusations of unfair trade practices in its dealings with competitor MCI. In 1982, after ten years of litigation and political wrangling, AT&T's virtual monopoly of the American telephone system was ordered dissolved. The consent decree, to take effect on January 1, 1984, mandated that the company divest itself of the principal assets of its Bell System operating companies, which were to be controlled instead by seven regional holding companies. Each region was to be divided into Local Access and Transfer Areas (LATAs) generally centered on a city or community and the Regional Holding Companies were to control all intra-LATA telecommunications services. AT&T was to retain control of all inter-LATA long distance services as well as telecommunications equipment manufacture and distribution. Michigan Bell, along with Bell operating companies from Wisconsin, Ohio, Illinois, and Indiana, became subsidiaries of the American Information Technologies Corporation (Ameritech) Regional Holding Company. The divestiture shook the telecommunications industry. Investors were uncertain how the newly formed holding companies would perform without the financial security of the giant corporation behind them.

Michigan Bell annual reports began this new corporate era with a tone of concern. Revenues dropped slightly in the first year of post divestiture operation as the company lost significant revenues from the transfer of equipment leasing services to AT&T. In addition, network access fees, which were designed to compensate the company for the use of its facilities by AT&T and other long distance carriers, did not yet make up for lost toll revenues. The Consent Decree stipulated that the Regional Holding Companies could provide only a limited range of services beyond traditional regulated telephone service. The challenge to Ameritech and its subsidiaries was to expand their market base within these regulations. One of the first successes for Michigan Bell was its Centrex service, which provided a number of telephone features such as call waiting and call transfer directly from Bell exchanges and thereby eliminated expensive telephone equipment. It soon became apparent that not only would the reborn Baby Bells survive on their own, they would thrive. Ameritech common stock price, which sold at about $12 a share during its first year of trading, doubled within less than two years and had reached $34 a share by the end of the decade.

After the initial challenges of divestiture, Michigan Bell revenues began to climb once again. Substantial gains were made in the business sector where new services increased both the number of lines in use and the charges per line. As parent Ameritech became both more diversified in its services and more confident of its direction, the division of its operations on a regional basis no longer seemed justifiable. In 1993, Ameritech undertook a major reorganization that assigned customers to business units based on the nature of the services provided rather than geographic location. At the same time, the company began a major campaign to increase awareness of the Ameritech brand name by replacing all references to the regional Bell companies with the Ameritech name. Bills, company trucks, hard hats and all company literature would now all bear the Ameritech logo. Michigan Bell and its sister companies continued to exist as distinct entities only for the purposes of regulation and stock-related filings.

Ameritech corporate policy was shaped by two main forces through the 1980s. As the company expanded its services, it ran up against, and sought to extend, the strict limitations that had been imposed by the AT&T divestiture Consent Decree. On the state level, Ameritech was regulated by five separate state commissions each with its own agenda, and all still operating under the tradition of rate setting based on a percentage of earnings that had been established at the turn of the century. Michigan Bell was the first of Ameritech's subsidiaries to make substantial headway with state regulators.

Indeed, with a newly elected, business-friendly Republican government, and an economy that was struggling to recover from an extended recession, Michigan Bell felt that it was in a position to push for a new basis for telephone regulation. In 1991, the Michigan government passed the Michigan Telecommunications Act that substantially reduced the Public Service Commission's authority over the introduction and pricing of many tele-

communication services. The new regulation was founded primarily on price caps rather than rates of return, freeing up company earnings for reinvestment in infrastructure and allowing the company to introduce a more flexible and competitive pricing structure. In this new regulatory environment, Michigan Bell was also free to introduce new services including interactive video and cable television provided the company could get permission from the Federal authorities to extend the provisions of the Consent Decree. The Michigan Telecommunications Act would become the model for similar regulatory schemes in the four other states in which Ameritech operated.

The United States District Court that had issued the original Consent Decree granted several waivers to the Regional Holding Companies during the late 1980s, permitting them to engage in the transmission of information services on a limited basis. In 1993, after a series of appeals, the waiver was extended to include the generation as well as the transmission of information. In 1995 four communities in Wayne County, Michigan, became the first potential customers of a new Ameritech Video Network when they signed an agreement, pending Federal approval, to obtain cable television services from Ameritech. Ameritech also continued to press the court for a lifting of the ban on the regional Bells entry into the long distance market.

While four of the other Regional Holding Companies took legal action to remove the prohibition, Ameritech began negotiations with the Justice Department to reach an agreement on the matter. In 1995, the Justice Department recommended that Ameritech be granted the right to provide limited long distance service in Detroit and Chicago on a trial basis in exchange for facilitating competition in the local exchange market. The door to local telephone competition in Michigan was opened for the first time in 1995 when the Michigan Public Service Commission authorized a small Michigan firm to compete with Ameritech in the Ann Arbor and Detroit areas. Although the details and pace of these changes remained under negotiation in late 1995, it seemed clear that as Michigan Bell entered the 21st century, Michigan telephone service was poised to once again enter a period of competition that had been unknown since the first growth in telephone service a century earlier.

Further Reading:

"Ameritech gets first real competition in local service," *Detroit Free Press,* February 24, 1995.
Bodwin, Amy, "Ameritech hopes name rings a bell," *Crain's Detroit Business,* August 30, 1993, p. 1.
Brooks, John, *Telephone: The First Hundred Years,* New York: Harper and Row, 1975.
Castine, John and Hiawatha Bray, "A New Line for Ameritech: Deal Would Allow Company to Provide Cable TV Service," *Detroit Free Press,* June 29, 1995, p. 1G.
History of the Telephone in Michigan, Detroit: Michigan Bell Telephone Co., 1969.
Kelly, Kevin, "Call Ameritech a baby bellwether," *Business Week,* April 17, 1995, p. 90.
Michigan Bell Telephone Company Annual Reports, Detroit: Michigan Bell Telephone Co., 1984–1994.
Tell, Lawrence J. "Footloose and Fancy Free: The Bell Operating Companies Are Doing Splendidly," *Barron's,* November 12, 1984, p. 8–9.

—Hilary Gopnik

National Sea Products Ltd.

Battery Point
Lunenburg, Nova Scotia BOJ 2CO
Canada
(902) 634-8811
Fax: (902) 634-4577

Public Company
Founded: 1945
Employees: 1,600
Sales: C$245.61 million
Stock Exchanges: Toronto Montreal
SICs: 2091 Canned & Cured Fish & Seafoods; 2092 Fresh or
Frozen Prepared Fish

National Sea Products Ltd. is a leading Canadian harvester, procurer, processor, and marketer of fish and seafood. Up until the early 1990s the company had been Canada's largest fish-processing company and one of the world's largest fishing enterprises. Since that time, National Sea has restructured and shifted its focus to procurement and marketing. National Sea's principal subsidiary is National Sea Products Inc., a manufacturer and distributor of retail frozen seafood products throughout the United States.

National Sea Products was formed in 1945. Its origins, though, can be traced back to 1899, when W. C. Smith & Company Limited was founded. That enterprise was established by fishermen in the village of Lunenburg on the coast of Nova Scotia. French Huguenots (Protestants, many of whom were persecuted and fled France) settled Lunenburg in the 1750s and eventually established a healthy fishing industry. W. C. Smith was formed as a salt fish operation. The business was successful, and in the 1920s the same group of shareholders decided to diversify into fresh fish and the burgeoning market for cold-stored fish. To that end, they formed Lunenburg Sea Products Limited in 1926.

In 1938, Lunenburg Sea Products and W. C. Smith & Company merged to form a single company. Then, in 1945, that organization merged with Maritime National Fish Company Limited of Halifax and some other companies. The resultant organization was dubbed National Sea Products Limited. It was officially amalgamated and recognized under the laws of Nova Scotia in 1967. During the 1950s, 1960s, and 1970s, National Sea expanded and became a powerhouse in the Canadian and North American fishing industries, offering everything from cod and

shrimp to scallops and lobster. It amassed a sizable fleet of fishing vessels along the Canadian Atlantic coast and became recognized as the largest Canadian fish processing company and even one of the world's largest fishing enterprises.

National Sea's greatest growth occurred during the 1970s. The company's owner at the time was H. B. Nickerson & Sons Ltd. Nickerson became convinced that National Sea would reap huge rewards when Canada declared a 200-mile coastal fishing zone in 1977. To take advantage of the enlarged zone, National Sea borrowed heavily and invested in new ships and processing facilities. When the declaration was made in 1977, National Sea boosted its fishing efforts and was able to increase volume sales substantially. Unfortunately, other companies boosted their hauls as well. The result was industry overcapacity. Fish prices collapsed, leaving National Sea and many other companies barely able to pay for operating costs. To make matters worse, interest rates shot up and National Sea staggered under its massive debt load.

By the early 1980s National Sea was teetering on the edge of bankruptcy. The situation had become so intolerable for the entire East Coast fishing industry, in fact, that the Canadian government decided to step in with a recovery plan. It took more than a year for the government to whip together a program to save the industry. By that time (1984) National Sea was gasping. It faced a staggering $250 million debt load and was sitting on $50 million to $60 million worth of warehoused fish that it couldn't sell. With National Sea and other fishing companies in deep trouble, the national government decided to nationalize the industry and bring it under government control. National Sea management scrambled, tapping all of its political and business connections, and barely managed to save the company from a government takeover.

Keeping National Sea a private company initially seemed to have been a good move. Indeed, after a six-year string of depressing losses culminating in a $19 million 1984 deficit, National Sea posted a $10.1 million profit in 1985 on sales of about $450 million. The turnaround was largely attributable to recovering prices and lower interest rates, which allowed National Sea to refinance much of its debt. However, an aggressive reorganization initiative contributed to National Sea's recovery. Although it had operated under various owners and leaders, National Sea had effectively functioned as a family-controlled company since its inception. In the early 1980s the company was being lead by David Hennigar, who was part of the Jodrey family. The Jodreys were among Nova Scotia's wealthiest and most powerful families. They also owned a large portion of National Sea's shares. Other big shareholders included the Sobey family and Bill Morrow, the grandson of one of National Sea's founders.

After the stifling setbacks of the late 1970s and early 1980s, National Sea's complexion began to change from that of a family-owned company to that of a public company. That shift was caused, in large part, by Gordon Cummings. Hennigar had hired Cummings in 1984, shortly after National Sea had launched a reorganization effort. Cummings, who had formerly been a senior partner at a management consulting firm, joined National Sea in 1984 and succeeded Hennigar as head of day-to-day operations. He was named president of the company in

1985. Cummings was brought in because of his complete under-standing of fishing industry finances as well as his proven track record in business.

Cummings had dropped out of high school at the age of 16 and taken a job as a mail clerk. Realizing that his future was limited, the ambitious Cummings began taking courses in his spare time. He eventually attained a college degree and even a masters degree in business administration in 1969. By 1974 the 33-year-old Cummings had become a partner at Woods Gordon Inc., a management consulting firm. He also became involved in regional politics, which helped him when he joined the politically connected National Sea in 1984. For example, Cummings managed to persuade Ottawa to allow National Sea to operate a high-tech, deep-sea factory freezer trawler capable of processing and freezing fish at sea (the company had been turned down for a license four times in the previous eight years). The license was expected at the time to add $4 million annually to the company's bottom line.

Cummings began a radical facelift of National Sea in 1984. Among his first moves was to sell off six of the company's 21 small processing plants, mostly to local operators, who Cummings believed could operate more efficiently. He eliminated some workers and restructured management as part of an effort to reduce the company's bloated bureaucracy. He moved the company's U.S. marketing headquarters, for example, from Florida to New Hampshire and installed an aggressive new sales team there. Importantly, Cummings recognized the need to diversify the company, reducing its traditional emphasis on harvesting and branching out into more marketing-driven arenas. To that end, National Sea launched a drive to become a major player in the North American market for frozen consumer fish products, such as battered fish sticks.

Among Cummings's most notable efforts was his bid to make National Sea a global company. Heading up that initiative was 30-year-old Henry E. Demone, who would later play a pivotal role at National Sea. Demone was a native of Lunenburg and a third-generation National Sea employee. In fact, both his father and grandfather had served as captains on the company's ships, and Demone's father, Earl, had served as the skipper of the most successful vessel in National Sea's fleet. Henry himself had gone to sea at the age of 17, working one summer with the crew of a National Sea trawler. After finishing first in his high school class and then getting his college degree, Demone's short career carried him around the world as a crew member on a German trawler and then as a sales manager in France for a Swedish food company.

In 1984 Demone was called back to help with the reorganization of National Sea. As vice-president of international marketing, Demone spearheaded National Sea's drive into France, Hong Kong, Australia, Argentina, and other areas. The goal was to make National Sea a global player in the fish distribution business. In fact, Demone's efforts, combined with other strategic moves engineered by Cummings, helped to rocket National Sea's profits more than threefold in 1986 to about $36 million. At the time, Cummings was heralded as the savior of National Sea and even the "Iacocca of Nova Scotia." Unfortunately, National Sea's good fortune evaporated as quickly as it had appeared. National Sea soon suffered a number of setbacks, including a decline in fish exports as a result of the appreciation of the Canadian dollar, a mussel scare, and a tuna-canning scandal.

During the late 1980s National Sea languished. Believing that his strategic course was generally correct, however, Cummings continued to expand internationally, invest, and diversify into new ventures. Going into 1987 National Sea was generating more than $450 million in annual sales, employing 8,000 workers, and supporting operations in all four Atlantic provinces and three U.S. states in addition to its growing overseas units. Unfortunately, a sharp reduction in Canadian fishing quotas thwarted National Sea's recovery. Overfishing, among other factors, contributed to a serious decline in the amount of fish that National Sea was allowed to catch. The company's stock price had rocketed to a record C$35 in 1987 from less than $5 a few years earlier. But then company began to suffer losses. By 1989 National Sea's stock price had plummeted to a lowly $9.

In fact, by 1989 National Sea still faced mounting losses and heavy debt, just as it had during the industry turmoil of the early 1980s. Frustrated with Cummings's long-term strategy for National Sea, Hennigar fired him as president in 1989 and brought in the 35-year-old Demone to lead the company. Demone steered National Sea on another radically different course during the early 1990s. Part of the new strategy was adopted out of necessity. Canadian offshore fishing quotas plummeted during the early 1990s and effectively squelched any opportunities available in National Sea's traditional harvesting business. In fact, the national quota plunged from 316,000 metric tons in 1990 to a strikingly low 34,700 metric tons in 1995; National Sea's quota crashed from 123,000 tons to just 14,400 tons.

As profits from harvesting businesses declined, Demone sought to increase profits from other segments while shoring up the company's bleeding balance sheet. To that end, he initiated an aggressive cost-cutting program. He sold off several of the company's ships and processing facilities and nearly halved National Sea's workforce to just 4,200 by 1992. Ironically, he began dismantling the globalization program that he had overseen during the mid- and late 1980s. The international pullback represented Demone's intent to refocus all of the company's resources on North America. Specifically, Demone planned to intensify National Sea's efforts in the consumer frozen foods market. Evidencing the shift was the fact that only 40 percent of National Sea's fish products were harvested on company vessels, compared to about 80 percent in the mid-1980s.

As National Sea jettisoned assets during the early 1990s, its sales fell, from C$607 million in 1990 to C$351 million in 1992 to just $266 million in 1993. Furthermore, the company posted net losses every year from 1988 to 1993. In 1993, write-offs related to discontinued operations contributed to a whopping C$42.5 million deficit for the year. Meanwhile, Demone continued to sell off assets related to traditional harvesting businesses and to reduce the company's workforce. In 1994, for instance, the company sold thirteen ships (including two deep sea freezer trawlers), its French subsidiary, and its shrimp processing plant in Florida.

With its restructuring and rationalization program substantially complete, National Sea posted its first positive net income in seven years in 1994. Going into 1995, the company was reduced to about 1,600 full-time employees, five processing plants, and

19 fishing vessels, only 13 of which were active. Its core business had changed from harvesting fish to marketing prepared, frozen, fresh, and packaged seafood. In fact, National Sea was the largest company in that Canadian industry in 1995. It marketed its foods under the High Liner and Sea Fresh trademarks in Canada, and under the Booth, Fisher Boy, and High Liner names in the United States. National Sea still exported products to France and Japan, but its short term market emphasis remained North America.

Principal Subsidiaries: National Sea Products Inc. (U.S.); Scotia Trawler Equipment Limited; Fisheries Resource Development Limited; Deep Sea Clam Company Limited.

Further Reading:

Campbell, Donald, ''Pool's CEO Focuses on Change,'' *Calgary Herald,* May 13, 1995, p. 1D.

Iler, Tim, ''New Man at the Helm,'' *Atlantic Business,* March 1986, p. 20.

Jones, Deborah, ''At Sea in Rough Water: Firm Struggles Through Atlantic Fishery Crises,'' *Financial Post,* May 29, 1993, p. 18.

Kimber, Stephen, ''Rescue at Sea,'' *Canadian Business,* October 1986, pp. 68–74

Pitts, Gordon, ''Battling the Gales at NatSea,'' *Financial Post,* February 8, 1992, p. B6.

—Dave Mote

NATURAL WONDERS™

Natural Wonders Inc.

4209 Technology Drive
Fremont, California 94538
U.S.A.
(510) 252-9600
Fax: (510) 252-6795

Public Company
Founded: 1986
Employees: 2,052
Sales: $137 million
Stock Exchanges: NASDAQ
SICs: 5947 Gift, Novelty and Souvenir Shops

Natural Wonders Inc. operates a chain of mall-based specialty gift stores that sell products related to the appreciation and enjoyment of nature and science. Merchandise ranges from jewelry and wind chimes to telescopes and games, and the stores are targeted toward upper-middle income adults and children. Natural Wonders was operating 145 stores in 36 states going into 1995.

Natural Wonders was started in 1986 by two entrepreneurs and veterans of the retail apparel industry: Robert S. Rubenstein and Stephen L. Jacobs. Rubenstein had formerly cofounded Pic-A-Dilly Stores and the Athletic Shoe Factory Stores. He had also served as a principal in the Hit or Miss retail chain. Jacobs had worked with Rubenstein at Pic-A-Dilly and Hit or Miss and had helped to open 300 new stores for the apparel-retailing Foxmoor chain. By the mid-1980s, Jacobs and Rubenstein had become restless and were looking for a new challenge.

Rubenstein and Jacobs found their new challenge in the northern California city of Los Gatos, California. There, Diann Reading had formed a successful specialty nature and ocean shop called Sand and Foam. Rubenstein and Jacobs believed that the Sand and Foam concept had a lot of potential and that similar stores could be replicated across the country. All they needed was a savvy marketing plan and some financial backing. Reading agreed to team up with the two retailers in 1986 with the long-term goal of taking the Sand and Foam concept nationwide. The team started with two northern California stores. Rubenstein and Jacobs drew on their extensive retailing backgrounds to tweak the stores' format, and they also managed to find some investors that were willing to gamble on their idea.

Among Rubenstein's first moves was to change the name of the stores from Sand and Foam to Natural Wonders. The name change reflected the founders' intent of capitalizing on the emerging market for nature specialty products. In fact, Rubenstein's plans for Natural Wonders were inspired, in part, by the burgeoning nature store chain The Nature Co. That successful shop started expanding nationwide in the mid-1980s and was enjoying big gains when Rubenstein started Natural Wonders. Its growth prompted other retailers like Rubenstein and Jacobs to consider the nature niche. "No question that the success of The Nature Co. helped sell us on the idea of Natural Wonders," Rubenstein was quoted as saying in the November 2, 1987, *Business Journal-San Jose.*

The Nature Co., which was in the San Francisco Bay area, was started in 1972 by a former Peace Corps volunteer. In 1983, the enterprise was purchased by the Boston-based CML Group. The deep-pocketed CML began taking the chain nationwide during the mid-1980s with shops as far away as Massachusetts, New York, and Minnesota. By 1987 The Nature Co. was operating 21 stores and was planning to step up expansion efforts in the near future. Natural Wonders differentiated itself from The Nature Co. with its emphasis on specialty gifts, as opposed to the educational and science merchandise highlighted by The Nature Co. "Their stores are more serious, more science oriented," Jacobs explained in the *Business Journal-San Jose* article. "We're less formal and more hands-on." Despite their differences, similarities between the two companies would eventually cause a rift that would be played out in the courts.

During 1986 and 1987, Rubenstein, Jacobs, Reading, and a small group of investors poured about $750,000 into Natural Wonders. That money was used to open two new mall stores. The shops stocked a variety of nature-related items ranging from small toys that sold for less than $1 to expensive telescopes. Natural Wonders sold a unique plastic worm that wiggled when it was placed on a table, for example, as well as a pair of expensive binoculars. Other items included gardening supplies, sea shells, rocks, and a selection of T-shirts, art, compact discs, and gifts and games for children. The stores were located in more upscale malls to complement their impulse-purchase gift orientation and to appeal to a relatively high-income crowd. Rubenstein compared his specialty retailing strategy at the time to that employed by the Sharper Image and Williams-Sonoma.

The private company did not release sales figures, but analysts estimated that Natural Wonders' sales were approaching $30 million by decade's end. Buoyed by the success of the first stores, Rubenstein was able to attract venture capital to fund ongoing expansion in 1988 and 1989—Jacobs left the company during that period and Rubenstein became president and chief executive. By late 1989 the company was operating a total of ten stores and had six more stores scheduled to open by the end of the year. The shops averaged 2,200 to 2,600 square feet and were typically located near clusters of stores within a mall. The successful retailing formula allowed them to garner sales-per-square-foot figures that were 40 percent to 50 percent above the average store in their respective malls.

All of the Natural Wonders outlets were in California in 1989, with five in the Bay area and the rest in southern California.

However, Rubenstein was beginning to eye the broader U.S. market. He began looking for store locations in Oregon, Washington, and Arizona, as well as in the Midwest and on the East Coast. Natural Wonders did begin expanding outside its core California market in 1990. In fact, the chain more than doubled in size during the year to 36 outlets. It became clear during 1990 that the Natural Wonders concept was working. Despite an economic recession, average annual net sales per square foot at Natural Wonders increased to a healthy $428 and the company's revenues surged to about $30 million. Meanwhile, Rubenstein searched for new store locations with plans to intensify expansion efforts.

Rubenstein had announced in 1989 that he expected to open 100 Natural Wonders outlets by 1994. In fact, the company was able to grow at a much faster rate. By 1991 there were 61 outlets, and by 1992 the Natural Wonders chain had swelled to an impressive 88 stores. The company's rapid growth rate was made possible, in part, by a public offering of Natural Wonders stock. The company used cash from that sale to build new stores and infrastructure. Early in 1993, for example, the company broke ground on a new national distribution center to replace the California-based distribution center. The new 323,000-square-foot facility was located in Kentucky to accommodate the chain's eastward move across the United States.

Natural Wonders' gains during the early 1990s were the result of its savvy marketing stratagem. By 1993 Natural Wonders' product mix had grown to include well over 2,000 items like globes, minerals, geodes, bird feeders, ceramics, science kits, and educational toys and games. In addition to the specialty gift items, the store carried an array of educational and science products for adults and for children aged six to 12 years. Besides an appealing inventory, the store attracted buyers with well-lit, floor-to-ceiling glass storefronts, an open floor plan that invited customers in to browse, and a hands-on environment that encouraged customers to pick up and explore different products.

New Age music or environmental sounds played through the stores, and a video monitor continuously played videotapes of nature scenes from the store's video collection. The stores kept advertising costs low by relying almost solely on their appealing environment to attract mall foot traffic. Furthermore, each store was supported by information systems located at the California headquarters. There, financial and merchandising information was gathered daily by polling sales information from each outlet's point-of-sale terminals. The data was used to generate various sales reports, identify buying patterns, and to manage inventory. Finally, Natural Wonders prided itself on trying to staff its shops with enthusiastic, informed salespeople that were trained to demonstrate products and engage customers.

Natural Wonders tagged a record 35 new stores onto its chain in 1993, bringing the total to 123. Sales shot up from $56 million in 1991 and $88 million in 1992 to a whopping $119 million during 1993. Unfortunately, the strain of rampant growth was beginning to show on the company's bottom line. The company had posted its first positive net income figure in 1990, and by 1992 earnings had surged to an encouraging $5.6 million. Despite sales gains in 1993, however, net income dipped to

about $4.9 million. Natural Wonders' stock price tumbled from a high of $27.50 early in 1993 to a lowly $8 by late summer. Company executives cited inventory mismanagement as the problem. They felt that the merchandise assortment had become too diverse and needed to be refocused. To that end, management initiated a new merchandising strategy in 1993 that jettisoned slow-moving, lower profit items like bird feeders, and emphasized high-margin, fast-moving ecology-oriented goods priced at $20 or less.

Another factor contributing to the company's profit slowdown in 1993 and 1994 was increased competition. Indeed, several retailers had hopped onto the nature retailing bandwagon during the early 1990s, including larger department stores that were offering merchandise similar to that sold by Natural Wonders. Importantly, Natural Wonders was also vying with its original nemesis, The Nature Co., in some key markets. The Nature Company had expanded at a pace similar to that of Natural Wonders and had become clearly uncomfortable with its competitor's gains. The Nature Company eventually sued Natural Wonders, claiming that Rubenstein had ripped off its retailing formula and infringed on its trademarks. Natural Wonders countersued, citing differences in its operating practices. The conflict was eventually settled out of court: All claims were dropped, and Natural Wonders agreed to pay the Nature Company a painful $1.1 million.

Natural Wonders hired a new merchandising manager late in 1993 to revamp its product mix. That manager tendered his resignation after only five months on the job, however, and the company continued to scramble to assemble a cohesive merchandising strategy. To make matters worse, the company's new distribution center went on line early in 1994, and Natural Wonders had trouble getting the facility to operate smoothly. Most of the start-up problems were eventually corrected, but not before creating significant delays in deliveries to several stores. All the while, increasing competition seemed to be eating away at the company's per-store margins. For example, after peaking in 1992, average per-square-foot sales at the company's outlets dropped 12 percent to $407 by 1994. That dynamic contributed to lower profit margins. Net earnings for Natural Wonders, in fact, fell to a disappointing $1.77 million in 1994.

Although comparable store sales drooped after 1992, Natural Wonders continued to expand at a steady, though slower, clip. The company added 22 new stores to its chain in 1994. By the end of the year Natural Wonders was operating 145 outlets in 36 states. States where the greatest number of stores were located included California, Illinois, Texas, Ohio, Washington, Michigan, Florida, and New Jersey. Because of lackluster performance by individual stores, however, management decided late in 1994 not to increase the number of outlets during 1995. Indeed, the company's 1994 annual report was refreshingly blunt about management's shortcomings during 1993 and 1994. It cited problems stemming from failures related to merchandising and inadequate long-term strategies.

Early in 1995 Natural Wonders initiated a reorganization. It eliminated approximately 20 employees at its corporate offices and distribution center, among other changes, and developed a plan to reduce the number of items in store inventories from 2,200 to about 1,600. In addition, Rubenstein stepped aside as president and chief executive, but remained as chairman of the board. He was succeeded by Kathleen M. Chatfield. The 42-year-old Chatfield was a retail industry veteran and had been with Natural Wonders since 1987. After taking the helm, Chatfield announced her intent to cut costs, reign in expansion, and work to improve per-store profitability.

Further Reading:

Barry, David, "Natural Wonders Plans More Stores," *Business Journal-San Jose,* October 2, 1989, p. 16.

Carlsen, Clifford, "Green Retailer Revamps Merchandise Just a Shade," *San Francisco Business Times,* September 3, 1993, p. 3.

——, "Natural Wonders Still Plagued by Merchandising Blunders; Same-Store Sales Still Declining, Merchandising Manager Resigns," *San Francisco Business Times,* February 4, 1994, p. 5.

Hoover's Handbook of Emerging Companies 1993–1994, Austin, Tex.: Reference Press, 1995.

Krey, Michael, "Sunnyvale Firm Sees Potential for Profit in Natural Setting," *Business Journal-San Jose,* November 2, 1987, p. 11.

Rubenstein, Robert S., "Natural Wonders Announces Settlement of Lawsuit with The Nature Co.," *Business Wire,* April 7, 1995.

Sauderland, John F., "Kathleen Chatfield Named CEO of Natural Wonders," *Business Wire,* February 13, 1995.

Shafer, Sheldon, "Natural Wonders Breaks Ground for Riverport Distribution Center," *Courier-Journal,* May 4, 1993, p. 3B.

Wichner, David, "Sold on Science: Nature Also Special Theme at Valley Specialty Stores," *Phoenix Gazette,* December 13, 1990, p. 1F.

—Dave Mote

NEVADA ✖ BELL.

Nevada Bell Telephone Company

P.O. Box 11010
Reno, Nevada 89520
U.S.A.
(702) 333-4000
Fax: (702) 367-5651

Wholly Owned Subsidiary of Pacific Telesis Group
Incorporated: 1913 as Bell Telephone Company of Nevada
Employees: 850
Sales: $160 million
SICs: 4813 Telephone Communications Except
   Radiotelephone

Nevada Bell was one of the telephone companies that changed forever due to the AT&T divestiture in 1984. When the Bell System divested its long-distance service from all local operations on January 1 of that year, Nevada Bell Telephone Company immediately came under new ownership. The Pacific Telesis Group, Nevada Bell's new parent company, had just been formed as one of the regional firms after the divestiture. Pacific Telesis helped Nevada weather the dramatic changes necessitated by the breakup, including numerous service changes for the company's customers. Over the years, Pacific Telesis has helped modernize Nevada Bell operations, and added many new products to an ever-growing list of services for customers, including such items as Teen Line, Voice Mail, and Custom Calling 2000.

Nevada Bell traces its history to the Sunset Telephone and Telegraph Company and the Pacific Telephone and Telegraph Company. During the late 19th and early 20th centuries, the telephone industry came to the western part of the United States. Numerous companies were formed throughout the region, including the state of Nevada, and the telephone soon became one of the integral parts of life in the West. Yet many of the early telephone companies were plagued by instability, and new companies were either going bankrupt, changing ownership, or buying more and more telephone exchanges.

One such company, the Sunset Telephone and Telegraph Company, started its early existence in Nevada with great promise by rapidly expanding its operations. Suddenly, without much notice, the company began to divest itself of all its holdings. As a result, all of its stock was purchased by the Pacific Telephone and Telegraph Company in 1906. Soon after the purchase,

Pacific Telephone sold the Carson City, Nevada, telephone exchange, one of the largest in the state at that time, to Nevada Consolidated Telephone and Telegraph Company. Pacific Telephone ran its operations primarily in the extreme western part of Nevada and did not significantly expand any of its network for years. In January 1913, however, the Pacific Telephone and Telegraph Company transferred the entirety of its operations in the state to Bell Telephone of Nevada, which was specifically incorporated to act as a holding company while the first transcontinental telephone wire was constructed in 1914.

The purchase of Pacific Telephone by Nevada Bell, as it was coming to be known, included the transfer of 695 miles of telephone wire throughout the state, in addition to numerous telephone plants and exchanges comprised of switchboards, wires, and poles. All together, the new company had acquired over 3,000 stations. But the event with the most impact on Nevada Bell was the construction of the Nevada portion of the transcontinental telephone line. The line was to connect the East and West coasts of the United States, and was one of the largest telephone construction projects ever undertaken within the United States. During one of the most stormy periods in Nevada's history, the construction of nearly 400 miles of telephone wire over mountains and deserts was completed on June 17, 1914. But it wasn't until January 1915 that the transcontinental telephone line was officially opened to provide service across the United States.

Although the construction of the transcontinental telephone wire brought a great deal of prestige to Nevada Bell, the company didn't build upon its success for another four years. However, in 1919, company management decided to initiate an expansion program, and started building telephone lines that crisscrossed the state. Nevada Bell also began to acquire telephone exchanges in the northern section of Nevada. In 1920, the company acquired the Utah, Nevada, and Idaho Telephone Company assets for approximately $64,000, and also brought the Carson City exchange of 437 telephones, which had previously been sold by the Pacific Telephone and Telegraph Company.

During the early and mid-1920s, there was a significant drop in Nevada Bell's activities. Neither new construction of telephone lines nor any additional acquisitions were made until 1929. In that year, the company constructed the Los Angeles-Salt Lake City telephone line from the California border to the state of Utah. Desert heat, snakes, a lack of water, and desolate countryside made the project one of the most difficult construction jobs ever contracted by Nevada Bell. However, this new line provided Las Vegas, and other parts of southern Nevada, with long-distance telephone service, a service that the northern part of the state had had for 30 years.

During 1930, Nevada Bell engaged in a flurry of activity, expanding and improving upon its services. Dial telephones began to replace the older exchange methods used since the turn of the century, and changing from common battery switchboards to dial switchboards cost the company's Reno office $565,000. At the same time, Nevada Bell purchased the entire operating system of White Pine Telephone Company, which owned an exchange telephone plant and connecting toll lines. The company also constructed a 119-mile telephone line from

Wendover to Ely, Nevada. Yet with the deepening of the Great Depression, plans for additional expansion and improvement of services came to an abrupt halt. For the entirety of the 1930s, Nevada Bell neither acquired new holdings nor constructed new telephone lines. In fact, with the economic situation getting worsening, the company concentrated on maintaining its existing services.

With the advent of World War II, Nevada Bell resumed its expansion activities. In 1942, the company laid two cables across the state as the Nevada portion of a new transcontinental telephone line. More importantly, however, during the same year the Defense Board Ruling Number One, issued by the U.S. Department of Defense, contracted Nevada Bell to construct the DBR line in western Nevada. Built for defense purposes to guard against a possible Japanese invasion on the American West Coast, the line provided common carrier communication service among the major cities in California, Nevada, Oregon, and Washington. Many of the places that the DBR ran through did not previously have any telephone service at all. Nevada Bell, therefore, was able to use the line to service many new areas in western Nevada.

After the war, Nevada Bell grew rapidly. In 1946, the company completed the first VHF (very high frequency) radio link between Death Valley Junction and the Spectre Mountain repeater station. By 1952, as part of AT&T's nationwide network, 13 microwave stations were built by Nevada Bell to provide communication services for a variety of cross country communications. In 1955, Nevada Bell assumed all the communications engineering projects for the Atomic Energy Commission located at the Mercury, Nevada, test site. Although the state of Nevada was slow in arranging for customers to receive television transmissions, when TV finally did come to the region, Nevada Bell constructed a SHF (super high frequency) radio link to provide television service to its customers. During the late 1940s and throughout the 1950s, Nevada Bell helped convert 15 communities to dial telephone service. In addition, new offices with modernized switchboards were built in Reno, Carson City, and Virginia City, Nevada. During approximately the same time, the company constructed a communications building for the U.S. military at Stead Air Force Base, and also provided the entire communications supplies used by NASA at the Nevada sites, which tracked the X15 rocket ship.

Nevada Bell entered the 1960s full of confidence and ready to take advantage of the growing market for communication services. For the first six years of the decade, Nevada Bell spent over $13 million to modernize and expand its services. In 1960, the company introduced direct distance dialing for its Reno customers, allowing them to direct dial all their calls across the United States, and then the company gradually introduced the service to other areas over the next few years. In the early 1960s, the company completed and began operation of numerous microwave sites, as well as VHF and SHF stations in Nevada. By 1962, over 1,100 people were employed by Nevada Bell, and the company reported over 68,000 telephones in service throughout the state. In 1964, more than 4,500 main stations were added to Nevada Bell's growing communications network, along with the addition of major exchanges in Pahrump and Lathrop Wells.

Starting with 1966, however, Nevada Bell suffered from the economic recession that affected the entire southwestern part of the country. Stead Air Force Base was deactivated, resulting in a decrease of nearly 2,000 main telephones from the previous year. In spite of this economic downturn, Nevada Bell forged ahead with service improvements. New equipment for Touch-Tone phones, direct distance dialing, and extended regional service was provided for the Carson City exchange. The company also received authorization to make its first acquisition of an independent telephone company in 40 years. The Nevada State Service Commission authorized the company's purchase of Lund-Preston Telephone Company, which served a number of agricultural communities for years in the White River Valley. This acquisition allowed Nevada Bell to initiate service for the population of an isolated ranching community. The company also constructed microwave stations between Las Vegas and Reno, the two largest cities in Nevada, so that long distance calls would not have to be rerouted through California. In 1968, Nevada Bell placed its one thousandth telephone in service and adopted the new Bell Telephone System color scheme of ochre and blue.

Nevada Bell's expansion and growth continued during the 1970s. In 1971, the company completed a project to offer toll station service to approximately 60 outlying ranches, and, one year later, the company installed a Number 2A Electronic Switching System in Sun Valley, Arizona. In 1973, a 4A switching center that provided direct long distance lines from Reno to major locations throughout the United States was completed, and in 1975, the company implemented a Traffic Service Position System (TSPS), which enabled customers who lived in isolated areas to direct dial all long distance calls they made. Within the old system, the operator was invaluable, but with TSPS more calls were handled with fewer operators, thereby lowering costs and retaining the same level of efficient service.

During the mid-1970s, the company initiated one of the most sweeping and thorough reorganization strategies of any telephone company in the United States. Nevada Bell eliminated the traffic, commercial, and plant department headings and replaced them with departments of administration, accounting, customer operations, network engineering, and network operations. Modernized electronic switching offices were opened in Stead and Reno, while the company opened its first phone center store in Carson City in 1979, and a second store in Reno near the end of the year. Large businesses and the development of casinos in the Reno area resulted in a growth from eight to 13 percent in main station facilities during this period. In addition, Nevada Bell's budget for new construction more than doubled during the last two years of the decade.

In the early 1980s, Nevada Bell provided many new services for its customers, including a change from directory assistance to number services, transferring all of the company's directory listings into a computer data base. This new process eliminated an operator's need to page through a paper directory in order to find a listing. With a keyboard and video display terminal, an operator could thus find a listing in about half as much time. In addition, the company introduced the Number 4 Electronic Switching System, which could process 150 phone calls per second.

The most important event during the 1980s, however, was the breakup of the Bell Telephone System, when AT&T was required by the U.S. court system to divest all of its local operations from all of its long-distance carrier services. A 70-year affiliation ended with the AT&T breakup on January 1, 1984, and Nevada Bell became a subsidiary of Pacific Telesis Group, a new regional company. As a result of the breakup, the service Nevada Bell provided for its customers was divided into two geographic locations, a northern and southern service area. Any phone calls made between those areas had to be arranged through a long-distance carrier such as Sprint, AT&T, or MCI. In fulfilling the U.S. court order which signaled the end of the Bell System, Nevada Bell began to offer other long distance carriers, such as MCI, access to local networks. Before the court order, customers in Nevada were required to dial as many as 12 extra digits to use long-distance carriers that were not AT&T. After the court order, however, customers could place calls using other long-distance carriers without having to dial any more numbers than when AT&T was used to make the call.

The late 1980s and early 1990s were years of significant change for Nevada Bell. The company initiated a comprehensive modernization plan in order to convert every access line into digitally-switched processes. Products like Teen Line, Custom Calling 2000, and Voice Mail were introduced by Nevada Bell to attract new customers. The company constructed a fiber optic ring surrounding Reno, and began to develop fiber optic technology for communications projects. Moreover, Nevada Bell has also upgraded and improved telephone services for rural communities, some of which remained very isolated in the wastelands of the state.

Like most of the other local telephone companies, Nevada Bell has successfully met the challenges posed by the breakup of the AT&T system in 1984. With its new research and development of fiber optic technology, Nevada Bell is working on the cutting edge of the telecommunications industry to provide its customers with high-quality service.

Further Reading:

Coy, Peter, ''The Baby Bells' Painful Adolescence,'' *Business Week,* October 5, 1992, pp. 124–132.

Gross, Joel, D., ''Baby Bells: An Exchange,'' *Barrons,* September 7, 1992, pp. 22–24.

Mason, Charles, F., ''RHCs Face Long, Tough Transition To World Of Competition,'' *Telephony,* July 13, 1992, p. 7.

——, ''Wake Up And Listen,'' *Telephony,* October 12, 1992, p. 44.

Nevada Bell's 80th Birthday: A Look Back, Reno: Nevada Bell, company document.

Nevada Bell History, 1913–1985, Reno: Nevada Bell, company document.

Slutsker, Gary, ''What Should We Be?,'' *Forbes,* September 28, 1992, pp. 132–136.

Smith, Geoffrey, N., ''Driving Down The Hypeway,'' *Financial World,* October 11, 1994, p. 8.

''Tend Your Own Backyards, Baby Bells,'' *Business Week,* October 5, 1992, p. 150.

—Thomas Derdak

NLLF

Newhall Land and Farming Company

23823 Valencia Boulevard
Valencia, California 91355
U.S.A.
(805) 255-4000
Fax:(805) 255-3960

Public Company
Incorporated: 1883
Employees: 265
Sales: $134.2 million
Stock Exchange: New York
SICs: 6552 Land Subdividers & Developers; 0174 Citrus Fruits

The Newhall Land and Farming Company is one of the oldest and most famous business operations in the state of California. Much of the development of the company parallels the development of the state itself. Newhall Land and Farming Company is involved in an extremely broad range of activities, including agricultural development, agricultural machinery rental, oil and gas production, livestock management, real estate development, commercial recreation activities such as designing golf courses and building theme parks, and land lease for the production of major Hollywood movies. From 1883 to the present, members of the Newhall family have held the majority of company shares.

The founder of Newhall Land and Farming Company, Henry Mayo Newhall, arrived in California during the autumn of 1848. Long before Newhall traveled to California, the Spanish has settled throughout its coastal region and established many missions that incorporated the land surrounding them. When Mexico won its independence from Spain, these missions and their vast estates were granted to private individuals who developed them into ranches. Known as Spanish Land Grants, the ranches were completely autonomous and self-sufficient.

The end of a way of life for the Mexican ranchers came suddenly with the California gold rush of 1848. The 24-year-old Newhall journeyed to California with $8,000 dollars in his pocket to seek his fortune in the Sierra foothills. But the young man found nothing, and before long his money had run out. He was offered a job at an auction house in San Francisco and worked his way up to become sole proprietor. The auction house grew rapidly, and Newhall sent for his wife to join him in

San Francisco. By the time he was 35, Newhall had become one of the most prominent men in San Francisco and entered into an arrangement that made him president of a firm that constructed the first railroad in the city. As luck would have it, the brand-new Southern Pacific Railroad purchased his venture. Newhall was a millionaire overnight.

In 1870, with his new money, Newhall began to search for other business opportunities. A whole new area of investment opened up when Newhall came across the Spanish Land Grants. The U.S. government had put pressure on the original Mexican owners to prove their title to the land. But the cost of litigation was too expensive for the rancheros, and, already burdened with a series of droughts that had starved most of their cattle, they were forced to borrow money to keep the land. Unable to pay the debts, the great ranches were possessed by the local sheriffs and placed on sale at the auction block. Newhall purchased a total of six land grants, varying in size from a small ranch of 2,600 acres to the largest, which covered a total of 48,000 acres. The two largest ranches included one located north of Santa Maria, another situated on the border between Ventura and Los Angeles counties. Newhall turned the second of these into his home. Naming it the Newhall Ranch, the property became the headquarters for his business holdings.

In 1875 the Southern Pacific Railroad was laying its new track from San Francisco to Los Angeles, and Newhall Ranch was directly in the path. Newhall gave Southern Pacific the right-of-way on his land and immediately entered into an agreement with the railroad to transport his ranch products to San Francisco. Five out his six ranches focused on raising cattle, but the new land baron transformed Newhall Ranch into an agricultural showplace. Clearing approximately 3,000 acres, Newhall cultivated more wheat than he expected. Not content with harvesting just wheat, the innovator experimented with different kinds of fruit trees in order to find out which one might be the best for commercial production.

Henry Mayo Newhall died in 1882, leaving the entirety of his estate to a wife and five sons, William, Edwin, Henry, Walter, and George. The Newhall sons incorporated their father's business holdings as the Newhall Land and Farming Company. All of the real estate and property located in San Francisco was deeded to Mrs. Newhall and could be sold as she determined. Each of the five sons were equal shareholders in the new company, which covered 220 square miles of California terrain. All of the sons had also agreed that land could be sold in order to provide for each of their respective family needs.

By the early 1890s most of the brothers were married with large families. Unfortunately, the income that allowed their father and mother to live in luxury did not meet the demands of four families seeking the same lifestyle. Cattle breeding on the various Newhall ranches had decreased and was not able to garner large amounts of needed cash. In addition, a lengthy drought destroyed both the wheat and fruit orchards at Newhall Ranch. The only source of profit was horse raising, which fetched $50 for every horse sent to San Francisco in order to pull horsecars. Land leases of small acreage to farmers brought in some money, and leases to oil companies also resulted in small payments but no discovery of oil. At a loss for what to do, the brothers decided to sell parcels of the company's land.

Advertising land sales in newspapers throughout California and on the East Coast as well as in England, the brothers began to sell off company land. The sale of land to maintain the lifestyles of the brothers and their families continued during the early years of the new century until William Mayo Newhall, the second son, became active in the company. A graduate of Yale University, Mayo, as he was called, put an end to the liquidation of company land. Immediately before the start of World War I, Mayo agreed to sell a small ranch in Monterey County but insisted that the money should be reinvested rather than distributed in dividends to shares owned by his brothers. Mayo then used the profits to clear land at the Newhall Ranch and grow citrus trees. The remainder of the money was used to purchase land in Sacramento Valley that was leveled and irrigated for lima bean crops.

In 1922 Mayo arranged to sell some of the company land to William Randolph Hearst, whose luxurious palace at San Simeon was adjacent to Newhall Company ranches. Hearst paid $1 million for approximately 38,000 acres, to be paid in installments of $100,000 per year for the next ten years. The Newhall Land and Farming Company grew during the mid-1920s due to the income generated from Mayo's investments in citrus trees and lima bean crops. Yet disaster befell the company when the St. Francis Dam broke on March 13, 1928. Owned by the city of Los Angeles, the dam was part of a huge reservoir that was located next to Newhall Ranch and supplied water to the entire region. When the dam broke, the company's livestock, orchards, and all its buildings were completely destroyed. The city of Los Angeles took responsibility for the catastrophe, established a commission, and began the process of reparations for damages incurred.

Compounding the problems of the dam break was the onset of the Great Depression in 1929. The company's land values dropped precipitously. In addition, Mayo's last surviving brother, George, died during the same year. George had acted as the company's banker and treasurer, but Mayo soon discovered that the family firm was completely bankrupt. The banks took control of the company's entire assets, and, with unpaid debts and no cash reserves, it looked as if Newhall Land and Farming Company was at the end of its existence. Yet Mayo was not a man to give up. Already in his late seventies, blind, and growing more frail each day, Mayo turned to his son-in-law, Atholl McBean, for help. McBean, a prominent businessman in San Francisco, had been adroit enough to save his entire fortune during the 1929 stock market crash.

Meeting with the company's board of directors in August 1930, McBean discovered that most of them wanted to sell its assets and liquidate the company. However, McBean was in favor of revitalizing the entire firm's operations. With reparations money from the city of Los Angeles for flood damages and the final payments from Hearst, he paid the company's debts and began a thorough reconstitution of the board of directors. During its first year under McBean's direction, Newhall Land and Farming Company lost over $125,000. By the third year the firm reported profits of just under $25,000; by 1935 the company was averaging profits of over $100,000 and had reinstated its stock dividend, which had been suspended since 1930.

In 1936 McBean leased part of the Newhall Ranch land to Barnscall Oil Company. Mayo Newhall was convinced that no oil was to be discovered on the company's property, but when oil was struck in early 1937 it boggled even the imagination of McBean. The land was so rich in "black gold" that 44 oil wells were drilled during the next few years, and the company began making millions of dollars from oil production. McBean put this money to good use during the late 1930s and throughout the war years by purchasing even more land and by cultivating and irrigating property already owned by the company. One of McBean's first major investments after the oil strike was the construction of cattle feed-yards. Newhall Land and Farming Company built its feed-yard in the middle of Newhall Ranch and fattened cattle for market by using the firm's own agricultural produce.

During the postwar years Newhall Ranch, located in the San Fernando Valley and situated on the main road between Los Angeles and San Francisco, was gradually surrounded by urban expansion. The city of Los Angeles appraised the land surrounding Newhall Ranch at what was regarded as its potentially greatest use, which meant that the company's corn and barley fields were the perfect locations for new homes and shopping malls. When the city began to tax the Newhall Land and Farming Company accordingly, McBean quickly realized that the company could not pay the raise in taxes by using the land for farming. As a result, McBean initiated a comprehensive program for land development.

In order to enhance the value of its land, the company during the 1950s hired urban planners to create a strategy for how to profitably change onion fields into homes, amusement parks, and business centers. With more and more real estate developers imploring the company to sell its land, the board of directors decided to plan and create an entirely new city, Valencia. A wholly owned subsidiary, California Land, was formed to oversee the process and, after a long period of planning and design, the actual construction started in the early 1960s. Schools, swimming pools, clubhouses, golf courses, a hospital, shopping centers, government offices, and a downtown center were all built quickly. By 1967 the first residents had moved into the town. With the plan completed, McBean retired from active management of the company and handed over responsibilities to the first administrators outside the family.

During the 1970s Newhall Land and Farming Company concentrated on developing the city of Valencia. Major construction included the Magic Mountain Amusement Park, along with a motorcycle park, more golf courses, and a recreational vehicle campground. Publicity garnered from the Magic Mountain project was enormous and contributed to the company's heightened profile as a land developer. In addition, the publicity identified Valencia as a fast growing yet stable residential community. Soon nearly 15,000 residents were living in Valencia and over 5,000 housing units had been built. The company sold its interest in Magic Mountain to Six Flags, Inc., in 1979 when management decided that administration of the park was too large of a task.

The 1980s became the best decade to date for the company. Over 9,000 cattle were fed on the firm's winter ranges, 23 different varieties of crops were cultivated on company lands throughout California, and a new business in renting agricultural machinery was growing rapidly. During the 1980s the company expanded its oil operations to encompass seven states and Canada. These properties, especially in Canada, were highly profitable for the firm. At the same time, Newhall Land and Farming Company began a lucrative leasing policy to Hollywood producers who wanted to use its land for filming movies and television shows. Over 250 such productions were made on company properties. Yet the most important part of the company's expansion policy involved its continual growth as a land developer. Newhall Land and Farming Company purchased land to develop golf courses, motels, shopping centers, and other commercial ventures not only in California but in states like Arizona.

Well known for its careful and successful development of Valencia, in 1994 Newhall Land and Farming Company unveiled a comprehensive plan to design a new residential and commercial site. Located in the Santa Clara Valley, the company proposed to transform an area of 19 square miles into a community for over 70,000 people. With plans for the development of ten schools, 25,000 houses, a business park, and six shopping centers, the site was much more ambitious and more expensive than the previous project at Valencia. The project was planned to be built in five phases and take a quarter-century to complete, although environmentalists and municipal officials raised con-

cerns about the company's plans for land that was occupied by two endangered species listed by the federal government.

Members of the Newhall family still sit on the company's board of directors, but most of the decisions are made by professional managers rather than family members.

Principal Subsidiaries: Valencia Company; Valencia Water Company.

Further Reading:

Dickason, James F., *The Newhall Land and Farming Company,* Newcomen Society: New York, 1983.
"Fourth-Quarter Net Slipped, Real-Estate Developer Says," *Wall Street Journal,* January 13, 1995, p. B9C(E).
Herron, Melissa, "Servicing the Sale," *Builder,* July 1995, pp. 69–76.
Kaplan, Tracey, "Plans for Planting Another Suburb," *Los Angeles Times,* July 12, 1994, pp. B1–B4.
Nelson, Cristina, "Soft Sell," *Custom Builder,* January-February 1994, pp. 19–21.
"Newhall Land and Farming Company," *Wall Street Journal,* July 25, 1995, p. B7(E).
"Newhall Land and Farming Company," *Wall Street Journal,* December 21, 1994, P. B9(E).
Schwolsky, Rick, "Delivering the Goods," *Builder,* July 1995, pp. 170–76.

—Thomas Derdak

Noble Roman's, Inc.

Noble Roman's Inc.

1 Virginia Avenue
Indianapolis, Indiana 46204
U.S.A.
(317) 634-3377
Fax: (317) 634-1234

Public Company
Incorporated: 1972
Employees: 1,300
Sales: $30.5 million
Stock Exchanges: NASDAQ
SICs: 5812 Eating Places; 6794 Patent Owners & Lessors

Operating a chain of casual dining restaurants in the Midwest, Noble Roman's Inc. is known primarily for its pizza and offers a broad selection of toppings and crust styles to be enjoyed at the restaurants as well as through carry-out and home delivery services. In 1995 the Noble Roman's chain included 80 restaurants located in Indiana, Ohio, Missouri, and Kentucky. While most of the restaurants were located in stand-alone buildings and were owned by the company, 14 were franchised in 1995.

Noble Roman's was started in Bloomington, Indiana, by Stephen Huse and Gary Knackstedt. Huse had graduated from the business school at Indiana University in Bloomington before taking a sales job in 1965 with Ransburg Corp. Eager to be on his own, Huse purchased an Arby's restaurant franchise in Bloomington and ran the operation for a few years. In 1969 he spearheaded the purchase of a struggling Bloomington pizza restaurant. During the early 1970s Huse and partner Knackstedt worked together to turn the restaurant around and then to expand in the Bloomington area with new Noble Roman's pizza outlets.

Huse and Knackstedt benefitted during the early and mid-1970s from overall growth in the fast food, and particularly pizza, business. As the population of the college town swelled with increasing numbers of students, sales of Noble Roman's unique pizzas surged. To help them take advantage of growth opportunities, Huse and Knackstedt were joined by investor Paul Mobley in the early 1970s. Mobley helped to fund Noble Roman's expansion throughout the 1970s. He also became increasingly involved in the company's management. In 1977, in fact, Mobley became president of the company. By that time, Knackstedt had left the venture to pursue other interests. Huse,

on the other hand, would remain chairman and chief stockholder in the company until 1986.

Noble Roman's continued to grow during the late 1970s and early 1980s, expanding outside of Bloomington's borders in central Indiana and later throughout Indiana and into Ohio. Throughout this period, the burgeoning restaurant chain rang up consistent, healthy profits. To garner more money for expansion, Mobley and Huse took the company public in 1982. They used proceeds from that stock offering to build new outlets and to branch out into other ventures. In addition, Noble Roman's management expanded the chain through franchising. Within a few years of the public offering the Noble Roman's chain had grown to include about 120 stores in Indiana and Ohio, 25 of which were company-owned stores.

After posting hefty profit gains for more than a decade, Noble Roman's fortunes began to turn in 1985. The company netted income of $146,000 in 1984, after which profitability began deteriorating rapidly. Part of the problem stemmed from the chain's decision to intensify its expansion efforts in Ohio through the buyout of several ailing Godfather's Pizza outlets. Godfather's called Noble Roman's executives in 1984 to see if they would be interested in buying their 21-store Dayton, Ohio, operations. Noble Roman's already had nine units in the area and was planning to open another five within the year. Executives initially rejected the offer, but finally agreed to purchase seven of the stores, which they planned to convert to Noble Roman's.

The deal was closed in March 1985, but problems immediately ensued. The management at Noble Roman's clashed with managers at the Godfather's stores. All seven of the store managers quit within a few months, and Mobley and fellow executives had trouble finding worthy replacements. To make matters worse, the deal had left Noble Roman's financially strapped and unable to invest funds necessary to revitalize the lagging Godfather's outlets. Rather than sell off the new stores, Mobley decided to hire the best managers he could find at whatever price he would have to pay. Even that effort proved to be inadequate because the stores had already developed a bad reputation locally; little could be done to make amends.

Noble Roman's finally shuttered six of the seven stores, as well as three existing Noble Roman's in Dayton and another failing store in Decatur, Indiana. As a result of the failed Godfather's deal and other setbacks within the company, Noble Roman's net income plunged in 1985 to a deficit of $1.5 million. The company lost another $700,000 in the first quarter of 1986 and suffered another big deficit the next quarter when it wrote off losses related to the ten stores it closed in 1985. Noble Roman's eventually recorded a crushing $3.7 million loss for 1986. Management was left scrambling for a solution to the crisis.

While Mobley and fellow executives worked to repair the ailing company, Noble Roman's founder, Steve Huse, distanced himself from the company. In fact, Huse's influence on day-to-day operations had been declining since he and Mobley took the company public in December 1982. When the company negotiated the Godfather's deal, Huse increasingly began to turn his attention to other interests. He continued to own half of American Diversified Foods, Inc., which owned 11 Arby's Roast Beef franchises in Indiana and was connected to the first Arby's franchise he had started in 1967. Huse also dabbled in real estate and had owned a group of billiards/electronic game halls for a time (the halls were sold to Bally Manufacturing Corp. in 1983).

In 1985, the time when Noble Roman's first began to encounter serious problems, Huse opened a new restaurant in Bloomington called Mustard's. The venture, which represented a culmination of restaurant ideas that Huse had picked up during various travels, was ultimately a success. Shortly after opening that restaurant Huse purchased the well-known and respected St. Elmo Steak House in Indianapolis. Moreover, although Huse remained the largest single shareholder of Noble Roman's stock, he had been reducing his stake in the company since 1977. Finally, in 1986, Huse resigned from his position as chairman of the board. He later started the Huse Food Group, a holding company with various restaurant and real estate interests, and served for a few years as president and chief executive officer of the Indianapolis-based Consolidated Products, Inc., which owned the venerable Steak n Shake chain of eateries.

Although Noble Roman's same-store sales improved during 1986, the company continued to struggle toward profitability. In an effort to buoy the company's sagging balance sheet, a group of company insiders led by Mobley purchased 12 stores from the company in 1987 for about $4.1 million. That left Noble Roman's with a chain of about 120 outlets, roughly 40 of which were owned by the company or by its executives. In addition, Mobley moved the company's headquarters from Bloomington to Indianapolis as part of an overall cost-cutting effort. He also reduced the headquarters staff from 30 to 23, closed some restaurants, and initiated several other measures that reduced the company's expenses by about $1.1 million annually. Mobley was joined in the effort by his 25-year-old son Scott, who joined the company in 1986.

During the late 1980s Noble Roman's went through a major reorganization. Managers became more responsible for their own budgets and improving efficiency in their operational area, and several stores changed ownership as part of an effort to boost cash flow and recover some of the $4.1 million that management invested in 1987. Importantly, Mobley made a decision to shift Noble Roman's focus away from the cut-throat, low-cost delivery segment and toward the upscale end of the pizza market. To that end, the restaurant introduced and began to emphasize its premium, high-profit products and to intensify its quality and service efforts. The menu was expanded to include pastas and other pizza-related products, and a late-night menu was introduced as well. Importantly, Noble Roman's also initiated a costly renovation program during the late 1980s designed to update the stores and give them a more upscale, progressive image.

As a result of the efforts of Mobley and his managers, Noble Roman's finances gradually recovered. The company's net loss of $500,000 in 1988 was reduced to a deficit of just $16,531 in 1990. Finally, in 1991 Noble Roman's returned to profitability with earnings of more than $200,000 on revenue of about $8.5 million. Throughout the period of recovery, however, some analysts remained skeptical of the company's strategy, citing several concerns. Even as late as 1989, for example, Noble Roman's was scrambling for cash to meet its burdensome liabilities, and observers noted that a variety of influences, such as a potential increase in the minimum wage, threatened to quash the company's gains. By the early 1990s, though, many skeptics were beginning to place more faith in Noble Roman's course of action. "I think they'll get this done," said stock analyst Ray Diggle in the *Indianapolis Business Journal* in January 1993. "Clearly, sales are doing exceptionally well. The company has done a good job of curtailing inventory costs. I think the company is poised for a period of solid growth."

After peaking at about 120 stores in the mid-1980s, the total number of Noble Roman's stores was reduced to about 75 by 1992. The reorganization and store reduction had allowed Noble Roman's to get back on track financially. In 1992, despite recessionary economic conditions, Noble Roman's increased its earnings to about $491,000 from sales of $9.1 million. In January 1993 the company bought back 27 of its restaurants from three companies that were franchising the outlets in Indiana. That left it with a total of 42 company-owned stores and 31 franchises. The purchase helped the chain to boost its sales to $24.2 million while profits grew to about $841,000. A drawback of the move was that it saddled Noble Roman's with a fat debt burden—long-term debt rocketed from $2.5 million to a lofty $8 million after the purchase. At the same time, Noble Roman's was still trying to pay off tax liabilities that had been accruing since the organization began experiencing problems in the mid-1980s.

Noble Roman's heavy debt and thin cash flow was reflected by its stock price, which had hovered around a low $3 during much of the early 1990s. That situation began to change in 1994, though, when Noble Roman's performance continued to improve and Mobley began paring the company's liabilities. In 1994 Noble Roman's added a total of five new restaurants to its chain and announced plans to tag an additional 30 stores onto its portfolio by 1996.

The company also benefitted from general industry trends. Indeed, although the pizza industry was growing, the big, low-cost delivery chains were not. Instead, smaller operators catering to the high-end segment were posting solid market share gains. Evidencing the validity of Noble Roman's upscale strategy, the chain reported record net income in 1994 of $1.5 million from revenues of $30.5 million.

Besides opening new stores in 1994 and 1995, Noble Roman's continued to buy outlets that were being operated as franchises. By mid-1995 Noble Roman's was operating 66 company-owned stores and 14 franchises, a state of affairs that gave it ownership and control of more than 80 percent of the outlets in its chain. That increased ownership, combined with savvy management, allowed Noble Roman's to boost its sales and profits 63 percent and 87 percent, respectively, between 1991 and 1994. That achievement earned Noble Roman's a spot on *Business Week*'s 1995 list of "small, hot-growth" companies in 1995. (To be eligible for the list, a company had to have revenues between $10 million and $150 million and a market value of less than $1 million.) Going into the latter part of the 1990s, Noble Roman's was planning to expand its midwestern chain to more than 120 outlets, increase per-store profits, and reduce its debt.

Further Reading:

Burton, Brian, "Improving the Recipe: A New Look at Noble Roman's, Inc.," *Indiana Business,* September 1986, p. 28.

Harton, Tom, "Following the Leader: Steak n Shake Parent Company Hires Two More Huse Group Execs," *Indianapolis Business Journal,* May 14, 1990, p. 9A.

Jeffrey, Don, "Huse Quits Noble Roman's; Founder Leaves 'To Pursue Other Interests'," *Nation's Restaurant News,* September 15, 1986, p. 2.

Kukolla, Steve, "Nobel Roman's Scores on Business Week List," *Indianapolis Business Journal,* May 22, 1995, p. 10A.

"Noble Roman's Inc. Profits Rise 78 Percent," *Nation's Restaurant News,* February 20, 1995, p. 16.

"Noble Roman's Would Reclaim 40 Franchises Through Stock Sale," *Indianapolis Business Journal,* July 6, 1992, p. 3.

Parent, Tom, "Noble Roman's Digging Out of Deep Dish," *Indianapolis Business Journal,* January 25, 1993, p. 1.

Rush, Jill, "Noble Roman's Still Losing Dough, But May Turn Corner This Week," *Indianapolis Business Journal,* July 3, 1989, p. 9A.

—Dave Mote

Octel Communications Corp.

1001 Murphy Ranch Road
Milpitas, California 95035-7912
U.S.A.
(408) 321-2000
Fax: (408) 321-2100

Public Company
Founded: 1982
Employees: 2,393
Sales: $406.2 million
SICs: 3661 Telephone and Telegraph Apparatus

Octel Communications Corp. is the leading manufacturer and provider of voice-mail products and services. The firm has grown enormously during its brief history as the voice-mail market has expanded dramatically.

Octel was founded by Robert Cohen, a product manager for a computerized instrumentation equipment company, and Peter Olson, an engineer. They met in 1981 when Cohen called Olson to fix a problem with a piece of electronic equipment that worked in the lab but not in the field. Cohen was so impressed with Olson's abilities that he suggested they start a company together.

The duo drew up a list of possible areas of specialization in the technology field and settled on voice mail because they thought it a good market niche. At the time, most voice-mail systems were made by giants like International Business Machines, whose products were large, expensive, and unpopular. Some smaller companies existed, but Olson and Cohen felt that they were not geared toward dealing with businesses in a professional manner. Olson and Cohen designed a product to fit this niche. Their business plan called for a voice-mail machine that would cost $10,000 to make and $50,000 to sell. They wanted it to take up no more space than a closet and to be compatible with the top ten telephone systems then being used. Competing voice-mail systems generally worked only with the manufacturer's telephone system, and none worked with all 80 PBX systems on the market. So whereas AT&T could sell its voice-mail system only to businesses owning an AT&T phone system, the Octel system could be sold to anybody.

With this business plan, Octel raised about $2 million in venture capital, effectively selling half of the company to various investors in the process. When finished, the firm's system took up as much room as a large suitcase and sold for $55,000. A competing system from IBM was the size of a small room and cost $250,000. Despite its small size, the Octel system was powerful; Olson had used advanced microprocessors made by Intel and Zilog and wired them to run in parallel.

After spending another $4 million, Octel had the system ready in early 1984. However, corporate purchasing departments usually took about a year to order new systems, a fact that was overlooked in Octel's business plan. By fall of that year the company had sold only about 10 systems. The firm had to cut costs and raise another $7 million in venture capital. By 1985, however, orders for Octel's system began arriving. Voice mail was becoming more popular in corporate America, and thanks to its universal compatibility the Octel system sold very well for a first product by a new company.

Voice-mail machines essentially are computers dedicated to the purpose of answering telephones and recording the human voice. Voice-mail systems translate voices into digital information and store it. To keep file sizes small, much of the information is stripped out, which can lead to a tinny quality that some users find objectionable. Also, telephone answering machines were relatively new, and many people were reluctant to leave messages with machines. However, voice mail offered many advantages. Because information is digital, messages can be copied or manipulated like other computer data. Thus an executive can send ten messages simultaneously or forward a message to someone else. Using touch-tone telephones, callers can select from menu options and route their calls without using a human operator. Octel's system also offered options such as slowing down or speeding up a message during playback and automatic call-forwarding. Corporations were first beginning to evaluate the benefits of such systems when Octel's system came to market, and its low price tag generated interest and orders.

The firm became profitable in 1986, considered a fast takeoff for a start-up technology firm. A 1987 ruling court ruling changed telecommunications regulations to allow the regional Bell telephone companies to begin offering telecommunications services like voice mail. They were, however, not allowed to manufacture their own equipment, and several decided to use Octel's equipment in their systems.

Propelled by its sales to the Bells, Octel became the largest manufacturer of voice-mail systems in 1988, just four years after offering its first product. Its sales grew from $19 million in 1986 to $48 million in 1987. The voice-mail market was booming, growing 50 percent a year by some estimates, to reach $270 million in 1987. In February 1988, Octel went public, raising $7 million by selling 15 percent of the company. The firm was looked over carefully by the financial community because it was one of the first high-technology companies to go public after the stock market crash of October 1987. Later that year, in a sign of the growing importance of both Octel and the voice-processing industry, electronics giant Hewlett-Packard bought 10 percent of Octel. Its new link with H-P gave the young company a marketing boost and a quick presence in Europe, where its products were to be sold under the Hewlett-Packard name. It also led to increased integration of Octel's products with Hewlett-Packard's electronic-mail and computer systems.

At the time, Octel was offering two voice-mail systems: Aspen systems were designed for large businesses and could contain up to 7,500 mailboxes; the VPC 100, for smaller customers, contained up to 100 mailboxes.

In 1990 Cohen resigned as chief executive officer, citing the need to spend more time with his family; he remained on Octel's board. Douglas Chance, a 24-year veteran of Hewlett-Packard who had served on Octel's board, became CEO. Octel earned $18 million on sales of $160 million for 1990; voice-mail sales for its nearest competitor, AT&T, were $140 million.

With computer technology constantly improving, Octel's systems were rapidly becoming more sophisticated, providing the link between employees (who could be at a touch-tone telephone anywhere in the world) and their employer's computer systems. Universities were using the firm's PowerCall system for student registration. With it, the schools recorded course descriptions for students, who could then check whether a particular class was available and register for it right over the phone. In 1991 Octel introduced a device that attached to voice-processing systems and turned telephones into terminals, allowing users to interact with computers through the number pads on their telephones. The system, called the Voice Information Processing Server, let callers access databases, voice messages, and electronic mail and carried caller data throughout the call so that information—an identification number, for instance—did not have to be reentered.

By 1992 Octel not only held 20 percent of the voice-mail market but had 36 percent of the market for voice-information services (in which telephone service providers buy voice-mail systems, then rent voice-mail services to customers). In fact, Octel was the first company to enter this business, which had exacting standards because of the high volume of calls that were processed and because the systems themselves were attached to equipment located in the central office of a telephone company. The quickly growing cellular telephone market accounted for many of the firm's voice information services sales. The firm had installed 6,500 voice-mail machines, many at Fortune 500 companies.

The firm announced plans to introduce a universal mail box, a system that would collect messages from many sources: voice mail from a subscriber's business, home, and cellular telephones, as well as paper mail. It would also receive data, like faxes, to be printed out or viewed later.

In late 1992 Octel bought Tigon, Ameritech Corp.'s Dallas-based voice messaging subsidiary. Ameritech agreed to buy voice-processing services from Tigon. Octel made Tigon a wholly owned subsidiary and renamed it Octel Network Services. Ameritech had bought Tigon in 1988 but could not operate it at enough of a profit. At the time of Octel's purchase, Tigon had large corporate customers in most major U.S. cities, as well as some in Japan, Taiwan, Britain, Australia, and Canada. Because of the purchase, Octel quickly became the world's largest voice mail outsourcing company. Octel Network Services managed clients' voice-mail networks and engaged in disaster recovery, operations management, systems administration, and project management. These operations brought Octel a large source of recurring revenue to help balance the one-time profit of selling a voice-mail system.

Ameritech became one of the most important clients for Octel Network Services, which operated the voice-mail services that Ameritech offered to residential and small-business customers. By 1994 400,000 Ameritech residential customers were using the system, with thousands joining up every month.

In 1993, with the use of faxes proliferating in corporate America, Octel released three products for its Voice Information Processor: Faxagent, Faxbroadcast, and Faxstation. Each consisted of a card and software. The same year, the firm began a joint venture in Israel, hoping to gain access to some of that country's technical specialists. Also in 1993 Robert Cohen rejoined the firm as president and CEO. Total revenue for the year came to $338.5 million.

Octel saw an opportunity in operating voice-mail systems in developing countries, and by the mid-1990s it had major installations operating in Brazil and China. In these countries millions of customers wanted their own telephones but could not get them; thus many simply bought their own mailbox and checked messages from pay phones. The firm hoped this system would catch on in developing countries and become a major source of revenue.

In early 1994 Octel took over the industry's first voice-mail company when it merged with VMX Inc. in a stock swap valued at about $150 million. Octel's first move was to write software allowing the two systems to network and to port VMXworks, a software application, to Octel's systems. Several VMX vice-presidents took similar titles in related areas at Octel.

Octel now had the two most popular user interfaces for voice mail. Analysts expected the acquisition to help Octel as voice processing became based less on the telephone and more on the personal computer. The purchase also brought on VMX's Rhetorex subsidiary, which designed and manufactured voice-processing components.

Octel had an installed base of 37,000 systems including those that came with the VMX deal. With new applications like fax products the firm hoped to capitalize on this market to make secondary sales. Meanwhile, Octel continued to win customers. In 1994 data-processing giant Electronic Data Systems, which had purchased voice-mail systems from Octel in the past, chose to use Octel's voice-processing services. The seven-year contract called for Octel to provide facilities management and services for over 100 Octel systems at Electronic Data Systems locations. Octel also signed long-term contracts with Kodak, Blockbuster Entertainment, and Texas Instruments.

In 1994 Octel finished its new corporate headquarters, a five-building complex in Milpitas, California, with 368,000 square feet of space. VMX employees also moved into the space.

With the increasing prevalence of electronic mail and the increasing power of personal computers, the creation of voice-mail products for the personal computer became more important. In 1994 Octel released Visual Mailbox, a software program that allowed users on local area networks to use personal computers to access voice mail and faxes. The computers did not need built-in multimedia support, although the software required users to be on a system using Octel's VMX 200/300 voice-mail system. Octel believed that voice mail would likely be provided on local area networks as they became more powerful and considered the moves an important way to prepare for future market changes. In 1995 Octel demonstrated add-ons for Microsoft's Exchange messaging server that enabled users to integrate voice, fax, and e-mail. Also in 1995 Bell Atlantic signed a three-year agreement to use Octel's OptiMail, which permitted the outsourcing of voice and fax messaging services.

In the mid-1990s Octel was the leading company in its field and many industry analysts believed it was well positioned for future growth. The telecommunications field was constantly evolving, however, and if regional Bell companies were allowed into manufacturing, some of the firm's biggest customers might rapidly become competitors.

Principal Subsidiaries: Octel Network Services; VMX Inc.

Further Reading:

Bylinsky, Gene, "How to Shoulder Aside the Titans," *Fortune,* May 18, 1992, pp. 87–88.

DiLorenzo, Jim, "Octel to Acquire VMX," *Telephony,* February 7, 1994, pp. 14–16.

Edwards, Mike, "Octel Brings Phones, Computers Closer Together with Voice Processing System," *Computing Canada,* May 9, 1991, pp. 43, 49.

Lee, Paula Munier, "Going Public After the Crash," *Small Business Reports,* October 1989, pp. 32–36.

"Octel Communications Corporation," *Wall Street Transcript,* July 17, 1989, p. 94, 284.

"Octel Communications Names New President and Chief Executive," *Wall Street Journal,* October 9, 1990, p. B13.

Pitta, Julie, "Panic!" *Forbes,* October 28, 1991, pp. 102–103.

Pollack, Andrew, "Hewlett-Packard Sets 10% Purchase of Octel," *New York Times,* August 12, 1988, p. D4.

—Scott M. Lewis

Odetics

Odetics Inc.

1515 South Manchester Avenue
Anaheim, California
U.S.A.
(714) 774-5000
Fax: (714) 774-9432

Public Company
Incorporated: 1969
Employees: 600
Sales: $87.7 million
Stock Exchanges: NASDAQ
SICs: 3572 Computer Storage Devices; 3821 Laboratory
  Apparatus & Furniture

Odetics Inc. designs, develops, manufacturers, and markets specialized information automation products and other high-tech machines. Product examples include magnetic tape cartridge and cassette handling subsystems for automated tape library systems and time-lapse VCRs used in commercial and industrial closed circuit television security and surveillance applications. The company relied heavily on sales to governments during the 1970s and 1980s before it began deemphasizing that market in the early 1990s. Odetics is distinguished by its unique corporate culture.

Odetics was started in 1969 by six engineers: Cran Gudmundson, Jerry Muench, Gordon Schulz, Jim Welch, Jim Reisinger, and Joel Slutzky. The men were all working at Leach Corp. in California when Slutzky approached the others about jumping ship to form a new company. The aerospace industry was booming and Slutzky believed that they could find a niche there. Specifically, he recognized the need for a high-quality, long-life magnetic tape recorder to store and forward digital data in space. In fact, the 29-year-old Slutzky had approached his managers at Leach about stepping up the company's efforts related to spaceborne tape recorders. "But they decided to expand into the more lucrative computer peripheral market," Slutzky said in a February 1987 issue of *Industry Week*. "So I went to five key people in the company and asked them if they were interested in starting their own company to build spaceborne recorders. They said yes."

Slutzky, who already had a wife, a son, and a daughter, quit his job and headed east to round up investment capital. To his surprise, he was quickly able to line up about $600,000 in

financing for the new venture. His partners eventually left their posts, as well, and together they formed Odetics. They sublet a corner of a building in Anaheim, California, and got to work developing an improved version of the spaceborne tape recorder that they had worked on at Leach. Because they were competing with the likes of corporate giants RCA, Borg-Warner, and Emerson, the engineers had to prove themselves in the market. Impressively, Odetics managed to squeak out a profit in its first full year of operation.

Because he had initiated the venture, Slutzky was the natural choice to head Odetics. Aside from his entrepreneurial nature Slutzky was a techno-wiz and self-admitted workaholic. His superb math aptitude had emerged at Senn High School in Chicago, where his teachers advised him to major in engineering at college. He picked up a couple of degrees in math and science at the University of Illinois and taught metallurgy for a while after graduation. He eventually moved into the private sector and ended up in California at North American Aviation, which was subsequently purchased by defense-industry behemoth Rockwell International. At North American, Slutzky worked on missile guidance systems before moving to Leach. Slutzky served as manager of mechanical engineering at Leach, where he helped design spaceborne tape recorders.

During much of the 1970s the Odetics engineers were eating, sleeping, and breathing spaceborne tape recorders. Their products earned the company a good reputation in the aerospace industry, and Odetics managed to post profits throughout the decade. After establishing a presence in the tape recorder niche, the company decided it was time to branch out into a new area. After extensive research and development, Slutzky and fellow executives settled on time-lapse video recording. The talented Odetics engineering staff developed a breakthrough technology that adapted the half-inch VHS VCR to time-lapse recording. The innovation worked in space and on earth and could be used in applications ranging from convenience stores and automated teller machines (for security purposes) to space flight.

Odetics was again battling established corporate giants when it targeted time-lapse video recording technology. Despite competition from venerable Japanese competitors Panasonic and Sony, the superior engineering at Odetics allowed the firm to capture 50 percent of the U.S. market within a few years. Thus, Odetics sustained its profitability into the early 1980s. Having achieved success in two markets, management decided to diversify into other product groups. To that end, Odetics decided to go public and made its initial public offering in 1981. Enthusiastic investors dumped millions of dollars into the company, and Odetics funded a new initiative during the early and mid-1980s. The company also used the cash to secure dominance in its original two markets.

Slutzky decided to target the burgeoning and fascinating field of robotics following the 1981 stock offering. Odetics's push into robotics was inspired by engineer and tinkerer Stephen Bartholet. Bartholet served as senior engineer at Odetics during the development of the company's first robot—Odex 1. Odex 1 was the culmination of Bartholet's lifelong fascination and garage tinkering with robotics. His enthusiasm eventually convinced Slutzky to devote millions of dollars in research and development toward the Odex project. The idea was to develop an "intelligent" robot that could be used to fight fires, clean up hazardous wastes and nuclear accidents, or do battle, among other tasks.

In 1984 Odetics unveiled its amazing Odex 1, a six-legged walking robot that weighed only 300 pounds. Its onboard computer could be operated remotely and the robot moved under its own power. To display the contraption's agility, engineers commanded Odex to walk to a truck, get on the truck, and then actually move the truck. The device's tremendous strength-to-weight ratio wowed observers and Odetics quickly snared orders from the army and navy, the Department of Agriculture, the National Aeronautics and Space Administration (NASA), and others. Odetics received the well-known Private Sector Award in 1984 for its work in robotics, and the original Odex 1 prototype was later put on display in the Smithsonian Institution.

During the next few years Odetics worked to hone its robotics technology and to develop other intelligent devices. Following a Stanford University marketing study, Odetics began gearing its robotics technology to serve a wide array of different markets. By 1986 Odetics had developed robot technology that could be used to fight fires in nuclear facilities and on ship decks and clean up nuclear, biological, and other dangerous wastes. The company expected those capabilities to generate particular interest for Superfund cleanups under the Department of Energy and Department of Defense. In addition to its robotics breakthroughs, Odetics' list of credits by the mid-1980s included taking pictures of Chernobyl's nuclear accident from space, making flight recordings on NASA's space shuttle, developing a special laser scanner for the Department of Agriculture, and building docking and birthing devices utilized by NASA.

Odetics generated revenues of $31.5 million in 1985 and net income of nearly $500,000. Sales rose to $33.1 million in 1986, although heavy investments in new robotics research diminished the company's earnings to a measly $33,000. Only by instigating a companywide salary deferral for the firm's 440 employees was Odetics able to sustain its legacy of profitability in that year. Because of the relatively slow sales and profit growth, some investors became disenchanted—one group even filed a lawsuit claiming that the company had misled investors about the risks associated with its projects. Slutzky maintained that Odetics was operating with its eye on the future by developing technologies for markets that would not fully bloom until the 1990s. "We are not here for the quarterly profits," he said in the *Industry Week* article.

Despite sporadic profit levels, no one could deny that the firm's technological feats were impressive. There were many reasons for those successes, but Slutzky's unique management style was likely the most important factor. Indeed, Slutzky had earned a reputation in U.S. industry as a maverick and nonconformist—and not because he was one of the few chief executives that sported a beard. The coffee tables in Slutzky's office reception area wore wing tips, shirts, and ties, and Slutzky once had kept his six-foot pet alligator in the office. Every year, Slutzky rented a theater for his "associates"—he banished the term "employee"—so that they could stage their own play productions. He even sponsored a sock hop during a work day. Associates dressed in 1950s-style garb and period music flowed from the public-address system all day.

Odetics also held an annual company Olympics, which featured wheelbarrow races and wienie-eating contests. Slutzky once encouraged a consciousness-raising event in which associates were allowed to write anonymous notes to their bosses and peers and tell them exactly what they thought of them. Slutzky held that the unusual work environment was necessary to relieve the stress of long hours and to cultivate a creative, spontaneous work atmosphere. Reflecting the company's singular philosophy were two flags hanging outside of company headquarters with the slogans; "An adventure in American Creativity" and "Long Live Liberty." The Odetics workforce did embody the American dream, with workers that had immigrated to the United States from 21 different countries. The company's employee-focused management philosophy earned it a place in the book *100 Best Companies to Work for in America* and was evidenced by an extremely low employee turnover rate (just five percent in the late 1980s and early 1990s).

By 1987 Odetics was manufacturing spaceborne tape recorders, time-lapse video cameras for security systems, audio recorders for courtrooms, automated television broadcast carts, and the six-legged, superstrong robot. Most of its sales were to government departments. Spurred by orders from the thriving defense sector, sales rose steadily during the late 1980s. By the early 1990s Odetics was generating more than $60 million in annual revenue. Unfortunately for the company, however, growth in government expenditures began to slow. The Department of Defense, particularly, slashed its procurement budget, leaving many contractors looking for work. To overcome the slowdown, Odetics managers scrambled to reorient their product mix for the private sector.

Slutzky and fellow executives decided to use previously developed Odetics technology to target the data storage industry. It invested heavily to invent a magnetic tape cartridge and cassette handling subsystem that could be used in automated tape library systems. Those systems were used to store mass amounts of computer data. Odetics also began manufacturing large library cart machines used by broadcast and cable-TV station operations to store video and other information. The company also beefed up its efforts to market time-lapse VCRs and related products used in commercial and industrial closed circuit television security and surveillance applications. As a result of the new strategy, the percentage of revenues attributable to government purchases plummeted to less than 50 percent in the early 1990s, then to only about 25 percent going into the mid-1990s. President Bush visited Odetics during his 1992 campaign, praising the company as a model of peacetime technology conversion.

Despite the firm's successful conversion to private-sector markets and its rising revenue base—the company was capturing revenues of $70 million by 1992—its stock price languished. Having reached a high of $12 in 1985, the stock price dropped and was mired around $8 by 1993. Part of the problem was that investors were still unsure of the company's ability to generate long-term profit gains. The doubts were not without merit; Odetics sales dropped about one percent during 1993 (fiscal year ended March 31) to $69.3 million, a slim $141,000 of which was netted as income. Nevertheless, Slutzky remained optimistic and the company continued to operate much as it had for the past 24 years (as evidenced by a spur-of-the-moment contest to win a free lunch by shooting a hockey puck past Slutzky in the company cafeteria in 1993).

New product introductions and recovering markets helped push firm sales up 20 percent in 1994 to $84.1 million, about $1.8 million of which was netted as income. Partly because of research and development expenditures, the company was forced to register its first income deficit since its founding in 1969 during the 1995 fiscal year ended March 31. The income slide intensified during the last quarter of 1994 and the first quarter of 1995, which helped to push the organization's stock price down to around $4 by mid-1995. Management remained optimistic however, and was banking on products that were in the works to sustain revenue growth and boost long-term profitability, particularly products related to data storage, communications, and multimedia. Its major product categories remained automated tape libraries, digital video processors, time-lapse video recorders, and digital data recorders. The company was employing about 600 workers going into the mid-1990s in Anaheim and at its El Paso, Texas, plant.

Principal Subsidiaries: Odetics U.K. Limited; ATL Products, Inc.

Further Reading:

Blake, Mike, ''Joel Slutzky Keeps Odetics' Feet on the Ground,'' *Orange County Business Journal,* October 13, 1986, p. 16.
Jacobs, Bruce A., ''Joel Slutzky Is Crazy (Like a Fox),'' *Industry Week,* February 9, 1987, p. 41.
Takahashi, Dean, ''High-Tech Spinoffs: Pathway to Innovation for Entrepreneurs,'' *Los Angeles Times,* August 18, 1991, p. 1D.
Woolley, Scott, ''Fun and Gains: Wacky Approach, 24 Straight Years of Profit for Odetics,'' *Orange County Business Journal*, June 21, 1993, p. 1.

—Dave Mote

The Ohio Art Company

One Toy Street
Bryan, Ohio 43506
U.S.A.
(419) 636-3141
Fax (419) 636-7614

Public Company
Incorporated: 1930
Employees: 300
Sales: $40.2 million (1994)
Stock Exchanges: American
SICs: 3944 Dolls, Toys, Games & Sporting & Athletic
   Goods

Headquartered in a small northwest Ohio town, The Ohio Art Company is best known for its classic toy, the Etch A Sketch. In stark contrast to the faddish toys that crowded the toy market during the late 20th century, the company's flagship product had endured 35 years, sold over 100 million units, and appealed to children in 65 countries worldwide. By the early 1990s the Etch A Sketch was manufactured in five countries and sold in 67 nations around the world. One of the oldest toymakers in the United States, Ohio Art manufactured about 200 other basic toys in the early 1990s. The company's slogan, "Making Creativity Fun," emphasized its focus on art- and craft-oriented toys. And though toys generated the majority of Ohio Art's annual sales, industrial components contributed about one-fourth of revenues in the early 1990s. After reaching an anticyclical peak of $56.93 million in 1992, Ohio Art's sales declined by over 25 percent to $41.07 million in 1994. Profits eroded even faster, by over three-fourths, from $3.44 million to $824,000 during the same period. Nevertheless, the sparsely traded company has never failed to pay an annual dividend.

Ohio Art traces its history to the first decade of the 20th century, when Henry Simon Winzeler made a dramatic career change. Trained as a dentist, Winzeler opened a private practice in the tiny town of Archbold, Ohio, in 1900. Inspired by an oval mirror in his aunt's clothing store, Winzeler decided to start manufacturing oval picture frames. With $300 borrowed from friends, Winzeler made preparations to begin production in a rented hall. He sold the dental office in 1908 and opened a grocery, using the market's profits to buy equipment for the

frame business. He continued to operate his "Hub Grocery" through early 1909.

Winzeler launched The Ohio Art Company in October 1908 with 15 employees. For the first two years, his oval metal frames were stamped in Toledo, then painted on-site in Archbold. In 1910 Winzeler bought his own stamping machine and consolidated production.

Sold primarily through the new breed of mass marketers like Woolworth's, Kresge's, and Sears, Roebuck & Co., Ohio Art's framed pieces featured religious scenes, still lifes, and landscapes. Within just two years production had expanded to 20,000 units each day. The company's most popular view featured a pair of cupids, one asleep, one awake. The Cupid images were copyrighted by Taber-Prand Company, and Ohio Art paid a royalty on each set. Ohio Art's 75th anniversary publication noted that "Winzeler offered $100,000 for the rights to these pictures, but his offer was rejected. In 1938, Taber-Prand went into bankruptcy and Winzeler's son, Howie, bought the rights for $10." Company figures estimated that over 50 million of the cupid sets were sold, meaning that the decoration graced over one-half of all homes in the early 20th century.

Rising demand spurred moves to progressively larger plants, until Ohio Art moved to the town of Bryan and a specially built plant in 1915. The addition of lithography equipment that same year expanded the company's capabilities. Ohio Art diversified cautiously at first, lithographing wood-grain finishes on its traditional metal frames. This product line grew to include advertising signage and scale faces.

Ohio Art also expanded through acquisition during this period. The 1916 purchase of Chicago's Holabird Manufacturing Company broadened the product line to include glass-framed calendars featuring popular Ohio Art prints.

The onset of World War I in 1914 interrupted toy imports from Germany and afforded domestic toymakers the opportunity to fill the void. In 1917 Ohio Art acquired both the C. E. Carter Company's Erie toy plant and the Battle Creek Toy Manufacturing Company. During this period, Ohio Art began making the lithographed metal windmills, sand pails, toy cars, wagons, circus trains, spinning tops, and drum sets that would be mainstays throughout the 20th century. The company honed its lithography skills with the production of metal tea sets that featured detailed depictions of nursery rhymes, alphabets, animals, and children's stories.

In 1927 H. S. Winzeler retired from Ohio Art to concentrate on his West Coast businesses. Although Winzeler continued to own the company, Lachlan M. ("Mac") MacDonald succeeded Winzeler as president and directed Ohio Art's 1930 incorporation. About 20 percent of the company's equity was sold to the public at that time, but the Winzelers retained a controlling stake. Fifteen-year-old son Howard W. ("Howie") Winzeler started working part-time at Ohio Art in 1930 and joined the firm full-time three years later.

Ohio Art maintained its fiscal strength throughout the Great Depression and was even able to acquire several other companies hobbled by the crisis. In 1930 alone the company bought out four firms: Mutual Novelty Manufacturing Company in Chicago, a producer of artificial icicles for decorating Christmas trees; Veelo Manufacturing Company, maker of dolls and stuffed animals; Delta Products, a manufacturer of electric appliances and car parts; and Household Appliance Manufacturing Company, a maker of clothes dryers. Craftsman Studios, a manufacturer of brass and copper tableware, was acquired in 1931. Two printing companies, Kenyon Company, Inc., and Detroit Publishing Company, were purchased the following year. When H. S. Winzeler died in 1939 Howie was appointed to fill the vacant seat on the board of directors. By the end of the year, he had also advanced to vice-president.

During World War II, when virtually all domestic production was harnessed for the war effort, even toymakers like Ohio Art were called upon to manufacture strategic products. The tiny northwest Ohio firm made parts for rockets, bombs, and aircraft throughout the war, and its contributions earned an "Excellence" award at war's end.

When Ohio Art resumed toymaking in the postwar era, it began using new plastics to make its traditional toys. Metal dollhouses featured plastic furniture, and tea sets, sand pails, and farm sets reappeared in plastic.

H. W. Winzeler, who advanced to Ohio Art's presidency in 1953, encountered what would become the company's flagship product at a European toy fair in 1959. That's when France's Arthur Granjean pitched his "L'Ecran Magique" ("magic writer") to the chief executive officer. Winzeler was reluctant to pay the apparently steep price Granjean demanded to license the product but bought the rights after a second presentation later that year.

Renamed the Etch A Sketch, the toy featured a glass "window" enclosed in a red plastic frame. A combination of aluminum powder and plastic pellets inside the window made it look like a flat gray screen. Young sketchers could create line images by turning the white knobs on the left and right of the screen, which, by a series of internal strings and pulleys, controlled the horizontal and vertical movement of a stylus that scraped the aluminum powder from the back of the glass, leaving a thin black line. To erase a drawing and start over, the sketcher simply turned the toy on its face and shook, coating the glass with a new film of aluminum powder.

Ohio Art launched the toy in time for the 1960 holiday season and supported Etch A Sketch (which itself resembled a television) with its first televised advertising campaign. With seals of approval from Good Housekeeping and Parents magazines, the Etch A Sketch soon became a toy store mainstay. Sears, Roebuck & Co. alone sold 10 million of the toys from 1960 to 1970.

Not content to rest, Ohio Art balanced the toy market's seasonally cyclical sales with the incorporation of Strydel, Inc., in 1962. Strydel applied Ohio Art's injection molding, lithography, and metal stamping capabilities to the production of metal and plastic industrial components like auto trim, film canisters, and reproductions of classic metal signs and trays, mostly premiums for Coca-Cola. Ohio Art was eventually producing 500 lithographed designs. In 1968 Ohio Art acquired Trinc Company, a truck leasing firm formerly owned by Ohio Art execu-

tives, and a controlling interest in Emenee Corporation, a manufacturer of toy musical instruments.

The founding Winzeler family sold its controlling stake in Ohio Art to William Casley Killgallon in 1977. The Winzelers had drawn Killgallon from a rival toy company to become sales manager in 1955. He advanced to a seat on the board within two years and was elected president in 1966 and board chairman in 1978. William Killgallon was joined by his son Bill (William Carpenter) in 1968; Bill succeeded his father as president and chief executive officer in 1978 and was joined at the company by his brother, Martin ("Larry") Killgallon. They consolidated Ohio Art's peripheral businesses as the diversified Products Division in 1978.

Although Ohio Art had utilized licensed characters to make its products more attractive and recognizable to children and parents since the late 1920s, licensing efforts intensified dramatically during the 1980s. Ohio Art continued to license perennially popular Disney characters—even offering an Etch A Sketch in the shape of Mickey Mouse—as well as trendy animated figures like Smurfs and Pac-Man. The company also introduced the Lil' Sport line of scaled-down basketball, baseball, and soccer toys during the late 1970s and early 1980s.

Ohio Art launched Etch A Sketch spin-offs during the 1980s, including plastic overlays with drawing games and puzzles, as well as travel and pocket Etch A Sketch models. The company's efforts to parlay its long-running (yet only moderately profitable) Etch A Sketch franchise culminated in the 1986 launch of the Etch A Sketch Animator. This electronic version of the classic toy could store several drawings at a time and play them back, effecting animation. At a retail price of about $50, the Animator was one of Ohio Art's most expensive offerings. The company's sales jumped 50 percent from about $31.3 million in 1985 to $47 million in 1986, and its profits quintupled to $2.5 million. However, those high-flying results came back to earth in the ensuing years, when competition from video games battered Animator sales. Ohio Art lost $3 million in 1989 and 1990 and finally ceased production of the Animator.

In a more low-tech vein, Ohio Art launched a color Etch A Sketch in 1993 that used the traditional two-knob drawing method but featured six colors and produced a color copy of each drawing. In honor of the toy's 35th birthday in 1995, Ohio Art introduced pocket models in jewel tones.

Ironically, the recession of the early 1990s helped Ohio Art to a certain degree, as many of its toys retailed for less than $20 and thus appealed to budget-conscious parents. Art, craft, and educational toys offered to "Make Creativity Fun." Sales and profits peaked at $56.93 million and $3.44 million in 1992. But as the United States slowly emerged from recession, Ohio Art's results headed downward again. Sales declined by over 25 percent to $41.07 million in 1994, and profits dropped by over three-fourths to $824,000 during the same period. The Killgallons, who continued to own a controlling interest in the company in the early 1990s, worked to regain Ohio Art's luster, reducing the workforce by about 15 percent, cutting inventory levels, and achieving efficiencies in administrative areas.

Principal Subsidiaries: Strydel, Inc.; Trinc Co.

Further Reading:

A 75 Year Headstart on Tomorrow, 1908–1983: The Ohio Art Company, Bryan, Ohio: Ohio Art Co., 1983.
Brown, Paul, ''Staying Power,'' *Forbes,* March 26, 1984, p. 186.
Cropper, Carol, ''Etch a Mickey,'' *Forbes,* March 30, 1992, p. 14.
Grimm, Matthew, ''U.S. Toy Makers Invade the Eastern Bloc,'' *Adweek's Marketing Week,* June 4, 1990, p. 4.

''Lego Wars: A Christmas Tale,'' *Newsweek,* December 28, 1987, p. 40.
''Ohio Art Sparks Creativity with Its Scope Activity Toys,'' *Playthings,* February 1993, p. 140.
Salas, Teresa, ''Manufacturers Plot to Tackle Toy Troubles,'' *Playthings,* February 1991, p. 66.
Slutsker, Gary, ''Etch a Future,'' *Forbes,* March 23, 1987, p. 72.

—April Dougal Gasbarre

Ohio Bell Telephone Company

45 Erieview Plaza
Cleveland, Ohio 44114
U.S.A.
(216) 822-9700
Fax: (216) 822-5522

Wholly Owned Subsidiary of Ameritech Corporation
Incorporated: 1880 as The Cleveland Telephone Company
Employees: 9,084
Revenues: $2.17 billion
SICs: 4813 Telephone Communications Except
    Radiotelephone; 4812 Radiotelephone Communications

Ohio Bell Telephone Company, as a part of the Ameritech Corporation, provides local-exchange and limited long-distance telephone communications in Ohio. In the mid-1990s, Ohio Bell was serving about three-fifths of Ohio's residents and maintaining over 3.4 million phone lines in the Cleveland area, the company's home base. Ohio Bell was also engaged in providing other communications services as well, including private line voice and data services, data transmission, and radio and television broadcasts.

In 1876 Alexander Graham Bell shouted to his colleague through a revolutionary communications device; one year later, Cleveland, Ohio, installed its first telephone. The first phone service in that city was provided by Western Union Telegraph Co., but that company soon withdrew from the business after a patent dispute with the Bell Telephone Company, the organization formed to oversee and market Alexander Graham Bell's technology. The exchange was then purchased by a Bell licensed company called the Cleveland Telephone Company. Incorporated in 1880, the Cleveland Telephone Company operated as the only local telephone company in the city for ten years.

Phone service in Cleveland grew rapidly. The city's original customer base of 76 had increased to almost 300 by 1880. Ten years later that number had multiplied nearly ten times to 2,979 subscribers. Given the relative expense incurred by phone service ($72 a year for businesses and $60 for homes), the invention's popularity came primarily from the wealthy and from businesses.

After local phone line needs were met in Cleveland, long distance service moved into the area as well, reaching Cleve-

land for the first time in 1883 via a Chicago-based Bell organization. By 1893 the American Telephone and Telegraph Company (AT&T) was providing long-distance service to Cleveland, marking the beginning of a relationship between AT&T and Cleveland Telephone that would remain for almost a century.

AT&T was originally formed by Bell Telephone as its long-distance subsidiary. As Bell Telephone grew at a tremendous rate throughout the country, it found that it needed additional money to fund the expansion. However, the amount of capital it could raise and the means of raising it were restricted by the state of Massachusetts, in which Bell Telephone was incorporated. So, Bell Telephone had its AT&T subsidiary (incorporated in New York where rules for expansion were more lenient) take over its local phone exchanges as well as continuing its role as long distance provider. With over $70 million in assets, AT&T became the parent company of the Bell System in 1899, and the Cleveland Telephone Company became a wholly-owned subsidiary of AT&T.

After the expiration of the Bell patents in 1894, independent phone companies began forming and the Cleveland Telephone Company met its first competition. The Cuyahoga Telephone Company, for example, offered lower rates than Cleveland Telephone and gave subscribers access to locations not reached by the Bell system. The new competition prompted Cleveland Telephone to lower its rates. However, customers of each company soon became frustrated when they found they couldn't place calls to those subscribing to the competitors' service. In fact, businesses found that communicating effectively with all their customers necessitated subscribing to the services of both companies. In 1901, to help with this problem, the two companies agreed to exchange services.

The real growth of the Cleveland Telephone Company began in the early 1900s with a name change and a series of acquisitions. In 1921, Cleveland Telephone became incorporated as The Ohio Bell Telephone Company, an identity that remained for over 70 years. Also during this time, it acquired the Central Union Telephone Company's Ohio locations, as well as the southern Ohio services of the Chesapeake and Potomac Telephone Company of West Virginia. Finally, a merger with Ohio State Telephone, the country's largest independent phone company, made Ohio Bell the dominant communications company in the state. During this time, Ohio boasted around 875,000 phones, and Ohio Bell operated 505,000 of that total. The company was valued at $100 million.

Although the expansion of phone lines slowed during the great Depression, use increased again in the late 1930s, and Ohio Bell continued to upgrade its services and expand its operations. In fact, Ohio Bell became the eighth largest of the Bell companies. In the Cleveland area alone, over 188,000 people used Ohio Bell's services in 1940. Ten years later the company operated about 600,000 phones in the city and surrounding suburbs, and by 1965 that number had reached one million. In the late 1960s, Ohio Bell replaced the exchange numbers used since 1897 with new seven-digit numbers, and some customers also began enjoying such new services as call transfer, three-way calling, and call-waiting.

Ohio Bell's parent, AT&T, was also growing at an amazing rate. Acquiring independent phone companies beginning in the early 1900s, AT&T was reporting income of over $1 billion by 1929. During the late 1930s and 1940s, AT&T grew by one million new customers every year. With over one million employees by the mid-1960s, the corporation provided phone communications to about 85 percent of the homes in service region. Thus, by the 1970s AT&T was the largest company in the world.

The telephone industry in the United States was clearly dominated by the Bell System and AT&T, and such control was viewed by many as the most effective way to operate telecommunications in the country. This view had been expressed, in fact, by AT&T president Theodore Vail, in the company's 1910 annual report: "The telephone system should be universal, interdependent and intercommunicating, affording opportunity for any subscriber of any exchange to communicate with any other subscriber of any other exchange.... Such control and regulation as will afford the public much better service at less cost than any competition or governmental-owned monopoly." And telecommunications had become a regulated industry in 1934 under the authority of the Federal Communications Commission (FCC), which believed that the industry should be directed by public interest and not by free market competition.

But by the 1970s, however, some began to question such control. Customers began to wonder whether the company was still working in their best interests, and companies with new telecommunications ideas wanted to compete. For example, an ambitious company called Microwave Communications, Inc. (MCI) sought to provide new and less expensive microwave technology for long distance services. When MCI received permission to offer limited service in the early 1970s, it promptly filed an antitrust suit against AT&T in 1974. A similar suit was also filed by the Justice Department during this time.

Following years in court in the biggest antitrust case in U.S. history, AT&T agreed to divest its operations in 1982. AT&T shed its local operating subsidiaries as part of the antitrust settlement, and Ameritech Corporation, a Chicago-based communications company, was established as one of the seven new regional holding companies. On January 1, 1984, The Ohio Bell Telephone Company became a wholly-owned subsidiary of Ameritech Corporation.

The period from the mid-1980s through the 1990s was a time of major restructuring and consolidation for Ohio Bell. In 1990, the company announced the reduction of about eight percent of their workforce, or approximately 1,000 jobs, through early retirement, hiring freezes, and resignations. Two years later, Ameritech consolidated management positions at all five of its Bell telephone companies: Ohio Bell, Illinois Bell, Indiana Bell, Michigan Bell, and Wisconsin Telephone. Thousands of positions in marketing, advertising, training, operations and accounting were eliminated or transferred into Ameritech Services Inc., the administrative division of the group. Additional cuts were made in later years.

During this crucial restructuring time, Jacqueline F. Woods became the new president of Ohio Bell and was faced with the challenge of assuring employees and customers that the recent changes were best for everybody. Nevertheless, many Ohio Bell workers worried about the future of their jobs and some customers were confused about who actually served their phone needs. Also during this time, management announced that the Ohio Bell name would be phased out and the state company would adopt the Ameritech name. The company thereafter became known among its customers as Ameritech Ohio, retaining the Ohio Bell name for financial reporting purposes only.

Increased competition in the 1990s prompted Ameritech Ohio to seek regulatory changes on the state level. Specifically, the company supported a plan to reform the way local-exchange companies were controlled. The Ohio Telephone Association (OTA), representing 42 local-exchange companies including Ameritech Ohio, proposed the changes, asking that local-exchange companies be subjected to lower taxes and allowed more freedom to set prices, especially with business phone rates. If approved by state officials, the changes would help Ameritech Ohio compete with competitive access providers (CAPs), who supplied businesses with fiber-optic lines that connected them to long-distance carriers at lower prices. CAPs were one of the most rapidly growing segments in the industry during this time. According to an Ameritech Ohio spokesperson in a 1992 *Business First-Columbus* article, "We are still operating under a regulatory system that was established at the start of the century. We need to change that system to reflect the fact that local telephone companies are no longer a monopoly business and face competition on all fronts." Moreover, Ameritech also petitioned the federal government for open communications markets for both local and long distance companies. Ameritech wanted competition, regarding it as an opportunity to grow and expand into new markets.

Technology brought exciting new services to the modern phone customer in the 1990s. Through a joint venture telecommunications experiment with new homeowners in a New Albany, Ohio, community, Ohio Bell, AT&T, and Georgia-based ICS, Inc. worked together to make daily communications life even easier. A fiber optics system called Integrated Services Digital Network (ISDN), installed in new homes, allowed residents to enjoy intercom services with other homes and locations in the community, caller identification, customized ringing patterns, a do-not-disturb feature, night service, as well as back-up power in case of power failure. The system also allowed home offices to access company computers and networks without interrupting other phone calls to the home. Other new equipment such as pagers, modems, and cellular phones made communications even easier and more convenient. Such advancements also gobbled up phone numbers, and in 1995, the state of Ohio added an additional area code to increase the availability of new numbers. While a changing regulatory environment and consolidation of services at Ameritech Ohio made their course difficult to predict, the company was pursuing a program of greater efficiency and growth, spurred by technological advancements in an increasingly interactive industry.

Further Reading:

Brooks, John, *Telephone: The First Hundred Years,* New York: Harper & Row Publishers, Inc., 1975.
Connole, Jon, "Ohio Bell Begins to Restructure, Cut 1,000 Jobs," *Crain's Cleveland Business,* August 6, 1990, p. 1.

Hall, Matthew, "Ma Bell Changes," *Business First-Columbus,* December 13, 1993, p. 15.

——, "Rival Pitching Tent in Bell's Back Yard: MetroComm Eyes Local-Exchange Market," *Business First-Columbus,* July 13, 1992, p. 17.

"Home Information Services Now on Trial," *Custom Builder,* September-October 1993, p. S19.

Lashinsky, Adam, "Ameritech Expected to Merge Bell Units," *Crain's Cleveland Business,* September 7, 1992, p. 1.

"Ohio Bell Realigns Network, Marketing," *Business First-Columbus,* July 9, 1990, p. 2.

Rose, William Ganson, *Cleveland: The Making of a City,* Cleveland: World Publishing Co., 1950.

The Telephone Situation in the State of Ohio, Cleveland: The Ohio Bell Telephone Co., 1924.

Thompson, Chris, "Bell Chief Awaits Test: New President to Lead Corporate Transition," *Crain's Cleveland Business,* March 1, 1993, p. 1.

Tunstall, W. Brooke, *Disconnecting Parties—Managing the Bell System Break Up: An Inside View,* McGraw-Hill Book Company, 1985.

—Beth Watson Highman

OmniSource Corporation

1610 N. Calhoun Street
Fort Wayne, Indiana 46808
U.S.A.
(219) 422-5541
Fax: (219) 422-9154

Private Company
Incorporated: 1946 as Superior Iron and Metal Company
Employees: 800
Sales: $420 million
SICs: 5093 Scrap & Waste Materials

OmniSource Corporation is one of the largest scrap metal processors in the nation, with more than 20 trading offices, processing divisions, and collection centers scattered throughout the Midwest and the South. OmniSource buys, collects, and processes scrap metals like copper, steel, iron, and aluminum, and then sells the material to manufacturers of finished metal products.

The company that became OmniSource traces its roots to the bed of a Russian immigrant's pickup truck. Irving Rifkin fled the Bolshevik revolution in 1920 and came to the United States to start a new life. ''My father, Irving Rifkin, journeyed to America searching for personal freedom and the opportunity to build a life and a family,'' related Irving's son Leonard in company literature. ''His future,'' the younger Rifkin observed, ''was guided by the philosophy that hard work, perseverance, and personal integrity would provide the foundation for future growth and success.''

Rifkin settled in New York City, where he ran a restaurant and deli business during the 1920s and throughout most of the Great Depression. In 1940 he decided to move to Lima, Ohio, to get involved with his uncle's scrap metal business. For three years Rifkin drove around Ohio in his pickup truck brokering scrap. He would buy discarded metals and try to sell them for a profit to scrap processors and metal manufacturers. He eventually tired of that job and, at the suggestion of another of his relatives, decided to start his own scrap business. Rifkin moved to Fort Wayne, Indiana, in 1943 and purchased his first scrap yard. He dubbed it Superior Iron and Metal Co., launching an operation that was destined to become a leader in the U.S. scrap metal industry.

Superior Iron and Metal grew slowly during the 1950s and 1960s as a result of Rifkin's hard work and determination. The

company supplied scrap for the war effort during World War II and managed in the 1950s and 1960s to establish a reputation as a dependable and fair buyer, processor, and seller of scrap. During that time, the metal scrap business was a relatively crude, unglamorous trade. Scrap was used by automobile or rail manufacturers, for example, to help make new iron and steel products. But the cost associated with making metals from freshly mined materials was not significantly greater, in most applications, than the cost of producing metal using scrap. That was largely because resources were abundant and because technologies related to making steel and integrating some types of scrap into the production process were crude.

By the early 1970s, Rifkin had grown Superior Iron and Metal into a successful, though small, regional scrap company. He had four scrap operations that served customers primarily in the upper Midwest and had expanded the operation, according to son Leonard, by focusing on long-term opportunities rather than short-term benefits. He had also differentiated his scrap business from others in the region by both processing and brokering the scrap. Indeed, while most of its competitors were involved in either the brokerage or processing end of the business, Superior profited by integrating both activities into its operations. Superior was also distinguished by its conservative Depression-era financial strategy, which emphasized low debt and minimal operating costs.

Superior had carved out a profitable niche in its locale by the late 1970s. Still, the metal scrap trade was a relatively low-margin, low-tech business. Scrap operations were generally associated with junk yards, barking dogs, and rusted cars. To keep costs down, scrap yards typically operated with old, beat-up trucks and antiquated cranes, shears, and balers. The days of the traditional scrap yard were numbered going into the late 1970s, however, because a variety of influences would soon transform the scrap business and elevate it to a new stature in the metal manufacturing industry. Leading Superior through that industry transformation would be Leonard Rifkin and his three sons.

The metal scrap business was impacted by some negative influences during the 1980s. One such influence was the increased use of synthetic metal substitutes for a variety of applications ranging from car bodies to home siding. Another was a significant decline in U.S. steel output caused primarily by low-cost imports. But pivotal positive developments outweighed those problems. Importantly, the scarcity of basic metal-making resources, including the electricity needed to make metal from base materials, became apparent beginning in the late 1970s. That point was highlighted during the energy crunch, created by the Organization of Petroleum Exporting Countries (OPEC) oil embargo, during the late 1970s and early 1980s. One result was a newfound emphasis on conserving and recycling some metals, particularly aluminum.

Also bolstering the scrap industry was an improvement in steel and iron manufacturing technology during the 1980s, as U.S. steel and iron makers took advantage of new equipment and techniques that allowed them to produce more efficiently. That drive for efficiency was largely the result of intense competition from Japan and other metal importers. In the past, U.S. manufacturers had utilized techniques that created a substantial amount of their own 'home scrap' that was generated during the production process. When new technology eliminated much of that residue, demand for outside scrap from companies like Superior increased.

Perhaps the biggest boon for scrap metal companies, however, was the advent of the minimill. Minimills differed from traditional integrated steel mills in that they typically started the production process using scrap materials, rather than with base materials like iron ore, limestone, and coke. The scrap was typically melted in advanced electric arc furnaces (EAFs), rather than traditional blast or basic oxygen furnaces, and 'continuously cast' into basic shapes. Minimills proliferated during the 1980s and early 1990s, given their big cost advantages over integrated mills. For example, minimills were not confined to operating near raw material supplies, so their transportation costs were lower. Furthermore, advanced manufacturing processes centered around the use of scrap reduced energy consumption and, in many cases, proffered higher quality steel.

Superior benefited from positive trends in the scrap metal industry during the 1980s. It drew on its established reputation in the Midwest to boost sales and even to increase its share of the market. To usher Superior into a new era, Leonard Rifkin brought sons Danny, Rick, and Marty, as well as son-in-law Barry Dorman, into the executive ranks. Superior also purchased other scrap operations as part of an effort to diversify its offerings and to extend its network throughout the Midwest and even into the southern United States. To that end, in 1985 the company changed its name to OmniSource, which was intended to suggest that the enterprise was a single source for all types of scrap metal products.

Besides broadening its geographic and product scope, OmniSource thrived by implementing various quality and customer service initiatives. Those efforts reflected the changing dynamics of the scrap market, which was becoming increasingly characterized by specific needs and services. OmniSource adopted a 'Total Quality Management' (TQM) program in its nonferrous metals division and later implemented the plan in its ferrous operations. The program was designed to foster an atmosphere of continuous improvement where employees were constantly focused on improving not only customer service, but also manufacturing methods, employee relations, and all other facets of the business. "Our customers have remained loyal to us because they know that when the call us, they are going to get prompt, efficient service," explained John Marynowski, company vice-president, in OmniSource's January 1995 *Scrap Rap Magazine.*

OmniSource augmented its customer focus with heavy investments in new technology that allowed the company to produce high-quality scrap products efficiently. OmniSource had been one of the first scrap companies in the industry to adopt a formal quality control program, and its processing installations had been adapted during the 1980s and early 1990s to incorporate, for example, the most advanced production and statistical process control methods. Its overall quality efforts had earned it recognition from major customers. In 1994, for example, OmniSource became one of only 12 suppliers, out of a total of 13,000, to receive Chrysler Corporation's Platinum Pentastar performance and service award two years in a row.

In addition to its scrap collection and processing centers, OmniSource was operating a state-of-the-art scrap brokerage service in the 1990s. While scrap had traditionally been traded on a local and regional basis according to demand in the area, by the early 1990s the scrap market had become international in scope. OmniSource developed a corporate trading network that covered a broad range of products including scrap, primary metal, fabricated metal shapes, and more. The company's trading offices in the Midwest and southern United States tracked prices and activities in domestic and foreign markets to allow OmniSource to fill direct orders from customers at the highest possible profit margins.

By boosting sales and market share from existing operations, and by acquiring other companies to augment the company's expanding scrap metal and metal brokerage network, OmniSource was able to boost sales past the $300 million mark by the early 1990s. The still private and family-owned company managed to boost revenues throughout the early 1990s, despite a general downturn in the U.S. economy. Revenues jumped to about $330 million in 1992 and then to roughly $350 million in 1993. Healthy markets and prices in 1994 sent OmniSource's sales spiraling to a record $420 million for the year.

By the mid-1990s, OmniSource was operating a network of more than 20 trading offices, processing divisions, and collection centers that catered to a wide variety of needs in scrap and related markets. OmniSource's Defiance Briquetting Division in Ohio, for example, consumed scrap to produce iron and steel briquettes for use in foundry and steel mill furnaces. OmniSource was a pioneer in briquetting, and its Defiance plant incorporated some of the most advanced technology in the industry used to ensure high quality. OmniSource also operated a separate granulating plant to efficiently and cleanly separate copper and aluminum from insulated wire, and to process millions of pounds of the metals into new wire every month. OmniSource's precious metals and refining division employed advanced technology to recover silver from sources such as x-ray films, exhausted photographic supplies, and electroplated materials.

In 1995 OmniSource was focusing on improving service and sales to its existing customer base, and adding new clients in its existing midwest markets. Still under the tutelage of Leonard Rifkin and his three sons and son-in-law, OmniSource continued to pursue the strategy of long-term growth, fiscal conservatism, and customer service initiated by founder Irving Rifkin.

Further Reading:

"Former Noranda Exec Gets OmniSource Post," *American Metal Market,* May 7, 1990, p. 13.

"Interview with John Marynowski," *Scrap Rap Magazine,* Vol. 5, No. 1, 1995, pp. 2–3.

Marley, Michael, "Chrysler's Bundles Go to Broker; OmniSource to Take Warren Auto Scrap," *American Metal Market,* November 19, 1991, p. 2.

Newman, Jeff, "The Indiana 100: OmniSource Built on Family Involvement," *Indianapolis Business Journal,* May 22, 1995, p. B24.

"OmniSource Awarded Pentastar Award," *Scrap Rap Magazine,* Vol. 5, No. 1, 1995, p. 5.

—Dave Mote

OREGON STEEL MILLS

Oregon Steel Mills, Inc.

1000 Broadway Building
Suite 2200
1000 S.W. Broadway
Portland, Oregon 97205
U.S.A.
(503) 223-9228
Fax: (503) 240-5250

Public Company
Incorporated: 1928 as Gilmore Steel Corporation
Employees: 3,019
Sales: $838 million
Stock Exchanges: New York
SICs: 3312 Blast Furnaces & Steel Mills

Oregon Steel Mills, Inc., produces a wide range of specialty and commodity steel products. Among minimill companies in the United States, Oregon Steel Mills (OSM) ranks second in sales, trailing only industry leader Nucor Corporation. OSM is organized into two divisions, Oregon Steel Division and CF&I Steel Division, which together operate two steel mills and five finishing facilities. The Oregon Steel Division produces steel plate, which is used to manufacture heavy equipment such as rail cars, storage tanks, bridges, and ships; and large diameter pipe, used primarily for transmitting oil and natural gas. Its Portland Steel Mill minimill provides the steel for its pipe mills in Napa, California, and Camrose, Alberta. Until late 1994, this division also operated a plate rolling mill in Fontana, California. The CF&I Division, centered on a minimill in Pueblo, Colorado, was acquired in 1993. It produces steel rail, rod, wire, and bar products, purchased mainly by customers in the railroad business. Both of OSM's minimills use scrap steel, rather than iron ore, as raw material for their steel production.

Gilmore Steel Corporation, as Oregon Steel Mills was known until 1987, was founded by William G. Gilmore in 1926. The company was incorporated in California two years later. Originally, Gilmore was a steel service center chain based in San Francisco. Its emphasis changed to steel production, however, following its purchase of a steel mill in Portland, Oregon. Gilmore remained a relatively small regional outfit through its first several decades of operation. By the early 1970s, the company was running two steel mills in Portland—one for reinforcing bars and one for steel plate. These two mills made up the

company's Oregon Steel Mills division. Gilmore's other operating unit was Gilmore Steel Contractors, a fabricating company that used steel supplied by the mills. Although Gilmore had become an important steel supplier to the Western states by the 1970s, it appeared to be a company past its prime. The facilities were old and inefficient, and competition from foreign companies was forcing Gilmore to run its mills far below capacity. Other headaches included the high cost of keeping the ancient equipment in compliance with new environmental regulations. OSM's steel bar mill in Portland closed for exactly that reason in late 1974.

Over the next few years, the problem of foreign competition came to the forefront. In 1977 Gilmore filed a complaint with the U.S. Customs Office in Washington, D.C., charging that several Japanese companies were flooding the West Coast market with steel plate priced unfairly low. According to Gilmore president and chief executive officer Walter Jameson, Japanese firms had already captured half of the region's market by dumping steel plate at prices below the cost of production.

Although Gilmore's anti-dumping petition against the Japanese companies was successful, steel-making on the West Coast remained a chancy endeavor, and by the end of the 1970s only a handful of steel companies were left in the region. Gilmore remained on shaky ground into the 1980s. In 1980 the high cost of natural gas caused the company to shut down a direct-reduced-iron plant that had been completed only ten years earlier. Although Gilmore controlled about 18 percent of the market for steel plate in the 11 westernmost states plus Alaska and Hawaii, pressure from foreign mills continued, leading Gilmore to initiate anti-dumping procedures against steel-makers from West Germany, Belgium, and South Korea.

In 1982 Thomas Boklund, a construction engineer who had been with the company for about ten years, was promoted to president and chief operating officer. Also that year Gilmore's biggest West Coast competitor, Kaiser Steel Corporation of Fontana, California, went out of business and sold off its remaining steel at bargain basement discounts, depressing prices throughout the region. Despite proclamations by some industry observers that Kaiser's demise spelled the end of the West Coast steel industry, Gilmore persevered. By 1983 OSM had raw steel capacity of 300,000 tons per year, although its facilities were rarely operating anywhere near capacity. For the year, the company shipped only 150,000 tons of steel, and lost $7 million on estimated sales of $47 million.

Boklund also had to confront severe labor difficulties. In September 1983, hourly employees at Gilmore represented by the United Steelworkers of America began a strike that would last almost a year. During the course of the strike, the company continued to operate using replacement workers, joined by about 80 union laborers who crossed the picket line. The strike was bitter, and the tension between union and management, as well as between strikers and replacements, was great. The strike finally ended after workers dropped some of their demands and the company agreed to rehire union workers as business improved.

Although the strike was devastating for business, it marked a turning point of sorts, after which the company was able to transform itself from a dinosaur struggling for survival into a streamlined aggressor tearing up the industry. When faced with a crew consisting mainly of raw beginners, management was forced to pay more attention to its training methods. A new system was initiated in which input from employees was more welcome than it had been in the past. Managers began taking classes on how to communicate more effectively with employees. A new, more participatory culture was created among the new employees.

Meanwhile, the owners of Gilmore, which included the family of company founder William Gilmore, a foundation named after him, and two corporations, had grown tired of losing money, and they wanted out. Gilmore managers, who had purchased ten percent of the company's stock through an employee stock-ownership plan (ESOP) in the 1970s, decided to acquire the entire company via a leveraged buyout. They were assisted by Midland-Ross Corporation (Boklund's former employer), which purchased 68 percent of Gilmore's stock, and then sold it to the management group. In 1984 Gilmore workers voted to decertify the union, after which all Gilmore employees were put on salary. Management then offered its workers an ESOP of their own. Profit sharing was also worked into the system, and management perks were eliminated. These measures succeeded in sealing up to a great degree the rift between management and labor. They also marked the first step in the remarkable turn-around process that took place at Gilmore over the next few years.

By 1985 Gilmore was the only steel plate producer in the West. Boklund was given the additional title of CEO that year. Now firmly in charge, Boklund initiated a program to modernize the company's aging equipment. A major factor in Gilmore's comeback was the installation in 1985 of a high-powered eccentric-bottom-tapping electric furnace, the first furnace of its type to be installed anywhere in the United States. It produced all of the Portland mill's liquid steel for the next decade. The new furnace improved the mill's efficiency dramatically, and allowed the company to focus on becoming one of the lower cost producers in the industry. With the melt shop finally operating at full capacity, Gilmore was able to turn its first profit in years in 1986. As of fiscal 1994, the company had earned a profit every year since then.

Several other factors contributed to Gilmore's resurgence in 1986. To keep the orders coming in briskly, Boklund launched an aggressive pricing policy. By keeping prices low, Gilmore not only kept its facilities operating at full tilt, but also discouraged competition from foreign companies. Gilmore also benefited from a strike at USX Corporation's Geneva Works plant near Provo, Utah, which had previously put about 10,000 tons of steel plate per month into the marketplace. By 1987 the company was completely rejuvenated and ready to expand. That year the company changed its name to Oregon Steel Mills, Inc., reflecting the fact that it had essentially transformed itself into a new company. In an effort to establish a captive market for its steel, Oregon Steel then spent $18.5 million to purchase the Napa, California, large-diameter-pipe mill that had been one of its steadiest customers as part of Kaiser Steel, which had shut down the Napa plant a year earlier. As part of Oregon Steel, the facility was resurrected and once again became the biggest user of steel plate from the company's Portland mill. It was also the

only pipe mill located west of Pittsburgh, and one of only three in the entire United States.

OSM went public in 1988, and, as a result, dozens of company employees who had participated in the ESOP became millionaires. That year the company shipped 350,000 tons of steel, and had annual sales of about $190 million. Building on the success of its Napa acquisition, OSM began to seek out other aging steel facilities that it believed could be turned into efficient units. In 1989 the company bought a plate-rolling mill in Fontana, California, from California Steel Industries, Inc., for $7.5 million. The Fontana mill was capable of producing steel plate wider than that made at Portland, which enabled the company to manufacture wider steel pipe at the Napa facility than was previously possible. The addition of the Fontana mill boosted OSM's annual plate capacity to 1.1 million tons.

As the only large-diameter pipe producer west of the Mississippi, OSM found itself in an excellent position by the beginning of the 1990s. Around that time, many natural gas companies in the region were either expanding their pipeline networks or replacing older, deteriorating pipes. If they were located anywhere in the West, OSM was a likely choice to supply the new pipe. In 1990 sales reached $334 million, a 44 percent increase over the previous year, and profits soared to $28 million. Since the largest sources of natural gas in North America were located in western Canada, the Gulf of Mexico, and Colorado, but the greatest concentrations of users were in the Northeast and California, demand for pipeline remained high. This demand fueled OSM's growth, with pipe accounting for about three-fourths of the company's earnings.

In 1992 OSM boosted its Canadian presence by purchasing 60 percent of a pipemaking plant in Camrose, Alberta, from Stelco, Canada's biggest steel maker. Stelco retained control of the remaining 40 percent of Camrose. That year, Robert Sikora was named president of OSM, with Boklund retaining the chairman and CEO positions. OSM's biggest acquisition to date came in 1993, when it purchased Colorado Fuel & Iron (CF&I), a bankrupt steel company with a minimill in Pueblo. The acquisition of CF&I, which became a division of OSM, more than doubled the company's steel tonnage output for the year. The Pueblo plant produced steel rod, bar, wire, tube, and rail. Shortly after the purchase, a modernization program was initiated at the Pueblo mill, and like OSM's other facilities, it was quickly transformed into one of the industry's more efficient units.

In 1994 OSM made moves to become an international player in the steel industry, largely in response to the sluggishness of the U.S. market. During that year, projects in Mexico, Thailand, and Tunisia accounted for the sale of more than 200,000 tons of OSM steel pipe. In addition, OSM purchased a 13 percent interest in an iron company based in Guyana that was planning to make hot-briquetted iron at a plant in Venezuela. OSM also formed a strategic alliance with Nippon Steel, the largest steelmaker in the world. The alliance consisted of two parts: Nippon Steel's purchase of a ten percent interest in CF&I and OSM's acquisition of Nippon Steel's head hardened rail technology. OSM also began construction on a new combination mill at its Portland site. The addition of the combination mill, scheduled to go into production in the second half of 1996, would allow the company to consolidate its steel plate rolling operations into one facility, thus paving the way for the closure of the Fontana, California, mill. Although OSM's net income slipped to $12.1 million for 1994 (from $14.8 million), new records were set in revenue ($838 million) and tonnage sold (nearly 1.7 million tons).

Over the course of a decade, OSM managed to transform itself from an aging, inefficient company that produced steel plate into an international leader with the flexibility to produce several specialty steel products, all with a high degree of efficiency. The company continued to search for additional international markets, as well as for sources of raw materials to serve as alternatives to the scrap metal that feeds most of the company's production. OSM also sought to continue expanding its line of specialty steel products, which carry high profit margins. Although steel is a volatile industry, OSM's remarkable turnaround suggests that it has become capable of riding out even the stormiest of economic cycles.

Principal Subsidiaries: Camrose Pipe Company (60%); CF&I Steel, L.P. (95.2%); Napa Pipe Corporation; Oregon Steel Mills-Fontana Division, Inc.

Further Reading:

"Another Steel ESOP," *Industry Week,* February 18, 1985, p. 26.

Autry, Ret, "Companies to Watch: Oregon Steel Mills," *Fortune,* May 20, 1991, p. 116.

Berry, Bryan, "A Construction Engineer Helps Build a Steelmaker," *New Steel,* August 1994, pp. 14–22.

Colon, Aly, "Japanese Dumping May Close Gilmore Steel, Trade Panel Told," *American Metal Market,* March 9, 1978, p. 2.

Haflich, Frank, "Costly EPA Compliance Jeopardizes Oregon Mill," *American Metal Market,* November 6, 1973, p. 1.

——, "Oregon Steel Holds Discounts," *American Metal Market,* November 15, 1983, p. 1.

——, "Aggressive Pricing, Less Rivalry Stem Red Ink Flow at Oregon Steel," *American Metal Market,* December 30, 1986, p. 1.

——, "Oregon Steel Closes Carbon Plate Mill Buy," *American Metal Market,* November 21, 1989, p. 1.

——, "Link With CF&I Seen Appealing to Oregon Steel," *American Metal Market,* January 29, 1992, p. 1.

Kindel, Stephen, "Oregon Steel: Playing the Piper," *Financial World,* August 20, 1991, pp. 12–14.

Marley, Michael, "Oregon Steel Rises to the Challenge," *Iron Age,* June 1989, pp. 41–45.

"Oregon Steel Concern Files Price Complaint against Japanese Firms," *Wall Street Journal,* March 3, 1977, p. 3.

"Pipe Dream," *Forbes,* April 3, 1989, p. 188.

Sullivan, R. Lee, "If You Stand Still, You Lose," *Forbes,* January 4, 1993, p. 170.

—Robert R. Jacobson

Overnite Transportation Co.

1000 Semmes Avenue
Richmond, Virginia 23224-2246
U.S.A.
(804) 231-8000
Fax: (804) 231-8732

Wholly Owned Subsidiary of Union Pacific Corp.
Incorporated: 1947
Employees: 14,300
Revenues: $1.04 billion
SICs: 4213 Trucking, Except Local; 4225 General
Warehousing and Storage

Overnite Transportation Co. is a major interstate trucking company serving all 50 states and portions of Canada and Mexico. It transports a variety of products, including machinery, textiles, plastics, electronics, and tobacco and paper products. Overnite specializes in less-than-truckload (LTL) business; it ranked fourth in that transport sector in the early 1990s and seventh overall in revenue among trucking firms. Although it remained the nation's largest nonunion trucking company in 1995, Overnite was being hard-pressed by an International Brotherhood of Teamsters organizing campaign. The company, acquired by Union Pacific Corp. in 1987, is a subsidiary of Overnite Holding, Inc.

J. Harwood Cochrane, founder of Overnite, was one of nine children raised on an 85-acre Virginia farm. He dropped out of the tenth grade to work at an assortment of jobs. In 1929, at the age of 17, he took a job delivering milk, first by horse-and-wagon and later by truck. Four years later he went into business with his brother in Richmond. The Cochrane brothers bought two trucks which they used to haul hay, fertilizer, and household goods and to make local pickups and deliveries. In January 1935 Cochrane struck out on his own, but soon lost his only two trucks in highway accidents. He had no insurance to cover the losses but received a secondhand Chevrolet truck furnished by his brother in payment of a debt. He was back in business in a few weeks.

Interviewed for *Nation's Business* in 1978, Cochrane recounted the difficulties of being a fledgling trucker during the Great Depression. There were no motels, and even if there had been any, neither he nor his employees could have afforded to stay in one. Only one truck had a sleeper cab. The rest of the time

Overnite's truckers huddled beside an oil lantern and inside a quilt to keep from freezing. Their meal options were limited; they stopped when they could at the few all-night diners in existence at the time, where they would get a cup of coffee and warm up. Most of the time, Cochrane recalled, he carried part of a loaf of bread and a jar of mayonnaise, picking up some bologna or cheese to make a meal. He paid for gas with post-dated checks or by leaving jacks or spare tires as collateral.

Although no friend of big government, Cochrane acknowledged that the Interstate Commerce Commission (ICC) had a beneficial—perhaps crucial—effect on his business when it began to regulate trucking in August 1935. It stabilized rates and assigned Overnite a route from Richmond to High Point, North Carolina, via Durham, North Carolina, with a return by Winston-Salem, North Carolina, and Danville, Virginia. The ICC also gave Cochrane a certificate to handle specified commodities like eggs, rugs, and bakery and dairy products into Charlotte and the surrounding area. Overnite became profitable in two years.

At one point during this period Overnite signed a bargaining agreement with the Teamsters, but after the first year Cochrane refused to renew his contract. "I told them I'd never sign another agreement," he recalled to a *Barron's* interviewer in 1984, "even if it meant cutting back to one truck and driving it myself." Nonunion help enabled Overnite to use truck drivers as warehousemen or office workers when the need arose, a practice that reduced the threat of layoffs during slack periods. Staff loyalty also was enhanced by designing runs to get drivers home to their families as often as possible.

After five years of bare survival, Overnite took its first step toward expansion in 1940 with the purchase of a small competitor. World War II enabled the company to make money transporting war supplies, and the Overnite fleet grew from seven to 31 trucks. These vehicles, however, were used vehicles with used tires, paid for out of earnings rather than bank loans because, according to Cochrane, "I was a second-class citizen. The railroads had everything sewed up." The situation changed in the late 1940s, when Southern cigarette producers and textile manufacturers began hiring truckers like Overnite. According to Cochrane, "At first these shippers used trucks only as a threat to beat down rail rates, but when they got a taste of the service we could offer, we kept the traffic."

Incorporated in 1947, Overnite reached net income of $100,000 the following year. It grew rapidly over the next decade, both by expansion and acquisition. It first issued shares to the public in 1957, and by 1963 it had acquired 24 companies. Operating revenue grew from $4.4 million in 1952 to $15.3 million in 1960. Net income grew from $147,632 in 1952 to $653,635 in 1958 before declining to $536,777 in 1960. In that year the company had 3,000 miles of routes in Virginia, North Carolina, South Carolina, Georgia, and Tennessee. It operated 34 terminals (four of them company-owned) and had a company-owned fleet of 296 trucks, 287 tractors, 641 trailers, and 39 automobiles. The company covered nearly two million miles and carried a total tonnage of over 750,000 pounds. Cochrane held 48 percent of the company's shares.

About 63 percent of Overnite's tonnage hauled in 1962 was classified as less-than-truckload, and this business accounted for about 70 percent of revenue. Such small hauls commanded higher rates than full loads. Overnite's relatively short runs (averaging about 195 miles) gave it a certain degree of freedom from railroad piggyback competition, which generally required runs in excess of 300 miles. The following year Overnite entered the public-warehouse business by completing a 125,000-square-foot storage facility next to its executive offices in Richmond. A wholly owned subsidiary, Foremost Warehouse Corp., was organized to run the venture.

In 1963 Overnite drivers were being paid 8.5 cents a mile, compared to the regional union rate of 9.5 to 10 cents. To keep Overnite's 1,100 drivers satisfied with their lot and resistant to Teamster organizing, Overnite had established an employee stock-purchase plan wherein payment was usually made through payroll deductions. High unemployment rates in the area also enhanced the company's position, enabling it to choose among 30 applicants for one driving job on one occasion. Overnite won a $363,000 judgment against the Teamsters for imposing a secondary boycott in 1959, and close liaison with local police chiefs kept the company free from the threat of union violence. In 1962 operating expanses consumed only 83 percent of revenue, compared to a national motor-carrier industry average of 96 percent. Overnite was able to keep this ratio under 90 percent until the 1990s.

Cochrane, however, felt his labor force could be more productive. In 1970 he discovered that Overnite was losing more than $1 million a year in claims on cargo lost or damaged by his employees. He instituted a cash-bonus system for terminal managers who cut claims expenses and opened the company's stock-purchase plan to all employees. By the end of the year claims had been reduced by about 80 percent. Profits rose from $2.2 million in 1969 to $3.9 million in 1970 and $7.4 million in 1971. Company directors authorized two stock splits and three dividend increases as the stock increased 125 percent in value in 1970 and 145 percent in 1971.

By then Overnite was rapidly on the move toward realizing a nationwide operation, purchasing companies operating over the interstate highway system as much as possible. In 1967 alone the company acquired 28 carriers in whole or part. Its purchase of nine other companies from 1971 to 1974 enabled it to move into the states of Alabama, Delaware, Florida, Indiana, Kentucky, Maryland, Ohio, Pennsylvania, and West Virginia, and into Washington, D.C. At the end of 1974 Overnite was operating 41 terminals located in or around 14 states. Operating revenue passed the $100-million mark in 1974, a year in which the company posted net income of $8.3 million.

In 1976 Overnite acquired four more companies and opened terminals in Memphis, Columbus, and Washington, D.C. Terminals were established in Chicago and St. Louis in 1977, the year the company began interstate service in Arkansas, Illinois, Kansas, Mississippi, Missouri, and New Jersey. The acquisition in 1978 of St. Louis-Kansas City Express Inc. enabled Overnite to expand its routes as far west as Kansas City. By this time the company was also serving six seaports: Baltimore, Charleston, Jacksonville, Norfolk, Savannah, and Wilmington, North Carolina. Net income reached a record $12.1 million in 1977, when

Overnite believed itself to be the nation's fifth largest carrier of general commodities as measured by net profits. It reached $17.1 million in net income in 1979 on operating revenue of $230.1 million.

This period of prosperity ended in 1980, when the trucking industry was freed from federal regulation. To fend off thousands of small competitors on its previously ICC-franchised routes, Overnite felt compelled to offer a 10-percent across-the-board rate reduction to its less-than-truckload customers, who accounted for more than 70 percent of revenue. Net income dipped to $7.6 million on revenue of $242.6 million, and the dividend dropped to 35 cents a share from $1.36 the previous year, the first year since the company's inception that Overnite's cash dividend did not increase from the previous year. Still, Overnite's operations continued to expand. The company added Texas and Louisiana to its routes in 1980 and established a presence in Michigan and Oklahoma in 1981.

Deregulation and the severe 1981-82 recession drove about 300 motor carriers out of business. Overnite, however, thrived once more. In 1984 its routes stretched north to Boston, south to Tampa, and west to Los Angeles. Some 107 terminals in and around 31 states and the District of Columbia provided food, fuel, and lodging to its drivers. Company managers maintained a tight rein on costs, buying no-frills White, Mack, and International Harvester trucks rather than more expensive Kenworths. All of its fleet rolled on inexpensive tires of a single size. Operating revenue reached $415 million in 1984, and net income was $33.9 million. Long-term debt was minuscule.

Much of Overnite's success in the 1980s could be traced to its emphasis on less-than-truckload shipments of under 10,000 pounds. Rates for LTL shipments were running about three times the price per ton of full-sized truckload freight. Overnite's network of shipping terminals, its extensive truck fleet, and its modern computer systems also helped it win customers who wanted just-in-time deliveries. This business practice had grown in popularity as companies sought to keep smaller inventories on hand. Labor costs of about $16 an hour in wages and benefits, compared to the Teamsters' $21 an hour, kept Overnite's profit margin in 1985 at 8.3 percent, double the average for major truckers.

In October 1986 Cochrane sold Overnite to Union Pacific Corp. for $1.2 billion, the largest amount ever paid for a trucking company. Cochrane, who stayed on to run the company, and other family members garnered $47.6 million from the deal. Union Pacific had made the purchase to combine Overnite's 4,000 trucks with its trailer-carrying railroad flatcars in a nationwide network. In 1993 Overnite established a special truck-rail division to link Canada and Mexico with the United States. Ford and Chrysler auto parts already had been moving in both directions in 48-foot containers trucked by Overnite and carried on double-stack Union Pacific trains.

Cochrane retired as chairman of Overnite in 1989 and was succeeded by Thomas W. Boswell. Boswell resigned in March 1995 following problems that ironically arose from a 28-day Teamster strike against rival carriers in 1994. Overnite took on more business as a result of the strikes, but had its reputation hurt as the size of its obligations resulted in slow deliveries and lost and damaged goods. In addition, as Overnite accepted more long-haul freight from its regular customers, some of its short-haul business was lost to regional competitors. "What should have been a windfall appears to have been a tactical blunder," said one trucking analyst. "They took on too much incremental volume during the strike and found out they couldn't serve those customers as profitably as they had assumed."

Overnite also faced a renewed Teamster organizing drive in 1995. By May it claimed to have won 14 of 34 local elections covering some 1,500 workers. The company, which twice raised wages after the organizing campaign got under way, contended that it had won 27 of 40 elections. Regional offices of the National Labor Relations Board, meanwhile, issued seven complaints alleging that Overnite managers had harassed and fired workers for union activities. It charged the company with 150 violations of labor law. The Teamsters claimed Overnite was paying its workers $14 an hour, compared to $17 an hour for Teamster workers. An Overnite spokesman said the company paid its top drivers $15.05 an hour.

As the company and the Teamsters battled, Overnite continued with its operations. Their services by the mid-1990s included next-day, intrastate, and regional shipping; entry to portions of Canada and Mexico; toll-free access to customer service; electronic shipment-tracking information; and on-site representatives at customer locations who facilitated partnerships with major customers. The company also pursued development of an integrated dispatching, yard-management, dock-management, and time-tracking system, using hand-held computers and mobile communications.

Overnite was serving 95 percent of the population of the United States in the mid-1990s. It had 173 service centers, located primarily in the eastern, southeastern, and central United States and on the Pacific Coast, and boasted a fleet of 5,300 tractors and nearly 19,000 trailers. The company also showed a continued concern with maintaining its stature. A newly established customer service and billing center serving all Overnite terminals was the first of its kind in the industry, accepting imaged bills of lading and sending invoices to customers every morning. Meanwhile, Overnite pursued agency partnerships with several small, high-quality carriers that served areas not directly covered by Overnite.

Overnite's operating revenues of $1.04 billion in 1994 marked the first time it had passed the $1-billion mark. Operating income declined to $67 million from $69 million in 1993 (on revenue of $939 million). The ratio of operating expenses to operating revenue was 91.3 percent, higher than in the past, but still the lowest of the major LTL carriers.

Further Reading:

"From One Secondhand Truck to a Giant Truckline," *Nation's Business,* July 1978, pp. 41–46.

Garcia, Art, "Spotlight on Overnite Transportation Co.," *Journal of Commerce,* March 20, 1978, pp. 2, 19.

Gissen, Jay, "No Union Dues, No Union Blues," *Forbes,* October 12, 1981, pp. 214–220.

"Growth of Territory, Brake on Costs Strengthen Overnite Transportation," *Barron's,* February 11, 1963, p. 23.

Machalaba, Daniel, "Union Pacific Unit Names President to Succeed Boswell," *Wall Street Journal,* January 11, 1995, p. B2.

McConville, Daniel J., "An Uncommon Carrier," *Barron's,* November 19, 1984, pp. 16, 41.

"Not Too Big, Not Too Small," *Business Week,* July 6, 1963, pp. 73–74.

Rea, Alison Bruce, "From Two Used Trucks to a $1.2-Billion Deal," *Fortune,* January 5, 1987, p. 67.

Stavro, Barry, "The Road Ahead Is Wide Open," *Forbes,* September 22, 1986, pp. 131–132.

"Teamsters Mount Campaign to Organize Overnite Transportation," *Traffic Management,* May 1995, pp. 17–18.

Watson, Rip, "Overnite Transportation Co. Launches New Truckload Unit," *Journal of Commerce,* March 17, 1993, p. 3B.

—Robert Halasz

Parisian, Inc.

750 Lakeshore Parkway
Birmingham, Alabama 35211
U.S.A.
(205) 940-4000
Fax: (205) 940-4987

Private Company
Incorporated: 1880 as the Parisian Dry Goods & Millinery
   Company
Employees: 6,500
Sales: $598 million
SICs: 5651 Family Clothing Stores

Parisian, Inc., is one of the most successful retail family cloth-ing store chains located in the southern United States. Selling clothes lines similar to those found in Dayton-Hudson, The Gap, The Limited, and Bloomingdale's, the company has been a highly regionalized operation, with stores primarily in Ala-bama, Tennessee, and Florida, but by the mid-1990s it was expanding nationwide. Parisian has been managed by the same family for nearly 70 years, and until the 1980s this stability helped the firm establish solid if not spectacular growth. How-ever, the 1980s were boom years for the company. With sales hovering at $96 million in 1980, revenues skyrocketed to over $500 million by the early 1990s. Company sales have continued to grow rapidly, and management planned to aggressively ex-pand operations.

The Parisian Dry Goods & Millinery Company of Birmingham, Alabama, was founded in 1880 by two sisters, Estella and Bertha Sommers. The store originally sold clothing and milli-nery at low prices. However, the Sommers sisters had financial difficulties from the start of their operation and were forced to move three times during a period of nine years. The two sisters sold their interest in the firm to Louis Gelders and G. W. Beringer in 1911, who renamed the store The Parisian Com-pany. Lauren Bloch was hired as the general manager and, in turn, Bloch purchased the store from Gelders and Beringer in 1918. The new owner renamed his operation Bloch's Parisian.

During the early 1920s, Carl Hess and his family had traveled from Germany to America in search of a better life. The Hess family settled in Memphis, and Carl worked a number of differ-ent jobs in the retail industry, including a position as buyer for a large department store in the center of the city. The owner of the store was a brother of Lauren Bloch, and when Bloch died his brother asked Hess if he wanted to acquire the Parisian Com-pany. Hess jumped at the opportunity, moved his family to Birmingham, and arranged for a partner, William Holiner, to help him finance and manage the business.

Throughout the 1920s, the Parisian Company grew slowly. Selling clothing items and millinery, the small company had a difficult time competing with the larger stores in downtown Birmingham. In 1928, Hess and Holiner decided to move the location of the store into a larger building, thinking that the additional space and attractive quarters would attract many new customers. Unfortunately, the relocation proved disastrous. Away from the busier streets and pedestrian thoroughfares, the company began losing money. By the time the Great Depres-sion swept across the United States, the company was in dire financial condition. Hess traveled to New York in order to purchase merchandise on credit; his wife became the head buyer of girls' clothing, and Holiner managed the company's day-to-day operations. Hess's efforts were to no avail, however. As the depression grew worse, the company was forced into receiver-ship in 1932.

Hess and Holiner turned to the First National Bank of Birming-ham for help, and the bank assisted the owners in buying back the company from the court. One of the first decisions made after the reacquisition was to move the store back to the center of the city's retailing district. By the end of the depression, the Parisian Company was slowly rebuilding its clientele and mak-ing a name for itself as a quality clothing store. When World War II started, both Hess and Holiner expected their profits to increase. But the government's regulation on ''excess profits'' required that taxes were to be paid on most of the company's earnings. In spite of this setback, Parisian Company was able to significantly expand its customer base during the war and established a firm financial framework.

When the war ended, the son of Carl Hess, Emil, and the son-in-law of William Holiner, Lenny Salit, joined the company. Emil Hess had earned an MBA from the Wharton School of Business at the University of Pennsylvania, and Salit had graduated from Dartmouth University and intended to pursue a career in retail-ing. With their fathers' consent, the two young men arranged a meeting for all the company managers and began to assess the strength and weaknesses of the business. Although the firm was growing, Emil's and Salit's analyses uncovered many prob-lems, including the absence of a regular customer base and the lack of brand-name merchandise.

Throughout the postwar period and the early 1950s, Emil Hess and Salit worked to correct the problems that they had identi-fied. The two men initiated a comprehensive and aggressive merchandising program to bring in brand-name products and implemented numerous policies to improve customer service. One of the most important of these policies involved the cre-ation of a six-month installment plan. Most of Parisian Com-pany's competitors offered their customers extended payment plans that carried interest charges of 1.5 percent per month, adding up to 18 percent per year. Hess's and Salit's alternative was to offer a six-month, interest-free credit account. With assurances from First National Bank of Birmingham, just as during the Great Depression, to provide funds necessary to cover increases in the company's receivables, the new credit account was a rousing success. Shoppers flocked to the store during the early 1950s, and with its revenues growing, the company was able to concentrate on developing more policies that enhanced customer service, such as free gift wrapping, free mailing throughout the United States (except during holiday seasons), and a no-fuss return policy. One of the first retail stores in America to provide these services to its customers, Parisian Company began to stand out as one of the most reliable and professional clothing stores in the state of Alabama.

During the late 1950s and early 1960s, the civil rights movement had a profound effect on the company. Birmingham, Alabama, was the center of social unrest during this period, and a very small group of businessmen, including Emil Hess, tried to alleviate some of the indignities suffered by African-Americans in the city's transportation system and government offices. All of their efforts, however, came to naught. When the Reverend Martin Luther King Jr. arrived in town, a boycott was brought against the retailers and merchants. Clothing stores such as the Parisian Company were asked by the African-American community to meet certain of their demands. The small group of businessmen lobbied hard on behalf of King's requests, and most of the stores in Birmingham's retail district complied.

Nonetheless, the experience of the downtown Birmingham boycott made a lasting impression on Emil Hess and his partner. As a result, in 1963 the two men decided to expand their operations and open a store in the city's suburban Five Points West Shopping Center. Although the owners' expectations were low, the customer response was overwhelming. Buoyed by the success of the company's first suburban store, the two men immediately decided to open another outlet in the Decatur Gateway Shopping Center. This second store also garnered an enormous response from suburban customers. The lessening of racial tensions convinced Hess and Salit to open two additional stores in Birmingham, the Vestavia store in 1965, and the Eastwood Mall store in the last year of the decade. One of the milestones for the company had been reached in 1968 when Parisian Company was named "Brand-Name Store of the Year." Management's commitment to stocking its stores with designer labels and brand-name clothing made it very popular with consumers and resulted in huge financial rewards.

In 1970 Donald Hess, the son of Emil Hess, joined the company. A graduate of Dartmouth, Donald worked as a buyer under the direct supervision of Lenny Salit. After Salit died in 1972, Donald was promoted to general merchandise manager. A short time later he was appointed president of Parisian Company by his father. Donald Hess continued the expansion strategy that Salit and his father had initiated during the 1960s. A new store was opened in the Parkway City Mall in 1976 in Huntsville, Alabama, and additional stores in 1977 in Montgomery, Alabama, and in 1978 in Florence, Alabama. Sales continued to increase during this period, and by the end of the decade Donald Hess decided to take a close look at how he could best build upon the foundation that his father and Lenny Salit had established.

What Donald Hess discovered about the company in 1980 was not surprising. Parisian was one of the leading fashion specialty stores in Alabama, known for its moderate to expensive price range and high-quality merchandise. The company concentrated on providing its customers with leading fashion designs. Every store owned by Parisian Company had an impressive array of different kinds of merchandise, including men's and women's accessories, cosmetics, and apparel. Most important of all, however, was the reputation Parisian Company had established for its extremely helpful and courteous customer service. Many people drove their cars 50 miles or more to shop the nearest store.

During the 1980s Parisian Company was becoming known as a primary tenant, rather than a secondary tenant, in the development and building of suburban shopping malls. During the late 1960s and throughout the 1970s the firm was one of the companies selected for a mall site only after a store like Sears, Penny's, or Dayton-Hudson had already signed a lease. By 1981, with the company's store in the University Mall in Tuscaloosa, Alabama, Parisian Company was a primary tenant and one of the first companies the developers of the mall sought out to lease space. Parisian Company was in the enviable position among retail stores to make development plans for almost any suburban mall become a reality. The opening of its store in the Bel Air Mall in Mobile, Alabama, in 1983, and the opening of an additional store in the Madison Square Mall in Huntsville, Alabama, in 1984, were indicative of Parisian Company's growing influence and prestige in the retail industry.

In order to raise the capital needed for Hess's continuing expansion program, the family decided to take the company public in 1983. Maintaining control of the firm by selling a minority interest, on November 11, 1983, over 1.5 million shares of company stock were sold at $14.50 per share. A secondary offering was made in 1986 at $26.00 per share, and this contributed additional equity in the amount of approximately $18 million. With this money, Hess was able to open new stores in Riverchase, Dothan, Pensacola, and Chattanooga. The first of the company's out-of-state stores was opened in Atlanta, Georgia, in 1986. Two of the most important indicators of performance within the retail industry are inventory turnover and sales per square foot. In 1985, with all of its stores operating at full capacity, the company reported an inventory turnover rate of 3.7. This meant that all the merchandise in Parisian Company stores totally changed in less than four months, one of the best turnover rates in the industry. During the same year, the firm reported sales of $255 per square foot of selling space on the store floor, approximately twice the national average for all department stores.

By 1988 Emil Hess was semiretired, and Donald Hess had assumed full responsibility as the company's president and chief executive officer. Even though he was the force behind taking Parisian public in 1983, there still wasn't enough money to fulfill his plans, and Donald Hess remained dissatisfied with the pace of the firm's expansion. As a result, in 1988 Hess brought in a partner whom he thought would contribute funding for expansion. The U.S. branch of Hooker Company, an Australian holding firm that had already purchased Bonwit Teller and B. Altman, acquired Parisian for $250 million and agreed to make $125 available to Hess for his expansion program. Unfortunately, the highly leveraged buyout for Hooker misfired when a recession hit the United States in the late 1980s and easy financing for such ventures abruptly ended. Hooker filed for bankruptcy and its U.S. holdings were sorely threatened.

Since most of its stores were located in the South, Parisian survived the recession and Hess bought Hooker's interest in the company for $31 million. But now the company was loaded with debt and, since Hess still wanted to continue his expansion program, he sold a 45 percent interest in the firm to Lehman Brothers in July 1990. Once again a private company, Parisian had the financial wherewithal to open new stores with the influx of approximately $35 million provided by Lehman. Nine new stores were opened with this money by 1992. Yet Hess seemed insatiable for even more Parisian outlets. In 1993 he decided to take the company public again to finance more store openings, but he was forced to withdraw the public offering when Wall Street brokers did not express enthusiasm for retail department stores. These setbacks did not affect Donald Hess at all. In 1994 Parisian opened five new stores, including locations in Detroit, Michigan, and Nashville, Tennessee.

Although not as cautious as his father, Donald Hess has built a solid reputation for Parisian, Inc., as one of the premier department stores, equal in quality to Dayton-Hudson, Nordstrom, or Lord & Taylor. Hess's expansion program has provided the company with a higher profile, and Parisian is no longer viewed as a chain of southern stores catering to a localized, southern clientele. Only time will tell whether Donald Hess's aggressive expansion program benefited the company over the long term.

Further Reading:

Born, Pete, "Parisian: $500 Million And Counting," *Women's Wear Daily,* February 12, 1993, p. 4.
—— "Parisian's Big Gamble," *Women's Wear Daily,* August 14, 1992, p. 9.
Feldman, Amy, "But It Wasn't Broken," *Forbes,* March 14, 1994, pp. 66–67.
Hess, Emil, and Donald Hess, *Parisian, Inc.,* Newcomen Society: New York, 1986.
Lloyd, Brenda, "Open Sesame," *Daily News Record,* September 4, 1992, p. 9.
"Parisian Plans 2 Indianapolis Units In 1993," *Daily News Record,* July 10, 1992, p. 4.
"Parisian Set to Take Itself Public Again," *Women's Wear Daily,* April 2, 1993, p. 13.
Rutberg, Sidney, "Pro Forma—The 'What If' Balance Sheet That Gives Companies a Second Chance," *Women's Wear Daily,* April 13, 1993, p. 4.
"Small World," *Women's Wear Daily,* March 24, 1992, p. 12.

—Thomas Derdak

The Peak Technologies Group, Inc.

The Peak Technologies Group, Inc.

600 Madison Avenue
26th Floor
New York, New York 10022
U.S.A.
(212) 832-2833
Fax: (212) 832-3151

Public Company
Incorporated: 1989 as Logon Holdings, Inc.
Employees: 553
Revenues: $114.1 million (1994)
Stock Exchanges: NASDAQ
SICs: 5065 Electronic Parts & Equipment, Not Elsewhere
   Classified

The Peak Technologies Group, Inc., is the major international full-service distributor and systems integrator of bar-code data-collection and wireless data-communications equipment and systems, focusing primarily on industrial applications and certain niche retail applications. The company's distribution and system integration operations also include information systems printing equipment, consumable supplies, and related accessories. Peak markets the systems and products of over 50 manufacturers, including those of the most advanced bar-code products, in addition to its own proprietary systems and products, and also designs, manufactures, and distributes several lines of miniprinters, principally for original equipment manufacturers. The company also offers maintenance, technical support and consulting services covering the products and systems it sells. Peak entered 1995 providing services to more than 18,000 customers—principally end-users in the form of large companies and government agencies as well as resellers—through 74 sales and maintenance sites in 33 states across the United States, the Canadian providence of Ontario, the United Kingdom, and France.

Peak's core businesses are largely involved in the distribution of high-performance computer peripheral equipment and systems, primarily automatic-identification data-collection equipment and systems based on bar-code labeling and scanning technologies. Automatic identification involves data entry into a computer without key strokes and is the predominate automatic-identification technology. This technology utilizes a series of bars and spaces of specific width groups that represent specific

numeric or alphanumeric characters that can be affixed to a product to allow for rapid and accurate product identification for management and tracking purposes. Bar-code labeling and scanning systems comprise labeling systems that create and affix labels, reading devices such as laser scanners or light pens that transfer scanned data to decoders, and data collection instruments that store, process and forward scanned information to a host computer. The company's remaining major product lines include office automation equipment (primarily printers), electronic publishing products, and other related equipment and supplies. The products Peak distributes are integrated to provide specific applications for manufacturing, warehousing, specialized retailing, hazardous waste tracking, health care uses, office automation, and other industrial and business uses.

Peak Technologies Group, originated in the late 1980s through the efforts of the investment partnership of Edwardstone Partners, whose principals included Nicholas R. H. Toms, a practicing attorney with the firm of Skadden, Arps, Slate, Meagher & Flom. Peak's foundation was set in May 1988 when an investor group led by Toms, along with two other Edwardstone affiliates, Hugo H. Biermann and Julian C. Askin, acquired Logon, Inc., a distributor of computer peripheral equipment and systems. In February 1989 Logon, Inc., was reorganized to create a newly incorporated holding company, Logon Holdings, Inc. (the predecessor of Peak), to facilitate future acquisitions and serve as the parent of an operating subsidiary, Logon, Inc., created at the same time. Toms (then chief executive of Edwardstone) became chairman, president, and chief executive of Logon Holdings, Biermann (president of Edwardstone) became vice-chairman, and Donald W. Rowley (Edwardstone's vice-president and chief financial officer) became vice-president and chief financial officer of Logon Holdings. Logon Holdings headquarters were established in New York City, in office space subleased from Edwardstone.

Peak Technologies Group was built through a combination of acquisitions (14 companies between May 1988 and October 1995) by Edwardstone (its founding stockholder), Logon Holdings (later renamed Peak Technologies Group), and affiliates of Edwardstone. The company's early strategic acquisitions, like that of Logon, Inc., focused on companies that had roots in microwave and radio frequency (RF) technologies, which led these Peak predecessor companies to become distributors of Printronix, an early leading manufacturer of high-performance matrix printers. (Printronix was one of the first peripheral manufacturers that sold its products mainly through a limited number of specialized regional distributors.) With a goal of becoming a national company, Peak targeted in the late 1980s and early 1990s companies that were early distributors of peripheral equipment in given territories; as a result it had an established customer base of other peripherals manufacturers and suppliers in respective regions.

In January 1990 Logon Holdings acquired, for $5.1 million, Peak Technologies, Inc. (PTI). Jack A. Bowser, president of PTI since its 1981 inception, retained his post and also became a member of the Logon Holdings board, bringing with him a decade's worth of experience in the development of printers and electronic systems and his 20 years in distribution operations. In May 1990 Logon Holdings and its affiliates acquired Texas-based Telpar, Inc., for $15.8 million. Telpar had initially been acquired by Edwardstone principals in 1986 before being sold in 1988 and then reacquired. Telpar, unlike other Peak acquisitions, was exclusively involved with the design, assembly, and distribution of miniprinters, including proprietary printer control boards made for customer-specific applications and sold principally to original equipment manufacturers (OEMs); additionally, it was a distributor of Epson and NCR miniprinter lines and Fujitsu thermal miniprinters. Logon Holdings sales climbed to $33.2 million in 1990 (compared to $11.8 million in 1989 and $7 million for eight months in 1988), lifting earnings to $4 million (compared to a loss of $314,000 in 1989 and earnings of $25,000 in 1988).

In May 1991 Logon Holdings changed its name to The Peak Technologies Group, Inc. In October of that year the operating subsidiary, Logon, Inc., was merged into the operating subsidiary, PTI, and that same month PTI acquired, for $3.1 million, the Distribution and Service Division of MESA Technology Corp. The acquired operations, offering a family of disc storage systems, became Peak's Mass Storage Division. Despite sales that climbed to $43.9 million in 1991, Peak Technologies Group lost $51,000 on the year, largely as a result of interest expenses stemming from the company's leveraged financial structure.

Peak's early acquisitions strategy was to develop a national distribution and service network for its products, thereby giving the company a more efficient organizational structure and the ability to service large customers on a broad geographic basis and the opportunity to obtain the most favorable prices from its own suppliers. Peak entered 1992 with operations in a dozen states, principally in the Northeast. In April 1992 the company expanded into the Southeast with the $4.9 million acquisition (with loans worth $2.5 million and the issuance of 507,000 shares of new common stock) of Gentry Associates, Inc., a Florida-based distributor of computer peripherals operating in ten southeastern states. Robert J. Theodore, Gentry's president since 1979, retained his position and also joined the Peak board and took control of Peak's marketing division. Gentry, a full-service distributor of Peak's core product lines, added 165 employees and sales of $24.8 million to Peak's operations and boosted Peak's distribution reach to 22 states, primarily east of the Mississippi River.

Concentrating on a nonretail customer base where bar-coding was just beginning to gain momentum, by mid-1992 Peak's customer base had grown to about 11,000, approximately two-thirds of which were large end-users such as major corporations utilizing bar-coding to track inventory and shipments; the remainder was made up of OEMs and systems integrators. By mid-1992 Peak had also completed the initial phase of integrating its first three acquisitions—Logon, PTI, and MESA—with inventory purchasing and control, maintenance dispatch and logistics, and data-processing and accounting operations, all centralized in Columbia, Maryland; maintenance operations management were headquartered in Arlington Heights, Illinois. The company also consolidated warehouse and office facilities in Teterboro, New Jersey, and Arlington Heights.

Following three years of geographic expansion through strategic acquisitions, in August 1992 Peak went public with an initial offering of 2.2 million shares of common stock, designed to raise more than $16 million. Proceeds were used to repay long-term and other acquisition-associated debt, and all preferred stock was either converted to common status or surrendered for cancellation. The timing of Peak's public offering took advantage of an increasing acceptance of automatic-identification and bar-code data-collection systems aimed at increasing productivity and quality; additionally, a growing number of industries were requiring suppliers to use specific bar-code labels and looking to full-service distributors such as Peak to provide installation and maintenance services.

In November 1992 Donald Rowley, a principal in Edwardstone, resigned as chief financial officer to pursue other interests through Edwardstone. Rowley was replaced by Edward A. Stevens, who had previously served as Peak's investor relations officer and vice-president as well as a director and vice-president of MESA's former parent (in 1995 Stevens joined the Peak board).

In December 1992 Peak gained the right to distribute the mass storage products of Hewlett-Packard Company (HP) throughout its service territory. As a result, Peak began distributing HP magnetic disk drives, magnetic tape drives, and optical disk drives in three midwestern and most southeastern states in order to supplement Peak's distribution of those products in New England, New Jersey, New York, and the mid-Atlantic states. By the end of the year Peak had become one of the fastest growing distributors of HP products.

Near the end of 1992 Peak expanded its distribution of bar-code products into Texas, utilizing the existing operations of Telpar, based in Dallas. During 1992 Peak also bolstered its status in a number of ways, becoming a leading distributor of industrial bar-coding and data-collection systems, the largest distributor of products made by such industry leaders as Zebra Technologies and Printronix, and one of the largest North American customers of products made by Dataproducts, Norand, Symbol Technologies, and Welch Allyn products. In 1992 Peak additionally began distributing Tektronix color page printers. By the end of 1992 Peak was providing services through more than 60 locations throughout the United States, and for the year its revenues rose 87 percent to $82 million, pushing earnings to $1.8 million.

In April 1993 Peak enhanced its geographic reach west of the Mississippi River by acquiring, for $1.5 million, Group Three Electronics, Inc., a distributor of bar-code and data-storage equipment and peripherals with operations in Seattle, Washington, and Torrance and Sunnyvale, California (this move complemented Peak's offices in Irvine and San Jose, California, which were opened in early 1993). In July 1993 Peak acquired through merger New England-based Concord Technologies, Inc., for 86,000 common shares valued at approximately $900,000. Concord, bringing with it service experience in high-end wireless data-collection and bar-code systems, provided Peak with additional service opportunities in New England and New York.

During the late 1980s and early 1990s Peak implemented one of its earliest proprietary bar-code scanning systems in New York City schools in response to truancy and building security concerns. In conjunction with the firm Vertex, Inc., Peak developed bar-coded student identification cards as part of its CLAS-SPORT Time and Attendance Security System, which was implemented in more than 40 New York schools and one Chicago-area school by the early 1990s. In 1993 Peak introduced several new proprietary bar-coding products: Wireless Warehouse, a comprehensive warehouse-management system to manage a variety of shipping, receiving, storing, and inventory functions; QRBar, a low-end system for gathering data to in turn generate advance shipping notices; Peak Link II, a high-end, Unix-based wireless system designed to provide compliance labeling, online ship verification, and advance ship notices for manufacturing and distribution applications; TAG, a user-friendly (terminal-resident application generator) system allowing for easy change of applications on a 16-bit handheld data-collection device without interfacing with a host computer; and IncrediBar, a Windows-based bar-code label-generation package compatible with all Peak-distributed bar-code printers.

In 1993 Peak was named the exclusive national sales and service center for Zebra Technologies. The company also opened up service centers in Kentucky, California, Oregon, and Georgia, and it reorganized its service and maintenance department, regionalizing service operations. Peak also improved revenue possibilities by instituting a trade-in policy, which allowed printer customers to trade in obsolete or low-performance printers and receive a reduced price on new printers. This policy also allowed the company to sell restored printers as a low-cost option and utilize spare parts salvaged from unrestorable trade-ins.

In 1993 a new management team took over Telpar, which that year introduced a new proprietary panel-mount printer useful for various sensitive applications such as automobile emissions inspections, breathalyzer tests, environmental control information, and medical printouts. In 1993 Telpar also expanded its sales force and geographic coverage into the Northeast and West Coast and increasingly began to move its miniprinter business into the bar-code market, principally through portable printers.

In December 1993 Peak, having decided to focus on the industrial bar-code market, discontinued the operations of what it saw as the volatile and less-than-completely compatible Mass Storage Division, acquired in 1991. The decision was designed to improve the company's focus and productivity and reduce its ongoing overhead. In connection with that decision, Peak restructured its remaining operations to focus on the automatic-identification market and around the core areas of bar-code systems, information systems printing, miniprinters, consumable replacement and spare products, and maintenance services.

Between Peak's initial public offering and the end of 1993 its workforce grew from 256 to 428 while its established installed base of wireless/RF systems grew to more than 1,700 terminals at over 185 customer locations. For 1993 Peak lost $7.4 million on increased sales of $86.3 million. Without restructuring charges and write-offs associated with the discontinuation of mass storage operations, Peak would have earned $3.7 million from continuing operations.

In 1994 Peak established what it believed was the industry's first wireless testing laboratory at its new centralized operations headquarters in Columbia, Maryland. During the same year, the company also reduced the square footage it occupied by 30 percent, placing all domestic distribution operations under one roof. The company also released a specialized retail application software package, Nucleus Stock Audit, designed to run on Symbol Technologies handheld terminals and allow retailers to generate quick and accurate inventory counts with little disruption to sales operations. In 1994 Telpar also rolled out a new series of kiosk miniprinters used for gaming, information kiosk, and other specialized applications.

In July 1994 Peak acquired NACO Electronics Corp., an established distributor of bar-code and information-systems printing equipment with operations in New York, New Jersey, and New England. VisionData, a NACO division, provided Peak with a distribution business serving resellers and system integrators and thereby providing Peak with additional opportunities to market Peak's hardware systems to end-users. The purchase price for NACO was $850,000 and 167,000 shares of common stock.

In November 1994 Peak made its first European acquisition, ENDATA Group Ltd. (renamed Peak Technologies UK Limited), a leading U. K. integrator of bar-code data capture and wireless data-transmission products. ENDATA brought to Peak six U.K. offices and made Peak the only systems integrator of its type offering full-service operations in both North American and European territories. As a result, ENDATA provided Peak with another way to differentiate itself from competitors: the ability to serve multinational companies seeking a standardized, global approach to data collection.

By the end of 1994 Peak had an installed base of wireless systems comprising 4,000 terminals at about 400 separate customer sites, making it the largest system integrator in the data-collection industry. During 1994 the company had opened eight new service centers as its maintenance operations increased revenues by 17 percent. Additionally, revenues from consumable products had risen, after the earlier introduction of a series of proprietary products, by 42 percent. For 1994, Peak earned $4 million on sales that increased 32 percent to $114 million.

In January 1995 Peak completed its goal of becoming a national concern when it acquired Innovative Products & Peripherals Corporation (IPPC), a Denver-based integrator of bar-code data-collection products with $12 million in annual sales. The acquisition placed Peak in every region of the country with active operations in 33 states.

Capitalizing on increased interest in bar-coding in industrial and international markets, in May 1995 Peak issued a secondary public offering of 1.38 million common shares of stock, generating $25.5 million that was used to pay off all of the company's then long-term debt and generate additional funds for general purposes and future acquisitions. Beginning in May 1995 Peak also continued its European expansion with a series of acquisitions: ISF, a French software company; Datapen Systems Ltd., based in Ascot, England; and BPC Numeric Arts Ltd., a Marow, England-based data-collection software developer and European-market reseller of Symbol Technologies and Zebra Technologies products. In 1995 Peak also debuted a new proprietary software product, HazTrack, a waste-management tracking system using wireless data-communications and bar-code technologies.

For the first half of 1995, Peak's six-month revenues climbed by 30 percent to $76.8 million while net income increased 64 percent to $2.3 million, with gains attributed to new products of key manufacturers supplying the company, including Printronix, and increased service contracts and sales of consumable supplies. Wall Street was not oblivious to Peak's gains; between October 1994 and July 1995 the company's stock value rose from $11 to $27.

In October 1995 Peak acquired Accuscan, Inc., an Atlanta-based software supplier of integrated bar-code and data-capture programs with operations in California, Florida, Georgia, Illinois, Maryland, New Jersey, North Carolina, and Texas. An integrator of Symbol Technologies products and a developer of its own proprietary software utilizing Symbol terminals, Accuscan provided Peak with a broader suite of products and opportunities to consolidate operations in overlapping geographical regions and improve its purchase-power relationship with Symbol. At the time of the acquisition the firm Brean Murray, Foster Securities Inc. estimated that the acquisition would boost Peak's annual revenues to $207 million and its earnings by more than 50 percent to $11.7 million by 1996.

Peak moved toward the close of 1995 with the goal of becoming the dominant distributor of bar code-based data-collection and wireless data communications systems worldwide, providing a single source for national and multinational customers' data-capture requirements. In the process of moving toward this goal, Peak was banking on snatching a bigger share of what was estimated to be a $5.8 billion global industry by 1998, an industry expected to grow by 18 percent annually through the end of the decade. Peak additionally anticipated benefiting from the burgeoning industrial segment of the bar-code market, which, compared to the retail segment, was far less penetrated.

In looking to its future, Peak expected growth to come through internal growth and through complementary acquisitions, and it expected to benefit from four continuing trends: the increasing use of bar-code automatic-identification and data-collection systems geared toward improving productivity and quality; the expanding use of mobile and wireless computing to handle data communications; the expanding number of industries requiring specific bar-code labels on products supplied to them; and the increasing preference for distributors like Peak capable of offering design, supply, installation, and maintenance services through North American and portions of Europe. Given these trends, Peak's prospects for future sales and earnings gains seemed favorable.

Principal Subsidiaries: Concord Technologies, Inc.; Gentry Associates, Inc.; Group Three Electronics, Inc.; Peak Technologies, Inc.

Further Reading:

Baker, Molly, ''Bar-Coding Field Spells Room to Grow,'' *Wall Street Journal,* June 5, 1995, pp. C1, C7.
Beall, Pat, ''Gentry's Parent Goes Public,'' *Orlando Business Journal,* August 14, 1992, p. 1.
Marcial, Gene G., ''Bar-Coding the World,'' *Business Week,* July 31, 1995, p. 71.
——, ''Scanning the World,'' *Business Week,* March 8, 1993, p. 81.
Willis, Gerri, ''IPOs Are Propelling Fast Growing Firms,'' *Crain's New York Business,* October 18, 1993, p. 17.

—Roger W. Rouland

PeopleSoft Inc.

1331 North California Boulevard
Walnut Creek, California 94596-4502
U.S.A.
(510) 946-9460
Fax: (510) 946-9461

Public Company
Founded: 1987
Employees: 750
Stock Exchanges: NASDAQ
Sales: $113 million
SICs: 7372 Prepackaged Software

PeopleSoft Inc. is a leading U.S. producer of software for financial management, human resources management, manufacturing, and other business applications. Going into the mid-1990s its primary customers were mid-sized and large corporations, including Hewlett-Packard and American Express. The company has grown explosively since its inception in 1987 by producing cutting-edge, problem-solving software for client/server systems.

Dave Duffield and Ken Morris are the progenitors of People-Soft. Both software developers had been working at Integral Corp. before jumping ship to start their own company. In fact, Duffield had founded Integral in 1982 and served as its chief executive until 1984. Integral started out providing consulting services but later moved into the lucrative market of mainframe computer software. Duffield was credited with helping to grow Integral into a $40 million (in sales) producer of human resources applications for use on mainframes.

By the mid-1980s, after taking Integral public, Duffield had effectively lost control of the company that he had founded. That loss of authority would ultimately cause Duffield to jump ship. The conflict arose when Duffield took an interest in the burgeoning personal computer networking industry. At the time, mainframes were still the dominant platform for large and mid-sized companies, and Integral had profited handsomely by chasing that big market. But early on Duffield recognized the potential of personal computer networks (dubbed client/server systems because the PCs were linked to a server system). He believed that Integral should shift its focus away from mainframes and toward client/servers, which he viewed as the wave of the future.

Integral's board of directors disagreed with Duffield, and so he decided to leave the organization. He even offered to sign a no-compete agreement with Integral in return for one year's salary, which would have kept him from competing with Integral in the human resources software industry. Integral's board foolishly rejected the offer, and Duffield started a new company that he called PeopleSoft. Duffield took fellow Integral employee Ken Morris with him, and together they began designing human resources software geared for client/server systems. In 1988 Morris and Duffield introduced the first high-end human resources software application ever designed for a client/server system.

Although PeopleSoft's first program was greeted by a willing market, the tiny firm was strapped for cash. To fund the start-up, Duffield took out a mortgage on his home; he and Morris tapped the nest egg to fund the development of their first program. That effort generated revenues of about $200,000 in 1988, the company's first year of sales. Importantly, the company scored a major coup in 1988 when it landed Eastman Kodak as its major customer. That gave a much-needed boost to PeopleSoft's bottom line.

Kodak, like many other corporations in the late 1980s, was beginning to realize the advantage of the client/server approach. A company could purchase a number of relatively inexpensive PCs, network them through a more expensive server, and have a system with capabilities similar to a mainframe. The obvious advantages were much lower costs and, in many cases, increased flexibility. At the same time, PeopleSoft's human resources software became a valuable tool for companies that were reorganizing and cutting costs during the recession of the early 1990s. Thus, as the client/server industry took off and PeopleSoft's innovative human resources program became known, sales shot up. In 1989 PeopleSoft generated an impressive $1.9 million in sales. That figure exploded to $6.1 million in 1990, about $420,000 of which was netted as income.

Despite big sales and profit gains, cash was short. PeopleSoft was trying to hire new staff, buy new computer systems, market its existing software, and develop new products—all on a shoestring budget. To make matters worse, Integral Corp. (where PeopleSoft's success had not gone unnoticed) was forcing PeopleSoft to spend money in court. In 1990 Integral and a San Francisco-based company called Tesseract Inc. filed separate lawsuits against PeopleSoft, claiming it had obtained proprietary trade information from them. They even sought injunctions to halt the sale of PeopleSoft products. A San Francisco judge denied the injunction requests and PeopleSoft was able to settle out of court in 1991, but only after expending significant legal fees from its tight budget.

Duffield, despite the cash drain, was not about to give up control of his company again to outside financiers, and he was able to secure a $1 million line of credit from a bank. That helped to offset some costs, but he needed more. In 1991 Duffield sold 11 percent of his company for $5 million to Norwest Partners, a venture capital firm. He used much of that cash to update the company's systems and also to help fund development of a new client/server program for financial management applications. In addition to the $5 million, PeopleSoft enjoyed net earnings in 1991 of $1.9 million from sales of $17.1 million.

By 1992 PeopleSoft was growing at a seemingly exponential pace. Its human resources applications were selling like hotcakes and it was gearing up to launch its awaited financial management programs. To fund the growth, Duffield finally decided to take the company public. In November 1992 PeopleSoft made its initial public offering, which brought $36 million into its coffers. Investor enthusiasm sent the stock's price cruising 64 percent higher than the original offer price on the same day. Six months later PeopleSoft netted a fat $50.4 million with a second offering. The wary Duffield still managed to keep about 50 percent ownership in the company. "We waited four years," Duffield said in the April 1993 issue of *Diablo Business.* "We didn't want to give away a big part of the company, and we didn't."

By 1992 PeopleSoft was controlling about 40 percent of the entire high-end market for human resources programs—some of PeopleSoft's human resources applications priced out at $600,000 or more. Because a plethora of companies were hopping into the client/server game by that time, however, the enterprise was banking on its freshly introduced financial applications to help it sustain rapid growth. The financial software industry was crowded with competitors, but PeopleSoft had staffed its programming department with some heavy hitters, and it believed that its experience in the client/server industry gave it an edge. Although financial program sales contributed only a few million dollars to PeopleSoft's revenue base in 1992, company sales and profits spiraled upward to $31.6 million and $4.8 million.

Duffield had hoped that his financial programs would eventually account for as much as one-half of company sales. The software was welcomed by the market and seemed to be living up to Duffield's expectations by late 1993. The line of financial programs was expanded to include applications for general ledger accounting, asset management, and accounts payable/receivable management. When sales from that line kicked in during 1993, revenues and profits vaulted to about $58.2 million and $8.4 million. Interestingly, that sales figure approximated the 1992 revenues for Integral, the company that Duffield had started and left six years earlier; soon, PeopleSoft would leave that mainframe software company in the dust.

An interesting sidebar to the PeopleSoft story during the late 1980s and early 1990s was the Raving Daves, a rock band made up of PeopleSoft employees. Named after the company's chief executive and founder, the Raving Daves provided insight into the quirky but effective culture at PeopleSoft. PeopleSoft was loosely structured and efficient. Employees were empowered to make important decisions and nobody had a secretary or receptionist—even Duffield answered his own telephone. The environment was designed to spawn creativity and innovation, as evidenced by the formation of the Raving Daves (a group of eight musicians and singers that were full-time PeopleSoft employees). The group became the centerpiece of the company's image advertising campaign in 1995.

PeopleSoft's unique management formula combined with the growth in client/server systems in 1993 and 1994 and propelled the company to prominence. The client/server market mushroomed, in fact, at a much greater rate than most analysts had predicted. PeopleSoft controlled a whopping 50 percent share of the entire human resources software market by 1994. By that time a horde of former mainframe software developers began leaping headfirst into the client/server market. But PeopleSoft benefited from what was known as "clean technology," meaning that its applications had been written specifically for client/server and had not been converted from a mainframe environment.

By 1994 PeopleSoft's client base had broadened to include corporate giants like Hewlett-Packard, Advance Micro Devices, Rolm, and Pacific Bell, among many others. Furthermore, overseas interest in the company's programs was proliferating. Exports jumped to about $1.6 million in 1993, with customers buying from as far away as Australia, France, England, and South America. Buoyed by increasing demand at home and abroad for PeopleSoft's human resources applications and, particularly, its financial applications, Duffield began considering new markets. He planned to eventually lead PeopleSoft into client/server software markets in manufacturing, health care, education, and government, to name a few.

The first new market that Duffield tried to crack was the giant manufacturing sector. Specifically, PeopleSoft began chasing manufacturers of automobiles, electronics, and consumer durables in 1995. The manufacturing market offered massive growth potential for the company, as client/server software sales to that segment were then growing at a rate of 78 percent annually (compared to a still-healthy 38 percent for the financial software market). Duffield believed that success with manufacturing software would allow PeopleSoft to quadruple its revenues within two years. To meet that challenge, PeopleSoft brought on board leading manufacturing software veterans like Roger Bottarini and Chris Wong.

Because of its ambitious foray into manufacturing software, PeopleSoft was again looking for funds to fuel the growing enterprise. Rather than sell off more of the company, Duffield cleverly arranged to have the project funded externally. PeopleSoft entered into a joint venture with its old financier, Norwest Venture Capital. Norwest fronted the development capital and PeopleSoft contributed the intellectual property (such arrangements had been pioneered in the capital-intensive biotechnology industry). As a result, PeopleSoft, which owned 49 percent of the venture, was able to get the program up and running much faster at much reduced risk.

As PeopleSoft entered the mid-1990s its share of the U.S. client/server packaged software market was about 20 percent and growing. Company sales shot up from $175 million in 1992 to $320 million in 1993 to a whopping $575 million during 1994. Likewise, net income bolted from $8.4 million in 1993 to $14.55 million in 1994—a jump of about 75 percent. Furthermore, results for the first half of 1995 showed an increase in sales and income of about 100 percent over the same period in 1994. PeopleSoft continued to garner most of its profits from client/server software for applications in human resources, benefits administration, claims administration, and payroll tasks, with emphasis on health care, higher education, and government markets. The company was supporting offices throughout North America and Europe, as well as in Singapore, South Africa, Brazil, and Australia.

Principal Subsidiaries: none.

Further Reading:

Berry, Michael, ''Software Supernova: After Sales Tripled in its Third Year,'' *Diablo Business,* April 1993, p. 12.

Burstiner, Marcy, ''Software Union: If You Can't Beat 'em, Join 'em,'' *San Francisco Business Times,* January 27, 1995, p. 3.

Clifford, Carlsen, ''Software Maker Aims High With New Products,'' *San Francisco Business Times,* April 10, 1992, p. 2.

Gadbois, Ray, ''PeopleSoft Inc. Announces PeopleSoft Financials Implementation Partnership Program,'' *Business Wire,* May 9, 1994.

Labate, John, ''PeopleSoft,'' *Fortune,* March 7, 1994, p. 85.

''PeopleSoft Inc.,'' *San Francisco Business Times,* November 18, 1994, p. 26.

Rauber, Chris, ''People Power Software Company: PeopleSoft Grows Beyond Human Resources Niche,'' *San Francisco Business Times,* April 29, 1994, p. 59.

Snyder, Bill, ''Band on the Run,'' *PC Week,* May 29, 1995, p. 5A.

Zecher, Linda, ''E. F. Codd Joins PeopleSoft Board of Directors,'' *Business Wire,* September 17, 1992.

—Dave Mote

PETsMART, Inc.

10000 North 31st Avenue, Suite C-100
Phoenix, Arizona 85051
U.S.A.
(602) 944-7070
Fax: (602) 395-6502

Public Company
Incorporated: 1986 as The Pet Food Warehouse
Employees: 7,900
Sales: $601 million
Stock Exchanges: NASDAQ
SICs: 5999 Miscellaneous Retail Stores, Not Elsewhere
    Classified; 0742 Veterinary Services Specialties

The largest operator of pet food, pet supplies, and pet services superstores in the United States, PETsMART, Inc., stands atop a roughly $15 billion industry it helped to create. With nearly 200 mammoth stores scattered throughout 24 states in 1995, PETsMART was recognized as an industry leader and pioneer, having originated the concept of a pet food and supply superstore eight years earlier. By aggressively pursuing expansion and stocking substantially more products in considerably larger stores than its competition, PETsMART quickly emerged as the dominant company of its kind. Although much of the chain's success was attributed to the size of its stores—all were larger than 18,000 square feet—and its vast selection of products—more than 11,000 items—PETsMART became the dominant force it represented during the mid-1990s through the astute leadership of Samuel J. Parker, the company's chairman of the board and chief executive officer. Under Parker's stewardship, PETsMART evolved into a one-stop pet shopping center offering pet grooming, adoption, and veterinary services, as well as sundry food and accessory products.

In 1987 a new concept in retailing pet food was born when Jim and Janice Dougherty opened the first store of their new company, The Pet Food Warehouse. As its corporate title suggested, The Pet Food Warehouse sold huge bags of pet food in a large, sparsely decorated, cement-floored store, giving consumers the opportunity to purchase food for their pets in bulk at discount prices. The warehouse retail concept was not new at the time, but it was the first time the high-volume, low-priced approach of retailing products to consumers had carried over to the pet industry, a roughly $7 billion-a-year industry during the mid-

1980s that was dominated by supermarkets and mass merchandisers, with myriad small pet stores snatching what little was left. The Doughertys, however, were intent on adding a new type of competitor to the industry, one that could take advantage of a burgeoning trend among consumers during the 1980s and fuel the growth of their fledgling enterprise.

Jim and Janice Dougherty incorporated their company in August 1986, using $1 million in start-up investment from Phillips-Van Heusen Corporation and other investors to open their first two stores in Phoenix, Arizona, the following year. Venture capitalists continued to fund the company's expansion after the first two stores were established, providing the financial support to establish five additional stores by 1989, as The Pet Food Warehouse began to take on the qualities of a retail chain. Although there was evidence that The Pet Food Warehouse was performing well—seven stores had been established in less than two years, and annual sales had risen to nearly $16 million—there was one important financial statistic that tinctured its success, particularly in the minds of the company's all-important investors: the regional chain was losing money. In 1989 The Pet Food Warehouse lost $1.8 million, prompting the group of investors supporting the company to make a dramatic change. That year, the board of investors voted for the removal of the Doughertys, retaining the two founders as consultants but excluding them from direct control over the company they had started less than two years earlier.

Although the Doughertys were gone, the concept of selling pet supplies in a large retail store at discount prices remained alive, at least in the hearts of the investors who still hoped The Pet Food Warehouse approach could yield a return on their investments. To replace the Doughertys, the company's financial supporters wanted someone with more retail management experience, and in Samuel J. Parker they gained a leader with considerable experience. A 19-year veteran of the Jewel supermarket chain, Parker had also served as president of Frame-N-Lens Optical and the GEMCO division of Lucky Stores, accruing sufficient executive management experience to attract the attention of The Pet Food Warehouse's anxious controlling investors.

Parker was hired as chairman of the company shortly after the removal of the Doughertys in 1989 and immediately began to exert his managerial control over the seven-unit chain. Although the Doughertys had originated the warehouse retail concept in the pet supply industry, Parker's refinement of the concept would produce the results that antsy investors hoped for, and he soon transformed the money-losing Pet Food Warehouse into PETsMART, Inc., one of the fastest growing companies of any kind in the United States during the early 1990s.

Once Parker was brought on board, sweeping changes were made: cement floors were replaced with tile floors, aisles were widened, and in-store lighting was brightened, creating a more hospitable environment for customers. Instead of merely selling pet food, Parker stocked the company's stores with a full array of pet accessories and supplies, attempting to beat the competition by offering a far greater selection of products at substantially reduced prices. What emerged early under Parker's reign was a hybrid version of the concept first developed by the Doughertys, a retail approach that incorporated the design of a warehouse store with the more conventional trappings of a retail store. In the rear of a PETsMART store, pet food was sold in austere surroundings; pet accessories were displayed on retail racking in the front, giving the customers who frequented each location the benefits of both worlds. Additionally, Parker established grooming and veterinary centers at PETsMART stores then set up a pet adoption service called "Luv-a-Pet," creating a one-stop pet store that offered services and supplies even the largest mass merchandiser or supermarket could not match.

As these important changes were being made, engendering an entirely different type of retail competitor, the need to add additional stores became paramount for Parker. Aggressive expansion across the nation would become an integral component of the success PETsMART enjoyed during the early 1990s, enabling the chain to saturate markets before competitors could establish a foothold and also positioning the Phoenix-based company as the strongest acquisitive force in an industry that would begin to consolidate in earnest between 1993 and 1994. To finance this expansion Parker relied on the same financial source as the Doughertys, urging the venture capitalists backing PETsMART to provide the capital for the establishment of PETsMART stores throughout the southwestern United States. By the end of 1989 five additional units had been opened, giving PETsMART a total of 12; by the end of 1990, the chain comprised 29 stores, averaging 25,000 square feet and stocking roughly 7,500 products.

As the number of stores increased, so did PETsMART's annual sales, recording prodigious leaps that testified to the public's willingness to frequent a pet supply superstore. During the first five years of Parker's stewardship, PETsMART recorded annual sales growth of 85 percent, quickly securing the company's ranking as the largest operator in its industry. From 1989's total of $15.9 million, annual sales surged to $29.3 million in 1990 and nearly doubled in 1991, when the company operated 48 stores by year's end, reaching $58.2 million. That the company demonstrated such robust growth during the economically recessive early 1990s was most impressive. While the PETsMART chain blossomed many businesses, particularly retail businesses, suffered mightily in the anemic economic climate. Thus, PETsMART's surge during the early 1990s testified to the soundness of the entire concept and encouraged Parker to continue his strategic expansion across the country and bolster the chain's market position.

In 1992 annual sales jumped to $106.6 million and for the first time the company registered a profit, generating $400,000 in net income after recording a series of financial losses. PETsMART's net income leaped to $2.4 million the following year on sales of $188 million, but when these financial figures were announced they were applauded by a considerably larger group of people than PETsMART employees, management, and the company's controlling investors. In July 1993 PETsMART made its first public offering, opting to become a public company after years of relying on investors to shoulder the burden of financing the company's expansion. At the time, plans for the development of additional stores were ambitious, dwarfing the rate of expansion recorded during the previous years, as Parker and PETsMART management set sights on establishing a host of new PETsMART stores in new locations. In mid-1993 the company operated 71 stores in 13 states; by the end of the year

Parker hoped to operate a total of 106 stores and broaden the chain's geographic coverage to include 20 states, then add 40 additional stores in 1994, as the race to blanket the country with PETsMART stores accelerated.

To finance this prodigious expansion the company needed capital, which the public offering would provide. Becoming a public company would also enable PETsMART to pay down its debt and give the company's controlling financiers a return on their investments, which had fueled PETsMART's expansion throughout its existence. The initial public offering yielded $125 million, giving the company the financial means to forge ahead and grab a larger share of the pet food and supplies industry.

By the time PETsMART went public in mid-1993, U.S. consumers were spending $8.5 billion annually on pet food and supplies, mostly in large supermarkets and mass-merchandising outlets. This had been true when The Pet Food Warehouse first emerged in Phoenix in 1987 and continued to characterize the industry as PETsMART battled to maintain supremacy, but the company had secured its place in the vast market by stocking products the industry's largest competitors did not. Nearly 50 percent of PETsMART's food sales were derived from items such as Science Diet and Iams, brands previously available only through veterinarians and small pet shops. And though this move alone distinguished the company from its competition, that distinction began to blur as the pet food industry entered the mid-1990s.

PETsMART's success had spawned a host of imitators across the country, each trying to capture a share of the pet food and supplies market with an approach similar to that pioneered by the Doughertys and refined by Parker. During the early 1990s each of these companies had broadened their geographic reaches, establishing new stores in new locations much like PETsMART, but as the mid-1990s neared, these companies and their respective expansion plans began to collide, creating a contentious environment within the industry that pitted one company against another. It was either acquire or be acquired in the pet food and supplies industry, with only the strongest competitors likely to withstand the ensuing battle for dominance.

As the largest operator of superstores specializing in pet food, supplies, and services, PETsMART occupied an enviable position for the acquisitive years ahead. Parker had pursued a plan of rapid expansion from the beginning of his tenure at PETsMART. Now, as competition became more intense in the wake of the company's initial public offering, his plans for growth would include swallowing competing companies as well as establishing PETsMART stores in new locations. Succinctly framing the company's attitude for the future, Parker informed *Forbes* at the end of 1993 that "we're in a race," but even as he uttered those words the fix was in.

The company opened 41 stores in 1993, lifting annual sales from $106.6 million to $187.9 million, and acquired Phoenix-based Pet Food & Supply and its five superstores. PETsMART subsequently folded the Pet Food & Supply chain, retaining one store, then entered 1994 looking to expand wherever the best real estate deals could be had. In January 1994 PETsMART announced its intentions to acquire the 31-unit Petzazz chain from the Weisheimer Companies through an $81.3 million stock swap, an acquisition expected to add $50 million in new business and facilitate PETsMART's entry into the Chicago market, where Petzazz already operated.

In 1995 PETsMART continued to make pivotal acquisitions, including the May purchase of Sporting Dog Specialties, Inc., the world's largest catalog retailer of pet and animal supplies and accessories, but the year's most important acquisition was the purchase of the company's closest rival, Atlanta-based Petstuff, Inc., and its 56 superstores. Announced in February, the acquisition of Petstuff further solidified PETsMART's commanding lead in the industry, giving the company control over much of the nation's pet food and supply market. As the company prepared for the late 1990s and expected growth in the market it already dominated, projections for the future were deservedly sanguine, raising hopes that the years ahead would be as successful as the early 1990s.

Further Reading:

Helverson, Richard, ''PETsMART: Teaching an Old Pet Care Business New Tricks,'' *Discount Store News,* December 6, 1993, p. 81.

Hooper, Amy, ''Retailers Greet Petstuff Demise with Mixed Feelings,'' *Pet Product News,* August 1995, p. 22.

Perez, Janet, ''Phoenix-Based PetSmart's Superstores Offer One-Stop Shopping for Pets,'' *Phoenix Gazette,* September 9, 1993, p. 9.

''Pet Consolidation in Offing: PETsMART Buys Petzazz; Enters Chicago, Portland, Ore.,'' *Discount Store News,* March 21, 1994, p. 3.

''PETsMART Inc.,'' *Wall Street Journal,* February 8, 1995, p. B4.

Reagor, Catherine, ''PetSmart Will Survive Attack on Pet Food Line by Wal-Mart,'' *Business Journal—Serving Phoenix and the Valley of the Sun,* September 30, 1994, p. 7.

Roth, Steve, ''PETsMART Plans to Open String of Metroplex Stores,'' *Dallas Business Journal,* August 24, 1990, p. 11.

Roush, Chris, ''Cash Squeeze Forced Petstuff to Sell Out to Petsmart,'' *Knight-Ridder/Tribune Business News,* May 3, 1995, p. 50.

Shepherd, Kim, ''Huge Pet Stores Cater to Booming Number of Animal Owners,'' *Knight-Ridder/Tribune Business News,* September 12, 1994, p. 9.

Sullivan, R. Lee, ''Puppy Love,'' *Forbes,* December 20, 1993, p. 138.

Swenson, Steve E., ''Bakersfield, Calif. Pet Supply Store Sues PETsMART for Deceptive Ads,'' *Knight-Ridder/Tribunes Business News,* September 20, 1995, p. 92.

Taub, Stephen, ''Diamond in the Ruff,'' *Financial World,* September 1, 1993, p. 16.

—Jeffrey L. Covell

Physician Sales & Service, Inc.

7800 Belfort Parkway, Suite 250
Jacksonville, Florida 32256
U.S.A.
(904) 281-0011
Fax: (904) 281-9555

Public Company
Incorporated: 1983
Employees: 1,229
Sales: $236.19 million (1995)
Stock Exchanges: NASDAQ
SICs: 5047 Physicians & Surgeons Equipment & Supplies

Within just a few years, Physician Sales & Service, Inc., has grown into the first national physician supply company in the United States. Following a series of acquisitions, PSS also became the leader in the $6 billion office-based physician supply market. Sales for the Jacksonville-based company reached $236 million in 1995, up from $66.1 million just four years earlier. With the strength of recent acquisitions, revenues for 1996 were predicted to approach $500 million.

Company founder Patrick Kelly grew up in a Richmond, Virginia, boys' home. His experience with both forgiving and strict guardians helped him to develop a penchant for risk-taking, which he brought to PSS. "People here will never get in trouble for making a mistake," he told *Inc.* in 1995. He also gained experience in the U.S. Army, where he issued weapons, and the practice of delegating decision-making to young people impressed and intrigued Kelly. Later this became vital to his own training and recruiting methods.

With the help of an investor, Kelly, then in his mid-30s, founded the company in the spring of 1983 in Jacksonville, Florida, with two partners, Bill Riddell, who served as executive vice-president for sales and marketing, and Clyde Young. Kelly, Riddell, and Young had worked previously as sales representatives at another medical supply business. In order to facilitate decision-making, Kelly received 31 percent ownership versus 23 percent for the other three.

Doctors' offices have limited storage capacity and are prone to occasional shortages of critical supplies. To differentiate itself, PSS began to offer next-day delivery of most items versus the usual wait of three to four days. This practice allowed PSS to charge premium prices, which financed technological improvements in its distribution and sales departments. For example, competitors relied on commercial shipping companies, but PSS bought its own trucks.

Kelly's initial goal was to make the same money at PSS as he had at his previous job. The company's growth in these years was encouraging, but it did not become phenomenal until, in 1988, Kelly was inspired by a motivational speaker to set a bold goal for PSS. Its mission: to become the first national physician supply company in a field of regional players. The goal was heralded on banners and stationery and in conversation. The ambitious statement encouraged and emboldened the company's young staff. In 1987 PSS achieved sales of $13 million from its five Florida-based branches, but sales surged to $31 million in 1989 from ten branches. In 1991 there were 32 branch offices.

The company has been quick to use new information technology to improve service. In 1993 a new wireless data-transmission system supplied by RAM Mobile Data and Compaq Concerto laptop computers was implemented at a cost of $1.5 million. However, as information technology vice-president Darlene Kelly (not related to Patrick Kelly) stated, "The investment more than paid for itself in less than a year." Sales for the average representative increased roughly $10,000 each month, grossing $3,000 for the company. The system was first used to input orders from the field electronically, opening the possibility of same-day delivery (for orders received by 11:00 a.m.) while increasing the time available for sales. Administrative work at the service center was also greatly reduced. By 1995 PSS was boasting a same-day fill rate on 94 percent of items carried, or 16,000 products. The "Instant Customer Order Network" (ICON) enabled a decentralized approach at PSS, empowering sales representatives to make pricing decisions in the field. ICON was later upgraded to include instantly accessible pricing and usage histories, which allowed representatives to offer physicians timely, informed advice on budget and inventory management. Manufacturers' equipment catalogs and cost analyses were also immediately available.

Sales representatives, called "PSSers," were more than necessary to bring customers the benefits of this service and technology. Since the beginning Patrick Kelly had always practiced careful management of his staff. Experienced professionals had been difficult to acquire due to the company's short history and the tendency for jilted employees to sue PSS. However, the company developed a successful recruiting and training program for its young sales staff, who in 1995 averaged 27 years in age.

Kelly and his colleagues visited colleges, searching for candidates with ambition and drive rather than experience. Young team members brought many advantages to growth-oriented PSS. With fewer family connections, they could work longer hours and accept relocation to new facilities. They were also more amenable to performance-oriented compensation. True to his military background, Kelly promoted from within and not necessarily by seniority. A thinning of the top ranks through expansion created a considerable demand for new high-level managers, all either groomed from within or brought in through mergers. The wide-open possibilities for advancement in exchange for hard work seemed quite attractive to the type of individual Kelly sought. In return for the efforts laid out by his staff, Kelly, who disdained bureaucracy, promised to place no barriers on their potential for success.

PSS trainees learned various areas of the company's operations: working in warehouses, making deliveries, studying sales techniques, and learning about the products. Eventually, "PSS University" was established in Jacksonville, Florida. After sixteen weeks the trainees who made it through the first phase (about 90 percent of those who signed up) spent an intense week studying the industry and PSS sales techniques. Full days in class—punctuated by written tests, role playing, and video critiques—were followed by dinner lectures emphasizing important points. PSS was eager to invest heavily in training—approximately $10,000 to $25,000 per salesperson—in order to foster phenomenal growth. The trainees reduced the need for full-time warehouse and customer-service employees.

Attrition in the training program reached 30 percent before the PSS Sales Interview Guide was drafted in 1989. Like the previous hiring strategy, it emphasized attitudes and behavior rather than experience. Qualities sought in salespeople were aggressiveness and energy. The sales-training dropout rate fell to ten percent after the more highly selective interview guidelines were implemented; job offers were made to only 70 candidates out of 800 that applied in 1990. Cash incentives were a part of the process for those who did the hiring: branch managers received $2,000 for each successfully trained candidate. Once hired and successfully trained, PSSers tended to remain loyal. In 1989 turnover was only five percent. Providing each employee a stake in the company's success was critical to this stability.

The job was demanding. In 1995 the average representative called on 200 clients. PSS salespeople were trained to keep clients informed of emerging developments in products and to develop consulting relationships that naturally would increase their persuasiveness in selling products. Incentives were impressive; every type of employee at PSS had the possibility of earning a bonus, which could be as much as several thousand dollars, based on branch profit rankings. To increase motivation, company numbers, including daily sales reports and monthly profit-and-loss statements, were kept highly visible. Kelly even took to passing out $20 bills during visits to branches, rewarding those who correctly answered a randomly chosen question from a book of 100 work-related questions. Similarly, surprise "Blue Ribbon" tours twice a year rated each branch on 100 standards for doing business.

The company needed a constant supply of leadership talent, yet it found the best salespeople suffered high turnover when promoted to management. Kelly's solution was to institute "Creativity Week," a meeting aboard Kelly's boat in which prospective leaders read management texts such as *The Seven Habits of Highly Effective People* and discussed hypothetical cases. During the cruise, additional students were picked up each day, and the original three became mentors. Since 1987 all PSS managers went through the program.

PSS organized many recreational activities to motivate its troops and sustain an environment of expectancy. Regional annual picnics treated staff to two or three days in a distant resort. The interbranch volleyball tournament that began at these picnics culminated in playoffs at the national sales meeting, which also featured golf, and there were half-day trips for corporate staff. The company's focus on performance was enlivened by the "PSS Challenge," which brought monthly performance meetings into recreational settings such as bowling alleys and ballparks. An integral part of the PSS Challenge was a game show-style contest in which teams tested their knowledge of a particular business subject. PSS also took care of advertising and promotion in house, an approach that helped give its branch mangers and sales representatives a feeling of ownership toward sales promotions.

Although the concentration on profits helped buffer the company against the potential drawbacks of rapid growth, it consistently ran into problems with nervous banks, which urged the company to build up more equity and to contain its sales growth. At least five banks dropped PSS until Kelly increased the company's equity. In 1983 his 21 employees invested $50,000 in PSS; the founding partners added $100,000. An employee stock-ownership plan, which in 1995 owned one-fifth of the company's stock (worth around $46 million), offered pretax payroll deductions and matching company contributions and was reported to be responsible for creating 40 millionaires. An employee stock-purchase plan, for after-tax sale of stock, was later added along with stock-option incentives. The venture capital firm of Tullis-Dickerson & Co. bought one-fifth of the company in 1989, and in 1994 its initial public offering at $11 per share raised almost $16 million, lowering its debt-to-equity ratio to around 1:1.

The PSS of the mid-1990s continued to boast a high level of customer responsiveness, featuring same-day service. PSS asked for no minimum order and provided simple statements free of hidden handling charges. Doctors in the United States became much more price-conscious after President Bill Clinton's health care reform efforts in 1993; PSS responded by dropping prices on popular items and establishing a "comprehensive savings plan," Network Plus, a type of buyer's club that offered hassle-free credit and lower prices. Profits suffered with the new emphasis on low costs, but eventually market share increased and lower expenses helped recover the difference. The company also expanded its relationship with its clients, offering biomedical equipment repair and consulting services in the areas of space planning; laboratory design; federal safety regulation compliance; sterilization, sanitation, and infection control; inventory management; and financial services. Sales reached $169.7 million in 1994, an increase of more than 250 percent over 1990. Each sales representative wrote $468,000 in sales, an increase of nearly 40 percent since 1990. New branches typically became profitable within 18 months and eventually earned eight percent profit on sales, which, during this period, were increasing 22 percent per year at the average branch.

In 1995 sales reached $236.19 million before the acquisition of Taylor Medical, which PSS bought for $65 million. The privately owned company, based in Beaumont, Texas, was PSS's third-largest competitor, with 18,000 customers in 23 states and annual revenues of $122 million. At the time, PSS serviced 57,000 medical offices in 48 states with its existing 56 service centers. The deal also gave PSS 175 sales representatives, increasing its total to 620. PSS had previously acquired Lancet Medical Ltd. of St. Louis, where PSS already had a service center. Lancet's 1994 sales were worth $1.5 million. PSS also signed an exclusive distribution agreement with Abbott Laboratories to distribute its Physician Office Laboratory line of diagnostic equipment; this was projected to bring PSS $65 million the first year, $100 million the next.

In 1994 Kelly had announced a new goal: $1 billion in sales by the end of 2001. Having attained its goal of becoming the first national physician supply company, and likely to reach $500 million in sales in 1996, PSS would seem to be more than halfway there.

Further Reading:

Case, John, ''The 10 Commandments of Hypergrowth,'' *Inc.,* October 1995, pp. 32–44.

Greco, Susan, et al., ''Do-It-Yourself Marketing: How Smart Companies Are Selling More and Spending Less,'' *Inc.,* November 1991, pp. 52–67.

Lammers, Teri, ''The Foolproof Interviewer's Guide,'' *Inc.,* December 1991, pp. 127–32.

''Physician Sales & Service: The First National Physician Supply Company,'' Jacksonville, Fla.: Physician Sales & Service, n.d.

Posner, Bruce G., ''Growing Your Own: What to Do When You Can't Afford to Hire Experienced People,'' *Inc.,* June 1989, pp. 131–32.

''PSS Acquires Taylor Medical, Making It Nation's Largest Physician Supplier,'' *Health Industry Today,* May 1995, p. 16.

Taylor, Thayer C., ''Sales Automation Cuts the Cord,'' *Sales & Marketing Management,* July 1995, pp. 110–15.

—Frederick C. Ingram

PLATINUM TECHNOLOGY

PLATINUM Technology, Inc.

1815 S. Meyers Road
Oakbrook Terrace, Illinois 60181
U.S.A.
(708) 620-5000
Fax: (708) 691-0710

Public Company
Incorporated: 1987
Employees: 600
Sales: $95.7 million
Stock Exchanges: NASDAQ
SICs: 7372 Prepackaged Software

PLATINUM Technology, Inc., is one of America's fastest growing software development companies. Based in a Chicago suburb, PLATINUM writes and sells an extensive line of software tools and utilities that ease the use of International Business Machine Corporation's DB2 mainframe relational database management system. As growth in the mainframe market slowed in the 1990s, PLATINUM jumped into the rapidly expanding client/server database market as well, supporting such operating systems as UNIX, DOS, Windows, and IBM's OS/2, and such databases as Informix, Microsoft SQL, Oracle, and Sybase. It shifted its focus to open enterprise systems management (OESM), which enables efficient data operations across wedded mainframe computer, minicomputer, and personal computer networks. In the mid 1990s PLATINUM also sold educational and training services and publications to support its software and the DB2 system. PLATINUM's more than 6,000 clients include AT&T, IBM, Sony Corporation, the University of California, the Federal Reserve Bank, and other government agencies. In 1995, PLATINUM completed a series of acquisitions that nearly tripled its size.

PLATINUM Technology was the brainchild of Andrew "Flip" Filipowski, former president and founder of the now-defunct DBMS Inc. The son of immigrants and a college dropout, Filipowski grew up in a working-class Chicago neighborhood. After a stint as a tutor with the Evelyn Wood Reading Academy but with no professional sales experience, Filipowski joined Cullinet Software Inc. (then known as Cullinane Corp.) as a salesman. He became the company's first million-dollar salesman and within five years rose to executive vice president. Cullinet was then the fastest-growing database management

systems developer in the country; however, because of the complexity of such systems, many customers experienced difficulties in operating their systems, resulting in inefficient and often ineffective operations. Filipowski identified the related needs for both software and training that would ease the use of such systems. In 1979, after Cullinet declined to develop the increasingly important special services market, Filipowski left to found DBMS Inc.

DBMS's software products acted as more manageable layers on top of standard database systems, much as Microsoft's Windows allowed the DOS operating system to become easier to use. In conjunction with its software sales, DBMS offered training programs and expert systems to help companies get the most out of their database systems. Originally aligned exclusively with Cullinet, Filipowski recognized that his company's fortunes were too closely tied with the other's, leaving DBMS vulnerable should Cullinet slip. DBMS soon began to support the other major database suppliers, Applied Data Research, Inc., and IBM. Later, DBMS would include workstation development tools among its product offerings. DBMS's strategy was to sell various software programs bundled as kits, which it offered at a steep discount. Because of the cost in time and effort in developing software, DBMS would purchase some of the components of its software kits, allowing it to bring its products more quickly to the marketplace. By 1986, DBMS had passed $20 million in annual revenues. However, by then changes in database technology were making much of DBMS's product line obsolete, and Filipowski prepared to update DBMS's technology. As he told *Crain's Chicago Business*, "it was like [DBMS was] selling spark plugs for the Edsel."

The United States was then in the throes of the takeover fever of the 1980s, and DBMS soon became the object of a hostile takeover by Shamrock Holdings Inc. Unable to agree with the new owners on the future of the company, relationships turned bitter. Shortly thereafter, Filipowski found himself surrounded by a cadre of armed guards and ejected from his own company. Within twenty-four hours, Filipowski started PLATINUM Technology, taking DBMS's top software developers and executives with him. Two years later, DBMS Inc. went into a slide and was bought up by Computer Associates International.

At that time, IBM was phasing out its earlier database management system in favor of its new DB2 relational database management system for its mainframes, which had been introduced in 1983. PLATINUM began writing software for the new system, reasoning that the introduction of DB2 would create a worldwide market for businesses that could help install and customize the system and then train employees on the new system. The DB2 technology, an electronic filing system, involved enormous amounts of information arranged in a vast array of file and data structures, which in turn taxed the operating capabilities and efficiencies of mainframe computers. PLATINUM offered data processing tools for the system, such as software that allowed data to be analyzed, modified, or transferred among databases while enhancing mainframe efficiency and performance during such tasks. PLATINUM also developed educational programs that trained personnel in DB2's installation and operation. In 1988, PLATINUM became a Business Partner in IBM's Authorized Application Specialist Program for DB2.

In its first year, PLATINUM recorded revenues of $1.5 million with a loss of $895,000. One year later, it earned a profit of nearly $400,000 on revenues of $6 million. Competition was high, however, principally from market-leader BMC Software Inc. Filipowski's initial strategy involved what *Business Week* dubbed "guerrilla tactics." Recognizing that BMC refused to sell its products under its list price, PLATINUM offered deep discounts on its line. Although PLATINUM's products were not yet perfected, with more bugs than its rival's products, customers were attracted by the savings PLATINUM offered, ranging in the hundreds of thousands of dollars. Filipowski exploited another weakness he found at BMC. Because BMC relied heavily on telemarketing to sell its products, PLATINUM created a direct-sales staff, who could also offer more extensive, personalized technical support to their customers. As Filipowski told *Fortune*, "We identify our competitors' 'religious behavior.' That's finding out what's sacred to them, what won't they change—say, a reliance on telemarketing. We attack by replicating their system or doing something else better. We work like the devil not to be religious. . . . That way, if anyone picks on us, we change. We survive." PLATINUM's strategy worked well, gaining them a foothold in the market and soon a steadily increasing market share.

A more important initiative came in response to the need for distribution of the PLATINUM line. With a potential customer base that included every one of the thousands of companies using DB2, Filipowski needed a way to provide individualized installation, training, and ongoing support of his products on a global scale. However, as a small company, PLATINUM did not have the resources to compete with larger, more established software and computer consulting companies. Rather than undergoing the lengthy and expensive process of opening additional offices and acquiring and training personnel to staff them, or licensing its products to franchises, Filipowski instead hit on the idea of building a network of affiliated companies. By recruiting a number of small consulting companies to sell its products under the PLATINUM name, PLATINUM could extend its reach across the United States and throughout the world, giving PLATINUM the appearance—and credibility—of a large company. In return, the smaller consulting firms would be better able to compete with larger firms while still maintaining their independence. As Filipowski explained to *INC.*, "the little guy's margins were constantly being squeezed."

By 1990, PLATINUM's network included more than 30 affiliates with nearly 3,000 employees. With each company, including PLATINUM, contributing into a fund, PLATINUM was able to create national and international advertising campaigns. PLATINUM telemarketers passed on potential sales to companies according to their established territory, and profits were split between PLATINUM and the affiliate making the sale and providing the service. At the end of 1990, PLATINUM itself had grown to 80 employees, it had licensed 1,900 products to 300 customers, and its revenues had doubled over the year before to $15 million, pushing its profits to nearly $3 million.

In April 1991 PLATINUM went public, selling 2.5 million common shares in its initial offering and netting $18 million. Part of these funds were used for the purchase of another company's related DB2 software. Then in June 1991, PLATINUM was named as one of four partners in IBM's developmental Sys-

temView systems management architecture. Along with Candle Corp., Bachman Information Systems, Inc., and Goal Systems International Inc., PLATINUM received access to IBM's research efforts on SystemView, allowing them not only a first look at the new system's specifications but also design input to allow SystemView to work more effectively with, and thereby increase demand for, their own products. IBM also agreed to market only PLATINUM's DB2 products in Japan. In return, PLATINUM would pay IBM 10 percent of earnings from PLATINUM's SystemView software products. Within months, PLATINUM's share of the then $170-million market had risen to 11 percent, behind BMC's 16 percent, and IBM's leading 32 percent share.

The following year, *Business Week* ranked PLATINUM at the number two spot on its list of the best small companies of 1991. PLATINUM posted revenues of $32.1 million and profits of $5 million, and in 1992 captured a 35 percent share in the DB2 software market, equaling BMC. Quality control problems, particularly glitches in its software, still presented some difficulties, but the company's continued discounted pricing and its vows to achieve statistical perfection for its software, had kept sales high. By then, PLATINUM's products were divided along three lines: PLATINUM Catalog Facility; PLATINUM Analyzers, and PLATINUM Utilities. All three lines focused on improving the utilization and performance of the DB2 mainframe system. By the end of 1992, PLATINUM's revenues had jumped to $49 million, with earnings of $9.3 million.

Changes in technology and the marketplace's application of new technology were beginning to have an impact on the mainframe software market. Rapid developments in the power and speed of personal computers had made them a more viable tool for data-driven applications. Companies were shifting from a dependence on mainframes to the use of more flexible and less expensive client/server systems, which comprise networked personal computers linked to a central server. IBM's sales of its mainframe computers dropped, causing stock prices of mainframe software developers, including PLATINUM, to fall. Although mainframe software sales soon rebounded, given the great number of mainframes already in existence around the world, PLATINUM moved to support the new technology by writing software and providing support for client/server systems. At the same time, the company continued to enhance its mainframe software portfolio, with a focus on the integration of mainframes with client/server networks. PLATINUM increased its software design staff to 76 people, twice its former size. However, Filipowski also used the strategy that had worked for the company before: He acquired third-party software rather than develop his own from scratch. In 1993 PLATINUM purchased Datura Corp. of Richmond, Virginia, a specialist in client/server software, for $6 million. This purchase began a period of rapid growth for the company, as PLATINUM sought to expand further the reach of its software capabilities. PLATINUM's client base had grown to 1,200 customers licensing 8,000 of its products. Its revenues had reached $62 million.

Price cuts on IBM mainframes in 1994 helped stem the tide of clients turning from the larger machines to client/server systems, providing PLATINUM some breathing room in which to develop its new product lines. Meanwhile, PLATINUM began its surge of acquisitions, picking up 13 companies over two years, including, in 1994, Datura; Aston Brooke Software, a provider of performance monitoring tools; and Dimeric Development Corporation, a developer of UNIX tools and utilities. Ranked 43rd among *Fortune*'s fastest-growing American companies, PLATINUM had extended its product line with PLATINUM Information Environment products, which included enterprisewide client/service software applications, and PLATINUM Client/Server Products, which comprised 18 tools and utilities for distributed database management systems across multiple operating platforms. Software products accounted for 63 percent of PLATINUM's $95 million in 1994 sales, with support and maintenance services and educational and training programs providing the remainder.

PLATINUM's acquisitions continued into 1995, when it announced the purchase of ten more companies, together costing an estimated $300 million. In addition to these acquisitions, PLATINUM also formed development and marketing alliances with Oracle, Sybase, and Informix, while continuing its association with IBM. PLATINUM's chief, Filipowski, was determined to reinvent the company, transforming it from its former narrow range of mainframe products to a wide-ranging vendor of MVS- and UNIX-based enterprisewide desktop network systems management tools, utilities, and support services. In tripling the size of the company, PLATINUM first investigated problem areas for corporate network users, then chose and approached the companies working in each segment. Response from each company was positive because most were small companies with limited abilities to market their products. Under the purchase agreements, all of the acquired companies' CEOs remained in place, and the companies continued to develop their respective products. In 1995, PLATINUM unveiled its PLATINUM Open Enterprise Management System, which provided full integration of PLATINUM and third-party software into a network system.

Despite a sustained period of net losses due to the scope of its acquisitions, PLATINUM continued to be viewed as one of America's fastest-growing and most promising companies.

PLATINUM's competition broadened, too, as it faced Computer Associates International Inc., Legent Corp., Tivoli Systems, Inc., along with long-time rival BMC Corp., and other industry powerhouses. Yet most analysts agreed that, even while confronting the difficulties of merging so many different companies and corporate cultures in a short time, PLATINUM's chief asset may well be Andrew "Flip" Filipowski.

Principal Subsidiaries: Advanced Software Concepts; Altai Inc.; Answer Systems; Aston-Brooke Software; AutoSystems Corporation; BrownStone Solutions; Datura Corporation; Dimeric Computing Corporation; Reltech Group; Software Interfaces; SQL Software Corporation; Trinzic Corporation; ViaTech Development Inc.

Further Reading:

"The Best Small Companies," *Business Week*, May 25, 1992, p. 97.
Kapp, S., "The Wrong Guy to Bet," *Business Marketing*, September 1986, p. 8.
Murphy, H. L., "Flip or Flop? Merger Frenzy at Platinum," *Crain's Chicago Business*, May 15, 1995, p. 1.
Murphy, H. Lee, "Platinum Gaining Momentum in New Computer Technology," *Crain's Chicago Business*, June 13, 1994, p. 22.
Oloroso Jr., A., "Hard-Charging Chief Makes Platinum Tech Compute," *Crain's Chicago Business*, September 23, 1991.
PLATINUM *Technology, Inc.*, "Revised Corporate Backgrounder," downloaded 9/95 from PLATINUM *Technology, Inc.* World Wide Web site.
"PLATINUM Technology," *Standard Nasdaq Stock Reports, November 30, 1994,* New York: Standard & Poor's, 1994.
"PLATINUM Technology," *Standard Nasdaq Stock Reports, September 18, 1991,* New York: Standard & Poor's, 1991.
Richman, T., "Recruiting Affiliates," *INC.*, December 1990.
Serwer, A. E., "Lessons From America's Fastest Growing Companies," *Fortune*, August 8, 1994, pp. 54–56.
Stedman, C., "Platinum's New Frontier," *Computerworld*, February 27, 1995, p. 71.
Therrien, L., "Why Platinum Looks Like Gold," *Business Week*, June 29, 1992, p. 93.

—M. L. Cohen

PriceCostco, Inc.

10809 120th Avenue N.E.
Kirkland, Washington 98033
U.S.A.
(206) 828-8100
Fax: (206) 828-8106

4649 Morena Blvd.
San Diego, California 92117
U.S.A.
(619) 581-4600
Fax: (619) 581-4773

Public Company
Incorporated: 1993
Employees: 40,000
Sales: $16 billion
Stock Exchanges: NASDAQ
SICs: 5141 Groceries, General Line; 5182 Wines & Distilled
Beverages

The merger of The Price Company and Costco Wholesale Corporation in 1993 created the nation's second largest membership warehouse chain. With 240 Price Club and Costco Wholesale warehouse stores, including clubs in Canada, Mexico, England, and Korea, and sales of over $16 billion in 1995, PriceCostco, Inc. had become a giant in the relatively young warehouse retailing industry, challenging the leadership of the Sam's Club chain owned by Wal-Mart, Inc. As of the mid-1990s, PriceCostco warehouse customers paid an annual fee in return for a low-cost, no-frills, limited selection of nationally branded and private label merchandise, including fresh foods and baked goods. Membership in PriceCostco clubs was limited to businesses, including individuals; members and employees of selected banks, credit unions, savings and loan and other associations; local, state, and federal government employees; and shareholders in the company. In exchange for the privilege of buying goods at prices only slightly higher than wholesale, business members paid a $30 annual fee and Gold Star (individual) members paid a $35 annual fee. With markups of 10 percent or less, PriceCostco clubs offset their low prices with a high inventory turnover rate, limited selection, no-frills self-service, volume purchasing, limited advertising, and other efficiency strategies, as well as with the annual fee charged to members.

The members-only warehouse club was the creation of Sol Price. In 1954, Price introduced the concept of one-stop shopping when he started Fedmart, a discount department store open to government employees, who paid a membership fee of $2 per family. Fedmart's first year was highly successful; over the next 20 years Fedmart grew to include 45 stores in a chain that generated more than $300 million in annual sales. However, Price sold Fedmart Corp. after losing leadership of the company in 1976. Fedmart folded seven years later.

In the mid-1970s, small business owners had no options other than to buy their products and supplies from regional wholesalers or cash-and-carry operations. Price set out to offer an alternative. In 1976, with $800,000 of his own, $1 million raised among local California small business owners, and an additional $500,000 from former Fedmart employees, Price, along with his son Robert, formed the Price Company and opened the first Price Club store in San Diego. Price's other son, Laurence, declined to join the new company.

Price Club represented a revolution in retailing. Its concept was simple: it would offer a small selection of products covering a broad range of goods and sell in bulk in order to keep prices low, usually at no more than a 10 percent markup over the wholesale cost. To maintain such discount prices, overhead was kept to a bare minimum. Products were stocked directly on the selling floor in minimally decorated warehouses built on cheap industrial land, sales help was almost nonexistent, and there would be no advertising, except to announce the opening of new stores. Selection was limited, offering the broad range but not the depth—and consequent inventory burden—of the typical department store. Products were bought in bulk directly from the manufacturers. Low margins were further offset by rapid inventory turnover, as high as 20 turns a year, allowing stores to pay suppliers quickly and achieve added early-payment discounts. Membership was initially limited to small business owners, whose fees would also offset overhead costs. Restricted membership reduced the risk of bad checks and shoplifting because members would be more financially secure than the general buying public. The store also refused to accept credit cards, in part to avoid the cost of their administration and credit card fees of as much as 1.5 percent.

Price's first year went poorly, however, with losses of $750,000 on sales of $16 million. Price responded by broadening its membership base to include members of selected credit unions and savings and loan associations and government, utility, and hospital employees. Additional stock sold to friends generated enough capital to keep the company in business, and, by 1978, Price had recovered sufficiently to open its second warehouse in Phoenix, Arizona. In that year, Laurence Price borrowed money from the Price Company to open a tire-mounting and battery installation shop next to a Price Club store. The new shop leased its space from Price, servicing the tires and car batteries sold there.

The Price Company continued to expand, opening two more stores, in Arizona and California, and, when it went public in 1980, was already generating annual sales of $150 million. Business boomed among customers who appreciated the no-frills approach in exchange for low prices, and their word-of-mouth remained the company's most important—and only—advertisement.

The typical Price Club was a marked contrast to the department stores of the day. Located in industrial districts on a city's outskirts, where land and building costs were low, a Price Club store was housed in little more than a large warehouse space, generally from 100,000 to 120,000 square feet. Goods, ranging from five-pound bags of rice and five-gallon jars of peanut butter to tires, televisions, and snowblowers, were loaded by forklift directly onto 18-foot-high shelves. Bulk packaging of smaller items appealed both to the small business owner and to families. Personnel and administration costs were also kept to a minimum by restricting store hours to a single-shift, eight-hour day. The stores had no expensive, trained sales staff, such as those found in department stores. In later years, the introduction of computerized scanning devices further reduced the need for personnel.

The rising inflation of the 1970s aided the success of the Price Club concept. Customers proved they were willing to travel to an out-of-the-way location for the best prices. Soon, Price began acquiring additional land and properties, forming a subsidiary, TPCR Corporation, to develop and operate land in excess of Price Club needs. Reasoning that increased traffic would offset increased competition, Price entered partnerships with developers, who would construct additional retail buildings, splitting rents with the Price Company. Price stepped up its expansion only slightly. By 1984 it had added 16 new stores, entering New Mexico and building two stores in Virginia. The East Coast proved a somewhat less accessible market, with suitably priced, commercially zoned land difficult to find. Consumers on the East Coast also faced heavier traffic when traveling to the stores' typically remote locations. The company's desire to own the land under stores they built themselves was another factor that kept the pace of its expansion slow. Nevertheless, Price moved into Maryland and formed a joint venture with Steinberg Corporation to operate Price Clubs in Canada. In 1985, Price posted profits of $45 million on sales of $1.9 billion.

By then, Sol Price's warehouse concept had grown to a $4 billion per year industry. In 1983, Price was suddenly faced with new competitors who were successfully copying the Price Club idea. Wal-Mart's Sam's Clubs quickly became a giant in the young industry, with added competition from Kmart's PACE Memberships Clubs, and from Costco, whose Seattle, Washington-based Costco Wholesale Clubs directly challenged Price's hold on the West Coast market. At the same time, traditional retailers began introducing elements of the Price concept, including bulk goods and heavy discounting, providing additional competition.

James D. Sinegal, co-founder of Costco, had worked with Sol Price at Fedmart before joining him at the Price Company. Sinegal left Price, having reached the level of executive vice president, and in 1983 formed Costco Wholesale Corporation with Jeffrey H. Brotman, a former oil exploration company executive. The first Costco, based heavily on the Price Club concept, opened in that year in Seattle, Washington. In less than two years, Costco went public, expanded into Canada, and became one of Price's fiercest competitors. Costco was also seen as the more creative merchandiser, becoming the first

warehouser to extend its product line to encompass such fresh foods as baked goods, meats, seafood, and produce. As much as two-thirds of its sales were based on such recession-proof items, which became an important element to its success in the economic downturn of the late 1980s. In later years, Costco would also expand into the do-it-yourself market. By 1988, Costco had achieved sales of $2 billion, and by 1993 Costco was ranked third in the industry, with 103 stores.

Despite the increased competition, Price's growth continued. In 1986 it posted earnings of $75 million on sales of $2.6 billion. The company's stock reached its all-time high of $55.75 per share. Industry observers, however, began to predict a shakeout in an industry that was becoming increasingly crowded. By 1986, Sam's Clubs had taken over the lead. Added trouble came in 1986 when, after a quarrel between Sol Price and Laurence Price, Price attempted to exercise its option to buy out Laurence Price's tire-mounting and battery-installation chain, which by then had grown to 20 centers and over $5 million in sales. Laurence Price filed for arbitration, winning a $3.7 million settlement, then filed a $100 million lawsuit against Price Company.

Price's conservative approach to expansion during this period was also criticized. "Instead of responding to the threat by pushing into and dominating new markets," *Business Week* reported, "Price Co. remained almost exclusively on the West Coast . . . [leaving] the rest of the country wide open for more aggressive competitors." Price's focus on owning its own real estate had slowed its expansion. More than half of the Price properties also included shopping center and mall developments. Developing its property and building its own warehouses became a heavy financial burden for the company, during a time when its competitors were pursuing far more rapid expansion plans. Price also lagged behind in industry developments as well, as Costco and other competitors moved to provide fresh foods and other products, expanding the one-stop shopping experience. By 1987, Costco had 39 stores and Sam's had 49 stores, passing Price's 35.

Sol Price resigned as chairman of the Price Company in 1988 and was replaced by Robert Price. By then, Price had grown to $4 billion in sales, and earnings were growing steadily each year. In the next year, Price paid its first and only cash dividend of $1.50 per common share, for a total of $75 million. By then, Price Clubs had extended to New Jersey, Connecticut, New York, and Quebec. However, Price Club's fortunes were beginning to fade. Attempts to venture into the home and office furniture market failed. In addition, despite a more aggressive expansion push in the early 1990s, many of the new Price Clubs were opened in California, adding, in 1991, 11 stores to the 29 already operating in that state. Staggered by a $630 million overhead burden, Price was also in effect cannibalizing its own stores. The following year, Price's earnings dropped for the first time since it had gone public.

In just 17 years, the warehouse club industry had grown to a $39 billion industry. However, the rapid growth of the 1980s slowed drastically in the 1990s as the U.S. market became saturated with stores. The increasing numbers of warehouse-concept stores specializing in single markets, such as pet foods or office supplies, were adding to the competition. The warehouse clubs were beginning to cannibalize each others' sales. Price moved into Mexico in a joint venture with Mexican retailer Controladora Comercial Mexicana in 1991, while adding stores in Colorado and British Columbia. But in order to finance its growth, Price was forced to spin off some $150 million of its real estate assets. Its expansion had come too late; competition from Sam's and PACE closed down its newly opened stores in New York and Pennsylvania.

Threats of a Costco takeover by Sam's Clubs, which by 1993 owned 434 stores and nearly half of the market, prompted Price to begin merger negotiations with Costco in 1992. Costco, too, was eager to avoid being swallowed up by Sam's and was equally frightened by the prospect of Price selling out to Sam's. Yet negotiations broke down when the parties could not decide on who would head the projected new company. When Price's earnings continued to drop, however, down 40 percent in the second quarter of 1993, Price finally entered into a deal with Costco. Sinegal would take the CEO position and Robert Price was named as chairman of the board. Called a partial merger, the two companies would continue to operate their respective headquarters, with the bulk of domestic responsibility going to Costco and international business to be headed by Price. Price shareholders, including the 13 percent share of the Price family, would retain 48 percent of the new company to Costco's 52 percent, the largest part of which, 24 percent, was controlled by the French Carrefour retailer. The merger allowed the two companies to consolidate their purchasing and shipping operations, share scanner and other technologies, and to dominate the West Coast market.

The new company, PriceCostco, Inc., continued Price's international expansion, developing more stores in Mexico, opening two stores in England, and licensing a Price Club in South Korea. However, hopes that the merger would halt sales declines did not materialize, and by 1994 sales for stores open more than a year had fallen by 3 percent, with a corresponding drop in earnings. Despite the initial optimism that had greeted the merger, the two management sides had never reached agreement on many crucial issues. The company continued to operate out of both headquarters. Soon, arguments arose over which direction PriceCostco should take. Robert Price sought to continue his company's real estate interests, whereas Sinegal pushed for further expansion of the warehouse chain. Disputes also arose over whether to continue funding the in-store Quest Electronic Catalogue, a computerized network that allowed customers to purchase products not stocked in the stores.

By the middle of 1994, the PriceCostco merger was being called premature. Disagreements between Sinegal and Robert Price finally resulted in a partial breakup announced in July 1994. PriceCostco's commercial real estate properties, as well as other assets, were spun off as Price Enterprises, Inc., to be headed by Robert Price. Apart from its commercial real estate, Price Enterprises took with it four warehouse locations; a 51 percent interest in the Quest catalogue; 51 percent of PriceCostco's Mexican partnership, which by then included nine stores; and 51 percent ownership of PriceCostco's international development projects in Central America, Australia, and New Zealand. Together, these assets represented less than 10 percent of PriceCostco's earnings. Sinegal remained as president and CEO of PriceCostco, while his long-time partner, Jeffrey Brotman, took over as chairman.

With PriceCostco's focus now firmly fixed on increasing its warehouse operations, new PriceCostco clubs opened in San Francisco and in the New York metropolitan area. Plans were announced for as many as 29 new clubs to open through 1996. During the same period, PriceCostco expected to close several overlapping Price and Costco stores that had remained after the merger. Meanwhile, the company increasingly looked overseas for its growth, with plans for added stores in Korea and England and for entry into Taiwan and Latin America. Per-store profits were once again on the rise, and the total number of PriceCostco stores was expected to grow to 245 by the end of 1995. Yet competition seemed only certain to intensify as this very American industry spread worldwide.

Further Reading:

Anderer, C., "Costco Seen Dominating Price Deal," *Supermarket News*, October 25, 1993, p. 12.

Barrett, A., "A Retailing Pacesetter Pulls Up Lame," *Business Week*, July 12, 1993, pp. 122–23.

Bryant, A., "Costco Set to Merge with Price," *New York Times*, June 17, 1993, pp. D1, 7.

Markowitz, A., "Merger Signals Clubs' Maturation," *Discount Store News*, July 5, 1993, pp. 1, 118.

Ortega, B., "Price/Costco's Spinoff Reflects a Difficult Marriage," *The Wall Street Journal*, July 19, 1994, p. B4 (E).

"PriceCostco Approves a Plan to Spin Off Assets," *New York Times*, July 30, 1994, p. 37 (L).

Spector, R., "Price/Costco Has Expansion in Its Future," *Women's Wear Daily*, February 8, 1995, p. 18.

White, G., and Kraul, C., "Price Co., Costco Warehouse Stores to Merge," *Los Angeles Times*, June 17, 1993, pp. A1, A38.

—Mickey L. Cohen

Raley's Inc.

P.O. Box 15618
Sacramento, California 95852
U.S.A.
(916) 373-3333
Fax: (916) 372-6226

Private Company
Incorporated: 1935
Employees: 8,500
Sales: $1.8 billion
SICs: 5411 Grocery Stores; 5912 Drug Stores & Proprietary
  Stores

Raley's Inc. is the most successful privately owned grocery store chain located on the western coast of the United States. Opened in 1935, at the height of the Great Depression when the Social Security Act was passed by the U.S. Congress, Alcoholics Anonymous was established, and *Mutiny on the Bounty* starring Clark Gable won the Oscar for Best Picture of the Year, it seemed an inauspicious time for a grocery store to commence operations. However, Tom Raley, founder of the enterprise, possessed an overwhelming confidence in his ability to succeed. His faith was not unfounded. By the mid-1990s, the little grocery store had grown into one of the most prominent chains in the entire nation, numbering over 81 stores with sales of over $1 billion.

The founder of Raley's Inc., Thomas P. Raley, was born in 1903 in Carrollton Hollow, Arkansas, the 13th in a family of 14 children. Raley's father, a Baptist preacher and farmer, gave his son the opportunity to become a farmer like himself, but when Tom graduated from high school he decided to attend Springfield Business College in Missouri. However, the young man grew increasingly dissatisfied with his studies and dropped out of school after six months. He went to work in a wheat field and, with four of his fellow workers, suddenly decided to travel west to seek his fortune.

Arriving in Los Angeles, California, Raley first worked as file clerk and then as a delivery man. Selling and hauling five-gallon jugs of water to local grocery stores, Raley soon tired of the routine and called the vice president of Safeway grocery stores for a new job. He was hired as a produce receiving clerk at one of the company's distribution centers, but his ambition still was not satisfied. When the president of Safeway made an inspection

visit, Raley introduced himself and asked for a chance to learn about the grocery business. The president, M. B. Skaggs, was surprised and impressed by Raley's aggressiveness and, within 13 months, appointed him to manage one of Safeway's store.

Throughout the late 1920s and early 1930s, Raley learned about the grocery business as he worked as a manager for various Safeway stores. By the mid-1930s, he was ready to start his own operation, and he purchased a site in Placerville, California. He arranged for a Sacramento contractor to build a 2,500-square-foot store, and Raley himself built the store's counters and shelves. With only $121 in his pockets, he was unable to purchase food stock for his empty shelves, so he asked M. B. Skaggs to provide a credit recommendation. Skaggs not only gave Raley a glowing recommendation, but guaranteed the young man's debts. The store opened in February of 1935, and Raley advertised his new grocery business as ''the nation's first drive-in market.''

The Placerville store soon garnered a reputation for fresh meat and produce, and by the end of the year the company reported a profit of $4,500. Business grew so quickly that Raley decided to open a second store in Sacramento, California. The beginning of World War II, however, slowed the company's growth. Fresh produce and meat became scarce, and such items as butter and coffee went on the government's list of rationed foodstuffs. Many of the company's male employees were drafted into military service, and Tom Raley was forced to work longer hours on the grocery floor himself. On top of all this, the store at Placerville burned down in 1942. However, Raley remained determined to succeed and opened new stores in Roseville and Grass Valley.

At the end of the war, life in the United States returned to normal, yet certain foods and dry goods still remained difficult to purchase. Sorghum was used as a substitute for sugar after the war, and bananas and honeydew melons were almost nonexistent on the shelves of grocery stores. Tom Raley was resourceful, however, and his grocery business thrived under these adverse circumstances. One of the most important changes in the grocery store business after World War II was the introduction of packaged mixes for cakes, pie crusts, and puddings. Before the war most women cooked from scratch with such items as flour, sugar, and other staples that lined grocery store shelves. With the advent of packaged mixes, women found they had more time for other activities. Merchants such as Raley's were only too willing to accommodate the rising demand for such goods. Another of the more important developments within the grocery industry was the creation of plastic wrap. Before the war, a customer would give an order to the store's butcher, and the butcher would cut a piece of meat to the desired specifications. However, the creation of plastic wrap by E.I du Pont de Nemours & Company revolutionized the perishable grocery market. Raley's was the first store in northern California to use plastic wrap for its meats, which heralded the arrival of the self-service meat counter.

The 1950s was a time of empire building for Tom Raley. Stores were opened and closed at an incredibly fast pace at places like Roseville, Carmichael, Grass Valley, Napa, and Vallejo. By 1953, Raley operated 7 grocery stores. Company employees worked long hours, anywhere from 10 to 14 hours per day and almost always six days a week. Raley hired those people whom he thought worked the hardest, equipped them with a pencil, a Garvey market, and a box cutter, and sent them off to one of his stores. Even under these conditions, employees were extremely dedicated and loyal to the company. In 1956, Raley's counted nine stores in operation and over $8 million in annual revenues.

During the 1960s, flush with cash and heady with the success of his grocery empire, Tom Raley decided to expand his operations and enter the hotel business. Along with three partners, Raley purchased the Mayfair Hotel in Los Angeles and the elegant MiraMar Hotel in Santa Barbara, California. Extensive renovations were required at both hotels, and the partners found themselves sinking more and more money into their venture. When the deal began to lose money, Raley's partners opted out of the agreement, but Raley refused to admit defeat. As the hotels continued to lose money, Raley's own grocery store chain began to suffer, and finally his entire empire was threatened. Undeterred, Raley opened two new 100,000-square-foot combined grocery and department stores. Realizing that he made a mistake, Raley made plans to reorganize the stores and bring his company back to profitability. Along with Charles Collings, a valued and trusted employee, Raley approached the San Francisco Board of Trade with a restructuring plan for his company. The plan was accepted by the Board and, slowly but surely, Raley and Collings saved the company from the worst financial crisis it had experienced up to that time.

Never one to dwell on past mistakes, when Tom Raley discovered that the Eagle Thrifty Drug store chain was put up for sale by the Gastanagas family, he immediately sent a team to negotiate its purchase. Whittling the price down from $6.5 million to $3.5 million, Raley acquired the company's 10 store chain in 1973. Since the late 1950s, Raley had conceived and implemented a strategy of placing drugstores next to his grocery stores whenever he had the opportunity. Although the two operations had their separate ordering, accounting, and marketing procedures, the physical proximity of the a grocery and drugstore was attractive to customers. With the acquisition of Eagle Thrifty Drug stores, Raley began to build combined grocery and drugs stores, and began to put in place a smooth-running management for both operations.

During the early 1980s, Raley's combined with Bel Air and Save Mart supermarkets to form a joint venture called Mid-Valley Dairy. The purpose of the enterprise was to reduce the expenses involved in purchasing dairy products from large milk processing plants. Larger grocery store chains were buying dairy products through retailer-owned processing plants, which resulted in a distinct disadvantage for Raley and other smaller retail owners. The joint venture partners acquired the Red Top Dairy production facility in Fairfield, California, funded a comprehensive renovation of the entire plant, and opened for business in 1981.

Just 20 days after starting operations, the remodeled plant burned to the ground, when a blowtorch accidentally severed a hydraulic line and the workman using it ran, leaving the still ignited blowtorch on the floor. The joint venture group brought a suit against the workman's company, but it took nearly five years for them to collect money for damages. In the end, a pretrial settlement provided the group with $23 million in dam-

ages, $11 million for the cost of the building and $12 million in compensation for lost profits.

The Mid-Valley joint venture group didn't wait, however, to start rebuilding their facility. Approximately two years after the fire, Mid-Valley Diary was rebuilt and housed the most sophisticated computerized fluid milk processing plant in the United States. One of the plant's most important achievements was the bottling and selling of milk in one-half gallon plastic containers, the first operation west of Arkansas to do so. The Fairfield plant provided Raley's, Bel-Air, and Save Mart with a competitive edge against larger stores. The joint venture group was so pleased with the results that they decided to open a second dairy processing plant in Turlock, California, in 1988. Products soon expanded from milk, butter, and ice cream to include purified drinking water, orange juice, and, in conjunction with Rainbow Bread Company, the sale of bread at competitive prices.

The founder and guiding light of Raley's, Tom Raley, died in 1992. Tom Raley was still active in various aspects of the company's management up to his death, and then Charles Collings assumed full control of the responsibilities as chief executive officer and president. During the change in leadership, Raley's decided to purchase one of its partners in the Mid-Valley joint venture. The acquisition of Bel Air Markets, a 17-unit local competitor, boosted Raley's annual volume up to sales of nearly $1.8 billion. Bel Air Markets consisted of a group of high-volume superstores that had developed a reputation throughout California for superb quality and excellent customer service. Allowing Bel Air to keep its name enabled Raley's to capitalize on the good name recognition of its new subsidiary.

In 1993, Raley's decided to expand its joint venture with the remaining partner of the Mid-Valley group, Save Mart Supermarkets, and construct a 100,000-square-foot frozen food distribution center. The joint venture group had already grown from its two dairy plants to include an ice cream plant and a dry goods warehouse. The purpose of the new facility was to get lower prices through larger volume discounts, and eliminate the wholesale agent for each part of the joint venture. The distribution facilities, in addition to a marketing and merchandising division, were handled by the joint venture's wholly owned subsidiary, Super Store Industries.

During the mid-1990s, Raley's began to move away from the image of a family-run business and implemented management and operational strategies that improved the position of the company as one of the giant superstore chains in California and Nevada. The company made it a priority to hire managers and executives from outside Raley's, in order to strengthen its professionalism and broaden the scope of its high-level employees. Raley's also initiated a new merchandising strategy that included in-store, sit-down cafes and customer service centers. With the acquisition of Bel Air Market, Raley's intended to augment its combination store format with an alternative superstore format.

Raley's devised three extremely innovative strategies that began to bear fruit in the mid-1990s. The first of these innovations involved the remodeling of the company's pharmacies to include a consulting area for customers and pharmacists. One of the reasons management embarked upon this innovation was to make it easier for company pharmacies to comply with California legislation that required drug counseling to be given with every new prescription. The second innovation was the development of a very broad health and beauty aid line of products in almost all of its stores. With this additional line of products, Raley's believed it could become more competitive with superstore giants such as Safeway and Kmart. Perhaps the single most innovative strategy Raley's has developed is the child care program. Called Play Care, six of Raley's stores offers child care services for its customers, which has resulted in higher sales volumes at those locations. Customers can shop while their children, from ages 2 through 8, are taken care of in supervised play areas for up to two hours.

In 1995, Raley's total revenues approximated $1.8 billion, and the company operated 81 stores. All of the company's stores are extremely well managed, and both sales and profits continue to climb. With its astute management keenly aware of the trends in merchandising, Raley's is on the road to successfully competing with such national superstore chains as Target and Walmart.

Principal Subsidiaries: Bel Air Markets.

Further Reading:

Bauer, Bob, ''Save Mart and Raley's Adding Frozen Depot,'' *Supermarket News,* December 27, 1993, pp. 31–32.
Flood, Ramona G., ''Raley's to Redesign, Expand Its HBC Line,'' *Supermarket News,* July 10, 1995, p. 31.
Hansen, Betty, *Raley's: A Family Store,* Sacramento: Raley's, Inc., 1989.
O'Leary, Chris, ''Raley's Finds Resistance to Automated Schedules,'' *Supermarket News,* July 4, 1994, p. 11.
''Raley's to Buy Bel Air,'' *Supermarket News,* June 1, 1992, p. 50.
Roberts, Gail, ''Raley's Computerizes Front-End Scheduling,'' *Supermarket News,* January 17, 1994, p. 31.
Slezak, Michael, ''Raley's Goes Deep,'' *Supermarket News,* August 1, 1994, pp. 41–48.
Zimmerman, Denise, ''Food Source to Use Open-System PCs,'' *Supermarket News,* November 28, 1994, p. 15.
Zwiebach, Elliot, ''Raley's New Direction,'' *Supermarket News,* May 3, 1993, pp. 1–4.

—Thomas Derdak

The Rank Organisation

The Rank Organisation Plc

6 Connaught Place
London W2 2EZ
England
71-706-1111
Fax: 71-262-9886

Public Company
Incorporated: 1937 as Odeon Theatres Holdings Ltd.
Employees: 39,700
Sales: £2.2 billion (US$3.3 billion)
Stock Exchanges: London Toronto Amsterdam Frankfurt
    Brussels NASDAQ
SICs: 7812 Motion Picture and Video Production; 5049
    Professional Equipment, Not Elsewhere Classified; 5065
    Electronic Parts & Equipment, Not Elsewhere Classified;
    3825 Instruments to Measure Electricity

The Rank Organisation Plc maintains a diversified array of holdings primarily in the film and television industries, but it also owns various holiday, recreation, and leisure businesses. Among these operations are the Odeon cinema chain in England; various holiday parks and centers in Europe; bingo parlors and casinos in England, Canada, and Spain; and Hard Rock Cafes around the world. Rank also owns a half-share of the Universal Studios Florida theme park in Orlando. Resting wholly outside this fairly interrelated group of enterprises is a partial share of Rank Xerox, a joint venture with the Xerox Corporation. Throughout much of its history, Rank Xerox has supplied a disproportionate share of Rank's profits.

The overall picture of Rank remains rather confusing until one understands that its history falls into two very distinct parts. When Joseph Arthur Rank (later dubbed Lord Rank) founded the conglomerate in 1935, he quickly assembled the dominant motion picture combine in Great Britain, with interests in everything from the manufacture of cameras to Lawrence Olivier's interpretation of *Henry V.* Twenty years later the nation's film business was suffering, so Rank made a deal with a little-known American company to market the company's products everywhere outside of the western hemisphere. That company was Xerox, and since then the only real task for the managers at Rank has been to decide how to intelligently utilize the endless profits generated by its partnership. Continually seeking to

diversify in order to lessen its fiscal dependence on Rank Xerox, the Rank Organisation has followed a wobbly course of expansion into a variety of areas without managing to correct its fundamental, though hardly fatal, imbalance, although it began to do so when it sold part of its stake in Rank Xerox in 1995.

The story of Rank's emergence as the leading film magnate in Great Britain is complex and closely bound up with the history of British film as a whole. Joseph Arthur Rank was born in 1888 to a wealthy Yorkshire flour miller—His father was the founder of today's Ranks Hovis McDougall, one of Britain's leading food companies. The younger Rank first became interested in film as a means to spread the truths of the Methodist religion, to which he was deeply devoted. Working with a group called the Religious Film Society, he paid for the 1934 production of *Mastership,* and shortly thereafter joined a like-minded millionaire, Lady Yule, in founding Pinewood Studios. Rank soon decided to leave religion in the pulpit. Taking advantage of his growing connections in the film world, he began to produce and distribute popular entertainment. The board of directors of Pinewood included members from the boards of the British and Dominion Film Corporation and British National Films Ltd., two of the country's leading production houses. British and Dominion also had an agreement with United Artists (UA), the American film company, whereby the latter distributed Dominion films in Great Britain. From this nucleus of financiers and film makers would grown one-third of Rank's empire; the production division.

In March 1936, Rank and four other men formed the General Cinema Finance Company (GCFC), with enough capital to allow its subsequent acquisition of General Film Distributors Ltd. (GFD), the basis of Rank's future distribution business. GFD's board included members of the British and Dominion board, which formed an important link between GFD and United Artists—as will become apparent, Rank was a lover of intricate corporate strategy. Also in 1936, Rank and a group of American and British investors brought a controlling interest in one of the American "majors," Universal Pictures. As a result, GFD became the distribution arm of Universal in Britain. Another thread in Rank's densely woven corporate cable was represented by A. H. Giannini, a member of the new Universal board of directors who also happened to be the president and chairman of United Artists. In this way, Rank tightened his links with the critically important Hollywood industry and its vast American market.

Having solidified his interests in production and distribution, Rank needed only a circuit of theaters to complete a vertically integrated film combine. As of 1936, the two leading circuits in Great Britain were Gaumont-British and ABPC (Associated British Pictures Corporation), but Odeon Theatres Ltd. was a rising power. In May 1937, Odeon had purchased a rival company's theaters to secure its position as the third major circuit, with some 250 cinemas in the country. Odeon was already half-owned by United Artists, making it a kind of second cousin to Rank's growing interests. Also closely allied to UA was the important London Film Productions Ltd., managed by Alexander Korda and the owner of large new studios at Denham. Toward the end of 1938, Rank began putting together these many pieces. In December he merged his Pinewood Studios with the extensive complex at Denham (creating D & P Studios). and in the following year GCFC added to its production capacity with the purchase of the Amalgamated studios at Elstree. Finally, and most significantly, Rank acquired an interest in Odeon Theatres by subscribing (via GCFC) to its issue of debentures.

Odeon Theatres was soon in grave financial difficulties. The holding company which controlled it, Odeon Cinema Holdings Ltd., turned to Rank for assistance, and he soon became a 50 percent owner along with United Artists (because of certain peculiarities in the company's rules, Rank was able to outvote his partner despite their equal stakes). At about the same time, GCFC was able to buy the holding company that ran the Gaumont-British theaters, giving Rank effective control over approximately 619 cinemas, or one-fifth of the total in Britain. Through a complicated series of holding companies, all of the above-named entities and some 80 subsidiaries were ultimately owned by Manorfield Investments Ltd., a private corporation in turn owned by Arthur Rank and his wife. This tidy arrangement allowed Rank to exert personal control over a vast segment of the British film industry, with commanding positions in all three of the industry's basic components—production, distribution, and exhibition. His dominance is perhaps best illustrated by the fact that of 63 new films made in Britain in 1948, more than half were produced by Rank's empire.

Many of Rank's acquisitions were made possible by the slump that overtook the business in 1938. Inspired by the success of Alexander Korda's 1933 hit, *The Private Life of Henry VIII,* English producers convinced themselves that they could compete with Hollywood in the high-budget blockbuster market. They were wrong, and the failure of numerous costly films during the next few years drove many companies to the brink of bankruptcy. Rank took advantage of the buyer's market to complete the integrated group of holdings outlined above, purchasing for about £1.7 million assets later estimated to have had a market value of £50 million.

Such conspicuous success attracted its share of resistance. After its 1941 buyout of Gaumont-British, the Rank Organisation had grown sufficiently large to merit the accusation of monopoly. In 1944, the government's Palache Report made several recommendations about how best to curb the growth of the combines while encouraging a healthy degree of independent production. Rank agreed to seek government approval before he bought more theaters, but as he already held a commanding lead over his nearest rivals, the agreement did little to change the industry's excessive concentration.

The government did, however, manage indirectly to bring about the decline of Rank's power. In an effort to redress the growing imbalance in U.S.-British trade, the Labor government instituted in 1947 the so-called Dalton duty, a prohibitively high tax on all foreign films distributed in the country. In retaliation, Hollywood refused to release any films at all in Great Britain, at which point the latter's film industry, led by the highly patriotic Rank, offered to step up production to fill the gap. The year 1948 marked the zenith of British production, with Rank showing the way. But in March the government abruptly reversed itself and lifted the duty, precipitating an avalanche of high-

quality American imports. More hastily produced British films were destroyed at the box office, none more so than Rank's. For the fiscal year ending June 1949, the group lost a painful £3.35 million.

1948 signaled the beginning of a long decline for the British film industry in general, and for Rank in particular. Despite his still-dominant position in all three aspects of the business, Rank could hardly continue to suffer the huge losses incurred after the 1948 debacle. But even after cutting his production drastically, Rank faced a complex of more formidable problems. The war years had actually boosted theater attendance, as war-weary British citizens sought escape. By 1950, however, relative prosperity encouraged a raft of new leisure resources, none more important than the automobile and the emerging television industry. The cumulative effect of these and other changes was a fall in theater attendance during the postwar years from 1.6 billion tickets sold in 1946 to only 400 million in 1963. The golden age of cinema had passed, and those producers who survived did so by moving quickly into other fields. Rank and his managing director, John Davis, proceeded to do just that, searching for allied industries in which to make use of the company's expertise and financial muscle. They really found only one such nugget in 20 years of prospecting, but it turned out to be a big one.

Rank's search for alternatives to the film business led him and Davis in two distinct directions, accounting for the oddly bifurcated nature of Rank's portfolio today. On the one hand, Davis tried to exploit the enemy, as it were, by expanding Rank interests into competing leisure and entertainment fields. He first closed down many of the large Odeon theaters; total Rank holdings fell from a postwar peak of 507 cinemas to around 350 by the end of the 1950s. The vacant theaters were either used as real estate for development by one of Rank's newly formed construction companies or were converted into bowling alleys, dance halls, and bingo parlors. The company also took a stab at the burgeoning record business in the late 1950s, and began investing in the new American-style motels and service areas needed alongside Britain's new system of highways. Most promising of all, Rank bought a piece of the television industry, taking a 37.5 percent interest in the Southern Television Corporation, which served several million homes by the end of the decade.

But none of these project proved more than briefly successful: Bowling alleys and large dance halls were largely passé by the early 1960s; the Rank record business failed utterly; Rank's motels and restaurants were not well situated; and even the television station failed to take off as Rank and Davis had expected. Rank had better luck in the other half of its diversification drive; precision industries and electronics.

Always involved in film producing and processing, Rank was well positioned to expand into new applications of similar technology. Among other companies, it acquired Taylor Hobson, a manufacturer of lenses and precision measuring instruments, and Cintel, an image processing concern. Soon thereafter, Rank began to make and sell television sets in its own retail outlets. The electronics program was much more successful than Rank's leisure ventures, but the company's future did not fully reveal itself until Rank Xerox began its spectacular rise in the early 1960s.

The connection between the two companies dates back ten years earlier, when Rank began making lenses for a new American manufacturer of copying machines called the Haloid Company. Its president, Joseph Wilson, had bought the rights to a dry-copy technique that could be used with nearly any type of paper—a great improvement over the later generation of copiers, which required specially treated paper and liquid toner. To take advantage of his find, called "xerography," Wilson needed a large amount of money and worldwide marketing strength. The Rank Organisation had both, and in 1956 an agreement was formed whereby Rank undertook to manufacture and sell (or lease) xerographic machines everywhere except in the Americas. A new company was formed, eventually to be called Rank Xerox (RX), of which Rank owned 48.8 percent of the equity but only one-third of the profit above a certain minimum. Xerox controlled and managed the joint venture while Rank supplied some cash, the manufacturing facilities, and a distribution network. In 1956 it was far from certain that this venture would turn into anything more than another good idea, and John Davis in particular must be credited with the foresight and courage needed to make the initial investment. Two other leaders in the field, IBM and Gestettner, had already declined to put their money on the line.

By the early 1960s Rank had entered the era of Rank Xerox: RX's sales soared from $7 million in 1962 to $276 million in 1969. Its success was so great that the Rank Organisation's other activities became of "academic interest only," as one financial analyst commented at the time. In 1965 the two divisions contributed equally to total Rank profit, but three years later RX profits were four times those generated by the rest of Rank (£33 million to £8.4 million). This treadmill continued to spin for quite a few years. While Rank muddled its way in and out of investments in both the leisure and technology fields, making a few pounds here and there, its Xerox associate churned out profits as if they too could be duplicated at the press of a button. By 1982, this tail-wags-dog situation had reached the point where the rest of Rank's many businesses contributed only 7 percent to the company's overall profit, while RX brought in 93 percent. Davis, Rank CEO from 1962 to 1977, seemed somewhat embarrassed by the reduction of his once-mighty empire to the role of coupon-clipper, and for that reason strove to establish the company in other areas. The results were not good. In 1971, Rank made $17 million on non-Xerox assets of about $204 million. 11 years later, it garnered only $7 million on assets worth twice that much. While RX forged ahead, Rank fell behind.

In the meantime, the world copier market caught up with Xerox. By the end of the 1970s, heavy Japanese competition cut into RX's profit and its market share. The combination of ineffective Rank management and a cooling RX sent investors into a panic. In 1976, institutional investors with large holdings in Rank pushed through a rules change enabling them to exercise closer control over the troubled company. By 1983 brokers were speculating that the organization might be taken over by corporate raiders and its substantial assets sold off to those who could manage them more profitably.

By 1988, however, Rank seemed to have rebounded under the management of its new CEO, Michael Gifford. All but one of its divisions reported a healthy increase in profits in 1988, and the balance of earnings between Rank and RX was closer to a 50–50 split. The holidays and recreation division had become the company's largest, and its collection of resorts and travel interests netted a robust £58 million on sales of £276 million in 1988.

Under Gifford's direction, Rank made additional investments and acquisitions in its core leisure, recreation, and holidays operations during the next several years. In 1988 Rank entered into a partnership with MCA to build the $600 million Universal Studios Florida theme park in Orlando. Rank invested £115 million for a 50 percent interest in the project, which opened in 1990 and by 1994 was attracting seven million visitors a year and generating £11.4 million in profits for Rank. In 1995 MCA and Rank began work on a $2 billion expansion that would include a second theme park called Islands of Adventure, scheduled to open in 1999.

In 1990 Rank offered to acquire Mecca Leisure Group for £512 million ($819 million). Mecca's management initially rejected the offer, then suddenly accepted it two months later. Mecca's holdings—hotels, theme parks, 85 bingo parlors, and 11 Hard Rock Cafes—fit in well with Rank's operations. Under Rank, some of these operations were expanded, such as the Hard Rock Cafes—That chain grew to 15 units by 1995—while others were closed or sold off, such as the hotels, the last of which Rank sold in 1994.

With these additions, Rank's revenue surged from £1.33 billion in 1990 to £2.11 billion in 1991. Over the next few years, revenue increased only slightly to £2.2 billion in 1994. Surprisingly, the increase in revenue did not reduce the firm's dependence on its Rank Xerox stake. The amount of profits owing to RX surpassed 50 percent once again by the mid-1990s. Rank made a move to lessen the role of RX in the company's future; In January 1995 it sold to Xerox 40 percent of its interest in RX for £620 million. Rank intended to use the funds to invest in leisure and recreation businesses.

This was perhaps a fitting time for a leadership transition at Rank since it was Gifford who had consistently focused on leisure and recreation during his reign at Rank and now had reduced its stake in its most important holding outside this area. Gifford announced in 1995 that he would retire in 1996. Rank searched for a new leader.

The question for Rank at this point in its history was whether it would invest its Rank Xerox money wisely, since what the firm did with its excess money had often been its downfall in the past. Signs indicated that Rank would increasingly concentrate on the leisure, recreation, and entertainment industries through the rest of the 1990s and that perhaps it would sell its entire stake in Rank Xerox to provide additional funding for expansion.

Principal Subsidiaries: Associated Leisure Limited; Butlin's Limited; Grosvenor Clubs Limited; Haven Leisure Limited; A. Kershaw & Sons, PLC (85%); Odeon Cinemas Limited; Pinewood Studios Limited; Rank Amusements Limited; Rank Brimar Limited; Rank Cintel Limited; Rank Film Distributors Limited; Rank Film Laboratories Limited; Rank Holdings (UK) Limited; Rank Holidays & Hotels Limited; Rank Leisure Limited; Rank Overseas Holdings Limited; Rank Precision Industries (Holdings) Limited (94%); Rank RX Holdings Limited (97%); Rank Taylor Hobson Limited; Rank Video Services Limited; Rank Xerox Limited (48.8%); Shearings Limited; Strand Lighting Limited; Top Rank Limited; Warner Holidays Limited; Film House Partnership (Canada); Rank Video Services G.m.b.H. (Germany); Rank Holdings (Netherlands) B.V.; Deluxe Laboratories Inc. (U.S.); Hard Rock Cafe International Inc. (U.S.); Rank America Inc. (U.S.); Rank Development Inc. (U.S.); Rank Leisure USA Inc.; Rank Orlando, Inc. (U.S.); Rank Taylor Hobson Inc. (U.S.); Rank Video Services America Inc. (U.S.); Resorts USA Inc.; Strand Lighting Inc. (U.S.).

Further Reading:

Armes, Roy, *A Critical History of the British Cinema,* New York: Oxford University Press, 1978, 374 p.

Daneshkhu, Scheherazade, ''From Hard Times to Hard Rock,'' *Financial Times,* September 27, 1995, p. 23.

Ferry, Jeffrey, ''Rank Returns to Its Roots,'' *Forbes,* August 6, 1990, pp. 60–61.

''Political and Economic Planning (PEP),'' *The British Film Industry,* London, 1952.

Rank Organisation Plc Annual Reports, London: Rank Organisation Plc, 1941–94.

Smith, Terry, ''The Good, the Bad, and the Ugly,'' *Management Today,* September 1995, pp. 54–60.

—Jonathan Martin
—updated by David E. Salamie

Bioscience

Roche Bioscience

3401 Hillview Avenue
Palo Alto, California 94304
U.S.A.
(415) 855-5050
Fax: (415) 855-5526

Wholly Owned Subsidiary of Roche Holding Ltd.
Incorporated: 1957 as Syntex Corporation
Employees: 10,300
Sales: $2.09 billion
Stock Exchanges: Basel Geneva Zurich
SICs: 2834 Pharmaceutical Preparations; 2819 Industrial
   Inorganic Chemicals, Not Elsewhere Classified; 8731
   Commercial, Physical & Biological Research

Roche Bioscience was formed in 1995 following the acquisition of Syntex Corp. by Roche Holding Ltd. in November 1994. Roche, a Swiss pharmaceutical company, is one of the largest in the world with 56,000 employees and sales of SFr 14.7 billion in 1994. Roche took advantage of Syntex's strong research foundation and its location in California's high-tech Silicon Valley to create an organization that would focus on bringing new pharmaceutical products to market through scientific research and strategic marketing. Roche Bioscience consists primarily of two business areas, a neurobiology unit and a musculoskeletal/auto-immune business unit, that are working to develop new drug treatments for prostate disease, incontinence, pain, osteoporosis, osteoarthritis, rheumatoid arthritis and other inflammatory conditions. After purchasing Syntex, Roche Holding Ltd. became the fourth largest drug maker in the world and the largest in terms of market capital. Syntex USA continued in existence as a legal entity for continuing patents and contracts previously held by Syntex Corporation.

Syntex was founded in 1944 in Mexico by two German refugees. The company concentrated its efforts on research and manufacturing bulk steroid chemicals. After World War II, the work of two new employees, George Rosenkranz and Carl Djerassi, was responsible for changing the direction of Syntex's business. Rosenkranz and Djerassi pioneered research in the synthesis of compounds that led to the development of oral contraceptives. Not recognizing the potential of this groundbreaking work, Syntex's original owners wanted to continue producing bulk chemicals rather than invest in new develop-

ments. Syntex's fortunes changed when a Wall Street financier, Charles Allen, Jr., decided to invest in the company. Allen was the senior partner of Allen & Company, one of the leading investment banking firms in the United States. Allen was respected for his financial prowess and also for his ability to predict industry trends and evaluate securities. When Allen decided Syntex was a good prospect, other Wall Street investors followed with the loyalty of an army behind its commander.

In 1951 Allen became half-owner of the Ogden Corporation. Several companies were added to Ogden Corporation as subsidiaries, including Syntex. The acquisition of Syntex, however, created tax problems. As a result, Syntex was sold in 1958 to Ogden stockholders for only two dollars a share. Allen & Company ended up with about 40 percent, or over one million, of the 4.5 million Syntex shares outstanding.

Syntex was registered as a Panamanian company. Tax advantages convinced company management to reestablish business in Central America where much of the company's products were shipped through Panama's free zone. When Rosenkranz, a Hungarian-born naturalized Mexican citizen, became the company president, he kept headquarters in Mexico City even as Syntex's growing U.S. concern shifted the company's geographic emphasis. The company's independent stature enabled it to reach an agreement with Eli Lilly and Company, one of the industry leaders. Syntex's experience with producing bulk steroid chemicals (sex hormones had been extracted from the Mexican barbasco root) prepared it to enter the growing contraceptive market. The arrangement with Lilly paid for half of certain research costs at Syntex in exchange for Lilly's rights to market the results of that research. Instead of asking for royalties or fixed-price contracts from other major drug firms, Syntex arranged an innovative agreement where it earned a percentage of what those firms earned. Thus Syntex gained quick access not only to Lilly, but to Johnson & Johnson, Schering and Ciba-Geigy, all major manufacturers of oral contraceptives.

The company achieved Wall Street notoriety in the early 1960s when stock prices reached as much as 100 times earnings. By 1964 Syntex became a case in point of the virtues and vices of "a bubbling speculative market." Since the company was financed by such a prominent Wall Street figure, since contraceptives had become more popular and, finally, since 150,000 shares on file for registration in Washington promised a future stock option program, Syntex's stock price increased from a low in 1962 of 11 to a high in 1964 of 190. This enthusiasm was bolstered by a three-for-one stock split and a *Wall Street Journal* cover story on birth control. To the horror of some financial experts, the company market value peaked at $855 million while sales for the year were only $16 million.

Problems began to arise during the 1970 Senate hearings on the adverse affects of birth control pills. Sales dropped ten percent and earnings fell almost 50 percent. The price of Syntex stock mirrored these trends. The price slipped from over $80 to less than $20 a share. Although prices did eventually climb to another high of $113, this would not be the last time Syntex stockholders would experience such a volatile period of stock market valuations. Syntex management realized that the Senate hearing had seriously threatened the company's viability. Action was necessary in order to ensure that future company profits were no longer dependent on one product, namely, the sale of contraceptives. As a result of that experience, Syntex embarked on an effort to expand into a full-line manufacturer of pharmaceuticals.

The company had begun marketing products under its own label in the mid-1960s. In 1973 an independent marketing team was established with 400 salespeople operating in the United States and in foreign subsidiaries. Product expansion continued into the topical corticoid market. Aarane, an antiasthma drug, was also introduced on the market. Syntex had a large success with Naproxen, a nonsteroidal anti-inflammatory drug used to relieve arthritis symptoms. One year after being released abroad, it became the best selling product in its field in Mexico.

Through acquisitions Syntex moved into the fields of animal health and dental equipment. By 1973 the dental division accounted for 6.5 percent of sales and the animal health division generated 22 percent of sales. One successful product in the animal health division was Synovex, a natural cattle hormone that captured more than 50 percent of the market when diethylstilbestrol (DES), a synthetic hormone, was banned by the Food & Drug Administration.

Sales figures increased as a result of Syntex's new product development and marketing efforts. In 1972, sales reached $130 million, a nearly 30 percent increase from 1971. Net income surpassed $18 million and Syntex boasted a 21 percent profit margin, the highest in the industry for that year. Oral contraceptives accounted for only 28 percent of sales and 35 percent of profits, whereas in 1966 they accounted for 47 percent of profits.

Syntex's Palo Alto research center became the focal point of the company's expansion. Located near Stanford University, Syntex's highly respected research center displayed a sign designating it the company's U.S. headquarters. Domestic operations accounted for 60 percent of Syntex's sales. Research Director Djerassi earned the company even greater respect when he strengthened the research organization by recruiting talent through post-doctoral fellowships.

By the mid-1970s Syntex's plan to expand its product line and increase profits with two new drugs, Aarane and Naprosyn, had not progressed according to schedule. Due to the fact that sales of steroid drugs had reached a peak, Syntex executives had planned on Aarane capturing up to 75 percent, or $40 million, of the market. However, Aarane sales had reached only $6 million annually by 1976. For this reason the sale of Naprosyn became a company imperative.

The new antiarthritic was released in the United States during May 1976. Although sales registered at a high of $20 million annually, the timing for the release of this drug could not have been less fortunate for Syntex executives. The FDA, under pressure from consumer and Congressional criticism, began to regulate drug testing procedures more strictly. The agency charged that lab tests for Naprosyn, conducted by an independent contractor, were invalid. The FDA argued that by failing to fully investigate laboratory tests revealing long-term animal toxicity, the administration of these tests had not adhered to proper federal guidelines.

With the price of Syntex stock declining, company president Albert Bowers traveled to Washington confident that he could delay the FDA's plan to hold a hearing on Naprosyn. While the FDA did agree to allow Syntex a 24-month period to conduct a replacement study in support of Naprosyn's safety, company earnings declined for five consecutive quarters as a factor of the FDA encounter. With the end of the FDA investigation in sight, however, renewed promotional efforts behind the sale of Naprosyn, as well as an overall operating increase, helped Syntex to resume its expansion and growth. At this time, the drug was being marketed throughout the world with the exception of Japan, which represented a major untapped market. With the Japanese government awaiting FDA approval, worldwide sales of Naprosyn promised large financial returns.

By 1978 Bowers boasted of a "strong resumption of growth in earnings" as both sales and profits reached record levels. With sales reaching $400 million, Bowers could point to Naprosyn as a large contributing factor to these impressive figures. The FDA, still awaiting test results on toxicity of the drug, continued to threaten Syntex with removal of the drug from the market should the results be unsatisfactory. With an approval for marketing the drug in Japan, however, and a new drug application submitted to the FDA for naproxen sodium (later to be sold as Anaprox, a drug useful not only in the treatment of soft tissue inflammation and dysmenorrhea, but also as an analgesic), Bowers announced a $1 billion sales goal for the mid-1980s.

In 1979, Syntex continued to report record earnings, but the year also marked a period of lawsuits. A large number of British women filed suit against Syntex contending they had been harmed by using the company's birth control pill. One plaintiff charged the company with withholding information about dangerous side effects of the pill after she suffered a severe stroke. She sought $1 million in damages because, her counsel argued, she was unable to lead a normal life. That same year Syntex agreed to settle out of court all pending lawsuits with Syntex shareholders and Industrial Bio-Test Laboratories, the independent lab responsible for the Naprosyn testing. The class action lawsuit alleged that IBT laboratories were inefficient in performing and reporting a study of the drug. While the company admitted no wrongdoing and was still awaiting FDA response to its resubmitted tests, a $2.75 million settlement fund was established. Syntex contributed $575,000 to the fund along with contributions from IBT and Syntex's insurance company.

The lawsuits did not seem to affect worldwide sales of the drug. By 1979, sales for Naprosyn reached $27.7 million in the second quarter and $56 million in the first half of the year. International sales of the drug accounted for 60% of total sales. A merger was completed by June of the same year with Den-Tal-Ez, a dental equipment manufacturer. With one lawsuit settled, good sales and expanding business, Syntex's future looked promising.

In the early 1980s, however, a new problem threatened Syntex's prosperity. The U.S. House of Representatives Subcommittee on Oversight and Investigations charged the company with failing to take action to protect the health of infants when reports linked Syntex-manufactured baby formulas to metabolic alkalosis. The company had removed salt from Neo-Mull-Soy and Cho-Free in response to evidence that salt intake by infants could possibly lead to hypertension when these infants became adults. Reports that babies who were given the formula were failing to gain weight and had lost their appetites led to a product recall in August of 1979. As a result, the National Institute of Health began a five-year follow-up study on the health of the afflicted children. In 1985, a $27 million verdict was awarded to two boys who sustained brain damage allegedly due to the salt removal from the formulas. The verdict represented the largest personal injury sum awarded in Illinois.

During this time, Albert Bowers replaced George Rosenkranz as the company's chief executive officer. With a Ph.D. in organic chemistry and 24 years with the company, Bowers was considered to be highly qualified for the position vacated by Rosenkranz. Bowers himself said that the move from the laboratory to the executive office was challenging, but that his strong background in chemical research was an invaluable asset in making him an effective leader.

Despite legal problems, Syntex continued to expand during the early and mid-1980s. The Den-Tal-Ez acquisition contributed to a third of total sales in 1980. Polycon contact lenses, still in the test stage, were predicted to earn $5 to $10 million in sales. Anaprox, the brand name for naproxen sodium, was selling quite well in foreign markets while awaiting FDA approval. The French pharmaceutical manufacturer Laroche Navarron was purchased and Syntex also announced plans to establish a subsidiary in Osaka.

Syntex also moved into the growing field of genetic engineering. The president of Syntex's diagnostics division viewed the laboratory work of several Seattle microbiologists and suggested a contract be drawn up where Syntex would pay $3 million for their research in exchange for the rights to manufacture and market tests developed for sexually transmissible diseases. When the agreement produced four successful products, a new venture was organized called Oncogen where Syntex and the microbiologists split profits 50–50. Later Bristol-Meyers was invited to join the venture by contributing $12 million. Eventually, however, the scientists sold their entire interest to Bristol-Meyers for $300 million. Bowers then proceeded to sell Syntex's portion of the venture to Bristol-Meyers and concentrated on in-house cancer research.

By 1988, Syntex had surpassed Bowers' goal of $1 billion in sales with revenues of $1.1 billion. Its naproxen and naproxen sodium products, sold as Naprosyn and Anaprox respectively, had performed so well that naproxen became the fifth best-selling prescription drug in the world and the third best in the United States and accounted for over 50 percent of Syntex's sales. However, a new problem faced the company: the patent on naproxen would expire in 1993, opening Syntex's best profit-maker to low-cost competition from generic drug manufacturers. Rather than reap the profits until the patent expired and accept a decrease in sales as the drug's market share shrank to name-brand loyal consumers, Syntex decided to invest in improving production techniques and reducing costs to stay competitive with the generic producers. Production costs had already come down 35 percent in real terms over the last seven years. To further improve efficiency, Syntex invested $9 million in a naproxen technology center in Boulder, Colorado, and planned to spend an additional $35 million over five years to

test three new processes for making the substance. The company also agreed at the time to form a joint venture with Procter & Gamble to manufacture and market an over-the-counter version of naproxen. These companies planned to have the nonprescription version approved by the FDA and in the marketplace before the expiration of Syntex's patent.

To diversify the source of future earnings after the expiration of the naproxen patent, Syntex saw the need to bring new money-making products to market and boost international sales. In 1988, *Financial World* reported that Syntex spent a higher percentage of sales on research and development than any other company, spending 17 percent compared to the industry average of 13 percent. In mid-1988, researchers presented the results of studies on a new drug being developed by Syntex, Ticlid. The drug, developed to prevent strokes by thinning the blood, was found to be more effective than aspirin in preventing strokes since patients with stroke-like symptoms who were subsequently treated with Ticlid had 21 percent fewer strokes than those treated with aspirin. Ticlid was also considerably more effective in women than aspirin. Although Ticlid would not be on the market until 1991, some analysts predicted a $750 million annual demand for the drug.

In 1989, Syntex had five new drug applications under review at the Food and Drug Administration. Several new drugs were close to market in several different treatment areas, including Cardene, a calcium channel blocker for use in treating angina and hypertension; Toradol, a high-strength non-addictive pain reliever; Nafarelin, for treating endometriosis; and Cytovene, an AIDS drug. Some of the drugs were meeting with challenges before the FDA, however, and critics attributed Syntex's difficulty in bringing new products to market to spreading too few resources too far.

Despite the promising new research and Syntex's renown as a research house, the company came in last in *Financial World*'s survey of research and development effectiveness over the past decade. Although Syntex had healthy earnings growth during this period, the success was primarily due to profits from Naprosyn sales which generated $700 million of $1.4 billion in sales in 1988. Earnings from new product sales had generated only $200 million. Some analysts attributed Syntex's research and development weakness to the fact that the company was the smallest player in the industry and its available capital too small to compete in the product development game. $200 million was considered the smallest amount of money necessary for research and development. Syntex just barely reached that level by dedicating 17 percent of sales to R & D. Without some big successes, that level of spending would begin to strain the company's finances, especially as the expiration of the naproxen patent approached. Moreover, Ciba-Geigy had recently introduced an anti-arthritic, Voltaren, that took 11 percent of the U.S. market in four months. In view of this crunch, analysts predicted that Syntex would be a prime take-over target.

At the time, the entire pharmaceuticals industry was beginning to undergo dramatic structural changes. Growing costs in research and development and in bringing new products to market required increasing amounts of capital. Companies were seeking opportunities to make their operations more efficient by spreading research dollars over a larger sales base. When

Smith-Kline Beckman and Beecham revealed that they were in merger talks, other mergers were anticipated. Syntex was often cited as a likely target, and the Swiss pharmaceutical manufacturer Hoffmann-LaRoche seemed a likely suitor. Roche was highly capitalized and already had a co-marketing agreement with Syntex. Moreover, Allen & Co. was reportedly trying to sell its remaining six percent share in Syntex, and Hoffmann-LaRoche was reputedly in negotiations for it.

In 1990, Syntex's Cytovene, a treatment for eyesight loss due to retinal tissue damage caused by an infection resulting from AIDS, was approved by the FDA. It was the first approval for such a drug in the United States. The next year, Syntex launched a joint venture with the non-profit Hong Kong Institute of Biotechnology. The venture, HKIB/Syntex, was formed to examine the potential for making drugs from substances used in traditional Chinese medicine preparations. The interest was spawned by increasingly disappointing results from the conventional Western method of creating new drugs by altering the molecular structure of existing drugs.

Syntex and Procter & Gamble's joint venture to produce an over-the-counter version of Naprosyn resulted in the introduction of Aleve in 1994. The FDA approved Aleve in January of that year, the first time in ten years a new over-the-counter pain reliever had been approved. Naprosyn would remain on the market as a prescription anti-arthritic and the non-prescription Aleve would be sold as an analgesic for headache, cold symptoms, toothache, muscle aches, mild arthritis and menstrual cramps. One analyst predicted that Aleve would be the third-best selling non-prescription analgesic by the end of 1995. The $100 million marketing campaign emphasized Aleve's former prescription status and its long-lasting effects. By the end of the fourth week in the stores, Aleve had an impressive 7.5 percent market share by volume, following third after Tylenol and Advil.

The advent of managed care and group purchasing organizations in the late 1980s created a continuing pressure on drug companies' profit margin. Companies responded by cutting sales forces, refining marketing strategies and reducing advertising. Another outgrowth of the squeeze on profits was the continued consolidation of the industry. Four large mergers were formed in 1994, including the purchase for $5.3 billion of Syntex by Roche Holding, the parent company of Hoffmann-LaRoche. The acquisition of Syntex made Roche the fourth largest pharmaceutical company in the world. Some observers

were surprised by the apparently inflated price Roche agreed to pay for Syntex, a premium of 57 percent over its publicly traded stock price. Other observers noted that Syntex's strong U.S. sales position and some promising new products would be valuable to Roche with its deep pockets.

From the merger of Roche and Syntex came Roche Bioscience, a research and product development venture located in Syntex's offices in Palo Alto, California. Syntex U.S.A. still existed as a legal entity for continuing contracts and patents. The new venture, Roche Bioscience, was designed with a flat management structure and integrated but separate research units to facilitate creativity, communication and rapid movement from concept to testing of new product ideas. With Syntex's research strength and U.S. positioning and Roche's financial backing and access to European markets, the new company seemed well-positioned to meet the challenges facing the industry at the end of the century.

Further Reading:

Benoit, Ellen, "Continental Drift," *Financial World,* May 2, 1989, pp. 38–39.

DeNitto, Emily, "American Home Applies Legal Pain to P & G's Aleve," *Advertising Age,* August 15, 1994, p. 4.

"FDA Gives Green Light to OTC Naproxen," *Chemical Marketing Reporter,* January 17, 1994, p. 5.

Gannon, Kathi, "OTC Naproxen Sodium Set to Shake OTC Analgesics," *Drug Topics,* February 7, 1994, p. 34.

Gwynne, Peter, "China's Healing Properties," *Far Eastern Economic Review,* May 16, 1991, p. 82.

Jabon, Jan, "Healthcare's Bitter Pill," *Advertising Age,* August 29, 1994, pp. 1, 8.

LePree, Joy, "Syntex Upsets Bulk Naproxen," *Chemical Marketing Reporter,* April 17, 1995, pp. 7, 14.

Parkinson, Gerald, "Syntex Prepares for the Future," *Chemical Week,* July 20, 1988, pp. 40–41.

Rhein, Reginald, Jr., "Science Finally Strikes Back at Strokes," *Business Week,* August 8, 1988, pp. 50–51.

Starr, Cynthia, "Syntex Laboratories Sets Its Sights on CMV Retinitis," *Drug Topics,* November 5, 1990, pp. 19–20.

Storck, William, ""Drug Firm Consolidation," *Chemical & Engineering News,* May 9, 1994, pp. 4–5.

Teitelman, Robert, and Anthony Baldo, "Grading R & D," *Financial World,* January 24, 1989, pp. 22-24.

Tully, Shawn, "Pill Pushers Get Merger Fever," *Fortune,* May 30, 1994, p. 14.

—updated by Katherine Smethurst

Rosenbluth International Inc.

2401 Walnut Street
Philadelphia, Pennsylvania 19103-4390
U.S.A.
(215) 977-4800
Fax: (215) 977-4026

Private Company
Founded: 1892
Employees: 3,000
Sales: $2.5 billion
SICs: 4724 Travel Agencies; 8742 Management Consulting
Services

Rosenbluth International, Inc. is the world's third largest travel management company. The company offers comprehensive corporate, vacation, and meeting travel services. A family-owned business for more than 100 years, Rosenbluth International has over 1,000 locations in more than 30 countries, and maintains its world headquarters in Philadelphia.

In 1892, Marcus Rosenbluth, a Hungarian immigrant, founded Rosenbluth Travel when he began selling steamship tickets from his Philadelphia neighborhood. For $50, his upstart company provided steamship passage from a European port to New York, helped passengers with their entry into the United States, and then arranged transportation from Ellis Island to Philadelphia.

The business relationship he maintained with his clients went beyond the sale of steamship tickets. Rosenbluth, who spoke nine languages, also became something of a family advisor to clients, giving them information and advice on such subjects as American citizenship. Once the immigrants settled and found jobs, many of them gave Marcus five and ten cents at a time until they had $50 in their account to bring over another family member to America. To help with this business dealing, Rosenbluth held a private banking license in addition to his travel agency license, but gave up the banking business in the 1930s to focus on travel.

Through two World Wars and the Great Depression, Rosenbluth Travel continued to focus on facilitating the immigration of thousands of Europeans entering America and gradually built a reputation for integrity and honesty. The founder's sons Joseph J. and Max Rosenbluth had also entered the busi-

ness, opening larger offices in their original neighborhood back in 1927. World War II, however, brought the company and the rest of the travel industry to a halt.

In 1949, the company moved out of its original neighborhood headquarters into a new office in Philadelphia's main business and shopping sector. That move and the travel industry's post-war development were significant milestones for Rosenbluth Travel. In the early 1950s, Americans became enthusiastic over the idea of leisure travel, and cruises and package trips to Florida became very popular. The package trip, introduced by major airlines of the day, effectively broadened the scope of the market, allowing middle income families to afford and enjoy leisure travel. From Florida, the market expanded further, to include trips to the Caribbean, Mexico, and Europe. Commenting on the company's history to that point in a *Travel Weekly* article, Harold Rosenbluth, grandson of Marcus Rosenbluth, observed: "We note that the families we brought over from Europe in steerage, we eventually sent back to Europe [for a vacation] in first-class cabins on the great ocean liners."

In the early 1950s, the founder's sons Max and Joseph J. Rosenbluth turned over the family business to their own sons, Harold and Joseph W. Rosenbluth, who represented the third generation of Rosenbluth leaders. Along with Joe's sister Cecile Block and her husband Eugene, they ran what Harold referred to as an "oversized mom and pop" emphasizing leisure travel.

Cousins Harold and Joe Rosenbluth both attended the University of Pennsylvania. But while Joe joined the family business immediately after graduation, Harold pursued a law degree and began to practice corporate law. After only a few years as a lawyer, however, Harold left law in 1953 to join his cousin Harold at Rosenbluth Travel.

The company had been steadily gaining a reputation for reliable and personal service, evidenced by their willingness to speak personally to maitre d's and other staff on behalf of their customers and even by meeting their customers at the docks as their cruises returned to New York. Harold and Joe also decided to create more markets for their travel services. In one of their earliest collaborative promotions, Red and Blue Tours, the men obtained a list of students at their alma mater, Penn, and, targeting those students who lived farthest away from school, began offering to arrange for their trips home.

In the mid-1960s, the agency began handling accounts for corporate travel; among its first corporate clients was General Electric Aerospace. In 1967, the company celebrated its 75th anniversary and moved into new headquarters on Philadelphia's Walnut Street. The following year, however, tragedy struck. Joe Rosenbluth was killed when his plane crashed on the way to Puerto Rico.

In the mid-1970s, Harold Rosenbluth prepared to turn the business over to his sons Hal and Lee, who had recently graduated from college. Recalling his father's attitude toward the eventual shift in leadership, Hall remarked in a *Travel Weekly* article that his father "always said that the success of this company is that each generation has known when to let go and let the next generation take over." At the time, as Harold had been quick to discern, potential breakthroughs in computer technology and the deregulation of the airline industry would shake up the travel industry.

Hal and Lee Rosenbluth began by working their way up through the ranks at Rosenbluth Travel. Hal, who eventually became chief executive officer and president, started as a gofer, running errands and stamping brochures. He then worked as a travel consultant before moving up to the corporate travel. Lee, who would become chief operating officer and executive vice-president, started as a reservation agent arranging for hotel rooms and car rentals before serving in the company's bookkeeping department.

During the late 1970s, the emergence of computers, the deregulation of the airlines, and the growth of corporate travel caused tremendous changes at Rosenbluth and in the industry in general. By rapidly adapting to these changes, installing a computer system in their offices, for example, the company was able to experience rapid growth and industry leadership. Annual sales at Rosenbluth Travel climbed from $4 million in 1960 to $35 million in 1970 to $120 million in 1980, before hitting the billion dollar mark in the late 1980s. Rosenbluth's work force increased accordingly, from eight employees in 1960 to over 3,000 in the mid-1990s.

By the early 1980s, Rosenbluth had opened the travel industry's first reservation center, had began actively pursuing corporate accounts, and had introduced an "Airfare Guarantee," under which the firm avowed to always offer the lowest applicable airfare or to refund the difference. Moreover, the company's forays into the corporate travel sector of the market proved tremendously successful, prompting expansion and a shifting of priorities.

Indeed, Rosenbluth's focus had shifted considerably since the late 1950s, when 100 percent of its business was generated from leisure travel. The introduction of corporate travel services as well as meeting organization services offered by Rosenbluth claimed an increasingly important percentage of its total business. In fact, by 1980, the company's reported that 75 percent of its business was for corporate clients, while 20 percent was attributed to leisure travel, and the remaining five percent to what it referred to as meetings and incentives. An important milestone during this time was the 1984 awarding of the Du Pont corporate travel account to Rosenbluth, the largest such contract ever awarded to a travel agency. Moreover by 1995, a full 95 percent of business at Rosenbluth would be attributed to such corporate clients as Bristol-Meyers Squibb, Chevron, Chase Manhattan, Eastman Kodak, General Electric, NBC, and Scott Paper.

Although the leisure segment of Rosenbluth represented less then ten percent of the business in the mid-1990s, it still remained a successful, viable part of the company, producing about $100 million in gross annual sales. Within a marketplace driven by price, the company adhered to his commitment to personal service, offering innovative programs like the "Vacation Promise," which assured that, given certain limitations, Rosenbluth would either remedy any problems clients experienced with land arrangements during Rosenbluth package trips or issue a refund to the client. A Family Vacation Center was also established, featuring a Kids Test Flight Room where

children about to embark on their first airplane flight might see the inside of an airplane and view a video describing a typical flight.

In the late 1980s, Rosenbluth began to expand its presence abroad, forming an international alliance of agencies in foreign countries. By 1992, Rosenbluth had 34 international associate agencies in 37 countries, including Austria, Belgium, France, Greece, Spain, Canada, Argentina, Egypt, Hong Kong, Japan, Saudi Arabia, and elsewhere. This brought the total number of Rosenbluth agencies to 1,280 worldwide. The company was also working on strengthening its presence in South America and opening negotiations in Russia. Global expansion, in fact, prompted the company to change its name to Rosenbluth International in 1992, on its 100th anniversary,

The use and development of computer systems and software also enhanced the growth of Rosenbluth. Regarded as a leader in automating the travel industry, Rosenbluth introduced the travel agency industry's first electronically linked trans-continental data distribution network. Rosenbluth was also the first firm to develop its own back office accounting and client reporting system, which offered corporate clients detailed reports on how their travel dollars were being spent. The company has also pioneered the development of software programs used in making airline reservations and in helping corporate clients evaluate car rental proposals and other travel expenses.

Striving to foster a good workplace environment for Rosenbluth employees, management began espousing an unusual precept: the customer comes second and the employee comes first. Toward that end, all employees are referred to as "associates," they were offered the best equipment and ongoing training programs, and their input on the company has been encouraged by upper management. Hal Rosenbluth co-authored a book about the importance of his organizational structure called *The Customer Comes Second and Other Secrets of Exceptional Service.*

The Rosenbluth management style has been successful for the company, and in 1993 Rosenbluth was named one of the "Ten Best Companies to Work for in America" by *Business and Society Review.* The company was judged on pay and benefits, opportunities for advancement, job security, pride in work and the company, the degree of openness and fairness, and the level of camaraderie among employees.

As the travel industry responded to a changing U.S. work environment and family structure, Rosenbluth continued to develop new and innovative ways to meet these changing needs. Specifically, Hal and Lee Rosenbluth predicted a need for additional corporate services beyond travel and were even considering branching out into janitorial, food, or data processing services. Nevertheless, with over a century of strong family leadership and a proven method of management, Rosenbluth International was poised to remain an industry leader in travel management services into the next century.

Further Reading:

Alter, Allan E., "Tracking System Aids Travelers," *Computerworld,* March 21, 1994, p. 12.

Case, John, "Many Happy Returns," *Inc.,* October 1990, pp. 30–44.

Feuer, Dale, "Rosenbluth Travel: Training in an Unstable Environment," *Training,* May 1986, pp. 63–68.

"Focus on Rosenbluth Travel," supplement to *Travel Weekly,* February 13, 1992, 34 p.

Levering, Robert, "The Ten Best Companies to Work for in America," *Business & Society Review,* Spring 1993, pp. 26–38.

Murphy, Liz, "Family Business: Who's Minding the Store?," *Sales & Marketing Management,* July 1987, pp. 53–55.

Rosenbluth, Hal, "Tales from a Nonconformist Company," *Harvard Business Review,* July/August 1991, pp. 26–36.

Weinstein, Jeff, "Service Lessons form Most-Admired Companies," *Restaurants & Institutions,* December 15, 1994, pp. 34–38.

—Beth Watson Highman

ROUNDY'S®

Roundy's Inc.

23000 Roundy Drive
Pewaukee, Wisconsin 53072
U.S.A.
(414) 547-7999
Fax: (414) 547-4540

Private Company
Founded: 1872 as Smith, Roundy & Co.
Employees: 5,000
Sales: $2.5 billion (1993)
SICs: 5141 Groceries General Line; 5411 Grocery Stores

Roundy's Inc. is the sixth-largest U.S. food wholesaler, supplying more than 1,800 supermarkets across the Midwest. Roundy's serves primarily independent grocers and also operates its own franchise, Pick 'n Save. The company is structured as a cooperative, owned primarily by the retailers it serves. Its member stores range from 5,000-square-foot "superettes" to giant warehouse stores. Roundy's pioneered the warehouse store concept with its successful Milwaukee Pick 'n Save chain. These stores range from 24,000 to 100,000 square feet, and stock from 4,000 to 5,000 items. Warehouse stores compete to offer the lowest prices in each market area by cutting costs in a variety of ways.

Roundy's founder, Judson A. Roundy, came to Milwaukee from Rhode Island. In 1872 he and two partners, Sidney Hauxhurst and William A. Smith, founded a wholesale grocery company called Smith, Roundy & Co. Smith went on to become governor of Wisconsin six years later. The company grew out of its first quarters and moved to a larger building at Milwaukee's Broadway and Buffalo Streets in 1885. This building was destroyed by a famous Milwaukee fire—the 3rd Ward Fire—in 1892. By 1895, the company completed new quarters at the same location.

The firm took on new partners and incorporated in 1902 as Roundy, Peckham & Dexter Co. Its president was Charles Dexter, who had been a partner since 1880 and who continued as president and chairman until his death in 1939. Roundy's began to offer its own private Roundy's brand beginning in 1922, when it introduced Roundy's Salt. The company expanded in the first half of this century until its stockholders numbered about 60, most of whom had inherited their holdings.

In 1953 the firm reorganized as a grocery cooperative, with only independent retailers allowed to hold Roundy's stock. Even the president and other top executives were required to sell their stock and assets unless they were themselves retailers. After this change, Roundy's management set out to offer services to independent grocers that would allow them to compete with large chains. Roundy's retailer-stockholders were offered bookkeeping and payroll services at low cost, and the company held seminars on grocery-related business topics, such as store security and job training.

Roundy's opened a grocery distribution center in Wauwatosa, Wisconsin, in 1955, which grew into a 450,000-square-foot complex on 10 acres of land. The company began to expand rapidly around this time, becoming one of the largest grocery distributors in Wisconsin. Sales reached $50 million in 1962 and then doubled to $100 million in the next nine years. The huge Wauwatosa warehouse stocked close to 9,700 items, including both Roundy's private label and national brand foods. Using rail sidings and over 40 truck loading docks in the early 1970s, the company moved more than 5,000 tons of merchandise a week. Roundy's private label had grown to include about 800 items, and sales in 1972 were close to $115 million. As early as 1972, Roundy's ordering was controlled by computer, and its processing system was also mechanized. Roundy's believed in using the most modern technology available to run its business and was often at the forefront of grocery innovation, particularly in its landmark warehouse stores.

In the recession that began in 1974, the warehouse stores became important. Roundy's management detected changing consumer attitudes as the economy worsened and decided to experiment with a new type of store that would appeal to the budget-conscious. Roundy's rented a vacant discount store in Milwaukee on a short-term lease and opened Pick 'n Save Warehouse Foods in March 1975. The store had minimal decoration and very few perishable items, including no fresh meat and very little produce. The store stood in sharp contrast to the traditional supermarket: packing crates and cases served as the main decor, and untiled floors and plywood walls emphasized the cost-cutting environment. Unique at the time, Pick 'n Save at first drew customers curious to shop in this innovative establishment. Customers used crayons to mark prices on items because the store saved labor by not price-marking, and customers also did their own bagging. The store catered to people doing large-volume shopping, stocking up for a week or two. Pick 'n Save became quite popular, and the store at times had long lines of customers waiting to get in. The warehouse concept proved so successful that Roundy's opened almost 20 more in the next five years, spreading from metropolitan Milwaukee across southern Wisconsin and northern Illinois. Other grocers imitated the warehouse concept as well.

Roundy's sales expanded in the late 1970s even as the economy pulled out of its slump, proving that the warehouse was not just a fad. However, the company's warehouse stores evolved to include more produce and a more finished decor. They began to have brightly painted walls and tiled floors, bringing the look closer to that of the traditional supermarket. But low price remained the essential difference that set the warehouse stores apart. The stores flourished by moving large volumes of stock, most of which was bought at "deal" prices. Low-priced merchandise coupled with the low overhead and inexpensive fixtures of the warehouse kept prices below competitors'. Labor costs were also kept very low. To avoid running a labor-intensive fresh meat counter, most stores offered smoked meats only, and stockwork was simple and fast because much merchandise was displayed on pallets at the ends of aisles. Sales per man hour at Pick 'n Save were said to be almost triple the average at traditional supermarkets, and one Roundy's executive claimed Pick 'n Save could sell 100 cases of groceries for the same labor cost a traditional store would take to sell only 10. Use of electronic scanner technology also allowed Roundy's warehouse stores to control costs. Information from scanners was used to determine exactly which brands and sizes sold best, which was crucial for management to know when buying deal merchandise. By keeping costs down, Roundy's warehouse stores offered consumers consistently low prices, and by 1980 a survey of Milwaukee-area stores found all Roundy's major competitors losing market share, while Roundy's Pick 'n Save chain gained.

Roundy's had 27 Pick 'n Save stores in Wisconsin by 1983. With four stores in the Chicago area, Roundy's strengthened its position in the Chicago market by purchasing Wayco Foods, a suburban grocery. The Wayco acquisition gained Roundy's a 218,000-square-foot warehouse near Chicago's O'Hare airport. Now with a base from which to service its Chicago stores, Roundy's made plans to open 10 to 15 more Pick 'n Saves in the area. This move put Roundy's in competition with other established warehouse-type chains, such as Cub Foods, owned by Super Valu Stores Inc. of Minnesota.

Roundy's continued to expand in the 1980s, with somewhat mixed success. Returns on sales began to slip in 1982, and in 1984 and 1985, revenues were stagnant. Profits fell, and in those two years Roundy's did not pay rebates (equivalent to stockholder dividends) to its member retailers. The company spent $40 million in 1984 to buy Scot Lad Foods, a grocery distributor in Lansing, Illinois. Although this acquisition doubled Roundy's sales, it also increased Roundy's debt. Sales by 1986 were $1.8 billion, coming from the Pick 'n Save chain, wholesale distribution, and stores Roundy's operated under the names Roundy's, Shop-Rite, and United Foods. However, the four Chicago Pick 'n Save stores were not doing well, and Roundy's decided to sell them off. Another venture, a gourmet food retailer, was also not doing well. Roundy's had spent between $1 and $2.5 million to open the gourmet store, called V. Richards, but the store did not quickly turn a profit.

Roundy's chairman and chief executive officer, Vincent R. Little, took early retirement in 1986 after 12 years at the post. After Little's exit, the new C.E.O. appointed two outside directors to Roundy's board and added two new trustees as well. The new directors and trustees came from outside the grocery business and so brought new perspectives on running a firm as large as Roundy's. After this management shift, Roundy's continued to expand through acquisitions. In 1988, the company bought Cardinal Foods Inc., an Ohio-based food distributor, and another Ohio firm, a health and beauty aid distributor called American Merchandising Associates Inc. A year later, Roundy's spent an undisclosed amount of cash on Viking Foods, Inc. This food distributor based in Muskegon, Michigan,

had 1988 sales of $100 million. Roundy's sales had increased significantly by 1988, up to $2.4 billion.

As Roundy's grew, it required more warehouse space to service its retailers. The company leased a new warehouse in Mazomanie, Wisconsin, in 1989, as it ran out of space in its old Wauwatosa facility. Roundy's grew by more than 20 percent between 1988 and 1991, and warehouse space continued to be a problem. In January 1991, the company announced plans to replace its 30-year-old Wauwatosa plant with a 1-million-square-foot warehouse center it would build in Waterloo, Wisconsin. Roundy's wanted to spend $50 million building a state-of-the-art warehouse facility to service more than 170 stores in Wisconsin and Illinois. However, this decision set off a storm of protest from the company's Wauwatosa workers, who were represented by the Teamsters Union. The company would not say whether its 900 employees at the Wauwatosa plant would be offered jobs at the new warehouse, which was about an hour's drive away. Because the Waterloo plant would also be in a different county from Wauwatosa, it would be outside the jurisdiction of the existing union contract. When the Teamster's Union contract expired in July 1991, negotiations on a new contract quickly broke down. Workers objected to Roundy's insistence on its right to relocate its entire warehouse operation at any time. To pre-empt a strike, Roundy's management decided to lock-out its workers. Workers picketed and called for a consumer boycott of stores supplied by Roundy's.

During the bitter contract dispute, another issue surfaced. Roundy's warehouse—like that of its major competitors in the area—was run by a computer, which filed orders from customer stores electronically and then calculated how long it should take human workers to fill each order. The computer set a productivity standard, and Roundy's workers were required under the old contract to achieve 85% of that standard. In its new contract negotiations, Roundy's demanded that workers achieve 100% of the computer's productivity standard. Workers complained that such a goal was impossible and that Roundy's was trying to gain an advantage over its competitors at their expense. Roundy's ended its lock-out after three weeks, then announced that it was changing its plans to build a new warehouse in Waterloo. The company would instead relocate the work done at the Wauwatosa warehouse even farther away, to Westville, Indiana. The company already had a warehouse in Westville, a small town between Gary and South Bend. Though drivers would have to go through Chicago to service Wisconsin stores, Roundy's claimed it had excess capacity in Westville, and the move was reasonable.

Roundy's and the Teamsters Union finally signed a five-year contract in late September 1991. The company abandoned its plans to move either to Westville or to Waterloo, and workers gained a small wage increase and a new productivity standard of 95 percent. Then in April 1992 Roundy's announced plans to add capacity at its Wauwatosa plant and move some work from a Fort Wayne, Indiana, warehouse to its other Wisconsin warehouse in Mazomanie. Without actually adding jobs in Wisconsin, this move did seem to emphasize Roundy's commitment to keeping work in its home state.

By 1994, Roundy's supplied more than 1,800 grocery stores, with distribution centers in Wisconsin, Illinois, Michigan, Indiana, and Ohio. Its Pick 'n Save chain continued to grow in the Milwaukee area. Roundy's had 42 in metropolitan Milwaukee in 1994, with a growing market share said to be between 39 and 47 percent. The newest stores were quite different from the original warehouse stores, though Pick 'n Save continued to be distinguished by low price. Whereas the early stores had no fresh meat and unadorned walls, one newer store boasted an $18,000 imported Italian cappuccino machine in its coffee bar and a reputation as a fine meat market. The stores were tailored to individual neighborhoods and to the owner's taste, and, except for sheer size, there was little to tie them to the bare bones warehouses of the 1970s.

Roundy's suggested in 1994 that it might make a public offering in order to fund future expansion. Then in October 1994, the company announced it would merge with Spartan Stores, another grocery wholesale cooperative based in Grand Rapids, Michigan. The merger of Roundy's, the nation's sixth-largest food wholesaler, and Spartan, the seventh largest, would have made the new combined corporation the third largest in the United States. However, the merger was called off a month later. The companies announced that they would pursue separate growth strategies, and a Roundy's vice president declared that the time was not right for the merger. Nonetheless, Roundy's did seem interested in further expansion, according to a statement by its president in the June 1994 *Progressive Grocer.* Whether that took the form of a different merger, a public offering, or more acquisitions, remained to be seen.

Further Reading:

"A Temporary Solution," *Progressive Grocer,* November 1990, p. 40.
Bennett, Stephen, "Good as Gold," *Progressive Grocer,* June 1994, pp. 42–44.
Daniel, Tina, "Growing Pains at Roundy's," *Milwaukee Journal,* July 27, 1986, pp. 1D, 4D.
Fauber, John, "Changes at Roundy's Expected to Stabilize Employment Here," *Milwaukee Journal,* April 19, 1992, p. D4.
——, "Jobs Hang in Balance at Roundy's," *Milwaukee Journal,* August 11, 1991.

"Food Stores Scrap Plans to Merge," *Wisconsin State Journal,* November 22, 1994.
Gunn, Erik, "Productivity Is Key to Roundy's Dispute," *Milwaukee Journal,* July 7, 1991.
Johnson, Paul, "Roundy's, Spartan Finalize Merger," *Wisconsin State Journal,* October 11, 1994.
Lank, Avrum D., "Roundy's Acquires Firm in Chicago Area," *Milwaukee Sentinel,* May 23, 1983.
Riddle, Jennifer, "Roundy's Makes Mazo Move," *Wisconsin State Journal,* March 9, 1989.
——, "Roundy's Plans Waterloo Move," *Wisconsin State Journal,* January 11, 1991.
"Roundy's Buys Michigan Food Company," *Capital Times,* April 18, 1989.
"Roundy's Inc.: Spartan Stores Plan Merger with the Food Wholesaler," *Wall Street Journal,* October 4, 1994, p. C17.
"Roundy's Locks Out Employees," *Capital Times,* July 1, 1991.
"Roundy's Marks Its Centennial," *Milwaukee Journal,* October 15, 1972, pp. 14–15.
"Roundy's Realigns Top Management," *Milwaukee Journal,* January 2, 1974.
"Roundy's Relocation Called Union Busting," *Wisconsin State Journal,* January 11, 1991.
"Roundy's Says It Wants to Talk," *Capital Times,* July 2, 1991.
"Roundy's Squares Off," *Chain Store Age Executive,* November 1990, pp. 124–25.
"Roundy's Suspends 15 Union Workers," *Capital Times,* July 23, 1991.
"Roundy's, Teamsters Talks Break Down," *Capital Times,* July 12, 1991.
"Roundy's Thinking of Moving Jobs," *Milwaukee Journal,* August 4, 1991.
"Roundy's to End Lockout Sunday," *Capital Times,* July 19, 1991.
"Roundy's to Move to Mazo," *Capital Times,* March 9, 1989.
"Roundy's Union OKs 5-Year Pact," *Capital Times,* September 23, 1991.
Tanner, Ronald, "Roundy's Latest: Barebones with a Difference," *Progressive Grocer,* February 1980, pp. 81–90.
"Three Teamsters Are Arrested," *Capital Times,* July 11, 1991.

—A. Woodward

ROYAL DOULTON

Royal Doulton Plc

Minton House, London Road
Stoke-on-Trent, Staffordshire ST4 7QD
England
01782 292292
Fax: 01782 292499

Public Company
Incorporated: 1854 as Doulton & Co.
Employees: 6,500
Sales: $339.94 million
SICs: 3262 Vitreous China Table & Kitchenware; 5023 Home
Furnishings; 3220 Glass & Glassware—Pressed or Blown

Royal Doulton Plc is the holding company of Royal Doulton Ltd., one of the world's best-known fine china companies, which designs and produces high-quality tableware and giftware under the popular brand names of Royal Doulton, Royal Crown Derby, Minton, and Royal Albert. In the mid-1990s, Royal Doulton claimed about ten percent of the world market for china and produced more than 40,000 different items. In addition to its commercial product lines available in higher-end specialty shops and department stores, the company has also accepted commissions to produce unique china service for royalty, wealthy individuals, embassies, luxury hotels, and England's House of Lords.

The history of Royal Doulton may be traced to the early 19th century, when John Doulton began an apprenticeship at London's Fulham Pottery, one of the most important of the early commercial potteries in England. Becoming an accomplished potter known for his hard work and innovation, Doulton found employment in Lambeth, along the south bank of the Thames River, at a small pottery business owned by Martha Jones, who had inherited it from her late husband. In 1815, Jones asked Doulton and another employee, John Watts, to enter into a partnership with her, and the three founded a business called Jones, Watts and Doulton. Producing utilitarian salt glaze and stoneware ceramics, stone jars, bottles, and flasks in its early years, the company eventually expanded its line to include mugs and jugs modeled in the likenesses of Napoleon and the Duke of Wellington, bottles for beer, gallipots (ointment pots), and blacking bottles. Allegedly, as a laboring child, Charles Dickens was said to have pasted labels on thousands of Doulton blacking bottles.

Five of John Doulton's sons joined him in the family business, but the second son, Henry, took his father's place in the pottery. Henry had become a master potter, learning all aspects of the business from the production stages through management, and he played an important role in product development and in improving working conditions at the Lambeth pottery. In the 1840s Henry Doulton established the world's first factory for making stoneware drainpipes, a significant development that helped England achieve improvements in health care by providing more sanitary conditions through the provision of piped water. As the pipe business continued to thrive, Henry opened an art studio in the early 1870s where he encouraged and employed talented artists.

Henry also became known for his interest in the welfare of workers, a rare concern at a time when industrialists capitalized on cheap labor. Potteries were generally hazardous places during this time, as arsenic was used in painting and lead in glazing. Workers often succumbed to a debilitating lung disease then known as "potter's rot." In addition, laborers had to carry an enormous amount of weight, lifting several tons of materials from depths of eight to ten feet. To help workers with this burden, Henry Doulton obtained a mechanical hydraulic lifting device to help eliminate some of the manual labor. He also believed encouraged scientific research to determine more modern and safe methods of production.

In 1877 Henry Doulton bought a factory at Burslem in Stoke-on-Trent, a city known as The Potteries and home of English bone china. Other famous potters located here included Wedgwood, Minton, Beswick, and Royal Adderly. Indeed, the area became the center for potters, given its wealth of raw materials including clay for earthenware, coal to heat the kilns, as well as lead and salt for glazing. The established potters in this area were initially annoyed, when Doulton moved in on their territory, and they predicted doom for the newcomer. Henry Doulton summed their attitude up thus: "In their view we Southerners know little about God and nothing at all about potting."

Through persistence and careful investment in staff and plant, Henry Doulton did succeed. The company's early success came from earthenware, decorated in the limited colors available from lead glaze at that time. Then, Doulton's art director John Slater and manager John C. Bailey encouraged Henry to pursue the idea of using bone china in production, a material that could be painted with more and brighter colors. By 1884, Henry Doulton had given his consent to the new medium, and the success of the results attracted to Doulton an outstanding team of modelers, decorators, and painters.

By the late 1880s, the company and its products had become internationally famous. In 1885 Henry was honored for his achievements, receiving the Albert Medal of the Society of Arts for his "encouragement in the production of artistic pottery." Only one Albert Medal was awarded each year, and previous recipients had included the poet Alfred, Lord Tennyson and Sir Rowland Hill, honored for his creation of the penny postage system. Henry's greatest honor, perhaps, came in 1887, when Queen Victoria awarded him knighthood; he was the first potter to ever be distinguished in this fashion. When Sir Henry Doulton died in 1897, he left behind a company that had diversified and established itself as one of the leaders in its field.

Sir Henry Doulton's son, Henry Lewis Doulton, who had been made a partner in the firm in 1881, became a leader at the company. In 1901, four years after his father's death, he received on behalf of the company the Royal Warrant of King Edward VII and was granted permission to add the word "Royal" to the Doulton name—a great and rare honor. As chairman and managing director, Henry Lewis Doulton guided the company through a difficult recession and period of war between 1900 and 1920.

Regarding product development, Henry Lewis Doulton was particularly interested in experimental glaze processes that produced unique, rare color effects. One such glaze, Rouge Flambé, a dramatic red and black glaze, remained unique to Royal Doulton, with a secret formula known only to three or four people in the company into the 1990s. The company also introduced new lines of character jugs, figurines, and decorative and utility china on earthenware and bone china bodies, and their popularity continued to grow.

In America, Royal Doulton became known as the finest English china. Indeed, Royal Doulton's presence in the American market was an important part of the company's growth and success, and remained Royal Doulton's most important overseas market in the mid-1990s. In 1945, a subsidiary, Royal Doulton USA Inc., was formed to help in the sales and marketing of the products in the United States.

Family leadership in the company continued. Ronald Duneau Doulton, a cousin of Henry Lewis Doulton, became one of the first directors of the business when it changed to a limited company, known as Doulton & Co. Limited, in January 1899. Lewis John Eric Hooper, son of Henry Lewis's sister, joined Royal Doulton in 1902. Under Eric's guidance much scientific research into the physical and chemical behavior of ceramic materials was carried out and new technology was developed and installed. His nephew, Orrok Sherwood Doulton, joined the company in 1935 and became director. Under his leadership, Royal Doulton captured the Queen's Awards for Industry, Technological Innovation, and Outstanding Export Performance.

Orrok Sherwood Doulton's sons, Mark and Michael, both joined the company. Michael Doulton joined the company in 1970, working under a fictitious name while learning the different aspects of pottery production. Since 1976 he acted as traveling ambassador for the company and with the formation of the Royal Doulton International Collectors Club, a group dedicated to the collection and preservation of Royal Doulton products, he served as honorary president since 1980. Although the Doulton family still remained an important and integral part to running the business, leadership extended outside the family in later years.

1968 saw the first series of acquisitions by Doulton and Co. Limited. It first purchased the world-renowned Minton China, a company founded by Thomas Minton in 1793. Minton dominated the industry during the middle of the 19th century and the company's innovations included the acid gold decorating process, the majolica-type body, the pâte-sur-pâte relief decoration technique, encaustic tiles, and parian statuary. In the same year, Doulton acquired Dunn Bennett, a company founded in 1876 when Thomas Wood-Bennett joined his father-in-law William Dunn to begin potting, concentrating on hotelware. In 1969,

Webb Corbett and Beswick became part of the Royal Doulton group. Webb Corbett was founded in 1897 to make English full-lead crystal; Beswick traced its history to 1890, when James Wright Beswick and his son began producing both table and ornamental ware.

The greatest merger in the history of ceramics came in 1972, when Pearson PLC purchased Doulton and Co. Pearson had a controlling interest in Allied English Potteries and combined the two tableware groups under the Royal Doulton Tableware name. Pearson's emergence in the pottery industry came about almost by accident. Originally, the Pearson empire was mainly concerned with constructional engineering and the development of oil fields. But after investing money into a struggling business called Booth's pottery during the 1920s, Pearson eventually became the controlling shareholder. Then, 20 years later, Pearson began increasing their pottery interests. In 1944, the company bought Colclough's of Longton, a business founded in 1893 that made moderately priced bone china teaware. Pearson combined its Booth pottery with that of Colclough's, forming a new entity called Booth and Colclough. In 1952, Pearson acquired the Lawley Group, a company controlling a national chain of specialist china and glass retailers and pottery manufacturers, including Ridgway and Adderly. Seven years later they purchased Swinnertons and Alcock, Lindley and Bloor, manufacturers of redware pots. Other names joining the group were Royal Crown Derby, Royal Albert, and Paragon. Following its string of pottery acquisitions, Pearson eventually changed their focus in the 1990s and divested many of its holdings. Royal Doulton plc was thus formed in December 1993 and was listed on the London stock exchange; according to analysts, the company had a market value of between £150 million and £200 million at the time.

The development of Royal Doulton's product lines are also integral to the company's history. In fact, some products developed in the company's early years remained popular in modern times. The Toby jug was one such example. First produced in the early 18th century, the Toby jug, or beverage mug, was designed to represent a seated male figure, stout and smiling, with the spouts at either side of the mug's rim serving as points on the character's tricorn hat. Royal Doulton produced the jugs at their Lambeth factory during the 19th and 20th centuries, and they reclaimed popularity in the 1930s when they were produced to represent famous characters from English songs, literature, and history. Since that time, Royal Doulton introduced updated versions of the mugs, featuring only the head of the character rather than its full body. Characters have included figures from American history as well as popular culture.

Figurines were also an important product line of Royal Doulton, and the company became known for the quality and attention to detail of its figurines. The earliest recorded figurative work produced by Royal Doulton is attributed to John Doulton, who made a flask depicting Queen Caroline around 1820. The tradition of producing figurines of people and animals continued throughout the years, and lines were constantly updated. Ideas for subjects came from a variety of sources, such as historic figures, popular nursery tales, or celebrated events. For example, figurines of the Royal family gained popularity in the 1980s, and a special edition was created in 1992 commemorating the 500th anniversary of Christopher Columbus's setting sail to discover the New World.

Tableware design and decoration began at the company in 1877, when Henry Doulton entered into a partnership with and later bought out Pinder & Bourne Company, a medium-sized producer of earthenware tableware. From earthenware the company moved into the area of fine china. As new decorative and manufacturing techniques emerged, fine china became available at more affordable prices. In 1960, the company introduced English Translucent China, a medium it pioneered and from which the costly ingredient of calcined bone had been eliminated. Through this new product, which became known as Royal Doulton Fine China, the company was able to offer the qualities associated with fine bone china at a modest cost to consumers. In 1974, the company revived the concept of its original Lambethware, creating a casual tableware with a country charm and practicality, being oven and freezer proof and unaffected by detergent or the dishwasher. Royal Doulton Tableware Limited grew to represent approximately one-third of the entire British tableware industry. Finally, by the 1990s, Royal Doulton was producing a wide variety of ceramic products for use in the chemical, textile, aircraft, engineering and atomic industries.

In the mid-1990s Royal Doulton management was focusing on achieving a greater degree of efficiency at its facilities. From 1987 to 1990, the company spent £10 million annually (approximately $16.4 million) to automate and mechanize their factories, resulting in even finer quality and manufacturing flexibility. The company maintained a dozen factories producing all types and grades of product at that time. Royal Doulton's superb products, excellent management, and outstanding reputation positioned the company among the top echelon of the industry. Their efforts to appeal to lower-priced markets, while maintaining their reputation for producing high-quality, traditional china, was likely to ensure their position as one of the leaders for many more years to come.

Principal Subsidiaries: Royal Doulton USA Inc.

Further Reading:

Doulton, Michael, *Discovering Royal Doulton,* Shrewsbury: Swan-Hill Press, 1993, 144 p.
Eyles, Desmond, *Royal Doulton: 1815–1965,* London: Hutchinson & Co., 1965.
Fallon, James, "Parent to Spin Off Royal Doulton," *HFD-The Weekly Home Furnishings Newspaper,* August 9, 1993, p. 44.
Neiss, Doug, "Royal Doulton Expands with Efficiency," *HFD-The Weekly Home Furnishings Newspaper,* April 30, 1990, p. 94.
Shenker, Israel, "From the Villages of Stoke-on-Trent: A River of China," *Smithsonian,* March 1989, pp. 131–138.

—Beth Watson Highman

Samsung Electronics Co., Ltd.

416, Maetan 3-Dong
Pardar-Gu Suwon 440–370
South Korea
(82) 331 27516114
Fax: (82) 331 27516111

Wholly Owned Subsidiary of Samsung Group (South Korea)
Founded: 1969
Employees: 51,926
Sales: US$14.94 billion
Stock Exchanges: Seoul
SICs: 3559 Special Industry Machinery Nec; 3561 Pumps &
    Pumping Equipment; 3571 Electronic Computers; 3578
    Calculating & Accounting Equipment; 3579 Office
    Machines Nec; 3670 Electronic Components &
    Accessories; 3585 Refrigeration & Heating Equipment;
    3594 Fluid Power Pumps & Motors; 3599 Industrial
    Machinery Nec

Samsung Electronics Co., Ltd., is the chief subsidiary of South
Korea's giant Samsung Group and one of the largest electronics
producers in Asia. Products built by Samsung Electronics include televisions and many other kinds of home appliances,
telecommunications equipment, and computers. Its most important product is semiconductors. Savvy management and heavy
investment in research and development in the late 1980s and
early 1990s were turning the company into a leading contender
in the global electronics industry.

Samsung Electronics was created in 1969 as a division of the
mammoth Korean chaebol Samsung Group. The unit was established as a means of getting Samsung into the burgeoning
television and consumer electronics industry. The division's
first product was a small and simple black-and-white television
that it began selling in the early 1970s. From that product,
Samsung Electronics gradually developed a diverse line of consumer electronics that it first sold domestically, and later began
exporting. The company also began branching out into color
televisions, and later into a variety of consumer electronics and
appliances. By the 1980s Samsung was manufacturing, shipping, and selling a wide range of appliances and electronic
products throughout the world.

Although the rapid growth of Samsung Electronics during the
1970s and early 1980s is impressive, it did not surprise ob-

servers who were familiar with the Samsung Group, which was
founded in 1938 by Byung-Chull Lee, a celebrated Korean
entrepreneur. Lee started a small trading company with a $2,000
nest egg and forty employees. He called it Samsung, which
means "three stars" in Korean. The company enjoyed moderate growth before the Communist invasion in 1950 forced Lee
to abandon his operations in Seoul. Looting soldiers and politicians on both sides of the conflict diminished his inventories to
almost nothing. With savings contributed by one of his managers, Lee started over in 1951 and within one year had grown his
company's assets twenty-fold.

Lee established a sugar refinery in 1953, a move that was
criticized at the time because sugar could be easily obtained
through American aid. But for Lee the act was important because it was the first manufacturing facility built in South Korea
after the Korean War. From sugar, wool, and other commodity
businesses, Lee moved into heavier manufacturing. The company prospered under Lee's philosophy of making Samsung the
leader in each industry he entered.

From manufacturing, Samsung moved into various service
businesses during the 1960s, including insurance, broadcasting,
securities, and even a department store. Lee experienced several
major setbacks during the period. For example, in the late
1960s, shortly before Samsung Electronics was created, Lee
was charged with an illegal sale of about $50,000 worth of
goods. The charges turned out to be the fabrication of a disgruntled government official to whom Lee had refused to pay a
bribe. Nevertheless, one of Lee's sons was arrested and Lee was
forced to donate a fertilizer plant to the government to win his
release. Despite that and other problems, Samsung continued to
flourish. Indeed, by the end of the 1960s the conglomerate was
generating more than US$100 million in annual revenues.

Shortly after Lee's son was arrested, Lee decided to break into
the mass communication industry by launching a radio and
television station, as well as by manufacturing televisions and
electronic components through the Samsung Electronics division. The industry was dominated at the time by several U.S.
and European manufacturers, and some Japanese companies
were beginning to enter the industry. Nevertheless, Lee was
confident that Samsung could stake its claim on the local market
and eventually become a global contender. During the early
1970s the company invested heavily, borrowed and coaxed
technology from foreign competitors, and drew on its business
and political connections to begin carving out a niche in the
consumer electronics industry. In addition to televisions, Samsung branched out into other consumer electronics products and
appliances.

Samsung Electronics's gains during the 1970s were achieved
with the assistance of the national government. During the
1950s and 1960s Samsung and other Korean conglomerates
struggled as the Rhee Sungman administration increasingly resorted to favoritism and corruption to maintain power. Student
revolts in the 1960s finally forced Rhee into exile. The ruling
party that emerged from the ensuing political fray was headed
by military leader Park Chung-Hee. His regime during the
1960s and 1970s was characterized by increasing centralization
of power, both political and industrial, as his government was
obsessed with economic growth and development. So, while

Park was widely criticized for his authoritarian style, his government is credited with laying the foundation for South Korea's economic renaissance.

In order to rapidly develop the economy, Park identified key industries and large, profitable companies within them. The government worked with the companies, providing protection from competition and financial assistance as part of a series of five-year national economic growth plans. By concentrating power in the hands of a few giant companies (the chaebols), Park reasoned, roadblocks would be minimized and efficiencies would result. Between 1960 and 1980 South Korea's annual exports surged from $33 million to more than $17 billion.

Samsung Electronics and the entire Samsung chaebol were beneficiaries of Rhee's policies. Several countries, including Japan, were barred from selling consumer electronics in South Korea, eliminating significant competition for Samsung. Furthermore, although Samsung Electronics was free to invest in overseas companies, foreign investors were forbidden to buy into Samsung. As a result, Samsung was able to quickly develop a thriving television and electronics division that controlled niches of the domestic market and even had an edge in some export arenas.

During the 1970s and 1980s Samsung Group created a number of electronics-related divisions, several of which were later grouped into a single entity known as Samsung Electronics Co. Ltd. Samsung Electron Devices Co. manufactured picture tubes, display monitors, and related parts. Samsung Electro-Mechanics Co. made VHF and UHF tuners, condensers, speakers, and other gear. Samsung Corning Co. produced television glass bulbs, computer displays, and other components. Finally, Samsung Semiconductor & Telecommunications Co. represented Samsung in the high-tech microchip industry. Rapid growth in those industries, combined with savvy management, allowed the combined Samsung Electronics Co., Ltd., to become Samsung Group's chief subsidiary by the end of the 1980s.

Samsung's entry into the semiconductor business was pivotal for the company. Lee had determined in the mid-1970s that high-tech electronics was the growth industry of the future, and that Samsung was to be a major player. To that end, he formed Samsung Semiconductor and Telecommunications Co. in 1978. To make up for a lack of technological expertise in South Korea, the South Korean government effectively required foreign telecommunications equipment manufacturers to hand over advanced semiconductor technology in return for access to the Korean market. This proved crucial for Samsung, which obtained proprietary technology from Micron of the United States and Sharp of Japan in 1983. Utilizing its newly acquired knowledge, Samsung became the first Korean manufacturer of low-cost, relatively low-tech, 64-kilobit dynamic random access memory (DRAM) chips.

Shortly after introducing its 64K chip, Samsung teamed up with some Korean competitors in a research project that was coordinated by the government Electronics and Telecommunications Research Institute. The result was a 1-megabit DRAM (and later a 4-megabit DRAM) chip. During the mid- and late 1980s, Samsung parlayed knowledge from the venture to become a significant supplier of low-cost, commodity-like DRAM chips to computer and electronics manufacturers throughout the world. Meanwhile, its other electronics operations continued to grow, both domestically and abroad. Samsung opened a television assembly plant in Portugal in 1982 to supply the European market with 300,000 units annually. In 1984 it built a $25 million plant in New York that could manufacture one million televisions and 400,000 microwave ovens per year. Then, in 1987, it opened another $25 million facility in England with capacity for 400,000 color televisions, 300,000 VCRs, and 300,000 microwave ovens.

Between 1977 and 1987 Samsung Group's annual revenues surged from $1.3 billion to $24 billion (or about 20 percent of South Korea's entire gross domestic product). Much of that growth was attributable to Samsung Electronics. Byung-Chull Lee died in 1987 and was succeeded by his son, Kun-Hee Lee. Kun-Hee Lee recognized the importance of the electronics division and moved quickly to make it the centerpiece of the Samsung Group. To that end, he consolidated many of the Group's divisions and eliminated some operations. He also introduced various initiatives designed to improve employee motivation and product quality. Kun-Hee Lee was credited with stepping up Samsung Electronics's partnering efforts with foreign companies as part of his goal to put Samsung at the forefront of semiconductor technology.

Sales at Samsung Group grew more than 2.5 times between 1987 and 1992. More importantly, Samsung drew from potential profit gains to more than double research and development investments as part of Kun-Hee Lee's aggressive bid to make Samsung a technological leader in the electronics, semiconductor, and communications industries. Besides partnering with U.S. and Japanese electronics companies, Samsung Electronics acquired firms that possessed important technology, including Harris Microwave Semiconductors and Integrated Telecom Technologies. In 1993 Kun-Hee Lee sold off ten of Samsung Group's subsidiaries, downsized the company, and merged other operations to concentrate on three industries: electronics, engineering, and chemicals.

Under the leadership of chief executive Kim Kwang-Ho, Samsung Electronics took the microchip world by storm when it introduced its 4-megabit DRAM chip in 1994. Sales of that chip helped to push Samsung's sales from US$10.77 billion in 1993 to US$14.94 billion in 1994. Profits, moreover, spiraled from US$173,000 to nearly US$1.3 billion. In addition, Samsung had staged a bold grab for domestic market share in 1995 by slashing prices for consumer electronics and home appliances by as much as 16 percent, and had wowed industry insiders when it unveiled an advanced thin-film-transistor display screen—used for laptop computers—at a world trade show in Japan.

Samsung Electronics's rapid rise and technical achievements put the company in the spotlight in the semiconductor industry. Its 4-megabit chip, in fact, had made it the leading global producer of DRAM chips by early 1995. Furthermore, Samsung Electronics was increasing its investment in development still further, as evidenced by a $2.5 billion outlay to develop a 64-megabit DRAM chip by 1998. In mid-1995, Samsung Electronics was hoping to generated profits of $2.3 billion on sales of

$19.3 billion—a revenue gain of nearly 30 percent over 1994. In addition to its DRAM chip pursuits, the company was working to establish a major presence in multimedia products, flat screens, and telecommunications gear.

Principal Subsidiaries: Samsung Semiconductors Inc.; Samsung Information Systems America Inc. (United States); Samtron Displays Inc.

Further Reading:

"A Giant with Wings?" *Business Korea,* December 1994, pp. 21–23.

Jameson, Sam, "Samsung Isn't Content to Be a Mere Giant," *Los Angeles Times,* July 5, 1990, Sec. D, p. 1.

Nakarmi, Laxmi, with Kevin Kelly and Larry Armstrong, "Look Out, World—Samsung Is Coming," *Business Week,* July 10, 1995, pp. 52–53.

Ota, Alan K., "Samsung Expands Overseas in Drive to Transform Itself," *Oregonian,* July 2, 1995, Sec. F, p. 9.

"Samsung Chairman Lee Kun-Hee: A Modern Day Fortuneteller?" *Business Korea,* August 1993, pp. 18–19.

"Samsung Group: Lee Kun-Hee's First Five Years," *Business Korea,* December 1992, p. 37.

"Samsung: Steering a New Course," *Business Korea,* February 1992, p. 26.

Selwyn, Michael, and Erwin Shrader, "Samsung Takes On the Giant," *Asian Business,* October 1990, pp. 28–34.

Sohn, Jie-Ae, "Samsung Group Embracing Breathtaking Changes," *Business Korea,* August 1993, pp. 15–18.

Steers, Richard M., with Yoo Keun Shin and Gerardo R. Ungson, *The Chaebol,* New York: Harper & Row, 1989.

Tanzer, Andrew, "Samsung of South Korea Marches to Its Own Drummer," *Forbes,* May 16, 1988, pp. 84–89.

—Dave Mote

✳ SBC Warburg

SBC Warburg

1 Finsbury Avenue
London EC2M 2PA
England
(0171) 606 1066
Fax: (0171) 382 4800

Public Company
Incorporated: 1934 as New Trading Company
Employees: 4,472
Total Assets: £22.58 billion
Stock Exchanges: London
SICs: 6711 Holding Companies; 6012 Recognized Banks;
6211 Stock Brokers, Dealers, & Flotation Companies

Founded by Siegmund Warburg, a scion of a German banking dynasty, SBC Warburg was established as a mutual aid society for Jewish refugees from Nazi Germany. After World War II it became known as a daring merchant bank whose bold initiatives frequently startled London's financial establishment. The company grew to be the United Kingdom's premier investment house and darling of the financial world; however, in the mid-1990s the bank encountered an exceptional string of setbacks that left it vulnerable to a takeover from a stronger bank, and in May 1995 Warburg formed an alliance with the Swiss Bank Corporation (SBC), Switzerland's third-largest bank.

The origins of Warburg can be traced back to 1559 in the small town of Warburg in Westphalia, Germany, where Simon von Cassel, prevented because he was Jewish from a free choice of professions, started a family money-lending business. From small beginnings the business prospered, and in time the family name was changed to Warburg. By 1902, the year that Siegmund Warburg was born, M. M. Warburg had become a banking dynasty, based in Hamburg but with interests worldwide. After his education, Siegmund Warburg joined the bank, gaining valuable experience in its offices in London, New York, and Boston before settling to pursue his career in Berlin.

With the rise of the Nazi Party, Siegmund Warburg left Germany for good, emigrating to London in 1934. There he set up the New Trading Company, which quickly attracted a number of German and Austrian refugees from the Nazis. The company financed the growth of small businesses and aided refugees in recovering the assets they had been forced to leave behind in their homelands. For more than ten years it was a small, shel-

tered Jewish enclave, bound together by a philosophy of reciprocal support and an atmosphere of friendly, even familial, camaraderie: the members were known as the ''uncles,'' and the company's internal language was German.

After the war, however, Siegmund Warburg and his partner, fellow German emigre Henry Grunfeld, transformed the New Trading Company into the merchant bank S. G. Warburg and Company and proceeded to tackle Britain's banking establishment on its own terms.

Over the next few decades S. G. Warburg steadily gained a name for itself. Occasionally the newcomer shocked the traditionalists of the banking community, most notably in 1958, when S. G. Warburg engineered the first hostile corporate takeover London had ever experienced. For its clients Reynolds Metal and Tube Investments, Warburg clandestinely acquired 10 percent of British Aluminium, then advised its clients on a hostile bid for the firm—a maneuver that many in the financial establishment found unsavory (though it subsequently became commonplace). In 1963 Warburg again broke new ground, taking a pioneering role in the launching of the Eurobond market with a £10 million loan for the Italian roadbuilder Autostrade Italiane.

Throughout the 1960s and 1970s, S. G. Warburg's image as an outsider, as the ''Jewish emigre'' bank, increasingly faded: by 1982, when Siegmund (now, tellingly, Sir Siegmund) died, the bank he had founded had become an integral part of the financial establishment.

Sir Siegmund did not leave a successor as such, but it was the man widely known as his ''adopted son,'' David Scholey, who piloted the bank through its next important phase. In 1986, with the so-called Big Bang, deregulation allowed London merchant banks for the first time in 200 years to diversify into the fields of broking and market-making. Under Scholey's direction, S. G. Warburg lost no time in taking advantage of the new freedom: in quick succession in 1986 and 1987, stockbrokers Rowe & Pitman, jobbers Akroyd & Smithers, and gilt market-makers Mullens & Co. were brought under the Warburg umbrella to create an integrated merchant banking and stockbroking firm.

Thus liberated by deregulation, and freed, as well, from the more cautious dictates of Sir Siegmund, who had never countenanced unnecessary risk-taking or over-extension, it seemed there was no stopping S. G. Warburg's ambitious and successful growth. The company was widely considered Britain's flagship investment bank.

As a leading investment banker with 30 offices in 23 countries, Warburg offered financial advice and services, through its 385 corporate finance executives, to corporations, governments, and investors worldwide. S. G. Warburg was the leading securities company in the United Kingdom, and among the top 20 internationally. In fiscal year 1993–94 the company represented 560 corporations and governments and traded with or in the interests of 2,000 institutional investors. Half of Britain's foremost 100 firms were Warburg's corporate finance clients. It was known as an adroit manager of corporate mergers, acquisitions, and restructurings, and was the world's third-largest adviser on such activities. Warburg was the world's largest research house, boasting more than 250 analysts producing macroeconomic, interest rate, currency, and company-specific information, including information on some 2,400 companies in 30 countries. The bank excelled in equity financing, managing more than $6 billion of international equity and equity-linked financings, and ranking sixth worldwide in international equity issuance. It was active also in fixed interest financing, offered securities distribution and trading, provided specialist financing in areas such as leasing, banking, and project finance, and supplied securities custody and administration services. Through its 75 percent stake in Mercury Asset Management (MAM) the bank governed one of the United Kingdom's most prominent and prosperous international investment management companies, providing services to 5,000 institutional and individual clients and 100,000 retail investors. In the international market, S. G. Warburg was the United Kingdom's strongest contender, better equipped than any other domestic bank to compete with the bigger investment houses of Wall Street. In all markets the bank enjoyed long-standing relationships with high-profile, often blue-chip clients. S. G. Warburg was, in short, what the *Independent* called "a standard bearer for the City and a model of sound, inspirational management and success."

It came as a profound shock, then, when suddenly, beginning in late 1994, an unusual series of events reversed S. G. Warburg's position. In October of that year the first faint alarm bells were heard when Warburg announced a profits warning: the profits of the group were less than half what they had been in the year before for the same period. Two months later, word leaked that Warburg was in the process of negotiating a merger with the U.S. investment bank Morgan Stanley. The merger, which would have created the world's largest investment bank, would have been advantageous to both parties. Warburg would have gained the clout it lacked in America, where it had been struggling for years to build a substantial presence with only limited success. Morgan Stanley would similarly have won a stronger position in Europe, and the U.S. bank was also very attracted to MAM.

When Morgan Stanley backed out of the deal, however, for reasons that were never fully explained, the abortive merger was seen not just an embarrassment but as a downright debacle, and Warburg's credibility was severely compromised. The *Independent* was typical in its assessment that Warburg had suffered "a public relations and strategy disaster from which the bank may take years to recover." The *Times* demurred, declaring, "City mutterings about Warburg inevitably stem from natural envy and a typically British denigration of success," but this was definitely the minority view.

The failed merger seemed to highlight Warburg's shortcomings, with the very fact that Warburg had desired a merger with Morgan Stanley in the first place viewed as a tacit admission that the bank was unable to succeed alone as a global operation. An expansionist strategy was considered difficult for a U.K. bank, because, unlike Wall Street firms, it did not have a large, profitable domestic market to draw on, and without the capital thus afforded could not hope to compete effectively.

After the attempted merger, Warburg's fortunes declined quickly. A month later, in January 1995, Warburg pulled out of the Eurobond market. Although the move was probably a wise one, as dollar issues dominated the market relative to sterling,

commentators remembered that it had been S. G. Warburg itself that had pioneered the Eurobond market and viewed its departure with alarm. In addition, it was remembered that Morgan Stanley, had it joined with Warburg, could have helped shore up the latter's flagging bond operations. Was this withdrawal an admission that Warburg could not compete alone in the fixed-interest market? In short, the move was another public relations disaster following much too closely on the last one.

Doubts about Warburg's future began to affect the bank internally, with morale at an all-time low. In February, key employees began to defect to rival houses. First to go were the joint heads of Warburg's equity capital markets, who joined Morgan Grenfell, a London-based investment bank owned by Deutsche Bank. Within days, several members of their team followed. To an investment house, where confidence is of paramount importance and staff a critical asset, it was a severe and shocking blow. "Readers beware," warned the *Sunday Times* somewhat snidely. "If you are walking past S G Warburg's Finsbury Avenue offices, take extra care. There is a danger you will be trampled by hordes of senior executives rushing from the building."

Someone was needed to take the blame, and the chief executive, Lord Cairns, duly resigned his post. His position was filled by chairman David Scholey, who postponed his own planned retirement to remain at the helm of the troubled bank. The maneuver proved of little help, however. In March Warburg curtailed its equities business in New York; in May the bank issued another profits warning. From the record pre-tax profits of the previous years, Warburg had sunk to what would have been a loss if not for MAM's good performance. A steady trickle of departing staff continued.

In May 1995 S. G. Warburg announced that it had formed an alliance with a stronger partner, the Swiss Bank Corporation (SBC), Switzerland's third-largest bank. In many ways the two complemented each other, with Warburg's strength in equities balanced by SBC's expertise in debt markets and derivatives and its position as a lead arranger in international bond issues. SBC was not strong in the American market, however, which was a long-cherished dream of Warburg's. Still, Scholey asserted confidently that SBC and Warburg fit together "like the clunk of a Rolls-Royce door." Some observers found the alliance less satisfying. "There is no point in pretending this is going to be anything but a rape," growled the *Independent*. "This could never have happened had Siegmund Warburg . . . still been at the helm," insisted the *Guardian*. "His legacy has been betrayed by his successors." More sympathetic but no less disapproving, the *Times* commented: "The death throes of SG Warburg are truly distressing to watch. For someone who remembers the heady days after Big Bang in 1986, when SG Warburg was the ultimate mover in the City, arrogant, powerful and effective, it seems scarcely credible that the current management is leading the bank off to the corporate equivalent of the knackers' yard."

SBC bought Warburg for £860 million, in a deal that did not include MAM: Warburg distributed its 75 percent stake of that company to its shareholders. For many it was the end of an era, as S. G. Warburg became SBC Warburg.

Warburg's future after the takeover remained unclear. Certainly the bank retained its core strengths in corporate finance and research. Indeed, the company was named in July 1995—for the fifth year in a row—as the leading research house in Extel's influential survey. Despite its troubles, Warburg could still point to countless successful projects undertaken for its blue-chip clients; whether those clients would choose to remain with Warburg, however, was an open question. Most significantly, the intentions of new owner SBC were unknown: it remained to be seen whether the house of Siegmund Warburg would find itself eventually subsumed into the larger corporation or would continue on to write new chapters in its interesting and distinctive history.

Principal Subsidiaries: Rowe & Pitman Ltd.; S. G. Warburg & Co. (Far East) Ltd. (Hong Kong); S. G. Warburg and Co. GmbH (Germany); S. G. Warburg & Co. Inc. (U.S.A.); S. G. Warburg & Co. (Japan) Ltd.; S. G. Warburg & Co. Ltd.; S. G. Warburg Futures & Options Ltd.; S. G. Warburg International; S. G. Warburg Options Inc. (U.S.A.); S. G. Warburg Securities Ltd.; S. G. Warburg Trust Co. Ltd.; S.G.W. Finance plc.

Further Reading:

"Banker Maturing over Four Centuries," *Daily Telegraph,* May 11, 1995.

"Coming Clean Has Left an Awful Lot of Mud," *Independent on Sunday,* December 18, 1994.

"Cowardice in the Face of Heavy Fire," *Guardian,* May 11, 1995.

"The Fall of the House of Warburg," *Independent,* February 17, 1995.

"The Fall of the House of Warburg," *Sunday Telegraph,* May 7, 1995.

"International Company News: Cold Logic Wins out at Warburg," *Financial Times,* January 10, 1995.

"The Knackers' Yard Beckons," *Times,* May 3, 1995.

"Lex Column: Warburg's Woes," *Financial Times,* February 11, 1995.

"Lord Cairns' Beau Geste," *Independent,* February 14, 1995.

"Old Guard to Rescue at Wounded Warburg," *Daily Mail,* February 14, 1995.

"Swiss Bank Stalks Warburg," *Guardian,* May 3, 1995.

"The Takeover of SG Warburg," *Financial Times,* May 22, 1995.

"Trading Places," *Sunday Times,* February 19, 1995.

"Warburg Breaks the Bond," *Financial Times,* January 11, 1995.

"Warburg Must Search out a New Direction," *Independent,* December 16, 1994.

"Warburg Must Set Course for a Complete Overhaul," *Sunday Times,* February 12, 1995.

"Warburg's Rise and Fall," *Sunday Business Post,* February 19, 1995.

"Warburg Sells out to Swiss," *Guardian,* May 11, 1995.

"Warburg Stays Top in Survey," *Times,* July 6, 1995, p. 23.

"Warburg to Pull out of Eurobonds after Losses," *Financial Times,* January 10, 1995.

"Warburg Whispering Swells," *Independent,* January 20, 1995.

—Robin DuBlanc

Schering-Plough Corporation

One Giralda Farms
Madison, New Jersey 07940-1000
U.S.A.
(201) 822-7000
Fax: (201) 822-7048

Public Company
Incorporated: 1970
Employees: 21,200
Sales: $4.65 billion
Stock Exchanges: New York
SICs: 2834 Pharmaceutical Preparations

Schering-Plough Corporation is one of the leading manufacturers of pharmaceuticals in the United States. With such successful prescription drugs as Garamycin and Claritin and such popular health and beauty brands as Coppertone and Dr. Scholl's, the company holds strong positions in both the consumer market and the health care professional market.

In 1971 Abe Plough, the founder and marketing genius behind Plough, Inc., a proprietary drug and consumer product company, approved of a merger between his company and the Schering Corporation. The 80-year-old man, with a colorful entrepreneurial history, was looking for a successor to run his firm. A solution was found in his unlikely friendship with Willibald Hermann Cozen, the German-born chief executive officer of Schering.

It was Cozen who actually designed the merger and, as a result, became the chief executive officer of Schering-Plough. The merger combined the comprehensive manufacturing of Schering's antibiotics, antihistamines, and other pharmaceuticals, and Plough's household consumer products with names as common as Coppertone and Di-Gel. With this diverse product line, Schering-Plough enjoyed steady growth and comfortable profit margins throughout its history.

Long before the merger, the Schering Corporation began as a drug manufacturer in Berlin. In 1894 the company started to export diphtheria medication to the United States, and an American branch of the German company opened in New York in 1929. Until the end of World War II, a sex hormone accounted for up to 75 percent of Schering's sales. The war, however, changed the course of the company's history forever. Frank

Brown, a New Deal lawyer with no previous experience in the pharmaceutical business, was dealt a hand that would bind his future to Schering.

Brown's legal career involved participating in government projects during the 1930s. He joined the Federal Deposit Insurance Corporation, a creation of Roosevelt's New Deal policies, and acted as legal counsel to Leo Crowley. During the war the United States seized the assets of all German-owned businesses operating within the country. Leo Crowley was appointed the Alien Property Custodian, and Brown was given the job of managing the Schering Company. He immediately filled vacated executive positions with associates from the FDIC. In 1943 Brown was formally appointed president of Schering, and under his direction the company soon proved a financial success.

Brown realized that research and development was the key to success in the pharmaceutical industry. To this end, Brown immediately began the development of a research department and, like many other pharmaceutical companies, conducted searches for those scientists and students on the verge of new discoveries or for noteworthy scientific contributions from medical colleges and universities across the country. Established in 1944, the Schering student competition fund has found many worthy recipients over the years.

Because the postwar years marked a reduced demand for sex hormones, the newly expanded research department could not have found a better moment to discover a new antihistamine. Marketed as a proprietary drug (a drug directly advertised to consumers) under the name Trimeton and marketed also as an ethical drug (a drug advertised to health care professionals) under the name Chlor-Trimeton, the antihistamine marked a turning point in the history of the Schering Corporation. By 1951, profits had quadrupled with sales reaching over $15 million.

That same year the U.S. attorney general put the company up for sale. A syndicate headed by Merrill Lynch outbid other prospective buyers and proceeded to sell $1.7 million of stock to the public. However, the investors asked Brown to remain on as company president. He accepted the offer and directed Schering to even greater profitability through the discovery of Meticorten and Meticortelone, two new corticosteroids that became the envy of the drug industry.

The discovery of synthetic cortisone dates back to 1949 when Merck & Co., an industry competitor, first made public its historic findings. Although the wonder drug's discovery rightfully belonged to Merck, the process for synthesizing the drug conflicted with several other patents for producing sex hormones. Schering was the owner of one of these patents, and through a "cross-licensing" agreement the company gained access to information about cortisone production.

Soon after production of cortisone began, Schering and its competitors raced to discover an improved line of the drug that would eliminate some of the side effects associated with the steroid. They all hoped to modify the cortisone molecule to find a more effective drug and, at the same time, eliminate hypertension, edema (water retention), and osteoporosis (a bone disease), all side effects connected with cortisone therapy. Using microorganisms to convert one chemical into another, Schering scientists discovered a drug in 1954 that fit the desired guidelines. Clinical testing of the drug brought excellent results. However, when Schering was confronted with the prospect of full-scale production, the company realized it had no previous experience in manufacturing by fermentation, the process used to make the new drug. So Schering first tried fermentation in a 150-gallon stainless steel container and later in a 1,000-gallon and finally a 22,000-gallon fermenter. This last container used $100,000 worth of cortisone and a few hundred gallons of microorganisms.

Having established a successful manufacturing technique, Schering released Meticorten in 1955 and Meticortelone soon afterwards. Almost unbelievably, sales for the drugs jumped to over $20 million by the end of the year, $1 million more than total sales in 1954. By the end of 1955 sales for these drugs reached a new high of almost $46 million and by 1957 exceeded $80 million.

Other pharmaceutical companies manufacturing steroids immediately attempted to profit from Schering's success. Lederle, Upjohn, and Merck all developed similar drugs, and soon Schering found itself embroiled in lawsuits over patent and licensing rights. Merck's product arrived on the market only three months after Schering's, but because Schering had spent heavily on advertising it managed to retain a major share of the market. Furthermore, while Schering was forced to arrange licensing agreements with other companies, Brown demanded what other companies regarded as overpriced royalty payments. Although this initiated new litigation, it also allowed Schering profits to remain at an all-time high while agreements were worked out in time-consuming court processes.

Unrelated to Schering's historical development, a consumer product company in Memphis, Tennessee, won recognition for its own success story. Abe Plough, founder of Plough, Inc., began his career in marketing in 1908. He borrowed $125 from his father to create a concoction of linseed oil, carbolic acid, and camphor and sold the potion door-to-door from a horse-drawn buggy as a cure for "any ill of man or beast." Plough's inventory expanded to include a mysteriously named C-2223. This relief for rheumatics became an immediate success; after four years Plough had sold 150,000 packages.

What he later claimed to be his shrewdest purchase occurred in 1915: Plough paid $900 for the inventory of a bankrupt drug company. He netted a profit of $34,000 peddling the stock in the back woods where there was still a large demand for oxidine chill tonic. In 1920 he bought the St. Joseph Company of Chattanooga, Tennessee, and began manufacturing children's aspirin. By the 1950s Plough realized that the huge sales figures for the popular aspirin was partially due to children taking overdoses of the product. To prevent this from reoccurring Plough ordered child-proof caps added to the aspirin at a time when safety regulations were almost nonexistent. He went on to purchase 27 other companies during the course of his lifetime. In addition to being talented at making important acquisitions, he was also very adept at marketing: 25 percent of all income from sales was routinely spent on advertising. The success of radio advertising, in particular, convinced Plough to buy five AM and FM stations. Plough was best known in his own

community for his philanthropic contributions. Upon his death in 1984 at age 92, flags throughout Memphis were lowered to half-mast.

Years before his death, however, the unlikely friendship between Willibald Hermann Cozen, chief executive officer of Schering in 1966, and Abe Plough was the antecedent to a company merger. At 17, after graduating from Kaiserin Augusta Gymnasium in Koblenz, Cozen began working for Schering A.G., the German parent company. When the U.S. company was seized during World War II and eventually sold to the public, Cozen became the chief executive officer of the new independent company.

When the merger of the two companies was finally completed, combined sales reached $500 million in 1971. This marked the fastest sales growth for any merger in the industry. Yet despite an earnings multiple of 46, Cozen, in his typically reserved style, spoke guardedly of continued expansion. The sales for Garamycin, an antibiotic introduced in 1966 as a treatment for urinary tract infections and burn victims, reached $90 million by 1972. This income accounted for almost half of both companies' growth for the period. The large profits, however, ironically concealed an "Achilles' heel." Garamycin's patent, scheduled to expire in 1980, signified the beginning of generic competition and the end of Schering-Plough's control over the manufacturing of this drug. The sound of competitors footsteps could be heard following closely behind; Cozen's cautious remarks on continued expansion were well founded.

In 1974 reduced sales for Garamycin already affected company profit margins. In 1975 the return on equity dropped from 31 to 27 percent and stock dropped ten percent from the previous year. Schering-Plough endured the ensuing decline in profits and increased funding for research and development. In 1974 several newly released drugs accounted for $100 million in sales. Similarly, Maybelline cosmetics, a Plough subsidiary, introduced a new line of makeup. The "Fresh and Lovely" cosmetic product line promised to catapult Maybelline into a competitive full-line makeup company.

These moves, however, were not remedies for the ailing profit margin. In 1979 Richard J. Bennet took over as chief executive officer and continued the efforts to solve the Garamycin conundrum. Schering-Plough had historically been a conservative company with no major debts, maintaining an asset-to-liability ratio of 2.2 to 1 and a $350 million cash excess after seven acquisitions. Yet Schering-Plough continued to look like a "one product" company because of its heavy reliance on Garamycin sales.

In 1979, 40 percent of all profits, or $220 million, was generated solely from Garamycin. Cozen's ineffective attempt to establish company profitability on the sales of a variety of drugs rather than a single product became Bennet's new challenge. Under his management the company released Netromycin, an antibiotic more potent that Garamycin but with fewer side effects. To ensure continued sales of Garamycin when the patent expiration date arrived, the company announced a discount plan to entice former customers into future contracts. Meanwhile, large sums of money continued to pour into the research facilities in the hope of discovering new drugs. Finally, in order to bolster consumer product sales, Schering-Plough purchased Scholl, Inc., (a well established footcare company) for $30 million.

Unfortunately, these maneuvers had only a limited effect on the company. Because doctors had already perfected methods for controlling Garamycin's side effects, they actually preferred to wait for generic and therefore cheaper versions of the drug rather than switch to Netromycin. Similarly, despite $75 million a year spent on research and development, no new discoveries were announced. Furthermore, while Scholl, Inc., had yearly revenues of $250 million and earnings of $12 million, its profits had barely kept pace with inflation since 1973.

Next to all of these disappointments, however, one consumer product did exhibit strong signs of financial success. Maybelline, once known as a manufacturer of "me-too" or imitation products, matured into an aggressive full-line cosmetic company. Bennet claimed in 1980 that Maybelline held 34 percent of the mascara market and 24 percent of the eyeshadow market. Estimated sales for 1980 jumped to $150 million from $75 million in 1976. But after Robert P. Luciano was appointed CEO in 1982, he refocused the company on health care, and Maybelline cosmetics and a household products group were sold.

On May 28, 1980, the day the patent on Garamycin expired, Schering-Plough executives appeared unperturbed. In fact, stock on that day jumped from 39⅛ to 45. Not only was Netromycin on the market, but 80 percent of the hospitals who were previous customers of Garamycin had signed up for the deferred discount plan. More importantly, however, Schering-Plough had paid $12 million for a 14 percent equity stake in a Swiss genetic engineering company called Biogen. Schering-Plough's interest in the company was significant because it provided them with worldwide rights to the synthesis of human leukocyte interferons using recombinant DNA. The possibilities for using the interferon, a chemical produced naturally in the body to fight viruses, were immense. It was hoped that the synthetic drug could be used to treat anything from cancer to the common cold. Moreover, gene-splicing promised to be highly cost-effective; this new method, on the cutting-edge of biotechnology, could produce the same amount of purer proteins in a week than old methods could in a year. Here was the long-awaited breakthrough.

By 1985, in an uncharacteristic move, Schering-Plough had made a more expensive investment in biotechnology than any of its competitors. Expenditures surpassed $100 million. In 1982 Schering-Plough, having reached an agreement to spend $31.5 million over 10 years, formed a partnership with West Berlin politicians to establish a research institute on genetic engineering in Berlin. At the same time, plans were announced to build a fermentation and purification plant in Ireland to market the first commercial interferon. Schering-Plough also purchased another biotech firm in Palo Alto, California, called DNAX Research Institute. Clearly, Schering-Plough announced to the world where the future of its company resided.

Although Schering-Plough was the first to market a commercial Interferon, patent problems with competitors gave Hoffmann-La Roche rights to market alpha interferons in the United States. On June 4, 1986, the Federal Drug Administration approved Schering-Plough's Intron A and Hoffmann-La Roche's Rofeon = A

for the U.S. market. Projected market sales for the interferon were $200 million in the United States and $150 million in Europe. By 1994, Intron A had sales of $426 million. Intron A's sales expanded in the United States and other international markets and grew to be the market leader worldwide. The company continued its study in the field of biotechnology, spending about one-quarter of their research dollars in this area. In 1995, the company expected to invest a total of nearly $650 million on research and development. According to Schering-Plough's 1994 annual report, "Biomedical innovation is truly the only viable, long-term solution for cost-effective quality care."

In the 1990s, Schering-Plough's largest and fastest-growing therapeutic category was in the area of asthma and allergy. Led by new product introductions, worldwide sales rose 24 percent in 1994 to approximately $1.46 billion. The most successful of these new drugs was Claritin (loratadine), a once-a-day, nonsedating antihistamine. Introduced in April 1993, Claritin was the third non-sedating antihistamine to reach the U.S. market. Despite its late arrival, in its first year on the market, Claritin had sales of nearly $200 million. It then captured the number one position in new prescriptions for plain antihistamines in less than a year and a half on the U.S. market, making it the largest single product for the company. Along with the November 1994 U.S. marketing clearance of Claritin-D, a twice-daily formulation combining the decongestant pseudoephedrine, the company expected to capture a significant share of the antihistamine/decongestant market.

Also in the 1990s, a fear of skin cancer and a depleting ozone layer turned sun care from a cosmetic segment to a health care one. With the introduction of Coppertone Kids and Shade UVAGuard, Schering-Plough proved to be a leader in the sun care market. It heavily promoted Shade UVAGuard, the sunscreen positioned as a drug that protects against year-round UVA and UVB rays, both of which cause skin cancer. Schering was also one of the first companies to market sunless tanning and sport products. 1994 marked the 50th anniversary of the Coppertone brand, and, during that year, the company helped launch a national UV (ultraviolet) Index in a joint pilot program with the U.S. Environmental Protection Agency and the National Weather Service to help educate consumers about the importance of proper sun protection. With its broad product lines, Schering-Plough captured major shares in important segments of the entire sun care market, and, in the fast-growing children's market, the company had a 60 percent share with its Coppertone Kids and Water Babies products.

An aging population, the popularity of self-medication, and active lifestyles were other trends that helped boost sales in Schering-Plough's foot care division and built its position as North America's leading foot care company. Schering-Plough's brands lead in every segment of the market, and, according to *Drug Topics* in 1995, Dr. Scholl's had a 72 percent share of the insole/insert category, an 86 percent share of the corn/callus/bunion category, and a 46 percent share of the odor/wetness/grooming category. The company, however, met increased competition from in-store and private label brands during this time.

Schering-Plough's efforts to be an environmentally responsible company received major recognition in 1994. After volunteering to participate in a pilot public-private partnership with the state of New Jersey to reinvent the state's environmental regulations, Schering Plough received New Jersey's and the nation's very first comprehensive, facilitywide environmental permit for its Kenilworth, New Jersey, facility. The one permit, which is unique in the United States, replaced more than 60 individual permits that regulated air emissions, waste water discharges, and solid waste management. Schering-Plough management found that the new permit increased the facility's operational flexibility and they expected to save about $300,000 annually in administrative, waste disposal, and raw materials costs. This strategy was hoped to be adopted by other states as the government challenged companies to accept greater responsibility and accountability for environmental programs.

According to a 1993 article in *Financial World,* Schering-Plough was generally thought to be a second-tier pharmaceutical company with uninspiring research, but with some winning products, and therefore a likely takeover product in the late 1980s. Since then, the company has turned in a remarkable 20 percent growth in per-share earnings. Analysts predicted that Schering-Plough shares would grow 2.5 times as fast as any other top U.S.-based drug company over the next few years. With the continued development of successful products like Garamycin and Claritin and supported by the popularity of household names like Coppertone and Dr. Scholl's, Schering-Plough should keep pace with the rapidly changing field of pharmaceuticals and remain a strong presence in the marketplace.

Principal Subsidiaries: Schering Corp.; Artra Cosmetics, Inc.; Schering Antibiotic Corp.; Plough Export, Inc.; Plough Trading Corp.; Schering Realty Corp.; Schering del Cribe, Inc.; Schering Pharmaceutical Corp.; Schering Export Corp.; White Laboratories, Inc.; The Emko Company; Plough Inc.; Plough Sales Corp.; Plough Advertising Corp.; Plough Broadcasting Co., Inc.; Coppertone Corp.; Schering Industries, Inc.; Schering Transamerica Corp.; Plough Laboratories, Inc.; Sheroid, Inc.; Schering Biochem Corp.; Manati Holdings Corp.; Burns-Biotec Laboratories Inc.; Wesley-Jessen, Inc.; Scholl, Inc.; Schering-Plough Investments, Ltd.; Essex Comercio, Importacao e Participacoes Ltda (Brazil); C.E. Fulford Limited (U.K.); Indus-

tria Quimica e Farmaceutica Schering, S.A. (Brazil); Plough (New Zealand) Ltd.; Schering Corp. (Puerto Rico); P.T. Essex Indonesia (90%); Scherico Ltd. (Switzerland); Schering Corp. Ltd. (Canada); Schering Corp. Centroamerica, S.A. (Panama); Schering Industrial Development Corp. (Puerto Rico); Schering Overseas, Ltd. (Bermuda); Galenacos, S.A. (Luxembourg); Scholl-Plough (S.A.) Pty. Ltd.; Plough de Mexico, S.A de C.V. (50%); Scherag (Pty.) Ltd. (South Africa); Scholl (Brazil) Comercio & Industria Ltd. (Brazil); Plough (Canada) Ltd.; Plough (Australia) Pty. Ltd.; Industria Quimica Plough (Chile) Ltda.; Plough Portuguesa Quimico Farmaceutica Lda. (Portugal; 50%); Pharmaco, Inc.; Coppertone (Japan; 50%); Plough Nederland B.V.; C.E. Fulford (India) Private Ltd.; White Laboratories of Canada Ltd.; Essex Laboratories (New Zealand); Laboratorio Procampo Ltda. (Brazil); Plough Produtos Farmaceuticies e Cosmeticies Limitada (Brazil).

Further Reading:

''Schering-Plough Banking on R&D,'' *Chemical Marketing Reporter,* July 11, 1994, pp. 7 (2).
''Step Up to Better Foot Care Sales,'' *Drug Topics,* March 20, 1995, pp. 68 (2).
''Touted Schering-Plough Feels the 'Clinton Effect,' '' *Chemical Marketing Reporter,* February 22, 1993, pp. 8 (2).
Hunter, Kris, ''Staff Cutbacks Begin at Schering-Plough,'' *Memphis Business Journal,* October 17, 1994, pp. 1 (2).
Kogan, Richard J., ''With Change Comes Opportunity,'' *Chemical Week,* April 26, 1995, p. 48.
Nayyar, Seema, ''Coppertone Adapts to a Changing World,'' *Brandweek,* February 22, 1993, p. 28.
Palmer, Jay, ''Say Yes to Drugs? How Schering-Plough Aims to Survive Hillary Clinton,'' *Barron's,* October 4, 1993, p. 14.
Shaffer, Marjorie, ''Schering-Plough: Against the Tide,'' *Financial World,* June 22, 1993, pp. 16 (2).
Starr, Cynthia, ''Schering's Claritin Promises Quick Onset, No Sedation,'' *Drug Topics,* June 7, 1993, pp. 22 (2).
Waldholz, Michael, ''Luciano to Quit Schering Post as Firm's CEO,'' *The Wall Street Journal,* April 26, 1995, p. B7.

—updated by Beth Watson Highman

Schottenstein Stores Corp.

1800 Molar Road
Columbus, Ohio 43207
U.S.A.
(614) 221-9200
Fax: (614) 443-5810

Private Company
Founded: 1917
Employees: 15,000
Sales: $1.2 billion (est. 1994)
SICs: 5311 Department Stores; 5712 Furniture Stores; 5331
   Variety Stores; 5399 Miscellaneous General Merchandise
   Stores

In its third generation under family management, Schottenstein Stores Corp. (SSC) ranks among the 250 largest private enterprises in the United States. In 1995 the family, led by 40-year-old Jay L. Schottenstein, chairman and chief executive officer, controlled over 92 percent of this retail department store company's equity. The firm spun off about one-third of its largest and best-known division, Value City Department Stores, in June 1991. By 1994 this unit alone boasted $864.9 million in annual sales, having achieved annual same-store revenue increases in spite of a U.S. recession during the late 1980s and early 1990s. Other Schottenstein interests included the Value City Furniture chain (with over 60 stores), four Schottenstein Department Stores, real estate holdings, Shiffren Willens jewelry stores, and Sara Fredericks boutiques.

Opportunism has long been a key to Schottenstein's retailing success. Historically, that meant the family's knack for spotting and taking advantage of retail liquidations. Ephraim L. Schottenstein, a Lithuanian immigrant, settled in Columbus, Ohio, and established this family tradition in the late nineteenth century. The patriarch got a modest start, buying overstocked and outdated goods from local retailers and selling them out of a horse and buggy. Within a few years, Schottenstein had worked up the "critical mass" to open his first shop. He launched his namesake department store in 1917. Ephraim was the patriarch of a family that would become known as "some of retailing's sharpest operators."

The business was nurtured by a second generation of Schottensteins, brothers Jerome, Saul, Alvin, and Leon. Not coincidentally, they joined the business just as the discount retail industry began gaining steam in the late 1940s. Jerome established a reputation as a hard worker while still in his teens. A 1992 retrospective in *Discount Store News* noted that he started "making buying decisions for the chain at an age when most of his peers would be going out on their first date." Known throughout the industry as "Jerry," he joined the executive ranks of the four-store Schottenstein chain in 1946 at the age of 20 and advanced to chairman and CEO in 1972.

Jerome directed the pivotal 1962 acquisition of Value City Stores, which had been established in 1909. According to a 1992 article in *Forbes,* Ephraim forbid the application of the family name on any store open on Saturday, the Jewish Sabbath. As a result, the Value City chain kept its name.

Led by Jerry, the Schottensteins earned a nationwide reputation as "pioneers of the retail liquidation industry" and "professional liquidators" by engineering buyouts of infamous failures. Perhaps the best-known example of the Schottenstein technique was the 1980 acquisition of E.J. Korvettes's entire 31-store inventory. Once a mighty budget retailer, Korvettes had suffered years of mismanagement before going bankrupt. Through an affiliate, M.H. Fishman & Co., Jerome Schottenstein purchased merchandise with a retail value of $58 million for $25 million and managed Korvettes's going-out-of-business sales. Known for his intuitive dealmaking, Schottenstein also participated in the much-publicized liquidation of 2,500 cars from the ill-fated DeLorean Motors enterprise.

That corporate culture of opportunism was reflected in Value City's oft-praised purchasing department. The chain's three dozen buyers averaged over a decade of experience each, a quality that helped earned them the personal connections vital to off-price and closeout buying. Vendors trusted the chain not to abuse their invaluable brand names. The Value City stores, which at 80,000 square feet were two to three times larger than other off-pricers', allowed for bulk purchasing and a wider variety of merchandise. Selection was so vast that Tony Lisanti, editor of *Discount Store News,* characterized Value City as "an off-price, value-driven mall, a collection of specialty stores under one roof." This dealmaking allowed Value City to sell national branded merchandise at substantial discounts (40 percent to 70 percent) from department store prices. More than one analyst likened the Value City shopping experience to a "treasure hunt."

The chain's influence in the off-price and closeout segment of retailing expanded quickly in the 1970s and 1980s. Value City set itself apart from competitors like TJX Companies' TJ Maxx, Mellville Corporation's Marshall's, Filene's Basement, and MacFrugals by offering both closeout and off-price merchandise lines under one roof. These two classes of discount merchandise can be distinguished by both the types of goods and the manner by which they are procured. The off-price category refers to soft goods, generally apparel, that are acquired at a discount by the retailer after the beginning of a fashion season. The term "closeout" generally applies to discontinued hard goods that are discounted by the manufacturer for quick sale.

About 60 percent of Value City's merchandise was apparel, 25 percent of the offerings were hard lines (including housewares, toys, and jewelry), and the remaining sales were generated through leased departments selling shoes and health and beauty aids. The chain was also distinguished from some of its competitors by its emphasis on high-quality brands, which constituted about one-fourth of VCD's merchandise. Only one-fourth of the chain's offerings were described as "budget quality."

Another, less obvious contributor to Value City's success has been technology. Computerized inventory controls, including electronic registers, bar-coding systems, and point-of-sale scanning, have helped this and other chains achieve peak efficiency by shrinking inventories, accelerating turnover, and reducing lead times. Automated distribution centers incorporated high-speed sorters and radio communications to enhance efficiency. Value City's internal computer network permitted "micromarketing," the tailoring of merchandise offerings for each individual store.

Schottenstein Stores Corp. grew along with the off-price discount segment throughout the late 1980s. According to a report prepared by the NPD Consumer Purchase Panel and cited in *Women's Wear Daily* in 1992, "off-price discounters gained about 56 percent of the total apparel market from 1985 to 1991, which translated into sales of about $7 billion." By 1989 SSC's 47 stores generated an estimated $771 million in annual sales.

In the spring of 1991 SSC offered a 25 percent stake in the Value City chain to the public. The stock sale, which forced the Schottensteins to publicize the financial records of their largest retail interest, raised $72.7 million for debt reduction and allowed the family to maintain its control of the board of directors and its executive positions. Before the year's end, a second stock flotation raised another $21.4 million for debt reduction. The shares, which initially sold for $19 each, rose to $50 before a 2-for-1 split in 1992.

But according to *Forbes,* a third stock flotation in April 1992 "flopped" because of investor concerns over conflicts of interest between SSC and Value City. The most obvious of these was the fact that the proceeds of the $50 million stock offering were intended to finance Value City's acquisition of GB Stores, Inc., a 13-store chain purchased by SSC in 1990 from the founding Glosser brothers. Moreover, SSC's 50 percent-owned Shonac Corp., which operated licensed shoe departments in Value City stores, generated another source of conflict. In the face of the failed stock offering, Value City took on new debt to retire $25 million in GB Stores debt and reimburse SSC for $23 million in assets. The GB units were slated for conversion to the more successful Value City format.

In 1991 SSC completed the acquisition of Retail Ventures Inc., the Pennsylvania-based operator of the 150-store American Eagle Outfitters chain. The concept featured private-label outdoorwear, footwear, and accessories. Founded in 1977, Retail Ventures had over $100 million in annual sales by the time SSC assumed full ownership. SSC had taken a 50 percent stake in the chain as early as 1980, when the founding Silverman family encountered a fiscal dilemma. Jay Schottenstein assumed the presidency of the division. Although most of the chain's units were located in the East and Midwest, Retail Ventures also had a nationally distributed mail-order catalog.

Jerry Schottenstein succumbed to cancer March 10, 1992, at the age of 66. According to a March 16, 1992, story in *Business*

First—Columbus, the hard-driving executive was "working in his office on the morning of the day he died." The family business mantle fell to son Jay L. Schottenstein, who had worked at the company since 1976 and eventually advanced to the board of directors in 1982 and a vice-chairmanship in 1986. Saul Schottenstein, the only surviving member of the second generation, stayed on as SSC president. George Iacono, who had come to SSC from Marshall's in 1984, advanced to the posts of president and general merchandise manager of Value City.

In the years following its partial spin-off, Value City and its executives generally garnered high praise. In 1992 *Fortune* noted that "Value City seems impermeable to the soggy retailing climate." Whereas most retailers were happy to tread water, Value City swam strongly forward, reporting same-store sales increases of ten percent. Under the slogan "Better Living for Less," the chain's sales doubled from 1987 to 1992, when they topped $600 million.

The chain also bucked a mid-1990s "retrenchment" in the off-price segment. "Off-pricers' market share hit an historic high of 12 percent of all women's apparel sales in 1994, compared with an estimated 11.4 percent in 1993," according to Isaac Lagnado, publisher of *Tactical Retail Monitor.* Although such stalwarts as Filene's Basement and TJ Maxx faltered when traditional department stores began to meet the off-price challenge, Value City's sales and operating profits continued their seemingly inexorable climb. In 1995 analyst R. L. Rotter gushed, "If there is such a thing as a 'Category Killer' in off-price and close-out retailing, VCD must be it." In anticipation of expanding the chain to 100 stores, the company built new distribution centers for its hard and soft lines in the early 1990s. Value City planned to open three new stores in the suburbs of Detroit, Chicago, and St. Louis by the end of 1995. Executives set their sights on surpassing the $1 billion mark by the turn of the century.

SSC revisited the public financial markets in 1994 with the sale of about 40 percent of American Eagle Outfitters Inc. to the public. The chain had suffered back-to-back losses totaling over $14 million in 1991 and 1992 but made operating income of $7.5 million on revenues of $168 million in 1993. Late in 1994 an SSC affiliate bought the 26-store Steinbach Inc. chain of department stores. Although terms of the acquisition were not publicized, it was known that Steinbach had revenues of approximately $225 million in 1993.

Several factors point toward a bright future for Schottenstein Stores Corp. and its affiliates. The firm's heritage of market savvy, both in terms of merchandising and corporate acquisitions, appears to be continuing under the direction of the newest generation of leadership. The company's commitment to discounting also seemed well placed in a consumer culture intent on quality and value. Finally, SSC's strategy of selling minority interests in its affiliates allowed the company to raise money for debt reduction and future acquisitions without relinquishing Schottenstein family control.

Principal Subsidiaries: Gee Bee Department Stores; Hochschild Value City Corp.; Schottenstein Stores Corp.; Discount

Housewares; Shiffren Willens Jewelers Inc.; Steinbach Inc.; Valley Fair Corp.; Value City Furniture.

Further Reading:

Arlen, Jeffrey, "Value City: Orchestrating Off-Price," *Discount Store News,* May 3, 1993, p. 18A.

Barmash, Isadore, *More Than They Bargained For: The Rise and Fall of Korvettes,* New York: Lebhar-Friedman Books, 1981.

"Companies to Watch: Value City," *Fortune,* March 23, 1992, p. 109.

Ginsberg, Stanley, "Opportunity Lost," *Forbes,* September 29, 1980, p. 38.

Koselka, Rita, "The Schottenstein Factor," *Forbes,* September 28, 1992, p. 104.

Lisanti, Tony, "Value City a Sign of Retail Vitality," *Discount Store News,* October 5, 1992, p. 8.

Mehlman, William, "Buyer Group Calls the Shots for Overachieving Value City," *Insider Chronicle,* March 2, 1992, p. 1.

"Off-Price Apparel Chains Pressed to Differentiate," *Discount Store News,* March 20, 1995, p. 6.

Phillips, Jeff, "Schottensteins Buy 153 Stores," *Business First—Columbus,* June 3, 1991, p. 1.

Phillips, Jeff, and William Jackson, "Schottenstein Passes Empire to Son, Jay," *Business First—Columbus,* March 16, 1992, p. 1.

Rotter, R. L., "Value City Department Stores—Company Report," Thomson Financial Networks Inc., April 3, 1995.

Schneiderman, Ira P., "Off-Price Discounters Double Dollar Volume From 1985 to 1991," *Women's Wear Daily,* November 4, 1992, p. 42.

Tosh, Mark, "Off-Price: A Change in Store," *Women's Wear Daily,* March 29, 1995, p. 14.

"Value City Aim: Absorb Gee Bee," *Discount Store News,* May 4, 1992, p. 1.

Walters, Rebecca, "American Eagle Going Public," *Business First—Columbus*, March 21, 1994, p. 1.

—April Dougal Gasbarre

Sealed Air Corporation

Sealed Air Corporation

Park 80 East
Saddle Brook, New Jersey 07662-5291
U.S.A.
(201) 791-7600
Fax: (201) 703-4205

Public Company
Incorporated: 1960
Employees: 3,700
Sales: $519 million
Stock Exchanges: New York
SICs: 3086 Plastics Foam Products; 3089 Plastics Products, Not Elsewhere Classified; 2674 Uncoated Paper and Multiwall Bags; 2676 Sanitary Paper Products; 5113 Industrial and Personal Service Paper

Sealed Air Corporation is one of the world's leading manufacturers of protective and specialty packaging materials. Some of the company's best-known products include Instapak, a system for injecting a protective, expanding polyurethane foam into shipping cartons and other containers; protective mailers and bags sold under the Jiffy brand name; and AirCap, which is the trade name for the bubble wrap that almost everybody loves to pop one cell at a time. In addition to a wide variety of other foam and air cushioning products, Sealed Air also makes food packaging products, such as its absorbent Dri-Loc pads found underneath meat, fish, and poultry sold in supermarkets. The company operated manufacturing facilities all over the world, including 27 locations in North America, 16 in Europe, and six in the Far East.

Sealed Air was founded by U.S. engineer Al Fielding and Swiss inventor Marc Chavannes, the two men who gave the world bubble wrap. Fielding and Chavannes first developed their Air-Cap material in 1957 but lacked the funding necessary to begin producing it commercially. After a few years of tinkering with manufacturing methods and hustling for seed capital, they launched Sealed Air in 1960. With $85,000 raised through an initial public stock offering, production of AirCap material began in earnest the following year. In its earliest form AirCap packaging material suffered from slightly leaky bubbles. In spite of the problems, however, the product gained popularity throughout the 1960s, and by the middle of the decade research efforts had led to the development of a special coating that

prevented the bubbles from losing air. By 1969 bubble wrap was beginning to catch on. For that year, Sealed Air reported sales of $4 million. This represented nearly the entire market for bubble wrap, since the product was still proprietary at the time.

In 1970 Sealed Air suffered a small deficit, despite continuing gains in sales. In the face of criticism from some members of the company's board, President Ted Bowers suddenly resigned. To replace him, the board turned to one of its members, T. J. Dermot Dunphy, an Irishman who had studied at Oxford and at Harvard Business School. Dunphy had arrived on the Sealed Air board after selling his own small packaging company, Custom-Made Packaging (which sold popsicle wrappers and the like), to Hammermill Paper. With cash on hand from that sale, Dunphy had asked friends at the investment firm Donaldson, Lufkin & Jenrette to find a public company for him to lead. Bowers's unexpected departure created that opportunity at Sealed Air.

Just prior to the beginning of the Dunphy era, Sealed Air had added a set of products to its line. By laminating AirCap cushioning material to kraft paper, the company developed its Mail Lite shipping envelopes, first sold in 1971. A smaller, cheaper version of Mail Lite called Bubble-Lite was introduced a few years later. The company also became international around this time, with the 1970 acquisition of Smith Packaging Ltd., later renamed Sealed Air of Canada, Ltd. Under Dunphy, the company's minor stumble of 1970 was quickly reversed, and by 1972 Sealed Air's sales had passed the $10 million mark. Another new product, PolyMask, was introduced in 1973. PolyMask, a pressure sensitive polyethylene film for protecting delicate surfaces against scratches, was the first Sealed Air product not based on its air bubble technology. For 1973, the company's after-tax profits topped $1 million for the first time. Of its $13.6 million in sales for that year, about 60 percent came from AirCap and about 20 percent from Mail Lite. The rest came mostly from the manufacture and distribution of a variety of packaging products by its Canadian subsidiary. The company's biggest customer was the electronics industry, which accounted for about 40 percent of sales.

Sealed Air made its first foray into Europe in 1973, acquiring ten percent of Sibco Universal, S.A., a French manufacturing firm. Over the next few years, Sealed Air bought the rest of Sibco. During the mid-1970s Sealed Air's researchers came up with another innovative use for the company's air cell technology. The Sealed Air Solar Pool Blanket was essentially a big sheet of bubble wrap that was placed on swimming pools. The Solar Pool Blanket allowed the sun's rays to heat the water and sharply reduced the evaporative loss of water and treatment chemicals. By 1977 the Solar Pool Blanket was generating six percent of company sales. As an offshoot of the pool blanket, the company also began making a roof-mounted solar water heater designed mainly for heating swimming pools.

The most important development of 1977 was the acquisition of Instapak Corporation, producers of a revolutionary "foam-in-place" cushioning system. The foam-in-place process, initially conceived in the 1950s by engineers at Lockheed Corporation, involves surrounding a product with urethane in a liquid form that would then quickly expand into a semirigid foam. The idea was finally made practical in 1969 by inventor Richard Sperry (whose grandfather, Elmer Sperry, invented the gyroscope). Instapak was made a division of Sealed Air, and it quickly became one of the company's most important products, generating almost as great a share of total sales as bubble wrap by the end of the decade. Foreign sales also increased dramatically during the second half of the 1970s, accounting for nearly a quarter of the company's total by 1977. By 1979 Sealed Air's annual sales had grown to more than $70 million.

By the beginning of the 1980s, foam-in-place was clearly a product destined for bigger things, and Sealed Air still had virtually no competition in the area. The pool blankets were also doing well, selling as fast as the company could make them. In 1981 Sealed Air added PolyCap to its product line. PolyCap was essentially a lower-cost, less durable version of AirCap, without the barrier coating, providing a less expensive option for products that required only a relatively short period of protection. Sealed Air broadened its product line further in 1983 by purchasing Cellu-Products Co., a Hickory, North Carolina, manufacturer of packaging materials, for $20 million. The Cellu-Products acquisition added thin-grade polyethylene foam, coated films, and other plastic and paper materials to the company's growing collection of packaging products. Although the recession of 1982 took a bite out of Sealed Air's revenue and earnings figures, the emergence of personal computers and other related electronic gizmos brought a new wave of business, and by 1983 the company's sales had grown to $124 million.

In an effort to diversify its product line further, and in part to prepare itself for the impending expiration of its bubble wrap patents, Sealed Air acquired several smaller companies during the middle part of the 1980s. In 1984 the company acquired Cortec Corporation, a small anticorrosive chemical firm. Cortec was sold off only a few years later, after being caught illegally shipping chemicals to Libya. Other acquisitions that yielded happier results included Static, Inc., in 1985; a Canadian spa manufacturer in 1987; and a Swedish packaging company in 1987. More important was the company's 1987 purchase of Jiffy Packaging, which manufactured padded mailers for items such as floppy disks and books. The addition of Jiffy solidified Sealed Air's dominant position in the protective mailer market. During this period, Sealed Air also began incorporating recycled materials into a number of its air bubble and paper packaging products, at a time when few companies in the industry were doing so.

By 1988 Sealed Air had annual sales of $346 million, and it earned $42 million in profit that year. All told, $127 million of the company's sales came from Instapak, which by this time had more or less replaced bubble wrap as the flagship product. The company boosted its presence in the food packaging business that year with the acquisition of a company that made absorbent pads for poultry. Meanwhile, Sealed Air's researchers, as well as freelancer Sperry (who had developed Instapak), kept busy at the drawing board. One new wrinkle was a pair of systems called Instapacker and VersaPacker, which could produce bags full of protective foam at the touch of a button.

Dunphy pulled off a remarkable financial maneuver in 1989. The company had been so profitable over the previous few years that it found itself with a huge cash surplus. Since Dunphy could not find any more companies that he felt were good acquisition candidates, he had no obvious outlets for this cash buildup. In order to avoid becoming too attractive a target for a takeover, as well as to create what he called a "controlled crisis" to shake his managers out of their complacency, Dunphy decided to give the money away. He announced a $40-per-share special dividend, amounting to a $328 million gift to shareholders. The move increased the company's long-term debt from $19 million to over $300 million, made up of a combination of bank loans and junk bonds.

Dunphy hoped that leveraging the company would push it to new heights of efficiency, and he was correct. The new debt situation necessitated changes in the way the company handled inventory and led to other cost-cutting measures. These changes enabled the company to begin repaying its debts ahead of schedule, creating further savings. At the same time, an unexpected reduction in the cost of raw materials resulted in yet more opportunities to work down part of the debt with extra cash. By the early 1990s it was clear that the gamble had paid off, and Sealed Air was ready to go shopping once again. In 1991 the company acquired a small company called KorrVu, which produced transparent suspension packaging. Sentinel Foam & Envelope Corporation, a packaging firm based in Philadelphia, was also acquired that year.

Sealed Air's sales figures stalled somewhat during the first part of the 1990s, advancing from $413 million in 1990 to only $452 million in 1993. Nevertheless, the company was able to generate solid profits each year. In order to boost revenue, Dunphy began concentrating heavily on worldwide expansion. Instapak was introduced in Mexico, and the company opened manufacturing facilities in Germany and Spain. Throughout, the company continued to emphasize research and development, and new products were unveiled at a steady pace. One such product was Floral, introduced in 1993. Floral was a foam that served as a base in artificial flower arrangements. Within a year of its first appearance, Floral was generating sales in the neighborhood of $5 million.

As the 1990s continued, Sealed Air made additional strategic acquisitions. In 1993 the company purchased the Shurtuff Division of Shuford Mills, Inc. Shurtuff's extremely durable plastic-based mailers meshed well with Sealed Air's existing protective mailer product line. On the product development front, the company developed a new inflatable packaging system called VoidPak. The acquisition department was very active in 1994. The company reinforced its European food pad business with the purchase of Hereford Paper and Allied Products Ltd., an English food pad manufacturing firm. Packaging companies based in Norway, France, and Italy were also acquired during the year. The French acquisition added two product lines, Sup-Air-Pack and Fill Air, to the company's collection of inflation-based systems, an area considered to hold great promise for the future. Toward the end of the year the company reorganized its management structure so that its important product lines were coordinated globally rather than country-by-country. This move reflected an increasing focus on the international market, which was expected to continue through the rest of the century. For 1994 sales numbers at Sealed Air made their first significant jump in several years, exceeding $500 million for the first time in company history. Earnings, at $31.6 million, reached record levels as well.

Sealed Air's biggest acquisition of this period came in January 1995, when it acquired Trigon Industries Ltd., a New Zealand company with operations in Australia, England, Germany, and the United States. With annual sales of $72 million, the addition of Trigon was expected to have an immediate and dramatic impact on Sealed Air's balance sheet as well as on its geographic reach. Trigon's products included food packaging systems, durable mailers and bags, and specialty adhesive products. With its successful global expansion program of the first half 1990s, Sealed Air appeared poised to extend to the worldwide market the commanding position it has enjoyed for many years in the domestic specialty packaging material industry.

Principal Subsidiaries: Aire Sellado, S.S. de C.V. (Mexico); Cascades Sealed Air Inc. (Canada, 50 percent); Danco (NZ) Ltd. (New Zealand, 95 percent); Delsopak S.A. (France); Emballasje Teknikk A/S (Norway); Europads Sarl (France); Hereford Paper and Allied Products Ltd. (England); Instapak France S.A.; PolyMask Corporation (50 percent); Polypride, Inc.; Sealed Air N.V. (Belgium); Sealed Air of Canada Ltd.; Sealed Air España, S.A.; Sealed Air Ltd. (England); Sealed Air (Far East) Ltd. (Hong Kong); Sealed Air GmbH (Germany); Sealed Air Holdings (NZ) Ltd. (New Zealand); Sealed Air Japan Ltd.; Sealed Air S.p.A. (Italy); Sealed Air (Korea) Ltd.; Sealed Air (Malaysia) Sdn. Bhd.; Sealed Air B.V. (Netherlands); Sealed Air (Puerto Rico) Inc.; Sealed Air (Singapore) Pte. Ltd.; Sealed Air Svenska AB (Sweden); Sealed Air Taiwan Ltd.; Sealed Air Thailand Ltd.; Sealed Air Trucking, Inc.; SPEC Srl (Italy); Static, Inc.; Trigon Industries Ltd. (New Zealand); Trigon Packaging Systems (NZ) Ltd. (New Zealand); Trigon Engineering Ltd. (New Zealand); Trigon Packaging Systems (Aust) Pty Ltd. (Australia); Trigon Packaging Corporation; Trigon Cambridge Ltd. (England); Trigon Packaging Systems (UK) Ltd.; Trigon Verpackungsysteme GmbH (Germany).

Further Reading:

"By the Throat," *Economist,* September 14, 1991, p. 78.
David, Gregory E., "Make My Day!" *Financial World,* January 17, 1995, pp. 38–39.
Dunphy, T. J. Dermot, *Sealed Air Corporation: Our Products Protect Your Products,* New York: Newcomen Society in North America, 1982.
Fadiman, Mark, "If the Bubble Bursts, Try Foam," *Forbes,* June 18, 1984, p. 104.
Gordon, Mitchell, "Sealed Air, Packaging Specialist, Headed for Eighth Straight Advance," *Barron's,* February 6, 1978, pp. 40–41;
—— "Sealed Air's Bag," *Barron's,* August 25, 1980, pp. 36–37.
"How This Bubble-Wrap Maker Boomed by Popping Its Own Bubble," *Money,* March 1994, p. 56.
"It's All in the Packaging," *Financial World,* May 1, 1980, pp. 48–49.
McGough, Robert, "Controlled Crisis," *Financial World,* February 6, 1990, pp. 74–75.
"Packaging That's Light But Strong Enables Sealed Air to Keep Growing," *Barron's,* December 2, 1974, pp. 44–45.
Smith, Geoffrey, "What Turnaround?" *Forbes,* October 1, 1979, pp. 89–92.

—Robert R. Jacobson

Shared Medical Systems Corporation

51 Valley Stream Parkway
Malvern, Pennsylvania 19355
U.S.A.
(610) 219-6300
Fax: (610)251-3124

Public Company
Founded: 1968
Employees: 4,370
Sales: $550.29 million
Stock Exchanges: NASDAQ
SICs: 7373 Computer Integrated Systems Design; 7374 Data
    Processing & Preparation

Shared Medical Systems Corporation (SMS) is a leading provider of computer-based information processing systems and associated services to the healthcare industry in North America and Europe. The company provides various data processing and management services to hospitals, clinics, physician groups, and miscellaneous healthcare corporations. SMS helped to pioneer the industry during the 1970s and was still enjoying heady gains in the mid-1990s.

SMS was formed in 1968 by three International Business Machines (IBM) salesmen, led by James Macaleer. Macaleer, a chemical engineering graduate of Princeton University, had worked his way up through the IBM Corporation as a salesman, and by the late 1960s he was serving as a medical marketing manager. He recognized a need for hospitals to automate their proliferating financial and patient-care information, and late in 1968 Macaleer and two fellow IBM salesmen left their jobs to launch SMS. Their goal was to sell systems that would solve some of the data management problems faced by the hospital market.

Macaleer and his associates started out selling computer systems to hospitals in the Delaware Valley. They encountered difficulties because the hospital personnel didn't know how to operate the complex machines and didn't have the skills to create or even use the software they needed. The partners altered their strategy and began offering only financial management systems to prospective clients. Their service was not unique; by the late 1960s, other companies were providing similar systems and services on a regional basis throughout the country. SMS differentiated itself from the pack, however, by offering its service on a national basis. They planned to eventually provide centralized data processing to a national network of hospitals.

Shared Medical's national expansion occurred quickly. The company's big break came when it landed an account with American Medicorp, a regional hospital corporation based in Bala Cynwyd, on the outskirts of Philadelphia. American Medicorp soon began buying other hospitals to add to its chain, expanding across the nation during the early and mid-1970s. As American Medicorp expanded it took SMS along with it, allowing the company to set up satellite terminals in its new hospitals.

SMS's satellite terminals were connected to a central mainframe system. Hospitals could connect to their centralized service on a time-share basis, avoiding the expense and trouble of purchasing and maintaining a separate mainframe system within the hospital. The arrangement was particularly advantageous for smaller hospitals or those on a tight budget that couldn't afford their own mainframe systems. During the mid-1970s SMS expanded from financial management services into the clinical areas of hospitals and eventually was offering a range of patient-care and financial management data administration services.

SMS gradually accumulated a substantial base of customers that allowed it to generate healthy profits from its investments in hardware and personnel. Besides a strong customer base, SMS benefitted from a savvy management team and fluid financing that allowed it to keep up with rapid growth in demand. Indeed, throughout much of the 1970s SMS sustained a revenue growth rate of approximately 20 percent annually. The company's strongest growth occurred following its initial public offering in 1976, when SMS was generating roughly $40 million in annual revenue. For several years SMS posted sales and profit gains averaging 20 percent to 25 percent annually. Revenues leapt to $131 million in 1981 and then to a $312 million by 1985. Earnings similarly soared from $6.8 million in 1977 to $16.6 million in 1981, and then to a $41.7 million in 1985.

SMS achieved this aggressive growth by parlaying its early American Medicorp coup into a nationwide network comprising hundreds of hospitals that were tapping into its time-share mainframe services. Several other companies followed SMS (and a few other pioneers) into the market, including IBM, which eventually became one of Shared Medical's major competitors by snatching up 35 percent of the hospital information systems market by the late 1980s. Nevertheless, SMS, with an elite sales force and heavy spending on research and development, managed to sustain its early industry lead and even to widen the gap over most of its competitors during the late 1970s and early 1980s. The company also began expanding internationally with offices in Europe and Japan. Going into the mid-1980s the company's market value was approaching a healthy $1.5 billion.

SMS entered the mid-1980s as the leader in the hospital information services industry. After posting increasing profits for more than a decade, however, the company began to come under heavy criticism for lackluster performance. Part of the problem was that the $2 billion industry was becoming increasingly crowded: by 1987 about 80 companies were vying for market share, and the market wasn't growing very quickly. Some companies had already fallen by the wayside, including the once-powerful BBO & Co., an Atlanta-based information services provider that had been one of SMS's main rivals. Losing money in its overseas operations, in 1986 SMS decided to close its unprofitable Japanese operations and was forced to take a $20 million write-off related to the maneuver.

According to critics, increasing competition in the marketplace was exacerbated at SMS by internal problems, including a failure to keep up with changing technology. The information services market had rapidly been shifting toward smaller platforms since the widespread acceptance of personal computers began in the early 1980s. System providers like IBM were increasingly installing personal computers and minicomputers as part of turnkey systems, rather than terminals connected to central mainframes. SMS had been slow to adapt to emerging market trends, according to some industry insiders, and had failed to keep pace with new software and service needs. In 1986, for example, SMS introduced its Independence system, a $3 million IBM mainframe-based system for financial and patient-care data that offered both in-house and shared-processing options. Although the system was advanced, orders were fewer than expected.

To make matters worse, it was estimated that less than half of the country's hospitals were big enough to warrant the type of large-scale computerization provided by SMS. And because of tightening budgets and newer, less expensive computer alternatives, that number was declining. Managers at Shared Medical countered criticism, citing market leadership and an intense effort to gear its products for new systems as evidence of its long-term potential, but declining sales and profits cast doubt on their claims. SMS's revenues increased 20 percent to $374 million 1986, but earnings fell from $42 million a year earlier to $32 million. In 1987, moreover, sales inched up only four percent, and net income effectively stagnated before dropping in both 1988 and 1989 to a low of $23 million. The company's stock price dropped by about 75 percent.

Analysts blamed the slide on mismanagement. "This is a very stubborn company," said analyst James Meyer. "It does what it thinks it should be doing, rather than listening to its customers." Adding fuel to critics' fire during the mid-1980s were two shareholder suits filed against SMS claiming that executives in the company had released misleading financial information that artificially inflated the company's stock price. They alleged that three executives had sold off large chunks of stock before releasing surprising information that indicated that SMS was experiencing significant financial, product, management, and marketing problems. SMS agreed late in 1988 to settle the two suits for about $5 million in cash, although it never admitted to any wrongdoing. The Securities and Exchange Commission filed another suit containing similar allegations late in 1991.

Despite the lawsuits and other problems, SMS continued to post profits throughout the late 1980s and to position itself for long-term growth. The company's performance during the early 1990s, in fact, belied claims that it was headed for a fall. Shared Medical's net income dropped to a several-year low of $22.6 million in 1990, but that figure rose to $25 million in 1991 as sales grew 9 percent to a record $438 million. SMS's stock price also began to recover, reflecting increased confidence on the part of investors in the company's potential. Sales surged again in 1992 before topping out in 1993 at more than $500 million. Earnings climbed back to a healthy $31 million.

The reasons for SMS's comeback were both internal and external. In 1989 the company introduced its successful Invision system, its next-generation information system for users of IBM and DEC computers, which offered both in-house and remote computing capability. Within a few years of Invision's introduction more than 80 new hospitals had signed up for the service and another 190 had upgraded from the Independence system. SMS and its Invision system benefitted during the early 1990s from an important industry trend: a return to remote data processing. After experimenting with on-site computing in the mid-1980s, healthcare organizations were coming to the realization that shared, off-site computing was generally more efficient. By 1993, in fact, about 80 percent of all hospitals were using shared systems, which meant more recurring revenues and greater profit opportunities for companies like SMS.

In addition to its success with Invision, SMS benefitted from gains in its professional services group and its international division, which posted a revenue increase of 40 percent in 1992, to $53 million. Furthermore, SMS was launching a number of new initiatives that were expected to generate substantial profits in the near future. For example, its strategic alliance program, launched in 1993, involved customers as investors in applications development. The program focused on hospital records automation, a growing market segment that SMS planned to lead by the mid-1990s. SMS was also making advancements in on-line medical record document imaging and diagnostic imaging products.

Besides improving its product and service offerings, SMS reorganized in an effort to eliminate underperforming operations and to improve overall profit margins. It closed its Canadian subsidiary in 1991, for example, as well as its physicians' practice management business. Those and other actions helped SMS to boost sales a solid ten percent in 1994 to $550 million, about $35 million of which was netted as income. About 92 percent of that revenue was attributable to service and system fees, while only eight percent came from the sale of hardware. Also in 1994, SMS announced its intent to acquire GTE Health Systems from its parent, GTE Information Services. The acquisition would bring a popular healthcare information system—the MedSeries 4—to SMS, and add 300 accounts to its customer base, further cementing the company's position as the leader in the healthcare information processing industry.

Principal Subsidiaries: SMS Europe.

Further Reading:

Abelson, Reed, "Shared Medical Rebounds; Hits 52-Week High of $50.38," *Philadelphia Business Journal,* February 9, 1987, Sec. 1, p. 12.
Armstrong, Michael W., "Shared Medical Optimistic It Will Rebound from 1987," *Philadelphia Business Journal,* January 25, 1988, Sec. 2, p. 4B.

——, "Shared Medical Reports Higher Net Income," *Philadelphia Business Journal,* February 29, 1988, Sec. 1, p. 19.

——, "SMS Adopts a 'Poison Pill' after Stockholder Grouses," *Philadelphia Business Journal,* May 13, 1991, Sec. 1, p. 1.

——, "SMS Shareholder Suit Settled for $5 Million," *Philadelphia Business Journal,* September 26, 1988, Sec. 1, p. 13.

——, "SMS, Three Execs Sued by SEC," *Philadelphia Business Journal,* October 28, 1991, Sec. 1, p. 8.

Chithlen, Ignatius, "A Niche Is Not Enough," *Forbes,* June 27, 1988, p. 73.

Cruickshank, Walter, "MICRO Healthsystems Names Graham O. King Chairman and C.E.O.," *Business Wire,* October 12, 1994.

George, John, "Shared Medical Software Runs Bedside Computers," *Philadelphia Business Journal,* July 30, 1990, Sec. 2, p. 7B.

Kyle, Terrence W., "Share Medical Systems to Acquire GTE Health Systems," *PR Newswire,* July 29, 1994.

Lehren, Andrew, "SMS Shareholders File Suit Alleging Misleading Data," *Philadelphia Business Journal,* September 14, 1987, Sec. 1, p. 1.

Pantages, Angeline, "Shared Medical Systems Corp.," *Datamation,* June 15, 1992, p. 134.

Sana, Siwolop, "Shared Med: LBO Fodder?" *Financial World,* December 13, 1988, p. 16.

—Dave Mote

Shelby Williams Industries, Inc.

1348 Merchandise Mart
Chicago, Illinois 60654
U.S.A.
(312) 527-3593
Fax: (312) 527-3597

Public Company
Incorporated: 1954
Employees: 1,728
Sales: $159.07 million
Stock Exchanges: New York
SICs: 2521 Wood Office Furniture; 2522 Office Furniture
    Except Wood

Shelby Williams Industries, Inc., is a leading supplier of furnishings for the contract furniture market. Shelby Williams and its subsidiaries design, manufacture, and distribute furniture, wall coverings and other textiles, and flooring and floor coverings to hotels and restaurants, casinos, country clubs, nursing homes, office buildings, colleges, and other institutions. With nearly 2 million square feet among nine manufacturing and distributing facilities in the United States and Mexico, 15 showrooms in the United States, and representation in 44 other countries, Shelby Williams and its 1,700 employees produced more than 1.25 million units for sales of close to $160 million in 1994. Exports to 63 foreign countries contributed roughly ten percent of its revenues. Among its many customers, Shelby Williams maintains long-term relationships with such corporations as Holiday Inns, Wendy's, and McDonald's. Shelby Williams has provided furniture for many of the world's luxury hotels, as well as for cruise ships such as the *Queen Elizabeth II* and the S.S. Norway line. After several years of a soft market, Shelby Williams rode the mid-1990s boom in the casino market.

Manfred Steinfeld, who remained chairman of Shelby Williams in 1995, was born in the farming village of Josbach, Germany, in 1925. The Nazi party began its rise several years later and, in 1939, Steinfeld's mother sent him to Chicago to live with an uncle. His mother and sister died in the Nazi concentration camps; a brother, sent to the former Palestine, died in the Israeli independence war. Steinfeld joined the U.S. 82nd Airborne as a parachutist and intelligence specialist and participated in the victory over the German army and the liberation of the concentration camps; in 1945, he was assigned to translate the terms of

Germany's unconditional surrender. By the end of the war Steinfeld had received the Bronze Star, the European Campaign medal with five stars, the Bronze Arrowhead, and the Purple Heart. He returned to Chicago and received a degree in business administration from Roosevelt University. After a stint as a research statistician, Steinfeld reenlisted for active duty in the Korean War. He returned to Chicago in 1952, working for Sam Horvitz, a noted restaurant designer. In 1954 Steinfeld and Horvitz bought up the assets of the defunct Great Northern Chair Company, a maker of Vienna bentwood chairs, for $10,000. The partners incorporated the new company under the name Shelby Williams. Horvitz became president, and Steinfeld was named vice-president and manager.

In its first year Shelby Williams employed 30 people and produced 50,000 chairs for sales of $350,000; by the following year production had doubled. The postwar boom had created a new market; previously, the contract market, so called because orders were placed by written contract, had been handled almost exclusively by large department stores. The rise in disposable income, and the corresponding increases in the numbers of people dining out and traveling, encouraged other manufacturers to enter the contract furnishings field. At the same time, department stores turned their focus to the growing numbers of individual consumers and dropped out of the contract market. As travel became less and less the preserve of the wealthy, new hotels—and a new breed of motels—sprang up across the country. Restaurants, especially fast-food restaurants, appeared in greater numbers. Innovations in restaurant design also encouraged the growth of firms offering design and manufacturing capabilities. The standardization of amenities introduced by hotel chains like Ramada Inn, Howard Johnson, and Holiday Inn, as well as restaurant chains like McDonald's, brought increasingly larger orders into the contract furniture firms.

By 1959 Shelby William's sales had jumped to $2.5 million. Its catalog had grown from 24 pages in its first year to 64 pages and included contemporary and Scandinavian designs. In response to the population boom on the West Coast, the company opened an assembly plant in Los Angeles. A break occurred for the young company when one of its main competitors, Thonet, the originator of bentwood manufacturing, left the burgeoning hotel and restaurant market. Shelby Williams rushed to fill the gap. From 1961 to 1964, Shelby Williams showrooms appeared in Dallas, Atlanta, Los Angeles, and in the Merchandise Mart in Chicago. The company expanded its product line beyond chairs to include tables and home furnishings with the 1962 acquisition of American of Chicago, the first in a long list of acquisitions. In 1963 Shelby Williams increased production capabilities with the opening of a plant in Morristown, Tennessee, which doubled in size within six months. During this time Horvitz left to return to design, and Steinfeld took over as chairman and president of Shelby Williams.

The company had achieved such steady growth that in 1965 Steinfeld took Shelby Williams public, reincorporating the company as a Delaware corporation. Its initial stock offering went for $10.75 per share. The following year the price had jumped to $15.75 per share, and in 1967, when the company was listed on the American Stock Exchange, its stock had reached $18.59 per share. Shelby Williams acquired Duo-Bed Corp. of Wichita, Kansas, a pioneer in the sleeper sofa, in 1965, and Madison Furniture Industries and its office furniture production plant in Canton, Mississippi, in 1966; the company extended its product range into the hospital and nursing home market in 1968 with the purchase of Goodman Bros. Mfg. Co. of Philadelphia.

By 1968 Shelby Williams sales totaled more than $18 million and its stock had reached a high of $36 per share. In that year Shelby Williams merged into Coronet Industries, Inc., a leading carpet manufacturer. Terms of the merger included an exchange of stock valued at just over $17 million, approximately four times the company's book value. Steinfeld remained as head of the company and Shelby Williams continued to operate autonomously. Its acquisitions continued: Chicago-based metal chair manufacturer Tri-Par Mfg. Co. in 1968; Morristown Foam and Fiber Corp. of Morristown, Tennessee, in 1970; and Stephen-Black Company of Los Angeles, another dual-purpose sleep furniture manufacturer, also in 1970.

Coronet Industries was acquired by RCA for a one-to-one exchange of stock in 1971. Steinfeld retained his leadership position in his company. Over the next several years RCA poured millions into Shelby Williams, increasing the scope of its operations, and introduced accounting and management disciplines that further increased the company's profits. The takeover came at a good time. The oil embargo and resulting recession of 1972–1975 severely cut into the contract furniture market; it seemed unlikely the Shelby Williams would have survived this period without the financial strength of RCA to back it.

In 1975, however, RCA decided to leave the contract furniture market. Steinfeld was offered the opportunity to buy back his own company. Gathering a group of investors, Steinfeld purchased Shelby Williams from RCA in 1976 for slightly more than $17 million in cash and notes, just $100,000 more than what he had received for the company less than ten years before. By then, however, Shelby Williams's sales had reached $44 million per year. The company was now a private company; in order to finance its debt, it sold off Goodman Mfg. in 1977. By 1979 company sales topped $67 million. Its catalog had grown to 240 pages, featuring more than 600 seating styles and serving customers throughout much of the world.

The company repaid its debt of approximately $9 million in promissory notes by 1979. Steinfeld prepared to take the company public once again; in 1983 Shelby Williams posted an initial common stock offering of 2 million shares at $10.75 per share, raising $7 million. Steinfeld controlled 51 percent of the company's stock, worth some $50 million. Its 1984 sales of $96 million made Shelby Williams the leader in the contract market, capturing as much as 20 percent of the hotel and restaurant furnishings segment. Two years later Steinfeld's stock, valued at $1 million in 1965, was worth $88 million on sales of $116 million. Apart from its U.S. showrooms, the company's licensees operated in Canada, the United Kingdom, and South Africa with distributor offices in France, Sweden, Germany, Ireland, and Hong Kong; the company also participated in a joint venture in Mexico. Foreign sales in 1983 reached $5.4 million.

Shelby Williams soon returned to acquiring other related manufacturers. Purchases included Preview Furniture Corp. in 1985;

Sellers & Josephson, Inc., in 1986; Thonet Industries Inc. and King Arthur Corp. in 1987; and Pacific Home Furnishings in 1988. The company's success could be attributed to a number of factors. With such a broad range of products in every price class it offered more variety than any of its competitors. Its emphasis on service above all was central to winning repeat business from its customers; part of its service was its focus on special orders, allowing its customers to build their own combination of furniture styles, fabrics, and fabric designs, rather than having to purchase from a fixed stock. During the 1980s the hotel industry underwent a construction boom, and large numbers of existing hotels, and hotel and restaurant chains, refurbished properties, resulting in large orders for Shelby Williams products. In addition, none of Shelby Williams's individual customers accounted for more than three or four percent of sales.

The end of the 1980s marked the end of this period of growth. The hospitality industry was becoming glutted with hotels and restaurants. Shelby Williams, with 70 percent of its sales owed to this industry, was also affected by the crimp in the market. The company shifted focus. Its purchase of Thonet Industries brought in that company's strong presence in the college dormitory and nursing home markets, where it posted roughly $25 million in sales. Shelby Williams also looked for strong growth in international sales, and its purchase of Pacific Home Furnishings of Hawaii, which distributed furniture, floor coverings, and textiles to the Far East, helped push the company's foreign exports to $8.5 million. On the domestic front, however, the food-service industry slumped. By 1988 Shelby Williams's sales had dropped to $154.7 million from $159.6 million the year before. The company announced its intention to increase sales in other market segments so that hospitality would account for around 50 percent of its sales. Other markets, however, were also tightening. Government orders, for example, were declining as spending budgets were slashed.

The slump continued across the industry into the 1990s. Shelby Williams's stock price dropped by as much as 39 percent in 1990 alone, to $6 per share. Meanwhile, many of the acquisitions from the previous years had not performed as well as expected. When Holiday Inns Inc.—Shelby Williams's largest customer with annual purchases of up to $6 million—was sold in 1990, its furniture orders were put on hold. Shelby Williams announced cost-cutting measures, including the construction of a manufacturing facility in Mexico; the company also heavily discounted its prices.

A factor in its favor, however, was the loyalty Shelby Williams—and especially Manfred Steinfeld—enjoyed among many longtime customers. Growing brands, such as Lettuce Entertain You Enterprises Inc., also remained committed to the Shelby Williams's brand of high-quality customer service. Nonetheless, the contract market continued to soften, and in November 1991 the company announced restructuring charges of $5.3 million and its intention to divest its international fabrics division. Staff cuts had also reduced the company from 1,800 employees to 1,476. In all, Shelby Williams posted a loss of $3.6 million on sales of $140 million during 1991.

The hotel and hospitality industry was slow to come out of the recession of the early 1990s. Shelby Williams's fortunes rose, however, with the sudden rise in demand from the casino industry. The 1990s saw the expansion and new construction of casino-hotels in Las Vegas and Atlantic City along with the opening of more and more riverboat gaming operations. Shelby Williams entered this market strongly, opening a showroom and creating a catalog devoted to casino furnishings. Within two years the company's casino sales reached $8 million, including the sale of 4,000 chairs for slot machines and blackjack tables in the giant MGM Grand Casino in Las Vegas. Other burgeoning markets included time-share condominiums and retirement communities. Shelby Williams sales continued to rise through 1994, when it posted $159 million in sales, with an additional backlog of more than $28 million. Manfred Steinfeld remained at the helm; the appointment of his son, Paul Steinfeld, as vice-chairman and chief operating officer signaled that Steinfeld's legacy would most likely maintain Shelby Williams's reputation for quality and service for years to come.

Principal Subsidiaries: King Arthur Tables; Thonet Industries, Inc.; Sellers & Josephson, Inc.; Preview Furniture Corp.; Madison Industries, Inc.; S.W. Textiles; PHF.

Further Reading:

Aston-Wash, Barbara, ''Chair-ished,'' *Knoxville News-Sentinel,* August 12, 1984.

Bowers, Larry C., ''Love of a Mother Rescued Son From Holocaust,'' *Chicago Tribune,* May 11, 1995, pp. A1, A8.

Byrne, Harlan S., ''Shelby Williams: Buoyed by New Casino Business, A Brighter Future is a Good Bet,'' *Barron's,* August 9, 1993, pp. 38–39.

Craig, David, ''Shelby Williams Chairman Jumps at Bargain Buying,'' *USA Today,* November 12, 1990, p. B6.

Cunningham, Peter, Shelby Williams Sits on Soft Market,'' *Crain's Chicago Business,* May 22, 1989, p. 20.

Elstrom, Peter J.W., ''Shelby Williams Tries Cost Cuts in Effort to Reverse Profit Slide,'' *Crain's Chicago Business,* June 11, 1990, p. 45.

''Have a Seat: At Your Local Eatery, It Could Be from Shelby Williams,'' *Barron's,* July 2, 1984, p. 39.

Merwin, John, ''The Amazing Chair Man,'' *Forbes,* November 19, 1984, p. 268.

Schmeltzer, John, ''2 Area Companies Plan Restructuring Charges,'' *Chicago Tribune,* November 5, 1991, p. 3.

Steinfeld, Manfred, ''The Shelby Williams Approach to Building a Unique Identity in a Low-Technology Market,'' *Journal of Business Strategy,* Spring 1987, pp. 87–89.

''Twenty-Five Years of Contract Furniture,'' Chicago: Shelby Williams Industries, 1979.

—M. L. Cohen

Shell Oil Company

One Shell Plaza
Post Office Box 2463
Houston, Texas 77252
U.S.A.
(713) 241-6161
Fax: (713) 241-7217

Wholly Owned Subsidiary of Royal Dutch/Shell Petroleum Inc.
Incorporated: 1922 as Shell Union Oil Corporation
Employees: 21,496
Sales: $21.58 billion
SICs: 1311 Crude Petroleum & Natural Gas; 2911 Petroleum Refining

One of North America's leading producers of oil, gas, and petrochemicals, Shell Oil Company has distinguished itself through its commitment to industry innovation. Its marketing expertise has enabled the company to compensate for its relatively low volume of crude oil production, as compared to its strongest competitors, by selling an equivalent amount of gasoline nationwide. Although the company conducts business primarily in the United States, Shell also explores for and produces crude oil and natural gas outside the country, both independently and through joint ventures with other subsidiaries of its parent organization, Royal Dutch/Shell Group. Shell Petroleum Inc. is a holding company that is 60 percent owned by Royal Dutch Petroleum Company and 40 percent owned by The Shell Transport and Trading Company.

The Royal Dutch/Shell Group began selling gasoline imported from Sumatra in the United States in 1912 to capitalize on the growth of the country's automobile industry and to compete with the Standard Oil Company. Starting with the formation of the Seattle-based American Gasoline Company, Royal Dutch/Shell Group also founded Roxana Petroleum Company in 1912 in Oklahoma to locate and produce crude oil. This was followed by the opening of refineries in New Orleans, Louisiana in 1916 and in Wood River, Illinois in 1918.

It soon became clear to Royal Dutch/Shell Group that with so much gasoline already available in nearby California, it was impractical to continue importing the product for sale in the Pacific Northwest. It therefore acquired California Oilfields, Ltd. in 1913 which, when coupled with a new refinery built two

years later in Martinez, California, gave the company the ability to fully integrate its operations. To reflect this new capability, the name of American Gasoline was changed to Shell Company of California in 1915. At this time, the company designed and built its first gasoline service station. Dubbed "the cracker-box," the station was originally constructed of wood. This structure was later replaced by a model made of prefabricated steel that required only a few days to erect.

The oil boom of the early 1920s, particularly at Shell's Signal Hill, California, site, provided the company with an opportunity to penetrate the Los Angeles area with sales of Shell gasoline and petroleum products manufactured in its new refineries nearby. In 1922 Shell Company of California and Roxana Petroleum merged with Union Oil Company of Delaware to form a holding company called Shell Union Oil Corporation. Approximately 65 percent of the holding company's shares were held by Royal Dutch/Shell Group.

By the late 1920s the company was actively laying pipeline across the country to transport oil from its Texas fields to the Wood River refinery. Shell Pipe Line Corporation, established in 1927 upon the acquisition of Ozark Pipe Line Corporation, also connected these fields to a new refinery built in Houston in 1929. This refinery was dedicated to manufacturing products destined for sale on the east coast of the United States and overseas. In 1929 Shell Petroleum Corporation, a forerunner of Shell Oil Company, purchased the New Orleans Refining Company, which later became one of Shell's largest manufacturing facilities.

Shell Development Company was formed in 1928 to conduct petrochemical research. The following year, after the discovery of chemicals that could be made from refinery by-products, the Shell Chemical Company began its manufacturing operation. By 1929 Shell gasoline was being sold throughout the United States. Although the economic problems of the early 1930s forced the company, along with the entire oil industry, to reassess and curtail its operations to some degree, Shell continued its chemical research. This resulted in the opening of two plants for manufacturing synthetic ammonia in 1931 and for making synthetic glycerine in 1937.

Upon developing the ability to synthesize 100-octane gasoline, Shell began supplying this fuel to the U.S. Air Corps in 1934 and gradually became one of the largest producers of aviation fuel. Due to the increased demands of the military during World War II, Shell shared this technology with the rest of the industry. It also helped the country overcome its wartime loss of natural rubber supplied by Java and Singapore by providing butadiene, a chemical required for the production of synthetic rubber products.

In 1939 Shell Oil Company of California merged with Shell Petroleum Corporation, whose name was subsequently changed to Shell Oil Company, Inc. Ten years later, the name was changed again to Shell Oil Company.

Until 1939, the company had offices in: San Francisco, California; St. Louis, Missouri; and New York City. The St. Louis office was closed in 1939, and San Francisco operations continued until 1949, when New York became the sole headquarters. Shell increased its oil exploration activities and expanded production to satisfy the growing fuel needs created by U.S. drivers' passion for big cars. New chemical plants were built that enabled Shell to become a leading producer of epoxy resins, ethylene, synthetic rubber, detergent alcohols, and other chemicals. Shell also pioneered the development of new fuel products during the 1950s, including jet fuel and high-octane, unleaded gasoline for automobiles.

In 1958, the company redesigned its service stations in an attempt to make them more compatible with surrounding areas. The ranch-style station was introduced at this time and continued as the company's primary retail outlet until the introduction of the self-service station in 1971. Shell provided additional retail support by launching several payment alternatives, including an offer to honor all other oil company credit cards and a travel-and-entertainment card bearing the Shell name. These developments helped Shell gain a significant share of the U.S. market for automobile gasoline.

By the 1960s growing environmental concerns led Shell to invest heavily in systems intended to reduce pollution and to conserve energy in its plants. In the following decade, the company began publishing a series of consumer-oriented booklets on such topics as car maintenance and energy conservation.

At the same time, the company turned its attention offshore and began drilling for oil and natural gas deposits in Alaska and the Gulf of Mexico. It soon became expert in using enhanced techniques to find and recover oil from U.S. fields. One of its biggest successes was the 1983 strike at the Bullwinkle prospect in the Gulf of Mexico. This recovery operation was expected to produce 100 million barrels of oil.

In 1970 Shell moved its headquarters to Houston. The company expanded into coal production in 1974 with the formation of Shell Mining Company. This business unit eventually operated mines in Wyoming, Illinois, Ohio, Kentucky, and West Virginia.

John F. Bookout assumed the presidency of the company in 1976 after the mandatory retirement of his predecessor, Harry Bridges. Bookout, a 25-year Shell veteran, had risen through the ranks of the company's oil and gas exploration and production division. Bookout took over during a period when high oil prices and flattening demand led other petroleum producers into ill-fated diversification attempts outside the oil industry. Rather than follow this path, Bookout elected to penetrate the oil industry more deeply and to emphasize increased efficiency in the company's ongoing operations. Beginning in 1978, for example, the company upgraded a number of its refineries and closed many of its less profitable service stations in order to concentrate on those in metropolitan areas with higher sales volume.

In 1979, Shell outbid several competitors to purchase California's Belridge Oil Company. The firm, which was subsequently renamed Kernridge Oil Company, gave Shell badly needed crude oil reserves at a time when opportunities for successful drilling ventures were declining. The company's technological expertise in steam-injected oil recovery enabled Shell to boost Kernridge's domestic production and reduce its reliance on more expensive foreign sources.

Beginning in January 1984, Royal Dutch/Shell Group launched a bid to acquire the remaining shares of Shell Oil Company. Attracted by Shell's U.S. oil reserves, the country's stable political situation, and a low corporate tax structure, cash-rich Royal Dutch/Shell viewed Shell as an increasingly worthy investment. The attempted buyout soon developed into a hostile battle over the amount that Royal Dutch/Shell had offered Shell shareholders. Its original offer of $55 a share was perceived as inadequate by Shell's directors and financial advisers, who placed the company's worth at closer to $75 a share, even though the offer represented a 25 percent premium over the stock's current selling price. By May, however, John Bookout and four other Shell executives agreed to tender their shares in exchange for Royal Dutch's sweetened offer of $60 a share. This agreement paved the way for the eventual completion of the takeover in June 1985.

In the following year, Shell came under the attack of an anti-apartheid coalition in the United States consisting of union representatives, activists, and members of various church groups that protested against Royal Dutch/Shell's involvement in South Africa. Through picketing in 13 cities, the coalition hoped to exert a negative impact on Shell's gasoline sales while also making the U.S. public aware of the parent company's coal, oil, and chemical operations in South Africa. A boycott launched by the AFL-CIO, United Mineworkers, and National Education Association in cooperation with the Free South Africa Movement was initiated to protest both alleged mistreatment of South African workers by Royal Dutch/Shell and the company's inaction against apartheid. Although Royal Dutch/Shell officials contended the company was a strong antiapartheid voice, by the end of 1988, Berkeley, California and Boston, Massachusetts had joined the fray trying to ban purchases of Shell products within city limits.

Shell encountered additional problems in 1989 over the cleanup of the Rocky Mountain Arsenal in Colorado. It was there that Shell had manufactured pesticides between the early 1950s and 1982, allegedly dumping carcinogens on the grounds. Also under scrutiny was the U.S. Army, which had used the Rocky Mountain plant to make nerve gas during World War II. Sued in 1983 by the state of Colorado under the federal superfund law, both the Army and Shell offered a plan to pay for cleaning up the site. The state subsequently deemed the proposal unsatisfactory. A California superior court ruled that insurance companies covering the company were not liable. Shell appealed that decision, but eventually reached an agreement with the U.S. government whereby Shell would pay 50 percent of the cleanup costs up to $500 million, 35 percent of costs between $500 million and $700 million, and 20 percent of costs in excess of $700 million. Through 1994, Shell had incurred $240 million in expenditures on the cleanup effort.

Led by President and Chief Executive Officer Frank H. Richardson, who succeeded John Bookout upon his retirement in 1988, Shell boasted strong cash flow and a decreasing level of long-term debt in the late 1980s. Underlying this rosy situation, however, were problems for Shell on the production side. In 1988, Shell was able to produce 531,000 barrels of oil a day, but by 1994 that figure had fallen to 398,000 a day. Shell had settled on the Gulf of Mexico as its prime area of exploration and development, an area that was disappointing during the period.

The recession of the early 1990s compounded Shell's difficulties by causing a decline in demand for petroleum products and pushing prices down. Like other U.S. oil companies, Shell saw its revenues steadily decline throughout the early 1990s—from $24.79 billion in 1990 to $21.09 billion in 1993.

In 1991, Shell decided it had to cut operating costs in order to generate enough money to boost its production. The company announced it would cut 10 to 15 percent of its work force as part of a corporate restructuring. Over the next two years more than 7,000 jobs were eliminated, reducing Shell's work force from 29,437 in 1991 to 22,212 in 1993.

Meanwhile, Shell engineers and workers were hard at work designing and constructing a $1.2 billion Auger platform in the deep waters of the Gulf of Mexico. With ten to 15 billion barrels of oil and gas lying under these waters, the question was not whether there was oil and gas to be found, but whether it could be extracted profitably. Located 135 miles offshore and in water of record depth of 2,860 feet, production began at the Auger platform in April 1994 and quickly reached 55,000 barrels a day, more than the anticipated peak of 46,000 barrels. Shell was the acknowledged leader in deep-sea drilling and its commitment to the Gulf had begun to pay off. Shell already had two more platforms in the works which were scheduled to begin production by 1997. The three projects were expected to generate 150,000 barrels a day, creating oil and gas worth $1 billion annually.

On the retail side, by 1994 Shell had 8,600 stations operating in 40 states and the District of Columbia and had strengthened its position as the top gasoline marketer in the United States. Shell's refinery activities in the early 1990s were highlighted by the beginning of construction of a $1 billion clean fuels project in Martinez, California, to be completed by 1997. Meanwhile, Richardson had retired in 1993 and was succeeded by Philip J. Carroll.

Shell's position in the mid-1990s was much healthier than earlier in the decade, due in large part to the success of its deep-water operations in the Gulf of Mexico.

Principal Subsidiaries: Pecten Arabian Company; Shell Finance Co.; Shell Leasing Co.; Shell Pipe Line Corp.

Further Reading:

Beaton, Kendall, *Enterprise in Oil: A History of Shell in the United States,* New York: Appleton-Century-Crofts, 1957, 815 p.

Bridges, Harry, *The Americanization of Shell: The Beginnings and Early Years of Shell Oil Company in the United States,* New York: Newcomen Society in North America, 1972, 26 p.

McWilliams, Gary, "The Undersea World of Shell Oil," *Business Week,* May 15, 1995, pp. 74–78.

Miller, William H., "Last of a Breed," *Industry Week,* July 18, 1988.

Sampson, Anthony, *The Seven Sisters: The Great Oil Companies and the World They Shaped*, 4th ed., New York: Bantam Books, 1991, 414 p.

Shell: 75 Years Serving America, Houston: Shell Oil Company, 1987.

Shell Oil Company: A Story of Achievement, Houston: Shell Oil Company, 1984, 16 p.

Smith, Gene, "Even First-Class Shell Must Change to Stay Competitive," *Oil Daily,* July 15, 1991, p. 2.

Wells, Barbara, *Shell at Deer Park: The Story of the First Fifty Years,* Houston: Shell Oil Company, 1979, 139 p.

—updated by David E. Salamie

SHOE CARNIVAL, INC.

Shoe Carnival Inc.

8233 Baumgart Rd
Evansville, Indiana 47711
U.S.A.
(812) 867-6471
Fax: (812) 867-4261

Public Company
Incorporated: 1978 as Russell Shoe Biz Inc.
Employees: 2,300
Sales: $250 million
Stock Exchanges: NASDAQ
SICs: 5661 Shoe Stores

Shoe Carnival Inc. is a leading retailer of family footwear in the United States. The company differentiates its shoe stores with value pricing and a carnival-like shopping atmosphere. Following rapid growth during the early 1990s, Shoe Carnival was operating about 90 stores in the Midwest and South in 1995.

Shoe Carnival was inspired by shoe salesman David Russell of Evansville, Indiana. Russell worked for 20 years selling shoes in the traditional fashion: He knelt in front of customers to measure their feet, carried boxes from the back room, and earned a commission from every pair of shoes he sold. Throughout his career, though, he had the feeling that there had to be a better way to sell shoes. Finally, in 1978, the 34-year-old Russell quit his job at Kinney Shoe Corp. to open his own shop. He combined his savings with money from his in-laws and opened a small shoe store that he dubbed "Shoe Biz." His idea was to create a selling environment completely different from the traditional, staid shoe store that was so common at the time. He wanted to create a shoe store that was fun. Thus, Shoe Biz offered thousands of boxes of shoes on self-service racks. Jukebox music that featured tunes from the 1950s blared away, though the music was often interrupted by announcements by the store manager, who was authorized to hawk footwear and cut deals with customers on the spot.

Russell's idea was a hit. Sales were so strong that he was able to open a second store in Evansville that he named Shoe Shower, although it and the other stores were later converted to the Shoe Carnival name. Russell also opened a third Shoe Carnival across the river from Evansville in Owensboro, Kentucky, in the early 1980s. Like the original store, the new stores enticed

shoppers with low-cost shoes and self-service shopping, a chaotic and entertaining shopping environment, and a sort of let's-make-a-deal atmosphere. Only "Elvis music or older" was allowed on the jukebox, and customers were encouraged to haggle over the price of the shoes. Managers were instructed to beat any price in town, and the stores featured an elevated stage where a store employee hawked specials on the intercom every few minutes. The deals occasionally involved spectacular giveaways that generated valuable press for the stores. The shop in Owensboro, for example, once gave away a cow, and one of the Evansville stores awarded $25,000 in cash to a customer.

Russell also grabbed attention with screaming advertisements. Once, Russell had to prove to the Better Business Bureau the validity of an advertising claim that he literally had "miles of boots" in stock. He measured a boot and multiplied the length by his inventory to discover that he was stocking exactly 5.7 miles of boots. Once the promotions got the customers into the stores, the carnival atmosphere was honed to get them into a buying mood. A free pair of tennis shoes might be offered to anyone who could hula-hoop for a minute, or to the first person who could bring an aspirin to the manager. Customers were also enticed by the sheer size of, and selection at, the stores. The shops eventually offered an average of more than 10,000 square feet of floor space, upon which name-brand stock was displayed on tall, self-service racks. By using a smaller number of salespeople, the company was able to keep prices low and generate profits through high-volume sales of name-brand shoes.

By 1984 Shoe Carnival was generating a lofty $8 million in annual sales from its three stores. Sales at the private company continued to grow and to catch the attention of other shoe industry players. In 1986, in fact, Russell sold a controlling interest in his company to Fisher-Camuto Corp., although he remained as chief executive in charge of the company's operation. Based in Stamford, Connecticut, Fisher-Camuto was the manufacturer of name-brand shoes including Gloria Vanderbilt, Enzo, Esties, and Nine West. Fisher-Camuto bought into the chain because it believed that it had access to the financing needed to expand Russell's proven concept outside of Evansville. To that end, in October and November of 1986 Fisher-Camuto financed the construction of three Shoe Carnival outlets in Indianapolis. The success of those new stores mimicked that of the Evansville-area outlets. Enthused, the Shoe Carnival organization opened a total of 15 additional outlets in major midwest markets in less than two years.

Realizing the potential of the Shoe Carnival concept, J. Wayne Weaver, with Russell's help, purchased Shoe Carnival from Fisher-Camuto in 1989 for a lowly $17 million. Weaver was serving as president and chief executive of Nine West at the time. After the buyout, Weaver became chairman of the again-independent Shoe Carnival (as well as chief executive of Nine West) and Russell retained his chief executive slot. Shoe Carnival continued to expand at a rapid clip under their tutelage. By the end of 1989, in fact, Shoe Carnival was sporting 30 stores spread throughout nine states in the Midwest and South—in Kentucky, Indiana, Illinois, Iowa, Michigan, Tennessee, Ohio, and Alabama. To support this growth, the chain employed a total of 1,500 part-time and full-time workers. At one point, Shoe Carnival was opening an average of one store per week.

Russell and Weaver planned to open only six or seven additional outlets in 1990, however.

Russell managed the expansion of Shoe Carnival during the late 1980s and early 1990s with the help of a close-knit management team that consisted of longtime friends and executives lured from competing shoe companies. The executives stayed close to the day-to-day operation of the stores, and Russell himself was occasionally seen packing merchandise in the company's Evansville distribution center, manning the microphone at Shoe Carnival outlets, and even handing out $1 bills to customers waiting in the check-out lines. Although his retail management experience was limited prior to the start-up of Shoe Carnival, few could argue with his success. The rapid expansion had not been without minor setbacks, however. "Initially, we expected to have the success of the Evansville store in every city," said Laura Ray, vice president of marketing, in the November 1989 *Indiana Business*. "But after the opening it tended to slow down a little. So it has been an education for us, getting customers used to the Carnival and our way of doing things. But overall we're pleased as punch with everything."

Shoe Carnival slowed its expansion during the early 1990s and concentrated on whipping its existing operations into shape. About ten new stores were added between 1990 and mid-1993. That grew the chain to a total of 41 outlets, most of which were in the Midwest. Throughout this period, Shoe Carnival was effectively a private company and was not required to release sales and earnings information. Early in 1993, though, the company converted from a Chapter S corporation to a public company. The change was made because Weaver and Russell wanted to generate expansion capital by way of a public stock offering. To that end, Shoe Carnival conducted an initial public offering that brought about $28 million into its coffers. That left Russell with about seven percent ownership in the company. Russell, who was also a significant owner of Nine West shares and several other interests, retained a 54-percent stake in the company. Subsequent stock offerings shortly thereafter brought additional funds into Shoe Carnival's war chest.

Shoe Carnival generated sales of about $127 million in 1992. Rapid growth following the initial public offering, however, would nearly double that figure within a few years. This revenue gain was primarily the result of new store openings. By the end of 1993, in fact, Shoe Carnival had opened a total of 57 stores in 15 states. Sales in that year climbed to $157 million, about $6 million of which was netted as income. Importantly, Shoe Carnival also realized improvements in its net profit margins and sales-per-square-foot of floor space, which were among the highest in the industry.

Going into 1994, then, Shoe Carnival was an emerging power in the U.S. family footwear industry. Athletic and women's shoes represented 33 percent and 29 percent, respectively, of company sales, while children's and men's shoes accounted for a combined 33 percent. Miscellaneous accessories like belts and purses made up the remainder of the company's revenues. Popular name brands sold at Shoe Carnival outlets included Nike, Reebok, Hush Puppies, Dexter, Florsheim, Rockport, and many more.

Shoe Carnival continued to add new stores to its chain during 1994. By the end of the year, in fact, there were 87 Shoe Carnival stores operating in 15 states. Besides increasing the store number, the company upgraded its Evansville distribution center to 108,000 square feet and installed a mechanized merchandise handling system. The new system allowed Shoe Carnival to reduce its store inventories and to more quickly deliver shoe styles that were hot sellers. That system was augmented by a new computerized point-of-sale system that connected all of the store's cash registers into the company's headquarters computer system. This arrangement enabled managers at both the store and headquarters levels to make decisions based on up-to-the-minute sales, inventory, and payroll data.

Meanwhile, store shenanigans and promotions continued to draw customers. For example, one long-time practice was for Shoe Carnival stores to offer deals at selected times by having an employee spin a big roulette wheel that was part of a Spin-'n-win game. The wheel was divided into specials such as "$1 off," "$2 off," or "free prize." The deal that came up on the wheel was the one offered to people that were in the store at the time. Another example of Shoe Carnival's unique promotional efforts was its kick-off of the sale of the popular Fila brand of shoes. Shoe Carnival brought in Pop-A-Shot electronic basketball games and invited customers to come in and shoot to win prizes, and in some cases to engage in shooting contests with well-known basketball players. Rounding out the carnival-like atmosphere in all of Shoe Carnival's stores were neon signs, colored lights, colorful displays, large mirrors, and 1950s jukebox music similar to what Russell played in the first Shoe Biz outlet in 1978.

Shoe Carnival's revenues rose 37 percent in 1994 to $214 million. At the same time, the company's sales-per-square-foot figure declined slightly and net income fell to just $1.2 million. The slide in net income was attributed to a number of factors. Several of the new stores that had been opened in Detroit, Alabama, and Georgia failed to live up to management's expectations. Additionally, Shoe Carnival's attempt to market private-label shoes was a flop. The company had hoped that they could boost profit margins by offering private-label women's shoes. But the shoes consumed valuable shelf space previously occupied by name brands, and Shoe Carnival lost money on the project. "We got a little bit out of our element," Russell said of the experiment in *Forbes* in 1994. Another part of the problem, according to some analysts, was that the shoe market was become increasingly crowded with other discount retailers that were eating into Shoe Carnival's piece of the pie.

To boost the profitability of existing stores, Shoe Carnival reduced its expansion plans for 1995, although it still expected to open up to 15 new outlets. Executives were also planning to further reduce sales of private-label shoes, and to trim the organization's inventory and overall operating costs. By mid-1995 management had made significant progress toward those goals. The company planned to sustain its basic strategy through the mid-1990s. Ongoing sales gains and a relatively meager debt load in 1995 boded well for Shoe Carnival's long-term prospects.

Further Reading:

Basch, Mark, "Weaver to Sell $11 Million of Shoe Stock," *Florida Times Union,* October 20, 1993.

Darlin, Damon, "Send in the Clowns," *Forbes,* August 1, 1994, p. 89.

Derk, James S., "The Shoe Carnival," *Indiana Business,* November 1989, p. 28.

"Glitz, Glitter, and, of Course, Shoes Galore," *Tribune Business Weekly,* August 11, 1993, p. 3.

Kent, Jennifer, "Shoe Carnival Coming," *Cincinnati Post,* May 26, 1993.

Massa, Sherri, "Shoe Carnival Swings Into Town With Low Prices, Crazy Gimmicks," *Indianapolis Business Journal,* January 19, 1987, p. 12.

Miller, Laura Novello, "Shoe Carnival Spins IPO Wheel to Finance Expansion," *Indianapolis Business Journal,* May 23, 1994, p. 9B.

"Shoe Carnival Reports Second Quarter Results," *PR Newswire,* August 24, 1995.

Wilson, Melinda, "The Shoe Carnival is Coming to Town," *Detroit News,* February 25, 1994, p. 1E.

—Dave Mote

SIEMENS

Siemens A.G.

Wittelsbacherplatz 2
D 80333 Munich
Germany
(0 89) 234-2812
Fax: (0 89) 234-2825

Public Company
Incorporated: 1966
Employees: 377,000
Sales: DM84.6 billion
Stock Exchanges: Berlin Hamburg Dusseldorf Munich
    Brussels Paris Zurich Basle Geneva Amsterdam Vienna
    London
SICs: 6719 Holding Companies, Not Elsewhere Classified;
    3674 Semiconductors & Related Devices; 3571 Electronic
    Computers; 3861 Photographic Equipment

Siemens A.G. is Europe's largest electrical and electronics
company, producing over 50,000 products manufactured at 400
sites in 40 countries. Referring to the company's history of
achieving success through well engineered refinements of other
people's inventions, one *Fortune* analyst noted that ''second is
best'' might well serve as Siemens' motto. But opportunism
is not the only interesting facet of Siemens' history, which is
also a story of a long family tradition and intimate involvement
with some of the most important events of the 19th and 20th
centuries.

Siemens & Halske was founded in Berlin in 1847 by Werner
Siemens and J. G. Halske to manufacture and install telegraphic
systems. Siemens, a former artillery officer in the Prussian army
and an engineer who already owned a profitable patent for
electroplating, was the driving force behind the company and
remained so for the rest of his life. The company received its
first major commission in 1848, when it contracted to build a
telegraph link between Berlin and Frankfurt.

Construction of telegraph systems boomed in the mid 19th
century, and Siemens & Halske was well equipped to take
advantage of the situation. In 1853, it received a commission to
build an extensive telegraph system in Russia. Upon its completion, the company opened an office in St. Petersburg under the
direction of Werner Siemens' brother Carl Siemens. In 1857
Siemens & Halske helped develop the first successful deep sea
telegraphic cable. This led to the transformation of the London

office into an independent company under the direction of
Wilhelm Siemens, another of Werner's brothers, the next year.
By 1865 the company's English operations had become sub-
stantial. Its name was changed to Siemens Brothers, still under
the direction of Wilhelm, who was eventually knighted as Sir
William Siemens.

In 1867 Siemens Brothers received a contract for an 11,000
kilometer telegraph line from London to Calcutta, which it
completed in 1870. In 1871 it linked London and Teheran by
telegraph. In 1874 Siemens Brothers launched its own cable
laying ship, the Faraday, which William Siemens co-designed.
The next year, it laid the first direct transatlantic cable from
Ireland to the United States.

In 1877 Alexander Graham Bell's new telephones reached Berlin for the first time. Immediately grasping their worth, Werner
Siemens quickly patented an improved version of the device
and began production. In the next decade, Siemens & Halske
also developed and began manufacturing electrical lighting and
power generating equipment after Werner Siemens discovered
the dynamo electric principle in 1866.

In 1888 Werner Siemens was ennobled by the German kaiser
for his achievements. Two years later he retired and his company became a limited partnership shared by his sons Arnold
and Wilhelm and his brother Carl. Werner Siemens died in
1892, but the House of Siemens continued to prosper. That
same year, Siemens & Halske built a power station at Erding in
Bavaria and founded an American subsidiary, Siemens &
Halske Electric Company, in Chicago. The latter, however,
closed in 1904. In 1895 Wilhelm Conrad Roentgen discovered
the X ray, and the very next year Siemens & Halske owned the
first patent for an X ray tube. In 1897 Siemens & Halske
decided to go public and reorganized with Carl Heinrich, now
Carl von Siemens after being ennobled by the Russian czar in
1895, as chairman of the supervisory board. He retired after
seven years in that post and was succeeded by his nephew
Arnold.

Siemens & Halske remained busy as the 19th century gave way
to the 20th. In 1903 it established Siemens Schuckertwerke
GmbH, a subsidiary devoted to electric power engineering. In
1909 Siemens & Halske developed an automatic telephone exchange serving 2,500 customers in Munich. But when World
War I broke out, orders for civilian electrical equipment slowed
considerably and the company began production of communications devices for the military. Siemens & Halske also produced explosives, gun locks for rifles, and, later in the war,
aircraft engines.

But perhaps the company's most successful contribution to the
German war effort was the fire control system it produced for
the navy's battlecruisers, which proved its worth at the Battle of
Jutland in 1916. There, the battlecruiser squadron of the High
Seas Fleet met its British counterpart for the only time during
the war. While the main fleets fought to a draw, the German
battlecruisers used their superior gunnery equipment to batter
their opponents, sinking two British ships and severely damag-
ing several others. It was a highlight for the German navy in a
battle from which it otherwise won no advantage.

On the balance, however, the war hurt Siemens & Halske badly. The Bolshevik government that seized power in Russia in 1917 also seized the assets of the company's St. Petersburg subsidiary, which were worth about 50 million rubles. Siemens Brothers was taken over by the British government in 1915 and sold to British interests the next year. The company was not returned to the Siemens family after the armistice, although it retained their name for business purposes. Siemens Brothers eventually re established links to its old parent and its general manager, Dr. Henry Wright, even became a member of the Siemens & Halske supervisory board in 1929. But Carl Friedrich von Siemens, a son of Werner's who had headed the British subsidiary for six years and had many English friends, was shocked by these events; "they have stolen our name," he lamented.

Arnold von Siemens died in 1918, before the end of the war. He was succeeded by his brother Wilhelm, who died the next year. Carl Friedrich then became chairman. Despite the precarious state of the German economy in the 1920s and a bias among foreign customers against doing business with a German company, the company continued to make its mark in electrical manufacturing. In 1923 it started producing radio receivers for the consumer market. In the same year, recognizing the growing importance of Japan as an industrial power and not wishing to concede that market to General Electric and Westinghouse, Siemens & Halske set up a Tokyo subsidiary, Fusi Denk, later known as Fuji Electric. In 1925 Siemens began construction of a power station on the Shannon River in Ireland, and in 1927 the company began work on another hydroelectric power station for the Soviet government, near Zaporozhe. Back home in Germany, Siemens & Halske financed and produced a railway network in suburban Berlin that began operation in 1928. By the end of the decade, the company was accounting for one third of the German electrical manufacturing industry's production and nearly the same proportion of its employees.

Siemens & Halske was bloodied by the Great Depression, but it survived. It was forced to halve its dividend in the early 1930s and lay off employees in large numbers, but remained on relatively sound financial footing until the Nazi government's rearmament project helped revive its fortunes in 1935. During the remainder of the decade, Siemens & Halske manufactured a wide range of equipment for all of Germany's armed services. One of its most significant technical contributions at this time, the development of an automatic pilot system for airplanes, was the result of a project initiated for the Luftwaffe.

The company's activities during this time are difficult to evaluate. One the one hand, according to family historian Georg Siemens, Carl Friedrich von Siemens was repelled by the Nazis' anti-Semitism from the start and only grew more disgusted with their goals and methods as time went on. Just before his death in 1941, he wrote to an assistant: "my work no longer brings me satisfaction or joy. Those who were once proud that their work was devoted to the task of serving progress and humanity, can now only be sad that the results of their work merely serve the evil of destruction. Whenever I start to think, 'why,' I should prefer to creep into a corner, so as not to see or hear any more." And yet there is no question that Siemens & Halske benefited from German rearmament during the late 1930s. Certainly the company did little or nothing to hinder Nazi militarism.

Carl Friedrich went into partial retirement in 1940 and appointed Hermann von Siemens, Arnold's eldest son, to succeed him. By this time, Siemens & Halske was devoting virtually all of its manufacturing capacity to military orders and would do so for the duration of the war. In 1944 it helped develop and manufacture the V 2 rocket. Its factories also suffered substantial damage from Allied bombing raids. And after the Soviet army conquered Berlin in 1945, Russian occupation authorities completely dismantled the Siemensstadt factory works and corporate headquarters.

In 1945 Hermann von Siemens, who had also been a director of Deutsche Bank, was arrested by American occupation authorities and interned for two years. There is also no question that the company employed slave labor during the war. Georg Siemens pointed out that every major German industrial concern used forced labor because of manpower shortages caused by the war, and asserted that Siemens & Halske treated its laborers better than most companies. But in 1947, allegations surfaced that three of the firm's directors had been active in importing slave laborers from occupied countries. In addition, testimony from Holocaust survivors also surfaced at this time that Siemens had supplied gas chamber equipment to the concentration camps. These allegations were never proven, however, and the company denied them both.

Hermann von Siemens resumed the chairmanship upon his release in 1948. The company had been devastated by the war and required years of rebuilding to get back on its feet. Its corporate headquarters were relocated to Munich in 1949. By the early 1950s, Siemens & Halske was once again producing railroad, medical, telephone, and power generating equipment, as well as consumer electronics products. In 1954 it established an American subsidiary in New York, Siemens Inc. Its first product sold to the American market was an electron microscope. In the mid-1950s Siemens & Halske entered the burgeoning fields of data processing and nuclear power. It introduced its first mainframe computer in 1955, and its first nuclear reactor went into service in 1959 at Munich Garching.

Hermann von Siemens retired in 1956 and was succeeded by Ernst von Siemens, Carl Friedrich's only son. In the mid 1960s, Siemens & Halske technology went to Mars after the company developed a disc seal triode that was used in the transmitter of the American space probe Mariner IV. In 1965 it scored another coup when its 03 high-speed passenger train went into service with the German Federal Railway. And in 1968, it began constructing a nuclear power station at Atucha, Argentina, the first such facility in South America.

The company underwent a major reorganization in 1966, bringing all of its subsidiaries directly under control of the parent company and reincorporating as Siemens A.G. By the end of the decade, worldwide sales had reached DM10 billion; in 1970 they reached DM12.6 billion. In 1971 Ernst von Siemens retired and his cousin Peter succeeded him as chairman.

The 1970s were prosperous years for Siemens. Despite a slower worldwide economy that cut into customer orders in some areas and forced the company to cut its workforce, sales grew to DM20.7 billion and net profits to DM606 million in 1976. When the summer Olympic Games came to Munich in 1972,

Siemens was its first official supplier of telecommunications and data processing equipment. In 1977 the company entered into a joint venture with the American engineering firm Allis Chalmers, called Siemens Allis Inc., to market turbine generators in the United States. In fact, Siemens' status as an electrical manufacturer rose to the point that *Fortune* wrote in 1978 that it had "replaced Westinghouse in General Electric's demonology." Siemens had replaced Westinghouse as the world's number two electrical manufacturing concern, ranking "as GE's major worldwide competitor in everything from motors and switchgear to generators and nuclear reactors." It had also raised its share of the West German mainframe computer market to 21 percent, cutting sharply into IBM's position as the Bundesrepublik's leading mainframe supplier.

In the late 1970s, Siemens stumbled when it initiated a research and development effort in microcircuit technology, against the advice of a consulting firm employed by the West German government to counsel the nation's industrial companies. It was thought that Siemens' slow and methodical practices would render it unable to keep up with the smaller, quicker Silicon Valley firms that were breaking ground in this area. Nonetheless, Siemens A.G., with its research and development budget of $1 billion (one eighth of all the money spent by West German industry on research at the time), eventually entered into a joint venture with Dutch rival Philips to develop advanced microcircuits. None of the company's efforts on this front proved successful, however. Its components division lost money through 1987 and Siemens was forced to buy chips from Toshiba to meet its commitments until its own became available in early 1988.

In 1981 Peter von Siemens retired and was succeeded by Bernhard Plettner. For the first time, the Siemens family relinquished day-to-day control over the company it had founded over a century ago. But the 67-year-old Plettner had worked for Siemens for all of his adult life, and Peter von Siemens felt that his own son, at the age of 44, was still too young and inexperienced for the top job.

Under Plettner and new CEO Karlheinz Kaske, Siemens embarked on an expensive and ambitious program of acquisitions and research and development to try to make itself into a world leader in high technology. Its effort to develop its own microchips was a part of that effort, as was the acquisition of IBM's struggling Rolm Systems subsidiary in 1988. That deal cost Siemens $844 million, but gave control of the third largest supplier of PBX telephone switching equipment in North America. Siemens' strategy during the 1980s was designed to pay off over the long term and produced few tangible benefits in the short run. The company spent $24 billion on both research and development and acquisitions between 1983 and 1988, and the tremendous cash drain produced both a significant drop in earnings and a cut in the dividend in 1988. As one analyst told *Business Week* in 1988, "Siemens will be an interesting story in the 1990s."

As the company entered the new decade, globalization became a vital part of its policy—and that meant a readjustment of the company's homogeneous culture. Europe was facing a recession and the Asian and South American markets offered huge opportunities for growth. To help guide the new direction of

Siemens, the company appointed Hermann Franz as chairman and Heinrich von Pierer as president and CEO. The appointment of Dr. Heinrich von Pierer as chief executive in 1992 reflected the need for a cultural change and the drive for higher profitability.

Siemens had always been dominated by engineers. When von Pierer, an economist and lawyer, was elected to head the company, it was seen as a commitment to greater commercialism for the company. Von Pierer's guidance stressed three fundamental trends: the first was that 85 percent of Siemens' business would be conducted either in global markets or in markets that showed an unmistakable trend toward globalization; second, that significant improvements in manufacturing depended on reducing manufacturing "depth"; and third, that software was the increasingly the crucial commercial factor.

Within the company, von Pierer caused a cultural revolution. He continued the reorganization begun by his predecessor, Kaske, and developed a program designed to make Siemens more competitive with Japanese companies by making it more responsive to market pressures. He replaced the hierarchical structure and engineering focus with a new emphasis on innovation and service. He gave managers in local markets free rein to cut costs and bid for projects, while also appointing a younger generation of managers in their 40s. Moreover, von Pierer cut Siemens' workforce by 7.5 percent and sold $2 billion in noncore businesses and slashed $3.6 billion in operating expenses by fiscal year end 1995. He continually asked if the company was flexible and changing enough, and at one point, included self-addressed postcards in the company magazine urging employees to send him their ideas.

Such measures were part of a strategy to get Siemens into new high-growth markets especially in Asia. Von Pierer planned to invest $3.4 billion in Asia by the year 2000 and to double sales to $14.3 billion, according to *Business Week* in 1995. He set up facilities in Asia and Eastern Europe to lower costs and reach new customers, and bought telecommunications units in the United States and Italy. He also planned further acquisition to move more production out of Germany. The strategy began to pay off. While net profits slipped 17 percent to $1.18 billion in 1994, earnings jumped eight percent in three months and analysts saw a 20 percent increase for the year. As of 1995, sales continued to increase and the declining profits for the company began to increase.

In another move toward globalization, an international partnership brought Siemens together with the world's largest computer maker and Japan's second largest chip maker. In 1992, Siemens joined forces with IBM and Toshiba Corp. to develop 256M-bit chips to create microprocessors with the power of supercomputers. The first chip was expected to be marketed in 1998. The estimated cost for the project was a billion dollars for designing the chip and another billion for setting up the manufacturing facilities. The Siemens, IBM, and Toshiba alliance was expected to become the industry norm given rising operation costs and the focus towards a "borderless" world economy.

Innovation has always been a part of Siemens' tradition. But new social pressures and rapidly changing technology throughout the world brought new challenges to Siemens as it faced the

21st century. To deal with this new business market, Siemens used its tradition of intelligence, resources, and systematic application to remain a strong international force. As von Pierer stated in Siemens' 1994 annual report: "Helping set the course of change has been a vital part of our business for nearly 150 years.... Fifteen years ago, barely half of our worldwide sales came from products that were less than five years old. This figure has now risen to more than two-thirds—solid proof that we are not just meeting increased demands for change, but are setting the pace for innovation."

Principal Subsidiaries: Siemens Nixdorf Informationssysteme AG; Osram GmbH; Vacuumschmelze GmbH; Duewag AG (97%); Siemens Matsushita Components GmbH & Co. KG (50%); Siemens S.A., Saint-Gilles (Brussels); Siemens A/S, Ballerup (Copenhagen); Siemens Osakeyhtiö, Espoo (Helsinki); Siemens S.A. Saint-Denis (Paris); Siemens A.E., Elektrotechnische Projekte und Erzeugnisse (Athens); Siemens plc, Bracknell (London); Siemens Ltd., Dublin; Siemens S.p.A., Milan; Siemens Nederland N.V., The Hague; Siemens A/S, Oslo; Siemens AG Österreich, Vienna (74%); Siemens S.A., Lisbon; Siemens AB, Stockholm; Siemens-Albis AG, Zurich (78%); Siemens S.A., Madrid; Simko Ticaret ve Sanayi A.S., Istanbul (51%); Siemens Nixdorf Information Systems S.A./N.V., Brussels; Siemens Nixdorf Information Systems S.A., Cergy (Paris); Siemens Nixdorf Information Systems Ltd., Bracknell (London); Siemens Nixdorf Informatica S.p. A., Milan (51%); Siemens Nixdorf Informatiesystemen B.V., Zoetermeer/Netherlands; Siemens Nixdorf Informationssysteme Ges.m.b.H., Vienna; Siemens Nixdorf Informationssysteme AG, Kloten (Zurich); Siemens Nixdorf Sistemas de Información S.A., Tres Cantos (Madrid); Osram S.A., Molsheim/France; Osram Ltd., Wembley (London); Osram Società Riunite Osram Edison-Clerici S.pA., Milan; Siemens U.S.; Siemens Electric Ltd., Mississauga (Ontario); Siemens S.A. de C.V., Mexico City; Osram S.A. de C.V., Tultitlan/Mexico; Siemens S.A., Buenos Aires; Siemens S.A., Sao Paulo (82%); Siemens S.A., Bogotá (94%); Siemens S.A., Caracas; Osram Argentina S.A.C.I., Buenos Aires (66%); Osram do Brasil-Companhia de Lâmpadas Eléctricas S.A., Osasco; Siemens Ltd., Richmond; Siemens Ltd., Bombay (51%); Siemens K.K. Tokyo (83%); Siemens Components (Advanced Technology) Sdn. Bhd., Malacca/Malaysia; Siemens Pakistan Engineering Co. Ltd., Karachi (64%); Siemens Componenets (Pte) Ltd. Singapore; Siemens Telecommunications Systems Ltd., Taipei (60%); Osram-Melco Ltd. Yokohama (51%); Siemens Ltd., Johannesburg (52%).

Further Reading:

Face to Face with Technology, Berlin: Siemens Aktiengesellschaft, 1991.
"Half Way There: Siemens," *The Economist,* July 4, 1992, p. 60.
Goodwin, Jack S., and Robert M. Fulmer, "Management Development at Siemens Electronics: Hitting a Moving Target," *Journal of Management Development,* September 1992, pp. 40–46.
Hussain, Ahrar, "Siemens—A Tradition of Excellence," *Economic Review,* August 1994, p. 109.
Lineback, J. Robert, "Siemens Braces for Rough Road Ahead," *Electronic News,* March 22, 1993, p. 18.
Miller, Karen Lowry, "Siemens Shapes Up: So Long Plodding Perfectionism. Hello, Aggressiveness," *Business Week,* May 1, 1995, pp. 52–53.
Panni, Aziz, "Sea Change at Siemens," *Management Today,* March 1994, p. 50.
Procassini, Andrew, "Alliances and Opportunities," *Electronic News,* September 28, 1992, p. 8.
Schares, Gail E., Jonathan B. Levine, and Peter Coy, "The New Generation at Siemens," *Business Week,* March 9, 1992, p. 46.
Scott J.D., *Siemens Brothers, 1858 1958,* Weidenfeld and Nicolson, 1959.
Siemens, Georg, *History of the House of Siemens,* trans. by A.F. Rodger and Lawrence N. Hold, Munich: Karl Alber, 1957.
Siemens, Werner von, *Inventor and Entrepreneur: Recollections of Werner von Siemens,* London: Lund Humphries, 1966.
"Technical Opportunities Beckon in Eastern Europe," *Design News,* September 20, 1993, p. 250.

—updated by Beth Watson Highman

Sime Darby Berhad

21st Floor, Wisma Sime Darby
Jalan Raja Laut
Kuala Lumpur 50350
Malaysia
(3) 291 4122
Fax: (3) 298 7398

Public Company
Founded: 1910 as Sime, Darby & Co., Ltd.
Employees: 32,000
Sales: $3.15 billion
Stock Exchanges: London Kuala Lumpur
SICs: 3011 Tires & Inner Tubes; 5012 Automobiles & Other
   Motor Vehicles; 5084 Industrial Machinery & Equipment;
   Commodity Contracts Brokers, Dealers; 6510 Real Estate
   Operators & Lessors

With 32,000 employees and about 200 companies under its control, Sime Darby Berhad is one of the largest multinational corporations in Asia. Its broadly diversified operations competed throughout the world in almost every industry ranging from insurance and finance to manufacturing and professional services. For example, Sime Darby's subsidiaries built petrochemical facilities, owned rubber plantations, operated hospitals, and assembled German, U.S., and English cars. The mammoth enterprise staggered in the mid-1980s but recorded hefty, consistent revenue and profit gains throughout the late 1980s and early 1990s.

The moniker ''Sime Darby'' was contrived in 1910 from the names of two European business partners; William Sime and Henry Darby. William Sime, a traveler and adventurer from Scotland, ventured to Malaysia when he was in his late thirties. Natural rubber—synthetic rubber was still being developed—had just been introduced to that country from Brazil. Sime and other entrepreneurs at the time recognized that the climate of Malaysia's jungle region was similar to that of Brazil's. Thus, rubber could just as easily be grown in that country and sold not only in Malaysia but throughout southeast Asia and the world. Sime suggested to his friend Henry Darby, an English banker, that they start a rubber plantation there. Darby agreed to help fund the effort and together they formed Sime, Darby & Co., Ltd.

Sime Darby initially encountered stiff opposition to its venture from locals, who were wary of outsiders coming in to operate a plantation in Malacca. To quell their contempt, Sime and Darby forged friendships with several members of the Chinese business community. The most notable of those business leaders was Tun Tan Cheng Lock. Lock would later lead the Malaya independence movement—in the 1990s, the Malay Peninsula was made up of parts of Burma, Thailand, and Malaysia. Among other distinctions, Lock ultimately was crowned a Knight Commander of the British Empire and also received Malaysia's highest award, which is called ''Tun.'' With the help of Lock and other business leaders, Sime and Darby were able to procure about 500 acres of rubber plantations in the dense jungles of Malacca.

Rubber markets surged during the 1910s and Sime Darby enjoyed healthy sales. The company expanded, becoming a manager for owners of other plantations and then moving into the trading end of the industry. Sime set up a branch office in Singapore in 1915 and shortly thereafter established a marketing office in London. Demand for rubber eventually outstripped Sime Darby's production capacity, and by the late 1920s the company found it necessary to clear more jungle. To do so, Sime Darby purchased a company called Sarawak Trading. Sarawak held the franchise for Caterpillar heavy earth-moving equipment. That important purchase signaled Sime Darby's expansion into the heavy equipment business, which would eventually become a major component of its expansive network.

Sime Darby made a fortune in the global rubber industry during the 1920s and 1930s. Growth in that industry began to fade, however, as natural rubber was gradually supplanted by synthetic rubber. Sales of natural rubber boomed during World War II as warring nations purchased all available supplies. However, the war also led to significant advancements in synthetic rubber technology. Thus, by the 1960s Sime Darby Holdings—the company was incorporated in the founders' home country of England in 1958 and its name was changed to Sime Darby Holdings Ltd.—was forced to begin looking elsewhere for revenues. To that end, Sime Darby became one of the first rubber plantations in the region to convert to the production of palm oil and cocoa oil.

Sime Darby's diversification turned out to be a smart move. Demand for its oils and other agricultural products surged during the late 1960s and 1970s, and the company began to accumulate excess cash. A good deal of it was used to acquire other companies, thereby expanding Sime Darby's reach into several other industries. Much of Sime Darby's success during that period was attributable to its acquisition of the giant Seafield Estate and Consolidated Plantations Berhad in the early 1970s. Through that operation Sime Darby became a leading force in the region's thriving agricultural sector. Besides growing the oil palms and cocoa, the company began processing the crops into finished products for sale throughout the world.

As its sales and profits spiraled upward during the early and mid-1970s, Sime Darby became a shiny feather in Britain's cap. To the surprise and chagrin of the British stockholders, however, the company was wrested from their control by the Malaysian government late in 1976. The intriguing events leading up to the takeover began in the early 1970s. During that time that, Sime Darby's chief executive, Denis Pinder, began investing the company's cash in new subsidiaries throughout the world.

The company's stock price soared as Sime Darby's sales spiraled upward. At the same time, some observers charged that Sime Darby was engaged in corrupt business practices (with critics coining the phrase "Slime Darby").

Allegations of corruption were confirmed in the eyes of some detractors when, in 1973, Darby's outside auditor was found stabbed to death in his bathtub. The Singapore police ruled the death a suicide, but Pinder still ended up in prison on misdemeanor charges. Pinder's successor took up where he left off, investing in numerous ventures, most of which were located in Europe. Unfortunately, many of those investments quickly soured. Some Malaysians felt that Sime Darby was taking profits from its successful domestic operations and investing them unwisely overseas. So, in 1976 the Malaysian government trading office bought up Sime Darby shares on the London stock exchange. It effectively gained control of the company and installed a board made up mostly of Asians.

Asian and British board members were able to agree that Tun Tan Chen Lock's son, Tun Tan Siew Sin, would be an acceptable replacement as chairman of Sime Darby's board. In 1978 Sime Darby was reincorporated in Malaysia as Sime Darby Berhad. Its headquarters was subsequently moved to Kuala Lumpur. Sime Darby jettisoned some of its poorly performing assets during the late 1970s and early 1980s under Lock's leadership. But it also continued investing in new ventures. It purchased the tiremaking operations of B.F. Goodrich Philippines in 1981, for example, and secured the franchise rights to sell Apple Computers in southeast Asia in 1982. The company also purchased a Malaysian real estate development company and used it to begin developing plantation lands.

By the early 1980s Sime Darby's push to diversify had given it a place in almost every industry, from agricultural and manufacturing to finance and real estate. Although it did diversify into heavy equipment, real estate, and insurance businesses, new management also plowed significant amounts of cash into the company's traditional commodity and plantation operations. Sime Darby became a favorite of investors that were looking for a safe bet. Indeed, the mammoth enterprise tended to minimize risks after the investment mistakes of the early 1970s and seemed content to operate as a slow-growth multinational behemoth that could withstand any market downturns. Even if it something did go wrong, the company had a war chest of nearly a half billion U.S. dollars from which it could draw.

Unfortunately, Sime Darby's staid strategy to negatively impact its bottom line. Sales dipped to M$2.78 billion in 1992 before plunging to M$2.17 billion in 1983. Sime Darby lumbered through the mid-1980s with annual sales of less than M$2.5 billion, and net income skidded from about M$100 million in the early 1980s to a low M$59 million in 1987. To turn things around, Sime Darby's board promoted Tunku Ahmad Yahaya to chief executive. Ahmad was a veteran of the company's executive ranks and was a favorite nephew of Malaysia's first prime minister, Tunku Abdul Rahman. Under Ahmad's direction, the giant corporation began a slow turnaround. Importantly, Ahmad was instrumental in luring Tun Ismail to Sime Darby's board. Ismail was a highly influential central-bank governor and the chairman of Sime Darby's biggest shareholder. Ismail became executive chairman of the company in 1988.

During the late 1980s Ahmad invested much of Sime Darby's cash horde into a bevy of new companies and ventures. Sime became a relatively big player in the global reinsurance business, for example, and tried to boost its activities related to heavy equipment and vehicle manufacturing. Most notably, Sime began pouring millions of dollars into property and tourism in key growth areas of Malaysia in an effort to get in on the development and tourism boom that began in that nation in the late 1980s. The success of that division prompted the company to also invest in tourism overseas. Through its UEP subsidiary, for instance, Sime Darby bought a full-service resort with condominiums in Florida and a hotel in Australia, among other enterprises. As the company dumped its cash into expansion and diversification, sales and profits bolted. Revenues climbed from M$2.53 billion in 1987 to M$4.98 billion in 1990 to a whopping M$6.20 billion in 1992. During the same period, net income careened from M$85 million to a tubby M$353 million.

Sime Darby realized a stunning 65 percent average annual growth in earnings during the late 1980s and early 1990s. Despite its gains, though, critics charged that the company had concentrated too heavily on traditional commodity industries and had failed to move into the 1990s with the rest of Malaysia. In fact, Sime Darby continued to garner about 43 percent of its sales from commodity trading activities in 1993 and only 18 percent from manufacturing. The rest came from heavy equipment distribution, insurance, and its property/tourism holdings. Although building strength in those businesses had added to the company's sales and profits during the late 1980s and early 1990s, the strategy had caused Sime Darby to fall behind more progressive holding companies in the region that were participating in booming high-tech, gaming, brokering, and manufacturing sectors. Many company insiders believed that Sime Darby would have to eliminate its heavy reliance on commodity industries if it wanted to sustain long-term growth.

Ahmad, the successful chief executive, also recognized the need for change at Sime Darby. The company's stock price began to fall in 1993 and its rapid revenue and profit growth began to subside in comparison to late-1980s levels. In 1993 Ahmad stepped back from control of the company when he named Nik Mohamed Nik Yaacob to serve under him as chief executive. Among Mohamed's first moves was to initiate the merger of the company's plantation assets, organized as Consolidated Plantations, and the parent company, Sime Darby. That effort signaled an end to the company's historical emphasis on commodities and reflected Mohamed's desires to increase activity in manufacturing, high-tech, and other fast-growth businesses and reduce Sime Darby's bureaucracy.

To that end, Sime Darby began increasing investments in businesses like power generation, oil and gas, and heavy equipment exporting. At the same time, Mohamed was faced with the formidable task of absorbing the flurry of acquisitions conducted during the previous six years and streamlining the company into some sort of cohesive whole. Despite restructuring activities, Sime Darby managed to boost sales to US$3.15 billion in 1994, about US$186 million of which was netted as income. Going into 1995, Sime Darby was still operating more than 200 companies and employing more than 30,000 people in 22 countries around the world.

Principal Subsidiaries: PSD Holdings (51 percent); Sime Sembawang Engineering (70 percent); Sime Tyres International; China Engineers; Sandestin Resorts (U.S.A.); Hastings Deering; Consolidated Plantations (50.1 percent); Sime UEP Properties (51.2 percent); Tractor Malaysia (71.7 percent); DMIB (51 percent); Sime Darbe Australia (Australia, 80.8 percent); Sime Singapore (Singapore, 89.1 percent); Sime Darbe Hong Kong (Hong Kong, 74.9 percent).

Further Reading:

Brown, Tom, ''Big Firm Moves Here,'' *Seattle Times,* June 18, 1991, p. 1F.
''Seeking Opportunities,'' *Far Eastern Economic Review,* March 3, 1994, p. 50.
Tsuruoka, Doug, ''Wake-Up Call,'' *Far Eastern Economic Review,* March 3, 1994, pp. 48–52.
——, ''Through the Wringer,'' *Far Eastern Economic Review,* March 3, 1994, p. 52.

—Dave Mote

Sonic Corporation

101 Park Avenue
Oklahoma City, Oklahoma 73102
U.S.A.
(405) 280-7654
Fax: (405) 280-7696

Public Company
Incorporated: 1959
Employees: 168
Sales: $123.75 million
Stock Exchanges: NASDAQ
SICs: 5812 Eating Places; 6794 Patent Owners & Lessors

Sonic Corporation franchises and operates the United States' largest chain of drive-in restaurants. At year-end 1995 there were 1470 Sonic restaurants, of which 1286 were owned and operated by independent franchisees—the remainder were majority-owned by Sonic Corp. Under the slogan "America's Drive-in," a Sonic restaurant features fast service and a limited menu of cooked-to-order items, including hot dogs, soft drinks, shakes, french fries, tater tots, and onion rings, with hamburgers accounting for 30 percent of sales. Sonic restaurants operate in 27 states, primarily in the Bible Belt and Sunbelt states and in small towns and communities with a population of less than 50,000.

The Sonic concept originated in Shawnee, Oklahoma in the early 1950s. Troy Smith, a veteran of World War II, operated a small diner called the Cottage Cafe, which, with only four booths and twelve counter seats, could not support him and his family. Smith sold the diner and opened a larger restaurant, called Troy's Panful of Chicken. But his attempts to expand into multiple locations were not successful, and by 1953 Smith's chicken restaurants had failed.

Smith next dreamed of running an upscale steakhouse. In 1953 he purchased land on the edge of Shawnee, a five-acre property that held a log cabin and included a root beer stand called the "Top Hat." Smith's original intent was to operate his steakhouse in the log cabin and to tear down the root beer stand to make more room for parking. In the meantime, the root beer stand, which sold hot dogs and hamburgers, contributed average sales of $700 in cash per week. Customers would park, walk up to the stand to get food, and eat in their cars.

The postwar boom in automobile purchases created an increasingly mobile public, and businesses developed to serve this new population. Fast-food restaurants began to appear across the country; in California, many operated as "drive-ins," with covered parking spaces and a wait staff that rollerskated to customers' cars. The drive-in concept soon spread across the country, particularly in the warm-weather states. While traveling in Louisiana, Smith stopped at one of these new restaurants. It had an intercom system with homemade speakers that allowed customers to remain in their cars while they placed their order. Smith contacted the inventor of that system and ordered intercoms for his Top Hat root beer stand. Smith also constructed parking canopies, which allowed him to control parking in the root beer stand's lot, and hired carhops to serve his customers. Sales at the stand jumped to $1,750 in the first week after the intercom system was installed, and Smith quickly lost interest in his steakhouse.

The Shawnee restaurant remained the sole Top Hat until 1956. In that year, Smith met Charles Pappe, a manager of a Safeway supermarket in the Oklahoma town of Woodward who was interested in starting his own restaurant. Pappe, visiting Shawnee, met Smith, and, as the two discussed Pappe's restaurant plans, Smith convinced him to dub his drive-in a Top Hat as well. They began to operate their restaurants under the slogan "Service at the Speed of Sound," and developed paper goods with the Top Hat name. By 1958 two more Top Hats opened, in Enid and Stillwater, Oklahoma.

Smith and Pappe made plans to step up their franchise business. They soon discovered, however, that the name Top Hat had already been copyrighted. The pair consulted the dictionary, where they found the word "sonic." The term fit neatly with their slogan. New signs and paper goods were developed, and in 1959 the Stillwater restaurant became the first to adopt the Sonic name.

The partners soon received requests from other entrepreneurs to open their own Sonic Drive-ins. Smith and Pappe assisted these new owner-operators with choosing locations and designing the restaurant layout and operations. Formal franchise agreements were drawn up for the new restaurants. The new owners paid a royalty fee of one penny per sandwich bag, purchased through a central supplier. These franchise agreements contained no provisions for advertising, territorial rights, or fixed menus. Instead, Smith and Pappe's business operated mostly on handshake deals. Sonic operators were still most likely to be local businessmen, owning in part or in full their restaurants, and restaurants were often family-run.

Sonic grew modestly through the 1960s. By 1967, the year of Charles Pappe's death, there were 41 Sonics in operation. Smith brought in two long-time Sonic restaurant franchisees, Matt Kinslow and Marvin Jirous, to run Sonic Supply, the company's supply and distribution division, while Smith continued to develop the company's franchise operations. Franchises appeared in Texas and Kansas, and, by 1972, there were 165 Sonic Drive-ins.

The company had grown too large for Smith, Kinslow, and Jirous to run alone. So, in 1973, Sonic restructured as a franchise company under the name Sonic Systems of America. Shortly thereafter it became Sonic Industries, Inc., which was a company comprised of ten key franchise owners that served as officers and directors of the new company. Smith became chairman of the board and Jirous was named president. Sonic purchased the rights to the name, logo, trademark, and slogan from Smith, and the supply company from Kinslow and Jirous. Each owner was also offered 1250 shares at $1 per share, and the volume of shares pushed the company to become an over-the-counter, publicly traded company. By year-end 1973, there were 200 Sonic Drive-ins. An additional 75 opened in 1974, and by 1975 Sonic was operating in 13 states.

The 1970s saw a dramatic growth in the number of Sonic restaurants. This growth was attributable to Sonic's second generation of owner-operators. Employees, many the sons and daughters of the original franchisees, were encouraged to become managers and supervisors and to open stores of their own. The company's franchise structure became increasingly complex. As former CEO and president C. Steven Lynn related to *Restaurant Business*, "[Troy Smith] would perhaps sell a one-unit franchise to a small town man. That man might train his high school buddy. . . . When he knew the business, another franchisee might recruit him to manage a second unit. All three might own a piece of the unit. . . . Nearly all of our franchisees own pieces of each others' stores, which were often structured as general partnerships."

Between 1973 and 1978 more than 800 new restaurants opened—during one two-year period, more than one new Sonic Drive-in opened each day. But the rapid expansion of the chain created a shortfall in the number of trained managers. Despite the establishment of a Sonic School manager training program in the mid-1970s, a number of restaurants began to fail. Rising inflation rates and higher gasoline prices as a result of the Oil Crisis of 1973 also placed pressure on the drive-in restaurant business. In addition, the company lacked a systemwide advertising program through most of the 1970s.

To boost advertising, the company established the Sonic Advertising Trust, requesting drive-ins to contribute 1.5 percent of their gross. Participation, however, was voluntary, and the first Sonic television commercials did not appear until 1977. By 1979 profits began to fall. A new advertising campaign, budgeted at only $5 million, could not reverse the decline, and by 1980 the company posted a net loss of almost $300,000. Overall revenues and per-store sales were down. In that year, 28 company-owned stores were closed, and by 1981 300 stores were had closed.

Jirous, Kinslow, and other original directors and officers left the company to focus on their own franchises. A new president was hired in 1981 but was replaced by Troy Smith in 1982. The following year, C. Stephen Lynn, formerly with Kentucky Fried Chicken and Century 21, took over the leadership of the company. Lynn identified a number of problems facing the company. Its licensing agreements—there were as many as 20 different agreements throughout the chain—did not bring in the revenue the company needed in order to provide support services across a system that had spread through 19 states. And many of the drive-ins were two decades old and had become shabby. Furthermore, many of the company's restaurants were losing money. Most importantly, the Sonic restaurants continued to operate more or less independently, with little cooperative purchasing and advertising.

Lynn worked to unify the company. By promising to cut food costs by three percent and to increase sales by 15 percent, he convinced 200 restaurants to consolidate their purchasing and to contribute one percent of sales to an advertising program. A new franchise agreement in 1984, adopted by nearly 90 percent of the franchisees, provided the company with ascending royalties, beginning at one percent of gross sales and rising to three percent, depending on store volume. By 1986, more than one-third of the stores in the chain were working cooperating. Per-store sales grew to an average of $350,000 per year, with new stores averaging up to $550,000.

In 1986, Lynn, along with a group of investors, performed a leveraged buyout for approximately $10 million and took the company private. Calling franchisees "partners," Lynn was able to increase chain-wide cooperation, forming advertising groups focused on key markets. Sonic put together a low-cost remodeling package, initially priced at $20,000, to encourage older restaurants to revitalize their image. At the same time, the new structure price was set at around $140,000. Lynn also moved to fix the Sonic menu to a limited number of basic items and regional specialties. Soon, Sonic was once again growing. In 1987 it built its 1000th restaurant.

Sonic's growth continued into the 1990s. It went public again in 1991, raising $52 million in its initial public offering. Lynn had increased cooperative advertising participation to 93 percent of the restaurants, which by then contributed an average of 2.25 percent of gross sales. Between 1990 and 1994 Sonic added nearly 400 new restaurants, tagging on more than 120 in 1994 alone. Systemwide sales rose from $454.6 million to $776.3 million, same-store sales rose from $446,000 to $585,000, and company revenues grew from $45.8 million to $99.7 million. In 1993, Sonic's market value was estimated at $200 million. Sonic had grown to the fifth-largest hamburger chain in the United States and was the top drive-in chain.

Sonic's growth remained relatively flat after 1992. After reaching a high of $33, its stock price slipped to around $23 per share in 1995. Per-store sales seemed stagnated between $515,000 and $585,000. Sonic, which traditionally owned its rural and suburban Southern markets, was facing increasing competition from drive-through chains such as Checkers and Rally's, while the giants of the industry—McDonald's and Burger King—with their ability to discount, began to invade the territory. Meanwhile, despite discussion of acquiring a northern-based partner, Sonic clung to its traditional market, making few inroads outside of the warm-weather Southern areas. The company faced additional trouble in 1994 when it was forced to take a $3.9 million writedown charge for discontinuing its five company-owned properties, including two closed restaurants in South Florida that had suffered as a result of the hurricane that devastated the area in 1992.

In 1994, after more than a year of often bitter talks with franchisees, Sonic renegotiated its franchising contracts. The new contract, good for twenty years with a ten-year option to renew, raised graduated royalties to four percent and increased advertising contributions to a fixed 2.5 percent while granting Sonic control over a systemwide advertising program. It also fixed a sole soft drink supplier. Sonic also collected conversion fees from franchisees signing new contracts. In return, the company agreed to give up its first right of refusal for franchisees wishing to turn over restaurants to their heirs or partners, and agreed to fewer audits of franchisees' books. Franchisees also gained wider territorial protection guarantees, with a protected trade radius of 1.5 miles in larger cities, and up to three miles in rural areas. About two-thirds of Sonic franchisees accepted the new contract.

The terms gave Sonic increases of $5 million in royalties and conversions, and allowed it to raise its advertising budget to $20 million. With the discontinuation of its Florida operations, Sonic saw its total revenues rise by 24 percent, to $123.75 million in 1995. At the beginning of that year, Lynn, who owned approximately 12 percent of the company, named Clifford Hudson, former executive vice-president and COO, to take over as president of the company. When Lynn left Sonic to become chief executive officer and president of the beleaguered Shoney's restaurant chain, Hudson was appointed chief executive officer as well.

The typical Sonic restaurant in 1996 remained true to the 1950s-style carhop concept: customers drove up to one of an average of 24 covered parking spaces, placed orders through an intercom, and were served at their car. Restaurants also offered drive-through service, with some restaurants operating as drive-throughs only. The absence of indoor dining allowed the company to maintain one of the highest margin restaurant operations in the country, with a new construction package costing less than $515,000 per unit and first-year sales of over $700,000. Average per-store sales were around $585,000 per year in 1995.

The company owned and operated, often through various franchise and partner agreements, 178 restaurants going into 1995. Company restaurants, together with franchise royalties and conversion fees, generated $123.75 million in revenues. Growth in the number of units was averaging 26 percent for franchised restaurants and 106 percent for company-owned restaurants over the five years from 1990 to 1994. Approximately two-thirds of franchisees were represented by the National Association of Sonic Drive-in Franchisees, which operated entirely separately from the company. Sonic entered the lste 1990s with a new executive team, including former executives from Coca-Cola Co., Taco Bell, McDonald's, and Wendy's, and plans for 125 new franchised and company-owned restaurants in 1996.

Principal Subsidiaries: Sonic Industries, Inc.; Sonic Restaurants, Inc.; Sonic Service Corp.

Further Reading:

Alva, Marilyn, ''Season of the Switch,'' *Restaurant Business,* February 10, 1995, pp. 56–64.
Gindin, Rona, ''Everything Old Is New Again,'' *Restaurant Business,* February 10, 1987, pp. 150–159.
Lynn, C. Stephen, ''Sonic: 40 Years of Success 1953–1993,'' *Newcomen Society,* address presented at a 1993 Oklahoma Meeting of the Newcomen Society of the United States, Oklahoma City, Okla., January 12, 1993.
Robertson, Nancy Love, ''The Long and Winding Road: Sonic Turns 40,'' *What's Cookin'; Sonic Industries News Magazine,* Spring 1994, pp. 9–16.

—Mickey L. Cohen

Southdown, Inc.

1200 Smith Street, Suite 2400
Houston, Texas 77002
U.S.A.
(713) 650-6200
Fax: (713) 653-6815

Public Company
Incorporated: 1930 as Realty Operators, Inc.
Employees: 2,400
Sales: $561.9 million
Stock Exchanges: New York
SICs: 3273 Ready-Mixed Concrete; 3241 Cement Hydraulic;
   6719 Holding Companies, Not Elsewhere Classified

One of the largest producers of cement and ready-mix concrete in the United States, Southdown, Inc. is also regarded as one of the industry's most efficient and modern producers. With eight manufacturing plants in California, Colorado, Florida, Kentucky, Ohio, Pennsylvania, Tennessee, and Texas, Southdown has distinguished itself as a leading competitor in an industry of vital importance to the construction industry, particularly large-scale public works projects. During the mid-1990s, more than half of the company's annual revenues and a substantially larger proportion of its operating earnings were generated from the production of cement, the primary binding agent in concrete. Southdown is also involved in the production of ready-mixed concrete, a building material used in myriad construction activities and the end-product of roughly 70 percent of the cement used in the United States. By gradually narrowing its focus on the production and marketing of these two products from the mid-1970s forward, Southdown established a solid position for itself in crucial cement and concrete markets across the country, particularly in Florida and southern California.

Although Texas-based Southdown was regarded as a major producer of cement and concrete during the 1990s, the company's historical roots stretch back to another state, to an entirely different line of business, and to a time when the company was known by a different name. Southdown's history charts an incongruous course; the company began its corporate life as a competitor in the sugar cane business, later diversified its interests by branching into a host of different business lines, then dismantled its conglomerate structure through a series of divestitures that left Southdown as narrowly focused as it was

during its early years, but focused on an entirely different type of business. In fact, the company that rose from plantation fields in Louisiana during the 1930s built the foundation for the prodigious cement and concrete producer of the 1990s, each distinct era woven together to create the multifarious history of Southdown, Inc.

Southdown was founded as Realty Operators, Inc. in the spring of 1930, beginning its corporate life in Louisiana as a sugar cane grower during the incipient stages of the United States' greatest economic calamity. The company survived the decade-long ravages of the Great Depression, spending its formative years in the crucible of economic turmoil, then rallied forward through the United States' greatest military effort, withstanding the disruptive yet economically vibrant years of the Second World War. In 1948, three years after the conclusion of the war, Realty Operators changed its name to Southdown Sugars, Inc., borrowing the Southdown name from the Southdown sugar cane plantation in Houma, Louisiana. Over the course of the next 20 years, Southdown Sugars increased its stature as a sugar cane company, benefitting from the most advantageous economic conditions since its formation. The company changed its name again in 1959 to Southdown, Inc., prophetically dropping "Sugars" from its corporate title as it prepared to enter the 1960s, the last decade the company would rely exclusively on sugar cane cultivation and production to drive its growth.

By the mid-1960s, Southdown had operated as a sugar cane company for nearly 40 years, amassing holdings in sugar cane plantations, sugar cane mills, and sugar cane refineries. Within a decade, however, Southdown would become much more than a sugar cane company. Through a series of acquisitions completed during the late 1960s and early 1970s, Southdown transformed itself into a conglomerate, using the foundation it had established in nearly four decades as a Louisiana sugar cane company to propel it into variegated business interests. The late 1960s and early 1970s were frenetic years for the company, made busy by the rapid absorption of companies and facilities involved in manufacturing activities far removed from its former mainstay sugar cane business. Southdown delved into the beverage business, acquiring wine, beer, and soft drink manufacturing facilities. It entered into candy production, developed vineyard and pistachio farms in California and Louisiana, and, most significantly, began acquiring cement manufacturing operations, marking the beginning of the company's involvement in what would become its primary business during the 1990s.

Southdown's diversification began with its entry into the oil and gas exploration business, which would remain a component of the company's business until the late 1980s. In 1966, Southdown formed a wholly-owned subsidiary, Southdown Exploration Inc., to superintend its oil and gas business, then in early 1967 acquired 40 percent interest in Burmah Oil Western Co. and Burmah Oil Western Exploration Co. With the addition of part interest in the two Burmah Oil companies, Southdown Exploration changed its name to Southdown Burmah Oil Co., which existed for roughly two years until all of the subsidiary's assets were transferred to another wholly-owned Southdown subsidiary, Pelto Oil Company.

Once Southdown had carved a new niche for itself in the oil and gas business, it jumped into a number of other businesses, acquiring, in 1969, McCarthy & Hildebrand Farms, Inc., Pearl Brewing Company, and 59 percent interest in Leonard T. Improvement Company. By far the most significant acquisition during the year, however, was the purchase of Southwestern Portland Cement Co., completed in late 1969. All the other properties purchased during the year would be divested in the years ahead, but the addition of Southwestern Portland Cement and its five cement plants introduced Southdown to the cement business.

Less than two years after acquiring Southwestern Portland Cement, Southdown restructured the company, organizing it as a wholly-owned subsidiary, then continued to diversify in the wake of its pivotal foray into cement manufacture. To its interests in beverage, cement, oil and gas exploration, and sugar cane, Southdown added cattle and agricultural operations in 1972, when the company's subsidiary, Southdown Land Company, acquired Chillagoe Land Company, which operated cattle-raising and farming operations on more than 500,000 acres in Australia. Next, the company organized Santa Clara Vintners, Inc. in cooperation with San Martin Vineyards Company to produce and market wines in California, rounding out Southdown's business interests to compose a conglomerate corporation that was substantially more diverse than the Southdown of the early 1960s.

In 1975, the company's Southdown Land Co. subsidiary, which had since been renamed Valhi, Inc., was organized as a separate company, spun-off to operate on its own as Southdown began to shed businesses and narrow its focus. When dissident shareholders gained control of the company the following year, Southdown's divestiture of its sundry business interests began in earnest, as a dramatic switch in the company's corporate strategy was implemented by new management. Effective on the last day of 1976, Southdown's new management decided to dispose of the company's soft drink and winery businesses, opting to concentrate on its cement and oil and gas operations. In early 1977, the net assets of the company's soft drink business, which had been controlled by three subsidiaries, were sold, followed by the divestiture of the company's winery business in May 1977. While these properties were being put on the block, Southdown's management decided to discontinue the milling and refining of operations belonging to Southdown Sugars, Inc., which had supported the company for nearly 40 years. Following the decision to exit the business that had defined the company during its formative decades, Southdown sold its Pearl Brewing Co. subsidiary in 1978, ending its involvement in the malt beverage business.

As the company entered the 1980s, it continued to winnow its business interests, selling Southdown Sugars, Inc. to Supreme Sugar Co. in 1980, and its candy business, conducted by its Judson Candies, Inc. subsidiary, in 1981. After these two divestitures, Southdown had completed its return to competing as a more narrowly focused company, with its financial future dependent on the successful development of its oil and gas business and its cement business. Three years after shedding its candy business, the company began moving toward strengthening its involvement in its two primary business lines, acquiring a cement plant in Colorado in 1984 as well as 78 percent interest in the Twin Lakes oil field in Chaves County, New Mexico, through its Pelto Oil Company subsidiary. In 1986, another

signal acquisition was completed when Southwestern Portland Cement Co., the cement subsidiary acquired in 1969, purchased the Los Angeles area ready-mix concrete operation belonging to Transmix Corp.

Next came Southdown's most important acquisition during the 1980s, the purchase of Moore McCormack Resources Inc. in 1988 for $528 million. The acquisition of Moore McCormack doubled the size of Southdown's cement manufacturing capacity, positioning the company within the cement industry as a substantially larger competitor and a burgeoning major player to be watched closely in the years ahead. Before the acquisition, Southdown principally had been a maker of cement and related products in the southwestern and western United States, but the addition of Moore McCormack Resources' facilities gave the company major cement manufacturing plants in the Southeast and in two key industrial states, Ohio and Pennsylvania, extending its geographic presence into crucial cement markets.

Following the completion of the Moore McCormack Resources acquisition, Southdown exited the oil and gas business by selling its Pelto Oil Company subsidiary to Energy Development Corp. in 1989, thereby staking the company's future on the successful development of its cement and concrete businesses. In 1990 the company sought to vertically integrate its cement operations by entering into the hazardous waste processing business, acquiring three processing companies in July and three additional processing companies in September. By collecting hazardous waste and processing it into hazardous waste derived fuel, Southdown could produce on its own a portion of the fuel required to feed its cement kilns, adding to the synergistic benefits already realized through its concrete manufacturing facilities. Although expectations were optimistic, the hazardous waste processing properties performed dismally during their first several years under Southdown ownership. Organized into Southdown's environmental services segment, the hazardous waste processing facilities recorded a $16 million dollar loss during their first two-and-a-half years of operation, leading Southdown to restructure the business segment in 1992. As part of the reorganization, four hazardous waste processing facilities were sold, but difficulties persisted, exacerbating Southdown's woes during the early 1990s.

In addition to losing money in its new environmental services business, Southdown was losing money elsewhere, incurring successive losses from its concrete products operations, as a national economic recession hobbled construction activity across the country and reduced the demand for concrete. Southdown's concrete products business lost $12.7 million in 1991, $11.6 million in 1992, and $1.6 million in 1993, but there was little the company could do to effect a recovery except wait for the economy to rebound and spur construction activity.

In 1994 the waiting came to an end when a resuscitated economy delivered its ameliorative affects to the country's construction industry and, as a consequence, to Southdown. Except for California, where construction activity continued to lag, all of the company's markets were buoyed significantly by the return to more prosperous times, particularly in Florida, where the construction market thrived as the mid-1990s neared. After three years of losses, Southdown's concrete products operations posted $9.3 million in operating earnings, while the company's cement operations recorded growth as well, generating $91.2 million in operating earnings, which represented an 11 percent increase over 1993's total.

In the wake of this encouraging news, Southdown exited its unprofitable environmental services business, announcing in November that it intended to divest its hazardous waste processing facilities and avoid competing in an industry reeling from excess capacity. As Southdown began to shed its waste processing properties and focus on developing plans for the remainder of the 1990s, future plans called for expansion in strategically important markets where the company already maintained a presence and for the modernization and expansion of particular cement and concrete manufacturing facilities. Toward this objective, the company purchased a cement import terminal in southern Florida in 1994 and announced its plans to revamp and expand its Ohio cement plant.

Principal Subsidiaries: Allworth Inc.; Florida Mining & Materials Concrete Corp.

Further Reading:

"Bright Outlook Ahead for Southdown, Inc.," *Investment Dealers' Digest,* August 26, 1969, p. 30.

Byrne, Harlan S., "Southdown Inc.: Oil and Gas, Cement Adds Up to Profitable Mix," *Barron's,* May 15, 1989, p. 109.

Jaffe, Thomas, "Is Southdown Heading North?," *Forbes,* July 13, 1987, p. 48.

Kovski, Alan, "Cement Company Paves a Route for Waste Disposal," *The Oil Daily,* November 20, 1990, p. 4.

Mehkman, William, " 'Home-Run' Potential Seen in Depressed Southdown," *The Insiders' Chronicle,* August 26, 1991, p. 1.

"The Next Job for a Managerial Wunderkind," *Business Week,* March 18, 1985, p. 93.

—Jeffrey L. Covell

Spartan Motors Inc.

1000 Reynolds Road
Charlotte, Michigan 48813
U.S.A.
(517) 543-6400
Fax: (517) 543-7728

Public Company
Incorporated: 1975
Employees: 540
Sales: 191.5 million
Stock Exchanges: NASDAQ
SICs: 3711 Motor Vehicles and Car Bodies

Michigan-based Spartan Motors Inc. is a world leader in the engineering and manufacturing of custom chassis for fire trucks, recreational vehicles, transit buses, school buses, and other specialty vehicles. Founded in 1975, Spartan went public in 1984 and has shown remarkable growth in sales and earnings through the 1980s and 1990s. Spartan Motor's management style, which stresses simplicity and frugality, has become as renowned in the automotive sector as their innovative chassis designs.

Spartan Motors was founded in 1975 by four longtime automobile industry workers, George W. Sztykiel, Bill Foster, Jerry Geary, and John Knox. Company president Sztykiel had worked for 19 years as an engineer at Chrysler Motors before moving to Diamond Reo Trucks in 1973, and he had developed his own very definite ideas about how a business should operate. Born in 1929, Sztykiel grew up in Poland where he lived through the German occupation and the subsequent communist takeover. In his characteristic anecdotal style, Sztykiel recounts memories of ostensibly well-equipped Germans falling to frostbite and exposure because their hobnailed boots conducted the cold while their Russian counterparts survived in crude straw-stuffed mukluks. The lesson that simplicity and improvisation often triumphed over sophistication would remain with Sztykiel throughout his professional life. This lesson, however, was hard to live by in the paper-bound administration of the giant Chrysler Corp. As an engineer, Sztykiel's sense of job satisfaction had come from designing superior products, but at Chrysler he found most of his time was spent processing the paperwork that such a large enterprise required before any decision could be made. ''I felt I was wasting my life,'' Sztykiel said in a 1992 profile in *Inc.* magazine.

Sztykiel's opportunity to follow his vision of the way a corporation should operate was unexpectedly offered to him when employer Diamond Reo Trucks went bankrupt in 1975. With a sick wife and two sons in college, Sztykiel was seemingly not in a position to take extensive risks; however, the moribund Michigan auto industry was also offering little in the way of opportunities, challenging or otherwise. Sztykiel's wife, confined to the hospital, begged him to find a job close enough to home to allow him to continue his daily visits, but 1975 was the nadir of the American auto industry's decline and there were simply no jobs available. Out of desperation more than entrepreneurship, Sztykiel and his three partners pooled all their savings, took out second mortgages on their homes, and built Spartan's first chassis in a converted commercial garage in Charlotte, Michigan. ''We had the luxury of having our house burn down at Diamond Reo,'' *Inc.* quotes Sztykiel as saying. ''We had the power of poverty.'' Although the partners had virtually no capital, they collectively had almost a century of experience in the automobile industry and they knew what hadn't been working for the established large truck chassis manufacturers. They had an idea of how they could do things differently but as yet no customers on whom to try their ideas. With no money to spend on advertising or glossy catalogues, the four men relied on word of mouth and the reputation each had established with customers while working for Chrysler and Diamond Reo. It was these connections that would eventually lead to their first customer.

FMC Inc. in Tipton, Indiana, had been manufacturing fire trucks using standard mass-produced truck chassis but had run into problems trying to adapt these chassis to the specialized requirements of the fire truck market. Not only did they have to make compromises about the design of the body to suit the chassis, but every time they made a modification in the chassis to accommodate indispensable fire-fighting apparatus they reduced the durability of the truck. FMC's management had dealt with the Spartan partners in their previous incarnation as automotive engineers with Chrysler and on hearing of the new venture thought that perhaps Spartan could help with their chassis problems. The partners lost no time in flying down to Indiana, where they quickly convinced the management to allow them to construct a sample chassis to the fire truck specifications. Back in Charlotte the four men scrambled to buy the necessary components, which they could not afford to have custom tooled for this single order. This bootstrapping assembly of standard components to produce a unique customized design would become the Spartan trademark. Upon seeing the prototype, FMC put in an order for twelve chassis and Spartan was officially in business.

Over the course of the next ten years Spartan Motors would take the necessary poverty of their first years and turn it into a virtue. Named after the Spartans of Ancient Greece who eschewed luxury in favor of thrift and discipline, the company was determined to retain a no-frills approach to management. Although in 1978 they moved out of the cinder-block garage that had served as their headquarters since their founding, their new offices and manufacturing space provided very little more in the way of comfort. The administrative offices at the new Spartan plant were packed together in a warehouselike space with flimsy partitions to serve as office walls. Sztykiel himself steadfastly refused to hire a secretary, saying that it would only create a need for more paperwork. Competition between management teams for budget assignments was avoided by the elimination of preset budgets altogether. Instead, every management decision was evaluated in terms of what it would bring to production. Sztykiel's son John, who would later become president of the company, commented in *Inc.*, "We are always asking ourselves, 'if we don't spend money on car phones, can we then use that money to hire somebody in the plant?'"

Spartan's approach to its employees also developed during these early lean years. Having lost their jobs to the auto recession themselves, the founders of Spartan were determined to build a devoted and hard-working workforce by offering bonuses pegged to profits and by avoiding lay-offs at all costs. In 1976, Sztykiel was forced to ask workers to take a 15 percent pay cut in order to prevent lay-offs and within months the workers had raised production by enough to allow the company to reinstate their full pay. Spartan also avoided hiring many expensive university-trained engineers, preferring instead to employ high school and vocational school graduates and training them on the job. Spartan's approach to engineering its chassis was particularly suited to on-site training: instead of lengthy on-paper design sessions, Spartan engineers brainstormed to solve design problems on the assembly-plant floor. According to one engineer, a substantial portion of the engineering on some designs was actually performed by assemblers.

During the company's first ten years of operation, Spartan continued to design and manufacture specialized chassis for the fire engine industry. In a field that had been geared towards standardization for almost 100 years, Spartan made customization its stock in trade. The use of standard components purchased in large quantities from a variety of suppliers allowed Spartan to keep the prices of its custom designs low. By putting the components together in a large variety of ways, however, the company was able to provide very different chassis to competing fire truck manufacturers. By the early 1990s, Spartan could offer fire truck manufacturers their choice of 10 different transmissions, more than a dozen engines and 30 rear-axle and suspension systems, not to mention 45 styles of cab in 57 different shades of red. In order to accommodate this variety, Spartan's assembly plant avoided an assembly line lay-out in favor of individual work stations arranged to permit continuous assembly of different chassis types. New specifications could be met without delay, allowing the company to respond quickly to market demands. A former engineer from one of Spartan's major competitors, Oshkosh Truck Corp., commented in a *Wall Street Journal* article that design changes at the large Wisconsin firm sometimes took from eight to nine months, whereas Spartan was producing new designs in half that time.

Spartan's unorthodox approach appealed to customers, and by 1983 the company's fire truck chassis were bringing in revenues of almost $12 million and income of $629,000. The four partners felt that it was time to expand both their product line and their floor space, but they ran into a crucial setback. As Sztykiel stated bluntly in an interview, "We ran out of money." The partners had sunk all of their assets into starting the company. The bank had already lent them three times their collateral and, in spite of the company's success, was unwilling to risk any more. In 1984 Spartan management made the crucial decision to go public with an initial public offering of 1,500 shares. With the infusion of new capital, Spartan now expanded their plant from 42,000 to 72,000 square feet and began to design chassis for new applications. By 1986, they were offering specialized chassis for the bus and motorhome market, as well as for the airport vehicles market. Although the new applications took a few years to produce profits, by 1988 Spartan was ready to expand their facility to include a motorhome chassis plant.

Although Spartan's original motorhome chassis incorporated standard gas-powered engines, toward the end of the 1980s Spartan engineers began to experiment with a diesel engine mounted in the rear of the chassis. Rear engine diesel chassis were quieter and provided a roomier cab than conventional designs, but they had always been prohibitively expensive for the motorhome market. Spartan engineers Tim Williams and Larry Karkau began tinkering with the traditional design and, with characteristic ingenuity, came up with a chassis that could cut the usual price almost in half. The only problem was that they would need custom-made parts to manufacture their design, which would greatly increase the cost of product development. Spartan had built its business by using standard components, and by this time the company had established a reputation with many component suppliers as being a dynamic and reliable customer. With this reputation behind them, Spartan engineers managed to convince component suppliers to share the risk of the new chassis design by assuming the cost of tooling the specialized parts. With development costs of only about $500,000, the EC-2000 rear engine diesel chassis would produce sales of $30 million by 1991 and would transform Spartan from a small, clever customizer to a significant force in the chassis industry.

When the EC-2000 was introduced in 1990 Spartan's annual sales had already reached $50 million, thanks largely to the company's innovative fire engine chassis. By 1991 sales of the new motorhome chassis pushed revenues up to almost $100 million and almost tripled the company's net income. Suddenly stock analysts began to sit up and take notice of the growing little company. Several profiles appeared and a number of "best pick" lists began to include Spartan as a good investment. Stock price, which had hovered around $3.00 a share in the late 1980s, suddenly soared, reaching $16.00 in 1991 and peaking at $25.00 by 1993.

Meanwhile, sales of Spartan's motorhome chassis continued to grow, and the company began to apply its rear engine diesel technology to other applications. In 1993, Spartan made its first significant move into the international market, founding Spartan de Mexico in Queretaro, Mexico, to produce bus chassis for the Mexican and South American markets. The growing firm felt that its newly developed bus chassis were the best bet for the international market. In 1994 they entered into a joint venture with SETCAR, a bus manufacturer based in Tunisia, to sell Spartan bus chassis in North Africa and the Middle East through a newly formed export company to be called Spartan International. Spartan also began to export its American-made bus chassis to a variety of European and Asian countries. Perhaps the most significant new venture for Spartan in the early 1990s was a licensing agreement with General Motors whereby GM would mass produce and market the low-cost Spartan Discovery motorhome chassis under the GMC name and Spartan would produce a higher-priced model that GM would sell and service. This relationship with one of the big automakers was a marked departure from Spartan's established philosophy of avoiding mass assembly-line production and the burdensome bureaucracy of the traditional auto industry and was a sign of the new role that Spartan was creating for itself in the industry.

When Spartan went public in 1984, the company employed about 100 people in a 42,000-square-foot manufacturing plant. By 1995, the Spartan workforce had increased to over 500, and the size of the Spartan facility in Charlotte, Michigan, had grown to 300,000 square feet. Clearly, the bootstrapping, improvisational approach to management that had been in large part responsible for Spartan's success could not function as reliably with so many employees and so many new product lines. Although budgets and paperwork had been unnecessary when president George Sztykiel could control every aspect of the operation, now more traditional management techniques were essential to monitor this growing enterprise. George's son John Sztykiel took over the presidency of Spartan in 1992 and by 1994 he began to hire a number of experienced professional managers to guide the company into this new phase of expansion. Even more significantly, in 1994 the company opened a dedicated research and development facility as part of its new plant expansion. Spartan's trademark ''on the floor'' design teams were to give way to the more efficient, but perhaps less sensitive, traditional R&D department.

Spartan Motors's sensational growth of the early 1990s began to taper off by the middle of the decade. Although Spartan's sales were still growing, analysts who had pumped the stock heavily in the early 1990s began to have reservations as the Mexican operations failed to generate an immediate profit and the agreement with GM got bogged down in a number of delays. Stock price fell from a high of $25 a share to a more realistic price of around $15. As Spartan moved into the last years of the century it remained to be seen whether management could successfully convert the feisty and innovative little customizer into a reliable, international manufacturing firm.

Principal Subsidiaries: Spartan de Mexico, SA de CV.

Further Reading:

''GM Inks Motorhome Pacts with Spartan,'' *Ward's Automotive Reports,* March 7, 1994, p. 5.
Selz, Michael, ''Quick Off the Mark: Agility Gives an Edge to Small Manufacturers,'' *The Wall Street Journal,* December 29, 1993, pp. A1–A2.
Teitelbaum, Richard S., ''Spartan Motors,'' *Fortune,* December 28, 1992, p. 55.
Welles, Edward O., ''The Shape of Things to Come,'' *Inc.,* February 1992, pp. 66–74.

—Hilary Gopnik

Spelling Entertainment Group, Inc.

5700 Wilshire Boulevard
Los Angeles, California 90036-3659
U.S.A.
(213) 965-5700

Public Company
Incorporated: 1959 as Pearce-Uible Co.
Employees: 700
Sales: $599.84 million
Stock Exchanges: New York Pacific
SICs: 7812 Motion Picture & Video Production; 7829
   Motion Picture Distribution Service; 7822 Motion Picture
   & Tape Distribution

The Spelling Entertainment Group, Inc., is a major producer
and distributor of multimedia entertainment. The company and
its subsidiaries produce network television for domestic and
international distribution, create and market interactive computer games, distribute feature films on video, and license related merchandise.

Spelling's history can be traced through its two predecessors,
the Charter Co. and Spelling Entertainment Inc. In 1991 Charter
acquired a controlling interest in Spelling, by which time both
companies were controlled by American Financial Corp. Under
the direction of namesake Aaron Spelling, Spelling Entertainment Inc. had produced some of the most popular television
programs of the 1970s and 1980s. Charter's odyssey had taken
it from a foundation in real estate, through a phase in the 1960s
and 1970s as a multi-billion-dollar conglomerate, to a 1980s
bankruptcy denouement.

Charter's phenomenal growth and ultimate demise have been
credited to Raymond K. Mason, who guided the company from
the early 1960s through the mid-1980s. After graduating from
the University of North Carolina in 1949, Mason returned to his
hometown, Jacksonville, to begin working at his father's real
estate, lumber, and insurance business. Founded in 1919, the
Mason Lumber Company had branched out into residential
construction in the 1930s and early 1940s and was generating
about $100 million in annual sales when the younger Mason
came on the scene.

In 1963, Guy Botts of the Charter Mortgage and Investment Co.
approached Mason with a merger proposal. Charter had origi-

nally been incorporated in 1959 as Pearce-Uible Co., a merger
of 14 real estate businesses in Florida. This firm, which expanded into mortgage banking with the subsequent acquisitions
of Commander Mortgage Company and Kirbo Mills McAlpine,
was rechristened Charter Mortgage and Investment Co. in 1962.
Charter and Mason merged in 1963. Guy Botts left the company
to accept the chairmanship of Barnett Banks, Inc., and went on
to guide that institution's growth into Florida's largest bank.
Raymond Mason assumed the chairmanship of the merged firm,
which was renamed simply The Charter Co. Over the ensuing
two decades, Mason assembled a multi-billion-dollar aggrega-
tion of oil, insurance, and communications companies. The core
mortgage operation would become the southeast United States'
largest mortgage company.

Charter made its first foray into the oil industry with a 1968
acquisition of 60 gasoline stations. Two years later, Mason
extended his reach "upstream" in the petroleum business with
the purchase of $70 million in oil refineries, gas stations, and
overseas shipping operations from Signal Oil & Gas Co. From
1971 to 1973, Charter acquired four other refineries and petroleum properties, largely through exchanges of stock. The bal-
looning conglomerate's assets increased by 1184 percent from
1969 to 1974, when annual sales crossed the $1 billion mark.

Charter developed a communications dynasty with the acquisi-
tions of Downe Communications, Inc., Redbook Publishing
Co., McCall Printing Co., and American Home Publishing Co.,
Inc. The company also owned six radio stations. By the end of
the decade, Charter published such well-known magazines as
Ladies Home Journal, Redbook, American Home, and *Sport.*

Late in the decade, Charter supplemented its insurance interests
with the acquisitions of Louisiana & Southern Life Insurance
Co. and two Crum and Forster subsidiaries. The insurance
business, although less profitable than the petroleum operations,
was a more consistent moneymaker. It helped to even out the
dramatic fluctuations of the oil business.

In the mid-1970s, when real estate values dropped, the magazines slumped, and Charter's oil properties in Venezuela were
nationalized, the company's profits slid 86 percent. Mason
managed to resurrect Charter through a combination of financial
savvy and plain old luck. He sold some assets and reorganized
the remainder, but, according to John Craddock of *Florida
Trend,* Charter was "saved by the Arab oil embargo that made
oil precious and refineries highly profitable." In the late 1970s,
Charter's stock rose from $6 to $50 per share.

Charter sold its oil-producing properties to focus on oil refining
in the late 1970s and got out of the slumping real estate market.
In 1978, Charter acquired Riffe Petroleum Co., a producer of
asphalt. A year later, Charter took a $500 million half-interest in
a 500,000-barrel-per-day Bahamian refinery and bought out the
troubled Carey Energy Corp., a bargain at $30 million in cash
and stock. The purchases catapulted Charter into the ranks of
America's top 20 oil companies, increased its sales from $2
billion in 1978 to $4.9 billion in 1979, and contributed to
earnings growth from $23 million to $365 million. Charter was
dubbed "a geyser of profits," and Mason was praised as "a
flamboyant president who often made surprising moves." Earnings had "routinely quintupled" every five years from 1963 to

1983, by which time Charter had 183 subsidiaries and ranked among Fortune's top 100 American companies.

Emboldened by the heady cash flow, Mason aimed ever higher, planning multi-billion dollar oil and life insurance acquisitions for the early 1980s. His scheme began to crumble however, when recession hampered both the publishing and petroleum legs of his tripod. Early in 1980, Charter acquired the struggling Philadelphia *Bulletin* for an estimated $35 million. The 132-year-old *Bulletin* had once been America's largest afternoon daily, but had begun to lose subscribers and advertisers in the last half of the 1970s. Charter was unable to turn the paper around; it came up $21.5 million short in 1981 and was losing almost $3 million each month when Charter, unable to sell it, shut it down in 1982. At the same time, Charter's *Ladies' Home Journal* was suffering similar ailments: from 1976 to 1980, its subscriber rolls declined from 6 million to 5.5 million, and it lost 17 percent of its advertising pages in the first six months of 1981 alone. Charter got out of the media business with the 1982 divestment of *Ladies' Home Journal* for $13 million in stock and *Redbook* for about $25 million in cash and notes.

Charter's petroleum refining business struggled through scandal and a cyclical downturn in the early 1980s. The conglomerate's oil returns were squeezed between the high price of crude oil (having sold its oil-producing properties, Charter had to buy crude on the open market) and the low prices its refined products were commanding. Charter's corporate ethics came under fire in 1979, when President Jimmy Carter's brother, Billy, offered to act as a liaison between the company and Libya in an effort to increase the crude supplies flowing to Charter. A company official accepted the offer, which promised "commissions" of $.5 to $.55 per barrel to Billy Carter. Although the deal never actually brought Charter a new supply of crude, it did bruise the company's reputation at a time when it could ill afford the disgrace.

In the midst of all these other problems, another scandal came to light: Charter subsidiary Independent Petrochemical's was accused of participating in the 1971 disposal of dioxin at Times Beach, Missouri. The site came to be known as the worst case of ground contamination since Love Canal. Charter set aside a $23 million reserve to cover the incident, which was finally settled in 1986.

The third leg of Charter's business, insurance, took a hit in 1983. Mid-year, insurance rater A.M. Best lowered its estimation of one of Charter's most lucrative products, its single-premium (tax) deferred annuities (SPDAs). During the first four years that Charter Security Life offered the products, its assets multiplied from $247 million to over $4.5 billion, and revenues skyrocketed from $20 million to $2 billion as Charter became the country's largest offerer of SPDAs. Analysts began to question the viability of the product when the second-ranking company took a nose-dive in 1982. In reaction to the rating, three of the brokerages that had been selling these insurance products— Dean Witter Reynolds Inc., Merril Lynch & Co., and Prudential-Bache Securities—stopped offering them. Late in 1983, Charter Security Life's quarterly revenues halved and the subsidiary experienced a $3.9 million quarterly deficit.

Although Charter's overall revenues increased from $4.2 billion in 1979 to $4.97 million in 1981, its net income slid from $365.33 million to $7.12 million. Charter's short-term debt multiplied from $29 million in 1982 to $150 million in September 1983, by which time its long-term debt stood at $400 million.

The company's downward spiral was prodded along by a flurry of negative publicity. Mason's reputation as an executive fell as quickly as Charter's bottom line. John Craddock of *Florida Trend* characterized him as an "incredible business genius" with "a monumental indifference to the day-to-day business of his companies." When the four top executives in charge of the nuts-and-bolts managing were killed in a tragic 1982 helicopter crash, Charter was left virtually rudderless. In fact, when Charter and 43 of its subsidiaries were forced by creditors into bankruptcy in April 1984, one of Mason's colleagues said that he was "the most surprised man on earth." That same year, *The Gallagher Report* (a weekly management newsletter) named Mason "one of America's ten worst corporate chairmen." In order to appease his detractors and Charter's creditors, Mason resigned the conglomerate's presidency and chief executive office before the end of 1984.

Financier Carl Lindner—who may have seen the writing on the wall before Mason—positioned himself as one of Charter's top creditors by trading his Charter stock (owned through the Cincinnati-based American Financial Corp.) for loans totaling $40 million right before the April 1984 bankruptcy. His status as a leading creditor made him a powerful participant in Charter's mid-1980s reorganization. His plan to get the floundering company out of bankruptcy offered to nullify Charter's financial obligations to him in exchange for a 41 percent stake in the company. Lindner chipped in another $146 million cash and loans to help pay off the $452 million Charter still owed to its other creditors.

In the meantime, the liquidations that had begun in the early 1980s gathered momentum as banks, shareholders, and other creditors clamored for their money. Charter sold its insurance division to Metropolitan Life Insurance Co. for $52 million late in 1982. The company's Northeast Petroleum Industries subsidiary, which had been acquired in February 1983 for $123.6 million, was sold to Cargill Inc. in 1986 for about $96 million. Charter also divested its New England retail fuel oil operations and its Houston oil refinery.

By 1987, Charter's annual revenues had shrunk to about $1.5 billion from a high of over $5 billion as the company scaled back, becoming an operator of over 400 convenience stores and more than 200 gas stations. Lindner moved Charter's headquarters to Cincinnati in 1988 after accumulating 53 percent of the company's stock and bringing it out of Chapter 11.

Charter acquired an 82 percent interest in Spelling Entertainment Inc. for $189.5 million in cash and notes in 1991. That stake had previously been held by another Carl Lindner business, Great American Communications.

A production company primarily focused on television, Spelling had been created in the 1960s by corporate namesake Aaron Spelling. Although Spelling was often derided as a "king of schlock" whose programs appealed to "television's lowest common denominator," there was no denying his commercial success. His multidecade string of hits included "Mod Squad,"

"Charlie's Angels," "The Love Boat," "Fantasy Island," and "Dynasty." His 1970s-era programs propelled the American Broadcasting Corporation to the top of the television ratings charts.

But by the late 1980s, Spelling appeared to have lost his "Midas Touch." Annual revenues were on the decline as the company had just one show on broadcast television and two others in production. Aaron Spelling Productions Inc. stock declined from its initial issue price of $14 in 1986 to $5 in 1988 as sales and earnings declined by double-digit percentages.

Spelling foreshadowed the merger with Charter in a 1988 interview with Mark Frankel of California Business. Spelling said that independent production companies such as his would "have to branch out and do other things besides just producing for television—become miniconglomerates—in order to make sure that we can keep doing what we do." He also targeted the foreign syndication market as an avenue for growth, acquiring Worldvision Enterprises Inc., a global distribution company, in 1989.

Charter completed its acquisition of Spelling with a mid-1992 exchange of stock valued at $44 million and raised money with the subsequent spin off the remaining oil business to its top managers. Renamed Spelling Entertainment Group, the merged companies continued to hold on to a few Charter assets through the mid-1990s.

Less than a year passed before Spelling Entertainment Group's corporate ownership structure changed again. In 1993, Lindner sold his controlling (53.4 percent) interest to Blockbuster Entertainment Corporation for $141.5 million. By the end of 1994, Viacom Inc. had bought Blockbuster and announced its intention to sell Blockbuster's stake in Spelling to help settle its own debts.

Spelling acquired Republic Pictures Entertainment and merged it with its Worldvision subsidiary in mid-1994, creating a library of 7,000 feature films, made-for-TV movies and miniseries, and 15,000 episodes of Spelling-produced television. Global syndication of these programs proved a steady source of revenue that fueled new production efforts.

Spelling's television production business rebounded in a big way in the early 1990s. "Beverly Hills 90210," a prime-time teen soap that featured Aaron Spelling's daughter, Tori, was the first of a string of early 1990s television hits that included spin-offs "Melrose Place" and "Models, Inc." These series became a mainstay of Rupert Murdoch's burgeoning Fox network.

Pursuant to that transaction, Spelling Entertainment acquired Virgin Interactive Entertainment plc from its parent. This producer of interactive games like "The 7th Guest" and "The Lion King" provided Spelling with another avenue for diversification in its growing array of businesses.

Spelling Entertainment fulfilled Aaron Spelling's vision of diversification in the early 1990s. From its core in television production, Spelling expanded into large-scale domestic and international distribution of television, film and video material, interactive games, and licensing and merchandising. By the end of 1994, Spelling's domestic television production and distribution contributed less than 25 percent of annual revenues. The diversification strategy appeared to pay off in increased annual sales and net income. Revenue nearly quintupled, from $122.75 million in 1991 to $599.84 million in 1994, and net income almost doubled (albeit erratically) from $12.96 million to $24.11 million.

Principal Subsidiaries: Charter Oil Company; Republic Entertainment Inc.; Spelling Entertainment Inc.; Virgin Interactive Entertainment Limited (United Kingdom) (90.5%).

Further Reading:

"Behind the Breakup at Charter," *Business Week,* March 5, 1984, p. 37.
Castro, Janice, "Last Rites for a Proud Paper," *Time,* February 8, 1982, p. 64.
"Charter Co.'s Chancey Dream," *Fortune,* August 25, 1980, p. 58.
Craddock, John, "The Unsinkable Raymond Mason Plans a Comeback," *Florida Trend,* January 1985, p. 54.
Engardio, Pete, "A Duel to Escort Charter from Chapter 11," *Business Week,* August 25, 1986, p. 76.
Fitzpatrick, Eileen, "Merger Partners Join Forces and Blend Strengths," *Billboard,* June 4, 1994, p. 89.
Frankel, Mark, "The Angst of Aaron," *California Business,* April 1988, p. 24.
Frook, John Evan, "Analysts Question Sale of Spelling in Near Future," *Los Angeles Business Journal,* March 26, 1990, p. 7.
Mason, Raymond K., *The History of the Charter Company: Its Challenges and Opportunities,* New York: Newcomen Society in North America, 1983.
Rosenberg, Hilary, "How Sound Is the Charter Company?" *Financial World,* February 7, 1984, p. 34.
Shaner, J. Richard, "Charter Survival Plan Pares It to Heavy Oils and Gasoline Retailing," *National Petroleum News,* March 1985, p. 25.
Trachtenberg, Jeffrey A., "Viacom to Shed Spelling Stake to Trim Debt," *Wall Street Journal,* August 11, 1995, p. A3.

—April Dougal Gasbarre

Spencer Stuart and Associates, Inc.

401 N. Michigan Avenue
Suite 3400
Chicago, Illinois 60611
U.S.A.
(312) 822-0080
Fax: (312) 822-0116

Private Company
Incorporated: 1956
Employees: 205
Sales: $50 million
SIC: 7361 Employment Agencies

Spencer Stuart & Associates, Inc. is one of the world's most famous executive search and consulting firms. The company is based in Chicago and has offices located around the globe in order to meet the burgeoning demand for management talent. Spencer Stuart & Associates is justifiably famous for the introduction of a new method for finding and placing managers. The *modus operandi* of the firm is to combine a management talent search with management consulting. Since the relationship between executive recruiting and management consulting is so close, Spencer Stuart & Associates combine the two well beyond the actual time of an executive's placement. This strategy, according to the company, helps both the executive and the client company form a closer, more satisfactory, working partnership and union.

On April 1, 1956, Spencer Stuart opened an executive search consulting firm on Michigan Avenue in Chicago, Illinois. Stuart had worked for many years at the well-known management consulting firm of Booz, Allen & Hamilton, also in Chicago. When he journeyed out on his own, Stuart was convinced that a new kind of executive search firm was needed, one that wasn't just a recruitment agency, but an executive search consulting firm. Executive search firms were a new kind of service during the late 1950s, and the changes that American corporations were experiencing at that time demanded a comprehensive, systematic, and thoroughly disciplined approach.

Listening very closely to his clients, Stuart profiled the company's organizational structure and corporate culture, prepared written descriptions of the required personnel so that there was no misunderstanding as to what kind of person was needed, developed a highly sophisticated search tailored to the specific client's industry, analyzed and appraised candidates for the management position, and designed a plan to assimilate the new executive within the client company so that the individual would become an effective participant in the firm's management structure as soon as possible.

Stuart's first assignment was to find an executive to manage a pharmaceutical firm in Caracas, Venezuela. The firm needed an individual who was fluent in Spanish, conversant with the methods of doing business in South America, familiar with the pharmaceutical industry, and whose family would be able to adapt to living in Venezuela. Stuart immediately hopped on a plane and found the right person for the job, one who was already living in Caracas. By 1958, business was booming and Stuart had spent more time on international assignments than working in the United States. Over 35 flights were taken to Europe and South America during that year, and the demand for his consulting services was growing so rapidly that Stuart established offices both in Mexico City and in Zurich, Switzerland.

By 1960, the company had completed executive search assignments in over 25 countries, including Denmark, Switzerland, Germany, England, France, Italy, Brazil, Venezuela, and other countries throughout Europe and South America. Client companies included firms from the food, machinery, construction equipment, cosmetics, banking, and pharmaceutical industries. Over 12 presidents of companies around the world had been found by Stuart's executive search firm. By 1961, new offices in London and New York were opened to meet the rapidly growing demand for the company's services. As new offices were opened in Paris, Brussels, Frankfurt, and Sydney, Australia, Spencer Stuart established a company policy that all the offices would be managed and operated by nationals.

Throughout the 1960s, Spencer Stuart pursued a long-range strategy of growth through expansion. The internal structure and decision-making process of the company was relaxed and informal, and management personnel would meet face-to-face in various locations around the world in order to discuss and refine policy and procedures, while also addressing problems and future opportunities. The company benefited through its association with larger corporations by drawing on different management philosophies to more clearly define the one most suitable for Spencer Stuart & Associates. Near the end of 1969, Stuart implemented an international management group within the company to improve worldwide communications among satellite offices and, at the same time, to prepare for his own departure.

By 1973, the company had nine offices in the United States, Europe, and Australia, staffed with approximately 55 full-time executive search consultants. At this point, Spencer Stuart decided to retire from his position as chief executive officer. The two partners who were chosen to replace Stuart included an Englishman by the name of Peter Brooke, and a Frenchman named Jean-Michel Beigbeder, both graduates of Harvard University's Business School. Stuart also decided to sell the entire share of his ownership in the company to the new managing partners.

The transition from one-man leadership to a professional management team took place smoothly, and Spencer Stuart & Associates began to grow both in size and in revenues. More importantly, the team of Brooke and Beigbeder began to capitalize on the new opportunities within the executive search industry. During the mid-1970s, management recruiting firms entered a period where the demand for their services grew rapidly. Corporations expressed a need for management talent that came from the outside. The idea of promoting executives from within a company was still in common practice, but not enough to meet the complex and stringent conditions of the business world demanded by management. Thus, rather than always promoting from within the organization, a company's needs could be met by hiring senior executives from the outside who brought experience and a novel perspective to the issues confronting the company. This new development in executive hiring went hand-in-hand with the idea that management mobility was a valid strategy to enhance one's career.

In addition to the increasing demand for external executive searches, there was a growing acceptance of management recruiting firms. Presidents and comptrollers of companies were just too busy to spend hours and hours reviewing and interviewing candidates for executive positions. As the demand for services provided by executive search firms grew, there was a sudden boom within the industry. By the mid-1970s, there were more than 900 executive search firms in the United States, many of them concentrating on providing services for a particular industry, geographical location, or function. Even though the majority of search firms were small, with between one and three consultants, there emerged six major executive recruiting firms based on annual revenues. Spencer Stuart was one of these firms. Without hesitating, management at Spencer Stuart had taken advantage of all the industry developments occurring during the 1970s and had built a reputation as one of the pre-eminent executive search consulting firms in the world.

By the late 1970s, as competition began to increase, Spencer Stuart & Associates embarked upon a strategy to expand its international practice. More offices were opened throughout Europe, but an intense effort was also made to develop the company's services in Canada, South America, Australia, and Southeast Asia. From 1974 to the end of the decade, the company expanded its offices from ten to over 25, most of these located in Europe and Asia. New markets, such as Africa, China, and the Middle East, also provided the company with opportunities to expand its executive search services. Noting also the growing opportunities in the American market, the company opened new offices in Dallas, Houston, Los Angeles, San Francisco, Cleveland, Atlanta, and Stamford, Connecticut. These offices were designed to provide more localized services to the regions within which they were located. With over 100 consultants and 35 research associates, Spencer Stuart & Associates had one of the largest staffs of executive search consulting firms in the world. Not surprisingly, from 1974 to 1981, the company's revenues grew annually by a margin of 25 percent, amounting to over 400 percent by the end of fiscal 1981.

By the early 1980s, a new president and managing partner had assumed the reins of Spencer Stuart & Associates. Thomas J. Neff began working at the company in 1976 and three years later was named its president. A graduate of Lafayette College, and having earned an MBA from Lehigh University, Neff completed a short stint in the U.S. Army as a first lieutenant and

then joined the famous Chicago firm of Booz, Allen & Hamilton. After a number of years at Booz, Allen, Neff joined the management consulting firm of MicKinsey & Company and worked at the firm's offices both in New York City and in Australia. By the time he arrived at Spencer Stuart & Associates, Neff had also gained valuable experience at the senior management level in the airline, packaged goods, and health care industries.

Under Neff's leadership, the company developed its international practice as well as its highly localized domestic executive search services. Spencer Stuart & Associates grew to include nine offices from coast to coast within the United States, and 11 offices in Europe, located in Amsterdam, Brussels, Dusseldorf, Frankfurt, Geneva, London, Madrid, Manchester, Milan, Paris, and Zurich. Offices were also located in Calgary and Toronto, Canada, Melbourne and Sydney, Australia, Sao Paulo, Brazil, and Hong Kong. Neff also supervised the addition of partners to the firm, from eight in 1974 to 27 by 1982. Most importantly, Neff emphasized the importance of developing the company's international practice by ensuring that the managing partners were an international mix of Americans, French, and British. This was true as well for the representation on the firm's Board of Directors, which drew people from Canada, France, Belgium, Australia, The Netherlands, the United Kingdom, and the United States.

The most important of Neff's contributions to the company during the 1980s, however, involved his development of executive search and management consulting ideas. As companies became more and more demanding in their expectations of what constituted a solution to a problem in management, Neff developed and refined the notion of management *consulting* in the executive search. Neff believed that it was important to focus on what happened during the period previous to and following the recruitment process, and the company began focusing on succession planning, preparing the Board of Directors for the new executive, designing compensation packages for executives that resolved all the issues surrounding economic security and job attraction, and the general problems involved in introducing a new executive into an organization. These concerns were intrinsic to the management consulting process, according to Neff, and contributed toward the success of the executive search. This detailed and thoroughgoing approach also helped Spencer Stuart & Associates become one of the most sought-after executive search firms in the nation during the 1980s. When a *Fortune 500* company needed a new president or chief executive officer, they turned to Spencer Stuart.

By the late 1980s and early 1990s, the two preeminent headhunting firms within the industry were Spencer Stuart & Associates and Heidrick & Struggles. Heidrick & Struggles was headed by Gerard R. Roche, and Roche had found such high-profile candidates as John Scully for Apple Computer Inc., Lawrence A. Bossidy for AlliedSignal Inc., and Stephen Wolf for UAL Corporation, the parent firm of United Airlines. Neff had also placed his share of top-notch candidates, including Louis V. Gerstner at R.J. Reynolds, Michael H. Walsh at Tenneco, and David W. Johnson at Campbell Soup. Both companies had set up divisions within which executive searches were conducted. Spencer Stuart & Associates' most active division included the investment management search practice and the entertainment search practice.

In 1992, both Spencer Stuart & Associates and Heidrick & Struggles were asked to find a successor for John Akers, the head of International Business Machines Corp. (IBM). This search caused a significant amount of controversy within the industry. Knowing that placement firms were bound by certain limitations (including the general agreement that prohibited headhunters from pursuing the executives they have already placed, and the restriction that such firms were not supposed to recruit from a company for two years after a placement had been made), IBM management hired both companies so that they could steal high-level executives from each other's previous clients. The strategy, according to IBM, was to purchase as broad a coverage of the market as possible. Thus Roche was able to pursue candidates off-limits to Neff, while Neff was able to pursue candidates off-limits to Roche. Although the new IBM executive, Louis V. Gerstner, Jr., was eventually found by Roche, both companies benefited by the enormous amount of publicity that the search generated in such popular business magazines as *Business Week, Fortune, Forbes,* and *The Economist.*

During the mid-1990s, Spencer Stuart & Associates was still considered one of the top two executive search consulting firms in the industry. The company's client list not only included American firms, but both large and small businesses around the world. With such an enviable placement record, and a client list that kept on growing, Spencer Stuart & Associates was carrying on the successful tradition started by Spencer Stuart in 1956.

Further Reading:

Byrne, John A., "Can Tom and Gerry Find a Big Cheese for Big Blue?", *Business Week,* February 22, 1993, p. 39.

Crawford, Kim, "The Rough Guide To Recruitment," *Marketing,* May 25, 1995, p. 28.

Fleming, Charles, "Hollywood Hunt is on for Executive," *Variety,* March 23, 1992, pp. 125–126.

"IBM Hires Two Firms to Help Search for a Chief," *The New York Times,* January 30, 1993, p. 37.

Sasseen, Jane, "Brief Encounters Management," *International Management,* September 1992, pp. 44–46.

Scism, Leslie, "Prudential May Seek Outsider to Succeed Chairman Winters When He Retires," *The Wall Street Journal,* September 28, 1994, p. B10.

"Spencer Stuart Launches Money Management Group," *Pensions & Investments,* July 11, 1994, p. 28.

Stuart, Spencer R., and Neff, Thomas J., *Spencer Stuart & Associates,* Newcomen Society: New York, 1981.

—Thomas Derdak

St. John Knits, Inc.

17832 Gillette
Irvine, California 92714
U.S.A.
(714) 263-9730
Fax: (714) 263-9798

Public Company
Incorporated: 1963
Employees: 2,420
Sales: $127.9 million
Stock Exchanges: New York
SICs: 2331 Women's and Misses' Blouses and Shirts; 2335
    Women's, Juniors' and Misses' Dresses; 2339 Women's
    and Misses' Outerwear, Not Elsewhere Classified; 5621
    Women's Clothing Stores

A swiftly rising competitor in the apparel industry, St. John Knits, Inc. designs and manufacturers women's apparel and accessories, selling clothing, bracelets, earrings, necklaces, and other fashion items through a chain of its own stores and through major department stores. Founded by a former model and her husband, St. John Knits operated for decades by marketing its designer clothing and accessories exclusively through department stores. In the 1990s the scope of the company's operations was widened when it began opening its own stores, creating a flourishing concern that stood well-positioned for consistent growth in the years ahead.

When she was 25 years old, Marie St. John was working as a model in Los Angeles, getting ready to marry her fiancé, Robert E. Gray, and about to start an enterprise that three decades later would prosper as a more than $125 million-a-year business. At the onset, the origins of the company resembled entrepreneurism in its classic form: a flourishing, multi-million-dollar company created from nothing, a half-by-chance, half-by-design bid to wedge an upstart, start-up company into a business world dominated by established corporate gentry, with the odds of success intimidatingly low, the sting of failure painfully close at hand.

For St. John and Gray, however, the fledgling years of their company, St. John Knits, were not quite as dramatic, at least in terms of the impending failure that lent entrepreneurism its dramatic flavor. Success came unexpectedly to the company, and it arrived early and easily, perhaps one of the reasons that from the outset St. John Knits pursued a course of moderate, methodical expansion. For years the company's management, led by St. John and Gray, kept St. John Knits' growth in check, refusing to mount an aggressive expansion program even as the St. John brand name became a status symbol for women across the country. Controlled growth would govern St. John Knits formative decades of development and still hold sway over the company's strategic plans during the 1990s, but the first few weeks in the company's history were harried days, frenetic days that first hinted at the riches Marie St. John and Robert Gray would later enjoy.

In 1962, at age 25, Marie St. John acted upon her disenchantment with the styles and prices of women's clothing hanging on the racks of retail establishments in the Los Angeles area by making her own knit clothes by hand. St. John began making clothes more in line with her sense of fashion: simple, straight knit skirts with matching short-sleeved tops. Quickly, St. John discovered that she was not the only one who preferred her self-designed clothes. Other models approached St. John, complementing her clothing and expressing an interest in purchasing their own, prompting St. John to purchase a $450 knitting loom. Using her loom, she began meeting the demand for her basic yet classic knit skirts and tops, and in the process kindled the spark that created the formation of St. John Knits.

Prompted by the demand for her personal line of clothing, St. John asked her fiancé for help in carrying out an idea of hers. Gray, auspiciously, was a self-employed salesman of women's apparel lines to department stores, but he was reluctant to use his professional experience to help fulfill his future wife's plan of selling her clothing to department stores. As he later reflected to a *Forbes* reporter, explaining his mindset in 1962, ''I took her dresses to retailers only to stop her nonsense and convince her that no one was going to buy them.'' Gray was flat wrong. For the next 35 years he would spend his days meeting the demand for his fiancée's clothing.

With nothing to prove but a lesson in the hardships of the retail clothing industry, Gray took St. John's samples to work with him and came back at the end of the day with 30-day delivery orders for 84 dresses signed on for by Bullock's and a fashionable local retailer. Retailers had been impressed by St. John's Chanel-inspired, timeless line of clothing that could endure the seasonal vagaries of fashion, but St. John had no time to be impressed. Eighty-four dresses had to be made in 30 days, a production volume that St. John later explained would take her, alone at her knitting loom, over a year to fulfill. Clearly, more elaborate plans had to be made, or the deadline would pass and, as it later became known, an incredibly lucrative opportunity would be missed.

St. John headed to the loom, while Gray proceeded to raise the financial means to make the production of 84 dresses a realistic aspiration. He borrowed $5,000, then purchased additional knitting looms and rented manufacturing space with the hope of meeting the unexpected, pressing demand for St. John's clothing. With the space and equipment secured, Gray set himself to the task of assembling the personnel to complete the job, hiring his mother, St. John's mother, and another knitter. Soon the family group began production, their hurried efforts marking the beginning of St. John Knits, Inc., incorporated in 1963 in the same month Gray and St. John were married.

Once the company completed production of its first wave of orders, less hectic days followed, with Gray assuming control over production, sales, and financial matters and St. John taking on the responsibility of designing the clothes for the company that bore her name. Early on, the couple decided they would design and sell four lines of clothing each year, ranging from tailored-look dresses, suits, and separates to more casual sportswear, with each line comprising 20 different items and styles. The couple also decided to pursue a moderate course toward expansion, opting for slow, measured growth and eschewing the potential pitfall of borrowing money to finance their business efforts, a strategy that would control St. John Knits' growth as the company's clothing lines became increasingly popular and began recording success outside the Los Angeles area.

By the end of St. John Knits' first year of business, the Irvine, California-based company had collected $92,000 in sales and earned $18,500, recording inaugural financial totals that had been achieved largely through word-of-mouth advertising, Gray's connections with retailers, and only a modicum of paid-for advertising. Instead of jumping the gun and allowing initial success to breed overambitious growth, Gray and St. John focused their efforts on developing the company's products, not on developing promotional campaigns, an approach that enabled Gray in particular to closely monitor St. John Knits' development. Gray also demonstrated his desire for control over the company's operations by opting against contracting a third-party manufacturer to produce the company's line of clothing. A popular practice among clothing companies was to locate the cheapest manufacturing source available, usually somewhere in the Far East; but Gray decided his and his wife's company would manufacture its own clothes in Irvine, allowing Gray maximum control over every of aspect of St. John Knits' operation.

With St. John spearheading the creative end of the business and Gray attending to the company's daily operation, St. John Knits' carved a lasting place for itself in the business world by selling to large, established retailers such as Jacobson's and Lord & Taylor, cultivating a relationship that would propel its growth for decades. Underpinning its respected standing among retailers were the company's distinctive lines of clothing, which began to attract a devout clientele drawn to Marie St. John's classically conservative fashion style. As one retail consultant explained, "For ladies who lunch, a St. John knit is almost like a uniform, a status symbol," which neatly described the company's typical retail customer and conveyed the essence of the clothes' success: generations of women made the inclusion of a St. John knit in their wardrobe a must.

Driven by the money spent by "ladies who lunch," St. John Knits' annual sales marched methodically upward, reaching $1 million by 1969 and arriving at the next financial benchmark, $10 million in sales, in 1980. Throughout the first two decades of St. John Knits' existence, the company's expansion had been financed entirely out of cash flow, with registered, in-the-books success fueling the gradual expansion of the company's operations and generating growth. Moreover, by avoiding outside financial assistance, Gray and St. John had retained absolute

control over their company and would continue to do so for nearly another decade. However, as the company's 30th anniversary approached, an opportunity presented itself that neither Gray nor St. John could resist. With their decision to take advantage of the opportunity, the couple relinquished some of their control, but the benefits of their decision were quickly demonstrated, ushering in a new era in St. John Knits' history.

In 1989, Munich-based Escada AG, a manufacturer of luxury women's apparel and accessories, offered to purchase an 80 percent stake in the company, presenting Gray and St. John with the chance to collect $45 million for ceding control to Escada. The German designer and maker of ready-to-wear designer sportswear had been founded in 1976 by Wolfgang Ley, a German businessman, and his designer wife, Margaretha, both of whom were intent on the aggressive expansion of their company throughout the world when they approached Gray and St. John. Aside from the similarities between the two companies—each was led by a businessman husband and a designer wife—Gray and St. John were attracted by the offer because the $45 million would enable them to open St. John Knits retail stores for the first time, opening up a vast new avenue for geographic and financial growth for their company. Accordingly, Gray and St. John agreed to the Leys' offer, and in 1990 Escada purchased an 80 percent interest in St. John Knits, leaving Gray and St. John at their company's helm to orchestrate the establishment of St. John Knits stores.

The first St. John Knits store opened in Palm Desert, California, followed by a string of other boutiques, including the opening of a store on prestigious Fifth Avenue in New York City and another in Munich, the company's first overseas boutique. While the company developed a retail branch of operations, it continued to sell its lines of clothing to department stores, the company's mainstay business for the previous three decades. St. John Knits' product lines had expanded by the early 1990s to include a line of brightly colored daywear and a line of evening wear, carried by three major department stores—Saks Fifth Avenue, Neiman Marcus Group, and Nordstrom, Inc.—which represented the company's largest customers. St. John Knits employees still handled nearly all of the production processes required to keep the company running, including the dying and spinning of yarn, the casting of buttons, and the manufacture of buckles, bracelets, earrings, necklaces, and other accessories, continuing a long-standing policy not abandoned after the company's acquisition by Escada.

Annual sales increased as the scope of the company's operations expanded, rising modestly from $57.9 million in 1990 to $65.8 million in 1991, then leaping to $80 million in 1992. In its 30th anniversary year, St. John Knits' annual sales eclipsed $100 million, much to the delight of the corporate offices in Irvine. With ten boutiques in operation and strong sales to major department stores robustly propelling the company forward, there were numerous reasons to rejoice in what St. John Knits had accomplished during its first 30 years of operation. However, against this ebullient backdrop the fate of the company unexpectedly became uncertain.

The reason for this uncertainty did not stem from St. John Knits, but from Escada. The German parent company had fallen on hard times, hobbled by declining sales and mounting debt. The company reported an operating loss of $61.3 million in 1992, a serious blow exacerbated by prodigious debt incurred from international expansion. Between 1990, when Escada purchased a majority interest in St. John Knits, and the end of 1992, the company's debt had tripled, and by the beginning of 1993 its stock had been stripped of nearly 90 percent of its value from the previous year, creating a desperate need for an infusion of cash. As a result, Wolfgang Ley, who had frequently referred to St. John Knits as ''the jewel of Escada'' sold his company's stake in the knitwear manufacturer in March 1993, marking the beginning of St. John Knits' operation as a publicly-owned company.

Gray and St. John retained 20 percent of the company's stock after the public offering, remaining in control of the company they had founded 30 years earlier and continuing to record enviable success in the wake of Escada's divestiture. In 1994, sales soared to $127.9 million, while the company's net income swelled to $14.9 million, an impressive increase from the $1.7 million posted in 1990. St. John Knits' legacy of success continued into 1995, with first quarter sales increasing 33 percent and profits jumping 42 percent, fueling expectations that the remainder of the 1990s would bring prosperous years of growth.

In September 1995, St. John Knits signed a lease to open a store on Wilshire Boulevard in Beverly Hills, aptly located between a Saks Fifth Avenue store and a Neiman Marcus store, the company's two largest department store customers. As St. John Knits moved forward to the anticipated March 1996 opening of the Beverly Hills store, the company's 17th, Gray and St. John

were attempting to target a younger customer than the typical St. John Knit customer, women in their 40s. To help engender this shift in the company's customer base, the couple was expected to pass the reins of leadership to their daughter Kelly Gray, a 28-year-old senior vice-president and creative director of the company who had begun working at St. John Knits at age 12. Kelly Gray was slated to assume control of the company in 1998, marking the beginning of a new era of leadership in the company's history and the beginning of a daughter's bid to build upon the success created by her parents, as she stewarded St. John Knits into the 21st century.

Principal Subsidiaries: St. John Trademarks, Inc.; St. John Knits International, Inc.

Further Reading:

Agins, Teri, ''Escada to Sell Its 80% Stake in St. John Knits,'' *Wall Street Journal,* January 13, 1993, p. A5
Block, Toddi Gutner, ''Do-It-Yourself Lady,'' *Forbes,* November 6, 1995, p. 245.
Dang, Kim-Van, ''St. John Knits Maps Expansion Plans,'' *Women's Wear Daily,* March 20, 1995, p. 24.
Marlow, Michael, ''St. John Finally Bags Beverly Site,'' *Women's Wear Daily,* September 22, 1995, p. 10.
Rutberg, Sidney, ''Escada aims for $100M from St. John Sale,'' *Women's Wear Daily,* January 19, 1993, p. 17.
Ryan, Thomas J., ''St. John Knits Lays Out Its Strategies for Maintaining Growth Rate at 20%,'' *Women's Wear Daily,* June 9, 1994, p. 6.
''St. John Knits,'' *Fortune,* July 12, 1993, p. 100.

—Jeffrey L. Covell

Stone Manufacturing Company

P.O. Box 3725
Greenville, South Carolina 29608
U.S.A.
(803) 242-6300
Fax: (803) 370-5640

Private Company
Incorporated: 1945
Employees: 1,800
Sales: $250 million
SICs: 2329 Mens & Boys Clothing, Nec; 2322 Mens & Boys
  Underwear & Nightwear

Stone Manufacturing Company is one of the leading producers of men and women's clothing in the United States, and owns one of the largest single apparel factories in the world. The company's Cherrydale plant, located in Greenville, South Carolina, manufacturers an entire range of products, including men's pants, shirts, shorts, sweaters, t-shirts, underwear, and sleeping garments. In recent years the company has also manufactured a popular line of women's clothing. Some of Stone Manufacturing Company's best-known brands include *Umbro,* a line of soccer clothing, *Women on the Run,* a line of running clothes for women, and *U.S. Action,* a line of sports clothes for both sexes.

Stone Manufacturing Company was the brainchild of Eugene E. Stone III. Stone was born in Spartanburg, South Carolina, and attended Fishburne Military School in Waynesboro, Virginia. He went on to Georgia Tech University in Atlanta and later graduated with a degree in geology from the University of South Carolina.

In 1929 Stone set out to strike it rich in the oil fields of East Texas. He joined the Seaport Oil Company working out of Houston and developed a close friendship with the man who started the company. At the time, drilling for oil seemed to be an easy route to success. Seaport Oil drilled seven wells and came up with seven oil gushers. However, Seaport Oil was just one of many companies that found oil, and, within a bare six months, the oil market was completely glutted. As a result, the price of a barrel dropped from a high of one dollar to a low of just six cents. Stone's dreams of wealth were shattered, and he returned to Greenville a poor but wiser man.

Back in Greenville, Stone soon found that conditions were even worse than in Texas. The entire nation was in the grip of the Great Depression, and South Carolina was particularly hard hit. Property values for both residential and commercial real estate had dropped dramatically, and wages were approximately one-third of what they had been before the Wall Street crash of 1929. Small farms in rural South Carolina had suffered the same fate as farms in the Dust Bowl of the plains states, and many families moved to cities in order to find work at factories or small businesses.

One of the small apparel manufacturing companies in Greenville was also struggling to survive. The firm was forced to reduce the wages of its employees so that it could continue business operations. An embittered worker sabotaged the firm's boiler and left the entire factory and all its personnel working in the cold. When Stone's father, the owner of the building, was asked to repair the boiler, the younger Stone, who had gained some experience fixing boilers in his student days, volunteered to tackle the problem. Stone fixed the boiler, the company resumed its normal operations, and the young man was offered a job at ten cents an hour for sixty-eight hours per week. Stone assumed the job with his usual enthusiasm, and despite the long hours found the time to court and marry Allene Wyman, known affectionately by her friends and family as "Linky." Stone and Linky left on their honeymoon with a guarantee from his boss that they would not only receive the two weeks' pay for his time off, but a new icebox upon their return.

When the Stones returned from their honeymoon they discovered that there would be neither a two-week paycheck nor an icebox. Stone immediately resigned, and with the skills he had acquired at the apparel manufacturing company, he opened the Stone Manufacturing Company on July 9, 1933. Stone hired five seamstresses and purchased eight sewing machines that formed the cornerstone of his company for the first few years. Stone himself did all the fabric cutting, as well as all the packaging and shipping. His wife was in charge of designing all the clothes.

The first order received by Stone Manufacturing Company was from Sterling Stores of Little Rock, Arkansas, for the production of 25 dozen pink bloomers of knit jersey made from cotton. Although the shipment got lost in transit, Sterling Stores gave Stone another chance and soon developed into one of his most loyal customers. Also during the company's first year of business, Stone made a sales call to G. C. Murphy Company, a retailer with stores throughout Pennsylvania. Before he finished showing the buyer his entire line of clothing, the buyer began filling out an order pad. After the meeting, Stone happily announced that the company had enough orders for the entire year.

During the mid-1930s, the nation was still in the midst of the Great Depression. Stone Manufacturing employees worked in cold, damp conditions since the company was only able to afford one potbellied stove for heat. Yet the firm produced high-quality clothes that people could afford, which was quite an accomplishment during the Depression. By 1935 the company was not merely surviving but making a profit, and Stone decided to buy a furnace for the clothing plant. One of the few apparel manufacturing firms in the country whose sales were always increasing during the 1930s, Stone Manufacturing Company was the envy of the entire industry.

In the late 1930s, due to its rapid growth, the company moved to a larger facility and at the same time expanded its product line. Stone Manufacturing was making dresses, aprons, slips, panties, dustcaps, and sunsuits. The sunsuits sold at Woolworth Department Stores for ten cents. The company held to a high standard of quality: for example, while most bloomers at the time were made with eight or nine stitches to the inch, Stone's bloomers were sewn with 15 stitches per inch. As a result, the clothing made by Stone Manufacturing gained the reputation of keeping its shape through continual wear and washing.

By the beginning of World War II, sales at Stone Manufacturing were growing approximately 30 percent per year. The U.S. Government contracted the company to make clothes for its soldiers in various theaters of war, and was given a production allotment. This allotment meant that one-quarter of the company's manufacturing facilities had to be set aside for producing clothing for the government. One of the firm's most important products during this time was mattress covers. These covers were so well made that sailors reportedly inflated them and used them as floats to wait for rescue boats when ships sank. By the time the war ended, Stone Manufacturing Company employed over 300 seamstresses.

After the war, Stone Manufacturing planned to take advantage of the demand for clothing necessitated by the return of servicemen to the United States. Stone himself thought that items such as the boxer shorts issued by the government and worn by military personnel during the war, popularly known as "skivvies," would transform the country's buying patterns. Stone purchased a new plant in Columbia, South Carolina, to foster its growth.

During the postwar years, as demand for its products grew, Stone Manufacturing began examining ways to improve the performance of the sewing machine. One of Eugene Stone's own inventions was the "clipper foot," a small attachment located next to the needle of the sewing machine to cut the thread after the seam was completed. This labor-saving device allowed the seamstress to continue sewing without having to stop and reach for a pair of scissors. Stone's invention was so efficient that sewing machine companies soon incorporated the "clipper foot" into the manufacture of their machines.

By 1949 Stone Manufacturing Company had grown so rapidly and had become so successful that it was profiled in *Life Magazine* as one of the leading clothing firms in the United States. The company had grown from a mere five employees in 1933 to over two thousand by the end of the 1940s. Production was so efficient that it had doubled a total of five times in just 13 years. The new plant in Columbia was fast becoming the largest manufacturing facility of men's and boy's underwear in the world. Women's clothing items, a specialty of Stone Manufacturing Company, were also produced in ever-greater quantities to meet the burgeoning demands of a populace entering America's economic boom.

During the 1950s, the company prepared to meet the growth in consumer demand by designing and constructing an entirely new manufacturing facility in Cherrydale, South Carolina.

When the plant began operation in 1951, it was heralded as the biggest apparel production facility in the world. At a time when planning, outfitting, and operating a clothing manufacturing plant with 300 sewing machines seemed nearly impossible, the company's new Cherrydale plant included over one thousand sewing machines.

The company's success continued into the 1960s. Stone Manufacturing broadened its product line to include more children's clothing such as T-shirts, pants, shorts, and underwear. The company's line of women's clothing also continued to expand, and began to gain a greater share of the domestic market. Men's clothing and boy's clothing, the firm's two mainstays, were enjoying their greatest popularity ever. Sales for men's underwear, especially the company's line of boxer shorts, were growing rapidly. Although far from the spotlight of Paris or New York fashions, Stone Manufacturing Company remained abreast of current trends within the fashion industry that affected the styles of clothing for both men and women.

With the advent of the 1970s, Stone Manufacturing Company expanded its line of children's wear and women's clothing. New product lines such as children's sweaters and women's jackets quickly gained the attention of consumers throughout the United States. In the mid-1970s, the physical fitness craze caught on in the United States, and Americans began to exercise on a more regular and vigorous basis. By the end of the decade, it was evident that this movement had become a permanent feature in the daily lives of millions of people. Management at Stone Manufacturing Company recognized the potential of such a new market and began to produce the simplest of exercise clothing—running shorts.

Soon Stone began to produce athletic socks, T-shirts, underwear, jerseys, sweatshirts, sweatpants, basketball shorts, and many other items. Soccer quickly became popular with young people across America, especially teens, and Stone Manufacturing Company launched its *Umbro* brand of soccer wear, which included jerseys, shorts, and knee-length socks. By the end of the 1980s, sales for the Stone activewear division were increasing rapidly.

By the mid-1990s, Eugene Stone III was gone and had been replaced by his son, Eugene E. Stone IV, who served as the company's chief executive officer. Like many other companies with a long history of family management, Stone Manufacturing Company has benefitted from the steady direction of its founders. If Stone's leadership remains flexible enough to continue to adapt to trends in the apparel industry, the company is assured of a prosperous future.

Principal Subsidiaries: Stone Manufacturing Company Lavonia; Stone Manufacturing Company Menswear.

Further Reading:

Curan, Catherine, "Wall St. Bullish on WR Shirts," *Daily News Record,* April 21, 1995, p. 1.
——, "Men's First Period Financial Results Better than Women's," *Daily News Record,* June 28, 1994, p. 2.
Gellers, Stan, "Designers Love Linen," *Daily News Record,* July 1, 1993, p. 6.

——, "Clothing Coming of Age," *Daily News Record,* May 22, 1992, p. 93.

Hancox, Clara, "What Will It Take to Survive into the Next Century," *Daily News Record,* June 28, 1993, p. 23.

Salfino, Catherine, "More Vendors See $ in the SSS Sports," *Daily News Record,* April 24, 1995, p. 6.

——, "Men's Apparel Execs Cheer Results of 1994 Federal Election," *Daily News Record,* November 10, 1994, p. 12.

Stone, Eugene W., III, *Stone Manufacturing Company,* Newcomen Society: New York, 1990.

"The Story of Stone Manufacturing," *Life Magazine,* August 1949, pp. 39–44.

Vargo, Julie, "Work Clothes Bring Fashion to the Street," *Daily News Record,* November 18, 1994, p. 3.

Walsh, Peter, "Outside Forces that Influenced Fashion," *Daily News Record,* May 22, 1992, p. 60.

—Thomas Derdak

Reach Higher

SUMMIT BANK

The Summit Bancorporation

One Main Street
Chatham, New Jersey 07928
U.S.A.
(201) 701-2666
Fax: (201) 701-0464

Public Company
Incorporated: 1974
Employees: 1,590
Total Assets: $5.5 billion
Stock Exchanges: NASDAQ
SICs: 6712 Bank Holding Companies; 6022 State
    Commercial Banks

The Summit Bancorporation is the holding company for Summit Bank, New Jersey's fourth largest bank. Through this subsidiary, the company oversees over 90 banking offices in 11 northern New Jersey counties, while also operating two affiliates—The Summit Mortgage Company and Beechwood Insurance Agency, Inc. Regarded as a forerunner in the area of fixed rate annuities and an innovator in the areas of customer service and market management, Summit Bancorporation aggressively sought to expand its market share in the mid-1990s.

Summit Bank began its long, successful history with an unsolicited piece of advice. A May 5, 1885 edition of *The Summit Record* stated, ''The gentlemen of Summit, New Jersey would do a good thing for the town by forming a stock company and starting a bank.'' With this appeal in mind, William Halls, Jr., John N. May, Sr., Joseph Palmer, G. Dillingham, and E.A. Chapman incorporated The Summit Bank on January 1, 1891, opening its doors on January 19, 1892. William Z. Larned served as its first president from 1891 to 1896, with ''capital paid in $50,000 and surplus and profits of $94,000'' and a staff consisting of ''one cashier, several full-time employees, and the bank directors meeting once every week.'' The city of Summit prospered, as did its bank, which moved into a larger facility in 1896, opening on May 2, 1899 with $384,482 in assets. The new bank featured 300 safe deposit boxes and six upstairs office rooms.

In 1909, the bank was reorganized as The Summit Trust Company, reflecting its intention to begin providing loan services to its customers. The first loan officer was named four years later, and, in 1926, the bank officially established a trust department.

Summit weathered the Great Depression, even managing to renovate its original building by adding on the rear of the building, erecting a new facade, and refurbishing the interior for a total cost of $175,000. In 1933, Summit Bank became a member of the Federal Reserve Bank System.

Summit remained a modest, one-bank operation until 1953, when it established its first branch office in New Providence. Another milestone in its history came in 1964, when Summit Trust merged with the Elizabethport Banking Company, becoming known as The Summit and Elizabeth Trust Company (SETCO). The combined operation boasted a total of six branch offices serving the New Jersey communities of Summit, New Providence, Berkeley Heights, and Elizabeth. In 1974 a bank holding corporation, Summit Bancorporation, was formed, with headquarters in Chatham, New Jersey, to oversee the operations of SETCO.

During the 1980s, New Jersey's strong economy made it one of the top banking areas in the country. In 1984, the bank reverted back to The Summit Trust Company name, as business thrived. Economic recession and a collapse in the New Jersey real estate market, however, led to unfavorable banking conditions in the late 1980s and by 1990 most major New Jersey banks were suffering from sharply declining asset quality, which was eroding capital ratios and earnings. In fact, in 1990 Summit reported a $12.8 million loss for the year.

Nevertheless, the following year Summit returned to profitability, reporting earnings of $21.2 million, and in March 1992 it announced plans to go public, issuing 2.3 million shares of common stock on the Nasdaq stock market. In 1993, Summit Bancorporation's commercial banking subsidiary reclaimed the name given to the original company, Summit Bank.

By the mid-1990s, Summit had hit its stride, with several acquisitions intended to expand its market and increase its earnings. Setting a goal of doubling its asset size in three to five years, Summit earned $11.3 million during the first quarter of 1994, a 14 percent increase over the same period the year before.

In February 1994, Summit purchased Crestmont Financial Corporation in a transaction valued at $91 million and geared toward increasing Summit's market share, competitive position, and retail franchise. In April of the same year Summit acquired Lancaster Financial Ltd. for 500,000 Summit common shares, a deal valued at $9.8 million. Purchase of this Parsippany-based mortgage company was viewed by many analysts as a good move in the long-term, because it would allow Summit Mortgages to expand its presence in New Jersey to include Bergen, Essex, Hunterdon, Middlesex, Morris, Passaic, and Union counties.

In mid-June 1995, Summit added another buy-out to its growing list, announcing that it had agreed to acquire Garden State BancShares, Inc. of Jackson, New Jersey, in an exchange of stock valued at $67 million, an acquisition that added clout to Summit's presence in Ocean County, New Jersey, moving it from a fifth position with an eight percent deposit share, to a strong number two position with about a 12 percent share.

Not all of Summit's acquisition attempts were successful. In September 1994, Summit announced that it would purchase Bankers Corporation of Perth Amboy, New Jersey, in a stock swap valued at $270 million. The deal was considered quite a coup because it would have given a hefty boost to Summit's market share ranking in Middlesex County—its only real opportunity to snag a sizable slice of deposits in that affluent area. This in turn would have made Summit a much more attractive candidate for acquisition.

But less than a month later, Summit and Bankers Corporation announced that they had broken off talks concerning a merger, a revelation that left many analysts baffled. The collapse of the deal was blamed on the premature disclosure of a letter of intent, leaked to traders and resulting in an upsurge in Bankers' stock price. Other analysts speculated that Bankers Corporation felt that their stock was undervalued and decided they could get a better offer elsewhere. Although terminated amicably, this failed merger was a significant setback to Summit in its quest to double its size.

During this time, Robert G. Cox was named to succeed Thomas D. Sayles, Jr. as chief executive officer at Summit. Sayles, who had been CEO at Summit Bancorp for 23 years, had groomed Cox for the position in a carefully developed plan of succession. Cox had joined Summit in 1973 as vice-president responsible for the mortgage department. In 1980, he was named president of Summit Bank, and in 1983 he was named its chief executive. Four years later, he became president and chief operating officer of the holding company. Sayles, who continued on as chairman at the $4.3 billion holding company and as a member of its executive committee, decided to take an early retirement at age 62, in part because he felt that new developments in the world of high finance, such as the increasing use of computer technology, required a younger and more technololgically savvy executive. This congenial and well thought-out passing of the baton was in all probability instrumental in Summit's future success.

Cox's succession ushered in a new era in Summit's history. In addition to focusing on continued growth, Cox looked to expand into uncharted territories, including the fixed-rate annuities market. After watching more and more of its customers withdrawing deposits to buy annuities from local brokers, Summit began selling fixed annuities in 1988, later expanding into mutual funds and variable annuities.

One of the bank's primary reasons for entering the market was for the management fees. Working in conjunction with money managers at Western National Life Company, its annuity underwriter, Summit was able to examine credit quality, durations, and other issues that went into choosing annuity investments, while at the same time improving services by lowering commissions and allowing customers to cash out earlier with fewer penalties. In April 1995, *American Banker* reported that the sales volume of fixed rate annuities had nearly doubled, from $18 million in 1992, to $35 million in 1994. Fixed Rate annuities made up over 35 percent of Summit's total investment sales.

In May 1995, Summit introduced its proprietary fixed annuity, aimed at increasing the bank's share of management fees and boosting its reputation in this area—a bold move that few other banks had emulated. In designing Summit's annuity, Jack D. Cussen, Summit Bancorp's executive vice-president, said he "approached it like a consumer," incorporating features such as a shorter surrender period that allowed investors to increase the rate of return twice during the life of the product in order to take advantage of any shifts in interest rates, according to the April 26, 1995 issue of *American Banker.*

Entrance into the fixed-annuity market was just one way Summit strove to gain a competitive edge. Cox kept an eye on acquiring smaller competitors, initiating in 1994 one of New Jersey's biggest deals, the $91 million purchase of $1 billion-asset Crestmont Financial Corp. This purchase was instrumental in enabling Summit to continue to meet its growth goals.

In addition to pursuing acquisitions, Cox hoped to establish a "retail store culture" in all of Summit's branches and at the executive level. Cox, described by analysts as "forward looking," brought in consultants to teach employees how to become better salespeople. With a new focus on cultivating customer relationships, Cox searched for better ways to handle customers at the branch level and to improve efficiency. Shunning high-pressure sales tactics, employees relied instead on internal and customer referrals.

Cox also looked to address the bank's efficiency ratio (the ratio of a bank's expenses, excepting interest, divided by its gross assets or net income), which had reached an undesirable high of 69 percent in 1991. Consolidation and other cuts in costs had brought Summit's cost efficiency ratio back down to 63 percent in 1994, but that still wasn't where Cox wanted it. Along this line, Cox and his executives established the "Vision 56" program, a restructuring plan that had the goal of reaching an efficiency ratio of 56 percent by 1996.

As part of this program, Cox also created three new business lines. The Retail Banking Group would oversee the branch delivery system, residential mortgage lending provided by The Summit Mortgage Company, consumer credit, sales of deposit products such as mutual funds, annuities and life insurance, as well as a full range of financial services for local businesses. The Commercial Banking Group served Summit Bank's corporate customers and provided credit products and other services, including trade finance and cash management services, and specialized lending for construction, commercial real estate and mortgage banking companies. Finally, The Private Banking and Asset Management Group would provide a broad range of investment credit and asset management services to high net worth and high income individuals and professionals. Asset management services were made available to businesses seeking corporate and employee benefit plans.

By the mid-1990s Summit had a large deposit share in some of New Jersey's fastest growing counties, and had the seventh largest market share in New Jersey, with 91 offices in 11 counties. This made it a highly desirable takeover target. In early February of 1995, Cox was evasive when asked about rumors of takeover and analysts predicted that the bank would remain independent in the short run.

But six months later, Summit announced its merger with UJB Financial Corp., a New Jersey-based financial services company with $15.9 billion in assets. The new corporation would operate under the Summit Bancorp name, and would report some $22 billion in assets, deposits of $17.6 billion, and shareholders equity of $1.7 million, creating New Jersey's second largest bank.

In a September 1995 press release, Cox said of the merger: "Summit has built an impressive retail franchise in New Jersey, while UJB Financial has scored successes by developing niche businesses, such as lending to health care professionals and hospitals and has a strong asset based lending activity. This transaction greatly enhances our business development strategies. We are forming a strategic partnership that rewards shareholders and offers customers a broader array of products and services."

Summit's second quarterly report for 1995 indicated record earnings of $17.9 million, representing a 33 percent increase over the $13.5 million earned in the second quarter of 1994, and reflecting the bank's continued improvement in the areas of operating efficiencies and asset quality. Consistent with its increase in productivity, Summit introduced its "Managing Local Markets" initiative during the first quarter of 1995. Market managers received training to design a marketing program that took advantage of unique demographics through the use of market segmentation and household profitability data.

In a survey conducted by Princeton's Research Strategies Corporation, 523 business leaders in Northern New Jersey were asked to rate eight factors in terms of their importance in evaluating banks and the quality of service received from them. Among regional or community banks Summit received the highest rating. It ranked first in every category from the quality of services offered to its role as a good corporate citizen. Moreover, following its strategic alliance with UJB, Summit Bancorp looked forward to continuing this reputation for good service as well as to exploring opportunities for increased revenues and greater shareholder value in the decade to come.

Principal Subsidiaries: Summit Bank.

Further Reading:

Kapiloff, Howard, "Summit Aims to Survive in Dog-Eat-Dog N.J.," *American Banker,* February 3, 1995.

Kaplan, Daniel, "Leak Sank Summit Merger, Bankers Savings Exec Says," *American Banker,* October 13, 1994.

Mehlman, William, "Summit Bancorporation," *The Insiders' Chronicle,* March 20, 1989.

Plasencia, William, "Summit, Thriving Among Giants, Aims Even Higher," *American Banker,* April 26, 1995.

Talley, Karen. "Summit Bancorp to Take Unusual Step of Helping to Manage Fixed Annuity," *American Banker,* March 1, 1995.

—Lynda D. Schrecengost

Sverdrup

Sverdrup Corporation

13723 Riverport Drive
Maryland Heights, Missouri 63043
U.S.A.
(800) 325-7910
Fax: (314) 298-0045

Private Company
Founded: 1928
Employees: 5,000
Sales: $673 million
SICs: 8711 Engineering Services; 8712 Architectural
  Services; 8713 Surveying Services; 8731 Commercial
  Physical Research; 8733 Noncommercial Physical
  Research; 8734 Testing Laboratories; 8741 Management
  Services; 8742 Management Consulting Services; 8744
  Facilities Support Services

Sverdrup Corporation is a broad-based engineering firm offering professional services in civil engineering and facilities, technology, and real estate development within the United States and abroad, boasting engineering experience in 65 countries. Founded in 1928, it was the only four-time winner of the American Consulting Engineers Council's Grand Conceptor Award, which honors engineering excellence. During the course of its more than 60 years, the company has engineered major bridges and tunnels; sports arenas; expansions for nine of the 20 largest U.S. airports; automated manufacturing and process plants; light rail and subways; corporate headquarters facilities; and cleanup of Superfund hazardous waste sites. In 1994, out of all U.S. engineering firms, Sverdrup was ranked 16th in engineering and architectural design, 19th in construction management, and 30th in design/build. It was also a leading provider of advanced engineering and technical services to support the operation of aerospace and industrial test centers.

The firm was founded as Sverdrup and Parcel in April 1928 by Leif J. Sverdrup and John Ira Parcel, a distinguished professor at the University of Minnesota. Sverdrup, a student of Parcel's and a Minnesota graduate in 1920, had been making a name for outstanding and thorough work at the Missouri Highway Department. He had become chief bridge engineer there in 1924. In 1927 the department didn't have the money to construct a bridge at Hermann, so construction of a toll bridge was chosen as the alternative. Sverdrup wrote to the Hermann Bridge Com-

pany, proposing to be the engineer that designed and supervised the construction of the bridge. He also wrote to Parcel, outlining his plan to start his own firm. He asked Parcel to be his partner.

Parcel had been at Minnesota for a long time and was reluctant to sever his ties completely, but eventually he decided to join the new company, taking an unpaid leave of absence from the university for one year in case things didn't work out. Sverdrup would own 60 percent of the firm, Parcel 40 percent. The firm opened its doors on April 1, 1928, two weeks before the Hermann job was approved.

While at the Missouri Highway Department Sverdrup met future partners D. C. Wolfe and E. R. Grant, and he asked them if they would join the company. Sverdrup subsequently hired design engineer Brice R. Smith from Missouri's leading supplier of bridge components. All would become partners by 1936. Initially the young firm struggled, with no contracts for major jobs lined up after the Hermann bridge, and by early 1929 it faced insolvency. There were lots of good leads, however, and neither Sverdrup nor Parcel wished to let anyone go, for they looked at dependable, well-trained employees as cash in the bank (a point of view the company maintained for many years). Just at the point of crisis, however, the company was selected to design a new bridge over the Missouri River, relocate U.S. Highway 54 at Lake of the Ozarks near the Bagnell Dam, and design the Grand Glaize bridge near the dam.

Given the long-term nature of civil engineering jobs, the stock market crash on October 25, 1929, created no immediate problems for Sverdrup and Parcel; in fact the following year was a successful one for the company. During that year Sverdrup decided that the company's continued success could only be guaranteed by spreading ownership among its employees, and so a policy of employee ownership was established for a limited number of principals. But on the whole the early 1930s were a period of instability for the company, with good years and bad. The depression finally caught up to Sverdrup and Parcel—only one bridge of consequence was contracted in 1931—but that contract associated the firm with a very significant future client: the U.S. Army Corps of Engineers.

Business remained bleak, however, and disaster again loomed when "the little job which saved the company" (as Sverdrup referred to it) came through at the end of 1931. Union Electric offered the company a contract to design a fish hatchery at Lake of the Ozarks (one of the provisions of the agreement with the state that allowed the Bagnell Dam to be constructed).

The company remained in trouble and Sverdrup could no longer support it with personal resources, for he had sold all his stocks and faced an acute shortage of cash. But a loan from an old St. Louis bank, backed by Sverdrup's pledge of his house and life insurance as collateral, made it possible for the firm to survive, and contracts for two more bridges came through. The New Deal's Public Works Administration (PWA), which made loans to states and municipalities for public works, also brought a degree of prosperity. By mid-decade, the firm had received commissions for two bridges from the PWA and increased its contact with the Corps of Engineers, developing several more bridges and picking up a pioneer hydropower project sponsored, but not completed, by the Corps along the Maine coast. In 1937 the company entered the electric transmission field, obtaining an initial commission from the Texas Rural Electrification Administration, and pulled in its first stadium job, for Sportsman's Park in St. Louis (a baseball stadium for the St. Louis Cardinals). "Jack Sverdrup continued to underscore the importance of the smaller jobs," said Franzwa. "He would someday parlay that knowledge of stadia into a number of the most famous sports arenas in the nation."

By the beginning of the 1940s the company had become one of the best bridge firms in the country. It broadened its scope significantly through its work with the Corps of Engineers in the Pacific theater during World War II, becoming one of the nation's most diversified engineering organizations by the mid-1940s. This transformation was carried out in the absence of company president Jack Sverdrup, who had accepted a commission in the Corps of Engineers and ended the war as major general in command of all engineering forces in the southwest Pacific and as adviser to General Douglas MacArthur.

One of the company's dramatic engineering feats during the war was the design and supervision of construction of Canol, a top-secret oil pipeline to Alaska laid across the Arctic wastes ("like a rock for eight months of the year, and a mushy tangle of primeval vegetation and sphagnum for the remainder"). The project's goal was to pump 3,000 barrels of crude oil through the line each day and to keep it flowing at temperatures that reached 70 degrees below zero. Employing 10,629 people at its peak, the project constructed 1,550 miles of pipe, 52 tanks, 14 air strips, and a number of roads and used 262,741 tons of supplies and 2,565 pieces of heavy equipment at a total cost of $133 million. Other Sverdrup wartime feats included the inventive construction of a chain of airfields into the Philippines and the design and construction of a 20-foot, 40,000-horsepower wind tunnel for the U.S. Army Air Corps. Bridge, railroad, and highway contracts constituted much of the company's continuing domestic work.

When the war ended in 1945, the company was well positioned to develop a variety of new roles including air technology research. This came thanks to the successful Sverdrup (who had refused President Harry Truman's request to become Secretary of Defense). The scope of work was so great that the company had to reorganize, and it was incorporated for the first time in 1946.

Recognizing the Germans' significant edge in aviation technology, U.S. officials proposed a new national supersonic facility, and Sverdrup and Parcel was chosen to prepare a national facilities master plan, conduct research and development, and provide architectural and engineering services at the new Arnold Engineering Development Center (AEDC). Sverdrup's responsibilities included the development of engine test facilities, flight test facilities, a missile testing range, rocket engine test cells, and even a chamber with photographic apparatus so sophisticated that a bullet could be photographed in full flight along with the shock pattern of the air it was cleaving.

The company continued its routine domestic work, developing bridges, electrical substations, a cement unloading dock (the first of many projects for the cement manufacturing industry), and a variety of other road and transportation projects. By the

late 1940s the company was well situated with long-range postwar jobs and abundant new work both within the United States and overseas. The firm's architectural section was also beginning to develop. One of the most exciting projects approved during this time was the Joint Long-Range Proving Ground at Cape Canaveral, Florida, which was to be the base for the missiles and satellites that would usher in the U.S. space age.

As the 1950s began Congress decided to privatize the AEDC, and Sverdrup and Parcel established a separate subsidiary organization called ARO (Arnold Research Organization) to operate it. ARO's early accomplishments, described as beyond state-of-the-art, included creating an enormous propulsion wind tunnel to test reciprocating engines, turbojets, and ram jets. Within two to three years, the subsidiary was four times the size of its parent corporation.

Sverdrup soon experienced large backlogs, and though it continued its efforts in its traditional market areas it also engaged in new directions, such as construction management. By 1953, however, despite the gargantuan nature of the ARO work and other jobs, growth began to slow. The company established a presence in Washington, developing relationships with federal agencies that might have an interest in quality engineering and architecture. In 1954 and 1955 the federal highway program was funded, and Sverdrup and Parcel got its share of the work. Among the most impressive jobs obtained by the company was the design and construction of bridges and tunnels that would enable vehicles to cross the mouth of the Chesapeake Bay. The company's highway efforts became so extensive that in 1955 they were spun off into a new company called the Sverdrup & Parcel Engineering Company. During this period work overseas continued to develop, albeit more slowly than the company's domestic efforts.

ARO continued to develop special structures for the nation's military, including, in 1957, a wind tunnel in which engines reached the speed needed to escape earth's gravity, as well as the design of a rotating-arm facility that tested the directional stability, maneuverability, and control of high-speed submarines and surface vessels. By 1959 ARO was operating AEDC facilities that had cost $220 million to design and build, and it was conducting much of the testing program for the nation's space program. Sverdrup and Parcel also continued to pick up new jobs that would develop into significant areas of company specialization in the future, such as the rehabilitation of Sportsman's Park.

During the 1960s the company operated energetically in a variety of areas. It continued its work with NASA and the air force and built rocket test stands that tested missiles for all branches of the armed services, including the Mercury systems that carried America's first men into space. In 1962 Sverdrup contracted to produce 27 study, criteria, and planning volumes for a NASA test facility in Mississippi to meet the goal of putting a man on the moon by 1970.

The company's involvement in the federal highway program was reaching its zenith, with perhaps the most impressive project being the Chesapeake crossing, which would construct and connect a 5,740-foot tunnel, another 5,450-foot tunnel, a

3,790-foot bridge, a 457-foot bridge, 8,300 feet of earth cause-way, and 64,500 feet of low-level trestle. The total length of the crossing was 17.5 miles, with another five miles of approach roads.

Sverdrup also developed a specialized reputation for its work with breweries and expanded its efforts with sports arenas, completing Busch Stadium in St. Louis in 1966 and completing many others by the end of the 1960s. The company also had time for special projects such as the design of track, supports, and a terminal building for the monorail system at the New York World's Fair and the design of a support system and skeleton for a life-sized replica of a blue whale for the Museum of Natural History in New York. The company considered, but did not develop, other projects including bridges over the Messina Strait from Sicily to Italy and over Long Island Sound and another canal across Panama.

By mid-decade the company was involved in projects in 32 states, the District of Columbia, the Panama Canal Zone, and 15 foreign countries. Nonetheless, Sverdrup found himself concerned that the company lacked midlevel strength and would be unable to fend for itself once the founding generation had passed on or retired. In 1965 Ira Parcel died; D. C. Wolfe and E. R. Grant retired in 1966. Only Sverdrup and Brice Smith were left.

Jack Sverdrup took steps to identify promising young people to lead the company in the future and also came to recognize that the company had developed a broader role with the passage of time—it was no longer a St. Louis firm with national branches but a national company headquartered in St. Louis. As the 1970s began, changes in federal priorities impacted the company. The federal highway program was winding down, and company executives recognized that new skills would be needed if business was to prosper. New efforts were undertaken in environmental engineering (including wastewater treatment), architectural and engineering design, railroads and subways, and geotechnical engineering.

The company also continued its efforts in its traditional areas of expertise (highways, tunnels, and bridges; projects for industry, including breweries; and the space program, including design of the space shuttle launch complex at Vandenberg). The company's international activities also boomed during this period. In 1975 company founder Jack Sverdrup died at the age of 78, raising concerns that the company might not be able to survive his passing. One year later, Brice Smith, the final remaining original partner, also died. In the words of a company official, however, "The company not only did not collapse, it didn't even sag."

Bob West, the new chairman, and Bill Rivers, president and CEO, recognized that with the rapid increase in company business a restructuring was necessary, and so in 1977 the Sverdrup Corporation was formed, composed of five operating companies—Sverdrup & Parcel and Associates, Inc., offering engineering, architectural, and planning services; ARO, Inc., providing facilities operation and high-technology engineering; SPIRE Corporation, for real estate and building development services; SPCM, Inc., providing construction management services; and Sverdrup & Parcel Consultants, Inc., handling most

work in the state of New York. The company also installed corporate principals who took charge of the long-range planning and marketing for each basic technical area in which the company was involved, including industrial, buildings and real estate, environmental, facilities operation, transportation, and public works.

The late 1970s and early 1980s brought considerable financial difficulties for Sverdrup, beginning with a conflict with the U.S. Air Force over the ARO contract to manage the AEDC. Beginning in 1978 the Air Force for the first time called for priced proposals on the contract renewal. Although ARO's contract was renewed for three years, in 1980 the Air Force split the AEDC contract into three parts and put all out for bid—and Sverdrup/ARO lost two out of three.

The recession of the early 1980s did not help the company, nor did the entry of the conservative Ronald Reagan administration in Washington, which was devoted to shrinking the federal budget and providing correspondingly less public works spending. Naturally, Jack Sverdrup's death had also resulted in an erosion of the company's relationship with the Corps of Engineers. Overall, company officials recognized they had to improve performance on a number of fronts, including entering areas that had been atypical for consulting engineers and pulling back somewhat from dependence on the public sector.

Thus the company decided to focus more intensely on construction management and design/build efforts, in which the firm not only designed a project but also built it. ARO changed its name to Sverdrup Technology and began a stronger effort to attract private-sector clients by asserting that it could engineer solutions on the frontiers of technology and also sought to regain credibility with the Air Force. By mid-decade the renamed unit had begun to grow.

A focus on traditional sources of revenue also maintained company stability. Sverdrup developed several rapid-transit projects in large eastern cities, new rail facilities for the nation's Northeast corridor, a major construction management project for the San Francisco airport, brewery improvements, wastewater treatment plants, and industrial parks. In 1981 it began work on the Fort McHenry Tunnel in Baltimore. It also engaged in a number of international projects. In 1983 the company received its first Grand Conceptor Award from the American Consulting Engineers Council for its Columbia River Bridge in Oregon. In 1984 it completed work on the Vandenberg space shuttle site.

During the mid-1980s the company again reorganized. In 1984, the company created an additional division—Sverdrup Investments—to create real estate and other developments for the firm. In 1985 Sverdrup restructured, replacing the cluster of companies created in 1977 with regional subgroups that offered the company's full scope of services to clients in smaller geographical areas. Sverdrup Technology remained a separate organization, however. Also in 1985 the company received a second Grand Conceptor Award for the Space Shuttle Complex, and by the end of the year its AEDC contract with the Air Force was extended for five years. (The company won its third Grand Conceptor Award just one year later for the Fort McHenry Tunnel in Baltimore.)

During the late 1980s and early 1990s the company received huge contracts from the public sector, including the State Department, Federal Aviation Administration, U.S. Air Force, and NASA. As the 1990s began Sverdrup also continued its efforts to provide a broad range of engineering services in the United States and abroad, engaging in a variety of innovative bridge, tunnel, dam, environmental technology, and other projects. In 1995 Sverdrup received a NASA award for its design of a simulator for astronaut training for Hubble Telescope repairs (NASA hailed it as a ''breakthrough'' that had permitted the successful completion of the mission). There were also state-of-the-art private-sector projects. Transportation continued as an important company interest, and a light rail system engineered by Sverdrup—MetroLink in St. Louis—received an unprecedented fourth Grand Conceptor Award from the ACEC in 1995.

Principal Subsidiaries: Sverdrup Technology Inc.; Sverdrup Investments Inc.; Sverdrup Environmental Inc.

Further Reading:

Franzwa, Gregory M., *Legacy: The Sverdrup Story,* St. Louis: Sverdrup Corporation, 1978.
—— *Challenge: The Sverdrup Story Continues,* St. Louis: Sverdrup Corporation, 1988.

—Bob Swierczek

SYBRON
INTERNATIONAL

Sybron International Corp.

411 E. Wisconsin Avenue
Milwaukee, Wisconsin 53202
U.S.A.
(414) 274-6600
Fax: (414) 274-6561

Public Company
Incorporated: 1968 as Sybron Corp.
Employees: 3,900
Sales: $439.70 million
Stock Exchanges: New York
SICs: 3842 Dental Equipment & Supplies; 6719 Holding
   Companies Not Elsewhere Classified

Sybron International Corp. is a leading manufacturer of products for the laboratory and professional orthodontic and dental markets in the United States and abroad. The enterprise has acted as a holding company since its inception in 1968. In 1995 Sybron was operating through four subsidiaries: Nalge Co., Erie Scientific Company, Barnstead/Thermolyne Corporation, and Sybron Dental Specialties.

Sybron's roots can be traced back to the founding of the Nalge Co., in 1949, in Rochester, New York. Emanuel Goldberg founded the company to produce one thing: polyethylene pipette jars used in laboratories. Sales were brisk and Goldberg incorporated the venture in 1954. From pipette jars, Nalge quickly expanded to produce a wide array of plastic items for industrial and laboratory use. By the mid-1960s Nalge, which is credited with pioneering the use of plastic in laboratory and industrial applications, was producing 180 different products in nearly 700 sizes. Because of its strength in its niche, Nalge became a takeover target for larger, more diversified companies.

In 1966 Goldberg agreed to sell his enterprise to Ritter-Pfaudler Corp., of Rochester, New York—Goldberg remained president of the company and operated it relatively autonomously until 1976. In 1968 Ritter-Pfaudler merged with a company called Taylor Instrument Co. The new organization was named Sybron Corp., which was effectively a holding company for the diversified subsidiaries. Throughout the 1970s and 1980s Sybron bought and sold numerous companies that complemented varying business strategies, but Nalge remained a core subsidiary. By 1976, the year that founder Goldberg retired, Nalge boasted

a work force of 250 and more than 240 products. Marshall Hyman took over as president of the Nalge subsidiary in 1976.

Besides Nalge, Sybron added a variety of businesses to its portfolio. By the mid-1980s, in fact, Sybron encompassed a diversified group of nearly 20 companies, most of which were engaged in the manufacture of various dental, laboratory, and specialty industrial products. The organization's sales and assets had rapidly ballooned and Sybron had become a Fortune 500 company. Its financial performance, however, began to wane. In fact, by the mid-1980s Sybron had become bloated and inefficient. The headquarters staff had swollen to a beefy 240 and Sybron had committed itself to more than $315 million in long-term debt.

In 1986 Sybron was purchased, by way of a leveraged buyout (LBO), by LBO specialist Forstmann Little & Co. in New York City. In cooperation with Sybron management, Forstmann purchased the company and initiated an aggressive restructuring program. Over a period of 18 months the new owners slashed corporate headquarters staff to just 24, jettisoned 12 entire operating divisions, and cut Sybron's debt load to just $65 million. By late 1987 Sybron had become a smaller, leaner, more profitable company specializing in the manufacture of laboratory and dental products. New management also took Sybron private again and, because of the elimination of many of its subsidiaries, quashed its Fortune 500 status.

The streamlined Sybron came under new ownership again in October of 1987. Donaldson, Lufkin & Jenrette Securities Corp., a New York Investment company, spearheaded the buyout, and was joined by Hicks & Haas, a Dallas merchant bank. In the end, about 30 percent of the company was owned by Sybron management and 56 percent was split evenly between the Donaldson and Hicks & Haas. The remainder of the company was publicly held in the form of stock, as the group had technically made Sybron a public company once again. Soon after the second LBO, the holding company moved its headquarters to Milwaukee, Wisconsin. Management further reduced headquarters staff to about 25 during the late 1980s and continued to slim the company's remaining five subsidiaries as part of an effort to improve overall operating margins.

Sybron's reorganization and financial turnaround during the late 1980s and through the early 1990s was largely attributable to the leadership of Kenneth F. Yontz, who eventually became chairman, chief executive, and president of Sybron. Yontz embodied the classic American success story. Raised in a blue-collar neighborhood in Sandusky, Ohio, Yontz was married at the age of 18 and had three children by the time he was 21. He started out working on a taillight assembly line at a Ford Motor Company plant in Michigan. When Ford offered to foot the bill for higher learning, Yontz jumped at the opportunity. ''I didn't want to be poor,'' Yontz said in the December 12, 1988, *Business Journal-Milwaukee*. ''I wanted a better lot in life. . . .'' Yontz drove a two-hour round trip three evenings a week to Bowling Green State University in Ohio. He got his bachelor of science degree in 1971 and later earned his masters degree in business administration at night at Eastern Michigan University.

Yontz was gradually promoted from the assembly line to a position as a finance manager. After receiving his masters degree he accepted a position in Chicago with Chemetron Corp., a manufacturer of fire suppression products and other industrial goods. Yontz moved quickly through the ranks before he was lured away in 1978 by Allen-Bradley, of Milwaukee, to serve as vice president. In 1984 Yontz was one of eight or nine managers that attempted an LBO of Allen-Bradley. The LBO attempt failed, but it succeeded in putting Yontz in touch with a Teddy Forstmann, a principal at the company that conducted the first LBO of Sybron. In 1986 Forstmann asked Yontz to head the newly acquired Sybron. Yontz left his comfortable position at Allen-Bradley and invested his entire net worth of $300,000 in Sybron to become a partner in the buyout.

When Yontz arrived at Sybron in 1986, the company was in trouble. Management ranks were bloated and the organization lacked direction. Furthermore, the former head of the company had attempted a leveraged buyout of his own that had severely damaged employee morale. To rectify the situation, Yontz lowered the boom quickly on most of the corporate staff and sent them packing. He then moved the company's headquarters to New Jersey to get a fresh start, and dumped most of the company's 17 operating subsidiaries. Yontz planned on leaving the company. But when the second LBO took place he agreed to stay on as president and chief executive if the new owners would allow him to move the company's headquarters to his family's home state of Wisconsin. Yontz and a skeletal staff of six or seven managers set up shop in Milwaukee. They later increased their group to an efficient team of about 25.

After Yontz and fellow managers pared its operations, Sybron's five subsidiaries were generating about $275 million annually going into the late 1980s. That figure increased to roughly $300 million in 1989 and then to nearly $330 million in 1990. During the early 1990s Yontz continued to try to reduce costs and boost sales and earnings. He also worked to minimize the substantial debt load that the company had accrued as a result of the LBO. To that end, Sybron made an initial public offering of stock in 1992 that raised $109 million. The cash also went to fund the acquisitions of some small companies, several of which were located in Europe. The European acquisitions reflected Sybron's five-year goal, started in 1991, to attain an equal amount of sales from domestic and foreign markets.

Sybron entered the 1990s with five operating subsidiaries that manufactured and marketed a number of dental and laboratory products, including microscope slides, reusable and disposable plastic labware, precision heating and stirring apparatus, and water purification systems. In several of those categories Sybron dominated the market. Still, among the most successful of Sybron's companies going into the 1990s was Nalge, the company that had been used to start Sybron. After Sybron began its turnaround in 1986, Nalge and other Sybron subsidiaries were given much more autonomy and allowed to return to their entrepreneurial roots. With Sybron bureaucrats out of their way, Nalge managers succeeded in boosting sales and profits at the subsidiary. By the early 1990s Nalge was controlling a fat 60 percent share of the American labware market; about 90 percent of the subsidiary's revenues came from the sale of plastic labware.

The driving force behind Nalge's strong performance in the early 1990s was David Della Penta, head of the division. Della Penta had joined Castle Co. in 1970, shortly after it had become part of Sybron. He shifted to different Sybron subsidiaries for the next ten years, holding various finance jobs. In 1981 he joined Nalge as vice president and controller. In 1986, new management began promoting him through the ranks until he became president of Nalge in 1990. Under Della Penta's direction, Nalge aggressively pursued exports and worked to shore up the company's product line. The division soon enjoyed gains, despite a U.S. and European recession during the early 1990s. Sales jumped from $70 million in 1989 to $82.5 million in 1991. Furthermore, in 1992 Nalge became one of just 55 companies to receive the E-Star award for excellence in exporting.

Sybron realized improvements in virtually all of its subsidiaries during the early 1990s. Overall sales increased from $330 million in 1990 (fiscal year ended September 30) to $383 million in 1992, and then to $440 million in 1994. During the same period net income rose from $3.1 million to $21.4 million, and then to $43 million in 1994. Furthermore, Sybron managed to decrease its long-term debt from $340 million in 1990 to about $224 million in 1994, partly as a result of the 1992 stock offering. Although Sybron had moved toward its goal of getting 50 percent of all sales from overseas, in 1994 it was generating only about one-third of its revenues from abroad. Its failure to increase that proportion was largely attributable, though, to surging domestic sales.

In 1995 Sybron was operating through four subsidiaries: Nalge, Erie, Barnstead/Thermolyne, and Sybron Dental Specialties. Nalge was primarily engaged in manufacturing reusable and disposable plastic labware products. Its Nalgene brand product line consisted of approximately 4,900 items ranging from beakers and flasks to cryogenic storage products. The company controlled between 60 percent and 65 percent of its market in the United States in 1995.

Erie Scientific Company was founded in 1934 and was subsequently acquired by Sybron. Headquartered in New Hampshire, Erie developed, manufactured, and marketed microscope slides and cover glass for sale in the United States and abroad in 1995. The Erie division maintained a wholly owned subsidiary in Switzerland that supplied its worldwide operations. The company was a leader in slide and cover glass technology and was developing a number of new technologies in the mid-1990s, such as disposable and electrically-charged glass products. Erie dominated about 90 percent of the market for its products in 1995.

Sybron's Barnstead/Thermolyne subsidiary was the successor to Thermolyne Corporation, founded in 1942, and Barnstead Company, founded in 1878. In 1995 the company developed, manufactured, and marketed precision-heating stirring and temperature control apparatus, water purification systems, liquid handling equipment, and replacement parts. The goods were sold primarily to laboratories. Like Nalge and Erie, Barnstead/Thermolyne was engaged in the research and development of a number of new products in the mid-1990s. Its major product categories controlled between 35 percent and 80 percent of their respective markets in the United States.

Sybron Dental Specialties comprised two companies: Kerr Corporation and Ormco Corporation. Kerr was founded in 1891 and in 1995 was developing, manufacturing, and marketing a broad range of consumable dental products, including amalgam alloys, cavity liners, endodontic instruments, laboratory products, and industrial jewelry products. Kerr's diverse product lines controlled between five percent and 35 percent of their markets. Ormco, founded in 1960, developed, produced, and marketed a broad line of orthodontic appliances and related products for U.S. markets. It served about 22 percent of the global market for such products in 1995.

In 1995 Sybron was enjoying steady gains in all of its subsidiaries. Profit increases were particularly healthy in Europe and Asia, and Sybron expected increases in both domestic and foreign markets through the mid-1990s. The company employed about 3,900 workers going into 1995, although that number was expected to increase following planned acquisitions during the year.

Principal Subsidiaries: Nalge Company; Sybron Dental Specialties, Inc.; Barnstead Thermolyne Corporation; Erie Scientific Company.

Further Reading:

"The CEOs of Wisconsin: Kenneth Yontz," *Business Journal-Milwaukee,* March 27, 1993, p. C43.

Cohen, Sidney H., "Sybron Chemicals Announces Acquisition," *PR Newswire,* July 26, 1994.

Dries, Michael, "Hot Shots—Wisconsin's Best-Performing Public Companies: Sybron Corp.," *Business Journal-Milwaukee,* July 31, 1993, p. C14.

Kirchen, Rich, "Original Sybron Investors Win Big in Selloff," *Business Journal-Milwaukee,* September 3, 1994, p. 6.

——, "Sybron Is Healthy Despite Having Been Raised on Junk," *Business Journal-Milwaukee,* March 19, 1990, p. 16.

——, "With Sales, Profit and Stock Up, Sybron I an IPO Success Story," *Business Journal-Milwaukee,* November 21, 1992, p. 13.

Le Beau, Christina, "A Worldwide Competitor's Family Touch: David Della Penta Believes in Keeping Things Close-knit at Home and on the Job at Nalge Co.," *Rochester Business Journal,* August 7, 1992, p. 10.

Olson, Jon, "Ken Yontz Came Home—With the Help of Two LBOs," *Business Journal-Milwaukee,* December 12, 1988, p. 10.

—Dave Mote

Syratech Corp.

175 McClellan Highway
East Boston, Massachusetts 02128
U.S.A.
(617) 561-2200
Fax: (617) 561-0275

Public Company
Incorporated: 1986
Sales: $242.2 million
Employees: 1,225
Stock Exchanges: New York
SICs: 3914 Silverware, Plated Ware & Stainless Steel Ware

Founded in 1986, Syratech Corp. is a leader in the tabletop- and giftware-products industry. Its subsidiaries include such prestigious silverware producers and marketers as Towle, International Silver, and Wallace Silversmiths. Syratech designs, manufactures, imports, and distributes holloware (goods such as trays, bowls, and pitchers), flatware (utensils such as knives, forks, and spoons), and numerous giftware products such as picture frames, photo albums, candlesticks, cosmetic accessories, and seasonal merchandise.

One of eight children of an immigrant Russian-Jewish grocer, Leonard Florence grew up living over the store in Chelsea, Massachusetts, a blue-collar suburb of Boston. He shined shoes to help support his family and never saw a piece of sterling silver in his youth. Florence attended Boston University on a scholarship provided by Dewey Stone, an industrialist. Upon his graduation in 1954, he was hired by Stone to help run one of his companies, Raimond Silver Manufacturing Co. of Chelsea, which at the time was losing money. Florence reduced staffing, dropped unprofitable items, and found an unexploited niche for Raimond making silver picture frames. When the company was sold in 1968 for $2.1 million, Florence received half the proceeds. He used the money to start his own company, Leonard Silver, which specialized in low-priced silverplated giftware. Company sales came to $269,000 in its initial year and profits to $14,000.

Leonard Silver first operated out of a Chelsea garage, with the entire staff pitching in to do chores: writing orders, polishing silver, and carrying boxes to be shipped. When the company erected an office building across the street, the staff helped pour concrete, thereby enabling Florence to fulfill his promise to

teach his employees the business "from the ground up." Leonard Silver sold silverplated holloware at one-half to one-third the prices charged for similar goods by competing firms and still made money. In 1979 Leonard Silver merged with Towle Manufacturing Co.

Unlike plebeian Leonard Silver, Towle (rhymes with "bowl"), had a pedigree going back to 1690, when William Moulton II set up shop in what became Newburyport, Massachusetts. Five generations of Moulton silversmiths followed before Anthony F. Towle and William P. Jones, apprentices of William Moulton IV, bought the business from him and Joseph Moulton IV in the 1860s. It was incorporated in 1880 as the Towle Manufacturing Co. The conservatively managed company was the one of the first to stress coordinated marketing of silver, china, and glass, and it made a steady profit even during the Great Depression. Although not reaching an annual net income of $1 million until the 1960s, it paid a dividend in every year after 1917. Towle's silver patterns included Chippendale, King Richard, and Old Master. As late as the 1970s its showroom was a 250-year-old Newburyport clapboard house, adjacent to the ivy-covered factory.

A survey of the $620 million tableware industry in 1970 found Towle to be one of the eight leading marketers. Among the others were International Silver Co. and Wallace Silversmiths Inc., later acquired by Syratech. By then Towle had been systematically diversifying its line of products from sterling (92.5 percent silver) flatware to silverplated (about ten percent silver) holloware in order to reduce its exposure to the fluctuating price of silver. Silverplated holloware, the fastest-growing area in silverware, was believed to account for around 40 percent of Towle's estimated sales in 1971. The company also was selling over 20 basic sterling flatware patterns under the Towle name through 3,000 retail outlets. It recorded after-tax profits of 9 to 10.5 percent of sales between 1966 and 1970.

Towle's solid performance and lack of long-term debt attracted a takeover attempt in 1974 from Nortek Inc., a diversified company only seven years old. In response, more than 800 residents in the Newburyport area signed an advertisement in the local newspaper expressing concern that Towle might move out if purchased by Nortek. Towle executives, who called their company the oldest in America doing business in the same place, voiced gratitude to their shareholders when Nortek's bid failed. The company's days as an independent entity were to prove numbered, however.

Leonard Silver, with sales of $38.7 million and earnings of about $2 million in 1977, claimed to be the nation's leading manufacturer of silverplated holloware when it took aim at Towle the following year. By contrast, Towle was the nation's second-largest manufacturer of sterling silver, its sterling flatware accounting for 80 percent of its sales volume of $35 million in 1977. According to Florence, he engineered a "reverse takeover" by threatening to make a tender offer to Towle's shareholders. In September 1978 Towle acquired Leonard Silver by issuing stock with a combined value of nearly $13.4 million. Leonard Silver stockholders received a share of Towle stock for each Leonard Silver share they held. Since Florence owned 40 percent of Leonard Silver, he emerged as Towle's largest stockholder and in essence elected himself Towle's president and chief executive officer.

The merger brought Florence the prestige of the Towle name, sterling flatware to fill in the high end of his line, and cash for his heavily indebted former company, now a Towle division. He immediately moved corporate headquarters to East Boston and redefined Towle by broadening its clientele. He made price, for the first time, a major consideration in selling the company's silverware, and only items that lent themselves to mass merchandising remained in production. To reduce overhead, salaried salespeople replaced jobbers, and silverplate was promoted through mail-order catalogues. Unlike sterling silver, silverplated holloware was recession-proof, Florence told a *Forbes* reporter in 1981. "No one's going to tell a bride, 'I can't give you a gift, there's a recession on. Come back next year.'" His oft-pronounced motto was, "Today Mrs. Jones wants to live like Mrs. Rockefeller," to which he added, "And I intend to let her think she can."

Florence not only introduced silverplated flatware under the Towle name, he also moved the company into china, glassware, stainless-steel flatware, dinnerware, barware, brass furnishings, pots and pans, ceramic gifts—even candles and silk flowers—by acquisition. In the following years Towle bought 14 companies. Nearly half of Towle's sales volume of about $200 million in 1980 came from nonsilver items. In 1981 a new 578,000-square-foot Towle automated distribution plant opened in Revere, Massachusetts.

Towle's old-line Yankee competitors accused Florence of cheapening the silverware industry through his sales promotions—many of which they subsequently imitated—and, they claimed, shoddy workmanship. He outraged them by his willingness to cut prices in order to bolster market share and by copying their designs. Dubbed the "King of Kitsch," he flaunted his parvenu trappings, which included four homes, a Rolls-Royce, Mercedes, and Jaguar, multiple gold chains, and a diamond-studded bracelet and Rolex gold watch. Florence compensated for these indulgences by habitually working seven days a week, spending nine months out of the year on the road, and sleeping, by his own account, only four hours a night. A New York department store executive told a trade-newspaper reporter, "Lenny Florence is successful because he has the ability to change with the times. The rest of the silver industry has been asleep for 100 years."

By 1980 Towle was the largest tabletop and giftware concern in the United States and the largest producer of silverware. It was selling 7,000 items, ranging from sterling silver tea sets commanding up to $10,000 to $20 vinyl ice buckets and $15 Muppet figurines and Kliban-cat clay coffee mugs. By 1984 Towle was selling 35,000 different items.

By late 1982, however, Towle was so heavily in debt that it had to sell 750,000 shares of newly issued common stock to a conglomerate, Anchor Hocking Corp., for $16.9 million in cash. Despite record sales of $285 million in 1983, earnings dropped sharply in 1982 and 1983, and in 1984 Towle lost $15.6 million. The problem stemmed partly from consolidating shipping operations in its state-of-the-art Revere facility. The computer system, unable to handle Towle's volume, broke down, and delays left the company unable to fill Christmas orders. More generally, analysts said, Towle emphasized growth without a corresponding attempt to integrate its acquisi-

tions into the parent company. As a result, one retailer told a *Boston Globe* reporter, "We're constantly confused about prices, programs, and deliveries."

Towle's board of directors forced Florence to resign in November 1985. It lost $67 million in 1985, and its debt reached $142 million. Paul J. Dunphy, the company treasurer and a former Arthur Hocking executive, succeeded Florence as president and chief executive officer. Towle filed for protection from its creditors under Chapter 11 of the federal bankruptcy code in March 1986. Its stock dropped in value to $3.25 a share, compared to a high of more than $31 a share in 1983.

Under Dunphy, Towle consolidated into three business divisions and began divesting itself of unprofitable operations. Its school-ring division, Old Harbor Candles affiliate, Deldan silk flowers unit, and Christmas Place ornaments lines were sold. Its brass furniture company was liquidated. Its practice of deep discounting was ended. The company lost $22 million in 1986, but the following year it became a subsidiary of First Republic Corp. of New York and emerged from bankruptcy. However, Towle again filed for Chapter 11 bankruptcy in 1989, acknowledging that its plan for anticipated "rather aggressive growth" had not materialized.

Florence, who with other family members still owned at least 12 percent of Towle at the time of his resignation, had raised $5 million and started a new company, Syratech. It bought money-losing Wallace International Silversmiths from Katy Industries Inc. in September 1986. Wallace Silversmiths Inc. and International Silver Co. had been merged into a single unit in 1983. The former company derived from Robert Wallace, who manufactured the first spoons made in the United States of German or nickel silver in 1835. Founded in 1898, International Silver Co. was at one time the world's largest manufacturer of silverware.

Syratech also bought Syroco, an unprofitable plastic-injection molding company that made decorative trim, in 1986. Florence moved it into plastic-resin patio furniture. Both units were profitable within a year. Acquiring Syroco enabled Syratech to keep its employees busy year-round, since outdoor furniture sold best in the spring while tableware sold best in the fall. In 1993 *Business Week* cited Syratech as one of 250 "companies on the move," and *Forbes* called it one of "the best small companies in America."

Florence reacquired four Towle units—Towle Canada, Towle Hong Kong, Towle Retail, and the Silversmiths division—in July 1990 for $20 million and merged them into Syratech. He told a *Forbes* interviewer in 1995, "In my humble opinion, Towle would not have gone into bankruptcy if they had let us stay the course. . . . I was let go wrongly, and I had to go out and prove it." At the beginning of 1993 Syratech went public, offering 2.2 million shares of common stock (about a quarter of the total) at an initial $17 per share. This stock issue raised $39 million. By then Syratech consisted of frame and gift companies as well as tableware and furniture and accessories. Of $127.7 million in sales in 1991, tableware and giftware accounted for 65 percent, furniture and accessories for 35 percent. In 1993 sales reached $210 million, and profits were nearly $18 million.

In 1995 Syratech sold Syroco to Marley plc, a British company, for $140 million. Syratech's sales had grown in 1994 to $242.2

million, of which Syroco accounted for 39 percent. Net income came to $19.9 million. Florence had a 28 percent stake in the company in 1994, while Katy Industries owned 29 percent. Long-term debt was only $2.3 million.

In 1995 Syratech was designing, manufacturing, importing, and distributing a variety of tabletop and giftware products, including sterling silver, silverplated, and stainless steel flatware and holloware, and seasonal items. Holloware and giftware items sold by the company included trays, coffee and tea services, goblets, pitchers, candlesticks and candelabra, picture frames, cosmetic accessories, vanity pieces, and Christmas and other seasonal merchandise.

Syratech was manufacturing sterling silver flatware in San German, Puerto Rico, in 1995, and was also fabricating silver there. Sterling silver and silverplated giftware products, including holloware, were being manufactured in North Dighton, Massachusetts. (The Newburyport plant was closed in 1994.) Products were also being purchased from about 160 foreign manufacturers. The company had warehouses in China, North Dighton, East Boston, and Kansas City, Missouri, and warehouse/distribution centers in Revere, Massachusetts, and Corona, California. There were showrooms in New York City, Los Angeles, Dallas, Atlanta, East Boston, and Hong Kong.

Syratech was selling its sterling silver and silverplated flatware and holloware under a number of trade names, including Tuttle, Wm. Rogers & Son, Leonard, Supreme Cutlery, Westmoreland, Melannco, International Christmas, and Holiday Workshops, as well as Towle, Wallace Silversmiths, and International. Its proprietary patterns and designs included King Richard and Old Master in the Towle line, Grand Baroque and French Regency in the Wallace line, Joan of Arc and Royal Danish in the International line, and Onslow in the Tuttle line.

Principal Subsidiaries: International Silver Co.; Leonard Florence (Leonard) Associates, Inc.; Syratech H.K. (Hong Kong); Syratech Holding Corp.; Syratech Silver Sales Corp.; Towle Holloware, Inc.; Towle Manufacturing Co.; Wallace International Silversmiths, Inc.

Further Reading:

Chakravarty, Subrata N., "I Do Just the Opposite," *Forbes,* July 6, 1981, pp. 130–31.
Connors, Mary, "Can He Keep It Growing?" *HFD,* August 4, 1980, pp. 1, 24–25.
"Gadfly of the Silversmiths," *Business Week,* July 28, 1980, pp. 81–82.
Hayes, John R., "Toilet Tissue or Fur Coats—What's the Difference?" *Forbes,* July 17, 1995, pp. 70–71.
Hogan, Edmund P., *An American Heritage: A Book about the International Silver Company,* Dallas: Taylor Publishing Co., 1977.
MacDonald, Dougald, "Towle Manufacturing, under Chapter 11, Weighs Cost of Breaking with Tradition," *New England Business,* May 19, 1986, pp. 36, 38.
"Marriage of Convenience," *Financial World,* October 1, 1980, pp. 24–25.
Marx, Linda, "Lenny Florence Knows All that Glitters Isn't Gold; He's the Poor Man's Silver Fox," *People,* May 17, 1982, pp. 113–15.
Patterson, Gregory A., "What Went Wrong at Towle," *Boston Globe,* December 17, 1985, pp. 29, 40.
Rainwater, Dorothy T., *Encyclopedia of Silver Manufacturers,* West Chester, Pennsylvania: Schiffer Publishing Ltd., 3rd rev. ed., 1986.
Reidy, Chris, "A Sterling Personality," *Boston Globe,* May 29, 1994, pp. 73, 75.
Smith, Anne Mackay, "King of Sterling: Towle's Chief Rattles Rival Silverware Firms by Selling to the Masses," *Wall Street Journal,* June 28, 1982, pp. 1, 13.
Therrien, Lois, "Silversmith Tries to Regain His Share," *Business Week,* February 18, 1985, p. 70.

—Robert Halasz

Tasty Baking Co.

2801 Hunting Park Avenue
Philadelphia, Pennsylvania 19129
U.S.A.
(215) 221-8500
Fax: (215) 223-3288

Public Company
Incorporated: 1914
Sales: $142.1 million
Employees: 1,200
Stock Exchanges: American
SICs: 2051 Bread and Other Bakery Products, Except
    Cookies and Crackers; 2052 Cookies and Crackers; 2064
    Candy and Other Confectionery Products; 2066 Chocolate
    and Cocoa Products

Tasty Baking Co. is a Philadelphia-based company that, in the mid 1990s, was manufacturing and selling about 75 varieties of single-portion food products, most of them confectionery. The company marketed its products, including cakes, pies, cookies, brownies, pastries, doughnuts, muffins, and pretzels, under the trademark TASTYKAKE. Tasty's products were being sold primarily to about 25,000 retail outlets in a six-state region ranging from New York to Virginia, but the company's distribution network was spreading south and west. At the same time Tastykake baked goods remained a Philadelphia institution, honored alongside other distinctly local food treats like cheese steaks, hoagies, and scrapple.

Tasty Baking was founded in 1914 by Philip J. Baur and Herbert C. Morris. Baur came from a German-American family that was in the process of selling its large Pittsburgh bakery, and Morris, a salesman, was from a well-established Cleveland family. Baur and Morris wanted to develop small cakes packed at a bakery plant, in contrast to the loaf cakes that were handled and cut into portions by retail grocers under the unsanitary conditions of the time. Since the sale of the Baur bakery forbade any Baur to open a bakery within 100 miles of Pittsburgh, the two decided to make Philadelphia their base. They found a deserted, burnt-out plant in North Philadelphia with its own railroad siding and set up shop there.

On February 25, 1914, the Tasty Baking Co. was incorporated with capital of $46,000, half provided by Baur and his father, the other half from Morris's father-in-law, Edward K. Sober.

Baur was responsible for production, Morris for sales. Morris's wife came up with the name of the new product, Tastykake. The early cakes were white, yellow, chocolate, raisin, molasses, and sponge. Sugar and flour were sifted by hand. After baking—at first in a single oven—the cakes were iced, cut into rectangles, wrapped, packed into boxes, and distributed to retailers who sold them for ten cents each. In its first year the company had impressive gross sales of $300,000; in 1918, sales reached $1 million.

By April 1915 Tasty Baking was serving stores as far away as Mt. Carmel and Reading, Pennsylvania, Trenton, New Jersey, and Wilmington, Delaware, as well as 13 Philadelphia routes. Morris would sell agents only as many cakes as he thought they could sell within the two days between the salesman's visits. The salesman replaced anything that had become stale with a new cake and took the stale one back to the plant, where it was destroyed. All business was transacted in cash. When the system broke down because the agents got behind on their payments, Tasty Baking decided to hire its own distributors and pay them a salary, commission, and car allowance. This arrangement remained in operation until the mid-1980s.

In 1922 Tasty Baking constructed a new, five-story plant on Hunting Park Avenue in North Philadelphia. Two additions were built within three years. The new plant led to new products: the Junior, a lemon sponge cake with icing on top; a chocolate cupcake; and the revolutionary Krimpet, a finger-sized butterscotch sponge cake baked in a fluted pan. The latter two products sold two for a nickel and became the company's best sellers. During this decade the Tastykake horse-drawn wagon was a familiar site on Philadelphia streets. Gasoline-fueled trucks and electric cars and trucks were also used, and Tasty products moved by rail and ship to more distant areas, but the last horse was not retired until 1941.

By 1930 the Hunting Park plant had five buildings and 350,000 square feet of floor space. Annual sales had climbed to $6 million. A lunchbox-size square apple pie called the Tasty-Pie proved a quick success. Newspaper advertisements, billboards, streetcar placards, and slides shown in movie theaters displayed Tastykake pastries or depicted children eating the products. The company weathered the Depression without layoffs by cutting their production costs. During World War II Tasty Baking employed 203 people, and company advertising promoted the sale of war bonds.

After Philip Baur died in 1951, his heirs purchased stock from the holdings of E. K. Sober's daughter (Herbert Morris's wife), giving the Baur family majority control of the private company. Vice-president Paul R. Kaiser assumed the presidency and Morris, who had served as president since the company's inception, became chairman of the board. In April 1954 Kaiser was able to report that the Tastykake territory had grown to cover parts of nine states and the District of Columbia. By the end of the decade annual sales had grown to nearly $22.9 million. Net income first passed the $1-million mark in 1955.

Under the slogan ''Automate or Abdicate'' Kaiser advanced a program of installing spiral metal chutes, powered conveyor belts, and auxiliary equipment. The baking cycle, which took up to 12 hours in 1935, was cut to as little as 45 minutes in 1956.

Acquisition of a Battle Creek wrapping machine began an era of automatic wrapping. A larger and more modern laboratory was completed in 1956.

During the 1950s Tasty Baking's traditional customers, mom-and-pop retail stores, began to give way to supermarkets. Radio and television were replacing the company's traditional reliance on billboards and posters. Tasty began sponsoring Philadelphia Phillies baseball telecasts, featuring commercials starring Joe E. Brown, Betty White, and Shari Lewis and her puppets. Over the next 25 years the company extended its sponsorship to baseball's Baltimore Orioles and Washington Senators, football's Philadelphia Eagles and hockey's Philadelphia Flyers, adding spokespersons ranging from musical impresario Dick Clark to Philadelphia sports heroes Bobby Clarke, Richie Ashburn, and Bill White.

One form of public relations the company badly needed, as the factory's neighborhood changed, was forging better ties to the black community. In 1960 a two-month boycott of Tastykake products organized by 400 black ministers ended only after Tasty Baking agreed to add blacks to its sales, clerical, and other previously all-white departments. Businesses and white residents continued to leave North Philadelphia, but the company chose instead to stay and fight decay. It organized the Allegheny West Foundation to rehabilitate housing, introduce new businesses, and support other forms of community development.

When Tasty Baking went public in 1961, its offered stock sold out the first day, the price rising immediately from $20 a share to $27 or $28. Officers and directors continued to hold nearly half the shares, however. In 1965 the company diversified for the first time by acquiring Phillips & Jacobs, Inc., a producer of industrial chemicals and wholesale printing supplies, for about $2.5 million in stock. The next year it added a Baltimore graphic-arts supply business, a potato-chip company, and a biscuit business. The following year it added Philadelphia and Atlanta graphic-arts companies.

By 1968 Tasty Baking was serving 30,000 stores in 12 states. Sales, in 1967, when net income was $2.8 million, reached $67.4 million, of which the baking operations accounted for 57 percent. Graphic arts accounted for 28 percent. The rest, 15 percent, came from the acquisition of potato-chip and pretzel manufacturers and three Ohio cookie distributors. The Baur family held 58 percent of the company's voting stock by 1968, management held 12 percent, and the public held 30 percent.

In March 1970 Kaiser told a group of Philadelphia financial analysts that the Tastykake division was distributing 35 varieties of small cakes and pies to 28,000 stores in 12 states on a three-day-a-week basis. He said the graphic-arts division was supplying 17,000 items to the printing and allied trades in 14 states. The cookie-distribution companies were marketing a complete line of cookies, crackers, and biscuits to 4,000 retail outlets in Ohio and western Pennsylvania. Despite this expansion, the ratio of net profits to sales fell in 1970 for the ninth consecutive year; it was only 2.8 percent, compared to 5.8 percent in 1962.

Concluding that the potato-chip and pretzel businesses were a drain on earnings, Tasty Baking sold them in 1970. In the same year, Tasty Baking expanded in a new direction by acquiring Larami Corp., a Philadelphia toy manufacturer, importer, and distributor. By 1972 the company's ratio of net profits to sales had improved slightly, but in the recession year of 1974 it was down to 2.6 percent: $3.5 million in net income on net sales of $132.1 million. In 1976, when net income peaked at $6.7 million on sales of $157 million, Tasty Baking made an unwise $5.5-million acquisition of Ole South Foods Co., a frozen-dessert manufacturer. Tasty eventually dissolved Ole South Foods in 1979; that year Tasty lost $2.2 million on net sales of $169.5 million—its first annual loss.

In 1981, Kaiser's last year as chief executive officer, Tasty Baking charted a new direction. The aging population of the Middle Atlantic states, he said, meant "There's been a decrease in the number of teens, and they're the big snack and cake eaters." The company introduced a chocolate-covered pretzel and also entered the breakfast-food market with Danish pastries and muffins. Finger-shaped cakes and cupcakes were packaged singly to attract more unit sales in single-person households. Tasty also entered agreements with distributors as far away as California. In a process learned from Ole South Foods, baked goods were frozen in Philadelphia, shipped under refrigeration, and thawed at their destinations. Larami Corp. formed a Hong Kong trading company to import premium nontoy gifts for direct-mail marketing by Tasty.

Kaiser's 28-year reign came to an end in April 1981, when dissident shareholders, upset by three consecutive quarters of losses, forced his resignation. Philip J. Baur, Jr., president of the Tastykake division and Kaiser's brother-in-law, succeeded him as chairman of the board. Nelson G. Harris, the company president since 1979, succeeded Kaiser as chief executive officer. Under new leadership, Tasty Baking retrenched. In October 1981 the company retreated from two of its major expansion projects, selling the toy manufacturer Larami and withdrawing from all but eight of its new markets in 40 states. In an October 1981 *New York Times* article, Harris explained, "We went too far too fast. The problems of distribution and transportation became prohibitive, and there was the problem of not advertising agressively enough."

Although 1982 was a recession year, Tasty Baking halted a five-year decline in unit sales. Net income rose from $1.7 million in 1982 to $2.4 million in 1983 and $2.9 million in 1984, when net sales reached $222.4 million. Long-term debt was reduced from $19 million to $7 million. Tastykake distribution stabilized at 21 states, including California, where the company was sponsoring baseball's San Diego Padres. (California was dropped in 1988, however.) Also during this time, subsidiary Phillips & Jacobs began serving the New York City market.

Tasty Baking reorganized its sales organization in 1985. While delivery persons had usually owned their own trucks and absorbed the cost of store returns, routes were now offered for sale to the driver-sales reps, who would become independent owner-operators of their territories. The company offered to finance the sales, with no down payment. According to Harris, the deliverymen "paid $50,000 or $60,000 and got something worth $110,000–$120,000. . . . We had 386 routes, and we sold them all. Today [in 1989] we have about 510 routes, and we've had 50 route splits."

The sale of its routes raised $16 million for Tasty Baking and also made drivers more dutiful in tending their accounts. Such dedication was essential to the company, because most Tasty products contained no preservatives or artificial flavors and thus had shelf lives as short as four days. Sales rose ten percent immediately. Meanwhile, Harris allotted more than $40 million to upgrade the Philadelphia plant. Between 1981 and 1988 revenues doubled to $264 million, while profits rose more than sevenfold, from $1.3 million to $9.5 million.

In 1989 Tasty Baking repackaged its Tastykake products in bright yellow instead of the traditional blue and white. It began a new line of cakes and pies in flavors that changed monthly and introduced a line of honey-graham cookies, called Tasty Bears, aimed at children aged six to 12. The following year the company introduced both Chocolate Royals, oversize cupcakes filled with chocolate mousse and topped with icing, and Tasty-Lights, a low-fat cupcake. It found that the former sold much better than the latter, leading division president Carl Watts to conclude, ''There's a segment that may not want a snack cake every day. But when they do, they want it to be as indulgent as can be.'' By the end of 1990, some 30 percent of Tasty's bakery revenues were coming from products introduced since 1982, including Honey Buns and Pastry Pockets. Watts succeeded Harris as chairman and chief executive officer of the company in 1992.

In 1991 Tasty Baking introduced its premium Gold Collection line. Several new products were introduced in 1992, including Tasty Mini Cupcakes, and Lemon and Jelly reduced-fat Krimpets cupcakes. That year Carrot Cake and Chocolate Chunk Macadamia Cookie cupcakes were added to the Gold Collection items. During 1993 new products included Dunkin' Stix, Pound Kake, and Blueberry Mini Muffins. Also in 1993, the company spun off Phillips & Jacobs to its shareholders, who received two shares of its common stock for every three shares of Tasty Baking common stock.

In 1994 Tasty Baking launched a record six new snack-cake products. These included Kreme Krimpies, a Krimpet-shaped, creme-filled sponge cake; Whirly Twirls, a chocolate roll cake with white creme filling and a dark chocolate coating; and P.B. Krunch, a crunchy wafer layered between strips of peanut butter covered with a rippled chocolate coating. The other three were seasonal products: Bunny Trail Treats, Sparkle Kakes, and Kringle Kakes, for Easter, the Memorial Day/Fourth of July period, and Christmas, respectively. St. Patty's Treats was to be

introduced in 1995 to complete the company's holiday coverage. Thirty-four percent of Tasty's snack-cake sales in 1994 came from Tastykake products that did not exist 10 years before.

Stripped of Phillips & Jacobs, Tasty Baking had net sales of $142 million in 1994 and net income of $5.8 million from continuing operations. Its long-term debt was $10.3 million in July 1994. Officers and directors controlled about 9 percent of the common stock, whereas institutions held 44 percent.

In 1995 Tasty Baking was selling its products in about 30 states. In addition to its approximately 25,000 retail outlets in the Middle Atlantic states, it was selling through direct alliances with major grocery chains in the Midwest, South, and Southwest. Cakes, cookies, and doughnuts sold for 25 to 69 cents per package, with family packages and jumbo packs ranging from $1.99 to $3.39. Pies, pastries, and brownies typically retailed for 69 cents apiece or per package. Three varieties of English muffins ranged from $1.49 to $1.69 per package. Customers could also order a variety of Tastykake gift packs by calling a toll-free number.

Principal Subsidiaries: TBC Financial Services, Inc.; TBC Service Co., Inc.

Further Reading:
Bullock, Jill M., ''Tasty Expects Benefits from New Packaging,'' *Wall Street Journal,* August 25, 1989, p. 4D.
''Expansion Setback Is Forcing Change at Tasty Baking,'' *New York Times,* October 22, 1981, p. 4D.
Gardner, Joel R., *Seventy-Five Years of Good Taste: A History of the Tasty Baking Company 1914–1989,* Philadelphia: Tasty Baking Co., 1990.
Helzner, Jerry, ''Local Mystique: Tasty Baking Hopes to Transport It to Most Big Markets,'' *Barron's,* April 30, 1984, p. 53.
Kaiser, Paul R., ''Tasty Baking Company,'' *Wall Street Transcript,* September 23, 1968, p. 14437.
——, ''Tasty Baking Company,'' *Wall Street Journal,* May 18, 1970, p. 20578.
Meeks, Fleming, ''Junk Food Blitz,'' *Forbes,* May 27, 1991, pp. 196–98.
Randolph, Deborah A., ''Tasty Baking Whips Up New Recipe in Effort to Bolster Its Sluggish Sales,'' *Wall Street Journal,* January 11, 1981, p. 34.
——, ''Tasty Baking Co. Dissidents Oust Kaiser, Omit Dividend and Cut Officers' Salaries,'' *Wall Street Journal,* April 27, 1981, p. 22.

—Robert Halasz

Telefonos de Mexico S.A. de C.V.

Parque Via 198
Col. Cuauhtemoc
Mexico City, DF 06599
Mexico
(5) 7033990
Fax: (5) 2545955

Public Company
Founded: 1947
Employees: 48,810
Sales: US$5.91 billion
Stock Exchanges: Mexico New York
SICs: 4810 Telephone Communications; 4822 Telegraph &
  Other Communications

Telefonos de Mexico S.A. de C.V. (Telmex) is Mexico's long-distance telephone monopoly and one of the largest companies in Mexico. It provides local and long-distance telecommunication services throughout Mexico and abroad to both residential and commercial customers. Telmex was operating as a government-owned-and-operated utility until the early 1990s, when the Mexican government began to privatize the organization. Under private ownership, Telmex was rapidly expanding and improving going into the mid-1990s.

Telefonos de Mexico was created in 1947 to purchase two telephone companies that were operating in Mexico: L.M. Ericsson, of Sweden, and the U.S.-based International Telegraph Corporation. Both companies had pioneered the telephone industry in Mexico and had succeeded in bringing basic services to larger cities in Mexico. Telmex was created to make the dominant phone service provider in Mexico a domestic company. The newly created organization acquired the Mexican division of L.M. Ericsson in 1947 before buying the Mexican subsidiary of International Telegraph in 1950. In effect, the merger gave Telmex a monopoly on the long-distance telephone industry in Mexico, although a number of smaller phone companies continued to provide local services. L.M. Ericsson and International Telephone managers continued to operate the Mexican enterprise.

From the start, the Mexican telephone service industry, like telephone industries in most other countries, was heavily influenced by the national government. That influence intensified during the 1950s and 1960s when the government decided that

it needed to push the development of a national phone system that would keep Mexico from falling too far behind the United States and Europe in communications capabilities. Importantly, in the 1960s the government imposed a telephone service tax on all long-distance calls. The money was earmarked for investment in the telephone sector, namely to help supply the billions of dollars needed to add telephone lines and switching stations throughout the country. Thus, throughout the 1950s and 1960s Telmex operated as a private enterprise that cooperated with the Mexican government to deliver phone services to the nation.

The Mexican government's role at Telmex continued to expand until 1972, when Mexico actually took control of the enterprise by purchasing 51 percent of Telmex's voting shares; the remainder of the shares in the company were owned by Mexican citizens and institutions as well as foreigners. From that point forward, Telmex in effect operated as a government-owned utility. The government regulated the prices that the company could charge, influenced its operating budget, and made other management decisions. However, Telmex still maintained some of its private-company flavor; Government appointees shared seats on Telmex's board with private individuals, and the government even retained most of Telmex's management after it took control of the company.

Throughout most of the 1970s Telmex operated much as it had as a private company. The chief executive of the company, a highly respected manager, served as head of Telmex throughout the 1970s and even during most of the 1980s. For most of that time, Telmex expanded its services at a rate of approximately six percent annually. At the same time, older parts of the system were gradually modernized. By 1980, close to 100 percent of Telmex's exchanges were automatic (not controlled by an operator), and the company was preparing to launch an ambitious plan to install only digital, rather than electro-mechanical, lines. Furthermore, Mexico's telephone service in comparison to other developing nations at the time ranked well in categories like the average number of inoperable lines or the amount of time required to install a new line.

Telmex also performed well in comparison to other state-owned companies in Mexico during the 1970s and early 1980s, largely because it was still partly a private company. At the same time, Telmex began to suffer from many of the problems that afflicted other state enterprises; political interference, inefficiency, labor union strength, and fiscal mismanagement. Indeed, although the utility had expanded service at a rate of about six percent annually, it could have grown at a much faster clip. A prime example of the problems the company faced was the telephone service tax that had been created in the 1960s. Over the years the government had raised the long-distance tax at a dizzying pace to the point that more than 50 percent of Telmex's revenues were eventually coming from the tax. At the same time, the government began drawing from the funds generated by the surcharge to pay for unrelated government programs. The unfortunate result was that Telmex, by the 1980s, had become a financing vehicle for the Mexican government.

The effects of bureaucratic influence at Telmex were undeniable by the mid-1980s. The company's overpaid work force had become bloated, yet service was barely improving. Although the Mexican telephone network compared positively with phone systems in places like Venezuela, Argentina, and Indonesia, its performance was dismal when compared to the systems in the United States, the European Community, and other wealthy regions. For example, a customer that requested a telephone line from Telmex would have to wait, on average, about three years for a hook-up—that compared to eight years in Venezuela, but just a few days in the United States, Japan, and most of Europe. In addition, the hook-up fee for a single business line could cost $500 or more. Furthermore, at any one time about ten percent of all the phone lines in Mexico were out of service. To make matters worse, the government had been increasing long-distance prices (through the tax) at a rapid pace, to the point where the cost of a call had become prohibitive for many customers.

Telmex's problems reflected lackluster national leadership. Between 1976 and 1982, for example, Mexico suffered under the inept direction of the Jose Lopez Portillo administration. Telmex remained profitable and always paid dividends because it was protected by the state, but it fell behind during the early 1980s in adopting some key technologies like 1-800 services and fiber-optics. Portillo was removed in 1982 and was followed by the Miguel de la Madrid administration. Madrid, realizing the urgency of the situation, took several drastic steps to improve the economy and decrease the nation's debt. Among his initiatives was a program designed to privatize many of Mexico's 1,155 state-owned enterprises, one of the largest of which was Telmex.

Both Mexico's economy and Telmex improved under the new administration. For instance, between the early and late 1980s the percentage of phone lines that were digital increased from zero to more than 20 percent. Toll-free 800 service was added in the late 1980s and even extended to calls to and from the United States. Throughout the period, Telmex continued to post profits and to pay dividends on its stock. At the same time, however, long-distance rates continued to rise. By the late 1980s a seven-minute phone call to the United States, for example, cost about $10. By that time the telephone tax was making up 60 percent of all of Telmex's revenues, and about half of the total tax proceeds were being consumed for other government programs. Furthermore, Telmex's powerful labor unions remained entrenched, making for an increasingly bloated and inefficient company.

The turning point for Telmex came in the early 1990s, shortly after Carlos Salinas was elected president of Mexico. Salinas had worked for the previous administration as the secretary of budget and planning, during which time he also served as government director on the board of Telmex. Salinas had supported the privatization program that had reduced the number of state-owned companies by more than half by the time he took office in the late 1980s. However, Salinas believed that Mexico was in need of much more radical economic changes. To that end, he announced plans in 1989 to make Telmex a private company again. The plan was to get Telmex operating on its own and then gradually allow other companies to begin competing for long-distance customers.

The reasons behind Salinas' decision to take Telmex private were multifold. Importantly, by privatizing giant Telmex soon after being elected, he would be sending a message to the global investment community that Mexico was serious about making its economy more competitive and free. A second reason for privatizing Telmex was to increase its efficiency. Indeed, having served on the company's board, Salinas knew that Telmex's potential for growth and profit were enormous but were being hampered by politics. By freeing the company from political strings, he hoped to markedly improve Telmex's performance and to enhance the country's communication infrastructure. Finally, Salinas knew that the sale of the government's 51-percent voting share—it represented about 20 percent of the company's total equity—could help cut Mexico's fat pile of debt by as much as US$2 billion.

Mexico began decentralizing the bureaucratic Telmex organization in 1989, in preparation for privatization. Then, in 1990, Telmex began accepting bids from investors who wanted to purchase the 20-percent equity stake in Telmex. Easily winning the bid contest was a consortium of three companies that, by outbidding their closest rival by more than $70 million, purchased the controlling interest in Telmex for US$1.76 billion. The three partners were Southwestern Bell (of the United States), France Telecom, and Mexico's Grupo Carso. Grupo Carso put up half of the US$1.76 billion and received a leading 10-percent equity stake in Telmex, while its partners financed the other half and shared the other 10 percent interest. The group agreed that Grupo Carso would have operating control of the company, Southwestern Bell would be responsible for improving operations and developing paging and cellular divisions, and France Telecom would concentrate on line expansion and modernization.

The head of Grupo Carso, Carlos Slim Helu, headed Telmex's new management team. After hearing about the privatization plan in 1989, Slim had approached executives at Southwestern Bell and France Telecom about teaming up to get control of Telmex. He reasoned that those two companies had the technological and management tools necessary to whip Telmex into shape and he had the political and economic clout. Indeed, at the time of the buyout, Slim's Grupo Carso was Mexico's sixth largest company, with a market value of about US$2.4 billion and only US$300 million in long-term debt. Known as unassuming and publicity shy, the 50-year-old Slim had amassed a US$1.9-billion personal fortune through his varied interests in mining, manufacturing, paper products, retailing, insurance, tourism, and other businesses. Incredibly, Slim, the son of a Lebanese immigrant, had started a small construction company that he built into the Grupo Carso empire.

When Telmex went private it was generating net profits of about US$1.1 billion from sales of roughly US$3.8 billion. Despite those impressive numbers, the government-supported monopoly was in serious need of repair. There were only six lines for every 100 Mexican citizens, for example, which compared to more than 50 lines per 100 citizens in the United States. More than 1.5 million people were on a waiting list to get service, and the typical wait was at least 18 months. The company was only generating revenues of about US$400 per line (compared to nearly twice that in the United States). Furthermore, about 10 percent of Telmex's lines were inoperable on a regular basis, despite a bloated work force by world telephone industry standards.

As part of the purchase agreement between the Grupo Carso consortium and the Mexican government, the new controllers of Telmex had to agree to rapidly increase and improve long-distance telephone service in Mexico. Specifically, the government designed a three-year plan for improvement that began in 1991 and directed Telmex to install about 8,500 miles of fiber-optic lines, replace 500,000 electro-mechanical lines with digital analog technology, bring phone service into all rural towns with a population of more than 500, and significantly reduce the waiting time to get new service installed. Furthermore, by 1996 Telmex was expected to interconnect with other carriers offering long-distance service, which would open the door for long-distance competition.

Telmex made significant progress toward its goals during the early 1990s. By late 1994, in fact, Telmex had replaced most of its obsolete lines and had converted old switching systems to 75 percent digital switching, one of the highest levels in the world. Furthermore, between 1992 and 1994 the company managed to increase the number of phone lines on its network at an average annual rate of 12.6 percent, bringing the number of phone lines per 100 citizens to 10. As a result, Telmex's sales rose to about US$6.6 billion in 1992 before jumping to US$7.9 billion in 1993. Although revenues declined to about US$6 billion in 1994, the company netted income of about US$1.6 billion. About 45 percent of Telmex's revenues came from local services, with the other portion attributable to domestic long-distance and international calls. Furthermore, Telmex invested about US$2.3 billion in its phone system in 1994 as part of an ongoing drive to improve service and prepare for competition in the long-distance market, which was scheduled to commence in 1997.

Further Reading:

Dabrowski, Andrea, ''Mexico's Privatization Plan Under Pressure,'' *Washington Post,* September 3, 1991, p. E1.
LaFranchi, Howard, ''Competition Lines Up for Long Distance Opening in Mexico,'' *Christian Science Monitor,* October 4, 1994, p. 9.
Lowe, Sandra, ''Party Line: Telefonos de Mexico Braces for More Competition,'' *San Antonio Business Journal,* November 4, 1994, p. B1.
Luxner, Larry, ''Special Report: Mexico Reaches for New Telecom Heights,'' *Telephony,* February 3, 1992, p. 22.
Poole, Claire, ''El Conquistador,'' *Forbes,* September 16, 1991, p. 68.
Ramamurti, Ravi, ''Telephone Privatization in a Large Country: Mexico,'' *The North-South Agenda,* May 1994, pp. 1–20.

—Dave Mote

Texaco Inc.

2000 Westchester Avenue
White Plains, New York 10650
U.S.A.
(914) 253-4000
Fax: (914) 253-7753

Public Company
Incorporated: 1926 as The Texas Corporation
Employees: 29,713
Sales: $33.35 billion
Stock Exchanges: New York Toronto London Zürich
   Brussels Geneva
SICs: 1221 Bituminous Coal & Lignite Surface; 1311 Crude
   Petroleum & Natural Gas; 2911 Petroleum Refining; 5541
   Gasoline Service Stations

Texaco is one of the world's largest oil companies, with exploratory, manufacturing, and marketing operations across the globe. Its primary petroleum-based products include automotive gasoline and oils, as well as aviation and heating fuels. Texaco expanded with the growth of the U.S. automobile industry in the early 20th century and quickly developed international production and marketing interests. By the 1960s it had established the largest sales network of any U.S. oil company, with operations concentrated in refining and marketing. The oil crisis of the 1970s cut off many of its international sources of crude oil and left it with limited reserves. Texaco was poised for recovery in 1984 when it entered into a court battle with Pennzoil Company over the acquisition of Getty Oil. Since settling with Pennzoil in 1988, Texaco has pursued an almost constant restructuring effort in an attempt to recapture its former profitability and prominence in the oil industry.

Texaco was founded during the early boom years of the Texas oil industry. In 1901 a gusher at the Spindletop oil field sent hundreds of entrepreneurs into Beaumont, Texas. Among them was Joseph S. "Buckskin Joe" Cullinan, an oilman who had begun his career working for Standard Oil Company in Pennsylvania. The Spindletop wells led to the rapid establishment of over 200 oil companies, pumping out as much as 100,000 barrels a day. Cullinan saw an opportunity in purchasing that crude for resale to refineries. With the help of New York investment manager Arnold Schlaet, he formed The Texas Fuel Company with an initial stock of $50,000. Cullinan and Schlaet

began soliciting additional investments in New York and Chicago. After raising $3 million, they reorganized their venture as The Texas Company.

Cullinan immediately began constructing a pipeline between Spindletop and the gulf coast of Texas. He built a refinery at the Texas coastal city of Port Arthur, and from there the company shipped its oil to Louisiana sugar planters, who used it to heat their boilers. In the fall of 1902, salt water leaked into the Spindletop wells and ruined many of the companies based there. The Texas Company survived with a timely discovery of oil at Sour Lake, 20 miles northwest of Spindletop. Other strikes soon followed in Oklahoma and Louisiana.

With Cullinan's oil expertise and the financing of his New York backers, The Texas Company soon became one of the nation's most prominent oil companies. Cullinan continued to drill wells in the southwest region, building more pipelines to connect them with Port Arthur. By 1908 the company was selling to all but five western states, and by 1913 its assets were worth $60 million. The nickname Texaco came from the cable address of the company's New York offices. Texaco gained popularity as a product name, and in 1906 the company registered it as a trademark. The well-known logo first appeared in 1909 as a red star with a green "T" in the center. The company formally changed its name to Texaco Inc. in 1959.

At the time of Texaco's founding, oil was used primarily for lighting and as fuel for factories and locomotives. Texaco met this demand with its first consumer product, Familylite Illuminating Oil, introduced in 1907. After 1910, however, the automobile revolutionized the oil industry. Demand for gasoline, formerly considered a waste by-product of kerosene, expanded rapidly. Texaco followed this trend, and by 1914 its gasoline production surpassed that of kerosene. The company went from distributing gasoline in barrels to underground tanks to curbside pumps, and in 1911 it opened its first filling station in Brooklyn, New York. By 1916, 57 such stations were in operation across the country. Powered by the growth of the automobile industry and the high demand for petroleum created by WWI, Texaco quadrupled its assets between 1914 and 1920.

After WWI, Texaco continued to concentrate on its automotive gasoline and oil production, introducing new products and expanding its national sales network. In 1920 two researchers at its Port Arthur refinery developed the oil industry's first continuous thermal cracking process for making gasoline. Named after its founders, the Holmes-Manley process greatly increased the speed of the refining process as well as the amount of gasoline that could be refined from a barrel of crude. Texaco marketed this gasoline through its retail network, pushing into the Rocky Mountain region between 1920 and 1926, and into West Coast markets with the acquisition of California Petroleum Company in 1928.

Products introduced during the 1920s included the company's first premium gasoline, as well as Texaco Aviation Gasoline and automobile motor oils. To market the lighter oils it refined from Texas crude, Texaco launched its first nationwide advertising campaign. The slogan "Clean, Clear, Golden" appeared at Texaco's filling stations, which displayed its motor oils in glass bottles. By 1928 Texaco owned or leased more than 4,000 stations in all 48 states.

The company's growth was also reflected in its corporate structure. Finding Texas's corporation laws too restrictive for doing business on such a large scale, Texaco decided to move its legal home. In 1926 it formed The Texas Corporation in Delaware, which then bought out the stock of The Texas Company and reorganized it as a subsidiary called The Texas Company of Delaware. The company also moved its headquarters from Houston to New York. The Texas Corporation acted as a holding company for The Texas Company of Delaware and The Texas Company of California—formerly The California Petroleum Company—until 1941, when it merged with both and formed a single company known as The Texas Company.

The Texas Corporation's earnings reached an all-time high in 1929, but then dropped precipitously after the stock market crash. Overproduction, economic recession, and low prices plagued the oil industry in the early 1930s. The company embarked on a strategy of introducing new products to stimulate demand. Texaco Fire Chief Gasoline was launched in 1932, and the company advertised it by sponsoring a nationwide Ed Wynn radio program. Havoline Wax Free Motor Oil, developed after the acquisition of the Indiana Refining Company in 1931, followed two years later, halting its losses by 1934. In 1938 The Texas Corporation, still nicknamed Texaco, introduced Texaco Sky Chief premium gasoline and also began promoting its Registered Rest Rooms program, assuring motorists that their service stations were "Clean across the Country." In 1940 Texaco began its landmark sponsorship of the New York Metropolitan Opera's Saturday afternoon radio broadcasts. This program, which is still running, is the oldest association between a U.S. company and an arts program.

While The Texas Corporation promoted its products and services at home, it undertook vigorous expansion abroad. During the 1930s it began exploration and production in Colombia and Venezuela. In 1936 it joined with the Standard Oil Company of California to create the Caltex group of companies, a 50–50 venture in the Middle East. The Caltex group consolidated the operations of both of these companies east of the Suez Canal. Texaco also purchased a 50 percent interest from Standard Oil of California in the California Arabian Standard Oil Company, later renamed the Arabian American Oil Company (Aramco). The Caltex and Aramco ventures vastly expanded Texaco's sources of crude, and also enabled it to integrate its operations in the Eastern Hemisphere.

The entry of the United States into WWII brought dramatic changes for The Texas Corporation. About 30 percent of its wartime production went to the war effort, primarily in the form of aviation fuels, gasoline, and petrochemicals. The company worked closely with Harold L. Ickes, federal petroleum administrator for the war effort, who organized the nation's oil companies into several nonprofit operations. The Texas Pipe Line Company, a subsidiary, oversaw the completion of two federally sponsored pipelines from Texas to the East Coast.

Texaco also joined War Emergency Tankers Inc., which operated a collective tanker fleet for the War Shipping Administration. Another such venture was The Neches Butane Products Company, which manufactured butadiene, an essential ingredient in synthetic rubber. This enterprise gave Texaco its start in the infant petrochemicals industry, and after the war it purchased a 25 percent interest from the Federal Government in the Neches Butane plant. Texaco acquired full ownership of this operation in 1980. The company furthered its interests in petrochemicals in 1944 when it formed the Jefferson Chemical Company with the American Cyanamid Company. Texaco later bought out American Cyanamid's interest in this venture and then merged it with its newly formed Texaco Chemical Company in 1980.

With the end of WWII, Texaco faced renewed customer demand at home. U.S. consumption of oil exceeded its production for the first time in 1947, and Texaco reacted by tapping new foreign sources for its crude oil. In 1945 Texaco's jointly owned Caltex companies increased their refining capacity on Bahrain, reaching 180,000 barrels per day by 1951. Texaco also formed the Trans-Arabian Pipe Line Company with three other oil companies to build a pipeline connecting Saudi Arabia's oil fields with the eastern Mediterranean. At home, Texaco increased its refining capacity with the Eagle Point Works near Camden, New Jersey. It also introduced several new automotive products, including Texaco Anti-Freeze and Texamatic Fluid for automatic transmissions.

During the 1950s and 1960s Texaco concentrated on expanding its global refining and marketing operations. The acquisition of the Trinidad Oil Company in 1956 and the Seaboard Oil Company in 1958, both of which held proven reserves in South America, expanded its interests in the Western Hemisphere. To increase its production in the Amazon Basin, the company built a jointly owned trans-Andean pipeline in 1969 and a trans-Ecuadorian pipeline in 1972. To increase its production in Europe, moreover, Texaco purchased the majority interest in the West German oil company Deutsch Erdol A.G. in 1966. It also reorganized the Caltex group in 1967, taking over one-half of the group's interest in 12 European countries that it had been serving from Saudi Arabia. This move allowed the company to expand its marketing operations in Europe, while leaving the Caltex companies free to concentrate east of the Suez Canal, where they enjoyed their greatest market penetration. Texaco brought its petrochemical business to Europe in 1966 with a plant in Ghent, Belgium, and to Japan three years later.

In the United States, Texaco expanded its interests by acquiring regional companies and increasing its refining capacity. The company strengthened its position on the East Coast by buying the Paragon group of companies in 1959 and the White Fuel Corporation in 1962. In 1962 it also acquired mineral rights to two million undeveloped acres in west Texas from the TXL Oil Corporation. The company's petrochemical production grew rapidly during this period, with the addition of a new unit at the Eagle Point works in 1960 and one of the world's largest benzene plants in Port Arthur in 1961. Texaco's operating volumes doubled between 1960 and 1970, with gross production surpassing three billion barrels per day in 1970.

Texaco's tremendous growth came to an abrupt halt in the 1970s. The Arab-Israeli War, the OPEC embargo, and the nationalization of foreign oil assets in many overseas nations cut Texaco's profit margins and endangered its sources of crude. Furthermore, federal price controls and mandatory allocation regulations restricted Texaco's ability to raise prices or withdraw from unprofitable markets. Its net income dropped from $1.6 billion in 1974 to $830.6 million a year later and remained at that level for the rest of the decade.

Tensions in the Middle East prompted a wave of nationalizations in the oil industry. In 1972 Saudi Arabia began to nationalize the assets of Aramco, in which Texaco owned a 50 percent interest, and took over all of its operations in 1980. Between 1973 and 1974 Libya nationalized the Texas Overseas Petroleum Company, a Texaco subsidiary. The decade ended with the Iranian revolution displacing Texaco's interests there and the Caltex group selling off part of its operations to the Bahrain government.

Texaco increased its exploration efforts and reorganized its marketing operations at home. Drilling activities increased both onshore and offshore in the southwest, as well as in new areas such as the North Sea and eastern Atlantic. The company also modernized its refineries in order to maximize the yield from each barrel of crude. Texaco made its most dramatic alterations in its retail network, abandoning the 50-state plan that had made it the United States's largest seller of oil. It began to withdraw from unprofitable markets, cutting operations in all or parts of 19 states in the Rocky Mountain, Midwest, and Great Lakes regions. It also reduced its number of service stations and opened more modern outlets in high-volume areas.

The 1980s began with the U.S. economy still suffering from recession, but the deregulation of the oil industry offered Texaco new flexibility in trying to recoup its fortunes. Under the direction of its new chairman, John K. McKinley, Texaco undertook a major restructuring plan in 1980. It decentralized its operations into three major geographic oil and gas divisions representing the United States, Europe and Latin America, and West Africa, as well as one worldwide chemical organization called the Texaco Chemical Company. The company expanded its exploration program and it also committed more resources to projects for developing alternative fuels, such as coal gasification and shale oil.

Retrenchment in its refining and marketing operations continued with the closing of six inefficient refineries by 1982 and the reduction of its retail outlets from 35,500 in 1974 to 27,000 in 1980. Texaco introduced a new logo in 1981, a red "T" inside a white star and red circle, to promote its high-volume System 2000 stations. These stations were a quick success, with more than 1,200 in the United States by 1987. The company also added a new operating division in 1982, Texaco Middle East/Far East, and made several important acquisitions to bolster its reserve base. By 1985 Texaco's net income was once again above $1 billion.

In the middle of this comeback, Texaco became involved in a legal battle. The 1984 purchase of the Getty Oil Company had promised to speed Texaco's recovery by adding an estimated 1.9 billion barrels of proven reserves to its assets. Pennzoil Company filed suit, however, claiming that Texaco had interfered with its plans to acquire three-sevenths of Getty's shares. In the resulting court case, a Texas State District Court in Houston ordered Texaco to pay Pennzoil $10.5 billion in damages. Arguing that important New York and Delaware state laws had been ignored in the case, Texaco obtained an injunction from a federal court in New York that temporarily halted the payment of damages while it appealed the decision.

In February 1987 the Texas Court of Appeals upheld the decision. In order to protect its assets while continuing its appeals, the company filed for protection under Chapter 11 of the United States Bankruptcy Code. Texaco spent most of 1987 in Chapter 11 while continuing its litigation. As a result, it incurred its first operating losses since the Great Depression, finishing the year $4.4 billion in the red. After the Texas Supreme Court refused to hear an appeal, New York financier Carl Icahn began buying Texaco's rapidly depreciating stock in an attempt to force it to settle with Pennzoil. A few weeks later Texaco agreed to pay Pennzoil $3 billion rather than appeal the decision to the Supreme Court, allowing it to begin planning for its emergence from Chapter 11.

However, Icahn continued to buy the company's stock, and in early 1988 he began a takeover bid. Texaco's board of directors had submitted a restructuring plan to the shareholders for meeting the company's debt obligations. Icahn favored, instead, the sale of the company. He launched the biggest proxy battle in business history when he tried to gain control of five seats on the board of directors, but he was ultimately defeated in a June 1988 shareholders' election. The board of directors then agreed to buy out Icahn's interest in Texaco.

With the Pennzoil case and the takeover attempt behind it, Texaco rebuilt its market position under the leadership of chairman and CEO James Kinnear by selling off assets and undertaking new joint ventures. From 1987 to 1989 it sold its operations in Germany and Canada, as well as fixed assets in the United States (including 2,500 gas stations) and the Middle East, raising $7 billion in the process. It also expanded drilling operations in the North Sea and offshore California, while continuing its exploration efforts in Asia, Africa, and South America.

In 1988 Texaco U.S.A. transferred approximately two-thirds of its refining and marketing operations to Star Enterprise, a joint venture established with Saudi Arabia's Aramco. Other moves have included the acquisition of Chevron's marketing operations in six European countries and the company's first commercial application of its coal gasification technology in an electric plant in the Los Angeles basin.

The recession of 1991–92 depressed demand for petroleum products and forced prices lower. As a result, Texaco's revenue dropped from $40.51 billion in 1990 to $37.16 billion in 1991 to $36.53 billion in 1992, while net income fell from $1.41 billion in 1990 to $1.29 billion in 1991 to $1.04 billion in 1992. By 1993, net income had improved to $1.07 billion, but revenue continued to fall, dropping to $34.07 billion. That same year Kinnear retired and was succeeded by Alfred C. DeCrane Jr.

Starting in 1993, DeCrane guided Texaco through yet another restructuring intended to improve its competitiveness. Like almost every other U.S. oil company going through restructuring at the time, Texaco reduced its work force. A cut of 2,500 workers, or eight percent, over a one-year period contributed to a $200 million reduction in overhead in 1994. DeCrane also wanted Texaco to focus on its core oil and gas operations, so he divested the company of its chemical business. In 1994 Texaco sold the Texaco Chemical Company to the Huntsman Corporation for $850 million. That year the company also sold more than 300 scattered, unprofitable oil- and gas-producing properties to Apache Corporation for $600 million.

With the funds generated through these moves, Texaco could now increase its budget for overseas exploration and production. Seeking to increase production by 125,000 barrels a day by the end of the decade, Texaco began to pursue opportunities in Russia, China, and Colombia. In order to minimize its exposure in such risky areas of operation as Russia, Texaco, like other oil companies, turned to joint ventures with its competitors. For instance, Texaco formed the Timan Pechora Company L.L.C. with Exxon, Amoco, and Norsk Hydro to negotiate a production-sharing agreement with Russia for the Timan Pechora Basin, which may hold more than two billion barrels of oil.

The much leaner Texaco of the mid-1990s had yet to return to its former prominence, but was in better shape than in many years. One positive sign was Texaco's reentry into the Canadian market in 1995 with its $30 million reacquisition of Texaco Canada Petroleum Inc. With the company committed to increasing its capital spending overseas from 45 percent of total capital spending to 55 percent by 1998, Texaco seemed determined to get its share of the oil available outside the United States. Whether that would be enough for Texaco to recapture its past glory in a decade of heated competition remained to be seen.

Principal Subsidiaries: Caltex Petroleum Corp. (50%); Four Star Oil & Gas Co.; Saudi Arabian Texaco Inc.; Star Enterprise (50%); TEPI Holdings Inc.; Texaco Cogeneration Co.; Texaco Exploration & Production Inc.; Texaco International Trader Inc.; Texaco Overseas Holdings Inc.; Texaco Pipeline Co.; Texaco Refining & Marketing Inc.; Texaco Trading & Transportation Inc.; TRMI Holdings Inc.; Texaco Brasil S.A. Produtos de Petroleo; Texaco Canada Petroleum Inc.; Texaco Denmark Inc.; Texaco Investments (Netherlands), Inc.; Texaco Overseas (Nigeria) Petroleum Co.; Texaco Panama Inc.; Texaco Britain Limited (U.K.); Texaco Limited (U.K.); Texaco North Sea U.K. Co.

Further Reading:

"Corporate Restructuring '90s Style: Merge and Purge, Lean and Mean," *National Petroleum News,* September 1994, pp. 16–18.

Folmer, L. W., *Reaching for a Star: Experiences in the International Oil Business,* Austin, Tex.: L. W. Folmer, 1993, 243 p.

James, Marquis, *The Texaco Story: The First Fifty Years 1902–1952,* New York: The Texas Company, 1953, 118 p.

Melcher, Richard A., Peter Burrows, and Tim Smart, "Remaking Big Oil: The Desperate Rush to Slash Costs," *Business Week,* August 8, 1994, pp. 20–21.

Petzinger, Thomas, *Oil & Honor: The Texaco-Pennzoil Wars,* New York: Putnam, 1987, 495 p.

Shannon, James, *Texaco and the $10 Billion Jury,* Englewood Cliffs, N.J.: Prentice Hall, 1988, 545 p.

Smart, Tim, "Pumping Up at Texaco," *Business Week,* June 7, 1993, pp. 112–113.

Texaco Today: The Spirit of the Star, 1902–1992, White Plains, N.Y.: Texaco Inc., 1992, 40 p.

Toal, Brian A., "The Man behind the Star," *Oil & Gas Investor,* February 1994, pp. 42–45.

—updated by David E. Salamie

Thomas J. Lipton Company

800 Sylvan Avenue
Englewood Cliffs, New Jersey 07632
U.S.A.
(201) 567-8000
Fax: (201) 894-7860

Wholly Owned Subsidary of Unilever United States
Incorporated: 1871
Employees: 5,000
Sales: $1.6 billion (estimated)
SICs: 2099 Food Preparations Not Elsewhere Classified

Thomas J. Lipton Company is the largest manufacturer of tea in the world. Lipton controlled about 50 percent of the U.S. brewed-tea market going into the mid-1990s and also held strong positions in markets for instant, fountain, and bottled tea products. Lipton, through various subsidiaries, is also involved in other food industries. It became the top North American manufacturer of ice cream novelty foods in the late 1980s, for example, and was the top seller of instant soup. Lipton was striving to become number one in all tea industry categories in the mid-1990s.

Thomas J. Lipton Company bears the name of its founder, an immigrant of Irish descent that sailed to the United States in 1865. Lipton's story is an intriguing rags-to-riches tale. The 15-year-old Lipton, who had fled his economically deprived homeland, arrived in New York with $8 in his pocket and not a friend on the continent. Had he arrived at almost any other time he might have found work in New York. However, the Civil War was just ending, war factories were closing down, and veterans were returning home to take any jobs that were available. Lipton walked the streets of New York for several days before he finally got an offer from an agent to go to work in the tobacco fields of war-ravaged Virginia.

For the next three or four years Lipton traveled up and down the eastern seaboard and the Mississippi River chasing any job that became available. Among other engagements, he worked in the South Carolina rice fields, as a carman outside New Orleans, as a plantation bookkeeper, and even as a firefighter in Charleston, South Carolina. Lipton returned to New York periodically to look for work, but inevitably was forced back to the depressed South, where labor was scarce. A vagabond with few friends, Lipton spent several difficult years trying to find steady, lucra-tive employment. His face was slashed by a crazed, knife-wielding Spaniard in the Carolinas, and once he stowed away on a coastal steamer when he did not have the fare to pay for the trip. Perhaps the greatest respite from his travails was when the proprietor of a plantation for which he worked took him into his home to be cared for by his wife. The employer only took him in, however, because an ugly hatchet accident severely damaged Lipton's foot.

Lipton finally did land a job in New York—as a department store clerk. He worked there for a year before returning to Scotland to go to work in his fathers Glasgow shop. He quickly became frustrated with his father's business practices, which he considered archaic compared to what he had witnessed in New York. So, in 1871, at the age of 21, Lipton invested his small savings in his own store. A few years later he opened a second shop. For the next several years Lipton worked tirelessly to build his business into a small empire. Lipton's mix of salesmanship, financial discipline, and determination helped him to accomplish more than many people thought was possible for a young man from such a common background. Within ten years Lipton was operating a chain of 20 profitable grocery stores.

Lipton's stores became well known in the area as much for their service and selection as for Lipton's promotionals. Indeed, Lipton continually employed a battery of marketing gimmicks that generated a loyal customer base for his stores. In 1881, in an effort that examples his flair for showmanship, Lipton imported, displayed, and sold the largest cheese that had ever been made. The "Jumbo" cheese consumed the milk of eight hundred cows and the labor of two hundred dairymaids. It was wheeled from the dock and down streets lined with cheering spectators. Right before Christmas, Lipton hit upon the idea of inserting gold coins into the cheese. When the cheese was cut up on Christmas Eve a police squad had to be called to control the crowd. Within two hours every ounce of the mammoth cheese had been sold. Giant cheeses subsequently became a fixture at Lipton's stores during the Christmas season.

In the 1880s Lipton's spiraling food business grew to more than 200 stores and Lipton became a multimillionaire. The adventurous Lipton became less involved in day-to-day management and instead began traveling abroad searching for new items to stock in his stores, and to quell his desire for travel. Tea became hugely popular in England during the 1880s, largely the result of an influx of inexpensive tea from India. Demand had grown to 40 million pounds by the late 1870s before doubling by the mid-1880s. Tea brokers in London had been pressing Lipton to stock their chests of tea in his food stores, but Lipton had resisted. When he finally decided to start selling tea, Lipton wanted to travel abroad and find his own tea supply, rather than relying on middlemen. He went to India in 1890 to peruse the tea plantations, initiating an important new chapter in his life.

Tea was selling for 50 cents per pound in 1890, which Lipton believed was too high a price for the working-class family. He believed that he could grow and sell tea himself for about 30 cents and still make a hefty profit simply by cutting out the middleman. By doing so, he would open the tea market up to a much broader spectrum of the population. Lipton also devised a clever marketing scheme to sell the tea. At the time, tea was sold out of large chests and weighed out for the customers. Buyers often had no way of knowing if the tea was fresh, or if the seller was giving them the proper amount. Lipton decided to sell tea in packets by the pound, half pound, and quarter pound. Besides being fresher, the tea would be easier to handle and more marketable in colorful, neat packaging. He even created an advertising slogan before he actually got into the tea business: ''Direct from the tea gardens to the teapot.''

The Lipton name would eventually become nearly synonymous with tea in the Western world. Interestingly, Lipton was a 40-year-old, self-made millionaire before he ever sold an ounce of the stuff. He initially got into the tea business as a sideline to his food retailing business, which by the early 1890s incorporated more than 300 stores. He quickly realized, though, that he had vastly underestimated the demand for his low-cost, packaged teas. Lipton seized the opportunity that lay before him. Instead of simply enjoying big demand for his tea, moreover, he aggressively marketed ''Lipton's Tea'' back in England with street parades, posters, Indian's marching through the streets, and signs perched on trains and buses. Sales mushroomed. Lipton's Glasgow warehouses were overrun, so he quickly moved his headquarters to London. Cash poured in so fast that Lipton lost track of how much money he had. Within a few short years the Lipton name had been transformed from a well-known store chain to a household icon.

By the late 1890s India was shipping a huge 120 million tons of tea annually. As demand boomed, Lipton's tea operations rocketed and quickly dwarfed the sales and profits gleaned from the Lipton grocery stores. Lipton was operating five tea plantations by the mid-1890s, but demand was simply too great, forcing him to open other plantations. By the early 1900s Lipton's tea empire had become vast, with stockyards not only in Europe but also in North America. In the United States, in fact, Lipton had returned victorious. He owned valuable properties in New York, as well as in other parts of the country, and even became an acclaimed public figure—He eventually returned to live in the United States for several years during the late 1910s. Meanwhile, back in England, Lipton became associated with several members of the Royal family, was knighted, and established himself as an international figure.

Lipton went public with its first stock offering in 1897. People clamored to buy into the now-public company. Lipton posted a profit of about £176,000 that year. As his business empire continued to grow, Lipton became active in other interests, particularly yachting. In fact, Lipton became as well known as a yachting enthusiast in many areas of the world as he was a businessman. He raced for the America's Cup and sailed in races throughout the world, all the while keeping an eye on his flourishing tea interests. Despite setbacks at the beginning and during World War I, Lipton survived and even prospered during the early 1920s. Unfortunately, Lipton's luck began to turn in the mid-1920s. The directors of his company forced him out of control when he was 76 years old, assigning him the figurehead title of ''Life President and Chairman.''

Lipton was obviously dissatisfied with the arrangement. He eventually agreed to remove himself from the company for a fee of $4 million—He reportedly signed the abdication papers in the stateroom of his beloved Shamrock yacht. Most of his remaining years were devoted to his second love: sailing. Lip-

ton was remembered as a ruthless, savvy, disciplined businessman and showman. He had almost no tolerance for imperfection and could be harsh. However, he also had a huge soft spot in his heart for the weak and disadvantaged, as evidenced by numerous charitable acts and gifts throughout his career. The demise of his tea empire was credited to Lipton's lack of perspective later in life. Lipton had become out of sync with the modern business world and had made several uncharacteristically poor judgments. He had also become paranoid, installing microphones in the furniture at his home to eavesdrop on guests and business associates, for example.

During the late 1920s and early 1930s, Lipton's new management team scrambled to reorganize the bloated tea and food company. Although the organization remained sound at its core, it needed to eliminate unnecessary operations and consolidate offices and divisions into a more cohesive whole. By 1930, earlier than most investors had expected, the company had returned to profitability and was even paying dividends on its shares. Lipton continued to post gains throughout much of the 1930s and 1940s, despite turbulence caused by economic problems and World War II. During those decades Lipton retained its status as a dominant supplier of bagged tea to the United States, northern Europe, and other parts of the world. Rampant growth in tea consumption, though, had long since stalled, and Lipton was forced to do battle in an increasingly competitive industry.

Following World War II, Lipton's tea operations became more focused on the U.S. market. Indeed, despite the proliferation of coffee, tea sales to the United States outstripped shipments to England as the U.S. population and economy soared during the post-war boom. Lipton changed ownership during the mid-1900s, and the company's headquarters were eventually moved to the United States. When growth in tea markets began to slow, Lipton branched out into a number of new food and beverage products. Importantly, the development of instant tea opened an entirely new market for Lipton. Similarly, Lipton developed a highly successful line of dried instant soups—Cup O' Soup—which came in packets and could simply be added to hot water. Lipton also introduced a line of gourmet teas and foods dubbed the Sir Thomas Lipton Collection.

Lipton's enterprising adaptation to shifting tea and beverage markets during the mid-1900s allowed it to post solid, steady gains. Indeed, between the early 1950s and the early 1980s Lipton enjoyed an unblemished record of revenue and profit growth—Much of that time was spent as a subsidiary of the multi-billion-dollar Anglo-Dutch Unilever NV. By the early 1980s, though, competition in Lipton's traditional markets was under attack from other established food and beverage companies. To keep pace with intensifying competition, Lipton stepped up efforts to diversify by adding a wide array of juices, tea drinks, sweeteners, salad dressings—Lipton owned the venerable Wish-Bone salad dressing brand name, for example—and other goods. Meanwhile, Lipton continued to dominate the tea industry. As the only major producer of both bagged and instant teas, Lipton controlled about 50 percent of the North American tea market.

Lipton went into the mid-1980s with roughly $1 billion in annual sales, about half of which were attributable to tea and soup sales. Throughout the decade the company continued to experiment with new food and beverage products and to cement its dominance of the tea and instant soup segment. To that end, Lipton posted healthy gains in the fast-growing instant tea industry by conducting a multimillion-dollar marketing blitz. Going into 1987 Lipton was serving 13 percent of the entire North American soup market, including both wet and dry soup products. Also in the late 1980s, Lipton became the largest manufacturer of frozen novelty products in the United States when it purchased the Popsicle and Disney brand frozen treat lines. In the early 1990s, moreover, Lipton bought out Klondike ice cream. That purchase helped push Lipton's overall revenue base to a whopping $1.4 billion in 1991.

During the early 1990s and going into the mid-1990s, Lipton was benefiting not only from its increasingly diversified food and beverage lines, but also from renewed growth in the tea industry. Driving growth in Lipton's core product line was demand for ready-to-drink fountain, canned, and bottled teas, and for gourmet bagged teas. Lipton introduced new products for both growing segments during the early 1990s and proclaimed its intent to command the surging ready-to-drink tea industry. To that end, Lipton teamed up with Pepsi to offer

seven bottled teas, three canned teas, and four fountain tea drinks. Lipton entered 1995 as the U.S. leader in novelty ice cream and instant soup industries and as a top seller of salad dressings, snacks, seasonings, gelatin products, and various side dishes. As it had since near the turn of the century, Lipton also dominated the global tea industry.

Principal Subsidiaries: Lawry's Foods; Gold Bond Ice Cream.

Further Reading:

Barns, Lawrence, "Lipton Goes on the Offensive," *Business Week,* September 5, 1983, pp. 102–3.
DeMarrais, Kevin G., "Lipton Adds to Ice Cream Empire: Buying Klondike and Popsicle Unit," *Record,* November 24, 1992, Section BUS.
Fannin, Rebecca, "From Soup to Soup," *Marketing & Media Decisions,* March 1986, pp. 60–64.
Kelley, Kristine Portnoy, "Lipton's Cup of Tea," *Beverage Industry,* June 1993, p. 46.
Sather, Jeanne, "Coffee-Crazed 1990s Are Tea Time for Seattle Firm," *Puget Sound Business Journal,* October 14, 1994, p. 14.

—Dave Mote

Thomas Nelson Inc.

Nelson Place at Elm Hill Pike
P.O. Box 141000
Nashville Tennessee 37214-1000
U.S.A.
(615) 889-9000

Public Company
Incorporated: 1961 as Royal Publishers Inc.
Sales: $265.1 million
Employees: 1,000
Stock Exchanges: New York
SICs: 2731 Book Publishing; 5112 Stationery and Office
Supplies

Thomas Nelson Inc. is the world's largest publisher of Bibles
and Bible-related materials. It also operates a large Christian
music recording label, makes gift products, and runs several
radio stations.

Thomas Nelson of Edinburgh, Scotland, founded Thomas Nelson and Sons when he published ''The Pilgrim's Progress'' in
1798. His son perfected the rotary press in 1850, and in 1854 the
firm opened a U.S. office in New York City. In 1885 it published
an English revision of the Kind James Version of the Bible. In
1901 it published the American Standard Version of the Bible.
With sales of the Bible central to its business, the firm built a
Bible bindery in 1946 in Camden, New Jersey. In 1952 Thomas
Nelson published a Revised Standard Version of the Bible.

A man important to the future of Thomas Nelson began selling
Bibles door-to-door while studying economics at the University
of South Carolina in the 1950s. A Christian Lebanese immigrant to the United States, Sam Moore went on to work at Chase
Manhattan Bank for a couple of years. However, he left the
bank to begin his own Bible-selling company called Royal
Publishers, Inc. in Nashville in 1959. He raised capital and used
it to buy Bibles and to hire college students whom he trained in
door-to-door selling methods.

Once his firm expanded out of the Nashville area, Moore began
publishing Bibles himself. In 1961 he took Royal public. The
firm prospered and began to gain attention in the world of
religious publishing. In 1969 a major opportunity presented
itself when British interdenominational Bible publisher Thomas
Nelson and Sons approached him about running its U.S. opera-

tions. Instead, Royal Publishing bought them. The $2.6 million
purchase price included the Nelson name, its Bible printing
plates, and its U.S. distribution network. The firm did not have a
printing plant, and Moore continued his practice of contracting
out print jobs.

The purchase of Thomas Nelson and Sons made Moore's firm,
now called Thomas Nelson, Inc., the largest Bible-publishing
company in the United States. In 1976 the firm published the
Bicentennial Almanac, which sold 600,000 copies at $20 each.
In 1978 it built a new distribution center in Nashville. In the
mid-1970s Moore spent $4 million having 150 scholars revise
the Bible. In 1982 this revision project resulted in the New King
James Version of the Bible, which sold so well that it made
Thomas Nelson the largest Bible-publishing company in the
world. Its principal market was a growing network of Christian
bookstores throughout the United States.

In 1983 the firm won an important new author when Moore
persuaded Robert H. Schuller, already known for his books and
television preaching, to let Thomas Nelson publish his next book,
Tough Times Never Last, but Tough People Do! Moore shuttled
Schuller around on a private jet during a three-week book-signing
tour, arranged for publicity in local papers, and helped the book
become a bestseller. It eventually sold over 500,000 hardcover
copies, many of them out of secular bookstores.

Also in 1983 Thomas Nelson bought a 240,000-square-foot
bindery and printing press located near Kansas City, Kansas.
Moore felt Thomas Nelson could print its own Bibles and
increase its profits. Given its success in religious publishing, the
firm decided to diversify into the secular publishing market as
well. Nelson paid $2 million for New York publisher Dodd,
Mead & Co., which owned the U.S. rights to Agatha Christie's
67 mystery novels and other properties. Both of these acquisitions proved to be mistakes. The U.S. dollar soared in value in
1984 and 1985, making printing inexpensive overseas. Nelson's
competitors printed Bibles in Britain and the Far East and
inundated the United States with Bibles selling at prices that
Thomas Nelson could not match. In addition, the New York
publishing business proved very different than publishing in
Nashville, and Nelson management soon realized that they did
not know how to succeed as a secular New York publisher. The
firm lost $5.4 million in 1986 on sales of $72 million and
amassed $40 million in debt.

The firm laid off about half of its work force of 600. It sold
Dodd, Mead and its printing plant and went back to contracting
out its printing. The moves saved the company, and by 1988 it
was profitable again. It again looked to diversify, but this time it
stayed closer to home. The firm realized that the Christian
bookstores it sold its Bibles to made about half of their money
from selling photo albums, prayer journals, and other gift items,
as well as from cassettes of Christian music. Thomas Nelson
quickly moved into these markets. Early tapes included Barbra
Streisand singing Christmas carols and Johnny Cash reading the
Bible. Although Nelson's products were similar to those of its
rivals, who had a head start in this market, the firm got its
products into stores because of its relationships with the bookstores' buyers—and because it offered steeper discounts than
its competitors. Gift and music sales only totaled $1.4 million in
1989, but they quickly grew, reaching $8 million in 1990.

Thomas Nelson earned $4.3 million in 1990 on sales of $74 million. By 1991 the firm had sold more than 22 million copies of its New King James Version, and had reduced its debt to $12.5 million. In late 1992, Thomas Nelson bought Word, Inc., a gospel music and inspirational book publishing company previously owned by Capital Cities/ABC, for $72 million in cash. The purchase virtually doubled the size of the company. It strengthened Nelson's music business by bringing it several successful singers, including Grammy winner Amy Grant. Nelson's book business benefited from the addition of bestselling authors Billy Graham and Pat Robertson. Just as importantly, Word's distribution complemented Nelson's. Word sold well internationally and had a strong direct marketing presence. The purchase left the firm with only one serious competitor in Christian book publishing, Zonderban Publishing House, owned by Rupert Murdoch's News Corp.

With "traditional values" and Christianity increasingly visible and powerful in the United States, Thomas Nelson felt it could now sell large numbers of its products in the mainstream mass market. Nelson had already gotten its King James Bibles into Wal-Mart and Kmart, and, with the acquisition of Word and the growth of Christian music, the firm was now able to get other products into the mass market. It began by convincing retailers to increase their offering of religious goods, such as Christian-themed children's books and Bibles, during the Christmas season. When these offerings proved successful, the stores gradually added Christian pop music, card games, and calendars. In January 1995, Thomas Nelson began showing a 4.5 minute promotional video in 440 Sam's Club stores. In it, Christian author and preacher Max Lucado advertised "A Time with God," a book, audio, and video package containing Bible verses accompanied by music by Thomas Nelson's music talent. This strategy proved successful; by 1995 Wal-Mart had expanded its Christian product line in 300 of its 2,100 stores.

Despite the pop-styling of most contemporary Christian music and the increased visibility of Christian issues in the United States, few mainstream radio stations would play Christian music. To get around this limit on its exposure, Thomas Nelson decided to build its own broadcast business. In 1994 it bought the Morningstar radio network in Texas, whose 39 stations had already been playing a lot of Christian music. Within a year, Thomas Nelson expanded the network to 105 affiliates and announced plans to enlarge it further. Perhaps aided by this radio exposure, consumer demand for Christian music continued to increase. In the mid-1990s, Blockbuster Entertainment Corp. stores doubled the shelf space they devoted to Christian cassettes and compact discs. By 1995, over a quarter of Christian music was sold through secular stores. Thomas Nelson hoped to sell half of its Christian music through secular retailers, though some industry analysts believed the genre would never achieve that kind of widespread popularity.

In 1994 Thomas Nelson bought Pretty Paper Inc. for 115,000 shares of common stock. Pretty Paper, which had sales of $5.6 million for 1993, became a wholly owned subsidiary. The purchase strengthened the company's line of gift items and its gift-item distribution network. Among other products, Pretty brought two collections of gift stationery, "Out in the Country" and "Potting Shed," both of which sold strongly. Thomas Nelson also sold gift products based on licensed cartoon characters from Looney Tunes and Paddington Bear.

With sales moving forward on all fronts, the firm made $11.7 million in 1995 on sales of $265.1 million. That year Nelson and Word published 11 books that made it to the top-20 Christian Booksellers Association Hardbound Bestsellers' List, more than any other publisher. The growth of Christian publishing had created entire new genres, such as the Christian thriller, in which characters underwent personal transformations without the sex and violence found in most mainstream thrillers. In 1995, Word sold hundreds of thousands of copies of such books by Pat Robertson and Charles Colson.

Thomas Nelson founded a new division called Royal Media, which included the Morningstar Radio Network and the Royal Magazine Group. The magazine group published four magazines: *Aspire,* which covered lifestyle issues and celebrities and was sold on newsstands; *A Better Tomorrow,* which was geared toward older readers; *Release,* which covered Christian recording artists and targeted those working in the Christian music industry; and *Release Ink,* which did the same for the Christian book industry. The Morningstar Radio Network had grown to 138 stations in 130 cities. Its digital programming was delivered by satellite 24 hours a day and consisted of two programming formats: adult contemporary Christian music and what the firm called "High Country." Nelson announced that it was considering a move into cable TV as well.

The firm's record and music division continued to expand, reaching sales of $89.7 million in 1995. Thomas Nelson acquired the Marantha! Music catalog of printed and recorded music products and signed a long-term agreement with Marantha covering future product development. Marantha specialized in a sub-genre called "praise and worship music" in which Thomas Nelson formerly had a weak presence. Despite its successful diversifications, Thomas Nelson continued to depend on the Bible as the mainstay of the company's offerings; in 1995 Thomas Nelson published more than 1,200 different Bibles and Bible-related products.

Principal Subsidiaries: Word, Inc.; Pretty Paper Company, Inc.

Further Reading:

Chithelen, Ignatius, "A Brush with the Devil," *Forbes,* August 19, 1991, pp. 61–62.
Rotenier, Nancy, "The Gospel According to Sam Moore," *Forbes,* April 12, 1993, pp. 122–23.
Sharpe, Anita, "Heavenly Niche," *Wall Street Journal,* February 6, 1995, pp. A1, A5.

—Scott M. Lewis

TIFFANY & CO.

Tiffany & Co.

727 Fifth Avenue
New York, New York 10022
U.S.A.
(212) 755-8000
Fax: (212) 605-4465

Public Company
Incorporated: 1868
Sales: $682.6 million
Employees: 3,306
Stock Exchanges: New York Chicago Pacific
SICs: 3229 Pressed & Blown Glass & Glassware, Nec; 3873
   Watches, Clocks, Clockwork Operated Devices & Parts;
   3911 Jewelry, Precious Metal; 5094 Jewelry, Watches,
   Precious Stones & Precious Metals; 5944 Jewelry Stores;
   5947 Gift, Novelty & Souvenir Shops

Tiffany & Co. has long been renowned for its luxury goods, especially jewelry, and has sought to market itself as an arbiter of taste and style. Tiffany's designs, manufactures, and sells jewelry, watches, and crystal glassware. It also sells other timepieces, sterling silverware, china, stationery, writing instruments, fragrances, leather goods, scarves, and ties. Many of these products are sold under the Tiffany name, at Tiffany stores throughout the world as well as through direct-mail and corporate merchandising. Goods are also sold wholesale to third-party distributors. Jewelry accounted for two-thirds of Tiffany's sales volume in fiscal year 1994.

In 1837 Charles Lewis Tiffany and John F. Young opened Tiffany & Young, with $1,000 in backing from Tiffany's father. Located on Broadway opposite Manhattan's City Hall Park, this store sold stationery and a variety of "fancy goods," including costume jewelry. Unlike other stores of the time, Tiffany featured plainly marked prices that were strictly adhered to, sparing the customer the usual practice of haggling with the proprietor. Tiffany also departed from the norm by insisting on cash payment rather than extending credit or accepting barter.

In 1841 Tiffany and Young took on another partner, J. L. Ellis, and the store became Tiffany, Young & Ellis. By 1845 the store was successful enough to discontinue paste and begin selling real jewelry, as well as the city's most complete line of stationery. Silverware was added in 1847. In addition to these main items, Tiffany's also sold watches and clocks, a variety of ornaments and bronzes, perfumes, preparations for the skin and hair, dinner sets, cuspidors, moccasins, belts, and numerous other sundries, including Chinese bric-a-brac and horse and dog whips.

The new partner's capital enabled Young to go to Paris as a buyer, and he later established a branch store there. When the French monarchy was overthrown in 1848, Young purchased some of the crown jewels and also a bejeweled corset reputed to belong to Marie Antoinette. A shrewd publicist, Tiffany was quick to exploit this coup. He teamed up with P. T. Barnum, to their mutual profit, on a number of ventures and presented a gem-studded miniature silver-filigree horse and carriage as a wedding present to Tom Thumb and his bride. He introduced sterling silver to the United States in 1852, a year after contracting John C. Moore to produce silverware exclusively for Tiffany's. In 1853 he bought out his partners, and the firm became Tiffany & Co.

Tiffany's was an emporium for military supplies during the Civil War, producing swords and importing rifles and ammunition. During the Gilded Age that followed, its main problem was not selling jewelry but finding enough to satisfy the demand. By then it also had established dominance over the American silverware market. In 1868 a London branch store was added and Tiffany & Co. was incorporated, with its proprietor as president and treasurer. Also in that year, Moore's workshop became part of the firm. The store, which had been inching uptown with the city itself, moved into a newly constructed, company-owned building adjoining Union Square in 1870.

Tiffany's prestige reached a new level when it won the gold medal for jewelry and grand prize for silverware at the Paris Exposition in 1878. Soon it was serving as a jeweler, goldsmith, and silversmith to most of the crowned heads of Europe. Its real clientele, however, came from the burgeoning ranks of America's wealthy, many with far more cash than taste. Tiffany's accommodated them all, no matter how ostentatious or whimsical their desires. The height (or depth) of vulgarity was reached when Diamond Jim Brady ordered, and Tiffany's duly produced, a solid gold chamber pot for Lillian Russell, with an eye peering up in the center of the bottom. It was estimated in 1887 that Tiffany's vaults held $40 million in precious stones. Among these was the largest flawless and perfectly colored canary diamond ever mined. This 128.5-carat "Tiffany Diamond," still held by the New York store, has been valued by the company at $22 million.

In 1894 a factory was established in New Jersey in Forest Hill, which was later annexed by Newark, for the manufacture of silverware, stationery, and leather goods. Charles Tiffany died in 1902, leaving an estate estimated at $35 million. He was the only Tiffany to run the company. Louis Comfort Tiffany, his eldest son to survive childhood, was an accomplished artist who sometimes made jewelry for Tiffany's but was best known for his Art Nouveau stained glass windows and lamps. In 1905 the store had moved into quarters at Fifth Avenue and 37th Street designed by Stanford White in the form of a Venetian palazzo, and two years later John C. Moore, great-grandson of the silversmith, became president.

Tiffany's sales volume rose from $7 million in 1914 to $17.7 million in 1919. This figure was seldom if ever matched during the 1920s, but profits remained high and dividends steadily. A share of stock bought in 1913 for $600 was worth the same in 1929, but split five-for-one in 1920 and also earned close to $10,000 in dividends over that period.

Even the rich cut back on luxury goods after the 1929 stock market crash. Tiffany's sales fell 45 percent to $8.4 million in 1930, dropped another 37 percent to $5.4 million in 1931, and yet another 45 percent to a rock bottom $2.9 million in 1932, when the federal government imposed an additional ten percent on the excise tax for jewelry. There were staff layoffs in 1933, 1934, 1935, 1938, and 1939. The company lost about $1 million a year throughout the decade, but, dipping into its capital reserve, never stopped paying a dividend, although it fell to $5 a share in 1940. In that year $3.6 million had to be taken from the reserve just to stay in business, and the London store was closed.

Also in 1940, Tiffany's moved uptown for the sixth and last time, to the southeast corner of Fifth Avenue and 57th Street, where it put up a $2.5 million Art Deco seven-story building. It was the first completely air-conditioned building in New York. Louis de B. Moore succeeded his father as president in that year. During World War II the Newark factory (which had made surgical instruments during World War I) was chiefly given over to military production. It made precision parts for anti-aircraft guns (which it made again during the Korean War) and fitting blocks for airplanes.

Tiffany's fortunes revived somewhat in this period, but in 1949 earnings came to only $19,368. Net profits were a mere $14,787 in 1952, when the Paris store was closed, and $24,906 in 1953. The company's $7 million in 1955 sales was no more than it had taken in during 1914. Conservative management and outdated styles were blamed by restive shareholders. One of these was Harry Maidman, a realtor attracted mainly by Tiffany's long-term lease to the land under its prime-location building. He quietly bought up at least 30 percent of the stock. Denied a seat on the board of directors, Maidman sold his shares in 1955 to the Bulova Watch Co. To prevent Bulova from taking control, Tiffany heirs and close associates sold Hoving Corp., owner of neighboring Bonwit Teller, 51 percent of the stock for $3.8 million.

Walter Hoving, who soon became chairman and chief executive officer of Tiffany's, had to report to the General Shoe Corp. (later Genesco, Inc.), which took a majority share of his own company in 1956. He did not win firm control of the store until 1961, when he assembled a group of investors that bought out Genesco and Bulova. Nevertheless, Hoving immediately put his stamp on Tiffany's by conducting the first bargain sale in the firm's history to clear out merchandise he considered gaudy or vulgar. He dropped diamond rings for men for that reason and discontinued leather goods, antiques, silver plate, brass, and pewter as not worthy of Tiffany's attention.

Hoving recruited a galaxy of stars to create a new standard of quality for Tiffany's products. Jean Schlumberger was hired to design its finest and most expensive jewelry. Henry Platt expanded the jewelry workshop's staff from eight to sixty, and later enlisted Elsa Peretti, Angela Cummings, and Paloma Picasso to create jewelry exclusively for Tiffany's. Van Day Treux, the new design director, revived vermeil (gold-plated sterling silver) and old patterns of silver flatware and commis-

sioned new china. Gene Moore, put to work dressing the store's windows, spent nearly 40 years creating striking and often provocative displays.

"Aesthetics," Hoving pronounced, "if properly understood, will almost always increase sales." To broaden the base of its clientele, the store added high-quality but lower-priced goods such as silver key rings for $3.50. By the early 1960s a third of the store's patrons were living 100 miles or more away. One of the firm's many longtime sales clerks said, "It's gotten so there are customers here whose names I don't even know." A San Francisco store was added in 1963, and branches in Chicago, Houston, Beverly Hills, and Atlanta soon followed.

The balance sheet reflected Tiffany's turnaround. Annual sales reached $21.9 million in fiscal year 1966 (ending January 31, 1967). Net profits rose every year, from $173,612 in 1955 to $1.7 million in 1966. That year about 65 percent of Tiffany's volume came from jewelry, 18 percent from silver, 14 percent from china and glassware, and the remaining three percent from stationery (engraved, not printed) and specialty items. The company made all its diamond jewelry and a small part of its gold jewelry in the Fifth Avenue store itself. Virtually all of it was designed by the staff. Nearly all of its sterling silver (carried by 150 franchised dealers as well as Tiffany stores) also was staff-designed, and 85 percent was being manufactured in the Newark plant. China and glassware were being made to company specifications. Tiffany's catalog (free until 1972) was the first major catalog entirely in color.

Business continued to grow in the 1970s. Sales increased from $23 million in 1970 to $35.2 million in 1974. Net income passed the $1 million mark in 1972 and reached $2.1 million the following year. In November 1978 Tiffany & Co. was sold to Avon Products Inc., the world's leading manufacturer and distributor of cosmetics and costume jewelry, for about $104 million in stock. Tiffany's sales had reached $60.2 million and net profits about $4 million in the previous fiscal year. Hoving remained chairman and chief executive officer until the end of 1980, when he retired.

Avon spent $53 million (raising some of it by selling some of its inventory of uncut diamonds) to open Tiffany stores in Dallas and Kansas City, expand its direct mail orders, introduce Tiffany credit cards, and streamline and computerize its back-office operations. But its ratio of operating profits to revenue fell from 17.6 percent to 6.5 percent between 1979 and 1983, mainly because it tried to compete with department stores in selling low-margin watches, china, and glassware. A 1984 Newsweek article noted that the Fifth Avenue store had stocked so many inexpensive items that it began looking like Macy's during a white sale, and that customers had complained about declining quality and service. In August 1984 Avon agreed to sell Tiffany to an investor group led by its chairman, William R. Chaney, for $135.5 million in cash. The company had earned only $984,000 in 1983 on sales of $124.2 million.

Under its new management Tiffany & Co. shifted direction again. It sought to reassure the affluent but socially insecure patron that Tiffany's taste remained "safe." The firm also cut costs by closing the Newark plant and its Kansas City store, cutting staff, and embarking on a program to wholesale its jewelry and silverware and the line of leather products that had been restored under Avon's management. Tiffany's lost $5.1 million in 1984 and $2.6 million in 1985, mainly because of heavy interest costs on borrowing to pay off Avon, but in 1986 it earned $6.7 million on net sales of $182.5 million, despite paying out $9.1 million for interest on its debt. During 1987 it earned $16.8 million on net sales of $230.5 million.

Tiffany's went public again in 1987, raising about $103.5 million by selling 4.5 million shares of common stock. About $43 million of this sum was earmarked to retire nearly all of the company's outstanding debt. The new public company no longer owned the Fifth Avenue building nor the land beneath it, which it had purchased for $2.8 million in 1963. (The air rights over the building had been sold in 1979 to Donald Trump, owner of neighboring Trump Tower, for $5 million.)

"Tiffany," a fragrance, was introduced in 1987 at $220 an ounce and marketed by department stores across the country. Wool and silk scarves were introduced the same year, shortly after neckties had been added and its line of handbags, evening purses, wallets, and briefcases expanded. A London store was reintroduced in 1986 and stores in Munich and Zurich opened in 1987 and 1988, respectively. Emphasizing its glitter, Tiffany's in 1988 displayed in five of its stores a collection of 22 individual pieces of jewelry made in its own workshop and valued at more than $10 million. All but one piece was sold. Paradoxically, perhaps, but profitably, Tiffany's emphasis on luxury drew in the masses; as many as 25,000 people visited the store on a Saturday during the holiday season.

Tiffany's catalog mailings reached 15 million in 1994. These publications were seen as a powerful sales and image tools for the stores as well as a source of profit in themselves. The company's direct-marketing effort also included business-to-business sales, which included a corporate gift catalog each year. Corporate customers purchased Tiffany products for business gift giving, employee service and achievement recognition awards, customer incentives, and other purposes.

The Far East played an important role in Tiffany's resurgence. Mitsukoshi Ltd., the "Bloomingdale's of Japan," which began stocking Tiffany items in its department stores and smaller shops in 1972, accounted for $26.5 million of Tiffany's $290 million in sales in 1988. Mitsukoshi bought ten percent of Tiffany's stock in 1989 to increase its earlier three percent stake. Tiffany's opened two stores in Hong Kong during 1988 and 1989, a third in Taiwan in 1990, and a fourth in Singapore in 1991.

Tiffany's suffered a serious setback in 1992 when sales to Mitsukoshi fell 35 percent, from an estimated $113 million in 1991. Hurt by a recession, Japanese consumers had cut back spending, catching the retailer with more inventory than it needed. In 1993 Tiffany's assumed direct responsibility for sales, merchandising, and marketing at Mitsukoshi's 29 Tiffany boutiques, taking a $32.7 million after-tax charge to buy them and run them on its own. This restructuring was largely responsible for a $10.2 million loss in 1993 despite sales of $566.5 million, a 16 percent gain. In spite of the setback, Tiffany's ranked sixth out of 28 public specialty retailers in return on

equity from 1989 to 1993, averaging an annual 18.8 percent over this period.

Also in 1992 the company, affected by curbed spending during the 1990–91 recession in the United States, again began to emphasize mass merchandising. A new information campaign stressed that the average Tiffany's purchase was under $200 and that diamond engagement rings started at only $850. It sent "How to Buy a Diamond" brochures to 40,000 people who called a toll-free number. To keep the company from losing its cachet, however, it continued to maintain its high-style image through books on Tiffany objects and in-store table setting displays. Avoiding calling Tiffany's a luxury-goods firm, Chaney described it as "a design-led business offering quality products at competitive prices."

During fiscal 1994 Tiffany's net sales rose to $682.8 million, of which U.S. retail accounted for 45 percent, international retail 41 percent (up from 32 percent two years earlier), and direct marketing 14 percent. (Despite this breakdown, "retail" also included wholesale sales.) Net income rebounded to $29.3 million. Long-term debt was $101.5 million at the end of 1994.

In mid-1995 Tiffany's was leasing 18 retail stores in the United States and was completing two more, in Short Hills, New Jersey, and Chevy Chase, Maryland. Another 11 were abroad. Tiffany's was also operating Faraone stores in Milan and Florence, many boutiques in Japanese stores, and one in Taiwan. Other parties operated four Tiffany boutiques in South Korea and one each in the Philippines, Abu Dhabi, Taiwan, Hong Kong, Hawaii, and Guam. Four Faraone boutiques were in Japanese department stores.

Of merchandise offered for sale by Tiffany's in fiscal 1994, 26 percent was produced by the company itself. Finished jewelry was produced in Tiffany's own workshop and also purchased from more than 100 manufacturers. The company acquired Howard H. Sweet & Son, Inc., a manufacturer of gold and silver jewelry and chains in fiscal 1989, and McTeigue & Co., a manufacturer of gold jewelry, in fiscal 1990. Cut and polished diamonds were being purchased from a number of sources. Diamond jewelry accounted for about 22 percent of Tiffany's net sales in fiscal 1994.

A single manufacturer produced Tiffany's silver flatware patterns from Tiffany's proprietary dies by use of its traditional manufacturing techniques. Likewise, engraved stationery was being purchased from a single manufacturer. A Paris workshop decorating hand-painted tableware was acquired in fiscal 1991. In the same year Tiffany's established a watch assembly, engineering, and testing operation in Lussy-sur-Morges, Switzerland. The following year the company acquired Judel Glassware Co., Inc., producer of crystal glassware in Salem, West Virginia. A distribution facility was being leased in Parsippany, New Jersey, and additional warehouse space in adjacent Pine Brook, New Jersey.

Principal Subsidiaries: Glassware Acquisition Inc.; Societe Francaise pour le Developpement de la Porcelaine d'Art S.A.R.L. (France); Tiffany and Co.; Tiffany & Co. (U.K.); Tiffany & Co. A.G. (Switzerland); Tiffany & Co. ICT, Inc.; Tiffany & Co. International; Tiffany & Co. Japan Inc.; Tiffany

& Co. K.K. (Japan); Tiffany & Co. of New York Limited (Hong Kong); Tiffany & Co. (New York) Pty. Ltd. (Australia); Tiffany & Co. Pte. LTD (Singapore); Tiffany & Co. Watch Factory S.A. (Switzerland); Tiffany-Faraone S.P.A. (Italy); Tiffco Jewelry and Chain Crafts, Inc.

Further Reading:

Carpenter, Charles H., *Tiffany Silver,* New York: Dodd, Mead, 1978.

Francke, Linda Bird, ''That Tiffany Touch,'' *New York,* December 22, 1980, pp. 23–26, 28.

Haden-Guest, Anthony, ''Tiffany's Big Gamble,'' *New York,* October 15, 1984, pp. 36, 38–41, 43.

Lacossitt, Henry, ''Treasure House on Fifth Avenue,'' *Saturday Evening Post,* January 24, 1953, pp. 30, 102, 104, 106; and January 31, 1953, pp. 30, 100, 109–110.

Pouschine, Tatiana, ''Tiffany: Act II,'' *Forbes,* November 11, 1991, pp. 70–73.

Prial, Frank J., ''The Tiffany Touch,'' *Wall Street Journal,* December 24, 1968, pp. 1, 8.

Purtell, Joseph, *The Tiffany Touch,* New York: Random House, 1971.

Slom, Stanley H., ''The Connoisseur: Walter Hoving Makes His Impeccable Taste a Tiffany Trademark,'' *Wall Street Journal,* October 27, 1975, pp. 1, 17.

Sparks, Debra, ''Attention Tiffany Shoppers,'' *Financial World,* July 19, 1994, pp. 32–35.

''Tiffany's Off on a Spree,'' *Business Week,* October 6, 1962, pp. 54–55.

Trachtenberg, Jeffrey A., ''Cocktails at Tiffany,'' *Forbes,* February 6, 1989, pp. 128, 130.

Wayne, Leslie, ''At Tiffany, A Troubled Transition,'' *New York Times,* October 16, 1983, Sec. 3, pp. 1, 30.

Zinn, Laura, and Uchida, Hiromi, ''Who Said Diamonds Are Forever?'' *Business Week,* November 2, 1992, pp. 128–29.

—Robert Halasz

T|N|T Freightways

TNT Freightways Corporation

9700 Higgins Road
Rosemont, Illinois 60018
U.S.A.
(708) 696-0200
Fax: (708) 696-2080

Public Company
Founded: 1984
Operating Revenues: $1.01 billion
Employees: 12,184
Stock Exchanges: NASDAQ
SICs: 3711 Motor Vehicles & Car Bodies; 4212 Local
   Trucking Without Storage; 4213 Trucking, Except Local;
   4226 Less-Than-Truckload (LTL) Transport; 4731
   Arrangement Transport Freight & Cargo; 6719 Holding
   Companies; 7549 Automobile Dead Storage &
   Maintenance Services

TNT Freightways Corporation is one of the most successful
trucking firms in North America, crisscrossing the country with
over 40,000 shipments each day by six regional carriers. Specializing in less-than-truckload (shipments under 10,000 lbs.)
overnight and second-day delivery, TNT's subsidiaries have
divided the United States into six overlapping parcels: Bestway
covers the Southwest from California to Texas; Dugan serves
the central United States, from the Dakotas to Texas and the
Gulf states and stretching into Georgia, Florida, and the Carolinas; Holland services the Southeast to the Great Lakes; Reddaway covers the entire West Coast with Alaska and Canada;
Red Star services the East Coast, Quebec, and Ontario and is
venturing into the Carolinas and Georgia; and United handles
the Pacific Northwest and Rocky Mountain states. Working
independently and in concert, TNT's divisions have continued
to conquer an ever-increasing share of the specialized, time-
sensitive trucking industry.

TNT's story began decades ago in the Southern Hemisphere. Sir
Peter Abeles, a Hungarian refugee who settled in Australia and
became a prominent entrepreneur, took a two-truck operation
named Thomas Nationwide Transport in the 1950s and over the
next 40 years turned it into a worldwide transportation conglomerate. Known as TNT Limited and based in Sydney,
Abeles's group of businesses came to include railcars, trucks,
and aircraft, with operations in 185 countries on six continents.

During the late 1980s and early 1990s the vast TNT empire
became unwieldy and fell victim to economic recession.

After losing $155 million in 1991, TNT Ltd. decided to spin off
several non-core assets, including its U.S. trucking interest. As
part of the deal, John "Cam" Carruth, who had headed TNT
Ltd.'s North American trucking operations since 1985, became
president and CEO of the newly independent TNT Freightways
Corp. In February 1992 TNT Freightways initiated the largest
initial public offering of a trucking company in U.S. history.
Luckily for TNT Freightways, trucking company stocks had
already risen by 12 percent in early 1992, making it an optimal
time for an IPO. The company's 14.4 million shares (75 percent
of its stock) were snapped up at a price of $19.50 in a matter of
days. The stock sale raised over $280 million, which TNT Ltd.
applied to its $1.5 billion debt load. An additional 1.3 million
shares netted the newly independent TNT Freightways more
than $24 million for what it called "general corporate pur-
poses." Although TNT Ltd. retained equity of more than 20
percent, TNT Freightways was now free to pursue its own
interests.

At the time of its IPO, TNT Freightways' six LTL trucking units
served most of the United States and some of Canada, with gaps
only in the Southeastern states. In addition to the regional
trucking operations were TNT Contract Logistics, TNT Distribution Services Inc., and TNT Auto Warehousing. TNT Contract Logistics, founded in 1990, provided a wide range of
logistics solutions for North American companies needing dedicated transport vehicles, warehousing, administrative, inventory management, and customer service functions. TNT Distribution Services Inc., also founded in 1990, handled assembly
and distribution services for the Chicago metropolitan area,
southeastern Wisconsin, and northwestern Indiana. And TNT
Auto Warehousing (known as the "little Detroit" of the Northwest), located on Puget Sound at the Port of Tacoma, accessorized and stored foreign and domestic vehicles for sale in the
United States or abroad, and provided a reconditioning service
for fleet and rental cars. TNT Auto Warehousing was later sold
in 1993 when the company decided to concentrate solely on
trucking and logistics operations.

Before going public, TNT Freightways' operating revenues
were $458.7 million for fiscal year 1989, with net income of
$14.4 million; in 1990 revenues rose more than 30 percent to
$597.9 million and net income to $15.9 million; and in 1991
operating revenue climbed about 13 percent to $675 million, but
net income fell by nearly half to $7.3 million in the midst of the
trucking industry's downturn. (Only TNT's operations in the
Southwest and Northeast registered actual losses.) In 1992 TNT
had regained its footing and once again posted gains in operating revenues, which totaled $800 million; net earnings, while
less than the previous year, were $6.9 million while many
competitors either closed down or were swallowed by stronger
rivals. TNT was able to register an impressive 16.3 percent
increase in its LTL revenue despite the woeful economic conditions.

In 1992 the company also launched Nationwide Logistics Corp.
to do for the trucking industry what TNT had already achieved
on a smaller scale for auto manufacturers. By offering one-stop,
long-term outsourcing through TNT's vast trucking networks,

Nationwide Logistics was designed to take over for the traffic departments many companies were forced to abandon during the recession. Though its competitors were plentiful (including divisions at ABF, Roadway, Ryder, Yellow Freight, and others), TNT believed the developing contract logistics field, with no established leader, had room for one more player. Nationwide Logistics Corp. was not meant to eclipse TNT Contract Logistics, but to complement its operations.

As TNT Freightways continued to make its mark in the United States and Canada, its former parent, TNT Ltd., had less and less interest in the trucking outfit. When word came down that TNT Ltd. was interested in selling its remaining shares, TNT Freightways was more than eager to reclaim them. In March 1993 TNT Freightways negotiated the purchase of TNT Ltd.'s remaining equity of over 5.5 million shares (about 20 percent) in the company, following the former parent's decision not to sell the stock in a public offering. By the end of the year, operating revenues had reached $898.9 million, just over 12 percent higher than in 1992, with income topping $27.3 million. Staffing had grown to more than 11,000 employees in the United States and Canada.

During the next year, 1994, TNT Freightways reached several critical milestones and was able to overcome an earthquake, severe weather conditions, and a potentially devastating strike. By 1994 TNT's regional truck lines served 90 percent of the continental United States, and the company was determined to raise this figure to 100 percent coverage, including Alaska and Hawaii. Since the Southeast wasn't adequately serviced, New Jersey-based Red Star Express (which covered the New England and mid-Atlantic states as well as Ontario and Quebec) announced plans to expand into the Carolinas and Georgia. Although Red Star's networks extended as far as a 29-door terminal in Richmond, Virginia, new operations were slated for Charlotte and Raleigh/Durham, North Carolina, with a possible third in South Carolina. Red Star also initiated partnerships with two siblings, Dugan and Holland, for more extensive coverage of the Southeastern states.

While its regional carriers were busy ironing out details for overlapping markets, TNT Freightways put the finishing touches on extended coverage to all 50 states. In January the company acquired Coast Consolidators, Inc., a freight forwarding company based in Los Angeles providing shipments to and from Hawaii. Later in the year TNT opened new transportation routes to Alaska and completed a new agreement for service in Puerto Rico.

Despite crippling snowstorms in the central and Northeastern states, first quarter results brought in record income of $5.9 million—46 percent higher than the previous year's figures—while LTL revenue as a whole climbed another 19.8 percent as each division continued to pull higher shipments and tonnage. In April, however, TNT's two largest LTL haulers, Red Star and the Michigan-based Holland Motor Express, were stymied by what became a 24-day International Brotherhood of Teamsters strike. Red Star and Holland had accounted for two-thirds of the company's revenues in 1993. After weeks of getting nowhere with 75,000 striking Teamsters, TNT was no longer willing to leave negotiations to a third-party agency and pulled out of the Washington-based TMI (Trucking Management Inc.)

to resolve the strike on its own. Fortunately, an agreement was reached just over three weeks after the strike began.

Despite disruptions from the California earthquake, record cold, winter storms, the Teamsters' strike, flooding along the Mississippi River, and special charges related to upcoming deregulation, TNT Freightways increased revenues by 13 percent over 1993 to break the $1 billion mark. Notable contributions were made by TNT's logistics businesses (which increased revenue by nearly 53 percent), and in particular by the three-year-old Contract Logistics, which exceeded $50 million on its own.

To protect its hard-won status as an independent billion-dollar company, TNT's board of directors adopted a poison pill provision in 1994 (which was set to expire on February 3, 2004). To maintain its growth rate, the company planned to continue increasing interregional shipment agreements between its six trucking divisions as well as cross-pollination with its four logistics businesses, and to further its globalization plans through an alliance with Direct Container Lines. Moreover, TNT hoped to speed delivery schedules and minimize handling costs through further territorial expansion and greater density within its already established networks.

TNT's Bestway Transportation, Dugan, Holland Motor Express, Reddaway Truck Line, Red Star Express, and United Truck Lines have become industry leaders known for their on-time delivery and dependability, while TNT's diversification into logistics with Coast Consolidators, Contract Logistics, Distribution Services, and Nationwide Logistics have taken computerized distribution and supply chain management to new levels of efficiency. By upping its territorial coverage and increasing its shipment size, TNT Freightways Corp.'s nearly 5,000 tractors and 11,000 trailers carried over 6.4 million tons of freight in 1994 and were well on their way to doubling this figure by the end of the decade.

Principal Subsidiaries: Nationwide Logistics Corporation; TNT Bestway Transportation Inc.; TNT Coast Consolidators Inc.; TNT Contract Logistics Inc.; TNT Distribution Services, Inc.; TNT Dugan, Inc.; TNT Holland Motor Express, Inc.; TNT Red Star Express, Inc.; TNT Reddaway Truck Line, Inc.; TNT United Truck Lines, Inc.

Further Reading:

Anderson, Veronica, "Trucker Keeps on Rolling," *Crain's Chicago Business,* April 11, 1994, pp. 46–47.
Commins, Kevin, "IPO Gives Area Trucking Firm New Firepower," *Crain's Chicago Business,* March 2, 1992, p. 41–42.
Hamilton, Dane, "TNT Freightways Begins Major Push for Customers of Logistics Subsidiary," *Journal of Commerce & Commercial,* February 1, 1993, p. 2B.
"Local News—TNT Freightways," *Chicago Tribune,* March 9, 1993, p. 8.
Luebke, Cathy, "TNT Bestway's Parent Goes Public, Breaks from Foreign Firm," *Business Journal* (Milwaukee), April 27, 1992, p. 5.
——, "TNT Freightways Corp.," *Business Journal* (Milwaukee), June 25, 1993, p. 115B.
"Motor Carriage—TNT Freightways Corp.," *Transportation & Distribution,* June 1994, p. 14.
"Motor Carriage—TNT Freightways Corp.," *Transportation & Distribution,* September 1993, p. 15.

"Nationwide Logistics Is New TNT Subsidiary," *Distribution,* March 1993, pp. 20–21.

"Profile: TNT North America," *Transportation & Distribution,* May 1991, p. 76.

"TNT Freightways Scores Strong Gains, but Weather Woes Create New Worries," *Journal of Commerce & Commercial,* January 4, 1993, p. 2B.

"TNT Freightways, Swift Soar as Overnite Stumbles," *Journal of Commerce & Commercial,* January 23, 1995, p. 2B.

"TNT Red Star Express Expands to Southeast," *Journal of Commerce & Commercial,* December 15, 1994, p. 2B.

"Transportation Report: Regional LTL Carriers Spun Off by TNT Limited," *Distribution,* March 1992, p. 16.

Wilhelm, Steve, "Our Little Detroit Gives Imports a Yankee Touch," *Executive Automotive Guide,* April 17, 1989, pp. 10–11.

—Taryn Benbow-Pfalzgraf

Todd Shipyards Corporation

1801 16th Avenue Southwest
Seattle, Washington 98134
U.S.A.
(206) 623-1635
Fax: (206) 233-0219

Public Company
Incorporated: 1916 as William H. Todd Corporation
Employees: 650
Sales: $69.09 million
Stock Exchanges: New York
SICs: 3731 Ship Building & Repair

Once the largest independent ship building company in the United States, Todd Shipyards Corporation operates one shipyard in Seattle, Washington, through its subsidiary, Todd Pacific Shipyards Corporation, which repairs, overhauls, converts, and constructs commercial and military vessels. During the early 1980s, Todd Shipyards, then based in New York, operated seven shipyards and collected nearly $800 million in annual sales, but by the end of the decade the company was in bankruptcy, hobbled by a dwindling number of U.S. defense-related contracts. Todd Shipyards came out of Chapter 11 protection in 1991, emerging as a considerably smaller company trying to rebuild its lost commercial business.

The history of Todd Shipyards nearly encompasses the breadth of ship building in the United States, beginning with one of the most memorable events in the country's Civil War. The superiority of iron over wood was first demonstrated in a duel that pitted what observers at the time described as ''a terrapin with a chimney on its back'' against ''a tin can on a shingle.'' The two awkward-looking vessels that elicited such disparaging comments were about to reshape ship building history. When the *S.S. Virginia,* the former *S.S. Merrimac* refitted by the Confederates with overlapping plates of two-inch armor, set out on her trial run in March 1862 and promptly sank two Union ships and ran aground three others, the navies of the world just as quickly were made obsolete. The Confederates' advantage over the rest of the world, however, lasted less than 24 hours, for the Union's iron-clad riposte was already on its way: the *S.S. Monitor,* an armor-hulled warship outfitted with the first revolving gun turret. When the two iron vessels faced off against each other the morning after the *Virginia*'s rout of the Union blockade at

the mouth of the St. James River, the contest ended inconclusively in a draw, but the effect on military ship building in the United States and throughout the world was definite. A new era of ship building had been inaugurated.

For their ability to respond to the *Virginia*'s awesome and novel power, the Union forces were indebted to John Ericsson, a Swedish naval architect who designed the *Monitor* and its singular revolving gun turret, and Cornelius DeLameter, whose company, DeLameter Iron Works, built the *Monitor*'s engines and propeller. Founded by William DeLameter in 1835, DeLameter Iron Works represented the earliest ancestral link to Todd Shipyards, the original corporate entity that after several name changes and exchanges in ownership became the William H. Todd Corporation, the direct descendent of Todd Shipyards.

The rapid changes that preceded the formal organization of the William H. Todd Corporation began when DeLameter Iron Works moved from its original location in Manhattan to Erie Basin in Brooklyn 1889. By the time of its relocation, DeLameter Iron Works was led by DeLameter's son-in-law, John N. Robins, who negotiated several acquisitions, revamped the company's corporate structure, then renamed the concern Erie Basin Dry Dock Company. Shortly after the name change, Robins hired William H. Todd to help manage the company's ship repair and ship building operations, conferring upon in his youthful manager a responsibility Todd was well-equipped to handle.

Todd had cut his teeth in the ship building business working as an apprentice boilermaker for Pusey & Jones Shipyard in Wilmington, Delaware, spending much of life learning the nuances of the ship building trade. At Erie Basin Dry Dock Co. he put his practical experience to work in a managerial capacity, achieving enough success to be named vice-president of the company in 1904, by which time the ship building and repair firm had been renamed again, becoming Robins Dry Dock and Repair Company. When Robins retired in 1909, Todd ascended to the top slot at the company, president. In 1915, Todd and several associates purchased Robins Dry Dock and Repair Co., the Tietjen & Lang Dry Dock Company of Hoboken, New Jersey, and Seattle Construction and Dry Dock Company, located in Seattle, Washington. With these companies, Todd formed the William H. Todd Corporation a year later, marking the formal beginning of Todd Shipyards' rise to the top of the ship building industry in the United States.

Formed midway through World War I, William H. Todd Corp. benefitted greatly from the pressing demand for ships, distinguishing itself as a prodigious shipbuilder and a company able to perform complicated ship conversions and major repair jobs. With its plants operating 24 hours a day, the company served as an integral producer of military vessels, supplying nearly 90 percent of the war's first convoy. By the end of the war, the rush of military orders had created a massive ship building company, employing 18,000 workers and supported by five plants on the Atlantic coast and two on the Pacific Coast. However, when the hostilities subsided, so did much of William H. Todd Corp.'s business. William Todd, however, had prepared for the postwar years of reduced ship building and repair by adding a products division to William H. Todd's corporate structure with the acquisition the White Fuel Oil Engineering Company in 1916.

The company leaned heavily on the business generated by White Fuel Oil to carry it through the more prosaic years following the conclusion of World War I, as its payroll shrank to 2,000.

By foreseeing the transition from coal to oil-burning equipment before the conversion became a pervasive trend, Todd ensured his company's success during peacetime, and for the next two decades, William H. Todd Corp.'s business steadily grew, driven by contracts to build and repair ships for the U.S. Navy and civilian contractors. In 1934, the company opened a tanker repair yard in Galveston, Texas, at Pelican Island, which became a primary division for the company in the decades ahead, and re-opened its shipyard in Seattle two years later, demonstrating a peacetime vibrancy that gave it a solid foundation for the frenetic years ahead, as the United States prepared to enter World War II.

During the 20th century's second great international struggle, Todd Shipyards played as pivotal a role as it had during the first. The company's scope of operations and payroll once again swelled during World War II, with its manufacturing facilities churning out 60 large cargo vessels for the British Purchasing Commission, and completing contract work awarded by the U.S. Navy and U.S. Maritime Commission, including an order for 350 Landing Craft, Infantry (LCI) vessels. By the end of the war, with nearly 57,000 workers filling its employment ranks, Todd Shipyards had completed the herculean task of building more than 1,000 ships and repairing or converting another 23,000 ships, earning 33 U.S. military awards for its contributions to the war effort.

One year after the conclusion of World War II, Todd Shipyards acquired the title to a plant at San Pedro, California, that the U.S. Navy had asked the company to manage in 1943. The San Pedro plant would eventually constitute Todd Shipyards' Los Angeles division, one of the three pillars, along with its facilities in Galveston and Seattle, that would support the company as it grew to become the largest independent shipbuilder in the country. During the 1950s and 1960s, as Todd Shipyards climbed the industry's ranks, the company derived its business from both civilian and military contracts, building its annual revenue total to approximately $175 million by the beginning of the 1970s.

An overwhelming majority of the company's business by the early 1970s was derived from the private sector, with government-funded contracts accounting for a mere 15 percent of Todd Shipyards' revenue volume. Holding sway as the largest independent shipbuilder in the country, Todd Shipyards' revenue volume climbed to nearly $400 million by the end of the decade, lifted in large part by contracts awarded by the U.S. military. Though the company's defense-related work would provide an impressive surge to its sales volume, boosting it to nearly $800 by the early 1980s, the increase in military work at the expense of losing civilian business supplied the chief ingredient for Todd Shipyards' disastrous decade ahead. During the 1980s, Todd Shipyards' century-and-a-half of ship building experience would be put to its greatest test yet, as the venerable shipbuilder quickly found itself in the crucible of bankruptcy.

Todd Shipyards' peak year before its downfall was in 1983, when during the fiscal year sales approached $800 million and its backlog of contracts for frigates amounted to $759 million.

By this time the company operated seven shipyards scattered across the country in Brooklyn, New Orleans, Houston, Galveston, Los Angeles, San Francisco, and Seattle, which were now geared for producing military vessels. Like other shipbuilders in the United States, Todd Shipyards had overhauled its production facilities so that it could capture the lion's share of the work generated by the Reagan Administration's defense buildup, which accounted for 80 percent of the company's annual sales. The country's naval fleet was expanding at a robust pace, propelling the growth of companies like Todd Shipyards, but when the government-funded orders for additional work began to wane, so did the fortunes of those companies that were over-reliant on an escalating defense budget. As the company whittled away at its nearly $800 million in backlogged contracts, counting the dwindling number of days it could look forward to sustaining its operations through government work, prognostications for the future grew increasingly bleak.

With its labor costs too high to recapture abandoned commercial work, Todd Shipyards was forced to scale down the range of its operations as the financial pressures bearing down on the company increased. A cost-reduction program was effected, part of which included the relocation of the company's corporate headquarters from New York to Jersey City, and the abandonment of its shipyards in New Orleans and Houston in 1985. As a hedge against its declining ship building business, the company purchased Aro Corp., an air-powered tool company, the same year it closed its New Orleans and Houston shipyards, but there was little the company could do to wrest free from mounting financial burdens. Repeatedly, the company was being underbid on major contracts with the U.S. Navy, while attempts to revive its floundering commercial business continued to meet with failure. At the end of March 1987, the company reported its financial figures for the previous year: sales were down to $417 million and, for the first time since William H. Todd took control of the company, it lost money, posting a $58 million loss for the year. Less than five months later, on August 17, 1987, Todd Shipyards filed for protection from creditors under Chapter 11 of the U.S. Bankruptcy Code.

Todd Shipyards remained in bankruptcy for more than three years, during which time a drastic downsizing program was implemented, as the company struggled to reorganize and pare away the remaining components of its once-illustrious ship building empire. The Los Angeles shipyard was closed in July 1989, its Aro Corp. pneumatic tools subsidiary was sold to Ingersoll-Rand Co. for $132 million in February 1990, and the closure of the company's Galveston shipyard was announced in May 1990, leaving, by the end of that year, a one-shipyard operation in Seattle: Todd Pacific Shipyard Corp. Although severe, the changes made between 1987 and the end of 1990 enabled Todd Shipyards to emerge from Chapter 11 in January 1991, ending the most dismal chapter in the company's history.

Looking toward the future, there were some signs of promise to encourage hope in Seattle. Out of Chapter 11, Todd Shipyards was lean and in the black. Its reliance on government contracts, which as recently as 1989 had accounted for 89 percent of the company's annual sales, had been reduced substantially, and now, as the company prepared to move forward by focusing on small commercial contracts, accounted for only half of its $187 million in annual sales. Lack of profitability, however would continue to hound the company for several more years as a contentious battle among dissident shareholders for control of Todd Shipyards took place. By 1994, when the air had cleared, the company was still losing money, reporting a $2.7 million loss for the year, but this loss at least was considerably less than the nearly $12 million loss reported the year before. More encouraging was Todd Shipyards success at diversification away from government work. Commercial revenues increased 115 percent during fiscal 1994, swelling to $52.4 million, while government work decreased 45 percent, falling to $16.2 million.

As Todd Shipyards entered the mid-1990s, it recorded a profit for the first time in three years, buoying hope that a recovery was on its way. The company recorded $3.8 million in net income on $69 million in sales in fiscal 1995, the same year it formed a radio subsidiary, Elettra Broadcasting Corporation, for its three FM radio stations in the Carmel area south of San Francisco. With work about to start on a $182 million contract to build three Washington State ferries, there were many challenges ahead for Todd Shipyards, as the company endeavored to build a new future commensurate with its storied past.

Principal Subsidiaries: Todd Pacific Shipyards Corp.; Montana Valley Land Company; TSI Management, Inc.; Elettra Broadcasting, Inc.

Principal Operating Units: Todd Seattle Shipyard

Further Reading:

Baldo, Anthony, "Todd Shipyards' False Buoyancy," *FW,* October 30, 1990, p. 18.
Chakravarty, Subrata N., "Aerospace and Defense," *Forbes,* January 2, 1984, p. 144.
"Curing the Navy Blues," *Financial World,* June 1, 1980, p. 25.
Hussey, Allan, F., "Full Ahead," *Barron's,* October 15, 1979, p. 48.
Jones, Sam L., "Todd Shipyards and Pacific Subsidiary File for Protections Under Chapter 11," *Metalworking News,* August 24, 1987, p. 14.
McDaniel, Linda, "Todd Shipyards: 140 Years of Shipbuilding," *Sealift,* August 1974, p. 14.
Payne, Seth, "Why a Navy Job May Go to the High-Cost Bidder," *Business Week,* April 1, 1985, p. 96.
Schifren, Matthew, "Mac Is Back," *Forbes,* September 14, 1992, p. 52.
Thomas, Dana L., "Wave of Prosperity," *Barron's,* October 9, 1972, p. 3.
"Todd Files in Bankruptcy," *Seattle Post-Intelligencer,* August 18, 1987, p. B3.
Wilhelm, Steve, "Fight for Control Scuttles Todd's Shipyard Work," *Puget Sound Business Journal,* September 4, 1992, p. 1
——, "Todd's Odd Medley: Radio and Shipyards," *Puget Sound Business Journal,* June 16, 1995, p. 1.

—Jeffrey L. Covell

TRW Inc.

1900 Richmond Road
Cleveland, Ohio 44124-3760
U.S.A.
(216) 291-7000
Fax: (216) 291-7629

Public Company
Incorporated: 1901 as Thompson Products Co.
Employees: 64,200
Sales: $9.09 billion
Stock Exchanges: New York Midwest Pacific Philadelphia
    London Frankfurt
SICs: 3714 Motor Vehicle Parts & Accessories; 3812 Search
    & Navigation Equipment; 7374 Data Processing &
    Preparation; 7323 Credit Reporting Services

Long a conglomerate, TRW Inc. is now primarily one of the world's leading automotive parts makers, with smaller operations in space and defense technology and information systems and services. TRW's automotive sector is led by its air bag systems, with power-steering systems and engine valves of secondary importance. The space sector has lately concentrated on satellites and satellite systems, including those for satellite phones. Its information services sector is best known for its credit-rating service.

TRW's conglomerate structure is deeply rooted in the company's history. In the early 1950s the Cleveland-based Thompson Products was looking for an acquisition. J. David Wright, the company's general manager, and Horace Shepard, a vice president, thought the auto valve and steering component maker needed more technical sophistication. Thompson, founded in 1901, had made a name for itself in automotive and aircraft engine parts and had become well known by sponsoring the famed Thompson Trophy Race, the aeronautical equivalent of auto racing's Indianapolis 500. However, in recent years the company was facing a decline in manned aircraft and saw opportunities in aerospace and electronics.

To break into the young high-tech industry, Wright and Shepard tried to buy Hughes Aircraft Co. Hughes was willing to listen to bids but scoffed at the Thompson offer, which was thought to be ten times too low. Just a few months later, two of Hughes Aircraft's top scientist-executives, Simon Ramo and Dean Woolridge, decided to leave Hughes to form a new electronic systems

company, and Thompson put up $500,000 to bankroll the venture. Not long afterward, Ramo-Woolridge Corporation was established in Los Angeles and quickly gained solid standing in the advanced technology business, being awarded the systems engineering and technical direction contracts for such important missile programs as Atlas, Minuteman, Titan, and Thor.

By 1958 Thompson Products had invested $20 million—20 percent of its net worth at the time—for a 49 percent interest in Ramo-Woolridge, and the two operations were merged as Thompson-Ramo-Woolridge. Though united on paper, the company maintained separate corporate headquarters, with Woolridge president in Los Angeles and Wright chairman in Cleveland. Ramo and Shepard, a former chief of production procurement for the Air Force, also had an active role in management.

The merger could hardly have started less auspiciously. In the midst of a recession, the Cleveland-based group was hit with a 14 percent drop in automotive business and a 34 percent drop in manned aircraft business. When business improved for the Cleveland division, the Los Angeles division got into trouble. Its venture into semiconductors collapsed in 1961, and the McNamara era was beginning at the Pentagon. The West Coast scientists, who had only known cost-plus-fixed-fee contracts, needed help. They had to learn how to go from spending money to making it. This education was hampered by hard feelings between the two groups. The electronics end was not living up to its promise of being the business of the future. In the first four years following the merger, profit margins, which had been at the 4 percent-plus level in the mid-1950s, dropped to an average of barely 2 percent.

With the company facing such mundane tasks as cost-cutting, Woolridge, who reportedly never really wanted to be a businessman anyway, resigned in 1962. As Woolridge was getting settled in at his new job as a professor at Caltech, Shepard was promoted to president and Ramo named vice-chairman. With Cleveland now in control of the company, the Los Angeles scientists were quickly reassured when the new management team instituted a number of reforms to get the company back on its feet, including writing off $3 million in inventory.

In 1963, Shepard and Wright began pruning unprofitable divisions. They sold most of the unprofitable Bumkor-Ramo computer division to Martin Marietta. The company retained partial ownership in Bumkor-Ramo but no longer played a large role in the company's plans. Shepard and Wright continued hammering out the company's plans for long-term growth, seeking specifically to raise profit margins. To this end, in 1964 they sold the microwave division and the division that made hi-fidelity components, intercoms, and language laboratories.

To shore up the company's auto parts division, they bought Ross Gear & Tool, a maker of mechanical and power steering units, and Marlin-Rockwell, a ball bearings manufacturer. The 7 percent profit margin of the new acquisitions, which had a combined profit of $5.7 million on sales of $76.5 million, helped boost TRW's overall margin to 4 percent in 1964, up a percentage point from the year earlier.

In 1965, in another look toward the future, Thompson-Ramo-Woolridge adopted a shorter, less cumbersome name, the now household initials TRW. Also in that year, the company's investment in aerospace and electronics became increasingly clear. In the previous decade, sales in space and electronics shot up from $14 million to $200 million. Despite that dramatic growth, the company's earnings still came mostly from its oldest business, auto parts. New and replacement parts accounted for 34 percent of TRW's $553 million in sales and 40 percent of its earnings. Chief among those products were its steering linkages, valves, and braking devices that it sold to General Motors, Ford, and Chrysler.

TRW's prospects improved in 1966. An auto parts boom helped the company's profitability. The Cleveland-based automotive group had a return of 6 percent on sales of $350 million. The equipment group, also in Cleveland, had an increase of sales to $200 million in aerospace and ordinance technology but lower profit margins because of start-up costs for unexpected demand in commercial aircraft. The Los Angeles-based TRW Systems had $250 million in sales and a 3 percent profit margin building and designing spacecraft and doing research. Totals were up to $870 million in sales for TRW, producing $36 million in profit for a 4.2 percent return. Even with the upturn in sales, the company was relying less on government contracts, down to about 44 percent from 70 percent ten years earlier.

With the company's finances on the upturn, the wrangling between Los Angeles and Cleveland declined. As *Business Week* reported, the discord was "under control, if not cured." The company continued tightening its operations in 1966. It bought United Car with $122 million in sales and sold its one consumer business, a hi-fi manufacturer.

TRW had grown into a conglomerate, a term disliked by company management. In 1969 TRW operated six groups that, in turn, administered 55 divisions. The company derived 32 percent of its revenues from aerospace products and systems and computer software, 28 percent from vehicle components for autos and trucks, 23 percent from electronic components and communication, and 17 percent from industrial products ranging from mechanical fasteners to automated controls.

To manage the increasingly far-flung company, TRW maintained strict management control over all operations. By encouraging communication between all levels of management and holding monthly manager meetings, TRW avoided the problems that had plagued other conglomerates. Another of TRW's successful management styles caught *Fortune*'s eye in 1966. The magazine covered in depth the happenings of a TRW management meeting in Vermont, where 49 of the company's top executives had gathered annually since 1952 at an old farmhouse to think about the company's future.

TRW continued beefing up its auto parts business, acquiring Globe Industries, a Dayton-based maker of miniature AC and DC electric motors. At the same time, TRW's electronics group had grown to more than 20 plants in the United States, Canada, and Mexico. The company continued to evade problems that had plagued other conglomerates, posting a slight pretax gain of 16.4 percent, above the industry average of 13.3 percent.

In 1969 TRW named a new president, Ruben F. Mettler. One of his first big projects was a contract for a laboratory that NASA would send on the Viking probe to Mars. TRW won the chal-

lenge to provide one black box weighing 33 pounds with complex instruments capable of making biological and chemical tests to detect the most primitive forms of life. The NASA contract was worth only $50 million, not a big financial risk for a multibillion dollar company like TRW, but the job was important for the company's prestige.

The auto parts business, in the meantime, was once again proving to be immune to cyclical trends in car output. The market for new parts was in a slump, but it was made up for by the accompanying increase in demand for replacement cars as consumers kept their cars on the roads longer. TRW also announced a move into business credit reporting, challenging Dun & Bradstreet.

The company's sound financial condition was unmistakable. For the five years preceding 1970, the company had average earning jumps of 27 percent annually and an average 23 percent increase annually in sales. But company officials conceded that the company could not keep growing at that rate forever. It had acquired 38 companies through 1968, a pace it would not be able to maintain indefinitely. The company looked for future growth to run about 10 percent.

The company's skillful management again became apparent in 1971, when TRW was forced to make cuts because of an aerospace recession. Its TRW Systems division had to cut the number of employees by 15 percent. Managers were not spared cuts either; 18 percent of the professional staff was laid off. The company's open management style enabled TRW to build a strong enough relationship with its employees that two-thirds of them were nonunion, perhaps preventing the labor squabbles that had appeared in other companies.

TRW made a risky venture in 1976, entering the tricky market of electronic point-of-sale machines. Those machines had boosted profits for retailers, but not for manufacturers. Its proposed 2001 system targeted the general market and cost $4,000 per unit, similar to competitors. TRW's move into POS was largely a defensive tactic. The electronic credit authorization business it had pioneered in the 1960s was coming under increasing competition. Then NCR, the overall leader in POS machines, launched a POS system incorporating credit checking in 1975. TRW attempted to enter the market with an established customer base by acquiring the service contracts for the 65,000 customers Singer had built up during its short, ill-fated move into the POS market. TRW remained cautious, however, only delivering 200 to 300 machines in 1976, mostly to the May Co. Altogether that year nonfood retailers ordered 24,500 POS terminals worth $94 million, and the market was picking up.

In 1976 TRW achieved the moment of glory it had long awaited with Viking's historic landing on Mars. The company took out full-page newspaper ads proclaiming "That lab is our baby." Appropriately, Mettler, 52, who had pushed for TRW to compete for the Viking contract, was named to succeed Horace A. Shepard as chairman and chief executive officer when Shepard retired the next year.

Aerospace ventures continued to play an important role in the company's finances. In 1977 TRW was still the chief engineer for U.S. intercontinental ballistic missiles. Aerospace and government electronic revenues were providing a cool $60 million in profits on revenue of $440 million. The electronics division had $300 million in sales. The data communications unit was also doing well with over $150 million in sales. It had established a retail credit bureau, a business credit system, and was an international maker of data communications equipment. However, auto and commercial parts were still accounting for twice as much in sales and five times as much in earnings.

In 1980 TRW and Fujitsu Ltd., Japan's largest computer maker, formed a joint venture. TRW had a 3,000-person service organization, reportedly the largest independent network in the United States for data process maintenance, with a special team to develop software. Each company invested $100 million, with Fujitsu keeping a 51 percent share and TRW 45 percent. TRW initiated the venture, seeking a foreign partner to perform maintenance work for its POSs. Fujitsu, which earned 68 percent of its revenue from data processing, was eager to expand overseas to increase its economy of scale to compete with IBM back home. Fujitsu named a majority of the directors of the new company so it could qualify for Japanese export and financing tax breaks, but TRW took charge of running it. One of new company's first moves was to buy TRW's ailing POS and ATM maker division. The company, hoping in the beginning to capture a large segment of the small and medium-sized computer market, predicted sales of $500 million to $1 billion by the decade's end.

Despite TRW's careful planning, the POS and Fujitsu deals both proved unsuccessful. The competition from established POS makers, particularly IBM and NCR, was too great. Nonetheless, TRW remained a strong, highly visible company. *Forbes* in 1983 called it "a paragon" for other conglomerates. It had by then grown to $5 billion in sales spread across 47 different businesses and had 300 locations in 25 countries. It had also grown to be the number one producer of valves for automobiles and aircraft plus a wide range of other products. With a 16 percent return on stockholders' equity as proof, *Forbes* called TRW one of the best-managed, most successful American companies. However, this outward success belied the company's growing inefficiency.

By the time Joseph T. Gorman was named president and chief operating officer of TRW in 1985 (he became chairman, president, and chief executive officer in 1988 when chairman Ruben Mettler retired), the company had grown bloated, inefficient, and overdiversified. It hit a low in 1985 when it lost $7 million on sales of $5.92 billion. Mettler and Gorman instituted a three-year restructuring plan that aimed to focus resources on core businesses, to slash staff, and to increase efficiency. The new TRW would focus on three main areas: automotive products, space and defense projects, and information systems and services. Among the noncore businesses divested were the firm's energy division. Staff was reduced from 93,200 in 1985 to 73,200 in 1988.

From 1986 to 1990, TRW's financial outlook improved somewhat with the new corporate structure. Although sales rose each year to a high of $8.17 billion in 1990, profits were stagnant and actually fell from 3.7 percent in 1988 to 3.6 percent in 1989 to 2.6 percent in 1990.

In 1989 TRW made a huge and risky commitment to what at the time was an unprofitable business: air bags. That year it purchased Talley Industries Inc.'s driver-side air bag unit for $85 million, plus royalties on any air bag sold in North America through the year 2001. TRW also began to invest in the development of passenger-side air bags. In total, the company invested more than half a billion dollars in its air-bag business by 1992. Until the fourth quarter of 1991, TRW lost money on air bags. Although Ford had chosen TRW as its sole supplier of the safety devices in 1989, TRW's fortunes suffered in 1990 because of a Ford recall of 55,000 vehicles with defective air bags and a massive fire at TRW's passenger-side air-bag plant (TRW air bags used sodium azide as its propellant, a chemical prone to explode in the manufacturing process). TRW's automotive business also suffered from a recession in the automotive industry in 1989 and 1990.

The space and defense sectors of TRW were also suffering from the end of the Cold War and the resultant leveling off in defense spending. With its two main sectors down, overall TRW sales for 1991 fell 3.1 percent to $7.91 billion. Gorman embarked on another restructuring late that year, incurring a $365 million charge that resulted in a $140 million loss for the year. This restructuring aimed to remake TRW into primarily an automotive products company, with reduced operations and investments in the space and defense and information sectors. With air bags now profitable and generating $600 million in annual revenue, the company aimed to take advantage of their increasing popularity with consumers and the mandatory inclusion of dual air bags in vehicles by the year 1998. Gorman also set his sights on overseas markets not only for air bags but also for TRW's power-steering systems and engine valves.

By 1994, TRW's automotive operations accounted for 63 percent of total sales, compared to 56 percent in 1992 (and 40 percent in the early 1980s), whereas space and defense accounted for only 31 percent, compared to 35 percent in 1992 (and 50 percent in the early 1980s). The defense operations were also reduced, with sales to the U.S. government falling to 28 percent of total sales, compared to the 45 percent figure of the late 1980s. Meanwhile, international sales accounted for 35 percent of total sales in 1994 (compared to 25 percent in 1985), led by sales to Japanese automakers of $800 million.

Although TRW appeared to have turned the corner with 1994 sales totaling $9.09 billion, an increase of 14.3 percent over 1993, the company's future was clouded. With a full 20 percent of revenue coming from air bags, TRW seemed particularly vulnerable to increasing air-bag competition, including advanced air-bag designs that do not use the dangerous sodium azide propellant. Further dampening the TRW outlook was a lawsuit brought by Talley Industries against TRW in 1994, which resulted in a $138 million judgment against them in 1995. Although its space and defense operations had been boosted by contracts to build satellites for the People's Republic of China and Korea, TRW's proposed $2 billion Odyssey satellite system (a joint venture with Montreal-based Teleglobe Inc. to be used for satellite phone service) was slowed when its patent application was stalled by the U.S. Patent Office in May 1995.

Principal Subsidiaries: ESL Inc.; TRW Automotive Products Inc.; TRW Components International Inc.; TRW Export Trading Corp.; TRW Financial Systems, Inc.; TRW International Holding Corp.; TRW System Services Co.; TRW Vehicle Safety Systems Inc.; TRW Canada Ltd.; TRW France S.A.; TRW GmbH fur Industrielle Beteilgungen (Germany); TRW Italia S.p.A.; TRW Steering Systems Japan Co. Ltd.; TRW U.K. Ltd.

Further Reading:

Berss, Marcia, ''Nothing Is in the Bag,'' *Forbes,* March 4, 1991, p. 97.
England, Robert Stowe, ''Less Sizzle, More Steak,'' *Financial World,* August 4, 1992, pp. 20–21.
Fehr-Snyder, Kerry, ''TRW Threatens to Fight $138 Million Trial Ruling: Talley Wins Lawsuit over Sale of Air-Bag Business,'' *Phoenix Gazette,* June 8, 1995, p. C1.
Flint, Jerry, ''The TRW Way,'' *Forbes,* July 31, 1995, pp. 45–46.
Mettler, Ruben F., *The Little Brown Hen That Could: The Growth Story of TRW Inc.,* New York: Newcomen Society, 1982, 24 p.
Nodell, Bobbi, ''Hughes, TRW Offset Defense Cuts with Telecommunications Projects,'' *Los Angeles Business Journal,* April 19, 1993, p. 52.
Phillips, Stephen, ''Just Don't Get in Joe Gorman's Way,'' *Business Week,* November 12, 1990, pp. 88–89.
Skeel, Shirley, ''Tracking Satellite Joe,'' *Management Today,* January 1990, pp. 60–66.
Thornton, Emily, ''To Sell in Japan, Just Keep Trying,'' *Fortune,* January 25, 1993, pp. 103–4.

—updated by David E. Salamie

Tyson Foods, Inc.

2210 West Oaklawn Drive
Springdale, Arkansas 72762-6999
U.S.A.
(501) 290-4000
Fax: (501) 290-4061

Public Company
Incorporated: 1947 as Tyson Feed & Hatchery, Incorporated
Employees: 62,880
Sales: $5.11 billion
Stock Exchanges: NASDAQ
SICs: 2015 Poultry Slaughtering & Processing; 2038 Frozen
  Specialties Not Elsewhere Classified; 0254 Poultry
  Hatcheries

During the Depression, when his son Don was still a toddler, John Tyson, an Arkansas farmer, began selling chickens. Don Tyson grew up along with the company and eventually transformed it into a giant in the poultry industry. The 1990s have seen Tyson Foods, Inc., become a significant player in the beef, pork, and seafood markets as well.

In 1935, John Tyson bought 50 ''springer'' chickens and hauled them to Chicago to sell at a profit. Two years later, he named his business Tyson Feed & Hatchery. Over the next 13 years the company prospered by buying and selling chickens, aided by the postwar boom which brought improved kitchen appliances and the first supermarkets. Gradually, however, Tyson became involved in raising chickens, which allowed him better control over the quality of what he sold. In 1947, the company was incorporated.

Five years later, Don Tyson graduated from college and joined the company as head of operations. Father and son were said to have made a dynamic team, the older Tyson more cautious and the younger one pushing forward. For example, Don convinced his father to raise rock cornish game hens, a market that Tyson would one day dominate.

For the next six years, Tyson focused on expanding production facilities, and, in 1958, the company opened a processing plant in Springdale, Arkansas, the site of the company headquarters. Tyson also introduced its first ice-pack processing line, which brought the company into a more competitive industry bracket.

By achieving more complete vertical integration, its dependence on other suppliers lessened.

During the early 1960s, many amateur chicken producers were lured into the market by the drop in feed-grain prices and the easy availability of credit. As a result, broiler production rose about 13 percent between 1965 and 1967. The glut that followed caused big price cuts and accounted for about $50 million in losses in the industry. Several small companies were forced out of business, but the demand for low-priced chicken soared. People were eating four times as much chicken as they did in 1950.

In 1963, Tyson went public and changed its name to Tyson's Foods, Incorporated. It also made its first acquisition, of the Garrett Poultry Company, based in Rogers, Arkansas. In 1966, John Tyson and his wife died in an automobile accident, and Don Tyson took over the business as president.

Technological improvements in the 1960s fundamentally changed the poultry industry. Broiler production had become one of the most industrialized, automated parts of American agriculture. Through the development of better feeds and better disease control methods, chickens were maturing more quickly. These improvements, combined with increased competition, meant lower prices for consumers, but, for processors, it meant lower earnings. In 1967, despite a 37 percent gain in sales, Tyson lost more than a dollar per share in earnings. Nonetheless, the company took advantage of a situation in which several smaller companies were floundering, and with its acquisition of Franz Foods, Inc., continued its pattern of buying out smaller poultry concerns. It also began to give its corporate name more visibility, printing ''Tyson Country Fresh Chicken'' on its wrappers instead of the name of the supermarket the chickens were sold to.

In 1968, Tyson went to court with two other processors when an Agriculture Department officer alleged that the processors had discriminated against Arkansas chicken farmers who were members of an association of poultry farmers. At that time, processors customarily hired farmers to raise their chickens; Tyson and the others had been accused of ''boycotting and blacklisting'' association members in 1962. In 1969, a federal appeals court ruled that the Agriculture Department had ''erred'' in treating the chicken processors like meatpackers and therefore did not have the authority under existing laws to take any action against them.

Also in 1969, Tyson acquired Prospect Farms, Inc., the company that became its precooked chicken division. That year Tyson produced more than 2 percent of the nation's chickens, 70 percent for retail sale and 30 percent for institutions. The company had grown from 15 to 3,000 employees and operated five chicken-processing plants and four protein-processing plants in northwest Arkansas and southwest Missouri.

During the 1970s, Tyson continued to grow and diversify. In 1970, a new egg facility was built, and, in 1971, a computerized feed mill and a plant in Nashville, Arkansas, were completed. Also in 1971 the company's name was changed from Tyson's Foods to Tyson Foods. In 1972, Tyson acquired the Ocoma Foods Division of Consolidated Foods Corporation, including three new plants, as well as Krispy Kitchens, Inc., and the poultry division of Wilson Foods. That year Tyson began selling the Ozark Fry, the first breaded chicken breast patty, and also bought a hog operation in Creswell, North Carolina, from First Colony Farms.

1972 was a shakeout year in the poultry business, and several large processors sold out to those with better prospects of survival, easing competition. Because of the rising prices of beef and pork, chicken consumption was increasing at a rapid rate, and new products and technological developments seemed to promise improved profits for the industry. Tyson was already a leader in introducing new products like its chicken patty, chicken hotdog, and chicken bologna—by 1979, it had 24 specialty products. Tyson also operated three plants that used the new deep chill (rather than ice-pack) process, in which the moisture of the bird was frozen at 28 degrees—one degree warmer than the temperature at which chicken meat freezes, leaving the meat still tender and doubling shelf life to about 25 days.

In the early 1970s Tyson closed its money-losing plant in Shelbyville, Tennessee, but reopened it in 1974 to produce more popular processed and precooked chicken products. In 1973, Tyson bought Cassady Broiler Company, another small poultry concern, and in the next year acquired Vantress Pedigree, Inc.

A civil antitrust lawsuit brought against Tyson and other broiler processors in 1974 for conspiring to fix, maintain, and stabilize broiler prices was settled in 1977. Tyson agreed to pay a $975,663 fine to about 30 chicken purchasers.

In 1978, Tyson acquired the rest of Wilson Foods Corporation. A year later the company sold its two North Carolina chicken-processing plants. In 1980, Tyson introduced its Chick 'n Quick line of products, which included a variety of chicken portions that were easy to prepare. By then Tyson was the largest grower of rock cornish game hens and one of the nation's largest hog producers. As it perfected its precooked chicken patty for restaurants, its institutional sales grew.

In 1983, Tyson implemented its new advertising slogan, "Doing our best . . . just for you" with television commercials on all three major networks in the United States. The company also acquired Mexican Original Products, Inc., a manufacturer of tortillas, taco shells, tostados, and tortilla chips.

By the early 1980s, consumers' nutritional concerns and the continuously high prices of beef and pork had caused the nation's poultry consumption to increase 30 percent since 1970. This increase was also partly due to innovative, easy-to-prepare products from companies like Tyson and the industry's ability to improve breeding and feed techniques. Some of Tyson's experiments had produced six-pound chickens in just six weeks. In 1984, Cobb, Inc., and Tyson began a joint venture called Arkansas Breeders, to breed and develop the Cobb 500, a female with fast growth, low fat, and high meat content.

In September 1984, Tyson acquired 90 percent of another poultry firm, Valmac Industries. By then, Tyson had expanded its operations into six states—Georgia, North Carolina, Missouri, Tennessee, Louisiana, and Arkansas—and many of its products were being distributed internationally. In 1986, *The Wall Street Transcript* named Don Tyson the gold award winner in the meat and poultry industry. The company acquired Lane Processing Inc., a closely held poultry processing firm that had been bankrupt since 1984.

In October 1988, Tyson made a takeover bid for Memphis-based Holly Farms Corporation, the national leader in brand-name chicken sales. Holly Farms had begun more than a century before as a cotton compressor. Over the years it had evolved into a chicken and food service firm with vast holdings and a 19 percent share of the brand-name chicken market. It had been the first processor to use its own name rather than the retail seller's on its packaging, which gave the company a long-standing credibility with consumers and made it a very attractive purchase. Holly Farms rejected the bid, nodding to Tennessee takeover laws, and agreed to merge with ConAgra, Inc., one of the nation's largest food companies and a leading poultry producer based in Omaha, Nebraska. Holly Farms also agreed to sell its poultry assets to ConAgra should the merger not come to fruition. In mid-November, Tyson sued Holly Farms and ConAgra to stop the merger. A few days later, a federal judge ruled that Tennessee's antitakeover laws were unconstitutional and could not be used to halt Tyson's bid, opening an eight-month fight between Tyson and ConAgra for control of Holly Farms.

Tyson's rapid growth in the fast-food chicken business had put a strain on its production facilities, and Tyson needed Holly Farms's chicken supply. More than half of Tyson's business now was with institutions and restaurants, and Tyson's name was not as popular as Holly Farms's in grocery stores. Finally in June 1989, Don Tyson agreed to pay $1.29 billion for Holly Farms, and the company was fully merged into Tyson later that year. In 1990, its first full year with Holly Farms under its wing, Tyson's sales increased 50.7 percent. The purchase of Holly Farms made Tyson the undisputed king of the chicken industry. It also gained a stronger position in beef and pork through Holly Farms's further-processing operations. Tyson's Beef and Pork Division grew substantially over the next several years and claimed 11 percent of the company's revenue by 1995.

In 1991, Leland E. Tollett, a college classmate of Don Tyson whom Tyson had brought into the firm in the late 1950s, was named president and chief executive officer; Tyson remained chairman of the board, but was slowly reducing his responsibilities.

Tyson next turned its attention to seafood in an effort to further diversify its operations. In 1992 Tyson acquired Arctic Alaska Fisheries Corporation, a vertically integrated seafood products company, and Louis Kemp Seafood Company, which was purchased from Oscar Mayer Foods Corporation. Tyson's resulting Seafood Division experienced some rocky initial years, and the firm was forced to take a write-down of $205 million on its seafood assets in 1994, the first major write-down in Tyson's history. The Seafood Division was subsequently revamped and then bolstered by the 1995 acquisition of the seafood division of International Multifoods Corp., which had $65 million in sales in 1994 and produced simulated crabmeat, lobster, shrimp, and scallops.

Arkansas Governor Bill Clinton's presidential election campaign and his subsequent term in office brought unwanted attention to the condition of Tyson's chicken processing plants and eventually embroiled the company in controversies. As governor of Arkansas, Clinton had strongly supported the chicken industry, and Don Tyson was a major contributor to Clinton's presidential bid. During the campaign several journalistic investigations of the chicken industry in Arkansas, such as one published in *Time*, revealed that many of the plants were unsanitary and dangerous and staffed by low-paid workers often subject to such difficult conditions as line speed-ups. Environmentalists had also charged that Clinton, while he was governor, had allowed the Arkansas poultry industry to dump tons of chicken waste in Arkansas streams.

After Clinton took office, the close ties between Tyson and the president aroused controversy first when reports stated that James Blair, Tyson's general counsel and a close friend of Bill Clinton and Hillary Rodham Clinton, had helped Hillary Clinton make a killing in the commodity markets. Then came reports in 1994 that Mike Espy, agriculture secretary under Clinton, had accepted a trip on a Tyson jet and football tickets from Tyson in exchange for favorable treatment from poultry inspectors. Espy subsequently resigned over this matter. Tyson denied any wrongdoing.

Tyson had traditionally expanded its chicken processing capacity through the purchase of existing facilities, but when it decided it needed to expand in 1994, no suitable plants could be found that were for sale. The company then decided to build—at a cost of about $400 million—four new poultry plants over a four-year period, each of which would be able to process 1.3 million chickens a week. That year Tyson also bought a controlling interest in Trasgo, S.A. de C.V., a Mexican joint venture started in 1988. Trasgo held the number three position in the growing chicken market in Mexico.

Also in 1994, Tyson acquired Culinary Foods, Inc., a maker of specialty frozen foods mostly for the food service market, and Gorges Foodservice, Inc., a further processor of beef for the food service market. Tyson failed, however, to acquire a much larger prize, WLR Foods Inc., a $700 million Virginia-based producer of high-quality turkey and chicken products sold primarily under the Wampler-Longacre brand. Similar to Tyson's experience with Holly Farms, WLR management fought Tyson's $330 million attempt to take over the company in early 1994, an attempt that then turned hostile. WLR instituted a takeover defense, which Tyson fought in federal district court as unconstitutional. This time, unlike the Holly Farms case, the judge ruled against Tyson in a decision that summer. Early in 1995, Tyson announced it would appeal the decision to the U.S. Circuit Court of Appeals.

The Seafood Division write-down had soured Tyson's 1994 results and it posted a $2 million loss, its first in years. Not to be deterred, the company continued its aggressive expansion in 1995 with the purchase of the chicken plants of Cargill, which had decided it could no longer compete with Tyson's chicken empire. This purchase added more than 2.5 million chickens per week to Tyson's processing capacity. Another 2.4 million chick-

ens per week were added later in the year with the acquisition of McCarty Farms Inc., a Mississippi-based closely held firm.

An important era for Tyson ended in April 1995 when Don Tyson retired as chairman, denying that the firm's recent controversies had prompted the move. Tyson remained involved in the firm as senior chairman, but day-to-day operations were handed over to Tollett, who became chairman in addition to his previous position as CEO, and Donald "Buddy" Wray, who became president in addition to his previous position as chief operating officer. Like Tollett, Wray was another college classmate of Tyson's and had joined the firm in 1961. John Tyson, Don's then-41-year-old son, was reportedly being groomed to eventually run the company and held the position of president of the Beef and Pork Division.

Its recent difficulties notwithstanding, Tyson Foods enjoyed a strong position in the mid-1990s as the leading chicken firm in the United States and a company enjoying tremendous growth. Sales had more than doubled from the pre-Holly Farms level of $2.54 billion of 1989 to $5.11 billion in 1994. Tyson was diversifying its operations to become more than just a poultry company, aiming to be a leader in all "center-of-the-plate" proteins. In 1994, poultry accounted for only 75 percent of Tyson's revenues. From this strong position, Tyson appeared ready to more aggressively pursue overseas opportunities, evidenced by the formation of a joint venture in the People's Republic of China in 1994, the opening of an office in Moscow in 1995, and the formation in 1995 of a subsidiary, World Resource, Inc., designed to help Tyson's customers throughout the world source products.

Principal Subsidiaries: Arctic Alaska Fisheries Corporation; Brandywine Foods, Inc.; Cobb-Vantress, Inc.; Culinary Foods, Inc.; Gorges Foodservice, Inc.; Louis Kemp Seafood Company; Tyson Export Sales, Inc.; World Resource, Inc.; Trasgo, S.A. de C.V. (Mexico; 50.1%).

Further Reading:

Behar, Richard, "Arkansas Pecking Order," *Time,* October 26, 1992, pp. 52–54.
Buckler, Arthur, "Tyson Foods Isn't Chicken-Hearted About Expansion," *Wall Street Journal,* January 18, 1994, p. B4.
Heath, Thomas, "A Booming Business Runs Afowl of Politics: Tyson Foods' Troubles Escalated Following Clinton's Election," *Washington Post,* July 23, 1995, p. H1.
Manning, Earl, "Don Tyson: The Chicken King Spreads His Wings," *Progressive Farmer,* March 1994, pp. 24–25.
McGraw, Dan, "The Birdman of Arkansas," *U.S. News & World Report,* July 18, 1994, pp. 42–46.
Ruggless, Ron, "Don Tyson: Chairman, Tyson Foods Inc., Springdale, Arkansas," *Nation's Restaurant News,* January 1995, pp. 213–14.
Schwartz, Marvin, *Tyson: From Farm to Market,* Fayetteville, Ark.: University of Arkansas Press, 1991, 158 p.
Stewart, D. R., "Tyson Forecasts Its Future in Faster Foods," *Arkansas Democrat-Gazette,* January 14, 1995, pp. D1–D2.
Tyson Corporate Fact Book, Springdale, Ark.: Tyson Foods, Inc., 1994, 40 p.

—updated by David E. Salamie

UNITED STATES
POSTAL SERVICE ™

United States Postal Service

475 L'Enfant Plaza S.W.
Washington, D.C. 20260
U.S.A.
(202) 268-2000
Fax: (202) 268-2175

Government-Owned Company
Founded: 1775
Employees: 728,944
Sales: $49.25 billion

The United States Postal Service is the executive branch of the U.S. government's largest independent agency. The service employs the country's largest civilian work force, which processes and delivers millions of pieces of mail every day. While increased competition in the mid-1990s was emerging from such independent courier services as Federal Express, UPS, Airborne Freight, and others, the service remained by far the most widely used mail delivery service in the United States.

On August 12, 1970, President Richard M. Nixon signed Public Law 91-375, which reorganized the federal Post Office Department as the United States Postal Service (USPS). Under the new law, which went into effect on July 1, 1971, the Service emerged as an independent agency of the executive branch, no longer under the control of Congress. Operational authority passed to a President-appointed and Senate-approved Board of Governors, and a managerial infrastructure, headed by the Postmaster General named by the Governors. No longer a cabinet member, the Postmaster General became the Service CEO. The law also gave the new agency the authority to issue public bonds to finance operations and to engage in collective bargaining between management and union representatives. It also established a postal rate-setting policy and procedure regulated by the independent Postal Rate Commission.

The reorganization and partial privatization of the Post Office Department was undertaken to solve difficulties that by the 1960s had made its traditional operation an ineffective and financially disastrous albatross for the American taxpayer. Because the rates charged for services no longer bore any relationship to their actual cost, the Post Office had come to depend heavily on federal subsidies, rendering it increasingly susceptible to the vicissitudes of partisan politics. Furthermore, the managerial organization had turned into a bureaucratic maze,

with a blurring of the lines of authority and fragmented control. Underfunding had also meant a continued reliance on antiquated facilities and equipment and mail-handling methods that, except for the introduction of the ZIP (Zoning Improvement Plan) Code in 1963, had not changed since the turn of the century, despite a vastly expanded volume of mail. The resulting inefficiency led to long delays in service, with jams that from time to time brought it to a virtual standstill, like that at the Chicago Post Office in 1966.

Along with the need to update both equipment and procedures, there was a clear need to reorganize management. In particular, labor-management relations had badly deteriorated in the 1960s. In March 1970, during Congressional deliberations on postal reforms, poor relations led to a six-day work stoppage involving about 152,000 employees at 671 locations. For many postal workers, the proposed changes, including a salary increase, were simply not substantial enough. However, the workers returned to their jobs when the Postmaster General agreed to giving the postal workers' unions a major part in planning reforms.

The restructuring of the Post Office Department as the U. S. Postal Service was a major overhaul of a federal department with roots in America dating back to the 17th century, when there was a need for correspondence between colonial settlements and trans-Atlantic exchange of information with England, the native country of most eastern seaboard settlers. The earliest mail services were disorganized and at best chaotic, with no uniform system in place until 1691, when Thomas Neale established a North American postal service under a British Crown grant and, in absentia, appointed Governor Andrew Hamilton of New Jersey his deputy postmaster general. Thereafter, under the control of the British Government, a centralized if erratic postal service operated in the colonies. In 1737, Deputy Postmaster General Alexander Spotswood, who had served as lieutenant governor of Virginia, named Benjamin Franklin, then 31, postmaster of Philadelphia. Franklin became joint postmaster general of the colonies and undertook important reforms that led to a more efficient, regular, and quicker mail service.

Mistrust of the royal postal service led to changes on the eve of the American Revolution. In 1774, the Crown dismissed Franklin because of his activities on behalf of the rebellious colonies. The colonists responded by setting up the separate Constitutional Post under the leadership of William Goddard. At the time of the first Continental Congress in 1775, Goddard's service provided inter-colonial service through 30 post offices operating between New Hampshire and Virginia.

The Continental Congress named Franklin chairman of a committee empowered to make recommendations for the establishment of a postal service. On July 26, 1775, the Congress approved the committee's plans, establishing the organization from which the U. S. Postal Service traces its direct descent and which, after the Bureau of Indian Affairs, is the second oldest federal department. The Congress wisely appointed Franklin the first Postmaster General. Although Franklin served just a brief period, until November 7, 1776, he is generally credited with being the chief architect of the modern postal service.

It was not until after the adoption of the Constitution in 1789 that a law passed on September 22, 1789 created the federal post office under the new government of the United States. It also established the Office of the Postmaster General. President Washington named Samuel Osgood to that post four days later. At the time there were 75 post offices and approximately 2,000 miles of post roads.

Additional legislation in the 1790s strengthened the U. S. Post Office by expanding its responsibilities and codifying its regulations. It remained in Philadelphia, the seat of the federal government, until 1800, when in just two wagons it moved all its furniture, records, and supplies to Washington, D.C., the nation's new capital.

The chief focus of the efforts of postal officials from the inception of the Post Office to the present day has been on ways to achieve a more efficient and effective mail service. Finding the best methods of transporting and directing mail have always been of primary concern. As a result, the Post Office has played a significant part in the development and subsidization of new modes of transportation. Willing to experiment in the handling and delivery of mail, the Post Office was quick to try out new inventions and policies, even some disastrous ones that led to scornful criticism and ridicule.

During the 19th century, a citizenry hesitant to accept things new and different watched comparatively rapid changes transform the postal service into a remarkable public convenience. By the start of the 1800s, the Post Office Department had bought several stagecoaches for transporting both mail and passengers on the nation's post roads. Its patronage led to better stagecoach design, insuring improved comfort and safety, and to better roads. Also, a full ten years before waterways became official post roads in 1823, the Post Office had begun using steamboats to transport mail between river-linked towns that shared no common road. By 1831, it had begun sending mail short distances via trains—the "iron horses" that many people denounced as demonic devices—and five years later awarded its first mail contract to a rail carrier.

Until replaced by automobiles and trucks at the beginning of the 20th century, horses remained major mail carriers, even over long distances, particularly during the period of westward expansion preceding the establishment of transcontinental telegraph and railway services. With the end of the Mexican War and the California gold rush of 1848, the need for effective communication between Atlantic and Pacific coastal cities quickly intensified. In that same year, the Post Office Department contracted a steamship company to carry mail to California. Ships from New York carried mail to Panama, where it was transported across the isthmus, then by ship again to San Francisco. The service was supposed to take between three and four weeks, a goal seldom realized in practice, and the Post Office sought alternative methods for getting the mail across North America in a more expeditious fashion.

In 1858, an overland service was contracted with a stage line, the Overland Mail Company, operating on a 2,800-mile route between Tipton, Missouri, and San Francisco. Semi-weekly stagecoaches began carrying mail in September of that year. The service was also prone to problems, however, and the advertised delivery time of 24 days in practice often ran into months. A solution was attempted by the Central Overland

California and Pike's Peak Express Company, which, without a contract with the Post Office, in 1860 began operating a mail carrier service between St Joseph, Missouri, and California. It was popularly known as the Pony Express. Changing mounts at established relay stations, riders could cover over a 100 miles per day. In March of 1861, the Pony Express carried President Lincoln's inaugural address over the route in under eight days, encouraging the Post Office to put the service under federal contract. It began operations under that arrangement in July 1861, but with the transcontinental telegraph hookup on October 24, 1861, the celebrated service, rendered instantly obsolete, was halted.

Some important procedural and organizational changes also marked the pre-Civil War development of the Post Office. In 1829, President Andrew Jackson invited Postmaster General William T. Barry to sit as a cabinet member, although Jackson had no formal authority for the move. Although Barry's predecessor, John McLean, had in fact begun calling the service the Post Office *Department* even earlier, it was not until 1872, after the Civil War, that Congress officially recognized it as such. A year after Barry took his cabinet seat under Jackson, the Office of Instructions and Mail Depredations was created as an investigative arm of the Post Office. It was headed by P. S. Loughborough, generally regarded at the first Chief Postal Inspector. Also, by 1840 all railroads in the United States had been designated as postal routes, which quickly expanded rail service, the main means of moving large quantities of mail well into the next century.

Initially, mail was not sent in envelopes. Writers would simply fold their letters and address them, then drop them off at post offices where their correspondents would pick them up. In larger cities, there was a local delivery system that charged an extra fee for carrying mail to homes and businesses. An important innovation was the postage stamp, first issued in 1847 and followed by its mandatory prepayment use in 1855. Prepaid postage helped facilitate a new system of free city delivery, which by 1863 was available in 49 cities.

During the Civil War, the Confederacy created its own Post Office Department, with John H. Reagan serving as Postmaster General. Although Reagan was appointed on March 6, 1861, it was a full two months before the Union Postmaster General, Montgomery Blair, stopped the federal mail service to the secessionist states. The war, with Union blockades of Confederate ports and its eventual invasion, seriously impeded postal service in the South. Even at the end of the war, with the restitution of the federal post, mail delivery was irregular. As late as November 1866, less than half of the post offices in the South had been fully restored to service.

After the Civil War, "post offices on wheels," or mail cars, came into a rapidly expanding use. They had first appeared during the war, in 1862, but it was not until August 1864 that an official Post Office route was put in operation between Chicago and Clinton, Iowa. Other routes quickly followed, providing mail sorting and handling services while trains were in transit. At first only letters were handled on the postal cars, but by 1869 all other types except parcels were being processed. The use of "post offices on wheels" would continue to grow well into the twentieth century. In 1930, when trains were still the most viable means of long-distance hauling, over 10,000 of them were used to carry mail to every city and rural town in the country. They would still be used into the 1970s, after the reorganization of the Post Office Department as the U. S. Postal Service, but very sparingly. The Transportation Act of 1958 had earlier insured their quick decline, so that by 1965 only 190 trains still carried and processed mail. The last to do so, which ran between New York and Washington, made its final run on June 30, 1977.

The invention of the horseless carriage and the airplane had much to do with declining use of mail cars and railroading in general. Both were extremely important in the changing face of the Post Office as it sought to provide service to the most isolated communities. Near the end of the 19th century, it inaugurated a system of rural free delivery (RFD) in a nation still in the process of shifting from an agrarian to an industrial society. Experiments with RFD were begun in West Virginia in 1896, despite vituperative complaints about its exorbitant cost and general impracticality. It was, however, a great boon to farm residents throughout America. It also stimulated the building and improvement of roads and highways, because service was only provided in places that had acceptable roads. So that local residents could qualify for RFD, town and county governments undertook these changes at public cost.

Improved roads were, of course, inevitable, thanks to the automobile. In the same year that it inaugurated RFD, the Post Office began experimenting with the "horseless wagon," and in 1901 awarded its first contract for a horseless carrier covering a short route in Buffalo. For the next decade the Post Office contracted such services through private companies, but in 1914, fed up with excessive charges and fraudulent practices, it requested and obtained the authority to establish its own motorized fleet of carriers. Two years before that, the Post Office had won another fight with private companies when it obtained permission to put in place its parcel post service, a move that stimulated the rapid growth of mail-order merchandising.

After World War I, which provided a proving ground for the flying machine, the Post Office undertook a serious expansion into airmail service. As early as 1911 it had experimented with the airplane, sponsoring several flights at fairs and meets in over two dozen states. In 1916, during the war, Congress even authorized a transfer of funds for the purpose, but it was not until 1918 that airmail service was begun in earnest. Using planes and pilots on loan from the Army Signal Corps, the Post Office began the first regular airmail service, between New York and Washington, D.C., on May 15 of that year. The date marked an important moment both in the history of the Post Office and commercial aviation.

The Post Office soon took complete control of the service, using its own planes and pilots, and despite reliance on primitive equipment and a lack of all navigational aids and weather data, compiled a remarkable safety record. The public was at first reluctant to pay the 24 cents charged for airmail letters, but interest picked up by 1920, when, on September 8, the last links were made to connect New York and San Francisco. By 1926, when the Post Office began contracting service with commercial airlines, it had won several awards for its pioneer work in night flying, the development of navigational aids, and the

general advance of aviation in the United States. The transfer of equipment and stations to the Department of Commerce and municipalities was completed by 1927, when the Post Office put all airmail service under contract to independent carriers.

The Post Office's methods of sorting and distributing of mail were, unfortunately, considerably less innovative. Despite some earlier experimentation with canceling and sorting machines, the old "pigeonhole" method of sorting and distributing mail remained in practice until the mid-1950s, when the Post Office began a serious effort to automate mail handling. It started issuing contracts for the development of a number of mechanical devices—from letter and parcel sorters to facer-cancelers and address readers.

Leading the way towards automation was a parcel sorting machine first used in Baltimore in 1956, but it was quickly followed by the importation and use of the Transmora, a foreign-manufactured, multi-position letter sorter. This was in turn superseded by an American machine, first tested in 1959, which remained in wide use into the 1970s. Other devices placed in service in the 1960s, when the mechanization program greatly accelerated, included Mark II facer-cancelers and a high-speed optical character reader (OCR) capable of sorting mail by the new ZIP Codes.

The ever increasing volume and change in the principal type of mail had made the changes mandatory. Most mail sent before World War II had been private correspondence, but by 1963, 80 percent had become business mail. The computer, an indispensable business tool, had already begun to play an important part in the rapid growth of business mail, so by the time that the Post Office was reorganized as the U. S. Postal Service in 1971, commercial matter was reaching the flood stage.

In fact, the most important problem faced by the newly created USPS was the upward spiraling volume of mail and the lack of adequate physical resources and equipment for handling it. Between 1970 and 1980, the volume of mail grew from just under 85 billion to 106.3 billion pieces, an increase of almost 20 percent. Alarmingly, it grew to 166.3 billion by 1990, and although the rate of growth abated thereafter, the problem of handling that quantity of mail remained formidable.

To deal with it, the U. S. Postal Service both updated equipment and sought new methods of improving its mail-handling efficiency. In 1978, it developed an expanded ZIP Code, which helped reduced the number of times mail had to be handled. In 1982, to exploit fully the revised ZIP Codes, the Postal Service installed its first computer-operated OCRs and barcode sorters (BCSs), and the next year introduced the ZIP + 4 code to further define address sectors in any geographical area. By 1985, the new equipment and ZIP Code refinements had made it possible for each key postal center to process 24,000 pieces of mail per hour, making it approximately four times as efficient as it had been using older sorting machines. By 1992, the Service also began replacing older facer-cancelers, the Mark II and M-36 models, with a more advanced facer-canceler system (AFCS), which, processing 30,000 pieces of mail per hour, proved twice as fast as the older models. Put in use, too, were multi-line optical character readers (MLOCRs), which, in conjunction with remote bar coding systems (RBCSs), were capable of sorting even hand-addressed envelopes after they have been sprayed with an identifying barcode. These automated mail-handling machines and procedures vastly improved the ability of the Service to handle the growing volume of mail efficiently.

Increased cost was the down side of improved efficiency, however. Between 1975 and 1985, the first-class letter rate rose from ten to 22 cents, and by 1995 it had increased to 32 cents, with proportional increases in other classes and types of mail. The greater expense to customers joined with a general slowdown in the economy quickly led to slower rate of growth in the volume of mail in the early 1990s. In fact, in 1991, it declined for the first time in 15 years.

The drop was also the result of growing competition, made possible, ironically enough, by the computer, the device that had played such an important role in the growth in the mail volume during the 1970s and 1980s. Fax machines, e-mail on the Internet, electronic money transfers, and increasingly competitive telecommunication rates offered viable and often preferred alternatives to the "snail" mail handled by the Postal Service. Many businesses that traditionally circulated advertisements via third-class mail, unhappy with the increasing rates, sought relief in telemarketing alternatives. Many mail order shippers also turned to Postal Service competitors like the United Parcel Service (UPS), which offered a quicker and more convenient package delivery service.

That competition caused the Service to undertake some restructuring. Of focal concern were customer needs and how these might best be met. In response, the Service instituted Customer Advisory Councils, made up of groups of interested citizens who worked closely with local postal managers to identify public concerns. There were 500 such councils in place by the summer of 1993. The Service also issued contracts with private firms to measure customer satisfaction with the mail service. Efforts to reduce bureaucracy and costs, improve customer relations, and stabilize postal rates followed. A downsizing program reduced the upper echelon personnel by one half, and, without layoffs or furloughs, cut other overhead positions by 30,000 through a policy of early retirements and other incentives. At the same time, it made strides towards it automation goals, which by 1994 were less than half realized. Estimates in that year were that 12,000 automation units would be in place and operating by 1977, a considerable increase over the 4,000 put in place between 1991 and 1994.

Downsizing and restructuring has helped the Postal Service considerably, but in the mid-1990s it still facee recurring prob-

lems that related to its massive size. For example, it was straddled with retirement benefit costs that total over ten percent of its sales, one of many reasons why it operated with an annual deficit. However, its size simply reflected the daunting nature of its task. The Postal Service handled 40 percent of the world's mail, processing about 580 million items per day. To do so, it employed the largest civilian work force in the nation, operated a transportation network using over 200,000 vehicles, and utilized over 250 million square feet of owned or leased office and storage space. If it were a private company, it would be one of the very largest in America, with a budget equal to about one percent of the Gross National Product. Moreover, despite its ungainly size, it remained doggedly efficient in its primary mission: to gets mail where it is supposed to go, and, usually, on time. According to its own 1994 assessment, the Postal Service will continue to "fine-tune" its size and organizational structure so as to be able to handle anticipated increases in the volume of mail efficiently as well as stabilize its operation. Its principal challenge will be to keep pace with the rapidly changing technology of the information revolution now in progress.

Further Reading:

Bruns, James H., *Mail on the Move,* Polo, Ill.: Transportation Trails, 1992.
Cullinan, Gerald, *The Office Department,* New York: Frederick A. Praeger, 1968.
——, *The United States Postal Service,* New York: Frederick A. Praeger, 1973.
Ferrara, Peter J, ed., *Free the Mail: Ending the Postal Monopoly,* Washington, D.C.: Cato Institute, 1990.
Fleishman, Joel L., ed., *The Future of the Postal Service,* New York: Frederick A. Praeger, 1983.
Jackson, Donald Dale, *Flying the Mail,* Alexandria, Vir.: Time-Life Books, 1982.
Long, Bryant A., and William J. Dennis, *Mail by Rail: The Story of the Postal Transportation Service,* New York: Simmons-Boardman Publishing Corp., 1951.
Scheele, Carl H., *A Short History of the Mail Service,* Washington, D.C.: Smithsonian Institute Press, 1970.
Sorkin, Alan L., *The Economics of the Postal System: Alternatives and Reform,* Lexington, Mass.: Lexington Books, 1980.
Summerfield, Arthur E., *U.S. Mail: The Story of the United States Postal Service,* New York: Holt, Rinehart and Winston, 1960.
The U.S. Postal Service: Status and Prospects of a Public Enterprise, Dover, Mass.: Auburn House Publishing Co., 1992.
U. S. Post Office Department, *A Brief History of the United States Postal Service,* Washington, D.C.: Government Printing Office, 1933.

—John W. Fiero

United Stationers Inc.

2200 East Golf Road
Des Plaines, Illinois 60016-1267
U.S.A.
(708) 699-5000
Fax: (708) 699-4716

Public Subsidiary of Wingate Partners (81%)
Incorporated: 1981
Employees: 4,000
Stock Exchanges: NASDAQ
Sales: $1.4 billion
SICs: 5112 Stationery & Office Supplies

United Stationers Inc. is the holding company for United Stationers Supply Co., the largest wholesale distributor of business
office products in North America. The company serves as a
liaison between manufacturers and retailers, distributing over
25,000 office products ranging from cleaning products to furniture to paper clips. United Stationers operates 30 regional warehouses and 28 smaller local distribution centers and sells to
traditional office supply retailers, office furniture retailers, mail
order houses, computer re-sellers, mass merchandise outlets,
and organizations of smaller retailers who band together to
profit from volume-buying discounts. United has remained
competitive in an increasingly difficult industry by focusing on
customer service. For the office products wholesale business,
this means providing retailers with the tools they need to profitably sell office supplies. In April 1995 Wingate Partners, a
Dallas-based private equity fund, purchased United Stationers
for approximately $258 million and merged it with its own
subsidiary, rival office-products wholesaler Associated Stationers. The merged companies continue under the name United
Stationers Inc.

Until the 1990s, United Stationers was primarily a family-run
business. Its roots trace back to 1921, when a trio of businessmen, Morris Wolf, Harry Hecktman, and Israel Kriloff purchased a 15-year-old office supply company in Chicago called
Utility Supply Co. Operating as an ''industrial loft stationer,''
Utility sold supplies such as paper, file folders, pens, and ink to
businesses in Chicago's downtown ''loop'' district by making
sales calls to nearby offices. The sales representatives would fill
the order at Utility's loft space on the top floor of an older

building, then return the next day to deliver the order. This was
the standard procedure for selling office supplies at that time.

Kriloff, a grocer, brought financial expertise to the business.
Wolf and Hecktman brought considerable salesmanship as well
as a customer base, having worked as salesmen for two of
Chicago's top office supply companies. When the three men
purchased the company, it was bringing in little more than
$12,000 in annual sales. By the end of their first year in business
together, the three partners had increased Utility's annual sales
ten-fold to $120,000. The company grew steadily through the
1920s, profiting from the booming U.S. economy of that decade. Although growth was slowed considerably after the stock
market collapse of 1929, the company was able to survive the
ensuing economic depression.

Following a trend started in 1892 by P. F. Pettitbone & Co., and
taken up by Utility's rival Horder's Associated Stationers Supply Co., Utility entered into another era of retailing in 1935
when it published its first catalog. ''Acting as an ever-present
representative of Utility Supply Co.,'' said company materials,
''The catalog could be sent to thousands of customers anywhere
in the country; successfully soliciting orders by mail or telephone.'' In 1937 Utility expanded again, opening its first retail
store in the heart of Chicago's bustling Loop. The company
reports that ''Business was good,'' so good that in 1939, when
Hecktman and Wolf bought Kriloff's share of the business,
Kriloff was able to take his retirement in Florida.

By this time Utility operated five retail outlets and had expanded its loft to serve as a warehouse for its retail outlets,
house administrative offices, and also to continue to serve customers through direct industrial sales.

Utility's foundation was shaken however, when the United
States became involved in World War II, creating a dearth of
office products because most raw materials were used in the war
effort. To keep the business afloat, Utility began offering general merchandise in its catalogs, at one time offering over 1,000
non-office products. Ultimately, the venture into non-office
supplies was unsuccessful, and by the end of World War II the
company was again concentrating solely on office products.

The postwar era was a period of tremendous growth for Utility.
The company mailed an extensive series of low-priced office
supply catalogs to retailers across the nation, developing a
reputation as ''the people from Chicago with the low prices.''
By 1948 the company was mailing as many as two million
catalogs per year and enjoying annual sales of $2 million. Forty
percent of sales were through mail order, 40 were through the
company's retail outlets, and the remaining 20 were through
direct industrial sales.

In the early 1950s the company made several major changes in
its sales operations. The most important was Morris Wolf's
decision to operate a segment of Utility as an office products
wholesaler, selling directly to independent office products retailers. There were two potential problems that Utility faced in
this decision. The first was the potential for conflict with its
existing retail and mail order businesses. Ultimately, Wolf
realized, the customers of Utility's wholesale business would
enter into direct competition with Utility's own retail businesses. The solution the company devised was to establish a

chain of franchised office supply stores, thus creating a "natural outlet" for their wholesale goods, and, they hoped, "expand both retailing and wholesaling." Franchises were opened in Milwaukee, Wisconsin, and Kankakee, Illinois; however, due to the scarcity of foot-traffic in these towns (as opposed to the high-density, heavily traveled Chicago Loop), the stores were unsuccessful. Attempts to boost franchise sales by sending sales representatives directly to potential industrial customers were also fruitless. By the late 1950s, Utility decided to discontinue its franchise operations and concentrate on wholesale, Chicago retail, and national catalog sales.

The second obstacle was the need to convince office products manufacturers that the Utility was serious about wholesaling, and not simply looking for a means of purchasing products at lower prices. Wilson Jones Co. was the first manufacturer to take interest in Utility as a wholesaler, which paved the way for other manufacturers to sell through the company.

Wholesaling became an even larger part of Utility's operations as office supply retailers began to appreciate the advantages of ordering from a wholesaler, as opposed to ordering directly from the manufacturer. Many office supply businesses were family operations that catered to a limited customer base. At that time, retailers were offered two options when purchasing goods for their stores: either buy them from a wholesaler or purchase them directly from manufacturers who frequently required dealers to buy large quantities of an item in order to receive a price discount. Although Utility's prices were slightly higher than manufacturers' discount prices, often it was to a retailer's advantage to buy small quantities from a wholesaler on an as-needed basis, as opposed to buying large quantities of an item when only a few were needed. The fact that many retailers needed only small quantities of certain items on an irregular basis served Utility's wholesale business well.

During the 1940s Howard Wolf, Morris Wolf's son, began working in the business and assumed the position of vice-president in charge of wholesale operations in 1952. Utility's burgeoning wholesale business grew. By 1956 the company had expanded to larger quarters, purchasing a building at 641 West Lake St. in Chicago, a move that doubled its warehouse and administrative office space. By 1960 the company's business volume had grown so much that Utility expanded into neighboring buildings, doubling its warehouse space again to over 300,000 square feet. In March 1960 Utility adopted the name United Stationers Supply Co. for its wholesaling business; its chain of retail stores retained the name Utility Stationery Stores.

Catalogs also served to boost sales of Utility's wholesale division. Early on, Utility realized that to generate its own sales, the independent retailers using Utility's business would need to generate sales. In 1959 Utility borrowed a concept from Horder's Associated Stationers Supply, its closest competitor, and began "syndicating" its office supply catalogs. For just under $2.50 each, retailers could buy 100 catalogs from Utility, with the store's name printed on the front cover. Utility took the concept a step further than its competitor, offering retailers a rebate on the price of catalogs based on a percentage of the products bought through the catalog from Utility Wholesale Supply Co. Benefits to retailers were twofold. The catalog

served as a marketing tool for retailers, and the more the retailer purchased from Utility, the less the overall cost of catalogs.

Utility's wholesale division grew rapidly during its first decade of operation. By 1966 coordination of activities was becoming a difficult and time-consuming task. Howard Wolf addressed the problem by purchasing an IBM 360/30 to track and record invoices, accounts receivable, and item demand. When the company began planning construction of a new warehouse in Forest Park, Illinois, Utility once again hired IBM to install a computerized inventory management system. The system was the first in the office products industry and represented a bit of a gamble for the company. However, the system was so successful that IBM proudly published numerous articles on the project.

In 1967, having grown their company's sales from $12,000 to $10 million, Morris Wolf and Harry Hecktman retired, and Morris's son Howard assumed the position of president and chief executive officer. The company's wholesale business grew quickly under the younger Wolf. By 1970 two-thirds of United's $15 million in annual sales came from its wholesale division. In addition to its catalog subscription program, Utility instituted a number of programs such as pricing services and promotional specials aimed at providing valued-added services to retailers. In addition, Utility began furnishing retailers with a computer system that provided a direct ordering link to its warehouses.

United also grew sales by expanding its catalog line. A promotional service launched in the early 1960s offered around 100 items at discount prices on color flyers printed with the retailer's name. Later Utility began publishing abridged catalogs targeted to specific groups or market segments. An office furniture catalog was introduced in 1967, a data processing catalog appeared in 1970, and in 1976, United's Basic Office Needs Directory debuted, offering a collection of frequently requested office supplies.

United continued to focus on its wholesale operations, expanding its business with the 1971 purchase of the wholesale division of Mutual Papers Co. of Detroit. United converted the newly acquired facilities into its first regional distribution center, directly linking operations at the Detroit warehouse with United's new computer system in Chicago. The venture was difficult and complex; however, after a year of operational difficulties that severely strained the company's financial resources, United's regional distribution center began to turn a profit. When United opened a third regional warehouse in Pennasauken, New Jersey, in 1973, the company experienced no start-up troubles.

The company then developed a number of Local Distribution Centers, low-cost redistribution points where shipment from its larger warehouses could be broken down for delivery to individual retailers nearby. This system assisted United in penetrating new markets and also offered lower costs to retailers as well as overnight delivery to most locations. In the mid-1970s, United established LCDs in St. Louis, Milwaukee, Kansas City, and Minneapolis/St. Paul, Boston, and New York.

In 1978 United sold its retail centers and began concentrating solely on expanding its wholesale business. Net sales that year were $106 million. Three years later, in August 1981, the company incorporated United Stationers Inc. (USI) to serve as a holding company for United Stationers Supply Co. USI went public on the NASDAQ exchange later that year and proceeds from the offering were used to construct a third regional distribution center in the Los Angeles area. Earnings in USI's first year as a public company were $4.8 million on sales of $200 million.

Sales grew steadily in the early 1980s, fueled by an increase in the number of white-collar workers and demands for computer-related office supplies. With its network of local and regional distribution centers, United was poised to profit from the demand, growing at a faster rate than both the wholesale and retail segments of the office supply industry. Increased sophistication of computers greatly aided in inventory management, allowing retailers to order goods through a computerized system and have them delivered by the following day.

The boom in the office supply industry was short-lived, however. Around 1985, office supply superstores and warehouse clubs began to threaten the existence of independent office products retailers, which made up United's traditional customer base. Independent retailers sold to two types of end markets. The first (and largest) was the corporate market, which was reached through outside sales representatives and catalogs, and remained unaffected by superstores. The second, smaller market comprised walk-in and small-purchase customers, whose business was more at risk of being attracted by the new superstores. United responded to the changing marketplace by developing marketing concepts to help independent retailers recapture some of the walk-in market segment. At the same time, the company sought to benefit from the changes by aggressively marketing to superstores and mail-order houses.

Sales in 1987 hit $720 million. However, the corporate market (which had remained unscathed by the growth of superstores) was beginning to shrink as many business began downsizing and laying off large percentages of their white-collar workforce. United responded by lowering prices and instituting volume-buying incentive programs and as well as targeting the specific needs of regional and local markets. To do this, the company continued to fortify its warehouse operations. By 1987 United had build nine more LCDs, providing access to markets in California, Texas, and the Eastern, Midwestern, and Southern regions of the United States. The following year, it opened a regional distribution center in southern Illinois, and another in upstate New York, bringing the total number of regional distribution centers to 14.

Sales from 1989 to 1991 hovered just below, but never broke, the $1 billion mark. The slumping office supply market was taking its toll on United, and in 1990 the company instituted a decentralization plan, laying off 15 percent of its staff at its headquarters near Chicago. The following year United expanded into the Canadian market by purchasing certain assets of an office supply wholesaler with warehouses in Canada and establishing its first foreign subsidiary, United Stationers Canada, Ltd. In 1992 sales broke the $1 billion level, fueled by the acquisition of Stationers Distributing Company, a general office products wholesaler with $425 million in sales and distribution centers across the United States. While much of the company's growth in the early 1990s was fueled by acquisition, United constantly sought new ways to market its products, creating a furniture division and a ''Custom Source'' division to market personalized products, as well as establishing its own line of office supplies, marketed under the ''Universal'' brand name. Sales in 1994 were $1.47 billion, slightly higher than 1993 sales. Net income declined 26.3 percent, due to unexpected expenses arising from merging Stationers Distributing's operations into its own.

In April 1995 Wingate Partners, a private equity fund, purchased United Stationers for approximately $258 million and merged it with its own subsidiary, office-products wholesaler Associated Stationers. While the merged companies assumed the United Stationers name, the purchase placed 81 percent of United's outstanding stock under Wingate's control, and effects of the merger have yet to be determined.

Principal Subsidiaries: Delaware Valley Pen Sales Inc.; MircoUnited, Inc.; United Stationers Supply Co.; United Stationers Canada, Ltd.

Further Reading:

''Acquired United Stationers Accepts Sweeter Deal, *Chicago Tribune,* February 15, 1995, Bus. Sec.
''Commitment to Success: The Story of United Stationers Inc.,'' Des Plaines, Ill.: United Stationers Inc., Summer 1987.
Gorman, John, ''Profits Aren't Stationary at Office Supplier, *Chicago Tribune,* July 15, 1985, Bus. Sec.
Taylor, Marianne, ''United Stationers Cuts Staff at Des Plaines Office,'' *Chicago Tribune,* March 22, 1991, Bus. Sec.
Young, David, ''Firm Seeks United Stationers Merger,'' *Chicago Tribune,* January 10, 1995, Bus. Sec.

—Maura Troester

URBAN OUTFITTERS

Urban Outfitters, Inc.

1809 Walnut Street
Philadelphia, Pennsylvania 19103
U.S.A.
(215) 564-2313
Fax: (215) 568-1549

Public Company
Incorporated: 1976
Employees: 1,100
Sales: $110.1 million
Stock Exchanges: NASDAQ
SICs: 2329 Men's/Boys' Clothing, Not Elsewhere Classified;
2339 Women's/Misses' Outerwear, Not Elsewhere
Classified

Urban Outfitters, Inc. is an American merchandiser, operating two chains of niche retail stores—Urban Outfitters and Anthropologie—as well the wholesale subsidiary Urban Outfitters Wholesale, Inc. Through its 20 Urban Outfitters stores in major U.S. metropolitan areas, the company offers casual clothing, accessories, and housewares aimed at the 18–30 age group. The three Anthropologie stores operating in 1995 cater to the over-30, upscale, suburban shopper, offering clothing, furniture, bedding, tablewares, and gifts. Urban Outfitters Wholesale designs, manufactures, and sells women's and men's clothing to over 1,000 specialty stores under four labels: Anthropologie, Co-Operative, Ecote, and Free People. Primary elements of the company's overall retail strategy include locating stores where their target customers are naturally concentrated; renovating and adapting existing structures to provide distinctive store environments; offering a broad mix of eclectic and fashionable brand name and private label apparel and home furnishings in the same store; and using innovative visual merchandising, striking store displays, and a distinctive mix of merchandise to present its wares.

Urban Outfitters was created in 1970 by two retail novices, anthropology graduate Richard Hayne and his former roommate at Lehigh University, Scott Belair. Hayne was just back from two years working with Eskimos in Alaska as a VISTA Volunteer; Belair was a second-year student at Wharton School of Business and needed a project for his entrepreneur workshop. Over beer one night, the two came up with the idea of a store for college and graduate students, selling inexpensive clothes and items for dorm rooms and apartments. Pooling $5,000, they opened the Free People Store in Philadelphia, near the campus of the University of Pennsylvania. The store offered inexpensive second-hand clothing, Indian fabrics, scented candles, T-shirts, drug paraphernalia, and ethnic jewelry, in 400 square feet decorated with packing crates and beat-up furniture. "I was that market," Hayne told Dan Shaw of the *New York Times* in 1994, adding that "everyone associated with the store was that market."

The store was a success. "Belair got an A on the project," according to Robert La Franco in a *Forbes* article, "and went on to Wall Street, where he [ran] his own bankruptcy workout business." Hayne stayed with the business, adding such merchandise as coffee mugs and glassware to the product line. In 1976 he moved to larger quarters near the university, changed the store's name to Urban Outfitters, and incorporated the company. In 1980, with sales around $3 million, Hayne opened a second store, in Cambridge, Massachusetts, close to several colleges.

In 1987 Hayne hired Kenneth Cleeland as chief financial officer. Cleeland, a graduate of George Washington University, had held financial positions with several wholesale and retail companies. At Urban Outfitters, he instituted financial controls to deal with shoplifting problems and Hayne's rather casual bookkeeping practices. Profits increased, and Cleeland helped Hayne borrow $3 million to open six new stores within three years.

New stores in the chain followed the original concept and were located in metropolitan areas near college students. By 1995, Urban Outfitters stores would be established in Madison, Wisconsin; Ann Arbor, Michigan; Boston; Minneapolis; Seattle; New York; Washington, D.C.; Chicago; and Portland. Moreover, the chain would also secure a presence in California, with five locations in college towns. Even when Hayne was tempted to drift from his original concept, store locations kept the company focused on its college-age market.

The new stores maintained Hayne's "counterculture" approach, and the company relied heavily on its buildings and interior displays to entice customers to enter, explore its stores, and buy its goods. "We always use renovated buildings," Hayne told *The Washington Post* in a 1993 feature. "Other stores will go into a mall and put their image into a space, where we use an existing space to enhance our image. None of our stores look alike. We go into these old buildings and adapt them for ourselves," he noted. In Washington, D.C., for example, the company took over a Woolworth's store, complete with worn wooden floors, exposed brick walls, and a steel staircase to the basement. The Ann Arbor store was established in an old theater, and other locations included a former bank and stock exchange. In 1993, Urban Outfitters stores averaged approximately 9,000 net selling square feet.

The decor within each stores was also unique, although the atmosphere remained similar throughout the chain—casual and fun. Much of this was due to the staff and the company's policy of listening to its customers. Hayne hired staff within the targeted age group and depended on their personal style to guide merchandising strategies. Staff decided on the music to be played, even bringing in their own compact disks, and department managers were made responsible for the look of their sections. "We have to come up with creative inventions for fixtures and displays," housewares manager Susan Duckworth, 27, explained in *The Washington Post,* adding that "It's the only place I've worked where you can bring an old crate to work, make something out of it and [the bosses] love it."

"We try to appeal to the mainstream and those who want to cross the line once in a while; we do stay abreast of fashion trends," Sala Patterson, an 18-year-old sales associate explained in the *Post* article. According to a 1995 *Forbes* story, Hayne spent $4 million a year on salaries and expenses for over 75 young fashion buyers who checked out neighborhoods in the United States, London, and Paris to report on hot fashion trends. The chain's unconventional atmosphere, merchandise, and music attracted students younger than 18 as well. As one 15-year-old explained to *The Washington Post,* "It's such a down-to-earth place, it's not a chain like the Gap and J. Crew. Everything's really different."

Urban Outfitters prepared its management, merchandising, and buying staff by recruiting recent college graduates and qualified store employees and sending them through a six- to nine-month "Management Development Program." While in the program, participants had a series of rotations between stores and the home office. A "Manager-in-Training" program offered the on-the-job experience needed to become departmental, assistant store, or store manager.

As the company grew, it took steps to keep its organizational structure relatively stable. Employees were eligible for profit sharing and stock options and took turns producing "Urban World," a quarterly in-house newsletter. Articles in the newsletter included reports from various branches and profiles of employees and customers, providing market research as well as internal communications. In 1993, the company initiated it "Shared Fate" program, designed to increase team management and give every employee the responsibility and authority to make decisions to increase productivity.

Recognizing that private label merchandise generally yielded higher gross profit margins than brand name merchandise, Hayne created the wholesale division in 1984 to design, produce, and sell its own line of junior sportswear. Michael Schultz joined the company in 1986 as president of Urban Wholesale, Inc. Schultz had previously served as president of Andrew Fezza International Division of Levi Strauss & Company and as a vice-president of merchandising at Pierre Cardin.

In 1990, the division replaced its signature Urban Outfitters collection brand with three separate labels: Ecote, Free People, and Anthropologie. The three apparel labels each targeted a different audience. Ecote produced solid and printed casual rayon dresses in styles ranging from baby dolls to A-lines and made up about 60 percent of the business in 1991. The Free People label produced sixties-inspired designs and hip casual-wear, while Anthropologie made young women's casual wear, primarily cotton, wool, and silk sweaters. Schultz expected Anthropologie to become the division's biggest label because it was the most adaptable. As reported in *Women's Wear Daily,* before the change, 70 percent of the division's sales were to department stores and 30 percent to specialty stores. In 1991, it

was just the opposite, as wholesale volume had grown 50 percent, from $10 million in 1989 to $15 million in 1990.

In 1993 and 1994 the Urban Wholesale division had revenue gains in excess of 76 percent and 56 percent, respectively. The company attributed this growth primarily to more and larger orders for the Anthropologie line from small and medium-sized specialty apparel stores. It should be noted that while much of the inventory of the company's stores was from the three labels, buyers for Urban Outfitters and Anthropologie did not automatically buy from the wholesale division. Urban Outfitters and Anthropologie accounted for 28.8 percent and .3 percent of Wholesale's total revenue in 1992, according to the company prospectus. By 1994, shipments of Urban Wholesale outside the U.S., particularly to Japan, was six percent of total sales. Merchandise made in the United States represented about 20 percent of the division's production.

As the number of stores grew and the wholesale division was revamped, company sales increased. In 1990, net sales amounted to $37.4 million. In 1991, sales increased 17.3 percent to $43.9 million. Most of the increase, 75 percent, was due to new stores opened in 1990 and 1991. The largest selling product category in Urban Outfitters stores was women's apparel. In 1992, it accounted for one-third of total sales, followed by footwear and accessories at 27 percent, men's apparel at 22 percent, and apartment wares and gifts at 18 percent.

In October 1992, Hayne opened the first Anthropologie store in a renovated automobile dealership in Wayne, Pennsylvania, outside Philadelphia, and named Glen Senk president. After 16 years of selling T-shirts, jeans, and work boots, and with his original chain doing well, Hayne thus took the company's strategy to older, more established shoppers living in the suburbs of major metropolitan areas. Anthropologie targeted customers who were focused on family, home, and career, with interests in travel, the arts, gardening, and reading. The Wayne store featured an espresso bar and placed greater emphasis on "hard-goods" such as furniture and a variety of home, garden, and tabletop products, including books and ceramics.

The decor of Anthropologie tended to be rustic and ecologically conscious. Product lines were intermixed and arranged in a variety of displays. For example, an antique bed might serve as the anchor for a section containing linens, towels, nightgowns, lingerie, soap, bath oils, picture frames. and mirrors. Another small area might feature children's clothes, books, toys, and note cards, while birdhouses and diaries of handmade paper might be found alongside men's sweaters and pants.

During 1992, company sales grew to $59.1 million, a 34.7 percent increase. The wholesale division introduced the Co-operative product line of fashion basics, consisting mostly of lower-priced cotton knit tops and sweaters. Profits also increased with the successful expansion of the company's higher-margin private label program.

During 1993, Hayne opened two more Urban Outfitters stores, in San Francisco and Costa Mesa. Comparable store sales increased by 18 percent and total sales exceeded $500 per selling square foot for the first time. The wholesale division opened a large sales office in New York. Prices at Urban Outfitters stores during 1993 ranged from $.75 for greeting cards to $450 for a

World War I-style leather bomber jacket. At the Anthropologie store, prices ranged from $1.00 for a greeting card to $1,500 for an antique Mexican cabinet. The company implemented its "Shared Fate" program for employees and initiated a company-wide profit sharing plan. Total sales for the year grew at 43 percent. In November, Urban Outfitters went public at $18 a share, raising over $13 million in capital through the initial public offering.

Hayne used the capital to continue his strategic plan of growth by adding new stores in the retail business and adding new customers and increasing sales to existing ones in the wholesale division. In 1994 he opened three new Urban Outfitters stores, two in Chicago and one in Pasadena, and indicated that he planned to open three or four new stores each year for next three years, some of which might be located outside the United States, in Canada and/or Europe. Based on the success of the Wayne, Pennsylvania, store, two more Anthropologie stores were opened in 1994, in Westport, Connecticut, and Rockville, Maryland, just outside Washington, D.C. In the company's annual report that year, Hayne indicated he hoped to open three to four additional Anthropologie stores each year and that the company would invest heavily in expanding the Anthropologie division. Overall company sales grew by 30 percent from 1993. Recognizing that high rates of growth would be difficult to maintain, the company set a goal of 20 percent annual growth.

In 1995, an Urban Outfitters store opened in Portland, Oregon, and lease signings were announced in Austin, Texas, and Tempe, Arizona, moving the company into the southwest for the first time. With steadily increasing sales during this time, the company gained a ranking as number 76 on the *Business Week* list of hot growth companies. As it neared the end of the century, the Urban Outfitters and Anthropologie chains appeared to be going strong, and, after a quarter century, Hayne and his staff were still successfully anticipating and responding to shifts in fashion trends and the changing tastes of their customers.

Principal Subsidiaries: Urban Outfitters Wholesale, Inc.; Anthropologie, Inc.

Further Reading:

Barrett, Amy, "Hot Growth Companies," *Business Week,* May 22, 1995.
Gilstrap, Peter, "Not-So-Radical Chic," *Washington Post Magazine,* September 12, 1993, p. 31.
Gordon, Maryellen, "Urban Outfitters' New Route," *Women's Wear Daily,* sportswear report supplement, January 2, 1991, p. 4.
Greenburg, Cara, "For School, Romance and Ripped Seams," *New York Times,* September 5, 1993, Sec. 9, p. 14.
La Franco, Robert, "It's All About Visuals," *Forbes,* May 22, 1995.
Shaw, Dan, "For Yubbies (Young Urban Bourgeois Bohemians)," *New York Times,* July 10, 1994, p. 31.
Zinn, Laura, et al, "Teens Here Comes The Biggest Wave," *Business Week,* April 11, 1994.

—Ellen D. Wernick

U.S. Bancorp

111 S.W. Fifth Avenue
P.O. Box 8837
Portland, Oregon 97208
U.S.A.
(503) 275-6111
Fax: (503) 275-6568

Public Company
Incorporated: 1968
Employees: 10,610
Total Assets: $21.8 billion
Stock Exchanges: NASDAQ
SICs: 6712 Bank Holding Companies; 6021 National
   Commercial Banks; 6022 State Commercial Banks

One of the 30 largest banking organizations in the United States, U.S. Bancorp is a regional multi-bank holding company for two retail and commercial banks, United States National Bank of Oregon and U.S. Bank of Washington. During the mid-1990s, United States National Bank of Oregon ranked as the largest bank in Oregon and the 52nd largest bank in the country, while U.S. Bank of Washington ranked as the third largest bank in its home state and the 99th largest nationally. Aside from these two principal subsidiaries, U.S. Bancorp owned numerous other subsidiaries involved in a variety of financial services, including mortgage banking, lease financing, consumer and commercial finance, discount brokerage, investment advisory services, and insurance agency and credit life insurance services. The breadth of U.S. Bancorp's business activities developed from the founding of United States National Bank of Oregon (originally incorporated as United States National Bank of Portland) in 1891 and its efforts to diversify its business by organizing U.S. Bancorp as a one-bank holding company in 1968.

U.S. Bancorp was organized as a holding company by the United States Bank of Oregon in the late 1960s, a time when many large banks across the country acknowledged and fostered their transformation into diversified financial services organizations by forming bank holding companies. The company's historical roots, however, stretch back nearly a century before the descriptive phrase ''diversified financial services organizations'' became part of banking nomenclature, reaching back into the late 19th century to a simpler age when the

business of banking comprised the rudimentary tasks of receiving deposits, cashing checks, and extending and collecting loans. Banking would develop into a much more sophisticated business by the time U.S. Bancorp first emerged in the late 1960s, but the company's true origins stemmed from the efforts of a handful of wealthy and influential businessmen during the early 1890s and their organization of The United States National Bank of Portland.

From out of the uncharted Portland wilderness, Oregon developed into a bustling commercial and industrial hub during the 19th century, its growth propelled by successive waves of settlers into the Pacific Northwest and the subsequent establishment of a spectrum of businesses and industries. As the community evolved from a secluded settlement into a burgeoning town, and finally into one of the principal cities underpinning the Pacific Northwest's economy, banks were there to promote and support its growth, serving as a crucial source of capital in a region far removed from the established financial centers in the eastern United States. Starting in 1859, when the first national bank in Portland, the Ladd and Tilton, was organized, Portland's business operators began to feed off the financial support of banks, using them as source for loans to develop their enterprises. As the town grew, requiring more and more capital to fund its development, the number of banks increased, totaling five in the state of Oregon by 1872, then jumping to 16 by 1880. Roughly a decade later, when more than 40 national banks were operating in Oregon, United States National Bank of Portland (U.S. National) was organized, founded by nine businessmen who created a banking institution that more than a century later would dominate the Pacific Northwest bank industry and rank as one of the largest financial services organizations in the country.

Led by Donald MacLeay, an immigrant from Scotland who made his fortune in the grocery and shipping business, and George Washington Ewing Griffith, a wealthy Kansas businessman, the founding directors, all of whom were born outside of Oregon, organized U.S. National on February 5, 1891, then opened the bank four days later in rented offices in downtown Portland. Although U.S. National operated without a vault during its inaugural year, the apparent lack of security did not dissuade customers from bringing their banking business to the city's newest bank. During the bank's first day, 15 customers opened new accounts, depositing a total of $21,886.30. By the end of its first year, fledgling U.S. National had become a thriving enterprise, holding $450,000 in deposits and capital stock and administering more than $350,000 in loans. It was an encouraging start for U.S. National, but before there was much chance for celebration, economic conditions in Oregon and throughout the nation soured, providing the bank with its first great test of resiliency while still in its infancy.

In 1893, two years after U.S. National began operating, a severe economic depression gripped the country, devastating more than 500 of the nation's banks and more than 16,000 businesses by the end of the year. Among the victims of the harsh economic conditions were a number of stable and respected Portland banks, but despite its status as neophyte in the area's banking community U.S. National beat back the debilitating affects of the economic downturn. The bank's deposits slipped from a high of more than $400,000 in 1892 to less than

$340,000 in 1896. But when the discovery of gold in the late 1890s swept away any lingering effects of the economic depression in the Pacific Northwest, U.S. National emerged stronger than ever before. For this strength the bank was indebted to the financial malaise of the early and mid-1890s, a deleterious period for many banks that left U.S. National occupying a more powerful position. Of Oregon's 41 national banks operating in 1892, only 27 remained after the depression, creating a more consolidated banking industry that buoyed U.S. National's position considerably. Of these 27 national banks that remained in business during the late 1890s, only four would survive to compete during the 20th century: Ainsworth National, Merchants National, First National, and the upstart U.S. National.

Less than a decade old at the turn of the century, U.S. National had already passed Ainsworth National in volume of business to rank as the third largest bank and was gaining ground on Merchants National to secure the industry's second position. Growth would come quickly during the first decades of the new century as bankers recouped their losses from the 1890s and shared in the prosperity of the times. During the first decade of the century, the number of national banks in Oregon increased from 27 to 75 and deposits quadrupled, as the city of Portland, with 200,000 residents by 1910, flourished economically. As one of the city's stalwart banks, U.S. National benefited greatly from the more robust economic conditions and was able to conclude several pivotal transactions that secured its inclusion among the region's leading banks. In 1902, U.S. National and Ainsworth National, the fourth largest bank, agreed to merge, creating a banking entity that kept the U.S. National corporate title and controlled resources valued at more than $2 million. Three years later, U.S. National merged with Wells Fargo Company's Portland bank, as growth and prosperity reigned, then in 1917 the bank merged with another large Portland bank, Lumbermens National. The merger with Lumbermens National increased U.S. National's deposits by $6.5 million and made it the second largest bank in the Pacific Northwest.

By the beginning of the 1920s, U.S. National had deposits of more than $36 million, having grown considerably during its first 30 years of operation. In the decades ahead, however, U.S. National would record growth of proportions that would dwarf its achievements during the bank's formative decades. In 1925, the bank set the tone for the magnitude of growth ahead when it merged with the venerable Ladd and Tilton. Aside from being the region's oldest bank, Ladd and Tilton represented a potent banking competitor, with more than $20 million in deposits and 30,000 depositors. Once Ladd and Tilton was merged into U.S. National, U.S. National received a substantial boost to its stature, becoming the largest bank north of San Francisco and west of Minneapolis, with resources totaling $64.6 million, deposits reaching $60 million, and a large base of depositors that numbered 75,000.

The 1920s were heady years for U.S. National, but as the events of the next decade unfolded, the bank faced economic conditions far more menacing than those surmounted during the 1890s. During the Great Depression more than half of the country's banks were financially ruined, thousands of businesses were devastated, and the ranks of unemployed swelled beyond precedent. Like the economic depression touched off in 1893, however, U.S. National withstood the pernicious effects

of financial collapse all around it, although deposits once again shrank during the period. Deposits reached a high of $71 million in September 1931, then over the next eight months fell by $10 million; however, by the late 1930s business began to recover and the bank's deposits eclipsed $100 million. Perhaps the most important occurrence during the otherwise crippling 1930s was the enactment of legislation enabling banks to establish branches, which U.S. National began doing in 1933 and would continue to do thereafter.

During the 1940s, U.S. National expanded its presence geographically by acquiring existing banks and converting them to U.S. National branches, such as the bank's 1940 purchase of the Medford National Bank, First National of Corvallis, and the Ladd and Bush Bank of Salem. Although the number of banking units comprising U.S. National's growing branch network rose only modestly during World War II, climbing from 26 to 29, deposits nearly tripled during the war years, leaping to $581 million by the end of 1945. Following the war, when an era of widespread prosperity gave large segments of the American population substantially more disposable income than ever before, the national banking industry underwent a dramatic shift, as banks across the country began focusing on the consumer with concerted intensity. Loans for consumer purchases proliferated, and U.S. National responded by augmenting its consumer credit department with a branch consumer credit department in 1949. Bank advertising during the era reflected the significant shift in focus, as advertisements began to emphasis the availability of loans for individuals and the use of bank credit, rather than encouraging thrift as the they had done since U.S. National's inception.

Between 1945 and 1955, 35 banking units were added to U.S. National's branch system, the bulk of which—29—were acquired through mergers and acquisitions, as the bank swallowed smaller competitors and outpaced larger competitors with its aggressive expansion across the state of Oregon. Aside from ranking as one of the larger state banks in the nation, U.S. National also began to distinguish itself as an industry pioneer during the 1950s by offering such innovative services as drive-up banking, erecting the first motor banking facility in Oregon in 1956, and leading the way with a computerized system to post checks in 1957.

In contrast to the 1950s, U. S. National expanded its branch network through internal means during the 1960s, creating new banking facilities rather than absorbing existing banking units through mergers or acquisitions. By 1965, the bank operated 100 branches across the state, a considerable presence that the bank's directors had acknowledged the previous year by changing the bank's name from United States National Bank of Portland to United States National Bank of Oregon. Other, more significant, changes were in the offing as the bank entered the late 1960s and began to formulate a plan for the future, in search of a way to contend with the mounting pressures affecting banks during the period.

The business of banking had become a complex and highly competitive endeavor by the 1960s, substantially more sophisticated than when U.S. National first opened its doors in 1891. In addition to a much broader range of financial services offered by commercial banks, the market for these services had become more competitive since World War II. Between 1945 and 1960, savings in commercial banks like U.S. National had doubled, whereas the amount in savings and loan associations had sextupled and the amount in credit unions had increased an enormous tenfold, absorbing business that would traditionally have gone to commercial banks.

In response, commercial banks began to form one-bank holding companies during the late 1960s, enabling them to acquire and organize other subsidiaries that could legally offer a broader range of services. With a broader range of financial services, banks hoped to beat back the competition and keep noncommercial banks from entering into financial activities that historically had been under the exclusive purview of commercial banks. On September 9, 1968, U.S. National followed the nationwide trend by forming U.S. Bancorp as a one-bank holding company, heralding the development of a vast financial services network and the extension of U.S. Bancorp beyond Oregon's borders.

Once able to delve into new businesses, U.S. Bancorp did so with fervor, organizing a host of financial services subsidiaries during the 1970s: Bancorp Leasing, Inc., which was organized to enhance service to business customers through lease financing; U.S. Bancorp Financial, Inc., a subsidiary formed to specialize in asset-based commercial financing; and Mount Hood Credit Life Insurance Agency, which was created to centralize and streamline credit-related insurance activities throughout the U.S. National system. Numerous other subsidiaries were formed in the wake of U.S. Bancorp's founding, transforming the U.S. National-U.S. Bancorp network into a genuine regional financial services organization.

By the beginning of the 1980s, U.S. Bancorp was well on its way to becoming one of the preeminent regional financial services organizations in the country. Decidedly acquisitive throughout the 1980s, the holding company started the decade by establishing The Bank of Milwaukee, a state-chartered bank, in 1980, making U.S. Bancorp a multi-bank holding company. During the year, the company also acquired State Finance and Thrift Company of Logan, Utah, and established Citizen's Industrial Bank in Littleton, Colorado, further bolstering its out-of-state presence in regions where U.S. National was not allowed to operate. By the end of the year U.S. Bancorp's territory included California, Texas, Washington, Utah, Idaho, Colorado, Montana, and its home state of Oregon, giving the company ample room to grow as the decade progressed.

With the acquisition of Spokane, Washington's Old National Bancorp and Seattle, Washington's Peoples Bancorp in 1987, U.S. Bancorp became the largest bank holding company based in the Northwest. During the late 1980s, the company continued to aggressively pursue smaller rival banks, hoping to achieve a dominant position in markets opened up earlier in the decade. Other large banking organizations followed a similar strategy,

creating a nationwide trend toward consolidation that left U.S. Bancorp as the last major independent bank in the Pacific Northwest by the early 1990s. With $19 billion in assets in 1992, the company ranked as the 32nd-largest bank in the United States.

During the next two years, U.S. Bancorp's management began to focus their efforts on achieving greater efficiency by streamlining the company's operations and eliminating nearly a quarter of its work force through layoffs and the divestiture of noncore subsidiaries. After two years of implementing severe downsizing measures, the company announced a momentous acquisition in 1995 that added substantially to U.S. Bancorp's already sizable holdings. Intent on strengthening its position in Idaho, where the company maintained only a token presence, U.S. Bancorp officials announced the $1.6 billion acquisition of West One Bancorp of Idaho in May, which the shareholders of both banking organizations agreed to in October. Once completed at the end of 1995, the deal would make U.S. Bancorp one of the 30 largest banking organizations in the country, with $30 billion in assets and $21 billion in deposits.

Principal Subsidiaries: United States National Bank of Oregon; U.S. Bank of Washington, National Association; U.S. Bank of California; U.S. Bank of Idaho, National Association; U.S. Bank of Nevada; First State Bank of Oregon; Heart Federal Savings and Loan Association; U.S. Bank of Southwest Washington; U.S. Savings Bank of Washington; U.S. Bank, National Association; Qualivest Capital Management, Inc.; U.S. Bancorp Securities; U.S. Bancorp Insurance Agency, Inc.; U.S. Bancorp Leasing and Financial; U.S. Bancorp Mortgage Company.

Further Reading:
Anderson, Michael A., "U.S. Bancorp's Interstate Bid Begins Anew," *Business Journal-Portland,* May 19, 1986, p. 1.
Bennett, Robert A., "Roger Faces Goliath," *United States Banker,* June 1992, p. 20.
Crockett, Barton, "U.S. Bancorp to Ax 52 Branches after Merger," *American Banker,* October 27, 1995, p. 4.
Fitch, Mike, "Mother Lode's Buyer Got Good Deal, Say Observers," *Puget Sound Business Journal,* November 6, 1989, p. 22.
Heind, John, "Buy or Be Bought," *Forbes,* May 18, 1987, p. 48.
Jaffe, Thomas, "Cheap Bank," *Forbes,* June 29, 1987, p. 122.
Manning, Jeff, "Bankruptcies May Be Lever for U.S. Bank," *Business Journal-Portland*, December 9, 1991, p. 1.
"Purchase by U.S. Bancorp to Create Northwest Giant," *New York Times,* May 9, 1995, p. D2.
"Shareholders Approve Merger of U.S. Bancorp & West One Bancorp," *PR Newswire,* October 3, 1995, p. 1.
Taylor, John H., "No Chest-Beater," *Forbes,* May 11, 1992, p. 172.
Zimmerman, Rachel, "Branch Closures Likely in U.S. Bank-West One Deal," *Puget Sound Business Journal,* August 25, 1995, p. 7.

—Jeffrey L. Covell

THE **Vanguard** GROUP
OF INVESTMENT COMPANIES ®

The Vanguard Group of Investment Companies

1300 Morris Drive
Wayne, Pennsylvania 19087
U.S.A.
(610) 648-6000
Fax: (610) 648-6000

Private Company
Incorporated: 1974
Employees: 2,300
Assets: $152 billion
SICs: 6282 Investment Advice

The Vanguard Group of Investment Companies is one of the most successful mutual funds in the United States. Managing over $155 billion worth of investors' money, the firm provides an entire family of mutual funds from real estate to bonds funds. One of the company's most important innovations was the Vanguard Index Trust, started in 1974. A portfolio of stocks that track the broad market, the Index Trust is the largest of all such portfolios in the investment community, with approximately $13.4 billion under its management. Vanguard was also the first mutual fund company to offer three maturities of municipal bonds, including short term, intermediate, and long term. Despite the volatility of the stock market during the late 1980s and early 1990s, customers continued to flock to Vanguard's family of mutual funds because it maintained one of the lowest expense ratios—the relation of management costs for a fund to the amount of assets in the fund—within the financial services industry.

Although the Vanguard Group of Investment Companies was started in 1974 by John C. Bogle, its predecessor goes back to 1929. The Wellington Fund was started by Walter L. Morgan in July of 1929. Morgan, a certified public accountant with a degree from Princeton University, was convinced that the ordinary investor with limited money needed a diversified investment portfolio managed by a professional staff, rather than just venturing out on his own and buying individual company stocks. Massachusetts Mutual Fund, America's first mutual fund, was established in 1924 in Boston, and Morgan immediately recognized the opportunity that such an investment service provided.

When Morgan formed the Wellington Fund, he based the firm's investment strategy on three principles: 1) that the fund was

unleveraged rather than leveraged, thus reducing the risk involved in using money that was borrowed; 2) that Wellington would be an open-end fund rather than a closed-end fund, and 3) that Wellington would be a balanced rather than a common stock fund, thereby reducing a customer's risk by including bonds as well as stocks in the individual's investment portfolio. These highly conservative decisions made in the midst of the most rampantly speculative era in stock market history served Morgan well. With the coming of the stock market crash in the autumn of 1929, the Wellington Fund not only remained in business but prospered. Capitalizing on its conservative investment philosophy, the fund's assets passed the $1 million mark by 1935 and grew steadily. By 1943, the Wellington Fund reported over $10 million in assets and by 1949, over $100 million.

Throughout the 1950s and early 1960s, Wellington Management Company, the formal organization with the responsibility of managing the Wellington Fund's assets, operated on four principles: a conservative investment philosophy, an emphasis on long-term investment performance, a single fund without any related or "sister" funds, and a comprehensive, well-organized sales and marketing campaign through brokers and investment advisors across the country.

As the years passed, however, what had worked for the company during the previous years was no longer viable for the era of burgeoning stock market investments. By the late 1960s, the company's strategy of a balance fund was out of favor with almost all investment advisors. The Wellington Fund, once the leader in balanced fund investing, fell to lower and lower performance levels. At the same time, Walter Morgan decided to retire from active management of the fund, and hired John C. Bogle, a Princeton University graduate. Morgan encouraged Bogle to revive the Wellington Fund by whatever means necessary, and the young man immediately established a strategy which included the acquisition of an aggressive growth fund, the entry into the investment counsel business, and hiring highly capable and experienced portfolio fund managers.

Carrying out Bogle's new plan as quickly as possible, The Wellington Company purchased Thorndike, Doran, Paine and Lewis, Inc., a well-established and successful investment firm in Boston, Massachusetts, that managed the Ivest Fund. The new acquisition also included an investment counsel business and four talented portfolio managers. The marriage of The Wellington Company's administrative and marketing operations to Thorndike, Doran, Paine and Lewis's investment expertise was concluded in 1967. It was assumed that Bogle would become the chief executive office of both company's and their respective funds. From the very start of the merger, events seem to conspire against its success. The stock market declined, both the Wellington Fund and Ivest Fund performed poorly, and business in general was on the downswing. Dissatisfaction began to arise among management and in 1974, because Bogle's associates from the Boston firm had a majority on the Wellington Management Company's board of directors, they summarily fired him.

Although Bogle was heartbroken over his dismissal and the loss of what he considered to be his company, he was determined to revive his fortunes. The Wellington Fund was required by United States federal law to have a board of directors independent of the managing company's board of directors. This latter group of directors voted to retain Bogle as chairman of the fund. Bogle then advocated to his board of directors that the Wellington Fund and Ivest Fund should be given complete independence of the Wellington Management Company. Yet the board of directors at the fund decided that Wellington Management Company should continue providing marketing and portfolio management services and also keep its name; at the same time the two funds, Wellington and Ivest, should be made independent of the Wellington Management Company and be given a new name. Bogle chose the name Vanguard, in honor of Lord Horatio Nelson's flagship *HMS Vanguard* during the Napoleonic Wars. Incorporated in 1974, The Vanguard Group of Investment Companies opened for business in July of 1975.

Bogle had advocated that the Wellington Fund and the Ivest Fund should be their own distributor. At first the board of directors rejected this proposal, but in 1977 it was decided that the two funds should get rid of Wellington Management Company as their distributor and designate Vanguard. The move resulted in an immediate cessation of the traditional broker-dealer distribution network that had always been used by the two funds and the total elimination of any sales charges. The conversion to what is now called a ''no load'' fund was due to the demand from consumers for lower prices in the management of their money. Initially, the company's cash flow reflected a loss of $125 million in 1976, but by 1977 Vanguard proudly reported a complete turnaround—its cash flow had jumped to a positive $50 million.

The 1980s were some of the brightest years for the company. Bogle decided to bring in-house the management of Vanguard's fixed income portfolio, which included six money market and municipal bond funds whose assets were approximately $1.8 billion. During this period, Vanguard's total assets rose from $500 million to almost $4 billion. The company's Windsor Fund, a mixed equities portfolio, was one of the best performing mutual funds in the nation during the entire decade, and its assets increased from $900 million to nearly $8 billion. Assets for the Vanguard Index Trust, the first index mutual fund in the world, skyrocketed from a mere $90 million to an astonishing $7.5 billion. By the end of the decade, Vanguard was acknowledged as the leading no-load mutual fund service which, in turn, led to more profitable returns and greater growth. The assets managed by the company had grown from $3 billion in 1980 to over $50 billion by the fall of 1990.

Vanguard's impressive growth during the 1980s was carried along by one of the most active and positive periods in the worldwide financial markets. During the early 1980s, both stocks and bonds started to produce tremendous returns on investments. On average throughout the decade, the bond market produced an annual rate of return of 13 percent, the highest in the history of the market. At the same time, the stock market came close to its historically highest rate of return, averaging an annual return of just over 18 percent. In addition, tax laws were changed in favor of retirement programs, and individual retirement accounts (IRAs) greatly enhanced the total asset base of the mutual fund industry. In fact, assets for the entire mutual fund industry leaped from $240 billion in 1981 to approximately $1.3 trillion by 1991, a sixfold increase. Although the company's portfolio managers were able and talented money

men, Vanguard doubtless rode the crest of the wave across all the financial markets. Assets managed by Vanguard in December of 1991 had increased to $75 billion and to an impressive $78 million in mid-January of 1992. Since its inception, Vanguard's asset base had grown at a phenomenal compounded growth rate of 35 percent annually.

The Vanguard Group of Investment Companies was in the vanguard of the mutual fund industry during the early and mid-1990s. The Vanguard Index Trust had grown into one of the largest equity mutual funds in the world, and the company set the standard for market indexing management. Consumerism led the way toward a cost-consciousness within the industry that has had lasting effects. Many of the mutual funds created during the early part of the decade were ''no-load'' direct marketing funds, following the lead that Vanguard had set years earlier. Ever mindful of the way extra costs decrease a customer's yields, in 1993 Vanguard introduced four new no-load funds with minimal expenses. Called the Admiral funds, these funds had an expense ratio, which includes money management fees and other costs, of a mere 0.15 percent of net assets. Compared with an average of 0.53 percent for United States Treasury money-market funds and 0.93 percent for United States Treasury bond funds, many investors were pleased with the bargain. This difference was telling, since only $100 in expenses would be paid by a customer who invested in the Vanguard Admiral U.S. Treasury Money Market Portfolio as opposed to $440 dollars in expenses in a Fidelity Spartan fund. The only drawback was that the Admiral funds required a minimum investment of $50,000.

In 1994, Vanguard enjoyed one of its best years. Although the market for bonds was highly volatile due to leveraged and risky kinds of derivatives and many mutual funds that specialized in bonds suffered as a result, Vanguard escaped the turmoil because of its supremely efficient bond fund management. In addition, when diversified stock funds lost 1.7 percent across the entire mutual fund industry, Vanguard's low costs and expenses enabled its stock funds to post an impressive 0.6 percent average gain. Not surprisingly, 16 out of Vanguard's 18 diversified stock funds performed better than the industrywide average. By the end of 1994, Vanguard's total asset base had increased to $132 billion.

In July of 1995, John J. Brennan was chosen to succeed John C. Bogle as chief executive officer of Vanguard. Brennan, only 40 years old at the time of the appointment, had worked at the company for 13 years and had acted as a Bogle's deputy since 1989. Brennan's vision included continuing the emphasis on index funds that his predecessor had started, along with the strategy of low-cost management of all the firm's mutual funds. Brennan also laid plans to invest in new technology that would allow people to transfer money from their bank to buy a Vanguard fund by using a personal home computer. In addition, he hoped to offset the competition from discount brokers by setting up a network so Vanguard would be able to sell non-Vanguard funds for a small transaction fee.

With the stock market climbing to record highs throughout 1995, both institutional investors and private investors began to pour money into mutual funds that were designed to follow the performance of market measures such as Standard & Poor's

500. These index funds became the leading performers during the year. Index funds that mimicked Standard & Poors' 500 reported increases of 19.9 percent during the first six months of 1995, compared to the average equity fund that only gained 16.6 percent during the same period. Vanguard's Index 500 Fund, with over $13 billion in assets, was the largest such portfolio. In the first half of 1995, the fund had taken in a net $1.5 billion of new money from investors. With the influx of such a large amount of money, the Index 500 became the company's largest stock fund.

At the end of 1995, Vanguard listed a wide range of mutual funds that investors could choose from, including money market funds, tax-exempt income funds, state tax-exempt income funds, fixed-income funds, balanced funds, growth and income funds, growth funds, aggressive growth funds, and international funds. A few of the company's most success mutual funds included the 500 Portfolio Fund, an index fund that invested in all the 500 stocks of Standard & Poor's 500 Composite Stock Price Index and which recorded an average annual return of 16.99 percent over the five-year period ending September 30, 1995; the Growth and Income Portfolio Fund, another index fund that reported an average annual return of 25.63 percent during the recent five-year period ending in September 1995; and the Vanguard Explorer Fund, an aggressive-growth fund that specialized in emerging companies with highly attractive growth potential and which recorded an average annual return of 22.84 percent over the five-year period ending in September 1995.

Further Reading:

Bogle, John, *Vanguard: The First Century,* Newcomen Society: New York, 1992.
Edgerton, Jerry, "Vanguard's New Skipper Will Push High-Tech Service and Index Funds," *Money,* July 1995, p. 53.
Grover, Mary Beth, "Feast or Famine," *Forbes,* July 4, 1994, p. 150.
Hardy, Eric S., and Zweig, Jason, "Vanguard's Achilles Heel," *Forbes,* May 8, 1995, p. 148.
Kaye, Stephen D., "Inside Vanguard," *U.S. News & World Report,* February 6, 1995, p. 70.
Misra, Prashanta, "The Vanguard Group Comes Begging for Less," *Money,* April 1993, p. 56.
Spiro, Leah Nathans, "Vanguard: Cutting Expenses, Boosting Returns," *Business Week,* March 1, 1993, p. 108.
Zweig, Jason, "Vanguard: The Penny-Pincher," *Forbes,* August 28, 1995, p. 164.

—Thomas Derdak

Verbatim Corporation

1200 W.T. Harris Boulevard
Charlotte, North Carolina 28262
U.S.A.
(704) 547-6500
Fax: (704) 547-6565

Wholly Owned Subsidiary of Mitsubishi Kasei Corporation
Incorporated: 1969 as Information Terminals Corporation
Employees: 1,300
Sales: $290 million
SICs: 3695 Magnetic & Optical Recording Media

One of the world's leading image and data storage media technology developers, Verbatim Corporation was one of the first manufacturers in the floppy disk industry, making its start several years after its founding in 1969. By virtue of a licensing agreement reached by the company's founder with International Business Machines (IBM), Verbatim began manufacturing floppy disks in the early 1970s, then went on to secure a dominant position in a market that would become intensely competitive. Based in Charlotte, North Carolina, Verbatim operated production facilities and sales offices throughout the world.

By the mid-1960s Reid Anderson had already devoted much of his life to his professional career. During the 1940s and 1950s, Anderson had spent 17 years working for Bell Laboratories developing electronic switching and storage devices, then moved on to NCR Corporation, spending two years there before arriving at the Stanford Research Institute, where he developed new products for an additional five years. Aged 46 when he ended his stay at Stanford Research Institute, Anderson was an unlikely candidate for entering into the frequently disappointing world of entrepreneurship, but in 1964 he did just that, leaving his position at Stanford Research Institute to start his own company. Although it would be another five years before Anderson pointed himself in the right direction, his first fateful steps in 1964 would lead to the founding of one of the world's preeminent companies in the computer disk industry.

While employed at Stanford Research Institute, Anderson had been working on developing new products for an assortment of companies, "essentially starting new businesses for various companies," as he would later reflect to *Forbes*. His entrepreneurial spirit aroused, Anderson used a transistorized metro-

nome-tuner he had designed to launch his own small business making metronomes for musicians like himself, an amateur clarinet player. The confluence of hobby and profession worked well, but after three years Anderson came to the realization that he had exhausted the market for metronomes in his area and, consequently, began looking for another business opportunity.

Following his three-year metronome venture, Anderson teamed up with a business consultant named Ray Jacobson and formed Anderson Jacobson, which produced acoustic data couplers, devices that permitted computer data to be transmitted over telephone lines. Before long, however, Anderson was drawn to the lucrative possibilities of another product. After recalling his years at Bell Laboratories when he worked on the development of magnetized tape in cassettes, Anderson was hopeful that the relatively new technology employed in the production of magnetized cassette tape would realize tremendous financial gains for a savvy entrepreneur. Anderson approached his business cohort about the idea of changing their product line, but Jacobson balked at the proposal, leaving it up to Anderson to launch the business himself.

The year was 1969 and Anderson was in his fifties, preparing to establish his own company after two less-than-spectacular efforts. He borrowed money from a bank and convinced several friends and relatives to loan him additional cash, giving him enough capital to found Information Terminals, which would be renamed Verbatim and develop into the largest manufacturer of magnetic computer floppy disks in the world. Before Anderson's fledgling company would begin its meteoric rise, however, one essential ingredient needed to be added: Information Terminals had been founded to manufacture data cassettes, not floppy disks. Anderson made the pivotal switch to that product four years after starting Information Terminals when he realized data cassettes would soon be outdated by faster 8-inch floppy disks. Floppy disks, which were used for recording, storing, and retrieving computerized data, were a revolutionary product first introduced by IBM in 1973. Anderson approached IBM, asking the behemoth company if he could license the new floppy disk technology, and IBM, more concerned with selling its expensive computers than selling five-dollar disks, agreed.

Annual sales at Anderson's Sunnyvale, California-based company before and after the licensing agreement with IBM provided ample and tangible proof of the boon floppy disk production represented. Sales in 1972 were a respectable $480,000, but two years later Anderson's signal licensing agreement with IBM had driven his company's annual revenue total to $4.3 million. Earnings had spiraled upward as well, enabling Verbatim to net more than half of what it had grossed two years earlier. Among the company's products were 8-inch floppy disks and 5.25-inch floppy disks, both of which would drive Verbatim's annual sales upward during the 1970s. By 1976, the company's annual sales had nearly tripled in two years' time, jumping to $12 million. Three years later, in 1979, the same year Verbatim became a publicly owned company, annual sales surged to $36 million, and the following year sales eclipsed the $50 million mark.

Verbatim's growth during the 1970s had been incredibly vigorous, transcending Anderson's hopeful expectations and outstripping all other floppy disk manufacturers, but as the 1980s began Verbatim became a victim of its own success. Rapid expansion had engendered a sprawling, loosely organized management structure. Uninhibited success, which had flourished for a decade, bred a debilitating complacency, and quickly the company found itself in trouble. Annual sales, which had swelled exponentially ever since Anderson approached IBM about obtaining a licensing agreement, recorded only a modest gain at the beginning of the 1980s, inching from $50 million in 1980 to $53 million in 1981, one year after earnings had plunged 43 percent.

At the heart of Verbatim's lackluster financial results were quality-control problems wrought by lackadaisical production management and over-confidence that the future would be as bright as the past. The company had let its guard down and customers started to complain, beginning in 1980 when problems with Verbatim's floppy disks began to surface. Specifically, Verbatim had used an incorrect chemical formulation for the material used to coat their disks' media base, which was exacerbated by additional problems with the protective liner used in the disks' jackets. As the number of complaints mounted, Verbatim reeled and its once stalwart financial growth shuddered to a stop.

The company announced a massive recall of its faulty disks, establishing a $1.5 million reserve against returns, but a recall solved only one of the many problems that had spread throughout Verbatim. To eradicate the complacency that had deleteriously affected the company, Verbatim's board of directors voted for wholesale changes, hiring Malcom Northrup, a technology manager at Rockwell International's semiconductor division, as chief executive in January 1981 and relegating Anderson to the chairman's office, which he would occupy temporarily before making his final exit from the company he had created. In the wake of this major change in leadership, Verbatim's manufacturing and testing procedures were improved and automated, giving birth to a new high-quality Datalife line of disks, which were sold with a five-year guarantee, the first in the industry.

With a new production management team installed and quality-control procedures revamped, Verbatim surged back, recording a robust gain in annual sales from $53 million in 1981 to $85 million in 1983, particularly encouraging in light of the recessionary economic conditions characterizing the early 1980s. By 1983, Verbatim was touting itself as the world's largest supplier of floppy disks, supported by production facilities in the United States, Ireland, Australia, and Japan. The company's embarrassing episode with its customers had taught management a lesson, leading Verbatim to completely restructure its sales and distribution network to develop retail business, focusing on the end-user rather than distributors, software companies, and other manufacturers. As an essential part of this important strategic shift, the company launched a $4 million promotional effort in 1983, aiming its sales pitch directly at secretaries, small-business owners, educators, researchers, and computer aficionados, an audience Verbatim had previously ignored.

After the sweeping changes were completed, Verbatim once again stood on stable ground. The company trailed only IBM in the market for 8-inch disks, but held a commanding lead in the larger 5.25-inch market, making it the overall industry leader as

the industry itself was set to expand substantially. In 1983 the floppy disk industry represented a $500 million market, a total that was expected to eclipse $1 billion by 1985 and reach $4 billion by the end of the decade. Considering Verbatim's number-one position in the industry and that floppy disk sales accounted for roughly 85 percent of its sales, growth prognostications such as those published in 1983 spurred expectations that the company would record commensurate growth. Ahead, however, were troubled years for Verbatim as floppy disk manufacturers became involved in a high-priced race to pioneer technological developments and as a global price war weeded out all but the strongest.

In 1985 Eastman Kodak Co., like numerous other large corporations, wanted to expedite its entry into the floppy disk business and share in the enormous profits that were expected to come. The company had introduced its own line of 8-, 5.25-, and 3.5-inch disks in late 1984, forming its Electronic Media Manufacturing division to superintend new business, but time was crucial and the company needed to quicken the pace. The acquisition of Verbatim presented Eastman Kodak with an opportunity to do so. In March 1985, Eastman Kodak announced its $174 million bid for Verbatim, promising to retain the company's management after its acquisition and to operate the floppy disk manufacturer as a wholly owned subsidiary.

Verbatim, meanwhile, had once again fallen on hard times, for painfully familiar reasons. Confusion about floppy disk media specifications for its largest customer, IBM, had led to the cancellation of future orders. This cancellation compounded the company's other ails, as laggard personal computer sales led to declining operating results for Verbatim. The company laid off 400 employees the week before Eastman Kodak announced its intention to acquire Verbatim, leading industry observers to speculate that Verbatim had sought Eastman Kodak out, hoping a parent company could alleviate some of its financial problems; however, it was never confirmed who approached whom first.

As the decade progressed, with Verbatim now operating as part of Eastman Kodak's Mass Memory unit, the floppy disk market became increasingly competitive, particularly because of the rapid rise of Japanese floppy disk manufacturers. By 1988, Verbatim had had enough and filed a complaint with the U.S. Department of Commerce alleging that Japanese companies were violating U.S. trade laws by selling their 3.5-inch disks at prices well below fair market value. In response to the federal inquiry triggered by Verbatim, three major Japanese manufacturers, Sony Corp., Maxell Corp., and Kao Corp., increased the competitive and pricing pressures they were exerting on U.S. manufacturers by opening production facilities in the United States and doubling production capacity. Adding further to Verbatim's difficulties were reported problems with the quality of its disks, which had been surfacing for a decade, preventing the company from securing large contracts with major software companies and computer manufacturers.

Against the backdrop of alleged dumping practices by Japanese manufacturers and Verbatim's increasingly precarious position, Mitsubishi Kasei Corporation, a Japanese chemical conglomerate that also manufactured optical disks and other information products, was assuming a more aggressive posture, hoping to establish a greater presence in both the U.S. and Japanese floppy disk markets as the 1990s began. Concurrently, Eastman Kodak was implementing a billion-dollar divestiture program aimed at shedding its noncore businesses. The common denominator in each company's divergent strategies was Verbatim, a nonessential component of the Eastman Kodak empire and an attractive asset for the acquisitive-minded Mitsubishi Kasei Corp. In a transaction valued at an estimated $200 million, Mitsubishi Kasei acquired Verbatim in 1990, making Mitsubishi Kasei the largest competitor in the U.S. market for floppy disks and a considerably stronger global competitor with the absorption of Verbatim's worldwide sales network.

With a new parent company supporting its growth, Verbatim entered the 1990s invigorated, intent on becoming a more well-rounded company. The acquisition of Carlisle Memory Products in 1992 and its entry in the memory card and CD-ROM markets helped to engender a significant transformation at Verbatim, as the company diversified from its mainstay floppy disk business to become what it termed the world's largest media manufacturer. In the three years since its acquisition by Mitsubishi Kasei, the company had introduced more new image and data storage products than any other company, introducing five new product lines, featuring 16 entirely new products, in 1993 alone. On the heels of this pervasive diversification, Verbatim formed a joint venture with Sanyo Laser Products in October 1994, creating one of the largest independent CD-ROM and audio-CD producers in North America.

Despite Verbatim's focus on developing innovative products and earning the reputation as one of the industry's premier manufacturers, competitive and pricing pressures continued to hound the company as it entered the mid-1990s. In November 1994, one month after forming its joint venture with Sanyo Laser Products, Verbatim laid off 100 employees—primarily production workers—at its Charlotte, North Carolina, facility. Conversely, the company established sales offices in Argentina, Chile, Columbia, and Venezuela in July 1994, hoping to capture a lucrative portion of the burgeoning South American computer market. Both Verbatim's retreat in Charlotte and its expansion in South America were indicative of the tenuous ground occupied by even the industry's largest players in the global battle for dominance, the rigors of which were not expected to lessen as Verbatim's management plotted their course for the remainder of the 1990s and beyond.

Further Reading:

Isaac, Daniel, ''Verbatim Left Adrift as Disk Probe Brings Industry Sea Change,'' *PC Week,* February 20, 1989, p. 65.
''Kodak Offers $174M in Bid for Verbatim,'' *Electronic News,''* March 18, 1985, p. 20.
''MKC Slims Down and Beefs Up,'' *Chemical Week,* April 4, 1990, p. 10.
Shipley, Chris, ''Verbatim Lays Off 400,'' *PC Week,* November 12, 1985, p. 184.
''Verbatim: Taking Charge of Change,'' *Managing Office Technology,* July 1993, p. 71.
Verna, Paul, ''Sanyo Forms Venture with Verbatim,'' *Billboard,* October 15, 1994, p. 86.
Weigner, Kathleen K., ''The One That Almost Got Away,'' *Forbes,* January 31, 1983, p. 46.
Wingis, Chuck, ''Verbatim Widens Its View of Expanding 'Floppy Disc' Field,'' *Advertising Age,* March 21, 1983, p. 4.

—Jeffrey L. Covell

Vienna Sausage Manufacturing Co.

2501 N. Damen Ave.
Chicago, Illinois 60647
U.S.A.
(312) 278-7800
Fax: (312) 278-4759

Private Company
Incorporated: 1893
Employees: 750
Sales: $95 million
SICs: 2013 Sausage & Other Prepared Meat Product; 2035
   Pickled Fruits & Vegetables Etc.; 2032 Canned
   Specialties; 2024 Ice Cream & Frozen Desserts

Vienna Sausage Manufacturing Co. and its subsidiaries produce and distribute its famous Vienna Beef hot dogs and nearly 900 other products, including deli meats, soups, condiments, breads, and desserts. Approximately 15 percent of its 1994 sales of $95 million were generated through retail channels: Vienna's primary market is foodservice, with sales to licensed Vienna Beef vendors forming the bulk of its business. In Chicago, where Vienna generates roughly 40 percent of its annual revenues, there are some 1,500 licensed Vienna Beef sellers. The company also owns and operates ten distribution centers in the Southwest and Southeast and exports its products to licensees in Germany, Japan, Hong Kong, Mexico, and Canada.

Sausage-makers Samuel Ladany and Emil Reichl emigrated to the United States from Austria-Hungary in 1890. The occasion of the World's Fair/Columbian Exposition in 1893 brought the pair to Chicago, where their products sold successfully enough to convince them to remain in that city. Ladany and Reichl opened their first facility, adopting the name Vienna Company to emphasize its link with the Austrian city, which was considered by many at the time to be the capital of sausage-making. Sausages, along with other kosher delicatessen products, such as frankfurters, knockwurst, pickled corned beef, salami, and bologna, formed the early core of Vienna's line. These products were sold in a retail store at the front of their shop.

The Vienna Company's sausages, in keeping with dietary laws associated with kosher food preparation, were 100 percent beef, distinguishing them from the more common pork and pork/beef blended sausages, and rigid supervision and inspection of their products assured consistency in quality. Soon the Vienna Company began selling to other retailers, and the company's reputa-

tion spread throughout Chicago. Peddlers' routes carried Vienna's products to a steadily growing list of clients. The company also became active outside of Chicago. The company began to hire jobbers, beginning in Detroit around the turn of the century, to distribute its products. The jobber maintained a stock of Vienna products to deliver to stores in his area, permitting quicker delivery and more widespread distribution. Before long Vienna's kosher products were sold throughout much of the country. Vienna soon expanded its line to included non-kosher foods as well.

The Great Depression had an unexpected effect on Vienna's business. Prices dropped as people had less and less money to spend. Frankfurters, for example, could be bought for as little as a penny apiece; buns, too, cost a penny. Vendors discovered that they could combine the two and sell the sandwich for a nickel. The hot dog market boomed. Vienna began to seek out hot dog vendors to sell its products, often finding them locations, providing signs, and teaching them selling techniques. In return, the vendors agreed to sell only Vienna products, and to advertise the Vienna name at their stands. By then, Vienna ruled Chicago's hot dog market and the hot dog had become Chicago's favorite ethnic food. More and more Vienna hot dog stands opened across the city, creating a loose franchise business. The company's sales grew steadily.

The start of the Second World War had a significant impact on the country's eating habits. Delicatessen meats had long been considered lunch or snack foods, and were sold primarily through delicatessens, butchers, and meat markets. The introduction of rationing during the war, coupled with food shortages, increased the share of delicatessen foods in people's diets; these foods also proved convenient for feeding the Armed Forces as the United States entered the war. By the end of the war, the change in American diets seemed permanent. More and more delicatessens and convenience and fast-food restaurants appeared. Vienna's fortunes rose with these trends. By this time, it had greatly expanded its original Halsted Street location, and a second refrigerated facility was leased nearby.

At the same time, large supermarket and chain stores were achieving their first success. These stores responded to the increasing demand for delicatessen products by adding these items to their stock. Advances in refrigeration were making it possible to store meats longer, and to sell products in smaller, self-service packages. Although Vienna virtually owned the Chicago hot dog stand market, it had not yet entered this new and increasingly important market. The announcement that New York-based Hygrade intended to enter the Chicago market forced Vienna to create a line of pre-packaged products for supermarkets. The company designed a new logo, featuring a large blue V and a frankfurter on a fork, which quickly became known nationwide, and developed a national advertising campaign to accompany the launch of its pre-packaged delicatessen line. Hygrade was forced to retreat from Chicago.

The success of this launch encouraged Vienna to expand its operations. Rather than continue to ship its products from Chicago, Vienna decided to open production facilities on the West Coast for its sales there. Renting space in Los Angeles, Vienna opened its first facility outside of Chicago in 1952. Production was limited at first to cured and pickled meat products, such as corned beef and beef tongue. The addition of smokehouses allowed the Los Angeles facility to produce pastrami, roast beef, and other meats. Strict control was maintained over the recipes and ingredients, so that Vienna's products on the West Coast would taste exactly the same as in Chicago. With its mild climate, which encouraged the year-round consumption of deli meats, the California market proved extremely lucrative for Vienna. The following year, Vienna took over its own distribution in the Southeast, by then another principal market, leasing cooler space and refrigerator trucks in Miami.

Steady increases in sales led Vienna to purchase land in Los Angeles and to construct a modern facility in 1964 in order to produce the full line of its all-beef products. Soon after, Vienna added a distribution center in San Francisco, which received Vienna products from Los Angeles and distributed them through Northern California, the Pacific Northwest, and Nevada. Less than five years later, Vienna's West Coast sales had outgrown its Los Angeles facility; a new wing was constructed for the factory in 1969.

Back in Chicago, Vienna had added a third facility for processing its products. By the start of the 1970s, however, operating the three plants was proving too costly and inefficient, as duplication of personnel, handling, and transporting stock and products among the three factories cut severely into the company's profits and compromised its competitiveness. In 1972 Vienna merged its operations into a single, newly constructed modern facility. At this time, the company dropped its kosher meat line, in part because of the limited growth potential of that market, and in part because the dietary laws surrounding kosher foods would have required maintaining a separate processing facility. Its kosher meat products were merged into Sinai Kosher Foods, with Vienna retaining a principal interest in that company. Sinai, and Vienna's share in it, was later purchased by Norris Grain Co., before being bought up again by Sinai management.

Its kosher foods, however, had provided Vienna with not only a national distribution network, but also a national reputation. The company capitalized on its name, opening distribution centers—generally large cooling warehouses—in Cleveland, Houston, Dallas, Phoenix, San Diego, and Tampa. Increases in its distribution business led Vienna to expand its product line into non-meat items. By the end of the 1970s, Vienna generated $50 million in annual revenues. Jules Ladany, who had taken over the company from his father, Samuel Ladany, died in 1979. The younger Ladany was succeeded by his son-in-law, Jim Eisenberg, who had joined the company in 1956. Three years later, Eisenberg, along with Jim Bodman, who had been with Vienna since 1964, reached agreement with the Ladany family for a leveraged buyout. Eisenberg was named chairman and Bodman became president.

The new management increased Vienna's expansion into non-meat products. Apart from the special high-sided poppy-seed buns that had become virtually a requirement for its hot dogs, the company established several subsidiaries and opened separate facilities for producing pizza, pickles, and pickled products, kosher foods such as matzo balls and blintzes, frozen prepared soups, and specialty desserts, as well as other delicatessen products and supplies. Vienna's emphasis remained on its core market of sandwich shops and delicatessens. Vienna also began licensing its products overseas, principally in Japan and Ger-

many. Its licensing agreement required that it products be made exactly the same and with the same high quality as in Chicago. In partnership with Japan Tobacco, Vienna formed The Chicago Co. in Tokyo to operate a chain of hot dog stands in that country. Vienna next expanded into Hong Kong, Singapore, Indonesia, Mexico, and Canada. Vienna's foreign ventures together contributed approximately three percent of its annual revenues.

In 1986 union pressures forced Vienna to stop boning its own meat. The company began purchasing boxed meat, but was dissatisfied with the quality. The following year, Vienna opened an abattoir, the Big Foot Cattle Co., in Harvard, Illinois, where it began slaughtering and hotboning the cattle—particularly bulls, the beef of choice for the Vienna Beef hot dog—for its products. The company's European sales snagged in 1989, however, with a ban by the European Community on hormone-raised animals. This meant Vienna's German licensee, Dieter Hein Co., could no long import the bull meat essential to maintain the taste and consistency of the Vienna Beef hot dog. Vienna experienced a further difficulty with a rise in hot dog "counterfeiters," that is, hot dog stands advertising the Vienna name while selling other cheaper and inferior-quality brands. Vienna instituted stricter inspections of these stands and tightened enforcement of its trademark, including filing several trademark infringement suits.

Entering the 1990s, Vienna had grown to a $100 million company offering nearly 900 products alongside its biggest selling franks. Ninety percent of its revenues were from foodservice vendors, including important sales to vendors at ball parks and stadiums in Chicago and other cities. The 1994 strikes of both Major League Baseball and the National Hockey League depressed Vienna's earnings. During the 1990s, also, consumers were becoming more and more aware of their diets, particularly their diets' fat content. In response, Vienna launched its "Deli-Lite Franks," featuring a nine percent fat content. Early sales, however, were disappointing. Other product innovations, such as Vienna Turkey Breast Pastrami, were more successful. The 1992 purchase of David Berg & Co. sausage manufacturers further strengthened Vienna's Chicago and Midwest position. Future plans called for Vienna to step up its advertising spending, which in 1993 accounted for less than two percent of its budget, in order to remain competitive against the country's larger retail suppliers. But the key to Vienna's future would remain its dedication to Chicago's—and much of the country's—favorite hot dog.

Principal Subsidiaries: Big Foot Cattle Co.; Bistro Soups, Ltd.; Chipico Pickles; Pie Piper Products, Ltd.; Sula Supply; Vienna Beef, Ltd.

Further Reading:

"The History of Vienna," Chicago: Vienna Sausage Manufacturing Co., 1993.
Mermelstein, Neil H., "Martha E. Cassens," *Food Technology,* August 1993, pp. 48–50.
Parsons, Heidi, "What's in a Name?," *Meat Processing,* August 1989.
Salvage, Bryan, "Vienna's Metamorphosis," *Meat Marketing & Technology,* March 1992, pp. 34–42.
Snyder, David, "Vienna Beefs Over Counterfeit Wiener Shops," *Crain's Chicago Business,* March 16, 1987, p. 3.

—M. L. Cohen

W. L. Gore & Associates, Inc.

551 Paper Mill Road
Post Office Box 9206
Newark, Delaware 19714-9206
U.S.A.
(302) 738-4880
Fax: (302) 731-9098

Private Company
Founded: 1958
Employees: 6,000
Sales: $800 million (est.)
SICs: 3089 Plastic Products Not Elsewhere Classified; 3643
Current-Carrying Wiring Devices

W. L. Gore & Associates, Inc., is a high-technology company that develops and manufactures, among other products, advanced synthetic fabrics used for aerospace, clothing, medical, automotive, chemical, electronic, and other applications. With operations spanning the globe, Gore's chief product in the mid-1990s was Gore-Tex, a patented high-performance fabric. Among other distinctions, W. L. Gore repeatedly has been cited as one of the best 100 companies to work for in America.

W. L. Gore & Associates is the progeny of renowned American entrepreneur, scientist, and inventor Wilbert L. (Bill) Gore. Gore began working for DuPont in 1941 when he was 29 years old. He helped to advance that company's research into polymers, resins, and plastics. On the advice of his wife, Vieve, Gore left his research job in 1958 to start his own company. Before his departure, Gore had been working on new DuPont-developed synthetic material called polytetrafluoroethylene (PTFE, or teflon). He hoped to build a company that developed and marketed new uses for the material. Gore and Vieve started the enterprise on a shoestring budget in the basement of their home.

Gore's first commercially viable products were wire and cable products insulated with teflon. Bill's son, Bob, was integral to those innovations. Bob, who was a chemical engineering student at the time, is credited with coming up with the concept that resulted in Gore's first patent for teflon-insulated wire and cable. For ten years, in fact, such products were the core of the Gore enterprise. The high-tech cables were respected in their industry niche and were even used in the Apollo space program for the first moon landing.

From their basement office, the Gores expanded into a separate production facility in their hometown of Newark, Delaware. Sales were brisk after initial product introductions. By 1965, just seven years after the business had started, Gore & Associates was employing about 200 people. It was about that time that Gore began to develop and implement the unique management system and philosophy for which his company would become recognized. Gore noticed that as his company had grown, efficiency and productivity had started to decline. He needed a new management structure, but he feared that the popular pyramid management structure that was in vogue at the time suppressed the creativity and innovation that he valued so greatly. Instead of adopting the pyramid structure, Gore decided to create his own system.

During World War II, while on a task force at DuPont, Gore had learned of another type of organizational structured called the lattice system, which was developed to enhance the ingenuity and overall performance of a group working toward a goal. It emphasized communication and cooperation rather than hierarchy of authority. Under the system that Gore developed, any person was allowed to make a decision as long as it was fair, encouraged others, and made a commitment to the company. Consultation was required only for decisions that could potentially cause serious damage to the enterprise. Furthermore, new associates joined the company on the same effective authority level as all the other workers, including Bill and Vieve. There were no titles or bosses, with only a few exceptions, and commands were replaced by personal commitments.

New employees started out working in an area best suited to their talents, under the guidance of a sponsor. As the employee progressed there came more responsibility, and workers were paid according to their individual contribution. "Team members know who is producing," Bill explained in a February 1986 issue of the *Phoenix Business Journal.* "They won't put up with poor performance. There is tremendous peer pressure. You promote yourself by gaining knowledge and working hard, everyday. There is no competition, except with yourself." The effect of the system was to encourage workers to be creative, take risks, and perform at their highest level. One of the key people to help the company succeed in the Apollo moon landing project, for example, came to Gore with only a 6th-grade education.

Gore reasoned that even under his management system organizations would begin to decline in effectiveness after reaching about 200 members. That was partly because too many people in a group caused a reduction in trust and cooperation. For that reason, he and Vieve decided to build a second manufacturing facility. In 1967 the company opened a new plant in Flagstaff, Arizona. The selection of Flagstaff reflected Gore's love of the outdoors, particularly for the western United States. The new plant helped the company to regain its productivity and creativity, and from that point forward Gore built a new facility each time the magic number of 200 was breached. Gore's unique and successful management system and philosophies proved valuable over time and became lauded as a model for management during the 1980s and 1990s.

The immense success of Gore's teflon-insulated wire and cable products, combined with savvy management during the middle and late 1960s, resulted in explosive growth at Gore. Indeed, during the late 1960s Gore established manufacturing and sales operations in Arizona, Scotland, and Germany and even launched a venture partnership in Japan. The company continued to post big gains during the 1970s as well. Perhaps more important to Gore's success during the 1970s and 1980s than the company's management system, however, was a pivotal product innovation that would help to make Gore one of the most successful private companies in the United States. That innovation came in 1969, about the time that Bill's son Bob became president of the company (Bob and his mother, the secretary and treasurer of the company, were the only two employees in the company with job titles).

Bob, who had gone to work at Gore after receiving his Ph.D. in chemistry, discovered that teflon could be quickly stretched to produce a material with many of the properties that scientists had been trying for years to create. Under the right conditions, the product could be stretched to form a material that was as strong as the original teflon and laced with microscopic holes, the size of which could be adjusted in the manufacturing process. The breakthrough was momentous because of the numerous properties exhibited by the material. For example, it shed water droplets like other synthetic materials but was also breathable and would allow small airborne moisture particles and body heat to move through the fabric. The obvious advantage: stretched teflon could be used to make waterproof clothing that was also breathable.

W. L. Gore & Associates applied for a patent for their invention in May 1970. The Gores dubbed the new material Gore-Tex. The patent was granted in 1976, by which time Gore was already marketing a number of products made with Gore-Tex. Among other advantages, Gore-Tex was chemically inert and resistant to infection. That made it an excellent material for dozens of medical applications—artificial arteries made with Gore-Tex, for example, eventually accounted for about 85 percent of all artificial arteries produced in the world. It was also beneficial for various uses ranging from household items to defense-industry goods. Gore-Tex was used to manufacture space suits and sporting apparel, for example, as well as dental floss and telecommunications gear. By the late 1980s, filters made with Gore-Tex were being used in virtually every intravenous bag in the world. In fact, Gore-Tex became the fabric of choice in most applications that necessitated a high flow rate along with maximum particle retention in both air and liquid filtration.

Gore experienced explosive growth during the 1970s and early 1980s, mostly as a result of the breakthrough success of Gore-Tex. The still-private company remained tight-lipped as always about its financial performance. Its success, though, was clearly evidenced by the rapid expansion of production facilities and sales and marketing offices. Gore was soon peddling its products throughout the world. Besides pushing Gore-Tex, the company continued to expand its other product lines and to develop new ideas. For example, Gore was called in to custom-manufacture teflon-insulated cable to help in the aftermath of the Three Mile Island nuclear accident. It also broadened its teflon-coated cable products to meet new needs in computer, telecommunications, aerospace, and medical industries. Still, Gore-Tex be-

came the company's cash cow and eventually grew to represent more than 80 percent of the organization's revenues.

By the mid-1980s Gore was churning out an estimated $200 million to $300 million in annual revenues and supporting a whopping 29 plants throughout the world; its workforce ballooned to 4,200 worldwide. In addition to his inventions, Bill Gore was being lauded as a leading contributor to the art and science of management. Bill Gore died on July 26, 1986, at the age of 74, of a heart attack suffered while hiking in the Wind River Range of Wyoming. Gore had been known for taking extended treks in the outdoors. On this particular occasion, he had been hiking with his wife and several grandchildren. ''If a man could flow with the stream, grow with the way of nature, he'd accomplish more and he'd be happier doing it than bucking the flow of the water,'' Vieve Gore recalled of her husband's business philosophy.

W. L. Gore & Associates continued to thrive following the death of its founder, despite ongoing disputes over its patent to Gore-Tex. Indeed, the company had been battling claims against its rights to the invention since the early 1970s. In 1982, in fact, a federal lawsuit in Cleveland resulted in the removal of Gore's patent rights, but the decision was soon overturned and the rights were restored. In 1984 Gore filed suit against a Tempe, Arizona, company called IMPRA Inc., claiming that IMPRA had violated Gore's patent in the manufacture of its artificial arteries. The judge's research showed that a Japanese company had tried to patent a material identical to Gore-Tex in 1963 and had gotten the patent in 1967. After several years of weighing the evidence, the judge decided in 1990 to terminate Gore's patent rights. Gore managed to keep patents for individual Gore-Tex products and manufacturing processes, however. At the time the decision was handed down, Gore was capturing an estimated $700 million annually from sales of Gore-Tex-related products.

The loss of the Gore-Tex patent predated the scheduled termination of patent rights by about three years. Thus, it opened the door for other companies to begin manufacturing Gore-Tex products earlier than they might have otherwise. Gore's product-development arm was healthy, though, and the company sustained its growth. In 1991 Gore announced plans to build two new 60,000-square-foot manufacturing facilities in Arizona at a cost of about $10 million. By the end of 1993 Gore was operating more than 40 facilities and employing about 6,000 workers. Interestingly, the plants were all located in nonmetropolitan areas because the Gores believed that such locations offered a higher quality of life for their employees. Evidencing the success of Gore's overall management philosophy, the company was named as one of the 100 best companies to work for two years in a row—a feat accomplished by only 29 other companies at the time.

Going into the mid-1990s W. L. Gore & Associates was operating 45 manufacturing and sales offices throughout the United States and in Germany, Scotland, and Japan. Gore-Tex products still accounted for the bulk of its sales. New Gore-Tex products being developed and introduced in 1994 and 1995 included Intervent, an allergen exclusion technology used, for example, in bedding; various surgical sutures used in vascular, cardiac, and general surgical procedures; and protective gear designed to reduce the spread of diseases like AIDS. The company was also developing and manufacturing various teflon-related electronics goods for industrial, defense, computer, telecommunication, and medical industries. Its four operating divisions in 1995 were Electronic Products; Fabrics; Industrial Products; and Medical Products. The still-private company did not release financial information but claimed to have achieved compound sales and profit growth rates exceeding 20 percent annually between 1975 and 1995.

Further Reading:

Day, Kathleen, "A Clothes Call with Danger: Microbe, Chemical Phobias Drive Up Demand for Protective Gear," *Washington Post,* March 11, 1995, p. 1C.
Fiscus, Chris, "Flagstaff Approves Gore Plan," *Arizona Business Gazette,* March 22, 1991, p. 1.
Jaffe, Susan Biddle, "Employee Freedom Is Gore Family Tradition," *Philadelphia Business Journal,* May 1, 1989, section 2, p. 6B.
Morrell, Lisa, "Tempe Medical-Products Firm Wins Round in Patent Lawsuit," *Arizona Republic,* May 15, 1990, p. 13C.
Nelton, Sharon, "In Appreciation of Innovators," *Nation's Business,* December 1986, p. 64.
Norris, Scott, "PDL&C Markets Gore-Tex Fabric to Military for Soldiers' Outerwear," *Rochester Business Journal,* September 24, 1990, p. 4.
Rhodes, Lucien, "William Gore 1912–1986," *Inc.,* November 1986, p. 22.
Sommer, Anthony, "Gore-Tex Patent Held as Invalid," *Phoenix Gazette,* May 15, 1990, p. 1C.
Stern, Jonathan, "Workers Manage Themselves Under Inventive Philosophy," *Phoenix Business Journal,* February 3, 1986, p. 11.
Wilke, Paul W., "Newark Root of W. L. Gore's Success," *Delaware Business Review,* January 31, 1994, p. 13.

—Dave Mote

The Wackenhut Corporation

1500 San Remo Avenue
Coral Gables, Florida 33146
U.S.A.
(305) 666-5656
Fax: (305) 662-7336

Public Company
Incorporated: 1958
Employees: 45,000
Sales: $748 million
Stock Exchanges: New York
SICs: 7381 Detective and Armored Car Services

The Wackenhut Corporation is an international provider of security, investigative, and correction facilities services for private industry and local, state, and federal agencies. In 1994, with nearly $748 million in revenues and a work force of 45,000, Wackenhut was the country's third largest security services firm, behind Borg-Warner Security Corporation (through its subsidiaries, Wells Fargo, Burns International, and Globe Security) and Pinkerton's, Inc. As of 1995, Wackenhut maintained offices in 40 states, including Washington, D.C., and in 49 other countries on six continents. Wackenhut provided security services to nuclear power facilities, U.S. embassies and missions, several Department of Energy and other U.S. government agency sites, and such installations as the Alaska pipeline. Wackenhut also provided airport security and crash and fire rescue services and was a pioneer in the privatization of fire, emergency rescue, police, and other municipal services. Through its subsidiary, Wackenhut Corrections Corporation, Wackenhut also built, secured, and managed several jail and prison facilities in the United States and abroad.

Wackenhut was founded in Miami in 1954 as Special Agent Investigators, Inc., by George R. Wackenhut, a former special agent of the Federal Bureau of Investigations (FBI), and three other former FBI agents. The company's initial focus was in investigative services; by 1955, however, the company began to provide physical security services as well, winning a contract with National Airlines of Miami, which lasted for the next 20 years. In 1958, George Wackenhut bought out his partners and incorporated the company as the Wackenhut Corporation, moving the company to Coral Gables, Florida. In that same year, Wackenhut received its first major contract from the Martin

Company (later known as Martin Marietta) to provide security and protection services; later contracts with Martin, in 1961 and 1963, brought Wackenhut security guards to Martin's Titan missile sites.

By 1959, the company was posting revenues of more than $1 million, and by 1961 the company employed more than 1,300 people. The acquisition of General Plant Protection Company in 1962 allowed Wackenhut to expand its operations beyond Florida, into California and Hawaii. One of the company's first government agency contracts followed in 1963, when the company, through its Wackenhut Services, Inc. (WSI) division, was hired to guard NASA's Lewis Research Center in Cleveland. The next year, Wackenhut won a $44-million, seven-year contract at the Kennedy Space Center. WSI began a contract for the Nevada nuclear testing site of the Atomic Energy Commission (later the Department of Energy) in 1965, with renewals through 1997. There, WSI deployed "a paramilitary operation," as noted by its vice president of Nevada Operations in *Security Management*, comprising "a very heavily armed force of individuals who receive specialized SWAT-type training, and armored vehicles and helicopters."

Wackenhut went public in 1966, listing initially with the American Stock Exchange, and, since 1980, on the New York Stock Exchange. That same year Wackenhut went international, opening an office in Venezuela, followed over the next several years by offices in Columbia, Ecuador, and Brazil. By 1971, Wackenhut had opened offices in Italy, France, and the Dominican Republic as well. This same period saw the company continuing to expand through acquisitions of other security services-related firms.

When construction on the 800-mile Alaska pipeline began in 1974, Wackenhut, through its subsidiary Ahtna AGA Security, Inc., provided guard and security services, and later, with the completion of the pipeline, continued to guard the pipeline and nearby oil reserves and facilities through the 1990s. In 1976, another division, Wackenhut International Inc., won a contract for providing the security design and installation at Jeddah (Saudi Arabia) International Airport, then the largest airport in the world. During this time Wackenhut sold off its U.S. divisions specializing in "central-station" security, where guards monitored properties from a centrally located office, a market that had proved unprofitable.

By the early 1980s, Wackenhut had grown to include more than 20,000 employees and over $200 million in revenue. At this time, the company sought to diversify its services, in part because of the low margins available through its guard and security services. Increasing competition, with over 10,000 security firms operating in the United States, were another factor in Wackenhut's efforts to diversify. Although the guard services would remain the company's core business, the company expanded to include strike support services, in which Wackenhut provided security and other services to allow companies to continue to operate while their workers were on strike. Another area Wackenhut attempted to develop was the privatization of emergency, police, and fire services, replacing communities' publicly funded services with its own trained personnel; however, this effort met with only limited success. In addition, Wackenhut continued to market its airport crash, fire, and rescue teams. Further acquisitions, in 1979 of Stellar Systems,

Inc., in California and in 1980 of Indentimat Corp. in New York, enabled Wackenhut to expand its high-technology security operations as well.

Wackenhut won several major government contracts in the 1980s. Its 1983 three-year, $81-million contract at the Savannah River Site in South Carolina was the largest paramilitary security contract ever awarded by the U.S. government. A $5 million, three-year contract in 1984 to create and manage the Department of Energy's Central Training Academy in Nevada continued to be held by the company through 1995, when it was renewed through the year 2000 for $58.6 million. Another significant, and lasting, contract began in 1986, when Wackenhut was awarded $25.3 million for security services at the DOE's Strategic Petroleum Reserve.

During the 1980s, financial pressures, as well as overcrowding, led to the privatization of increasing numbers of state and federal correction facilities. Wackenhut ventured into this new market when WSI was hired to design, construct, and operate an Immigration and Naturalization Service detention center in Colorado in 1987. In the next year, Wackenhut formed Wackenhut Corrections Corporation (WCC) as a wholly owned subsidiary and received contracts for two 500-bed facilities in Texas. WCC went public in 1994, selling approximately 26 percent of its stock, with the remainder under Wackenhut Corp.'s control. By the end of 1994, the number of prison beds under its direction had totaled 14,000. With annual revenues of $105 million, consultant and construction fees generating an additional $80 million, and profit margins as high as ten percent, corrections became one of the most successful areas of Wackenhut's business. Facilities under WCC's control included prisons in Australia, England, and Puerto Rico, as well as in six states in the United States, with ten facilities in Texas alone. A contract in December 1994 for the construction and management of a 1,300-bed medium-security prison in Florida provided WCC with $50 million, its largest contract as of that date.

Despite continued rises in revenues, Wackenhut's profit margin decreased at the beginning of the 1990s to 1.3 percent, a decline from the 2.5 percent in the early 1980s. *Florida Trend* ascribed this decline to Wackenhut's focus on long-term, rather than short-term, opportunities as it entered new markets and new services. In contrast to its chief competitors, where the security guard market accounted for 90 percent of their business, Wackenhut had diversified to the extent that its security services generated only 43 percent of its revenues. Government services, including airport and municipal fire and rescue, accounted for 35 percent, with an additional 10 percent of revenues arising from its DOE and corrections contracts. Wackenhut had become less dependent on the traditionally low-margin guard business, while supporting its newer projects with this core. Accordingly, Wackenhut's emphasis on diversification has been praised by Find/SVP of New York as "a conscious decision to forego short-term profits in favor of long-term gains." During this time, also, Wackenhut sold off two of its less profitable divisions, Stellar Systems, Inc., in 1991, and, in 1994, Wackenhut Monitoring Systems, which had lost $1.5 million in 1993.

Additional difficulty for Wackenhut came in 1992 when it was named in a lawsuit, along with the Alyeska Pipeline Service Company, the consortium of oil companies operating the Alaska pipeline, for illegally spying on an environmental activist. A government report prepared by Democratic members of the House Interior and Insular Affairs Committee further charged Wackenhut and Alyeska with attempting to interfere with the congressional investigation into their activities. However, the report's conclusions were challenged by Republican House members, and the lawsuit was settled for undisclosed terms and with neither Alyeska nor Wackenhut admitting guilt. Apart from the bad publicity and a $10,000 fine from the State of Virginia, the incident was described, in *Florida Trend*, as a "short-term problem for a company whose thinking is slanted toward the long term."

By the mid-1990s, Wackenhut's organizational structure comprised three main components: domestic operations; government services; and international Operations. Domestic operations provided—in addition to the traditional uniformed guard and other physical security services—such services as loss prevention analysis and system design, employee and prospective employee screening, and insurance inspections, fraud investigations, strike support, and transportation of assets. The rise in airplane hijackings in the 1970s and the continued threat of terrorism brought Wackenhut into the country's airports, where their guards were charged with screening passengers prior to boarding. The Nuclear Services Division of Domestic Operations were providing physical services to 16 nuclear power generating plants by 1995. The Domestic Operations Group also oversaw Wackenhut's Alaska Pipeline activities. With the increasing privatization of correction facilities, Wackenhut Support Services and Creative Food Management, which offered specialized food services to correctional institutions, increased revenues from $3 million in 1989 to $25 million in 1994.

Wackenhut's Government Services Group included the wholly owned subsidiaries Wackenhut Services, Inc. (WSI), which was formed in 1964 specifically for Wackenhut's government contract business; and Wackenhut Education Services, Inc., through which Wackenhut operates Job Corps Centers for the U.S. Department of Labor. Wackenhut Corrections Corp.'s activities are also included under the Government Services Group. In addition to the Nevada Nuclear Test Site, the Savannah River Site, the Strategic Petroleum Reserve, and the nuclear manufacturing plant in Rocky Flats, Colorado, WSI expanded beyond the Department of Energy to other government agencies, particularly the U.S. Army, for which WSI provided security, maintenance, hazardous waste disposal, and fire protection at three ammunition plants. WSI continued to provide private police, fire, and emergency services to municipalities as well as in major airports; a July 1995 contract with the state of Hawaii awarded Wackenhut nearly $35 million for security at eight airports over the next three years. The trend toward privatization included education as well. In 1984, the DOE contracted WSI to establish and then operate its Central Training Academy in New Mexico, and in 1985 the company began its first Job Corps Centers operations.

The International Operations Group of Wackenhut, through its subsidiary Wackenhut International Incorporated, has extended Wackenhut's domestic services to six continents and more than 50 countries, including placing security guards at 18 U.S. embassies and missions. New markets opened for Wackenhut in the 1990s with the fall of the Berlin Wall and the increasing normalization of relations with China. Wackenhut opened offices in Russia and in the Czech Republic and began to develop contacts with mainland China through its Hong Kong office. Additional expansion came as the company entered India and Pakistan and gained new embassy security contracts with the U.S. State Department. The 1994 acquisition of 60 percent ownership in SEGES extended Wackenhut into the Ivory Coast, described in the company's 1994 annual report as a "strategic move." Other services offered by the International Operations Group included central alarm station services, executive protection, armored car services, vehicle location and recovery, and privatized forestry, toll collection, corrections, and police and fire support.

As late as 1995, the Wackenhut Corporation remained under the control of George R. Wackenhut, its founder, who functioned as chairman of the board and chief executive officer and held 50 percent of the company's stock. In the early 1990s, however, George Wackenhut turned the presidency of the company over to his son, Richard R. Wackenhut, who also functioned as the company's chief operating officer. The company had also seen a shift in management, away from a personnel traditionally recruited from among retired police and military officers, to those with business school and established business backgrounds, with an average age in the mid-forties. The privatization of corrections facilities remained an important Wackenhut market, and the company continued to look to the privatization of government functions for new markets for its services. With a reduction in its long-term debt, from $57 million in 1993 to $39 million in 1994, and a credit agreement allowing the company

as much as $60 million in new loans, Wackenhut was poised to continue its program of expansion and diversification.

Principal Subsidiaries: Ahtna AGA Security, Inc.; Wackenhut Airline Services, Inc.; Wackenhut Corrections Corporation; Wackenhut Educational Services, Inc.; Wackenhut International, Inc.; Wackenhut Services, Inc.; Wackenhut Sports Security, Inc.

Further Reading:

Bork, Robert H. Jr., "Big George Wackenhut," *Forbes,* November 21, 1983, pp. 203–6.
Bryce, Robert, "Prison Business Booms in the US," *Christian Science Monitor,* August 12, 1993, p. 8.
"Critic Settles Suit Against Alaska Pipeline," *New York Times,* December 21, 1993, p. 23.
DeGeorge, Gail, "Wackenhut Is Out to Prove That Crime Does Pay," *Business Week,* December 17, 1990, pp. 95–96.
Dorfman, John R., "Caught Flat-Footed," *Forbes,* April 12, 1982, pp. 74–78.
Hersch, Valerie, "The Gumshoes Are Gone," *Florida Trend,* June 1992, pp. 65–67.
Kenworthy, Tom, "Alaska Oil Pipeline Company and Security Firm Criticized," *Washington Post,* July 24, 1992, p. 2.
Millman, Joel, "Captive Market," *Forbes,* September 16, 1991, p. 190.
Parker, Susie T., "Targets of Probe File Suit Against Alyeska Pipeline," *Oil Daily,* July 28, 1992, pp. 1, 8.
Sullivan, Allanna, "Congressional Report Urges Prosecution of Wackenhut and Alyeska Over Spying," *Wall Street Journal,* July 24, 1992, p. 12.

—M. L. Cohen

Waffle House Inc.

P.O. Box 6450
Norcross, Georgia 30091
U.S.A.
(770) 729-5700
Fax: (770) 729-5758

Private Company
Incorporated: 1955
Employees: 6,000
Sales: $79.2 million (1993 est.)
SICs: 5812 Eating Places

Waffle House Inc. (not to be confused with Waffle House of Indiana) operates a chain of about 1,000 Waffle House Restaurants located in 20 states. The restaurants, which are either company-owned or franchised, pride themselves on serving good food fast, at a reasonable price, in a diner atmosphere. The menu includes everything from waffles and eggs to steaks and salads. Family-owned, Waffle House Inc. is known for being an extremely private company.

Waffle House, according to information released in 1995 for the company's 40th anniversary, began as the dream of two neighbors who envisioned a company dedicated to both its customers and employees. The partners wanted to create a place where friends and neighbors could get together to enjoy good food served with a friendly smile. On Labor Day in 1955 they opened the first Waffle House restaurant in Avondale Estates, Georgia, a suburb of Atlanta. The first Waffle House restaurant was a smash, and the owners soon opened other Waffle House eateries throughout Georgia.

Waffle House made a name for itself during the late 1950s and 1960s by living up to its promise of ''Good Food Fast,'' which became one of the company's mottos. Waffle House located many of its restaurants along interstates, and truckers and travelers came to know that the Waffle House sign meant good food and friendly service. The company eventually spread outside of Georgia's borders and into neighboring states including Alabama, Louisiana, North Carolina, South Carolina, and Florida. As the U.S. interstate system expanded throughout the Southeast during the 1950s and 1960s, new Waffle House outlets were added along major arteries like Interstate 75, which trails from the southern tip of Florida through Tennessee to northern Michigan, and Interstate 85, which traverses Virginia and ex-

tends southwest into Alabama. Waffle House eventually built up a network of several hundred restaurants throughout the Southeast.

Waffle House also began franchising its name and concept to individual operators, which allowed the company to expand without assuming heavy debt and without having to sell shares to the public. Keeping Waffle House private was very important to its owners, because taking the company public would have required them to release financial and operating information. ''There are three types of companies,'' explained Bryan Elliott, analyst at Robinson-Humphrey, in the September 19, 1988, *Atlanta Business Chronicle.* ''There are public companies that trade stock and have to share information. Then there are private companies that don't trade stock but are somewhat open about their operations and numbers. And then there are the companies that won't even acknowledge that they exist. And that is Waffle House. They are a very, very private and tight-lipped company.'' For that reason, details about the growth and expansion of Waffle House and about the lives of its founders and executives are scant.

During the 1970s and 1980s, the roadside restaurant market became dominated primarily by two styles of eateries: fast-food chains like McDonald's and Burger King, and large sit-down restaurants like Shoney's and Cracker Barrel. The traditional diner-style eatery, in contrast, declined in popularity, with the chief exception of Waffle House. Indeed, Waffle House restaurants in the 1990s looked much the same as they did 40 years before. An exposed grill was located behind a long counter, at which customers could sit on stools. Other guests were seated in the booths that lined the restaurant. Waffle House continued to advertise solely through word-of-mouth, relying on its loyal clientele instead of promotion to reach new customers.

Even the Waffle House menu of southern fare had changed little since the 1950s. The restaurants still emphasized their famous T-bone steak, waffle, and egg meals, and claimed to have ''America's Best'' coffee. Meals that became a tradition at Waffle House included the ''King Size T-bone & Eggs'' dinner, which included a ten-ounce steak, hashbrowns, and two eggs or a salad—for just $8.99 in 1995. Other signature menu items included pecan waffles, Bert's chili, raisin toast, and cheese 'n' eggs. Waffle House took particular pride in its hashbrowns, which it served six different ways: ''scattered'' (on the grill); ''smothered'' with onions; ''covered'' with cheese; ''chunked'' with hickory-smoked ham; ''topped'' with chili; and ''diced'' with fresh tomatoes.

Besides its proven menu items, Waffle House prided itself on cooking all of its meals to order, and on using only the best ingredients in its food. Waffle Houses used only Kraft cheese, Minute Maid orange juice, and Heinz sauces, for example. The company also distinguished itself by staying open 24 hours a day and 365 days each year, which let highway travelers know that they were always welcome. In addition to proclaiming itself ''America's Best Place to Eat''—a slogan that supplanted ''Good Food Fast''—Waffle House touted its organization as ''America's Best Place to Work.'' Workers were referred to as associates, rather than employees, and the company sought to provide good jobs and careers for them.

Although Waffle House's operating strategy had changed little by the 1980s, the size of the chain had. In 1987 Dun & Bradstreet reported that Waffle House had 351 franchisees in addition to its network of company-owned stores. It was also reported that Waffle House employed a work force of 4,500 people, had a financial worth of roughly $60 million, and had total assets of about $81.2 million. *Nation's Restaurant News* estimated that in 1987 Waffle House had generated about $210 million in sales, up from about $175 million a year earlier, including receipts from franchise units. Excluding franchise sales, company revenues were about $87.5 million, which was up only slightly from a 1976 estimate of $84.6 million.

Waffle House remained a closely held company, with virtually all of the ten million shares of stock owned by company employees and the company still being run by the Rogers family. Joe W. Rogers, Jr., served as president. (His father, Joe W. Sr., had co-founded the company and presided over its expansion during the 1950s, 1960s, and 1970s.) M. Michael McCarthy, who joined the company in 1973, served as secretary-treasurer. J. Michael Upton, a former general manager of Old Hickory House, was a vice-president, as was Robert Bowman, who had worked with Arthur Andersen & Co. before joining Waffle House in 1976.

Going into the late 1980s Waffle House was operating in ten states; Alabama, Arizona, Louisiana, Florida, Georgia, Mississippi, Oklahoma, North Carolina, South Carolina, and Texas. It was also operating two subsidiary companies; WHI Inc., a real estate holding company that had its own vending machine subsidiary called Metro Distributors Inc.; and LaVista Equipment Supply Co., a designer and retailer of restaurant equipment. The real estate company reflected Waffle House's hefty property holdings: unlike many other chains, Waffle House owned much of the property on which its restaurants were built. According to Dun & Bradstreet in 1987, retained earnings had increased and the company's total debt was in line with its net worth. McCarthy confirmed in 1988 only that company sales were up in 1987 as a result of new restaurant openings, higher menu prices, and increased sales per store.

Waffle House grew rapidly partly as a result of its franchising. Announcements in 1988 made by Waffle House management, however, cast doubt on the financial success of the franchising strategy. Nancy Wilson, an employee in the franchising division, told the *Atlanta Business Chronicle* that the company planned to cease all new franchising efforts, making the statement as part of an effort to exclude Waffle House from the newspaper's list of top Georgia franchises. Joe Rogers, Jr., refused to confirm the report, stating, "It's our policy never to share information with the press."

Some industry insiders at the time cited the rumor that Waffle House had stopped franchising as evidence that the chain was stagnating in a rapidly changing restaurant industry and that it needed to update its image and menu. However, Waffle House didn't change much during the next few years, nor did executives squelch the franchising program. In fact, Waffle House expanded at a rapid clip during the late 1980s and early 1990s, opening restaurants in existing markets and branching out into Arkansas, Colorado, Illinois, Indiana, Kentucky, Missouri, New Mexico, Ohio, Tennessee, and Virginia. Interestingly, the stores in Indiana were named "Waffle and Steak" because the Waffle House name was already being used when Waffle House Inc. entered that state. Waffle House celebrated its 40th anniversary in 1995 by opening Unit #1000, the chain's 1000th store. The shop was located just a few blocks from the site of the original Waffle House #1 that had opened its doors in 1955.

Principal Subsidiaries: WHI Inc.; LaVista Equipment Supply Co.

Further Reading:

Cooper, Ron, "More Waffle Houses Making Themselves at Home in Area," *Business First-Louisville,* December 6, 1993, p. 1.

Fullam, Peter, "SunQuest Systems Reveals Plans," *Indianapolis Business Journal,* October 20, 1986, p. 1.

Welch, Mary, "Is Waffle House Cooking Up Changes? Restaurant Halts Franchise Growth," *Atlanta Business Chronicle,* September 19, 1988, p. 3A.

—Dave Mote

WEST BEND.

West Bend Co.

400 Washington Street
West Bend, Wisconsin 53095-0278
U.S.A.
(414) 334-2311
Fax: (414) 337-6800

Wholly Owned Subsidiary of Premark International, Inc.
Incorporated: 1911 as the West Bend Aluminum Co.
Sales: $200 million
Employees: 1,600
SICs: 3634 Electric Housewares and Fans; 3914 Silverware,
   Plated Ware and Stainless Steel Ware

West Bend Co. is a major manufacturer of small electric appliances, water-purification systems, and high-quality stainless-steel cookware. Its appliances include breadmakers, electric skillets, slows cookers, woks, corn poppers, beverage makers, and electronic timers, primarily under the West Bend trademark. In the mid-1990s it ranked among the top five small-appliance manufacturers in the United States.

When a pocketbook manufacturing company burned down in 1911, many residents of West Bend, Wisconsin, were thrown out of work. Young Bernhardt C. Ziegler, a local entrepreneurial dynamo who had organized his own full-fledged fire-insurance company while still in high school, set out to find a substitute industry for the townspeople. Impressed by the growth of aluminum novelty and cookware companies in eastern Wisconsin, he recruited six other men who, with himself, each put down $1,000 to incorporate the West Bend Aluminum Co. on September 27, 1911. Five of the seven founders were businessmen. The other two, Carl and Bob Wentorf, were skilled tool-and-die makers who had been working for an aluminum cookware company but had been threatened with dismissal because a third brother had left the firm to join another Wisconsin aluminum cookware company. They immediately began work on the tools and dies needed by West Bend.

The founders rented an old button factory on the west bank of the Milwaukee River for $8.50 a month and three weeks later had a lathe, shaper, and drill press in place. A draw press capable of turning out about 15 kinds of utensils was ordered from Brooklyn, New York, and 3,000 pounds of aluminum from a firm in Pennsylvania. Six to ten men were employed in the factory initially. The first items to bear the West Bend name

were saucepans in four sizes, a frying pan, a pie pan, and a water dipper. The company first exhibited its products at a 1913 hardware association meeting in Milwaukee.

Ziegler was named general manager of West Bend in 1914. He immediately put into effect a perpetual inventory and cost system. Also in that year, the company moved across the river to a new 14,000-square-foot plant on filled land. Net sales, which came to $73,244 in 1913, climbed to $124,304 in 1914 and $241,160 in 1915. Growth continued in the following years, and in 1918 a large three-story addition to the plant was completed. In 1920 sales passed the million-dollar market, reaching $1,598,562.

West Bend's anchor customer during these early years was Sears, Roebuck and Co., which until 1926 was wholly a mail-order firm. Up through 1919 Sears purchased between 40 and 50 percent of the company's production. Most of the rest was sold to different jobbers under their brand names. During World War I, West Bend won a contract to produce army mess kits, but just as production began, the war ended. After the war West Bend introduced its line in department stores, but the market was dominated by two bigger companies.

A new product emerged in 1921 at the suggestion of a West Bend salesman. Called the Waterless Cooker, this large pot with inset pans was stamped out of heavyweight aluminum and sold with a cast-iron base for cooking on a wood or coal stove. The lid of the cooker was fitted with clamps that prevented the escape of steam during cooking, making the addition of water unnecessary. The Waterless Cooker was advertised as a utensil in which a complete meal could be prepared in one pot. It was sold through commissioned house-to-house salesmen.

By 1929 West Bend ranked third in the nation in sales of aluminum cookware. In 1932 it introduced a "Flavo-Seal" line of heavy-gauge cookware made of up roasters, saucepans, and skillets and designed, like the Waterless Cooker, to cook foods without adding water. Two years later the company began to sell the Flavo-Seal line through retail stores as well as commissioned salesmen. These utensils were successful, and a new three-story addition had to be added to the factory in 1937 to handle increased demand.

Another successful product was a copper stein West Bend introduced for a Milwaukee brewery in 1932. Soon the company was meeting orders for copper steins from other breweries and giftware orders from other accounts for ashtrays, serving trays, and lamps. Copperware sales were stimulated by the low price of the metal—only one quarter that of aluminum in the depths of the Great Depression. West Bend's net sales, which had passed $3 million in 1928, dropped below $1 million in 1932 (for the first time since 1921). Sales did not again reach the $3-million mark until 1940, but West Bend made a profit every year, including 1932.

West Bend developed a new drip coffeemaker, which did not require filter paper, in 1922. The popularity of the "Flavo-Drip" led to the development of a rangetop percolator called the "Flavo-Perk." The company also introduced various sizes of portable coffee urns to its coffeemaking line. In 1949 the Flavo-Perk became electric, and the following year it was converted to fully automatic operation under the name "Flavo-matic."

Among its other early electric appliances, West Bend unveiled a portable drip coffee urn, the Speedmaster electric teakettle, Aluminum Glo lamps, and the Cadet water heater for automobiles.

In 1941, as the United States was being drawn into World War II, aluminum was earmarked for military production only, threatening West Bend's production. However, West Bend won a naval contract to produce 20mm brass antiaircraft cartridge cases. During the war the company produced more than 300 different items under defense contracts, including powder tanks and rocket containers. By the end of the war it had earned six Navy "E" awards for outstanding achievement.

During the war West Bend executives purchased the Kissel automobile plant in nearby Hartford, Wisconsin. After the war the plant was converted from military production to the manufacture of the first air-cooled outboard motor. It was sold, beginning in 1947, exclusively through Sears under the "Elgin" name and by West Bend under the "West Bend" and "Shark" names. A factory was added in Barrie, Ontario, in 1957 for Canadian distribution. Chrysler Corp. bought West Bend's outboard-motor and industrial-engine division in 1965 for an undisclosed sum. West Bend of Canada then became strictly a distribution center for the company's Canadian sales rather than a production facility.

Meanwhile, the West Bend plant also returned to civilian production and resumed its refinement and development of home appliances. It developed a color finishing process for aluminum and introduced new products like popcorn poppers. However, when the Korean War broke out in 1950, aluminum, as well as copper and steel, again became a restricted material. Although West Bend continued limited manufacture of products for civilian consumption, it also produced such military items as cartridge cases, powder tanks, rocket containers, and gas-mask canisters. After the war ended in 1953, West Bend continued defense production, notably with an army contract to make ammunition. In 1961 it dropped "Aluminum" from its name to reflect its use of a variety of materials, such as plastics, copper, steel, and brass.

West Bend expanded both its product lines and plant capacity during the 1960s. It introduced Gem Coat- and Teflon-finished cookware products; buffet appliances, including the Kabob 'n Grill, the Automatic Buffet Chef, and the Smokeless Broiler-Rotisserie; and a new line of decorative pantryware and insulated serveware. The company expanded its West Bend facility and added a new plant in Sheridan, Arkansas. It also acquired NFC Engineering Co., manufacturer of Thermo-Serv insulated plastic dishes, in 1965.

West Bend remained privately held until it was acquired in 1968 by Rexall Drug and Chemical Co. In its last 12 months as an independent company, from mid-1967 to mid-1968, West Bend earned $4.3 million on sales of $69 million. In payment Rexall issued to West Bend stockholders common and preferred shares valued in October 1968 at more than $80 million. Rexall later changed its name to Dart Industries and, after a 1980 merger with Kraft, Inc., to Dart & Kraft Inc.

During the 1970s West Bend introduced a new line called "specialty electrics," which included such appliances as an electric pizza baker and grill, an electric yogurt maker, an automatic egg cooker, and the "Fryette" electric deep fryer. Other products included drip coffee makers, an electric wok, microwave-oven cookware, and vertical-wheel humidifiers. The drip coffee makers were endorsed and promoted by the Pat Boone family and were manufactured for JC Penney, Sears, and Montgomery Ward, as well as under the West Bend name.

In 1982 West Bend dropped its original product line, retail cookware, although it continued to manufacture cookware for distributors and door-to-door sales. It also discontinued its humidifier line. The company expanded its scope the following year, however, by acquiring the rights to the Total Gym exercise system of home-fitness products, constructed of chrome-plated heavy-gauge steel tubing. Other fitness companies were purchased shortly thereafter. West Bend also bought the Borg-Erickson Corp.'s Borg Scale bathroom-scale business in 1985 for less than $15 million. Tom Kieckhafer, vice president for sales and marketing, explained these actions to *HFD*, a trade weekly, in October 1985 as "redeploying our assets into areas where there is a better return." Industry estimates put West Bend's annual sales volume at $200 million.

The company's big success story of the early 1980s was the introduction of its cordless iron, which proved to be its top product in sales dollars and units during 1984. In 1985 the iron again was West Bend's top product in dollars, although corn poppers were first in units sold. Typically, the company was seeking niches, generally smaller than the iron market, in which it could gain a dominant share. "We're number one in woks," Kieckhafer (a West Bend long-time employee who became president of the company in 1989) told the *HFD* interviewer, "we're number one in the corn popper category when you combine hot air and oil units, we're number two in slow cookers, and number one in party percolators and coffee urns." The company also had developed a family of electronic timers that had become steady volume producers.

In 1986 West Bend became part of Premark International, Inc., a corporation split off from Kraft, Inc. In the following year the home-fitness and bathroom-scale businesses were placed in a new Premark unit called Precor. West Bend Water Systems was created in 1989 to meet increased demand for quality water-treatment devices. The company purchased a water-distillation company, Environmental Products Corporation, of St. Catharines, Ontario, and introduced its high-grade, stainless-steel water distillers direct to the home under the Lifetime and Dol-Fyn brand names.

Meanwhile, West Bend continued to be active in the small-appliance market. In late 1991 it introduced Curl Crazy, an electric vegetable cutter that automatically sliced potatoes, zucchini, apples, and other foods in curly or spiral shapes. Introduced in 1993, West Bend Automatic was the first breadmaker manufactured in the United States, according to the company. The company had moved quickly to enter this hot new niche, completing the Automatic project in only 35 weeks, from concept to shipping. The company still managed to incorporate many desirable features in the breadmaker, including a choice of six bread settings, a programmable timer to delay baking up to 13 hours, a pan with a nonstick coating, and temperature indicators meant to avoid the common problem of killing the yeast.

Also in 1993, West Bend introduced a three-speed hand mixer. This appliance, established at the urging of Wal-Mart, exemplified the company's willingness to collaborate closely with leading retailers in introducing products to the marketplace. Like West Bend's three other most recent appliances, the mixer was manufactured in the company's own factory. Defying the conventional wisdom, West Bend was increasingly making its own products domestically rather than overseas for greater flexibility in adjusting to the volume of sales orders.

Industry sources estimated the company's annual sales at about $175 million in 1993 and its share of the electric small-appliance market at about 12 percent. During 1994 West Bend expanded its breadmaker, drip coffeemaker, and mixer lines. The company enjoyed record sales and segment profit in 1994. Sales of breadmakers were particularly strong.

In 1995 West Bend belonged to Premark's Consumer Products Group. The company's main manufacturing facility was its 1.5-million-square-foot plant in West Bend. The firm also operated manufacturing facilities in Barrie and St. Catharines, Ontario. West Bend de Mexico, a Premark subsidiary, operated a factory in Renosa, Mexico. A 210,000-square-foot distribution center was located near the West Bend plant, and two other centers were being rented in Sparks, Nevada, and Jackson, Mississippi. Its small appliances were being sold primarily in the United States and Canada, directly to mass merchandisers, department stores, hardware stores, warehouse clubs, and catalog showrooms. West Bend's stainless-steel cookware was being marketed under 23 separate product lines and several brand names, including Lifetime, Inkor, Kitchen Craft, Lustre Craft, Royal Queen, and European Lady. It was also being sold to consumers in 31 countries by independent distributors through dinner parties and other direct-sales methods.

Further Reading:

Purpura, Linda, ''West Bend Spud Slicers to Bow,'' *HFD,* September 30, 1991, p. 108.
Ratliff, Dawn, ''Bending Over Backwards,'' *HFD,* November 29, 1993, pp. 44–45.
Rock, James Martin, ''The Wisconsin Aluminum Cookware Industry Prior to World War II.'' Ph.D. dissertation, Northwestern University, 1966, pp. 109–112, 175–77, 185, 190–92.
——, ''A Growth Industry: The Wisconsin Aluminum Cookware Industry, 1893–1020,'' *Wisconsin Magazine of History,* Winter 1971–72, pp. 87–99.
Simmons, Tim, ''West Bend's Success: Market Prescience,'' *HFD,* October 14, 1985, p. 127.
''West Bend Makes Its Bread Machine Here,'' *HFD,* August 23, 1991, p. 51.

—Robert Halasz

Williamson-Dickie Manufacturing Company

P.O. Box 1779
Fort Worth, Texas 76101
U.S.A.
(817) 336-7201
Fax: (817) 336-5183

Private Company
Incorporated: 1922
Sales: $481 million
Employees: 4,000
SICs: 2325 Men's & Boys' Separate Trousers & Slacks;
  2326 Men's & Boys' Work Clothing

Williamson-Dickie Manufacturing Company is well known throughout the United States for its durable work clothes. In fact, the company has dominated the American work clothes market for years, and is confident enough to issue an unconditional guarantee on the quality of its products. During the late 1980s and early 1990s, however, imported clothes won over many American consumers and began to threaten Williamson-Dickie's market share.

During the latter part of the nineteenth century, C. N. Williamson, and his cousin, E. E. Dickie, founded the Mallory Hat distributorship. Partners for over 25 years, the two men distributed men's hats throughout the state of Texas. In 1920, while the partners were still distributing hats, C. D. Williamson, more often known as "Don," and brother to C. N. Williamson, began to work for a Fort Worth clothing manufacturer by the name of U.S. Overall Company. Coincidentally, C. N. Williamson and E. E. Dickie were primary stockholders in the company, and also sold the firm's merchandise on a part-time basis. When Dickie arranged a sale of items that the president of U.S. Overall did not feel the company could manufacture, the president agreed to sell his stock to C. N. Williamson and E. E. Dickie. Quite suddenly, a new company named Williamson-Dickie was established.

The two older partners asked Don Williamson to become the new company's general manager, chief operating officer, and chief executive officer. C. N. Williamson became president and offered help in the financial area, while Dickie became vice-president and offered to help with sales. Under Don's direction, the company soon outpaced the hat business, and the three men began to concentrate solely on developing the garment company.

Don Williamson's supervision of the company, and its early successes, were based on his idea that corporate management was a science. Most of the books written on managing a business during the 1920s and 1930s suggested that an ambitious entrepreneur work hard, devote long hours, and conduct his financial dealings within a morally sound framework. Don Williamson, however, thought that this approach was naive, so he developed his own management principles in a book entitled *Executive Operations Technique.* With help from Edwin Booz, the head of Booz, Allen, and Hamilton, a well-known consulting firm, Don Williamson was able to clearly identify a number of steps in running a successful business: Expose Conditions, Develop Ideas, Unify Views, Determine Plans, Produce Actions, and Review Results. According to Williamson, if a new employee studied these principles of management, he would be well on the way to understanding successful business practices. By the early 1940s, the company had implemented a regular series of seminars on executive management for all new middle- to high-level employees based on Williamson's principles.

During World War II, the company procured numerous contracts with the U.S. government to manufacture clothes for various units of the military, and after the war Williamson-Dickie introduced a more extensive line of work clothes, including jeans, jackets, overalls, and shirts. The company's most successful product was the khaki pant. Otherwise known as the "chino," and first worn by Texas oilfield workers, the khaki pant became a standard during the 1950s. Soon students, professors, golfers, and others from every walk of life were wearing khaki pants.

As a result of its popular work clothes, Williamson-Dickie's revenues and profitability skyrocketed. Next the company entered the industrial laundry business, cleaning and pressing work clothes and renting matching shirts and pants worn as employee uniforms. The volume of Williamson-Dickie's laundry business increased so rapidly that its officers reasoned that significant costs could be cut with if a permanent press process could be developed, which would allow them to clean work clothes without pressing them.

Executives at Williamson-Dickie contacted Harris Laboratories, located in Washington, D.C., to develop a permanent crease that could be processed into a cotton workpant. As the developer of Toni Home Permanents, a permanent wave for hair, Harris Laboratories was confident that they could develop a permanent crease for pants as well.

After just one year of research, the company developed a permanent press that actually worked; unfortunately, the treatment that allowed cotton pants to form a permanent press so weakened the material that after one or two washings the garment practically disintegrated. Irate customers complained to Williamson-Dickie about shredding pants, while also complimenting the company on the beautiful crease on the front of the trousers. Undismayed by this temporary setback, Williamson-Dickie and Harris Laboratories worked together to blend polyester with cotton to give the fabric more strength. From that time forward, permanent press became the standard for workpants, and Williamson-Dickie issued an unconditional guarantee on the quality and durability of all the company's work clothes.

During the late 1950s the company expanded its marketing efforts in Europe and the Middle East. American oilfield workers contracted for jobs in the Middle East introduced clothes manufactured by Williamson-Dickie that became popular throughout the entire region. In 1960 the company opened a manufacturing plant in Belize; one year later, however, Hurricane Hattie destroyed the entire operation. After the factory was rebuilt, jeans and work clothes from the Belize factory were exported to England, and later, as the plant grew and became more efficient, clothing items manufactured in Belize were sold in the United States.

At this time, one of Williamson-Dickie's competitors began importing into the United States a garment made in a Caribbean nation that severely undercut Williamson-Dickie's prices on one of its most popular items. Executives at Williamson-Dickie concluded that the competing company must be using the "American Goods Returned" section of the Tariff Act to reduce the import duty paid on the garment, allowing the competitor to sell the item at a lower cost than Williamson-Dickie's imports. Williamson-Dickie teamed up with three other American apparel manufacturers to lobby for a change in the Tariff Act regarding re-importing goods; their provision—in Sections 806.30 and 807—allowed American apparel companies to manufacture clothes in Mexico or the Caribbean with U.S. fabrics and fibers, and then return the garments for sale within the United States, paying duty only on the value of the foreign labor. This provision in the Tariff Act created a huge American apparel industry in Mexico and the Caribbean, which, due to low labor costs in these regions, was able to remain competitive in the face of low-priced imports clothes from China, Taiwan, and Korea.

During the early 1970s Williamson-Dickie purchased the General Diaper Corporation, one of the largest diaper manufacturers in the United States. General Diapers was in the process of switching over to the manufacture of disposable diapers; in addition, the company opened two industrial laundry facilities in New Orleans and Houston, acquired a plastics company that made film for the health care product market, and acquired a dental supply firm. This diversification provided Williamson-Dickie with additional revenues to help increase its share of the work clothes market.

During the mid and late 1970s, Williamson-Dickie began to dominate the work clothes market. As the Williamson-Dickie brand continued to grow more and more popular with the general public, the company expanded its product line to include such garments as matching shirt and pant work clothes, jackets, coveralls, overalls, painter pants, jeans, thermal underwear, bandannas, sweatshirts, socks, caps, work boots, flannel shirts, work gloves, and belts. The company also opened a number of stores in the southern United States that sold uniforms and matching accessories, including postman and policeman uniforms, holsters, footwear, and special uniform underwear.

Leadership at Williamson-Dickie had completely changed by the 1970s, with the original founders having retired and nonfamily members hired to manage the operations of the company. Dickie Industrial Services was created during the 1970s to formalize the company's operation of industrial laundry services throughout the South, Southwest, and West Coast regions of the United States. With 14 facilities, Williamson-Dickie was the leader in renting and laundering uniforms for employees from every walk of life, including security guards, police officers, fire fighters, fast food restaurant workers, laboratory technicians, and many more.

During the 1980s the General Diaper Company changed its name to the Blessings Corporation and focused its efforts on manufacturing plastic products for the health care and agricultural industries; developing its Publishing Division, which provided informational materials for new mothers; and growing its Geri-Care Division, which made health care products for the elderly. The company's industrial laundries operation and the apparel divisions were highly lucrative. By the end of the decade, Williamson-Dickie reported an annual growth rate of nearly 15 percent, and the company's manufacturing facilities, although concentrated in mostly southern states, were also thriving in California, New Jersey, and a number of Caribbean countries.

The advent of the 1990s saw an increased competition within the international apparel industry, with many American clothing manufacturers, including Williamson-Dickie, threatened by international imports. At the same time, these companies benefitted from a new and unexpected demand for their products by young urban customers, who made work clothes a fashion trend. With increasing sales to this market segment, Williamson-Dickie was able to move beyond its traditional blue-collar customers.

The company opened its first factory store outlet, in Orlando, Florida, during the mid-1990s. The store featured the company's brand-name work clothes, along with other sportswear and accessories. Williamson-Dickie entered another new channel by placing its work clothes—including painter's pants, coveralls, and long-tail T-shirts—in home improvement warehouse chains, and also contracted with Itochu of Japan for the latter company to distribute work clothes to Japanese consumers. While many other American apparel manufacturers have been badly damaged by overseas competition, Williamson-Dickie has proved extremely adept at creating new and highly profitable markets for its clothes.

Principal Subsidiaries: Blessings Corporation.

Further Reading:
Hancox, Clara, "And Now—For the Last Time—What Will It Take to Survive into the Next Century?" *Daily News Record,* June 28, 1993, p. 23.
Jarnagin, DeAnna, "Home Improvement Hits Prime Time," *Daily News Record,* April 24, 1992, p. 3.
Parola, Robert, "Workwear Grows New Fashion Muscle," *Daily News Record,* May 19, 1993, p. 4.
Salfino, Catherine, "More Vendors See $ in the SSS Sports," *Daily New Record,* April 24, 1995, pp. 6–15.
Vargo, Julie, "New Dickies Outlet Plays to Worker and Hip-Hopper," *Daily News Record,* February 18, 1994, p. 4.
——, "Work Clothes Bring Fashion to the Street," *Daily News Record,* November 18, 1994, p. 3.
Walsh, Peter, "Itochu of Japan," *Daily News Record,* December 8, 1993, p. 16.
Williamson, C. Dickie, *Williamson-Dickie Manufacturing Company,* Newcomen Society: New York, 1985.
"Williamson Dickie Introduces International Pro Rodeo Cowboy Jean," *Daily News Record,* April 19, 1995, p. 4.

—Thomas Derdak

Wisconsin Bell, Inc.

727 North Broadway
Milwaukee, Wisconsin 53202
U.S.A.
(414) 549-7102
Fax: (312) 207-1601

Wholly Owned Subsidiary of Ameritech Corporation
Founded: 1882 as Wisconsin Telephone Company
Employees: 4,651
Sales: $1.13 billion
SICs: 4813 Telephone Communications Except
   Radiotelephone

Wisconsin Bell, Inc., is the legal name of what has publicly been known as Ameritech Wisconsin since 1993. The largest provider of local telephone service in the state of Wisconsin, Wisconsin Bell focuses its attention on larger population centers, leaving less populous areas to Wisconsin's many small, independent telephone companies.

Wisconsin Bell was founded in 1882 as the Wisconsin Telephone Company by Charles H. Haskins, Benjamin K. Miller, and Harry C. Haskins. Charles Haskins, who had written a book on principals of electricity, became intrigued by the potential of the telephone shortly after its invention in 1876. The following year he created Milwaukee's first telephone exchange with 15 customers.

With Charles Haskins serving as its first president, Wisconsin Telephone set up its headquarters on Broadway in Milwaukee and installed its first switchboard in a building across the street. Customers contacted the switchboard by spinning a magneto crank attached to their telephones. Despite this primitive equipment, the company began stringing together its territory (which included the Upper Peninsula of Michigan and all of Wisconsin except Douglas and Grant Counties) with telephone wires. In 1883 the firm installed its first aerial telephone cable in Milwaukee. By the end of the 1880s 60 Wisconsin cities and towns had telephone service, with yearly telephone rates averaging $50 a year.

Wisconsin Telephone was part of the Bell system, with a license from Alexander Graham Bell's American Bell Telephone Company. When Bell's patents expired in the early 1890s, independent telephone companies were created and Wisconsin Tele-

phone experienced its first serious competition. The company fought it, led by new president Henry Payne and aided by its exclusive access to the Bell system's long-distance lines. Customers of rival companies who wanted to make long-distance calls had to go to a Wisconsin Telephone office to do so. Despite the competition, Wisconsin Telephone grew to nearly 20,000 customers by 1900.

Technical improvements appeared continuously throughout the telephone industry. Wisconsin Telephone began using dry-core, paper-insulated cable in 1894, replacing its less reliable cotton and paraffin cables. The firm already had long-distance service to Chicago, and after a Chicago-New York line opened in 1892 Wisconsin Telephone customers were able to call New York. In 1896 Wisconsin Telephone installed the first dial telephone system in the United States at Milwaukee City Hall.

With the rapid growth of the U.S. telephone, electrical, and railroad systems, states began to regulate public utilities. Independent telephone companies accused the Bell system of being a monopoly; partly as a result of that the Wisconsin legislature gave the state's Railroad Commission regulatory power over telephone companies. However, getting rate increases approved was far easier than it is today and regulation did not seem to hurt the company—it began buying up competitors, and its rate of growth actually increased. Meanwhile, the firm improved its infrastructure. It laid underground cables and conduits, rewired subscriber stations, and beefed up inspection of long-distance lines. To encourage use of its long-distance services, Wisconsin Telephone created a plan for businesses much like the "800" services. By 1910 the firm had over 100,000 telephones in service.

This growth necessitated structural changes within the company. In 1910 the plant, traffic, and commercial departments were given separate managers. The following year the Bell system organized its companies by region. Wisconsin Telephone became part of the Central Group along with four other Bell companies, encompassing parts of Illinois, Indiana, Ohio, and Michigan. This arrangement lasted for 11 years before the companies were left entirely on their own again. To keep up with growth, the company also built three more central offices in Milwaukee during the 1910s.

Service quality went down from 1916 to 1918 as many of Wisconsin Telephone's employees were given military leave to fight in World War I. Immediately after the war new buildings or additions to central offices were made throughout the firm's territory, including Appleton, Madison, and Eau Claire.

A string of intense winter storms hit Wisconsin during the 1920s, causing numerous service disruptions. One storm in February 1922 knocked out communications between Milwaukee and the Appleton and Eau Claire district headquarters. Repairs took two months. Despite these difficulties the firm continued to grow, reaching 9,000 employees in 1929. It reorganized again, this time into commercial, plant, and traffic departments, and began a large construction campaign.

The Great Depression hit the company hard. The numbers of telephones in service and calls being made plummeted. Between 1929 and 1931 the firm cut back by about 2,000 stations and put many of its employees on a staggered work schedule to avoid massive layoffs. Even so, the number of employees dropped to 5,800 by 1933. In 1932 the Wisconsin Public Service Commission reduced the firm's exchange rates by 12.5 percent. Wisconsin Telephone filed suit, claiming the rate reduction was arbitrary, and litigation continued throughout the 1930s. The firm also got into a conflict over its taxes with the Wisconsin Tax Commission and ended up having to pay $1.4 million in back taxes in 1936.

The firm was trying to convert its entire territory to dial telephones but was slowed down by these losses of revenue. It did create public relations departments at its offices throughout Wisconsin to examine customer complaints and attitudes. In 1939 the firm also helped lay the first coaxial cable in the United States between Stevens Point and Minneapolis, allowing for more reliable service. By this point the firm was recovering from the Great Depression, and the number of phones in service had reached 377,000, more than in 1930. In 1940 alone Wisconsin Telephone connected 17,000 more telephones, a record increase.

With the outbreak of World War II in 1941, Wisconsin Telephone, and the entire U.S. telephone system, adopted special security measures and cooperated with the Office of Civil Defense. Because military needs had a higher priority than civilian needs, equipment and supply shortages developed. Over 2,000 employees were hired to help meet growing military communications needs. By 1944 the firm's supply of telephones had been used up, and nearly 20,000 calls for service could not be met. Employee turnover soared, and many operators and service people were inexperienced. Wisconsin Telephone overturned its policy of ending a woman's employment when she got married and rehired about 650 former employees.

By the end of the war in 1945 the firm was behind by 28,500, and it took two years to catch up. As a result, the firm had 12,000 employees that year, the highest in its history. In 1946 and 1947 the firm experienced labor problems. Local calls could only be made from company offices during a month-long strike in April 1947. The following month the firm increased its payroll by $2.5 million per year.

The firm boomed during the 1950s, a decade of unprecedented telephone use, installing 420,000 telephones, constructing 83 buildings, and laying out $286 million for construction. The company continued modernizing, doing away with most of its remaining hand-crank telephones. To further increase demand for telephones, a station wagon was painted to depict different colors of telephone desk sets and driven around the firm's territory. In 1957 the firm's one-millionth telephone was installed in the office of Wisconsin Governor Vernon Thomson. Wisconsin Telephone also issued its first long-term debt ($30 million worth of 35-year debentures) to help pay for its record construction budget of $47 million.

In the 1960s the entire Bell system began offering a greater variety of telephones, and Wisconsin Telephone made money selling products like the Princess phone. That same year, Wisconsin Telephone installed its first outdoor walk-up coin phones. In 1964 it began offering touch-tone telephones, and in 1965 it began the WATS service, which allowed businesses to call out of their immediate area for a package price.

Competition was increasing in the telecommunications industry, and Wisconsin Telephone founded a marketing department in 1961 to help it sell new services, particularly to businesses. The firm established a Direct Distance Dialing Bureau in 1963 to allow long-distance calls without operator assistance. In 1968 the firm was hit by its first strike since 1947. The 18-day strike resulted in a $6 million settlement. By the end of the decade Wisconsin Telephone had 1.7 million phones in service and was spending about $80 million a year on construction.

The energy crisis of 1973 caused Wisconsin Telephone to decrease heating in its buildings, run a Milwaukee shuttle bus for its employees, and shrink the firm's fleet of vehicles. Meanwhile, communications technology continued to improve. Wisconsin Telephone expanded its use of electronic switching stations. These stations, brought out by AT&T in 1966, connected phone calls automatically and with great speed. They helped make possible the vast increases in the volume of telephone traffic in the 1970s and 1980s. With these increases in traffic came increased rates. In 1981, for example, the firm won approval for a $42.7 million annual rate increase.

In 1983 the firm, along with the entire Bell system, went through the most important reorganization in its history. Charges that AT&T was a monopoly that suppressed competition dated to the early years of the Bell system. However, in 1974, the U.S. Justice Department, goaded by some of AT&T's competitors, filed an antitrust lawsuit asking for the dismemberment of the company. Litigation lasted for years and finally resulted in an agreement that AT&T would break up the Bell system. This occurred on January 1, 1984, when Wisconsin Telephone became part of Ameritech, a new regional Bell operating company that also included Illinois Bell, Indiana Bell, Michigan Bell, and Ohio Bell. Partly to herald this event, Wisconsin Telephone changed its name to Wisconsin Bell in 1983.

Meanwhile, advances in telecommunications technology accelerated, and with them business opportunities. In 1983 Wisconsin Bell announced it would jointly offer interactive CATV services with Telenational Communications. In 1985 Wisconsin Bell began the process of buying digital central office switches from Siemens Public Switching Systems. These switches made a variety of new services possible.

In 1986 Wisconsin Bell built, with AT&T, an advanced government communications system. The sophisticated digital network linked 50,000 employees at 1,800 state and local government locations. AT&T built the spine, and Wisconsin Bell supplied local access. These advances did not necessarily make jobs more secure. In 1986 the firm offered early retirement to 263 managers, or 11 percent of its management staff of 2,333.

Other services stemming from technology advances followed. In 1988 the firm installed 350 pay phones able to read long-distance calling cards. This let customers make long-distance calls without using a mound of change. Sensing opportunity in the proliferation of telephone-answering machines, the firm began testing its own voice-mail message service in 1989. By 1988 Wisconsin Bell was using computerized systems to track maintenance for its fleet of 1,800 vehicles.

In 1989 Wisconsin Bell became the first of the Ameritech Bells to use only electronic switches. The firm's last electromechanical switches were replaced by digital switches made by Siemens. Of Wisconsin Bell's 1.6 million telephone lines, between 25 and 30 percent went to digital switches; the rest used analog switches.

Not all of Wisconsin Bell's technology advances centered on telephones and their switches. By 1990 many larger telephone cables used sophisticated temperature and humidity regulating systems. To keep air-core cables dry and operating efficiently, compressed dry air was pumped through them. Otherwise, minute amounts of rain or groundwater crept into defects in the cable sheath and caused shorts. A complex system of microprocessors and manifolds kept the air flowing. Revenue for 1990 came to $1.06 billion.

In September 1993 Ameritech retired the Wisconsin Bell brand name. Bills for local telephone service appeared bearing the Ameritech name at the top, instead of Wisconsin Bell. Consumers no longer encountered the name Wisconsin Bell because the firm was referred to in its telephone books, the press, and in marketing efforts simply as Ameritech or Ameritech Wisconsin. The company's legal name remains Wisconsin Bell, however. The same type of name change was carried out at the other state Bells in the Ameritech group, so that Ameritech could promote the Ameritech name.

The change did not affect Wisconsin Bell's rates or services, but it did reflect Ameritech strategies that had a potentially huge effect on Wisconsin Bell and its local phone service. By 1993, revenue had only increased to $1.13 billion since 1990. The local phone business was a steady source of revenue but did not grow quickly. Ameritech had its eye on the long-distance market, which was far more lucrative, as well as on other profitable communications services such as cable television. Ameritech proposed giving up its local telephone monopoly, allowing direct competition in its markets, in exchange for access to the long-distance market. Throughout the mid-1990s Wisconsin Bell watched as neighbor Illinois Bell, the chosen laboratory for the first such market experiment, negotiated regulatory and legislative hurdles, trying to work out the details of this market change.

As a result, in the mid-1990s Wisconsin Bell was a well-run company with a steady stream of revenue. However, its market seemed likely to change in the coming years, with more risks but also more potential for profit and growth.

Further Reading:

Cosgrove, James G., ''Wisconsin Brings Network Management Under Control,'' *Telephony,* November 10, 1986, pp. 50–53.
Mackie, Richard W., ''Wisconsin Bell Goes With the Flow,'' *Telephony,* May 7, 1990, pp. 34–37.
''Wis. Bell Goes All Electronic,'' *Telephony,* December 18, 1989, p. 16.

—Scott M. Lewis

Wolters Kluwer NV

Stadhouderskade 1
P.O. Box 818
NL-1000 AV Amsterdam
The Netherlands
(31) 20-6070400
Fax: (31) 20-6070490

Public Company
Incorporated: 1882
Employees: 8,700
Sales: D 2,736
Stock Exchanges: Amsterdam
SICs: 2731 Book Publishing & Printing; 2700 Book
   Publishing

Wolters Kluwer NV is one of the worldwide leaders in publishing, and the Netherlands' second-largest publisher after Reed Elsevier, with approximately $1.5 billion in 1994 sales. Under the slogan ''Partner in Information and Education,'' Wolters Kluwer and its subsidiaries are primarily active in the specialized publishing markets of business, law, tax, medicine, education, science, professional training, and electronic publishing, while maintaining only a limited presence in general consumer and trade publishing. With operations in selected Western and Eastern European countries and in the United States, Wolters Kluwer has pursued a growth strategy dominated by strategic acquisitions, including the $250 million acquisition of J. B. Lippincott & Company in 1990.

The Wolters Kluwer of the 1990s traces its origins to four Dutch publishing families of the nineteenth century: Wolters, Noordhoff, Kluwer, and Samson. During that century, the Industrial Revolution, combined with constitutional and legal reforms that more closely united the formerly loose association of Dutch provinces, prompted a growing demand for educational and informational literature. Many publishers, print shops, and typographers responded to this demand, numbering some 600 by the end of the 1880s. Until the twentieth century, however, publishing in the Netherlands remained the province of small-scale, often family-run businesses with fewer than ten employees. The first large publishing house, the Elsevier Bookselling and Publishing Company, appeared in Amsterdam in 1881, but remained an exception for some time to come.

J. B. Wolters founded the Schoolbook publishing house—later to be called the J. B. Wolters Publishing Company—in the provincial capital city of Groningen in 1836, providing educational and instructional materials for a country just beginning the transformation to a modern industrial economy. Wolters was childless, and upon his death in 1860, his brother-in-law, E. B. ter Horst, took over the company. Under ter Horst the company began a period of expansion, adding a printing shop and bindery to its editorial functions. Ter Horst brought his son, E. B. ter Horst, Jr., into the company in 1885, and ter Horst Jr. was made a partner in the company eight years later. Disagreements between father and son led the senior ter Horst to leave the company soon afterwards. Ter Horst Jr. led the company until his death in 1905. By then, the company's fortunes had fallen, to the point where the heirs to the company, ter Horst Jr.'s half-brothers F. R. and A. ter Horst, considered closing the company. Instead, the brothers reorganized the company from a partnership into a corporation, and for the first time brought in directors from outside the family. F. R. ter Horst, formerly a banking professional, became the company's managing director, overseeing the editorial portions of its textbook and academic publishing activities from his home in The Hague. The company's production facilities remained in Groningen.

In 1915 a separate office was opened in The Hague. Two years later Dr. Anthony M. H. Schepman, who was married to a niece of F. R. ter Horst, joined the J. B. Wolters Company and was soon named a director of the company, a position he held for more than forty years. Under the joint leadership of ter Horst and Schepman, the company continued to expand its operations. In 1920 the company opened an office in what is now known as Jakarta, Indonesia, in the Dutch East Indies, to provide books for the Dutch-speaking population there. Setbacks for the company came with the Depression of the 1930s, and the introduction of modern Dutch spelling, which removed many Germanisms from the Dutch grammar and spelling and rendered many of Wolters' titles obsolete. These setbacks resulted in a shutdown of its Hague offices. The Second World War, during which Schepman was interned as a member of the Dutch elite in a German concentration camp, added to the company's difficulties. After the war, and especially after Indonesia achieved its independence in 1949, the company enjoyed a period of enhanced prosperity. Wolters also moved into the Flemish-speaking areas of Belgium, especially with the promotion of Algemeen Beschaafd Nederlands (or ABN, a standardization of the language similar to Standard Received English) over the many Dutch and Flemish dialects still spoken throughout both countries. However, in 1954, the Republic of Indonesia moved to prohibit the importation of Indonesian-language books printed outside the country. The J. B. Wolters-Djarkata division attempted to set up printing facilities in Indonesia, but in 1959, Indonesia nationalized many of the foreign companies operating there, including J. B. Wolters-Djarkata.

By then, a postwar wave of mergers across Dutch industry had begun to affect the publishing industry as well. The era of the small family publishing house was fading. The Noordhoff publishing house, founded in 1858 by P. Noordhoff to serve the educational and vocational market, was located directly next door to Wolters' offices in Groningen, and was still managed by the Noordhoff family. Driven by the increasingly competitive nature of the Dutch publishing industry, Noordhoff approached

Wolters about merging the two companies. Wolters, nearly three times the size of Noordhoff but facing the same competition from much larger publishing companies, agreed. The merger of the two houses was accomplished in 1968, literally by the breaking down of the wall that had long separated their offices. The next phase in Wolters' history followed four years later, when it merged with the Information and Communication Group, which had been formed from an earlier merger with the Samson publishing family.

Nicolaas Samson's publishing career began as an offshoot of his civil service career in the Dutch village of Hazerswoude. As the recent modernization of Dutch law was slowly reaching from the larger cities to the outlying provinces, the need arose for new administrative materials and forms, which Samson provided. Samson's operated first in an office of the town hall, but by 1883 he had moved his publishing activities, including printing shop, bindery, and warehouse, to offices next to his home in Alphen aan den Rijn. In 1886 Samson left the civil service to operate his publishing business full time. At first Samson's business concentrated on administrative forms, but he soon added periodicals and books for the administrative market. In 1888 Samson's oldest son, Jacobus Balthus, joined the company; he was joined by his younger brothers Nicolaas and Willem in 1914 and 1915. After a brief period of financial difficulty, Samson's sons took over the company and expanded its operations.

Samson died in 1917. By then, the company had achieved a national reputation; it also maintained strong ties with the government. The company added educational materials and related forms and services to its list in 1920. Samson continued to prosper, yet always remained close to its core business. In 1970 Samson merged with the publisher A. W. Sijthoff, forming the Information and Communication Union (ICU), which merged with Wolters-Noordhoff two years later. The new company adopted the ICU name but in 1983 changed its name again, to Wolters-Samson.

The final branch of Wolters-Kluwer was founded in the 1880s in Deventer, in the eastern Netherlands, by Æbele E. Kluwer. Kluwer began as a bookseller. By 1891 he had published his first book, on arithmetic, called *The Thinker,* which was directed at the secondary school market. For many years, Kluwer concentrated on the educational and academic market, including children's books. In 1892 Kluwer published one of the first trade papers aimed at the educational market, called *De Sollicitant.* Several years later he initiated a successful series of picture books. Another of Kluwer's publication was *De Nederlandsche Jager,* a trade periodical for hunters. Within a decade, Kluwer expanded to include business information and technical works, and soon after into tax and professional publications as well. In 1909 Kluwer published *De Vakstudie* tax series, which provided purchasers with periodic supplements of updated information. By 1920 Kluwer was publishing similar works for other professional areas, by then in a more easily updated looseleaf binder form. These series were extremely profitable for the company, fueling its expansion and remaining one of its most important markets. Kluwer's sons, Evert, Nico, and Æben joined the firm between 1914 and 1921, and his daughters and their husbands also became involved in the company. Kluwer died in 1929, leaving the company to his sons. Kluwer Publish-

ers remained a family concern, growing to become the Netherlands' third-largest publisher, with subsidiaries in the United States and elsewhere, with revenues of 966 million guilders, by 1986.

The Netherlands were largely untouched by the wave of hostile takeovers that marked the 1980s. That changed in 1987, when Elsevier, the country's largest publishing house, announced its intention to buy up Kluwer's stock. A year earlier, Elsevier had initiated talks with Kluwer to suggest a merger between the two companies. Kluwer rejected the plan, pointing to differences in corporate cultures. In June 1987, Elsevier announced a bid of 390 guilders per Kluwer share, which had been worth only 266 guilders per share two weeks before. Kluwer responded by issuing another 2.5 million common shares and beginning talks with Wolters Samson about a possible friendly merger between the two companies. Kluwer's preference for a merger with the smaller house of Wolters Samson was explained by the greater similarity between the two companies' corporate cultures, and in the similarity in their publishing focus. Shortly thereafter, Kluwer issued an additional two million shares of preferential stock to Wolters Samson, vowing to do whatever necessary to stop Elsevier's takeover bid. By August 3rd, however, Elsevier had won control of 48.2 percent of Kluwer's stock, spending 25 million guilders in the final days to acquire it. However, by August 14th, Wolters Samson was able to announce that it had acquired 50.9 percent of Kluwer's outstanding common stock, effecting the merger of their two companies. The new company, called Wolters Kluwer NV, moved its headquarters to Amsterdam. In the final count, Elsevier retained approximately 33 percent of the new company's shares; in 1990 it announced that its intentions to sell these shares, surrendering, for the time being, the idea of a merger between the two companies.

With the merger, Wolters Kluwer became the Netherlands' second-largest publisher. With international holdings including the U.S. subsidiaries Kluwer Law Book Publishing Company, Raven Press, Aspen Systems, and others, Wolters Kluwer entered a period of foreign acquisitions. Over the next two years the company extended into France, West Germany, and Spain. By 1989, roughly 44 percent of its revenues were earned in foreign markets. The pending formation of the European market opened a lucrative arena for the company's well-developed tax and legal publishing arms. The company increased its focus on these areas, dropping several of its Dutch trade and consumer publishers, including Bert Bakker and Martinus Nijhoff International. Its acquisitions continued, with purchases of the IPSOA Editore of Italy, Kieser Verlag of Germany, Tecnipublicaciones of Spain, and Tele Consulte of France. In 1990 the company moved to strengthen its share of the U.S. medical market, completing the $250 million purchase of the two-hundred-year-old J. B. Lippincott and Company from HarperCollins. By that year, Wolters Kluwer included nearly 100 companies, posting annual revenues of more than two billion guilders.

Lippincott had been founded in 1836, when Joshua B. Lippincott opened the J. B. Lippincott & Co. in Philadelphia; Lippincott's 1849 purchase of the Grigg, Elliot & Co., then the world's largest book distributor, allowed him to extend his company's anniversary to the other company's 1792 founding date. The company grew quickly, with medical publications featuring prominently among its titles. The company incorporated in

1885; Lippincott died the following year, leaving the firm to his three sons. By the end of the century, Lippincott was the one of the three largest U.S. publishers. In addition to its medical list, it published for the educational market; however, it was best known for its trade books, which accounted for approximately 50 percent of its business. In the 1950s, however, the company reasserted its interest in other markets, particularly in medical and nursing book and journals. It also expanded its educational and college offerings, placing less and less emphasis on trade books. A major event occurred in 1972, when, finding itself undercapitalized, the company was forced to go public, with the Lippincott family retaining majority ownership. The new corporation launched a period of aggressive expansion, entering new markets and extending its established divisions. By 1977, however, rising costs and other factors had increased the company's debt-to-equity ration to 2/1. The following year, Lippincott was purchased by Harper & Row. Lippincott's activities were pared down to a core focused around medical and nursing books and journals. This formula proved successful; by the time Lippincott was purchased by Wolters Kluwer, its revenues had risen by 500 percent.

The opening of European borders in 1992 meant increasing numbers of new laws and regulations that would need to be translated into many languages. Wolters Kluwer stepped up the internationalization of its activities, concentrating on the most highly developed countries of the European Union. By 1993 its international sales represented 62 percent of its yearly revenues. Its European sales outside of the Netherlands accounted for 45 percent of its total revenues, the United States for 11 percent, and the Netherlands for 37 percent. Wolters Kluwer continued acquiring companies, including Liber in Sweden in 1993. The company established its first Eastern European subsidiary, IURA Edition, in Bratislava, Slovakia, and announced intentions for further Eastern European expansion. Electronic media, including computer diskettes, CD-ROMs, and CD-I technology, had become another growing area for Wolters Kluwer, accounting for six percent of its sales in 1994.

As Wolters Kluwer entered 1995, it showed no sign of slowing the pace of its acquisitions. Companies acquired in that year included Jugend & Volk (Austria); Dalian (France); Fateco Förlag and Juristförlaget (Sweden); Deutscher Kommunal-Verlag Dr. Naujoks & Behrendt (Germany); and Colex Data (Spain). Also in that year Lippincott and Raven Press, a medical publisher, were merged to form Lippincott-Raven Publishers. With operations in 16 countries, and more than 8,000 employees, Wolters Kluwer had become a true multinational in less than decade. However, industry analysts continued to predict an eventual merger between Elsevier and Wolters Kluwer by the beginning of the next century.

Principal Subsidiaries: Wolters Kluwer Belgium; Wolters Kluwer France; Wolters Kluwer Central and Eastern Europe; Wolters Kluwer Italy; Wolters Kluwer US; Wolters Kluwer Sweden; Wolters Kluwer UK; Wolters Kluwer Spain; Wolters Kluwer Academic Publishers; Wolters Kluwer Professional Training (Switzerland); Kluwer Law International; Wolters Kluwer Business Publishing; Wolters Kluwer Educational Publishers; Wolters Kluwer Law and Taxation; Wolters Kluwer Trade Publishing; Lippincott-Raven Publishers (U.S.); Bohmann Druck and Verlag Gesellschaft (Austria, 70%); Teleroute Austria; Aspen Publishers (U.S.); IURA Edition (Slovakia); ABC (Poland); Müszaki (Hungary).

Further Reading:

Feldman, Gayle, ''Going Dutch,'' *Publishers Weekly,* June 21, 1991, pp. 19–26.
Freeman, J. Stuart, Jr., *Toward a Third Century of Excellence: An Informal History of the J. B. Lippincott Company on the Occasion of Its Two-Hundredth Anniversary,* Philadelphia: J. B. Lippincott Company, 1992.
Hagerty, Bob, ''Esoteric Publisher Avoids the Obvious,'' *Wall Street Journal (Europe),* April 25, 1990, p. 7.
de Vries, Johan, *Four Windows of Opportunity: A Study in Publishing,* Wolters Kluwer (Amsterdam), 1995.

—M. L. Cohen

Worthington Foods, Inc.

900 Proprietors Road
Worthington Ohio 43085
U.S.A.
(614) 885-9511
Fax: (614) 885-2594

Public Company
Incorporated: 1939 as Special Foods Inc.
Employees: 461
Sales: $88.2 million (1994)
Stock Exchanges: NASDAQ
SICs: 2075 Soybean Oil Mills; 2099 Food Preparations Not
  Elsewhere Classified

Worthington Foods, Inc., has grown from a tiny manufacturer
of specialty foods into a leader of the U.S. markets for vegetarian foods and meat alternatives. The company continued to hold
a leading 65 percent share of the meat alternatives market in
1994 despite intense competition from America's largest food
conglomerates. By the mid-1990s, Worthington Foods offered
four branded lines of healthy foods: Morningstar Farms targeted
the mass market, while Worthington, LaLoma, and Natural
Touch were geared specifically toward the health food and
Seventh-day Adventist markets. The introduction of such new
products as Spicy Black Bean Burger, Better 'n Burger, and
Ground Meatless in 1995 helped the company expand its presence in the institutional food service and restaurant markets.
Worthington Foods' net income declined by over one-third
from $2.79 million in 1992, when the company made its initial
public stock offering, to $1.79 million in 1993, but rebounded
strongly to $4.33 million in 1994.

The business traces its heritage to 1939, when Dr. George T.
Harding III founded Special Foods in Worthington, Ohio. Harding adhered to Seventh-day Adventist dietary strictures, which
proscribe consumption of pork, ham, shellfish, caffeine, and
tobacco, among other foods and beverages. Most followers
eschew meat and other animal products altogether. Formally
established in 1863, the Seventh-day Adventist Church's concern for bodily health led to the establishment of hospitals,
sanitariums, and medical schools (as well as elementary and
secondary schools, colleges, and universities) throughout the
United States and eventually around the world.

Harding established Special Foods to supply vegetarian foods to
his father's nearby sanitarium (health spa). He also hoped that
the existence of a reliable supply of vegetarian foods would
encourage the development of a mid-Ohio Adventist community. With companies like Michigan's Battle Creek Foods Company, Tennessee's Madison Foods, and California's Loma
Linda Foods (owned by the General Conference of Seventh-day
Adventists) as models, Harding, his wife Mary Virginia, and
four other investors bought and refurbished a fire-damaged
house and started production in 1939.

Special Foods' early products were fashioned after "nut
meats," first concocted by Dr. John Kellogg, the first Adventist
to become a medical doctor. They combined roasted peanuts
with gluten (derived from flour) and seasonings to form meatless, yet high-protein main courses like PROAST, a substitute
for dark meat, and NUMETE, a substitute for light meat. A
1989 company history acknowledged that Special Foods' early
manufacturing practices were "primitive:" a garden hose was a
key piece of equipment, for example.

Nevertheless, Special Foods attracted a following. Bill Robinson, one of the company's founding investors and a former
salesman for Battle Creek Foods, was its first employee. He
coordinated sales to Seventh-day Adventists and health food
shops such that by 1941 the company was selling $20,000 worth
of vegetarian foods each year. Robinson soon emerged as Special Foods' top manager. He brought in James Hagle to assist
with and later assume general managerial duties in 1942.

Hagle came on board just in time to guide the company through
the challenging, yet rewarding, World War II era. Government
rationing during this period both hindered and helped Special
Foods. Tin shortages compelled the use of glass packaging,
which was heavier and more expensive to ship than Special
Foods' usual metal cans. The suspension of imports from Germany cut off supplies of yeast and other specialty flavorings,
but the company managed to procured these ingredients from
the Anheuser-Busch Company. Rationing of red meat, however, helped boost demand for Special Foods' growing array of
meat substitutes, known in the industry as "meat analogs." The
firm's 50th anniversary history noted that even New York's
Waldorf Astoria Hotel was serving CHOPLETS, a mock veal
cutlet. Hagle encouraged the growing interest with advertisements in health food magazines and through direct mail. The
company sometimes sacrificed profits to ship its products across
the country in the hopes that wartime consumers would keep
buying in peacetime. By the war's end, Special Foods' sales had
burgeoned to nearly $300,000 annually, the company had built
a new manufacturing and warehousing facility, and its offices
were moved to a separate building.

However, when World War II's food rationing ended, Special
Foods' customer base evaporated, leaving it with excess employees and equipment. Although the company struggled
through the immediate postwar era and suffered its first loss in
1947, it did not scale back operations. Instead, Hagle worked to
regain the company's wartime vigor by instituting research and
development and boosting marketing efforts. Hagle hired Allan
Buller, a former supply sergeant, to serve as assistant manager
and brought on Warren Hartman to guide product development
efforts. These changes were capped with the 1945 name change

to Worthington Foods, Inc. In 1948, founder George Harding was engaged as president of Loma Linda University, a Seventh-day Adventist institution in California. Hagle advanced to Worthington Foods' presidency, and Allan Buller became secretary-treasurer and general manager.

Worthington Foods' first new postwar product was a meatless wiener, a hand-packed, canned hot dog with a plastic casing. Demand for the new main dish, called Veja Links, ran so high that the company had to purchase an automatic linking machine to keep up with orders. Other new offerings included sandwich spread, soy milk, a vegetable gelatin, and sesame oil.

The company also augmented its product line through two major acquisitions. The first came in 1950, when Worthington Foods bought International Nutrition Laboratories. Founded by Dr. Harry Miller, this Ohio company produced soy-based foods, including Miller's Cutlets (renamed Vegetarian Cutlets). News of Dr. John H. Kellogg's death was followed quickly by an offer to sell his 91-year-old Battle Creek Food Company to Worthington Foods late in the decade. The two additions supplemented Worthington Foods' fledgling national sales network and helped push annual revenues over the $1 million mark.

Worthington Foods supported its growing distribution to mainstream supermarkets through the establishment of several warehouses across the United States. The company's facilities were often established near Seventh-day Adventist institutions in order to cater to that core market. By 1967, Worthington Foods boasted storage buildings in Portland, Oregon; San Leandro, California; Orlando, Florida; Beltsville, Maryland; South Lancaster, Massachusetts; and other locations.

Before the end of the decade, Worthington Foods midwifed the birth of an innovation in food technology that provided the company's entree into the mass market. It came from a highly unlikely source: the automotive industry. Scientist Robert Boyer had experimented before and during World War II with production of manmade fabrics and plastics from soybeans. The protein spinning process he used reduced soy protein to a liquid, then extruded it through tiny holes to form solid fibers. Although Boyer's soy fibers were not strong enough to form a material that could be used by automakers or the military, their texture closely resembled that of meat. The scientist made up several samples that looked like ham, beef, and lamb and set out to find a food manufacturer that could help him make them taste like those meats. After pitching his idea to such major food companies as Ralston Purina Company, Swift, and General Mills, Inc., Boyer took his samples to Worthington Foods, where they were met with an enthusiastic reception.

Unable to fund the massive capital investments necessary to build and operate a soybean mill, Worthington Foods contracted with Ralston-Purina to process soy meal into soy fiber and committed itself to purchasing the 10,000-pound-per-day output. New soy fiber-based products included White Chik, a chicken substitute; Prosage, a sausage analog; Stripples, a bacon-flavored product; and the self-explanatory Beeflike. Holiday Roast featured a plastic wishbone.

Unlike Worthington Foods' other meat analogs, which were canned, the soy fiber products could not withstand the high temperatures involved in shipping. This exigency forced the

food manufacturer to become America's first producer of frozen meat analogs. The company made major investments in freezer trucks as well as freezers at the plant, warehouses, and even in supermarkets, which were not generally equipped to handle frozen food at that time.

Worthington's revolutionary product development of the 1960s coincided with a global scarcity of protein. A 1969 report on vegetable protein prepared and published by Stanford University ranked Worthington Foods ahead of such major food and grain conglomerates as Central Soya and Archer Daniels Midland by virtue of its diverse line of "market-ready products."

Worthington Foods made and received a number of merger and acquisition overtures in the wake of the Stanford Report. The late 1960s were consumed with bargaining over operational and moral issues. Worthington entertained offers from Beatrice Company, Hershey Foods Corporation, Quaker Oats Company, W.R. Grace & Co., long-time partner Ralston Purina, and even The Coca-Cola Company. Coca-Cola's proposal was declined in part because of the beverage company's emphasis on caffeinated soft drinks. Ironically, however, Worthington Foods was also unable to agree on terms of a merger with Adventist Church-owned Loma Linda Foods. Worthington Foods accepted a takeover offer from Miles Laboratories in 1970 and became Miles' Worthington Division through an exchange of stock. Aside from the fiscal arrangements, Miles complied with Worthington's Sabbath-keeping requirements and its ongoing service to the Seventh-day Adventist market.

Worthington thrived during its decade under Miles' patronage. Sales doubled from $6 million to $12 million, production volume quadrupled, and the research and development department expanded tenfold. Worthington also benefited greatly from the marketing and distribution expertise Miles had garnered over decades of promoting such familiar products as One-A-Day vitamins and Alka-Seltzer antacid. Supported by multi-million-dollar annual advertising budgets and Miles' own food brokerage networks, Worthington flourished. During this period, Worthington launched its Morningstar Farms line of cholesterol-free vegetarian foods for the grocery trade, while the well-established Worthington brand continued as the trademark for products sold in Adventist and health food stores. The Morningstar Farms label spawned a new product, cholesterol-free Scramblers, a frozen substitute for whole eggs, in the mid-1970s.

In 1978, Miles was itself acquired by Germany's Bayer AG in a friendly takeover. Still led by Hagle and Buller, Worthington's management engineered a precarious buyback offer comprised of bank loans, bonds sold to Miles, and personal loans and investments. Some of Worthington's top executives bet their life's savings on the success of the "reborn" company. Sixty-five-year-old vice-president Allan Buller, for example, remortgaged his home and liquidated his retirement funds to participate in the buyback, which was completed in October 1982.

Worthington Foods suffered a small loss in 1982, but returned to profitability in 1983. That year, Hagle recruited Dr. Dale Twomley from Andrews University (an Adventist institution) to serve as Worthington's vice-president for development. With an eye toward succeeding Allan Buller as chief executive,

Twomley spent the ensuing three years learning the ins and outs of the meat analog business.

By the time Twomley advanced to president and CEO in 1986, Worthington Foods' annual sales had grown to $28 million. They more than doubled within Twomley's first five years at the helm, to over $70 million in 1991, as Worthington benefited from Americans' changing dietary habits. Over the course of the 1980s, Americans' consumption of red meat declined by over 12 percent, and the number of people who classified themselves as vegetarians or semi-vegetarians multiplied eight times. Nationwide sales of soy-based foods grew from $178 million in 1980 to $664 million in 1992. Due to growing health concerns regarding cholesterol, Morningstar Farms Scramblers had become Worthington's best-selling product and the $125-million egg-substitute segment's number-two seller by the end of the 1980s.

Worthington Foods' internal growth was supplemented with the 1990 acquisition of Loma Linda Foods' LaLoma Inc. meat-substitute and breakfast cereal businesses. The venerable California-based company had sold its infant formula business and Loma Linda trademark to Nutricia Netherlands Inc., a Dutch health food manufacturer with about $500 million in annual sales, in 1988.

After operating in a niche market for 50 years, Worthington began to encounter stiff competition from such mammoth food companies as Archer-Daniels-Midland Co., RJR Nabisco Holdings Corp., and Pillsbury Company in the late 1980s and early 1990s. These giants' market savvy and supermarket clout gave them a decided advantage over the tiny Ohio specialist. Morningstar Farms had several "weapons" in its arsenal: superior flavor, freezer-to-microwave convenience, low cholesterol, and no animal fats. Believing that "superior taste will win the race," Worthington missed the early 1990s crusade against fat.

Rival companies' fat-free burgers and egg substitutes began to erode Morningstar Farms' market share and overall profits: net income declined from $2.79 million in 1992 to $1.79 million in 1993. The company raised $21 million through a 1992 initial public offering to fund production increases, reformulations of old products, and new product launches. The company reduced levels of fat in its traditional meat analogs by one-fourth to one-half, thereby lowering the products' calories as well. New meat alternatives, including Garden Vege Patties, Chik Patties, Prime Patties, and Deli Franks, helped the company garner increased sales without cannibalizing the old products. Worthington Foods also created a foodservice division in 1990 to cater to the restaurant and institutional markets. The growing popularity of vegetarianism made Worthington's products appealing to many of these nontraditional outlets. During the early 1990s, the company won contracts with such major fast food companies as Burger King, Denny's, International House of Pancakes, and Subways. After declining from $20.17 million in 1989 to $18.82 million in 1991, Worthington's meat analog sales grew to $22.48 million by 1994.

Worthington Foods' record sales of $88.2 million and record earnings of $4.3 million in 1994 seemed but a foretaste of its future. Soyatech, a market research firm, projected America's total annual soyfood sales to increase from $664 million in 1992 to nearly $1.5 billion by the turn of the twenty-first century. If Worthington could retain its leading share of the meat analog market, it would share in this potential bonanza.

Further Reading:

Herold, June R., "Worthington Buying Anti-Cholesterol Cereal Line," *Business First-Columbus,* November 13, 1989, p. 3.
"A History of Worthington Foods," Worthington, Ohio: Worthington Foods, Inc., 1989.
Phalon, Richard, "Thin in the Wrong Places," *Forbes,* June 8, 1992, p. 62.
Reid, Robert, "Worthington Foods Prospers From Fitness Fads," *Business First-Columbus,* December 11, 1989, p. 15.
Whalen, William J., "Is The End Near? A Look at Seventh-day Adventists," *U.S. Catholic,* April 1994, p. 14.

—April Dougal Gasbarre

Wyle Electronics

15370 Barranca Parkway
Irvine, California 92718
U.S.A.
(714) 753-9953
Fax: (714) 753-9909

Public Company
Incorporated: 1953 as Wyle Laboratories
Employees: 2,000
Sales: $792 million
Stock Exchanges: New York
SICs: 5046 Commercial Equipment Not Elsewhere
    Classified; 5065 Electronic Parts & Equipment Not
    Elsewhere Classified; 8711 Engineering Services

Wyle Electronics is one of the leading U.S. marketers of high-technology electronic products and components, specializing in semiconductors, computer systems, and related services. The company's wide distribution network encompasses 30 locations across the United States. Wyle started out providing engineering and testing services but sold that division of the company in 1994 to focus solely on its thriving electronics distribution operations.

Wyle Electronics was created in 1994 as the successor to Wyle Laboratories. Wyle Laboratories, in turn, was incorporated in 1953 as the successor to a venture started in the late 1940s. In 1949 that enterprise was created to take advantage of the burgeoning market for specialized engineering testing services. The company built a highly advanced testing facility in Norco, California, and secured major contracts primarily with the U.S. government to test military and aerospace equipment. During the 1950s, in fact, Wyle tested components for the first intercontinental ballistic missiles. When contracts related to that business began to wane, Wyle turned to the emerging U.S. space program for work. Among other distinctions, Wyle's laboratories and highly skilled engineers played an important role in testing equipment for the Saturn rocket used in the Apollo moon program.

Norco secured a profitable niche in high-tech testing during the 1950s and 1960s. By the early 1960s, in fact, Wyle was generating revenues of about $30 million annually. Besides testing missiles, rockets, and other aerospace equipment, the company began branching out into other arenas. Importantly, early in the 1960s Wyle entered into the electronics marketing and distribution business. Although that segment would serve simply as a sideline for several years, it would eventually surpass the testing division in sales and would became Wyle's core business. In addition to getting into other related industries, Wyle continued to expand its Norco testing facilities. In the 1970s, for example, Wyle began offering testing services for high-speed trains and for equipment being developed for nuclear plants.

Although Wyle Laboratories was a leader in its unique niche, the company suffered from sporadic revenue and profit levels. That volatility was the result of the company's heavy reliance on government contracts and defense spending. Partly in an effort to minimize that volatility, Wyle placed an increasing emphasis on its electronics distribution business. During the late 1970s, in fact, sales from that segment surged past $100 million annually, and the importance of Wyle's testing services began to decline in comparison. Wyle's electronics business enjoyed big sales gains during the 1970s, but by the late 1970s and early 1980s its profit performance was spotty. In fact, Wyle was having problems throughout its organization. The laboratory testing services division encountered a number of setbacks and the electronics business, despite the fact that it was generating about $140 million annually in revenues, lacked focus and was floundering.

To whip the electronics marketing group into shape, Wyle hired an outsider named Charles Clough. Clough was hired away from Texas Instruments, where he had gained experience that was valuable to Wyle. He was hired in as president of the division and as an executive vice-president of the company. Two years later he was made a member of the board. When Clough arrived at Wyle, he felt that the electronics group had become too diversified, both geographically and in the number of products its was offering. He decided to eliminate all efforts east of the Mississippi and concentrate on the western United States, particularly in California. He also chose to concentrate on the two high-growth product segments at the time: semiconductors and computer systems. That decision turned out to be a fruitful one, as both the computer and semiconductor markets exploded during the early 1980s.

Wyle began to experience a turnaround in 1983 and 1984, largely as a result of Clough's efforts. Importantly, during his first three years at Wyle, Clough succeeded in securing a number of franchises from manufacturers to market and distribute their products as complete systems with peripheral manufacturers' products like printers and modems. Among the big name companies with which he was eventually able to reach agreements were NCR, Digital Equipment, Motorola, Intel, and Wyse. Evidencing the importance of his role and of the electronics division, Clough was elevated to president of Wyle Laboratories in 1985. Industry turbulence, combined with restructuring and divestiture of some of Wyle operations, reduced the company's sales from about $275 million in 1985 to less than $200 million in 1986. Furthermore, Wyle posted net losses in both 1986 and 1987. Sales were back to $265 million by 1988, however, and both sales and profits headed for record gains during the late 1980s and early 1990s.

Wyle's comeback in 1988 was partially attributable to its scientific services and systems division, which represented the original core of the company. That group was benefiting from increased defense spending and specific government contracts that were generating hefty cash flow. Notable was a $27 million contract that Wyle had secured for engineering and testing support on the Titan 34D rocket motor recovery program. Wyle was also in the running for two big space contracts and was even building a 60,000-square-foot, $6.5-million facility in Huntsville, Alabama (adjacent to the Marshall Space Flight Center), in anticipation of capturing at least one of the contracts. More important than contributions by the scientific services and systems division, though, were gains in the flourishing electronics marketing group.

Indeed, by 1988 Wyle had become the largest semiconductor distributor in the western United States. The company had accumulated a customer base of 14,700, not one of which represented more than two percent of the division's total sales. Importantly, Clough had smartly focused the company's efforts on the burgeoning market for customer-specific semiconductors, or applications specific integrated circuits (ASICs). ASICs differ from conventional semiconductor devices in that they are designed for specific applications. In comparison to their off-the-shelf cousins, ASICs are typically smaller, more expensive, more efficient and flexible, and simpler to install. Increased use of ASICs was reflective of growing demand for more specialized, noncommodity semiconductor devices. They also brought higher profit margins and signaled the beginning of the redemption of the U.S. semiconductor industry after years of market share gains by Japanese competitors.

By late 1988 Wyle had snared 65 percent of the fast-growing ASICs distribution business in the United States. Sales rose upward to nearly $320 million in 1989, and Wyle began to once again expand its distribution business east of the Mississippi. By that time, Clough had been promoted to chief executive of Wyle. In 1988 he replaced 62-year-old Stanley Wainer, who had served as Wyle's chief executive since 1979 and had recruited Clough from Texas Instruments. Within a year of the management change, Wyle's electronics group had undeniably surpassed the scientific services and systems division in terms of sales, profits, and future growth potential. Reflecting the profit potential of the distribution business were large contracts, such as a $20 million agreement reached in 1988 to supply Prudential Insurance Co. with custom-tailored computer systems. As sales of systems and semiconductors improved, moreover, Wyle began tagging on a growing number of complementary support services that brought additional dollars to the company's bottom line.

Buoyed by a rapid rise in shipments of ASICs, Wyle enjoyed heady demand growth for electronics products throughout the late 1980s and early 1990s. Also boosting that division beginning in the early 1990s was a new business called 'kitting.' Under that program, Wyle supplied the entire kit of materials and components needed by a customer, inspected and packaged to that company's specifications. In contrast to the electronics distribution business, the scientific services division languished. Hurting sales in that segment was a big decrease in U.S. defense spending and a lull in new testing and engineering contracts. As they had been doing since the late 1980s, managers of the scientific services group tried to capture additional revenue by chasing the market for cleaning up and closing military bases

and other government facilities. Still, the division stagnated and by 1990 was supplying little more than 20 percent of Wyle's total revenues.

In 1992 Clough promoted former Texas Instruments coworker Ralph Ozorkiewicz to president and chief operating officer of Wyle, which left Ozorkiewicz in charge of both the electronics marketing and scientific services groups. Ozorkiewicz was credited with launching Wyle's kitting program and, among other achievements, establishing a successful quality and customer satisfaction program. Ozorkiewicz had earned his engineering degree at University of Missouri before serving ten years at Texas Instruments and then a stint with Kierluff Electronics. By 1995 the 48-year-old Ozorkiewicz would succeed 66-year-old Clough as chief executive of the company, while Clough remained as chairman.

Under Clough's and Ozorkiewicz's leadership, Wyle's electronics division continued to prosper going into the mid-1990s. In fact, Wyle established itself as one of the top distributors of high-tech electronic components and systems in the country. Important to the company's growth was the trend toward outsourcing, in which Wyle's customers were increasingly contracting Wyle to handle add-on services such as semiconductor design and materials management. Wyle's distribution and services network swelled to include 30 facilities around the country that were generating company-wide sales of about $450 million by 1993. In 1994, moreover, Wyle achieved impressive growth as the market for semiconductors and computer equipment exploded. Revenues reached $792 million in 1994 as operating profits hit record levels. Unfortunately, Wyle was forced to record a $381 million net loss for the year.

Wyle's net loss in 1994 reflected write-offs related to the company's disposition of its scientific services and systems division. Indeed, in December of that year, Wyle completed the sale of the division to a buyout group that included some members of the new company's management team and was headed by a former secretary of the U.S. Treasury. The division was sold for $30 million and the resultant company was headed by F. Stephen Wyle, son of the company's founder. Although it had languished in comparison to Wyle's electronics division, the scientific services group was still a force in its unique industry. The Norco complex, where Wyle had started out in the 1950s, maintained state-of-the-art facilities that could, among other tasks, put a battle tank through its paces in an environmental chamber, simulate forces created in an earthquake, and test steam valves used in nuclear plants. The company also sported some of the industry's best talent. Managers of the new company planned to chase growth markets, such as the disposal of unexploded ordnance and hazardous waste cleanup.

Ozorkiewicz stepped into Clough's chief executive shoes in April 1995. He planned to sustain the growth strategy that had made Wyle an industry powerhouse during the 1980s and early 1990s: focus on marketing, distribution, and servicing high-quality, high-technology electronic products and components. In mid-1995 Wyle was stocking approximately 30,000 items from over 50 electronic component and computer product suppliers including industry giants like Intel, Texas Instruments, Motorola, Micron Technology, Digital Equipment, and others. In addition, from its system enhancement center in Garden

Grove, California, and from its Liberty Contract Services division, the company provided a wide range of value-added services, such as computer system configuration and networking, and semiconductor design and inventory management.

Principal Subsidiaries: Wyle Distribution Group-Santa Clara, Inc; Redwing of California, Inc.

Further Reading:

Deters, Barbara, "Wyle Plans to Grow in Valley: Computer Firm Could Add 300 Jobs," *Arizona Republic,* December 23, 1993, p. C1.

Flores, J.C., "Wyle Laboratories Profits Rise in Fourth Quarter, But Earnings Decline for the Year," *Los Angeles Business Journal,* March 12, 1990, p. 45.

Foley, John, "Ozorkiewicz Named President and Chief Operating Officer of Wyle Laboratories," *PR Newswire,* June 9, 1992.

Holland, Van, "Ozorkiewicz Elected CEO of Wyle; Clough Will Retire and Continue as Chairman," *PR Newswire,* January 16, 1995.

——, "Wyle Announces Completion of the Sale of its Scientific Services & Systems Group," *PR Newswire,* December 23, 1994.

McAuliffe, Don, "Wyle Laboratories Testing Unit To Be Bought," *Press Enterprise,* October 25, 1994, p. D1.

Rees, David, "New CEO at Wyle Laboratories Considers Expanding Marketing Effort to East Coast," *Los Angeles Business Journal,* June 13, 1988, p. 4.

—Dave Mote

subsequently removed when the metal solidifies. Forged metal has always been considered to have more beneficial properties than cast metal.

As Wyman-Gordon's reputation for high-quality forged metals began to spread along the eastern coast of the United States, the company began to garner contracts from new industries such as the bicycle, railroad, and automobile businesses. The company began to forge metal parts including pedals, sprockets, and spindles for bicycles, as well as automatic couplers for railroad cars. The most important contracts, however, which came between 1902 and 1904, involved forging crankshafts for 35 young companies that were producing the newfangled "horseless carriages."

With the beginning of World War I, Wyman-Gordon was contracted by the United States government to provide forgings for airplane engines. The Curtis Jenny, a large biplane with a 90-horsepower engine, was the first project for which the company provided crankshafts and other forgings. Soon Wyman-Gordon was manufacturing various engine and airframe forgings for almost every airplane used by the U.S. military during World War I.

After the war, and continuing throughout the 1920s and 1930s, the company developed a close relationship both with the commercial and military airplane industries. Wyman-Gordon became the leading and most sought-after producer of engine and component forgings for airplane engines and airframes. Parts not only for engines, but crankshafts, propellers, and landing gear formed the nucleus of the company's products during these two decades. With increasing requests for its heavy-duty, durable forgings, the company expanded its factory in Worcester and opened a new facility in Harvey, Illinois.

World War II helped Wyman-Gordon achieve even greater prominence within the industry. The company was contracted by almost every American airplane manufacturer to supply engine parts and airframe components. During the war, every plane in combat included either engine parts, a crankshaft, structural airframe components, propeller mechanisms, or landing gear parts that were forged by Wyman-Gordon. By the end of World War II, the company had forged more aviation parts and components than that of the entire rest of the industry combined.

As World War II began to wind down, the aviation industry changed dramatically with the development of the jet engine. Wyman-Gordon had built its reputation on forgings for propeller airplanes, which sometimes included over 120 forgings for a single propeller mechanism. The early jet engines, by contrast, included perhaps a dozen large forgings with no propeller. In addition, forgings made for airplanes before the jet age were only required to meet standards for tensile strength. New jet engines required forgings to meet not only the standards of tensile strength, but also standards involving greater durability, heat tolerance, and lighter weight.

During the 1950s, Wyman-Gordon met the challenges posed by the development of the jet engine with characteristic efficiency. The company retooled its facilities and kept up with the torrid pace of ever-changing jet engine designs. Engineers at the firm worked on forgings for turbines and compressors, calculated

Wyman-Gordon Company

P.O. Box 8001
Grafton, Massachusetts 01536
U.S.A.
(508) 756-5111
Fax: (508) 839-7500

Public Company
Incorporated: 1883
Operating Revenues: $380 million
Employees: 2,200
Stock Exchanges: New York
SICs: 3463 Nonferrous Forgings; 3462 Iron & Steel Forgings

Wyman-Gordon Company is one of the largest manufacturers of forgings, castings, engine components, and composite structures for the aerospace, mining, agricultural, construction, and forestry industries. The company lists an impressive string of accomplishments, including the following: it was the first to commercially develop the science of "heat treating," the first to manufacture a titanium support beam for the landing gear of the new 747 airplane, and the first to produce the largest closed-die forging of titanium in the world.

In 1883 H. Winfield Wyman and Lyman F. Gordon, recent graduates of Worcester Polytechnic Institute, started a company for the purpose of forging loom crankshafts. The Wyman-Gordon Company factory consisted of a small wooden building with five board-drop hammers, two Bradley Helv hammers, and two die sinking pieces of equipment. A 50-horsepower Wheelock steam engine provided power for the machines, and a total of eight people worked in the firm. Horace Wyman and Albert Gordon, the fathers of the two young men, both worked in management at Crompton Loom Works, and were instrumental in helping the new company procure contracts for loom crankshafts made of iron and other various forgings for micrometer frames and pistol parts.

The company's process of forging, an ancient art, is a well-known procedure for shaping various kinds of metal. The forging consists of a piece of metal that has been heated and worked between dies to create a shape. The part of the process that involves "working" the metal actually gives the piece a certain ductility and toughness that is not gained by any other process. Castings, on the other hand, are achieved by pouring molten iron, for example, into a previously shaped container that is increased speeds and stresses on various metals used in aviation designs, and helped airplane manufacturers improve the operating temperature for jet engine forgings. In the early 1950s, during the Korean War, the company was producing a lower number of forgings for jet engines than for the earlier piston-driven engines, but the value per part was much higher.

The growing demand for additional power, in combination with the request for lighter-weight forgings, led to the development of new alloys. Wyman-Gordon was at the forefront of these developments as one of the few facilities in the United States capable of forging titanium. The first major forging involving the metal was for compressor discs used in Pratt & Whitney engines. These engines were part of the design for the Century Series fighter planes which flew combat missions during the Korean War. Additional titanium components were sold to Westinghouse and General Electric for use in engines designed for both commercial and military use. During the mid-1950s, Wyman-Gordon forged titanium components for engines that powered the B-52 bomber, the Boeing 707, and the KC-135 transport aircraft. Structural applications of the titanium alloy were used by the company to cast the engine for the Minuteman Missile.

The company's production facilities grew at a rapid rate to meet the demands for new alloys and highly technical applications of these metals. Outside North Grafton, a short way from Worcester, Wyman-Gordon constructed a series of three hydraulic presses with an 18,000 ton capacity, a 35,000 ton capacity, and a 50,000 ton capacity. The 50,000 ton capacity hydraulic press was the largest forging press ever built in the United States. The company also developed new techniques to produce alloys such as titanium, including forging superalloys at extremely high temperatures within a vacuum and compacting metals in powder form under such high pressures of intensely heated gases that they take the shape desired.

By the early 1960s, Wyman-Gordon facilities and technical expertise were recognized throughout the industry as the best in the United States. At this time, the U.S. Air Force asked the company to design and produce an airframe for the SR-71 aircraft. Company engineers responded by developing an alloy that was nearly 60 percent stronger than any of the known alloys employing titanium. When Boeing asked Wyman-Gordon to produce a giant titanium support beam for the landing gear of its new 747, Wyman-Gordon used its 50,000 ton hydraulic press to create the largest closed-die titanium forging ever achieved in the industry. The company went on to produce over 1,000 more of these forgings in later years. During the Vietnam War, engineers at the firm developed titanium forgings for the F-4 fighter plane, and also produced more forged titanium rotor hubs for helicopters than any other American company.

During the early 1970s, Wyman-Gordon produced an increasing number of titanium forged engine components for the Titan and Minuteman missiles. The U.S. Airforce development of the F-14 and F-15 fighter planes also required an increased number of titanium forged engine components and structural airframe parts. At this time, Wyman-Gordon was the leading supplier of forged titanium engine parts, including such items as fan discs and compressors. In fact, the company's presence was so dominant within the industry that every commercial and military jet airplane, and every model of helicopter and missile, included a titanium forging produced at one of the Wyman-Gordon plants.

In 1978 the company received requests for forged titanium parts for 280 different types of aircraft from commercial airplane manufacturers. Two years later, requests for forged titanium parts had ballooned to include more than 700 different types of aircraft. Unfortunately, however, producers of titanium sponge and melters remained skeptical about the growing demand for titanium and refused to increase their capacity. As a result, companies that forged titanium were placed on an extremely limited allocation system. Since Wyman-Gordon was the largest forger of titanium engine parts in the United States, the company was hard hit by the unexpected turn of events. Determined not to let this happen again, Wyman-Gordon decided to enter the field of titanium manufacturing and production.

In the early 1980s, at a cost of only $12 million, Wyman-Gordon acquired a majority stake in International Titanium, Inc., in Moses Lake, Washington. With technical advice provided by Wyman-Gordon engineers, International Titanium began to produce titanium sponge using the most up-to-date technology. Continuing its strategy of vertical integration, management constructed a brand new Aerospace Alloys Center in Millbury, Massachusetts. At a cost of $11 million, this facility enabled Wyman-Gordon engineers to melt and alloy the sponge delivered from International Titanium. This new facility was built near the company's Grafton plant, and soon provided nearly half of all the titanium ingot used by Wyman-Gordon's plants. The company now controlled all the essential technologies involved in producing titanium components, including sponge manufacturing, melting and alloying, and the forging process. As a result, customer orders began to increase due to customers' confidence that Wyman-Gordon could provide an uninterrupted supply of titanium forged parts.

The increase in orders for titanium parts forged by Wyman-Gordon was short-lived however. By the late 1980s, the decrease in orders from commercial airline companies, and the end of the Cold War which resulted in declining defense expenditures, began to undermine Wyman-Gordon's traditional base of support. The company responded by laying off employees and reducing administrative and organizational costs. Yet even worse times were ahead. By early 1993, the aerospace industry business had declined by a whopping 40 percent since the lucrative days of the mid-1980s.

Although new orders, such as Britain's contract with Lockheed for a fleet of C-130J cargo-carriers, a U.S. Air Force contract with McDonnell-Douglas for a number of C-17s, and projections for an annual increase in commercial airlines by the end of the decade promised a long-awaited resurgence for companies doing business with the aerospace industry, they were not enough to return Wyman-Gordon to profitability. Faced with grim financial prospects, management decided to acquire Cooper Industries' Cameron Forged Products Division in order to create a giant nickel alloy and titanium forging producer. The two companies held approximately 20 percent of the American titanium market, and the merger was reported to be the largest in the declining aerospace industry. In addition, Wyman-Gordon joined with Pratt & Whitney and Western Aerospace Ltd. to create Western Australian Specialty Alloys Proprietary Ltd.

The new firm was formed to enter the superalloys market, but came under immediate criticism from competitors who claimed that the market was already saturated and that the joint venture would only hurt the industry. Wyman-Gordon management responded that their investment was for the long term, and could not be affected by the industry's short-term problems.

Principal Subsidiaries: Precision Founders, Inc.; Sierra Cast, Inc.; Wyman-Gordon Investment Castings, Inc.; Wyman-Gordon Composite Technologies, Inc.; Wyman-Gordon Scaled Composites, Inc.; Wyman-Gordon Precision Composites, Inc.

Further Reading:

Albert, Steven, "Why Wyman Now?" *Forbes,* June 20, 1994, p. 272.

Burgert, Philip, "Western Australia Venture Draws Flak," *American Metal Market,* July 22, 1993, pp. 11–15A.
Carter, Joseph R., *Wyman-Gordon Company,* Newcomen Society: New York, 1993.
"Cooper Industries Is Sellings Its Cameron Forged Unit," *New York Times,* September 18, 1993, p. 35L.
"Pratt Joins Australian Deal," *New York Times,* March 7, 1992, p. 41L.
"Wyman-Gordon Company," *Automotive News,* January 24, 1994, p. 45.
"Wyman-Gordon Company," *Wall Street Journal,* January 19, 1995, p. B2E.
"Wyman-Gordon Shareholders Approve Cameron Deal," *New York Times,* May 25, 1994, p. D4L.
"Wyman-Gordon to Acquire a Cooper Industries Division," *New York Times,* January 18, 1994, p. D4L.

—Thomas Derdak

Yellow Corporation

10777 Barkley Avenue
P.O. Box 7563
Overland Park, Kansas 66207
U.S.A.
(913) 967-4300
Fax: (913) 344-3433

Public Company
Incorporated: 1993
Employees: 33,400
Sales: $2.9 billion
Stock Exchanges: NASDAQ
SICs: 4731 Arrangement Transport Freight & Cargo; 4213
   Trucking, Except Local

Yellow Corporation, a holding company for Yellow Freight System, Inc., is one of the top three long-haul trucking companies in the United States. Yellow Corp. was known as Yellow Freight, and specialized in long-haul, less-than-truckload (LTL) services, until 1993, when the purchase of Preston Trucking Company expanded its business into regional and inter-regional trucking services. This prompted Yellow to reorganize as a holding company and change its name to reflect its broadened interests in trucking and related services.

The First World War proved the usefulness and flexibility of trucks in moving large quantities of goods and supplies wherever they were needed on the front lines. Soon after the war, the truck became a fixture U.S. cities. A. J. Harrell, who ran a bus line and franchise of Yellow Cab in Oklahoma City, recognized the importance and potential profitability of transporting goods, rather than people. In 1924 Harrell traded his cabs for trucks, and established the Yellow Transit trucking company.

The initial years of Yellow Transit were limited to local and short-run less-than-truckload (LTL) shipments, that is, shipments of less than 10,000 pounds, in Oklahoma City and the surrounding area, and between Oklahoma City and Tulsa. The roadway system in the United States, originally built for travel by horse and carriage, and still barely hardy enough for the automobile, could not yet provide dependable long-distance routes for the far heavier truck. Cities were only just recognizing the importance of linking with each other and with their outlying, especially farming, areas. For the time being, the railroads continued to dominate the nation's long-distance, bulk

transport freight business. Yet demand for transporting small volume, more fragile, and perishable shipments had begun to grow, and, as the country entered the Great Depression, companies came to appreciate the greater flexibility of trucks. Unlike the railroads, trucks could carry small loads to almost any location at any time, allowing companies to deliver inventory faster than ever before. The collapsing economy had left many people without work, and many rushed to join the young trucking industry. More and more trucking companies appeared, many comprising little more than a single truck, in the rush to meet the demand. Throughout the 1930s, the trucking industry boomed.

The first highways appeared during this time. Improvements in construction techniques made the new roads faster and stronger, and an early, crude highway system connected longer distances. Advancements in automotive technology, and particularly the perfection of the powerful and efficient diesel engine, made long-distance hauling not only more attractive, but practical as well. Yellow Transit soon expanded beyond its local routes into state-to-state shipping, reaching south into Texas and north into Missouri. By confining itself largely to north-south routes, Yellow avoided direct competition with the primarily east-west orientation of the railroads. Throughout the 1930s, Yellow continued to grow, adding more and more vehicles, routes, and subsidiaries.

Yellow continued to grow through the 1940s, extending operations into Kansas, Illinois, Indiana, Kentucky, and other mid-south states. By the end of the decade, Yellow operated through 51 small subsidiaries, nearing yearly revenues of $7 million. The trucking industry had begun to mature by then, and the era of small, independent truckers was giving way to larger, more efficient trucking corporations. Yellow found itself unable to compete, as its growth was limited by rising leasing rates and it became financially strapped from paying out dividends. After A. J. Harrell sold the company in 1951, it was forced to declare bankruptcy.

The following year, Yellow was purchased by George E. Powell and other investors. A banker in Kansas City, Powell had also been vice-chairman at Riss & Company, a leading Midwest trucking company. Joining Powell from Riss were his son, George Powell, Jr., and others. Within five months Powell and his team had reorganized Yellow into a more efficient and innovative company, raising it from bankruptcy into the black. Now with bases in Kansas City and Oklahoma City, Yellow turned its focus to long-haul routes, dropping its short-haul businesses. With the post-World War II boom to the economy, and with a new emphasis on cost accounting, customer service, and information flow, Yellow began buying up trucking companies whose routes would allow it to expand into the north and east. The Kansas City operation began to function as a hub to direct the growing network.

A major development in the trucking industry occurred in 1956, when legislation was passed creating the Federal Interstate Highway System (FIHS). With the end of the Second World War, the demand for automobiles boomed, and dramatic increases in the volume of transported goods would eventually develop trucking, and truck purchases, into a central element in the country's economy. The FIHS was planned to link into every city with a population of 50,000 or more across the United States, calling originally for 40,000 miles but ultimately reaching 45,000 miles. Freeways were to be constructed according to strict specifications, and, with their high quality, limited access, and free flow, were ideal for the long-haul trucking industry. The FIHS signaled the nation's commitment to the automobile for serving its transportation and shipping needs. Yellow was quick to capitalize on this latest boost to the trucking industry, and by 1957 had reached revenues of $15 million. In that year, Yellow purchased Michigan Motor Freight Lines, its largest purchase to date, further extending its network of routes across the country.

Meanwhile, advancements in tractor-trailer design were creating lighter, stronger, and more efficient trucks. Because of roadway weight limits, and because of rate regulations fixed by the Interstate Commerce Commission (ICC), new income was attainable primarily through increasing the amount of goods each truck could carry, as well as by cutting costs. The lighter, more efficient trucks and trailers allowed trucking companies to ship larger truckloads at less expense, and Yellow's strategy of continuously investing in the latest truck designs, while ridding itself of outdated vehicles and equipment, allowed it to achieve faster service at lower cost than its competitors. As it outpaced many smaller, older operations, Yellow began a period of aggressive acquisition. These acquisitions were especially important to Yellow's growth. The ICC controlled the creation of truck routes, and in order to extend across the country, Yellow would have had to petition that agency for its desired routes. However, by buying up other trucking companies, Yellow obtained their existing routes, and in this way added hundreds of trucking routes to its network. Into the 1960s, Yellow's rapid growth had made it the nation's 13th largest trucker, with annual sales of $40 million.

In 1965 Yellow purchased Watson-Wilson Transportation System, launching a new period in the growth of the company. Watson-Wilson was larger than Yellow, with revenues nearing $70 million per year. More importantly, it controlled routes stretching from Chicago to the West Coast. Nevertheless, the company had not kept up with technology advances and changes in the industry, and by the early 1960s was failing. Yellow's purchase of Watson-Wilson, for approximately $13 million, doubled its size. Subsequent acquisitions of Norwalk Truck Lines and other companies extended Yellow throughout the north- and southeast, bringing Yellow a fully connected, coast-to-coast operation. The company changed its name to Yellow Freight System in 1968 and posted revenues topping $200 million by the end of the decade, making it the nation's third-largest trucking company.

An important part of the company's operations were its nine "break-bulk" centers. Serving as hubs along the various legs of Yellow's network, these centers received shipments from one leg, broke down the products according to their following destinations, then loaded the trucks traveling those routes of the network. Break-bulk centers, apart from being labor-intensive, required a high degree of coordination among shipment arrivals and departures in order to achieve maximum speed and efficiency at the lowest cost. Yellow accomplished this with the 1971 installation of a computer-monitoring system, based in the Kansas City command center, placing it at the forefront of the industry. The use of computer technology allowed Yellow to track each shipment precisely, improving information flow within the company and with its customers as well, while gaining a finely tuned coordination of shipment arrivals and departures at its break-bulk centers.

These innovations, and tight discipline, brought the company's operating ratio to among the lowest in the industry. Further acquisitions, of Adley Express in 1973, Republic Freight Systems in 1975, and Braswell Motor Freight in 1977, strengthened its route network into the Pacific Northwest, the Southeast, and throughout the Southwest. By then, Yellow had reached 44 states, operated more than 220 terminals, and, despite dramatic rises in fuel prices since the 1973 Arab oil embargo, sustained an average 32 percent return on equity. During this time, George Powell stepped down as chairman, and his son George Jr. took over. Despite a misadventure into oil and gas exploration—the company opened Overland Energy Company in 1976, which lost some $60 million by the end of the decade—Yellow underwent a period of sustained growth throughout 1970s.

The 1980 deregulation of the trucking industry, amid a wave of deregulation activity brought on by the Reagan administration, caught Yellow by surprise. Gone were the restrictions on truck routes, and with it the $34 million per year Yellow earned through licensing fees charged to other companies to use its routes. When deregulation came, Yellow discovered that its terminals, depots, and break-bulk centers had fallen behind advances in the industry, at a time when these facilities had become more crucial to the LTL market than ever before. Yellow's main competitors, Consolidated Freightways and Roadway Express, had gained the edge on both break-bulk handling and broader route systems, each with a wider, larger array of state-of-the-art terminals and depots. By the end of 1981, Yellow had laid off 20 percent of its workers.

Yellow's profits continued to fall through 1983. However, Powell Jr., and his son, George Powell III, who had entered the family's business some years earlier, began a crash program to upgrade its facilities, converting 17 terminals into additional break-bulk centers in two years. Yellow also increased its LTL freight contracts to encompass nearly two-thirds of its business, and by 1985, Yellow had expanded its number of terminals to 600. The intense competition that followed deregulation closed many trucking companies, and by 1986, Yellow was once again assured of its number three position in the industry. With only Alaska left unrepresented in the United States, Yellow created a terminal there in 1987. As it entered the 1990s, Yellow, now led by George Powell III, turned to international expansion, into Mexico, Puerto Rico, and Canada.

Yellow's sales had passed $2 billion. Yet discounting across the industry, a series of Teamster strikes, higher fuel and labor costs, and a slow softening of the LTL market began to cut into Yellow's profits. Yellow boosted its competitive edge with a series of innovations, including computer software to enable its customers to track their shipments, and the introduction of its Metroliner two-day service and its guaranteed Express Lane service, which offered expedited shipments. Yellow entered Mexico in 1991, forming Yellow Freight Mexicana, and further increased its Canadian presence.

Yellow also began to eye entry into the growing regional LTL market, reasoning that its customers wanted a company that could handle both their regional and national needs. In 1992 Yellow bought the ailing Preston Trucking Company, a regional and inter-regional LTL carrier, for $24 million and the assumption of that company's $116 million in debts and loans. After restructuring, including a temporary nine percent pay cut to its workers, Preston was profitable again by 1993. The purchase of Preston brought Yellow into the important regional markets of the Northeast and South. However, drivers at both Yellow Freight and Preston were represented by the Teamsters union, leaving Yellow increasingly vulnerable to the threat of strikes. In 1992 Yellow formed a Texas subsidiary, Yellow Transportation, extending its regional business in that important state. Significantly, Yellow Transportation leased its trucks and hired only non-union drivers. In 1993 Yellow Freight restructured as a holding company for its subsidiaries, changing its name to Yellow Corporation.

Yellow's steady growth had slowed, however, as it entered the mid-1990s. A 24-day Teamster strike in 1994 resulted in more than $25 million in losses for Yellow, while the rough winter of that year further slowed the trucking industry and depressed profits. LTL demand continued to slow, and discounting among truckers became more and more competitive. A five percent wage increase instituted in April 1995—a result of the Teamsters strike from the year before—further ate into Yellow's earnings. But good weather, tight cost controls, and a five percent rate hike enabled Yellow to eke out a small profit that year. Yellow increasingly sought international expansion, forming a successful joint venture with Frans Maas Beheer BV, a Netherlands-based transportation and logistics firm, and draft-ing plans to enter the Pacific Rim. With nearly $3 billion in sales and the third George Powell at the helm, Yellow was certain to continue as a driving force in the trucking industry.

Principal Subsidiaries: Preston Trucking Company (including Preston Trucking, Saia Motor Freight Line, and Small Transportation); Yellow Freight System, Inc.; Yellow Logistics Services, Inc.; Yellow Technology Services, Inc.; Yellow Transportation, Inc.

Further Reading:

Baird, J., "Yellow Quietly Rolls into Texas, Sets up Non-Union Regional Unit," *Journal of Commerce and Commercial,* August 4, 1992, p. B2.

Bonney, J., "Yellow Freight Eyes Pacific Rim," *American Shipper,* January 1995, p. 62.

Coletti, R., "Yellow Freight: To the Victor, the Spoils?" *Financial World,* January 8, 1991, p. 18.

Isidore, Chris, "Cost Controls Spur Yellow Corp. to an Unexpected Profit," *Journal of Commerce and Commercial,* April 20, 1995, p. 3B.

——, "Yellow, M.S., PST Warn Earnings May Disappoint," *Journal of Commerce and Commercial,* June 9, 1995, p. B3.

McCartney, Robert J., "Kansas Firm Agrees to Buy Preston Corp. for $24 Million," *Washington Post,* November 21, 1992, p. C1.

"Preston's Quick Turnaround," *Distribution,* November 1993, p. 18.

Watson, Rip, "Teamsters Strike Costs 2 Carriers $90 Million," *Journal of Commerce and Commercial,* June 16, 1994, p. 1A.

——, "Yellow Freight Is 1st LTL to Announce Price Rises for '95," *Journal of Commerce and Commercial,* November 22, 1994.

"Yellow Corporation Announces Second Quarter Results," *PR Newswire,* July 20, 1995.

—M. L. Cohen

Zebra Technologies Corporation

Zebra Technologies Corporation

333 Corporate Woods Parkway
Vernon Hills, Illinois 60061-3109
U.S.A.
(708) 634-6700
Fax: (708) 913-8766

Public Company
Founded: 1969
Employees: 488
Sales: $119.5 million
Stock Exchanges: NASDAQ
SICs: 2752 Commercial Printing—Lithographic; 3555
   Printing Trades Machinery; 3577 Bar Code (Magnetic Ink)
   Printers; 3955 Carbon Paper & Inked Ribbons

The mysterious series of lines and numbers called bar coding has provided a thumbprint of products since the 1970s, conveying instant information on model, price, weight, and dozens of other product characteristics. As a manufacturer and international distributor of bar code and automatic identification labeling, Zebra Technologies Corporation develops and builds high-resolution thermal transfer printers to apply bar codes and provides the labels themselves and the ribbons with which to print them. Zebra's strong growth (an average of 34.4 percent from 1991 to 1994) make it a success story that has broken into the ranks of *Forbes's* Top 200 Best Small Companies, and a perennial favorite of the *Chicago Tribune, Crain's Chicago Business, Business Week, Fortune, International Business* and others.

In 1969 engineers Edward L. Kaplan and Gerhard Cless contributed $500 each to found Data Specialties Inc., a manufacturer of high-speed electromechanical products such as hole-punching and tape-reading machines. Kaplan had graduated with honors from the Illinois Institute of Technology and received a prestigious National Defense Education Act fellowship (which he relinquished after deciding not to earn a Ph.D.), while Cless had attended the University of Esslingen in Germany, where his mechanical engineering skills had earned him ten patents. While employed full-time as project engineers at Teletype Corp., they began to design machinery after hours.

After a client expressed interest in their work, they pooled their savings and came up with two punch machine prototypes using paper tape. Receiving an order for 500, Kaplan and Cless bor-

rowed $20,000 to produce the machines and worked nights in a Chicago loft to complete the order. Hiring 15 part-time workers to assemble parts during the day and on weekends, Kaplan and Cless then received a second, multimillion-dollar order for 2,000 machines from a client in the banking industry in response to an ad they had placed in a Florida trade publication.

Thrilled, Kaplan and Cless quit their day jobs and pushed hard to complete the initial order—of which only a fraction were finished and paid for. As the remainder of the machines awaited assembly, the client suddenly canceled. Kaplan and Cless then concentrated on designing machines for the second contract, creating a revolutionary punch machine that could print passbook and bookkeeping entries as well as customer receipts, all at the same time. They later discovered, however, that the client wanted only the prototypes so it could manufacture the machines on its own; the client then sued the engineers for breach of contract when they wouldn't hand them over. Unable to afford any retaliatory legal action, Kaplan and Cless were forced to relinquish the machines' designs in return for the lawsuit being dropped.

Citing the incident as ''devastating but one of those lessons that can't be taught,'' Kaplan and Cless were left with a loft full of parts for 475 punch machines and no money from their first three months of business. The two hammered out a new $1.5 million business plan to design and produce printing machinery, then set about raising the necessary capital. Able to come up with only $70,000, they hired themselves out as consultants and continued working on a paper punch machine to collect data while attached to other instruments. The partners decided that Kaplan would handle the management, marketing, and money side of Data Specialties' business and Cless the technological aspects. Kaplan then borrowed his father's car for a jaunt to the East Coast to drum up business. After eating and sleeping in the car the entire trip, the partners were almost ready to give up, but decided they would give their venture another two weeks before calling it quits. Within days an order came in from an Ohio-based division of Monsanto Corp., followed by two more orders in the next several weeks.

By the end of 1970, Data Specialties Inc. was located in Highland Park, Illinois, and had reached revenues of $90,000; in 1971 total sales climbed by 360 percent to $330,000. Then Bell and Howell Co. came calling with a major contract, contingent upon inspection of Data Specialties Inc.'s manufacturing plant—which didn't exist. Thinking fast, the engineers took apart already-assembled machines and spread them throughout their 1,320-square foot office space, hired a secretary and workers to reassemble the machines for the day, and enlisted their wives to call every ten minutes impersonating customers. Their creativity and virtual factory paid off, as Bell and Howell and many other clients signed with Data Specialties over the next few years, eventually earning the company a 50 percent share of the paper tape punch and related machinery market.

When the paper tape industry began to falter due to new technology like bar coding, the partners decided to pursue the latter. Although bar coding had been around since the 1970s, the industry was still in its infancy with just a handful of competitors. The odd-looking black and white stripes were first favored by grocers using UPC (Universal Product Code) labels as a means of speeding up the check-out and payment process, then bar codes caught on in the retail clothing industry. Data Specialties introduced its first bar code printer, The Zebra, at a Dallas trade show in 1982, and despite some minor glitches, the machine was far more advanced than those of competitors. "It had the capability to create on-demand bar coding," Cless explained, "that could revolutionize the industry." The fledgling company began selling its wares to businesses, especially health care and pharmaceutical companies, at home and overseas.

In 1986, to combat scanning problems due to poor resolution from off-shaped or uneven-surfaced products, the company built its first "thermal transfer" printer using heated printer heads that melted characters from a waxy ribbon onto labels made from paper, plastic, foil, or other smooth materials. Unlike standard bar codes, thermal transfer labels were able to withstand temperatures as high as 400 degrees Fahrenheit or as cold as minus 110 degrees Fahrenheit. Although there were other printing processes using heat, thermal transfer didn't require specially treated labels, lasted much longer, and soon became an industry standard for affixing labels to items of all shapes and sizes—such as U.S. Steel's strip steel coils and bars and hospitals' blood bags and specimens.

With the success of its Zebra printer and other products, Kaplan and Cless changed the company's name from Data Specialties to Zebra Technologies Corporation in 1986. Over the next few years, the company began transferring its Japanese manufacturing (which began in the early 1980s through a partnership) back to the United States, to maximize profit and decrease product defect rates. While manufacturing in Japan had initially been beneficial, the fall of the dollar by nearly half, government embargoes, and import duty increases had taken their toll on Zebra, and both Kaplan and Cless wanted to regain control of their manufacturing. Yet the years in Japan had given Zebra an important technological edge, which when combined with Cless's German background and their location in the United States, gave the company a valuable international orientation.

The next year Kaplan and Cless's hard work was recognized when the company was awarded the prestigious 1988 High Technology Entrepreneur Award from Peat Marwick Main & Co., a Chicago-based accounting and consulting firm. Zebra finished the year with $30 million in sales and income of $5.5 million; the following year, 1990, sales jumped nearly 30 percent to $38 million. In 1991 the partners decided to take their company public, and in August 1991 Zebra successfully completed an IPO of 2.8 million shares at $15.50 each; within hours, the stock traded at $18. By year's end in 1991 analysts estimated the bar code industry at $380 million with Zebra having captured over 25 percent of the market. There were more than 23,000 of Zebra's bar code printing systems installed at some 5,000 sites worldwide, pumping the company's net sales up to $45.6 million, including nearly 36 percent from international sources. As Zebra prospered the company increased its funding in R&D proportionately, spending nearly $2.4 million.

By 1992 Zebra was considered the premier manufacturer of high-performance demand printing materials used in factory assembly lines to label a wide variety of consumer goods. With over 30,000 machines installed worldwide, Zebra's product line of 20 thermal-transfer printing systems and 12 different symbologies had

earned a reputation for excellence as well as durability, especially in harsh conditions. As a result, Zebra was ranked number seven on *Forbes's* "200 Best Small Companies" in November. The company then ended the year with net sales of $58.7 million and earnings of $11.8 million, due in part to its increasing supplies business, which accounted for a quarter of 1992's sales. By the end of that year 90 percent of Zebra's operations were housed at its 67,000-foot Vernon Hills facility, which added another 37,000 square feet to accommodate the growth.

In March 1993, Zebra's second public offering of 2.6 million shares (at $22.75 each) went off without a hitch. The company now had 45,000 machines in circulation, and Zebra's engineers began looking in another direction. While its printers were intricately crafted, high-performance machines (which became known as the trademarked Performance Line), the company continued to research ways to make their printers more technologically advanced, less expensive, and accessible to a wider client base. In general, Zebra's customers were divided into two market segments and two subdivisions—the first between the industrial and retail markets (nearly 90 percent of retailers used bar codes, while only 20 percent of the industrial market had been tapped in 1993), and the second between clients whose primary purpose was compliance with bar-coding standards vs. those who used the bar codes for the detailed information the labels could provide about production, including tracking inventory and routing deliveries.

While some clients easily spent over $10,000 for a sophisticated, custom-made printer (prices ranged from about $1,600 to $12,000) others required as many as a dozen printers and supplies for factory assembly lines. With this in mind, in 1993 Zebra launched its Value-Line of economically priced products, consisting of completely reengineered and redesigned printers and accessories. While the technology of the entry-level Value-Line was still state-of-the-art, the products themselves were smaller and easier to assemble (with the number of parts reduced by up to 40 percent), lightweight (due to their use of structural plastic), manufactured in up to 25 percent less time, and, consequently, lower-priced by nearly half. When the Stripe S-300 and S-500 were introduced in the fall of 1993, sales were impressive. Yet romancing the mid- to lower-priced market didn't affect Zebra's higher-end markets—its specialized Performance Line machines continued to be purchased by its regular clients (which mainly consisted of Fortune 500 companies) and steadily attracted new ones as well.

While laser and ink-jet technology became hot topics of discussion in the bar code industry, Zebra's thermal transfer printing continued to reflect record gains: 1993's net sales rose to $87.4 million and income to $18.2 million, both well over the 27 percent in sales and 19 percent in profits predicted by analysts. Stock value, too, increased to $23.25 per share, and Zebra raised its R&D spending to $4.6 million to fine-tune its product line still further. Except for a setback in 1994's second quarter after manufacturing slowed due to extreme weather and the California earthquake, Zebra's growth continued unabated—again with record high sales of $107.1 million (up 22.5 percent from 1993), helped in part by the introduction of new products and significantly by an increase of almost 53 percent in international sales (which accounted for about 40 percent of Zebra's total sales). New products included an accessory called the Verifier, which identified unscannable or faulty labels; the STRIPE cutter, which sliced labels as they were printed for immediate application; and several new label surfaces resistant to not only excess heat and cold, but to abrasions, chemicals, light and moisture.

As the bar code industry saw its best year yet in 1994, due to clients like Kmart, Wal-Mart, and Lowe's, who demanded merchandise with bar coding—the company achieved number one status with its popular and durable Performance Line in the higher-priced market while possessing a healthy 33 percent share (second only to Datamax Corp. with a 40 percent share) in the economy segment. By the end of the first quarter in 1995, Zebra's overseas sales grew by 89 percent as a result of a weakened dollar and increased penetration of markets in the United Kingdom and other countries. Operations in High Wycombe and Preston, England, helped speed delivery to the company's international customers. The High Wycombe facility, completed in 1994, comprised 17,000 square feet and became Zebra's international headquarters, while the operation in Preston, near Manchester, occupied nearly 20,000 square feet and served as the company's European distribution center. Back in the United States, Zebra built a 50,000-square foot addition to its manufacturing facility and added another 11,500 square feet to its corporate headquarters in Vernon Hills. As square footage expanded worldwide, the company's work force approached a new high of 500.

By mid-1995 Zebra's $119.5 in sales had doubled from just three years earlier and the company was ranked number 72 on *Business Week's* list of "100 Best Small Corporations and Hot Growth Companies" in May. Zebra invested $5.8 million (up 26 percent from 1993) into R&D to explore new possibilities in engineering and design as well as materials and adhesives. The company's internal structure was overhauled after several senior employees left to work for competitors. With very little long-term debt and plenty of cash and marketable securities (estimated at over $54 million), the increasingly acquisition-minded Kaplan began hinting at diversification when he told *Equities Magazine Inc.,* "We're not married to the thermal transfer printer market." In July 1995, Kaplan and Cless purchased the Utah-based Vertical Technology Industries, a company specializing in bar code software. Kaplan turned day-to-day operations over to new president Jeffrey Clements (former CEO of Miller Fluid Power Corp.) while Cless continued in his role as executive vice-president of engineering and technology.

With distribution in 60 countries throughout Africa, Asia, Europe, the Middle East, the Pacific Rim, and Central, North and South Americas, Zebra Technologies' bar code printers have produced labels for myriad products, including millions of Microsoft's floppy diskettes, Motorola's cellular phone batteries, Philips Consumer Electronics' audio and video components, and even postage stamps and labels in 35 post offices in Taipei. "We have never seen a company that could not benefit from our technology," Kaplan told *Fortune* in 1993, and he and his partner Cless have been proved right repeatedly since founding their company in 1969.

Principal Subsidiaries: Zebra Technologies Europe Limited; Zebra Technologies Preston Ltd.; Zebra V.T.I., Inc.

Further Reading:

"Bar-Code Firm Will Go Public," *Chicago Tribune,* July 13, 1991, p. 3.
"The Generalist vs. The Specialist: How to Decide Which Printer Is Best for Your Application," *Modern Office Technology,* February 1992, p. 44.
Hamilton, Walter, "Zebra Tech Links Success to Entering Key New Markets," *Investor's Business Daily,* July 14, 1995, n.p.
Lyons, Daniel J., "Bar-Code Printers Produce Coded Labels," *PC Week,* January 6, 1992, pp. 77, 80.
Maclean, John N., "Weak Earnings Sink Zebra Stock," *Chicago Tribune,* April 23, 1994, p. 1.
——, "Zebra Says Ribbon Woes Are Ending," *Chicago Tribune,* May 11, 1994, p. 3.
Marcial, Gene G., "Bar-Coding the World," *Business Week,* July 31, 1995, p. 71.
Moskal, Brian S., "Zebra Tames New-Product Development," *Industry Week,* September 6, 1993, pp. 19–20.
O'Maolchoin, Sean, "Zebra Finds Its Stripes in Bar Codes," *Equities Magazine Inc.,* April 1995, n.p.
Palmer, Ann Therese, "Zebra Looks to Management Revamp to Help Bolster Growth," *Crain's Chicago Business,* March 6, 1995, p. 42.
——, "Zebra Strategies Anything but Tame," *Chicago Tribune,* April 13, 1992, pp. 1, 6.
——, "Different Stripes," *Chicago Tribune,* January 3, 1993, pp. 1, 6, 7.
Rae, Sriknmar S., "Tomorrow's Rosetta Stones," *FW,* November 22, 1994, pp. 70–72.
Ringer, Richard, "Market Place: Zebra Technologies Finds a Downside in Its Prosperity," *New York Times,* August 2, 1993, p. C4.
Sherrod, Pamela, "4 High-Tech Innovators Honored," *Chicago Tribune,* November 21, 1988, p. B1.
Teitelbaum, Richard S., "Companies to Watch: Zebra Technologies," *Fortune,* Janurary 25, 1993, p. 105.
Zipser, Andy, "Where Stripes Are," *Barron's,* January 20, 1992, pp. 42–43.

—Taryn Benbow-Pfalzgraf

INDEX TO COMPANIES AND PERSONS

Listings are arranged in alphabetical order under the company name; thus Eli Lilly & Company will be found under the letter E. Definite articles (The) and forms of incorporation that precede the name (A.B. and N.V.) are ignored for alphabetical purposes. Company names appearing in bold type have historical essays on the page numbers appearing in bold. Updates to entries that appeared in earlier volumes are signified by (upd.). The index is cumulative with volume numbers printed in bold type.

Beecham, Joseph, **III** 65
Beecham Research Laboratories Ltd., **III** 65
Beecham, Thomas, **III** 65
Beecham's Pills, **III** 65
Beeching, Richard, **V** 422
Beechwood Insurance Agency, Inc., **14** 472
de Beer, Tom, **IV** 92
Beerman, Arthur, **10** 281–82
Beerman Stores, Inc., **10** 281
Beers, Henry, **III** 181
Beeson, R.C., **7** 266
Beeson, Tom, **13** 110
Begelman, David, **II** 136; **12** 74
Begelman, Mark, **8** 405
Beggs, John I., **6** 601–02
Beggs, Lyman M. (John), **12** 439
Beghin Say S.A., **II** 540
Behar, Howard, **13** 494
Behl, Maureen, **11** 216
Behn, Hernand, **I** 462–63; **11** 196–97
Behn, Sosthenes (Col.), **I** 462–63; **11** 196–97
Behr-Manning Company, **8** 396
Behrakis, George, **I** 667
Behrendt, Peter, **12** 162
Behrens, Herman A., **III** 229
Behringwerke AG, **14** 255
Beijerinvest Group, **I** 210
Beijing Machinery and Equipment Corp., **II** 442
Beise, Clark, **II** 227
Beit, Alfred, **IV** 94
Beitz, Berthold, **IV** 88–89
Bejam Group PLC, **II** 678
Beker Industries, **IV** 84
Bekkum, Owen D., **6** 530
Bel Air Markets, **14** 397
Belairbus, **I** 42; **12** 191
Belasco, Warren I., **III** 94
Belcher, Benjamin, Jr., **13** 86
Belcher, Donald D., **12** 25
Belcher New England, Inc., **IV** 394
Belcher Oil Co., **IV** 394
Belden Corp., **II** 16
Belding, Don, **I** 12–14
Belfast Banking Co., **II** 318
Belfrage, Kurt-Allan, **III** 426–27
Belgacom, **6 302–04**
Belgian De Vaderlandsche, **III** 309
Belgian Rapid Access to Information Network Services, **6** 304
Belgian Société Internationale Forestière et Minière, **IV** 65
Belgochim, **IV** 499
Belgrano, Frank N., **II** 289
Belize Sugar Industries, **II** 582
Belk Stores Services, V 12–13
Belk, William Henry, **V** 12
Belknap, Hobart, **9** 96
Bell, **III** 674
Bell & Howell, **I** 463; **IV** 642
Bell, A. Scott, **III** 361
Bell Aerospace, **I** 530
Bell Aircraft, **I** 529; **11** 267
Bell Aircraft Company, **13** 267
Bell, Alexander Graham, **II** 97; **IV** 663; **6** 338, 341; **9** 366–67; **10** 377; **12** 115
Bell, Alexander Melville, **6** 305
Bell and Howell Company, **9** 33, **61–64**; **11** 197; **14** 569
Bell, Andrew, **7** 165

Bell Atlantic Corporation, **V 272–74**; **9** 171; **10** 232, 456; **11** 59, 87, 274; **12** 137; **13** 399
Bell, C. Gordon, **13** 201–02
Bell Canada, **6 305–08**; **12** 413
Bell Canada Enterprises Inc. *See* BCE, Inc.
Bell, Charles H., **II** 501–02; **10** 323
Bell Communications Research (Bellcore), **13** 58
Bell, David, **9** 281–82
Bell, Donald J., **9** 61
Bell, Drummond, **I** 378
Bell Fibre Products, **12** 377
Bell, Glen, **7** 505–06
Bell, Gordon, **III** 132, 134; **6** 234–35
Bell, Griffin, **I** 490
Bell Industries, **13** 47
Bell, James S., **II** 501; **10** 322
Bell, Joseph M., Jr., **6** 534–35
Bell Laboratories, **II** 33, 60–61, 101, 112; **8** 157; **9** 171; **11** 327, 500–01; **12** 61; **14** 52, 281–82
Bell, Lawrence D., **I** 529
Bell Pharmacal Labs, **12** 387
Bell Resources, **I** 437–38; **III** 729; **10** 170
Bell System, **II** 72, 230; **6** 338–40; **7** 99, 333; **11** 500
Bell Telephone Company, **I** 409; **6** 332, 334
Bell Telephone Company of Pennsylvania, **I** 585
Bell Telephone Company of Canada, **V** 269, 308–09. *See also* Bell Canada.
Bell Telephone Laboratories, Inc., **V** 259–64; **10** 108
Bell Telephone Manufacturing, **II** 13
Bell, Thaddeus F., **8** 274
Bell, Tim, **I** 33
Bell, Tom, **IV** 246
Bell, William, **I** 300–01; **8** 24–25
Bell's Asbestos and Engineering, **I** 428
Bell-Northern Research, Ltd., **V** 269–71
Bellak, John, **12** 442
Bellamy, Francis, **6** 582
Belle Alkali Co., **IV** 409; **7** 308
Belledune Fertilizer Ltd., **IV** 165
Bellefonte Insurance Co., **III** 29
Bellemead Development Corp., **III** 220; **14** 108
Belli, Melvin, **I** 400
Bellinger, John D., **11** 114–15
Bellisario, Marisa, **V** 326
Bellman, Harold, **10** 7
Bellofram Corp., **14** 43
Bellonte, Maurice, **V** 471
Bellows, John, **12** 554
Bellows, Randall, **13** 159
BellSouth Corporation, **V 276–78**; **9** 171, 321; **10** 431, 501
Belmin Systems, **14** 36
Belmont Electronics, **II** 85–86; **11** 412
Belmont Plaza, **12** 316
Belmont Savings and Loan, **10** 339
Belmont Springs Water Company, Inc., **I** 234; **10** 227
Belo, Alfred H., **10** 3
Belo Productions, Inc., **10** 3, 5
Beloit Corporation, **8** 243; **14 55–57**
Beloit Woodlands, **10** 380
Belridge Oil Co., **IV** 541
Belzberg family, **III** 424
Belzberg, Hyman, **III** 763
Belzberg, Samuel, **II** 661; **III** 763
Belzberg, William, **III** 763

Belzburg family, **10** 422
Belzer Dowidat, **IV** 199
Belzer group, **IV** 198
Bembridge, B.A., **I** 715
Bemis, A. Farwell, **8** 54
Bemis Company, Inc., **8 53–55**
Bemis, F. Gregg, **8** 54
Bemis, Judson (Sandy), **8** 54–55
Bemis, Judson Moss, **8** 53–54
Bemis, Stephen, **8** 54
Bemrose group, **IV** 650
Ben & Jerry's Homemade, Inc., **10 146–48**
Ben Franklin, **V** 152–53; **8** 555
Ben Franklin Savings & Trust, **10** 117
Ben Hill Griffin, **III** 53
Ben Johnson & Co. Ltd., **IV** 661
Ben Line, **6** 398
Benatar, Leo, **12** 151
Bencsik, Doris, **11** 69
Bendelari, Arthur, **8** 156
Bender, John, **7** 434
Bender, Marglin, **I** 116
Bender, Robert E., **V** 156, 158
Bendetsen, Karl, **IV** 264
Bendetsen, Karl B., **12** 130
Bendicks, **I** 592
Bendix Aviation Corp., **I** 141; **II** 33; **9** 16–17; **10** 260; **13** 357
Bendix Corp., **I** 68, **141–43**, 154, 166, 192, 416; **III** 166, 555; **7** 356; **8** 545; **10** 279; **11** 138; **13** 356
Bendix Helicopters Inc., **I** 141
Bendix Home Appliances, **I** 141
Bendix, Vincent, **I** 141
Beneduce, Alberto, **I** 465
Benedum, Mike L., **IV** 415
Beneficial Corporation, **II** 236; **8 56–58**, 117; **10** 490
Beneficial Finance Corporation. *See* Beneficial Corporation.
Beneficial National Bank USA, **II** 286
Beneficial Standard Life, **10** 247
Benesse Corporation, **13** 91, 93
Benetton, **8** 171; **10** 149
Benetton, Carlo, **10** 149
Benetton, Gilberto, **10** 149
Benetton, Giuliana, **10** 149
Benetton Group S.p.A., **10 149–52**
Benetton, Luciano, **10** 149–50, 152
Benetton U.S.A. Corporation, **10** 150–51
Bengal Iron and Steel Co., **IV** 205–06
Benhamou, Eric, **11** 519–20
Benjamin Allen & Co., **IV** 660
Benjamin, Curtis G., **IV** 635–36
Benjamin, John, **III** 114
Benjamin Moore and Co., **13 84–87**
Benjamin, Robert, **II** 147
Benn Bros. plc, **IV** 687
Bennack, Frank A., Jr., **IV** 627
Bennet, Richard J., **I** 684
Bennett Biscuit Co., **II** 543
Bennett, Carl, **12** 54–55
Bennett, Clarence F., **III** 627
Bennett, Donald, **7** 450–51
Bennett, Dorothy, **12** 54–55
Bennett, Elbert G., **11** 117–19
Bennett, F.I., **III** 508
Bennett, Floyd, **I** 54
Bennett, Harry, **12** 54
Bennett, Martin, **I** 196
Bennett, Mike, **12** 320
Bennett, Peter, **III** 554–55; **V** 212
Bennett, R. B., **6** 585

Compuware Japan Corporation, **10** 244

Comsat, **II** 425; **12** 19; **13** 341

Comstock Canada, **9** 301

Comstock, William A., **11** 339

Comte, **I** 121

Comyn, D.G., **III** 751–52

Con Ed. *See* Consolidated Edison of New York, Inc.

Con-Ferro Paint and Varnish Company, **8** 553

ConAgra, Inc., II 493–95, 517, 585; **7** 432, 525; **8** 53, 499–500; **12 80–82 (upd.)**; **13** 138, 294, 350, 352; **14** 515

ConAgra Red Meat Companies, **13** 350, 352

ConAgra Turkey Co., **II** 494

Conahay & Lyon, **6** 27

Concord International, **II** 298

Concordia, **IV** 497

Concrete Industries (Monier) Ltd., **III** 735

Conde, Mario, **II** 198

The Condé Nast Publications Inc., IV 583–84; **13 177–81**

Cone, Bernard, **8** 121

Cone, Caesar, **8** 120–21

Cone, Fairfax, **I** 12–15

Cone, Herman, **8** 120

Cone, Julius, **8** 120–21

Cone Mills Corporation, 8 120–22

Cone, Moses, **8** 120

Cone, Ron, **13** 126

Conelectron, **13** 398

Conestoga National Bank, **II** 316

Confaloniere, Fedele, **IV** 588

Confederation of Engineering Industry, **IV** 484

Confidata Corporation, **11** 111

Confindustria, **I** 162

Congas Engineering Canada Ltd., **6** 478

Congdon, R. C., **6** 447

Congoleum Corp., **12** 28

Congress Financial Corp., **13** 305–06

Congressional Information Services, **IV** 610

Conic, **9** 324

Conifer Group, **II** 214

Conill Corp., **II** 261

Coniston Partners, **I** 130; **II** 680; **III** 29; **6** 130; **10** 302

Conkling, Edgar, **8** 155

Conkling, Stephen, **8** 155

Conley, Kelvin, **III** 728

Conlin, William P., **13** 128

Conn, John, **11** 62

CONNA Corp., **7** 113

Connally, John, **11** 25

Connecticut Bank and Trust Co., **II** 213–14

Connecticut Electric Service Co. *See* Connecticut Light and Power Co.

Connecticut General Corp., **III** 223, 225–26

Connecticut General Life Insurance Co., **III** 223, 225–26

Connecticut Life Insurance Co., **III** 314

Connecticut Light and Power Co., 13 182–84

Connecticut Mutual Life Insurance Company, **III** 225, **236–38**, 254, 285

Connecticut National Bank, **13** 467

Connecticut River Banking Company, **13** 467

Connecticut Telephone Company. *See* Southern New England Telecommunications Corporation.

Connecticut Trust and Safe Deposit Co., **II** 213

Connecting Point of America, **6** 244

Connelly, John F., **I** 601–02; **13** 188–90

Conner, Finis F., **6** 230–31

Conner, Henry Workman, **12** 517

Conner Peripherals, Inc., 6 230–32; **10** 403, 459, 463–64, 519; **11** 56, 234

Conner Technology, Inc., **6** 231

Connie Lee. *See* College Construction Loan Insurance Assoc.

Connolly Data Systems, **11** 66

Connolly, John, **III** 603

Connolly, Walter J., Jr., **II** 214–15

Connor, John T., **I** 415

Connor, Joseph E., **9** 423

Connor, William, **7** 342

Connors Brothers, **II** 631–32

Conoco, **6** 539; **11** 97

Conoco Chemicals Co., **I** 402; **IV** 401

Conoco Coal Development Co., **IV** 401

Conoco, Ecuador Ltd., **IV** 389

Conoco Inc., I 286, 329, 346, 402–04; **II** 376; **IV** 365, 382, 389, **399–402**, 413, 429, 454, 476; **7** 346, 559; **8** 556

Conoco Oil, **8** 152, 154

Conoco UK Ltd., **11** 400

Conorada Petroleum Corp., **IV** 365, 400

Conover Furniture Company, **10** 183

Conover, James, **6** 465

Conrad, Anthony L, **II** 90

Conrad International Hotels, **III** 91–93

Conrail. *See* Consolidated Rail Corporation.

Conseco Capital Management, Inc., **10** 247

Conseco Capital Partners, **10** 247

Conseco Capital Partners II, L.P., **10** 248

Conseco Entertainment Inc., **10** 248

Conseco Inc., 10 246–48

Consgold. *See* Consolidated Gold Fields of South Africa Ltd. *and* Consolidated Gold Fields PLC.

Considine, Frank, **I** 608

Consigovy, Thierry, **13** 204

Consolidated Aircraft Corporation, **9** 16, 497

Consolidated Aluminum Corp., **IV** 178

Consolidated Brands Inc., **14** 18

Consolidated Cable Utilities, **6** 313

Consolidated Cement Corp., **III** 704

Consolidated Cigar Co., **I** 452–53

Consolidated Coal Co., **IV** 82, 170–71

Consolidated Coin Caterers Corporation, **10** 222

Consolidated Controls, **I** 155

Consolidated Copper Corp., **13** 503

Consolidated Denison Mines Ltd., **8** 418

Consolidated Diamond Mines of South-West Africa Ltd., **IV** 21, 65–67; **7** 122–25

Consolidated Distillers Ltd., **I** 263

Consolidated Edison, I 28; **6** 456

Consolidated Edison Company of New York, Inc., **V 586–89**

Consolidated Electric & Gas, **6** 447

Consolidated Electronics Industries Corp. (Conelco), **13** 397–98

Consolidated Foods Corp., **II** 571–73, 584; **III** 480; **12** 159, 494

Consolidated Freightways, Inc., V 432–34; **6** 280, 388; **12** 278, 309; **13** 19; **14** 567

Consolidated Gold Fields of South Africa Ltd., **IV** 94, 96, 118, 565, 566

Consolidated Gold Fields PLC, **II** 422; **III** 501, 503; **IV** 23, 67, 94, 97, 171; **7** 125, 209, 387

Consolidated Grocers Corp., **II** 571

Consolidated Insurances of Australia, **III** 347

Consolidated Marketing, Inc., **IV** 282; **9** 261

Consolidated Mines Selection Co., **IV** 20, 23

Consolidated Mining and Smelting Co., **IV** 75

Consolidated National Life Insurance Co., **10** 246

Consolidated Natural Gas Company, V 590–91

Consolidated Oatmeal Co., **II** 558

Consolidated Papers, Inc., 8 123–25; **11** 311

Consolidated Power & Light Company, **6** 580

Consolidated Power & Telephone Company, **11** 342

Consolidated Press Holdings, **8** 551

Consolidated Products, Inc., 14 130–32, 352

Consolidated Rail Corporation, II 449; **V 435–37**, 485; **10** 44; **12** 278; **13** 449; **14** 324

Consolidated Rand-Transvaal Mining Group, **IV** 90

Consolidated Specialty Restaurants, Inc., **14** 131–32

Consolidated Steel, **I** 558; **IV** 570

Consolidated Stores Corp., **13** 543

Consolidated Temperature Controlling Co., **II** 40; **12** 246

Consolidated Theaters, Inc., **14** 87

Consolidated Tyre Services Ltd., **IV** 241

Consolidated Vultee, **II** 7, 32

Consolidated Zinc Corp., **IV** 58, 122, 189, 191

Consolidated Zinc Proprietary, **IV** 58–59

Consolidated-Bathurst Inc., **IV** 246–47, 334

Consolidation Coal Co., **IV** 401; **8** 154, 346–47

Consoweld Corporation, **8** 124

Constable, Archibald, **7** 165

Constance, S.J., **I** 288

Constantineau, Richard, **II** 652

Constar International Inc., **8** 562; **13** 190

Constellation, **III** 335

Constellation Insurance Co., **III** 191

Constellation Reinsurance Co., **III** 191–92

Construcciones Aeronauticas S.A., **I** 41–42; **12** 190

Construcciones y Contratas, **II** 198

Construtora Moderna SARL, **IV** 505

Consul Restaurant Corp., **13** 152

Consumer Value Stores, **V** 136–37; **9** 67

Consumer's Gas Co., **I** 264

Consumers Cooperative Association, **7** 174

Consumers Distributing Co. Ltd., **II** 649, 652–53

Consumers Electric Light and Power, **6** 582

The Consumers Gas Company Ltd., 6 476–79

Davies, F.A., **IV** 536
Davies, Joseph, **IV** 672
Davies, Marion, **IV** 626
Davies, Paul L., **I** 442–43; **11** 133–34
Davies, R.E.G., **I** 114
Davies, Ralph K., **6** 353
Davies, Robert, **I** 371; **9** 358, 501
Davies, William Ltd., **II** 482
Davila, William S., **7** 570
Davis & Henderson Ltd., **IV** 640
Davis, A.C., **III** 670
Davis, A. Dano, **II** 684
Davis and Geck, **I** 301
Davis, Arthur Vining, **IV** 10, 14
Davis, Bernard, **12** 560
Davis, Bette, **II** 143, 175–76
Davis, Bob, **8** 518
Davis, Charles S., **III** 438–39
Davis Coal & Coke Co., **IV** 180
Davis, Culver M., **II** 669
Davis, D.W., **II** 654
Davis, David R., **I** 70; **11** 277
Davis, Delmont A., **10** 130
Davis, Donald D., **II** 501; **10** 322
Davis, Donald W., **III** 628–29
Davis, E. Asbury, **III** 396
Davis, Edmund (Sir), **IV** 21
Davis, Edward K., **IV** 10–11, 14
Davis, Edwin Weyerhaeuser, **8** 429
Davis, Erroll, **6** 606
Davis Estates, **I** 592
Davis, Frank S., **11** 120
Davis, George Ade, **6** 539
Davis, J.E., **II** 683–84
Davis, J. Luther, **6** 588–89
Davis, Jacob, **II** 644
Davis, Jefferson, **10** 268
Davis, Jerry, **12** 20
Davis, Jim, **11** 95
Davis, John, **II** 158–59; **IV** 381
Davis Manufacturing Company, **10** 380
Davis, Martin S., **I** 451, 453; **II** 156
Davis, Marvin, **II** 170–71
Davis, Nathanael V., **IV** 11–12
Davis, Norman, **III** 738
Davis, Peter, **IV** 667
Davis, Richard, **11** 466
Davis, Robert D., **II** 684
Davis, Sandra, **12** 180
Davis Wholesale Company, **9** 20
Davis, William, **IV** 686
Davis, William M., **II** 683
Davis-Standard Company, **9** 154
Davison Chemical Corp., **IV** 190
Davison, Ian Hay, **III** 280
Davison, Robert Park, **9** 506–07
Davison, Stanley, **II** 211
Davisson, Clinton, **13** 57
Davy Bamag GmbH, **IV** 142
Davy McKee AG, **IV** 142
Dawe's Laboratories, Inc., **12** 3
Dawnay Day, **III** 501
Dawson Mills, **II** 536
Day & Zimmermann Inc., **6** 579; **9** 162–64
Day Brite Lighting, **II** 19
Day, Cecil B., **11** 178
Day, Charles, **9** 162
Day, Doris, **II** 175
Day, Guy, **11** 49–50
Day International, **8** 347
Day Runner, Inc., **14** 157–58
Day, William, **III** 247–48
Day-Glo Color Corp., **8** 456

Day-Lee Meats, **II** 550
Day-N-Nite, **II** 620
Daybridge Learning Centers, **13** 49
Daybridge/Children's World, **13** 299
Dayco Products, **7** 297
Days Corp., **III** 344
Days Inns of America, Inc., **III** 344; **11** 178; **13** 362, 364
Daystar International Inc., **11** 44
Daystrom, **III** 617
Daytex, Inc., **II** 669
Dayton Citizens' Electric Co. *See* Dayton Power & Light Company.
Dayton Engineering Laboratories, **I** 171; **9** 416; **10** 325
Dayton Flexible Products Co., **I** 627
Dayton, George Draper, **V** 43–44
Dayton Hudson Corporation, **V** 43–44; **8** 35; **9** 360; **10** 136, 391–93, 409–10, 515–16; **13** 330; **14** 376
Dayton Lighting Co. *See* Dayton Power & Light Company.
Dayton Power & Light Company, **6** 467, 480–82
Dayton Walther Corp., **III** 650, 652
Daytron Mortgage Systems, **11** 485
DB. *See* Deutsche Bundesbahn.
DBMS Inc., **14** 390
DCA Food Industries, **II** 554
DCL BioMedical, Inc., **11** 333
DCMS Holdings Inc., **7** 114
DDB Needham Worldwide, **14** 159–61
DDI Corporation, **7** 118–20; **13** 482
De Angelis, Anthony "Tino", **II** 398; **10** 62
De Beers Botswana Mining Company Limited, **IV** 66; **7** 124
De Beers Consolidated Mines Limited / De Beers Centenary AG, **I** 107; **IV** 20–21, 23, 60, 64–68, 79, 94; **7** 121–26 (upd.)
De Beers Industrial Diamond Division, **IV** 66
De Benedetti, Carlo, **II** 295; **III** 144–45; **IV** 587–88, 615; **11** 205
De Benedetti, Franco, **III** 144–45
De Campi, John Webb, **I** 196
de Castro, Esdon, **8** 137–39
De Chalmont, Guillaume, **I** 399
de Chambrun, Rene, **12** 57–58
De Grenswisselkantoren NV, **III** 201
De Groote Bossche, **III** 200
De Havilland, **7** 11
De La Rue PLC, **10** 267–69
De Laurentiis Entertainment Group, **III** 84
De Laval Chadburn Co., **III** 419, 420
De Laval Cream Separator Co., **III** 418–19
De Laval Dairy Supply Co., **III** 419
De Laval Separator Company, **7** 235–36
De Laval Steam Turbine Company, **III** 419; **7** 235
De Laval Turbine Company, **7** 236–37
De Leuw, Cather & Company, **8** 416
De Lorean, John Z., **I** 173
De Nederlandse Bank, **IV** 132
De Payenneville, Gaston, **III** 210
de Pouzilhac, Alain, **13** 204
De Pree, D.J., **8** 255–56
De Pree, Hugh, **8** 256
De Pree, Max, **8** 256
De Ster 1905 NV, **III** 200
De Tomaso Industries, **11** 104
De Trey Gesellchaft, **10** 271
De Villiers, Wim (Dr.), **IV** 90, 92

De Vos, Richard M., **III** 11–14
De Walt, **III** 436
De-sta-Co., **III** 468
Dealer Equipment and Services, **10** 492
Dealey, George Bannerman, **10** 3
DeAllesandro, Joseph P., **III** 197
Deamer, Adrian, **IV** 651; **7** 390
Dean & Barry Co., **8** 455
Dean, Clarence R., **V** 652
Dean Foods Company, **7** 127–29
Dean, Howard M., **7** 127–28
Dean, James, **13** 413
Dean, R. Hal, **II** 562; **13** 426
Dean, Sam, Sr., **7** 127
Dean Witter & Co., **II** 445; **IV** 186
Dean Witter, Discover & Co., **12** 96–98
Dean Witter Financial Services Group Inc., **V** 180, 182
Dean Witter Reynolds, **7** 213; **12** 96
Dean-Dempsy Corp., **IV** 334
Dear, Albert, **IV** 582
Dear, Walter, **IV** 582
Dearden, William E., **II** 511
Deary, William, **8** 428
Deasy, Henry (Maj.), **III** 508
Deasy, W.J., **7** 356
DeBartolo, Edward, **12** 356
DeBartolo, Edward J., **8** 159–61
DeBartolo, Edward J., Jr., **8** 161
Debartolo, Edward J., Sr., **12** 390
Debenhams, **V** 20–22
Debron Investments Plc., **8** 271
DEC. *See* Digital Equipment Corp.
Decca Ltd., **II** 81, 83
Decca Records, **II** 144
Decherd, Robert, **10** 4
Decision Base Resources, **6** 14
Decker, Alonzo G., **III** 435–36
Decker, Alonzo G., Jr., **III** 436
Decker, William C., **III** 683
Decoflex Ltd., **IV** 645
Decolletage S.A. St.-Maurice, **14** 27
Dedeurwaerder, Jose, **I** 136, 190
Dee Corp., **I** 549; **II** 628–29, 642
Dee, Robert F., **I** 692
Deeds, Edward, **III** 151; **6** 265; **9** 416
Deeks McBride, **III** 704
Deely, J. T., **6** 474
Deep Oil Technology, **I** 570
Deep Rock Oil Co., **IV** 446
Deep Rock Oil Corp., **IV** 446
Deep Rock Water Co., **III** 21
Deepsea Ventures, Inc., **IV** 152
Deepwater Light and Power Company, **6** 449
Deer Park Spring Water Co., **III** 21
Deere & Company, **I** 181, 527; **III** 462–64, 651; **10** 377–78, 380, 429; **11** 472; **13** 16–17, 267
Deere & Mansur Works, **III** 462
Deere, Charles, **III** 462
Deere, John, **III** 462; **10** 377
Deere-Hitachi Construction Machinery, **III** 464
Deering Co., **II** 330
Deering, Ernest, **IV** 118
Deering Harvester Co., **IV** 660
Deering Milliken, **8** 13
Deering-Milliken, **V** 366–67
Defense Plant Corp., **IV** 10, 408
Defforey, Denis, **10** 204–05
Defforey, Jacques, **10** 205
Defforey, Louis, **10** 204–05
DeForest, Lee, **III** 534

Deft Software, Inc., **10** 505
DEG. *See* Deutsche Edison Gesellschaft.
Degener, Carl, **II** 163
Degener, Herbert, **II** 164
Degolia, E.B., **9** 548
DeGolyer, Everette, **IV** 365
DeGroat, C.H., **10** 328
Degussa AG. *See* Degussa Group.
Degussa Carbon Black Corp., **IV** 71
Degussa Corp., **IV** 71
Degussa Group, I 303; **IV 69–72**, 118
Degussa s.a., **IV** 71
Deihl, Richard H., **II** 182; **10** 343
Deikel, Ted, **9** 218–19, 360
Deinhard, **I** 281
Dejouany, Guy, **V** 633–34
DeKalb AgResearch Inc., **9** 411
Dekker, Nicholas, **III** 241–42
Dekker, Wisse, **II** 80; **13** 402
Del Monte Corporation, **II** 595; **7 130–32**; **12** 439; **14** 287
del Valle Inclan, Miguel Angel, **V** 415
Del Webb Corporation, **14 162–64**
Del-Rey Petroleum, **I** 526
Delafield Industries, **12** 418
Delagrange, **I** 635
Delahye Ripault, **II** 356
Delaney, Don, **6** 79
Delaware Charter Guarantee & Trust Co., **III** 330
Delaware Lackawanna & Western, **I** 584
Delaware Management Holdings, **III** 386
Delaware North Companies Incorporated, **7 133–36**
Delbard, **I** 272
Delbrück, Adalbert, **I** 410
Delchamps, **II** 638
Delco, **6** 265
Delco Electronics, **II** 32–35; **III** 151
Deledda, Grazia, **IV** 585
Delestrade, René, **III** 393
Delfont, Bernard, **I** 532
Delhaize Freres & Cie, ''Le Lion,'' **II** 626
Delhi Gas Pipeline Corporation, **7** 551
Delhi International Oil Corp., **III** 687
Deli Universal, **13** 545
Delicious Foods, **13** 383
Delimaatschappij, **13** 545
Dell Computer Corp., **9 165–66**; **10** 309, 459; **11** 62
Dell, Michael, **9** 165
Dell Publishing Co., **13** 560
Della Femina, Jerry, **13** 204
Della Femina, McNamee, **13** 204
della Vida, Samuel, **III** 206
Dellwood Elevator Co., **I** 419
Delmar Chemicals Ltd., **II** 484
Delmar Paper Box Co., **IV** 333
Delmarva Properties, Inc., **8** 103
Delmonico Foods Inc., **II** 511
Delmonico International, **II** 101
Deloitte & Touche, **9 167–69**, 423
Deloitte, Haskins, & Sells. *See* Deloitte & Touche.
Deloitte Touche Tohmatsu International, **9** 167–68
Deloitte, William Welch, **9** 167
DeLong Engineering Co., **III** 558
DeLong-McDermott, **III** 558
Deloraine, Maurice, **I** 464
DeLorean Motor Co., **10** 117; **14** 321
Delorme, Jean, **I** 358
Delorme, Paul, **I** 357
Delort, Jean-Jacques, **V** 10

Delphax, **IV** 252
Delprat, **IV** 58
Delprat, Guillaume, **IV** 44–45
Delta Acceptance Corporation Limited, **13** 63
Delta Air Corporation. *See* Delta Air Lines, Inc.
Delta Air Service. *See* Delta Air Lines, Inc.
Delta Air Lines Inc., **I** 29, 91, 97, **99–100**, 102, 106, 120, 132; **6** 61, **81–83 (upd.)**, 117, 131–32, 383; **12** 149, 381; **13** 171–72; **14** 73
Delta Air Service. *See* Delta Air Lines, Inc.
Delta Apparel, Inc., **8** 141–43
Delta Biologicals S.r.l., **11** 208
Delta Communications, **IV** 610
Delta Faucet Co., **III** 568–69
Delta Lloyd, **III** 235
Delta Manufacturing, **II** 85
Delta Mills Marketing Company, **8** 141, 143
Delta Motors, **III** 580
Delta Savings Assoc. of Texas, **IV** 343
Delta Steamship Lines, **9** 425–26
Delta Woodside Industries, Inc., **8 141–43**
DeLuxe Check Printers, Inc., **7** 137
Deluxe Corporation, **7 137–39**
DeLuxe Laboratories, **IV** 652
Deluxe Upholstering Ltd., **14** 303
Delvag Luftürsicherungs A.G., **I** 111
DelZotto, Angelo, **9** 512
DelZotto, Elvio, **9** 512–13
DelZotto, Leo, **9** 512
Demag AG, **II** 22; **III** 566; **IV** 206
Demerara Company, **13** 102
DeMille, Cecil B., **II** 154–55
Deminex, **IV** 413, 424
Deming Company, **8** 135
Deming, W. Edward, **8** 383
Deming, William Edwards, **III** 61, 545, 548; **IV** 162; **12** 450–51
Demka, **IV** 132–33
Demonque, Marcel, **III** 703–04
Dempsey & Siders Agency, **III** 190
Dempsey, Jerry E., **V** 753
Den Fujita, **9** 74
Den, Kenjiro, **I** 183
Den norske Creditbank, **II** 366
Den Norske Stats Oljeselskap AS, **IV 405–07**, 486
Den-Tal-Ez, **I** 702
Denain-Nord-Est-Longwy, **IV** 227
Denault Ltd., **II** 651
Denenberg, Herbert, **III** 326
Deneuve, Catherine, **10** 69
Denham, Robert E., **13** 449
Denison Corp., **III** 628
Denison, Merrill, **I** 275
Denison Mines, **12** 198
Denius, Homer, **II** 37–38
Denki Seikosho, **IV** 62
Denney-Reyburn, **8** 360
Dennison, Aaron, **IV** 251
Dennison and Co., **IV** 251
Dennison, Andrew, **IV** 251
Dennison Carter, **IV** 252
Dennison, Charles, **IV** 251
Dennison, Eliphalet Whorf (E.W.), **IV** 251–52
Dennison, Henry B., **IV** 251
Dennison, Henry Sturgis, **IV** 251–52
Dennison Manufacturing Co., **IV** 251–52, 254
Dennison National, **IV** 252

Denny, Arthur, **9** 539
Denny, Charles, **10** 18–20
Denny's Japan, **V** 88–89
Denny's Restaurants Inc., **II** 680; **III** 103; **12** 511; **13** 526
Denshi Media Services, **IV** 680
Dent & Co., **II** 296
Dent, Hawthorne K., **III** 352–53
Dent, Joseph Malaby, **13** 428
Dental Houses/Dentsply, **10** 272
The Dentists' Supply Co. *See* Dentsply International Inc.
Dentsply International Inc., **10 270–72**
Dentsu Inc., **I 9–11**, 36, 38; **9** 30; **13** 204
Dentsu, Ltd., **6** 29
Denver & Rio Grande Railroad, **12** 18–19
Denver Chemical Company, **8** 84
Denver Consolidated Electric Company. *See* Public Service Company of Colorado.
Denver Gas & Electric Company, **IV** 391; **6** 558
Denver Gas & Electric Light Company. *See* Public Service Company of Colorado.
Denver Gas Company. *See* Public Service Company of Colorado.
Denver, John, **12** 228
Department 56, Inc., **14 165–67**
Department Stores International, **I** 426
Depew, Chauncey M., **10** 72
Deposito and Administratie Bank, **II** 185
Depositors National Bank of Durham, **II** 336
Depuy Inc., **10** 156–57
Der Anker, **III** 177
Deramus, William N., **6** 400
Deramus, William N., III, **6** 400–01
Derby Commerical Bank, **II** 318
Derbyshire Stone and William Briggs, **III** 752
Dercksen, Gerrit Jan, **III** 308
Deritend Computers, **14** 36
Derr, Kenneth, **IV** 387
Deruluft, **6** 57
Derwent Publications, **8** 526
Des Moines Electric Light Company, **6** 504
Des Voeux, William (Sir), **IV** 699
DESA Industries, **8** 545
DesBarres, John P., **V** 740
Deseret National Bank, **11** 118
Desert Partners, **III** 763
Design Craft Ltd., **IV** 640
DeSimone, L.D., **8** 371
Desmarais Frères, **IV** 557, 559
DeSoto, Inc., **8** 553; **13** 471
Desoutter, **III** 427
Despret, Maurice, **II** 202
Destec Energy, Inc., **12 99–101**
Destray, Ellen, **10** 383
Det Danske Luftartselskab, **I** 119
Det Norske Luftartselskab, **I** 119
Deterding, Henri, **IV** 379, 530–31
Detra, Ralph W., **III** 643
Detroit Aircraft Corp., **I** 64; **11** 266
Detroit Automobile Co., **I** 164
Detroit Ball Bearing Co., **13** 78
Detroit Chemical Coatings, **8** 553
Detroit City and Gas Company. *See* MCN Corporation.
Detroit City Gas Company. *See* MCN Corporation.
Detroit Copper Co., **IV** 176
Detroit Copper Mining Co., **IV** 177

Eastern Corp., **IV** 703
Eastern Electricity, **13** 485
Eastern Enterprises, **IV** 171; **6 486–88**
Eastern Gas and Fuel Associates, **I** 354; **IV** 171
Eastern Indiana Gas Corporation, **6** 466
Eastern Kansas Utilities, **6** 511
Eastern Machine Screw Products Co., **13** 7
Eastern Operating Co., **III** 23
Eastern Pine Sales Corporation, **13** 249
Eastern States Farmers Exchange, **7** 17
Eastern Telegraph, **V** 283–84
Eastern Texas Electric. *See* Gulf States Utilities Company.
Eastern Tool Co., **IV** 249
Eastern Wisconsin Power, **6** 604
Eastern Wisconsin Railway and Light Company, **6** 601
Eastex Pulp and Paper Co., **IV** 341–42
Eastham, Edward, **6** 548
Eastham, William K., **III** 59
Eastman Chemical Company, **14 174–75**
Eastman Chemical Products, Inc. **III** 475; **7** 161; **8** 377
Eastman Co., **III** 474; **7** 160
Eastman Dry Plate and Film Co., **III** 474; **7** 160
Eastman Dry Plate Co., **III** 474; **7** 160
Eastman, George, **III** 474–76; **7** 160–62; **9** 422; **12** 231
Eastman Kodak Company, **I** 19, 30, 90, 323, 337–38, 690; **III** 103; **III** 171–72, **474–77**, 486–88, 547–48, 550, 584, 607–09; **IV** 260–61; **6** 288–89; **7 160–64 (upd.)**, 436–38; **8** 376–77; **9** 62, 231; **10** 24; **12** 342; **14** 174–75, 534
Eastman Photographic Materials Co., **III** 474; **7** 160
Eastman Radio, **6** 33
Eastman Technology, **III** 475
Eastmaque Gold Mines, Ltd., **7** 356
Eaton Axle Co., **I** 154
Eaton, Bob, **7** 462
Eaton, Cole & Burnham Company, **8** 134
Eaton Corporation, **I 154–55**, 186; **III** 645; **10 279–80 (upd.)**; **12** 547
Eaton, Cyrus, **6** 605; **7** 446; **13** 157
Eaton, Earl, **11** 543
Eaton, Frank, **9** 92
Eaton, Joseph Oriel, **I** 154; **10** 279
Eaton, Robert, **7** 461
Eaton Yale & Towne, **I** 154
Eavey Co., **II** 668
Eayres, Ellen Knowles, **IV** 622; **12** 223
Ebamsa, **II** 474
EBASCO. *See* Electric Bond and Share Company.
Ebasco Service Inc., **V** 612
Ebasco Services, **III** 499; **IV** 255–56
Ebbers, Bernard, **8** 310
EBC Amro Ltd., **II** 186
Eberhard Faber, **12** 115
Eberhard Foods, **8** 482
Eberle, William D., **III** 664–65
Eberstadt, Rudolph, Jr., **8** 366–67
Ebert, Horatio B., **III** 613
EBIC. *See* European Banks' International Co.
Eble, Charles, **V** 587–88
EBS. *See* Electric Bond & Share Company.
EC Erdolchemie GmbH, **7** 141
ECC Construction, **III** 689
ECC Construction Materials, **III** 689
ECC Group plc, **III 689–91**

ECC International Ltd., **III** 689–91
Eccles, George S., **11** 117–19
Eccles, Marriner S., **11** 117–18
Eccles, Samuel, **I** 267
Eccles, Spencer, **11** 119
Echevarrieta, Horacio, **6** 95
Echigoya Saburobei Shoten, **IV** 292
Echlin Corp., **I 156–57**
Echlin, Earl, **I** 156; **11** 83
Echlin Inc., **11 83–85 (upd.)**
Echlin, Jack, **I** 156; **11** 83
Echo Bay Mines Ltd., **IV 75–77**
Echols, O.P., **I** 76; **11** 363
Les Echos, **IV** 659
Eckel, Paul, **I** 28
Ecker, Frederick H., **III** 292
Ecker, Frederick W., **III** 292
Eckerd College, **9** 187
Eckerd Corporation, **9 186–87**
Eckerd Family Youth Alternatives, **9** 187
Eckerd, J. Milton, **9** 186
Eckerd, Jack, **9** 186
Eckerd Optical, **9** 186
Eckert, J. Presper, **III** 165
Eckert, Michael, **12** 304
Eckert, Robert A., **12** 372
Eckert, Wesley E., **9** 161
Eckert-Mauchly Corp., **III** 166
Eckhouse, Joseph L., **7** 202
Eckman, John, **I** 666–68
Ecko Products, **I** 527
Ecko-Ensign Design, **I** 531
Eckrich, Donald P., **7** 82
Eclipse Machine Co., **I** 141
Eco Hotels, **14** 107
Ecolab Inc., **I 331–33**; **13 197–200 (upd.)**
Econo-Lodges, **13** 363
Econo-Travel Corporation, **13** 362
Economics Laboratory. *See* Ecolab Inc.
Economo family, **III** 347
Economy Book Store, **10** 135
Economy Grocery Stores Corp., **II** 666
Ecopetrol. *See* Empresa Colombiana de Petróleos.
EcoSystems Software, Inc., **10** 245
ECS S.A, **12 138–40**
Ecusta Corporation, **8** 414
Edah, **13** 544–45
Edamoto, Kenzo, **13** 456
Eddie Bauer Inc., **9 188–90**; **9** 316; **10** 324, 489, 491; **11** 498
Eddie Bauer Ltd., **II** 503; **V** 160
Eddins, H.A. "Tex", **7** 410
Eddy Bakeries, Inc., **12** 198
Eddy Paper Co., **II** 631
Edeka Co-op Bank, **II** 621–22
Edeka Import and Export, **II** 621
Edeka Zentrale A.G., **II 621–23**
Edelman, Asher, **11** 274; **12** 118
Edelman, Asher B., **I** 170; **6** 146; **7** 514; **11** 68–69; **13** 361
Edelstahlwerke Buderus AG, **III** 695
Edelstein, Michael, **I** 471, 522
Edenhall Group, **III** 673
Edenton Cotton Mills, **12** 503
EDF. *See* Electricité de France.
Edgar, Charles L., **12** 45
Edgar, Jim, **6** 201
Edgar, N.S., **IV** 75
Edgars, **I** 289
Edgcomb Metals, **IV** 576
Edgcomb Steel Co., **IV** 575
Edgell Communications Inc., **IV** 624
Edgell, Robert L., **IV** 623–24; **12** 224–25

Edgerly, Martin Van Buren (Col.), **III** 285
Edgerly, William, **8** 492
Edgerton, David, **II** 613
Edgerton, Harold E., **8** 163
Edgewater Hotel and Casino, **6** 204–05
Edina Realty Inc., **13** 348
Edinburgh (Duke of), **IV** 708
Edison Brothers Stores, Inc., **9 191–93**
Edison Co., **III** 433
Edison Electric Appliance Co., **II** 28; **12** 194
Edison Electric Co., **I** 368; **II** 330; **6** 572
Edison Electric Illuminating Co., **II** 402; **6** 595, 601; **14** 124
Edison Electric Illuminating Company of Boston, **12** 45
Edison Electric Light & Power, **6** 510
Edison Electric Light Co., **II** 27; **6** 565, 595; **11** 387; **12** 193
Edison General Electric Co., **II** 27, 120, 278; **12** 193; **14** 168
Edison, Harry, **9** 191–92
Edison, Irving, **9** 192
Edison Machine Works, **II** 27
Edison Phonograph, **III** 443
Edison, Sam, **9** 192
Edison, Thomas, **11** 402; **12** 193, 544
Edison, Thomas A., **I** 409, 597; **II** 27–28, 120; **III** 683; **V** 695; **6** 465, 483, 555, 574, 595; **9** 274; **10** 115
Editions Albert Premier, **IV** 614
Editions Bernard Grasset, **IV** 618
Editions Dalloz, **IV** 615
Editions Nathan, **IV** 615
Editorial Centro de Estudios Ramón Areces, S.A., **V** 52
Editoriale L'Espresso, **IV** 586–87
Editoriale Le Gazzette, **IV** 587
EdK. *See* Edeka Zentrale A.G.
Edman, Jan, **II** 366
Edmark Corporation, **14 176–78**
Edmond Garin, **III** 418
Edmonston, D.C., **II** 297
Edmonton City Bakery, **II** 631
Edmunds, Henry, **I** 194
Edogawa Oil Co., **IV** 403
EdoWater Systems, Inc., **IV** 137
Edper Equities, **II** 456
EDS. *See* Electronic Data Systems Corporation.
Edstrom, J. Sigfrid, **II** 1–2
Education Funds, Inc., **II** 419
Education Systems Corporation, **7** 256
Educational & Recreational Services, Inc., **II** 607
Educational Credit Corporation, **8** 10
Educational Supply Company, **7** 255
Educational Testing Service, **12 141–43**
EduQuest, **6** 245
Edward Ford Plate Glass Co., **III** 640–41, 731
Edward J. DeBartolo Corporation, **V** 116; **8 159–62**
Edward Lloyd Ltd., **IV** 258
Edward P. Allis Company, **13** 16
Edward Smith & Company, **8** 553
Edward VII, King (England), **I** 251
Edwardes, Michael (Sir), **I** 429; **7** 332
Edwards, **13** 445
Edwards & Jones, **11** 360
Edwards, Albert Gallatin, **8** 3–4
Edwards, Albert Ninian, **8** 4
Edwards, Benjamin Franklin, **8** 3–4
Edwards, Benjamin Franklin, III, **8** 3–5

Greyhound Corp., **I 448–50**; II 445; **6** 27; **8** 144–45; **10** 72; **12** 199
Greyhound Dial, **8** 145
Greylock Mills, III 213
Grezel, Pierre, **IV** 174
Gribben, George, I 37
Grice, Robert, **13** 286
GRiD Systems Corp., II 107
Gridley, George, **13** 6
Grier, Herbert E., **8** 163
Griesheim Elektron, **IV** 140
Grieve, Pierson M., I 332–33; **13** 198–99
Grieveson, Grant and Co., II 422–23
Griffin and Sons, II 543
Griffin, Elton, III 672–73
Griffin, Joseph, **12** 527
Griffin, Marcus, **6** 109
Griffin, Marvin, Jr., **10** 222
Griffin, Matthew, **9** 194–95
Griffin, Merv, **9** 306; **12** 420
Griffin Pipe Products Co., **7** 30–31
Griffin Wheel Company, **7** 29–30
Griffin, William, **10** 287
Griffith, D.W., I 537; II 146
Griffith, Franklin, **6** 548–49
Griffith-Boscawen, Arthur, I 288
Griffiths, Edgar H., II 90
Griffiths, G. Findley, **8** 273–74
Griffon Cutlery Corp., **13** 166
Grigg, C.L., **9** 177
Grigg, Elliot & Co., **14** 555
Grigg, F. Nephi, **13** 382–83
Grigg, Golden T., **13** 382
Grigg, James, I 223
Griggs, Herbert, II 217
Grillet, Charles, I 488
Grillet, Nicolas, **10** 470
Grimshaw, Norman, **9** 92
Grindlays Bank, II 189
Gringoir/Broussard, II 556
Grinnell Corp., III 643–45; **11** 198; **13 245–47**
Grinnell, Frederick, **13** 245
Grinnell, Russell, **13** 245
Grinstead, Stanley, I 247
Grinstein, Gerald, **V** 428
Grip Printing & Publishing Co., **IV** 644
Grisanti, Eugene P., **9** 292
Griscom, Tom, **11** 153
Grisewood & Dempsey, **IV** 616
Grissom, Virgil, **11** 428
Grissom, Virgil I., I 79
Griswald, Gordon, **6** 456
Grocer Publishing Co., **IV** 638
Grocery Store Products Co., III 21
Grocery Warehouse, II 602
Groebler, Alfred, III 694
Groen Manufacturing, III 468
Grogan-Cochran Land Company, **7** 345
Grolier, **IV** 619
Grones, Alex, I 186
Grönfeldt, Mr., I 664
Groot-Noordhollandsche, III 177–79
Groovy Beverages, II 477
Grosch, Ernst, III 695
Gross, Courtland, **11** 267
Gross, Courtlandt, I 65
Gross, Patrick W., **11** 18
Gross, Robert, I 64–65; III 601; **11** 266–67
Gross Townsend Frank Hoffman, **6** 28
Grosset & Dunlap, Inc., II 144; III 190–91
Grossman, Jacob, **13** 248

Grossman, Joseph, **13** 248
Grossman, Louis, **13** 248
Grossman, M.J., **III** 375–76
Grossman, Maurice, **13** 249–50
Grossman, Reuben, **13** 248
Grossman, Sidney, **13** 248
Grossman's Inc., 13 248–50
Grossmith Agricultural Industries, II 500
Grosvenor, Edwin, **9** 366
Grosvenor, Gilbert H., **9** 366–67
Grosvenor, Gilbert M., **9** 367–68
Grosvenor Marketing Co., II 465
Grosvenor, Melville Bell, **9** 367
Grotoh, Keita, **V** 487
Groton Victory Yard, I 661
Grotrian, Herbert (Sir), **IV** 685
Ground Services Inc., **13** 49
Group Bull, **12** 246
Group Hospitalization and Medical Services, **10** 161
Group Lotus, **13** 357
Groupe AG, III 201–02
Groupe Air France, 6 92–94
Groupe Ancienne Mutuelle, III 210–11
Groupe Barthelmey, III 373
Groupe Bull. *See* Compagnie des Machines Bull.
Groupe Bull, **10** 563–64
Groupe Casino. *See* Etablissements Economiques de Casino Guichard, Perrachon et Cie, S.C.A.
Groupe Danone, **14** 150
Groupe de la Cité, IV 614–16, 617
Groupe de la Financière d'Angers, **IV** 108
Groupe Jean Didier, **12** 413
Groupe Salvat, **IV** 619
Groupe Victoire, III 394
Groupement des Exploitants Pétroliers, **IV** 545
Grousbeck, Irving, **7** 98–99
Groux Beverage Corporation, **11** 451
Grove, Andrew, II 44–46; **10** 365–67
Grove, Ernest L., Jr., **10** 306
Grove Manufacturing Co., I 476–77; **9** 393
Grover, Lewis C., III 302
Grow Chemical Corp., **12** 217
Grow Group Inc., 12 217–19, 387–88
Grow, Robert, **7** 193–94
Growmark, I 421; **11** 23
Grua, Rudolph, **10** 314
Grubb, L. Edward, **IV** 111
Gruene Apotheke, I 681
Gruhl, Alfred, **6** 602
Grum, Clifford, **IV** 343
Grumman Corp., I 58–59, **61–63**, 67–68, 78, 84, 490, 511; **7** 205; **8** 51; **9** 17, 206–07, 417, 460; **10** 316–17, 536; **11 164–67 (upd.)**, 363–65, 428
Grumman, Leroy, I 61–63, 490; **11** 164, 166
Grün & Bilfinger A.G., I 560–61
Grün, August, I 560
Grundhofer, Jerry A., **11** 466–67
Grundhofer, John F. (Jack), **12** 165
Grundig, I 411; II 80, 117; **13** 402–03
Grundig Data Scanner GmbH, **12** 162
Grundig, Max, II 117
Grune, George, **IV** 664
Grunenthal, I 240
Gruner + Jahr, **IV** 590, 593
Gruntal and Co., III 263
Gruntal Financial Corp., III 264
Grupo Carso, **14** 489
Grupo Corvi S.A. de C.V., **7** 115

Grupo Industrial Alfa, II 262; **11** 386
Grupo Televisa, S.A., **9** 429
Grupo Tudor, **IV** 471
Grupo Zeta, **IV** 652–53; **7** 392
Gruppo IRI, **V** 325–27
Grusin, Harry Jack. *See* Gray, Harry.
GSG&T, **6** 495
GSI. *See* Geophysical Service, Inc.
GSU. *See* Gulf States Utilities Company.
GTE Corporation, II 38, 47, 80; **V 294–98**; **9** 49, 478–80; **10** 19, 97, 431; **11** 500. *See also* British Columbia Telephone Company.
GTE Data Services, **9** 171
GTE Health Systems, **14** 433
GTE Information Services, **14** 433
GTE North, **14** 259
GTE Products Corp., III 475
GTE Sprint Communications, **9** 478–79
GTE Telenet Information Services, III 118
GTO. *See* Global Transport Organization.
GTS Duratek, Inc., **13** 367–68
Guangzhou M. C. Packaging, **10** 130
Guaranty Bank & Trust Company, **13** 440
Guaranty Federal Savings & Loan Assoc., **IV** 343
Guaranty Federal Savings Bank, **IV** 343
Guaranty Properties Ltd., **11** 258
Guaranty Savings and Loan, **10** 339
Guaranty Trust Co. of New York, II 329–32, 428; **IV** 20
Guardian, III 721
Guardian Bank, **13** 468
Guardian Federal Savings and Loan Association, **10** 91
Guardian Mortgage Company, **8** 460
Guardian National Bank, I 165; **11** 137
Guardian Royal Exchange, III 350
Guardian Royal Exchange Plc, 11 168–70
Gubanich, John A., **6** 444
Gubay, Albert, **11** 239
Guber, Peter, II 137, 149; **12** 75
Gucci, **12** 281
Guelph Dolime, **IV** 74
Guerney, Samuel, III 372
Guernsey Banking Co., II 333
Guest, Charlotte (Lady), III 493
Guest, John, III 493
Guest, Josiah (John) (Sir), III 493
Guest, Keen & Co., III 493
Guest, Keen & Nettlefolds Ltd., III 493–95
Guest, Keen and Nettlefolds plc, III 495. *See also* GKN plc.
Guest Keen Baldwins Iron and Steel Co., III 493–94
Guest, Keen Iron and Steel Co., III 494
Guest, Keen, Williams Ltd., III 493
Guest, Thomas, III 493
Gueyraud et Fils Cadet, III 703
Gueyraud, Felix, III 703
Gugelmann, Fritz, I 122
Guggenheim Brothers, **IV** 32
Guggenheim, Daniel, **IV** 31–33
Guggenheim family, **IV** 31–32, 176; **7** 261
Guggenheim, Isaac, **IV** 32
Guggenheim, Meyer, **IV** 31
Guggenheim, Murry, **IV** 32
Guggenheim, Simon, **IV** 32–33
Guggenheim, Solomon, **IV** 32
Guichard, Antoine, **12** 152–53
Guichard, Geoffroy, **12** 152
Guild Press, Inc., **13** 559

Hydro-Quebéc, 6 501–03
Hydrocarbon Services of Nigeria Co., **IV** 473
Hydroponic Chemical Co., **III** 28
Hydrox Corp., **II** 533
Hygeia Sciences, Inc., **8** 85, 512
Hygienic Ice Co., **IV** 722
Hygrade Containers Ltd., **IV** 286
Hygrade Foods, **III** 502; **7** 208; **14** 536
Hyland Laboratories, **I** 627
Hyland, Lawrence, **II** 33
Hyman, George, **8** 112–13
Hyman, Morton P., **11** 376
Hyndley (Lord), **IV** 38
Hyosung Group, **III** 749
Hyper Shoppes, Inc., **II** 670
Hyperion Press, **6** 176
Hypermart USA, **8** 555–56
Hyplains Beef, **7** 175
Hypo-Bank. *See* Bayerische Hypotheken-
   und Wechsel-Bank AG.
Hypobaruk, **III** 348
Hypro Engineering Inc., **I** 481
Hysol Corp., **I** 321; **12** 103
Hysol Grafil Composite Components Co., **I** 321
Hyster, **I** 424
Hyster-Yale Materials Handling, Inc., **7** 369–71
Hystron Fibers Inc., **I** 347
Hyundai, **12** 211
Hyundai America, **III** 515; **7** 231
Hyundai Cement Co., **III** 515; **7** 231
Hyundai Corp., **III** 515–16; **7** 231–32; **13** 280
Hyundai Electrical Engineering Co., **III** 516; **7** 232
Hyundai Electronics Industries Corporation, **III** 517; **7** 233; **10** 404
Hyundai Engine and Machinery Co., **III** 516; **7** 232
Hyundai Engineering & Construction Co., **III** 515–17; **7** 231, 233
Hyundai Group, I 207, 516; **II** 53–54, 122; **III** 457–59, **515–17; 7** 231–34 **(upd.); 12** 546
Hyundai Heavy Industries Co., **III** 516–17; **7** 232
Hyundai Housing and Industrial Development Co., **III** 516; **7** 232
Hyundai Information Systems, **7** 234
Hyundai Merchant Marine Co., **III** 516; **7** 232
Hyundai Mipo Dockyard Co., **III** 516; **7** 232–33
Hyundai Motor America, **7** 234
Hyundai Motor Co., **III** 515–17, 596; **7** 231, 233; **9** 350
Hyundai Motors, **12** 293–94
Hyundai Precision & Industry Co., **III** 516; **7** 232
Hyundai Shipbuilding and Heavy Industries Co., **III** 516; **7** 232
Hyundai Wood Industries Co., **III** 516; **7** 232

I.C.H. Corp., **I** 528
I.C. Johnson and Co., **III** 669
I.D. Systems, Inc., **11** 444
I-DIKA Milan SRL, **12** 182
I.G. Chemie, **I** 337
I.G. Dyes. *See* IG Farben.
I.G. Farben. *See* I.G. Farbenindustrie AG.

I.G. Farbenindustrie AG, **I** 305–06, 309–11, 337, 346–53, 619, 632–33, 698–99; **II** 257; **III** 677, 694; **IV** 111, 485; **8** 108–09; **11** 7; **13** 75–76
I.J. Stokes Corp., **I** 383
I.M. Pei & Associates, **I** 580; **III** 267
I.M. Singer and Co., **II** 9
I. Magnin Inc., **8** 444
I/N Kote, **IV** 116
I/N Tek, **IV** 116
I.R. Maxwell & Co. Ltd., **IV** 641; **7** 311
I-T-E Circuit Breaker, **II** 121
Iacocca, Lee, **I** 145, 167, 188; **III** 544; **7** 205; **11** 54, 139
Iba, Teigo, **I** 519; **II** 360; **IV** 215; **11** 478
IBC Holdings Corporation, **12** 276
Ibe, Kyonosuke, **II** 361
Iberdrola, **V** 608
Iberia, **I** 110
Iberia, Compañia Aérea de Transportes, S.A. *See* Iberia Líneas Aéreas de España S.A.
Iberia Líneas Aéreas De España S.A., 6 95–97
Ibero-Amerika Bank, **II** 521
Iberstein, Robert, **III** 258
Iberswiss Catering, **6** 96
Ibex Engineering Co., **III** 420
IBH Holding AG, **7** 513
IBJ. *See* The Industrial Bank of Japan Ltd.
IBJ International, **II** 301
IBM. *See* International Business Machines Corporation.
IBM Credit Corp., **II** 440; **12** 148
IBM France, **12** 139
IBM Japan, **III** 139; **6** 428
IBM World Trade Corp., **III** 148
IBM-Japan, **12** 484
Ibn Saud, King (Saudi Arabia), **IV** 386, 536–37
IBP, inc., II 515–17; 7 525
Ibstock Johnsen, **III** 735
Ibstock plc, 14 248–50
Ibuka, Masaru, **II** 101–02; **12** 453–54
Ibuki, Kazuo, **II** 322
IC Industries Inc., I 456–58; III 512; **7** 430; **10** 414, 553
ICA AB, II 639–40
ICA Banan A.B., **II** 640
ICA Eol A.B., **II** 639
ICA Essve A.B., **II** 639
ICA Frukt och Grönsaker A.B., **II** 639
ICA Hakon A.B., **II** 639
ICA Mortgage Corporation, **8** 30
ICA Rosteri A.B., **II** 640
ICA Technologies, Ltd., **III** 533
ICA-förlaget A.B., **II** 640
Icahn, Carl, **I** 123, 127, 426; **II** 408; **IV** 523, 553, 574; **7** 551; **8** 106; **12** 87, 311, 487, 489; **13** 41
ICE, **I** 333
Ichihara, Akira, **V** 143
Ichikawa, Shinobu, **I** 492
Ichimura, Kiyoshi, **III** 159; **8** 278
ICI. *See* Imperial Chemical Industries plc.
ICI Americas, Inc., **8** 179, 222
ICI Colours, **9** 154
ICI Membranes, **11** 361
ICI Paints, **8** 222
Ickes, Harold L., **IV** 121, 552
ICL plc, II 65; **III** 141; **6 240–42; 11** 150
ICL-KMECS, **6** 242
ICM Mortgage Corporation, **8** 436
ICOA Life Insurance, **III** 253

ICS. *See* International Care Services.
ICX, **IV** 136
ID, Inc., **9** 193
Idaho Frozen Foods, **II** 572–73
Idaho Power & Light Company, **12** 265
Idaho Power Company, 12 265–67
Idaho Railway, **12** 265
Idaho-Oregon Light & Power Company, **12** 265
IDB Broadcast, **11** 183–84
IDB Communications Group, Inc., 11 183–85
IDB Mobile, **11** 183
IDB Systems, **11** 183–84
IDB WorldCom, **11** 183–85
Ide, Chandler, **6** 353
Ide Megumi, **III** 549
Ideal Basic Industries, **III** 701–02; **8** 258–59; **12** 18
Ideal Corp., **III** 602
Ideka, Mochimasa, **III** 383–84
Idema, Walter D., **7** 493–94
Idemitso Petrochemicals, **8** 153
Idemitsu & Co., **IV** 434
Idemitsu Geothermal Development Co. Ltd., **IV** 435–36
Idemitsu Japanese Sea Oil Development Co. Ltd., **IV** 435
Idemitsu, Keisuke, **IV** 435
Idemitsu Kosan K.K., II 361; **IV 434–36**, 476
Idemitsu Myanmar Oil Exploration Co. Ltd., **IV** 519
Idemitsu Oil & Gas Co. Ltd., **IV** 435
Idemitsu Oil Development Co. Ltd., **IV** 435, 519
Idemitsu Petrochemical Co. Ltd., **I** 330; **IV** 435, 519
Idemitsu, Sazou, **IV** 434–35
Idemitsu Tanker Co. Ltd., **IV** 435
Idestam, Knut Fredrik, **IV** 314
IDG Communications, Inc, **7** 238
IDG World Expo Corporation, **7** 239
IDO. *See* Nippon Idou Tsushin.
Idris, King (Libya), **IV** 480–81
IEL. *See* Industrial Equity Ltd.
IFI, **I** 161–62; **III** 347
IFS Industries, **6** 294
IG Farben. *See* I.G. Farbenindustrie AG.
IGA, **II** 624, 649, 668, 681–82; **7** 451
Iggesund Bruk, **IV** 317–18
IGT-International, **10** 375–76
IGT-North America, **10** 375
Ihamuotila, Jaakko, **IV** 471
IHI, **I** 534
IHI Granitech Corp., **III** 533
Iida & Co., **I** 493
Iida, Seizo, **II** 439; **9** 384
Iida, Shinshichi, **V** 193
Iiguchi, Jiro, **V** 680
IinteCom, **III** 169
IISCO-Ujjain Pipe and Foundry Co. Ltd., **IV** 206
Ikawa family, **IV** 266
IKEA Group, V 82–84
IKEA International A/S of Denmark, **V** 82
IKEA-Belgium, **V** 65
Ikeda, Ichiro, **II** 277
Ikeda, Kikunae, **II** 463
Ikeda, Nariaki, **II** 291
Ikeda, Seihin, **I** 507
Ikeda, Shigeaki, **II** 325
Ikeura, Kisaburo, **II** 301
Ikuta, Hiizu, **I** 220

Intrac Handelsgesellschaft mbH, **7** 142
Intradal, **II** 572
Intraph South Africa Ltd., **6** 247
IntraWest Bank, **II** 289
IntroGene B.V., **13** 241
Intuit Inc., **13** 147; **14 262–64**
Invacare Corporation, **11 200–02**, 486
Invep S.p.A., **10** 150
Inveresk Paper Co., **III** 693; **IV** 685
Invergordon Distillers, **III** 509
Inversale, **9** 92
Investors Diversified Services, Inc., **II** 398;
   6 199; **8** 348–49; **10** 43–45, 59, 62
Investors DS, **10** 44
Investors Group, **III** 261
Investors Management Corp., **10** 331
Investors Overseas Services, **10** 368–69
Invista Capital Management, **III** 330
Iolab Corp., **III** 36
Ionpure Technologies Corporation, **6**
   486–88
Iowa Beef Packers, **II** 515–16; **IV** 481–82
Iowa Beef Processors, **II** 516–17; **13** 351
Iowa Light, Heat and Power, **6** 523
Iowa Manufacturing, **II** 86
Iowa Power, **6** 525
Iowa Public Service Company, **6** 524–25
Iowa Resources, Inc., **6** 523
IP Gas Supply Company, **6** 506
IP Services, Inc., **IV** 597
IP Timberlands Ltd., **IV** 288
IP&L. *See* Illinois Power & Light
   Corporation.
Ipalco Enterprises, Inc., **6 508–09**
IPC Magazines Limited, **IV** 650; **7
   244–47**
Ipko-Amcor, **14** 225
IPSOA Editore, **14** 555
Ira J. Cooper, **8** 127
Iran Air, **6** 101
Iran Pan American Oil Co., **IV** 466
Irani, Ray, **IV** 481
Iranian Offshore Oil Co. of the Islamic
   Republic, **IV** 467
Iranian Oil Exploration and Producing Co.,
   IV 466–67
Iranian Oil Refining Co., **IV** 466
Iraq Petroleum Co., **IV** 363, 386, 429, 450,
   464, 558–60
Irby, Tom, **11** 61
Irby-Gilliland Company, **9** 127
Ireland, Charles, **10** 44
Ireland, Charles Lincoln, **7** 572, 575
Ireland, Charles T., **II** 133; **6** 158
Ireland, Charles W., **7** 573
Ireland, Norman, **IV** 259
Ireland, Richard, **12** 442–43
Irgens, Finn T., **III** 598
IRI. *See* Instituto per la Ricostruzione
   Industriale.
IRIS Holding Co., **III** 347
Irish Paper Sacks Ltd., **IV** 295
Irish Sugar Co., **II** 508
Iron and Steel Corp., **IV** 22, 41, 92,
   533–34
Iron Cliffs Mining Company, **13** 156
Iron Mountain Forge, **13** 319
Iron Ore Company of Canada, **8** 347
Iroquois Gas Corporation, **6** 526
Irrgang, William, **13** 315–16
Irvin, Tinsley, **10** 38
Irvin, William E., **11** 554
Irving Bank Corp., **II** 192
Irving, David, **7** 578

Irving, John, **III** 372
Irving Trust Co., **II** 257
Irvington Smelting, **IV** 78
Irwin Lehrhoff Associates, **11** 366
Irwin Toy Limited, **14 265–67**
Irwin, Will G., **I** 146; **12** 89
Irwin, William G., **9** 274
Isabela Shoe Corporation, **13** 360
Iscor. *See* Iron and Steel Corporation.
Isenberg, Eugene M., **9** 364
Isenberg, Leslie, **11** 366
Isetan Company Limited, **V 85–87**
Isetan Finance Company, Ltd., **V** 87
Isetan Research Institute Company, Ltd., **V**
   87
Iseya Tanji Drapery, **V** 85
Isham, Ralph H. (Col.), **IV** 636
Ishibashi, Kanichiro, **V** 234
Ishibashi, Shojiro, **V** 234
Ishida, Taizo, **III** 637
Ishigami, Minoru, **IV** 298
Ishii, Susumu, **9** 379, 386
Ishikawajima Airplane Manufacturing Co.,
   III 532
Ishikawajima Automobile Manufacturing
   Co., **III** 532
Ishikawajima Automobile Manufacturing,
   Ltd., **9** 293
Ishikawajima Heavy Industries, **12** 484
Ishikawajima Heavy Industry Co., Ltd., **III**
   513, 532–33
Ishikawajima Hirano Shipyard, **III** 532
Ishikawajima Shibaura Turbine Co., **III**
   532
Ishikawajima Shipyard Co., Ltd., **III** 532
Ishikawajima Systems Technology Co., **III**
   533
**Ishikawajima-Harima Heavy Industries
   Co., Ltd.**, **I** 508, 511, 534; **II** 274; **III
   532–33**
Ishimoto, Shizue, **IV** 147
Ishizaki Honten, **III** 715
Ishizuka, Yozo, **III** 604–05
Isis Distributed Systems, Inc., **10** 501
Island Holiday, **I** 417
Isobe, Ritsuo, **6** 30
Isoda, Ichiro, **II** 361
Isolite Insulating Products Co., **III** 714
Isosceles PLC, **II** 628–29
Isotec Communications Incorporated, **13**
   213
Isover, **III** 676
ISS International Service System, Inc., **8**
   271
Issenmann, Nico, **6** 11
Istanbul Fertilizer Industry, **IV** 563
Istituto di Ricostruzione Industriale (IRI),
   13 28, 218
Istituto per la Ricostruzione Industriale,
   I 207, 459, **465–67**; **II** 191–92, 270–71;
   IV 419
**Istituto per la Ricostruzione Industriale
   S.p.A.**, **11 203–06**
Istock, Verne G., **11** 341
Isuzu Motors, Ltd., **II** 274; **III** 581, 593;
   7 8, 219; **9 293–95**; **10** 354
IT International, **V** 255
Itabira Iron Ore Co. Ltd., **IV** 54
ITABRASCO, **IV** 55
Itakura, Joji, **II** 326
Italcarta, **IV** 339
Italcementi, **IV** 420
Italiatour, **6** 69
Italmobiliare, **III** 347

Italstate. *See* Societa per la Infrastrutture e
   l'Assetto del Territorio.
Italtel, **V** 326–27
Itaú Winterthur Seguradura S.A., **III** 404
Itek Corp., **I** 486; **11** 265
Itel Corporation, **II** 64; **III** 512; **6** 262,
   354; **9** 49, **296–99**
Ithaca Gas & Electric. *See* New York State
   Electric and Gas.
Ithaca Gas Light Company, **6** 534
ITM International, **IV** 239
Ito Bank, **II** 373
Ito Carnation Co., **II** 518
Ito, Denzo, **II** 518
Ito Food Processing Co., **II** 518
Ito Gofuku Co. Ltd., **V** 129
Ito Ham Co. Ltd., **II** 518
Ito Ham Provisions Co. Ltd., **II** 518
Ito, Jirozaemon, **V** 130
Ito, Kenichi, **II** 518
Ito, Masatoshi, **V** 88
Ito Meat Processing Co., **II** 518
Ito, Morimatsu, **V** 129
Ito Processed Food Co., **II** 518
Ito, Tatsuji, **IV** 714
Ito, Yasuhisa, **V** 89
Ito, Yudo, **V** 129
Ito-Yokado Co., Ltd., **II** 661; **V 88–89**
Itochu and Renown, Inc., **12** 281
Itochu of Japan, **14** 550
Itoh. *See* C. Itoh & Co.
Itoh, Chubei, **I** 431, 492
Itoh, Chubei, II, **I** 431, 492
Itoh, Junji, **I** 106
Itoham Foods Inc., **II 518–19**
Itokin, **III** 48
ITT. *See* International Telephone and
   Telegraph Corporation.
ITT Corp., **III** 98, 164, 166, 645, 684; **9**
   10–11, 324; **11** 516. *See also*
   International Telephone & Telegraph
   Corporation.
ITT Grinnell Corp., **13** 246
ITT Sheraton Corporation, **III 98–101**
ITW. *See* Illinois Tool Works Inc.
ITW Devcon, **12** 7
Iue, Kaoru, **II** 91–92
Iue, Satoshi, **II** 92
Iue, Toshio, **II** 55, 91–92
Iue, Yuro, **II** 91
IURA Edition, **14** 556
IVAC Corp., **I** 646; **11** 90
IVACO Industries Inc., **11** 207
Ivanhoe, Inc., **II** 662, 664
IVAX Corporation, **11 207–09**
Iveagh (Earl of), **I** 251
Iveco, **I** 148; **12** 91
Iverson, F. Kenneth, **7** 400–02
Ives, **I** 623
Ives, J. Atwood, **I** 245; **6** 487–88
Ivory, James, **III** 360
Ivy, Robert E., **I** 682
Iwadare, Kunihiko, **II** 66–67
Iwai & Co., **I** 492, 509–10; **IV** 151
Iwai, Bunsuke, **I** 509
Iwamura, Eiro, **IV** 125
Iwasa, Yoshizane, **II** 292
Iwasaki family, **II** 57; **III** 577
Iwasaki, Koyata, **I** 503; **12** 341
Iwasaki, Toshiya, **III** 666
Iwasaki, Yanosuke, **I** 265, 503; **IV** 713; **12**
   341
Iwasaki, Yanosuki, **12** 341

Katz, Emmanuel, **6** 32
Katz, Eugene, **6** 32
Katz, George R., **6** 32
Katz, Gustave David, **12** 286–87
Katz, Nathan, **I** 665
Katzenberg, Jeffrey, **6** 176
Katzman, James A., **6** 278
Kauffman, Erwing Marion, **I** 648–49; **9** 328
Kauffman-Lattimer, **III** 9–10
Kaufhalle AG, **V** 104
Kaufhof, **II** 257
Kaufhof Holding AG, V 103–05
Kaufhof Mode und Sport GmbH, **V** 104
Kaufman and Broad Home Corporation, 8 284–86; 11 481–83
Kaufman, Armin, **III** 645
Kaufman, Don, **8** 284
Kaufman, Donald, **11** 481
Kaufman, Henry, **II** 448; **13** 448
Kaufman, Mitchell B., **9** 133
Kaufman, Stephen, **10** 113
Kaufman, Victor, **II** 137; **12** 75
Kaufmann, Abraham, **III** 290
Kaufmann's, **V** 132–33
Kaufmann's Department Stores, **6** 243
Kaukaan Tehdas Osakeyhtiö, **IV** 301
Oy Kaukas Ab, **IV** 300–02
Kaukas Oy, **IV** 302
Kaunda, Kenneth D., **IV** 18, 239–41
Kauppaosakeyhtiö Kymmene Aktiebolag, **IV** 299
Kauppiaitten Oy, **8** 293
Kautex Werke Reinold Hagen AG, **IV** 128
Kautex-Bayern GmbH, **IV** 128
Kautex-Ostfriedland GmbH, **IV** 128
Kawachi Bank, **II** 361
Kawada, Ganyemon, **I** 519; **11** 478
Kawai, Ryoichi, **III** 545–46
Kawai, Yoshinari, **III** 545
Kawakami, Gen'ichi, **III** 657
Kawakami, Kaichi, **III** 657
Kawamata, **11** 350
Kawamata, Katsuji, **I** 183
Kawamoto, Nobuhiko, **10** 354
Kawamura, Teijiro, **V** 473
Kawanto, Nobuhiko, **III** 549
Kawasaki Aircraft Co., **III** 539
Kawasaki Aircraft Heavy Industries, **III** 539
Kawasaki Denki Seizo, **II** 22
Kawasaki Dockyard Co., Ltd., **III** 538–39; **IV** 124
Kawasaki Heavy Industries, Ltd., I 75; **II** 273–74; **III** 482, 513, 516, **538–40,** 756; **IV** 124; **7** 232; **8** 72
Kawasaki Kisen Kaisha, Ltd., V 457–60
Kawasaki Rolling Stock, **III** 539
Kawasaki, Shozo, **III** 538; **IV** 124
Kawasaki Steel Corporation, I 432; **II** 274; **III** 539, 760; **IV** 30, **124–25,** 154, 212–13; **13** 324
Kawasaki, Yaemon, **6** 430
Kawasaki Zosenjo, **V** 457–58
Kawase, Jiro, **III** 715
Kawashima, Hiroshi, **III** 658
Kawashima, Kiyoshi, **I** 175
Kawashimaya Securities Co., **II** 433
Kawashimaya Shoten Inc. Ltd., **II** 433
Kawazoe, Soichi, **I** 183–84; **11** 350
Kawecki Berylco Industries, **8** 78
Kawneer Aluminum GmbH., **IV** 18
Kawneer Co., **IV** 18
Kawneer G.m.b.H., **IV** 18

Kawsmouth Electric Light Company. *See* Kansas City Power & Light Company.
Kay County Gas Co., **IV** 399
Kay, Jean, **I** 45
Kay's Drive-In Food Service, **II** 619
Kay-Bee Toy and Hobby Shops, Inc., **V** 137
Kaye, Marvin, **III** 504
Kayex, **9** 251
Kaynar Manufacturing Company, **8** 366
Kayser Agricultural Chemicals, **8** 229
Kayser Aluminum & Chemicals, **8** 229
Kayser, Paul, **12** 144
Kayser-Roth, **8** 288
Kaysersberg, S.A., **IV** 290
Kazan, Elia, **II** 175
Kazarian, Paul B., **9** 485
KBLCOM Incorporated, **V** 644
KC Holdings, Inc., **11** 229–30
KCPL. *See* Kansas City Power & Light Company.
KCS Industries, **12** 25–26
KCSI. *See* Kansas City Southern Industries, Inc.
KCSR. *See* Kansas City Southern Railway.
KDT Industries, Inc., **9** 20
Keady, William L., **III** 763
Kean, Bruce R., **III** 674
Keane, Stephen J., **11** 274
Kearns, David T., **6** 290
Keating, Charles, **III** 191; **9** 199; **10** 340
Keating, Paul, **IV** 652; **7** 391
Keaton, Buster, **II** 146
Keay, John (Sir), **III** 690–91
Keck, Donald, **III** 684
Keck, George, **I** 129; **6** 128–29
Keebler Co., **II** 594
Keebler, Godfrey, **II** 594
Keefe Manufacturing Courtesy Coffee Company, **6** 392
Keefe, Thomas J., **8** 322
Keeler, William, **IV** 522–23
Keen, Arthur, **III** 493
Keen, Arthur T., **III** 493
Keen, Robinson and Co., **II** 566
Keene, W.C.L., **III** 272
KEG Productions Ltd., **IV** 640
Kehaya, Ery, Sr., **13** 490–91
Kehaya, Ery W., **13** 491
Kehaya, Grace Whitaker, **13** 490
Kehrl, Howard, **7** 461
Kei, Hara, **III** 408
Keiffer, E. Gene, **9** 183–84
Keihan JUSCO, **V** 96
Keil Chemical Company, **8** 178
Keil, Jeffrey C., **11** 416–17
Keio Teito Electric Railway Company, V 461–62
Keir, John S., **IV** 252
Keisei Electric Railway, **II** 301
Keiser, Robert, **7** 415
Keith, John, **V** 401
Keith, Kenneth, **I** 82
Keith, Max, **I** 233; **10** 226
Keith, Minor, **II** 595
Keith of Castleacre (Lord), **III** 164
Keith, Robert J., **II** 556; **13** 408
Keith, William H., **9** 222
Keith-Albee-Orpheum, **II** 88
Kekkonen, Urho (Dr.), **IV** 469
Kelce, David, **7** 33
Kelce, Merl, **IV** 170; **7** 32
Kelce, Russell, **IV** 170; **10** 447–48
Kelce, Ted, **IV** 170

Kell, Eliza, **I** 267
Kelleher, Herbert D., **6** 119–21
Keller, Gottfried, **III** 376, 410
Keller, J.P., **12** 406
Keller, Mark, **9** 112
Kelley & Partners, Ltd., **14** 130
Kelley, Gaynor N., **7** 425, 427
Kelley, Jack, **8** 256
Kelley, Wendell J., **6** 506–07
Kelley, William V., **7** 29
Kellock, **10** 336
Kellogg, Amherst W., **III** 321
Kellogg Company, I 22–23; **II** 463, 502–03, **523–26,** 530, 560; **10** 323–24; **13** 3, **291–94 (upd.)**
Kellogg Food Co., **II** 523
Kellogg, John Harvey, **II** 523; **13** 291–92
Kellogg, John L., **II** 523–24; **13** 291–92
Kellogg, Leonard Lamb, **6** 523
Kellogg, Robert H., **III** 237–38
Kellogg Toasted Corn Flake Co., **II** 523
Kellogg, Will Keith, **II** 523–25; **13** 291–92
Kellogg's, **12** 411
Kellum, John, **9** 369
Kellwood Asia Ltd., **8** 289
Kellwood Company, V 181–82; **8 287–89**
Kelly & Associates, **III** 306
Kelly & Cohen, **10** 468
Kelly Assisted Living Services, Inc., **6** 37
Kelly, Donald, **I** 441; **II** 468–69
Kelly, Douglas and Co., **II** 631
Kelly, Edwin S., **8** 290
Kelly Girl Service, Inc. *See* Kelly Services Inc.
Kelly Health Care, **6** 36–37
Kelly Home Care. *See* Kelly Health Care.
Kelly, James, **IV** 682
Kelly, James B., **I** 584
Kelly Nason, Inc., **13** 203
Kelly, Richard, **6** 35
Kelly, Russell. *See* Kelly, William Russell.
Kelly Services, Inc., 6 35–37, 140; **9** 326
Kelly, Walt, **IV** 672
Kelly, William Russell, **6** 35–36
The Kelly-Springfield Tire Company, 8 290–92
Kelm, Erwin, **II** 617; **13** 137
Kelman, Bryan, **III** 687, 737–39
Kelsey, Harold, **9** 245
Kelsey, John, **7** 258
Kelsey Wheel Company, **7** 258
Kelsey-Hayes Corp., **I** 170; **III** 650, 652; **7** 258–60
Kelsey-Hayes Group of Companies, 7 258–60
Kelsey-Hayes Wheel Company, **7** 258
Kelso & Co., **III** 663, 665; **12** 436
Kelty, Gibbons L., **13** 168
Kelty Pack, Inc., **10** 215
Kelty, William, **13** 168
KemaNobel, **9** 380–81; **13** 22
KemaNord, **9** 380
Kemet Corp., 14 281–83
Kemi Oy, **IV** 316
Kemira, **III** 760
Kemira, Inc., **6** 152
Kemira-Ube, **III** 760
Kemoularia, Claude de, **II** 259
Kemp's Biscuits Limited, **II** 594
Kemp-Welch, John, **II** 476–77
Kempe, Carl, **IV** 317–18
Kempe, Erik, **IV** 318
Kempe, Frans, **IV** 317

Khomeini, Ruholla (Ayatollah), **I** 261; **III** 137
Khoo, Tan Sri, **II** 358
Khosla, Vinod, **7** 498
Khouri, Barbara, **12** 94
Khrushchev, Nikita, **I** 277; **13** 365
Kia Motors, **I** 167
Kia Motors America, **12** 293–94
Kia Motors Corp., 12 293–95
Kianka, Frances, **I** 46
Kidd, Walter, **11** 493–94
Kidde Inc., I 475–76; **III** 503; **7** 209
Kidde, John, **I** 476
Kidde, Walter, **I** 475–76
Kidder, C. Robert, **9** 179–80, 344
Kidder, Peabody & Co., **II** 31, 207, 430; **IV** 84; **7** 310; **12** 197; **13** 465–67, 534
Kidder Press Co., **IV** 644
Kids ''R'' Us, **V** 203–05; **9** 394
Kids Foot Locker, **14** 293, 295
Kidston Mines, **I** 438
Kiekhaefer Corp., **III** 443
Kiely, W. Leo, **13** 11
Kien, **13** 545
Kienzle Apparate GmbH, **III** 566
Kiernan, Peter D., **9** 229
Kierulff Electronics, **10** 113
Kieser Verlag, **14** 555
Kiewit Diversified Group Inc., **11** 301
Kiewit, Peter, **8** 422–24
Kifer, E. H., **6** 473
Kijkshop/Best-Sellers, **13** 545
Kikawada, Kazutaka, **V** 730–31
Kikkoman, **I** 9
Kikkoman Corporation, 14 287–89
Kikuchi, Minori, **III** 386
Kikuchi, Shojiro, **V** 483
Kikumoto, Naojiro, **II** 325
Kilbourne, E. C., **6** 565
Kilburn & Co., **III** 522
Kilby, Jack S., **II** 113; **11** 506
Kilgo Motor Express, **6** 370
Kilgore, Barney, **IV** 602
Kilgore Ceramics, **III** 671
Kilgore Federal Savings and Loan Assoc., **IV** 343
Kilgour, Charles H., **6** 316
Killam, Izaak Walton, **6** 585–86
Killen, Robert, **6** 481
Kilmartin, John, **10** 409
Kilmer, Fred B., **III** 35; **8** 281
Kilmer, Joyce, **III** 35
Kilpatrick, Lester L., **13** 126–27
Kilpatrick, Robert D., **III** 226
Kilroy, Howard, **12** 529
Kilsby Tubesupply, **I** 570
Kim, Suk Joon, **III** 749
Kim, Suk Won, **III** 748–50
Kim, Sung Kon, **III** 747–48
Kim, Woo Choong, **III** 457–59
Kimball, David, **III** 644; **9** 251
Kimball Europe P.L.C., **12** 297
Kimball, Frederick, **V** 484
Kimball Furniture Reproductions, Inc., **12** 297
Kimball Healthcare Co., **12** 297
Kimball Hospitality Furniture, Inc., **12** 297
Kimball International, Inc., 12 296–98
Kimball International Transit, Inc., **12** 296
Kimball, Justin Ford, Dr., **10** 159
Kimball Music Center, **12** 296
Kimball Office Furniture, **12** 297
Kimball Piano, **12** 296
Kimball, W.W., Company, **12** 296

Kimbell Inc., **II** 684
Kimberley Central Mining Co., **IV** 64; **7** 121
Kimberly & Clark Co., **III** 40; **IV** 648
Kimberly, Clark & Co., **III** 40
Kimberly, John A., **III** 40
Kimberly, Michael J., **13** 61
Kimberly-Clark Australia Ltd., **IV** 249
Kimberly-Clark Corporation, I 14, 413; **III** 36, **40–41**; **IV** 249, 254, 297–98, 329, 665; **8** 282
Kimco Realty Corporation, 11 228–30
Kimco, S.A. de C.V., **12** 297
Kimes, Beverly Rae, **I** 151
Kimmel, Martin S., **11** 228
Kimmel, Sidney, **11** 216–18
Kincaid Furniture Company, **14** 302–03
Kindelberger, James, **I** 78–79
Kindelberger, James Howard, **11** 427–28
Kinden Corporation, **7** 303
KinderCare Learning Centers, Inc., 13 298–300
Kinear Moodie, **III** 753
King, Albert E., **III** 360
King, Alexander, **IV** 672
King Bearing, Inc., **13** 79
King, Cecil Harmsworth, **IV** 666; **7** 342–43
King, Charles, **9** 306
King, Chuck, **I** 184; **11** 351
King Cullen, **II** 644
King, Don, **6** 211
King Features Syndicate, **IV** 626
King Folding Box Co., **13** 441
King Fook Gold and Jewellery Co., **IV** 717
King, Frank, **II** 289
King, George E.B., **13** 124
King, J.B., **III** 762
King, John (Lord), **I** 94
King, Mackenzie, **6** 360
King, Martin Luther, Jr., **I** 420, 449; **II** 634
King, Michael, **9** 306
King, Olin, **9** 463–64
King Ranch, Inc., 14 290–92
King, Rodney, **12** 477
King, Roger, **9** 306–07
King, Rollin, **6** 119
King Soopers Inc., **12** 112–13
King, W. Frank III, **6** 255
King World Productions, Inc., 9 306–08
King World's Camelot Entertainment, **9** 306
King's Lynn Glass, **12** 528
King-Seeley Thermos, **II** 419
Kingfisher plc, V 106–09; **10** 498
Kingly, William C., **II** 312
Kings County Lighting Company, **6** 456
Kings County Research Laboratories, **11** 424
Kings Mills, Inc., **13** 532
Kingsbury, J.E., **III** 162
Kingsford Corp., **III** 21
Kingsford-Smith, Charles (Sir), **I** 54
Kingsin Line, **6** 397
Kingsley, Darwin, **III** 316
Kingsley, Francis G., **V** 139–40
Kingsmill, W.H. (Lt. Col.), **IV** 723
Kingsport Pulp Corp., **IV** 310
Kinigstein, Joseph, **12** 37
Kinki Nippon Railway Company Ltd., V 463–65
Kinko's, **12** 174
Kinnear, Thomas C., **II** 344
Kinnevik, **IV** 203–04

Kinney, Alva, **II** 493; **12** 80
Kinney, E. Robert, **II** 502–03; **10** 323–24; **13** 243–44
Kinney National Service Inc., **II** 176; **IV** 672
Kinney, Samuel, **IV** 346
Kinney Services, **6** 293
Kinney Shoe Corp., V 226; **11** 349; **14** 293–95
Kinney Tobacco Co., **12** 108
Kinoshita Sansho Steel Co., **I** 508
Kinross, **IV** 92
Kinsella, John, **I** 23
Kintec Corp., **10** 97
Kintigh, Allen E., **6** 536
Kipfmuller, Emil, **II** 163
Kirby, **III** 214. *See also* Scott Fetzer Company.
Kirby, Allan, Jr., **10** 44
Kirby, Allan P., **IV** 180; **10** 43–44
Kirby Forest Industries, **IV** 305
Kirby, Fred, **10** 43
Kirby, Fred, II, **10** 44–45
Kirby, Fred M., **V** 224–25
Kirby, Luke, Jr., **12** 54–55
Kirby, Robert, **II** 121–22; **12** 545–46
Kirch Group, **10** 196
Kirch, Leo, **IV** 591
Kircher, Donald P., **II** 10
Kircher, John, **IV** 401
Kirchner, Moore, and Co., **II** 408
Kirchoff, Donald J., **II** 491–92
Kirdorf, Adolph, **I** 542
Kirdorf, Emil, **I** 542
Kirin Brewery Co., I 258, **265–66**, 282; **10** 78, 80; **13** 258, 454
Kirin-Seagram Ltd., **I** 266
Kirk, Desault B., **II** 14
Kirk Stieff Company, **10** 181; **12** 313
Kirkstall Forge Engineering, **III** 494
Kirkwood, Robert C., **V** 225
Kirman, Ernest, **II** 594
Kirn, W.H., **I** 622
Kirsch Co., **II** 16
Kirschner, Sidney, **11** 338
Kirstein, Louis, **V** 26
Kirwan, Thomas, **III** 249
Kishimoto & Co., **I** 432, 492
Kishimoto Shoten Co., Ltd., **IV** 168
Kissel, R., **IV** 140
Kissel, Wilhelm, **I** 138; **11** 31
Kissinger, Henry, **II** 248; **III** 197; **13** 146
Kisskalt, Wilhelm, **III** 300
Kistler, Lesh & Co., **III** 528
Kistler, William, **III** 429
Kistner, Erik, **I** 625
Kita Karafunto Oil Co., **IV** 475
Kita Nippon Paper Co., **IV** 321
Kitagawa & Co. Ltd., **IV** 442
Kitagawa, Yohei, **IV** 442
Kitaura, Kiichiro, **II** 440; **9** 385
Kitchell Corporation, 14 296–98
Kitchen, Lawrence, **I** 66; **11** 268
KitchenAid, III 611, 653–54; **8 298–99**
Kitchenbell, **III** 43
Kitchens of Sara Lee, **II** 571–73
Kittery Electric Light Co., **14** 124
Kittinger, **10** 324
Kittredge, Rufus J., **9** 61–62
Kittredge, William, **IV** 661
Kivekas, Lauri, **II** 302
Kiwi Packaging, **IV** 250
Kjøbenhavns Bandelsbank, **II** 366
KJPCL. *See* Royal Interocean Lines.

LIGHTNET, **IV** 576
Lightwell Co., **III** 634
Lignum Oil Co., **IV** 658
Liguori, Frank N., **6** 42–43
LILCO. *See* Long Island Lighting
  Company.
Liliuokalani, **I** 565
Lillard, John, **IV** 703
Lillehei, C. Walton, **8** 351
de Lilliac, René Granier. *See* Granier de
  Lilliac, René.
Lillian Vernon Corp., 12 314–15
Lillie, John M., **6** 355
Lilliput Group plc, **11** 95
Lilly & Co. *See* Eli Lilly & Co.
Lilly, David, **7** 534–35
Lilly, Eli, **I** 645; **11** 89
Lilly, Eli, Jr., **11** 89
Lilly, Josiah, **I** 645; **11** 89
Lilly, Josiah, Jr., **I** 645; **11** 89
Lillybrook Coal Co., **IV** 180
Lillywhites Ltd., **III** 105
Lily Tulip Co., **I** 609, 611
Lily-Tulip Inc., **8** 198
Limbaugh, Rush, **11** 330
Limburger Fabrik und Hüttenverein, **IV**
  103
Limited Express, **V** 115
The Limited, Inc., V 115–16; 9 142; **12**
  280, 356
Limmer and Trinidad Ltd., **III** 752
LIN Broadcasting Corp., II 331; **6** 323; **9**
  320–22; **11** 330
Lin Data Corp., **11** 234
Lincoln, Abraham, **II** 247, 284; **III** 239,
  275, 315, 505; **IV** 604, 647, 668, 682; **8**
  222; **11** 186; **13** 465
Lincoln American Life Insurance Co., **10**
  246
Lincoln Benefit Life Company, **10** 51
Lincoln Electric Co., II 19; **13 314–16**
Lincoln Electric Motor Works, **9** 439
Lincoln First Bank, **II** 248
Lincoln Income Life Insurance Co., **10** 246
Lincoln, James Finney, **13** 314–15
Lincoln, John, **9** 439
Lincoln, John C., **13** 314
Lincoln, Leroy A., **III** 292
Lincoln Liberty Life Insurance Co., **III** 254
Lincoln Life Improved Housing, **III** 276
Lincoln Motor Co., **I** 165
Lincoln National Corporation, **III**
  274–77; **6** 195; **10** 44
Lincoln National Life Insurance Co., **III**
  274–76
Lincoln Philippine Life Insurance Co., **III**
  276
Lincoln Property Company, 8 326–28
Lincoln, Robert, **11** 385
Lincoln, Robert Todd, **III** 274
Lincoln Savings, **10** 340
Lincoln Savings & Loan, **9** 199
Lincoln Telephone & Telegraph
  Company, 14 311–13
LinCom Corp., **8** 327
Lindbergh, Charles, **12** 487
Lindbergh, Charles A., **I** 78, 89, 125; **II**
  151; **III** 27, 251; **IV** 370; **7** 35; **9** 416;
  11 427
Lindblom, C.G., **III** 478
Linde A.G., I 297–98, 315, **581–83**; **10**
  31–32
Linde Air Products Co., **I** 582; **9** 16, 516;
  11 402

Linde Company, **11** 402–03
Lindemann, Karl, **6** 398
Lindemann's, **I** 220
Linden, Arthur, **II** 2
Linder, David, **V** 442
Lindex, **II** 640
Lindh, Björnz-Eric, **I** 211
Lindner, Carl Henry, **I** 453; **II** 596, 619;
  III 190–92; **7** 84–86; **8** 537; **9** 452; **10**
  73
Lindner, Carl, **III**, **10** 74
Lindner, Richard E., **III** 190
Lindner, Robert D., **III** 190
Lindsay Parkinson & Co., **I** 567
Lindstrom, Raymond, **13** 435–36
Lindustries, **III** 502; **7** 208
Linear Corp., **III** 643
Líneas Aéreas Postales Españolas, **6** 95
Linehan, Joel, **III** 430
Linen, James A., **III**, **IV** 674; **7** 527
Linen, Jonathon, **9** 470
Linens 'n Things, **13** 81–82
Linfood Cash & Carry, **13** 103
Linfood Holdings Ltd., **II** 628–29
Ling Electric Co., **I** 489
Ling Electronics Inc., **I** 489
Ling, James J., **I** 489–91
Ling Products, **12** 25
Ling-Temco-Vought. *See* LTV Corporation.
Lingren, G. Douglas, **13** 274
Linjeflyg, **I** 120
Link, Gordon, **6** 16
Link House Publications PLC, **IV** 687
Link-Belt Corp., **I** 443; **IV** 660
Linkletter, Art, **IV** 83; **7** 187
Linquist, E. Gunnard, **12** 6
Lint, Amos, **I** 201
Lintas: Worldwide, I 18; **6** 30; **14**
  314–16
Linton, Robert E., **II** 407–08; **8** 388–89
Lintott Engineering, Ltd., **10** 108
Lion Corporation, III 44–45
Lion Dentrifice Co., Ltd., **III** 44
Lion Fat & Oil Co., Ltd., **III** 44
Lion Manufacturing, **III** 430
Lion Oil, **I** 365
Lion Products Co., Ltd., **III** 44
Lion Soap Co., Ltd., **III** 44
Lion's Head Brewery, **I** 290
Lionel, **12** 494
Lionex Corporation, **13** 46
Lipetzky, Paul A., **13** 348
Lipman, Frederick, **II** 382
Lipman, Frederick L., **12** 535
Lipper, Kenneth, **I** 631
Lippert, Al, **12** 530–31
Lippert, Felice, **12** 530–31
Lippincott & Margulies, **III** 283
Lippincott, Philip E., **IV** 330–31
Lippincott-Raven Publishers, **14** 556
Lipson, Norman S., **II** 649
Lipton, 1i 450
Liptons, **II** 609, 657
Liquid Carbonic, **7** 74, 77
Liquor Barn, **II** 656
Liquorland, **V** 35
Liquorsave, **II** 609–10
LIRCA, **III** 48
Lisbon Coal and Oil Fuel Co., **IV** 504
Liscaya, **II** 196
Lissarrague, Pierre, **I** 46
Lister, Joseph, **III** 35
Litchfield, Paul W., **V** 244–46
Litco Bancorp., **II** 192

Litho-Krome Corp., **IV** 621
Litronix, **III** 455
Little, Arthur D., **IV** 92
Little, Brown & Company, **IV** 675; **7** 528;
  10 355
Little Caesar International, Inc., 7
  278–79; **7** 278–79
Little Chef Ltd., **III** 105–06
Little General, **II** 620; **12** 179, 200
Little Giant Pump Company, **8** 515
Little Leather Library, **13** 105
Little, Royal, **I** 529–30; **8** 545; **13** 63
Little Tikes Co., III 614; **12** 169; **13**
  317–19
Little, W. Norris, **9** 466
Littlewoods Mail Order Stores, **V** 117
Littlewoods Organisation PLB, V 117–19
Littlewoods Warehouses, **V** 118
Litton, Charles, **I** 484; **11** 263
Litton Industries Credit Corp., **III** 293
Litton Industries Inc., I 85, 452, 476,
  484–86, 523–24; **II** 33; **III** 473, 732; **IV**
  253; **6** 599; **10** 520–21, 537; **11 263–65**
  (upd.), 435; **12** 248, 271–72, 538–40
Litton Resources Group, **III** 473
Litwin Engineers & Constructors, **8** 546
Litzsinger, Mark, **12** 173–74
Litzsinger, P. Richard, **12** 173
Litzsinger, Todd, **12** 173
Livanos, **III** 516
Lively, Tom, **8** 87–88
Liveright, Horace, **13** 428
Liverpool (Lord), **II** 306
Liverpool and London and Globe Insurance
  Co., **III** 234, 350
Liverpool and London Fire and Life
  Insurance Co., **III** 349
Liverpool Fire and Life Insurance Co., **III**
  350
Liversidge, Horace P., **11** 388
Livesey, George, **V** 559–60
Livia, **I** 154; **10** 279
Livia, Anna, **IV** 295
Living Centers of America, **13** 49
Living Videotext, **10** 508
Livingston Communications, **6** 313
Livingston, Crawford, **II** 395; **10** 59
Livingston, Fargo and Co., **II** 380, 395; **10**
  59
Livingston, Homer, **II** 284
LivingWell Inc., **12** 326
Liz Claiborne, Inc., 8 329–31
Ljungberg, Erik Johan, **IV** 336
Ljungström, Gunnar, **I** 197; **11** 438
LKB-Produkter AB, **I** 665
Llewellyn, John S., Jr., **7** 404
Lloyd A. Fry Roofing, **III** 721
Lloyd Adriatico S.p.A., **III** 377
Lloyd Aereo de Bolivia, **6** 97
Lloyd, Charles, **II** 306
Lloyd, Charles, II, **II** 306
Lloyd, Edward, **III** 278; **IV** 257
Lloyd, Harold, **II** 155, 307, 309
Lloyd, Ian, **I** 196
Lloyd Italico, **III** 351
Lloyd, James, **II** 306
Lloyd, John, **III** 508
Lloyd, Louis, **11** 418
Lloyd, Sampson Samuel, **II** 306–07
Lloyd, Sampson, II, **II** 306–07
Lloyd, Sampson, III, **II** 306
Lloyd Webber, Andrew, **6** 162
Lloyd's Electronics, **14** 118
Lloyd's of Connecticut Inc., **14** 18

Lorenzo, Frank, **I** 98, 103, 123–24, 130; **6** 129
Lorillard, **V** 396, 407, 417
Lorillard Industries, **I** 488; **12** 317
Lorimar Telepictures, **II** 149, 177
Lorman, William, **V** 552
Lorraine-Escaut, **IV** 227
Lorrell, Mark A., **I** 43
Lortie, Pierre, **II** 652
Lorvic Corp., **I** 679
Los Angeles Can Co., **I** 599
Los Angeles Drug Co., **12** 106
Los Angeles Gas and Electric Company, **V** 682
Los Angeles Steamship Co., **II** 490
Los Gaitanes (Count of), **II** 197
Los Lagos Corp., **12** 175
Los Nietos Co., **IV** 570
Lothian (Marquis of), **III** 358
Lothringer Bergwerks- und Hüttenverein Aumetz-Friede AG, **IV** 126
Lothringer Hütten- und Bergwerksverein, **IV** 126
Lotus, **12** 335
Lotus Cars Ltd., 14 320–22
Lotus Development Corp., IV 597; **6** 224–25, 227, **254–56**, 258–60, 270–71, 273; **9** 81, 140; **10** 24, 505
Lotus Publishing Corporation, **7** 239
Lotus Radio, **I** 531
Loucks, Hoffman & Company, **8** 412
Loucks, Vernon R., **I** 628
Loucks, Vernon R., Jr., **10** 142–43
Loudon, Arnout A., **13** 21
Loughead Aircraft Manufacturing Co., **I** 64
Loughead, Allan, **I** 64, 76
Loughead, Malcolm, **I** 64
Loughhead, Robert L., **IV** 237
Louis B. Mayer Pictures, **II** 148
Louis C. Edwards, **II** 609
Louis, J.C., **I** 235, 279
Louis Kemp Seafood Company, **14** 515
Louis Marx Toys, **II** 559; **12** 410
Louis Philippe, King (France), **III** 616; **IV** 226
Louis Rich, Inc., **II** 532; **12** 372
Louis Vuitton, I 272; **10 397–99**
Louis Vuitton Moët Hennessy, **III** 48; **8** 343
Louis XIV, King (France), **II** 474; **III** 675
Louis XVIII, King (France), **IV** 617
Louisiana & Southern Life Insurance Co., **14** 460
Louisiana Bank & Trust, **11** 106
The Louisiana Land and Exploration Company, IV 76, 365, 367; **7 280–83**
Louisiana Land Offshore Exploration Co., **7** 281
Louisiana-Pacific Corporation, IV 282, **304–05**; **9** 260
Louisville Cement Co., **IV** 409
Louisville Gas and Electric Company. *See* LG&E Energy Corporation.
Louisville Home Telephone Company, **14** 258
Lourie, Donald B., **12** 410
Lourle, Donald B., **II** 559
Louthan Manufacturing Company, **8** 178
Love, Howard M. (Pete), **V** 152–53
Love, J. Spencer, **V** 354
Lovelace, Griffin M., **III** 238
Lovelace Truck Service, Inc., **14** 42
Lovering China Clays, **III** 690
Lovering family, **III** 690–91

Low, Abiel A., **III** 240
Lowe Bros. Co., **III** 745
Lowe, James, **V** 122
Lowe, L. S., **V** 122
Lowe, Leo, **I** 661
Lowe, William C., **7** 206
Lowe's Companies, Inc., V 122–23; 11 384; **12** 234, 345
Lowell Bearing Co., **IV** 136
Lowell, John, **III** 312
Lowell Shoe, Inc., **13** 360
Löwenbräu, **I** 220, 257; **II** 240
Lowenstein, Louis, **II** 673–74
Lowney/Moirs, **II** 512
Lowry, Edward, **III** 258
Lowry, Grosvenor, **II** 27; **12** 193
Lowry, Robert J., **12** 517
Loy, Myrna, **13** 86
Loyalty Group, **III** 241–42
Loyalty Life, **III** 243
Loynd, Richard B., **III** 531; **9** 134
Lpuschow, Gunter, **I** 138
LRL International, **II** 477
LSI. *See* Lear Siegler Inc.
LSI Logic Corporation, 13 323–25
LTA Ltd., **IV** 22
LTV Corporation, I 62–63, **489–91; 7** 107–08; **8** 157, 315; **10** 419; **11** 166, 364; **12** 124
Luberef, **IV** 538
Lubert, Ira, **10** 232
Lubitsch, Ernst, **II** 155, 175
Lubrizol Corp., I 360–62
Lucander, Bruno Otto, **6** 87
Lucas Aerospace, **III** 555–56
Lucas Applied Technology, **III** 556
Lucas Automotive, **III** 556
Lucas Battery Co., **III** 556
Lucas Bols, **II** 642
Lucas Defence Systems, **III** 556
Lucas Digital Ltd., **12** 322
Lucas, Donald L., **6** 272–73
Lucas Electrical Co., **III** 554–55
Lucas, George, **II** 144; **12** 322–24
Lucas Girling, **I** 157
Lucas, Harry, **III** 554
Lucas Industrial Systems, **III** 556
Lucas Industries Plc, III 509, **554–57**
Lucas Instruments, **III** 556
Lucas, John H., **6** 510
Lucas, Joseph, **III** 554
Lucas, Oliver, **III** 554–55
Lucas, William F., **I** 226–27; **10** 180–81
LucasArts Entertainment Co., **12** 322
Lucasfilm, **9** 368, 472
Lucasfilm Ltd., 12 322–24
Lucchini, **IV** 228
Luce, Charles F., **V** 588
Luce, Clare Boothe, **IV** 674; **7** 527
Luce, Henry, III, **IV** 675; **7** 528
Luce, Henry Robinson, **IV** 661, 673–75; **7** 526–28
Luciano, R.P., **I** 685
Lucier, Francis P., **III** 436
Lucking, W.T., **6** 546
Luckman, Charles, **I** 513
Lucks, Roy, **7** 131
Lucky Chemical Co., **II** 53–54
Lucky Continental Carbon, **II** 53
Lucky Lager Brewing Co, **I** 268
Lucky Stores, **II** 605, 653
Lucky Stores Inc., **6** 355; **8** 474; **12** 48
Lucky Strike, **II** 143

Lucky-Goldstar, II 53–54; III 457; **13** 574. *See also* Goldstar Co., Ltd.
Ludlow Corp., **III** 645
Ludlow, Daniel, **II** 247; **13** 145
Ludmer, Irving, **II** 663–64
Ludvigsen, Elliot, **I** 154; **10** 279
Ludwick, Andrew K., **10** 510, 512
Ludwig, Daniel K., **IV** 522, 570
Ludwig I, King (Bavaria), **II** 238, 241
Ludwig II, King (Bavaria), **II** 241
Luecke, Joseph E., **III** 270–71
Lüer, Carl, **IV** 140
Luerssen, Frank, **IV** 115
Lufkin Rule Co., **II** 16
Luft, Klaus, **III** 155
Luftag, **I** 110
Lufthansa. *See* Deutsche Lufthansa A.G.
Lufthansa A.G., **6** 59–60, 69, 96, 386
The Luggage Company, **14** 224
Luigs, C. Russell, **9** 266
Luisi, Marie, **I** 21
Luiso, Anthony, **7** 242–43
Lukas, Stephen **I** 678
Luke, David, **IV** 351
Luke, David L., III, **IV** 353–54
Luke, David L., Jr., **IV** 351–53
Luke, John, **IV** 351
Luke, John A., **IV** 354
Luke, Thomas, **IV** 351
Luke, William, **IV** 351
Lukens Inc., 14 323–25
Lukey Mufflers, **IV** 249
Lukman, Rilwanu, **IV** 473–74
Lum's, **6** 199–200
Lumac B.V., **I** 387
Lumbermen's Investment Corp., **IV** 341
Lumbermens Mutual Casualty Co., **III** 269–71
La Lumière Economique, **II** 79
Lummus Co., **IV** 469
Lumonics Inc., **III** 635
Lundberg, Kenneth, **IV** 576
Lundberg, William, **I** 136
Lundeen, Robert, **I** 325; **8** 149, 519
Lundgren, Terry, **12** 356
Lundqvist, Bengt, **I** 626
Lundqvist, Emil, **IV** 336
Lundy, J. Edward, **I** 166; **11** 138
Lunenburg Sea Products Limited, **14** 339
Lunevale Products Ltd., **I** 341
Lunn Poly, **8** 525–26
Luntey, Gene, **6** 457
Luotto-Pankki Oy, **II** 303
Lupton, John T., **13** 162–63
Lurgei, **6** 599
LURGI. *See* Metallurgische Gesellschaft Aktiengesellschaft.
Lurgi Paris S.A., **IV** 141
Luria Bros. and Co., **I** 512–13
Luria Brothers, **6** 151
Lurie, Robert, **8** 229–30
Lurton, H. William, **7** 255–56
Lutens, Serge, **III** 63
Luter, Joseph W., III, **7** 477
Luther's Bar-B-Q, **II** 556
Luthringer, Marshall S., **6** 470
Lutteroth, Herman (Baron), **III** 345
Lutz, Norman E., **7** 479
Lux, **III** 478
Lux, John H., **9** 24
Lux Mercantile Co., **II** 624
Lux, Samuel, **II** 624
Luxor, **II** 69; **6** 205
Luxury Linens, **13** 81–82

Minet Europe Holdings Ltd., **III** 357
Minet Holdings PLC, **III** 357
Minhinnik, John, **IV** 437
Mini Stop, **V** 97
Mining and Technical Services, **IV** 67
Mining Corp. of Canada Ltd., **IV** 164
Mining Development Corp., **IV** 239–40
Mining, Kuhara, **12** 237
Mining Trust Ltd., **IV** 32
MiniScribe, Inc., **6** 230; **10** 404
Minister of Finance Inc., **IV** 519
Minivator Ltd., **11** 486
Minneapolis General Electric of Minnesota, **V** 670
Minneapolis Heat Regulator Co., **II** 40–41; **12** 246
Minneapolis Millers Association, **10** 322
Minneapolis-Honeywell, **8** 21
Minneapolis-Honeywell Regulator Co., **II** 40–41, 86; **12** 247
Minnesota Cooperative Creameries Assoc., Inc., **II** 535
Minnesota Linseed Oil Co., **8** 552
Minnesota Mining & Manufacturing Company (3M), **I** 28, 387, **499–501**; **II** 39; **III** 476, 487, 549; **IV** 251, 253–54; **6** 231; **7** 162; **8** 35, **369–71 (upd.)**; **11** 494; **13** 326
Minnesota Paints, **8** 552–53
Minnesota Power & Light Company, **11 313–16**
Minnesota Sugar Company, **11** 13
Minnesota Valley Canning Co., **I** 22
Minnetonka Corp., **II** 590; **III** 25
Minnig, Max, **I** 405
Minoli, Federico, **10** 151
Minolta Camera Co., Ltd., **III 574–76**, 583–84
Minolta Camera Handelsgesellschaft, **III** 575
Minolta Corp., **III** 575
Minomura, Rizaemon, **I** 505–06, **II** 325
Minorco, **III** 503; **IV** 67–68, 84, 97
Minstar Inc., **11** 397
Minute Maid Corp., **I** 234; **10** 227
Minute Tapioca, **II** 531
MIPS Computer Systems, **II** 45; **11** 491
Mirabito, Paul, **I** 142; **III** 166; **6** 282
Mirage Resorts, Inc., **6 209–12**
Miramar Hotel & Investment Co., **IV** 717
Mircali Asset Management, **III** 340
Mircor Inc., **12** 413
Mirkin, Morris, **9** 94
Miron, Robert, **IV** 583
Mirrlees Blackstone, **III** 509
Mirror Group Newspapers Ltd., **7** 312
Mirror Group Newspapers plc, **IV** 641; **7** 244, **341–43**
Mirror Printing and Binding House, **IV** 677
Misceramic Tile, Inc., **14** 42
Misr Airwork. *See* AirEgypt.
Misrair. *See* AirEgypt.
Miss Clairol, **6** 28
Miss Selfridge, **V** 177–78
Missenden, Eustace, **V** 421
Misset Publishers, **IV** 611
Mission Energy Company, **V** 715
Mission First Financial, **V** 715
Mission Group, **V** 715, 717
Mission Insurance Co., **III** 192
Mission Land Company, **V** 715
Mississippi Chemical Corporation, **8** 183; **IV** 367
Mississippi Drug, **III** 10

Mississippi Gas Company, **6** 577
Mississippi Power & Light, **V** 619
Mississippi River Corporation, **10** 44
Missouri Book Co., **10** 136
Missouri Gas & Electric Service Company, **6** 593
Missouri Pacific Railroad, **10** 43–44
Missouri Public Service Company. *See* UtiliCorp United Inc.
Missouri Utilities Company, **6** 580
Missouri-Kansas-Texas Railroad, **I** 472; **IV** 458
Mistral Plastics Pty Ltd., **IV** 295
di Misurata, Giuseppe Volpi (Count), **III** 208
Mita, Katsushige, **I** 455; **12** 238
Mitarai, Takeshi, **III** 120–21, 575
Mitchell & Mitchell Gas & Oil, **7** 344–35
Mitchell, Billy, **I** 67
Mitchell, Charles, **IV** 392
Mitchell, Charles E., **I** 337; **II** 253–54; **9** 123
Mitchell Construction, **III** 753
Mitchell, David W., **III** 16
Mitchell, Dean H., **6** 532
Mitchell, Edward F., **6** 554
Mitchell Energy and Development Corporation, **7 344–46**
Mitchell, George P., **7** 344–46
Mitchell, Gerald B., **I** 153; **10** 265
Mitchell Home Savings and Loan, **13** 347
Mitchell Hutchins, **II** 445
Mitchell International, **8** 526
Mitchell, Johnny, **7** 344
Mitchell, Rodger J., **11** 106
Mitchell, Roger, **10** 385
Mitchell, Sidney Z., **V** 546–47, 549, 564; **6** 565, 595
Mitchell, Sir Godfrey Way, **12** 201–02
Mitchell, Tom, **8** 466–67
Mitchell, W., **IV** 19
Mitchell, William, **II** 655
Mitchells & Butler, **I** 223
Mitchum Co., **III** 55
Mitchum, Jones & Templeton, **II** 445
MiTek Industries Inc., **IV** 259
MiTek Wood Products, **IV** 305
MitNer Group, **7** 377
Mitsubishi, **V** 481–82; **7** 377
Mitsubishi Aircraft Co., **III** 578; **7** 348; **9** 349; **11** 164
Mitsubishi Atomic Power Industries, **III** 579; **7** 349
Mitsubishi Bank, Ltd., **II** 57, 273–74, 276, **321–22**, 323, 392, 459; **III** 289, 577–78; **7** 348
Mitsubishi Bank of California, **II** 322
Mitsubishi Cement Co., **III** 713
Mitsubishi Chemical Industries Ltd., **I** 319, **363–64**, 398; **II** 57; **III** 666, 760; **11** 207
Mitsubishi Corporation, **I** 261, 431–32, 492, **502–04**, 505–06, 510, 515, 519–20; **II** 57, 59, 101, 118, 224, 292, 321–25, 374; **III** 577–78; **IV** 285, 518, 713; **6** 499; **7** 82, 233, 590; **9** 294; **12 340–43 (upd.)**
Mitsubishi Development Corp., **IV** 713
Mitsubishi Electric Corporation, **II** 53, **57–59**, 68, 73, 94, 122; **III** 577, 586; **7** 347, 394
Mitsubishi Electric Manufacturing, **II** 58
Mitsubishi Estate Company, Limited, **IV 713–14**

Mitsubishi Estate New York Inc., **IV** 714
Mitsubishi family, **III** 288
Mitsubishi Gas Chemical Company, **I** 330; **8** 153
Mitsubishi Goshi Kaisha, Ltd., **III** 538, 577–78, 713; **IV** 713; **7** 347
Mitsubishi Heavy Industries, **9** 349–50
Mitsubishi Heavy Industries, Ltd., **II** 57, 75, 323, 440; **III** 452–53, 487, 532, **577–79**, 685; **IV** 184; **7** 347–50 **(upd.)**; **8** 51; **10** 33; **13** 507
Mitsubishi Internal Combustion Engine Manufacturing Co., **III** 578; **7** 348; **9** 349
Mitsubishi Iron Works, **III** 577; **7** 348
Mitsubishi Kasei Corp., **III** 47–48, 477; **8** 343; **14** 535
Mitsubishi Kasei Industry Co. Ltd., **IV** 476
Mitsubishi Marine, **III** 385
Mitsubishi Materials Corporation, **III 712–13**
Mitsubishi Metal Corp., **III** 712–13
Mitsubishi Mining & Cement, **III** 712–13
Mitsubishi Mining Co., **III** 712–13; **IV** 554
Mitsubishi Motor Sales of America, Inc., **8** 374
Mitsubishi Motors Australia Ltd., **9** 349
Mitsubishi Motors Corporation, **III** 516–17, 579; **7** 219, 349; **8** 72; **9 349–51**
Mitsubishi Motors of America, **6** 28
Mitsubishi Oil Co., Ltd., **IV 460–62**, 479, 492
Mitsubishi Paper Co., **III** 547
Mitsubishi Petrochemical Co., **I** 364; **III** 685
Mitsubishi Petroleum, **III** 760
Mitsubishi Pulp, **IV** 328
Mitsubishi Rayon Co. Ltd., **I** 330; **V 369–71**
Mitsubishi Rayon Company, **8** 153
Mitsubishi Sha Holdings, **IV** 554
Mitsubishi Shipbuilding Co., **II** 57; **III** 513, 577–78; **7** 348
Mitsubishi Shipbuilding Co. Ltd., **9** 349
Mitsubishi Shoji Trading, **IV** 554
Mitsubishi Shokai, **III** 577; **IV** 713; **7** 347
Mitsubishi Trading Co., **IV** 460
Mitsubishi Trust, **II** 323
Mitsubishi Trust & Banking Corporation, **II 323–24**; **III** 289
Mitsubishi Yuka Pharmaceutical Co., **I** 364
Mitsui, **13** 356
Mitsui and Co., **I** 282; **IV** 18, 224, 432, 654–55; **V** 142; **6** 346; **7** 303
Mitsui Bank, Ltd., **II** 273–74, 291, **325–27**, 328, 372; **III** 295–97; **IV** 147, 320; **V** 142
Mitsui Bussan K.K., **I** 363, 431–32, 469, 492, 502–04, **505–08**, 510, 515, 519, 533; **II** 57, 66, 101, 224, 292, 323, 325–28, 392; **III** 295–96, 717–18; **IV** 147, 431; **9** 352–53
Mitsui Chemical, **IV** 145, 148
Mitsui family, **III** 288; **IV** 145, 715
Mitsui Gomei Kaisha, **IV** 715
Mitsui Group, **9** 352
Mitsui, Hachiroemon, **I** 505
Mitsui Harbour and Urban Construction Co., Ltd., **IV** 715
Mitsui Home Co., Ltd., **IV** 715–16
Mitsui House Code, **V** 142
Mitsui Light Metal Processing Co., **III** 758

Monk, Alec, **II** 628–29
Monk-Austin Inc., **12** 110
Monks, Bob, **13** 497
Monnerat, Jules, **II** 545; **7** 380
Monochem, **II** 472
Monod Jérome, **V** 657
Monogram Aerospace Fasteners, Inc., **11** 536
Monogramme Confections, **6** 392
Monolithic Memories, **6** 216
Monon Corp., **13** 550
Monon Railroad, **I** 472
Monoprix, **V** 57–59
Monroe Auto Equipment, **I** 527
Monroe Calculating Machine Co., **I** 476, 484
Monroe Cheese Co., **II** 471
Monroe, Marilyn, **II** 143; **III** 46
Monroe Savings Bank, **11** 109
Monrovia Aviation Corp., **I** 544
Monsanto, **9** 466
Monsanto Chemical Co., **I** 365; **9** 318
Monsanto Company, **I** 310, 363, **365–67**, 402, 631, 666, 686, 688; **III** 741; **IV** 290, 379, 401; **8** 398; **9 355–57 (upd.)**, 466; **12** 186; **13** 76, 225
Monsanto Oil Co., **IV** 367
Monsavon, **III** 46–47
Montagu (Lord), **I** 194
Montagu, Basil, **III** 272
Montagu, Samuel, **II** 319
Montague, Theodore G., **II** 471–72
Montale, Eugenio, **IV** 585
Montan Transport GmbH, **IV** 140
Montana Enterprises Inc., **I** 114
Montana Power Company, **6** 566; **7** 322; **11 320–22**
Montana Refining Company, **12** 240–41
Montana Resources, Inc., **IV** 34
Montana-Dakota Utilities Co., **7** 322–23
Montaup Electric Co., **14** 125
Monte, Woodrow, **I** 688
Montecatini, **I** 368; **IV** 421, 470, 486
Montedison SpA, **I 368–69**; **IV** 413, 421–22, 454, 499; **14** 17
Montefibre, **I** 369
Montefina, **IV** 499
Montefiore, Moses (Sir), **III** 372
Monterey Mfg. Co., **12** 439
Monterey's Tex-Mex Cafes, **13** 473
Montfort of Colorado, Inc., **II** 494
Montgomery, Bernard, **I** 178
Montgomery, Dan H., **11** 440
Montgomery, Dan T., **8** 113
Montgomery, James, **10** 339–40
Montgomery, Parker, **I** 667–68
Montgomery, Robert H., **9** 137
Montgomery Ward & Co., Incorporated, **III** 762; **IV** 465; **V 145–48**; **7** 353; **8** 509; **9** 210; **10** 10, 116, 172, 305, 391, 393, 490–91; **12** 48, 309, 315, 335, 430
Montgomery Ward Auto Club, **V** 147
Montgomery Ward Direct, **V** 148
Montgomery Ward Vision Center, **13** 165
Montreal Bank, **II** 210
Montreal Engineering Company, **6** 585
Montreal Gas Company, **6** 501
Montreal Island Power, **6** 502
Montreal Light, Heat & Power Company, **6** 501–02
Montreal Light, Heat & Power Consolidated, **6** 502
Montres Rolex S.A., **8** 477; **13 353–55**
Montrose Chemical Company, **9** 118, 119

Montrose Chrome, **IV** 92
Monument Property Trust Ltd., **IV** 710
Monumental Corp., **III** 179
Monus, Michael J. ''Mickey'', **12** 390–91
MONY Life of Canada, **III** 306
MONYCo., **III** 306
Moody family, **III** 91
Moody, James L., **12** 220–21
Moody, Robert, **8** 28–29; **12** 168
Moody, Shearn, **8** 28
Moody, William Lewis, Jr., **8** 27–28
Moody's Investors Service, **IV** 605
Moog, Art, **13** 357
Moog, Bill, **13** 356–57
Moog Inc., **13 356–58**
Moon-Hopkins Billing Machine, **III** 165
Mooney, E.J., **12** 347
Moore, B.C., **10** 154
Moore, Benjamin, **13** 84
Moore Business Forms de Centro America, **IV** 645
Moore Business Forms de Mexico, **IV** 645
Moore Business Forms de Puerto Rico, **IV** 645
Moore, Chistopher W., **11** 552–53
Moore, Clyde R., **11** 516
Moore Corporation Limited, **IV 644–46**, 679
Moore, Crawford, **11** 553–54
Moore, E. Allen, **III** 627
Moore, Everett, **8** 201
Moore, F. Rockwood, **6** 595
Moore Formularios Lda., **IV** 645
Moore, Francis C., **III** 240
Moore, Frank B., **V** 753
Moore, George, **II** 254; **9** 124
Moore, Gordon, **II** 44–46; **10** 365–67
Moore Group, **IV** 644
Moore, James, **11** 62
Moore, James L., **10** 223
Moore, John H., **I** 268
Moore, L.R., **6** 510
Moore, M. Thomas, **13** 158
Moore, Mary Tyler, **13** 279
Moore McCormack Resources Inc., **14** 455
Moore, Philip, **11** 468
Moore, R. Stuart, **12** 307
Moore, Robert, **III** 98; **13** 84
Moore, Samuel J., **IV** 644–45
Moore, Stephen D.R., **9** 140
Moore, Tom, **13** 78
Moore, William, **V** 224–25
Moore, William H., **II** 230–31; **10** 73
Moore, Willis, **9** 367
Moore-Handley Inc., **IV** 345–46
Moores, John, **V** 117–18
Moorhead, James T., **9** 516
Moorhouse, **II** 477
Mooty, John, **10** 374
Moran, Dan, **IV** 400
Moran Group Inc., **II** 682
MoRan Oil & Gas Co., **IV** 82–83
Morana, Inc., **9** 290
Morand, Paul, **IV** 618
Morcott, Southwood ''Woody'', **10** 265
More, Avery, **10** 232–33
Morehead May, James T., **I** 399
Moreland and Watson, **IV** 208
Moret, Marc, **I** 673
Moretti-Harrah Marble Co., **III** 691
Morey, Parker, **6** 548
Morgan & Cie International S.A., **II** 431
Morgan, Bill, **I** 568
Morgan, C. Powell, **7** 95

Morgan, Cary, **I** 61; **11** 164
Morgan Construction Company, **8** 448
Morgan Edwards, **II** 609
Morgan, Edwin B., **II** 380; **12** 533
Morgan Engineering Co., **8** 545
Morgan family, **III** 237
Morgan, Graham, J., **III** 763
Morgan Grampian Group, **IV** 687
Morgan Grenfell (Overseas) Ltd., **II** 428
Morgan Grenfell and Co., **II** 427
Morgan Grenfell and Co. Ltd., **II** 428
Morgan Grenfell Group PLC, **II** 280, 329, **427–29**; **IV** 21, 712
Morgan Grenfell Inc., **II** 429
Morgan Grenfell Laurie, **II** 427
Morgan Grenfell Securities, **II** 429
Morgan Guaranty International Banking Corp., **II** 331; **9** 124
Morgan Guaranty International Finance Corp., **II** 331
Morgan Guaranty Trust Co., **13** 49, 448
Morgan Guaranty Trust Co. of New York, **I** 26; **II** 208, 254, 262, 329–32, 339, 428, 431, 448; **III** 80; **10** 150
Morgan Guaranty Trust Company, **11** 421; **14** 297
Morgan, Harjes & Co., **II** 329
Morgan, Henry, **II** 430–31
Morgan, J.P., **12** 28, 45
Morgan, J.P. & Co. Inc. *See* J.P. Morgan & Co. Incorporated.
Morgan, James, **7** 13
Morgan, James C., **10** 108
Morgan, John Pierpont (J.P.), **I** 47, 61; **II** 229, 312, 329–32, 427, 430, 447; **III** 247; **IV** 110, 400, 572; **V** 146; **6** 605; **7** 261, 549; **9** 370; **10** 43, 72, 162; **11** 164; **13** 123, 447
Morgan, John Pierpont, Jr. (Jack), **II** 227, 330, 427; **IV** 573; **7** 550
Morgan, Junius Spencer, **II** 329–30, 427–28
Morgan, Lewis, Githens & Ahn, Inc., **6** 410
Morgan Mitsubishi Development, **IV** 714
Morgan, Richard T., **12** 226
Morgan Stanley & Co., Inc., **II** 330, 408, 430–31
Morgan Stanley Group, Inc., **I** 34; **II** 211, 403, 406–07, 428, **430–32**, 441; **IV** 295, 447, 714; **9** 386; **12** 529
Morgan Stanley International, **II** 422
The Morgan Stanley Real Estate Fund, **11** 258
Morgan Yacht Corp., **II** 468
Morgan's Brewery, **I** 287
Morgens, Howard, **III** 52; **8** 433
Morgenthau, Hans, **II** 227
Morgridge, John, **11** 58–59
Mori Bank, **II** 291
Mori, Kaoru, **V** 455
Moria Informatique, **6** 229
Moriarity, Roy, **10** 287
Morino Associates, **10** 394
Morino, Mario M., **10** 394
Morison, William, **I** 497; **12** 332
Morita & Co., **I** 103
Morita, Akio, **II** 5, 56, 101–03; **7** 118; **12** 453–55
Morita family, **II** 103
Morita, Ko, **IV** 656
Morita, Kuzuaki, **II** 103; **12** 455
Moritz, Michael, **I** 145
Morley, Roger, **10** 62

Münchener Rückversicherungs-
Gesellschaft. *See* Munich Re.
Mundt, Ray, **I** 412–13; **III** 10
Mungana Mines, **I** 438
Munich Re, **II** 239; **III** 183–84, 202,
299–301, 400, 747
Munich-American Reinsurance Co., **III**
401
Municipal Assistance Corp., **II** 448
Munising Paper Co., **III** 40; **13** 156
Munising Woodenware Company, **13** 156
Munksund, **IV** 338
Munn, Stephen, **8** 80
Munoz, Jose, **7** 556
Munro, J. Richard, **IV** 675; **7** 528
Munroe, George B., **IV** 178–79
Munsell, Harry B., **6** 511
Munson, Donald W., **8** 322
Muntasir, Omar, **IV** 453
Munter, Herb, **I** 47
Murai, Tsutomu, **I** 221
Murakami, Kohei, **IV** 656
Muramoto, Shuzo, **II** 274
Murchison, Clint, **V** 737; **7** 145; **10** 43
Murchison, Clint, Jr., **10** 44
Murchison, John, **10** 44
Murdoch, Keith, **7** 389
Murdoch, Keith (Sir), **IV** 650, 652
Murdoch, Keith Rupert, **7** 252–53
Murdoch, Robert, **12** 231
Murdoch, Rupert, **II** 156, 169, 171, 176;
IV 264, 611, 619, 630, 641, 650–53,
666, 684, 687, 703; **V** 524; **6** 16, 73; **7**
336, 389–92; **8** 527, 551; **9** 119, 429; **10**
288; **12** 86, 358–60, 561
Murdock, David, **II** 492; **9** 215–16
Murdock, David H., **8** 424; **9** 176
Murdock, Melvin Jack, **8** 517–18
Murdough, Thomas G., **13** 317–18
Murfin Inc., **8** 360
Murless, Gordon, **9** 462
Murmic, Inc., **9** 120
Murphy, Charles H., Jr., **7** 362–63
Murphy, Charles H., Sr., **7** 362
Murphy Farms, **7** 477
Murphy, Henry C., **II** 312; **V** 428
Murphy, Jeremiah, **II** 388
Murphy, John, **I** 269–70; **12** 337
Murphy, John J., **III** 473
Murphy, Michael, **I** 98
Murphy Oil Corporation, **7 362–64**
Murphy, Ray, **III** 248
Murphy, Richard J., **III** 535
Murphy, Thomas, **10** 420; **13** 449
Murphy, Thomas S., **II** 131
Murphy, W.B., **II** 479–80
Murphy, W.H., **I** 473
Murphy-Phoenix Company, **14** 122
Murray, Allen E., **IV** 465; **7** 353
Murray, Annie, **III** 20
Murray Bay Paper Co., **IV** 246
Murray Corp. of America, **III** 443
Murray Goulburn Snow, **II** 575
Murray, J. Alec G., **13** 492
Murray, J. Terrence, **9** 229–30
Murray, John, **7** 548
Murray, Kenneth Sutherland, **I** 314–15
Murray, Pascall, **II** 476
Murray, Phillip, **IV** 114
Murray, T.G., **III** 672–73
Murray, William C.R., **III** 20
Murrayfield, **IV** 696
Murrow, Edward R., **II** 132; **6** 157

Murtaugh Light & Power Company, **12**
265
Murto, William H., **III** 124; **6** 221
Musashino Railway Company, **V** 510
Muscatine Journal, **11** 251
Muscocho Explorations Ltd., **IV** 76
Muse Air Corporation, **6** 120
Muse, M. Lamar, **6** 119–20
Music Corporation of America, **II** 143–44
Music Plus, **9** 75
Music-Appreciation Records, **13** 105
Musica, Philip, **I** 496; **12** 331
Musicland Stores Corporation, **9
360–62**; **11** 558
Muskegon Gas Company. *See* MCN
Corporation.
Musotte & Girard, **I** 553
Mussadegh, Muhammad, **IV** 379, 440, 466,
483, 559
Musser, Warren V., **10** 232, 473–74
Mussolini, Benito, **I** 161, 459, 465; **II** 271;
III 208, 346; **IV** 632; **11** 102, 203; **13**
28, 218
Mutoh Industries, Ltd., **6** 247
Mutual Benefit Financial Service Co., **III**
304
Mutual Benefit Life Insurance Company,
III 243, **302–04**
Mutual Gaslight Company. *See* MCN
Corporation.
Mutual Life Insurance Co. of the State of
Wisconsin, **III** 321
**Mutual Life Insurance Company of New
York**, **II** 331; **III** 247, 290, **305–07**,
316, 321, 380
Mutual Medical Aid and Accident
Insurance Co., **III** 331
Mutual of Omaha, **III** 365
Mutual Oil Co., **IV** 399
Mutual Papers Co., **14** 522
Mutual Safety Insurance Co., **III** 305
Mutual Savings & Loan Assoc., **III** 215
Mutualité Générale, **III** 210
Mutualité Immobilière, **III** 210
Mutualité Mobilière, **III** 210
Mutuelle d'Orléans, **III** 210
Mutuelle de l'Quest, **III** 211
Mutuelle Vie, **III** 210
Mutuelles Unies, **III** 211
Muysken, J., **IV** 132
Muzak Corporation, **7** 90–91
Muzzy, J. Howard, **I** 158; **10** 292
Muzzy-Lyon Co., **I** 158–59
Mwinilunga Canneries Ltd., **IV** 241
MXL Industries, **13** 367
MY Holdings, **IV** 92
Myanmar Oil and Gas Enterprise, **IV** 519
MYCAL Group, **V** 154
Mycrom, **14** 36
Myers, Burt, **10** 373
Myers, Charles F., **V** 354–55
Myers, Jerry, **7** 494
Myers, John Ripley, **III** 17; **9** 88
Myers, Malcolm, **8** 80
Myers, Mark B., **6** 290
Myers, Ted, **12** 124
Myers, William E., **7** 479
Mygind International, **8** 477
Myklebust, Egil, **10** 439
Mylan Laboratories, **I 656–57**
Myllykoski Träsliperi AB, **IV** 347–48
Mylod, Robert J., **11** 304–06
Myokenya, **III** 757

Myokenya Home Fixtures Wholesaling
Co., Ltd., **III** 757
Myson Group PLC, **III** 671
Mysore State Iron Works, **IV** 205

N M Electronics, **II** 44
N.A. Otto & Cie., **III** 541
N.A. Woodworth, **III** 519
N.C. Cameron & Sons, Ltd., **11** 95
N.C. Monroe Construction Company, **14**
112
N.K. Fairbank Co., **II** 497
N.M. Rothschild & Sons, **IV** 64, 712
N.M.U. Transport Ltd., **II** 569
N.R.F. Gallimard, **IV** 618
N.V.Philips Gloeilampenfabriken. *See*
Philips Electronics N.V.
N.W. Ayer & Son, **I** 36; **II** 542
N.Y.P. Holdings Inc., **12** 360
Nabisco, **9** 318. *See also* RJR Nabisco *and*
Nabisco Brands, Inc.
Nabisco Brands, Inc., **II** 475, 512,
542–44; **7** 128, 365–67; **12** 167. *See
also* Nabisco Foods Group *and* RJR
Nabisco.
Nabisco Foods Group, **7 365–68 (upd.)**
Nabisco, Inc., **14** 48
Nabors Drilling Limited of Canada, **9** 363
Nabors Industries, Inc., **9 363–65**
Nabors Manufacturing, **9** 93
NACCO Industries, Inc., **7 369–71**
Nacional Financiera, **IV** 513
Naddaff, George, **12** 42–43
Nadeau, Bertin, **II** 653
Nader, Ralph, **I** 366, 393, 610, 633, 646,
654; **9** 518; **11** 24, 90, 403
Nadhir, Saad J., **12** 43
NAFI. *See* National Automotive Fibers,
Inc.
Nafziger, Ralph Leroy, **12** 274
Nagano Seiyu Ltd., **V** 188
Nagaoka, Takeshi, **V** 479
Nagaro, Takeshi, **III** 713
Nagasaki Shipyard, **I** 502
Nagasakiya Co., Ltd., **V 149–51**
Nagase & Company, Ltd., **8 376–78**
Nagase family, **III** 38
Nagase, Hideo, **8** 378
Nagase, Shozo, **8** 378
Nagase-Alfa, **III** 420
Nagel, Friedrich, **V** 466
Nagel Meat Markets and Packing House, **II**
643
Nagoya Bank, **II** 373
Nagoya Electric Light Co., **IV** 62
Naguib, Mohammed, **6** 85
Naigai Tsushin, **6** 29
Naigai Tsushin Hakuhodo, **6** 29
Naikoku Tsu-un Kabushiki Kaisha, **V** 477
Naikoku Tsu-un Kaisha, **V** 477
Naito, Tashio, **I** 10
Nakabe, Ikujiro, **II** 578
Nakabe, Kaneichi, **II** 578
Nakada, Otakazu, **IV** 714
Nakagawa, Seibei, **I** 382; **13** 454
Nakagawi, Takeshi, **II** 540
Nakahara, Nobuhei, **IV** 554
Nakahashi, Tokugoro, **V** 473
Nakai Ltd., **IV** 292
Nakai, Reisaku, **IV** 157
Nakai, Saburobei, **IV** 292
Nakai Shoten Ltd., **IV** 292
Nakajima, Kumakichi, **III** 490
Nakajima, Michio, **III** 455

Oji Paper Manufacturing Co., **IV** 320–21, 327
OK Bazaars, **I** 289
Okada, Shigeru, **V** 143
Okada, Takuya, **V** 96–98
Okadaya Co. Ltd., **V** 96
Okamoto, Norikazu, **III** 409
Okamoto, T., **9** 294
Okawa, Heizaburo, **IV** 320
Okazaki, Kaheito, **6** 70
Oki & Co., **II** 72
Oki America, Inc., **II** 73
Oki Electric Co., Ltd., **II** 72
Oki Electric Industry Company, Limited, **II** 68, **72–74**
Oki, Kibataro, **II** 72–73
Oki Shokai, **II** 66
Oki Univac Kaisha, Ltd., **II** 73
Okidata, **9** 57
Okinoyama Coal Mine, **III** 759
Oklahoma Airmotive, **8** 349
Oklahoma Entertainment, Inc., **9** 74
Oklahoma Gas and Electric Company, **6** **539–40**
Oklahoma Natural Gas Company, **6** 530; **7** 409–10
Oklahoma Natural Gas Transmission Company, **7** 409–11
Oklahoma Oil Co., **I** 31
Oklahoma Publishing Company, **11** 152–53
Okonite, **I** 489
Okoso, Yoshinori, **II** 550
Okubo, Shoji, **7** 219–20
Okuma, Shigenobu, **I** 502, 506; **V** 449; **12** 340
Okumura, Tsunao, **II** 439; **9** 385
Okura & Co. America, Inc., **IV** 168
Okura & Co., Ltd., **IV** **167–68**
Okura, Kihachiro, **IV** 167
Okura Mining Co., **IV** 167
Okura Public Works Co., **IV** 167
Okura-gumi, **I** 282; **IV** 167–68
OLC. *See* Orient Leasing Co., Ltd.
Olcott & McKesson, **I** 496
Olcott, Charles, **II** 614
Old Colony Trust Co., **II** 207; **12** 30
Old Dominion Power Company, **6** 513, 515
Old El Paso, **I** 457; **14** 212
Old Kent Financial Corp., **11** **371–72**
Old Line Life Insurance Co., **III** 275
Old Mutual, **IV** 23, 535
Old National Bancorp, **14** 529
Old Quaker Paint Company, **13** 471
Old Republic International Corp., **11** **373–75**
Old Stone Trust Company, **13** 468
Oldfield, Mike, **12** 514
Oldham Estate, **IV** 712
Olds, Irving S., **IV** 573; **7** 550
Olds Motor Vehicle Co., **I** 171; **10** 325
Olds Oil Corp., **I** 341
Olds, Ransom Eli, **I** 171; **III** 438; **7** 400; **10** 325
Oleochim, **IV** 498–99
Olesen, Douglas, **10** 140
OLEX. *See* Deutsche BP Aktiengesellschaft.
Olex Cables Ltd., **10** 445
OLEX Deutsche Benzin und Petroleum GmbH, **7** 141
OLEX Deutsche Petroleum-Verkaufsgesellschaft mbH, **7** 140

OLEX-Petroleum-Gesellschaft mbH, **7** 140
D'Olier, Franklin, **III** 338
Olin Corporation, **I** 318, 330, **379–81**, 434; **III** 667; **IV** 482; **8** 23, 153; **13** **379–81 (upd.)**
Olin, Franklin, **I** 379; **13** 379
Olin, John, **I** 379–80; **13** 379–80
Olin Mathieson Chemical Co., **I** 695
Olin Mathieson Chemical Corp., **11** 420
Olin, Spencer, **I** 379; **13** 379
Olinkraft, Inc., **II** 432; **III** 708–09; **11** 420
Olins Rent-a-Car, **6** 348
Olinvest, **IV** 454
Olive Garden Italian Restaurants, **10** 322, 324
de Oliveira, Eduardo Fernandes (Dr.), **IV** 504
Olivetti. *See* Ing. C. Olivetti & C., S.p.A.
Olivetti, **V** 339; **6** 233, 235; **11** 59
Olivetti, Adriano, **III** 144–45
Olivetti, Camillo, **III** 144
Olivetti Information Services, **III** 145
Olivetti Office, **III** 145
Olivetti Systems and Networks, **III** 145
Olivetti Technologies Group, **III** 145
Olivier, Laurence, **II** 157
Olivine Industries, Inc., **II** 508; **11** 172
Olmsted, George W., **V** 652
Olofsson, **I** 573
Olohana Corp., **I** 129; **6** 129
Olsen Dredging Co., **III** 558
Olsen, Fred, **7** 531–32
Olsen, Ken, **6** 233–36
Olsen, Kenneth, **III** 132–34
Olsen, Thomas, **7** 531
Olshan, Kenneth S., **6** 51–52
Olson & Wright, **I** 120
Olson, Arthur, **11** 353
Olson, Bruce F., **7** 503
Olson, Carl G., **III** 518
Olson, Frank A., **I** 130; **6** 130; **9** 283–84
Olson, Gene, **8** 462
Olson, H. Everett, **II** 488–89
Olson, Hugo, **7** 502–03
Olson, Robert A., **6** 510–11
Olsonite Corp., **I** 201
Olsson, Elis, **8** 102
Olsson, George C.P., **7** 404
Olsson, Sture, **8** 102
Olsten Corporation, **6** **41–43**; **9** 327
Olsten, William, **6** 41–43
Olsten's Temporary Office Personnel. *See* Olsten Corporation.
Oltz, Harry M., **10** 371–73
Olun, Serge, **13** 5
Olveh, **III** 177–79
Olympia & York, **8** 327
Olympia & York Developments Ltd., **IV** 245, 247, 712, **720–21**; **6** 478; **9** 390–92 **(upd.)**
Olympia Arenas, Inc., **7** 278–79
Olympia Brewing, **I** 260; **11** 50
Olympia Floor & Tile Co., **IV** 720
Olympiaki, **III** 401
Olympic Airways, **II** 442
Olympic Fastening Systems, **III** 722
Olympic Packaging, **13** 443
Olympus Sport, **V** 177–78
Omaha Cold Store Co., **II** 571
Oman Oil Refinery Co., **IV** 516
Omega Gas Company, **8** 349
Omega Gold Mines, **IV** 164
Omex Corporation, **6** 272

OMI International Corp., **IV** 34; **9** 111
OMI Investments Inc., **9** 111–12
Omlon, **II** 75
Ommium Française de Pétroles, **IV** 559
Omni Construction Company, Inc., **8** 112–13
Omni Hearing Aid Systems, **I** 667
Omni Hotels Corp., **12 367–69**
Omni Products International, **II** 420
Omni-Pac, **12** 377
Omni-Pac Embalajes, SA, **12** 377
Omnibus Corporation, **9** 283
Omnicare, Inc., **13** 150
Omnicom Group, **I** **28–32**, 33, 36; **14** 160
OmniSource Corporation, **14 366–67**
Omron Tateisi Electronics Company, **II** **75–77**; **III** 549
Omura, Hikotaro, **V** 199
ÖMV Aktiengesellschaft, **IV** 234, 454, **485–87**
ÖMV Handels-Aktiengesellschaft, **IV** 486
On Cue, **9** 360
On-Line Software International Inc., **6** 225
Onan Corporation, **8** 72
Onbancorp Inc., **11** 110
Oncogen, **III** 18
Ondal GmbH, **III** 69
Ondetti, Miguel A., **I** 696
Ondulato Imolese, **IV** 296
One Hundredth Bank, **II** 321
One-Hundred Thirtieth National Bank, **II** 291
Oneida Bank & Trust Company, **9** 229
Oneida County Creameries Co., **7** 202
Oneida Gas Company, **9** 554
Oneida Ltd., **7 406–08**
ONEOK Inc., **7 409–12**
Ong, John D., **V** 233; **11** 158
Onitsuka Tiger Co., **V** 372; **8** 391
Online Distributed Processing Corporation, **6** 201
Online Financial Communication Systems, **11** 112
Ono family, **I** 506
Onoda California, Inc., **III** 718
Onoda Cement Co., Ltd., **I** 508; **III** **717–19**
Onoda U.S.A., Inc., **III** 718
Ontario Hydro, **6 541–42**; **9** 461
Ontel Corporation, **6** 201
Oode Casting, **III** 551
Oode Casting Iron Works, **III** 551
Oode, Gonshiro, **III** 551–52
Oosterhoff, J., Jr., **III** 177
Opel, Fritz, **V** 241
Opel, Georg, **V** 241
Opel, John, **III** 149; **6** 252
Open Board of Brokers, **9** 369
Oppenheimer. *See* Ernest Oppenheimer and Sons.
Oppenheimer & Co., **I** 667; **II** 445
Oppenheimer, Ernest (Sir), **IV** 20–23, 64–66, 79, 191; **7** 121–23
Oppenheimer family, **IV** 20–21, 23
Oppenheimer, Harry, **IV** 22–23, 64, 66, 68, 79–80, 90; **7** 121, 123, 125
Oppenheimer, Nicky, **IV** 68; **7** 125
Oppenlander, Robert, **I** 100; **6** 82
Opperman, Dwight D., **7** 580
Opryland USA, **11** 152–53
OPTi Computer, **9** 116
Opti-Ray, Inc., **12** 215
Optilink Corporation, **12** 137
Optimum Financial Services Ltd., **II** 457

Pak-a-Sak, **II** 661
Pak-All Products, Inc., **IV** 345
Pak-Paino, **IV** 315
Pak-Well, **IV** 282; **9** 261
Pakhoed Holding, N.V., **9** 532
Pakkasakku Oy, **IV** 471
Paknet, **11** 548
Pakway Container Corporation, **8** 268
PAL. *See* Philippine Airlines, Inc.
Pal Plywood Co., Ltd., **IV** 327
Pala, Gino N., **12** 115–16
Palatine Insurance Co., **III** 234
Palestine Coca-Cola Bottling Co., **13** 163
Paley, William, **6** 157–59
Paley, William S., **II** 132–34
Pall Corporation, 9 396–98
Pall, David, **9** 396
Palley, Stephen W., **9** 307
Palm Beach Holdings, **9** 157
Palmafina, **IV** 498–99
Palmer, Ben, **8** 462–63
Palmer, Chauncey, **III** 325
Palmer, Derek, **I** 224
Palmer, Dick, **II** 32
Palmer G. Lewis Co., **8** 135
Palmer, H. Bruce, **III** 303
Palmer, Henry L., **III** 321–22
Palmer, Jim, **12** 285
Palmer, John, **V** 496
Palmer, Lowell M., **I** 695
Palmer, Potter, **III** 237
Palmer, Reginald, **13** 63
Palmer, Robert B., **6** 236
Palmer, Stanton, **7** 479
Palmer Tyre Ltd., **I** 428–29
Palmerston (Lord), **I** 468
Palmieri, Alan, **12** 43
Palmieri, Aldo, **10** 150, 152
Palmolive Co., **III** 23
Palms, Eddie, **12** 43
Palo Alto Research Center, **10** 510
Pamour Porcupine Mines, Ltd., **IV** 164
Pamplemousse, **14** 225
Pamplin, Robert B., **IV** 281–82; **9** 259–260
Pan Am. *See* Pan American Airways Inc.
Pan Am Corp., **I** 116
Pan Am World Services, **III** 536
Pan American Airways Inc., **9** 231, 417
Pan American Banks, **II** 336
Pan American Grace Airways, **I** 547–48
Pan American International Oil Corp., **IV** 370
Pan American Petroleum & Transport Co., **IV** 368–70
Pan American Petroleum Corp., **IV** 370
Pan American World Airways, Inc., I 20, 31, 44, 64, 67, 89–90, 92, 99, 103–04, 112–13, **115–16**, 121, 124, 126, 129, 132, 248, 452, 530, 547; **6** 51, 65–66, 71, 74–76, 81–82, 103–05, 110–11, 123, 129–30; **9** 231; **10** 561; **11** 266; **12** 191, **379–81 (upd.)**, 419; **14** 73
Pan European Publishing Co., **IV** 611
Pan Ocean, **IV** 473
Panacon Corp., **III** 766
Panagra, **I** 547–48
Panama Refining and Petrochemical Co., **IV** 566
PanAmerican Airlines, **13** 19
Panarctic Oils, **IV** 494
Panasonic, **9** 180; **10** 125; **12** 470
Panatech Research & Development Corp., **III** 160

Panavia Consortium, **I** 74–75
Pandair, **13** 20
Pandel, Inc., **8** 271
Panettiere, John M., **12** 41
Panhandle Eastern Corporation, IV 425; **V 691–92; 10** 82–84; **11** 28
Panhandle Eastern Pipe Co., **I** 377
Panhandle Eastern Pipeline Co., **I** 569; **14** 135
Panhandle Oil Corp., **IV** 498
Panhandle Power & Light Company, **6** 580
Panhard, **I** 194
Panhard-Levassor, **I** 149
AB Pankakoski, **IV** 274
Panmure Gordon, **II** 337
Pannill Knitting Company, **13** 531
Pannill, William L., **13** 531
Panny, William, **I** 142
Panocean Storage & Transport, **6** 415, 417
Panola Pipeline Co., **7** 228
Panosh Place, **12** 168
Pansophic Systems Inc., **6** 225
Pantepec Oil Co., **IV** 559, 570
Pantera Energy Corporation, **11** 27
Pantheon Books, **13** 429
Panther, **III** 750
Panther Express International Company, **6** 346
Pantry Pride, **I** 668; **II** 670, 674; **III** 56
Pants Corral, **II** 634
Pao, Yue-Kong (Sir), **I** 470; **III** 517
Pape and Co., Ltd., **10** 441
Papelera Navarra, **IV** 295
Papeleria Calparsoro S.A., **IV** 325
The Paper Factory of Wisconsin, Inc., **12** 209
Paper Makers Chemical Corp., **I** 344
Paper Mate Co., **III** 28
Paper Recycling International, **V** 754
Paper Stock Dealers, Inc., **8** 476
Paperituote Oy, **IV** 347–48
Paperwork Data-Comm Services Inc., **11** 64
Papeterie de Pont Sainte Maxence, **IV** 318
Papeteries Aussedat, **III** 122
Papeteries Boucher S.A., **IV** 300
Les Papeteries Darblay, **IV** 258
Les Papeteries de la Chapelle, **IV** 258
Les Papeteries de la Chapelle-Darblay, **IV** 258–59, 302, 337
Papeteries Navarre, **III** 677
Papierfabrik Salach, **IV** 324
Papierwaren Fleischer, **IV** 325
Papierwerke Waldhof-Aschaffenburg AG, **IV** 323–24
Papyrus, **IV** 336
Paquette, Joseph F., Jr., **11** 389
Para-Med Health Services, **6** 181–82
Parade Gasoline Co., **7** 228
Paragon, **IV** 552
Paramax, **6** 281–83
Paramount Communications, Inc., **II** 154–55; **IV** 671–72, 675; **7** 528; **9** 119, 429; **10** 175
Paramount Paper Products, **8** 383
Paramount Pictures Corporation, I 451–52; **II** 129, 135, 146–47, **154–56**, 171, 173, 175, 177; **IV** 672; **9** 428; **12** 73, 323
Paramount-Publix, **II** 155
Paravision International, **III** 48; **8** 343
Parcelforce, **V** 498
PARCO, **V** 184–85
Parcor, **I** 676

Pardonner, William, **7** 465
Parducci, Les, **12** 531–32
Pare, Paul, **V** 401
Parente, Marco, **III** 206
Paresky, David, **9** 505
Paretti, Harold J., **I** 117
Parfet, Ray T., **I** 707; **8** 547
Parfums Chanel, **12** 57
Parfums Christian Dior, **I** 272
Parfums Rochas, **I** 670; **III** 68; **8** 452
Parfums Stern, **III** 16
Pargas, **I** 378
Paribas. *See* Compagnie Financiere de Paribas.
Paribas/Parfinance, **III** 48
Paridoc and Giant, **12** 153
Paris, Alessio, **III** 206, 345
Paris Playground Equipment, **13** 319
Parisian, Inc., 14 374–76
Park Chung Hee, **I** 516; **II** 54; **III** 747–48; **IV** 183; **12** 293
Park Consolidated Motels, Inc., **6** 187; **14** 105
Park Hall Leisure, **II** 140
Park Inn International, **11** 178
Park Ridge Corporation, **9** 284
Park Tae Chun (Maj. Gen.), **IV** 183–84
Park View Hospital, Inc., **III** 78
Parkdale Wines, **I** 268
Parke, Davis & Co., **I** 674, 711–12; **10** 550–51
Parke-Bernet, **11** 453
Parker, **III** 33
Parker Appliance Co., **III** 601–02
Parker, Art, **III** 601–02
Parker, Barry J.C., **9** 142–43
Parker, Bob, **11** 544
Parker Bros., **II** 502; **III** 505; **10** 323
Parker Drilling Company of Canada, **9** 363
Parker, Fernley, **9** 92
Parker, Foster, **13** 119
Parker, George B., **IV** 607
Parker, George S., **9** 326
Parker, Gordon, **7** 289
Parker Hannifin Corporation, III 601–03
Parker Hannifin NMF GmbH, **III** 602
Parker, Helen, **III** 601–02
Parker, Herbert L., **II** 18
Parker, Hugh, **9** 343
Parker, J. Harleston, **III** 267
Parker, Jack, **11** 5
Parker, John, **III** 751
Parker, Kenyon S., **III** 272
Parker, Lewis R., **8** 13
Parker, Morgan, **9** 96
Parker, Patrick, **III** 602–03
Parker Pen Corp., **III** 218; **9** 326
Parker Peter, **V** 423
Parker, Wayne A., **6** 539
Parkinson Cowan, **I** 531
Parkinson, J. David, **11** 516
Parkinson, Joseph L., **11** 307
Parkinson, Thomas, **III** 248
Parkinson, Ward, **11** 307
Parkmount Hospitality Corp., **II** 142
Parks Box & Printing Co., **13** 442
Parmalee, Harold J., **8** 538, 540
Parmelee, Henry S., **13** 245
Parola, Olli, **IV** 350
Parr, David, **11** 24
Parr, Jack, **12** 284
Parr's Bank, **II** 334; **III** 724
Parretti, Giancarlo, **9** 149

Société Générale North America, **II** 355
Société Générale pour favoriser l'Industrie
    nationale, **II** 294
Société Générale pour favoriser le
    Développement du Commerce et de
    l'Industrie en France S.A., **II** 354–55
Société Industrielle Belge des Pétroles, **IV**
    498–99
Société Internationale Pirelli S.A., **V** 250
Société Irano-Italienne des Pétroles, **IV** 466
Société Le Nickel, **IV** 107–08, 110
Societe Mecanique Automobile de l'Est, **7**
    37
Societe Mecanique Automobile du Nord, **7**
    37
Société Métallurgique, **IV** 25
Société Métallurgique de Normandie, **IV**
    227
Société Métallurgique des Terres Rouges,
    IV 25–26
Société Minière de Bakwanga, **IV** 67
Société Minière des Terres Rouges, **IV**
    25–26
Société Nationale de Recherche de Pétrole
    en Algérie, **IV** 545, 559; **7** 482
Société Nationale de Transport et de
    Commercialisation des Hydrocarbures,
    IV 423
Société Nationale des Chemins de Fer
    Français, V 512–15
Société Nationale des Pétroles d'Aquitaine,
    I 303; **IV** 453, 544–46; **7** 481–84
Société Nationale Elf Aquitaine, I
    303–04, 670, 676–77; **II** 260; **IV** 174,
    397–98, 424, 451, 453–54, 472–74,
    499, 506, 515–16, 518, 525, 535,
    544–47, 559–60; **V** 628; **7 481–85**
    (upd.); 8 452; **11** 97
Société Nationale pour la Recherche, la
    Production, le Transport, la
    Transformation et la Commercialisation
    des Hydrocarbures, **IV** 423–24
Société Nord Africaine des Ciments
    Lafarge, **III** 703
Societe Parisienne pour l'Industrie
    Electrique, **II** 93
Société pour l'Eportation de Grandes
    Marques, **I** 281
Société pour l'Étude et la Realisation
    d'Engins Balistiques. *See* SEREB.
Société pour L'Exploitation de la
    Cinquième Chaîne, **6** 374
Societe Vendeenne des Embalages, **9** 305
Societe-Hydro-Air S.a.r.L., **9** 27
Society Corporation, 9 474–77
Society for Savings, **9** 474
Society National Bank, **9** 474
Society National Bank of Mid-Ohio, **9** 475
Society of Lloyd's, **III** 278–79
SOCO Chemical Inc., **8** 69
Socombel, **IV** 497
Socony. *See* Standard Oil Co. (New York).
Socony Mobil Oil Co., Inc., **IV** 465; **7** 353
Socony-Vacuum Corp., **IV** 463–64; **7** 172,
    352
Socony-Vacuum Oil Co., Inc., **IV** 428–29,
    464–65, 485, 504, 537; **7** 171, 352
Sodak Gaming, Inc., **9** 427
Sodastream Holdings, **II** 477
Soden, James, **10** 529–30
Söderlund, Gustaf, **IV** 203
SODIAAL, **II** 577
SODIMA, II 576–77
SODIMA CLB, **II** 576

SODIMA Frais, **II** 576
SODIMA International S.A., **II** 576
Sodyeco, **I** 673
Soeharto, **IV** 492
Soekor, **IV** 93
Soeparno, Moehamad, **6** 90
Sofia, Zuheir, **11** 182
Sofiran, **IV** 467
Sofrem, **IV** 174
Softbank Corp., 12 562; **13 481–83**
Softsel Computer Products, **12** 334–35
SoftSolutions Technology Corporation, **10**
    558
Software AG, **11** 18
Software Arts, **6** 254
Software Dimensions, Inc., **9** 35
Software, Etc., **13** 545
Software International, **6** 224
Software Plus, Inc., **10** 514
Software Publishing Corp., **14** 262
Softwood Holdings Ltd., **III** 688
Soga, Chubei, **I** 518
Soga, Riemon, **I** 518; **III** 634; **IV** 214; **11**
    477
Soga, Tomomochi, **I** 518; **11** 477
Soga, Tomonobu, **I** 518; **11** 478
Soga, Tomosada, **I** 518
Soga, Tomoyoshi, **I** 518
Sogebra S.A., **I** 257
Sogen International Corp., **II** 355
Sogexport, **II** 355
Soginnove, **II** 355–56
Sohio Chemical Company, **13** 502
Sohken Kako Co., Ltd., **IV** 327
Sohl, Hans-Günther, **IV** 222
Soinlahti Sawmill and Brick Works, **IV**
    300
Sokel, David, **9** 301
Sokolov, Richard S., **8** 161
Sola Holdings, **III** 727
Solair Inc., **14** 43
La Solana Corp., **IV** 726
Solana, Luis, **V** 339
Solar, **IV** 614
Solar Electric Corp., **13** 398
Solberg, Carl, **I** 69
Solchaga, Carlos, **V** 608
Solectron Corp., 12 161–62, **450–52**
Solel Boneh Construction, **II** 47
Soles, W. Roger, **11** 214–15
Soletanche Co., **I** 586
Solid Beheer B.V., **10** 514
Solid State Dielectrics, **I** 329; **8** 152
Solinsky, Robert, **I** 607–08
Sollac, **IV** 226–27
Solmer, **IV** 227
Solomon, Harry, **II** 513
Solomon, Howard, **11** 141–43
Solomon, James, **11** 45–46
Solomon, Martin, **10** 369–70
Solomon, Stephen D., **I** 393
Solomon Valley Milling Company, **6** 592
Solon Automated Services, **II** 607
Solso, Theodore M., **12** 92
Solters, Larry, **13** 509
Solvay & Cie S.A., I 303, **394–96**,
    414–15; **III** 677; **IV** 300
Solvay, Alfred, **I** 394
Solvay Animal Health Inc., **12** 5
Solvay, Ernest, **I** 394–95
Solvay, Jacques, **I** 395
Solvent Resource Recovery, Inc., **9** 109
Solvents Recovery Service of New Jersey,
    Inc., **8** 464

SOMABRI, **12** 152
SOMACA, **12** 152
Somerfield, Stafford, **IV** 650; **7** 389
Somervell, Brehon Burke, **I** 354
Somerville Electric Light Company, **12** 45
Sommar, Ebbe, **IV** 315–16
Sommer, Charlie, **I** 366
Sommer, Julius, **IV** 140
Sommer, Steven, **I** 244
Sommers Drug Stores, **9** 186
Sommers, O. W., **6** 474
SONAP, **IV** 504–06
Sonat Coal Gas, Inc., **6** 578
Sonat Energy Services Company, **6** 578
Sonat Gas Gathering, Inc., **6** 578
Sonat Gas Supply, Inc., **6** 578
Sonat, Inc., 6 577–78
Sonat Marine, **6** 577
Sonat Marketing Company, **6** 578
Sonat Minerals, Inc., **6** 578
Sonat Minerals Leasing, Inc., **6** 578
Sonat Offshore Drilling, Inc., **6** 577
Sonat Subsea Services, **6** 578
Sonatrach, **V** 626; **12** 145. *See also*
    Entreprise Nationale Sonatrach.
Sondey, Edward, **6** 457
Sonecor Systems, **6** 340
Sonesson, **I** 211
Sonic Corporation, 14 451–53
Sonnabend, Abraham, **10** 44
Sonne, Karl-Heinz, **III** 543
Sonneborn Chemical and Refinery Co., **I**
    405
Sonneborn, Henry, **I** 405–06
Sonnen Basserman, **II** 475
Sonoco Products Company, 8 475–77; 12
    151
Sonoco Products Corporation, **12** 150
Sonoma Mortgage Corp., **II** 382
Sonometrics Inc., **I** 667
Sony Chemicals, **II** 101
Sony Corp. of America, **II** 103
Sony Corporation, I 30, 534; **II** 56, 58,
    91–92, **101–03**, 117–19, 124, 134, 137,
    440; **III** 141, 143, 340, 658; **6** 30; **7**
    118; **9** 385; **10** 86, 119, 403; **11** 46,
    490–91, 557; **12** 75, 161, 448, **453–56**
    (upd.); 13 399, 403, 482, 573; **14** 534
Sony Kabushiki Kaisha. *See* Sony
    Corporation.
Sony Overseas, **II** 101–02
Sony USA, Inc., **II** 135, 137; **12** 75
Sony-Prudential, **III** 340
Sonzogno, **IV** 585
Soo Line, **V** 429–30
Soo Line Mills, **II** 631
SOPEAL, **III** 738
Sophia Jocoba GmbH, **IV** 193
SOPI, **IV** 401
Sopwith Aviation Co., **III** 507–08
Sopwith, Thomas (Tommy) (Sir), **III**
    507–09
Soravie, **II** 265
Sorbus, **6** 242
Sorcim, **6** 224
Soreal, **8** 344
Sorg, Paul J., **IV** 595
Soriano, Andres, **6** 106
Soros, George, **8** 519; **13** 235
Sorrell, Martin, **I** 21; **6** 53
Sorrells, John H., **IV** 607
SOS Co., **II** 531
Sosa, Bromley, Aguilar & Associates, **6** 22
Sosnoff, Martin, **6** 201

Specialty Papers Co., **IV** 290
Specialty Products Co., **8** 386
Spectra-Physics AB, **9** 380–81
Spectra-Physics Inc., **9** 381
Spectral Dynamics Corporation. *See* Scientific-Atlanta, Inc.
Spectrum Concepts, **10** 394–95
Spectrum Dyed Yarns of New York, **8** 559
Spectrum Health Care Services, **13** 48
Spectrum Technology, Inc., **7** 378
Speed-O-Lac Chemical, **8** 553
SpeeDee Marts, **II** 661
Speedy Muffler King, **10** 415
Speer, Edgar B., **IV** 574; **7** 551
Speer, Roy M., **V** 77
Speich, Rudolf, **II** 369
Speidel Newspaper Group, **IV** 612; **7** 191
Speigel Inc., **9** 190, 219
Spelling Entertainment, **9** 75
Spelling Entertainment Group, Inc., 14 460–62
Spence, Richard C., **V** 435
Spencer Beef, **II** 536
Spencer Gifts, **II** 144
Spencer, Percy, **II** 85–86; **11** 412
Spencer, Roy A., **13** 559
Spencer Stuart and Associates, Inc., 14 463–65
Spencer, Tom, **V** 124
Spencer, Walter O., **III** 745; **13** 470
Spencer, William, **IV** 437
Spenco Medical Corp., **III** 41
Spenser, Mark, **II** 250
Spero, Joan E., **I** 464
Sperry, **13** 511
Sperry & Hutchinson Co., **12** 299
Sperry Aerospace, **6** 283
Sperry Aerospace Group, **II** 40, 86; **12** 246, 248
Sperry Corporation, **I** 101, 167; **III** 165, 642; **6** 281–82; **8** 92; **11** 139; **12** 39. *See also* Unisys Corporation.
Sperry Milling Co., **II** 501; **10** 322
Sperry Rand Corp., **II** 63, 73; **III** 126, 129, 149, 166, 329, 642; **6** 241, 261, 281–82
Spethmann, Dieter, **IV** 222
Sphere, **8** 526
Sphere Inc., **13** 92
Spicer, Clarence, **I** 152; **10** 264
Spicer Manufacturing Co., **I** 152; **III** 568
Spie Batignolles SA, **13** 206
Spie-Batignolles, **I** 563; **II** 93–94
Spiegel, **III** 598; **V** 160
Spiegel, Arthur, **10** 489–90
Spiegel, Inc., 8 56–58; **10** 168, **489–91**; **11** 498; **13** 179
Spiegel, Joseph, **10** 489
Spiegel, M.J., **10** 490
Spiegel, Modie, **10** 489
Spielberg, Steven, **II** 144; **12** 228, 323–24
Spielvogel, Carl, **I** 18, 27
Spillers, **II** 500
Spin Physics, **III** 475–76; **7** 163
SPIRE Corporation, **14** 477
Spirella Company of Great Britain Ltd., **V** 356
Spitz, S.J., **9** 291–92
Spizzico, Giacinto, **IV** 588
Spock, Benjamin (Dr.), **IV** 671
Spoerle Electronic, **10** 113
Spokane Falls Electric Light and Power Company. *See* Edison Electric Illuminating Company.

Spokane Falls Water Power Company, **6** 595
Spokane Gas and Fuel, **IV** 391
Spokane Natural Gas Company, **6** 597
Spokane Street Railway Company, **6** 595
Spokane Traction Company, **6** 596
Spom Japan, **IV** 600
Spoor Behrins Campbell and Young, **II** 289
Spoor, William H., **II** 556–57; **13** 408–09
Spoornet, **6** 435
Sporck, Charles E., **6** 261–63
Sporck, Charles L., **II** 63–64
Sporloisirs S.A., **9** 157
Sporn, Philip, **V** 547–48
Sporting Dog Specialties, Inc., **14** 386
Sporting News Publishing Co., **IV** 677–78
Sports Experts Inc., **II** 652
Sports Inc., **14** 8
Sportservice Corporation, **7** 133–35
Sportsystems Corporation, **7** 133, 135
Sprague, Benjamin, **7** 465–66
Sprague, Bill, **7** 466
Sprague Co., **I** 410
Sprague Devices, Inc., **11** 84
Sprague Electric Company, **6** 261
Sprague Electric Railway and Motor Co., **II** 27; **12** 193
Sprague, Frank Julian, **II** 27; **12** 193
Sprague, Peter, **II** 63
Sprague, Peter J., **6** 261, 263
Sprague, Richard, **7** 465
Sprague, Warner & Co., **II** 571
Sprague, William, Jr., **7** 466
Spray-Rite, **I** 366
Sprayon Products, **III** 745
Sprecher & Schub, **9** 10
Sprecher, Melvin, **7** 592
Spriggs, Frank S., **III** 508
Spring Forge Mill, **8** 412
Spring Grove Mill, **8** 412
Spring Industries, Inc., V 378–79
Spring Valley Brewery, **I** 265
Springbok Editions, **IV** 621
Springer, Axel Cäsar, **IV** 589–91
Springer family, **IV** 591
Springer, Ferdinand, **IV** 641; **7** 311
Springer, Friede, **IV** 590–91
Springer, Jerry, **11** 330
Springer, Julius, **I** 410
Springer Verlag GmbH & Co., **IV** 611, 641
Springer, William C., **11** 173
Springfield Bank, **9** 474
Springhouse Corp., **IV** 610
Springhouse Financial Corp., **III** 204
Springorum, Friedrich, **IV** 104
Springorum, Fritz, **IV** 104
Springs, Elliott White, **V** 378–79
Springs, Leroy, **V** 378
Springsteen, Bruce, **II** 134
Sprint. *See* US Sprint Communications.
Sprint Communications. *See* US Sprint Communications.
Sprint Communications Company, L.P., 9 478–80
Sprint Communications Corporation, L.P., **11** 500–01
Sprint Corp., **9** 478, 480; **10** 19, 57, 97, 201–03; **11** 183, 185
Sprint/Mid-Atlantic Telecom, **10** 203
Sprott, J.S., **I** 201
Spruce Falls Power and Paper Co., **III** 40; **IV** 648

Spruce, J. K., **6** 474
Spun Yarns, Inc., **12** 503
Spur Oil Co., **7** 362
SPX Corporation, 10 492–95
SQ Software, Inc., **10** 505
SQL Solutions, Inc., **10** 505
Squibb Beech-Nut, **I** 695–96
Squibb Corporation, I 380–81, 631, 651, 659, 675, **695–97**; **III** 17, 19, 67; **9** 6–7; **13** 379–80
Squibb, Edwin Robinson, **I** 695
Squibb Pharmaceutical Company, **8** 166
Squires, Charles P., **11** 342
Squires, John, **6** 230
SR Beteilgungen Aktiengesellschaft, **III** 377
SRI International, **10** 139
SRI Strategic Resources Inc., **6** 310
SS Cars, Ltd. *See* Jaguar Cars, Ltd.
Ssangyong Cement (Singapore), **III** 748
Ssangyong Cement Industrial Co., Ltd., III 747–50
Ssangyong Computer Systems Corp., **III** 749
Ssangyong Construction Co. Ltd., **III** 749
Ssangyong Corp., **III** 748
Ssangyong Engineering Co. Ltd., **III** 749
Ssangyong Heavy Industries Co., **III** 748
Ssangyong Investment & Securities Co., **III** 749
Ssangyong Motor Co., **III** 750
Ssangyong Oil Refining Co. Ltd., **III** 748–49; **IV** 536–37, 539
Ssangyong Paper Co., **III** 748–49
Ssangyong Precision Industry Co., **III** 748
Ssangyong Shipping Co. Ltd., **III** 748
Ssangyong Software & Data Co., **III** 749
Ssangyong Trading Co. Ltd., **III** 748
SSC&B, **I** 17
SSC&B-Lintas, **14** 315
SSC&B: Lintas Worldwide, **I** 16
SSI Medical Services, Inc., **10** 350
SSMC Inc., **II** 10
St. Alban's Sand and Gravel, **III** 739
St. Andrews Insurance, **III** 397
St. Charles Manufacturing Co., **III** 654
St. Clair Industries Inc., **I** 482
St. Clair Press, **IV** 570
St. Croix Paper Co., **IV** 281; **9** 259
St. Davids (Lord), **III** 669
St. George Reinsurance, **III** 397
St. Helens Crown Glass Co., **III** 724
St. Joe Minerals, **8** 192
St. Joe Minerals Corp., **I** 569, 571
St. Joe Paper Company, 8 485–88
St. John Knits, Inc., 14 466–68
St. John's Wood Railway Company, **6** 406
St. Joseph Co., **I** 286, 684
St. Jude Medical, Inc., 6 345; **11 458–61**
St. Lawrence Cement, **III** 702
St. Lawrence Cement Inc., **8** 258–59
St. Lawrence Corp. Ltd., **IV** 272
St. Lawrence Steamboat Co., **I** 273
St. Louis and Illinois Belt Railway, **6** 504
St. Louis Refrigerator Car Co., **I** 219
St. Louis Troy and Eastern Railroad Company, **6** 504
St. Paul (U.K.) Ltd., **III** 357
St. Paul Bank for Cooperatives, 8 489–90
St. Paul Fire and Marine Insurance Co., **III** 355–56
St. Paul Guardian Insurance Co., **III** 356

INDEX TO INDUSTRIES

Index to Industries

ACCOUNTING

Deloitte & Touche, 9
Ernst & Young, 9
L.S. Starrett Co., 13
McLane Company, Inc., 13
Price Waterhouse, 9

ADVERTISING & OTHER BUSINESS SERVICES

A. C. Nielsen Company, 13
Ackerley Communications, Inc., 9
Adia S.A., 6
Advo, Inc., 6
Aegis Group plc, 6
American Building Maintenance Industries, Inc., 6
The Associated Press, 13
Bates Worldwide, Inc., 14
Bearings, Inc., 13
Berlitz International, Inc., 13
Burns International Security Services, 13
Chiat/Day Inc. Advertising, 11
D'Arcy Masius Benton & Bowles, Inc., 6
DDB Needham Worldwide, 14
Dentsu Inc., I
Equifax, Inc., 6
Euro RSCG Worldwide S.A., 13
Foote, Cone & Belding Communications, Inc., I
Grey Advertising, Inc., 6
Hakuhodo, Inc., 6
Interpublic Group Inc., I
Japan Leasing Corporation, 8
JWT Group Inc., I
Katz Communications, Inc., 6
Kelly Services Inc., 6
Ketchum Communications Inc., 6
Leo Burnett Company Inc., I
Lintas: Worldwide, 14
The Ogilvy Group, Inc., I
Olsten Corporation, 6
Omnicom Group, I
Pinkerton's Inc., 9
Saatchi & Saatchi PLC, I
ServiceMaster Limited Partnership, 6
Shared Medical Systems Corporation, 14
Skidmore, Owings & Merrill, 13
Sotheby's Holdings, Inc., 11
Spencer Stuart and Associates, Inc., 14
TBWA Advertising, Inc., 6
Ticketmaster Corp., 13
The Wackenhut Corporation, 14
Wells Rich Greene BDDP, 6
WPP Group plc, 6
Young & Rubicam, Inc., I

AEROSPACE

Aerospatiale, 7
Avions Marcel Dassault-Breguet Aviation, I
Banner Aerospace, Inc., 14
Beech Aircraft Corporation, 8
The Boeing Company, I; 10 (upd.)

British Aerospace PLC, I
Cessna Aircraft Company, 8
Fairchild Aircraft, Inc., 9
G.I.E. Airbus Industrie, I; 12 (upd.)
General Dynamics Corporation, I; 10 (upd.)
Grumman Corporation, I; 11 (upd.)
Gulfstream Aerospace Corp., 7
N.V. Koninklijke Nederlandse Vliegtuigenfabriek Fokker, I
Learjet Inc., 8
Lockheed Corporation, I; 11 (upd.)
Martin Marietta Corporation, I
McDonnell Douglas Corporation, I; 11 (upd.)
Messerschmitt-Bölkow-Blohm GmbH., I
Moog Inc., 13
Northrop Corporation, I; 11 (upd.)
Pratt & Whitney, 9
Rockwell International Corporation, I; 11 (upd.)
Rolls-Royce plc, I; 7 (upd.)
Sequa Corp., 13
Sundstrand Corporation, 7
Textron Lycoming Turbine Engine, 9
Thiokol Corporation, 9
United Technologies Corporation, I; 10 (upd.)

AIRLINES

Aeroflot Soviet Airlines, 6
Air Canada, 6
Air New Zealand Limited, 14
Air-India, 6
Alaska Air Group, Inc., 6
Alitalia—Linee Aeree Italiana, SPA, 6
All Nippon Airways Company Limited, 6
America West Airlines, 6
American Airlines, I; 6 (upd.)
British Airways PLC, I; 14 (upd.)
Cathay Pacific Airways Limited, 6
Comair Holdings Inc., 13
Continental Airlines, I
Delta Air Lines, Inc., I; 6 (upd.)
Deutsche Lufthansa A.G., I
Eastern Airlines, I
EgyptAir, 6
Finnair Oy, 6
Garuda Indonesia, 6
Groupe Air France, 6
HAL Inc., 9
Iberia Líneas Aéreas de España S.A., 6
Japan Air Lines Company Ltd., I
Koninklijke Luchtvaart Maatschappij, N.V., I
Korean Air Lines Co. Ltd., 6
Malaysian Airlines System BHD, 6
Mesa Airlines, Inc., 11
Northwest Airlines, Inc., I; 6 (upd.)
Pan American World Airways, Inc., I; 12 (upd.)
People Express Airlines, Inc., I
Philippine Airlines, Inc., 6
Qantas Airways Limited, 6

Saudi Arabian Airlines, 6
Scandinavian Airlines System, I
Singapore Airlines Ltd., 6
Southwest Airlines Co., 6
Swiss Air Transport Company, Ltd., I
Texas Air Corporation, I
Thai Airways International Ltd., 6
Trans World Airlines, Inc., I; 12 (upd.)
Transportes Aereos Portugueses, S.A., 6
United Airlines, I; 6 (upd.)
USAir Group, Inc., I; 6 (upd.)
VARIG, SA, 6

AUTOMOTIVE

Adam Opel AG, 7
Alfa Romeo, 13
American Motors Corporation, I
Arvin Industries, Inc., 8
Automobiles Citroen, 7
Automobili Lamborghini S.p.A., 13
Bayerische Motoren Werke A.G., I; 11 (upd.)
Bendix Corporation, I
Borg-Warner Automotive, Inc., 14
The Budd Company, 8
Chrysler Corporation, I; 11 (upd.)
Cummins Engine Co. Inc., I; 12 (upd.)
Daihatsu Motor Company, Ltd., 7
Daimler-Benz A.G., I
Dana Corporation, I; 10 (upd.)
Eaton Corporation, I; 10 (upd.)
Echlin Inc., I; 11 (upd.)
Federal-Mogul Corporation, I; 10 (upd.)
Ferrari S.p.A., 13
Fiat S.p.A, I; 11 (upd.)
Ford Motor Company, I; 11 (upd.)
Fruehauf Corporation, I
General Motors Corporation, I; 10 (upd.)
Genuine Parts Company, 9
Harley-Davidson Inc., 7
Hino Motors, Ltd., 7
Honda Motor Company Limited (Honda Giken Kogyo Kabushiki Kaisha), I; 10 (upd.)
Isuzu Motors, Ltd., 9
Kelsey-Hayes Group of Companies, 7
Kia Motors Corp., 12
Lotus Cars Ltd., 14
Mack Trucks, Inc., I
Mazda Motor Corporation, 9
Midas International Corporation, 10
Mitsubishi Motors Corporation, 9
Navistar International Corporation, I; 10 (upd.)
Nissan Motor Company Ltd., I; 11 (upd.)
Officine Alfieri Maserati S.p.A., 13
Oshkosh Truck Corporation, 7
Paccar Inc., I
The Pep Boys—Manny, Moe & Jack, 11
Peugeot S.A., I
Porsche AG, 13
Regie Nationale des Usines Renault, I
Robert Bosch GmbH., I
Rolls-Royce Motors Ltd., I

Rover Group plc, 7
Saab-Scania A.B., I; 11 (upd.)
Saturn Corporation, 7
Sealed Power Corporation, I
Sheller-Globe Corporation, I
Spartan Motors Inc., 14
SPX Corporation, 10
Superior Industries International, Inc., 8
Suzuki Motor Corporation, 9
Toyota Motor Corporation, I; 11 (upd.)
TRW Inc., 14 (upd.)
Volkswagen A.G., I; 11 (upd.)
AB Volvo, I; 7 (upd.)
Winnebago Industries Inc., 7

BEVERAGES

Adolph Coors Company, I; 13 (upd.)
Allied-Lyons PLC, I
Anheuser-Busch Companies, Inc., I; 10 (upd.)
Asahi Breweries, Ltd., I
Bass PLC, I
Brauerei Beck & Co., 9
Brown-Forman Corporation, I; 10 (upd.)
Canandaigua Wine Company, Inc., 13
Carlsberg A/S, 9
Carlton and United Breweries Ltd., I
Cerveceria Polar, I
Coca Cola Bottling Co. Consolidated, 10
The Coca-Cola Company, I; 10 (upd.)
Corby Distilleries Limited, 14
Distillers Company PLC, I
Dr Pepper/7Up Companies, Inc., 9
E & J Gallo Winery, I; 7 (upd.)
Foster's Brewing Group Ltd., 7
G. Heileman Brewing Company Inc., I
General Cinema Corporation, I
Grand Metropolitan PLC, I
Guinness PLC, I
Heineken N.V, I; 13 (upd.)
Heublein, Inc., I
Hiram Walker Resources, Ltd., I
Kikkoman Corporation, 14
Kirin Brewery Company Ltd., I
Labatt Brewing Company Ltd., I
Miller Brewing Company, I; 12 (upd.)
Moët-Hennessy, I
Molson Companies Ltd., I
Pepsico, Inc., I; 10 (upd.)
Pernod Ricard S.A., I
Sapporo Breweries, Ltd., I; 13 (upd.)
The Seagram Company, Ltd., I
Snapple Beverage Corporation, 11
South African Breweries Ltd., I
Starbucks Corporation, 13
The Stroh Brewing Company, I
Whitbread and Company PLC, I

BIOTECHNOLOGY

Biogen Inc., 14
Centocor Inc., 14
Immunex Corporation, 14

CHEMICALS

A. Schulman, Inc., 8
Air Products and Chemicals, Inc., I; 10 (upd.)
Akzo Nobel N.V., 13
American Cyanamid, I; 8 (upd.)
ARCO Chemical Company, 10
Atochem S.A., I
BASF A.G., I
Bayer A.G., I; 13 (upd.)
Betz Laboratories, Inc., I; 10 (upd.)
Boc Group PLC, I
Brenntag AG, 8

Cabot Corporation, 8
Celanese Corporation, I
Chemcentral Corporation, 8
Ciba-Geigy Ltd., I; 8 (upd.)
Crompton & Knowles, I
The Dexter Corporation, I; 12 (upd.)
The Dow Chemical Company, I; 8 (upd.)
DSM, N.V, I
E.I. Du Pont de Nemours & Company, I; 8 (upd.)
Eastman Chemical Company, 14
Ecolab, Inc., I; 13 (upd.)
Ethyl Corporation, I; 10 (upd.)
Ferro Corporation, 8
First Mississippi Corporation, 8
Formosa Plastics Corporation, 14
G.A.F., I
Georgia Gulf Corporation, 9
Great Lakes Chemical Corporation, I; 14 (upd.)
Hercules Inc., I
Hoechst A.G., I
Hoechst Celanese Corporation, 13
Huls A.G., I
Huntsman Chemical Corporation, 8
IMC Fertilizer Group, Inc., 8
Imperial Chemical Industries PLC, I
International Flavors & Fragrances Inc., 9
Koppers Inc., I
L'air Liquide, I
Lawter International Inc., 14
Lubrizol Corporation, I
M.A. Hanna Company, 8
Mitsubishi Chemical Industries, Ltd., I
Mitsui Petrochemical Industries, Ltd., 9
Monsanto Company, I; 9 (upd.)
Montedison SpA, I
Morton International Inc., 9 (upd.)
Morton Thiokol, Inc., I
Nagase & Company, Ltd., 8
Nalco Chemical Corporation, I; 12 (upd.)
National Distillers and Chemical Corporation, I
NCH Corporation, 8
NL Industries, Inc., 10
Nobel Industries AB, 9
Novacor Chemicals Ltd., 12
NutraSweet Company, 8
Olin Corporation, I; 13 (upd.)
Pennwalt Corporation, I
Perstorp A.B., I
Praxair, Inc., 11
Quantum Chemical Corporation, 8
Reichhold Chemicals, Inc., 10
Rhône-Poulenc S.A., I; 10 (upd.)
Rohm and Haas, I
Roussel Uclaf, I; 8 (upd.)
Sequa Corp., 13
Solvay & Cie S.A., I
Sumitomo Chemical Company Ltd., I
Terra Industries, Inc., 13
Union Carbide Corporation, I; 9 (upd.)
Univar Corporation, 9
Vista Chemical Company, I
Witco Corporation, I

CONGLOMERATES

Accor SA, 10
AEG A.G., I
Alcatel Alsthom Compagnie Générale d'Electricité, 9
Alco Standard Corporation, I
Allied-Signal Inc., I
AMFAC Inc., I
Aramark Corporation, 13
Archer-Daniels-Midland Company, I; 11 (upd.)

Barlow Rand Ltd., I
Bat Industries PLC, I
Bond Corporation Holdings Limited, 10
BTR PLC, I
C. Itoh & Company Ltd., I
Cargill Inc., 13 (upd.)
CBI Industries, Inc., 7
Chemed Corporation, 13
Chesebrough-Pond's USA, Inc., 8
Colt Industries Inc., I
Delaware North Companies Incorporated, 7
The Dial Corp., 8
Elders IXL Ltd., I
Farley Northwest Industries, Inc., I
FMC Corporation, I; 11 (upd.)
Fuqua Industries, Inc., I
Gillett Holdings, Inc., 7
Grand Metropolitan PLC, 14 (upd.)
Great American Management and Investment, Inc., 8
Greyhound Corporation, I
Gulf & Western Inc., I
Hanson PLC, III; 7 (upd.)
Hitachi Ltd., I; 12 (upd.)
IC Industries, Inc., I
Ingram Industries, Inc., 11
Instituto Nacional de Industria, I
International Controls Corporation, 10
International Telephone & Telegraph Corporation, I; 11 (upd.)
Istituto per la Ricostruzione Industriale, I
Jardine Matheson Holdings Ltd., I
Katy Industries, Inc., I
Kesko Ltd (Kesko Oy), 8
Kidde, Inc., I
KOC Holding A.S., I
Lancaster Colony Corporation, 8
Lear Siegler, Inc., I
Leucadia National Corporation, 11
Litton Industries, Inc., I; 11 (upd.)
Loews Corporation, I; 12 (upd.)
Loral Corporation, 8
LTV Corporation, I
Marubeni K.K., I
MAXXAM Inc., 8
McKesson Corporation, I
Menasha Corporation, 8
Metromedia Co., 7
Minnesota Mining & Manufacturing Company, I; 8 (upd.)
Mitsubishi Corporation, I; 12 (upd.)
Mitsui Bussan K.K., I
NACCO Industries, Inc., 7
National Service Industries, Inc., 11
Nissho Iwai K.K., I
Norsk Hydro A.S., 10
Ogden Corporation, I
Pentair, Inc., 7
The Rank Organisation Plc, 14 (upd.)
Samsung Group, I
Sime Darby Berhad, 14
Sumitomo Corporation, I; 11 (upd.)
Swire Pacific Ltd., I
Teledyne, Inc., I; 10 (upd.)
Tenneco Inc., I; 10 (upd.)
Textron Inc., I
Thorn Emi PLC, I
Time Warner Inc., IV; 7 (upd.)
Tomkins plc, 11
Toshiba Corporation, I; 12 (upd.)
Transamerica Corporation, I; 13 (upd.)
Triarc Companies, Inc., 8
TRW Inc., I; 11 (upd.)
Unilever PLC, II; 7 (upd.)
Veba A.G., I
Virgin Group PLC, 12
W.R. Grace & Company, I
Wheaton Industries, 8

Whitman Corporation, 10 (upd.)
Whittaker Corporation, I
WorldCorp, Inc., 10

CONSTRUCTION

A. Johnson & Company H.B., I
The Austin Company, 8
Baratt Developments PLC, I
Bechtel Group Inc., I
Bilfinger & Berger Bau A.G., I
Bouygues, I
Brown & Root, Inc., 13
Centex Corporation, 8
Cianbro Corporation, 14
The Clark Construction Group, Inc., 8
Dillingham Corporation, I
Eurotunnel PLC, 13
Fairclough Construction Group PLC, I
Fluor Corporation, I; 8 (upd.)
George Wimpey PLC, 12
John Brown PLC, I
John Laing PLC, I
Kajima Corporation, I
Kaufman and Broad Home Corporation, 8
Kitchell Corporation, 14
The Koll Company, 8
Kumagai Gumi Company, Ltd., I
Lennar Corporation, 11
Lincoln Property Company, 8
Linde A.G., I
Mellon-Stuart Company, I
Michael Baker Corp., 14
Morrison Knudsen Corporation, 7
NVR L.P., 8
Ohbayashi Corporation, I
The Peninsular & Oriental Steam
   Navigation Company (Bovis Division), I
Perini Corporation, 8
Peter Kiewit Sons' Inc., 8
Pulte Corporation, 8
The Ryland Group, Inc., 8
Taylor Woodrow PLC, I
Trammell Crow Company, 8
Tridel Enterprises Inc., 9
The Turner Corporation, 8
U.S. Home Corporation, 8
Wood Hall Trust PLC, I

CONTAINERS

Ball Corporation, I; 10 (upd.)
Continental Group Company, I
Crown, Cork & Seal Company, Inc., I, 13
Gaylord Container Corporation, 8
Inland Container Corporation, 8
Keyes Fibre Company, 9
The Longaberger Company, 12
Longview Fibre Company, 8
Metal Box PLC, I
National Can Corporation, I
Owens-Illinois, Inc., I
Primerica Corporation, I
Sonoco Products Company, 8
Toyo Seikan Kaisha, Ltd., I

DRUGS

A.L. Pharma Inc., 12
Abbott Laboratories, I; 11 (upd.)
ALZA Corporation, 10
American Home Products, I; 10 (upd.)
Amgen, Inc., 10
A.B. Astra, I
Baxter International Inc., I; 10 (upd.)
Bayer A.G., I; 13 (upd.)
Becton, Dickinson & Company, I
Block Drug Company, Inc., 8
Carter-Wallace, Inc., 8

Chiron Corporation, 10
Ciba-Geigy Ltd., I; 8 (upd.)
D&K Wholesale Drug, Inc., 14
Eli Lilly & Company, I; 11 (upd.)
F. Hoffmann-Laroche & Company A.G., I
Fisons plc, 9
Fujisawa Pharmaceutical Company Ltd., I
G.D. Searle & Company, I; 12 (upd.)
Genentech, Inc., I; 8 (upd.)
Genetics Institute, Inc., 8
Genzyme Corporation, 13
Glaxo Holdings PLC, I; 9 (upd.)
Johnson & Johnson, III; 8 (upd.)
Marion Merrell Dow, Inc., I; 9 (upd.)
McKesson Corporation, 12
Merck & Co., Inc., I; 11 (upd.)
Miles Laboratories, I
Mylan Laboratories, I
National Patent Development Corporation,
   13
Novo Industri A/S, I
Pfizer Inc., I; 9 (upd.)
Pharmacia A.B., I
R.P. Scherer, I
Roche Bioscience, 14 (upd.)
Rorer Group, I
Roussel Uclaf, I; 8 (upd.)
Sandoz Ltd., I
Sankyo Company, Ltd., I
Sanofi Group, I
Schering A.G., I
Schering-Plough Corporation, I; 14 (upd.)
Sigma-Aldrich, I
SmithKline Beckman Corporation, I
Squibb Corporation, I
Sterling Drug, Inc., I
Syntex Corporation, I
Takeda Chemical Industries, Ltd., I
The Upjohn Company, I; 8 (upd.)
Warner-Lambert Co., I; 10 (upd.)
The Wellcome Foundation Ltd., I

ELECTRICAL & ELECTRONICS

ABB ASEA Brown Boveri Ltd., II
Acuson Corporation, 10
Advanced Technology Laboratories, Inc., 9
Alpine Electronics, Inc., 13
Alps Electric Co., Ltd., II
AMP Incorporated, II; 14 (upd.)
Analog Devices, Inc., 10
Andrew Corporation, 10
Arrow Electronics, Inc., 10
Atari Corporation, 9
Autodesk, Inc., 10
Avnet Inc., 9
Bicoastal Corporation, II
Bose Corporation, 13
Cabletron Systems, Inc., 10
Cobra Electronics Corporation, 14
Compagnie Générale d'Électricité, II
Cooper Industries, Inc., II
Dallas Semiconductor Corp., 13
Digi International Inc., 9
Dynatech Corporation, 13
E-Systems, Inc., 9
Emerson Electric Co., II
Exar Corp., 14
Foxboro Company, 13
Fuji Electric Co., Ltd., II
General Electric Company, II; 12 (upd.)
General Electric Company, PLC, II
General Instrument Corporation, 10
General Signal Corporation, 9
GM Hughes Electronics Corporation, II
Goldstar Co., Ltd., 12
Gould Electronics, Inc., 14
Harris Corporation, II

Honeywell Inc., II; 12 (upd.)
Hubbell Incorporated, 9
Hughes Supply, Inc., 14
Intel Corporation, II; 10 (upd.)
Itel Corporation, 9
Kemet Corp., 14
KitchenAid, 8
KnowledgeWare Inc., 9
Koor Industries Ltd., II
Kyocera Corporation, II
Loral Corporation, 9
LSI Logic Corporation, 13
Lucky-Goldstar, II
Marquette Electronics, Inc., 13
Matsushita Electric Industrial Co., Ltd., II
Methode Electronics, Inc., 13
Mitsubishi Electric Corporation, II
Motorola, Inc., II; 11 (upd.)
National Semiconductor Corporation, II
NEC Corporation, II
Nokia Corporation, II
Oki Electric Industry Company, Limited, II
Omron Tateisi Electronics Company, II
The Peak Technologies Group, Inc., 14
Philips Electronics N.V., II; 13 (upd.)
Philips Electronics North America Corp.,
   13
Pittway Corporation, 9
The Plessey Company, PLC, II
Potter & Brumfield Inc., 11
Premier Industrial Corporation, 9
Racal Electronics PLC, II
Raychem Corporation, 8
Rayovac Corporation, 13
Raytheon Company, II; 11 (upd.)
RCA Corporation, II
Read-Rite Corp., 10
Reliance Electric Company, 9
Samsung Electronics Co., Ltd., 14
Sanyo Electric Company, Ltd., II
Schneider S.A., II
SCI Systems, Inc., 9
Sensormatic Electronics Corp., 11
Sharp Corporation, II; 12 (upd.)
Siemens A.G., II; 14 (upd.)
Silicon Graphics Incorporated, 9
Solectron Corp., 12
Sony Corporation, II; 12 (upd.)
Sumitomo Electric Industries, Ltd., II
Sunbeam-Oster Co., Inc., 9
Tandy Corporation, II; 12 (upd.)
TDK Corporation, II
Tektronix, Inc., 8
Telxon Corporation, 10
Teradyne, Inc., 11
Texas Instruments Incorporated, II; 11
   (upd.)
Thomson S.A., II
Varian Associates Inc., 12
Victor Company of Japan, Ltd., II
Vitro Corp., 10
Westinghouse Electric Corporation, II; 12
   (upd.)
Wyle Electronics, 14
Zenith Data Systems, Inc., 10
Zenith Electronics Corporation, II; 13
   (upd.)

ENGINEERING & MANAGEMENT SERVICES

Analytic Sciences Corporation, 10
The Austin Company, 8
Brown & Root, Inc., 13
CDI Corporation, 6
CRSS Inc., 6
Day & Zimmermann Inc., 9
EG&G Incorporated, 8

INSURANCE

LEGAL SERVICES

MANUFACTURING

Toys "R" Us, Inc., V
The United States Shoe Corporation, V
United Stationers Inc., 14
Uny Co., Ltd., V
Urban Outfitters, Inc., 14
Value Merchants Inc., 13
Vendex International N.V., 13
Venture Stores Inc., 12
Viking Office Products, Inc., 10
W H Smith Group PLC, V
W.W. Grainger, Inc., V
Waban Inc., 13
Wal-Mart Stores, Inc., V; 8 (upd.)
Walgreen Co., V
Wherehouse Entertainment Incorporated, 11
Wickes Companies, Inc., V
Woolworth Corporation, V

RUBBER & TIRE

The BFGoodrich Company, V
Bridgestone Corporation, V
Carlisle Companies Incorporated, 8
Compagnie Générale des Établissements Michelin, V
Continental Aktiengesellschaft, V
Cooper Tire & Rubber Company, 8
General Tire, Inc., 8
The Goodyear Tire & Rubber Company, V
The Kelly-Springfield Tire Company, 8
Pirelli S.p.A., V
Sumitomo Rubber Industries, Ltd., V
The Yokohama Rubber Co., Ltd., V

TELECOMMUNICATIONS

Acme-Cleveland Corp., 13
ADC Telecommunications, Inc., 10
AirTouch Communications, 11
Alltel Corporation, 6
American Telephone and Telegraph Company, V
Ameritech, V
Ascom AG, 9
AT&T Bell Laboratories, Inc., 13
BCE Inc., V
Belgacom, 6
Bell Atlantic Corporation, V
Bell Canada, 6
BellSouth Corporation, V
British Columbia Telephone Company, 6
British Telecommunications plc, V
Cable and Wireless plc, V
Canal Plus, 10
Carolina Telephone and Telegraph Company, 10
Centel Corporation, 6
Century Communications Corp., 10
Century Telephone Enterprises, Inc., 9
Chris-Craft Industries, Inc., 9
Cincinnati Bell, Inc., 6
DDI Corporation, 7
Deutsche Bundespost TELEKOM, V
Directorate General of Telecommunications, 7
DSC Communications Corporation, 12
Executone Information Systems, Inc., 13
France Télécom Group, V
General DataComm Industries, Inc., 14
GTE Corporation, V
Havas, SA, 10
Hong Kong Telecommunications Ltd., 6
IDB Communications Group, Inc., 11
Illinois Bell Telephone Company, 14
Indiana Bell Telephone Company, Incorporated, 14
Infinity Broadcasting Corporation, 11
Koninklijke PTT Nederland NV, V

LDDS-Metro Communications, Inc., 8
LIN Broadcasting Corp., 9
Lincoln Telephone & Telegraph Company, 14
McCaw Cellular Communications, Inc., 6
MCI Communications Corporation, V
Mercury Communications, Ltd., 7
Metromedia Companies, 14
MFS Communications Company, Inc., 11
Michigan Bell Telephone Co., 14
Multimedia, Inc., 11
Nevada Bell Telephone Company, 14
Nippon Telegraph and Telephone Corporation, V
Northern Telecom Limited, V
NYNEX Corporation, V
Octel Communications Corp., 14
Ohio Bell Telephone Company, 14
Österreichische Post- und Telegraphenverwaltung, V
Pacific Telecom, Inc., 6
Pacific Telesis Group, V
Paging Network Inc., 11
PictureTel Corp., 10
Posti- ja Telelaitos, 6
QVC Network Inc., 9
Rochester Telephone Corporation, 6
Schweizerische Post-, Telefon- und Telegrafen-Betriebe, V
Scientific-Atlanta, Inc., 6
Società Finanziaria Telefonica per Azioni, V
Southern New England Telecommunications Corporation, 6
Southwestern Bell Corporation, V
Sprint Communications Company, L.P., 9
Swedish Telecom, V
SynOptics Communications, Inc., 10
Telecom Australia, 6
Telecom Eireann, 7
Telefonaktiebolaget LM Ericsson, V
Telefónica de España, S.A., V
Telefonos de Mexico S.A. de C.V., 14
Telephone and Data Systems, Inc., 9
Tellabs, Inc., 11
U S West, Inc., V
United States Cellular Corporation, 9
United Telecommunications, Inc., V
Vodafone Group plc, 11
Wisconsin Bell, Inc., 14

TEXTILES & APPAREL

Adidas AG, 14
Albany International Corp., 8
Amoskeag Company, 8
Benetton Group S.p.A., 10
Birkenstock Footprint Sandals, Inc., 12
Brown Group, Inc., V
Burlington Industries, Inc., V
Cato Corporation, 14
Charming Shoppes, Inc., 8
Coach Leatherware, 10
Coats Viyella Plc, V
Collins & Aikman Corporation, 13
Cone Mills Corporation, 8
Courtaulds plc, V
Crystal Brands, Inc., 9
Danskin, Inc., 12
Delta Woodside Industries, Inc., 8
Dominion Textile Inc., 12
Edison Brothers Stores, Inc., 9
Esprit de Corp., 8
Fieldcrest Cannon, Inc., 9
Fruit of the Loom, Inc., 8
The Gitano Group, Inc. 8
Greenwood Mills, Inc., 14
Guilford Mills Inc., 8

Hartmarx Corporation, 8
The Hartstone Group plc, 14
Hermès S.A., 14
Interface, Inc., 8
Irwin Toy Limited, 14
J. Crew Group Inc., 12
Jockey International, Inc., 12
Kellwood Company, 8
Kinney Shoe Corp., 14
L.A. Gear, Inc., 8
L.L. Bean, Inc., 10
Laura Ashley Holdings plc, 13
Lee Apparel Company, Inc., 8
The Leslie Fay Companies, Inc., 8
Levi Strauss & Co., V
Liz Claiborne, Inc., 8
Milliken & Co., V
Mitsubishi Rayon Co., Ltd., V
Nike, Inc., V; 8 (upd.)
OshKosh B'Gosh, Inc., 9
Oxford Industries, Inc., 8
Polo/Ralph Lauren Corporation, 12
Reebok International Ltd., V; 9 (upd.)
Russell Corporation, 8
Shelby Williams Industries, Inc., 14
Springs Industries, Inc., V
Starter Corp., 12
Stone Manufacturing Company, 14
Stride Rite Corporation, 8
Teijin Limited, V
The Timberland Company, 13
Toray Industries, Inc., V
Tultex Corporation, 13
Unifi, Inc., 12
United Merchants & Manufacturers, Inc., 13
Unitika Ltd., V
VF Corporation, V
Walton Monroe Mills, Inc., 8
The Warnaco Group Inc., 12
Wellman, Inc., 8
West Point-Pepperell, Inc., 8
Williamson-Dickie Manufacturing Company, 14

TOBACCO

American Brands, Inc., V
Brown and Williamson Tobacco Corporation, 14
Dibrell Brothers, Incorporated, 12
Gallaher Limited, V
Imasco Limited, V
Japan Tobacco Incorporated, V
Philip Morris Companies Inc., V
RJR Nabisco Holdings Corp., V
Rothmans International p.l.c., V
Standard Commercial Corporation, 13
Tabacalera, S.A., V
Universal Corporation, V
UST Inc., 9

TRANSPORT SERVICES

Air Express International Corporation, 13
Airborne Freight Corp., 6
Alamo Rent A Car, Inc., 6
Alexander & Baldwin, Inc., 10
Amerco, 6
American President Companies Ltd., 6
Anschutz Corp., 12
Atlas Van Lines, Inc., 14
Avis, Inc., 6
BAA plc, 10
British Railways Board, V
Budget Rent a Car Corporation, 9
Burlington Northern Inc., V
Canadian National Railway System, 6
Canadian Pacific Limited, V

Carlson Companies, Inc., 6
Carnival Cruise Lines, Inc., 6
Carolina Freight Corporation, 6
Chargeurs, 6
Chicago and North Western Holdings
   Corporation, 6
Compagnie Générale Maritime et
   Financière, 6
Consolidated Freightways, Inc., V
Consolidated Rail Corporation, V
Crowley Maritime Corporation, 6
CSX Corporation, V
Danzas Group, V
Deutsche Bundesbahn, V
DHL Worldwide Express, 6
East Japan Railway Company, V
Emery Air Freight Corporation, 6
Enterprise Rent-A-Car Company, 6
Evergreen Marine Corporation Taiwan
   Ltd., 13
Federal Express Corporation, V
Fritz Companies, Inc., 12
GATX, 6
Hankyu Corporation, V
Hapag-Lloyd AG, 6
The Hertz Corporation, 9
Illinois Central Corporation, 11
J.B. Hunt Transport Services Inc., 12
Kansas City Southern Industries, Inc., 6
Kawasaki Kisen Kaisha, Ltd., V
Keio Teito Electric Railway Company, V
Kinki Nippon Railway Company Ltd., V
Koninklijke Nedlloyd Groep N.V., 6
Kuhne & Nagel International A.G., V
La Poste, V
Leaseway Transportation Corp., 12
London Regional Transport, 6
Mayflower Group Inc., 6
Mitsui O.S.K. Lines, Ltd., V
National Car Rental System, Inc., 10
NFC plc, 6
Nippon Express Co., Ltd., V
Nippon Yusen Kabushiki Kaisha, V
Norfolk Southern Corporation, V
Ocean Group plc, 6
Odakyu Electric Railway Company
   Limited, V
Österreichische Bundesbahnen GmbH, 6
Overnite Transportation Co., 14
Overseas Shipholding Group, Inc., 11
The Peninsular and Oriental Steam
   Navigation Company, V
Penske Corporation, V
PHH Corporation, V
Post Office Group, V
Preston Corporation, 6
Roadway Services, Inc., V
Ryder System, Inc., V
Santa Fe Pacific Corporation, V
Schenker-Rhenus AG, 6
Seibu Railway Co. Ltd., V
Seino Transportation Company, Ltd., 6
Société Nationale des Chemins de Fer
   Français, V
Southern Pacific Transportation Company,
   V
Stinnes AG, 8
The Swiss Federal Railways
   (Schweizerische Bundesbahnen), V
Tidewater Inc., 11
TNT Freightways Corporation, 14
TNT Limited, V
Tobu Railway Co Ltd, 6
Tokyu Corporation, V
Totem Resources Corporation, 9
Transnet Ltd., 6
TTX Company, 6
Union Pacific Corporation, V

United Parcel Service of America Inc., V
United States Postal Service, 14
Yamato Transport Co. Ltd., V
Yellow Corporation, 14
Yellow Freight System, Inc. of Delaware,
   V

UTILITIES

The AES Corporation, 10; 13 (upd.)
Air & Water Technologies Corporation, 6
Allegheny Power System, Inc., V
American Electric Power Company, Inc., V
American Water Works Company, 6
Arkla, Inc., V
Associated Natural Gas Corporation, 11
Atlanta Gas Light Company, 6
Atlantic Energy, Inc., 6
Baltimore Gas and Electric Company, V
Bayernwerk A.G., V
Big Rivers Electric Corporation, 11
Boston Edison Company, 12
British Gas plc, V
British Nuclear Fuels plc, 6
Brooklyn Union Gas, 6
Canadian Utilities Limited, 13
Carolina Power & Light Company, V
Cascade Natural Gas Corporation, 9
Centerior Energy Corporation, V
Central and South West Corporation, V
Central Hudson Gas and Electricity
   Corporation, 6
Central Maine Power, 6
Chubu Electric Power Company,
   Incorporated, V
Chugoku Electric Power Company Inc., V
Cincinnati Gas & Electric Company, 6
CIPSCO Inc., 6
Citizens Utilities Company, 7
City Public Service, 6
CMS Energy Corporation, V, 14
Cogentrix Energy, Inc., 10
The Coleman Company, Inc., 9
The Columbia Gas System, Inc., V
Commonwealth Edison Company, V
Commonwealth Energy System, 14
Connecticut Light and Power Co., 13
Consolidated Edison Company of New
   York, Inc., V
Consolidated Natural Gas Company, V
Consumers Power Co., 14
Consumers Water Company, 14
Consumers' Gas Company Ltd., 6
Destec Energy, Inc., 12
The Detroit Edison Company, V
Dominion Resources, Inc., V
DPL Inc., 6
DQE, Inc., 6
Duke Power Company, V
Eastern Enterprises, 6
El Paso Natural Gas Company, 12
Electricité de France, V
Elektrowatt AG, 6
ENDESA Group, V
Enron Corp., V
Enserch Corporation, V
Ente Nazionale per L'Energia Elettrica, V
Entergy Corporation, V
Equitable Resources, Inc., 6
Florida Progress Corporation, V
FPL Group, Inc., V
Gaz de France, V
General Public Utilities Corporation, V
Générale des Eaux Group, V
Gulf States Utilities Company, 6
Hawaiian Electric Industries, Inc., 9
Hokkaido Electric Power Company Inc., V
Hokuriku Electric Power Company, V

Hongkong Electric Company Ltd., 6
Houston Industries Incorporated, V
Hydro-Québec, 6
Idaho Power Company, 12
Illinois Bell Telephone Company, 14
Illinois Power Company, 6
IPALCO Enterprises, Inc., 6
The Kansai Electric Power Co., Inc., V
Kansas City Power & Light Company, 6
Kenetech Corporation, 11
Kentucky Utilities Company, 6
KU Energy Corporation, 11
Kyushu Electric Power Company Inc., V
LG&E Energy Corporation, 6
Long Island Lighting Company, V
Lyonnaise des Eaux-Dumez, V
Magma Power Company, 11
MCN Corporation, 6
MDU Resources Group, Inc., 7
Midwest Resources Inc., 6
Minnesota Power & Light Company, 11
Montana Power Company, 11
National Fuel Gas Company, 6
National Power PLC, 12
N.V. Nederlandse Gasunie, V
Nevada Power Company, 11
New England Electric System, V
New York State Electric and Gas, 6
Niagara Mohawk Power Corporation, V
NICOR Inc., 6
NIPSCO Industries, Inc., 6
North West Water Group plc, 11
Northeast Utilities, V
Northern States Power Company, V
Nova Corporation of Alberta, V
Oglethorpe Power Corporation, 6
Ohio Edison Company, V
Oklahoma Gas and Electric Company, 6
ONEOK Inc., 7
Ontario Hydro, 6
Osaka Gas Co., Ltd., V
Pacific Enterprises, V
Pacific Gas and Electric Company, V
PacifiCorp, V
Panhandle Eastern Corporation, V
PECO Energy Company, 11
Pennsylvania Power & Light Company, V
Peoples Energy Corporation, 6
Philadelphia Electric Company, V
Pinnacle West Capital Corporation, 6
Portland General Corporation, 6
Potomac Electric Power Company, 6
PowerGen PLC, 11
PreussenElektra Aktiengesellschaft, V
PSI Resources, 6
Public Service Company of Colorado, 6
Public Service Company of New Mexico, 6
Public Service Enterprise Group
   Incorporated, V
Puget Sound Power and Light Company, 6
Questar Corporation, 6
Rochester Gas and Electric Corporation, 6
Ruhrgas A.G., V
RWE Group, V
San Diego Gas & Electric Company, V
SCANA Corporation, 6
Scarborough Public Utilities Commission,
   9
SCEcorp, V
Scottish Hydro-Electric PLC, 13
Severn Trent PLC, 12
Shikoku Electric Power Company, Inc., V
Sonat, Inc., 6
The Southern Company, V
Southern Electric PLC, 13
Southern Indiana Gas and Electric
   Company, 13
Southwestern Public Service Company, 6

WASTE SERVICES

NOTES ON CONTRIBUTORS

Notes on Contributors

COBB, Loretta. Free-lance writer.

COHEN, M. L. Novelist and free-lance writer living in Chicago.

COVELL, Jeffrey L. Free-lance writer and corporate history contractor.

DERDAK, Thomas. Free-lance writer and adjunct professor of philosophy at Loyola University of Chicago; former executive director of the Albert Einstein Foundation.

DUBLANC, Robin. Free-lance writer and copyeditor in Yorkshire, England.

FIERO, John. Free-lance writer, researcher, and consultant; Professor of English at the University of Southwestern Louisiana in Lafayette.

GASBARRE, April Dougal. Archivist and free-lance writer specializing in business and social history in Cleveland, Ohio.

GOPNIK, Hilary. Free-lance writer.

HALASZ, Robert. Former editor in chief of *World Progress* and *Funk & Wagnalls New Encyclopedia Yearbook;* author, *The U.S. Marines* (Millbrook Press, 1993).

HARLEY, Judith. Free-lance writer, editor and owner of Oxford Communications, a publishing company.

HIGHMAN, Beth Watson. Free-lance writer.

INGRAM, Frederick. Business writer living in Johnson City, Tennessee; contributor to the *Encyclopedia of Business,* the *Encyclopedia of Consumer Brands,* and *Global Industry Profiles.*

JACOBSON, Robert R. Free-lance writer and musician.

LEWIS, Scott. Free-lance writer and editor.

LINTON, David. Free-lance writer.

McMANUS, Donald. Free-lance writer.

MOTE, Dave. President of information retrieval company Performance Database.

PACKEL, John F., II. Teacher and drummer living in New York City; publisher of *Green: Personal Finance for the Unashamed.*

PFALZGRAF, Taryn Benbow. Free-lance editor, writer, and consultant in the Chicago area.

ROULAND, Roger. Free-lance writer whose essays and journalism have appeared in the *International Fiction Review,* Chicago *Tribune,* and Chicago *Sun-Times.*

SALAMIE, David E. Part-owner of InfoWorks Development Group, a reference publication development and editorial services company.

SCHRECENGOST, Lynda D. Free-lance writer and editor specializing in promotional and educational materials.

SMETHURST, Katherine. Free-lance writer.

SWIERCZEK, Bob. Journalist and policy analyst; currently writing for several publications in Washington, D.C.

TROESTER, Maura. Free-lance writer based in Chicago.

WERNICK, Ellen D. Free-lance writer and editor.

WOODWARD, Angela. Free-lance writer.

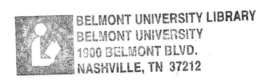